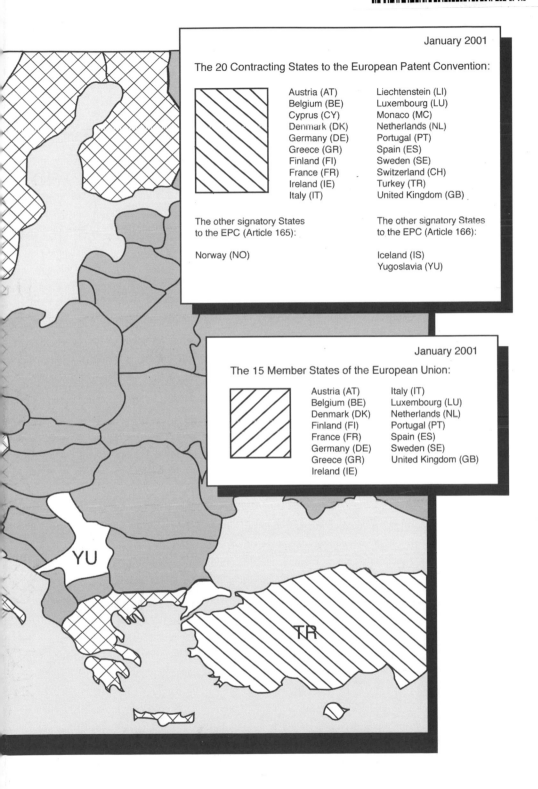

January 2001

The 20 Contracting States to the European Patent Convention:

Austria (AT)	Liechtenstein (LI)
Belgium (BE)	Luxembourg (LU)
Cyprus (CY)	Monaco (MC)
Denmark (DK)	Netherlands (NL)
Germany (DE)	Portugal (PT)
Greece (GR)	Spain (ES)
Finland (FI)	Sweden (SE)
France (FR)	Switzerland (CH)
Ireland (IE)	Turkey (TR)
Italy (IT)	United Kingdom (GB)

The other signatory States
to the EPC (Article 165):

Norway (NO)

The other signatory States
to the EPC (Article 166):

Iceland (IS)
Yugoslavia (YU)

January 2001

The 15 Member States of the European Union:

Austria (AT)	Italy (IT)
Belgium (BE)	Luxembourg (LU)
Denmark (DK)	Netherlands (NL)
Finland (FI)	Portugal (PT)
France (FR)	Spain (ES)
Germany (DE)	Sweden (SE)
Greece (GR)	United Kingdom (GB)
Ireland (IE)	

YU

TR

THE EUROPEAN PATENT SYSTEM

The Law and Practice
of the
European Patent Convention

AUSTRALIA
LBC Information Services—Sydney

CANADA and **USA**
Carswell—Toronto

NEW ZEALAND
Brooker's—Auckland

SINGAPORE and **MALAYSIA**
Sweet & Maxwell Asia
Singapore and Kuala Lumpur

ISBN 0-421-58600-1

9 780421 586000

THE EUROPEAN PATENT SYSTEM

The Law and Practice of the European Patent Convention

SECOND EDITION

by

GERALD PATERSON M.A. (OXON)

Barrister-at-Law, Gray's Inn, London;
Former Member of the Enlarged Board of Appeal and
Chairman of a Technical Board of Appeal,
European Patent Office, Munich

LONDON
SWEET & MAXWELL
2001

Published by
Sweet & Maxwell Limited of
100 Avenue Road, London NW3 3PF;
Phototypeset by Mendip Communications Limited, Frome, Somerset;
Printed and bound in Great Britain
by MPG Books Ltd, Bodmin, Cornwall

**A catalogue record for this book is available
from the British Library**

ISBN 0 421 58600 1

The author has in respect
of this work asserted generally
his right of identification under the
U.K. Copyright, Designs and
Patents Act 1988, s.77.

*Acknowledgment:
Statutory material used
in this publication is
Crown copyright*

PREFACE

The European patent system has established itself impressively, pressed forward by the increasing number of European patent applications filed every year, and by the need to process the grant of such applications, and subsequent oppositions, in accordance with a uniform practice.

Twenty-three years after the European Patent Office ("EPO") opened in 1978, its scale of operations is such that industry worldwide needs to be aware, through its advisers, of the current state of the law in connection with the grant of European patents, as well as its trends. The aim of this book is to continue to meet that need, and to provide guidance to patent practitioners, by presenting an objective picture of the jurisprudence which has so far been developed through the many decisions issued annually by the Boards of Appeal of the EPO. There are currently more than a thousand appeals filed each year, and a corresponding number of decisions are issued.

As far as possible, decisions of the Boards of Appeal which have been published in the Official Journal of the European Patent Office ("O.J. EPO") before January 1, 2001 have been taken into account, as well as some decisions which have not been so published, and some which will be published in the near future.

Since the first edition of this book was published in 1992, there has been considerable development in the case law of the Boards of Appeal, especially in that governing the procedure before the EPO, and in particular in relation to the procedure governing oppositions and opposition appeals. This was the most important area of uncertainty at the time when the first edition was published. This uncertainty arose from the text of the EPC itself, which had created a hybrid procedural system for oppositions, containing aspects of both investigative and adversarial procedure. The development of a proper balance between these two procedural traditions within Europe was left to the Boards of Appeal, and primarily as a result of a series of decisions on questions of law which were referred to the Enlarged Board of Appeal, most of the procedural uncertainties in this respect have been resolved. In general terms, especially in opposition appeal proceedings, in contrast to the purely administrative nature of first instance procedure, the judicial character of the Boards of Appeal has been recognised, with the consequence that the appeal procedure should be appropriate to an administrative court. Thus the principle of "party disposition" is applicable to opposition appeal procedure, which as a consequence of its judicial character is less investigative than an administrative procedure.

The above procedural developments have required a reorganisation of the chapters which concern procedure, compared to the first edition. They are discussed in detail primarily in Chapters 3 and 4. The practical advantages of such developments lie in a greater procedural certainty in opposition appeals, and less procedural complication and delay in the overall opposition procedure.

In parallel with the above procedural developments within the EPO, the central importance within the European patent system of the case law and practice of the Boards of Appeal in relation to substantive patent law, especially concerning the requirements for patentability, has been increasingly recognised during the last ten years. Concomitantly, the need for a better system of jurisdiction within the European patent system has also been recognised, in order to ensure a better level of harmonisation of the practice within the Boards of Appeal (and the EPO generally) concerning substantive patentability with the decisions of national courts within the Contracting States. In the absence of a common appeal court which would provide judicial harmonisation between the EPO and the individual national courts, the emergence of different interpretations of the substantive European patent law by individual national courts and the Boards of Appeal is bound to occur. The situation is complicated by the fact that the national courts are responsible for the determination of infringe-ment and enforcement issues relating to European patents granted by the EPO.

Much has been written during recent years concerning the creation of a system of jurisdiction within Europe which would be appropriate for the harmonisation and development of all aspects of the European patent system. Not least, a Green Paper on "the Community patent and the patent system in Europe" was issued by the European Commission in 1997, which attempted to propose adjustments to the judicial arrangements set out in the Community Patent Convention ("CPC": see Chapter 14) in the context of a unitary Community patent. Its proposals were not received with particular favour, however. Recently, a proposal for a Community Patent Regulation has been published by the European Commission, which contains improvements to such judicial arrangements.

A future European patent system needs a court structure whose courts would determine issues of infringement and validity at the same time, in the context of a common procedural system. Such a court structure would need to include a supreme European appeal court, and each of the first instance courts would need to include some judges with a proper level of experience in patent matters. Beyond all this, measures to accommodate the problems associated with the numerous European languages need to be included in such a system. It remains to be seen whether, and if so when, an acceptable system of jurisdiction for the European patent system can be devised which would carry forward the harmonisation which has already been achieved within the EPO.

A further imminent development of the European patent system concerns the amendment of the European Patent Convention ("EPC"). An EPC revision conference of all the Contracting States was held in Munich in November 2000, prior to which a comprehensive review of the provisions of the EPC had been undertaken. The text of the proposed revisions, which contains the proposed amendments to the EPC, has been published. Details and comments upon the proposed revisions to the EPC have been included throughout this book whenever appropriate, in paragraph numbers with a suffix "A" (see also "Revision of the European Patent Convention: Background and outline of proposals" issued by the EPO in January 2001, and reproduced in Appendix 24).

The proposed amendments are intended to modernise the EPC cautiously in the light of twenty years of practical experience, and in the light of legal and technical developments. The need for conformity with the TRIPS agreement, the future Community patent and the forthcoming Patent Law Treaty (which harmonises a number of formal requirements) has been taken into account.[1]

The revised text of the EPC will require ratification by all the Contracting States and will therefore not come into force for several years. Further revision conferences are planned, in particular in order to consider further substantive amendments to the EPC concerning the protection of biotechnological inventions, and computer programs and business methods.[2]

Crown copyright is acknowledged in extracts from *Reports on Patent, Design and Trade Mark Cases* ("R.P.C."), which are reproduced with permission from the Patent Office on behalf of Her Majesty's Stationery Office.

The views which have been expressed in this book are entirely those of the author.

Gerald Paterson
Hampstead, London
January 1, 2001

---

[1] See the Notice of President of the EPO dated March 24, 2000, O.J. EPO 2000, 195.
[2] See Appendix 24.

INTRODUCTION

The European Patent Convention (EPC) provides a centralised system for granting European patents. Upon filing a European patent application at the European Patent Office, the applicant is required to designate the Contracting States to the Convention in which protection is desired. Upon grant, a European patent has the effect of a bundle of national patents in each of such designated Contracting States. After grant, apart from the centralised opposition procedure before the European Patent Office which in accordance with the Convention may be commenced within nine months from grant, a European patent is no longer within the competence of the European Patent Office; the resulting bundle of national patents may only be challenged and enforced individually within the national jurisdictions of the designated States.

Since the first edition of this book was published in 1992, Ireland, Finland, Cyprus and Turkey (November 1, 2000) have become Contracting States to the EPC, so that there are at present 20 such Contracting States.

Furthermore, agreements have been made between the European Patent Organisation and a number of European States that are not Contracting States, whereby the protection conferred by a granted European patent maybe extended to such States. At the time of writing extension agreements have entered into force for Slovenia, Lithuania, Latvia, Albania, Romania and Macedonia.

Under the extension system, extension of protection to each such State is deemed to be requested for any European patent application filed on or after the entry into force of an extension agreement for each such State, subject to payment of an extension fee within a time limit. Upon grant, a European patent has the effect of a national patent in such States.

This book is primarily concerned with the interpretation of the European Patent Convention in the case law and practice which has been developed by the Boards of Appeal of the European Patent Office in Munich, through their decisions in appeals under the European Patent Convention concerning both European patent applications and oppositions by third parties to patents granted pursuant to such applications.

The departments of the European Patent Office which make decisions the subject of such appeals are the Legal Division, the Receiving Section, the Examining Divisions and the Opposition Divisions. These are "first instance" departments.

The Receiving Section is in the branch of the European Patent Office at The Hague, and is responsible for the examination on filing and the examination as to formal requirements of each European patent application. A European Search Report is then drawn up by a Search Division, also based at The Hague.

An Examining Division is thereafter responsible for the substantive examination of each such application, as to whether the application or the invention to which it relates meets the requirements of the European Patent Convention, in particular the requirements for patentability, so that a European patent can be granted.

Within nine months from grant of a European patent, any person may file an opposition to the granted patent, on one or more grounds which are specified in the Convention. An Opposition Division is responsible for the examination of such an opposition.

If a party to proceedings before a first instance department is "adversely affected" by a decision of such a department, he may appeal to a Board of Appeal ("the second instance"). Following examination of such an appeal, the Board of Appeal issues reasons for its decision on the appeal in writing.

This book commences with a chapter discussing the interpretation of the European Patent Convention within its legal framework.

Subsequent chapters describe in particular the detailed procedure before the first instance departments of the EPO and before the Boards of Appeal, and the requirements for patentability. The discussion is centred upon decisions of the Boards of Appeal which have been issued in relation to each such topic.

The penultimate chapter discusses the determination of the extent of the protection which is conferred by a European patent, both in proceedings before the European Patent Office having regard to relevant Board of Appeal decisions, and also in infringement proceedings before some national courts.

The final chapter considers the jurisdictional relationship between proceedings before the departments of the European Patent Office, patent proceedings before national courts, and proceedings before the Common Appeal Court, as envisaged by the Community Patent Convention (which is not yet in force).

Where appropriate, a comparison has been made between the jurisprudence of the Boards of Appeal and the law as stated by the courts in the United Kingdom.

In this connection, however, an important difference between the system of precedent applied within the Boards of Appeal and that applied by courts within the United Kingdom must be noted. A conventional textbook of national law in the United Kingdom would normally attempt to state the law as at a particular date, having regard to judgments issued prior to that date. This is possible because of the system of precedent which operates within the United Kingdom, whereby a court is bound to follow previous judgments on a point of law, not only of higher courts within the United Kingdom, but effectively also of courts at the same level. In contrast, within the European Patent Office, and under the European Patent Convention, individual Boards of Appeal are not bound to follow previous decisions of other Boards of Appeal on a point of law; they normally will, but they may not. Even the first instance departments of the European Patent Office are not bound under the Convention to follow previous decisions of the Boards of Appeal on points of law, although they almost always do. The function of the Enlarged Board of Appeal is to "ensure uniform application of the law" through its decisions. The system of precedent provided under the Convention by the Enlarged Board of Appeal and its relationship with individual Boards of Appeal is discussed further in Chapter 4.

Nevertheless, as discussed in Chapter 1, the individual decisions of the Boards of Appeal provide an essential guide to the system of law and practice under the European Patent Convention.

A Note on the Identification of Decisions

Every decision issued by a Board of Appeal is identified by a letter, a number and the year in which is was issued. The different categories of decision issued by the Boards of Appeal with which this book is concerned are identified by letters as follows:

Enlarged Board of Appeal	— G
Legal Board of Appeal	— J
Technical Boards of Appeal	— T

Almost every decision issued by a Board of Appeal is also identified by a "headword", consisting of the name of the applicant or patentee, and a short title.

The European Patent Office has adopted the practice of referring to individual decisions generally by number, rather than by headword or name of the applicant or patent proprietor. This practice has been followed in the text of this book. In the United Kingdom, however, by long tradition, legal judgments are identified by the names of the parties. Following this tradition, decisions of the Boards of Appeal are commonly referred to and identified in the United Kingdom by the name of the applicant or patentee, rather than by their numbers.

In order to help the identification of individual decisions referred to in this book, every numbered decision in the text is referred to in a footnote with its headword and with a reference to its place of publication, if any. Decisions which have not been published either in the Official Journal or in the European Patent Office Reports are accompanied by their date of issue. A decision which is scheduled for publication in the Official Journal but is not yet so published is additionally marked with a (P).

The tables of EPO cases at the beginning of the book correlate the numbers of the decisions with their headwords. The decisions are set out first in numerical and then in alphabetical order so that references may be located whether one knows the number or only the name of a particular decision. Tables of cases are also provided at the end of each chapter to facilitate finding decisions within the particular subject area of that chapter.

CONTENTS

CHAPTERS

TABLE OF CASES

Enlarged Board of Appeal Cases

Chronological and Numerical Order

Board of Appeal Cases—Legal Board

Chronological and Numerical Order

Board of Appeal Cases—Technical Boards

Chronological and Numerical Order

Enlarged Board of Appeal Cases

Alphabetical Order

Board of Appeal Cases—Legal Board

Alphabetical Order

Board of Appeal Cases—Technical Boards

Alphabetical Order

European National and European Cases

TABLE OF STATUTES

lv

TABLE OF TREATIES, CONVENTIONS AND PROTOCOLS

TABLE OF DIRECTIVES AND REGULATIONS

TABLE OF ABBREVIATIONS

1989 Agreement	Agreement Relating to Community Patents (Luxembourg, December 1989)
All E.R.	All England Reports
BGH	Bundesgerichtshof, German Federal Court of Justice
Brussels	Brussels Convention on Jurisdiction and the Enforcement of Judgments
Budapest	Budapest Treaty on the International Recognition of the Deposit of Micro-organisms
CA	Court of Appeal (U.K.)
Ch.	Law Reports, Chancery Division
C.M.L.R.	Common Market Law Reports
COPAC	Common Appeal Court (under CPC)
CPC	Community Patent Convention
EPC	European Patent Convention
EPO	European Patent Office
E.P.O.R.	European Patent Office Reports
F.S.R.	Fleet Street Law Reports
G	Prefix to EPO Decision numbers indicating Enlarged Board of Appeal Decisions
GRUR	Gewerblicher Rechtsschutz und Urheberrecht (The Protection of Industrial Property and Copyright)
Guidelines	Guidelines for Examination in the EPO
HL	House of Lords (U.K.)
ISA	International Search Authority
IPEA	International Preliminary Examination Authority
J	Prefix to EPO Decision numbers indicating Legal Board of Appeal Decisions
Lloyds Rep.	Lloyds List Reports
O.J. EPO	Offical Journal of the EPO
(P)	Used in case citations to indicate that a Decision is due to be published in the O.J. EPO
Paris	Paris Convention for the Protection of Industrial Property
PCT	Patent Co-operation Treaty
Protocol	CPC Protocol on Litigation
RPBA	Rules of Procedure of the Boards of Appeal
R.P.C.	Reports of Patent, Design and Trade Mark Cases
RPEBA	Rules of Precedure of the Enlarged Board of Appeal
Strasbourg	Strasbourg Convention on the Unification of Certain Points of Substantive Law on Patents for Invention
T	Prefix to EPO Decision numbers indicating Technical Boards of Appeal Decisions
1949 U.K. Act	Patents Act 1949 (12, 13 & 14 Geo. 6, c. 87)
1977 U.K. Act	Patents Act 1977 (c. 37)

UPOV Convention	International Convention for the Protection of New Varieties of Plants
Vienna	Vienna Convention on the Law of Treaties
WIPO	World Intellectual Property Organisation
W.L.R.	Weekly Law Reports

CHAPTER 1

INTERPRETATION OF THE EUROPEAN PATENT CONVENTION

Contents

All references are to paragraph numbers

1

Cases Referred to in Chapter 1

A. Introduction

The European patent system has so far been primarily concerned with the **1–01** granting of European patents and, therefore, with their validity, but not with their enforcement. It is based upon the codification of patent law which came into force in 1977 as the European Patent Convention,[1] which provides the main structure for this book. The main objects of the EPC are:

> "to strengthen co-operation between the States of Europe in respect of the protection of inventions, ... that such protection may be obtained in those States by a single procedure for the grant of patents and by the establishment of certain standard rules governing patents so granted".

Such co-operation and standardisation inevitably involves each Contracting State giving up, to some extent, the right to determine exactly what the law is, even though such law affects the legal rights within each Contracting State. The codification of law which is embodied in the EPC is necessarily the result of compromise, and its roots are based in a joint European interest rather than individual national interest.

Ratification of the EPC does not bind a Contracting State to bring its **1–02** national law into conformity with the EPC. However, most of the 19 current Contracting States, including the United Kingdom, have changed their national laws so that they do so conform. Thus the United Kingdom Patents Act 1977 (the "1977 U.K. Act") replaced the earlier 1949 Patents Act and came into effect in 1978 *inter alia* in order to "establish a new law of patents" and "to give effect to certain international conventions on patents", in particular the EPC. The EPC has not only caused a change in the written law as set out in the Patents Act, however. Its impact is also felt upon the way in which such written law is interpreted by the courts.

Before 1978, the United Kingdom patent law stretched steadily backwards through statutes and cases to its staring point at the Statute of Monopolies in 1623. Each Contracting State similarly had its own separate national patent law. The European patent system under the EPC has essentially rendered such earlier national laws obsolete, except to the extent that such earlier national laws may throw light upon the proper interpretation of the EPC and corresponding current national laws.

When considering the relationship between the new European patent **1–03** law and previous national laws, Lord Denning's vivid metaphor concerning the relationship of the Treaty of Rome to English law comes naturally to mind: "... the Treaty is like an incoming tide. It flows into the estuaries and up the rivers. It cannot be held back." (*H.P. Bulmer Ltd v. J. Bollinger SA.*)[2]

As far as European patent law is concerned, the flow is in both

---

[1] Convention on the Grant of European Patents (European Patent Convention)—signed Munich, 1973; reproduced in full at Appendix 1 with proposed revised text in Appendix 1a. Herein referred to as the EPC.
[2] [1975] R.P.C. 321, CA.

directions. Aspects of various previous national patent laws (including much German and somewhat less English law) have been fed into European patent law. Some provisions of European patent law as codified in the EPC have been taken from previous national laws with virtually no modification. Other provisions of the EPC have been derived from previous national laws, but with considerable modification, and still others are entirely new. Basically, then, the system of patent law under the EPC can be regarded as a new piece of legislation with mixed parentage. This new legislation has to be assimilated into the national patent laws in each Contracting State.

B. The European Patent Convention and its Associated Legislation

(1) The European Patent Organisation: the EPO and the Administrative Council

1–04 The EPC establishes a European Patent Organisation which consists of the European Patent Office (EPO) and the Administrative Council (Article 4 (1) and (2) EPC) and which has administrative and financial autonomy (Article 4(1) EPC). According to Article 4(3) EPC "The task of the Organisation shall be to grant European patents. This shall be carried out by the EPO supervised by the Administrative Council."

The EPO is directed by its President, who is responsible for its activities to the Administrative Council (Article 10 EPC), and is administratively organised as five Directorates-General (DG). The five Directorates-General are DG 1 (Search) DG 2 (Examination/opposition), DG 3 (Appeals), DG 4 (Administration) and DG 5 (Legal/International affairs). Each Directorate-General has a Vice-President, and all five are within the responsibility of the President, and assist him in directing the EPO (Article 10(3) EPC), subject to the very important exceptions with respect to the Boards of Appeal regarding their independence as discussed hereafter.

The European Patent Organisation is primarily responsible for implementation of the EPC. The EPO is responsible for the interpretation of the EPC in relation to the granting of European patents. The Administrative Council and the President of the EPO have some legislative powers under the EPC, as discussed below.

(2) Legislation by and under the EPC

(a) Legislative components of the EPC

1–05 According to Article 164(1) EPC, the Rules of the Implementing Regulations (commonly referred to as the "Rules"), the Protocol on Recognition, the Protocol on Privileges and Immunities, the Protocol on Centralisation and the Protocol on the Interpretation of Article 69 EPC are all integral parts of the EPC.

According to Article 164(2) EPC, in the case of conflict between the provisions of the EPC itself, (*i.e.* Articles 1 to 178 EPC) and those of the Rules, the provisions of the EPC itself shall prevail.

(b) Amendment of the EPC

(1) The EPC itself, and its Protocols. According to Article 172 EPC, the **1–06** EPC may be revised by a Conference of the Contracting States, which is prepared and convened by the Administrative Council. In order to be validly constituted, at least three-quarters of the Contracting States must be represented at such a conference. In order to adopt a revised text, there must be a majority of three-quarters of those Contracting States who are represented and who vote at the Conference. Abstentions are not considered as votes.

Since the EPC entered into force, the first such Conference took place in December 1993, at which Article 63 EPC was amended. A further such Conference took place in November 2000 and proposals for the revision of the EPC have been published. Further such Conferences are planned in the coming years.[3]

According to Article 33(1)(a) EPC, the Administrative Council is competent to amend the time limits laid down in the EPC. This general power of amendment of time limits is qualified in that the time limit for filing a request for examination under Article 94 EPC may only be amended by the Administrative Council under the condition laid down in Article 95 EPC (namely "if it is established that European patent applications cannot be examined in due time").

According to the proposed revision of the EPC, the above qualification of **1–06A** Article 33(1)(a) EPC concerning Article 94 EPC will be removed.

(2) The Implementing Regulations (the "Rules"). According to Article **1–07** 33(1)(b) EPC, the Administrative Council is competent to amend the Rules of the Implementing Regulations. Many such amendments have been made.

(c) Subordinate legislation under the EPC: the Ancillary Regulations

(i) Powers of the Administrative Council. According to Article 33(2) **1–08** EPC, the Administrative Council is competent, in conformity with the EPC, to adopt and to amend the following provisions:

(a) the Financial Regulations;
(b) the Service Regulations and related provisions;
(c) the Pension Scheme Regulations and increases in pensions;
(d) the Rules relating to Fees;
(e) its Rules of Procedure.

The Rules relating to Fees were first passed in October 1977, and have been amended by the Administrative Council many times since then.

[3] See Appendix 24.

1–09   **(ii) Powers of the President of the EPO.** The EPC delegates to the President of the EPO, either directly or through subordinate legislation adopted by the Administrative Council, extensive power to issue "decisions" and "notices", and to make agreements, which govern the activities of the EPC and consequently have the character of subordinate legislation implementing the EPC.

(d) Publication of the Ancillary Regulations

1–10 A comprehensive collection of regulations implementing the EPC is published by the EPO. This mainly contains:

(i) Decisions of the Administrative Council.
(ii) Decisions and communications of the President of the EPO.
(iii) Legal Advice from the EPO.
(iv) Agreements between the EPO and national offices or WIPO.[4]

C. Other Related Sources of European Patent Law

1–11 Current European patent law has as its main source the series of international conventions or treaties (especially the EPC) by which the Member States have agreed upon a common codification of various provisions of patent law. The manner of interpretation of such internationally agreed law has itself been codified in the Vienna Convention on the Law of Treaties (see paragraph 1–58 below).[5]

The primary sources of European patent law are as follows.

(1) International Conventions relating to the EPC

1–12 The essential background to international patent law is the Paris Convention.[6] The essential background to substantive European patent law is the Strasbourg Convention.[7] The Patent Co-operation Treaty[8] is internationally procedurally important. The Community Patent Convention[9] (CPC) was conceived at the same time as and in parallel with the EPC but it is not yet in force and its future is still uncertain (see Chapter 14).

The main contents of these international Conventions, and their

---

[4] World Intellectual Property Organisation.
[5] Convention on the Law of Treaties—signed Vienna, 1969; see Appendix 18. Herein referred to as the Vienna Convention.
[6] Convention for the Protection of Industrial Property—signed Paris, 1883, amended Stockholm, 1967; Appendix 14 contains those parts of this Convention which are relevant to patents. Herein referred to as the Paris Convention.
[7] Convention on the Unification of Certain Points of Substantive Law on Patents for Invention—signed Strasbourg, 1963; reproduced in full at Appendix 16. Herein referred to as the Strasbourg Convention.
[8] Patent Co-operation Treaty—signed Washington, 1970. Herein referred to as the PCT.
[9] Convention for the European Patent for the Common Market (Community Patent Convention)—signed Luxembourg, 1975, amended Luxembourg, 1985 and 1989; reproduced in full at Appendix 19. Herein referred to as the CPC.

relationship to the EPC, will be discussed in section D, paragraphs 1–27 *et seq.* below.

(2) The Guidelines

The "Guidelines for Examination in the European Patent Office" (the **1–13** Guidelines) are published by and obtainable from the EPO. They were adopted by the President of the EPO in accordance with his functions and powers as set out in Article 10(1)(a) EPC, *i.e.* that "he shall take all necessary steps, including … the publication of guidance for the public, to ensure the functioning of the EPO". They became effective on June 1, 1978, the day when the EPO commenced operation, and have been amended on a number of occasions since then. During the initial years of operation of the EPO, in conjunction with the text of the EPC itself and the "working papers" leading to the EPC, the Guidelines represented virtually the only guide to the practical working of the European patent system within the EPO. They were, therefore, vital to the functioning of this new system at first instance, because they provided the initial flesh upon the bones of the system set out in the EPC. As first published, they represented an initial statement of interpretation of all the practical aspects of the EPC.

Subsequent revised editions of the Guidelines (the latest having been published in July 1999 and amended in May 2000) continue to represent the basic practice of the first instance departments of the EPO, and normally such departments can be expected to follow what is there set out, so far as applicable to a particular case. As mentioned above, they are frequently amended, particularly in response to practical experience within the first instance departments, in response to changes in the Articles and Rules of the EPC (under the authority of the Administrative Council, see Article 33 EPC), and in response to decisions of the Boards of Appeal.

The relationship between the Guidelines and first instance departments (in this particular case, the Examining Division), and the role of the Boards of Appeal in relation to the contents of the Guidelines, has been summarised as follows:

"[A Board of Appeal's] position with regard to the Guidelines for Examination is governed by Article 23(3) EPC. In application of that Article, the Guidelines do not bind any Board of Appeal. Article 15(2) of the Rules of Procedure of the Boards of Appeal prescribes only that if in its decision, a Board gives a different interpretation of the Convention to that provided for in the Guidelines, it shall state the grounds for its action if it considers that this decision would be more readily understood in the light of such grounds. A knowledge of the Guidelines is therefore presupposed but they are not binding upon any Board of Appeal. The question whether an Examining Division has applied the Guidelines correctly or not in a particular case is, however, quite different. As is stated in the introduction to them, the Guidelines should be considered only as general instructions, intended to cover normal occurrences. The Examining Division therefore has a certain discretion to depart from the general directives in a particular case. It must, however, in its actions remain within the bounds defined by the EPC. In view also of the provisions of Article 23(3) EPC that the Boards in their decisions shall comply only with the provisions of the Convention, the Board considers that its function is to judge on the facts of the case whether the Examining Division has acted in accordance with the provisions of the EPC" (T162/82).[10]

1–14 This position is recognised and set out in the General Introduction to the Guidelines:

"For the ultimate authority on practice in the EPO, it is necessary to refer firstly to the EPC itself including the Implementing Regulations [*i.e.* 'the Rules'] (together with the agreed Conference Minutes on interpretation), and secondly to the interpretation put upon the EPC by the Boards of Appeal and the Enlarged Board of Appeal."

The reference in the above statement to the necessity to refer to the agreed Conference Minutes in conjunction with the EPC itself should be qualified by reference to the discussion of the role of the preparatory documents, including such Conference Minutes, in the interpretation of the EPC at paragraph 1–83 below.

(3) Legal Advice[11]

1–15 A more detailed explanation of the practice within the EPO in certain procedural areas is given by a series of notices entitled "Legal Advice", which are published in the Official Journal of the EPO.

The purpose of such Legal Advice is not to interpret the substantive law relating to patentability, but is confined to discussing and explaining particular questions on procedural points which have been found to cause difficulties in practice. They are not intended to constitute either instructions or guidelines: each such Legal Advice explains that it is not binding on the EPO. Nevertheless, the Legal Advice notices have played, and continue to play, a useful role as an extra source of procedural law explaining the practice which can be expected from the EPO, at least in the first instance departments.

Some of the earlier notices have been superceded, for example by amendments to the EPC or Rules, and have therefore been cancelled.[12]

---

[10] T162/82 *SIGMA/Classifying areas* O.J. EPO 1987, 533.
[11] "Legal Advice" by the EPO. The headnotes and Official Journal references of all such notes which have been issued to date and which have not been cancelled are contained in Appendix 6.
[12] See O.J. EPO 1998, 359.

(4) Board of Appeal Decisions

(a) The status of decisions

As the number of decisions issued by the Boards of Appeal has increased, **1–16** and especially as the number of decisions which are published in the Official Journal has also increased, so such decisions have become the main source of law on the interpretation of the EPC, as well as being the "ultimate authority" within the EPO (see paragraph 1–14). Thus the substance of the subsequent chapters in this book is based upon and derived from such decisions—mainly, but not entirely, from decisions which have been published in the Offical Journal of the EPO.

The case law of the Boards of Appeal is normally followed within first instance departments, although it is not binding upon them. A Board of Appeal decision is only binding in respect of the particular case decided— see Article 111(2) EPC.

As discussed in Chapter 4 at paragraphs 4–02, 4–24, the Boards of Appeal have varying compositions of members of mixed nationality. Thus, decisions of the Boards of Appeal represent a fusion of European concepts of patent law.

(b) The publication of decisions

The Official Journal publishes decisions of the Boards of Appeal pursuant **1–17** to Article 129(b) EPC, which requires the EPO to publish periodically an Official Journal containing *inter alia* "any other information relevant to the EPC or its implementation".

While perhaps in legal theory all decisions of the Boards of Appeal have equal weight, whether published or unpublished in the Official Journal, nevertheless in practice a greater weight is generally attached to those decisions that are (or are scheduled to be) published in the Official Journal.

In the normal course of events, the proposal to publish a particular decision in the Official Journal is made by the Chairman of the Board concerned, in conjunction with the other members. Nevertheless, such a proposal may occasionally be varied following suggestions or consultations within the Boards of Appeal.

(c) Headnotes of published decisions

When a Board proposes to publish a particular decision, a headnote is **1–18** initially prepared within that Board.

The function of the headnote of a decision published in the Official Journal is not always intended to be the same as the function of headnotes in law reports in the United Kingdom and elsewhere. Sometimes such a headnote does contain the *ratio decidendi* of the decision: sometimes it is a considerable generalisation upon the precise reasoning of the decision in the English sense, and is set out rather in the form of a "teaching". On occasions, the headnote contains limits upon the applicability of the reasoning of the decision which are not necessary for the purpose of the decision itself, but are by way of explanation of the views of the Board that issued the decision.

As a rule, a headnote issued by a Board of Appeal is intended to emphasise the generally applicable points of law dealt with within the decision, and to make such jurisprudence more readily retrievable. At the same time, such points of law are commonly associated with the specific facts of the case so as to indicate inherent restrictions upon such generality.

While it would be clearly desirable for a more uniform approach to the contents of headnotes to be adopted by the Boards of Appeal, variations in content such as are described above are a consequence of bringing a new multinational appeal system into operation. In any event, such "official" headnotes themselves constitute an important source of law.

(d) Publication of decisions elsewhere

1–19 Decisions which are not proposed for publication in the Official Journal by the Boards responsible for issuing them may still be recognised by others as containing material which is worthy of publication. Thus, many Board of Appeal decisions which have not been published in the Official Journal have been published in English in "European Patent Office Reports" (E.P.O.R.), together with many decisions which have been (or are to be) published in the Official Journal. All decisions published in E.P.O.R. have headnotes "in the English style" in place of the "official" headnotes for such decisions in the Official Journal. In view of the provenance of the "official" headnotes, however, it would be desirable to include them in the E.P.O.R. reports.

Furthermore, many Board of Appeal decisions (both published and unpublished in the Official Journal) have been published in German in "Gewerblicher Rechtsschutz und Urheberrecht" (G.R.U.R.).

All decisions of the Boards of Appeal are published in the sense that they are made available to the public upon request, and are placed on the shelves of the library in the EPO (unless they contain confidential subject-matter).

(e) "Case Law"

1–20 An important source of reference for Board of Appeal decisions is entitled "Case Law of the Boards of Appeal of the European Patent Office", and is published by and obtainable from the EPO. The third edition (1998) covers all decisions issued between 1978 and 1997 (and includes some 1998 decisions).

The "Case Law" was developed from the annual reports of the Board of Appeal case law which have been produced and published as "special editions" forming part of the Official Journal of the EPO since 1987. It includes a summary of all the more important decisions of the Board of Appeal, both published and unpublished, and is arranged in chapters including sub-headings covering different aspects of substantive and procedural law and practice under the EPC.

(5) Decisions of national courts

The decisions and judgments of national courts of Contracting States **1–21** concerning the interpretation of their national laws are an important source of European patent law especially in cases where such national laws are similar or identical in wording and content to the corresponding parts of the EPC. However, the harmonisation of national decisions with Board of Appeal case law still raises a number of problems. In particular·

(a) only a relatively small number of national courts have issued decisions on such points of law, in comparison with the increasing number of decisions issued by the Board of Appeal;
(b) especially if only one or two national decisions on a point of law have been issued, it may be difficult for Boards of Appeal to apply such decisions;
(c) in some cases, the issued national decisions on a point of law are inconsistent;
(d) in any event, it is currently difficult to obtain information concerning relevant national decisions which have been issued in the national courts of the Contracting States (and such information, if available, may need to be translated into the official language of the EPO).

A few important national judgments and decisions concerning European patent law are published regularly in the Official Journal, but these are not comprehensive.

The relationship in law and practice between decisions of national courts and of the Boards of Appeal and the need for harmonisation in this respect is considered separately below (paragraphs 1–61 *et seq*).

(6) Previous national patent laws

As such, previous national patent laws are usually of little direct value as **1–22** an aid to interpretation of the EPC. Even when the wording of such a national law is the same as corresponding wording in the EPC, the context is different. Furthermore, it is not always easy to know whether or not a change of wording from a previous national law was intended to change the law as a matter of substance. For example, concerning the relationship between the content of the claims and that of the description of a patent application, secion 4(4) of the 1949 U.K. Act prescribed that claims "must be *fairly based* on the matter disclosed in the specification", whereas section 14(5) of the 1977 U.K. Act corresponds to Article 84 EPC and prescribes that claims "shall be *supported* by the description" (emphasis added): see paragraphs 7–83 *et seq*. below. One example where the previous German national law was used by a United Kingdom court to interpret Article 64(2) EPC and the corresponding section 64(1) of the 1977 U.K. Act is discussed in Chapter 13 at paragraph 13–24.

(7) Preparatory papers for the EPC

1–23 The preparatory papers for the EPC formed a relatively important source of law in the earlier years of operation of the EPC, because (as discussed in paragraph 1–13 above) during this period, prior to the issue of relevant decisions on the Boards of Appeal, ancillary sources of law to the EPC itself were few in number.

The current status of these preparatory papers as a source of law is discussed separately at paragraph 1–83 below, in the context of interpretation of the EPC.

(8) Commentaries

1–24 Books and commentaries on European patent law (including those by living authors) have a higher legal status and authority under the European patent system than under English law. Such works by living persons are not excluded as "inadmissible", as in English law. All such works are given appropriate weight and authority, on their merits.

A comprehensive and authoritative commentary on the EPC by Singer was first published in German in 1989 under the title *Europäisches Patentübereinkommen* (Carl Heymanns Verlag). A revised and updated English edition was written by Raph Lunzer and published in 1995 by Sweet and Maxwell. A new and expanded second edition has been written by a number of authors and edited by Margarete Singer and Dieter Stauder ("Singer/Stauder"), and has been published in German in 2000 by Carl Heymanns Verlag. A further comprehensive and authoritative commentary is contained in the sixth edition of Schulte's *Patentgesetz* (Carl Heymanns Verlag AG), to be published in 2001 in German, which is a combined commentary upon the German patent law and the EPC.

Van Empel's *The Granting of European Patents* (A. W. Sijthoff-Leyden), published in English in 1975, contains much useful information on the history leading to the implementation of the EPC in its present form, and the reasons behind many of its provisions.

(9) General principles of law

1–25 This source of law is considered separately at paragraphs 1–70 *et seq.* below.

(10) European Union Regulations and Directives

1–26 Such Regulations and Directives (under Article 95 of the E.C. Treaty) are binding upon the Member States of the European Union, but do not directly affect the provisions of the EPC or its implementation within the EPO. They are likely to be used increasingly as an effective means of changing and harmonising European patent law. In so far as such Directives contain provisions which differ to a greater or lesser extent from provisions of the EPC as interpreted by the EPO, including the Boards of Appeal, they are clearly at least highly persuasive as indicating either the need for a different interpretation of the provisions of the EPC, or the need to change such provisions.

A Regulation is binding in its entirety and directly applicable in all E.C. Member States, whereas a Directive obliges Member States to adopt all measures necessary to ensure that it is effective.

Directive 98/44[13] dated July 6, 1998 on the legal protection of biotechnological inventions has clarified, amplified and to some extent changed the provisions of Article 53 EPC. As a consequence new Rules 23b–e EPC have been added to the Implementing Regulations of the EPC by the Administrative Council, nominally under the Council's power to amend such Rules pursuant to Article 33(1)(b) EPC. The effect of the Directive and the corresponding new Rules is considered in Chapter 9 at paragraphs 9–72 *et seq.*

A further Directive concerning the patenting of computer software and business methods is planned.

Furthermore, following the Green Paper on the Community Patent and the Patent System in Europe which was issued in 1997 (see paragraph 1–53 below and Chapter 14 at paragraph 14–01), a proposal for a Community Patent Regulation has been published by the Commission of the European Union, and is currently under consultation (see paragraph 1–53 and Chapter 14 at paragraph 14–01).

D. International Conventions Relating to the EPC

(1) The Paris Convention (1883)

(a) Introduction

This was the first Convention to provide for international co-operation in **1–27** the field of industrial property law, including patent law. Although in relation to patents it deals with a relatively small number of points, it must be recognised as providing the foundation for all the later international co-operation over patent rights, in particular the EPC itself.

Furthermore, although certain of its provisions do not seem so significant now, this is partly because they have become taken for granted. For example, the provisions of Articles 2 and 3 of the Paris Convention ("Paris") concerning the reciprocal treatment of nationals of, and those with interests in, Union countries are fundamental to the international patent system as it is known today. More importantly, the priority system established by Article 4 Paris has remained central to all subsequent national and international patent legislation (as to the priority provisions of the EPC, and their interpretation by reference to Article 4 Paris, see Chapter 10).

Since 1883 there have been a series of revisions to the original text, as a result of successive Revision Conferences. The last Revision Conference

---

[13] Directive 94/44 of the European Parliament and Council of July 6, 1998 on the legal protection of biotechnological inventions, O.J. EPO 1999, 101: see Appendix 23.

took place at Stockholm in 1967. Those parts of the current Stockholm text which are most relevant to European patent law are reproduced in Appendix 14.

The value of the Paris Convention is reflected in the ever-increasing number of member countries ("Union countries"—see Article 1(1)).

Article 19 Paris provides for the making of special agreements between Union countries, "in so far as these agreements do not contravene the provisions of this Convention". This Article provided the mechanism for a number of later international Conventions, including the EPC.

(b) Provisions relating to patents—a summary

1–28 *Articles 2 and 3*—reciprocal treatment. By Article 2 Paris, Union countries must apply their own laws as regards patent protection to the nationals of other Union countries. Article 3 Paris extends this reciprocity of treatment to nationals of non-Union countries who are either domiciled in a Union country, or have "real and effective industrial or commercial establishments" in a Union country.

1–29 *Article 4*—priority. This sets out the scheme for priority rights, which is fully discussed in Chapter 10. Beyond this, however, Article 4b Paris provides for the filing of divisional applications, either if required when examination shows the presence of more than one invention, or upon an applicant's own initiative, while preserving the filing date and the right to priority. The conditions for authorisation of such divisional applications are a matter for national (and European) law: see Article 76 and Rule 25 EPC.

1–30 *Article 4 bis*—independence of national patents. This provides that patents in individual countries for the same invention shall be independent of each other "in an unrestricted sense". In particular, patents in different countries claiming priority from the same earlier application (see Chapter 10) are independent of each other both as regards validity and as regards duration.

While up until now this provision has been taken for granted as being appropriate and necessary for the protection of individual national sovereignty and interest, it would seem that in the future, as European patent law becomes more integrated (in particular, under the CPC), the independence of patents in the European Contracting States as regards the grounds for invalidation and revocation will become less important.

1–31 *Article 4 ter*—naming of inventor. The right of an inventor to be mentioned as such in his patent is incorporated into European patent law in Article 62 EPC.

1–32 *Article 4 quater*—no effect from restrictions on sale. This provision protects the right to have a national patent granted even when the national domestic legislation restricts the sale of the patented subject-matter, and provides indirect guidance as to what is not "contrary to *ordre public*" (Article 53(a) EPC, see Chapter 9 at paragraphs 9–62 *et seq.*).

Article 5—abuse of patent rights, compulsory licences.　　　**1–33**

    A.　This provides that a patent cannot be forfeited by reason of the
patentee importing the patented articles. However, abuse of the
patent right, for example by failure to work a patent in a particular
country, may be prevented under national laws by provisions for
the grant of compulsory licences, and ultimately, if compulsory
licences do not prevent such abuse, by forfeiture of the patent.

    D.　Marking of goods may not be required as a condition for patent
protection.

Article 5 bis—renewal fees. This provides that all countries must provide **1–34**
a period of at least six months' grace for the payment of renewal fees,
subject to payment of such surcharge as national laws may require.
Furthermore, national laws may provide for restoration of patents which
have lapsed through non-payment of renewal fees.

In respect of the renewal fees for European patent applications, Article
86(2) EPC provides for payment of an "additional fee" within six months of
th due date. Failure to pay a renewal fee plus the additional fee within the
six months' grace period results in the European patent application being
deemed to be withdrawn—Article 86(3) EPC. However, re-establishment
is possible under Article 122 EPC.

After grant of a European patent, the payment of renewal fees is a matter
of national law—Articles 86(4) and 141 EPC.

Article 5 ter—restrictions on infringement on vessels, etc. This provides **1–35**
that the use of patented inventions on vehicles, vessels, aircraft, etc., which
are temporarily within a particular country does not constitute infringement of patent rights within that country.

This provision is clearly in the public interest in the maintenance of
freedom of international transportation.

Article 5 quater—product-by-process patents. This is an important **1–36**
provision dealing with the rights of a patentee in respect of a process
patent, as regards the importation of products of that process.

It is here provided that such a patentee "shall have all the rights, with
regard to the imported product, that are are accorded to him by the
legislation of the country of importation, on the basis of the process patent,
with respect to products manufactured in that country".

Under the European patent system, Article 64(2) EPC provides that "if
the subject-matter of the European patent is a process, the protection
conferred by the patent shall extend to the products directly obtainable by
such process".

The provision is essentially directed to processes for the manufacture of
products as such, which is in line with the natural meaning of Article 5
quater Paris (G2, 6/88).[14]

[14] G2, G6/88 *MOBIL OIL/BAYER/Friction reducing additive* O.J. EPO 1990, 93, 114; [1990]
E.P.O.R. 73, 257.

The ultimate effect of Article 64(2) EPC is essentially that the sale and use of products made directly by a process the subject of a European patent constitutes infringement of that European patent, as well as the use of the process itself; and the rights of a European patent proprietor must be construed accordingly.

Consequently, in accordance with Article 5 *quater* Paris, a European patent proprietor must also be considered as having rights as regards the mere importation of such products into designated Contracting States.

1–37   *Article 11*—temporary protection in respect of exhibitions. This provides an obligation upon Union countries to provide "temporary protection" under their national law in respect of inventions which are exhibited at "official or officially recognised international exhibitions". Together with the priority system set out in Article 4 Paris, this was one of the basic provisions of the Paris Convention in its original 1883 version. The need to encourage international displays of the latest inventions as early as possible without loss of patent protection (provided certain conditions are fulfilled) was thus recognised as being in the international interest.

This Article leaves the means by which temporary protection is provided to national laws. Under the European system, protection is provided under Article 55 EPC for a period of up to six months prior to the filing of a European patent application in respect of the invention which is exhibited, in that such a disclosure of the invention is non-prejudicial to such an application: the disclosure "shall not be taken into consideration" under Article 54 EPC, as part of the state of the art—see Chapter 11 at paragraph 11–34 below.

1–38   *Article 12*—industrial property office. Every Union country is obliged to establish a central office and industrial property service for the publication of information concerning patents, in particular a periodical official journal containing the names of the proprietors of patents granted, with a brief designation of the inventions patented.

Under Article 129 EPC, the EPO publishes the European Patent Bulletin containing this and other prescribed information.

1–39   *Article 13*—Assembly by Union countries. Each country within the Paris Union is represented by a delegate in an Assembly. The Assembly has a large number of administrative functions, including in particular, directing the International Bureau set up as secretariat under the World Intellectual Property Organisation (WIPO) Convention (1967) in respect of the preparation of Revision Conferences. The last Revision Conference was held in Stockholm in 1967. Preparations for a further Revision Conference have been continuing since 1974.

(2) The Strasbourg Convention (1963)

(a) Historical background

This Convention ("Strasbourg") was prepared within the framework of **1–40** the Council of Europe, which was formed in 1949, and which provided the forum during the 1950s for considerable discussion of proposals for the further internationalisation of patent law. There were two possible areas of harmonisation—the procedural requirements and the substantive requirements. As to the former, by 1953 a Formalities Convention[15] was signed by a number of European States. The main provisions of this Convention were to establish the maximum requirements for obtaining a filing date for a patent application, and the maximum requirements for a patent application during later stages of its prosecution. These formal requirements have subsequently been incorporated into the EPC and the PCT, and the Contracting States to the EPC have consequently terminated the Formalities Convention as such.

As to the harmonisation of substantive requirements of patent law, during the late 1950s these were discussed in relation to the European Community and the removal of trade barriers within it. The existence of separate national patents for the same invention was seen as a mechanism whereby trade barriers could be maintained, contrary to the newly emerging European interest in a common market. Thus during the early 1960s, the first drafts for a European patent came into being, in the context of the European Community. It was at this time that considerable agreement was reached within the Community as to the future harmonisation of substantive patent law.

Although for political reasons (*i.e.* the failure of the application by the United Kingdom to join the Community in the early 1960s) the concept of a Community Patent did not mature at this stage, nevertheless, important areas of substantive patent law were agreed within the larger forum of the Council of Europe when the Strasbourg Convention was signed by nine European States. It eventually came into force on August 1, 1980.

(b) Relationship of its provisions to the EPC

The substantive provisions of the Strasbourg Convention are of basic **1–41** significance to the EPC, because they have all been incorporated into the EPC with little change of wording, as will be seen below.

The wide aims of this Convention as set out in its preamble should also be noted. In particular, it is recognised that the unification of points of substantive patent law is likely to assist industry and inventors in a European context, and not just within national boundaries for the furtherance of national interests. The preamble even recognises that unification will contribute towards the future creation of an international patent. Indeed, Article 10 Strasbourg provides that after its entry into force,

---

[15] European Convention relating to the Formalities required for Patent Applications (Formalities Convention), signed Paris, 1953.

accession is not limited to European states, but is open to any member of the Paris Convention (the preamble provides that it is a special agreement under the Paris Convention).

A comparison of the corresponding Articles of the Strasbourg Convention and the EPC is set out in the following table.

Strasbourg	EPC	Subject
1	52(1)	Patentable inventions
2	53	Exceptions to patentability
3	57	Industrial application
4(1) to (3)	54(1) to (3)	Novelty
4(4)	55	Non-prejudicial disclosures
5	56	Inventive step
6	—	(Not relevant to the EPC)
7	54(3)	Subsidiary formal aspect of novelty
8(1) and (2)	83	Disclosure of the invention
8(3)	69(1)	Extent of protection
9–14	—	(Formal matters)

The wording of each of the above substantive provisions of the Strasbourg Convention is essentially identical to the corresponding EPC provisions.

(3) The Patent Co-operation Treaty: PCT (1970)

(a) Background

1–42   Prior to the 1960s, the major need for harmonisation of national granting procedures so as to avoid the costly and time-consuming repetition of making separate applications in different countries, coupled with separate searching and examination, had been well recognised. This had indeed become the main thrust of the work done within the European Community during the early 1960s. When further progress became politically impossible in that context in about 1965, the forum shifted to the International Bureau (since 1967, the secretariat of WIPO—see paragraph 1–39), and by 1970 the PCT was both drafted and signed.

The PCT primarily provides a basis for international harmonisation and integration at the application, search and examination stages, and is essentially procedural in content. It is an international treaty, not just concerning European states, and as such does not directly form part of the developing European patent law. However, its provisions are closely interlocked with those of the EPC, in particular by virtue of Articles 150–158 EPC.

(b) Contents

1–43   Chapter I PCT, comprising Articles 3 to 30 PCT, prescribes *inter alia* the form and content of an "international application", and provides for the carrying out of an "international search" and the consequent preparation of an "international search report by an international Search Authority" (*i.e.* one of certain nominated national patent offices or the EPO). The "international publication" of an international application is required "promptly after the expiration of 18 months from the priority date of that application" (Article 21(2) PCT). The application must designate at least one Contracting State.

Chapter II PCT, comprising Articles 31 to 42 PCT, provides for the carrying out upon request of what is designated an "international preliminary examination", and the consequent preparation of an "international preliminary examination report", by an International Preliminary Examination Authority (again, one of the nominated national patent offices or the EPO).

(c) Significant provisions

1. Probably the most fundamental provision of the PCT, which **1–44** currently establishes its importance, is that set out in Article 11(3) PCT, namely that the filing date of the international patent application filed under the PCT "shall be considered to be the actual filing date in each designated State".

This provision carries the concept of priority originally developed by the Paris Convention a step further. Whereas the Paris Convention provides for the automatic existence of a priority right attaching to a patent application whenever filed in a Union Country, for a period of 12 months thereafter, the PCT provides an applicant under the PCT with an automatic right to convert his international application (which may itself claim priority under the Paris Convention) into a national application within 20 months from the priority date of the international application. By this stage, the applicant has received the International Search Report made under Articles 15 to 18 PCT and is accordingly in a position to make further decisions as to the scope of his invention and the extent of international protection required.

2. In theory, the international search report prepared under Chapter **1–45** I PCT could provide the basis for all further substantive examination of an application. In practice, a further search is made in the patent offices of countries which carry out an examination of a patent examination. Thus, there is at present no mutual international recognition of international search reports prepared under the PCT.

3. Furthermore, in theory, a substantive examination such as that **1–46** carried out under Chapter II PCT could provide a universal basis for subsequent decisions concerning the grant of patents in designated Contracting States. However, the provisions of the PCT in this respect are somewhat tentative. The examination under Chapter II PCT is specifically referred to as a "preliminary"

examination, and is merely optional for international applicants using the PCT. Its objective is "to formulate a preliminary and non-binding opinion" on the novelty, inventive step, and industrial applicability of the subject-matter of the application (Article 33(1) PCT). In practice, there is no mutual recognition between patent offices of the content of a preliminary examination report.

(4) The European Patent Convention: EPC (1973)

Historical context and significant concepts

1–47   Between 1968 and 1973, work on the harmonisation of the European patent system was resumed, greatly stimulated by the signing of the PCT. A number of highly significant concepts emerged at this stage, which ensured the international acceptability of the EPC and enabled the current European system to be brought into effect:

1–48   **(1) The two-Conventions concept.** As will be apparent, pressure for greater unification of the European patent system was occurring both inside and outside the European Community. With the envisaged enlargement of the Community, the interests of countries (such as the United Kingdom) not yet within it could not be ignored. Thus the finalisation of a Community patent system became less pressing than the conclusion of a Convention which would harmonise the granting procedure and provide for centralised examination. The development of two Conventions in parallel thus emerged—the EPC and the CPC.

1–49   **(2) The concept of the coexistence of European Conventions with national laws.** Starting from the concept of a Community patent, it was recognised at an early stage that the Member States could not realistically at a single instant abandon their separate national systems and accept a Community system in their place. The proposed coexistence of a Community patent with national patents was then extended to the coexistence also of a European examination and granting procedure with existing national granting procedures.

The coexistence of the European patent system with existing national systems has been generally recognised as the main reason for its international acceptability.

1–50   **(3) The "bundle of patents" concept.** The unification of the examination and granting procedure in turn led to the concept of conversion of such European-examined patents at grant into individual national patents, to be thereafter administered and enforced within national jurisdictions. This concept is fundamental to the EPC as it emerged.

In this way, Contracting States to the EPC could regard the EPC essentially as a means to overcome the problem of multiple national applications which previously existed, while maintaining a level of sovereignty over the "national" patents so granted.

(4) The concept of early publication. The EPC includes as part of its **1–51**
procedural scheme the requirement for early publication of a European
patent application, namely "as soon as possible after the expiry of a period
of 18 months from the date of filing, or, if priority has been claimed, as from
the date of priority" (Article 93 EPC).

This requirement is in contrast to previous European national patent
laws, and has far-reaching significance:

(a) It serves the highly important function of making the information
contained in European patent applications available at an early
stage.

(b) However, since a decision concerning the possible grant of a
European patent can rarely be made so quickly, an applicant for a
European patent is in effect forced to publish the subject-matter of
his application without knowing whether his application will be
successful: it must become a hostage to fortune.

(c) Publication of the application before the scope of the claims is
finalised is nevertheless effectively a notification to the public that
any subject-matter disclosed in a patent application (but *only* such
disclosed subject-matter) may eventually become protected by
the patent as granted.

(5) The Community Patent Convention: CPC (1975)

(a) Historical background and present status

The initial work upon a Common Market patent began at an early stage **1–52**
among the original six members of the Community, as mentioned above in
the context of the Strasbourg Convention. By 1962 a draft Community
Convention had been prepared but, for the political reasons mentioned in
paragraph 1–40, no further progress was possible at that time.

During the preparatory work on the EPC between 1968 and 1973, work
upon the concept of a Community patent was resumed, and the need to
conclude a second Convention to follow the EPC and to bring such a patent
into being was agreed between the Member States of the Community in
1969.

The Community Patent Convention was signed in Luxembourg in 1975
by the then nine Member States, but for political reasons relating to certain
Member States the CPC did not then come into force.

A Conference took place in Luxembourg in 1985, with the intention that **1–53**
the text of the Convention should be finalised in a form in which it could
enter into force, but essentially the same political reasons again prevented
real progress being made in this respect.

An "Agreement relating to Community Patents" dated December 15,
1989 (the "1989 Agreement") was established at a conference in Luxembourg in 1989. This 1989 Agreement was signed by all the Member States,
but was not ratified by a sufficient number of States to enter into force.

A Green Paper on the Community patent and the patent system in

Europe was issued by the European Commission in 1997. A proposal for a Community Patent Regulation has recently been published (see Chapter 14 at paragraph 14–01).

(b) Significant provisions in relation to the EPC

1–54 The main significance of a Community patent granted under the CPC in comparison with a European patent granted under the EPC is the fact that whereas a European patent on grant has the effect of a bundle of national patents (paragraph 1–50 above), a Community patent upon grant becomes a single unitary supra-national patent covering (eventually) all the Member States of the European Community. In this way, the Community patent is intended to take its place within the general structure of Community Law.

The CPC builds upon the essentially pre-grant harmonisation and integration of European patent law provided by the EPC, and continues such integration during the full life of a Community patent after grant.

Thus the EPC and the CPC were intended to be to a large extent complementary to one another, and the contents of each were originally drafted with the other in mind. This is a relevant factor in relation to the interpretation of some aspects of the EPC (see for example paragraph 3–11).

(6) The TRIPS Agreement, 1994[16]

1–55 This Agreement has created and strengthened the international obligations of Member States to provide a minimum level of intellectual property protection and enforcement. Some of the main provisions relating to patents are clearly derived from the corresponding provisions of the EPC: for example, the provisions in Article 27 concerning patentable subject-matter.

In relation to the revocation of patents, Article 32 provides that "An opportunity for judicial review of any decision to revoke or forfeit a patent shall be available." Compliance with this provision by the appeal system under the EPC has been questioned and challenged, notably in *Lenzing AG's European Patent (U.K.)*[17]; but the challenge was dismissed, because of the lack of direct effect of the TRIPS Agreement, and because of the effect of the EPC, but also because "the Boards of Appeal of the EPO do provide a means of judicial review within Article 32 of TRIPS".

(7) Conclusion

1–56 The above historical summary of the significant international Conventions leading up to and including the EPC and the CPC is not simply a matter of academic interest, but demonstrates the very different legal background of

---

[16] Agreement on Trade-Related Aspects of Intellectual Property Rights: partly reproduced in Appendix 22.
[17] [1997] R.P.C. 245.

the EPC (and of the corresponding provisions of the 1977 U.K. Act), as compared to previous statutory provisions of United Kingdom and other national patent laws.

Recognition of the existence of this different, international, background to the codified provisions of European patent law is essential to an understanding of the interpretation of the provisions of the EPC and their national counterparts, and of the way in which such interpretation is currently developing.

Furthermore, the summary demonstrates the slow but steady tendency towards harmonisation and integration of patent law, both in respect of the rationalisation of procedure and in respect of substantive requirements for patentability.

E. Interpretation of the EPC

(1) Introduction

In interpreting the provisions of the EPC, a basic difference from the **1–57** interpretation of a United Kingdom statute such as the 1949 U.K. Act has to be recognised. Under English law, there exists a well developed body of law in accordance with which a United Kingdom statute has to be construed. No such body of law exists which can be applied to the interpretation of an international treaty such as the EPC. Some relevant international law exists, but this area of law is in an early stage of development.

(2) The Vienna Convention (1969)

Articles 31 to 33 of this Convention ("Vienna") contain a clear and **1–58** relatively concise statement as to how a treaty such as the EPC should be interpreted (see Appendix 18). The text of Articles 31 and 32 Vienna was summarised by the Enlarged Board of Appeal in Decision G5/83,[18] so far as concerned interpretation of the EPC, as follows:

"1. The treaty must be interpreted in good faith.
2. Unless it is established that the Contracting States intended that a special meaning should be given to a term, the terms of the treaty shall be given their ordinary meaning in their context and in the light of the object and purpose of the EPC.
3. The context, for this purpose, is:

— the text (including the Preamble and Implementing Regulations) and
— any agreement made between all the parties in connection with the conclusion of the traty (*e.g.* the Protocol to Article 69 EPC).

[18] G1, 5, 6/83 *EISAI/Second medical indication* O.J. EPO 1985, 64; [1979–85] E.P.O.R.: B: 241.

4. There shall also be taken into account:

    — any subsequent agreement between the parties regarding interpretation or application of the provisions
    — any subsequent practice which establishes the agreement of the parties regarding interpretation
    — any relevant rules of public international law.

5. The preparatory documents and the circumstances of the conclusion of the treaty may be taken into consideration:

    — in order to confirm the meaning resulting from the application of the previous rules or
    — to determine the meaning, when applying those rules either leaves the meaning ambiguous or obscure or leads to a manifestly absurd or unreasonable result."

1–59   The Vienna Convention is not specifically applicable to the EPC, because it only entered into force for a number of countries on January 27, 1980 and not for all the Contracting States to the EPC. Under Article 4 Vienna "the [Vienna] Convention applies only to treaties which are concluded by States after the entry into force of the present Convention with regard to such States".

Nevertheless, it has been widely recognised that the Vienna Convention provides a useful codification of what already was recognised as the proper approach to the interpretation of treaties under public international law, and on this basis the Boards of Appeal have applied the above Articles of the Vienna Convention to questions of interpretation of the EPC (G5/83).[19]

(3) Interpretation of the EPC in its context—in the light of its object and purpose

1–60   1. The "context", for the purpose of interpretation of the EPC, is limited in scope—see 3. above—to the following specific items:

        (i) The Preamble
        (ii) The Rules
        (iii) Agreements ancillary to the conclusion of the EPC (*e.g.* the Protocol to Article 69 EPC).

        As to (i), the wording of the Preamble my sometimes be particularly important in that it indicates the extent to which the EPC is intended to harmonise European patent law, *i.e.* by "a single procedure for the grant of patents", and by "the establishment of certain standard rules governing patents so granted". Thus the division between before and after grant is firmly

---

[19] G1, 5, 6/83 *EISAI/Second medical indication* O.J. EPO 1985, 64; [1979–85] E.P.O.R.: B: 241.

established. Whereas before grant there is a "single procedure" leading to grant (governed by the EPC), after grant only "certain standard rules" are established by the EPC: the remaining law applicable to granted patents is thus left to the Contracting States (see Article 2 EPC).

2. In interpreting provisions of the EPC in individual cases, the extent to which a Board of Appeal may take into account and be influenced by the context, object and purpose of such provisions in addition to consideration of its literal meaning depends upon various factors, including in particular whether the literal meaning is entirely appropriate to the circumstances of the case before it.

3. The "object and purpose" of the EPC can be considered as rather more broad than as specifically set out in the Preamble. Clearly a main object and purpose of the EPC is to provide an efficient, fair and workable procedure, and such considerations are often inherently taken into account.

(4) Harmonisation: an additional factor influencing interpretation

(a) Introduction

In contrast to the traditional kind of treaty regulating legal relations **1–61** between States, the EPC "directly creates and defines rights and duties for individuals and corporate bodies". For such a treaty, it is also necessary "to pay attention to questions of harmonisation of national and international rules of law" (G5/83).[20]

In other words, while the generally accepted method of interpreting international treaties as reflected in the Vienna Convention are in principle applicable to the EPC, nevertheless in appropriate circumstances the desire for harmonisation can influence the way in which the EPC is interpreted both by the Boards of Appeal and by national courts.

(b) The "second medical use" cases

G5/83 and corresponding national judgments provide a clear example of a **1–62** group of parallel cases in which the desire for harmonisation openly affected decision-making. The "second medical use" patentability question came before various national courts and the Enlarged Board of Appeal at about the same time (see Chapter 11 at paragraphs 11–105 *et seq.* below).

The Enlarged Board of Appeal. While the case was pending before the **1–63** Enlarged Board and before it had reached a decision, the German Federal Court of Justice (Bundesgerichtshof, "BGH") had decided in *Hydropyridine*[21] that in German law a claim to "the use of a substance to treat an illness" could protect a second (or further) medical use. In contrast, a

---

[20] *Ibid.*
[21] *Hydropyridine*, BGH Case No. X ZB 4/83 O.J. EPO 1984, 26.

practice statement ("Legal Advice") issued by the Swiss Federal Intellectual Property Office dated May 30, 1984[22] had recognised the patentability of a claim to "the use of a substance for the manufacture of a medicament for a second medical use" (the "swiss form of claim"). The Enlarged Board declined to follow the reasoning and conclusion of the BGH on the basis that it was difficult to follow the practice of only a single Contracting State, but observed that if other courts in other Contracting States were to follow the reasoning of the BGH the Enlarged Board might reconsider the question.

The Enlarged Board held that the "Swiss form of claim" was novel and patentable, while recognising the legal problem of interpretation that this involved (see Chapter 11 at paragraphs 11–86 *et seq.*).

Subsequently, corresponding cases were brought before the national courts in the United Kingdom and Sweden and the Appeal Division of the Dutch Patent Office, with the following results:

1–64   **The United Kingdom.** The Patents Court of the United Kingdom in *John Wyeth's Application*[23] referred to the statement of the Enlarged Board concerning the BGH *Hydropyridine*[24] decision, and specifically disagreed with the German decision. However, with regard to the Swiss form of claim, the Courts recognised that under the relevant United Kingdom law (*i.e.* sections 1–4 of the 1977 U.K. Act—see Appendix 21), the "better view" was that such a claim lacked novelty. Nevertheless, the court went on to consider and to follow the reasoning of the Enlarged Board to the effect that such a claim was novel. The entire basis of this judgment was "the desirability of achieving conformity" under the EPC and the corresponding provisions of the 1977 U.K. Act (such intended conformity being expressly recognised in section 130(7) of that Act).

1–65   **Sweden.** The Swedish Court of Patent Appeals in *Hydropyridine*[25] also recognised that "it was possible to question whether the approval of patent claims" in the Swiss form was justifiable. Nevertheless, it went on to state that:

> "Any refusal of the possibility of obtaining a [Swedish] patent on the basis of this type of claim within the field of drugs would, however, result in the extremely unfavourable situation described in the 'travaux préparatoires' to the 1978 [Swedish] legislation whereby it would be possible on the basis of differences in the conditions of patentability—or in their application—to obtain a European patent for Sweden in cases in which a national Swedish patent cannnot be granted. There are obviously good reasons why such a situation should be avoided."

---

[22] Legal Advice from the Swiss Federal Intellectual Property Office, May 30, 1984; O.J. EPO 1984, 581.
[23] *John Wyeth and Brother Ltd/Schering A.G.'s Applications* O.J. EPO 1986, 175; [1985] R.P.C. 545.
[24] See n.21 above.
[25] *Hydropyridine*, Court of Patent Appeals, Sweden, O.J. EPO 1988, 198.

The decision contained considerable discussion of the background against which Sweden acceded to the EPC, and the recognition there of the desirability of legal harmonisation for the benefit of trade, industry and inventors. A report by the Court of Patent Appeals prior to accession was referred to, which stated that "harmonisation of patent practice does not mean that national patent authorities must slavishly follow everything done at the EPO. It should thus still be possible to justify departures from the practice of the EPO on the grounds of weighty pertinent considerations."

Nevertheless, no sufficiently weighty considerations were found to be present such as to justify rejection of the Swiss form of claims to a second use. No view was expressed upon the allowability of the alternative form of claims, corresponding in form to those allowed by the German BGH.[26]

The Netherlands. The Appeal Division of the Netherlands Patent Office, **1–66** however, took a different course.[27] It recognised that uniformity of the law was desirable, but referred to an earlier decision of the Appeal Division stating that:

> "harmonisation of case law does not mean the a pronouncement by the European Patent Office concerning the construction to be put on a particular Article of the European Patent Convention would have to be followed by the Netherlands Patent Office when considering a similar situation under the (Netherlands Patents Act), simply because it happened to have been made first. Both bodies should rather take note of each other's interpretation and the arguments supporting it, so that if the interpretations differ they can try—by each weighing up the arguments of the other—to arrive at the same interpretation".

The Appeal Division had to apply the national law, which was not the same as the relevant provisions of the EPC. It referred to the established case law in Holland, whereby a requirement for novelty was that an inventive idea should be expressed concretely in the form of new measures or processes, and held that the form of claims before them could not be allowed without making further distinction from the prior art (*i.e.* they lacked novelty). It carefully analysed the above identified decisions and judgments in Germany, the United Kingdom, Sweden and in the Enlarged Board of Appeal, as well as relevant "working papers" leading to the EPC, and could not justify any other result from such analysis.

The above decisions on this point of substantive patent law give a clear indication of the fine balance between strict application of the law and European harmonisation of patent law with which the Boards of Appeal

---

[26] Following grant of a Swedish patent including the Swiss form of claims, the patent was opposed and the allowability of such claims was challenged again. The allowability of such claims was confirmed by the Supreme Administrative Court of Sweden in its Decision delivered on November 13, 1991.

[27] Decision ("Second medical use/NL") dated September 30, 1987 Appeal Division, Netherlands Patent Office, O.J. EPO 1988, 405.

and national courts are confronted. Clearly, a unified patent law is the eventual aim of the Contracting States, and this can only be achieved at the present stage of development of the European Patent System if the Boards and national courts strive for harmonisation. On the other hand, harmonisation and unification must be achieved on a correct legal basis (or at least upon a basis which is legally accepted as universally as possible).

(c) Other examples of recognition by national courts of the need for harmonisation of interpretation

1–67   **(i)**   In *Tollwutvirus*,[28] (concerning the patentability of micro-organisms *per se* and the requirements for reproducibility of such inventions—see Chapter 7 at paragraphs 7–35 *et seq.* below), the German Federal Court of Justice (BGH) stated as follows:

> "The EPO takes a different view than the former case law of this Court in conjunction with the interpretation and application of Articles 52, 53, 83 EPC which corresponds to Sections 1, 1a and 2b of the 1978 Patent Act (Sections 1, 2, 35 of the 1981 Patent Act) and allows the deposit of a sample which can be multiplied to suffice for the reproducibility of an application directed to a micro-organism as such . . .
>
> Since the harmonisation of national and European provisions of substantive patent law should serve the creation of largely identical patent law, care must also be taken that the interpretation in the national and international area be as uniform as possible. In the point of law to be decided in this case, the EPO in accordance with the preceding reasons has the better arguments and it is not to be expected that it will change its position. Thus, for reasons of a desirable uniform interpretation of the law, it appears necessary also that this Court should abandon its earlier case law under the 1978/1981 Patent Act which has been adapted to the EPC."

1–68   **(ii)**   In *Asahi Kasei Kogyo K.K.'s Application*[29] (concerning the necessity for an "enabling disclosure" in the state of the art in connection with loss of novelty—see Chapter 11 at paragraph 11–67 below), the House of Lords in the United Kingdom referred to the "considerable persuasive authority" of certain Board of Appeal and Enlarged Board of Appeal decisions, "having regard to the provisions of Section 130(7) [of the 1977 U.K. Act] and the desirability of avoiding, so far as possible, divergent jurisprudence on the interpretation of broadly parallel provisions".

1–69   **(iii)**   In *Re. N V Philips Gloeilampenfabrieken*,[30] (concerning the patentability of methods used in conjunction with computer programs—see

[28] *Tollwutvirus*, BGH Decision X ZB 4/86 O.J. EPO 1987, 429.
[29] [1991] R.P.C. 485.
[30] Supreme Administrative Court of Sweden, delivered June 13, 1990.

Chapter 9 at paragraphs 9–11 *et seq.* below), the Supreme Administrative Court of Sweden sitting *en banc*, stated that whereas previous Swedish case law had deviated from that of Board of Appeal decisions, the principles on patentability that had been expressed in the Board of Appeal decisions were consistent with the Swedish Patent Act: "Sweden's ratification of the EPC requires that the Court should, in the internal application of Swedish law and to the extent consistent with the legislation, observe the case law of the EPO in its application of corresponding provisions of the EPC."

(5) General principles of law as an aid to interpretation

(a) Introduction

A national patents act comes into force in the context of a complete system **1–70**
of law governing, *e.g.* rights of property, contractual rights, the law of tort, procedural rights and remedies, and all such matters. In contrast, a treaty such as the EPC is brought into being and exists without such a specific surrounding context; there is no specific body of international law surrounding the EPC in the way that a specific body of national law surrounds a national patents act. The concepts of international law are necessarily more elusive.

In the course of operation of the procedural and substantive law created by the EPC, issues arise from time to time to which the EPC itself provides no direct answer. Gaps in the legislative structure thus need to be filled. Furthermore, situations may arise in which the literal application of the wording of the EPC (or of the absence of wording) appears to lead to manifest unfairness. In such circumstances, it becomes necessary to rely upon what are called the "general principles of law" as an aid to interpretation of the EPC:

> "General legal principles are a recognised source of legal information and can help in the interpretation of written law. They are applied by the national courts of Contracting States to fill gaps in the law or to deviate from a strictly literal interpretation of existing provisions where such interpretation would lead to inequities" (G1/86).[31]

The most relevant analogy to this legal situation is in the context of **1–71**
European Community Law. In a similar fashion, various issues have arisen in cases before the European Court of Justice which cannot be properly answered by direct reference to Community legislation: the Court has therefore introduced the concept of such general principles of law into its jurisprudence. Reliance upon such "general principles" provides a recognisably proper foundation for the reasoning of a judgment; a fair result in a particular case may be reached on the basis of such principles in circumstances where the existing written legislation provides little guidance.

[31] G1/86 *VOEST ALPINE/Re-establishment of opponent* O.J. EPO 1987, 447; [1987] E.P.O.R. 388.

Justification for such "judicial law-making" is fairly easily derived from various provisions of the E.C. Treaty. The EPC expressly provides such a law-making power in respect of procedural matters in Article 125 EPC, which states that: "In the absence of procedural provisions in [the EPC], the EPO shall take into account the principles of procedural law generally recognised in the Contracting States."

1–72   Such general principles of law have been applied in decisions of the Boards of Appeal both:

> 1.   to aid interpretation of the EPC, and
> 2.   to justify reaching a just result in disputes arising between the EPO and parties to proceedings before it.

These two applications are really quite distinct. The second application is more closely analogous to the application of the principles of equity in English law. Nevertheless, both applications have in common the desire to justify reaching what would generally be regarded as a fair conclusion.

(b) The principle of good faith

1–73   The Boards of Appeal have used this term to describe one of the general principles of law. In Community law the term "legal certainty" is used to refer to a broad general principle of law, which includes in one aspect the principle of "legitimate expectations". This latter concept is derived from German law ("Vertrauensschutz"). According to this principle, actions (or omissions) by an institution (here the EPO) must not violate the legitimate expectations of those concerned: an expectation is not legitimate unless it is reasonable.

> "One of the general principles of law which is well established in European Community Law and which is generally recognised among the Contracting States and within the jurisprudence of the Boards of Appeal is the protection of legitimate expectations. In the present case, this principle is applicable having regard to the good faith existing between the EPO and its users. In the application of this principle to procedure before the EPO, measures taken by the EPO should not violate the reasonable expectations of parties to such proceedings" (G5/88,[32] G2/97[33]).

1–74   This principle of good faith governs the relations between the EPO and parties to EPO proceedings in relation to procedural matters laid down in the EPC and its Rules (J10/94)[34], and requires communications to be clear and unambiguous, and to be worded so as to rule out any misunderstanding on the part of a reasonable addressee (J3/87)[35]. The principle also

---

[32] G5, 7, 8/88 *MEDTRONIC/Administrative agreement* O.J. EPO 1991, 137; [1991] E.P.O.R. 225.
[33] G2/97 *UNILEVER/Good faith* O.J. EPO 1999, 123; [2000] E.P.O.R. 73.
[34] J10/84 *TEXAS/Amendments* O.J. EPO 1985, 71; [1979–85] E.P.O.R.: A: 213.
[35] J3/87 *MEMTEC/Membranes* O.J. EPO 1989, 3; [1989] E.P.O.R. 175.

applies to courtesy services provided by the EPO. Where such a service has been rendered, a party is entitled to rely upon its contents if the communication from the EPO was the direct cause of the action taken and on an objective basis, it was reasonable for the party to have been misled by the information (J27/92[36]). The principle applies to both written and oral communications (J.../87,[37] J27/92[38]).

No disadvantage to the interests of a party should result from his having been misled by conduct which could fairly to be regarded as misleading to a reasonable addressee (J.../87[39]).

For example, if "during a long period of time, the EPO by its conduct leads the parties and the public to the legitimate belief that no loss of rights has taken place, the EPO cannot later refer to a loss of rights which occurred several years previously without offending against the prohibition of '*Venire contra factum proprium*' and therefore contravening the principle of good faith" (J14/94[40]; see also J18/96[41]).

In such circumstances, the late payment of a renewal fee may—by way of exception—be considered as having been made in time, if the EPO had not informed the applicant of the outstanding payment, had accepted later renewal fees without objection, and had continued the examination proceedings for several years (J14/94[42]). **1–75**

Nevertheless, the principle of good faith does not impose any obligation upon the EPO to warn a party of procedural deficiencies within the area of the party's own responsibility, and there is no legitimate expectation for a party to receive a warning from the EPO with respect to such a deficiency (G2/97[43]).

In some cases there may be an obligation upon the EPO to warn a party of omissions or errors which could lead to a loss of rights. For example, an applicant should "have his attention drawn to deficiencies in his application for re-establishment of rights which are obviously easy to correct (fee not paid and substantially not supplied) if correction of the deficiencies can be expected within the two month time limit" (T14/89[44]: see also J13/90[45]). However, "a party may not expect a warning in respect of any deficiency occurring in the course of the proceedings" (J2/94[46]), if the documents filed by a party give no evident indication which would make a clarification or reminder necessary. For example, there is no obligation for a Board of Appeal to notify an appellant that an appeal fee is missing "if there is no indication—either in the notice of appeal or in any other **1–76**

---

[36] J27/92 *MAXTOR/Media storage system* O.J. EPO 1995, 288; [1995] E.P.O.R. 688.
[37] J.../87 *Incapacity* O.J. EPO 1988, 323; [1989] E.P.O.R. 73.
[38] J27/92. See note 36 above.
[39] J.../87 See note 37 above.
[40] J14/94 *THE EXPANDED METAL COMPANY/Principle of good faith* O.J. EPO 1995, 824; [1996] E.P.O.R. 327.
[41] J18/96 *N.N./Filing date* O.J. EPO 1998, 403; [1999] E.P.O.R. 327.
[42] J14/94. See note 40 above.
[43] G2/97 *UNILEVER/Good faith* O.J. EPO 1999, 123; [2000] E.P.O.R. 73.
[44] T14/89 *UHDE/Re-establishment* O.J. EPO 1990, 432; [1990] E.P.O.R. 656.
[45] J13/90 *CASTLETON/Omitted payment not completed* O.J. EPO 1994, 456; [1994] E.P.O.R. 76.
[46] J2/94 *UCFE (FRANCE)/Restitution* [1998] E.P.O.R. 195.

document filed in relation to the appeal—from which it could be inferred that the appellant would, without such notification inadvertently miss the time limit for payment of the appeal fee" (G2/97,[47] which reviews previous relevant decisions; see also T161/96[48] in relation to under payment of the opposition fee).

(c) Equality of treatment

1–77   "The Contracting States to the EPC recognise the principle that all parties to proceedings before a court must be accorded the same procedural rights ... this derives from the general principle of equality before the law and thus before the courts which administer that law" (G1/86[49]).

(d) The right to a fair hearing

1–78   There are various aspects to the concept of a fair hearing:

1–79   **(1) Right to be informed of and comment upon the case to be met.** In one aspect, namely the right of a party to be informed of and to comment upon the case it has to meet, the right to a fair hearing is one of the recognised general principles of law accepted by the European Court of Justice. The Court has stated as a general rule of Community law that "a person whose interests are perceptibly affected by a decision taken by a public authority must be given the opportunity to make his point of view known".[50]

The principle is specifically reflected in Article 113(1) EPC, which states that:

> "The decisions of the EPO may only be based on grounds or evidence on which the parties concerned have had an opportunity to present their comments, and which is of fundamental importance for ensuring a fair procedure between the EPO and parties conducting proceedings before it" (G4/92,[51] J20/85,[52] J3/90[53]).

"(The) term grounds or evidence in Articles 113(1) EPC should not be narrowly interpreted" (T951/92[54]). In particular, the word "grounds" should be interpreted as referring to the essential reasoning, both legal and factual, which may lead to a loss of rights by a party. Article 113(1) EPC is intended to ensure that before an adverse decision is issued, a party has been clearly informed by the EPO of the essential legal and factual reasons on which such an adverse decision may be based, so that he may have a

---

[47] G2/97 *UNILEVER/Good faith* O.J. EPO 1999, 123; [2000] E.P.O.R. 73.
[48] T161/96 *MALLINKRODT/Underpayment of opposition fee* O.J. EPO 1996, 331; [1999] E.P.O.R. 388.
[49] G1/86 *VOEST ALPINE/Re-establishment of opponent* O.J. EPO 1987, 447; [1987] E.P.O.R. 388.
[50] *Transocean Marine Paint Association v. European Commission* (Case 17/74) [1974] E.C.R. 1063.
[51] G4/92 *PRESIDENT OF THE EPO/Basis of decisions* O.J. EPO 1994, 149; [1994] E.P.O.R. 392.
[52] J20/85 *ZENITH/Missing claims* O.J. EPO 1987, 102; [1987] E.P.O.R. 157.
[53] J3/90 *FISHER SCIENTIFIC/Postal strike* O.J. EPO 1991, 550; [1992] E.P.O.R. 148.
[54] T951/92 *NEC/Opportunity to comment* O.J. EPO 1996, 53; [1996] E.P.O.R. 371.

proper opportunity to comment upon such reasons or otherwise to take appropriate action to avoid such an adverse decision (see also paragraph 5–73).

Numerous Board of Appeal decisions have relied upon Article 113(1) EPC when deciding whether there has been a "substantial procedural violation" within the meaning of Rule 67 EPC during proceedings before the EPC (see Chapter 4 at paragraphs 4–169 *et seq.*). For example:

> "Due process of law required by Article 113 EPC has not been applied when a decision to refuse an application is based essentially on documents which, though supplied by the applicant in support of his case, are used against him to produce an effect on which he has not had an opportunity to make observations" (T18/81[55]).

Similarly, the fundamental principle set out in Article 113(1) EPC "is not **1–80** observed in a case in which the EPO has made an examination of the facts of its own motion (under Article 114(1) EPC) unless the parties concerned have been fully informed about the enquiries made and the results thereof and then given sufficient opportunity to present their comments before any decision is issued" (J3/90[56]).

Furthermore, any investigation of facts by the EPO of its own motion must be done "in a wholly objective manner".

The right to be heard under Article 113(1) EPC may be surrendered by a party, for example if a party declares *"that it will take no further part in the proceedings"*. Such a declaration:

> "can ... only be construed as [the party's] unequivocal decision to voluntarily surrender their rights laid down in Article 113(1) and to no longer avail themselves of the opportunity to present their comments on any objections, facts, grounds of evidence which could potentially be introduced into the proceedings by [another party] or the Board and which could later turn out to be decisive for the revocation of the patent, *even if they were given the opportunity to do so"* (T892/94[57]: see also Chapter 5 at paragraph 5–64).

(2) An impartial tribunal—the rule against bias. This is another aspect **1–81** of the right to a fair hearing. Article 24 EPC contains relevant provisions as regards the Boards of Appeal; this matter is discussed further in relation to the first instance departments and the Boards of Appeal in Chapter 5 at paragraphs 5–18 *et seq.*

(e) Duty to give reasons

This is one of the general principles of law recognised in Community law. **1–82**
The EPC expressly requires that all decisions issued by the EPO, both at

---

[55] T18/81 *SOLVAY/Olefin polymers* O.J. EPO 1985, 86, 166; [1979–85] E.P.O.R.: B: 325.
[56] J3/90 *FISHER SCIENTIFIC/Postal strike* O.J. EPO 1991, 550; [1992] E.P.O.R. 148.
[57] T892/94 *ROBERTET/Deodorant compositions* O.J. EPO 2000, 1; [1999] E.P.O.R. 516.

first instance (Rule 68(2) EPC) and by the Boards of Appeal (Rule 66(2) EPC) shall be written and shall include reasons.

In particular:

> "When a decision hinges upon the exercise of a discretion, the reasons should be given. In accordance with general principles of law, such discretion must be exercised having regard to the factors which are relevant to the issue in question. Thus, such reasons should take into account those factors which are legally relevant to the issue in question, and should not simply consider whether the facts of the case are exactly the same as in a previously decided case. Such factors are determined by considering the purpose of the exercise of the discretion in its context, and in the context of the EPC as a whole" (T182/88[58]).

(f) The principle of proportionality

1–82a "In accordance with general principles of law, as applied in the context of administrative law, a procedural means used to achieve a given end (*e.g.* a sanction following a procedural non-compliance) should be no more than that which is appropriate and necessary to achieve that end; this is commonly referred to as the principle of proportionality" (T869/90,[59] T111/92[60]).

This principle has occasionally been referred to in the context of applications for re-establishment (See Chapter 6 at paragraph 6–60).

(6) The preparatory documents of the EPC as a supplementary aid to its interpretation

1–83 As the Vienna Convention recognises (see paragraph 1–58 above), the preparatory papers of the EPC (the preliminary drafts, minutes of conferences, etc.) are a legitimate aid to the interpretation of the EPC in certain circumstances. In the initial years after the EPO entered into force, there was naturally a tendency within the EPC to rely heavily upon such preparatory documents when interpreting the EPC.

However, the limited circumstances in which it is proper to take such documents into consideration are set out in Article 32 Vienna, and the importance of preliminary drafts and working papers leading to the EPC should not be over-emphasised when considering how it should be interpreted (G1/84,[61] T26/88[62]).

The approach in Article 32 Vienna

> "... obviously accords with common sense, in that the text of a treaty is

---

[58] T182/88 *UNIVERSITY OF CALIFORNIA/Dimeric oligopeptides* O.J. EPO 1990, 287; [1989] E.P.O.R. 147.

[59] T869/90 TEXACO/Restitution [1994] E.P.O.R. 581.

[60] T111/92 *SONY/Restitution*, August 3, 1992 .

[61] G1/84 *MOBIL OIL/Opposition by proprietor* O.J. EPO 1985, 299; [1986] E.P.O.R. 39.

[62] T26/88 AKZO/Automatic revocation O.J. EPO 1991, 30; [1990] E.P.O.R. 21.

the primary source of law, and that is what tells practitioners and the public what the law is.

The working papers are not widely available. If the Convention itself can be sensibly interpreted so as to lead to a clear, fair and practically workable result which is in accordance with its object and purpose, recourse to the working papers is normally unnecessary. In any event, it is to be recognised that passages in the working papers leading up to a treaty may sometimes be misleading in relation to the proper interpretation of that treaty as finally agreed.

It is to be noted that the European Court of Justice has very rarely had recourse in its judgments to the working papers leading to the various treaties and conventions which it has to interpret.

In accordance with the generally accepted international practice referred to above, judgments of the European Court of Justice commonly interpret treaties such as the Treaty of Rome in the light of its object and purpose. In the Board's view, this approach should normally be followed when interpreting the EPC" (T26/88[63]).

Occasionally, however, the preparatory papers provide a valuable source in order either to solve an ambiguity, or to confirm the proper interpretation of its wording. One recent example of a decision of the Enlarged Board of Appeal which did rely upon the background surrounding the drafting of the EPC, including the preparatory papers, is G1/98[64] which is concerned, *inter alia* with interpretation of the term "plant varieties" (see Chapter 9 at paragraph 9–88).

F. Interpretation of United Kingdom National Patent Law in the Light of the EPC

Section 130(7) of the 1977 U.K. Patents Act contains a well-known and **1–84** unusual provision which is as follows:

"Whereas by a resolution made on the signature of the Community Patent Convention the governments of the member states of the European Economic Community resolved to adjust their laws relating to patents so as (among other things) to bring those laws into conformity with the corresponding provisions of the European Patent Convention, the Community Patent Convention and the Patent Co-operation Treaty, it is hereby declared that the following provisions of this Act, that is to say ..."

and then it enumerates a number of sections of the 1977 U.K. Act which "are so framed as to have, as nearly as practicable, the same effects in the United Kingdom as the corresponding provisions of the European Patent

---

[63] *Ibid.*
[64] G1/98 *NOVARTIS II/Transgenic plant* O.J. EPO 1998, 509; [2000] E.P.O.R. 303.

Convention, the Community Patent Convention and the Patent Co-operation Treaty have in the territories to which those Conventions apply".

1–85   The wording of such sections is frequently considerably different from the corresponding provisions of the EPC. This is undesirable.[65] The approach to the interpretation of such sections of the United Kingdom patent law was considered in *Smith Kline and French Laboratories Ltd. v. R. D. Harbottle (Mercantile) Ltd.,*[66] where reference is made to a passage in a speech of Lord Diplock in *The Jade*[67]:

> "if there be any difference between the language of the statutory provision and that of the corresponding provision of the (relevant) Convention, the statutory language should be construed in the same sense as that of the Convention if the words of the statute are reasonably capable of bearing that meaning".

This approach was adopted by the Court of Appeal in *Asahi Kasei Kogyo K.K.'s Application,*[68] where it was also pointed out that there are various sections in the 1977 U.K. Act (such as section 15) which have counterparts in the EPC but which are not listed in section 130(7).

1–86   So far as the 1977 U.K. Act is concerned, in *Genentech's Patent,*[69] the following two suggestions were made by the Court of Appeal in relation to its interpretation:

> "First, as to the reported cases. Because the industrial revolution happened when and where it did, and because some of the most penetrating legal minds, both on and off the bench, have directed themselves to the evolution of patent law, the United Kingdom is fortunate to possess a wealth of reported authority on this topic which is probably unrivalled elsewhere. It is not, therefore, surprising that in a case so difficult as the present the parties have combed the books and brought before us dozens of citations in an effort to throw light on the various problems. Of course, this is not a matter for criticism, and I warmly acknowledge the diligence and skill with which the authorities have been assembled and deployed. Yet I believe that we should approach them with caution.
>   We are concerned here with a new statute which differs in important respects from the former law, not only as regards procedure, but also in the balance which it strikes between the interests of the researcher and of the public. We should not assume that the new Act is just the old English law re-written, or that statements of principle of passing observations on individual questions can now be

---

[65] See *Beloit Technologies Inc. v. Valmet Paper Machinery Inc.* [1995] R.P.C. 705 at 737.
[66] [1980] R.P.C. 363, at 372, 373.
[67] [1976] 1 All E.R. 920.
[68] [1991] R.P.C. 485.
[69] [1989] R.P.C. 203.

culled from the reported cases and applied without reserve, however eminent the sources from which they are drawn. This is all the more so given that the source of the Act is a treaty, and moreover a treaty written in three languages of equal status.

Whilst it would be senseless to ignore the obviously English parentage of some of the expressions used in the English text, it would also be a mistake to assume that the Act, which must be interpreted by other national courts and by the tribunals of the European Patent Office, can best be illuminated by researching the arcana of the English patent law, distilled from decades of reported cases by the very special analytical processes of the common law. I think it is safer to concentrate on what the new statute says."

Furthermore, in *Gale's Application*[70] the Court of Appeal explained its approach to the interpretation of the 1977 U.K. Act as follows: **1–87**

"One of the purposes of the 1977 Act was to give effect to the European Patent Convention. Thus, section 77(1) provides that a European patent (UK), by which is meant a European patent designating the United Kingdom, shall as from a prescribed date be treated for the purposes of parts 1 and 3 of the Act as if it were a patent under the Act granted in pursuance of an application made under the Act. Section 77(4) provides that where a European patent (UK) is revoked in accordance with the European Patent Convention, the patent shall be treated for the purposes of parts 1 and 3 of the Act as having been revoked under the Act.

The Act had a further purpose. The Act did not merely enact the statutory provisions necessary for the provisions of the Convention regarding European patents to take effect in this country. The Act also had a harmonisation objective. On the signature of the Convention for the European Patent for the Common Market, referred to in the Act as the Community Patent Convention, and not to be confused with the European Patent Convention, the governments of the member states of the European Community resolved to adjust their laws relating to patents so as to bring those laws into conformity with the corresponding provisions in the European Patent Convention and other conventions. Accordingly, when construing and applying section 1(1) and (2) of the Act, the court must have regard to the legislative intention with which those subsections were framed, namely, that they were framed so as to have, as nearly as practicable, the same effect in the United Kingdom as the corresponding provisions in Article 52(1), (2) and (3) of the European Patent Convention have in the territories in which that Convention applies. That is the effect of section 130(7) in the present case.

From this brief reference to the European Patent Convention one

---

[70] [1991] R.P.C. 305.

point which emerges is that it is of the utmost importance that the interpretation given to section 1 of the Act by the courts in the United Kingdom, and the interpretation given to Article 52 of the European Patent Convention by the European Patent Office, should be the same. The intention of Parliament was that there should be uniformity in this regard. What is more, any substantial divergence would be disastrous. It would be absurd if, on an issue of patentability, a patent application should suffer a different fate according to whether it was made in the United Kingdom under the Act or was made in Munich for a European patent (U.K.) under the Convention. Likewise in respect of opposition proceedings.

It is for these reasons that I shall refer below to certain decisions of the Board of Appeal of the European Patent Office. When interpreting the Act an English court should have due regard to decisions of the Board of Appeal and take them into account, although the English court is not bound by them. Indeed, this must be one of the matters Parliament had in mind when providing, in section 91(1)(c), that judicial notice shall be taken of decisions or expressions of opinion by the relevant convention court on questions arising under the relevant convention. "Relevant convention court" is defined, in section 130, in terms which include the Board of Appeal of the European Patent Office. Of course, this should be a two-way flow. No doubt, in appropriate cases, the European Patent Office has regard to, and takes into account, decisions of the courts of this country as well as decisions of the courts of other contracting states, and will continue to do so."

1–88   The Court of Appeal's reference to a "two-way flow" between decisions of the Boards of Appeal and of the national courts of Contracting States reflects what is set out in the various decisions and judgments which are referred to in paragraphs 1–61 *et seq.* above.

Furthermore, in *Merrell Dow Pharmaceutical Inc. v. H. N. Norton & Co. Ltd*,[71] the House of Lords stated that:

"It is therefore the duty of the United Kingdom Courts to construe Section 2 (of the 1977 U.K. Act) so that, so far as possible, it has the same effect as Article 54 EPC. For this purpose, it must have regard to the decisions of the EPO on the construction of the EPC. These decisions are not strictly binding upon courts in the United Kingdom but they are of great persuasive authority: first, because they are decisions of expert courts (the Boards of Appeal and the Enlarged Board of Appeal of the EPO) involved daily in the administration of the EPC and secondly because it would be highly undesirable for the provisions of the EPC to be construed differently in the EPO from the way they are interpreted in the national courts of a Contracting State."

It follows from the above that the best way of ensuring that the

[71] [1996] R.P.C. 76, HL.

provisions of the 1997 U.K. Act are interpreted as having the same meaning as the corresponding provisions of the EPC (especially when so intended by section 130(7) of the 1977 U.K. Act) is to work directly from the provisions of the EPC.

Consequently,

"it will be better for all concerned with patent matters in the U.K. (and, I hope, through Europe) to work on the basis that the corresponding provisions of [the EPC, and where appropriate, the CPC] are of direct effect (*Bristol-Myers Squibb v. Baker Norton Pharmaceuticals*".[72])

Cases Referred to in Chapter 1

Board of Appeal Decisions

G1, 5, 6/83   EISAI/Second medical indication O.J. EPO 1985, 64; [1979–85] E.P.O.R. B: 241.

G1/84   MOBIL OIL/Opposition by proprietor O.J. EPO 1985, 299; [1986] E.P.O.R. 39.

G1/86   VOEST ALPINE/Re-establishment of opponent O.J. EPO 1987, 447; [1987] E.P.O.R. 388.

G2, 6/88   MOBIL OIL/Friction reducing additive O.J. EPO 1990, 93, 114; [1990] E.P.O.R. 73, 257.

G5, 7 & 8/88   MEDTRONIC/Administrative agreement O.J. EPO 1991, 137; [1991] E.P.O.R. 225.

G4/92   PRESIDENT OF THE EPO/Basis of decisions O.J. EPO 1994, 149; [1994] E.P.O.R. 392.

G2/97   UNILEVER/Good Faith O.J. EPO 1999, 123; [2000] E.P.O.R. 73.

G1/98   NOVARTIS II/Transgenic plant O.J. EPO 1998, 509; [2000] E.P.O.R. 303.

J10/84   TEXAS/Amendments O.J. EPO 1985, 71; [1979–85] E.P.O.R.: A: 213

J20/85   ZENITH/Missing claims O.J. EPO 1987, 102; [1987] E.P.O.R. 157.

J3/87   MEMTEC/Membranes O.J. EPO 1989, 3; [1989] E.P.O.R. 175.

J.../87   Incapacity, O.J. EPO 1988, 323; [1989] E.P.O.R. 73.

J3/90   FISHER SCIENTIFIC/Postal strike O.J. EPO 1991, 550; [1992] E.P.O.R. 148.

J13/90   CASTLETON/Omitted payment not completed O.J. EPO 1994, 456; [1994] E.P.O.R. 76.

J27/92   MAXTOR/Media Storage system O.J. EPO 1995, 228; [1995] E.P.O.R. 688.

J2/94   UCFE (FRANCE)/Restitution [1998] E.P.O.R. 195.

J14/94   THE EXPANDED METAL COMPANY/Principle of good faith O.J. EPO 1995, 824; [1996] E.P.O.R. 327.

---

[72] [1999] R.P.C. 253 at 258–9.

J18/96   NN/Filing date O.J. EPO 1998, 403; [1999] E.P.O.R. 327.

T18/81   SOLVAY/Olefin polymers O.J. EPO 1985, 166; [1979–85]
         E.P.O.R.: B: 325.

T162/82 SIGMA/Classifying areas O.J. EPO 1987, 533; [1987] E.P.O.R.
         375.

T26/88   AKZO/Automatic revocation O.J. EPO 1990, 4; [1990]
         E.P.O.R. 21.

T182/88 UNIVERSITY OF CALIFORNIA/Dimeric oligopeptides O.J.
         EPO 1990, 287; [1989] E.P.O.R. 147.

T14/89   UHDE/Re-establishment O.J. EPO 1990, 432; [1990] E.P.O.R.
         656.

T869/90 TEXACO/Restitution [1994] E.P.O.R. 581.

T111/92 SONY/Restitution August 3, 1992.

T951/92 NEC/Opportunity to comment O.J. EPO 1996, 53; [1996]
         E.P.O.R. 371.

T892/94 ROBERTET/Deodorant compositions O.J. EPO 2000, 1; [1999]
         E.P.O.R. 516.

T161/96 MALLINKRODT/Under payment of opposition fee O.J. EPO
         1996, 331; [1990] E.P.O.R. 388.

Decisions of National Courts

Asahi Kasei Kogyo K.K.'s Application [1991] R.P.C. 485, HL.

Bulmer (H. P.) Ltd. v. Bollinger (J.) S.A. [1974] Ch. 401; [1975] R.P.C. 321,
   CA.

Eschercheim, The; Jade, The [1976] 1 W.L.R. 430; [1976] 1 All E.R. 920.

Gale's Application [1991] R.P.C. 305.

Genentech Inc.'s Patent [1989] R.P.C. 203.

"Hydropyridine" June 13, 1986, Court of Patent Appeals, Sweden; O.J.
   EPO 1988, 198.

"Hydropyridine", BGH Case No. X ZB 4/83; O.J. EPO 1984, 26.

John Wyeth and Brother Ltd's Application/Schering A.G.'s Application
   O.J. EPO 1986, 175; [1985] R.P.C. 545.

Lenzing AG's European Patent (U.K.) [1997] R.P.C. 245.

Merrell Dow Pharmaceutical Inc. and Anr. v. H. N. Norton & Co. Ltd
   (House of Lords) [1996] R.P.C. 76.

"re NV Philips Gloeilampenfabrieken", Supreme Administrative Court of
   Sweden, delivered June 13, 1990.

"Second medical use/NL"—decision dated September 30, 1987, Appeal
   Division, Netherlands Parent Office: O.J. EPO 1988, 405.

Smith Kline Laboratories Ltd v. R. D. Harbottle (Mercantile) Ltd [1980]
   R.P.C. 363.

"Tollwutvirus", BGH Decision X ZB 4/86; O.J. EPO 1987, 429.

Transocean Marine Paint Association v. E.C. Commission (Case 17/74)
   [1974] E.C.R. 1063; [1974] 2 C.M.L.R. 459, European Court.

CHAPTER 2

PROCEDURE BEFORE GRANT

Articles 75 to 86, 90 to 98 EPC

Contents

All references are to paragraph numbers

Cases Referred to in Chapter 2

A. Introduction

The requirements for filing a European patent application are discussed in **2–01**
Section B of this chapter. After a European application is filed it is
examined to ensure that it conforms with both the formal and substantive
requirements of the EPC.

Initially, an application is examined by the Receiving Section pursuant
to Articles 16, 90 and 91 EPC to ensure that the documents purporting to
constitute a European patent application comply with the requirements of
Article 80 EPC for the accordance of a filing date, and also to ensure that
other formal requirements are met. The Receiving Section is also responsible (under Article 16 EPC and pursuant to Article 93 EPC) for the
publication of the application and of the European search report, which is
drawn up by the Search Division, and sent to the applicant pursuant to
Article 92 EPC. Section C of this chapter is concerned with the examination
of the formal contents of an application which is carried out by the
Receiving Section immediately following its filing, and Section D is
concerned with the drawing up of the European search report.

Following the filing of a request for examination by the applicant **2–02**
pursuant to Article 94 EPC, an Examining Division becomes responsible
for the substantive examination of the application (Articles 18, 96 and 97
EPC). Section E of this chapter is concerned with the procedure before the
Examining Division.

Proceedings before the EPO for grant of a patent come into existence
when an application is filed, and remain in existence, unless the application is withdrawn, until the application is refused or granted. During
such proceedings the EPO has sole competence in respect of all matters
relating to the application. A decision to grant a patent takes effect on the
date on which the European Patent Bulletin mentions the grant (Article
97(4) EPC) and from then on, subject to the filing of opposition proceedings, competence over the granted European patent is transferred to the
designated Contracting States (Articles 2(3) and 64(1) EPC). Certain
procedural matters may arise at any time during such proceedings for
grant before the EPO, and these are discussed in Section F.

B. Filing a European Patent Application

(1) Place of filing

(a) EPO

In accordance with Article 75(1)(a) EPC, and with two Decisions of the **2–03**
President of the EPO,[1] an application may be filed at any one of the filing
offices of the EPO, which are in Munich, The Hague and the sub-office in

---

[1] Decisions of the President of the EPO dated May 10, 1989 and March 18, 1991; O.J. EPO 1989,
    218 and O.J. EPO 1991, 223.

Berlin. The EPO has filing offices in Munich at both office buildings, Isar and Pshorrhofe.

The EPO also has a sub-office in Vienna, but this is not a filing office. An application received at this sub-office is forwarded to the office at Munich or The Hague as appropriate by internal mail, and its date of receipt at the EPO (that is, its filing date—see paragraph 2–12) is the date of its arrival at a filing office in Munich or The Hague, as the case may be.

(b) Competent national authorities

2–04   In accordance with Article 75(1)(b) EPC, in addition to the EPO filing offices, an application may be filed at "the central industrial property office or other competent authority" of a Contracting State, if the law of that State so permits. An application which is filed at such a competent national authority is forwarded to the EPO by that authority "in the shortest time compatible with the application of national law concerning the secrecy of inventions in the interests of the State" (Article 77(1) EPC). Thus, applications which are obviously not liable to secrecy should be forwarded within six weeks of filing (Article 77(2) EPC), and applications which require further examination as to secrecy should be forwarded within four months of filing or fourteen months after the priority date, if claimed (Article 77(3) EPC). An application which is made secret is not forwarded to the EPO (Article 77(4) EPC). An application which does not reach the EPO before the end of 14 months from filing, or 14 months from the priority date, if claimed, shall be deemed to be withdrawn (Article 77(5) EPC). If an application is deemed to be withdrawn under Article 77(5) EPC, neither further processing (Article 121 EPC) nor re-establishment of rights (Article 122 EPC)—see Chapter 7—are available. In such a situation an applicant may convert the European application into a national patent application pursuant to Article 135 EPC (see J3/80[2]).

Although a European application may be filed at a competent national authority, all subsequent documents filed in the ensuing examination proceedings must be filed at the EPO itself (see paragraph 2–03).

A divisional application may not be filed at a national authority (Article 76(1) EPC).

(2) Manner of filing

2–05   Under Rule 24 EPC, an application may be filed in writing either *directly* or *by post*. Furthermore, other means of communication may be permitted by the President of the EPO, subject to conditions governing their use; in particular, written confirmation may be required.

Filing an application *by facsimile* is permitted at the EPO by a Decision dated May 26, 1992,[3] subject to written confirmation of the application

---

[2] J3/80 *CHUBB/Failure to forward a European patent application* O.J. EPO 1980, 92; [1979–85] E.P.O.R.: A:23.
[3] Decision of President of the EPO dated May 26, 1992, O.J. EPO 1992, 299.

documents at the invitation of the Receiving Section of the EPO within a non-extendable period of one month. An application may be filed by facsimile at competent national authorities of Contracting States that so permit. An application may *not* at present be filed at the EPO by any other means; in particular, telegram, telex, teletext, diskette or similar data carriers may not be used. An application so filed is not an application and is not allocated a filing date.

(3) Date of filing

(a) Receipt of application documents

When application documents are filed, either at the EPO or at a competent **2–06** national authority, they are marked with the date of receipt, pursuant to Rule 24(2) EPC, and a receipt is issued to the applicant which includes the application number, the nature of the documents, and the date of receipt.

Wherever application documents are filed, their date of receipt at the EPO or competent authority is used to determine the filing date (J18/86[4]). Provided the application documents meet the minimum requirements of Article 80 EPC (see paragraph 2–12 below) the date of receipt is the filing date of the application.

(b) Post-dating to designate a new Contracting State

It is possible to post-date an application to a filing date subsequent to the **2–07** receipt of the application documents in order to allow the designation of a State which had not quite become a Contracting State at the date of receipt of the application documents, if it is clear that the applicant at the filing date desired such post-dating.

Thus if an application is filed before the accession date for a Contracting State, and *after* such accession date the applicant pays a designation fee for such State and requests post-dating of the application, such post-dating will not be allowed. "Re-dating an application cannot be justified on the grounds that the later date would permit the granting of a European patent for a new Contracting State" (J14/90[5]).

On the other hand, however, if an application is filed before the accession date, and at the time of filing the Contracting State is identified in the application as an intended designated State, and the designation fee for such State is paid at the filing date, "such express designation may, after checking with the applicant, be interpreted as meaning that the applicant does not want a filing date earlier than the date on which the EPC enters into force for the state concerned" (J18/90[6]).

---

[4] J18/86 *ZOUEKI/Filing date* O.J. EPO 1988, 165; [1988] E.P.O.R. 338.
[5] J14/90 *FLACHGLAS/Denmark—tacit* O.J. EPO 1992, 505; [1992] E.P.O.R. 553.
[6] J18/90 *CANON/Denmark—expressly* O.J. EPO 1992, 511; [1992] E.P.O.R. 553.

(4) Who may file an application: representation

2–08   Any person may file a European application (Article 58 EPC). As to establishing the identity of an applicant, and the legal entitlement to apply, see respectively paragraphs 2–24 *et seq.* and 2–78 *et seq.* below.

There may be more than one applicant (Article 59 and Rule 26 EPC), and a common representative will then be appointed (either by the applicants under Rule 26(3) EPC or under Rule 100 EPC).

The requirements for representation of parties to proceedings before the EPO are set out in Article 133 EPC and are considered in Chapter 5 at paragraphs 5–13 *et seq.* below. As there stated, as a general principle, a person not having either a residence or a place of business within a Contracting State ("a non-European person") must act through a professional representative in such proceedings. However, as an exception, such a person may himself file a European application without acting through a professional representative, just as a person with either a residence or a place of business within a Contracting State may himself file a European application.

An application must be signed either by the applicant or by his professional representative (see Rule 26(2) EPC).

(5) Language of an application

2–09   See Chapter 5 at paragraphs 5–03 *et seq.*

C. Procedure Before the Receiving Section: Formal Examination

2–10   The duties of the Receiving Section, first in examining an application on filing, in particular to determine its filing date, and secondly in examining an application to ensure that all formal requirements are met, are set out in Articles 90 and 91 EPC.

(1) Formal contents of an application

(a) Introduction

2–11   According to Article 78 EPC a European patent application shall contain:

> "(a) a request for the grant of a European patent;
> (b) a description of the invention;
> (c) one or more claims;
> (d) any drawings referred to in the description or the claims;
> (e) an abstract."

Article 79(1) EPC requires that the request for grant shall contain the designation of the Contracting States in which protection is desired (see sub-paragraph (c) below) and Rule 26 EPC governs the formal contents of the request for grant.

The substantive contents of an application, namely the description, claims and drawings (Article 78(b)(c) and (d) EPC) are governed by Articles 83 and 84 EPC (see Chapter 7 below). Implementing Rules 27 to 35 EPC govern the formal aspects of such substantive contents and of the abstract (as well as some substantive aspects—see Chapter 7).

According to the proposed revision of the EPC, Article 79(1) EPC will be **2–11A** amended so as to read as follows:

> 79(1): "All the Contracting States party to this Convention at the time of filing of a European patent application shall be deemed to be designated in the request for grant of a European patent."

See paragraph 2–15A below.

(b) Accordance of a filing date: minimum contents under Article 80 EPC

According to Article 80 EPC, in order to be allocated a filing date an **2–12** application need only contain:

(a) an indication that a patent is sought—(see paragraph 2–14 below)
(b) the designation of at least one Contracting State (see paragraphs 2–15 *et seq.* below)
(c) information identifying the applicant (see paragraph 2–26 below)
(d) a description and one or more claims (see paragraphs 2–28 *et seq.* below) in a language as defined in Article 14(1) and (2) EPC.

Clearly, the allocation of a filing date corresponding to the date on which documents which are intended to constitute a European application are filed at the EPO can be of crucial importance to the validity of such application. The *minimum contents* of an application which are required in order that items (a) to (d) of Article 80 EPC are satisfied are discussed below.

According to the proposed revision of the EPC, Article 80 EPC will be **2–12A** amended to read:

> 80: "The date of filing of a European patent application shall be the date on which the requirements laid down in the Implementing Regulations are fulfilled."

Such requirements will then be easily adapted to correspond to the requirements for according a date of filing under the forthcoming Patent Law Treaty.

(2) Contents of the request for grant

2–13 The formal requirements for the contents of a request for grant are set out in Rule 26 EPC. Some specific requirements are discussed below, as well as the minimum contents which are necessary in order to meet such requirements.

(a) Request for grant: minimum contents under Article 80(a) EPC

2–14 Rule 26(2)(a) EPC requires "a petition for the grant of a European patent", that is, an express request for grant.

However, Article 80(a) EPC defines the minimum contents as "an indication that a patent is sought". On general principles such an "indication" could be implied from the filing of other application documents, by analogy with J25/88[7] in connection with an application which contains no express designation of a Contracting State. If other documents including a description and claims are filed, it is "almost self-evident" that a European patent is sought.

(b) The designation of Contracting States

2–15 **(i) Introduction.** Article 79(1) EPC and Rule 26(2)(b) EPC require that the request for grant shall contain "the designation of the Contracting State or States in which protection of the invention is desired". Publication of the application (including the request for grant) under Article 93 EPC gives notice to the public of the States where the invention may be protected.

Article 79(2) EPC provides that "The designation of a Contracting State shall be subject to the payment of a designation fee". Such fees must be paid within a normal time limit of six months of the date on which the European Patent Bulletin mentions the publication of the European search report (that is, the same date as that on which the examination fee becomes due under Article 94(2) EPC); but the payment of such designation fees is subject to a grace period under Rule 85a EPC. Under Rule 85a(1) EPC such fee may be validly paid within a grace period of "one month of notification of a communication pointing out the failure to observe the time limit, provided that within this period a surcharge is paid". Under Rule 85a(2) EPC, designation fees in respect of which the applicant has dispensed with such notification may be validly paid within a grace period of "two months of expiry of the normal time limits" under Article 79(2) EPC, provided that within this period a surcharge is paid (as to calculation of such an "aggregate time limit", see Legal Advice 5/93 rev.[8]).

2–15A According to the proposed revision of the EPC, Articles 79(1) and (2) EPC will be amended to read as follows:

79(1): "All the Contracting States party to this Convention at the time

---

[7] J25/88 *NEW FLEX/Date of filing* O.J. EPO 1989, 486; [1990] E.P.O.R. 59.
[8] O.J. EPO 1993, 229; see Appendix 6.

of filing of a European patent application shall be deemed to be designated in the request for grant of a European patent."
79(2): "The designation of a Contracting State may be subject to the payment of a designation fee ..."

It is also proposed that the time limit for the payment of designation fees in Article 79(2) EPC and the last two sentences of Article 79(3) EPC be deleted and their substance moved to the Implementing Regulations.

These proposed amendments follow on from the pre-crossed, precautionary designation of all Contracting States becoming an express designation of all Contracting States in 1997 (see paragraph 2–16 below). In 1999 a ceiling for the payment of designation fees, fixed at seven designation fees, has resulted in an ever-increasing number of applicants effectively designating all Contracting States.

(ii) Precautionary designation. In order to avoid the possibility of 2–16 applicants—by mistake—omitting to designate States where protection is desired, since 1986 the "Request for Grant Form 1001" has included a pre-printed precautionary designation of all States, and dispenses with notification by the EPO under Rules 85a(1) EPC of non-payment of the designation fees of any States within the normal time limit under Article 79(2) EPC. This practice of precautionary designation was introduced in recognition of the fact that it is difficult for applicants to decide upon the States to be designated at the time of filing an application, and enables applicants to postpone such decision until payment of designation fees become due.

Originally Article 79(2) EPC required designation fees to be paid twelve months after filing an application, and at the latest 13 months after the priority date (if claimed). Thus for a direct European application the designation fees were payable shortly after filing, and usually together with the filing and search fees; whereas Euro–PCT applicants are required to pay designation fees only upon entry into the European phase, that is, 21 or 31 months after the priority date, and after receipt of the international search report or international preliminary examination.

Under the amended version of Article 79(2) EPC which came into force on July 1, 1997, a direct European applicant may postpone the decision as to which designation fees to pay (and thus which States to designate) until after the European search report has been received and considered, in the same way as a Euro–PCT applicant.

A discussion of the early background concerning the designation of States is contained in Legal Advice 7/80[9] (now cancelled).

A discussion of the amended version of Article 79(2) EPC is contained in a Notice dated March 1, 1997[10].

(iii) Specific designation. If the request for grant specifically designates 2–17 certain Contracting States, corresponding designation fees are payable

[9] O.J. EPO 1980, 395.
[10] O.J. EPO 1997, 107.

within the normal time limit under Article 79(2) EPC or within the grace period (together with surcharge) under Rule 85a(1)EPC. If "the designation fee has not been paid in due time in respect of any designated State the designation of that State shall be deemed to be withdrawn" (Article 91(4) EPC; and Rule 104c(2) EPC):

> "Without prejudice to Article 67(4) EPC [concerning the rights conferred by a European patent application after publication], the designation of a Contracting State . . . in a European patent application does not retroactively lose its legal effect and is not deemed never to have taken place if the relevant designation fee has not been paid within the applicable time limit" (G4/98,[11] overruling J22/95[12])

2–18 The deemed withdrawal of such a designation takes effect upon expiry of the applicable time limits (Article 79(2), Rules 15(2), 25(2) and 107(1) EPC). Consequently, a divisional application can designate any state which has been designated in the earlier application unless and until any such designation in the earlier is deemed to be withdrawn by reason of failure to pay the designation fee in due time (Article 76(2) EPC, G4/98,[13] and see paragraph 2–57).

2–19 **(iv) Absence of any explicit designation: minimum contents under Article 80(b) EPC.** The practice of precautionary designation can be "legally classified as a presumption of a general wish of applicants to designate all Contracting States in the initial stage of filing" an application. Consequently:

> "For the purposes of according a filing date under Article 80(b) EPC there is no need for an explicit designation of any particular Contracting State. In the absence of such a designation, the documents filed by the applicant shall be considered to contain a precautionary designation of all Contracting States" (J25/88[14]).

2–20 **(v) Matching fees to designated States.** Payment of designation fees should specify for which States payment is made, so as to establish the purpose of the payment in accordance with Article 7(1) RF.

If the purpose of a payment is unclear, an invitation to specify the purpose of the payment within a set period is issued, under Article 7(2) RF. If a payment is insufficient to cover all the States which have been specifically designated, the fees are deemed to have been paid in the order of designation for the number of States covered by the payment, pursuant to Article 9(2) RF.

---

[11] G4/98 Designation fees O.J. EPO(P).
[12] J22/95 AUMAC/Designation of contracting states in a divisional application O.J. EPO 1998, 569.
[13] See note 11.
[14] J25/88 NEW FLEX/Date of filing O.J. EPO 1989, 486; [1990] E.P.O.R. 59.

(vi) Parallel grace periods for specific and precautionary designations: 2–21 expiry of time limit. If specific States are designated in the request for grant, but insufficient fees are paid within the normal time limit under Article 79(2) EPC, notification of failure to pay is sent by the EPO pursuant to Rule 85a(1) EPC, so that the grace period under Rule 85a(1) is brought into operation. At the same time the precautionary designation of all States in the request for grant causes the grace period under Rule 85a(2) EPC to be brought into operation. Depending upon the date on which the notification of failure to pay pursuant to Rule 85a(1) EPC is sent, the grace period under Rule 85a(1) EPC may expire before or after the grace period under Rule 85a(2) EPC.

In such a situation, designation fees can still be validly paid up to the end of whichever grace period expires last (J5/91[15]).

(vii) Withdrawal of designations. The withdrawal of a designation is **2–22** allowed at any time before grant of an application, but the corresponding designation fee is not refunded (Article 79(3) EPC). Furthermore, a designation fee in respect of a Contracting State that has been withdrawn cannot be re-allocated to a different designation.

The circumstances in which a retraction of a withdrawal of a designation by way of correction of a mistake under Rule 88 EPC is allowable are considered in Chapter 6 at paragraph 6–17 below.

According to the proposed revision of the EPC, Article 79(3) EPC will be **2–22A** amended by deletion of the second and third sentences which provide that the withdrawal of all designations is deemed to be a withdrawal of the European patent application, and that designation fees shall not be refunded, respectively.

(c) Extension of European patent applications to European non-Contracting States

Extension agreements have currently entered into force for Slovenia, **2–23** Lithuania, Latvia, Albania, Romania and Macedonia, whereby the protection conferred by a European patent application or patent may be extended to such States.

Under the extension system which is implemented by such agreements, extension of protection to each such State is deemed to be requested for any European patent application filed on or after the respective date of entry into force of the extension agreement for each such State, subject to payment of an extension fee within a time limit. For direct European patent applications, the time limit is the same as for paying a designation fee (see paragraph 2–16). For Euro–PCT applications, the time limit is prescribed in Rule 104b(1) EPC.

Full details of the extension system (with particular reference to

---

[15] J5/91 *KONGSKILDE /Legal loophole* O.J. EPO 1993, 657; [1994] E.P.O.R. 205.

Slovenia) are set out in a note entitled "Extension of European patents to Slovenia"[16].

(d) The applicant

2–24 **(i) Naming the applicant.** Rule 2(2) EPC requires that the request for grant shall contain "the name, address and nationality of the applicant and the State in which his residence or principal place of business is located" (the latter information being relevant in connection with representation— see Chapter 5 at paragraph 5–14 below).

Article 58 EPC provides that a European application "may be filed by any natural or legal person" and Article 60(1) EPC provides that "the right to a European patent shall belong to the inventor or his successor in title". However, Article 60(3) EPC provides that: "For the purpose of proceedings before the EPO, the applicant shall be deemed to be entitled to exercise the right to a European patent." Thus the person who is named as the applicant in the documents constituting an application will be assumed by the EPO to be entitled to the European patent, without "any need to investigate the existence of the entitlement" (J18/93[17]).

2–25 **(ii) Determination of the lawful applicant.** The procedure if a third party wishes to assert his entitlement to apply for a European patent in place of or in addition to the named applicant is discussed in paragraphs 2–78 *et seq.* below.

2–26 **(iii) "Information identifying the applicant": minimum contents under Article 80(c) EPC.** The requirement of Article 80(c) EPC is met for the purpose of according a filing date "whenever it is possible beyond reasonable doubt the identity of the applicant on the basis of all data contained in the documents filed . . ." (J25/86[18]). For example, an applicant may be sufficiently identified even if his first name is stated incorrectly (J25/86).

If the wrong applicant is originally named by mistake, it may be possible to correct the mistake under Rule 88 EPC—see Chapter 6 at paragraph 6–12 below.

On the other hand, if the applicant documents as originally filed simply state that the applicant's identity "will be communicated later", a date of filing will be accorded on the date when the applicant's identity is first received by the EPO (J21/87[19]).

(e) A priority declaration (if applicable)

2–27 If priority is claimed from an earlier application in respect of the same invention (Article 87 EPC, see Chapter 9), a declaration of priority must be

---

[16] O.J. EPO 1994, 75.
[17] J18/93 *CARDIAC/Correction of mistake* O.J. EPO 1997, 326; [1998] E.P.O.R. 38.
[18] J25/86 *WARHEIT/Identity of applicant* O.J. EPO 1987, 475; [1988] E.P.O.R. 40.
[19] J21/87 *MATSUBARA/Identification of the applicant* December 21, 1987.

included in the request for grant "indicating the date on which and the country in or for which the earlier application was filed" (Rule 26(2)(g) EPC).

The circumstances in which a priority declaration may be corrected after filing, under Rule 88 EPC, are considered in Chapter 6 at paragraphs 6–19 *et seq.* below.

(3) A "description and one or more claims": minimum contents under Article 80(d) EPC

(a) What constitutes a claim?

The requirement of Article 80(d) EPC for "one or more claims" to be **2–28** included in the application documents if a filing date is to be allocated, and in particular the meaning of the word "claim" in this context, is not entirely clear.

In one case, an application was filed which included a description and drawings, but which did not include any claims (in the normal sense of a set of definition statements). Since Article 84 EPC requires that "The claims shall define the matter for which protection is sought", it is clearly arguable that if the description includes statements which can be regarded as "defining the matter for which protection is sought", Article 80(d) EPC is thereby satisfied. In the course of an appeal the following questions were referred to the Enlarged Board:

"(1) For a filing date to be established in respect of a European patent application is it is necessary for the filed application to contain, in addition to a description, at least one claim which is formulated separate from the description and is recognisable as such?

(2) If the answer to question (1) is no, for a filing date to be established within the meaning of Article 80 EPC, is it sufficient if there is at least one claim which, as such, is derivable from the invention as described?

(3) If the answer to question (2) is yes, to what extent must a claim which is not expressly formulated as such be derivable?

(a) is it necessary for at least one claim to be directly and clearly recognisable from the text of the description; or

(b) is it sufficient for the description to disclose an invention in such a way that it is possible to recognise subject-matter to be protected for which a claim could be formulated" (J20/94[20]).

Before the Enlarged Board had considered these questions, however, the application in suit was withdrawn, so the above questions remain unanswered.

[20] J20/94 *According of a filing date* O.J. EPO 1996, 181 [1996] E.P.O.R. 593.

(b) In a language as defined in Article 14(1) and (2) EPC

2–29 "The requirements under Article 80 EPC for according a filing date are not fulfilled if the description and claims are filed in two different official languages." In such a case it would be "impossible to determine the language of the proceedings from the documents as filed, which would be in direct conflict with Article 14(3) EPC" (J18/96[21]).

On the other hand; textual matter on the drawings may be in a different language from that of the description and claims:

> "The Convention does not make the accordance of the date of filing dependent on whether text matter in the drawings is in the same language as that of the description and claims in accordance with Article 14(1) and (2) EPC.... There is nothing to prevent the application being amended on the basis of a translation of this text matter into the language of the proceedings" (T382/94[22]).

D. The European Search Report: Search Fees

(1) Introduction

2–30 In accordance with Article 92 EPC, if an application has been accorded a date of filing and has not been withdrawn or deemed to be withdrawn under Article 90(3) EPC, the Search Division draws up the European search report.

(2) Unity of invention: non-unitary application

2–31 Article 82 EPC requires that an application "shall relate to one invention only or to a group of inventions so linked as to form a single general inventive concept".

Pursuant to Rule 46(1) EPC, if an application as filed is considered by the Search Division not to comply with Article 82 EPC and therefore to be a non-unitary application, a partial search report is drawn up on the subject-matter of the invention which is first mentioned in the claims. Furthermore, the applicant is informed that if the search report is to cover the other inventions which are disclosed in the application, an additional search fee must be paid for each such invention, within a time limit of between two and six weeks.

(3) Effect of payment of further search fees

2–32 The payment of additional search fees as so requested ensures that after receipt of the search report covering all such inventions, the applicant may choose which invention to put forward in the claims of the application, and he may file divisional applications (see paragraph 2–56 *et seq.* below) in

[21] J18/96 *N.N./Filing date* O.J. EPO 1998, 403; [1999] E.P.O.R. 9.
[22] T382/94 *CARL ZEISS/Documents as filed* O.J. EPO 1998, 24; [1998] E.P.O.R. 200.

respect of the other inventions which have been covered by the search report. Although each such divisional application is subject to payment of a further search fee in accordance with Article 76(3) EPC, each such further search fee is refundable fully or in part under Article 10 of the Rules relating to Fees, depending upon the extent to which the Search Division benefits from the earlier search report on the parent application.

(4) Determination of non-unity by Examination Division

If the applicant is requested by the Search Division to pay one or more **2–32a** further search fees under Rule 46(1) EPC in respect of a non-unitary application as set out above, there is no possibility of appeal from such a request. However, if the applicant has paid further search fees in response to such request, during the subsequent substantive examination he may request a refund from the Examining Division (or from the Board of Appeal in any appeal), on the basis that the finding by the Search Division of non-unity was not justified (Rule 46(2) EPC).

Furthermore "in a case where an applicant fails to pay further search fees when requested to do so by the Search Division under Rule 46(1) EPC, Rule 46 EPC does not prohibit a review by the Examining Division of the correctness of the Search Division finding of lack of unity of invention" (T631/97[23]).

(5) Effect of non-payment of further search fees

According to the procedural system governing search and examination of **2–33** an application prior to grant, and having regard to the requirement of unity of invention in Article 82 EPC, it is clear that "in order to proceed to grant an application is required to contain claims relating to one invention only". Furthermore, "the invention which is to be examined for patentability must be an invention in respect of which a search fee has been paid prior to the drawing up of the European search report". Rule 46 EPC is intended to ensure that "an appropriate extent of search is completed in respect of each individual application before it is substantively examined by the Examining Division". Therefore:

> "An applicant who fails to pay the further search fees for a non-unitary application when requested to do so by the Search Division under Rule 46(1) EPC cannot pursue that application for the subject-matter in respect of which no search fees have been paid. Such an applicant must file a divisional application in respect of such subject-matter if he wishes to seek protection for it" (G2/92[24]—as to divisional applications, see paragraphs 2–56 et seq. below).

[23] T631/97 TOSHIBA/Doped regions O.J. EPO 2001, 13.
[24] G2/92 Non-payment of further search fees O.J. EPO 1993, 591; [1994] E.P.O.R. 278.

(6) The EPO as International Searching Authority

2–34 The EPO acts as International Searching Authority under Article 17 PCT in relation to Euro–PCT applications. Pursuant to Article 17(3)(a) PCT and Rule 40.1 PCT the EPO may in this capacity invite an applicant under the PCT to pay additional search fees with respect to an international application which it considers does not comply with the requirement of unity of invention.

Under Rule 40.2 PCT an international applicant may pay such additional fees under "protest", and such protest is examined by "a three-member board or other special instance. ... or any competent higher authority." Under Article 154(3) EPC the Boards of Appeal are responsible for deciding upon such a protest. The EPO first conducts a review as to whether the invitation to pay the additional fee(s) was justified. If it is considered unjustified, the additional fees are refunded. If it is considered justified, the applicant is invited to pay a "protest fee". If such fee is duly paid, the protest is referred to a Board of Appeal (Rule 40.2(e) PCT and Rule 104a(3) EPC).

In deciding upon such protests, the Boards of Appeal apply the PCT, not the EPC (although the relevant provisions are almost identical). Decisions on such protests may be published in the Official Journal of the EPO, however.

E. Procedure Before the Examining Divisions: Substantive Examination

(1) Introduction

2–35 In accordance with Article 94(2) and (3) EPC, a request for examination must be filed within six months after the date on which the European Patent Bulletin mentions the publication of the European search report in respect of an application. Otherwise (subject to the one month grace period following a notification provided by Rule 85(b) EPC) the application is deemed to be withdrawn. Since the grace period is not "set" by the EPO, further processing of the application under Article 121 EPC is not available if the grace period is not complied with (J47/92[25]).

When a request for examination is duly filed (or in the case where the request for examination has been filed before the European search report was transmitted to the applicant, when the applicant has indicated that he desires to proceed further with the application) responsibility for further substantive examination of the application passes to an Examining Division (Articles 16 and 18(1) EPC). Pursuant to Article 94(1) EPC, the Examining Division examines whether the application and the invention to which it relates meet the substantive requirements of the EPC, and if not, in accordance with Article 96(2) and Rule 51(2) and (3) EPC, the applicant is

---

[25] J47/92 *SILVER SYSTEMS/Further processing* O.J. EPO 1995, 180; [1995] E.P.O.R. 495.

invited to file observations in reply to a communication issued by the Examining Division.

During the examining procedure, therefore, as well as during any subsequent appeal proceedings, the procedural rights of an applicant in prosecuting an application are important.

(2) Composition of an Examining Division

According to Article 18(2) EPC, an Examining Division consists of three **2–36** technical examiners, one being the chairman. Furthermore, if an Examining Division considers that the nature of the decision on a particular application so requires, the Division can be enlarged by the addition of a legally qualified examiner.

The examination prior to a final decision is conducted by one member of the Division, the primary examiner. A decision on an application is taken by majority vote. In the event of parity of votes (if there are four members), the chairman's vote is decisive (Article 18(2) EPC). A decision on an application must be taken, and signed, by persons who are existing members of the Examining Division at the date of the decision. If this is not the case, the decision is set aside as void (because of a substantial procedural violation in the making of the decision) in the event of an appeal (T714/92[26]).

(3) Communications and observations in reply

(a) Contents of a communication under Article 96(2) EPC

(i) Grounds of objection to grant. Article 96(2) states that if examination **2–37** of an application reveals that the requirements of the EPC are not met, "the Examining Division shall invite the applicant, in accordance with the Implementing Regulations and as often as necessary, to file his observations ...".

Rule 51(3) provides that "Any communication pursuant to Article 96(2) EPC shall contain a reasoned statement covering, where appropriate, all the grounds against the grant of the European patent."

Rule 51(3) EPC involves two requirements:

(1) "the applicant shall be informed, if appropriate, of *each require-ment of the EPC* which is considered as not being met";
(2) "for each requirement of the EPC which is referred to, the applicant should be informed of the *legal and factual reasons* which are considered to lead to the conclusion that the requirement of the EPC is not met" (T951/92[27]) (emphasis added).

It follows that an application cannot be refused unless at least one communication has been issued by the Examining Division which meets

[26] T714/92 *POHJOLA* September 18, 1992.
[27] T951/92 *NEC/Opportunity to comment* O.J. EPO 1996, 53; [1996] E.P.O.R. 371.

the requirements of Rule 51(3) EPC. If a decision refusing an application is issued following a communication which does not include a "reasoned statement" in accordance with Rule 51(3) EPC, this constitutes a "substantial procedural violation" under Rule 67 EPC, and the decision should be set aside on appeal, and the appeal fee should be reimbursed (*e.g.* T951/92[28], T596/97[29]).

2–38   **(ii) The "requirements of the Convention": not Article 167 EPC.** Under Article 167 EPC, a Contracting State may, upon accession to the EPC, make reservations for a limited period with respect to its national law (for example, some recent Contracting States do not allow claims to chemical or pharmaceutical products). Any such reservations are not considered as constituting requirements of the EPC under Article 96(2) EPC, and there is no obligation to draw attention to such reservations in a communication under Rule 51(3) EPC. In practice, the applicant's attention is drawn to the possibility of filing separate sets of claims for designated States which have made such reservations in every communication under Rule 51(4) EPC (see paragraph 2–67 below), as voluntary assistance to the applicant (G7/93[30]).

2–39   **(iii) Invitation to reply.** Article 96(2) EPC also requires the Examining Division, when raising one or more grounds of objection to the grant of a patent, to invite the applicant to file observations in reply within a fixed period, normally of between two and four months. An applicant has a right to reply within this fixed period. Alternatively, an applicant may ask for an extension of time for replying. Rule 51(2) EPC requires that in any invitation under Article 96(2) EPC, "the Examining Division shall, where appropriate, invite the applicant to correct the disclosed deficiencies and, where necessary, to file the description, claims and drawings in an amended form".

    The procedure relating to filing amendments is considered in paragraphs 2–48 *et seq.* below.

(b) Observations in reply

2–40   Such observations in reply should be filed within the fixed period unless an extension of time is requested, and should deal fully with all the objections to grant which have been raised in the communication under Article 96(2) EPC. At the same time, any appropriate facts and evidence in support of the application and any proposed amendments to the application should be filed (see paragraph 2–48 below). Furthermore, if the applicant wishes to argue that the application should be allowed at oral proceedings pursuant to Article 116 EPC, a request for oral proceedings should preferably be filed with the observations in reply (see Chapter 5 at paragraphs 5–45 *et seq.*).

    If a request for oral proceedings is filed, such oral proceedings will be

---

[28] *Ibid.*
[29] T596/97 HITACHI/*Centrifugal fluid machine*, June 10, 1998.
[30] G7/93 WHITBY II/*Late-filed amendments* O.J. EPO 1994, 775; [1995] E.P.O.R. 49.

appointed unless the application is considered allowable (either with text as originally filed or with text as proposed to be amended). If oral proceedings are appointed, a further communication under Rule 71a EPC will be issued with the summons to oral proceedings (see paragraph 5–51).

(c) Failure to reply in due time

Article 96(3) EPC provides that "If the applicant fails to reply in due time to **2–41** [an invitation under Article 96(2) EPC], the application shall be deemed to be withdrawn." (This sanction is subject to a request for further processing under Article 121 EPC—see paragraph 6–02, and if appropriate, an application for re-establishment under Article 122 EPC—see Chapter 6 at paragraphs 6–27 et seq. (J12/92[31], J29/94[32])).

The phrase "fails to reply in due time to any invitation" in Article 96(2) EPC "has to be construed in the light of the purpose of the invitation which is to afford the applicant an opportunity to exercise his right to present comments in accordance with Article 113(1) EPC. Hence a letter which neither exercises nor waives that right is not a reply for the purposes of Article 96(3) EPC" (T685/98[33]).

If the applicant "fails to reply in due time" for the purposes of Article 96(3) EPC, an Examining Division "has no power to refuse the application under Article 97(1) EPC", and a purported refusal is *ultra vires*, because the penalty for failing to reply is laid down in Article 96(3) EPC, namely that "the application shall be deemed to be withdrawn" (T685/98[34]).

Furthermore: "In unclear cases there can be no presumption that an applicant has waived his right to be heard under Article 113(1) EPC" (T685/98[35]).

If an application has been "deemed to be withdrawn" under Article 96(3) EPC the transfer of such application can still be recorded in the Register of European patents if re-establishment of rights has been applied for under Article 122 EPC (J10/93[36]).

(d) Contesting a refusal of extension of time

"If a request for extension of time limit filed in good time has been **2–42** rejected under Rule 84, second sentence, EPC and the applicant considers this unjust, the ensuing loss of rights can only be overcome by a request for further processing under Article 121 EPC. At the same time, he may request reimbursement of the fee for further processing. This secondary request will have to be decided on in connection with the final decision. Under Article 106(3) EPC, the decision on the

---

[31] J12/92 BLAIZAT/Restoration of rights: further processing April 30, 1993.
[32] J29/94 GARCIA/Deemed withdrawal O.J. EPO 1998, 6; [1998] E.P.O.R. 342.
[33] T685/98 GPT/Clock synchronisation O.J. EPO 1999, 546; [1999] E.P.O.R. 560.
[34] Ibid.
[35] See note 33.
[36] J10/93 COLLAPSIBLE BOTTLE OF AMERICA/Transfer O.J. EPO 1997, 91; [1997] E.P.O.R. 491.

secondary request can be appealed together with the final decision. The appeal may also be confined to contesting the decision on the secondary request" (J37/89[37]).

(e) Further communication or adverse decision?

2–43   **(i) When a communication is necessary.** The requirement of Article 96(2) EPC that "the Examining Division shall invite the applicant ... as often as necessary to file his observations ..." is to be interpreted as follows:

> "the use of the word 'necessary' in this context implicitly recognises that in certain circumstances there will be a legal obligation upon an Examining Division to invite further observations from the applicant before issuing a decision" (T640/91[38]).

In particular there is a legal obligation for an Examining Division to invite further observations if failure to do so would result in a contra-vention of Article 113(1) EPC, which states that a decision of the EPO "may only be based on grounds or evidence on which the parties concerned have had an opportunity to present their comments".

In this connection, "the term 'grounds or evidence' in Article 113(1) EPC should not be narrowly construed".

For example:

> "In the context of the examining procedure ... Article 113(1) EPC is intended to ensure that before a decision refusing an application for non-compliance with a requirement of the EPC is issued, the applicant has been clearly informed by the EPC of the essential legal and factual reasons on which the finding of non-compliance is based, so that he knows in advance of the decision both that the application may be refused and why it may be refused, and so that he may have a proper opportunity to comment upon such reasons and/or to propose amendments so as to avoid refusal of the application" (T951/92[39]).

2–44   Furthermore:

> "If a communication under Rule 51(3) EPC and pursuant to Article 96(2) EPC does not set out the essential legal and factual reasoning which would lead to a finding that a requirement of the EPC has not been met, then a decision based upon such a finding cannot be issued without contravening Article 113(1) EPC unless and until a communi-cation has been issued which does contain such essential reasoning. If

---

[37] J37/89 *MATSUSHITA/Rejection of extension of time limit* O.J. EPO 1993, 20; [1993] E.P.O.R. 356.
[38] T640/91 *NIPPON/Examination procedure* O.J. EPO 1994, 918; [1995] E.P.O.R. 243.
[39] T951/92 *NEC/Opportunity to comment* O.J. EPO 1996, 53; [1996] E.P.O.R. 371.

a decision is issued in the absence of a communication containing such essential reasoning Article 96(2) EPC is also contravened since in order to avoid contravening Article 113(1) EPC it was necessary to issue a further communication ..." (T951/92[40]).

Thus, for example, a further communication under Article 96(3) is "necessary" if the first communication (or each previous communication) fails to set out "the essential legal and factual reasons" of non compliance with the EPC on which a decision of refusal is or would be based (see T951/92). If a decision includes several grounds, Article 113(1) EPC must be fulfilled with respect to each ground (T802/97[41]—see Chapter 5 at paragraph 5–73).

If an applicant provides bona fide submissions and/or technical information in reply to a communication of the Examining Division substantially changing the points at issue, the Examining Division has a legal obligation under Article 96(2) EPC to inform the applicant of the objections under the EPC arising from the new situation and to invite him to provide further observations before issuing a decision to refuse the application (T921/94[42]).

In both of the above two examples, failure to send a further communication before issuing a decision constitutes a "substantial procedural violation" (see Chapter 4 at paragraphs 4–166 *et seq.*).

(ii) The exercise of discretion under Article 96(2) EPC. Following a first **2–45** communication and observations from the applicant in reply (which may, for example, contest the objections raised by the Examining Division and/or propose amendments to meet the objections), if the Examining Division still considers that requirements of the EPC are not met, (and in the absence of circumstances which make it "necessary" to issue a further communication inviting further observations as discussed above), in order to satisfy the requirements of Article 113(1) and Rule 51(3) EPC it has a discretion in each individual case as to whether to issue a further communication with concomitant invitation to reply thereto, or an adverse decision.

The Guidelines state that "The examiner should be guided at the examination stage by the overriding principle that a final position (grant or refusal) should be reached in as few actions as possible, and he should control the procedure with this always in mind." The aim of the Examining Division in accordance with the public interest as well as the interest

[40] *Ibid.*
[41] T802/97 *LAMBDA ELECTRONICS* July 24, 1998.
[42] T921/94 *CIBA/Aminoanthraquinone derivatives*, October 30, 1998.

of individual applicants is "to carry out the substantive examination thoroughly, efficiently and expeditiously" (T84/82[43]).

The exercise of such discretion depends primarily upon whether or not there is a reasonable prospect that such an invitation could lead to the grant of the patent application (T84/82[44], T162/82[45], T640/91[46]).

Thus:

> "the expression 'as often as necessary' in Article 96(2) EPC indicates that the Examining Division has a discretion which has to be exercised objectively in the light of the circumstances of each case. In particular, it has to be interpreted as meaning that further invitations to file observations after the first one are required if there is a reasonable prospect that further discussion with the applicant could lead to reconciling conflicting opinions of the applicant and the Examining Division as to the allowability of the application or to the submission of amendments which might meet the objections raised" (T162/82[47]).

2–46   Communications in other circumstances are not excluded, but in the interest of orderly and economic examining procedures, there is no obligation for an Examining Division to send a communication which, on a reasonable objective basis, could be considered superfluous and unlikely to lead to a positive result (T162/82[48]). On the other hand, the necessity for a further communication prevails "as long as progress towards grant can be envisaged in the light of submissions made" (T84/82[49]).

There must obviously be a limit, however, to the number of opportunities which an applicant should be given to file observations in support of his application:

> "Article 113(1) EPC does not require that the applicant be given a repeated opportunity to comment on the argumentation of the Examining Division so long as the decisive objections against the grant of the European patent remain the same" (T161/82[50]).

Furthermore:

> "It is in principle not the function of the Examining Division to assess either the degree of collaboration from an applicant or his good faith, when deciding whether or not to invite further observation in the exercise of its discretion under Article 96(2) EPC" (T640/91[51]).

[43] T84/82 *MACARTHYS/Chloral derivatives* O.J. EPO 1983, 451; [1979–85] E.P.O.R.: B: 507.
[44] *Ibid.*
[45] T162/82 *SIGMA/Classifying areas* O.J. EPO 1987, 533; [1987] E.P.O.R. 375.
[46] T640/91 *NIPPON/Examination procedure* O.J. EPO 1994, 918; [1995] E.P.O.R. 243.
[47] See note 45.
[48] See note 45.
[49] See note 43.
[50] See note 45.
[51] See note 46.

(iii) Avoiding refusal after one communication. It follows from the 2–47 above discussion that even an applicant who is genuinely aiming to overcome the grounds raised against grant, by argument and/or by amendment, may in appropriate circumstances only be given one opportunity to reply before a decision refusing the application is issued.

Nevertheless, when applications are refused after only one opportunity to respond to the objections to grant which have been raised, it is no doubt natural for applicants to consider on occasions that the refusal was arbitrary, and that further dialogue might have resolved the situation without recourse to the filing of an appeal.

There are two ways of alleviating this situation which are open to an applicant when filing his first observations in reply:

(a) Requesting oral proceedings (as to which see Chapter 5 at paragraphs 5–45 *et seq.*);
(b) Filing amendments by way of one or more auxiliary requests (see paragraphs 2–28 *et seq.* and 5–29).

In this connection:

"even if it is possible for the Examiner to envisage amendments which might enable progress towards grant, the burden lies upon an applicant (if he so wishes) to propose amendments (including by way of auxiliary requests) which overcome the objections raised by the Examining Division, in his observations in reply to the first communication in which such objections are raised" (T300/89[52]).

(4) Amendments

(a) When allowable

The procedural admissibility of an amendment of an application is 2–48 governed by Article 123(1) and Rule 86 EPC. Thus, Article 123(1) EPC sets out an overriding principle that "In any case, an applicant shall be allowed at least one opportunity of amending the description, claims and drawings of his own volition." Beyond this, however, the admissibility of an amendment depends upon the stage of the procedure, as follows:

(i) Before receipt of the European Search Report—no amendments. 2–49 Pursuant to Rule 86(1) EPC, no amendment may be made before receipt of the European Search Report issued pursuant to Article 92(2) EPC ("except where otherwise provided", *i.e.* in particular, under Rule 41 EPC in order to remedy deficiencies of a formal nature).

(ii) After receipt of the European Search Report—amendment as of 2–50 right. The following opportunities to amend are provided:

[52] T300/89 3M/*Amendments* O.J. EPO 1990, 9; [1991] E.P.O.R. 502.

(1) After receipt of the search report and before receipt of a communication from the Examining Division, amendment is as of right (Rule 86(2) EPC).

(2) Similarly, after receipt of the first communication from the Examining Division, the applicant may amend once as of right at the same time as he replies to such communication (Rule 86(3) EPC).

2–51 **(iii) After further communications—amendment discretionary.** Thereafter, "no further amendment may be made without the consent of the Examining Division" (Rule 86(3) EPC, second sentence).

However, in any second or further communication under Article 96(2) EPC, the Examining Division "shall, where appropriate, invite the applicant to correct the disclosed deficiencies and, where necessary, to file the description, claims and drawings in an amended form" (Rule 51(2) EPC).

2–52 **(iv) Exercise of discretion to allow amendment.** The principles by which such discretion is exercised in practice are basically the same in proceedings before the Examining Division and on appeal. In particular, it is an overriding principle that an amendment which is proposed in reply to objections to grant (at any stage of the proceedings) will be accepted provided it is clearly allowable, both formally (*i.e.* having regard to Article 123(2) EPC), and in the sense that it overcomes the objections to patentability which have been raised.

In normal practice, if in reply to a communication from the Examining Division which raises objections to grant, the applicant proposes amendments which go a long way towards meeting the objections, a further opportunity to amend will be allowed provided that allowable amendments can be envisaged. It is in fact quite common for allowable amendments to be suggested to applicants for their consideration during pre-grant proceedings, although the practice varies in this respect.

However, it is also clearly within the discretion of the Examining Division, in a case where one or more proposals to amend have been made in reply to a communication raising objections to grant, but where the amendments do not come close to meeting the objections, to issue a decision refusing the application.

In this event, the applicant's only remedy is to appeal.

(v) Amendments during oral proceedings. See Chapter 5 at paragraph 5–67.

(b) Auxiliary requests

2–53 The general practice in relation to the filing of main and auxiliary requests, which is applicable in proceedings before the Examining Division, is discussed in Chapter 5 at paragraph 5–29.

When one or more auxiliary requests are filed in addition to the main request, the EPO is bound to these requests (Article 113(2) EPC), and to their order. Before a decision can be made in relation to an auxiliary request, the main request and all preceding auxiliary requests must be examined and decided upon—so long as such preceding requests have not been withdrawn, and are therefore still pending (T1105/96[53]).

Furthermore, an applicant "has a right both to file one or more auxiliary requests in addition to a main request, and to maintain all such requests (that is not to withdraw or abandon them), even if the Examining Division communicates its view that all except the last (possibly with further amendment) are inadmissible or unallowable, and he is then entitled to a reasoned appealable decision in respect of each such request" (T1105/96[54]).

If an auxiliary request is indicated to be allowable, the rejection in advance of such request unless all preceding requests are abandoned is unlawful and a substantial procedural violation within Rule 67 EPC (T1105/96[55]).

Although an applicant may *file* a number of auxiliary requests, since each such request is a request for amendment its admissibility is a matter of discretion under Rule 86(3) EPC (see paragraph 2–51 above). Thus in response to a communication raising objections to grant, an *appropriate* number of auxiliary requests may be filed, but the Examining Division has a discretion to refuse to admit an inappropriate number of such requests.

(c) Decision only on requested text

As discussed in paragraph 5–73, in accordance with Article 113(2) EPC and EPO is bound by the text of requests for amendment made by an applicant. **2–54**
Thus if a decision is issued on the basis of a text of the application which differs from the text requested by the applicant, such decision is contrary to Article 113(2) EPC and has to be set aside because it involves a substantive procedural violation (T647/93[56]).

(d) Summary

As discussed above, the procedure before the Examining Division in relation to amendments and auxiliary requests is, of necessity, reasonably **2–55**
flexible. The aim of this procedure is to progress towards a set of claims which is allowable as quickly as possible having regard to the nature of the case, provided the application contains patentable subject-matter at all. The stage at which the Examining Division may issue a decision refusing the application necessarily varies from case to case.

---

[53] T1105/96 *HAMAMATSU/Requests* O.J. EPO 1998, 249; [1998] E.P.O.R. 26.
[54] *Ibid.*
[55] *Ibid.*
[56] T647/93 *HITACHI MAXELL/Procedural violation* O.J. EPO 1995, 132; [1995] E.P.O.R. 195.

(5) Divisional applications

(a) Introduction

2–56 After filing a European patent application, an applicant may file a divisional application in respect of subject-matter which is divided out of the earlier, parent application. A divisional application may be filed "only in respect of subject-matter which does not extend beyond the content of the earlier application as filed" (Article 76(1) EPC). This requirement is the same as that which applies *mutatis mutandis* to the amendment of an application after filing; see paragraphs 8–02 *et seq.* below. The practice which is applicable to such amendments is also applicable to divisional applications, and vice-versa.

A divisional application "shall be deemed to have been filed on the date of filing of the earlier application and shall have the benefit of any right to priority" (Article 76(1) EPC).

A divisional application may be filed by an applicant either of his own motion, or in order to meet an objection of lack of unity of invention under Article 82 EPC during the examination procedure.

The EPC does not prohibit the presence in a divisional application of an independent claim—explicitly or as a notional claim derived by partitioning an actual claim—which is related to an independent claim in the parent application in such a way that the "parent" claim includes all the features of the "divisional" claim combined with an additional feature (T587/98[57]).

(b) Designation of Contracting States

2–57 A divisional application "shall not designate Contracting States which were not designated in the earlier application" (Article 76(2) EPC).

In a case where the earlier application originally designates a Contracting State but the designation fee in respect of such State is not paid in due time, the designation of that State is deemed to be withdrawn (Article 91(4) EPC).

> "The deemed withdrawal of the designation of a Contracting State ... takes effect upon expiry of the time limits mentioned in Article 79(2), Rules 15(2), 25(2) and 107(1) EPC, as applicable, and not upon expiry of the period of grace provided by Rule 85a EPC" (G4/98[58])

Consequently, in such a case, a divisional application may designate a Contracting State which has been designated in the earlier parent application, up until the time when the deemed withdrawal of the designation in the earlier application takes effect as set out above (G4/98[59], overruling J22/95[60]).

---

[57] T587/98 KOMAG/*Divisional claim conflicting with parent*, O.J. EPO 2000, 497.
[58] G4/98 *Designation fees* O.J. EPO(P).
[59] *Ibid.*
[60] J22/95 AUMAC/*Designation of contracting states in a divisional application* O.J. EPO 1998, 569.

According to the proposed revision of the EPC Article 76(2) EPC will be amended so as to read: **2–57A**

> 76(2): "All the Contracting States designated in the earlier application at the time of filing of a European divisional application shall be deemed to be designated in the divisional application".

(c) Latest date for filing a divisional application

(i) The general rule: not after approval of text under Rule 51(4) EPC
Rule 25(1) EPC states that:

> "Up to the approval of the text, in accordance with Rule 51(4) EPC, in which the European patent is to be granted, the applicant may file a divisional application on the pending earlier European patent application." **2–58**

As to approval of the text under Rule 51(4) EPC (see paragraph 2–67 below) Rule 25(1) EPC implements Article 76(1) EPC and is compatible with it, and accordingly a divisional application cannot be filed after such date of approval of the text (G10/92[61], overruling J11, 16/91[62]).

(ii) Not after withdrawal of approval of text. Furthermore, although approval of the text under Rule 51(4) EPC may be withdrawn within the fixed period set in the communication under Rule 51(4) EPC in order to request further amendment (T1/92:[63] see paragraph 2–67 below), "The mere fact that approval can be withdrawn does not however mean that the applicant who withdraws approval then acquires the right to file a divisional application. Nor can the applicant by withdrawing the approval, alter the fact that it was once given" (G10/92[64]). Thus where approval of the text has been given: **2–59**

> "Withdrawal of this consent for the sole purpose of filing a divisional application is not effective to re-open the period in which a divisional application can be filed" (J29/96[65]).

(iii) Absence of Rule 51(4) EPC communication following oral proceedings in an appeal: divisional application after approval of text. In appeal proceedings following refusal of an application by an Examining Division, a Board of Appeal may decide to grant the application with a text as requested by the applicant during the appeal proceedings (for example, during oral proceedings). In such a case, the practice of the Board of Appeal is to issue a decision remitting the case to the Examining Division **2–60**

[61] G10/92 *Divisional application* O.J. EPO 1994, 633; [1995] E.P.O.R. 265.
[62] J11, 16/91 *DOW/Deadline for filing divisional application* O.J. EPO 1994, 28; [1994] E.P.O.R. 235.
[63] T1/92 *LELAND STANFORD/Approval* O.J. EPO 1993, 685.
[64] See note 61.
[65] J29/96 *N.N./Divisional application* O.J. EPO 1998, 581; [1998] E.P.O.R. 358.

with an order to grant the patent with such text as specified, and the patent is thereafter granted in the absence of a communication under Rule 51(4) EPC.

In such a case, "the approval of a text in which the patent is to be granted is implied, in the absence of special circumstances, in the appellant's request to take a decision on the text he submitted to the Board". Furthermore: "Such approval which is not expressed in the form specified by Rule 51(4) EPC does not exclude the filing of a divisional application filed after remittal to the first instance" (J8/98[66]).

(d) Amendment of a divisional application: Articles 76(1) and 123(2) EPC

2–61   "A divisional application has to comply with the requirements of both Article 76(1) EPC and 123(2) EPC. Article 76(1) EPC governs the filing of a divisional application and therefore whether it is entitled to the filing date of the parent application and has the same benefit of right to priority as the parent application. Article 123(2) EPC governs amendments to the divisional application subsequent to its filing" (T873/94[67]).

(6) Consolidation of European and Euro–PCT applications

2–62 A European application may be consolidated with a Euro–PCT application under certain conditions which are set out in Legal Advice 10/92. In particular, the filing and priority dates must be the same. Although the Legal Advice states that "the text of the description and the claims must be identical", this requirement is too stringent, and consolidation may be allowed with somewhat different texts to the claims, for example (J17/92[68]).

(7) Abandonment of particular subject-matter

2–63 The principles governing the withdrawal of a patent application are discussed in paragraphs 2–73 *et seq.* below.

Similar principles apply to abandonment of particular subject-matter within a patent application, for example certain claims and the corresponding description. Thus:

"if on the true interpretation of a statement made by an applicant or patentee, it may be considered that a particular subject-matter has been expressly abandoned together with the complete deletion of the appropriate claim and in addition all support therefor in the specification, the same cannot be reinstated again in the application" (T61/85[69]).

[66] J8/98 *N.N./Divisional application* O.J. EPO 1999, 687.
[67] T873/94 *TOSHIBA/Amended divisional application* O.J. EPO 1997, 456; [1998] E.P.O.R. 71.
[68] J17/92 *WARNER/Consolidation* November 22, 1996.
[69] T61/85 *ICI/Polyester crystallisation* [1998] E.P.O.R. 20.

Furthermore:

"If an applicant cancels claims included in a European patent application, but fails to state at the same time that their deletion is without prejudice to the filing of a divisional application, the Examining Division will be obliged to refuse its consent to the subsequent filing of a divisional application" (J15/85[70]).

This is because: 2–64

"At the date of abandonment of [certain claimed subject-matter], the parent application had been published so that the public had access to the file. The public was thus immediately entitled to assume that, since there was no reference to filing of a divisional application, the applicant had irrevocably abandoned and would not thereafter seek to obtain protection for the [abandoned claimed subject-matter]"

The irreversibility of such an abandonment is one of the consequences of the early publication of a European patent application.

If particular subject-matter in the description and/or claims is either deleted from the application before grant, or indicated in the description as no longer belonging to the claimed invention, such subject-matter is regarded as having been substantively abandoned at the date of grant, and therefore cannot thereafter be reinstated in the application after grant, during opposition proceedings. This follows in particular from Article 123(3) EPC (see Chapter 8 at paragraphs 8–62, 8–72a) (T1149/97[71]).

(8) Suspension of proceedings for grant

(a) Pending Enlarged Board of Appeal proceedings

"Whenever a decision of the Examining Division depends entirely on   2–65
the outcome of proceedings before the Enlarged Board of Appeal on a legal question or point of law raised according to Article 112 EPC—and this is known to the Examining Division—the further examination of the application must be suspended until the matter is decided by the Enlarged Board of Appeal" (T166/84[72]).

(b) Pending proceedings concerning entitlement to grant

Rule 13(1) EPC provides for suspension of proceedings for grant: "If a third   2–66
party provides proof to the EPO that he has opened proceedings against the applicant for the purpose of seeking a judgment that he is entitled to the grant of the European patent." The EPO "shall stay the proceedings" unless the third party consents to continuation.

---

[70] J15/85 X/Abandonment of claim O.J. EPO 1986, 395; [1987] E.P.O.R. 118.
[71] T1149/97 SOLARTRON/Fluid transducer O.J. EPO 2000, 259.
[72] T166/84 TAKEDA/Postponement of examination O.J. EPO 1984, 489; [1979–85] E.P.O.R.: C: 981.

If a third party provides satisfactory proof of relevant proceedings and seeks suspension, "the suspension must be ordered, provided that the ... application has not been withdrawn or is not deemed to have been withdrawn" (T146/82[73]).

Rule 13(3) EPC provides that the EPO may set a date for continuing the examination proceedings, which may subsequently be varied (T146/82).

The procedure following a request for a stay of proceedings is considered in paragraphs 2–83 *et seq.* below.

(9) Preparation for grant: late amendments

(a) Requesting and giving approval of the text: Rule 51(4) EPC

2–67 Before deciding to grant a patent, the Examining Division must inform the applicant of the proposed text in which it intends to grant the patent, and it must request the applicant's approval of such text, within a fixed period of between two and four months, which shall be extended once by up to two months upon request (Rule 51(4) EPC). If no approval is communicated to the Examining Division in due time, the application is refused (Rule 51(5) EPC).

The communication requesting approval must clearly identify the text to be approved.

"A valid approval of the text intended for grant requires that it is clear which text the applicant has approved. This is not the case if the communication under Rule 51(4) EPC refers to an enclosed text which is not actually annexed" (J29/95[74]).

After the Rule 51(4) EPC communication has been issued, amendments to the text may still be requested under Rule 86(3) EPC, within the fixed period. If the Examining Division does not consent to amendments requested during this period, it must give its reasons, and it must invite the applicant to submit observations within a specified period, before taking its decision (Rule 51(5) EPC).

An approval of the text may be withdrawn within the fixed period set in a Rule 51(4) EPC communication, in which case Rule 51(5) EPC applies (T1/92[75]).

If amendments are proposed during the fixed period set in a Rule 51(4) EPC communication and are considered allowable by the Examining Division, there is no need for a further communication under Rule 51(4) EPC. Approval of the text may be established "on the basis of the amendments and of the texts communicated to the applicant to which no amendments have been submitted" (J29/95[76]).

[73] T146/82 *TAG/Suspension of proceedings* O.J. EPO 1985, 267; [1979–85] E.P.O.R.: B: 618.
[74] J29/95 *AXIS/Divisional application* O.J. EPO 1996, 489; [1997] E.P.O.R. 1.
[75] T1/92 *LELAND STANFORD/Approval of text* O.J. EPO 1993, 685; [1997] E.P.O.R. 424.
[76] See note 74.

(b) Procedure following approval of the text: Rule 51(6) EPC

After approval of the text pursuant to a Rule 51(4) EPC communication, the **2–68** applicant is invited to pay fees for grant and printing and to file translations of the claims into the other two official languages within a non-extendable fixed period of between two and three months (Rule 51(6) EPC). Failure to comply with such request within the fixed period results in the application being deemed to be withdrawn (Rule 51(8) EPC).

Following issue of a communication under Rule 51(6) EPC and until issue of a decision to grant the patent, amendment of the text may still be requested and is within the discretion of the Examining Division under Rule 86(3) EPC (G7/93[77]). This discretion must be properly exercised. Thus:

> "When exercising such discretion following issue of a communication under Rule 51(6) EPC, an Examining Division must consider all relevant factors. In particular it must consider and balance the applicant's interest in obtaining a patent which is legally valid in all of the designated States, and the EPO's interest in bringing the examin-ation procedure to a close by the issue of a decision to grant the patent. Having regard to the object underlying the issue of a communication under Rule 51(6) EPC, which is to conclude the granting procedure on the basis of the previously approved text, the allowance of a request for amendment at that late stage in the granting procedure will be an exception rather than the rule" (G7/93[78]).

If oral proceedings under Article 116(1) EPC are requested in connection with a request for amendment which is made after issue of a communi-cation under Rule 51(6) EPC, an oral hearing must be appointed before a decision refusing such amendments is issued (T556/95[79]: see Chapter 5 at paragraph 5–44).

(c) Latest date for amendment compared to filing a divisional application

Although the filing of a divisional application bears some similarity with **2–69** amending an application it should be noted that whereas up until issue of a decision to grant the patent it is always a matter of discretion under Rule 86(3) EPC whether to allow a request for amendment, nevertheless under Rule 25(1) EPC a divisional application may only be filed up to the approval of the text under Rule 51(4) EPC. There is no discretion to allow filing of a divisional application after approval of the text under Rule 51(4) EPC. This applies even if the approval of the text is withdrawn within the fixed period set in the Rule 51(4) EPC communication (see paragraph 2–59 above).

---

[77] G7/93 *WHITBY II/Late-filed amendments* O.J. EPO 1994, 775; [1995] E.P.O.R. 49.
[78] *Ibid.*
[79] T556/95 *CHAUM/Undeniable systems* O.J. EPO 1997, 205; [1997] E.P.O.R. 394.

(10) Decision to grant or refuse

(a) Decision to grant

2–70   "The decision to grant the European patent shall state which text of the European patent application forms the basis for the grant of the European patent" (Rule 51(11) EPC).

"The decision to grant a European patent shall not take effect until the date on which the European Patent Bulletin mentions the grant" (Article 97(4) EPC).

(b) Decision to refuse

2–71   "The Examining Division shall refuse a European patent application if it is of the opinion that such application or the invention to which it relates does not meet the requirements of the Convention, except where a different sanction is provided for by this Convention" (Article 97(1) EPC).

(c) Requirements for a decision

2–72 See Chapter 5 at paragraph 5–74.

F. Miscellaneous Procedural Matters Before Grant

(1) Withdrawal of an application

(a) Introduction

2–73 An application may be withdrawn by the applicant at any time before the date of grant, which is the date on which the European Patent Bulletin mentions the grant (Article 97(4) EPC). For example, an application may be withdrawn before publication under Article 93 PC, or after a decision to grant is made under Article 97(2) EPC, but before the date of grant.

The effect of withdrawal is retrospective in that the application is deemed never to have conferred any protection from the date of publication upon the applicant under Article 64 EPC (Article 67(4) EPC). The date of withdrawal must be entered in the Register of Patents (Rule 92(m) EPC) must be published in the Patent Bulletin (Article 129(a) EPC). As explained in detail in Legal Advice No. 8/80,[80] for reasons of legal certainty "it is essential for the point in time at which the said legal effects result from a notice of withdrawal to be clearly established". Thus, in order to avoid any uncertainty, "the withdrawal of a European patent application is binding on an applicant". Moreover, further processing of an application under Article 121 EPC (see Chapter 6 at paragraph 6–02 below) is not possible following withdrawal of an application.

---

[80] O.J. EPO 1981, 6; see Appendix 6.

(b) What constitutes a withdrawal

Since the withdrawal of an application has such an irreversible effect, it is **2-74** important to be able to determine when a withdrawal has actually been made. In this connection two possible courses should be distinguished, namely:

(i) "active" withdrawal, which is intended to be immediately effective;

(ii) "passive" abandonment, where it is intended that the applicant will take no further action in connection with the application, with the result that the application will in due course lapse through non-payment of a renewal fee.

This distinction has been explained as follows:

"in the operation of the European patent system there is a recognised difference between passive abandonment and active withdrawal of a European patent application. Each case in which there is a dispute as to the applicant's intentions has to be considered on its own facts" (J15/86[81]).

In view of the immediate and conclusive nature of a withdrawal of an **2-75** application, the distinction between these two courses of action is of vital importance. Furthermore, a request for withdrawal "should only be accepted without question if it is completely unqualified and unambiguous" (J11/80[82]).

"Where there is any doubt as to the actual intent of a patent applicant who has made a declaration which could be construed as a withdrawal of the application, that declaration may be so construed only if the related facts confirm that such was the applicant's true intent" (J11/87[83]).

However,

"Effective withdrawal ... does not depend on whether the applicant has used the term 'withdrawal'. The language used must be interpreted having regard to the surrounding circumstances from which it must be clear that the applicant really wants immediate and unconditional withdrawal rather than passive abandonment. ..." (J7/87[84]).

Particular cases:

---

[81] J15/86 *AUSONIA/Withdrawal of application* O.J. EPO 1988, 417 [1989] E.P.O.R. 152.
[82] J11/80 *ROHM/Withdrawal of European patent application* O.J. EPO 1981, 141; [1979–85] E.P.O.R.: A: 48.
[83] J11/87 *DORIS/Abandonment of application* O.J. EPO 1988, 367; [1989] E.P.O.R. 54.
[84] J7/87 *SCHWARZ ITALIA/Abandonment* O.J. EPO 1988, 422; [1989] E.P.O.R. 91.

(1) "We hereby withdraw the above-mentioned patent application. Publication of the application should not take place" (J11/80[85]). This letter was received by the EPO at a point in time when preparations for publication were complete and could not be cancelled. The letter was interpreted (on appeal) as a conditional request for withdrawal, *i.e.* conditional upon the application not being published, and since publication had taken place, the request for withdrawal was not effective.

(2) "Applicant wishes to abandon this application" (J6/86[86]). This letter was filed subsequently to disapproval of the text Rule 51(4) EPC, and was held to constitute an active withdrawal of the application.

(3) "We advise you that our client has decided to abandon the case in re . . ." (J7/87[87]). This letter was held (on appeal) not to be an active withdrawal since it could fairly be interpreted as passive abandonment.

(c) Withdrawal to avoid publication

2–76 An application will not be published if it is withdrawn before "the termination of the technical preparations for publication" (Rule 48(2) EPC). Such termination is fixed as ten weeks before expiry of eighteen months from the date of filing or the date of priority (Decision dated December 14, 1992[88]). If a declaration of withdrawal is filed by such date, the applicant has a right to prevent publication. If a declaration of withdrawal is filed after that date, the EPO will try to prevent publication if circumstances permit (Notice dated December 14, 1992[89]), but if preparations for publication are complete or nearly so, the EPO cannot necessarily stop the publication (Guidelines C.VI,15,5a).

(d) Retraction of a withdrawal

2–77 Legal Advice No. 8/80[90] emphasises that the necessity for legal certainty in connection with the withdrawal of an application virtually excludes the possibility of retraction of a withdrawal once made. It concludes that "the EPC views the notice of withdrawal as basically irrevocable".

Thus, "in the public interest, it must be too late to ask for retraction of a letter of withdrawal once withdrawal of the . . . application has been notified to the public in the European Patent Bulletin".

However, correction of a withdrawal of an application may be possible under Rule 88 EPC: see Chapter 6 at paragraph 6–18.

---

[85] J11/80 *ROHM/Withdrawal of a European patent application* O.J. EPO 1981, 141; [1979–85] E.P.O.R.: A: 48.
[86] J6/86 *RIKER/Withdrawal* O.J. EPO 1988, 124; [1988] E.P.O.R. 277.
[87] J7/87 *SCHWARZ ITALIA/Abandonment* O.J. EPO 1988, 422; [1989] E.P.O.R. 91.
[88] Decision of the President of the EPO O.J. EPO 1993, 55 dated December 14, 1992.
[89] Notice from the EPO concerning withdrawal of the application to prevent publication O.J. EPO 1993, 56 dated December 14, 1992.
[90] O.J. EPO 1981, 6; see Appendix 6.

(2) Determination of the lawful applicant: related procedure

(a) Introduction: determination by a national court

As a matter of law, in accordance with Article 60(1) EPC, the right to a **2–78** European patent belongs to the inventor or his successor in title. Consequently, only such a person is entitled to apply to the EPO for a European patent. As a matter of fact, however, an application may in practice be filed by a person who is not the inventor or his successor in title and who is therefore an unlawful applicant. In such a case, the application is filed contrary to the rights of the lawful applicant in respect of an invention which is the subject of a European application. The person who is named as the applicant in the documents constituting an application will be assumed by the EPO to be entitled to the European patent and the EPO has no obligation or power to investigate the legal entitlement to the patent (see paragraph 2–24 above).

Under the Protocol on Recognition, which is an integral part of the EPC **2–79** (Article 164(1) EPC), the national courts of the Contracting States are responsible for determining disputes concerning the entitlement to the grant of a patent upon a European application, before grant. The Protocol on Recognition "gives the courts of the Contracting States jurisdiction to decide claims to entitlement to the right to the grant of a European patent, provides a system for determining which national court shall decide such claims in individual cases, and requires the mutual recognition of decisions in respect of such claims, within the Contracting States to the EPC" (G3/92[91]).

"In relation to any particular claim by an alleged lawful applicant against an actual applicant for a European patent, the particular Contracting State whose courts have jurisdiction to decide the claim is determined by the system of jurisdiction set out in Articles 2 to 8 Protocol. For any such claim, this system of jurisdiction designates the courts of one (and only one) Contracting State as the proper forum in which the claim must be decided" (G3/92[92]).

Thus a third party who believes that he is the lawful applicant for a European patent in place of the named applicant may apply to the appropriate national court for a decision to that effect.

(b) Suspension of proceedings for grant pending national court proceedings

Rule 13(1) EPC states that: **2–80**

> "If a third party provides proof to the EPO that he has opened proceedings against the applicant for the purpose of seeking a judgment that he is entitled to the grant of a European patent, the EPO shall stay the proceedings for grant unless the third party consents to

---

[91] G3/92 *LATCHWAYS/Lawful applicant* O.J. EPO 1994, 607; [1995] E.P.O.R. 141.
[92] *Ibid.*

the continuation of such proceedings. Such consent must be com-municated in writing to the EPO; it shall be irrevocable. However, proceedings for grant may not be stayed before the publication of the European patent application."

Thus, subject to satisfactory proof as to the opening of proceedings, and provided proceedings for grant are still in existence (as to which see below), an application for a stay must be granted (T146/82[93]). However, under Rule 13(3) EPC, when the EPO decides to grant a stay of grant proceedings, it may set a date on which it intends to continue the proceedings. However, "the date may be varied, or the order staying the proceedings may be discharged on the subsequent request of the applicant or of the third party who applied for the order" (T146/82[94]).

2–81   **(i) Timing of request for stay.** The final sentence of Rule 13(1) EPC makes it clear that proceedings for grant may not be stayed before the publication of the application pursuant to Article 93 EPC. Furthermore, proceedings for grant can only be stayed pursuant to Rule 13(1) EPC if they are in existence at the point in time when a third party provides proof to the EPO that he has opened entitlement proceedings. Thus if the application has been withdrawn, deemed to be withdrawn or refused before such proof is provided, clearly the proceedings for grant cannot be stayed. Similarly, proceedings for grant cannot be stayed if the application has already been granted at the time when such proof is provided to the EPO.
        A decision to grant a European patent pursuant to Article 97(2) EPC takes effect on the date on which the European Patent Bulletin mentions the grant (Article 97(4) EPC)—(not on the date when the decision-making process following written examination proceedings is completed: *cf.* G12/91[95]).
        Thus a request for a stay of the grant proceedings is admissible if a third party provides such proof to the EPO before the date of mention of grant under Article 97(4) EPC (J7/96[96]).

2–82   **(ii) Proof that a third party has "opened proceedings".** The wording of Rule 13(1) EPC suggests that a third party must provide the EPO with proof that he has taken the necessary first step in commencing legal proceedings before a national court of a Contracting State in order to establish that he is entitled to the grant of a European patent, not the named applicant. For example, in relation to proceedings under section 12 of the 1977 U.K. Act before the United Kingdom Patent Office (which is a "court" for the purposes of the Protocol on Recognition), a copy of the completed Patents Form 2/77 constituting a reference to the Comptroller of Case in support of such reference should be sufficient "proof" that a third party

[93] T146/82 *TAG/Suspension of proceedings* O.J. EPO 1985, 267; [1979–85] E.P.O.R.: B: 618.
[94] *Ibid.*
[95] G12/91 *NOVATOME II/Final decision* O.J. EPO 1994, 285; [1994] E.P.O.R. 309.
[96] J7/96 *INSTANCE/Suspension of proceedings* O.J. EPO 1999, 443; [1999] E.P.O.R. 198.

has "opened proceedings" (see, *e.g.* J7/96[97]), and upon receipt of such documents the EPO should stay the proceedings for grant. In this connection it may be noted that Patents Form 2/77 is entitled "Initiation of proceedings before the Comptroller".

It should be added that in the context of Rule 13(1) EPC it should not be necessary for a third party to provide proof to the EPO that the named applicant has received a copy of the above documents as filed at the United Kingdom Patent Office.

(iii) Procedure following a request for a stay: the status of the named 2–83 **applicant.** The procedure following a request for a stay of grant proceedings by a third party, both at first instance before the Legal Division of the EPO and in the event of an appeal to the Legal Board of Appeal, in particular as regards hearing the named applicant, was considered in J28/94[97a]. The decision explains that if the conditions of Rule 13(1) EPC are met a stay of proceedings is automatic and immediate, this being justified by the fact that a stay is a preventive measure in favour of the third party who is requesting it, in order to prevent the named applicant from withdrawing the application for example. Thus the named applicant is not regarded by the Legal Division as a party who has to be heard before the grant proceedings are stayed. On the other hand if the Legal Division decided not to stay the proceedings for grant, the third party requesting the stay could appeal such decision.

If the proceedings or grant are stayed, the named applicant could ask that the stay be removed (for example, because of lack of sufficient proof of the opening of proceedings). If the Legal Division decided to remove the stay, the third party could appeal that decision. If the Legal Division decides not to remove the stay, the named applicant could appeal that decision.

If the Legal Division refuses a request for a stay by a third party, or 2–84 removes a stay which it has previously granted, in the event of an appeal by the third party, the named applicant is a "party as of right to appeal proceedings initiated by the third party", and may therefore "challenge the justification" for a stay, even though he was not heard by the Legal Division (J28/94[98]).

If, following a request by a third party for a stay, the Legal Division either does not grant a stay or removes a stay which has been granted, the European application might proceed to grant. In such a case, and in the event of an appeal against the decision to refuse or remove the stay, having regard to the suspensive effect of an appeal (see Chapter 4 at paragraph 4–53) the EPO should publish a cancellation of the mention of grant in the European Patent Bulletin, either of its own motion (J7/96[99]) or if necessary upon order of the Legal Board of Appeal (J28/94[100]).

[97] *Ibid.*
[97a] J28/94 *SOLUDIA/Stay of grant proceedings* O.J. EPO 1995, 742; [1997] E.P.O.R. 379.
[98] *Ibid.*
[99] See note 97.
[100] See note 98.

The above procedure is somewhat complex, but is analogous to the determination of the admissibility of an opposition (if a notice of opposition is prima facie admissible, it is regarded as admissible, without prejudice to the right of the patent proprietor to contest such admissibility, both at first instance and on appeal—see Chapter 3 at paragraph 3–36).

(c) Procedure following determination that a third party is the lawful applicant

2–85   If a national court decides that a person other than the named applicant for a European application is legally entitled to the grant of a European patent pursuant to that application, under Article 61(1) EPC the lawful applicant may within a period of three months after the national court decision becomes final, for the Contracting States to which the decision applies:

"(a)   prosecute the application as his own application in place of the applicant,

(b)   file a new European patent application in respect of the same invention,

(c)   request that the application be refused."

Clearly options (a) and (c) envisage that the application is still pending. However; option (b) does not depend upon the application being still pending, as discussed below.

(d) Procedure under Article 61(1)(b) EPC if the application is no longer pending

2–86   "When it has been adjudged by a final decision of a national court that a person other than the applicant is entitled to the grant of a European patent application in respect of the same invention under Article 61(1)(b) EPC, it is not a pre-condition for the application to be accepted that the earlier usurping application is still pending before the EPO at the time the new application is filed" (G3/92[101]).

In G3/92,[102] a third party who had been informed of an invention in confidence by the inventor's company filed a European application which was duly published and then deemed to be withdrawn because of failure to pay the examination fee. Subsequently the inventor's company filed a European application, but the European search report cited the earlier application by the third party. The inventor's company commenced proceedings under section 12 of the United Kingdom Patents Act 1977 before the United Kingdom Patent Office (which is a "court" for the purpose of the Protocol on Recognition, under Article 1(2) of the Protocol), which issued a decision that the inventor's company was the lawful

---

[101] G3/92 *LATCHWAYS/Lawful applicant* O.J. EPO 1994, 607; [1995] E.P.O.R. 141.
[102] *Ibid.*

applicant. The lawful applicant then filed a new European application pursuant to Article 61(1)(b) EPC, but this was rejected by the Receiving Section on the basis that the earlier application by the third party (the "unlawful applicant") was no longer pending, this being said to be a prerequisite for the application of Article 61 EPC.

The Enlarged Board held that it was not a precondition that the original **2–87** usurping application be pending before the EPO at the time a new application is filed by the lawful applicant under Article 61(1)(b) EPC. Thus the lawful applicant was allowed to file a new European application in its own name in respect of the same subject-matter as has been disclosed in the application which had been filed by the unlawful applicant and published and withdrawn about four years previously. The new application was allocated the filing date of the earlier application by the unlawful applicant pursuant to Article 61(2) EPC. Consequently the content of the earlier application does not form part of the prior art with respect to the new application.

G3/92[103] recognises that if a lawful applicant was not able to file a new application under Article 61(1)(b) EPC in such circumstances, an unlawful applicant could ensure his own freedom to use the invention which he had misappropriated simply by filing an application and then withdrawing it after publication, which "cannot have been intended under the Protocol on Recognition". On the other hand, the decision also recognises the possibility of prejudice to third parties who are misled by the withdrawal of the earlier application into using the invention on the assumption that it is in the public domain, and suggests that such special circumstances could be taken into account by a national court, either in the context of proceedings deciding upon the right to entitlement to a European patent, or in the context of any subsequent infringement proceedings.

The decision contains a dissenting minority opinion pursuant to Article 12a RPEBA (see Chapter 4 at paragraph 4–196).

(4) Renewal fees for European Patent Applications: time-limits

The payment of such fees, which are due for the third and subsequent years **2–88** after filing, is governed by Article 86 EPC. In particular Article 86(2) EPC provides that a renewal fee may be validly paid together with an additional fee, within an additional period of six months after each due date. If the renewal fee and any additional fee have not been paid in due time, the application is deemed to be withdrawn (Article 86(3) EPC). This additional period has to be calculated, taking into account Rule 83 EPC concerning the calculation of time limits. Consequently:

"When calculating the six-month period for the payment of a renewal fee with additional fee under Article 86(2) EPC, Rule 83(4) EPC should be applied *mutatis mutandis* in the light of Rule 37(1), first sentence,

[103] *Ibid.*

EPC. This means that the six-month period does not end on the day of the subsequent six month corresponding 'in number' to the due date according to Rule 37(1), first sentence, EPC but on the day which is equivalent to this due date by virtue of its being 'the last day of the month'. For the purposes of calculating the additional period under Article 86(2) EPC, therefore, Rule 83(4) EPC, in the context of Rule 37(1) first sentence EPC, results in a period running 'from the last day of the month to the last day of the month' " (J4/91[104]).

Furthermore,

"Legal Advice No 5/80. Calculation of aggregate time limits" (O.J. EPO 1980, 149), is not applicable to the start of the additional period under Article 86(2) EPC. This means that the period starts on the last day of the month referred to in Rule 37(1), first sentence, EPC, even in the circumstances described in Rule 85(1),(2) and (4) EPC. It follows that the occurrence of such circumstances at the beginning of the period does not result in the end of the period being postponed beyond the end of the sixth month and into the seventh month" (J4/91[105]).

Cases Referred to in Chapter 2

Board of Appeal Decisions

G12/91	NOVATOME II/Final decision O.J. EPO 1994, 285; [1994] E.P.O.R. 309.
G2/92	Non-payment of further search fees O.J. EPO 1993, 591; [1994] E.P.O.R. 278.
G3/92	LATCHWAYS/Lawful applicant O.J. EPO 1994, 607; [1995] E.P.O.R. 141.
G10/92	Divisional application O.J. EPO 1994, 633; [1995] E.P.O.R. 265.
G7/93	WHITBY II/Late filed amendments O.J. EPO 1994, 775; [1995] E.P.O.R. 49.
G4/98	Designation fees O.J. EPO(P).
J3/80	CHUBB/Failure to forward a European patent application O.J. EPO 1980, 92; [1979–85] E.P.O.R.: A:31.
J11/80	ROHM/Withdrawal of a European patent application O.J. EPO 1981, 141; [1979–85] E.P.O.R.: A:48.
J15/85	X/Abandonment of claim O.J. EPO 1986, 395; [1987] E.P.O.R. 118.
J6/86	RIKER/Withdrawal O.J. EPO 1988, 124; [1988] E.P.O.R. 277.

[104] J4/91 AHMAD/*Additional period for renewal fee* O.J. EPO 1992, 402; [1994] E.P.O.R. 365.
[105] *Ibid.*

J15/86   AUSONIA/Withdrawal of application O.J. 1988, 417
          [1989] E.P.O.R. 152.
J18/86   ZOUEKI/Filing date O.J. EPO 1988, 165; [1988] E.P.O.R.
          338.
J25/86   WARHEIT/Identity of application O.J. EPO 1987, 475;
          [1988] E.P.O.R. 40.
J7/87   SCHWARZ ITALIA/Abandonment O.J. EPO 1988, 422;
          [1989] E.P.O.R. 91.
J11/87   DORIS/Abandonment O.J. EPO 1988, 367; [1989]
          E.P.O.R. 54.
J21/87   MATSUBARA/Identification of applicant December 21,
          1987.
J25/88   NEW FLEX/Date of filing O.J. EPO 1989, 486; [1990]
          E.P.O.R. 59.
J37/89   MATSUSHITA/Rejection of extension of time limit O.J.
          EPO 1993, 20; [1993] E.P.O.R. 356.
J14/90   FLACHGLAS/Denmark—tacit O.J. EPO 1992, 505; [1992]
          E.P.O.R. 553.
J18/90   CANON/Denmark—expressly O.J. EPO 1992, 511; [1992]
          E.P.O.R. 553.
J4/91   AHMAD/Additional period for renewal fee O.J. EPO
          1992, 402; [1994] E.P.O.R. 365.
J5/91   KONGSKILDE/Legal loophole O.J. EPO 1993, 657; [1994]
          E.P.O.R. 205.
J11, 16/91 DOW CHEMICAL/Deadline for filing divisional appli-
          cation O.J. EPO 1994, 28; [1994] E.P.O.R. 235.
J12/92   BLAIZAT/Restoration of rights; further processing April
          30, 1993.
J17/92   WARNER/Consolidation November 22, 1996.
J47/92   SILVER SYSTEMS/Further processing O.J. EPO 1995,
          180; [1995] E.P.O.R. 495.
J10/93   COLLAPSIBLE BOTTLE OF AMERICA/Transfer O.J.
          EPO 1997, 91; [1997] E.P.O.R. 491.
J18/93   CARDIAC/Correction of mistake O.J. EPO 1997, 326;
          [1998] E.P.O.R. 38.
J20/94   HINTERHOLZER/According of a filing date O.J. EPO
          1996, 181; [1996] E.P.O.R.
J28/94   SOLUDIA/Stay of grant proceedings O.J. EPO 1995, 742;
          [1997] E.P.O.R. 379.
J29/94   GARCIA/Deemed withdrawal O.J. EPO 1998/6; [1998]
          E.P.O.R. 342.
J22/95   AUMAC/Designation of contracting states in a div-
          isional application O.J. EPO 1998, 569.
J29/95   AXIS/Divisional application O.J. EPO 1996, 489; [1997]
          E.P.O.R. 1.
J7/96   INSTANCE/Suspension of proceedings O.J. EPO 1999,
          443.

J18/96   N.N./Filing date O.J. EPO 1998, 403.
J29/96   N.N./Divisional application O.J. EPO 1998, 581; [1998]
              E.P.O.R. 358.
J8/98   N.N./Divisional application O.J. EPO 1999, 687; [2000]
              E.P.O.R. 283.

T84/82   MACARTHYS/Chloral derivatives O.J. EPO 1983, 451;
              [1979–85] E.P.O.R.: B:507.
T146/82   TAG/Suspension of proceedings O.J. EPO 1985, 267;
              [1979–85] E.P.O.R.: B:618.
T161/82   AMP/Electrical contact O.J. EPO 1984, 551; [1979–85]
              E.P.O.R.: C:660.
T162/82   SIGMA/Classifying areas O.J. EPO 1987, 533; [1987]
              E.P.O.R. 375.
T166/84   TAKEDA/Postponement of examination O.J. EPO 1984,
              489; [1979–85] E.P.O.R.: C:981.
T61/85   ICI/Polyester crystallisation [1998] E.P.O.R. 20.
T300/89   3M/Amendments O.J. EPO 1990, 9; [1991] E.P.O.R. 502.
T640/91   NIPPON/Examination procedure O.J. EPO 1994, 918;
              [1995] E.P.O.R. 243.
T1/92   LELAND STANFORD/Approval—disapproval O.J. EPO
              1993, 685.
T714/92   POHJOLA September 18, 1992.
T951/92   NEC/Opportunity to comment O.J. EPO 1996, 53; [1996]
              E.P.O.R. 371.
T647/93   HITACHI MAXELL/Procedural violation O.J. EPO 1995,
              132; [1995] E.P.O.R. 195.
T382/94   CARL ZEISS/Documents as filed O.J. EPO 1998, 24;
              [1998] E.P.O.R. 200.
T873/94   TOSHIBA/Amended divisional application O.J. EPO
              1997, 456; [1998] E.P.O.R. 71.
T921/94   CIBA/Aminoanthraquinone derivatives October 30, 1998
T556/95   CHAUM/Undeniable systems O.J. EPO 1997, 205; [1997]
              E.P.O.R. 394.
T1105/96   HAMAMATSU/Requests O.J. EPO 1998, 249; [1998]
              E.P.O.R. 26.
T596/97   HITACHI/Centrifugal fluid machine June 10, 1998.
T631/97   TOSHIBA/Doped regions O.J. EPO 2001, 13.
T802/97   LAMBDA ELECTRONICS July 24, 1998.
T1149/97   SOLARTRON/Fluid transducer O.J. EPO 2000, 259.
T587/98   KOMAG/Divisional claim conflicting with parent, O.J.
              EPO 2000, 497.
T685/98   GPT/Clock synchronisation O.J. EPO 1999, 346.

CHAPTER 3

OPPOSITION TO A GRANTED PATENT

Articles 99 to 105 EPC

Contents

All references are to paragraph numbers

Cases Referred to in Chapter 3

A. Introduction: The Nature of Opposition Proceedings

(1) Centralised revocation proceedings

3–01   When a European patent is granted, in accordance with Article 54(1) EPC it confers the same right upon the proprietor as would be conferred by a bundle of national patents in the designated Contracting States. In accordance with Article 2(2) EPC it has the effect of and is subject to the same conditions as a national patent in each such State. Any infringement of a European patent is dealt with by the national law, in accordance with Article 64(3) EPC.

Upon grant of a European patent, there is therefore a transfer of competence in respect of the rights which are conferred by it from the EPO to the designated Contracting States, who are thereafter responsible for its administration and enforcement.

Opposition proceedings constitute an exception to this general rule of transfer of competence. The opposition procedure under Articles 99–105 EPC is a procedure whereby, during a limited period of time (namely nine months from grant), a centralised action for revocation of the complete bundle of national patents constituting the European patent may be brought before and decided by the EPO (T117/86[1] and T9/87[2]).

Since opposition proceedings are in reality revocation proceedings, the word "opposition" in this context can be considered to be a misnomer, in so far as what is being "opposed" is something that has already happened, namely, grant of a patent.

The cost and time advantages of such a centralised revocation procedure as compared to separate revocation proceedings in the national courts of Contracting States are of obvious practical significance.

(2) The nature of opposition proceedings

3–02   Initially, opposition proceedings which were commenced in the early 1980s were treated within the EPO rather as an extension of examination proceedings, with considerable emphasis upon the investigative powers of the EPO under Article 114(1) EPC, which states that:

> "In proceedings before it, the European Patent Office shall examine the facts of its motion; it shall not be restricted in this examination to the facts, evidence and arguments provided by the parties and the relief sought".

The "*inter partes*" aspect of opposition proceedings was played down: an early decision of the Enlarged Board of Appeal states that:

> "it would be wrong to regard [opposition proceedings] as essentially

---

[1] T117/86 *FILMTEC/Costs* O.J. EPO 1989, 40; [1989] E.P.O.R. 504.
[2] T9/87 *ICI/Zeolites* O.J. EPO 1989, 438; [1990] E.P.O.R. 46.

contentious proceedings between warring parties, where the deciding body takes a neutral position, as would be the case in revocation proceedings before a national court" (G1/84[3]).

The nature of opposition proceedings remained controversial, however, and even G1/84[4] recognised that "opposition procedure is not designed to be, and is not to be used as, an extension of examination procedure". The separate nature of opposition procedure began to be emphasised: for example:

"the opposition procedure is an independent procedure which takes place after the grant procedure: it is a separate procedure, in which a patent wrongly granted may be limited or revoked. . . . the opposition procedure is not part of the grant procedure" (T198/88[5]).

Especially controversial aspects of opposition procedure concerned the **3–03** powers of an Opposition Division or a Board of Appeal to enlarge the scope of the issues in dispute; for example, by examining the validity of claims not attacked by an opponent (T9/87[6]), or by introducing grounds of opposition and/or evidence in support not raised by an opponent in the notice of opposition, either upon request of an opponent, or of its own motion (T198/88,[7] T182/89[8]).

A turning point in the handling of oppositions by the EPO came in 1993 with cases G9/91[9] and G10/9l,[10] which concerned two questions of law which were consolidated, decided and issued simultaneously, and which set out the principles on which Opposition Divisions and Boards of Appeal should act when deciding the extent of examination of an opposed patent (for example, which claims to investigate) (G9/91[11]), and the grounds of opposition to be examined (G10/91[12]). These matters are considered below, in paragraphs 3–44 *et seq.* and also in Chapter 4 in relation to opposition appeals. In order to decide such principles, the Enlarged Board of Appeal necessarily had to examine the concepts underlying opposition proceedings within the framework of the EPC. In particular it was emphasised (in contrast to the earlier G1/84[13] decision quoted above) that "opposition proceedings under the EPC, being *post-grant* opposition proceedings, involve a concept which differs considerably from that of classical pre-grant opposition and in fact has several important features

[3] G1/84 MOBIL OIL/Opposition by proprietor O.J. EPO 1985, 299; [1986] E.P.O.R. 39.
[4] Ibid.
[5] T198/88 SCHWIETE/Concrete reconstruction O.J. EPO 1991, 254; [1991] E.P.O.R. 455.
[6] T9/87 ICI/Zeolites O.J. EPO 1989, 438; [1990] E.P.O.R. 46.
[7] See note 5.
[8] T182/89 SUMITOMO/Extent of opposition O.J. EPO 1991, 391; [1990] EPOR 438.
[9] G9/91 ROHM AND HAAS/Power to examine O.J. EPO 1993, 408; [1993] E.P.O.R. 485.
[10] G10/91 Examination of oppositions/appeals O.J. EPO 1993, 420; [1993] E.P.O.R. 485.
[11] See note 9.
[12] See note 10.
[13] See note 3.

more in common with the concept of traditional revocation procedure". Furthermore, "opposition proceedings under the EPC are in principle to be considered as contentious proceedings between parties normally representing opposite interests, who should be given equally fair treatment" (G9, 10/91[14]).

The concept of opposition proceedings as outlined in G9, 10/91,[15] especially the contentious and adversarial nature of such proceedings, has a number of important consequences in connection with a number of different aspects of opposition procedure under the EPC, as will be discussed in the remainder of this chapter.

(3) Two stages of examination: admissibility and substantive examination

3–04   Opposition proceedings are commenced by the filing of a notice of opposition whose contents are first examined to ensure that they comply with the minimum requirements for admissibility. If the opposition is admissible, the substantive procedure is commenced.

(4) Effect of inadmissibility

3–05   "When an opposition has been declared inadmissible, its substance cannot be examined, nor is it possible for the EPO to examine the facts of its own motion in accordance with Article 114(1) EPC" (T328/87)[16].

If an Opposition Division decides that an opposition is inadmissible, such a decision may be subject to an appeal. If an Opposition Division decides that an opposition is inadmissible, its decision should not contain its views on the substantive grounds raised in the opposition. Such procedure is inconsistent with the principle that the opposition proceedings are legally terminated by a finding of inadmissibility (T925/91[16a]).

(5) Opposition procedure generally: accelerated processing

3–06   The procedure governing opposition proceedings is dealt with comprehensively in part D of the Guidelines. The EPO has also published a Note entitled "Opposition Procedure in the EPO"[17] which gives useful guidance.

The time taken for an opposition to be examined and decided in the EPO is a frequent criticism. The Guidelines D,VII.1.2 set out the general principles applied to the sequential processing of oppositions, and they also refer to certain exceptional circumstances when a particular opposition may be given priority, namely:

    (a) if the earlier examination proceedings were of considerably longer duration than usual,

---

[14] G9, 10/91 *ROHM AND HAAS/Power to examine; Examination of oppositions/appeals* O.J. EPO 1993, 408, 420; [1993] E.P.O.R. 485.
[15] *Ibid.*
[16] T328/87 *ELECTROLUX/Admissibility* O.J. EPO 1992, 701; [1993] E.P.O.R. 191.
[16a] T925/91 *EXXON/Combustion effluents* O.J. EPO 1995, 469; [1996] E.P.O.R. 77.
[17] O.J. EPO 1989, 417; reproduced in full at Appendix 12.

(b) if the opposition proceedings have already extended over a considerably longer period than usual,

(c) if a party to the proceedings has submitted a detailed and reasoned request for the proceedings to be speeded up and has given special grounds for his request which, after careful consideration of the interests of all parties, justifies a departure from the timetable of the sequence of tasks,

(d) if other matters to be dealt with, *e.g.* divisional applications, hinge upon the final decision concerning the opposition,

(e) if the next procedural step can be dealt with relatively quickly.

Additionally, a Notice dated May 19, 1998[18] sets out the special procedure to be followed if an infringement action in respect of an European patent is pending before a national court in a Contracting State, and if a party to the opposition proceedings requests accelerated processing.

B. Composition of an Opposition Division

(1) Possible overlap with the Examining Division

Both an Examining Division and an Opposition Division comprises three **3–07** technical examiners. The appointment of examiners to form an Opposition Division to decide upon a particular case is governed by Article 19(2) EPC: at least two of the three examiners "shall not have taken part in the proceedings for grant of the patent to which the opposition relates"; furthermore, an examiner who has taken part in such examination proceedings "shall not be the Chairman". In certain cases, an Opposition Division may also include a legally qualified examiner, "if the nature of the decision so requires". For example, a legally qualified examiner is normally included if oral evidence is to be taken.

It should be noted that Article 19(2) EPC does not prohibit an examiner of the Examining Division that was responsible for the grant of a patent also being an examiner (but not the Chairman) in the Opposition Division which is responsible for deciding an opposition in respect of the same patent. Furthermore, the same examiner may be the "primary examiner" in both the Examining Division and the Opposition Division; that is the examiner who is entrusted with the conduct of the examining proceedings and/or the opposition proceedings, under Article 18(2) and 19(2) EPC, respectively.

Such an overlap between the compositions of the Examining Division and the Opposition Division responsible for deciding upon the validity of a particular patent appears to be undesirable. If an opponent wishes to rely

---

[18] Notice of the President of the EPO dated May 19, 1998 concerning accelerated processing of oppositions where infringement proceedings have been instituted, O.J. EPO 1990, 324; reproduced in full at Appendix 13.

upon similar grounds of objection against the patent to those which were considered during the pre-grant examination proceedings, he might suspect that the primary examiner who was responsible for granting the patent will be influential in the direction of maintaining the patent, as primary examiner in the opposition proceedings. However, it is economically attractive for the EPO to use the same examiner as primary examiner in both proceedings.

Article 19(2) EPC should ideally be amended in order to prevent such an overlap by providing that an Opposition Division should be composed of different examiners from those who participated in the Examining Division before grant.

(2) Composition contrary to Article 19(2) EPC

3–08 If the composition of an Opposition Division which decides an opposition is contrary to Article 19(2) EPC, on appeal the decision of such an Opposition Division will be set aside as void, and the case ordered to be re-examined by a properly constituted Opposition Division (T251/88[19]).

(3) Objection for suspected partiality

3–09 See Chapter 5 at paragraph 5–25.

C. Filing an Opposition

(1) Who may file an opposition

(a) Any person: no "interest" required

3–10 Any person may file a notice of opposition to a European patent, *i.e.* any natural or legal person (Article 99(1) EPC). The notice of opposition must *inter alia* state the name of the opponent (Rule 55(a) EPC).

There is no requirement that an opponent must show an interest in the subject-matter of the patent (T798/93[20]). Thus "the motives of the opponent are in principle irrelevant (otherwise no doubt the phrase 'any person' would have been rendered as 'any person interested') ..." (G1/84[21]).

The meaning of the words "any person" in Article 99(1) EPC, and the identity of a person named as opponent, has nevertheless been controversial, as discussed below.

(b) No self-opposition by the patent proprietor

3–11 An early question of interpretation which arise in connection with Article 99(1) EPC was whether the patent proprietor himself comes within the term "any person".

---

[19] T251/88 *IRSID/Opposition Division* [1990] E.P.O.R. 246.
[20] T798/93 *ROAD TRAIN/Identification of real opponent* O.J. EPO 1997, 363; [1998] E.P.O.R. 1.
[21] G1/84 *MOBIL OIL/Opposition by proprietor* O.J. EPO 1985, 299; [1986] E.P.O.R. 39.

When a patent proprietor becomes aware of potential objections to the validity of his European patent for the first time after grant (for example, objections based upon prior art which was not considered during the examination proceedings), he may wish to amend the patent to take account of such objections (for example, by restricting the scope of the claims of the patent). However, the EPC does not contain at present any provision which allows a proprietor to initiate proceedings before the EPO in order to request amendment of a granted European patent by means of a centralised amendment procedure before the EPO (but see paragraph 3–12A below and Chapter 8 at paragraph 8–04a). The CPC does contain such provisions (see Chapter 14 at paragraph 14–18), but is not yet in force (see Chapter 1 at paragraph 1–53).

The question whether a proprietor could file an admissible opposition against his own patent, for the purpose of requesting amendment of that patent within such centralised proceedings, was first referred to the Enlarged Board of Appeal in G1/84.[22] On the basis of the view taken by that composition of Enlarged Board as to the nature of opposition proceedings under the EPC (see paragraph 3–02 above) it was held that an opposition "is not inadmissible merely because it has been filed by the proprietor": in other words, a proprietor could oppose his own patent in order to request amendments to it.

Subsequently, G9, 10/91[23] took a fundamentally different view of the nature of opposition proceedings from G1/84 (see paragraph 3–03 above), and essentially the same question was referred back to the Enlarged Board in G9/93.[24] A second referral of the same question of law to the Enlarged Board is envisaged by Article 16 RPBA, which states:

> "Should a Board consider it necessary to deviate from an interpretation or explanation of [the EPC] contained in an earlier opinion or decision of the Enlarged Board of Appeal, the question shall be referred to the Enlarged Board of Appeal".

G9/93 endorsed the concept of opposition proceedings which is set out 3–12 in G9, G10/91, namely that opposition proceedings are contentious proceedings between opposing parties, (*inter partes* proceedings), and recognised that this concept "does not fit with the idea expressed in G1/84, that opposition proceedings can be initiated by a single party (*ex parte* proceedings)". Consequently "having regard in particular to the nature and purpose of opposition proceedings", the words any person "in Article 99(1) EPC can ... only be reasonably interpreted as referring to the public at large which is being given the opportunity to challenge the validity of the patent ..."; and to include the patent proprietor in this concept would be

---

[22] G1/84 *MOBIL OIL/Opposition by proprietor* O.J. EPO 1985, 299; [1986] E.P.O.R. 39.
[23] G9, 10/91 *ROHM AND HAAS/Power to examine; Examination of oppositions/Appeals* O.J. EPO 1993, 408, 420; [1993] E.P.O.R. 485.
[24] G9/93 *PEUGEOT AND CITROEN II/Opposition by patent proprietor* O.J. EPO 1994, 891; [1995] E.P.O.R. 260.

artificial, because the Rules clearly assume that "the opponent is a person other than the patent proprietor and that opposition proceedings are always *inter partes* (*cf.* in particular Article 99(4) and 101(2) and Rule 57 EPC)" (G9/93[25]).

Accordingly:

"A European patent cannot be opposed by its own proprietor" (G9/93[26]).

This situation is unsatisfactory in the absence of centralised amendment proceedings (see paragraph 3–12A below).

3–12A   According to the proposed revision of the EPC, new Articles 105a, b and c EPC will provide for limitation or revocation of a European patent at the request of the proprietor (see Chapter 8 at paragraph 8–04a). Such centralised amendment proceedings at the request of the proprietor would obviate the need for a proprietor to oppose his own European patent, and would be consistent with G9/93.[27]

(c) Nominal opponent on behalf of a third party: no abuse of process

3–13 The admissibility of an opposition in circumstances where an opponent may be acting on behalf of a third party has been controversial. For example, previous decisions have stated that a professional representative may not file an opposition in his own name when he is acting in his professional capacity on behalf of a client (T10/82),[28] but that a professional representative may file an opposition in his own name and on his own behalf, to supplement his professional training (T798/93).[29] Furthermore, previous decisions have suggested that if a doubt exists as to the true identity of the opponent, an opposition is inadmissible (T635/88),[30] and that an opponent may be required to provide a written sworn statement in order to dispel such a doubt (T635/88,[31] T289/91,[32] T590/93[33]).

The controversy has been removed, and current practice has been established by G3, 4/97[34] as follows:

"An opposition is not inadmissible purely because the person named as opponent according to Rule 55(1) EPC is acting on behalf of a third

---

[25] *Ibid.*
[26] *Ibid.*
[27] *Ibid.*
[28] T10/82 *BAYER/Admissibility of opposition* O.J. EPO 1983, 407 [1979–1985] E.P.O.R.: B: 381.
[29] T798/93. *ROAD TRAIN/Identification of real opponent* O.J. EPO 1997, 363; [1998] E.P.O.R. 1.
[30] T635/88 *DE ERVEN G. DE BOER BV./Opponent-identifiability* O.J. EPO 1993, 608; [1994] E.P.O.R. 858.
[31] *Ibid.*
[32] T289/91 *HOECHST/ACE inhibitors* O.J. EPO 1994, 689; [1995] E.P.O.R. 32.
[33] T590/93 *KOGYO/Photosensitive resins* O.J. EPO 1995, 337; [1995] E.P.O.R. 478.
[34] G3, 4/97 *INDU PACK, GENENTECH/Opposition on behalf of a third party* O.J. EPO 1999, 270.

party. Such an opposition is, however, inadmissible if the involvement of the opponent is to be regarded as circumventing the law by abuse of process.

Such a circumvention of the law arises in particular, if: **3–14**

- the opponent is acting on behalf of the patent proprietor;
- the opponent is acting on behalf of a client in the context of the activities which taken as a whole, are typically associated with professional representatives, without possessing the relevant qualifications required by Article 134 EPC" [see Chapter 5 at paragraphs 5–15].

However, a circumvention of the law by abuse of process does not arise purely because:
- a professional representative is acting in his own name on behalf of a client;
- an opponent with either a residence or principal place of business in one of the EPC contracting states is acting on behalf of a third party who does not meet this requirement" (G3,4/97).
"In determining whether the law has been circumvented by abuse of process, the principle of the free evaluation of evidence is to be applied. The burden of proof is to be borne by the person alleging that the opposition is inadmissible. The deciding body has to be satisfied on the basis of clear and convincing evidence that the law has been circumvented by abuse of process" (G3,4/97[35]).

Furthermore:

"The admissibility of an opposition on grounds relating to the identity of an opponent may be challenged during the course of the appeal, even if no such challenge has been raised before the opposition division" (G3,4/97[36]; see Chapter 4 at paragraph 4–62a).

(d) Joint opposition: opponents acting in common

According to Rule 100(1) EPC, third parties may act in common in filing **3–15** notice of opposition (or intervention—see paragraphs 3–64 *et seq*.). The procedure is similar to that which applies when there is more than one applicant for a patent (see Chapter 2 at paragraph 2–08). Thus if a notice of opposition names several opponents and does not name a "common representative" the first named opponent is considered as common representative. But if one of the opponents is "non-European" and is consequently obliged to appoint a professional representative under Article 133(2) EPC, this representative "shall be considered to be the common representative unless the first named [opponent] has appointed a professional representative".

Clarification of the procedure relating to such a joint opposition has been

---

[35] *Ibid.*
[36] *Ibid.*

requested from the Enlarged Board of Appeal by referral of the following questions of law under Article 112 EPC:

"1. Is an opposition admissible which otherwise meets the requirements of Article 99 EPC and Rule 55 EPC if it is filed jointly by two or more persons and only one opposition fee is paid?

2. If the answer to question 1 is in the affirmative and a common representative was named under Rule 100(1) EPC in the notice of opposition, is an appeal valid even if it is not filed by this person?

3. If the answers to Questions 1 and 2 are in the affirmative, which other requirements, if any, have to be met by a joint opposition or a joint appeal in order to safeguard the rights of the patent proprietor?" (T272/95[37]).

At the time of writing the decision of the Enlarged Board in response to these questions is awaited (G3/99[38]).

(e) Exclusive licensee as opponent

3–16 If an opponent holds an exclusive licence under the opposed patent, there may be an implied obligation not to challenge the patent. However:

"Invoking a no-challenge obligation is incompatible with the object and purpose of the centralised European opposition procedure, and in most cases does not lead to what is otherwise an admissible opposition being declared inadmissible" (Decision of an Opposition Division[39]).

(2) Time limit for filing opposition

3–17 In order to comply with the requirements of Article 99 and Rule 55 EPC, a notice of opposition must be filed within nine months "from the publication of the mention of the grant of the European patent" (Article 99(1) EPC), which is in effect the date of grant of the patent by virtue of Article 97(4) EPC.

The final sentence of Article 99(1) EPC provides that the notice of opposition "shall not be deemed to have been filed until the opposition fee has been paid". If the opposition fee is not paid within the nine-month period, the opposition is inadmissible (T152/85[40]).

(3) Place of filing

3–18 Documents relating to proceedings before the EPO may be filed either at the EPO itself in Munich or at its branch in The Hague or at the filing office in the Berlin sub-office of the EPO.[41]

---

[37] T272/95 *HOWARD FLOREY INSTITUTE/Admissibility of joint opposition or joint appeal* O.J. EPO 1999, 590.
[38] G3/99 *HOWARD FLOREY INSTITUTE* O.J. EPO (P); *referral at* O.J. EPO 1999, 589.
[39] Decision of an Opposition Division O.J. EPO 1992, 747.
[40] T152/85 *SANDVIK/Unpaid opposition fee* O.J. EPO 1987, 191; [1987] E.P.O.R. 258.
[41] Decision of the President of the EPO, May 10, 1989 O.J. EPO 1989, 238.

(4) Contents of the notice of opposition

(a) Introduction: minimum formal and substantive contents

A notice of opposition must include both formal and substantive contents. **3–19** Formal contents are concerned with such matters as identifying the patent and the opponent (and his representative, if any). The substantive contents are concerned with setting out the extent to which the patent is opposed, the grounds of opposition, and sufficient initial information in support of such grounds.

A notice of opposition must include certain minimum formal and substantive contents to satisfy the requirements for admissibility of the opposition. Unless such requirements are satisfied, the opposition will be held inadmissible, in which case the substantive grounds of opposition will not be examined, and the proceedings will be terminated (paragraphs 3–04, 3–05 above).

A notice of opposition is therefore first examined formally for admissibility. If the opposition is admissible, the substantive examination procedure is commenced.

(i) Formal contents. Rule 55 EPC prescribed that a notice of opposition **3–20** must contain a number of formal particulars. Such formal contents may be divided into two categories, according to whether or not such contents are essential for admissibility within the nine-months opposition period.

(b) Formal contents essential within the nine-month period

(i) Identity of opponent. "If the identity of an opponent has not been **3–21** established before expiry of the period allowed for opposition, the opposition is inadmissible" (T25/85[42]). However, this conclusion is not apparent from the wording of Rules 55 and 56 EPC (T317/86).[43] In particular, Rule 56(1) EPC specifically refers to "sufficient identification of the patent" as being necessary for admissibility within the nine-month opposition period, but does not refer to the identity of the opponent in this respect.

(ii) Identity of the opposed patent. The first sentence of Article 99(1) **3–22** EPC provides for notice of opposition "to the European patent granted" within the nine-month period. Furthermore, Rule 55(b) provides that the notice of opposition shall contain "the number of the (opposed) European patent ... , and the name of the proprietor and title of the invention." A notice of opposition is inadmissible if within the nine-month period it "does not provide sufficient identification of the [opposed] patent". (Rule 56(1) EPC)

A patent is sufficiently identified under Rule 56(1) Rule EPC if the particulars in the notice enable the EPO without undue effort to identify

---

[42] T25/85 *DEUTSCHE GELATINE-FABRIKEN, STOESS & CO./Opponent-identifiability* O.J. EPO 1986, 81; [1986] E.P.O.R. 158.
[43] T317/86 *SMIDTH/Title of invention* O.J. EPO 1989, 378; [1989] E.P.O.R. 415.

with certainty the contested patent before expiry of the opposition period. Particulars in the notice other than those specified in Rule 55(b) EPC may be used to aid such identification (T317/86[44]).

(c) Formal contents not essential within the nine-month period

3–23 Rule 55 EPC requires that a notice of opposition contains:
    (a) "the name and address of the opponent" and
        "the State in which his residence or principal place of business is located" (in accordance with Rule 26(2)(c) EPC).

These requirements are clearly primarily for the purpose of identification of the opponent, as well as in order that it can be decided whether the opponent requires a professional representative (see Chapter 5 at paragraph 5–14 below);

    (b) "the number of the [opposed] European patent";
        "the name of the proprietor";
        "the title of the invention".

Again, these requirements are primarily for the purpose of identification of the opposed patent and its proprietor.

If such requirements are noted as not complied with, the deficiencies may be remedied within a period fixed by the Opposition Division, which may expire outside the nine-month limit. Failure to correct the deficiencies within the fixed period will result in the opposition being rejected as inadmissible.

(d) Substantive contents

(i) Minimum contents essential for admissibility

(1) The extent to which the patent is opposed

3–24 Rule 55(c) EPC requires the notice of opposition to contain "a statement of the extent to which the European patent is opposed"; for example, which claims are opposed. Thus it should be clear from the notice of opposition whether the opposition is directed against the entire patent or only a part of it (for example, only the process claims).

In some cases, even in the absence of an explicit statement of such extent, it may be implicitly clear from the content of the notice that the entire patent is opposed. Nevertheless, since the power of an Opposition Division or a Board of Appeal to examine and decide on the maintenance of a European patent in opposition proceedings depends upon the extent to which the patent is opposed in the notice of opposition (G9/91[45]—see paragraphs 3–41 *et seq.* below):

---

[44] *Ibid.*
[45] G9/91 *ROHM AND HAAS/Power to examine* O.J. EPO 1993, 408; [1993] E.P.O.R. 485.

"If the extent to which a patent is opposed is in serious doubt, the opposition may be rejected as inadmissible" (T376/90[46]).

(2) Grounds for opposition

Rule 55(c) EPC requires that the notice of opposition contains a statement **3–25** of "the grounds on which the opposition is based".

The only possible grounds of opposition are set out in Article 100 EPC, namely:

    (a) the subject-matter is not patentable, under Articles 52 to 57 EPC; therefore including:
        (i) excluded subject-matter, Articles 52 and 53 EPC;
        (ii) lack of novelty, Article 54 EPC;
        (iii) lack of inventive step, Article 56 EPC;
        (iv) not susceptible of industrial application, Article 57 EPC;
    (b) insufficiency of disclosure, under Article 83 EPC;
    (c) wrongful addition of subject-matter before grant, under Article 123(2) EPC.

In the context of Articles 99 and 100 and Rule 55(c) EPC, a "ground for **3–26** opposition" means an individual legal basis for objection to the maintenance of a patent. Thus Article 100(a) EPC contains a collection of different legal objections, that is grounds of opposition, and is not directed to a single ground of opposition. Similarly, Article 100(b) and (c) EPC each relate to a single legal basis of objection, or ground of opposition (G1/95[47]). For an opposition to be admissible it must identify at least one ground of opposition. For an opposition to be admissible within the framework of Article 100(a) EPC it must necessarily be based on at least one of the legal bases, or grounds of opposition, set out in Articles 52 to 57 (G1/95[48]).

It may be noted that the same grounds as set out in Article 100(a), (b) and (c) EPC are available as grounds for revocation of a European patent by the national courts of Contracting States, under Article 138(1)(a), (b) and (c) EPC. Additional grounds for revocation by national courts are also set out in Article 138(1) as follows:

"(d) if the protection conferred by the European patent has been extended [Article 123(3) EPC];
(e) if the proprietor of the European patent is not entitled under Article 60(1) EPC" (see Chapter 2 at paragraphs 2–78 et seq.).

It should also be noted that neither Article 100 EPC nor Article 138 EPC allows the requirements of Article 84 EPC (concerning clarity of claims and their support by the description—see Chapter 7) to be relied upon as

---

[46] T376/90 *SUMITOMO/Polymer solution* O.J. EPO 1994, 906; [1995] E.P.O.R. 232.
[47] G1, 7/95 *DE LA RUE/ETHICON/Fresh grounds for opposition* O.J. EPO 1996, 615, 626; [1996] E.P.O.R. 601.
[48] *Ibid.*

grounds for opposition to or revocation of a European patent after grant (see Chapter 7 at paragraphs 7–73, 7–73A).

(3) Support for grounds of opposition (substantiation)

(a) General principles

3–27 Rule 55(c) EPC further requires that the notice of opposition contains "an indication of the facts, evidence and argument presented in support" of each ground on which the opposition is based.

There is no clear distinction between "facts" and "evidence". Reference to the corresponding French and German texts shows that the division into such categories is not intended to be precise and mutually exclusive. A party may present facts, or evidence to establish facts. However, "the distinction between the presentation of facts and evidence, on the one hand, and the presentation of argument on the other hand, is of basic importance under the EPC" (G4/95[49]). Each of these two categories will require separate consideration in the context of various aspects of opposition procedure.

The use of the words "an indication" in Rule 55(c) EPC means that it is not essential for an opponent to file all the evidence in support of the alleged grounds of opposition with the notice of opposition or within the nine months opposition period (T328/87[50]), although he may do so. However, it is essential that a *sufficient indication* of the facts, evidence and argument should be set out in the notice of opposition, if it is to be admissible. The timing of the filing of facts and evidence in opposition proceedings is considered in paragraphs 3–51 *et seq.* below.

3–28 The basic principle in relation to the contents of a notice of opposition is that it should state "the legal and factual reasons" why the alleged grounds of opposition should succeed (T550/88[51]). The requirement of Rule 55(c) EPC is only satisfied if the contents of the notice of opposition are sufficient for the opponent's case to be properly understood on an objective basis, both by the patent proprietor and by the Opposition Division without further investigations (T222/85,[52] T2/89[53]).

The notice of opposition as filed and within the nine-month period should summarise the entire case of the opponent as to why the patent should not be maintained in its form as granted (T297/88[54]).

If the only facts and evidence which are indicated in the notice of opposition cannot as a matter of law support the alleged grounds of opposition, the opposition is inadmissible (T550/88[55]). If none of the alleged grounds of opposition is properly supported in the manner set out

[49] G4/95 *BOGASKY II/Representation* O.J. EPO 1996, 412; [1996] E.P.O.R. 333.
[50] T328/87 *ELECTROLUX/Admissibility* O.J. EPO 1992, 701; [1993] E.P.O.R. 191.
[51] T550/88 *MOBIL OIL/National prior right* O.J. EPO 1990, 10; [1990] E.P.O.R. 391.
[52] T222/85 *PPG/Ungelled polyesters* O.J. EPO 1988, 128; [1987] E.P.O.R. 99.
[53] T2/89 *BASF/Opposition grounds* O.J. EPO 1991, 51; [1991] E.P.O.R. 391.
[54] T297/88 *BAYER/Nimodipin II* December 5, 1989.
[55] See note 51.

above, the opposition is inadmissible. If at least one of the alleged grounds of opposition is properly supported, the opposition is admissible.

If an opponent substantiates a ground of opposition against a single claim of each request of the patent proprietor which is on file, "and if he succeeds in establishing that one claim of each such request is not allowable, the patent will be revoked. Thus an opponent is under no obligation to 'overkill' requests put forward by the proprietor by substantiating grounds of opposition against more than one claim of [each] such request" (T926/93[56]).

(b) Sufficient support distinguished from strength of case

It follows from the above principles that, at least in theory, a notice of opposition could be rejected as inadmissible, although if properly drafted and based upon the same facts and evidence the opposition would have succeeded. Thus: **3–29**

> "On the one hand, an unconvincing ground of opposition might have been clearly presented and argued. Conversely, a deficient submission may be rejected as inadmissible even though if properly drafted it would have succeeded. The desirability that European patents are granted for patentable inventions only must in this context be balanced against the desirability of an efficient procedure in opposition proceedings ..." (T222/85[57]).

Whether an opposition is admissible under Rule 55(c) EPC must be distinguished from the question of the strength of the opponent's case (T2/89[58]).

(c) Substantiation of prior use

"Prior public use is only adequately substantiated if specific details are given of what was made available to the public, where, when, how and by whom" (T93/89[59]). "When an opposition is based on ground of prior use, the requirements of Rule 55(c) EPC are only fulfilled if the notice of opposition indicates, within the opposition period, all the facts which make it possible to determine the date of prior use, what has been used, and the circumstances relating to the alleged use" (T328/87[60]). **3–30**

(d) Decided cases

The above principles are illustrated with reference to the facts of decided cases: **3–31**

[56] T926/93 MITSUBISHI/Gas laser device O.J. EPO 1997 447; [1998] E.P.O.R. 94.
[57] T222/85 PPG/Ungelled polyesters O.J. EPO 1988, 128; [1987] E.P.O.R. 391.
[58] T2/89 BASF/Opposition grounds O.J. EPO 1991, 51; [1991] E.P.O.R. 391.
[59] T93/89 HOECHST/Polyvinyl ester dispersion O.J. EPO 1992, 718.
[60] T328/87 ELECTROLUX/Admissibility O.J. EPO 1992, 701; [1993] E.P.O.R. 191.

(1) The only alleged ground of opposition was lack of novelty under Article 54(3) EPC and the only "facts and evidence" in support of this ground comprised certain "national prior rights". Since a national prior right is not a "European patent application" within the meaning of Article 54(3) EPC, such national prior rights were not part of the state of the art. The opposition was inadmissible. (T550/88[61]).

3–32   (2) The only document cited to support the only alleged ground of lack of inventive step has been published after the filing date; however, the document identified on its front page a corresponding patent document with identical contents which has been prior published. The opposition was admissible. (T185/88[62]).

3–33   (3) The alleged grounds of lack of novelty and inventive step were supported merely by reference to a number of prior documents.

The opposition was inadmissible for the following reasons:

"In the absence of any specific guidance in the present case as to what particular statements in the cited documents are alleged to destroy the novelty of the claimed invention or to form the basis for an argument on obviousness, the Opposition Division and the Respondent are at a loss as to where to start with their examination of the Appellant's allegation in respect of the parameters set out in Claim 1. In the Board's judgment, the notice of opposition is therefore insufficient at the level of facts and evidence in this respect. What the Appellant did was no more than to invite the Opposition Division to carry out further searches in these documents ex officio, in the hope that it would formulate some arguments of its own accord on the basis of its findings. This task, however, was that of the Appellant within the available time for filing the notice of opposition. Oppositions must be filed and pursued in good faith so as to avoid procrastination and uncertainty. Keeping back any relevant information from the Opposition Division, which is already available to the opponent, is not in accordance with this principle" (T222/85[63]).

3–34   (4) An allegation of lack of novelty based upon a prior document is not properly substantiated in accordance with Rule 55(c) EPC if several different subject-matters are described in the prior document, and "it is neither indicated nor readily recognisable which of them is supposed to incorporate all the features of a contested claim" (T448/89[64]).

[61] T550/88 MOBIL OIL/National prior right O.J. EPO 1990, 10; [1990] E.P.O.R. 391.
[62] T185/88 HENKEL/Surface active agents O.J. EPO 1990, 451; [1990] E.P.O.R. 649.
[63] T222/85 PPG/Ungelled polyesters O.J. EPO 1988, 128; [1987] E.P.O.R. 99.
[64] T448/89 SIEMENS/Stimulating electrode O.J. EPO 1992, 172; [1992] E.P.O.R. 149.

(5) Similarly, an allegation of lack of inventive step is not properly substantiated by a general reference to all the documents mentioned in the European search report (T448/89[65]).

D. Examination for Admissibility: Preparation for Substantive Examination

When a notice of opposition is first filed, it is formally examined for **3–35** admissibility by a Formalities Officer of the Opposition Division. In the case of deficiencies (see paragraph 3–23 above), a communication may be sent under Rule 56 EPC, and a decision rejecting the opposition as inadmissible may be issued, on an *ex parte* basis. Except in clear cases, possible deficiencies under Rule 55(c) EPC will be referred to the Opposition Division.

In the event that the notice of opposition is not rejected as inadmissible under Rule 56 EPC, it is communicated to the proprietor under Rule 57(1) EPC and the patent proprietor may then contest the admissibility of the opposition in his observations in reply. Such contentions, including inadmissibility under Rule 55(c) EPC, are decided in *inter partes* proceedings by the Opposition Division itself.

If an opposition is not rejected as inadmissible on an *ex parte* basis, a **3–36** finding of inadmissibility during the subsequent *inter partes* proceedings is not precluded in the light of an objection from the patent proprietor (T222/85[66]).

"The admissibility of an opposition must be checked ex officio in every phase of the opposition and ensuing appeal proceedings [see also Chapter 4 at paragraph 4–62a]. .... Admissibility of the opposition has to be judged on the basis of the content of the notice of opposition as filed, taking account of additional documents filed before the expiry of the opposition period as far as they remedy any deficiency fatal to the admissibility. Such a defect cannot be remedied outside the period for opposition (Rule 56(1) EPC).

> "The overall purpose of the admissibility requirement is to allow the proprietor of the patent and the opposition division to examine the alleged ground for revocation without recourse to independent enquiries" (T522/94[67]).

Following the preliminary examination for admissibility the case is **3–37** prepared for the examination stage. This preparation is governed by Rule 57 EPC. Thus:

---

[65] *Ibid.*
[66] See note 63.
[67] T522/94 TECHMO/*Powered vehicle for operation of ladles* O.J. EPO 1998, 421; [1999] E.P.O.R. 75.

(a) The notice of opposition is sent to the proprietor, and he is invited to file observations and/or amendments to the text of the patent where appropriate, within a fixed period. (Rule 57(1) EPC).

(b) In the case of several notices of opposition being filed by several opponents each notice is sent to the other opponents (Rule 57(2) EPC).

(c) Any observations and amendments filed by the proprietor in response to the invitation under (a) are sent to all opponents, who are invited to reply to the proprietor's submissions within a fixed period if the Opposition Division "considers it expedient" (Rule 57(3) EPC).

If the facts and evidence indicated in the notice of opposition have not been submitted within the nine months period, the opponent is invited to file such facts and evidence within two months. Subsequently, the proprietor is invited to file observations (including facts and evidence) under (a) above.

As mentioned above, the patent proprietor may contest the admissibility of the notice of opposition, as part of his observations to the invitation under Rule 57(1) EPC and this is then decided as part of the *inter partes* proceedings. As to the effect of a finding of inadmissibility, see paragraph 3–05 above.

E. Substantive Examination

3–38 Procedure during the examination stage before the Opposition Division is governed by Article 101(2) and Rules 57, 57a and 58 EPC.

(1) Extent of the substantive examination

(a) Introduction

3–39 Article 101(1)EPC provides that "the Opposition Division shall examine whether the grounds for opposition laid down in Article 100 EPC prejudices the maintenance of the European patent". Furthermore, Article 114(1) EPC, which is one of the "Common provisions governing procedure" set out in Part VII EPC ("Common Provisions"), provides that the EPO "shall examine the facts of its own motion: it shall not be restricted in this examination to the facts, evidence and arguments provided by the parties and the relief sought". However, as discussed in paragraph 3–25 above, Article 99(1)EPC and Rule 55(c) EPC require an opponent to specify in the notice of opposition which grounds of opposition (as set out in Article 100 EPC) are relied upon, and to indicate the legal and factual reasons in support of each such ground within nine months of grant.

Prima facie, these provisions of the EPC appear to be inconsistent with one another. In particular, it would appear to be inconsistent that an opponent should be required to comply with Rule 55(c) EPC in respect of each ground of opposition relied upon, within nine months, and that subsequently, after expiry of the nine month period, an Opposition Division may, pursuant to Articles 101(1) and 114(1) EPC, either upon request of an opponent or of its own motion:—

> (i) consider the validity of claims not attacked by the opponent;
> (ii) examine grounds of opposition other than those relied upon by the opponent in the notice of opposition;
> (iii) consider facts, evidence and arguments which were not "indicated" in the notice of opposition.

As mentioned in paragraph· 3–03 above, the early practice of the **3–40** Opposition Divisions tended towards a re-examination procedure, so that the extent of the opposition as set out in the Notice of Opposition was frequently expanded in accordance with (i) to (iii) above. Within the Boards of Appeal these inconsistent provisions led to different interpretations of them and consequent inconsistent appeal decisions (*e.g.* T9/87,[68] T493/88,[69] T182/89[70]).

Questions of law concerning the powers of the Opposition Divisions and of the Boards of Appeal in these respects were referred to the Enlarged Board of Appeal (G9/91[71] and G10/91[72]). The answer to such questions depended upon the view taken as to the nature of opposition proceedings under the EPC, which is discussed in paragraphs 3–02, 3–03 above. Since, as there stated "opposition proceedings under the EPC are in principle to be considered as contentious proceedings between parties normally representing opposite interests" (G9, 10/91[73]) it follows that Rule 55(c) EPC only made sense if interpreted as having the *double function* of:

> (1) "governing (together with other provisions) the admissibility of the opposition"; and of
> (2) "establishing at the same time *the legal and factual framework, within which the substantive examination of the opposition in principle shall be conducted*" (G9, 10/91[74]).

This statement of principle as to the double function of Rule 55(c) EPC within the framework of opposition procedure is of fundamental importance to the conduct of such procedure, in proceedings both before an Opposition Division and before a Board of Appeal.

(b) Extent of the patent to be examined

Normally a patent is opposed in its entirety, and the notice of opposition **3–41** makes this clear. Occasionally, however, only certain subject-matter is

[68] T9/87 *ICI/Zeolites* O.J. EPO 1989, 438; [1990] E.P.O.R. 46.
[69] T493/88 *CEA-FRAMATOME/Spacer grid* O.J. EPO 1990, 5; [1991] E.P.O.R. 393.
[70] T182/89 *SUMITOMO/Extent of opposition* O.J. EPO 1991, 391; [1990] E.P.O.R. 438.
[71] G9/91 *ROHM AND HAAS/Power to examine* O.J. EPO 1993, 408; [1993] E.P.O.R. 485.
[72] G10/91 *Examination of oppositions/appeals* O.J. EPO 1993, 420; [1993] E.P.O.R. 485.
[73] G9, 10/91 *ROHM AND HAAS/Power to examine; Examination of oppositions/appeals* O.J. EPO 1993, 408, 420; [1993] E.P.O.R. 485.
[74] *Ibid.*

attacked in the notice of opposition (for example, in T9/87 only claims 1, 2 and 11 of the patent were opposed: the remaining claims were deliberately not opposed). In this circumstance the question arises whether the EPO can examine and decide on the validity of unopposed claims to different subject-matters (for example, process claims compared to product claims). In this context, the following questions were referred to the Enlarged Board:

> "1. Is the power of an Opposition Division or, by reason of Rule 66(1) EPC of a Board of Appeal, to examine and decide on the maintenance of a European patent under Articles 101 and 102 EPC dependent upon the extent to which the patent is opposed in the notice of opposition pursuant to Rule 55(c) EPC?
>
> 2. If the answer to the first question should be affirmative, are there any exceptions to such dependence?" (G9/91[75])

3–42 1. Having regard to the double function of Rule 55(c) EPC, the Enlarged Board pointed out that the requirement "to specify the extent to which the patent is opposed" within the nine month opposition period" would obviously be pointless if later on other parts of the patent could freely be drawn into the proceedings. This would also be contrary to the basic concept of post-grant opposition under the EPC. Consequently the subject-matter of those parts of the patent which are not opposed is not subject to an opposition in the sense of Articles 101 and 102 EPC, and there are no "proceedings" in the sense of Articles 114 and 115 EPC in existence concerning such non-opposed subject-matter.

Thus the first question was answered in the affirmative. In particular, the power of an Opposition Division .... "to examine and decide on the maintenance of a patent depends upon the extent to which the patent is opposed in the notice of opposition ..." (G9/91[76]).

3–43 2. As to the second question, the Enlarged Board held that:

> "subject-matter of claims depending on an independent claim, which falls in opposition ... proceedings may be examined as to their patentability even if they have not been explicitly opposed, provided their validity is prima face in doubt on the basis of already available information" (G9/91[77]).

In other words, the subject-matter of dependent claims may be implicitly opposed when an independent claim is explicitly opposed.

(c) Grounds of opposition to be examined

3–44 In this connection the following question was referred to the Enlarged Board:

[75] *Ibid.*
[76] *Ibid.*
[77] G9/91 *ROHM AND HAAS/Power to examine* O.J. EPO 1993, 408; [1993] E.P.O.R. 485.

"When examining an opposition, does the Opposition Division have to examine all the grounds for the opposition given in article 100 EPC or is the examination restricted to the grounds for opposition presented by the opponent?" (G10/91[78]).

As a preliminary matter in answering this question the problem underlying it was distinguished from the questions considered in G9/91[79] on the basis that "in the case of the extent to which the patent is opposed, it is a matter of the formal competence of an Opposition Division or a Board of Appeal", whereas in the case of possible consideration of other grounds of opposition, the problem *concerns the procedural principles* to be applied, in a case where the patent is already under attack.

In the first place it was held that Articles 101 and 102 could not properly **3–45** be interpreted as requiring that an Opposition Division should examine all possible grounds of opposition set out in Article 100 EPC, but that they were intended to refer to the *total possible* framework of the opposition. Similarly, Article 114(1) EPC "is no legal basis for an obligatory review of grounds of opposition not covered by the notice of opposition". Consequently:

> "An Opposition Division ... is not obliged to consider all the grounds for opposition referred to in Article 100 EPC, going beyond the grounds covered by the statement under Rule 55(c) EPC" (G10/91[80]).

In the second place, with reference to the second half of the referred question, it was held that:

> "In principle, the Opposition Division shall examine only such grounds for opposition which have been properly submitted and substantiated in accordance with Article 99(1) in conjunction with Rule 55(c) EPC. Exceptionally, the Opposition Division may in application of Article 114(1) EPC consider other grounds for opposition which, prima facie, in whole or in part would seem to prejudice the maintenance of the European patent" (G10/91[81]).
>
> Thus Article 101(1) EPC is interpreted as merely "covering *the total possible* framework of the examination" of the opposition (G10/91[82]), and not as creating an obligation to examine all grounds of opposition set out in Article 100 EPC.

Relating to the above interpretation, according to the proposed revision **3–45A** of the EPC Article 101(1) and (2) EPC will be amended to read:

[78] G10/91 *Examination of oppositions/appeals* O.J. EPO 1993, 420; [1993] E.P.O.R. 485.
[79] See note 77.
[80] See note 78.
[81] *Ibid*.
[82] See note 78.

101(1) EPC: "If the opposition is admissible, the Opposition Division shall examine, in accordance with the Implementing Regulations, whether at least one ground for opposition under Article 100 EPC prejudices the maintenance of the European patent. During this examination, the Opposition Division shall invite the parties, as often as necessary, to file observations on communications from another party or issued by itself."

101(2) EPC: "If the Opposition Division is of the opinion that at least one ground for opposition prejudices the maintenance of the European patent, it shall revoke the patent. Otherwise it shall reject the opposition."

3–46   Thus an Opposition Division has a discretion under Article 114(1)EPC to introduce further grounds of opposition after the nine months opposition period, which were not specified by the opponent in the notice of opposition, and which appear to prejudice maintenance of the patent, either upon request from an opponent or of its own motion. This discretion is an exception to the principle that the statement pursuant to Rule 55(c) EPC establishes "the legal and factual framework, within which the substantive examination of the opposition in principle shall be conducted" (see paragraph 3–40 above), and should only be exercised "in cases where, prima facia, there are clear reasons to believe" that the maintenance of the patent is prejudiced (G10/91[83]).

Furthermore:

"If an Opposition Division wishes to introduce a new ground of opposition into the proceedings in addition to the ground(s) substantiated in the notice of opposition, either of its own motion or upon request by an opponent, the patent proprietor must be informed (normally in writing) not only of the new ground of opposition, but also of the essential legal and factual reasons (*i.e.* its substantiation) which could lead to a finding of invalidity and revocation. Thereafter the patent proprietor must have a proper opportunity to present comments in reply to the new ground and its substantiation" (T433/93[84]).

(d) Documents to be examined

3–47 Beyond the documents which are relied upon by each opponent in support of the opposition, an Opposition Division may rely upon further documents when examining an opposition, as indicated below.

3–48   **(i) European search report documents.** An Opposition Division does not have any duty to reconsider documents which were cited in the European search report but were not cited by the opponent, but may introduce them into opposition proceedings if it has "strong reasons to

[83] *Ibid.*
[84] T433/93 *ATOTECH/Re-hearing* O.J. EPO 1997, 509; [1998] E.P.O.R. 135.

consider that such documents do in fact provide evidence in support of a ground of opposition that is of such relevance that it could effect the outcome of the opposition proceedings" (T387/89[85]).

(ii) Documents referred to in the opposed patent. A document which is **3–49** indicated in the patent as the closest or important prior art for the purposes of elucidating the technical problem set out in the description forms part of the opposition proceedings even if not expressly cited in the notice of opposition (T536/88[86]).

However, a document which was considered in the examination procedure is not automatically considered in opposition or opposition appeal proceedings even if quoted and acknowledged in the patent (T198/88[87]).

In practice such a document which is important from the point of view of assessing inventiveness will be considered in opposition proceedings at least as part of the background of the case.

(e) Summary

In accordance with the principles set out in G9, 10/91,[88] the adversarial **3–50** nature of opposition proceedings before the EPO is taken fully into account. Prior to grant, a European patent application should have been fully examined by an Examining Division so as to ensure as far possible that a granted patent meets all the requirements of the EPC, and further re-examination by the EPO within the framework of opposition proceedings is in principle inappropriate and contrary to the procedural scheme of the EPC. Consequently, the extent of examination of the validity of a European patent in opposition proceedings should normally be limited to a consideration of what the opponent has alleged against the maintenance of the patent.

Although in general terms it is in the public interest that European patents should be maintained only if they comply with all the requirements of the EPC, nevertheless, following a full pre-grant examination by the EPO, it is also contrary to the general interest of procedural expediency that post-grant opposition proceedings should be regarded as an opportunity for the EPO to re-examine the granted patent. Consequently, after grant of a European patent, an opponent can be taken as representing the public interest as to whether or not the patent should be maintained. The public interest at this point in time is essentially equivalent to the interested commercial interests.

While it can be accepted that the proprietor of a European patent will normally have little interest in maintaining the patent if it is clearly invalid

---

[85] T387/89 *MEDTRONIC/Cardioverter* O.J. EPO 1992, 583; [1993] E.P.O.R. 113.
[86] T536/88 *BADISCHE KARTONUND PAPPENFABRIK/Dust-tight folding carton* O.J. EPO 1992, 638; [1993] E.P.O.R. 202.
[87] T198/88 *SCHWIETE/Concrete reconstruction* O.J. EPO 1991, 254; [1991] E.P.O.R. 455.
[88] G9, 10/91 *ROHM AND HAAS/Power to examine; Examination of opposition/appeals* O.J. EPO 1993, 408, 420 [1993] E.P.O.R. 485.

(at whatever point in time that this becomes apparent—see Chapter 4 at paragraph 4–108), nevertheless in accordance with general procedural principles the extent of opposition proceedings (and any subsequent appeal proceedings) should be essentially defined by the notice of opposition at the commencement of such proceedings.

(2) The filing of facts and evidence

(a) Time of filing

3–51 As stated at paragraph 3–27 above, it is not *necessary* for an opponent to file all the facts and evidence in support of each alleged ground of opposition within the nine months opposition period, in order that the opposition should be held admissible: an "indication" of the facts and evidence is sufficient in the notice of opposition.

Furthermore, the EPC does not set out any time limit for filing facts and evidence in support of a ground of opposition. In fact, "the prescribed procedure does not contain any detailed regulation as to how and when facts and evidence should be filed by the parties to an opposition. The filing of facts and evidence is left to the discretionary control of the EPO" (G4/95[89]).

According to the practice of the Opposition Divisions as set out in the Note "Opposition procedure in the EPO"[90]:

> "facts and evidence should be adduced at an early stage in proceedings before the Opposition Division—see in particular paragraphs 8 to 13. An opponent should normally file evidence in support of his opposition within the nine-month opposition period or within a short period (two months) thereafter, and the proprietor must file his evidence in reply within a fixed period after that" (G4/95[91]).

The underlying principle is one of "early and complete presentation of the parties' case as opposed to the piecemeal and tardy introduction of the arguments and support evidence" (T326/87[92]).

(b) "Late filed" facts and evidence

3–52 Since the filing of facts and evidence is not governed by any time limit under the EPC, the exact meaning of "late filed" comes into question. Article 114(2) EPC provides that the EPO (and thus an Opposition Division) "may disregard facts or evidence which are not submitted in due time by the parties concerned". Thus the filing of facts and evidence is under the discretionary control of the Opposition Division. "However, if late-filed facts or evidence are obviously crucial to the decision, they have to be taken into consideration no matter what stage the procedure has

---

[89] G4/95 *BOGASKY/Representation* O.J. EPO 1996, 412; [1996] E.P.O.R. 333.
[90] O.J. EPO 1989, 417; reproduced in full at Appendix 12.
[91] See note 89.
[92] T326/87 *DU PONT/Polyamide compositions* O.J. EPO 1992, 522; [1991] E.P.O.R. 47.

reached" (paragraph 12 of the above identified Note). This practice has been supported by the Boards of Appeal both before and after the issue of G9, 10/91[93] (see *e.g.* T156/84,[94] T1002/92[95]). In particular, late-filed facts and evidence which go beyond what is "indicated" in the notice of opposition "should only exceptionally be admitted into the proceedings ... if, prima facie, there are clear reasons to suspect that such late-filed material *would prejudice* the maintenance 'of the patent'" (T1002/92[96]).

Thus the *main principle* governing the admissibility and consideration of late–filed facts and evidence is that of sufficient *relevance*. Consequently, an Opposition Division "must ascertain the relevance of evidence submitted ... before deciding to admit or reject it. Only in exceptional circumstances need they not do so" (T142/97[97]).

If late-filed facts and/or evidence are admitted into opposition proceedings, costs may be awarded against the party responsible for their late filing (Article 104 EPC: see Chapter 4 at paragraphs 4–156 *et seq.*)

(c) Other aspects of evidence

The topic of evidence is considered generally in Chapter 5 at section G 3–53 (paragraphs 5–32 *et seq.*). Oral evidence is considered in the context of oral proceedings at section H (paragraphs 5–54 *et seq.*).

(3) Communications and observations

Procedure during the examination stage before an Opposition Division is 3–54 governed by Article 101(2) and Rules 57, 57a and 58 EPC.

Following the exchange of the parties' observations as set out in paragraph 3–37 above, the Opposition Division may issue a communication which "where necessary ... shall contain a reasoned statement", and "where appropriate ... shall cover all the grounds against the maintenance of the European patent" (Rule 58(3) EPC).

However:

> "The provisions of Article 101(2) and Rule 58(3) EPC cannot be interpreted as meaning that the Opposition Division is obliged in every case to issue at least one communication" (T275/89[98]).

(a) Observations by the parties: control by the EPO

There is a general discretionary power for an Opposition Division to 3–55 control the extent of the observations filed by parties during the examination of an opposition:

[93] G9, 10/91 *ROHM AND HAAS/Power to examine; Examination of oppositions/appeals* O.J. EPO 1993, 408, 420; [1993] E.P.O.R. 485.
[94] T156/84 *AIR PRODUCTS/Pressure swing adsorption* O.J. EPO 1988, 372; [1989] E.P.O.R. 47.
[95] T1002/92 *PETTERSON/Queueing system* O.J. EPO 1995, 605; [1996] E.P.O.R. 1.
[96] *Ibid.*
[97] T142/97 *STOCKLI/Apparatus for separating disc-shaped objects* O.J. EPO 2000, 358.
[98] T275/89 *KLOSTERMANN/Steel radiator* O.J. EPO 1992, 126; [1992] E.P.O.R. 260.

"Article 101(2) EPC provides that 'the Opposition Division shall invite the parties, as often as necessary, to file observations ... on communications from another party or issued by itself.' Furthermore, Rule 57(1) and (2) EPC is concerned with the initial stage of opposition proceedings, immediately following the filing of the notice(s) of the opposition, and clearly provides the patentee with an opportunity as of right to file observations in reply to such notice(s) of opposition. Thereafter, however, by way of contrast, Rule 57(3) EPC emphasises that following communication of the patentee's observations (and any amendments) to the other parties, such other parties shall only be invited by the Opposition Division to reply to such observations 'if it considers it expedient'.

It is clearly most desirable in the interest of the smooth and efficient conduct of opposition proceedings, and accordingly in the public interest, that observations by parties should be properly limited to what is necessary and expedient. This in turn requires the exercise of a proper control by the Opposition Division ... over the admissibility of observations by parties as well as of documents filed in support of such observations. Of course, the extent to which further observations from parties are necessary or expedient depends upon various factors, including the complexity of the issues raised, and can only be decided in the context of each individual case. Nevertheless, it should be recognised that, in appropriate cases, ... the Opposition Division ... [has] the power, and indeed the duty, to refuse to admit observations and/or supporting documents for consideration ..." (T295/87[99]).

(b) Invitation to file observations on late-filed submissions before decision

3–56 In some cases further facts, evidence and arguments which are filed by an opponent after the patent proprietor has replied to the notice of opposition have been sent to the proprietor without an express invitation to file further observations, and have been followed by the issue of a decision adverse to the proprietor, based upon such late submissions and in the absence of observations from the proprietor. However:

"Following the late filing of new evidence by an opponent, if the EPO intends to consider such evidence in view of its relevance to the decision to be taken, then in the absence of observations upon such evidence by the patent proprietor, it is necessary within the meaning of Article 101(2) EPC to invite the proprietor to present his comments by filing observations, before the case can be decided on the basis of such evidence. This necessity follows both from Article 113(1) EPC and from the general principles of procedural law applicable under Article 125 EPC". (T669/90[100]: contrary to T22/89[101])

[99] T295/87 *ICI/Polyetherketones* O.J. EPO 1990, 420; [1991] E.P.O.R. 56.
[100] T669/90 *ATT/Inviting observations* O.J. EPO 1992, 739; [1992] E.P.O.R. 397.
[101] T22/89 *ALCAN/Aluminium alloys* June 26, 1990.

(c) The content of communications

While preliminary expressions of opinion by the Opposition Division are **3–58** often included in communications for the purposes of clarifying and expediting the proceedings, a communication should not suggest how a party could improve his case. Thus:

> "the expression of preliminary conclusions in communications in *inter partes* proceedings is, in itself, objectionable, unless their sole purpose is to clarify matters and/or to curtail the length and complexity of proceedings. It is *a fortiori* undesirable, and inconsistent with the [previously cited] jurisprudence and general principles, for communications in such cases to contain express or even implied invitations to one party to improve his case in a specific manner" (T173/89[102]).

Similarly:

> "While it is permissible, and even desirable, in proceedings before the EPO for the EPO to draw attention to any discrepancies between the arguments presented and the documents which are supposed to support these arguments, this should always be done in as neutral and objective a way as possible. It is definitely not proper to request the filing of statement under oath having a content suggested by the Opposition Division or any other instance. This involves the risk of leading witnesses and could seriously undermine the probative value of such statements. Such practice should therefore be avoided" (T804/92[103]).

(4) Amendments to the patent

(a) When appropriate and necessary: discretionary control

Rule 57(1) EPC requires that when a notice of opposition is communicated **3–59** to the patentee, it "shall invite him ... to file amendments, where appropriate, to the description, claims and drawings" within a fixed period. Thus, it seems that at this stage in an opposition the patentee has a right to file "appropriate" amendments to the patent. The meaning of "appropriate" in this context is considered below.

Thereafter, during an opposition, Rule 58(2) EPC provides that in any communication to the patentee "he shall, where appropriate, be invited to file, where necessary, the description, claims and drawings in amended form."

Subsequent to the communication to the proprietor of the notice of **3–60** opposition, and in the absence of an invitation to amend, the filing of

---

[102] T173/89 *ICI/Gamma-sorbital* [1991] E.P.O.R. 62.
[103] T804/92 *THERMO PRODUKTER/Energy saving refrigeration apparatus* O.J. EPO 1994, 862; [1995] E.P.O.R. 89.

amendments, further amendments or auxiliary requests for amendment is a matter within the discretion of the Opposition Division.

> "In opposition proceedings (including related appeal proceedings) the question whether to allow the patent proprietor's proposals for amendments to the description or claims is left to the Opposition Division or Board of Appeal, which must exercise due control in the matter.
>
> Although Rules 57 and 58 EPC directly concern only those criteria to be applied by the Opposition Division when the question of *inviting* the patent proprietor to make amendments arises, they indicate clearly and conclusively ... that even if not explicitly invited by the Opposition Division the patent proprietor may expect his proposals for amendments to be allowed only if it decides after exercising due discretion that it *regards* them as appropriate and/or necessary *in the above sense*. It would not be consistent with the general sense of these rules to interpret them as meaning that the Opposition Division could invite the patent proprietor to make amendments only if they were appropriate and necessary, but that he (the proprietor) actually had the more far-reaching legal right to have inappropriate and unnecessary amendments incorporated" (T406/86[104]).

3–61   Consequently, "proposed amendments may be disregarded in particular if submitted late in the proceedings. *i.e.* when examination of the opposition or appeal is already substantially complete" (T406/86[105]).

The practice in relation to auxiliary requests is discussed in Chapter 5 at paragraph 5–29.

A new Rule 57(a) EPC entered into force on June 1, 1995, which states that "Without prejudice to Rule 87 the description, claims and drawings may be amended, provided that the amendments are occasioned by the grounds of opposition specified in Article 100, even if the respective ground has not been invoked by the opponent."

Thus earlier decisions which refused to allow amendments which were not clearly related to an alleged ground of opposition are no longer applicable, (*e.g.* T127/85,[106] T295/87,[107] T550/88[108]).

3–61A   According to the proposed revision of the EPC, new Articles 105A, B and C will provide for limitation or revocation of a European patent at the request of the proprietor (see Chapter 8 at paragraph 8–04A and paragraph 3–12A above).

It would seem that Rule 57(a) EPC was introduced into the Implementing Regulations to compensate for the lack of any other possibility of

---

[104] T406/86 *WACKER/Trichloroethylene* O.J. EPO 1989, 302; [1989] E.P.O.R. 338.
[105] *Ibid.*
[106] T127/85 *IRECO/Blasting compositions* O.J. EPO 1989, 271; [1989] E.P.O.R. 358.
[107] T295/87 *ICI/Polyetherketones* O.J. EPO 1990, 470; [1991] E.P.O.R. 56.
[108] T550/88 *MOBIL OIL/National prior right* O.J. EPO 1990, 10; [1990] E.P.O.R. 391.

centralised amendment by the patent proprietor before the EPO after grant. If Articles 105A, B and C EPC are introduced into the EPC, Rule 57(a) EPC no longer seems to be appropriate. Rule 57(a) EPC is contrary to the concept and nature of opposition procedure as set out in paragraphs 3–02 and 3–03 above (see G9,10/91[109]).

(b) Examination of objections arising from amendments

Article 102(3) EPC provides that "If the Opposition Division is of the **3–62** opinion that [in view of the amendments made during the opposition proceedings] the patent and the invention to which it relates meet the requirements of the EPC," it shall maintain the patent as amended.

> "In all cases in which amendments are requested by the patentee and are considered to be free from objection under Article 123 EPC, Article 102(3) EPC confers upon the Opposition Division and the Board of Appeal jurisdiction, and thus the power, to decide upon the patent as amended in the light of the requirements of the EPC as a whole. The jurisdiction is thus wider than that conferred by Articles 102(1) and (2) EPC, which expressly limit jurisdiction to the grounds of opposition mentioned in Article 100 EPC. When substantive amendments are made to a patent ... both instances have the power to deal with grounds and issues *arising from those amendments* even though not specifically raised by an opponent pursuant to Rule 55(c) EPC" (emphasis added) (T227/88[110]).

Furthermore: **3–63**

> "when amendments are made to a patent during an opposition, Article 102(3) EPC requires consideration ... as to whether *the amendments* introduce any contravention of any requirement of the EPC, including Article 84 EPC. Article 102(3) EPC does not allow objections to be based upon Article 84 EPC if such objections do not *arise out of the amendments* [emphasis added]. ... In support of this conclusion, it would seem to be somewhat absurd if the making of a minor amendment could enable objections outside Article 100 EPC to be raised which have no connection with the amendment itself" (T301/87[111]).

However, the requirement of unity of invention under Article 82 EPC is not one of the "requirements of the EPC" which the amended patent must meet (G1/91[112]).

The above effect of Article 102(3) EPC is confirmed as follows:

---

[109] G9,10/91 *ROHM AND HAAS/Power to examine; Examination of oppositions/appeals* O.J. EPO 1993, 408, 420; [1993] E.P.O.R. 485.
[110] T227/88 *UNILEVER/Detergent Compositions* O.J. EPO 1990, 292; [1990] E.P.O.R. 424.
[111] T301/87 *BIOGEN/Alpha-interferons* O.J. EPO 1990, 335; [1990] E.P.O.R. 190.
[112] G1/91 *SIEMENS/Unity* O.J. EPO 1992, 253; [1992] E.P.O.R. 356.

"It should . . . be confirmed that in case of amendments to the claims or other parts of a patent in the case of opposition or appeal proceedings, such amendments are to be fully examined as to their compatibility with the requirements of the EPC, (*e.g.* with regard to the provisions of Article 123(2) and (3) EPC" (G9, 10/91[113])

It is the *amendments* which have to be examined for compatibility with the EPC (*i.e.* whether the amendments introduce objections). Thus for example, an Opposition Division cannot raise an objection of lack of clarity under Article 84 EPC (which is not a ground of objection under Article 100 EPC), unless such objection arises out of the amendment.

(5) Intervention by an assumed infringer

3–64 Article 105 EPC provides a special procedure whereby, after the nine-month period under Article 99 EPC for filing an opposition has expired, an alleged infringer may become a party to the proceedings, by filing a notice of intervention.

(a) Proof required

3–65 In order to be allowed to intervene, the intervener must prove either:

(a) that proceedings for infringement of the European patent have been instituted against him; or

(b) that the patent proprietor has requested that he cease the alleged infringement of the patent, and that he (the intervener) has instituted proceedings for a ruling that he is not infringing the patent.

3–65A According to the proposed revision of the EPC, Article 105 EPC will be amended by re-drafting it to clarify its meaning. In particular, the word "court" will be deleted. The procedural details relating to intervention will be transferred to the Implementing Regulations.

(b) Time limit for filing a notice of intervention

3–66 A notice of intervention must be filed at the EPO within three months from, the date on which infringement proceedings, or proceedings for a declaration of non-infringement (paragraphs 3–65 above), were instituted.

The applicable starting point for calculating the three-month period is always the date of institution of the first proceedings. Thus if the patent proprietor commences an action for infringement and the alleged infringer subsequently institutes an action for a declaration of non-infringement, the three month-period runs from commencement of the infringement action (T296/93[114]). This applies even if the subject of the alleged infringement changes (T144/95[115]).

---

[113] G9, 10/91 *ROHM AND HAAS/Power to examine; Examination of oppositions/appeals* O.J. EPO 1993, 408, 420; [1993] E.P.O.R. 485.
[114] T296/93 *BIOGEN/HBV* O.J. EPO 1995, 627; [1995] E.P.O.R. 1.
[115] T144/95 *UNILEVER/Dishwashing process* February 26, 1999.

(c) Intervention after final decision of the Opposition Division: only if appeal exists

A necessary pre-requisite for the filing of a notice of intervention is that **3–67** there must be opposition proceedings in existence at the time of filing (either proceedings before an Opposition Division or opposition appeal proceedings before a Board of Appeal) (G4/91[116]; G1/94[117]).

Thus, following issue of a final decision by an Opposition Division, and in the absence of an appeal by one of the parties to the proceedings before the Opposition Division, a notice of intervention which is filed subsequent to such decision (for example during the two-month period for appeal under Article 108 EPC) has no legal effect (G4/91[118]).

Furthermore, in the absence of an appeal from the decision of the **3–68** Opposition Division an alleged infringer cannot file a notice of appeal in addition to a notice of intervention within the two-month appeal period in order to initiate opposition appeal proceedings, because he is not a party to the proceedings before the Opposition Division. "The possibility that an assumed infringer may *initiate* proceedings by the filing of a notice of intervention is not envisaged by Article 105 EPC" (emphasis added) (G4/91[119]).

> "A decision ... which decides upon the issues raised by the opposition is a final decision in the sense that thereafter the Opposition Division has no power to change its decision" (G4/91[120]).

A decision following solely written proceedings before an Opposition Division becomes effective on the date when the written decision is handed to the internal courier service of the EPO for issue to the parties (G12/91[121]), and a notice of intervention which is filed after that date is inadmissible (in the absence of an appeal filed by a party to the Opposition Division proceedings) (T631/94[122]).

(d) Contents of the notice of intervention: subsequent procedure

The notice of intervention must contain "a written reasoned statement", **3–69** and must satisfy the same requirements for admissibility as a notice of opposition (see paragraphs 3–19 *et seq.*). In particular "It shall not be deemed to have been filed until the opposition fee has been paid" (Article 105(2) EPC).

Thereafter the intervention must be "treated as an opposition", except that in accordance with Rule 57(4) EPC, the Opposition Division may dispense with the requirements of Rule 57(1) to (3) EPC (*i.e.* in respect of

---

[116] G4/91 *DOLEZYCH II/Intervention* O.J. EPO 1993, 707; [1993] E.P.O.R. 120.
[117] G1/94 *ALLIED COLLOIDS/Intervention* O.J. EPO 1994, 787; [1994] E.P.O.R. 491.
[118] See note 116.
[119] See note 116.
[120] See note 116.
[121] G12/91 *NOVATOME II/Final decision* O.J. EPO 1994, 285; [1994] E.P.O.R. 309.
[122] T631/94 *WAGNER SINTO/Moulding machine* O.J. EPO 1996, 67; [1996] E.P.O.R. 401.

inviting observations from the proprietor and subsequent replies from the opponents).

(6) Observations by third parties

3–70 Third parties may file observations in writing concerning the patentability of an invention which is the subject of an opposed European patent, during opposition or intervention proceedings, pursuant to Article 115 EPC. The procedure is discussed in Chapter 5 at paragraph 5–31.

The filing of such observations may be useful if a third party (having failed to file a notice of opposition) wishes to support grounds of opposition already under examination during pending opposition proceedings, or if he become aware of additional grounds of objection which are not being examined in the pending proceedings.

(7) Transfer of an opposition

(a) By assignment

3–71   "An opposition pending before the EPO may be transferred or assigned to a third party as part of the opponent's business assets together with the assets in the interest of which the opposition was filed.

The term 'business' must be understood in a broad sense as describing an economic activity which is or could be carried on by the opponent and which constitutes a specific part of his business assets" (G4/88[123]).

Whether an opposition can be transmitted or assigned independently of the existence of an interest in instituting the opposition has not been decided, and is open to question.

(b) To an heir or successor in title

3–72   "The transmission of the opposition to the opponent's heir acknowledge implicitly in Rule 60(2) EPC which stipulates that the opposition proceedings may be continued even without the participation of the deceased opponent's heirs. [Guidelines, DI1,4] also allows, by analogy, for the opposition to be transmitted to the opponent's universal successor in law" (G4/88[124]).

(c) Transfer of the right to appeal

3–73 The right to file an appeal against the maintenance of a European patent in opposition proceedings may be transferred to a third party as part of the opponent's business assets (T563/89[125]).

---

[123] G4/88 MAN/Transfer of opposition O.J. EPO 1989, 480; [1990] E.P.O.R. 1.
[124] Ibid.
[125] T563/89 NAKAMURA September 3, 1991.

(d) Transfer during opposition appeal proceedings

"A party's rights in a case may be transferred at any stage of **3–74** opposition appeal proceedings, provided they are transferred together with the business assets or the assets in the interests of which the appeal was filed" (T659/92[126]).

(8) Withdrawal of an opposition

An opposition may be withdrawn at any time either during proceedings **3–75** before an Opposition Division or during opposition appeal proceedings. The effect is different in each of these two cases however:

(a) Withdrawal during Opposition Division proceedings

If an opposition is withdrawn during proceedings before an Opposition **3–76** Division, the "opposition proceedings may be continued by the EPO of its own motion" pursuant to Rule 60(2) EPC. This is a matter for the discretion of the Opposition Division.

After withdrawal of an opposition, the opposition proceedings should be continued if they have reached such a state that they are likely to result in a limitation or revocation of the European patent without further assistance from the Opponent and without the Opposition Division itself having to undertake extensive investigations.

In the light of this obligation the Opposition Division should, in principle, continue opposition proceedings when a communication pursuant to Rule 58(4) EPC was already sent to the parties before the opposition was withdrawn. The dispatch of the communication shows clearly that the Opposition Division was of the definite opinion that the European patent could not be maintained in the granted form. Under these circumstances it is in the public interest to continue the opposition proceedings after the withdrawal of the opposition even if the proprietor would have disagreed with the amended text proposed by the EPO, all the more so where the proprietor explicitly declared his agreement (T197/88[127]).

(b) Withdrawal during an opposition appeal

The effect of withdrawal of an opposition by an opponent during **3–77** opposition appeal proceedings depends upon whether the opponent is an appellant or a respondent in such proceedings, and is discussed in Chapter 4 at paragraphs 4–128 *et seq.* Rule 60(2) EPC is not applicable in opposition appeal proceedings (G8/93[128]).

---

[126] T659/92 SCHWEISFURTH/*Transfer of opposition* O.J. EPO 1995, 519; [1996] E.P.O.R. 314.
[127] T197/88 ICI/*Continuation of opposition proceedings* O.J. EPO 1989, 412; [1990] E.P.O.R. 243.
[128] G8/93 SERWANE II/*Withdrawal of opposition in appeal* O.J. EPO 1994, 887; [1995] E.P.O.R. 271.

(9) Surrender or lapse of the opposed patent during opposition proceedings

3–78   "If the European patent has been surrendered or has lapsed for all the designated States, the opposition proceedings may be continued at the request of the opponent filed within two months as from a notification by the EPO of the surrender or lapse" (Rule 60(1) EPC).

There is no legal obligation for the EPO to ascertain the legal status of the patent in this context (T194/88[129]).

Furthermore, Rule 60(l)EPC does not apply unless confirmation of surrender or lapse is received by the EPO from the authorities of all the designated States (T 194/88[130]).

(10) Assignment of the opposed patent during opposition proceedings

3–78a   "If the European patent is transferred during opposition proceedings the new patent proprietor entered in the Register of Patents takes the place of the previous patent proprietor both in the opposition and in the appeal proceedings. His entitlement may not be questioned in these proceedings" (T553/90[131]). Article 60(3) EPC is applicable ("the applicant shall be deemed to be entitled to exercise the right to the European patent").

The right to be entered on the Register of Patents may be contested before the Legal Division of the EPO (Article 20 EPC), and its decision may be appealed to the Legal Board of Appeal. The right to a European patent may also be contested before a national court, pursuant to the Protocol on Recognition (see also Chapter 2 at paragraphs 2–78 *et seq.*).

(11) Concurrent opposition and national revocation proceedings

3–79   From the moment when a European patent is granted (*i.e.* from "the date on which the European Patent Bulletin mentions the grant"—Article 97(4) EPC) not only can any person file an opposition at the EPO (within the nine-month period), but also revocation proceedings may be commenced in national courts. In the United Kingdom, this follows from section 77(1) of the U.K. 1977 Act, which states that ". . . a European patent (UK) shall, as from the publication of the mention of its grant in the European Patent Bulletin, be treated . . . as if it were a patent under this Act . . .". The revocation proceedings may be commenced either directly under section 72, or by way of defence to infringement proceedings commenced by the patent proprietor under section 61.

Such opposition proceedings and national revocation proceedings may, therefore, become pending at the same time. The filing of an opposition at

---

[129] T194/88 *MARANGON AND FIGLIO* November 30, 1992.
[130] *Ibid.*
[131] T553/90 *MARLBORO/Transfer* O.J. EPO 1993, 666; [1994] E.P.O.R. 440.

the EPO does not suspend the effect of grant of the European patent. The question may then arise whether one or other of these proceedings should be stayed pending completion of the other, in order to avoid duplication, or for other reasons.

This situation occurred in the United Kingdom Patents Court in **3–80** *Amersham International plc v. Corning Ltd and another.*[132] Shortly after grant of the European patent, infringement proceedings were commenced, and the defendants asked the Patents Court to stay the court proceedings pending decision in the opposition, on the basis that they undertook to be bound by such decision in the United Kingdom, and would not dispute validity in the United Kingdom if the patent was maintained in the opposition proceedings.

The Patents Court refused to stay its proceedings, primarily on the ground that the EPO was not an "alternative forum" for the purpose of granting a stay under English law, but also as a matter of discretion if the EPO was assumed to be an alternative forum in that context. The reasons for such an exercise of discretion are summarised in the headnote as follows:

"(i) Revocation of a European patent should primarily be a matter for the national court.
(ii) The convenient, desirable and usual practice in patent infringement litigation is for both infringement and validity to be tried and decided in the same proceedings. This was of juridical advantage to the plaintiffs.
(iii) If the stay were granted but the European opposition eventually failed, it was possible that the plaintiffs' claim for infringement would have been delayed by four to five years or more.
(iv) Both parties could well afford the costs of proceedings in both the High Court and the European Patent Office. Moreover the costs of litigation were small, in comparison with the value of the likely market in products subject of the patent."

In a Decision[133] of the German Federal Patent Court (Bundespatent- **3–81** gerichthof), it was held that:

"Pending European grant or opposition proceedings have no prejudicial effect on parallel opposition proceedings before the German Patent Office and cannot constitute grounds under Section 148, Code of Civil Procedure, for a stay of national proceedings."

Nevertheless, in other Contracting States it appears to be more common for national proceedings concerning a European patent to be stayed pending the outcome of opposition proceedings before the EPO.

---

[132] *Amersham International plc v. Corning Ltd and another* O.J. EPO 1987, 558; [1987] R.P.C. 513.
[133] Case No. 4W (pat) 50/85, O.J. EPO 1987, 557.

The possibility of concurrent opposition proceedings before the EPO and national proceedings in respect of the validity (and infringement) of the same European patent could lead to the unsatisfactory consequence of conflicting results in the different jurisdictions (*e.g.* a European patent may be held valid in national proceedings but revoked in EPO opposition proceedings or vice versa).

> "It is desirable for that to be avoided. Therefore the [U.K.] Patents Court will stay the English proceedings pending a final resolution of the European proceedings, if they can be resolved quickly and a stay will not inflict injustice on a party or be against the public interest. Unfortunately, that is not always possible as resolution of opposition proceedings in the EPO takes from about 4–8 years." (*Beloit Technologies v. Valmet Paper Machinery*, CA[134]).

(12) The decision

(a) Kinds of decision: interlocutory and final decisions

3–82 The final outcome of opposition proceedings will involve one of three possibilities:

(a) the patent may be revoked (Article 102(1) EPC);
(b) the opposition may be rejected, and the patent maintained unamended (Article 102(2) EPC);
(c) the patent may be maintained in amended form (Article 102(3) EPC).

Article 106(3) EPC provides that:

> "A decision which does not terminate proceedings as regards one of the parties can only be appealed together with the final decision, unless the decision allows separate appeal."

Such interlocutory decisions are frequently issued before an opposition is finally disposed of. For example, an Opposition Division may issue a decision refusing amendment of the patent as requested by the proprietor, on the basis of Article 123(2) EPC (prohibition of added subject-matter— see Chapter 8 at paragraphs 8–05 *et seq.* below), and thus revoking the patent as having no valid text. This decision may be the subject of a separate appeal, and if such appeal is allowed, the Opposition Division may proceed with examination of other grounds of opposition (*e.g.* lack of inventive step).

---

[134] *Beloit Technologies v. Valmet Paper Machinery Inc.* [1995] R.P.C. 533.

(b) Oral and written decisions

If requested, oral proceedings will be appointed in respect of such **3–83** intermediary matters, as well as before the final decision is issued by the Opposition Division in respect of the proceedings.

The decision of an Opposition Division is normally announced orally when oral proceedings are held. The written decision is then subsequently notified to the parties. If no oral proceedings are appointed, a written decision is issued to the parties.

(c) Finality of a decision

Both an interlocutory decision allowing separate appeal under Article **3–84** 106(3) EPC, and a decision of an Opposition Division which decides upon all the substantive issues raised by the opposition and therefore decides the opposition in accordance with Article 102(1), (2) or (3) EPC, is a "final" decision in the sense that thereafter, the Opposition Division has no power to change its decision. The effect of such a final decision (whether announced orally or in writing) can only be changed by appeal proceedings (G4/91,[135] T390/86[136]).

(d) Special considerations concerning maintenance in amended form

Article 102(3) and Rule 58(4) and (5) EPC contain provisions governing the **3–85** maintenance of European patents in amended form which are intended to ensure, in particular, that the patent is maintained with a text which has been approved by the proprietor, as required by Article 113(2) EPC.

(i) Approval/disapproval of the proposed amended text. Thus Article **3–86** 102(3) and Rule 58(4) EPC require that, before an Opposition Division decides to maintain the patent in amended form, the parties must be informed of the proposed amended text, and given an opportunity to present observations on such text within a period of two months if they disapprove of the text.

The main purpose of this provision is to ensure that the patent proprietor approves of the text in which the patent is intended to be maintained, as required by Article 113(2) EPC. While an opponent may also object to the proposed text pursuant to Rule 58(4) EPC he is under no obligation to do so, and his failure to do so does not affect his right of appeal. The opponent's opportunity to disapprove of the text is additional to his right of appeal (G1/88[137]).

(ii) Interlocutory decision on amended text. Article 102(3) EPC also **3–87** requires in effect that when a patent is maintained in amended form, a new patent specification has to be printed, and to this end, the payment of a printing fee within a prescribed time limit is required, together with

---

[135] G4/91 *DOLEZYCH II/Intervention* O.J. EPO 1999, 707; [1993] E.P.O.R. 120.
[136] T390/86 *SHELL/Changed composition of division* O.J. EPO 1989, 30; [1989] E.P.O.R. 162.
[137] G1/88 *HOESCHT/Opponent's silence* EPC O.J. EPO 1989, 189; [1989] E.P.O.R. 421.

translations of any amended claims (Rule 58(5) EPC). These requirements are important in that if they are not complied with, the patent is revoked.

Bearing in mind the possibility of an appeal from a decision of this kind by the Opposition Division, the practice has been to designate this type of decision as interlocutory in the sense of Article 106(3) EPC.

> "The EPO very early on adopted the device of an interlocutory decision, for which there is no express provision, in order to establish in the first place the text of the amended specification. Only after this interlocutory decision has come into force are the fee for printing and a translation of the claims ... requested pursuant to Rule 58(5) EPC. Once these requirements have been fulfilled, what is then a non-appealable final decision on maintenance of the patent as amended is given. ..." (G1/88[138]).

3–88   **(iii) Application of Rule 58(4) EPC after oral proceedings.** The requirement in Rule 58(4) EPC (that the parties should be informed of the intention to maintain the patent in amended form and given a period of two months in which to file disapproval of the text and observations is applicable when such intention to maintain the patent in amended form is reached during oral proceedings:

> "in proceedings before the Opposition Division ... the parties should always be informed in accordance with Rule 58(4) EPC even if oral proceedings have been held" (T219/83[139]).

This is in contrast with the corresponding procedure before the Boards of Appeal (see Chapter 4 at paragraphs 4–146 *et seq.*).

(e) Revocation at the request of the proprietor

3–89   If, for whatever reason, the proprietor of a European patent decides during opposition proceedings that he no longer wishes to maintain his patent, he may make a request to that effect during the opposition proceedings, and the patent will then be revoked (T73/84,[140] T186/84,[141] T237/86,[142] T459/88[143]).

(f) Costs in opposition proceedings

3–89A   The general principle is set out in Article 104(1) EPC as follows:

> "Each party to the proceedings shall meet the costs he has incurred ...

---

[138] G1/88 *HOECHST/Opponent's silence* O.J. EPO 1989, 189; [1989] E.P.O.R. 421.
[139] T219/83 *BASF/Zeolites* O.J. EPO 1982, 211; [1986] E.P.O.R. 247.
[140] T73/84 *SMS/Revocation at the instigation of the patent proprietor* O.J. EPO 1985, 241; [1979–85] E.P.O.R.: C: 944.
[141] T186/84 *BASF/Revocation at proprietor's request* O.J. EPO 1986, 79; [1986] E.P.O.R. 165.
[142] T237/86 *SMS/Abandoned patent* O.J. EPO 1988, 261; [1988] E.P.O.R. 397.
[143] T459/88 *MAN/Admissibility of appeal* O.J. EPO 1990, 425; [1991] E.P.O.R. 72.

unless a decision of an Opposition Division or Board of Appeal, for reasons of equity, orders ... a different apportionment of costs incurred during taking of evidence in oral proceedings".

The principles governing apportionment of costs are considered in the context of appeal proceedings in Chapter 4 at paragraphs 4–156 *et seq.*

(g) Change in composition of Opposition Division between oral and written decision

The written decision which is issued following announcement of an oral **3–90** decision during oral proceedings before an Opposition Division should normally be signed by the same members of the Opposition Division who participated in the oral proceedings, and in the absence of a sufficiently good reason why this has not been done, a decision which is not so signed would be set aside as void and the case remitted for re-examination *ab initio* by the Opposition Division (T390/86,[144] T243/87[145]).

On the other hand, if exceptionally a member of an Opposition Division was prevented by incapacity from signing a written decision following oral proceedings, for example, the decision could be signed by another member in the name of the incapacitated member (T243/87[146]).

(h) Correction of errors in decisions

Rule 89 EPC provides that "only linguistic errors, errors of transcription **3–91** and obvious mistakes [in decisions] may be corrected."

"A decision cannot be cancelled by the instance which issued it, but can only be corrected under Rule 89 EPC (T212/88[147])."

Such a correction "can only be instigated by the Opposition Division itself (normally by a further decision giving the ground of correction)" (T212/88[148]), and has a retrospective (*i.e.* declaratory) effect (*cf.* Rule 88 EPC—see Chapter 8 at paragraph 8–82).

See also Chapter 6 at paragraphs 6–75 *et seq.*

Cases Referred to in Chapter 3

Board of Appeal Decisions

G1/84   MOBIL OIL/Opposition by proprietor O.J. EPO 1985, 299; [1986] E.P.O.R. 39.

G1/88   HOECHST/Opponent's silence O.J. EPO 1989, 189; [1989] E.P.O.R. 421.

---

[144] T390/86 *SHELL/Changed composition of division* O.J. EPO 1989, 30; [1989] E.P.O.R. 162.
[145] T243/87 *LESAFFRE/Composition of Opposition Division* [1990] E.P.O.R. 136.
[146] *Ibid.*
[147] T212/88 *BP/Theta-1* O.J. EPO 1992, 28; [1990] E.P.O.R. 518.
[148] *Ibid.*

G4/88 MAN/Transfer of opposition O.J. EPO 1989, 480; [1990]
E.P.O.R. 1.

G1/91 SIEMENS/Unity O.J. EPO 1992, 253; [1992] E.P.O.R. 356.

G4/91 DOLEZYCH II/Intervention O.J. EPO 1993, 707.

G9, 10/91 ROHM AND HAAS/Power to examine; Examination of
oppositions/appeals O.J. EPO 1993, 408, 420; [1993]
E.P.O.R. 485.

G12/91 NOVATOME II/Final Decision O.J. EPO 1994, 285; [1994]
E.P.O.R. 309.

G8/93 SERWANE II/Withdrawal of opposition in appeal O.J. EPO
1994, 887; [1995] E.P.O.R. 271.

G9/93 PEUGEOT AND CITROEN II/Opposition by patent
proprietor O.J. EPO 1994, 891; [1995] E.P.O.R. 260.

G1/94 ALLIED COLLOIDS/Intervention O.J. EPO 1994, 787; [1994]
E.P.O.R. 491.

G1/95 DE LA RUE/Fresh grounds for opposition O.J. EPO 1996,
615; [1996] E.P.O.R. 601.

G4/95 BOGASKY II/Representation O.J. EPO 1996, 412; [1996]
E.P.O.R. 333.

G7/95 ETHICON/Fresh grounds for opposition O.J. EPO 1996, 626;
[1997] E.P.O.R. 89.

G3, 4/97 INDUPACK/GENENTECH/Opposition on behalf of a third
party O.J. EPO 1999, 245 and 270.

G3/99 HOWARD FLOREY INSTITUTE; O.J. EPO (P).

T10/82 BAYER/Admissibility of opposition O.J. EPO 1983, 407;
[1979–85] E.P.O.R. 381.

T219/83 BASF/Zeolites O.J. EPO 1986, 211; [1986] E.P.O.R. 247.

T73/84 SMS/Revocation at the instigation of the patent proprietor
O.J. EPO 1985, 241; [1979–85] E.P.O.R.: C: 944.

T156/84 AIR PRODUCTS/Pressure swing adsorption O.J. EPO 1988,
372; [1989] E.P.O.R. 47.

T186/84 BASF/Revocation at proprietor's request O.J. EPO 1986, 79;
[1986] E.P.O.R. 165.

T25/85 DEUTSCHE GELATINE-FABRIKEN, STOESS & CO./
Opponent-identifiability O.J. EPO 1986, 81; [1986] E.P.O.R.
158.

T127/85 IRECO/Blasting compositions O.J. EPO 1989, 271; [1989]
E.P.O.R. 358.

T152/85 SANDVIK/Unpaid opposition fee O.J. EPO 1987, 191; [1987]
E.P.O.R. 258.

T222/85 PPG/Ungelled polyesters O.J. EPO 1988, 128; [1987] E.P.O.R.
99.

T117/86 FILMTEC/Costs O.J. EPO 1989, 40; [1989] E.P.O.R. 504.

T237/86 SMS/Abandoned patent O.J. EPO 1988, 261; [1988] E.P.O.R.
397.

T317/86 SMIDTH/Title of invention O.J. EPO 1989, 378; [1989]
E.P.O.R. 415.

T390/86   SHELL/Changed composition of division O.J. EPO 1989, 30; [1989] E.P.O.R. 162.

T406/86   WACKER/Trichloroethylene O.J. EPO 1989, 302; [1989] E.P.O.R. 328.

T9/87   ICI/Zeolites O.J. EPO 1989, 438; [1990] E.P.O.R. 46.

T243/87   LESAFFRE/Composition of Opposition Division [1990] E.P.O.R. 136.

T295/87   ICI/Polyetherketones O.J. EPO 1990, 470; [1991] E.P.O.R. 56.

T301/87   BIOGEN/Alpha-interferons O.J. EPO 1990, 335; [1990] E.P.O.R. 190.

T317/87   KIESERLING & ALBRECHT/Spinning Lathe (unpublished).

T326/87   DU PONT/Polyamide composition O.J. EPO 1992, 522; [1991] E.P.O.R. 47.

T328/87   ELECTROLUX/Admissibility O.J. EPO 1992, 701; [1993] E.P.O.R. 191.

T185/88   HENKEL/Surface active agents O.J. EPO 1990, 451; [1990] E.P.O.R. 649.

T197/88   ICI/Continuation of opposition proceedings O.J. EPO 1989, 412; [1990] E.P.O.R. 243.

T198/88   SCHWIETE/Concrete reconstruction O.J. EPO 1991, 254; [1991] E.P.O.R. 455.

T212/88   BP/Theta-1 O.J. EPO 1992, 28; [1990] E.P.O.R. 518.

T227/88   UNILEVER/Detergent compositions O.J. EPO 1990, 292; [1990] E.P.O.R. 424.

T251/88   IRSID/Opposition Division [1990] E.P.O.R. 246.

T297/88   BAYER/Nimodipin II December 5, 1989.

T459/88   MAN/Admissibility of appeal O.J. EPO 1990, 425; [1991] E.P.O.R. 72.

T493/88   CEA—FRAMATOME/Spacer grid O.J. EPO 1991, 380; EPO 1990, 5; [1991] E.P.O.R. 393.

T536/88   BADISCHE KARTON UND PAPPENFABRIK/Dust-tight folding carton O.J. EPO 1992, 638; [1992] E.P.O.R. 202.

T550/88   MOBIL OIL/National prior right O.J. EPO 1990, 10; [1990] E.P.O.R. 391.

T635/88   DE ERVEN G. DE BOER BV./Opponent identifiability O.J. EPO 1993, 608; [1994] E.P.O.R. 358.

T2/89   BASF/Opposition grounds O.J. EPO 1991, 51; [1991] E.P.O.R. 391.

T22/89   ALCAN/Aluminium alloys June 26, 1990.

T93/89   HOECHST/Polyvinyl ester dispersion O.J. EPO 1992, 718; [1992] E.P.O.R. 155.

T173/89   ICI/Gamma-Sorbitol [1991] E.P.O.R. 62.

T182/89   SUMITOMO/Extent of opposition O.J. EPO 1991, 391; [1990] E.P.O.R. 438.

T275/89   KLOSTERMANN/Steel radiators O.J. EPO 1992, 126; [1992] E.P.O.R. 260.

T387/89   MEDTRONIC/Cardioverter O.J. EPO 1992, 583; [1993]
          E.P.O.R. 113.
T448/89   SIEMENS/Stimulating electrode O.J. EPO 1992, 361; [1992]
          E.P.O.R. 540.
T563/89   NAKANURA September 3, 1991.
T580/89   ROHM AND HAAS/Power to examine, August 29, 1991 (P).
T716/89   UNILEVER/Right to be heard O.J. EPO 1992, 132.
T89/90   SPRECHER UND SCHUH, November 27, 1990 (P).
T376/90   SUMITOMO/Polymer solution O.J. EPO 1994, 906; [1995]
          E.P.O.R. 232.
T553/90   MARLBORO/Transfer O.J. EPO 1993, 666; [1994] E.P.O.R.
          440.
T669/90   ATT/Inviting observations O.J. EPO 1992, 739; [1992]
          E.P.O.R. 397.
T289/91   HOECHST/ACE inhibitors O.J. EPO 1994, 649; [1995]
          E.P.O.R. 32.
T925/91   EXXON/Combustion effluents O.J. EPO 1995, 469; [1996]
          E.P.O.R. 77.
T659/92   SCHWEISFURTH/Transfer of opposition O.J. EPO 1995, 519;
          [1996] E.P.O.R. 314.
T804/92   THERMO PRODUKTER/Energy saving refrigerator O.J. EPO
          1994, 862; [1995] E.P.O.R. 89.
T1002/92 PETTERSSON/Queueing system O.J. EPO 1995, 605; [1996]
          E.P.O.R. 1.
T296/93   BIOGEN/HBV O.J. EPO 1995, 627; [1995] E.P.O.R. 1.
T433/93   ATOTECH/Re-hearing O.J. EPO 1997, 509; [1998] E.P.O.R.
          135.
T590/93   KOGYO/Photosensitive resins O.J. EPO 1995, 337; [1997]
          E.P.O.R. 478.
T798/93   ROAD TRAIN/Identification of real opponent O.J. EPO 1997,
          363; [1998] E.P.O.R. 1.
T926/93   MITSUBISHI/Gas laser device O.J. EPO 1997, 447; [1998]
          E.P.O.R. 94.
T382/94   CARL ZEISS/Documents as filed O.J. EPO 1998, 24.
T522/94   TECHMO/Powered vehicle for operation of ladles O.J. EPO
          1998, 421; [1999] E.P.O.R. 75.
T631/94   WAGNER SINTO/Moulding machine O.J. EPO 1996, 67;
          [1996] E.P.O.R. 401.
T144/95   UNILEVER/Dishwashing process February 26, 1999.
T272/95   HOWARD FLOREY INSTITUTE/Admissibility of joint oppo-
          sition or joint appeal O.J. EPO 1999, 590.
T142/97   STOCKLI/Apparatus for separating disc-shaped objects O.J.
          EPO 2000, 358.

Decision of an Opposition Division O.J. EPO 1992, 747.

Decisions of National Courts.

Amersham International plc v. Corning Ltd; [1987] R.P.C. 513.
Beloit Technologies v. Valmet Paper Machinery Inc. [1995] R.P.C. 533.
Case No. 4W (pat) 50/85, German Federal Patent Court, O.J. EPO 1987, 557
Hydropyridine June 13, 1986 Court of Patent Appeals, Sweden O.J. EPO 1988, 198.

CHAPTER 4

APPEALS

Contents

All references are to paragraph numbers

Cases Referred to in Chapter 4

A. Introduction

4–01 With a steadily increasing number of decisions being issued by the Boards of Appeal each year on all aspects of the EPC, it is apparent that such decisions provide a dynamic and rapidly developing source of European patent law.

The EPC provides an appeal as of right from all decisions made by the departments of the EPO which constitute the first instance—namely, the Receiving Section, the Examining Division, the Opposition Division, and the Legal Division. The second and final instance is in all cases provided by the Boards of Appeal.

This chapter examines first the way in which the Boards of Appeal are organised, and then the appeal procedure, including the way in which the Boards of Appeal operate. A final section (paragraphs 4–175 *et seq.*) examines the operation of the Enlarged Board of Appeal which, as will be seen, is not a further instance of appeal above the other Boards of Appeal. Its decisions, however, have a higher legal authority than those of the Boards of Appeal, and are the highest legal authority within the structure of the Boards of Appeal and the EPO.

4–02 Especially within an international organisation such as the EPO, which is not subject to any supervisory national laws, the safeguard provided by such a right of appeal is an essential one, and the responsibility of the Boards of Appeal is heavy. Without such a right of appeal to a properly constituted body which provides an independent review of any decision at first instance on its merits, there would be no check upon the power exercised by the EPO, and the way would be open for the making of decisions on an arbitrary basis, without proper reasoning based upon the provisions of the EPC as correctly interpreted.

The procedural law and practice under the EPC relating to the organisation and operation of the Boards of Appeal, and the development of this by means of decisions of the Boards of Appeal, is particularly important for the maintenance of a European patent system which generates confidence in its users. Individual states commonly have a well established procedure and practice in relation to patent appeals. In contrast, although the number of appeals before the Boards of Appeal has increased rapidly to a current level of about 1100 a year, the practice in relation to such appeals is based upon relatively short experience of new provisions. Nevertheless, such practice is now generally well established, following a series of decisions which have been issued in recent years by the Enlarged Board of Appeal.

Members of the Boards of Appeal have been appointed from the majority of the 20 Contracting States. This international element in the composition of the Boards of Appeal necessarily underlies the way in which they operate. The relevant provisions of the EPC were in part derived from different previous national systems, but they are also partly new. There has been considerable scope for different interpretations of the EPC, and also for the introduction of variations in practice from Board to

Board, and from time to time. This is clearly undesirable in the long term, but almost inevitable in the short term pending establishment of a settled practice by the Enlarged Board of Appeal.

As mentioned above, the Boards of Appeal decide upon all appeals from **4–03** decisions of the first instance departments of the EPO concerning European patent applications and patents.

For the sake of completeness, it should be mentioned that the Boards of Appeal are also responsible for deciding upon "protests" in respect of findings of non-unity of invention for the purpose of carrying out an international search under the Patent Co-operation Treaty (PCT), pursuant to Articles 154(3) and 155(3) EPC (see Chapter 2 at paragraph 2–34).

Legally qualified members of the Boards of Appeal may also sit upon the Disciplinary Board of Appeal, in conjunction with two members of the Institute of Professional Representatives, which decides upon:

(a) appeals against decisions of the Disciplinary Committee of the Institute of Professional Representatives and of the Disciplinary Board of the EPO imposing disciplinary measures on professional representatives;

(b) appeals against decisions of the Examination Board in connection with the European Qualifying Examination (admission to the Examination and failure to pass it).

This book is not concerned with the above special functions of the Boards of Appeal.

B. Organisation of the Boards of Appeal

(1) Position of the Boards of Appeal within the European Patent Organisation

Pursuant to Article 15 EPC, the Boards of Appeal (including the **4–04** Enlarged Board of Appeal), are administratively organised as one of five Directorates-General (DG) within the EPO (see Chapter 1), and the members of the Boards of Appeal and the Enlarged Board of Appeal are therefore permanent employees of the EPO (except for the external members who are appointed under Article 160(2) EPC—see paragraph 4–09A)

This arrangement is essentially intended to provide ease of administration, and the Boards of Appeal are intended to operate entirely independently from the remainder of the EPO. This independence of operation is guaranteed as far as possible by the independent status of the individual members of the Boards of Appeal, which is discussed below (see paragraphs 4–06 *et seq.*).

The Boards of Appeal have a Vice-President who is responsible to the **4–05** President of the EPO for their operation (Article 19(3) EPC). The present Vice-President of the Boards of Appeal is also a legal member of the Boards of Appeal, and may, therefore, act as a member of individual Boards of Appeal, either as a member or as a Chairman. He is currently appointed Chairman of the Enlarged Board of Appeal. The present Vice-President of the Boards of Appeal thus occupies a dual position involving both administrative and judicial responsibilities.

However, the EPC does not require that the Vice-President of the Boards of Appeal should also be appointed as Chairman of the Enlarged Board of Appeal, or even as a chairman or member of the Boards of Appeal. Initially, and until 1985, the Chairman of the Enlarged Board was a separate appointment from that of Vice-President, and the administrative power of the Vice-President was therefore separated from the judicial function of the Chairman of the Enlarged Board.

(2) Independence

(a) Introduction

4–06 Independence in a judge or any other person exercising a judicial function is essentially an attitude of mind.

The Boards of Appeal are composed of both legally qualified and technically qualified members (as are the German Federal Patents Court and the Swedish Court of Patent Appeals) who sit together to decide individual cases, as discussed below. As the Boards of Appeal and the Enlarged Board of Appeal are set up within the EPO by virtue of Article 15 EPC, in common with the departments of first instance, the members of the Boards are also employees of the EPO. As mentioned previously, however, this is essentially for ease of administration: the Boards of Appeal are intended to operate entirely independently, not only from the departments of first instance which make the decisions that are the subject of appeals, but also from the President of the EPO and its administration. The independent status of the individual members of the Boards of Appeal is provided by the EPC, and is essential to the maintenance of public confidence in the appeal system.

4–07   In the context of the making of decisions by members of the Boards of Appeal, there are a number of important factors concerning their independence:

(a) They must be independent in their decision-making from the organisation which pays them, namely the EPO;
(b) They must be independent of other Directorates-General of the EPO, especially the first instance departments;
(c) They must be independent of their national backgrounds;
(d) They must only apply the law in accordance with the EPC.

All of these aims are promoted by provisions of the EPC itself, as well as by provisions of the Service Regulations of the EPO. As a result, the independence of members of the Boards of Appeal is similar to that of national judges.

(b) Provisions of the EPC

Article 23(3) EPC provides that "in their decisions the members of the **4–08** Boards shall not be bound by any instructions and shall comply only with the provisions of the EPC." This is a statement of their status in law.

The position of the Boards of Appeal is different from national courts insofar as they are included within an organisational structure whose head, the President of the EPO, is also responsible for the departments within other directorates who are in turn responsible for the issue of the first instance decisions, the subject of proceedings before the Boards of Appeal.

In order to safeguard the independence of the members of the Boards of Appeal during decision-making, the EPC provides additional measures relating both to their appointment and to their term of office.

(i) Appointment to the Boards of Appeal. Article 11 EPC deals with the **4–09** appointment of "senior employees" of the EPO, namely the President and Vice-Presidents and the members (including the Chairmen) of the Boards of Appeal. As to the latter, under Article 11(3) EPC they are appointed (and re-appointed) by decision of the Administrative Council. The degree of influence of the President of the EPO in relation to such appointments is defined as follows: the initial appointment can only take place by a Council decision after a "proposal" by the President, but any re-appointment takes place upon a Council decision after the President has been "consulted". Essentially, therefore, appointment of the membership of the Boards of Appeal should be decided by the national delegations that comprise the Administrative Council.

"External members" of the Boards of Appeal and the Enlarged Board of **4–09A** Appeal are currently appointed under Article 160(2) EPC, which provides for such appointments "during a transitional period". However, in accordance with the proposed revision of the EPC, Article 160 EPC will be deleted from the EPC, so that external members will no longer be appointed to the Boards of Appeal. Legally qualified members from national courts or authorities will be appointed members of the Enlarged Board of Appeal under a new provision to be inserted into Article 11 EPC (see paragraph 4–190A).

(ii) Disciplinary authority. Article 11(4) EPC provides that it is the **4–10** Administrative Council which exercises disciplinary authority over the Boards of Appeal (as well as the Vice-Presidents of the EPO): this is in contrast to all other employees of the EPO, over whom the President exercises disciplinary authority under Article 10(2)(h) EPC.

(iii) Term of office and security of tenure. Article 23(1) EPC provides for **4–11** a fixed term of office of five years, which is renewable. Such a period of office is short compared for example with the appointment for life of most national judges. Nevertheless, security of tenure during the five-year period is strong, as also provided by Article 23(1) EPC: a Board member may not be removed from office, "except if there are serious grounds for such removal", and unless the Administrative Council takes a decision to this effect, on a proposal from the Enlarged Board of Appeal. Thus, the President of the EPO has no power to remove a member of the Boards of Appeal from his appointed office during the term of his appointment.

There are practical reasons for the EPC providing such a short term. In particular, at the time when the EPC was drafted and signed, the success of the EPO could not be guaranteed and it was, therefore, difficult to provide a long term of office or a life term with the possibility of little or no work.

In practice, at the present time the need for increasing numbers of members of the Boards means that reappointment is normally to be expected, even if it is not automatic.

(c) Provisions in the Service Regulations

4–12 In addition to the provisions of the EPC discussed above, the Service Regulations for permanent employees of the EPO provide special obligations for members of the Boards of Appeal.

In particular, each member of the Boards of Appeal must swear an oath or give an undertaking upon appointment to perform his duties "in accordance with the EPC and the principles of procedural law generally recognised in the Contracting States; to act, in taking decisions, to the best of his knowledge and in all conscience, without respect of persons, and to act solely in the interests of truth and justice" (Article 15(1) Service Regulations).

Furthermore, a member must conduct himself, both in the performance of his duties and otherwise, "in such a manner as not to detract from confidence in his independence" (Article 15(2) Service Regulations).

(d) Judicial status of the Boards of Appeal and their members

4–13 Although the Boards of Appeal are not constituted as a court of justice, members of the Boards of Appeal are public officers appointed to administer the law. In a broad sense, therefore, members of the Boards of Appeal can fairly be considered as judges in their function of administering the law and deciding cases in accordance with the law, even though they do not sit in a body which is formally constituted as a court.

Thus:

> "Those EPC provisions governing the independence of members of the Boards of Appeal (Article 23 EPC) their competence and method of work and the nature of the decisions they take, indicate that the Boards act as courts with the task of ensuring that the provisions of the EPC do not conflict with the law when applied in practice ..." (G1/86).[1]

Furthermore, having considered *inter alia* the provisions discussed in

---

[1] G1/86 *VOEST ALPINE/Re-establishment of opponent* O.J. EPO 1987, 447; [1987] E.P.O.R. 388.

paragraphs 4–08 *et seq.* above, the United Kingdom Patents Court in *Lenzing*[2] stated that "the legal position of the Boards of Appeal complies completely with English notions of a judicial tribunal" and that "the members [of the Boards of Appeal] are independent in their judicial function and that independence is guaranteed by the EPC itself. They are judges in all but name."

3. Rules of Procedure

(a) Introduction

The procedure of the Boards of Appeal when deciding individual cases, **4–14** both internally and externally in relation to each party to an appeal, is governed partly by provisions of the EPC and partly by the Rules of Procedure of the Boards of Appeal ("RPBA")[3] and of the Enlarged Board of Appeal ("RPEBA").[4] The relevant provisions of the EPC, including the EPC itself and the Rules, were part of the original texts which entered into force in 1977. It was intended that following the entry into force of these texts, further rules of procedure governing the proceedings before the Boards of Appeal would be brought into effect under the mechanism of Article 23(4) EPC, whereby the Boards of Appeal essentially propose and adopt their own procedural Rules (see below), subject to the approval of the Administrative Council. This is in accordance with the principle of judicial independence which is embodied in Article 23(3) EPC and which extends to the procedure which is either preparatory to or otherwise related to the making of decisions by the Boards of Appeal (G6/95[5]).

The Administrative Council may amend the original text of the Rules of the EPC, including those which govern the procedure of the Boards of Appeal, under Article 33(1)(b) EPC (see Chapter 1 at paragraph 1–07).

(b) Adoption

The Rules of Procedure of the Boards of Appeal ("RPBA") and of the **4–15** Enlarged Board of Appeal ("RPEBA") are adopted separately, in accordance with Article 23(3) EPC and Rule 11 EPC. The RPBA are adopted by the "authority" which is identified and described in Rule 10(2) EPC, which is known as the "Presidium" of the Boards of Appeal, and which is composed of the Vice-President and Chairmen of the Board of Appeal, plus three elected members of the Boards of Appeal. The RPEBA are adopted by the Enlarged Board itself. Both the RPBA and the RPEBA are adopted subject to the approval of the Administrative Council. Such Rules of Procedure are binding upon the Boards of Appeal (see Articles 19 RPBA and 14 RPEBA), subject to the EPC.

[2] *Lenzing AG's European Patent (U.K.)* [1997] R.P.C. 245.
[3] O.J. EPO 1980, 171; O.J. EPO 1983, 7; O.J. EPO 1989, 361. Reproduced in full at Appendix 4, below.
[4] O.J. EPO 1983; 3; O.J. EPO 1989, 362. Reproduced in full at Appendix 5, below.
[5] G6/95 *GE CHEMICALS/Interpretation of Rule 71a(1) EPC* O.J. EPO 1996, 649; [1997] E.P.O.R. 265.

(c) Status compared to the EPC Rules: G6/95[6]

4–16 A question of law concerning a potential conflict between an amended Rule of the EPC (Rule 71a (1) EPC) and the RPBA had to be resolved by the Enlarged Board. In particular, if the amended Rule 71a(1) EPC (which entered into force on June 1, 1995) was interpreted as applying to the Boards of Appeal as well as the first instance departments of the EPO it would be directly contradictory to and in conflict with Article 11(2) RPBA, which was adopted pursuant to Article 23(4) EPC. However, having regard to the principle of judicial independence embodied in Article 23 EPC the Enlarged Board considered that "the Administrative Council must be presumed to know the limits of its own power", and that it was "therefore reasonable to assume that the Administrative Council did not intend to amend Rule 71 EPC so as to provide a conflict with a Rule of Procedure of the Boards of Appeal". Accordingly, Rule 71a(1) EPC was interpreted as being applicable to the first instance departments of the EPO but not to the Boards of Appeal (see paragraph 5–51 (G6/95[7])).

(4) Composition of the individual Boards

(a) Legal and Technical Boards of Appeal

4–17 Most appeals are from decisions of the Examining Division and the Opposition Division, and most of these are decided by a Board of Appeal composed of two technical members and one legal member, which is known as a Technical Board of Appeal. Some appeals concern procedural and legal issues, and are decided by a Board of Appeal composed of three legal members, which is known as the Legal Board of Appeal.

Decisions at first instance can in principle be divided into two broad categories: those concerned essentially with procedural points, and those concerned with substantive grounds of objection to the validity of a patent application or patent. Appeals from procedural decisions are purely legal in nature, whereas the majority of appeals from substantive decisions commonly raise a mixture of legal and technical issues, although the technical aspects normally predominate.

This division between the two categories—legal and technical—is reflected in accordance with Article 21 EPC in the compositions of individual Boards of Appeal.

There are four first instance departments whose decisions are subject to appeal: the Receiving Section, the Legal Division, the Examining Divisions, and the Opposition Divisions (Article 21(1) EPC).

[6] *Ibid.*
[7] *Ibid.*

(b) Decisions of the Receiving Section and Legal Division

The decisions of the Receiving Section and the Legal Division are always **4–18** concerned solely with procedural and legal matters, and appeals from such decisions are decided by the Legal Board of Appeal (Article 21(2) EPC).

(c) Decisions of the Examining Divisions

Most appeals from decisions of the Examining Divisions are concerned **4–19** with the refusal or grant of a European patent and are decided by the Technical Boards of Appeal (Article 21(3)(a) and (b) (EPC). Other such appeals are decided by the Legal Board of Appeal (Article 21(3)(c) EPC).

The distinction between a decision of an Examining Division which "concerns" refusal or grant of a patent (Article 21(3)(a) EPC), and one which does not, may be a fine one. Thus an appeal from a decision which refused a request for correction of a decision to grant a patent pursuant to Rule 89 EPC (two pages of the text of the description had been omitted by error) should be decided by a Technical Board of Appeal, because a decision to grant necessarily "concerns" the grant of a patent if the subject of the decision under appeal is the text in which the patent is to be or has been granted, since this text defines the rights conferred by the patent; whereas an appeal from a decision which refused to allow a request for correction of the text of a patent application under Rule 88 EPC should be decided by the Legal Board of Appeal, because such a decision is interlocutory and does not terminate the grant procedure (G8/95[8]).

(d) Decisions of the Opposition Divisions

Appeals from decisions of the Opposition Division are never decided by **4–20** the Legal Board of Appeal, but always by a Technical Board of Appeal (Article 21(4) EPC), even if the issues to be decided are purely procedural or legal.

(e) Decisions of Formalities Officers on behalf of Examining Divisions or Opposition Divisions

A number of procedural matters before the Examining Divisions and the **4–21** Opposition Divisions are entrusted for decision to Formalities Officers (EPO employees who need neither legal nor technical qualifications) of those Divisions, by Notices[9] pursuant to Rule 9(3) EPC. Appeals from such decisions are decided by a Technical Board of Appeal (G2/90[10]).

---

[8] G8/95 *US GYPSUM II/Correction of decision to grant* O.J. EPO 1996, 481; [1997] E.P.O.R. 66.
[9] Notices dated June 15, 1984, O.J. EPO 1984, 317, 319. Notice dated February 1, 1989, O.J. EPO 1989, 178. Reproduced at Appendix 7.
[10] G2/90 *KOLBENSCHMIDT/Responsibility of the Legal Board of Appeal* O.J. EPO 1992, 10; [1992] E.P.O.R. 125.

(f) Competence of the Legal and Technical Boards: summary

4–22 The scheme of Article 21 EPC is clearly intended to provide individual compositions of the Boards of Appeal which include technical and/or legal members in accordance with the subject-matter of the issues in each particular appeal. In general, it achieves this: however, there are certain circumstances, presumably not fully envisaged when Article 21 EPC was drafted, where this is not achieved, and a mixed composition of legal and technical members, including a majority of technical members, is required to decide a purely legal point. In particular, applications for re-establishment which are made during examination or opposition proceedings are decided at first instance by a Formalities Officer and, in the event of an appeal, by a mixed composition Technical Board including only one legal member.

In any event, the reality is that there is no clear line of demarcation between legal and technical issues depending simply upon whether they are procedural or substantive. Even essentially procedural questions such as the admissibility of an opposition or appeal may contain a considerable element of technical subject-matter.

Article 21 EPC is weighted in the direction of always requiring the inclusion of technical members in the composition of a Board of Appeal if there is any possibility of the issues raised before it including technical subject-matter.

(g) Allocation of business: designation of members

4–23 The Legal Board of Appeal and individual Technical Boards of Appeal are each composed of a Chairman and a number of other members.

A Chairman of a Technical Board of Appeal may be either technically or legally qualified. Currently, most Chairmen of Technical Boards of Appeal are technically qualified; there are three legally qualified Chairmen.

The membership of the individual Boards of Appeal is designated in accordance with a business distribution scheme which is drawn up pursuant to Rule 10(1) EPC and which is published in the first issue of the Official Journal each year.

There are currently seven Technical Boards of Appeal for Chemistry, six Technical Boards for Mechanics, two Technical Boards for Electricity, and three Technical Boards for Physics. Individual appeals from the Examining Division and the Opposition Division are assigned to specific Technical Boards of Appeal according to the classification of the technical subject-matter of the application or patent concerned. Such assignments may be changed by agreement between Chairmen having regard to the technical nature of the appeals.

In accordance with Article 1(2) RPBA, the Chairman of each Board designates the members of his Board who are to be responsible for each appeal which is assigned to his Board, as and when it is received by the Registry of the Boards of Appeal.

(h) Nationality of members

As previously mentioned in paragraph 4–02, nationals of most of the 20 **4–24**
Contracting States have currently been appointed as members of the
Boards of Appeal. While occasionally an individual Board of Appeal for a
particular case may include two nationals of one Contracting State, a Board
of Appeal consisting of more than two nationals of a Contracting State is in
practice avoided wherever possible. In the majority of cases, a Board of
Appeal is composed of three different nationalities.

(i) Enlargement of Technical Boards to five members

(i) Automatic enlargement. Article 21(3)(b) and (4)(b) EPC provide for **4–25**
automatic enlargement of Technical Boards of Appeal, from three to five
members, in certain cases. There are then two legally qualified and three
technically qualified members. Such an enlargement must take place when
the appeal is from an Examining Division or an Opposition Division
consisting of four members; that is, when the first instance has itself been
enlarged from the usual three technical members so as to include a legal
member as well. When enlargement of a Technical Board of Appeal is
automatic the five members are appointed when the appeal is first filed.

(ii) Discretionary enlargement. A Technical Board may also decide to **4–26**
enlarge itself to five members under Article 21 (3)(b) and (4)(b) EPC if it
considers that "the nature of the appeal so requires".
In the following circumstances in particular, Technical Boards have
commonly enlarged themselves to five members in the exercise of such
discretion:

- (a) where the technical subject-matter of the appeal involves a
  mixture of technologies (*e.g.* chemical and electrical); (in such a
  case the appeal might initially be assigned to a Chemical Board of
  Appeal, for example, which would include two chemically
  qualified members, and that Chemical Board would decide to
  enlarge itself so as to include an electrically qualified member, and
  necessarily a second legally qualified member);
- (b) where the legal or technical issues in the appeal are of such
  importance or difficulty as to justify an enlargement of the Board;
  in particular, it may be considered desirable to bring in a second
  legal member by way of enlargement if the legal issues are
  important or difficult. According to Article 8 RPBA, "the decision
  to enlarge the Board shall be taken at the earliest possible stage in
  the examination of the appeal." The three originally appointed
  members remain within the enlarged Board.

(5) Precedent within the Boards of Appeal

(a) Non-binding precedent

4–26a   There is nothing in the EPC which requires individual Boards of Appeal, when deciding upon appeals from decisions of first instance departments of the EPO, to follow interpretations of the law under the EPC as set out in previous decisions of individual Boards of Appeal. Nevertheless, an unofficial system of precedent commonly operates within the Boards of Appeal, under the general principle that similar cases should be decided in the same way. A particular Board having its own permanent chairman will naturally wish to maintain its own consistent jurisprudence. Furthermore, if a previous Board in an earlier decision has interpreted the EPC in a particular way, later Boards will usually follow that interpretation unless there are good reasons not to do so. In this way, a line of jurisprudence becomes established within the Boards of Appeal, and a practice ("case law") is developed.

The existence of such a system of non-binding precedent within the Boards of Appeal is clearly desirable and in the public interest, in that it provides a reasonable degree of legal certainty.

This loose system of precedent is reinforced by Article 15(1) RPBA, which reads as follows:

> "Should a Board consider it necessary to deviate from an interpretation or explanation of the EPC given in an earlier decision of any Board, the grounds for this deviation shall be given, unless such grounds are in accordance with an earlier opinion or decision of the Enlarged Board of Appeal. The President of the EPO shall be informed of the Board's decision."

The Rules of Procedure bind the Boards of Appeal (Article 18 RPBA) subject to the supremacy of the EPC.

The direction to all Boards of Appeal which is set out in Article 15(1) RPBA, to give grounds for any deviation from an interpretation or explanation of the EPC in any earlier decision, is intended to provide a practical check upon different Boards of Appeal giving varying interpretations or explanations of the EPC in an incidental manner. It is relatively simple to deviate from an interpretation of the EPC in an earlier decision without explaining why: but to give the grounds for the deviation is generally not so easy. That would normally involve giving reasons why the deviating Board considers that the interpretation or explanation in the earlier decision is wrong.

The reason for the President of the EPO being informed of a Board's decision which deviates from an earlier decision is in order that he may take advice as to whether a question of law should be referred to the Enlarged Board of Appeal under Article 112(1)(b) EPC (as to which see paragraph 4–187 below). Thus:

"it is clearly desirable that whenever a Board of Appeal is aware that its decision in the course of an appeal involves a different interpretation of the law, on a point of substance and importance, from that applied in a decision of a previous Board, attention is drawn to this fact in its decision, in a manner which is appropriate to the circumstances of the case, and reasons are given for the different interpretation, in order that the President can take appropriate action" (G1/89[11]).

Although Article 15(1) RPBA is binding upon the Boards of Appeal, there is, in reality, an increasing possibility that decisions containing conflicting interpretations or explanations of the EPC may be issued: both because of the ever-increasing total number of Board of Appeal decisions that have been issued, and because of the greater rate at which such decisions are issued, as a result of the increasing number of Boards of Appeal which are operating. It therefore becomes more and more difficult for individual Boards to be aware of all earlier and concurrent decisions containing such interpretations or explanations.

(b) Precedent in relation to independence

As previously discussed (see paragraph 4–08), all individual members of **4–26b** the Boards of Appeal are required in their decisions to comply only with the provisions of the EPC (Article 23(3) EPC). The supremacy of the EPC over the RPBA is recognised in Article 18 RPBA, which states that:

"These Rules of Procedure shall be binding upon the Boards of Appeal, provided that they do not lead to a situation which would be incompatible with the spirit and purpose of the EPC."

This broad statement of the supremacy, not only of the literal meaning of the EPC but also of its "spirit and purpose", in combination with the independent status of the Boards of Appeal and their individual members, should ensure that the system of precedent and practice described above does not become too rigid and prevent development and change in the law applied by the Boards of Appeal, when and where necessary, within the framework of the EPC itself.

The need for legal certainty as provided by the system of precedent has to be balanced against the need for appropriate review of previous interpretations of the law under the EPC, and the need to change such interpretations when appropriate. The maintenance of some degree of flexibility, at least in order to allow for changing circumstances in technology and otherwise, is particularly important in view of the fact that the EPC itself is difficult to alter (see Chapter 1 at paragraph 1–06).

For the above reasons, in the context of a particular case a Board of Appeal need not follow a previous interpretation of the EPC in one or more

---

[11] G1/89 X/*Polysuccinate esters* O.J. EPO 1991, 155; [1991] E.P.O.R. 239.

previous decisions, but may deviate from such previous interpretation as envisaged in Article 15(1) RPBA.

In this event, the existence of decisions by different Boards of Appeal giving differing interpretations of the EPC obviously causes legal uncertainty, and is generally undesirable. A principal function of the Enlarged Board of Appeal is to resolve such differences of interpretation when they arise, if it is sufficiently important for this to be done.

C. Appeal Procedure

(1) Introduction

4–27   The EPC provides four general stages of procedure in appeal proceedings before a Board of Appeal:

   (a) Filing the appeal and examination for admissibility.
   (b) Written procedure concerning examination for allowability.
   (c) Oral proceedings (which are optional).
   (d) Making and issuing the decision.

Exceptionally, an additional stage may take place before the decision is made, namely reference of one or more points of law to the Enlarged Board of Appeal (see paragraphs 4–175—4–180 *et seq.* below).

A brief guide to appeal procedure is contained in a note entitled "Guidance for parties to appeal proceedings and their representatives"[12], issued by the Boards of Appeal.

(2) Filing an admissible appeal

(a) Filing an appeal

4–28   **(i) The subject of an appeal—a first instance decision: communications and notification distinguished.** An appeal can only be filed in respect of a "decision" of one of the four first instance departments of the EPO— namely the Receiving Section, the Examining Divisions, the Opposition Divisions, and the Legal Division (Article 106(1) EPC). The Boards of Appeal are only responsible for the examination of appeals from such first instance departments (Article 21(1) EPC). (They are also responsible for deciding upon "protests" under Article 154(3) EPC—see paragraph 4–03 above, but such protests are not appeals within the meaning of Article 106 EPC *et seq.*)

A "decision" of a first instance department must be distinguished from both a communication and a notification. A decision decides one or more issues. A communication normally invites a reply. A notification normally gives notice of some event (such as loss of rights), without inviting observations in reply.

Communications are frequently issued by the EPO, especially during

---

[12] O.J. EPO 1996, 342. Reproduced in full at Appendix 8.

examination and opposition proceedings. For example, under Articles 96(2) and 101(2) EPC a communication commonly express a point of view which is adverse to a party to such proceedings, and invites observations in reply. Such a communication is never binding upon the department of the EPO which issued it, and cannot be the subject of an appeal. The contents of such a communication never constitute a decision within Article 106(1) EPC (T222/85[13]).

Similarly, under Articles 97(2) and 102(3) EPC, and pursuant to Rules **4-29—** 51(4) and 58(4) EPC, a communication will inform an applicant or patentee **4-31** of the text in which it is intended to grant or maintain a patent, in order to establish that the applicant or patent proprietor approves such text (see Chapter 2 at paragraph 2–67 and Chapter 3 at paragraph 3–86). Such a communication always indicates an intention to decide the matters in issue in such proceedings, and is not a decision within Article 106(1) EPC (T5/81[14]).

There are also many occasions during first instance proceedings when notifications are issued to parties to the proceedings, under Article 119 EPC (and see Rules 69 and 77 to 82 EPC). Such notifications must also be clearly distinguished from decisions which are subject to appeal.

While the above-mentioned classes of documents should normally be clearly identified as such, the title of such a document (or lack of it) is not necessarily decisive as to its true nature. The legal status of a document (for example, whether it constitutes a decision within Article 106(1) EPC) depends upon its substance rather than its form or title (J8/81,[15] T934/91,[16] J2/93[17]).

> "An appeal may relate only to a decision subject to appeal within the meaning of Article 106(1) EPC and not to the preparatory measures referred to in Article 96(2) and Rule 51(3) EPC" (T5/81[18]).

(ii) Interlocutory decisions—separate appeal allowable. Article 106(3) **4-32** EPC provides that "A decision which does not terminate proceedings as regards one of the parties can only be appealed together with the final decision, unless the decision allows separate appeal."

This provision is particularly important in connection with decisions pursuant to Article 102(3) EPC, in which the Opposition Division decides to maintain a patent in amended form. In such cases, a separate appeal is in practice allowed (see paragraph 3–87 above).

---

[13] T222/85 *PPG/Ungelled polyesters* O.J. EPO 1988, 128; [1987] E.P.O.R. 99.
[14] T5/81 *SOLVAY/Production of hollow thermoplastic objects* O.J. EPO 1982, 249; [1979–85] E.P.O.R.: B: 287.
[15] J8/81 *CATERPILLAR/Form of decision* O.J. EPO 1982, 10; [1979–85] E.P.O.R.: A: 92.
[16] T934/91 *KONICA/Meaning of decision* O.J. EPO 1994, 184; [1993] E.P.O.R. 219.
[17] J2/93 *ETA/Decision subject to appeal* O.J. EPO 1995, 675.
[18] T5/81 *SOLVAY/Production of hollow thermoplastic objects* O.J. EPO 1982, 249; [1979–85] E.P.O.R.: B: 287.

4–33— **(iii) No decision within Article 106(1) EPC: appeal inadmissible.** An
4–34 appeal may be filed against a document which purports to be a decision, or
which is thought to be a decision, and upon examination of the document a
Board of Appeal may decide that it is not a decision within Article 106(1)
EPC on its proper interpretation, but a communication or notification and
therefore not subject to appeal. The appeal will then be held inadmissible
(T934/91[19], J29/92[20]), but the appeal fee is not refunded (J37/97[21]).

(b) Parties to an appeal

4–35 **(i) The appellant.** An appeal may only be filed by a party to proceedings
before one of the four named first instance departments of the EPO (Article
106(1) EPC) who is "adversely affected" by a decision of such first instance
department (Article 107 EPC).

4–36 **(ii) Meaning of "adversely affected".** In principle, a party to first
instance proceedings before the EPO can only be adversely affected by a
decision if what is decided (the "order" of the first instance department) is
contrary to what that party has requested.
For example:

> "an applicant can only be adversely affected by a decision to grant the
> patent when such a decision is inconsistent with what he has
> specifically requested" (J12/85[22]).

Similarly:

> "An applicant ... may be 'adversely affected' ... by a decision to grant
> a patent, if it is granted with a text not approved by the applicant in
> accordance with Article 97(2)(a) and Rule 51(4) EPC" (J12/83[23]).

4–37 In opposition proceedings a patent proprietor whose patent is maintained by the Opposition Division in accordance with his sole request is not
adversely affected and has no right of appeal (T506/91[24]). This applies even
if, in the light of the reasons given in the decision, the patentee considers
that the amendments which he proposed were not necessary (T722/97[25]).
Furthermore, an opponent who agrees before the Opposition Division that
if certain amendments are made by the patent proprietor he no longer
objects to maintenance of the patent, is not adversely affected by a decision
which maintains the patent so amended, and has no right of appeal
(T156/90[26]).

---

[19] See note 16.
[20] J29/92 MERCK/*Premature appeal inadmissible* December 9, 1992.
[21] J37/97 ALGERNON PROMOTIONS October 15, 1998.
[22] J12/85 KUREHA/*Inadmissible appeal* O.J. EPO 1986, 155; [1986] E.P.O.R. 336.
[23] J12/83 CHUGAI SEIYAKU/*Inadmissible appeals* O.J. EPO 1985, 6; [1979–85] E.P.O.R.: A: 196.
[24] T506/91 WOODCAP/*Appeal of proprietor* [1994] E.P.O.R. 197.
[25] T722/97 JACOBS/*Admissibility of appeal*, January 11, 1999.
[26] T156/90 BLUEWATER/*Admissibility*, September 9, 1991.

A party does not have a right to appeal if he disagrees with the reasoning leading to a decision upon an issue. Thus: "under Article 106(1) EPC appeals lie from decisions rather than from the grounds of such decisions" (T611/90[27]).

For example, in one case two documents alleged to destroy novelty were **4-38** said to have been published during the convention priority year, in opposition proceedings. The proprietor contended (1) that his claims were entitled to priority, and (2) even if not entitled to priority, the claims were still novel; and requested maintenance of his patent as granted. The Opposition Division decided that the claims were not entitled to priority, but were novel. The opponents appealed, and the proprietor was uncertain of his right to challenge the adverse finding on priority. It was held that:

> "the patentee was not adversely affected by the decision [of the Opposition Division] as such, because the decision to maintain the patent as granted was what the patentee had requested. Thus, even though some of the reasoning in the decision (namely that concerning priority) was contrary to the contentions of and therefore adverse to the patentee, he could not file an appeal against the decision" (T73/88[28]).

The question arises, however, as to whether in such a case a patentee could specifically request a decision to the effect that he was entitled to claim priority from his priority application; and in the event of an adverse decision at first instance on this specific request, whether the patentee would be entitled to appeal even if his patent was maintained as granted. This question has not yet been decided by a Board of Appeal.

(iii) Multiple appellants. More than one party to opposition proceed- **4-39** ings may be adversely affected by a first instance decision. For example, if a patent is maintained in amended form in accordance with an auxiliary request (see Chapter 5 at paragraphs 5-29, 5-30), the patentee is adversely affected by the decision not to maintain the patent as granted, and the opponent is adversely affected by the decision not to revoke the patent.

Similarly, in any opposition by several opponents in which the patent is maintained, all the unsuccessful opponents are adversely affected by such a decision. In such cases, any "adversely affected" party may file an appeal (Article 107 EPC, first sentence).

(iv) Status of a party "as of right": respondents. Article 107 EPC, second **4-40** sentence states that "Any other parties [*i.e.* those who are not appellants] to the proceedings shall be parties to the appeal proceedings as of right".

However, a party to first instance proceedings who is adversely affected by a decision of the Opposition Decision but who does not file an appeal, cannot challenge such decision (*i.e.* the "order" of such decision). Similarly, a party who is not adversely affected by such a decision, in other words, a

---

[27] T611/90 *MITSUI/Fresh case* O.J. EPO 1993, 50; [1991] E.P.O.R. 481.
[28] T73/88 *HOWARD/Snackfood* O.J. EPO 1992, 557; [1990] E.P.O.R. 112.

"party as of right" to appeal proceedings in accordance with Article 107 EPC (a respondent) may participate in the appeal proceedings and may support the decision under appeal, but may not challenge the first instance decision which is the subject of the appeal proceedings. (Similarly, the Board of Appeal may not "challenge" the first instance decision.)

Thus:

> "If the patent proprietor is the sole appellant against an interlocutory decision maintaining a patent in amended form, neither the Board of Appeal nor the non-appealing opponent as a party to the proceedings as of right under Article 107, second sentence, EPC, may challenge the maintenance of the patent as amended in accordance with the interlocutory decision.

4–41
> If the opponent is the sole appellant against an interlocutory decision maintaining a patent in amended form, the patent proprietor is primarily restricted during appeal proceedings to defending the patent in the form in which it was maintained by the Opposition Division in its interlocutory decision. Amendments, proposed by the patent proprietor as a party to the proceedings as of right under Article 107, second sentence, EPC, may be rejected as inadmissible by the Board of Appeal, if they are neither appropriate nor necessary" (G9/92[29]).

For example, amendments which do not arise from the appeal may be rejected as inadmissible (G9/92, G4/93[30]; but see paragraphs 4–103 to 4–105 below as to the allowability of amendments in this situation).

G9/92[31] includes a minority opinion pursuant to Article 12a RPEBA (see Chapter 4 at paragraph 4–196). Consequently, a party to first instance opposition proceedings who is adversely affected by the decision of the Opposition Division (within the meaning of Article 107 EPC as discussed above), and who wishes to challenge such decision, must file an admissible appeal. If he does not file an appeal, he cannot contend that the decision under appeal should be changed, even though he is a party to the appeal proceedings.

4–42
A party "as of right" cannot continue the appeal proceedings, if the sole appellant (or appellant) withdraws his appeal (G2/91[32], G7,8/91[33]: and see paragraphs 4–128 *et seq.* below).

Although a respondent may not challenge the order of the decision under appeal, he may during the appeal proceedings challenge adverse reasoning leading to the decision (*e.g.* a finding of loss of priority right—see Chapter 10). For example:

---

[29] G9/92 *BMW/Non-appealing party* O.J. EPO 1994, 875; [1995] E.P.O.R. 169.
[30] *Ibid.*
[31] *Ibid.*
[32] G2/91 *KROHNE/Appeal fees* O.J. EPO 1992, 206; [1992] E.P.O.R. 407.
[33] G7, 8/91 *BASF/BELL/Withdrawal of appeal* O.J. EPO 1993, 346, 356; [1993] E.P.O.R. 440, 445.

"In the event of an appeal being filed by an opponent . . . if the patentee wishes to contend that such adverse reasoning was wrong he should set out his grounds for so contending in his observations in reply to the statement of grounds of appeal" (T73/88[34]).

(v) No "cross-appeal" possible. "The EPC does not provide for the 4-43 possibility of a cross-appeal by a respondent" (G9/92, G4/93[35]).

In other words, as discussed above, a party to opposition proceedings who is adversely affected by the first instance decision must appeal, within the two month period under Article 108 EPC, if he wishes to challenge such decision. No additional period of time is provided so as to allow such a party to wait to see if another adversely affected party will file an appeal, and if so file a cross-appeal in response. The two month time limit cannot be extended (except by way of re-establishment under Article 122 EPC—see Chapter 6 at paragraphs 6–27 *et seq.*), and must be observed by all appellants. Thus an adversely affected party can wait until the last day of the period for filing an appeal to see if another adversely affected party files an appeal, and if not, he must decide whether to file an appeal, with the possibility that another party will also file an appeal on the last day.

(c) Formal requirements for filing an admissible appeal

(i) Existence of an appeal: examination for admissibility   4-44
An appeal is brought into existence when a notice of appeal is filed, and the appeal fee paid, within the two-month time limit under Article 108 EPC. The requirements for filing a notice of appeal are considered below.

Rule 65 EPC prescribes that a Board of Appeal shall reject an appeal as inadmissible if the requirements of Article 106 and 108 and Rule 64 EPC are not complied with. These requirements will also be discussed below.

The purpose of the examination for inadmissibility is to determine whether the appeal may go forward for substantive examination and decision. Unless an appeal is admissible, the Board of Appeal may not examine whether the appeal is allowable (Article 110(1) EPC).

(ii) Time limits   4-45
A decision of a first instance department is sent to the parties by registered post with advice of delivery—Rule 78(1) EPC. Notification of the decision is deemed to take place in all cases on the tenth day following its posting (*i.e.* even if it was in fact received earlier than the tenth day), unless the registered letter fails to arrive or arrives after the tenth day—Rule 78(3) EPC. In the event of any dispute as to notification, the burden of proof lies on the EPO "to establish that the letter has reached its destination or to establish the date on which the letter was delivered to the addressee, as the case may be."—Rule 78(3) EPC.

A notice of appeal must be filed, and the appeal fee paid, within two months after the date of notification of the decision under appeal—Article

[34] T73/88 HOWARD/*Snackfood* O.J. EPO 1990, 5; [1990] E.P.O.R. 112.
[35] See note 29.

108 EPC. The notice of appeal is deemed not to have been filed until the appeal fee is paid.

The two-month period is calculated in accordance with Rule 83(2) EPC by reference to the date of notification determined as above. Under this Rule the two-month period commences the day after the date of notification. Thus, for example, if a decision is issued on March 1, and is received by a party within 10 days, the date of notification is deemed to be March 11, and a notice of appeal must be filed by May 11 (subject to Rule 85(1) EPC).

Similarly, a statement of grounds of appeal must be filed within four months after the date of notification of the decision, calculated in the same way.

4–46 **(iii) Beginning of the time limits.** Although Article 108 EPC provides that the notice of appeal must be filed within two months *after* the date of notification of the decision appealed from, nevertheless

"Article 108 EPC does not in any way forbid the filing of an appeal before notification of the decision, but merely prescribes that it cannot be filed later than two months after this notification" (T389/86[36]).

4–47 **(iv) Notice of appeal.**

(a) *Introduction.* The essential contents of a notice of appeal are set out in Rule 64 EPC, which is mandatory, as follows:

(a) the name and address of the appellant (see Rule 26(2)(c) EPC);
(b) a statement identifying;

    (i) the decision which is impugned,
    (ii) the extent to which amendment or cancellation of the decision is requested.

On their face, these requirements appear to be in the nature of formalities, and there is, therefore, a danger that they are regarded as relatively unimportant. When interpreting these requirements and considering whether they have been met in particular cases, their wording should be considered in conjunction with their purpose, in the context of the EPC. Such an approach is in line with that which has been taken by the Boards of Appeal when interpreting analogous formal requirements within the EPC: for example, the requirements of Rule 55 EPC concerning the contents of a notice of opposition (see paragraph 3–40).

4–48 The purpose of requirement (a) is clearly to identify the appellant and his address, in order that postal correspondence with him can take place. The appellant may be identified by reference to the decision under appeal (T1/97). In the event of non-compliance with this requirement within the two-month time limit of Article 108 EPC, under Rule 65(2) EPC the Board of Appeal is required to invite the appellant to remedy the deficiencies

[36] T389/86 BEHR/Time limit for appeal O.J. EPO 1988, 87; [1988] E.P.O.R. 381.

within a specified period. Only after continued non-compliance beyond such specified period may the Board reject the appeal as inadmissible.

The purpose of requirement (b)(i) is to identify the decision which is to be challenged, within the two-month time limit for appeal under Article 108 EPC, in order that the date of notification of the decision can be determined and the expiry date of the two-month period calculated. Thus, if the decision which is impugned is not sufficiently identified, under Rule 65(1) EPC the Board will reject the appeal as inadmissible unless the deficiency is rectified within the two-month appeal period. Rectification in this situation would seem to require sufficient identification at least for the calculation of the two-month period.

Requirement (b)(ii) is intended to ensure that the extent of the issues **4–49** raised in the appeal proceedings is defined. Furthermore, since by virtue of Article 106(1) EPC, an appeal has "a suspensive effect" (for the meaning of which see paragraph 4–53 below), this obligation to define the extent to which amendment or cancellation of the first instance decision is requested will also determine the extent to which the first instance decision is and is not "suspended." This is a matter of legal certainty. Under Rule 65(1) EPC, if this requirement is not complied with within the two-month appeal period of Article 108(1) EPC, the Board of Appeal must reject the appeal as inadmissible.

"For a notice of appeal to be valid, it must at least contain an explicit declaration of the wish to contest a particular decision by means of an appeal" (T371/92[37]; J16/94[38]).

Similarly:

"A notice of appeal ... is inadmissible if it does not contain an explicit and unequivocal statement expressing the definite intention to contest an appealable decision" (T460/95[39]).

Furthermore:

"An appeal filed as a subsidiary request, *i.e.* subject to the condition that the main request be allowable by the first instance, is ... inadmissible" (T371/92[40]).

On the other hand:

"The extent of the appeal within the meaning of Rule 64(b) EPC is sufficiently identified if a European patent application has been refused by the decision impugned and it is stated in the notice of

[37] T371/92 *FINA/Appeal not filed* O.J. EPO 1995, 324; [1995] E.P.O.R. 485.
[38] J16/94 *APPLIED RESEARCH SYSTEM/Notice of appeal* O.J. EPO 1997, 331; [1998] E.P.O.R. 49.
[39] T460/95 *SOMAB/Notice of appeal* O.J. EPO 1998, 587.
[40] See note 37.

appeal that an appeal is being lodged against that decision in its entirety. In such a case it can initially be assumed that the appellant adheres to the submission on which the impugned decision was based" (T7/81[41]).

When drafting a notice of appeal, it is clearly desirable to ensure that all the literal requirements of Rule 64 EPC are in fact complied with, in order to avoid any risk of rejection of the appeal on the ground of inadmissibility.

Requirement (b)(ii) is particularly important because it defines the extent of an appeal.

4–50   (b) *Extent of the appeal proceedings: principle of party disposition.* The requirement that a notice of appeal must state "the extent to which amendment or cancellation of the decision is requested" is intended to ensure that the extent of the issues raised in the appeal proceedings is defined right at the outset of the proceedings when the notice of the appeal is filed within the two month time limit following issue of a first instance decision.

The statement of "the extent to which amendment or cancellation of the decision is requested" is the "appeal request" of the appellant.

"Proceedings under the EPC in respect of European patent applications and patents are, with some exceptions, initiated by a party. The initial 'request' determines the extent of the proceedings. This is known as the principle of *party disposition (ne ultra petita)*" (G9/92[42]).

"The aim of an appeal is to eliminate an 'adverse effect' (Article 10 EPC) … the subject of the appeal proceedings is always the appeal itself" (G9/92[43]).

Thus "the statement pursuant to Rule 64(b) EIPC of the 'extent to which amendment or cancellation of the decision is requested' defines the legal framework of the appeal proceedings" (T501/92[44]).

Consequently, it will be seen below (paragraphs 4–99, 4–100) that subsequent requests by any party to appeal proceedings which would alter the extent of the proceedings as defined in the notice of appeal cannot be examined.

4–51   **(v) Language.** See Chapter 5 at paragraphs 5–03 *et seq.*

4–52   **(vi) Non-existence of an appeal: refund of appeal fee.**
As noted above, under Article 108 EPC a notice of appeal "shall not be deemed to have been filed until after the fee for appeal has been paid,"—even if the notice of appeal has in fact been filed before the appeal fee is paid.

However, if a notice of appeal has been filed and the appeal fee has been paid within the two-month appeal period of Article 108 EPC, an appeal is thereby brought into existence. Thereafter, a refund of the appeal fee

---

[41] T7/81 *CIBA-GEIGY/Dyeing of linear polymides* O.J. EPO 1983, 98; [1979–85] E.P.O.R.: B: 301.
[42] G9/92, *BMW/Non-appealing party* O.J. EPO 1994, 875; [1995] E.P.O.R. 169.
[43] *Ibid.*
[44] T501/92 *ARTHUR G. RUSSELL/Alphanumeric display* O.J. EPO 1996, 261; [1996] E.P.O.R.

cannot be obtained by withdrawing the appeal (T41/82[45]) or by failing to file a statement of grounds of appeal (T13/82[46], T89/84[47]).

If the notice of appeal is physically filed within the two-month period, but the appeal fee is not paid in due time but is paid late, it is refunded because no appeal is brought into existence (see, *e.g.* J21/80[48], J16/82[49]).

Similarly, if an appeal fee is paid in due time, but the notice of appeal is not filed within the two-month period, the appeal fee is refunded on the same basis (T371/92[50]).

This type of case is quite different from the type of case discussed in paragraph 4–29 above, where no appeal exists because no decision exists from which an appeal lies.

(vii) Suspensive effect of an appeal.   4–53

As mentioned earlier (paragraph 4–49 above), according to Article 106(1) EPC an appeal has "suspensive effect", which "deprives the contested decision of all legal effect until the appeal is decided" (J28/94[51]). This provision is derived from German law, and it means that the consequences of the decision under appeal (*e.g.* revocation of a patent) do not ensue so long as the appeal is pending. This is in contrast to the position under English law, where a decision under appeal takes effect unless and until the first instance or appeal court orders otherwise.

(viii) The statement of grounds of appeal.   4–54

(a) *Substantive contents.* In contrast to the essential contents of a notice of appeal, which are specified in Rule 64 EPC, the EPC does not specify the essential contents of the statement of grounds of appeal. Article 108 EPC merely prescribes that "a written statement setting out the grounds of appeal must be filed" (within the four months period).

While the filing of such a statement within the prescribed time limit is a formal requirement, the contents of such a statement have to be substantive in nature. Article 108 EPC provides an additional two months, beyond the two-month period prescribed for filing a notice of appeal, during which the grounds of appeal must be filed, and thus clearly envisages that the grounds of appeal should contain something more than what is required to be included in the notice of appeal (namely, a statement that a part or the whole of the first instance decision, which is impugned, should be set aside).

(b) *Minimum content.* The requirement for the contents of a statement of   4–55
grounds of appeal is not merely formal, but involves "a presentation of the appellant's case."

[45] T41/82 SANDOZ/Reimbursement of appeal fee O.J. EPO 1982, 256; [1979–85] E.P.O.R.: B: 446.
[46] T13/82 BROWN, BOVERI/Statement of grounds of appeal O.J. EPO 1983, 411; [1979–85] E.P.O.R.: B: 405.
[47] T89/84 TORRINGTON/Reimbursement of appeal fees O.J. EPO 1984, 562; [1979–85] E.P.O.R.: C: 949.
[48] J21/80 HEISEL/Late payment of appeal fee O.J. EPO 1981, 101; [1979–85] E.P.O.R.: A: 65.
[49] J16/82 THEURER/Assistant; substitute O.J. EPO 1983, 262; [1979–85] E.P.O.R.: A: 137.
[50] T371/92 FINA/Appeal not filed O.J. EPO 1995, 324; [1995] E.P.O.R. 485.
[51] J28/94 SOLUDIA/Suspensive effect O.J. EPO 1995, 742.

The statement should set out:

"the substance of the appellant's case: that is, the reasons why the appeal should be allowed and why the decision under appeal should be set aside ... A well drafted statement of grounds should contain reasoning that is full but concise. And, in general, it is obvious that the less reasoning that a statement contains the greater will be the risk that the appeal will be rejected as inadmissible" (J22/86[52]).

Similarly:

"it is the established case law of the Boards of Appeal that grounds of appeal should state the legal and factual reasons why the decision under appeal should be set aside and the appeal allowed" (T145/88[53]).

For example, a case concerning inventive step:

"It is not sufficient for the appellants merely to refer in general terms to passages from the literature showing the state of the art and to the Guidelines for Examination in the EPO without making their inferences adequately clear" (T220/83[54]).

4–56   In a case where, following proceedings before an Opposition Division in which the patent was maintained in amended form, the proprietor failed to pay the printing fee and file translations of the amended claim in due time pursuant to Rule 58(5) EPC:

"A written statement announcing only that the appellant will complete an omitted act, in this case the filing of the translation of the revised claims, within the four-month period allowing for submitting the grounds of appeal, does not comprise [reasons why the decision should be set aside] and therefore does not constitute a valid statement of the grounds of appeal" (T22/88[55]).

It is, of course, important that the grounds of appeal should deal with the actual ground(s) on which the decision under appeal is based. Thus, in a case where an opposition was rejected as inadmissible by the Opposition Division, on the ground that the notice of opposition contained insufficient support for the ground of opposition alleged, the grounds of appeal did not deal with this issue, but merely attempted to supplement the ground of opposition. The appeal was accordingly held to be inadmissible as well (T213/85[56]).

---

[52] J22/86 MEDICAL BIOLOGICAL/Disapproval O.J. EPO 1987, 280; [1987] E.P.O.R. 87.
[53] T145/88 NICOLON/Statement of grounds O.J. EPO 1990, 4; [1991] E.P.O.R. 356.
[54] T220/83 HÜLS/Grounds for appeal O.J. EPO 1986, 249; [1987] E.P.O.R. 49.
[55] T22/88 SECRETARY OF STATE FOR DEFENCE/Grounds for appeal O.J. EPO 1993, 143; [1993] E.P.O.R. 353.
[56] T213/85 GEORG FISCHER/Grounds of appeal O.J. EPO 1987, 482; [1988] E.P.O.R. 45.

(c) *Contents depend upon the case.* When the issues intended to be raised in **4–57** the appeal are the same as those which were raised at first instance and which were decided at first instance adversely to the appellant, it follows from the above that it is certainly not enough merely to assert that the decision under appeal is wrong.

Moreover, it is generally not enough to leave the reasons why the decision under appeal should be set aside to inference. It is normally necessary to state specific reasons why the decision is wrong, either in its statements of the facts or in its application of the law, or both.

Nevertheless:

"The question whether a particular statement alleged to be a statement of grounds of appeal in a particular case meets the requirements of Article 108 EPC can only be decided in the context of that particular case; and the context of a particular case will normally include the contents of the decision under appeal" (J22/86[57]).

In general the same broad principles are applicable to the sufficiency and therefore the admissibility of a statement of grounds of appeal as are applicable to a notice of opposition, *mutatis mutandis* (see for example T222/85[58] and Chapter 3 at paragraphs 3–27 *et seq.*).

(d) *Reference to previous submissions at first instance.* The question **4–58** sometimes arises as to whether grounds of appeal which simply refer back to submissions which were made during the first instance proceedings are sufficient to satisfy the requirements of Article 108 EPC. This is specifically disapproved in "Guidance for Appellants and their Representatives."[58a]

Thus in one case the notice of appeal merely stated that "the grounds of appeal are as set out in the opposition as well as set out during the oral proceedings ...". The decision states that:

"the appellant has left it entirely to the Board and the respondent to conjecture in what respect the appellant may consider the decision under appeal to be defective. This is just what the requirement that grounds for appeal be filed is designed to prevent. Especially in a case such as the present one, where the submissions made during the opposition are voluminous, it is essential for the appellant to set out the specific factual and/or legal reasons on which he is relying. Otherwise, the respondent is at a loss to know how to prepare his case and the Board cannot direct the appeal proceedings in an efficient way" (T432/88[59]).

The appeal was, therefore, rejected as inadmissible.

---

[57] J22/86 *MEDICAL BIOLOGICAL/Disapproval* O.J. EPO 1987, 280; [1987] E.P.O.R. 87.
[58] T222/85 *PPG/Ungelled polyesters* O.J. EPO 1988, 128; [1987] E.P.O.R. 99.
[58a] O.J. EPO 1996, 342. See paragraph 4–27. Reproduced in full at Appendix 8.
[59] T432/88 *OKI/Grounds for appeal* [1990] E.P.O.R. 38.

In another case, however, an appeal was held to be admissible in similar circumstances, on the basis that examination of the submissions before the Opposition Division made the grounds of appeal clear, as a matter of substance (T140/88[60]).

Such a course is clearly dangerous in so far as it may not be apparent from the submissions to the first instance in a particular case what the substantive grounds of appeal really are.

4–59   (e) *Fresh case in the appeal.* In a particular class of appeal cases, the circumstances of the case change between the time when the first instance decision is issued and the time when the grounds of appeal are filed. This commonly occurs when an applicant/appellant in effect admits that the adverse first instance decision was correct for the claims on which the decision was based, but submits a proposed amended set of claims for consideration in the appeal (*e.g.* in the statement of grounds of appeal).

In such circumstances:

"There is nothing in the wording of (Articles 106 to 108 and Rule 64 EPC) supporting the idea that the task of a Board of Appeal should be strictly limited to considering whether or not the decision of the first instance is correct on the basis only of facts and arguments presented before that instance ... Nor is there anywhere else in the EPC any support for this idea. On the contrary, it is clearly foreseen that, depending on the particular circumstances of each individual case, new facts and arguments may be presented in the appeal proceedings and considered by the Board of Appeal ..." (T105/87[61]).

4–60   Furthermore:

"The minimal requirements of Article 108 EPC are satisfied when the notice of appeal can be interpreted as containing a request for rectification of the decision concerned on the grounds that due to the fact that the conditions set forth in a former communication of the EPO were not fulfilled, the decision was no longer justified" (J2/87[62]).

Similarly:

"An appeal is to be considered sufficiently well-founded to satisfy the requirements of Article 108 EPC if it refers to a new circumstance which, if confirmed, will invalidate the contested decision" (J.../87[63]).

In that case the new circumstance referred to was that Rule 90 EPC

---

[60] T140/88 *MEDTRONIC* February 13, 1990.
[61] T105/87 *INLAND STEEL* February 25, 1988.
[62] J2/87 *MOTOROLA/Admissibility* O.J. EPO 1988, 330; [1989] E.P.O.R. 42.
[63] J.../87 *Incapacity* O.J. EPO 1988, 323; E.P.O.R. 73.

(interruption of proceedings on the ground of incapacity: see Chapter 6 at paragraphs 6–63 *et seq*) was considered to be applicable to the case.

In another case the decision at first instance was adverse to the **4–61** opponent, who therefore filed a notice of appeal. Subsequently, but prior to the filing of a statement of grounds of appeal by the opponent, the proprietor/respondent himself requested revocation of his patent. In this circumstance, a statement of grounds of appeal which merely referred to the fact of the patentee's request for revocation was held to be admissible, on the basis that it would be superfluous to refer to any other fact (T459/88[64]).

In an opposition appeal, an opponent's grounds of appeal requested cancellation of the decision under appeal on the basis of a fresh case (alleged prior use) under a previously alleged opposition ground (lack of novelty). It was held that:

"An appeal raising a case entirely different from that on which the decision under appeal was based is still admissible [within the meaning of Rule 65 EPC] if it is based on the same opposition grounds" (T611/90[65]).

However, an appeal may be admissible for the purpose of Rule 65 EPC but the admissibility of the subject-matter of the appeal under Article 114(2) EPC is still a matter of discretion for the Board. Thus:

"An appeal unconnected with the reasons given in the appealed decision (lack of inventive step) and directed only to a new ground for opposition (lack of novelty) based on a new document is contrary to the principles laid down in [G9, 10/91][66], according to which an appeal should be within the same legal and factual framework as the opposition proceedings. It is tantamount to a new opposition and is thus inadmissible" (T1007/95[67]).

Having regard to the principles set out in G9, 10/91[68] (as to which, see in **4–62** particular Chapter 3 at paragraph 3–40, and paragraphs 4–71 *et seq*. below):

"facts, evidence and arguments constituting an entirely fresh factual case on appeal should normally be disregarded pursuant to Article 114(2) EPC unless convergence of the debate is guaranteed *e.g.* by a manifestly unanswerable challenge to the validity of the opposed patent necessarily resulting in restriction or revocation of the patent. Furthermore the conclusiveness of this challenge should normally be manifest from the statement of appeal" (T389/95[69]).

---

[64] T459/88 *MAN/Admissibility of appeal* O.J. EPO 1990, 425; [1991] E.P.O.R. 72.
[65] T611/90 *MITSUI/Fresh case* O.J. EPO 1991, 50; [1991] E.P.O.R. 481.
[66] G9, 10/91 *ROHM AND HAAS/Power to examine/Examination of oppositions/appeals* O.J. EPO 1993, 408, 420; [1993] E.P.O.R. 485.
[67] T1007/95 *PERSTORP/Appeal inadmissible* O.J. EPO 1999, 733.
[68] See note 66.
[69] T389/95 *MOTOROLA/Mobile phone* October 15, 1997.

Finally, there may be exceptional cases where the contents of a statement of grounds of appeal are hardly relevant, but where the decision under appeal shows that the first instance procedure leading up to that decision was clearly wrong and misleading. In such circumstances, the grounds of appeal may be considered to be admissible "even though the grounds contained in such statement can fairly be described as minimal" (J22/86[70]).

4-62a **(ix) Admissibility of a notice of opposition during an opposition appeal.**
"The admissibility of an opposition must be checked ex officio in every phase of the opposition and ensuing appeal proceedings" (T522/94[71]).

"The admissibility of an opposition on grounds relating to the identity of an opponent may be challenged during the course of the appeal, even if no such challenge has been raised before the Opposition Division" (G4/97[72]— see also Chapter 3 at paragraph 3–14).

(d) Interlocutory revision

Article 109 EPC

4-63 **(i) Introduction.** An unusual provision compared to United Kingdom law is set out in Article 109(1) EPC, whereby the notice of appeal and the statement of grounds of appeal are, upon filing, initially considered by the first instance department whose decision is impugned. If that department "considers the appeal to be admissible and well founded, it shall rectify its decision." Thus an opportunity is provided for a first instance department to have second thoughts on its decision, after having seen the grounds of appeal. This provision provides a strong incentive in appropriate cases to set out as clearly as possible in the statement of grounds of appeal the legal and factual reasons why the decision under appeal should be set aside.

This provision is derived from German and Swiss patent law. "The essential aim of ... interlocutory revision is to withhold from the appeal instance those cases in which the patent office itself recognises that the decision must be corrected when the grounds of appeal are taken into consideration" (J32/95[73]).

Interlocutory revision is not possible "where the appellant is opposed by another party to the proceedings" (Article 109(1) EPC, second sentence).

In other words, interlocutory revision is possible either in *ex parte* examination proceedings, or in opposition proceedings if the opposition is withdrawn by the opponent(s) and the patent proprietor appeals (see paragraph 4–137).

4-64 Rule 67 EPC provides *inter alia* that "reimbursement of appeal fees shall be ordered in the event of interlocutory revision ... if such reimbursement

---

[70] J22/86 *MEDICAL BIOLOGICAL/Disapproval* O.J. EPO 1987, 280; [1987] E.P.O.R. 87.
[71] T522/94 *TECUMO/Opposition admissibility* O.J. EPO 1998, 421; [1992] E.P.O.R. 75.
[72] G4/97 *GENENTECH/Opposition on behalf of third party* O.J. EPO 1999, 270.
[73] J32/95 *GENERAL MOTORS/Power of Examining Division to refuse reimbursement of appeal fee* O.J. EPO 1999, 713.

is equitable by reason of a substantial procedural violation". Furthermore, "reimbursement shall be ordered by the department whose decision has been impugned and, in other cases, by the Board of Appeal."

The practice of the first instance departments is set out in the Guidelines, E.X1.8. If interlocutory revision is ordered following a substantial procedural violation, reimbursement may be ordered if it is equitable. If interlocutory revision is ordered following amendments filed with the appeal which meet the decision under appeal, reimbursement will not be ordered.

However:

> "Under Rule 67 EPC, in the event of interlocutory revision, the department whose decision has been impugned does not have the power to refuse a requested reimbursement of the appeal fee. Such power lies with the Board of Appeal. If the department whose decision is contested considers the requirements of Article 109 EPC ... as being fulfilled, but not the requirement of Rule 67 EPC ..., it shall rectify its decision and remit the request for reimbursement of the appeal fee to the Board of Appeal for decision" (J32/95[74]).

Article 109(2) EPC provides that "if the appeal is not allowed within **4–65** three months after receipt of the statement of grounds, it shall be remitted to the Board of Appeal without delay, and without comment as to its merits".

The period for rectification of the decision was recently extended from one month to three months to allow the possibility of greater use being made of this provision. "... if further separate issues—such as reimbursement of the appeal fee—arise out of the appeal, the instance in charge of the case is obliged under Article 109(2) EPC to take a separate decision on rectification [within such period] as soon as it realises that a decision on any further issue cannot be taken within that period" (T939/95[75]).

(ii) A "well-founded" appeal. (1) An appeal is clearly well founded if, **4–66** upon examination of the statement of grounds of appeal, the first instance department itself recognises that the decision under appeal should not after all be supported, on its merits; in other words, when the first instance department is persuaded by the grounds of appeal or otherwise has second thoughts and is therefore prepared to set aside its own previous decision as mentioned above.

(2) Furthermore:

> "an appeal is to be considered well-founded if the amendments submitted by the appellant clearly meet the objections on which the decision [under appeal] relies. That there are other objections which have not been removed but which were not the subject of the

---

[74] *Ibid.*
[75] T939/95 *NCR/Time limit for rectification* O.J. EPO 1998, 481; [1999] E.P.O.R. 167.

contested decision cannot preclude the application of Article 109 EPC" (T139/87[76]).

Similarly:

"an appeal may be considered as well founded ... if the appellant no longer seeks grant of the patent with a text corresponding to that which was rejected by the Examining Division, and if substantial amendments are proposed which are clearly intended to overcome the objections raised in the decision under appeal. Rectification of the previous decision ... does not preclude a further adverse decision in respect of the amended text" (T47/90[77]).

In such a case, interlocutory revision *must* be ordered (T139/87[78]).

"Substantial" amendments are those which require a substantial further examination in relation to both the formal (*i.e.* Article 123(2) EPC) and substantive requirements of the EPC" (T63/86[79]).

4–67   Thus, where the amendments proposed to the text of the patent by the main request in the appeal are sufficiently substantial for a Board of Appeal to remit the case to the first instance under Article 111(1) EPC, they are also in principle sufficiently substantial for the first instance department to rectify its own decision which is under appeal by way of interlocutory revision. In either case, the consequent further examination of the case by the Examining Division may lead to a further decision which may or may not be favourable to the appellant.

Interlocutory revision in these circumstances means that in the event of another adverse decision by the first instance department, the appellant again has the right to appeal, thus preserving the possibility of consideration of the merits of the case by two instances.

4–68   **(iii) Failure to apply interlocutory revision.** Normally, if the Examining Division does not rectify its decision by way of interlocutory revision, an applicant cannot complain and has no remedy, even if he has specifically requested this in the grounds of appeal. In the absence of interlocutory revision, the Board of Appeal may still remit the case to the Examining Division (see paragraph 4–121 below).

For example, if the notice of appeal requests grant of the patent in a text which had been specified in a communication under Rule 51(4) EPC during examination proceedings, the Examining Division should rectify the decision under Article 109. Failure to do so constitutes a procedural violation, but since the text of the Rule 51(5) EPC communication is not

[76] T139/87 BENDIX/*Governor valve* O.J. EPO 1990, 68; [1990] E.P.O.R. 234.
[77] T47/90 SUMITOMO/*Remittal* O.J. EPO 1991, 486; [1991] E.P.O.R. 513.
[78] See note 76.
[79] T63/86 KOLLMORGEN/*Consent for amendments* O.J. EPO 1988, 224; [1988] E.P.O.R. 316.

approved until the filing of the appeal, it would not be equitable to reimburse the appeal fee (T898/96[80]).

In certain circumstances, a failure to apply interlocutory revision can amount to a substantial procedural violation justifying refund of the appeal fee. For example, following the failure by the Examination Division both during examination proceedings and at the interlocutory revision stage "to appreciate the logical significance of a clear submission made by a party to the proceedings" (T268/85[81]).

3. Substantive examination of an appeal

(a) Introduction

(i) **General characteristics.** Following due filing of the notice of appeal **4–69** and the statement of grounds of appeal, the consideration in respect of interlocutory revision under Article 109 EPC, and the examination for admissibility under Rule 65 EPC, an appeal is ready for substantive examination and decision under Articles 110 and 111 and Rule 66 EPC.

There are two basic categories of appeal proceedings—*ex parte* proceedings (*i.e.* examination appeal) and *inter partes* (*i.e.* opposition appeal) proceedings, which will be considered separately where necessary. By far the majority of cases before the Boards of Appeal are appeals from decisions of the Examining Divisions and the Opposition Divisions which are examined and decided by Technical Boards of Appeal (Article 21 EPC). The procedure in appeals from decisions of the Examining Divisions and the Opposition Divisions is formally similar to the respective procedures before those departments themselves (Rule 66(1) EPC, but see paragraph 4–72 below).

The procedural system in relation to appeals is not directly comparable **4–70** to any national system. It includes aspects of both inquisitorial and adversarial procedure, and is essentially a hybrid system. Furthermore, oral proceedings are optional either at the request of a party or at the instance of the Board of Appeal (see Chapter 5 at paragraphs 5–39 *et seq.* below). In view of the optional nature of oral proceedings, the procedure is necessarily arranged so as to provide for elucidation and clarification of the issues in the appeal as far as possible in writing, prior to the making of a decision in the case. Such clarification of the issues in writing has the advantages of sometimes avoiding the need for oral proceedings which might otherwise be required, and if there are oral proceedings, helping to keep these reasonably short. This is especially desirable having regard to the international nature of many of the cases, and the consequent need for parties and their representatives sometimes to travel a considerable distance in order to attend oral proceedings.

Furthermore, the prior clarification of the issues in writing normally

---

[80] T898/96 *HITACHI* January 10, 1997.
[81] T268/85 *STAMICARBON/Polymer filaments* [1989] E.P.O.R. 229.

enables the decision to be made and announced at the conclusion of the oral proceedings (see Chapter 5 at paragraph 5–76 below).

In practice, less than half the appeals filed are currently decided without any oral proceedings and therefore solely on the written documents in the case. Opposition appeal proceedings commonly include oral proceedings. The importance of the option of oral proceedings in the practice of the Boards of Appeal should not be underestimated, as will be discussed below.

4–71 **(ii) Judicial nature and function of an appeal.** The various provisions which have been discussed in paragraph 4–06 above (especially Article 23 EPC) which govern the independence of the members of the Boards of Appeal, as well as "their competence and method of work and the nature of the decisions they take, indicate that the Boards act as courts with the task of ensuring that the provisions of the EPC do not conflict with the law when applied in practice" (G1/86[82]). "The appeal procedure must be regarded as a procedure proper to an administrative court" (G7, 8/91[83]). Thus "the appeal procedure is to be considered as a judicial procedure" (G9, 10/91[84]).

Consequently, the Boards of Appeal provide "judicial review" of decisions which are the subject of an appeal: in particular, they provide judicial review of a first instance decision to revoke a patent, in compliance with Article 32 TRIPS (see Chapter 1 at paragraph 1–55) (*Lenzing A.G's European Patent (U.K.[85])*).

4–72 It follows from the scheme of Articles 106 to 111 EPC that "the essential function of an appeal is to consider whether a decision which has been issued by a first instance department is correct on its merits ... It is not normally the function of a Board of Appeal in appeal proceedings to examine and decide upon issues in the case which have been raised for the first time during appeal proceedings" (T26/88[86]). Thus in opposition appeal proceedings "The purpose of the appeal procedure *inter partes* is mainly to give the losing party the possibility of challenging the decision of the Opposition Division on its merits" (G9, 10/91[87]). Consequently, appeal proceedings are not the mere continuation of first instance proceedings. "Appeal proceedings are wholly separate and independent from the first instance proceedings. Their function is to give a judicial decision upon the correctness of a separate earlier decision of the first instance department" (T34/90). "The appeal procedure is basically a review of the decision under appeal, not a re-examination of the application or patent" (T534/89[88]).

The above described judicial characteristics and court-like nature of

---

[82] G1/86 *VOEST ALPINE/Re-establishment of opponent* O.J. EPO 1987, 447; [1987] E.P.O.R. 388.
[83] G7, 8/91 *BASF/BELL/Withdrawal of appeal* O.J. EPO 1993, 346, 356; [1993] E.P.O.R. 440, 445.
[84] G9, 10/91 *ROHM AND HAAS/Power to examine; Examination of opposition/appeals* O.J. EPO 1993, 408; [1993] E.P.O.R. 485.
[85] *Lenzing A.G.'s European Patent (U.K.)* [1997] R.P.C. 245.
[86] T26/88 *AKZO/Automatic revocation* O.J. EPO 1991, 30; O.J. EPO 1990, 4; [1990] E.P.O.R. 21.
[87] See n. 84 above.
[88] T534/89 *EMS/Inadmissible late filing* O.J. EPO 1994, 464; [1994] E.P.O.R. 540.

appeal proceedings have important consequences in various aspects of appeal procedure, as will be considered in detail below. In particular, the principle of "party disposition" is a characteristic of court procedure which is generally applied in appeal proceedings. In accordance with this principle, the parties to the proceedings primarily control the course of the proceedings and the issues that are to be decided.

"Proceedings under the EPC in respect of European patent applications and patents are with some exceptions initiated by a party. The initial 'request' determines the extent of the proceedings. This is known as the principles of party disposition (*ne ultra petita*)" (G9/92, G4/93[89]).

The extent of application of Rule 66(1) EPC, which provides that "unless otherwise provided, the provisions relating to proceedings before [the first instance department] shall be applicable to appeal proceedings *mutatis mutandis*", consequently is affected by such characteristics and nature, as will be seen below (see for example paragraph 4–130).

(iii) Powers of Board of Appeal when deciding a case: convergent 4–73
procedure. In the context of a Board of Appeal deciding on an appeal, Article 111(1) EPC provides that: "The Board of Appeal may either exercise any power within the competence of the department which was responsible for the decision appealed or remit the case to that department for further prosecution."

When deciding an appeal, a Board of Appeal therefore has a broad discretion under Article 111 EPC either to decide matters in issue, or in appropriate circumstances to remit the case to the first instance in relation to certain issues. Having regard to the judicial nature and function of an appeal as discussed above, this discretion should clearly normally be exercised so as to ensure that parties to appeal proceedings before the EPO have each issue in a case examined and decided by two instances. "It is not normally the function of a Board of Appeal in appeal proceedings to examine and decide upon issues in a case which have been raised for the first time during appeal proceedings" (T26/88[90]). "If a fresh ground is admitted, the case should, having regard to the purpose of the appeal procedure as stated above, be remitted to the first instance for further prosecution, unless special reasons present themselves for doing otherwise" (G9, 10/91[91]). The circumstances in which such discretion to remit may call to be exercised are considered further below (see paragraphs 4–92 *et seq*.).

Thus if a new issue is introduced into a case during appeal proceedings, a Board of Appeal will normally remit the case to the first instance, under Article 111 EPC. Such remittal inevitably increases the overall length of time taken by the proceedings considerably, which is undesirable. Consequently, it will be seen below that in order to avoid such lengthening

[89] G9/92 *BMW Non-appealing party* O.J. EPO 1994, 875; [1995] E.P.O.R. 169.
[90] T26/88 *AKZO/Automatic revocation* O.J. EPO 1991, 30.
[91] G9, 10/91 *ROHM AND HAAS/Power to examine; Examination of oppositions/appeals* O.J. EPO 1993, 408, 420; [1993] E.P.O.R. 485.

of EPO proceedings (especially opposition proceedings), it is necessary and justified for the Boards of Appeal to be restrictive in allowing new material of a substantive nature into appeal proceedings—especially so at a late stage in appeal proceedings. If the issues to be decided are allowed to expand during an appeal, procedural complication and delay are inevitable. Appeal proceedings should therefore be *convergent* in nature.

4–74 **(iv) Extent of the substantive examination: principles.** Having regard to the nature and function of appeal proceedings as discussed generally in paragraph 4–71 above, the question arises both in *ex parte* examination appeals and in *inter partes* opposition appeals as to how far a Board of Appeal may go in examining and deciding an appeal, both as a matter of legal competence or power and as a matter of practice. Can a Board of Appeal consider and decide upon issues which were not decided in the first instance decision, and if so, in what circumstances?

The question is complicated by the fact that following the conclusion of first instance proceedings, the subject-matter of the claims in dispute may change as a result of amendments being proposed by the applicant or proprietor, to a greater or lesser extent. Furthermore, additional relevant facts or evidence may become available, whether or not the subject-matter of the claims changes. Consequently, the subject-matter of the issues in dispute may change.

In this section these matters will be considered as a matter of principle. In relation to both the legal powers of the Boards of Appeal and their practice, the relevant considerations are different depending upon whether the appeal is *ex parte* or *inter partes*.

4–75 (a) *Ex parte proceedings: examination appeals.*

Proceedings before an Examining Division are concluded by a decision refusing the application under Article 97 EPC on the ground that one or more requirements of the EPC are not met. The decision to refuse the application is thus the subject of the appeal. Following the principle of party disposition discussed above, the filing of an appeal against such decision determines the extent of the appeal: that is, whether or not the application should be refused. However:

> "In contrast to opposition appeal proceedings the judicial examination in *ex parte* proceedings concerns the stage *prior* to grant and lacks a contentious nature ... In *ex parte* proceedings therefore, the Boards of Appeal are restricted neither to examination of the grounds for the contested decision nor to the facts and evidence on which the decision is based, and can include new grounds in the proceedings. This applies to both the patentability requirements which the Examining Division did not take into consideration in the examination proceedings and those which it indicated in a communication or in a decision to refuse the application as having been met" (G10/93[92]). In other

---

[92] G10/93 *SIEMENS II/Sensor* O.J. EPO 1995, 172; [1997] E.P.O.R. 227.

words "the Board of Appeal has the power to examine whether the application or the invention to which it relates meets the requirements of the EPC" (G10/93[93]).

Thus in *ex parte* appeal proceedings, an applicant who appeals against a **4–76** decision to refuse an application on the ground of lack of novelty, for example, may succeed in relation to the ground of lack of novelty but may lose the appeal on the ground of inventive step, or even sufficiency, for example. *"Reformatio in peius"* is applicable.

Nevertheless:

> "The power to include new grounds in *ex parte* proceedings does not however mean that Boards of Appeal carry out a full examination of the application as to patentability requirements. This is the task of the Examining Division. Proceedings before the Boards of Appeal in *ex parte* proceedings are primarily concerned with examining the contested decision. If, however there is reason to believe that a condition for patentability may not have been satisfied, the Board either incorporates it into the appeal proceedings or ensures by way of referral to the Examining Division that it is included when examination is resumed" (G10/93[94]).

The exercise of a Board of Appeal's discretionary power under Article 111(1) EPC either to decide such a new ground itself or to remit the case for further prosecution is considered in paragraph 4–94 below.

(b) *Inter partes proceedings: opposition appeals.* **4–77**

The nature of opposition proceedings generally has been considered in Chapter 3 at paragraph 3–02, and the extent of the substantive examination by an Opposition Division is considered in paragraphs 3–39 *et seq.* It is there emphasised that:

(a) "opposition proceedings under the EPC are in principle to be considered as contentious proceedings between parties representing opposite interests, who should be given equally fair treatment" (G9, 10/91[95]).

(b) one of the two functions of the statement in a notice of opposition which is required under Rule 55(c) EPC is to establish *"the legal and factual framework* within which the substantive examination of the opposition in principle shall be conducted" (G9, 10/91[96]—emphasis added). Consequently, the extent of the opposition is estab

[93] *Ibid.*
[94] G10/93 *SIEMENS II/Sensor* O.J. EPO 1995, 172; [1997] E.P.O.R. 227.
[95] G9, 10/91 *ROHM AND HAAS/Power to examine; Examination of oppositions/appeals* O.J. EPO 1993, 408, 420; [1993] E.P.O.R. 485.
[96] *Ibid.*

lished once and for all by the notice of opposition as filed within the nine-month opposition period (T105/94[97]).

These principles which underlie opposition proceedings are generally applicable not only to proceedings before an Opposition Division but also in opposition appeals. However, the way in which these principles are applied in appeal proceedings differs from first instance proceedings, principally because of the judicial nature of appeal proceedings (paragraph 4–71 above) but also because of the later stage at which appeal proceedings take place.

4–78   Thus:

> "The purpose of the appeal procedure *inter partes* is mainly to give the losing party the possibility of challenging the decision on its merits. It is not in conformity with this purpose to consider grounds for opposition on which the decision of the Opposition Division has not been based. Furthermore ... the appeal procedure is to be considered as a judicial procedure ... Such procedure is by its very nature less investigative than an administrative procedure [*i.e.* procedure before an Opposition Division]" (G9, 10/91[98]).

Consequently, the possibilities for expanding the "legal and factual framework" of an opposition beyond what is set out in the notice of opposition during appeal proceedings, for example by filing new grounds of opposition, new facts and evidence, and major amendments, become increasingly restricted during the appeal procedure. In other words, opposition and opposition appeal procedure is a *convergent* procedure, in the sence that the issues to be decided during such procedure should in principle therefore be narrowed rather than expanded.

The application of these general principles to the admission of requests by parties, further grounds of opposition, late-filed amendments and late-filed facts and evidence in support of the opposition is considered in detail below.

(b) The written examination stage

4–79   **(i) Introduction: characteristics of the written stage.**
The written examination stage begins at some time after the statement of grounds of appeal has been filed and the admissibility of the appeal determined, and in the case of an opposition appeal following filing of any observations by the respondent (see paragraph 4–96 below). At this point the case is considered initially by the rapporteur of the Board of Appeal (see below).

The written examination stage is completed, if no oral hearing has been

---

[97] T105/94 *MOLNLYCKE* July 29, 1997.
[98] See note 95.

requested, by the issue of the written decision or otherwise when oral proceedings are held.

It is the written examination stage of an appeal, governed by Article 110 **4–80** and Rule 66(1) EPC, which gives the appeal procedure its most distinctive characteristics, which are:

(a) The work of the "rapporteur"
(b) The flexibility of the procedure
(c) The control of the procedure by the Board.

As to (a), the procedure set out in Article 110 and Rule 66(1) EPC has been developed by means of the Rules of Procedure of the Boards of Appeal. In particular Article 4(1) RPBA requires: "that the chairman of each Board shall designate a member or himself as 'rapporteur'." Article 4(2) RPBA provides that "The rapporteur shall carry out a preliminary study of the appeal," and he may prepare and sign communications to the parties on behalf of the Board.

As to (b), Article 110(2) EPC provides that "the Board of Appeal shall invite the parties, as often as necessary, to file observations, within a period to be fixed by the Board of Appeal, on communications from another party or issued by itself."

The flexible nature of the appeal procedure at this stage is apparent.

As to (c), the examination stage of an appeal is primarily the responsibility of the rapporteur, as follows from Article 4(2) RPBA referred to above, although he works in consultation with the other members of the Board and prepares communications to the parties under the direction of the Chairman. Thus, the time taken by and the course of the examination stage can be controlled by the rapporteur and tailored to the nature and requirements of each individual case, depending upon the complexity of the issues raised and the amount of any further information or evidence which may be requested.

In the majority of cases, if the statement of grounds of appeal and the **4–81** observations in reply from any respondent are well drafted, not more than one communication from the rapporteur should be necessary before the appeal can be decided. However, if a proprietor proposes amendments to the patent in response to a first communication, for example, the admissibility of such amendments may necessitate a further communication. In many cases, no communication may be necessary.

The importance of a comprehensively drafted grounds of appeal can now be recognised. Whatever the minimum contents of a statement of grounds of appeal may be (as discussed in paragraphs 4–55 to 4–57 above), it is apparent that a full, concise and well reasoned grounds of appeal can maximise the chances of success in an appeal. Similarly, the contents of a respondent's observations in reply to the grounds of appeal in opposition proceedings are equally important. The rapporteur's attention will then be focused upon the most relevant issues and documents at an early stage.

4–82   **(ii) Amendments in appeal proceedings.**
(a) *General principles.* Rules 51 and 86(3) FPC, which are applicable *mutatis mutandis* to appeal procedure under Rule 66(1) EPC, govern the admissibility of amendments in examination appeal proceedings (T63/86[99]). Rules 57 and 57a EPC in conjunction with Rule 66(1) EPC similarly govern the admissibility of amendments in opposition appeals. In both cases, therefore, the admissibility of amendments is discretionary (T63/86,[100] T840/93[101]). The exercise of such discretion may depend upon the content of the proposed amendments and the timing of the proposed amendments.

Following refusal of an application or revocation of a patent (or refusal of preferred requests), by a first instance decision, newly formulated claims are commonly presented in the course of subsequent appeal proceedings, usually with the statement of grounds of appeal. The note "Guidance for parties to appeal proceedings and their representatives"[102] states that:

> "A party wishing to submit amendments to the patent documents in appeal proceedings should do so as early as possible. It should be borne in mind that the board concerned may disregard amendments which are not submitted in good time prior to oral proceedings (as a rule four weeks before the day set for the oral proceedings).
>
> Auxiliary requests should be filed as early as possible" (as to auxiliary requests, see Chapter 5 at paragraph 5–29).

4–83   The above statement applies to both examination and opposition appeals, and sets out the general principles which are applicable in appeal proceedings.

It should be emphasised that the admissibility of proposed amendments which are filed at any time during appeal proceedings is always a matter of discretion. Thus:

> "A patentee who has lost before the Opposition Division ... has the right to have the rejected requests considered by the Appeal Board. If however the patentee wants other requests to be considered, admission of these requests into the proceedings is a matter of discretion of the Appeal Board, and is not a matter of right ... For exercising the discretion in favour of the patentee ... there must be good reasons" (T840/93[103]).

The consequences of filing amendments in appeal proceedings necessarily depends upon the nature and content of the proposed amendments,

---

[99] T63/86 *KOLLMORGEN/Consent for amendments* O.J. EPO 1998, 224; [1988] E.P.O.R. 316.
[100] *Ibid.*
[101] T840/93 *PROCTOR II/Oral composition* O.J. EPO 1996, 355; [1997] E.P.O.R. 56.
[102] O.J. EPO 1996, 342; see Appendix 8.
[103] T840/93 *PROCTOR II/Oral composition* O.J. EPO 1996, 355; [1997] E.P.O.R. 56.

as well as upon whether the appeal is in examination or opposition proceedings. For example, in both kinds of appeal proceedings the filing of proposed amendments may result in the case being remitted to the first instance under Article 111(1) EPC, if the proposed amendments result in a substantial change to the claimed subject-matter. However, the considerations which are applicable to the exercise of the discretion to remit the case under Article 111(1) EPC may be different in examination and opposition appeals. Consequently the filing of amendments in examination and opposition appeals is considered separately below.

(b) *Late-filed amendments: "if clearly allowable"*. In both examination and **4–84** opposition appeals, proposed amendments which are filed at a late stage in appeal proceedings, for example, either shortly before or during oral proceedings, may be refused if they are not "clearly allowable". Thus:

> "In relation to appeal proceedings, the normal rule is as follows: if an appellant wishes that the allowability of alternative sets of claims, which differ in subject-matter from those considered at first instance, should be considered (both in relation to Article 123 EPC and otherwise) by the Board of Appeal when deciding on the appeal, such alternative sets of claims should be filed with the grounds of appeal, or as soon as possible thereafter".

When deciding on an appeal during oral proceedings, a Board may **4–85** justifiably refuse to consider alternative claims which have been filed at a very late stage, for example during the oral proceedings, if such alternative claims are not "clearly allowable" (T153/85[104]).

This statement was made in the context of an examination appeal, but is applicable to and has been frequently applied in both examination and opposition appeals. The reasoning in support of the above "normal rule" is that:

> "In all normal circumstances an appellant has ample time and opportunity, both during the proceedings at first instance and during the appeal proceedings, to consider and formulate the full range of claims that he may desire, well prior to the oral hearing" (T153/85[105]).

Similarly, it has been stated in the context of an opposition appeal that: **4–86**

> "For the avoidance of doubt in future cases, the Board takes the opportunity of saying that it is only in the most exceptional circumstances, where there is some clear justification both for the amendment and for its late submission, that it is likely that an amendment

---

[104] T153/85 *AMOCO/Alternative claims* O.J. EPO 1998, 1; [1998] E.P.O.R. 116.
[105] *Ibid*.

not submitted in good time before oral proceedings will be considered on its merits in these proceedings by a Board of Appeal" (T95/83[106]).

Consequently a proposed amendment which is clearly allowable, both under Article 123 EPC and in relation to other requirements of the EPC, will normally be allowed even at a late stage of appeal proceedings. However, a proposed amendment whose allowability is on its face doubtful, or whose allowability may depend upon the result of further investigations, will not normally be allowable if filed at such a late stage in the appeal. In general, the later a proposed amendment is filed, the greater the risk that it may not be regarded as admissible.

Examples of the exercise of discretion in relation to late-filed amendments are considered below in the context of both examination and opposition appeals.

4–87 **(iii)** *Ex parte* **proceedings: examination appeals.**

(a) *Introduction.* Substantive examination of an appeal by a Board of Appeal begins in *ex parte* proceedings at some time after the statement of grounds of appeal has been filed and the admissibility of the appeal determined, when the rapporteur carries out a preliminary study of the appeal (Article 4(2) RPBA).

4–88 (b) *Communications and observations in reply.* If, after examination of the statement of grounds of appeal, the Board intends to allow the appeal, no communication on behalf of the Board is necessary, and a decision favourable to the appellant may be issued directly.

If, after such consideration, the Board is not able to issue a favourable decision directly, two kinds of communication are possible, depending upon whether or not oral proceedings have been requested.

4–89 1. *No request for oral proceedings filed: a communication under Article 110(2) EPC.* Grounds of objection to grant are normally contained in such a communication, and it is then necessary to invite observations in reply within a fixed period of time, normally two to four months (which period may be extended).

A reply to such a communication (together with any appropriate facts and evidence in support of the application) must be filed in due time. Article 110(3) EPC provides that if the applicant fails to reply in due time to an invitation under Article 110(2) EPC, "the application shall be deemed to be withdrawn." Further processing may be requested under Article 121 EPC (see Chapter 6 at paragraph 6–02).

This provision does not apply to an appeal from a decision of the Legal Division (Article 110(3) EPC).

---

[106] T95/83 *AISIN/Late submission of amendment* O.J. EPO 1985, 75; [1979–85] E.P.O.R.: C: 815.

2. *Request for oral proceedings filed: a communication in preparation for oral proceedings under Article 11(2) RPBA.* If oral proceedings have been requested, a communication may be sent in preparation for such proceedings, accompanied by the summons to oral proceedings. In this case, there is no specific invitation to file observations in reply pursuant to Article 110(2) EPC but the appellant is normally notified that any observations in reply should be filed at least one month before the date of oral proceedings. Alternatively, the appellant's comments upon the Board's communication may be made at the oral hearing itself.

If a Board of Appeal sends a communication in preparation for oral **4–90** proceedings, the parties "are obliged to comply with it, in particular as far as the final date for reply is concerned" (T97/94[107]).

As a further possible alternative, a Board of Appeal may simply summons the appellant to oral proceedings. As explained in paragraph 4–16 above, Rule 71a EPC does not apply to appeal proceedings, and a Board of Appeal is not obliged to send a communication with the summons.

(c) *Amendments in ex parte appeals.* Following refusal of an application by **4–91** an Examination Division, and in the light of the reasons for such refusal as set out in the decision of refusal, newly formulated claims or other amendments may be and commonly are presented with the statement of grounds of appeal or subsequently, for example in response to a communication from the Board of Appeal. Such amendments are normally admissible in *ex parte* proceedings, especially if filed before substantive examination of the appeal has begun, or in response to a communication from the Board. Such amendments will therefore be fully examined for allowability.

At a late stage in the appeal proceedings, however, for example either shortly before or during the oral hearing, proposed amendments may be refused if they are not "clearly allowable", as already explained in paragraph 4–84 above. In practice, this means that a proposed amendment which clearly overcomes all objections and results in a description and claims which meet the requirements of the EPC will be allowed even at a very late stage during the oral hearing. Similarly, "cosmetic" amendments which improve clarity and are clearly allowable will not be refused even at a very late stage. However, new proposals for amendment which are filed for example at a late stage during oral proceedings and which require major substantive consideration may be refused (especially if a further search is required).

In general terms, the later a proposed amendment is filed, the more "clearly allowable" it should be (T570/96[108]). It is in the public interest that

---

[107] T97/94 *CECA/Timetable for procedure* O.J. EPO 1998, 467; [1992] E.P.O.R. 65.
[108] T570/96 *ALLIED COLLOIDS* August 20, 1998.

an amendment should not be allowed to prolong the appeal proceedings unduly.

For example, in a case where an auxiliary request was proposed and admitted during oral proceedings and the case was remitted to the Examining Division for examination of inventive step, it was recognised that the delay involved in such a course "could be in the interest of the applicant . . ., and contrary to the interest of other potential workers in the same field" (T381/87[109]).

4–92   (d) *Remittal to the Examining Division.*
    1 Following a substantial amendment.   When amended claims are filed during appeal proceedings, either with the grounds of appeal or at a later stage, which are intended to replace the claims which were refused by the first instance, the Board of Appeal has to exercise its discretion under Article 111(1) EPC, either to decide upon the allowability of the new claims, or to remit the case to the first instance.

Obviously, one major factor in the exercise of this discretion must be the substantiality of the proposed amendments. Minor amendments, primarily of a clarifying nature for example, which do not affect the basis on which the decision under appeal was made, clearly do not justify remittal to the first instance. On the other hand, substantial amendments to the claims constituting the main request of the appellant may justify such remittal.

4–93   Another major factor in the exercise of this discretion is the stage at which the amendments are proposed. The later the amendments are proposed in appeal proceedings, and the more involved the Board of Appeal is in the case, the less likely it is that remittal will be ordered.

It is thus quite common for such new claims to be examined and decided upon by a Board of Appeal, sometimes after a suggestion has been made for further amendments such as will satisfy the Board. While this course may be time-efficient, it has the disadvantage that the new claims are effectively only examined by one instance.

> "In a case where substantial amendments to the claims are proposed an appeal, which require substantial further examination, the case should be remitted to the Examining Division, so that such examination should be carried out, if at all, by the Examining Division after the latter has exercised its discretion under Rule 86(3) EPC . . .
>
> In this way the applicant's right to appeal to a second instance is maintained, both in relation to the exercise of discretion under Rule 86(3) EPC, and (if such discretion is favourably exercised) in relation to the formal and substantive allowability of the amended claims" (T63/86[110]: see also T47/90[111]).

---

[109] T381/87 *RESEARCH CORPORATION/Publication* O.J. EPO 1990, 213; [1989] E.P.O.R. 138.
[110] T63/86 *KOLLMORGEN/Consent for amendments* O.J. EPO 1988, 224; [1988] E.P.O.R. 316.
[111] T47/90 *SUMITOMO/Remittal* O.J. EPO 1991, 486.

2   For decision upon issues not yet examined.   It sometimes happens   **4–94**
that the Examining Division issues a decision refusing the application
upon one particular ground, and leaves other issues outstanding. If the
appeal is allowed, the case will normally be remitted to the Examining
Division for examination of the outstanding issues (see T19/90[112] for
example).

As discussed in paragraphs 4–75 and 4–76, a Board of Appeal may
exceptionally introduce new grounds, facts or evidence during examination appeal proceedings, and thus effectively introduce a new possible
basis for refusing the application. In such a situation, the case will normally
be remitted to the Examining Division under Article 111 EPC for
examination and decision in relation to such new basis for refusal, in order
to ensure two instances of examination, unless the applicant agrees to the
Board of Appeal examining and deciding the new objection itself.

3   Following a relevant Enlarged Board decision.

"In a case where a legal position has been fundamentally clarified by   **4–95**
decision of the Enlarged Board of Appeal and a new type of claim for
particular inventions has been allowed, the Board remits the case to
the Examining Division, regardless of whether claims of that type
have already been filed" (T17/81[113]).

In the case in question, the application had been refused because it
contained unallowable "medical use" claims, before the issue of G5/83[114]
(see Chapter 11 at paragraphs 11–86 *et seq.*).

(iv) *Inter partes* **proceedings: opposition appeals.**   **4–96**
(a) *Introduction.* In *inter partes* proceedings, following the filing of the
statement of grounds of appeal, and the determination of admissibility
each respondent is invited to file observations upon such statement of
grounds within a fixed period (usually four months, but this may be
extended). The substantive examination of the appeal begins after such
observations have been filed, or after the time limit for filing such
observations has expired, when the rapporteur carries out a preliminary
study of the appeal (Article 4(2) RPBA). A communication may then be
drafted.

(b) *Communications and observations in reply.*

"If a Board deems it expedient to communicate with the parties   **4–97**
regarding a possible appreciation of substantive or legal matters, such
communication shall be made in such a way as not to imply that the
Board is in any way bound by it" (Article 12 RPBA).

[112] T19/90 *HARVARD/Onco-mouse* O.J. EPO 1990, 476; [1990] E.P.O.R. 501.
[113] T17/81 *BAYER/Nimodipin I*, O.J. EPO 1985, 130, [1979–85] E.P.O.R.: B: 320.
[114] G5/83 *EISAI/Second medical indication* O.J. EPO 1985, 64; [1979–85] E.P.O.R.: B: 241.

Where no request for oral proceedings has been made, a main consideration for a Board sending a communication to the parties is to ensure compliance with Article 113(1) EPC, namely to give the parties an opportunity to comment upon the grounds and evidence upon which the decision may be based.

If oral proceedings have been requested:

> "The Board may send with the summons to oral proceedings a communication drawing attention to matters which seem to be of special significance, or to the fact that questions appear no longer to be contentious, or containing other observations that may help concentration on essentials during the oral proceedings" (Article 11(2) RPBA).

4–98   As explained in Chapter 5 at paragraph 5–51 above, Rule 71a RPC does not apply to appeal proceedings, and there is consequently no obligation for a Board of Appeal to send a communication to the parties with the summons to oral proceedings.

As to the contents of such a communication:

> "all instances of the EPO and in particular the Boards of Appeal are required to abide by the principle of impartiality, and accordingly to refrain ... from giving one-sided assistance in *inter partes* matters" (T173/89[115]).

Nevertheless, it is normal in many circumstances to indicate preliminary views on a case in order that the parties are clearly informed in advance of the hearing of points which may be taken against them, and thus should be in a position to present their cases at the oral hearing as well as possible.

4–99   (c) *Requests to be examined.*

As explained in paragraphs 4–49 *et seq.* above, the extent of appeal proceedings, that is, the issues to be decided, is determined in general terms by the statement of "the extent to which amendment or cancellation of the decision [under appeal] is requested" (Rule 64(v) EPC) in the notice of appeal or by each such statement in the case of more than one notice of appeal being filed (G9/92, G4/93[116]).

Consequently, "requests" should only be examined by a Board of Appeal if they fall within the scope of an "appeal request" by such party.

In the majority of opposition appeals, the Opposition Division decision is fully in favour of either the proprietor, or one or more opponents. For example, if the opposed patent is maintained in accordance with the main request of the proprietor (for example, the patent is maintained as granted), the opponent or opponents will request cancellation of the decision to maintain the patent and revocation of the patent. If the patent is

---

[115] T173/89 *ICI/Gamma-sorbitol* [1991] E.P.O.R. 62.
[116] G9/92 *BMW/Non-appealing party* O.J. EPO 1994, 875; [1995] E.P.O.R. 169.

revoked, the proprietor will request cancellation of such decision and maintenance of the patent (for example, in accordance with one or more requests for amendment); and if the patent is maintained as granted, the opponent(s) will request cancellation of the decision and revocation of the patent.

In some cases, however, the patent is maintained in amended form in **4–100** accordance with an auxiliary request of the patent proprietor. In such a case, the proprietor is "adversely affected" by the decision now to allow the main request and each opponent is adversely affected by the decision not to revoke the patent.

As explained in paragraphs 4–40 to 4–42 above, if any party to the proceedings wishes to challenge such a decision, he must file an appeal, and he must state in the notice of appeal "the extent to which amendment or cancellation of the decision is requested". The parties to the appeal proceedings may thereafter only make requests which are consistent with the extent of the appeal proceedings as defined by the (admissible) notice(s) of appeal which have been filed.

In such a case, for example, if only the proprietor appeals and requests maintenance of the patent in accordance with the main request before the Opposition Division, in the appeal proceedings an opponent may not request revocation of the patent and any such request would be rejected as inadmissible. Similarly, if only an opponent appeals and requests revocation of the patent, the proprietor may not request maintenance of the patent in accordance with the main request, and any such request would be rejected as inadmissible.

In the latter situation, the extent to which the patent proprietor may request amendments which were not requested during the proceedings before the Opposition Division is considered, in paragraphs 4–103 to 4–105 below.

(d) *Amendments in inter partes appeals.*   **4–101**
The general principles which are applicable to the filing of amendments during appeal proceedings have been discussed in paragraphs 4–82 *et seq.* above.

1 Amendments within the extent of the appeal.   **4–102**
i *Proprietor as appellant.* If the Opposition Division revoked the opposed patent, the patent proprietor during the course of his appeal may request amended claims at least within the scope of the requests which were examined and refused by the Opposition Division (G9/92, G4/93[117]).

ii *Proprietor as a party as of right (Article 107 EPC).* If the Opposition **4–103** Division maintained the patent in amended form in accordance with an auxiliary request of the proprietor, and one or more opponents file appeals and request revocation of the patent, but the proprietor does not file an appeal, the proprietor may file further auxiliary requests with claims

---

[117] G9/92 *BMW/Non-appealing party* O.J. EPO 1994, 875; [1995] E.P.O.R. 169.

within the scope of the claims which were maintained by the Opposition Division (G9/92, G4/93[118]).

In such a case however, the extent to which the proprietor may file further main or auxiliary requests which are not within the scope of the claims as maintained in the Opposition Division decision requires careful consideration.

The general principle is that "the patent proprietor is primarily restricted ... to defending the patent in the form in which it was maintained by the Opposition Division ... Amendments, proposed by the patent proprietor as a party to the proceedings as of right under Article 107 EPC may be rejected as inadmissible by the Board of Appeal if they are neither appropriate nor necessary". This is the case "if the amendments do not arise from the appeal. (Article 101(2) EPC, Rules 58(2) and 66(1) EPC; T406/86[119]; T295/87[120])" (G9/92, G4/93[121]).

4–104   The basis for this conclusion derives from the principle that an appellant should not be placed in worse position as a result of his appeal than he was as a result of the decision under appeal. "The idea that irrespective of whether the opposing party appeals, an appellant might have to take the risk of its appeal endangering the result which it achieved before the first instance, is ... not found in the EPC" (G9/92, G4/93[122]).

However, since the issue of G9/92, G4/93 a new Rule 57a EPC has come into effect (June 1995). This provides that "the description, claims and drawings [of the patent] may be amended, provided that the amendments are occasioned by grounds for opposition specified in Article 100 EPC, even if the respective ground has not been invoked by the opponent". According to one view, in the light of Rule 57a EPC the requirements of G9/92, G4/93[123] are satisfied if an amendment arises from a ground of opposition under Article 100 EPC, even if it does not arise out of the appeal (T1002/95[124]).

4–105   In order to clarify this legal situation, the following question has been referred to the Enlarged Board of Appeal:

> "Must an amended claim which would put the opponent and sole appellant in a worse situation than if he had not appealed—*e.g.* by deleting a limiting feature of the claim—be rejected?" (T315/97[125]).

At the time of writing the decision of the Enlarged Board (G1/99[126]) is awaited.

However, it would appear that Rule 57a EPC should not be interpreted

---

[118] *Ibid.*
[119] T406/86 *WACKER/Trichloroethylene* O.J. EPO 1989, 302; [1989] E.P.O.R. 338.
[120] T295/87 *ICI/Polyether ketones* O.J. EPO 1990, 479; [1991] E.P.O.R. 56.
[121] See note 117.
[122] See note 117.
[123] See note 117.
[124] T1002/95 *FURUKAWA* February 10, 1998.
[125] T315/97 *3M/Reformatio in peius* December 17, 1998 O.J. EPO (P).
[126] G1/99 Not yet issued. O.J. EPO (P).

so as to override the discretion of a Board of Appeal as to the admissibility of amendments during appeal proceedings, and that a Board of Appeal should therefore exercise such discretion by not admitting amendments during appeal proceedings which place an opponent/sole appellant in a worse position than if he had not appealed, because a request for such amendments by the patent proprietor goes beyond the extent of the appeal as defined in the opponent/sole appellants notice of appeal.

According to the proposed revision of the EPC, a new post-grant 4–105A amendment procedure will be introduced (Articles 105a, b and c EPC—see Chapter 8 at paragraph 8–04A). Such a procedure would appear to make Rule 57a EPC inappropriate and unnecessary in any event.

2 Late-filed amendments. The decided cases illustrate various circum- 4–106 stances where late-filed amendments have not been admitted in the exercise of a Board's discretion. For example:

(i) In a case where oral proceedings had not been requested by either party, proposed amendments which were filed at a point in time when "examination of the appeal under Article 110 EPC had been practically completed and a decision had already been drafted", and which were in response to the opponent's observations, were not admitted, because their admission would "slow down the proceedings and could also affect the rights of third parties, which would be contrary to the public interest", and because the amendments were not clearly allowable (T406/86[127]).

(ii) An auxiliary request which was filed near the end of oral proceedings, in which the main claim of such request contained subject-matter from a subclaim which had not previously been attacked by the opponent or otherwise put forward by the proprietor for consideration in relation to inventive step was rejected as inadmissible, because there was no reason for the opponent to have attacked such subject-matter previously, and examination of such subject-matter would delay the proceedings (T926/93[128]).

(iii) In an opposition appeal concerning a divisional patent, new requests filed shortly before oral proceedings containing claims to subject-matter which had not been considered by the Opposition Division were rejected as inadmissible, because other divisional applications were still pending and because "it is inappropriate to admit ... new requests which are neither immediately allowable nor bona fide attempts to overcome objections raised" (T840/93[129]).

[127] T406/86 WACKER/Trichloroethylene O.J. EPO 1989, 302; [1989] E.P.O.R. 593.
[128] T926/93 MITSUBISHI/Gas laser device O.J. EPO 1997, 447; [1998] E.P.O.R. 94.
[129] T840/93 PROCTOR II/Oral composition O.J. EPO 1987, 447; [1987] E.P.O.R. 239. O.J. EPO 1996, 335.

(iv) New main and auxiliary requests filed the day before oral proceedings may not be admitted in the absence of good reason. In particular:

"A lack of communication between the proprietor and its licensee does not afford sufficient justification upon which the Board can exercise its discretion to admit requests filed at an extremely late stage in the appeal" (T583/93[130]).

4–107   **3 Examination of objections arising out of amendments.** As during proceedings before an Opposition Division (see Chapter 3 at paragraphs 3–62 and 3–63) when amendments are filed during an opposition appeal, a Board of Appeal has the power under Article 102(3) EPC, and indeed the obligation, to examine whether the amendments introduce any contravention of any requirement of the EPC, including Article 84 EPC (T227/88,[131] T301/87,[132] G9, 10/91[133]). However following the filing of amendments a Board of Appeal does not have the power under Article 102(3) EPC and the relevant passage in G9, 10/91 would be somewhat absurd in the context: for example if a minor amendment in the middle of the description would allow new objections to be made to the claims which have no connection with the amendment itself (T301/87[134]).

4–108   (e) *Fresh grounds of opposition.*
1 When admissible. The introduction of fresh grounds of opposition which are raised for the first time by an opponent (or a Board of Appeal) during appeal proceedings is governed by Article 114(1) EPC. Having regard to the judicial nature of the appeal procedure, it "is by its very nature less investigative than an administrative procedure" (such as the procedure before an Opposition Division), and "it is therefore justified to apply this provision [Article 114(1) EPC] generally in a more restrictive manner in such procedure than in opposition procedure". Thus, fresh grounds of opposition "may in principle not be introduced at the appeal stage" (G10/91[135]).

This "reduced the procedural uncertainty for patentees having otherwise to face unforeseeable complications at a very late stage in the proceedings", bearing in mind that opponents may subsequently commence revocation proceedings before national courts (G10/91[136]).

"However, an exception to the above principle is justified in case the patentee agrees that a fresh ground for opposition may be considered: *volenti non fit injuria.* It may in some cases be in his own interest that such a ground is not excluded from consideration in the centralised procedure

---

[130] T583/93 *HYMO CORPORATION/Water-soluble polymer dispersion* O.J. EPO 1996, 496; [1997] E.P.O.R. 129.
[131] T227/88 *UNILEVER/Detergent compositions* O.J. EPO 1990, 292; [1990] E.P.O.R. 424 .
[132] T301/87 *BIOGEN/Alpha-interferons* O.J. EPO 1990, 335; [1990] E.P.O.R. 190.
[133] G9, 10/91 *ROHM AND HAAS/Power to examine; Examination of opposition/appeals* O.J. EPO 1993, 408, 420; [1993] E.P.O.R. 485.
[134] See note 132.
[135] See note 133.
[136] See note 133.

before the EPO." Nevertheless, "such a ground should only be raised by a Board of Appeal or, if raised by an opponent, be admitted into the proceedings, if it is considered by the Board to be already *prima facie* highly relevant". Furthermore, "if the patentee does not agree to the introduction of a fresh ground ... such a ground may not be dealt with in substance in the decision of the Board of Appeal or at all. Only the fact that the question has been raised may be mentioned" (G10/91[137]).

2 Meaning of "fresh grounds". 4–109

i General principles. The term "a fresh ground of opposition" as used in G10/91[138] "must be interpreted as having been intended to refer to a new legal basis for objecting to the maintenance of the patent, which was not both raised and substantiated in the notice of opposition, and which was not introduced into the proceedings by the Opposition Division" (G1, 7/95[139]).

Thus "Article 100(a)EPC contains a collection of different legal objections (*i.e.* legal bases), or different grounds of opposition, and is not directed to a single ground for opposition" (G1, 7/95[140]).

Accordingly:

> "In a case where a patent has been opposed on the grounds set out in Article 100(a) EPA, but the opposition has only been substantiated on the grounds of lack of novelty and lack of inventive step, the ground of unpatentable subject-matter based upon Article 52(1), (2) EPC is a fresh ground for opposition and accordingly may not be introduced into the appeal proceedings without the agreement of the patentee" (G1/95[141]).

ii Novelty/inventive step. In accordance with the above principles, the **4–110** objections of lack of novelty and lack of inventive step under Articles 54 and 56 EPC are different legal bases within Article 100(a) EPC Thus:

> "In a case where a patent has been opposed under Article 100(a) EPC on the ground that the claims lack inventive step in view of documents cited in the notice of opposition, the ground of lack of novelty based upon Articles 52(1), 54 EPC is a fresh ground for opposition and accordingly may not be introduced into the appeal proceedings without the agreement of the patentee. However, the allegation that the claims lack novelty in view of the closed prior art document may be considered in the context of deciding upon the ground of lack of inventive step" (G7/95[142]).

[137] G10/91 *Examination of oppositions/appeals* O.J. E.P.O. 1993, 420; [1993] E.P.O.R. 485.
[138] *Ibid.*
[139] G1, 7/95 *DE LA RUE, ETHICON/Fresh grounds for opposition* O.J. EPO 1996, 615, 626; [1996] E.P.O.R. 601.
[140] *Ibid.*
[141] *Ibid.*
[142] *Ibid.*

4–111   This is because:

> "if the closest prior art document destroys the novelty of the claimed subject-matter, such subject-matter obviously cannot involve an inventive step. Therefore, a finding of lack of novelty in such circumstances inevitably results in such subject-matter being unallowable on the ground of lack of inventive step" (G7/95[143]).

It follows from the above that in a case where a patent has been opposed only on the ground of lack of novelty having regard to certain prior art an allegation of lack of inventive step having regard to such prior art is a fresh ground of opposition and may not be introduced into the appeal proceedings without the agreement of the patentee.

The question whether a new objection to the effect that the claims lack novelty in view of prior art other than the closest prior art document (either previously cited in support of the ground of lack of inventive step or newly cited in the appeal proceedings) constitutes a "fresh ground for opposition" was left unanswered in G7/95[144] because it did not arise for decision in the appeal proceedings from which the question of law was referred. However, it would appear that a new objection of lack of novelty based upon a part of a previously cited document which had not been relied upon in support of the objection of lack of inventive step, or based upon a newly cited document in the appeal proceedings, ought in principle normally to be regarded as a fresh ground for opposition, and consequently inadmissible in the absence of the agreement of the patentee.

4–112   *iii   Wrongful amendment before grant: Article 100(c) EPC.*   If amendments to the patent were allowed before grant, and were not objected to under Article 100(c) EPC in the notice of opposition, the raising of such a ground of objection for the first time in appeal proceedings constitutes a fresh ground for opposition which cannot be examined without the patentee's consent (T443/96[145]).

4–113   *iv   Grounds not decided by the Opposition Division.*   Following the general principles set out in paragraph 4–108 above, a ground of opposition which was raised and substantiated in the notice of opposition but which was left undecided by the Opposition Division may be introduced into subsequent appeal proceedings without the patentee's agreement. This is the case even if the opponent did not maintain the ground of opposition during the proceedings before the Opposition Division (T274/95[146]).

If a new ground for opposition (not properly raised and substantiated in the Notice of Opposition or is only sought to be properly raised in the appeal) is unsuccessfully sought to be introduced during the proceedings before an Opposition Division, within the meaning of Rule 55(c) EPC (see

---

[143] *Ibid.*
[144] *Ibid.*
[145] T433/96 *MITSUI* December 10, 1997.
[146] T274/95 *MARS/Re-introduced ground of opposition* O.J. EPO 1997, 99; [1997] E.P.O.R. 34.

Chapter 3 at paragraphs 3–27 *et seq.*) it is a fresh ground of opposition within the definition of that term which is set out in G1, 7/95[147] and in paragraph 4–108 above, and accordingly it should not be raised in appeal proceedings without the agreement of the patentee (T105/94[148]; contrary to T986/93,[149] decided before G1, 7/95[150]).

Lack of novelty based upon prior use which is relied upon in the notice of opposition of a first opponent which is held inadmissible, such prior use not having been considered by the Opposition Division, constitutes a fresh ground for opposition if raised during an appeal by a second opponent (T154/95[151]).

(f) *Filing facts and evidence in an opposition appeal.*   **4–114**

1 General principles. As discussed in paragraph 3–51 facts and evidence should normally be adduced at an early stage in proceedings before the opposition division.

> "Appeal proceedings are normally examined and decided on the basis of facts and evidence filed during the proceedings before the Opposition Division. While the filing of facts and evidence by parties to opposition and opposition appeal proceedings is not precluded at any stage such proceedings, the admissibility of facts and evidence filed at a late stage in such proceedings is always a matter of discretion for the EPO (see Article 114(2) EPC)" (G4/95[152]).

Clearly the exercise of such discretion in opposition appeal proceedings depends on the circumstances of each individual case. Nevertheless certain principles have been expressed in decided cases.

As discussed in paragraph 4–120 below, if new facts and/or evidence are admitted during an opposition appeal, the case may be remitted to the Opposition Division. Furthermore, costs may be awarded against the opponent (paragraph 4–160).

2 Late-filed facts and evidence.   **4–115**

i Relevance. If new facts or evidence are filed during appeal proceedings, the general practice is to examine objectively its relevance and to admit such late-filed facts or evidence if it is considered to be sufficiently relevant that it might affect the outcome of the appeal. On the other hand, if such objective examination reveals that the new material, either on its own or in combination with the facts and evidence already filed, is unlikely to change the outcome of the appeal, the late-filed facts and evidence will be

---

[147] G1, 7/95 *DE LA RUE/ETHICON/Fresh grounds for opposition* O.J. EPO 1996, 615, 626; [1998] E.P.O.R. 601.
[148] T105/94 *MOLNLYCKE* July 29, 1997.
[149] T986/93 *EATON CORPORATION/Central tyre inflation sytem* O.J. EPO 1996, 215; [1996] E.P.O.R. 486.
[150] See note 147.
[151] T154/95 *GUILBERT EXPRESS* January 27, 1998.
[152] G4/95 *BOGASKY II/Representation* O.J. EPO 1996, 412; [1996] E.P.O.R. 333.

rejected as inadmissible on this basis. (T156/84[153]). This practice applies particularly to new documents which are filed in support of grounds of opposition which were properly substantiated in the notice of opposition. However: "The introduction of ... new documents at the appeal stage of opposition proceedings may not be allowable ... depending upon the degree of relevance and the lateness" (T271/84[154]).

In particular: "Written state of the art which is only mentioned and offered for inspection by an opponent after the parties have presented their main submissions during oral proceedings may be regarded by the Board as late-submitted under Article 114(2) EPC and does not need to be added to the file" (T501/96[155]).

The above principles apply to evidence of common general knowledge which "like any other evidence in support of an opponent's case, should be filed at an early stage in the proceedings before the Opposition Division (G4/95[156]), and may be rejected as inadmissible in the Board's discretion if filed for the first time during appeal proceedings" (T85/93[157]).

4–116 *ii New facts and evidence outside the notice of opposition: if "highly relevant".* If late-filed facts and evidence (and recited arguments) go beyond the indication of facts, evidence and arguments presented in the notice of opposition, and therefore go beyond "the legal and factual framework within which the substantive examination of the opposition in principle shall be conducted" (G10/91[158]: paragraph 4–77), they "should only very exceptionally be admitted into the proceedings: if such new material is *prima facie* highly relevant in the sense that it is highly likely to prejudice maintenance of the European patent in suit" (T1002/92[159]).

Beyond such high relevance in such a case, the exercise of discretion "is also subject to broader considerations ... [namely] the avoidance of procedural complications and uncertainty for patentees ... having regard also to the fact that a European patent may subsequently be the subject of revocation proceedings before national courts" (T1002/92[160]).

4–117 *iii Avoidance of complication and delay: experiments/prior events etc.* Late filed evidence which may require considerable investigation and cause consequent delay will normally be rejected as inadmissible, because:

> "The discretionary power ... serves to ensure that proceedings can be concluded swiftly in the interests of the parties, the general public and the EPO, and to forestall tactical abuse. If a party fails to submit the facts, evidence and arguments relevant to their case as early and

---

[153] T156/84 AIR PRODUCTS/*Pressure swing adsorption* O.J. EPO 1988, 372; [1989] E.P.O.R. 47.
[154] T271/84 AIR PRODUCTS/*Removal of hydrogen sulphide and carbonyl sulphide* O.J. EPO 1987, 405; [1987] E.P.O.R. 23.
[155] T501/96 March 3, 2000.
[156] G4/95 BOGASKY II/*Representation* O.J. EPO 1996, 412; [1996] E.P.O.R. 333.
[157] T85/93 PITNEY BOWES/*Apparatus for determining fees* O.J. EPO 1998, 183; [1997] E.P.O.R. 561.
[158] G10/91 *Examination of oppositions/appeals* O.J. EPO 1993, 420; [1993] E.P.O.R. 485.
[159] T1002/92 PETTERSON/*Queueing system* O.J. EPO 1995, 605; [1996] E.P.O.R. 1.
[160] *Ibid.*

completely as possible without adequate excuse, and admitting the same would lead to an excessive delay, the Boards of Appeal are fully justified in refusing to admit them ..." (T951/91[161]).

In the case in question intended experimental evidence was held inadmissible even before it was filed, on the above basis.

It is particularly important that facts and evidence relating to the proof of alleged prior events such as prior use or prior oral disclosure are filed in proper time, so that the patent proprietor can investigate the alleged facts and prepare a reply without delay. The more that time passes, the more difficult it may become to investigate the facts surrounding prior events.

"Anyone who claims a prior public use, merely in passing, after expiry of the opposition period and who fails to provide further details until well into the appeal proceedings must be deemed not to have submitted in due time (Article 114(2) EPC) especially where the prior use is by the appellants themselves" (T93/89[162]).

iv Limits of ex officio *examination: Article 114 EPC.* The obligation **4–118** upon a Board of Appeal under Article 114(1) EPC to "examine the facts of its own motion" is necessarily restricted having regard also to Article 114(2) EPC (The EPO "may disregard facts or evidence which are not submitted in due time by the parties concerned") which "sets the legal limit upon the inquisitorial duties of the Board under Article 114(1) EPC" (T326/87[163]).

For example:

"Under Article 114(1) EPC, when alleged facts which had been put forward without proof as novelty destroying, occurred a long time ago and the question is no longer pursued by the parties, the Board is not obliged to investigate the matter *ex officio*" (T60/89[164]).

Similarly:

The obligation under Article 114(1) EPC "does not extend so far as investigating an allegation of prior public use, where the party who formerly made that allegation has withdrawn from the proceedings, and it is difficult to establish all the relevant facts without his co-operation ... the obligation ... is not unlimited in its scope, but is confined by considerations of reasonableness and expediency" (T129/88[165]).

---

[161] T951/91 *DU PONT/Late submission* O.J. EPO 1995, 202; [1995] E.P.O.R. 398.
[162] T93/89 *HOECHST/Polyvinyl ester dispersion* O.J. EPO 1992, 718; [1992] E.P.O.R. 155.
[163] T326/87 *DU PONT/Polyamide composition* O.J. EPO 1992, 522; [1991] E.P.O.R. 47.
[164] T60/89 *HARVARD/Fusion proteins* O.J. EPO 1992, 268; [1992] E.P.O.R. 320.
[165] T129/88 *AKZO/Fibre* O.J. EPO 1993, 598; [1994] E.P.O.R. 176.

4–119 *v* *Abuse of procedure: "inadmissible regardless of relevance".*

> "An assertion of public use, based on the opponent's own activities and submitted after the expiry of the opposition period and in the absence of good reasons for the delay, represents an abuse of the proceedings and a breach of the principle of good faith which all parties are expected to observe … this kind of assertion … is to be disregarded under Article 114(2) EPC irrespective of its potential relevance" (T17/91[166]).

Similarly:

> "When abuse of procedure is manifest in view of the fact that a party deliberately abstained from raising an issue even when the evidence in its support was available, it would be contrary to the principle of good faith to admit such evidence by applying Article 114(2) EPC in favour of that party" (T534/89[167]).

In such cases, the sanction of an award of costs caused by such late filing is inappropriate and insufficient, even if the late-filed material is highly relevant:

> "Whereas the apportioning of costs between parties may be appropriate in cases of neglect or ignorance, when a late submission is caused by deliberate manipulation, the justification for exercising the discretion under Article 114(2) EPC against a party who wilfully acted contrary to good faith should be considered" (T534/89[168]).

Thus an opponent who is guilty of abuse of procedure should be left to pursue his case against the patent before national courts.

4–120 (g) *Remittal to the Opposition Division.* Under Article 111(1) EPC, following initial examination of an appeal, the Board of Appeal has the power to remit the case to the first instance for further prosecution. There are a number of particular circumstances where this power is exercised, primarily in order to ensure that issues are examined and decided by two instances:

4–121 **1 Following substantial amendment.** When amended claims are filed during an opposition appeal, either with the grounds of appeal or at a later stage, which are intended to replace the claims which were refused by the Opposition Division, the Board of Appeal has to exercise its discretion under Article 111(1) EPC, either to decide upon the allowability of the new claims, or to remit the case to the first instance.

Similar principles apply as with *ex parte* appeals (see paragraph 4–92). Thus minor clarifying amendments clearly do not justify remittal, but

---

[166] T17/91 *GILLETTE/Razor blades* August 26, 1992.
[167] T534/89 *EMS/Inadmissible late filing* O.J. EPO 1994, 464; [1994] E.P.O.R. 540.
[168] *Ibid.*

major substantive amendments which change the claimed subject-matter to a major extent may justify remittal in order to ensure examination by two instances. On the other hand, if such major amendments are filed at a late stage, a Board may prefer not to admit them, rather than to admit them with the inevitable and considerable delay which would result from remittal (T926/93[169]).

2 Following admission of a fresh ground of opposition. If a fresh 4–122 ground for opposition is admitted (see paragraph 4–108) "the case should, having regard to the purpose of the appeal procedure, ... be remitted to the first instance for further prosecution, unless special reasons present themselves for doing otherwise" (G10/91[170]).

3 Following new facts or evidence If new and relevant facts or 4–123 evidence (such as new documents) are introduced into opposition appeal proceedings, Boards of Appeal normally remit the case to the Opposition Division so as to ensure two instances of examination. For example:

> "It is immediately clear ... that the impugned decision of the department of first instance cannot stand. Examination as to patentability needs to be resumed on a new basis and the technical problem to be solved by the invention determined in the light of a new citation. That is primarily the task of the department of first instance.
>
> Were the Board itself to undertake this examination on the new basis and taking into account the state of the art as newly established, this would necessarily have the effect of bypassing one level of jurisdiction, which in turn would be contrary to the principle of equity followed by the Board.
>
> However, thus allowing the introduction of documents submitted after the period for opposition has expired could lead to abuses difficult to control.
>
> The Board accepts that to allow such documents necessarily means considerably lengthening the procedure and that certain limits must be set. In the Board's opinion those limits were not exceeded in the present case, for the reasons given ... since the inconvenience resulting from the lengthened procedure is here offset by the obligation imposed by Article 114(1) EPC on all departments of the EPO to conduct an examination of their own motion" (T273/84[171]).

Similarly: 4–124

> "If a document is sufficiently relevant in this sense to be admitted, then, in the exercise of the Board's discretion under Article 111(1) EPC, the case, together with the document admitted, should normally be referred back to the first instance so as to allow the case to be examined in the light of the new document at two levels of jurisdiction so as not

[169] T926/93 *MITSUBISHI/Gas laser device* O.J. EPO 1997, 447; [1998] E.P.O.R. 94.
[170] G10/91 *Examination of oppositions/appeals* O.J. EPO 1993, 420; [1993] E.P.O.R. 485.
[171] T273/84 *RHÔNE-POULENC/Silico-aluminate* O.J. EPO 1986, 346; [1987] E.P.O.R. 44.

to deprive the patent proprietor of one such level of jurisdiction. Such a procedure is clearly desirable when the Board considers that the newly introduced document is of such relevance that it puts the maintenance of the patent at risk, whilst if this is not the case, then it is open to the Board to deal with the matter itself" (T326/87[172]).

Remittal will be ordered in particular if a fresh case is raised in the appeal, for example, a new allegation of prior use in support of the previously alleged ground of lack of novelty.

"If there is such an entirely fresh case, it may, subject to the other circumstances of the case, be inappropriate for an Appeal Board to deal itself with its allowability. The public's and the parties' interest in having the proceedings speedily concluded may then be overridden by the requirement that appeal proceedings should not become a mere continuation of first instance proceedings" (T611/90[173]).

4–125   Similarly:

"Where fresh evidence, arguments or other matters filed late in the appeal raise a case substantially different from that decided by a first instance, the case should be referred back to the first instance where this is demanded by fairness to the parties" (T97/90[174]).

On the other hand, the normal rule that the case is remitted to the Opposition Division if new and relevant facts or evidence is filed during an appeal may exceptionally not be followed in the absence of any request for remittal or other response whatsoever from the patent proprietor (T258/84[175]).

4–126   **4   For adaptation of the description to amended claims.**   If a Board of Appeal decides to maintain the patent with amended claims in accordance with an auxiliary request, it may decide upon the text of the description itself if this can be done quickly and incontroversially during oral proceedings for example, but if such adaptation is likely to take considerable time, the case is normally remitted to the Opposition Division pursuant to Article 111(1) EPC so that the parties can consider this matter fully, and so that the Opposition Division can control the final text of the amended patent (with the possibility of further appeal on such adaptation).

4–127   **(v) Completion of the written examination stage.** The examination stage under Article 111 EPC in both *ex parte* and *inter partes* appeals is completed when each party has filed observations on communications from the Board of Appeal or other parties (or when the time limit for filing

---

[172] T326/87 *DU PONT/Polyamide compositions* O.J. EPO 1992, 522; [1991] E.P.O.R. 47.
[173] T611/90 *MITSUI/Fresh case* O.J. EPO 1993, 50; [1991] E.P.O.R. 481.
[174] T97/90 *TAKEMOTO YUSHI/Lubricating agents* O.J. EPO 1993, 719; [1993] E.P.O.R. 135.
[175] T258/84 *ÉTAT FRANÇAIS/Portable hyperbar box structure* [1987] E.P.O.R. 154.

such observations has expired). The rapporteur will then consult with the other members of the Board as regards deciding the appeal. If there has been no request for oral proceedings, the written decision may then be drafted. Alternatively, if oral proceedings have been requested, a summons to oral proceedings may be issued (see Chapter 5 at paragraph 5–50).

(c) Withdrawal of an appeal

(i) Introduction.

"In general, an appeal ... can be withdrawn without the consent of the **4–128** Board concerned. Part of an appeal can be withdrawn in a case in which the part in question relates to a specific issue which formed a distinct part of the decision" (J19/92[176]).

An appeal may be withdrawn at any time after it has filed until the appeal proceedings are terminated by the announcement or issue of a decision. However, the appeal fee cannot be refunded.

As discussed in paragraph 4–72 above, the principle of "party disposition" applies to appeal proceedings. According to this principle, "a public authority or a court normally may not continue proceedings if the procedural act which gave rise to the proceedings (such as the filing of an appeal) has been retracted, unless procedural law specifically permits continuation". (G7, 8/91[177]). Examples of such specific exceptions in the EPC are the prohibition on withdrawal of a request for examination under Article 94(2) EPC and the consequences of withdrawing an opposition which are set out in Rule 60(2) EPC.

Consequently, in application of this principle to withdrawal of an appeal, the effect of such a withdrawal is that:

"Insofar as the substantive issues settled by the contested decision at first instance are concerned, appeal proceedings are terminated, in *ex parte* and *inter partes* proceedings alike, when the sole appellant withdraws the appeal" (G7, 8/91[178]).

Thus upon withdrawal of an appeal by the sole appellant, whether **4–129** patent proprietor or opponent, the appeal proceedings are immediately and automatically terminated so far as the substantive issues are concerned. The suspensive effect of the appeal which is provided by Article 106(1) EPC is also automatically terminated, with the result that the substantive decision of the first instance department which was the subject of the appeal becomes immediately and automatically effective and final.

Consequently, it is obviously of great importance that an appellant

[176] J19/92 *TORAY/Partial withdrawal of appeal* O.J. EPO 1984, 6.
[177] G7, 8/91 *BASF/BELL/Withdrawal of appeal* O.J. EPO 1993, 346, 356; [1993] E.P.O.R. 440, 445.
[178] *Ibid.*

should only withdraw his appeal if that is what he really wants. Once withdrawn, an appeal cannot be reinstated.

The application of the principle of party disposition to the withdrawal of an appeal in accordance with G7, 8/91[179] is consistent with the previous practice of the Boards of Appeal.

4-130   In this connection, although Rule 60(2) EPC allows the EPO to continue opposition proceedings after withdrawal of an opposition, this provision in conjunction with Rule 66(1) EPC does not provide an exception to the principle of party disposition, in view of the different legal natures of opposition and opposition appeal proceedings:

> "whereas the opposition procedure is a purely administrative procedure, the appeal procedure must be regarded as a procedure proper to an administrative court, in which an exception from general procedural principles, such as the principle of party disposition, has to be supported by much weightier grounds than in administrative procedure" (G7, 8/91[180]).

Similarly, the concept of protection of the public interest does not justify an exception to the party disposition principle:

> "In the European patent system, the public interest is primarily safeguarded by the fact that within nine months from ... grant ..., any person may give notice of opposition to the patent. In principle, therefore it must be assumed that the patent does not disturb those who have not filed opposition. It is therefore at variance with the thinking on which the European patent system is based to continue the appeal proceedings where the appeal ... has been withdrawn merely in order to safeguard the interests of those who filed no opposition at all" (G7, 8/91[181]).

The effects and practical consequences of withdrawal of an appeal in various circumstances are considered below.

4-131   **(ii) Withdrawal of an *ex parte* appeal.** Withdrawal of an appeal by an applicant/appellant immediately and automatically removes the suspensive effect of the appeal, (Article 106(1) EPC see paragraph 4–49 above) and the decision of the first instance department becomes immediately effective and final (for example, a decision of an Examining Division to refuse an application becomes final and cannot thereafter be changed).

4-132   **(iii) *Inter partes* appeal: withdrawal by the sole appellant.** Withdrawal of an appeal by a sole appellant, whether patent proprietor or opponent, immediately and automatically terminates the appeal and removes its

[179] *Ibid.*
[180] G7, 8/91 *BASF/BELL/Withdrawal of appeal* O.J. EPO 1993, 346, 356; [1993] E.P.O.R. 440, 445.
[181] *Ibid.*

suspensive effect, so that the substantive decision of the Opposition Division which is the subject of the appeal becomes immediately effective and final and cannot be changed. This applies whatever the stage of the appeal when it is withdrawn.

Consequently, if the sole appellant withdraws his appeal by a document (*e.g.* a facsimile) filed at a particular time on a particular day, a notice of intervention (see paragraphs 4–141 *et seq.* below) which is filed later on the same day is inadmissible.[182]

For example, if the patent proprietor has requested an amended claim as his main request in the appeal, to replace the text of the claim as maintained by the Opposition Division, and the sole appellant/opponent subsequently withdraws the appeal, the proprietor can no longer pursue his main request in the appeal, and the patent will immediately be maintained with text in accordance with the decision of the Opposition Division. From the moment that the appeal is withdrawn, "the Board of Appeal has no power to consider the patent within the meaning of Article 113(2)EPC. The terms of that provision as regards obtaining the patent proprietors' agreement to the text of the patent therefore do not apply" (G7, 8/91[183]).

In general terms:

"Insofar as the substantive issues settled by the contested decision at first instance are concerned, a Board of Appeal may not continue opposition appeal proceedings after the sole appellant who was the opponent in the first instance has withdrawn his appeal" (G7, 8/91[184]).

(iv) *Inter partes* appeal: withdrawal by one of multiple appellants. 4–133
Withdrawal of an appeal by one of multiple appellants restricts the extent of the appeal proceedings to examining the issues raised by the appeal requests of the remaining appellant(s). An appellant who withdraws his appeal remains a party as of right under Article 107 EPC.

(v) Withdrawal of an opposition during appeal proceedings. 4–134
(a) *By an opponent/appellant.* If an opponent/appellant states during appeal proceedings that he withdraws his opposition, this is treated as equivalent to withdrawal of his appeal (G8/93[185]).

(b) *By an opponent/appellant who is one of multiple appellants.* If the 4–135 opponent/appellant in question is one of multiple appellants, the effect of withdrawal of the opposition is as set out in (iv) above; that is, a corresponding restriction upon the extent of the appeal.

(c) *By an opponent/sole appellant.* However, if the opponent/appellant in 4–136 question is the sole appellant, the effect of such a withdrawal is as set out in (iii) above. Consequently:

---

[182] T517/97 *UNILEVER/Intervention* O.J. EPO 2000, 515.
[183] G7, 8/91 *BASF/BELL/Withdrawal of appeal* O.J. EPO 1993, 346, 356; [1993] E.P.O.R. 440, 445.
[184] *Ibid.*
[185] G8/93 *SERWANE II/Withdrawal of opposition in appeal* O.J. EPO 1994, 887; [1995] E.P.O.R. 271.

"The filing by an opponent, who is sole appellant, of a statement withdrawing his opposition immediately and automatically terminates the appeal proceedings, irrespective of whether the patent proprietor agrees to termination of those proceedings, and even if in the Board of Appeal's view the requirements under the EPC for maintaining the patent are not satisfied" (G8/93[186]).

4–137   (d) *By an opponent/respondent.* If an opponent who is a respondent to the appeal proceedings states that his opposition is withdrawn, this has no immediate effect on the appeal, because the existence and extent of the appeal depends upon the "appeal request" of the appellant, which is unaffected by such withdrawal.

Thus:

"Whereas under Rule 60(2) EPC opposition proceedings may be continued at the discretion of the EPO where the opposition is withdrawn, withdrawal of the opposition in appeal proceedings has no immediate significance if the Opposition Division has revoked the European patent. The Board of Appeal must then re-examine the substance of the Opposition Division's decision of its own motion ... evidence may be cited which has been submitted by an opponent before the opposition was withdrawn" (T629/90[187]).

The same clearly applies if the Opposition Division has maintained the patent in accordance with an auxiliary request and contrary to the main request of the proprietor/appellant.

4–138   **(vi) Further decision on outstanding procedural matters.** As explained in paragraph (i) above (paragraph 4–129), in the event of withdrawal of an appeal by a sole appellant, the substantive issues raised by the appeal may no longer be considered. However, any outstanding ancillary procedural issues may still be examined and decided in the appeal proceedings, which therefore remain in existence until any such outstanding issues are decided.

For example, in a number of cases outstanding requests for an apportionment of costs under Article 104 EPC have been decided after withdrawal of a sole appeal (*e.g.* T117/86,[188] T323/89[189]). Similarly, requests for reimbursement of the appeal fee under Rule 67 EPC have been decided (J12/86,[190] T41/82[191]).

If a sole appeal is withdrawn after a notice of intervention has been filed under Article 105 EPC, the admissibility of the notice of intervention has still to be determined (T195/93[192]). If the notice of intervention is

---

[186] *Ibid.*
[187] T629/90 *SEDLBAUER/Holding device* O.J. EPO 1992, 654; [1993] E.P.O.R. 147.
[188] T117/86 *FILMTEC/Costs* O.J. EPO 1989, 401; [1989] E.P.O.R. 504.
[189] T323/89 *KONISHIROKU/Photographic material* O.J. EPO 1992, 169; [1992] E.P.O.R. 210.
[190] J12/86 *LINVILLE/Refund of appeal fees* O.J. EPO 1988, 83 (Headnote).
[191] T41/82 *SANDOZ/Reimbursement of appeal fee* O.J. EPO 1982, 256; [1979–85] E.P.O.R.: B: 446.
[192] T195/93 May 4, 1995.

admissible, the issues raised by such notice have to be examined and decided.

(vii) Determination of an appellant's right to withdraw.

"If the sole appellant declares the appeal withdrawn, the Board of **4–139** Appeal may decide ... whether the appeal has been validly withdrawn or whether the appeal proceedings should not continue on the grounds that the status of opponent in the opposition appeal proceedings, and thus entitlement to withdraw an appeal, had passed to a third party before the appeal was withdrawn" (T659/92[193]).

(viii) Determination of the meaning and extent of a request to withdraw. It has been emphasised in paragraph 4–129 above that an appeal should only be withdrawn if that is definitely intended, because a withdrawal may not subsequently be retracted.

In a case where an appellant in an examination appeal had appealed against a decision of the Examining Division to refuse amendments filed after a Rule 51(4) EPC communication had been issued (see paragraph 2–67), the appellant stated that the appeal was withdrawn and requested grant of a patent in accordance with such Rule 51(4) EPC communication. This statement was interpreted as withdrawal of that part of the appeal concerned with the requested amendments, but not of the appeal as such (T1073/92[194]).

(d) Accelerated processing of an appeal

Depending upon the circumstances of a case, a Board of Appeal has a **4–140** discretion to examine a particular appeal out of turn and thus to accelerate the processing of and decision in respect of that appeal.

A Notice dated May 19, 1998[195] concerning accelerated processing before the Boards of Appeal provides that the Boards of Appeal "can speed up an appeal as far as the procedural regulations allow", either in response to a request from a party or *ex officio* (by way of exception). "Whether or not a particular case is regarded as urgent will depend on the nature of the case and not merely on whether accelerated processing is requested by the parties".

A request for accelerated processing "should contain reasons for the urgency together with relevant documents; no particular form is required".

Examples of circumstances which "could justify an appeal being dealt with particularly rapidly" are set out in the Notice[196]:

  (i) infringement proceedings brought or envisaged;
  (ii) a licensing decision hinges on the outcome of the appeal;

---

[193] T659/92 SCHWEISFURTH/Transfer of opposition O.J. EPO 1995, 519; [1996] E.P.O.R. 314.
[194] T1073/92 ALZA/Withdrawal of appeal, February 11, 1993.
[195] Notice from the Vice-President DG3 dated May 19, 1998 concerning accelerated processing before the Boards of Appeal. O.J. EPO 1998, 362; reproduced in full at Appendix 13 below.
[196] Ibid.

(iii) the opposition the subject of the appeal received accelerated processing in the first instance proceedings (see Chapter 3 at paragraph 3–06).

It is obviously essential that a party desiring accelerated processing should provide appropriate information to the EPO to support his request.

(4) Intervention during an opposition appeal

4–141 The procedure in relation to intervention by an assumed infringer in proceedings before an Opposition Division is considered in Chapter 3 at paragraphs 3–64 *et seq*. An assumed infringer may intervene in opposition appeal proceedings:

"Intervention of the assumed infringer under Article 105 EPC is admissible during pending appeal proceedings and may be based on any ground for opposition under Article 100 EPC" (G1/94[197]).

Consequently, provided that opposition appeal proceedings are in existence and pending before a Board of Appeal, an assumed infringer may intervene during such proceedings by filing a notice of intervention in a "written reasoned statement" and paying an opposition fee, in accordance with Article 105(2) EPC. Thereafter, as with a notice of intervention which is filed during proceedings before an Opposition Division, the intervention shall be treated as an opposition (except that the requirements of Rule 57(1) to (3) may be dispensed with (Rule 57(4) EPC)).

4–142   If the sole appellant withdraws his appeal, a notice of intervention which is filed later in the same day as the appeal was withdrawn is inadmissible, because the appeal proceedings are no longer in existence (T517/97[198]; see also paragraph 4–132 above). Different views have been expressed as to whether an intervener in an opposition appeal must also pay an appeal fee (T27/92,[199] T1011/92[200]). However, it would seem that an intervener in an opposition appeal is not "adversely affected by the decision of the Opposition Division within the meaning of Article 107 EPC, and accordingly has neither a right nor an obligation to pay an appeal fee at the time that he files a notice of intervention" (T144/95[201]).

The procedure relating to intervention during an opposition appeal has not yet been clearly established. However, since an admissible intervention is to be treated as an opposition, it would seem that the issues raised in the notice of intervention, in particular the grounds of opposition, must first be decided by an Opposition Division (whether or not the provisions of Rule 57(1) to (3) EPC are dispensed with).

[197] G1/94 *ALLIED COLLOIDS/Intervention* O.J. EPO 1994, 787; [1994] E.P.O.R. 491.
[198] T517/97 *UNILEVER/Intervention* O.J. EPO 2000, 515.
[199] T27/92 *KA-TE SYSTEMS/Intervention* O.J. EPO 1994, 853; [1994] E.P.O.R. 501.
[200] T1011/92 *VON KÜNSSBERG* September 16, 1994.
[201] T144/95 *UNILEVER/Dishwashing process* February 28, 1999.

In so far as there may be overlap between the grounds of opposition **4–143** which are the subject of the appeal proceedings and the grounds of opposition which are substantiated in the notice of intervention, it would then be appropriate to stay the appeal proceedings until the Opposition Division has decided upon the grounds raised in the intervention. In this connection the possibility of dispensing with the application of Rule 57(1) to (3) EPC which is envisaged in Rule 57(4) EPC would appear to be designed to enable the Opposition Division to issue a decision upon the notice of intervention quickly.

The separate nature of the existing opposition appeal proceedings and the later intervention proceedings means that if, following the filing of a notice of intervention the earlier opposition appeal is withdrawn, the intervention proceedings remain pending (T195/93[202]).

(5) The Decision

(a) Making the decision

In accordance with Article 21 EPC, the composition of every Board of **4–144** Appeal is always an odd number. Articles 13 and 14 RPBA provide that when necessary, namely if the members of a Board are not all of the same opinion, decisions on issues in a case are taken by majority vote.

Deliberations within a Board are secret, and normally only the members of the Board therefore participate. The Chairman of a Board "may authorise other officers to attend," but in practice this is limited to the authorisation of an assistant to a particular Board to participate in such deliberations.

The order of voting is regulated by Article 14(2) RPBA, in particular the rapporteur (see paragraph 4–80 above) votes first, and the Chairman votes last (even if he is also the rapporteur). Abstentions are not permitted.

These provisions make it clear that so far as the making of a decision in a case is concerned, the vote of a Chairman of a Board has the same weight as the other members, although it may clearly be the decisive vote as it is made last. In this respect, the Chairman is *"primus inter pares."* This follows also from Article 23(3) EPC: "In their decisions the members of the Boards shall not be bound by any instructions and shall comply only with the provisions of the EPC."

(b) Issuing the decision

(i) Timing. The appeal procedure is terminated by the issue of the **4–145** decision on the case. In the event of oral proceedings, "the decision may be given orally," in which case "subsequently, the decision in writing shall be notified to the parties" (Rule 68(1) EPC).

In practice, at the conclusion of oral proceedings normally only the bare decision on the issues is announced, corresponding to the "order" in the

---

[202] T195/93 May 4, 1995.

written decision, and formal minutes of the oral proceedings, which include a statement of such decision or order, are signed by the Chairman and the registrar of the Board in accordance with Rule 76(3) EPC and sent immediately to the parties. The reasons for the decision are sent later in writing.

In practice, the minutes of oral proceedings before a Board of Appeal are minimal with respect to the requirements of Rule 76(1) EPC and in comparison with the minutes of oral proceedings before first instance departments. However, a full summary of "the essentials of the oral proceedings", including the submissions of the parties, is always set out in the written decision. As previously mentioned, in accordance with Article 11(3) RPBA the policy is that the procedure should lead to a situation in which the case is ready for decision at the conclusion of oral proceedings. Thus, in the majority of appeals the result is announced orally. However, in appropriate cases a Board may reserve its decision.

In accordance with general principles, at the oral proceeding each party has ample opportunity to present arguments intended to influence the Board one way or the other, and to watch the effect of such arguments, in public. In all normal circumstances the natural point in time for the Board to make up its mind about the case is at the conclusion of the oral proceedings, when the submissions made and the exchange of ideas with the Board of Appeal are still fresh in the mind. Whether or not oral proceedings have taken place, the written decision is drafted by the rapporteur, agreed with the other members of the Board and issued to each party. Every written decision must be in accordance with all the formal and substantive requirements of Rule 66(2) EPC.

4–146 **(ii) Maintenance with amended text—special considerations.** In an opposition appeal, if the final decision of the Board of Appeal is to maintain the patent in an amended text, in the absence of oral proceedings the parties are informed in writing of the intention to maintain the patent in amended form and are given an opportunity to comment (*cf.* Rule 58(4) EPC in conjunction with Rule 66(1) EPC; T219/83[203]).

On the other hand, if oral proceedings are held, the parties normally have an adequate opportunity to comment upon a proposal to amend. "Rule 58(4) EPC is intended to ensure that due account is taken in opposition proceedings of the principles of due process set out in article 113(1) EPC" (T219/83[204]). Consequently:

> "it has to be considered in each individual case whether or not the parties ought to be informed in accordance with Rule 58(4) EPC" (T219/83[205]).

Similarly:

---

[203] T219/83 *BASF/Zeolites* O.J. EPO 1986, 211; [1986] E.P.O.R. 247.
[204] *Ibid.*
[205] *Ibid.*

"After oral proceedings in connection with an opposition, the parties must be sent a communication pursuant to Rule 58(4) EPC only if they cannot reasonably be expected to state their observations concerning the maintenance of the European patent in the amended form definitively during the oral proceedings" (T185/84[206]).

This is now the normal practice of the Boards of Appeal in such circumstances. A written communication under Rule 58(4) EPC after oral proceedings is normally dispensed with.

(c) Form of the written decision

The form of a written Board of Appeal decision is governed by Rule 66(2) **4–147** EPC. In practice the substance of the decision consists of a first section entitled "Summary of facts and submissions", a second section entitled "Reasons for the decision", and an "Order" at the end which sets out the decision upon each of the issues which were raised by the appeal.

The composition of the Board of Appeal responsible for a decision is set out on the title page, with the chairman first and the rapporteur second.

In practice the Legal Board of Appeal and all Technical Boards of Appeal always issue a single decision on behalf of the Board as a whole, whether or not the voting is in fact unanimous. No dissenting opinions are ever issued, and it is therefore not possible to ascertain whether or not all the members of a particular Board were in favour of a decision issued on its behalf (but compare the Enlarged Board of Appeal—see paragraphs 4–196 *et seq.* below).

(d) Binding nature of a decision following remittal

Article 111(2) EPC states: **4–148**

"If the Board of Appeal remits the case for further prosecution to the department whose decision was appealed, that department shall be bound by the *ratio decidendi* of the Board of Appeal, insofar as the facts are the same".

(i) Examination appeals. Consequently, for example, if a Board of **4–149** Appeal in an examination appeal refuses claims in accordance with the main request, and remits the case for further prosecution on the basis of an auxiliary request, the Examining Division has no power to examine the main request. If the auxiliary request is held to be allowable, the Examining Division is bound to issue a Rule 51(4) EPC communication on the basis of such text (T79/89[207]).

In such a case, "the legal effect of Article 111 EPC is that examination of the allowability of the rejected claim subject-matter cannot thereafter be re-opened either by the Examining Division during its further examination

---

[206] T185/84 *BASF/Paint line supply system* O.J. EPO 1986, 373; [1987] E.P.O.R. 34.
[207] T79/89 *XEROX/Finality of decision* O.J. EPO 1992, 283; [1990] E.P.O.R. 558.

of the case, or by the Board of Appeal in any subsequent appeal proceedings" (T79/89[208]).

In any further such appeal "the Board of Appeal necessarily has no power to re-open examination in respect of such claims, because it can only exercise any power which is within the competence of the Examining Division (Article 111(1) EPC)" (T79/89[209]).

A decision by a Board of Appeal on an issue which arises in an examination appeal (for example, the priority date of application) is *res judicata* in such examination proceedings and cannot thereafter be reconsidered in any subsequent appeal in such examination proceedings concerning the application (T934/91[210]; T690/91[211]).

4–150   **(ii) Opposition appeals.** If, for example the Board of Appeal in an opposition appeal orders that "the case should be remitted to the Opposition Division with the order to maintain the patent on the basis of the ... main request", in order that the Opposition Division should control the adaptation of the text of the description to the allowed claims, such a decision is "binding in the sense that neither the wording nor the patentability of these claims may be further challenged in subsequent proceedings before the EPO. A finding of fact upon which this decision rests, *i.e.* a finding which is *conditio sine qua non* for the decision, is equally binding ... [and] not open to reconsideration pursuant to Article 111(2) EPC" (T843/91[212]).

This interpretation of Article 111(2) EPC follows from "the general principle of legal certainty, *i.e.* the general interest of the public in the termination of legal disputes (*"interest reipublicae ut finis sit litium"*) as well as the right of the individual to be protected from the vexatious multiplication of suits and prosecutions" (T843/91).

4–151   Thus in such a case, the only issue that can be decided by the Opposition Division following remittal by the Board of Appeal is the outstanding issue of adaptation of the description to the amended claims which were allowed by the Board of Appeal. Similarly, that is the only issue which can be examined and decided by a Board of Appeal in any subsequent appeal from the decision of the Opposition Division upon such adaptation of the description (T757/91,[213] T843/91[214]).

Any decision of a Board of Appeal in an opposition appeal upon an issue which is raised in such an appeal is *res judicata* and final. Such a decision cannot thereafter be challenged in the same EPO proceedings.

For example, a decision by a Board of Appeal to apportion or fix costs between the parties (see paragraphs 4–156 *et seq.* below) cannot thereafter

---

[208] *Ibid.*
[209] *Ibid.*
[210] T934/91 *KONICA/Meaning of decision* O.J. EPO 1994, 184; [1993] E.P.O.R. 219.
[211] T690/91 *CELLTECH/Chymosin* January 10, 1996.
[212] T843/91 *EASTMAN KODAK COMPANY/Photographic elements* (1) O.J. EPO 1994, 818 [1995] E.P.O.R. 116.
[213] T757/91 *ESB/Second appeal* [1995] E.P.O.R. 595.
[214] See note 212.

be challenged in subsequent proceedings before the Opposition Division (T934/91[215]).

(e) An examination appeal decision is not res judicata *in subsequent opposition proceedings*

> "A decision of a Board of Appeal on appeal from an Examining **4–152** Division has no binding effect in subsequent opposition proceedings or an appeal therefrom, having regard both to the EPC and *'res judicata'* principle(s)" (T167/93[216]).

This follows because one or more opponents are parties to the subsequent opposition and opposition appeal proceedings but were not parties to the earlier examination appeal proceedings. Furthermore the EPC provides an examination stage (Article 96 and 97 EPC) and an opposition stage (Articles 99 to 102 EPC). These provisions in conjunction with Article 113(1) EPC "preclude any implicit public policy preventing a matter being considered a second time in judicial proceedings, that is *estoppel per rem judicatum* from being applicable" (T167/93[217]).

The principle of *res judicata,* as generally recognised in the Contracting States, applies to a finding which has been:

> "(a) judicially determined;
> (b) in a final manner;
> (c) by a tribunal of competent jurisdiction;
> (d) where the issues of fact are the same;
> (e) the parties (or their successors in title) are the same; and
> (f) the legal capacities of the parties are the same" (T167/93[218]).

Furthermore, Article 111(1) EPC set out a very narrow binding effect of a Board of Appeal decision, and there is nothing in the EPC to suggest that the principle of *res judicata* should apply in such a situation, where the parties are not the same.

Furthermore, no possibility of an appeal from a decision of a Board of **4–153** Appeal is provided by the EPC (although points decided by the Boards of Appeal may subsequently be referred to the Enlarged Boards of Appeal for opinion or decision). In particular, there is no provision for any further appeal to a court outside the EPO.

This is the case even though a Board of Appeal has a discretionary power under Article 111(1) EPC effectively to act as the only instance in some cases. As already stated, Article 111(1) EPC provides that a Board of Appeal has a discretion during appeal proceedings before it to "exercise any power within the competence of [a first instance department]."

[215] T934/91 *KONICA/Meaning of decision* O.J. EPO 1994, 184; [1993] E.P.O.R. 219.
[216] T167/93 *PROCTER AND GAMBLE/Bleaching agents* O.J. EPO 1997, 229; [1997] E.P.O.R. 471.
[217] *Ibid.*
[218] *Ibid.*

"even when a request is made before a Board of Appeal whose subject-matter does not correspond to any request made before and decided upon by the first instance, a Board of Appeal has the power to act as the first and only instance in deciding upon such a request, without the possibility of further appellate review" (T79/89[219]).

(f) Finality of a decision

4–154   **(i) No subsequent review possible.** Once a decision has been issued by a Board of Appeal—whether orally or in writing—it is final and cannot be cancelled or changed (except under Rule 89 EPC "Correction of errors in decisions"—see Chapter 5 at paragraph 5–80). The EPC does not provide any possibility for review of a Board of Appeal decision.

This is also the case even if a decision which is issued by a Board of Appeal involves a substantial procedural violation: for example if a party's right to a fair hearing has been contravened (see Chapter 1 at paragraph 1–78)

Consequently, any attempt by a party to appeal proceedings to have a decision issued by a Board of Appeal set aside or otherwise reviewed, by application either within the Boards of Appeal or otherwise within the EPO generally (for example by application to the President of the EPO) is regarded as an inadmissible request (G1/97[220]).

"In the context of the European Convention, the jurisdictional measure to be taken in response to requests based on the alleged violation of a fundamental procedural principle and aimed at the revision of a decision taken by a Board of Appeal with the force of *res judicata* should be the refusal of the request as inadmissible.

The decision concerning inadmissibility is to be issued by the Board of Appeal which took the decision forming the subject of the request for revision. The decision may be issued immediately and without further procedural formalities" (G1/97[221]).

Similarly such a decision is not subject to the supervising jurisdiction of the national courts of the Contracting States (see, *e.g. Lenzing*[222] and a Judgment of the Bavarian Administration Court, Munich[223]).

4–154A   Nevertheless, in a case where a substantial and fundamental procedural violation has occurred during appeal proceedings, it is clearly desirable that a decision whose validity is undermined by such violation should be reviewed, and if necessary set aside.

According to the proposed revision of the EPC, a further function and responsibility will be given to the Enlarged Board of Appeal, namely:

---

[219] T79/89 *XEROX/Finality of decision* O.J. EPO 1992, 283; [1990] E.P.O.R. 558.
[220] G1/97 *ETA/Request with a view to judgment revision* O.J. EPO 2000, 322.
[221] *Ibid.*
[222] *Lenzing AG's European Patent (U.K.)* [1997] R.P.C. 245.
[223] Judgment of the Bavarian Administrative Court, Munich, July 8, 1999; O.J. EPO 2000, 205.

Article 22(c) EPC: "deciding on petitions for review of decisions of the Board of Appeal under Article 112a EPC".

Such a petition will be governed by a new Article 112a EPC (see paragraph 4–201A).

(ii) No estoppel in relation to challenging validity in a national court. 4–155
As previously stated, if a European patent is revoked during proceedings before a Board of Appeal, such patent is regarded as never having been in force; and no challenge to the decision of the Board of Appeal is possible. In other words, if a European patent is revoked, "the revocation works for all designated States—a central 'knock-out' system" (*Lenzing*[224]).

However, if following opposition or opposition appeal proceedings the European patent is maintained, no cause of action estoppel arises, because the decision to maintain the patent is not "a final and conclusive decision as to the validity of the patent". Validity in such a case is "finally decided in revocation proceedings by the courts of the Contracting States" Furthermore:

"The court [in a Contracting State] could revoke a European patent (U.K.) on the same grounds that had been raised in an opposition in the EPO. Conclusions in the opposition were not binding upon the parties in revocation proceedings" (*Buehler AG. v. Chronos Richardson Ltd*[225]: see also "Zahnkranzfräser"[226]).

(g) Costs in opposition appeals

The general principle with respect to costs, before both the Opposition 4–156
Division and the Boards of Appeal, is set out in Article 104(1) EPC as follows:

"Each party to the proceedings shall meet the costs he has incurred … unless a decision of an Opposition Division or Board of Appeal, for reasons of equity, orders … a different apportionment of costs incurred
[i] during taking of evidence
[ii] or in oral proceedings."

(i) "During taking of evidence". 4–157
The phrase "taking of evidence" in Article 104(1) EPC "refers generally to the receiving of evidence during opposition proceedings", whatever the form of such evidence (T117/86[227]). Thus the phrase is not limited in this context to the taking of "oral evidence of parties, witnesses or experts" or

---

[224] See note 222.
[225] [1998] R.P.C. 609.
[226] *BGH Case No. XZR* 29/93; G.R.U.R. 757, 759.
[227] T117/86 *FILMTEC/Costs* O.J. EPO 1989, 40; [1989] E.P.O.R. 504.

carrying out an inspection, in accordance with the procedure set out in Rule 72 EPC.

> "The term 'taking of evidence' is used in two ways in the EPC. Sometimes it denotes the procedure following an EPO decision pursuant to Rule 72 EPC on the need to hear parties, witnesses or experts to carry out an inspection. This is not the sense of the term 'taking of evidence' as used in Article 104(1) EPC, in which it refers to any of the means of giving or obtaining evidence set out in Article 117(1). EPC" (T323/89[228]).

4–158   **(ii) "In oral proceedings".**
The phrase "in oral proceedings" has been interpreted broadly, so as to cover costs incurred in or relating to the attendance of oral proceedings, Thus, parties may be awarded their costs incurred "as a result of" the oral proceedings (*e.g.* T10/82[229]). In appropriate cases, however, an award of costs could of course be more limited in scope.

4–159   **(iii) "For reasons of equity".**
Awards of costs under each of the above headings can only be made "for reasons of equity":

4–160   (a) *During taking of evidence:*
Thus "costs should be awarded if a party to proceedings can be held to have caused unnecessary expense that could well have been avoided with normal care" (T323/89[230]). In cases in which an award has been made in respect of costs incurred during taking of evidence, the late filing of facts and evidence by an opponent has normally been the basis of the award.

> "Irrespective of whether or not facts or evidence which are presented after expiry of the nine-month period are admitted into the proceedings, such late-filed material may clearly cause the incurring of additional costs by another party, which would not have been incurred if such material had been presented within the nine-month period. Such late-filed facts or evidence may, therefore, justify an order for apportionment of costs" (T117/86[231]).

4–161   (b) *In oral proceedings:*
(1) If a party is summoned to oral proceedings, but fails to attend without giving notice to opposing parties or the Board of Appeal, costs against that party may be awarded with respect to any unnecessary costs incurred as a result of the failure to attend (*e.g.* T338/90,[232] T930/92[233]).

> "There is an equitable obligation upon every party who is summoned

---

[228] T323/89 *KONISHIROKU/Photographic material* O.J. EPO 1992, 169; [1992] E.P.O.R. 210.
[229] T10/82 *BAYER/Admissibility of opposition* O.J. EPO 1983, 407; [1979–85] E.P.O.R.: B: 381.
[230] See note 228.
[231] T117/86 *FILMTEC/Costs* O.J. EPO 1989, 40; [1989] E.P.O.R. 504.
[232] T338/90 *DOW* October 21, 1993.
[233] T930/92 *HITACHI/Ion beam processing* O.J. EPO 1996, 191; [1997] E.P.O.R. 20.

to oral proceedings to inform the EPO as soon as it knows that it will not attend as summoned. This is the case whether or not that party has itself requested oral proceedings, and whether or not a communication has accompanied the summons to oral proceedings" (T930/92[234]).

Furthermore:

"If a party who has been summoned to oral proceedings fails to attend as summoned without notifying the EPO in advance that it will not attend, an appointment of costs in favour of another party who has attended as summoned may be justified for reasons of equity in accordance with Article 104(1) EPC" (T930/92[235]).

For example, if both parties have requested oral proceedings and one fails to attend such proceedings without notification to the EPO or at all, the costs of the other party attending the oral proceedings may be awarded against the party who failed to attend, if the oral proceedings were unnecessary in the absence of such party (T338/90[236], T930/92[237]).

(2) Furthermore, the late filing of new facts or evidence in support of an **4–162** opposition which causes additional costs in oral proceedings, may justify an award of costs:

"an opponent who cites new prior art with a considerable delay ... with no special reason justifying the delay, runs the risk of having to bear some or all of the proprietor's costs incurred in attending oral proceedings which cannot bring the case to an end because of the new citation" (T867/92[238]).

Similarly:

"If a party to proceedings communicates to the Board shortly before the oral proceedings facts that are significant to its decision and which would have rendered oral proceedings unnecessary, it may be equitable to require him to pay the costs incurred by the other party as a result of the oral proceedings" (T10/82[239]).

However, consideration of the strength of an appeal:

"could never be a reason for ordering a different apportionment of

---

[234] *Ibid.*
[235] *Ibid.*
[236] See note 232.
[237] See note 233.
[238] T867/92 *KONICA/Late citation* O.J. EPO 1995, 126; [1995] E.P.O.R. 683.
[239] T10/82 *BAYER/Admissibility of opposition* O.J. EPO 1983, 407; [1979–85] E.P.O.R.: B: 381.

costs ... This is because Article 116(1) EPC guarantees the right of any party to request oral proceedings *i.e.* to argue his case orally before the relevant instance of the EPO. It may be that a party feels that he can present his case better orally than in writing, even if he has no new arguments" (T383/87[240]).

4–163   (iv) Requesting costs.

A request for costs should normally be made in writing.

If made at an oral hearing, the request should be made as part of a party's submissions:

> "The practice before the Boards of Appeal is that all requests by parties, including any requests as to costs, should be made before any decision is announced in oral proceedings. In this connection, it is relevant that an apportionment of costs under Article 104 EPC is not dependent upon the result of a case as announced in the decision, but depends upon 'reasons of equity'. This is in contrast to proceedings in the United Kingdom, for example, where costs commonly follow the result of the decision" (T212/88[241]).

4–164   (v) Fixing the costs.

The Boards of Appeal have the power to apportion and also to fix costs: "Article 104(1) and (3) and 111(1) EPC, having due regard to Article 113(1) EPC." In other words, "the Boards of Appeal are competent to fix the quantum of costs, either in a specific amount, or in terms of a specific fraction of the costs" (T934/91[242]).

> "Under Rule 63(1) EPC apportionment of costs must be dealt with in the decision. This may be done by awarding all the additional costs or a fraction thereof against the party ... who caused them" (T323/89[243]; T117/86[244]). If a fixed amount is set, "this has the advantage of dispensing with the need for the costs to be established pursuant to Rule 63(2) EPC" (T323/89[245]).

4–165 The procedure for fixing the amount of an award of costs, in accordance with the credibility of the evidence adduced, is set out in Rule 63 EPC.

In particular: "such apportionment shall only take into consideration the expenses necessary to assure proper protection of the rights involved" (Rule 63(1) EPC).

Consequently, in addition to the remuneration of the professional representative of that party, the expenses incurred by an employee of that party in order to instruct the professional representative before and during

---

[240] T383/87 *MOBIL OIL/Thermoplastic film* April 26, 1989.
[241] T212/88 *BP/Theta-1* O.J. EPO 1992, 28; [1990] E.P.O.R. 518.
[242] T934/91 *KONICA/Meaning of decision* O.J. EPO 1994, 184; [1993] E.P.O.R. 219.
[243] T323/89 *KONISHIROKU/Photographic material* O.J. EPO 1992, 169; [1992] E.P.O.R. 210.
[244] T117/86 *FILMTEC/Costs* O.J. EPO 1989, 40; [1989] E.P.O.R. 504.
[245] See note 243.

oral proceedings may be taken into consideration under Rule 63(1) EPC if such instruction was "necessary to assure proper protection of the rights involved" (T930/92[246]).

(h) Refund of an appeal fee: substantial procedural violation

(i) Introduction. 4–166

As mentioned in paragraphs 4–64 above, the appeal fee may be refunded in the event of interlocutory revision under Article 109 EPC, in accordance with Rule 67 EPC. Rule 67 EPC also provides for reimbursement of the appeal fee if:

(1) the appeal is allowable; and
(2) reimbursement "is equitable by reason of a substantial procedural violation".

These requirements are discussed below.

If an appeal is admissible and there is no interlocutory revision under Article 109 EPC, and if the appeal is subsequently held not to be allowable, a Board of Appeal has no power to order refund of an appeal fee. This is because:

"the restrictive language of Rule 67 EPC is plainly inconsistent with the idea that a Board of Appeal has a wide discretion to order reimbursement of appeal fees" (T41/82[247]).

(ii) Procedural violation distinguished from error of judgment. 4–167

In order to fall within Rule 67 EPC, there must have been a procedural violation, as opposed to an error of judgment, in relation to a case:

"A finding in a decision that there had not been a request for oral proceedings, although wrong, did not constitute ... a substantial procedural violation" (T19/87[248]).

Thus a case where the first instance department wrongly interpreted the wording used by a party as not constituting a request for oral proceedings (error of judgment) must be distinguished from a case where a request for oral proceedings has clearly been made by a party, but oral proceedings have nevertheless not been appointed (procedural violation).

Furthermore:

"The Guidelines not having the binding authority of a legal text, a failure by the Examining Division to follow them is not to be regarded

---

[246] T930/92 *HITACHI/Ion beam processing* O.J. EPO 1996, 191; [1997] E.P.O.R. 20.
[247] T41/82 *SANDOZ/Reimbursement of appeal fee* O.J. EPO 1982, 256; [1979–85] E.P.O.R.: B: 446.
[248] T19/87 *FUJITSU/Oral proceedings* O.J. EPO 1988, 268; [1988] E.P.O.R. 393.

as a procedural violation within the meaning of Rule 67 EPC unless it also constitutes a violation of a rule or principle of procedure governed by an [Article or Rule] of the EPC" (T42/84[249]).

In the absence of an established case law concerning a particular procedure under the EPC, use of an incorrect procedure does not constitute a substantial procedural violation (T156/84[250] and T234/86[251]).

4–168   **(iii) A "substantial" violation.**
A trivial procedural violation by the EPO cannot justify reimbursement of an appeal fee. Thus:

> "An alleged violation affecting a part of a decision other than its ratio decidendi cannot be a substantial violation within the meaning of Rule 67 EPC" (T5/81[252]).

4–169   **(iv) Examples of "substantial procedural violation".**
(a) *Violation of Article 113(1) EPC.* Article 113(1) EPC provides that decisions of the EPO "may only be based on grounds or evidence on which the parties concerned have had an opportunity to present their comments".

The appeal fee must be reimbursed if Article 113(1) EPC has not been complied with (J7/82[253], T197/88[254]).

Consequently, before a decision is issued which is adverse to a party, such party must have a proper opportunity to comment upon the actual case against him; furthermore, the case put forward by that party must be properly considered.

> "Article 113(1) EPC is intended to ensure that before a decision refusing an application for non-compliance with a requirement of the EPC is issued, the applicant has been clearly informed by the EPO of the essential legal and factual reasons on which the finding of non-compliance is based, so that he knows in advance of the decision both that the application may be refused and why it may be refused, and so that he may have a proper opportunity to comment upon such reasons and/or to propose amendments so as to avoid refusal of the application" (T951/92[255]).

---

[249] T42/84 *EXXON/Alumina spinel* O.J. 1988, 251; [1998] E.P.O.R. 387.
[250] T156/84 *AIR PRODUCTS/Pressure swing adsorption* O.J. EPO 1988, 372; [1989] E.P.O.R. 47.
[251] T234/86 *SOMARTEC/Therapy with interference currents* O.J. EPO 1989, 79; [1989] E.P.O.R. 303.
[252] T5/81 *SOLVAY/Production of hollow thermoplastic objects* O.J. EPO 1982, 249; [1979–85] E.P.O.R.: B: 287.
[253] J7/82 *CATALDO/Cause of non-compliance* O.J. EPO 1982, 391; [1979–85] E.P.O.R.: A: 108.
[254] T197/88 *ICI/Continuation of opposition proceedings* O.J. EPO 1989, 412; [1990] E.P.O.R. 243.
[255] T951/92 *NEC/Opportunity to comment* O.J. EPO 1996, 53; [1996] E.P.O.R. 371.

For example:

"Due process of law required by Article 113 EPC has not been applied when a decision to refuse an application is based essentially on documents which, though supplied by the applicant in support of his case, are used against him to produce an effect on which he has not had an opportunity to make observations" (T18/81[256]).

Similarly, where the EPO has examined facts of its own motion, Article **4–170** 113(1) EPC requires that the parties concerned are "fully informed about the enquiries made and the results thereof and then given sufficient opportunity to present their comments before any decision is issued".

"If certain facts [presented by an applicant] prove to be inaccurate, [the EPO] must invite the parties to present their comments."

Furthermore:

"Article 113(1) EPC requires that an express opportunity to present observations be given to the parties by the Opposition Division after remittal to it of a case by a Board of Appeal for further prosecution on the basis of new evidence, even if submissions with respect to this new evidence have already been made during the preceding appeal proceedings" (T892/92[257]).

A party must not be misled by the EPO into believing that it is unnecessary to file observations in reply to submissions from an opposing party. Thus:

"If the EPO sends a communication which (on a reasonable interpretation) misleads a party into believing that it is not necessary to file observations in reply to new evidence and related argument filed by an opposing party, and if such new evidence and argument then forms the basis for a decision adversely affecting the first party, the latter has not had 'an opportunity to present its comments' within the meaning of Article 113(1) EPC" (T669/90[258]).

As to the proper consideration of a party's case: **4–171**

"The right to be heard in accordance with Article 113(1) EPC guarantees that grounds put forward are taken into consideration. That principle is contravened if a translation ... in an official language of a Japanese document cited in due time is disallowed" (T94/84[259]).

---

[256] T18/81 *SOLVAY/Olefin polymers* O.J. EPO 1985, 166; [1979–85] E.P.O.R.: B: 325.
[257] T892/92 *KONICA/Remittal* O.J. EPO 1996, 664; [1995] E.P.O.R. 238.
[258] T669/90 *ATT/Inviting observations* O.J. EPO 1992, 739; [1992] E.P.O.R. 397.
[259] T94/84 *DUCO/Paint layers* O.J. EPO 1986, 337; [1987] E.P.O.R. 37.

Similarly:

"Failure to take submissions into consideration which is a result of a delay with the EPO and not attributable to the parties ... calls for reimbursement of the appeal fee" (T231/85[260]).

4–172 (b) *Violation of Article 11 3(2) EPC.* Article 113(2) EPC provides that the EPO "shall consider and decide upon the European patent application or the European patent only in the text submitted to it, or agreed, by the applicant for or proprietor of the patent".

This provision is also "a fundamental procedural principle, being part of the right to be heard, and as of such prime importance that any infringment of it must, in principle, be considered to be a substantial procedural violation" (T647/93[261]).

Thus a decision which is based upon a text of the patent which does not include requested amendments constitutes a substantial procedural violation (T647/93[262]).

4–173 (c) *Failure to apply interlocutory revision.* Failure to order interlocutory revision under Article 109 EPC following the filing of significant amendments by the applicant may constitute a substantial procedural violation (T268/85). Such is the case, for example, if the applicant points out in the grounds of appeal that Article 113(2) EPC had been violated by the Examining Division in its decision, but the Examining Division fails to order interlocutory revision (T647/93[263]).

If the notice of appeal requests grant of a patent with a text which has previously been the subject of a communication under Rule 51(4) EPC (which was not then approved by the applicant), failure to order interlocutory revision is a substantial procedural violation, but reimbursement of the appeal fee is not equitable (T898/96[264]).

4–174 (d) *Other examples.* (1) It is the duty of the Opposition Division, having communicated its intention to organise oral proceedings to inform the parties as soon as possible of a withdrawal of the request for oral proceedings by one of the parties and the subsequent change of attitude of the Opposition Division towards holding oral proceedings:" Issue of a decision without holding oral proceedings constitutes a substantial procedural violation in such circumstances" (T811/90[265]).

(2) "Rejection of a request [*e.g.* an auxiliary request] without any reason being given in the decision itself or at least in a preceding communication referred to therein" is a violation of Rule 68(2) EPC which justified

[260] T231/85 *BASF/Triazole derivatives* O.J. EPO 1989, 74; [1989] E.P.O.R. 293.
[261] T647/93 *HITACHI MAXELL/Procedural violation* O.J. EPO 1995, 132; [1995] E.P.O.R. 195.
[262] *Ibid.*
[263] *Ibid.*
[264] T898/96 *HITACHI* January 10, 1997.
[265] T811/90 *AE PLC/Exclusion of documents from public inspection* O.J. EPO 1993, 728; [1994] E.P.O.R. 271.

reimbursement of the appeal fee (T234/86[266]—see Chapter 5 at paragraph 5–74; see also T755/96[267]—Chapter 5 at paragraph 5–51).

(3) However:

"The failure of the EPO to enclose the text of Articles 106 to 108 EPC with the decision [contrary to Rule 68(2) EPC] neither invalidates the decision nor does it constitute a substantial procedural violation" (T42/84[268]).

D. The Enlarged Board of Appeal

(1) Introduction

In accordance with Article 112 EPC, the dual purpose of the Enlarged Board of Appeal is to provide for uniform application of the law within the Boards of Appeal, and to decide important points of law which arise under the EPC. It provides the highest hierarchical level of judicial authority within the EPO, but:

4–175— 4–180

"The Enlarged Board of Appeal is not a third instance within the EPO, but part of the second instance constituted by the Boards of Appeal" (T79/89[269]).

There are two possible mechanisms by which a question of law may be referred to the Enlarged Board under Article 112 EPC; these mechanisms are discussed in paragraphs 4–187 *et seq.* below.

(2) Function of the Enlarged Board

According to Article 22 EPC, the Enlarged Board of Appeal is responsible for:

4–181

(a) deciding points of law referred to it by Boards of Appeal;
(b) giving opinions on points of law referred to it by the President of the EPO.

A decision under Article 22(a) EPC and an opinion under Article 22(b) EPC are of equal authority; it is merely the mechanism by which the points of law are referred to the Enlarged Board which is different in the two cases, as to which, see below.

According to the proposed revision of the EPC, a third function will be given to the Enlarged Board by a new Article 22(c) EPC, namely:

4–181A

[266] T234/86 SOMARTEC/Therapy with interference currents O.J. EPO 1989, 79; [1989] E.P.O.R. 303.
[267] T755/96 RESEARCH TRIANGLE INSTITUTE/Camptotheorin derivatives O.J. EPO 2000, 174.
[268] T42/84 EXXON/Alumina spinel O.J. EPO 1988, 251; [1998] E.P.O.R. 387.
[269] T79/89 XEROX/Finality of decision O.J. EPO 1992, 283; [1990] E.P.O.R. 558.

"deciding on petitions for review of decisions of the Boards of Appeal under Article 112a" (see paragraph 4–201A below).

(3) Procedure for referring questions of law to the Enlarged Board

4–182   There are at present two ways in which the Enlarged Board of Appeal can be convened (a third way is provided under the proposed revision of the EPC—see paragraph 4–181A above):

(a) By a Board of Appeal

4–183   Under Article 112(1)(a) EPC, an individual Board of Appeal may refer one or more questions of law to the Enlarged Board during the course of particular appeal proceedings before it, either of its own motion, for example in circumstances such as discussed above, or upon the request of a party to the appeal proceedings.

4–184   **(i) Time for making a request for referral.**

"After a Board of Appeal has issued a decision in respect of certain issues, it has no power under Article 112(1)(a) EPC in the same proceedings to refer a question of law to the Enlarged Board of Appeal which arose in connection with issues which it has already decided, even though other issues are still pending before the Board of Appeal in proceedings on the same case" (T79/89[270]).

Furthermore:

"The proper interpretation of Article 112(1)(a) EPC in its context is such that a Board of Appeal may only refer questions of law to the Enlarged Board 'during proceedings on a case' and before it decides upon the issues in the appeal in relation to which such questions of law are considered to arise. This is clear from Article 112(1)(a) EPC itself, which envisages the presence of reasons for rejection of requests for referral of questions in the 'final decision' of the Board of Appeal. . . . Furthermore, in the event that a Board does refer questions to the Enlarged Board, Article 112(2) EPC makes it clear that the parties are also parties to the Enlarged Board proceedings, and Article 112(3) EPC prescribes that the decision of the Enlarged Board is binding on the Board of Appeal: this can only make sense if questions are referred to the Enlarged Board before a Board of Appeal has decided the issues in the appeal in connection with which the questions of law arise" (T79/89[271]).

4–185   **(ii) Form of a request.** If a party considers that a particular case should be referred pursuant to this provision, he may request a Board of Appeal to

---

[270] T79/89 *XEROX/Finality of decision* O.J. EPO 1992, 283; [1990] E.P.O.R. 558.
[271] *Ibid.*

refer questions of law to the Enlarged Board. To improve the chances of his request being acceded to, he should not merely make a bare request: he should also state his reasons in support of his request. These will normally include:

(a) the point of law which is said to arise: this can conveniently be put in the form of the draft question(s) which the party wishes to be referred to the Enlarged Board, and

(b) the reasons why the point of law is important and needs to be referred in order to ensure uniform application of the law.

If the Board of Appeal rejects such a request, Article 112(1) EPC requires that it must give its reasons in its final decision; there is no sanction provided if it does not give any reasons, however.

(iii) Decision of referral and subsequent procedure. As an alternative **4–186** to issuing a decision which deviates from earlier decisions, a Board of Appeal may, in the context of a case before it, refer a question of law directly to the Enlarged Board of Appeal of its own motion, for example if it does not wish to follow a previous interpretation of the EPC in an earlier decision.

Furthermore, a point of law of considerable importance may arise for the first time before a particular Board of Appeal, which may consider it preferable to refer the question to the Enlarged Board for decision, instead of deciding the point itself.

If a Board of Appeal decides to refer one or more questions to the Enlarged Board, either of its own motion or upon request from a party, it issues a written decision (see Article 17 RPBA) setting out a summary of facts and the background to the questions which are to be referred, and the reasons for the referral. The context of the referred questions is thus stated. The appeal proceedings before that Board of Appeal are then stayed during the appeal procedure before the Enlarged Board and until the issue of its decision by which the referred questions are decided (Article 22(1)(a) EPC).

The parties to the appeal proceedings before the referring Board of Appeal are automatically parties in the proceedings before the Enlarged Board (Article 112(2) EPC). As to the procedure before the Enlarged Board, see paragraphs 4–196 *et seq.* below.

The decision which is issued by the Enlarged Board under this procedure is binding on the Board of Appeal which referred the question in respect of the particular appeal concerned (Article 112(3) EPC).

(b) By the President of the EPO

Under Article 112(1)(b) EPC, the President of the EPO may refer an **4–187** important point of law to the Enlarged Board "where two Boards of

Appeal have given different decisions on that question", in circumstances such as discussed above, in order to ensure uniform application of the law. Since the two previous decisions are already final, such a reference to the Enlarged Board has no effect upon the cases which were the subject of such previous decisions.

The procedure in the event of a referral by the President of the EPO is governed by the same Rules of Procedure as in a referral by a Board. The Enlarged Board is responsible for issuing an "opinion" on the point of law, rather than a decision, and is thus acting in effect as an advisory body, because no particular case is brought before it and there are no parties involved; but as previously mentioned, there is no difference in principle between the effect of an opinion and a decision of the Enlarged Board.

The President of the EPO has no power to refer a question of law to the Enlarged Board of Appeal unless two Boards of Appeal have given different (*i.e.* conflicting) decisions on that question of law. If the President refers a question of law to the Enlarged Board of Appeal, but two Boards of Appeal have not given different (*i.e.* conflicting) decisions on that question of law, the question is inadmissible, and the Enlarged Board of Appeal has no power to issue an opinion on that question (G3/95[272]).

(4) Composition of the Enlarged Board

4–188 The Enlarged Board of Appeal for a particular case consists of five legally qualified members and two technically qualified members of the Boards of Appeal (Article 22(2) EPC), *i.e.* a total of seven members, and operates under a Chairman (who is one of the legally qualified members).

Under Article 1 (RPEBA), a business distribution scheme is drawn up for each working year, which determines the specific composition of the Enlarged Board for each case. The scheme is published in the first issue of the Official Journal each year.

Currently, the practice is that the business distribution scheme appoints a "permanent" composition of the Enlarged Board for each year, there being not more than one member of any one nationality in such composition.

4–189 Compared with national courts, international judicial organs such as the Enlarged Board tend to be larger. Thus, an individual chamber of the House of Lords in England, sitting for an individual case, is composed of five Law Lords: this is the largest normal composition of a court in the United Kingdom. International courts such as the European Court of Justice (15 members—one judge per Member State) and the European Court of Human Rights (seven members) are larger.

There are several possible reasons for such a large composition for the Enlarged Board, in common with other international judicial organs. In the first place, a large Board may increase public confidence in its decisions, and helps to promote a greater authority. In one respect, the increase in confidence and authority is simply a question of there being strength in

[272] G3/95 *Inadmissible referral* O.J. EPO 1996, 169; [1996] E.P.O.R. 505.

numbers. In another respect, the larger the composition, the larger the potential spread of nationalities, and thus the greater the chance of a composition having a reasonable representation from a number of different Contracting States. In this regard, the current business distribution scheme of the Enlarged Board provides that normally only one member of each nationality is included in the Enlarged Board for each particular case.

Public confidence in the decisions of all the Boards of Appeal, but **4–190** especially in the decisions (and opinions) of the Enlarged Board as the highest authority on matters of law within the EPO, is particularly important having regard to the persuasive nature of such decisions upon national courts (see Chapter 1 at paragraphs 1–84 *et seq.*) and given the international nature of the industrial and public community which it serves.

As discussed previously, it is impossible for the EPC to provide direct answers for all the problems which may arise in the course of the EPO's operations, and the EPC is therefore inevitably incomplete. Legal answers must when necessary be deduced by reference to general principles of law within the Contracting States, which are in turn developed from the various national legal systems. A large composition for the Enlarged Board provides a greater spread of knowledge and experience of such national systems and therefore of the general principles of law which may be developed.

(a) Inclusion of national judges in the Enlarged Board

During recent years certain national judges have been appointed external **4–190A** members of the Enlarged Board under Article 160(2) EPC (see paragraph 4–09A above), and have taken part in a number of Enlarged Board cases at the invitation of the Chairman. In accordance with the proposed revision of the EPC, Article 160(2) EPC will be deleted, and under a new Article 11(5) EPC:

> "The Administrative Council, after consulting the President of the EPO, may also appoint as members of the Enlarged Board of Appeal legally qualified members of the national courts or quasi-judicial authorities of the Contracting States, who may continue their judicial activities at the national level. They shall be appointed for a term of three years and may be re-appointed."

Thus national judges may be appointed members of the Enlarged Board on a part-time basis.

The involvement of national judges in important cases before the Enlarged Board will provide valuable input, will help the international recognition of the Enlarged Board, and should help the harmonisation of the European patent system.

(b) Composition for deciding on petitions for review

4–190B According to the proposed revision of the EPC, when deciding on petitions for review of decisions of the Boards of Appeal under new Article 22(1)(c) EPC (paragraph 4–201a below), the Enlarged Board may be composed of less than seven members as laid down in the Implementing Regulations (Article 22(2) EPC).

(5) Procedure of the Enlarged Board

4–191 This is governed primarily by the "Rules of Procedure of the Enlarged Board of Appeal" (RPEBA).

These Rules of Procedure are adopted by the Enlarged Board itself, and are subject to the approval of the Administrative Council (Article 23(4) and Rule 11 EPC). They are generally similar to those of the Boards of Appeal, *mutatis mutandis*. For example, by Article 4 RPEBA one or more rapporteurs are appointed in respect of the referred questions of law, and such rapporteurs are responsible for the preparation of communications and the eventual drafting of the decision.

A number of important amendments to the RPEBA have been made since the original Rules were adopted in 1982:

(a) Article 11a RPEBA—EPO President's right to comment

4–192 This new Article entered into force in July 1989, and reads as follows:

> "The Board may, on its own initiative or at the written, reasoned request of the President of the European Patent Office, invite him to comment in writing or orally on questions of general interest which arise in the course of proceedings pending before it. The parties shall be entitled to submit their observations on the President's comments."

This procedure enables the President to obtain the views of the relevant department of the EPO on questions of general interest, and to communicate such views to the Enlarged Board. The Enlarged Board will then hear the parties' comments on such views, before deciding a case. The President, however, does not thereby become a party to the proceedings.

Although Article 11a RPEBA is applicable to both mechanisms under Article 112(1) EPC by which questions of law may be referred to the Enlarged Board (paragraphs 4–183 *et seq.* above), it is particularly important under Article 112(1)(a) EPC when a Board of Appeal refers a question; previously the President had no opportunity to express views on the referred question in that situation.

4–193 The primary purpose of the Article is clearly to enable the President to present his point of view having regard to the practice of the EPO generally (especially the first instance departments, but the Article is not limited in this respect (he may be invited to comment "on questions of general interest").

Any such invitation from the Enlarged Board and reply from the President becomes part of the file of the case, and is available for public inspection under Article 128 EPC.

Unfortunately, while this Article enables the Enlarged Board to obtain valuable additional views and information before it decides upon the referred questions, the procedure under Article 11a RPEBA is inevitably time consuming, because the President must be given a reasonable time in which to repond to an invitation from the Enlarged Board, and thereafter the parties must be given a reasonable time in which to comment upon the President's submissions. Thereafter all such views must of course be taken into account before deciding upon the referred questions, and dealt with in the eventual decision on the case.

(b) Article 11b RPEBA—third party statements

This new Article entered into force in June 1994, and reads as follows: **4–194**

> "Statements by third parties.
> (1) In the course of proceedings before the Board, any written statement concerning points of law raised in such proceedings which is sent to the Board by a third party may be dealt with as the Board thinks fit.
> (2) The Board may announce further provisions concerning such statements in the Official Journal of the EPO if it seems appropriate."

No such further provisions have so far been announced.

Before the adoption of this provision, the Enlarged Board had no power to deal with such statements which it received from interested parties. The Article fulfils a practical need in this respect. Questions of law which are referred to the Enlarged Board are frequently of great importance to parties and potential parties to proceedings before the EPO, as well as to other persons such as professional representatives. Article 11b RPEBA allows all such persons to express their views upon the referred questions, even though they are not parties to the pending proceedings before the Enlarged Board.

In one sense, this additional Article can be regarded as a counter-balance to Article 11a RPEBA above, which gives the President of the EPO a right to comment when so invited.

Such a provision is liberal compared to the practice under most national **4–195** jurisdictions. For example, interventions by a third party has only rarely been permitted in proceedings before the House of Lords in the United Kingdom. However, it is well established that third party intervention may be permitted by the European Court of Justice and by the European Court of Human Rights.

Neverthless, the importance of the Enlarged Board's jurisdiction within the European patent system seems to fully justify this provision. Third parties have frequently made use of the opportunity to submit their views to the Enlarged Board (especially in cases concerning the protection of biotechnological inventions—G3/95[273] and G1/98[274]).

If such a third party statement raised "grounds or evidence" for the first time which could effect the answer to a referred question under Article 112(1)(a) EPC, in accordance with Article 113 EPC it would be necessary for the parties to the proceedings to be given an opportunity to present their comments upon such grounds or evidence, before a decision was issued.

Such a third party statement may be dealt with by the Enlarged Board "as it thinks fit". Thus overall procedural control remains with the Enlarged Board, and the proceedings should not be unduly prolonged by the filing of such statements.

(c) Article 12a RPEBA—minority opinion

4–196   This new Article also entered into force in June 1994, and reads as follows:

> "Reasons for decision
> The decisions of the Board shall be in accordance with the votes of the majority of its members. If a majority of the members of the Board agrees, the reasons for such decision may also indicate the opinions held by a minority of the members.
> Neither the decision nor its reasons may indicate either the names of the members forming any such minority or the size of the minority."

4–197   The possibility of a "minority opinion" being issued as part of the decision or opinion of the Enlarged Board in answer to a referred question, but only if the majority of the Board agrees to the minority opinion being issued, goes less than halfway towards the practice in the United Kingdom, the United States and many other countries to allow (or even to require) dissenting opinions to be expressed whenever they exist. However, less than half of the Contracting States to the EPC allow such a practice within their national jurisdictions. Individual dissenting (or concurring) opinions form part of the "common law" tradition and are increasingly but more rarely found in continental Europe.

Internationally, since 1920 the International Court of Justice in The Hague has allowed individual opinions (either dissenting or concurring) to be added to the Court's judgment; but the European Court of Justice does not allow individual opinions to form part of the Court's judgment.

Before Article 12a RPEBA came into force, the absence of any minority opinions was considered important in order to establish a clear strong line of Enlarged Board decisions and opinions. Before this Article was adopted, its desirability was carefully considered. A main argument against such minority opinions is that they are said to weaken the standing of an Enlarged Board decision. On the other hand, the inclusion of such minority

---

[273] G3/95 *Inadmissible referral* O.J. EPO 1996, 169; [1996] E.P.O.R. 505.
[274] G1/98 *NOVARTIS/Transgenic plant* O.J. EPO 1998, 509; [2000] E.P.O.R. 303.

opinions is a more honest reflection of the independent views of individual members, because it would be unrealistic to expect the seven members of an Enlarged Board always to hold the same opinion on referred questions, since many of such referred questions are very controversial, which is why they are referred to the Enlarged Board. Furthermore, it is well recognised that the publication of minority opinions can play an important role in the future development of case law. Especially from this point of view, it would appear to be desirable to remove the control of the majority over the inclusion of minority opinions from Article 12a RPEBA ("...if a majority of its members agree ...").

(6) Binding effect of an Enlarged Board decision or opinion

(1) As stated previously, if a question of law is referred to the Enlarged **4–198**
Board of Appeal by an individual Board of Appeal during the course of appeal proceedings before it, either of its own motion or following a request from a party to the appeal, the decision of the Enlarged Board which answers the referred question is binding on the Board of Appeal which referred the question "in respect of the appeal in question" (Article 112(3) EPC).

(2) Beyond this, however, every Enlarged Board opinion or decision has **4–199**
a binding effect upon subsequent individual Boards of Appeal, having regard in particular to Article 16 RPBA which states:

> "Should a Board consider it necessary to deviate from an interpretation or explanation of the EPC contained in an earlier opinion or decision of the Enlarged Board of Appeal, the question shall be referred to the Enlarged Board of Appeal."

This provision does not quite provide a system of precedent as far as opinions or decisions of the Enlarged Board of Appeal are concerned, but it does prevent a Board of Appeal from deciding a case either for or against a party if the reasons for such a decision are based upon an interpretation of the EPC which is contrary to an interpretation or explanation of the EPC in an opinion or decision of the Enlarged Board. Instead of so deciding, the Board of Appeal must refer a question of law to the Enlarged Board under Article 112(1)(a) EPC (see paragraphs 4–183 *et seq.*): the question of law which is so referred should be framed so that the answer to be provided by the Enlarged Board will decide whether the interpretation or explanation as set out in the previous Enlarged Board decision, or the interpretation of the referring Board which deviates therefrom, is correct.

In practice, a Board of Appeal is unlikely to follow the procedure of Article 16 RPBA except in unusual circumstances. To date, only one Board of Appeal has "considered it necessary to deviate" from an interpretation or explanation of the EPC by the Enlarged Board of Appeal (T788/90,[275] G9/93[276]—see Chapter 3 at paragraphs 3–11 *et seq.* above).

4–200   Although Article 16 RPBA does provide a kind of precedent system for the Boards of Appeal in relation to the Enlarged Board of Appeal, there is an important distinction between this system of precedent and the more strict system of precedent required by English law. In English law, if for example a judge in the High Court deviates from an interpretation of the law in an earlier judgment of the Court of Appeal, the party to the proceedings before the High Court judge has a right of appeal to the Court of Appeal, who could then be expected to set aside the judge's decision. Under the EPC and RPBA, however, there is nothing that a party could do as of right if a Board of Appeal deviated from a previous decision of the Enlarged Board of Appeal (whatever the reason for the deviation, whether accidental or intentional) or if the party considered that the Board of Appeal had so deviated.

Thus the fact that Article 16 RPBA is binding upon the Boards of Appeal does not provide any protection in the form of a remedy for a party to proceedings before a Board of Appeal if that particular Board of Appeal fails to follow a previous interpretation or explanation of the EPC by the Enlarged Board.

(7) The extent of the Enlarged Board's jurisdiction

4–201 The limited extent of the Enlarged Board's jurisdiction as defined in Articles 22 and 112 EPC has the practical consequences that important and controversial questions of law under the EPC sometimes take a long time to be referred to the Enlarged Board, with consequent legal uncertainty. Such a limited jurisdiction has disadvantages. There is an obvious disadvantage for parties who may lose cases before the first instance departments of the EPO or before individual Boards of Appeal, without having the question decided (perhaps in their favour) by the Enlarged Board first. Such a period of uncertainty, during which inconsistent decisions may be issued by the EPO, is contrary to one of the purposes of the Enlarged Board's jurisdiction ("to ensure uniform application of the law").

During more than fifteen years of operation of the Enlarged Board, it seems that in general, the most important and controversial questions of law do eventually reach the Enlarged Board for decision. Nevertheless, the above disadvantage could be at least partially alleviated if the jurisdiction of the Enlarged Board was extended so as to allow the Enlarged Board to give leave for a party to proceedings before an individual Board of Appeal to appeal to the Enlarged Board from a decision of such an individual Board of Appeal either on an important point of law, or in order to ensure

---

[275] T788/90 *PEUGEOT AND CITROËN/Opposition by patent proprietor* O.J. EPO 1994, 708.
[276] G9/93 *PEUGEOT AND CITROËN II/Opposition by patent proprietor* O.J. EPO 1994, 891; [1995] E.P.O.R. 260.

uniform application of the law, in accordance with the purposes underlying Article 112 EPC. Such an extension of jurisdiction would provide the possibility of a further judicial level of appeal in relation to decisions of the EPO in appropriate cases. If the Enlarged Board's jurisdiction was extended in that way, the current Rules of Procedure of the Enlarged Board, including the additional Articles discussed above, should ensure that the Enlarged Board is sufficiently and properly informed from all points of view of all relevant aspects of the point of law which would be the subject of such an appeal to the Enlarged Board.

Such an extension of the Enlarged Board's jurisdiction could not be achieved by amendment of its Rules of Procedure, however; it could only be achieved by a future amendment of Articles 22 and 112 EPC.

According to the proposed revision of the EPC, the jurisdiction of the Enlarged Board will be increased so as to include: **4–201A**

"deciding on petitions for review of decisions of the Boards of Appeal under Article 112a".

Under a proposed new Article 112a EPC:

"(1) Any party to appeal proceedings adversely affected by the decision of the Board of Appeal may file a petition for review of the decision by the Enlarged Board of Appeal:
(2) The petition may only be filed on the grounds that:

(a) a member of the Board of Appeal took part in the decision in breach of Article 24 EPC, or despite being excluded pursuant to a decision under Article 24 EPC;
(b) the Board of Appeal included a person not appointed as a member of the Boards of Appeal;
(c) a fundamental violation of Article 113 EPC occurred;
(d) any other fundamental procedural defect defined in the Implementing Regulations occurred in the appeal proceedings;
(e) a criminal act established under the conditions laid down in the Implementing Regulations may have had an impact on the decision."

Such a petition for review "shall not have suspensive effect" (Article 112(3) EPC).

Such a petition for review must be filed in a reasoned statement and must be filed within two months after notification of the decision of the Board of Appeal in the case of a petition filed on one of the grounds set out in (2)(a) to (d) above; or "within two months of the date on which the criminal act has been established and in any event not later than five years from notification of the decision of the Board of Appeal" in the case of a petition based on (2)(e) above. (Article 112a(4) EPC).

If such a petition is allowed, the decision under review would be set aside, and proceedings before the Boards of Appeal would be re-opened in accordance with the Implementing Regulations (Article 112a(5) EPC).

Under Article 112a(6) EPC, any person in a designated Contracting State who in good faith has "used or made effective and serious preparations for using an invention [the subject of the petition] in the period between the decision of the Board of Appeal under review and publication of the mention of the decision of the Enlarged Board of Appeal on the petition, may without payment continue such use in the course of his business or for the needs thereof".

Cases Referred to in Chapter 4

Board of Appeal Decisions

G5/83	EISAI/Second medical indication O.J. EPO 1985, 64; [1979–85] E.P.O.R.: B: 241.
G1/86	VOEST ALPINE/Re-establishment of opponent O.J. EPO 1987, 447; [1987] E.P.O.R. 388.
G1/89	X/Polysuccinate esters O.J. EPO 1991, 155; [1991] E.P.O.R. 239.
G2/90	KOLBENSCHMIDT/Responsibility of the Legal Board of Appeal O.J. EPO 1992, 10; [1992] E.P.O.R. 125.
G2/91	KROHNE/Appeal fees O.J. EPO 1992, 206 [1992] E.P.O.R. 407.
G4/91	DOLEZYCH II/Intervention O.J. EPO 1993, 707; [1993] E.P.O.R. 120.
G6/91	ASULAB II/Fee reduction O.J. EPO 1992, 491; [1993] E.P.O.R. 231.
G7/91	BASF/Withdrawal of appeal O.J. EPO 1993, 356; [1993] E.P.O.R. 440.
G8/91	BELL/Withdrawal of appeal O.J. EPO 1993, 346; [1993] E.P.O.R. 445.
G9/91	ROHM AND HAAS/Power to examine O.J. EPO 1993, 408; [1993] E.P.O.R. 485.
G10/91	Examination of oppositions/appeals O.J. EPO 1993, 420; [1993] E.P.O.R. 485.
G9/92	BMW/Non-appealing party , O.J. EPO 1994, 25; [1995] E.P.O.R. 169.
G3/93	Priority interval O.J. EPO 1995, 18; [1994] E.P.O.R. 521.
G8/93	SERWANE II/Withdrawal of opposition in appeal O.J. EPO 1994, 887; [1995] E.P.O.R. 271.
G9/93	PEUGEOT AND CITROËN II/Opposition by patent proprietor O.J. EPO 1994, 891; [1995] E.P.O.R. 260.
G10/93	SIEMENS II/Sensor O.J. EPO 1994, 172.
G1/94	ALLIED COLLOIDS/Intervention O.J. EPO 1994, 541; [1995] E.P.O.R. 97.

G1/95	DE LA RUE/Fresh grounds for opposition O.J. EPO 1996, 615; [1996] E.P.O.R. 601.
G3/95	Inadmissible referral O.J. EPO 1996, 169; [1996] E.P.O.R. 505.
G4/95	BOGASKY II/Representation O.J. EPO 1996, 412; [1996] E.P.O.R. 333.
G6/95	GE CHEMICALS/Interpretation of Rule 71a(1) O.J. EPO 1996, 649; [1997] E.P.O.R. 265.
G7/95	ETHICON/Fresh grounds for opposition O.J. EPO 1996, 626.
G8/95	US GYPSUM II/Correction of decision to grant O.J. EPO 1996, 481; [1997] E.P.O.R. 66.
G1/97	ETA/Request with a view to judgment revision O.J. EPO 2000, 322.
G4/97	GENENTECH/Opposition on behalf of third party O.J. EPO 1999, 270.
G1/98	NOVARTIS II/Transgenic plant O.J. EPO 1998, 509; [2000] E.P.O.R. 303.
G1/99	Not yet issued O.J. EPO (P).
J21/80	HEISEL/Late payment of appeal fee O.J. EPO 1981, 101; [1979–85] E.P.O.R.: A: 65.
J8/81	CATERPILLAR/Form of decision O.J. EPO 1982, 10; [1979–85] E.P.O.R.: A: 92.
J7/82	CATALDO/Cause of non-compliance O.J. EPO 1982, 391; [1979–85] E.P.O.R.: A: 108.
J16/82	THEURER/Assistant; substitute O.J. EPO 1983, 262; [1979–85] E.P.O.R.: A: 137.
J12/83	CHUGAI SEIYAKU/Inadmissible appeals O.J. EPO 1985, 6; [1979–85] E.P.O.R.: A: 196.
J12/85	KUREHA/Inadmissible appeal O.J. EPO 1986, 155; [1986] E.P.O.R. 336.
J12/86	LINVILLE/Refund of appeal fee O.J. EPO 1988, 83.
J22/86	MEDICAL BIOLOGICAL/Disapproval O.J. EPO 1987, 280; [1987] E.P.O.R. 87.
J2/87	MOTOROLA/Admissibility O.J. EPO 1988, 330; [1989] E.P.O.R. 42.
J.../87	Incapacity O.J. EPO 1988, 323; [1989] E.P.O.R. 73.
J3/90	FISHER SCIENTIFIC/Postal strike O.J. EPO 1991, 550; [1992] E.P.O.R. 148; see also J4/90 (MARELLO/Postal strike) [1990] E.P.O.R. 576.
J19/92	TORAY/Partial withdrawal of appeal O.J. EPO 1984, 6.
J29/92	MERCK/Premature appeal inadmissible December 9, 1992.
J2/93	ETA/Decision subject to appeal O.J. EPO 1995, 675.
J16/94	APPLIED RESEARCH SYSTEM/Notice of appeal O.J. EPO 1997, 331; [1998] E.P.O.R. 49.
J28/94	SOLUDIA/Suspensive effect O.J. EPO 1995, 742.

J32/95   GENERAL MOTORS/Power of Examining Division O.J.
          EPO 1999, 713.
J37/97   ALGERNON PROMOTIONS October 15, 1998.

T5/81   SOLVAY/Production of hollow thermoplastic objects O.J.
          EPO 1982, 249; [1979–85] E.P.O.R.: B: 287.
T7/81   CIBA-GEIGY/Dyeing of linear polyamides O.J. EPO 1983,
          98; [1979–85] E.P.O.R.: B: 301.
T17/81   BAYER/Nimodipin I O.J. EPO 1985, 130; [1979–85]
          E.P.O.R.: B: 320.
T18/81   SOLVAY/Olefin Polymers O.J. EPO 1985, 166; [1979–85]
          E.P.O.R.: B: 325.
T10/82   BAYER/Admissibility of opposition O.J. EPO 1983, 407;
          [1979–85] E.P.O.R.: B: 381.
T41/82   SANDOZ/Reimbursement of appeal fee O.J. EPO 1982,
          256; [1979–85] E.P.O.R.: B: 446.
T22/83   FUJITSU/Acoustic wave generator (unpublished).
T95/83   AISIN/Late submission of amendment O.J. EPO 1985, 75;
          [1979–85] E.P.O.R.: C: 815.
T219/83   BASF/Zeolites O.J. EPO 1986, 211; [1986] E.P.O.R. 247.
T220/83   HÜLS/Grounds for appeal O.J. EPO 1986, 249; [1987]
          E.P.O.R. 49.
T42/84   EXXON/Alumina spinel O.J. EPO 1988, 251; [1988]
          E.P.O.R. 387.
T89/84   TORRINGTON/Reimbursement of appeal fees O.J. EPO
          1984, 562; [1979–85] E.P.O.R.: C: 949.
T94/84   DUCO/Paint layers O.J. EPO 1986, 337; [1987] E.P.O.R. 37.
T122/84   HOECHST/Metallic paint coating O.J. EPO 1987, 177;
          [1987] E.P.O.R. 218.
T142/84   BRITAX/Inventive step [1987] E.P.O.R. 148.
T156/84   AIR PRODUCTS/Pressure swing adsorption O.J. EPO
          1988, 372; [1989] E.P.O.R. 47.
T167/84   NISSAN/Fuel injector valve O.J. EPO 1987, 36; [1987]
          E.P.O.R. 344.
T185/84   BASF/Paint line supply system O.J. EPO 1986, 373; [1987]
          E.P.O.R. 34.
T258/84   ÉTAT FRANÇAIS/Portable hyperbar box structure [1987]
          E.P.O.R. 154.
T271/84   AIR PRODUCTS/Removal of hydrogen sulphide and car-
          bonyl sulphide O.J. EPO 1987, 405; [1987] E.P.O.R. 23.
T273/84   RHÔNE-POULENC/Silico-aluminate O.J. EPO 1986, 346;
          [1987] E.P.O.R. 44.
T153/85   AMOCO/Alternative claims O.J. EPO 1988, 1; [1988]
          E.P.O.R. 116.
T213/85   GEORG FISCHER/Grounds of appeal O.J. EPO 1987, 482;
          [1988] E.P.O.R. 45.

T222/85   PPG/Ungelled polyesters O.J. EPO 1988, 128; [1987]
           E.P.O.R. 99.
T226/85   UNILEVER/Stable bleaches O.J. EPO 1988, 336; [1989]
           E.P.O.R. 18.
T231/85   BASF/Triazole derivatives O.J. EPO 1989, 74; [1989]
           E.P.O.R. 293.
T268/85   STAMICARBON/Polymer filaments [1989] E.P.O.R 229.
T292/85   GENENTECH/Polypeptide expression O.J. EPO 1989, 275;
           [1989] E.P.O.R. 1.
T63/86   KOLLMORGEN/Consent for amendments O.J. EPO 1988,
           224; [1988] E.P.O.R. 316.
T117/86   FILMTEC/Costs O.J. EPO 1989, 40; [1989] E.P.O.R. 504.
T234/86   SOMARTEC/Therapy with interference currents O.J. EPO
           1989, 79; [1989] E.P.O.R. 303.
T389/86   BEHR/Time limit for appeal O.J. EPO 1988/87; [1988]
           E.P.O.R. 381.
T390/86   SHELL/Changed composition of division O.J. EPO 1989,
           30; [1989] E.P.O.R. 162.
T406/86   WACKER/Trichloroethylene O.J. EPO 1989, 302; [1989]
           E.P.O.R. 338.
T19/87   FUJITSU/Oral proceedings O.J. EPO 1988, 268; [1988]
           E.P.O.R. 393.
T105/87   INLAND STEEL February 25, 1988.
T139/87   BENDIX/Governor valve O.J. EPO 1990, 68; [1990] E.P.O.R.
           234.
T295/87   ICI/Polyetherketones O.J. EPO 1990, 470; [1991] E.P.O.R.
           56.
T301/87   BIOGEN/Alpha-interferons O.J. EPO 1990, 335; [1990]
           E.P.O.R. 190.
T323/87   RHÔNE-POULENC/Official language O.J. EPO 1989, 343;
           [1989] E.P.O.R. 412.
T326/87   DU PONT/Polyamide composition O.J. EPO 1992, 522;
           [1991] E.P.O.R. 47.
T381/87   RESEARCH CORPORATION/Publication O.J. EPO 1990,
           213; [1989] E.P.O.R. 138.
T383/87   MOBIL OIL/Thermoplastic film April 26, 1989.
T22/88   SECRETARY OF STATE FOR DEFENCE/Grounds for
           appeal O.J. EPO 1993, 143; [1993] E.P.O.R. 353.
T26/88   AKZO/Automatic revocation O.J. EPO 1991, 30; O.J. EPO
           1990, 4; [1990] E.P.O.R. 21.
T73/88   HOWARD/Snackfood O.J. EPO 1990, 5; [1990] E.P.O.R.
           112.
T93/88   UNILEVER/Oral proceedings August 11, 1988.
T129/88   AKZO/Fibre O.J. EPO 1993, 598; [1994] E.P.O.R. 176.
T136/88   VAN DER LELY; October 11, 1989.
T140/88   MEDTRONIC; February 13, 1990

T145/88   NICOLON Statement of grounds O.J. EPO 1990, 4; [1991]
            E.P.O.R. 356.
T197/88   ICI/Continuation of opposition proceedings O.J. EPO 1989,
            412; [1990] E.P.O.R. 243.
T212/88   BP/Theta-1 O.J. EPO 1992, 28; [1990] E.P.O.R. 518.
T227/88   UNILEVER/Detergent compositions O.J. EPO 1990, 292;
            [1990] E.P.O.R. 424.
T283/88   ABBOTT/Oral proceedings September 7, 1988; [1989]
            E.P.O.R. 225.
T320/88   EXXON/Arranging oral proceedings O.J. EPO 1990, 359;
            [1989] E.P.O.R. 372.
T432/88   OKI/Grounds for appeal [1990] E.P.O.R. 38.
T459/88   MAN/Admissibility of appeal O.J. EPO 1990, 425; [1991]
            E.P.O.R. 72.
T609/88   AMOCO July 10, 1990.
T60/89   HARVARD/Fusion proteins O.J. EPO 1992, 268; [1992]
            E.P.O.R. 320.
T79/89   XEROX/Finality of decision O.J. EPO 1992, 283; [1990]
            E.P.O.R. 558.
T93/89   HOECHST/Polyvinyl ester dispersion O.J. EPO 1992, 718;
            [1992] E.P.O.R. 155.
T173/89   ICI/Gamma-sorbitol [1991] E.P.O.R. 62.
T323/89   KONISHIROKU/Photographic material O.J. EPO 1992,
            169; [1992] E.P.O.R. 210.
T357/89   BASF/Withdrawal of appeal August 19, 1991 (P).
T534/89   EMS/Inadmissible late filing O.J. EPO 1994, 464; [1994]
            E.P.O.R. 540.
T695/89   BELL/Withdrawal of appeal September 9, 1991.
T716/89   UNILEVER/Right to be heard O.J. EPO 1992, 132.
T3/90   BRITISH TELECOMMUNICATIONS; April 24, 1991 (P).
T19/90   HARVARD/Onco-mouse O.J. EPO 1990, 476; [1990]
            E.P.O.R. 501.
T34/90   UNILEVER/Viscosity reduction O.J. EPO 1992, 454; [1992]
            E.P.O.R. 466.
T47/90   SUMITOMO/Remittal O.J. EPO 1991, 486; [1991] E.P.O.R.
            513.
T97/90   TAKEMOTO YUSHI/Lubricating agents O.J. EPO 1993,
            719; [1993] E.P.O.R. 135.
T156/90   BLUEWATER/Admissibility September 9, 1991.
T272/90   KOLBENSCHMIDT/Competence of Legal Board of
            Appeal O.J. EPO 1991, 205.
T290/90   SAVIO PLASTICA/Fee reduction October 9, 1990.
T338/90   DOW October 21, 1993.
T367/90   ASULAB/Reduction of fee July 2, 1991 (P).
T611/90   MITSUI/Fresh case O.J. EPO 1993, 50; [1991] E.P.O.R. 481.
T629/90   SEDLBAUER/Holding device O.J. EPO 1992, 654; [1993]
            E.P.O.R. 147.

T669/90 ATT/Inviting observations O.J. EPO 1992, 739; [1992] E.P.O.R. 397.

T788/90 PEUGEOT AND CITROËN/Opposition by the patent proprietor O.J. EPO 1994, 708.

T811/90 AE PLC/Exclusion of documents from file inspection O.J. EPO 1993, 728; [1994] E.P.O.R. 271.

T17/91 GILLETTE/Razor blades August 26, 1992.

T506/91 WOODCAP/Appeal of proprietor April 3, 1992.

T690/91 CELLTECH/Chymosin January 10, 1996.

T751/91 ESB/Second appeal [1993] E.P.O.R. 595.

T843/91(a) EASTMAN KODAK COMPANY/Partiality O.J. EPO 1994, 832.

T843/91 EASTMAN KODAK COMPANY/Photographic element (1) O.J. EPO 1994, 818; [1995] E.P.O.R. 116.

T934/91 KONICA/Meaning of decision O.J. EPO 1994, 184; [1993] E.P.O.R. 219.

T951/91 DU PONT/Late submission O.J. EPO 1995, 202; [1995] E.P.O.R. 398.

T27/92 KA-TE SYSTEMS/Intervention O.J. EPO 1994, 853; [1994] E.P.O.R. 501.

T371/92 FINA/Appeal not filed O.J. EPO 1995, 324; [1995] E.P.O.R. 485.

T501/92 ARTHUR G RUSSELL/Alphanumeric display O.J. EPO 1996, 261; [1996] E.P.O.R. 479.

T659/92 SCHWEISFURTH/Transfer of opposition O.J. EPO 1995, 519; [1994] E.P.O.R. 314.

T867/92 KONICA/Late citation O.J. EPO 1995, 126; [1995] E.P.O.R. 683.

T892/92 KONICA/Remittal O.J. EPO 1994, 664; [1995] E.P.O.R. 238.

T930/92 HITACHI/Ion beam processing O.J. EPO 1996, 191; [1997] E.P.O.R. 20.

T951/92 NEC/Opportunity to comment O.J. EPO 1996, 53; [1996] E.P.O.R. 371.

T1002/92 PETTERSON/Queueing System O.J. EPO 1995, 605; [1996] E.P.O.R. 1.

T1011/92 VON KÜNSSBERG September 16, 1994

T85/93 PITNEY BOWES/Apparatus for determining postage fees O.J. EPO 1998, 183; [1997] E.P.O.R. 561.

T167/93 PROCTER AND GAMBLE/Bleaching agents O.J. EPO 1997, 229; [1997] E.P.O.R. 471.

T583/93 HYMO CORPORATION/Water-soluble polymer dispersion O.J. EPO 1996, 496; [1997] E.P.O.R. 129.

T590/93 KOGYO/Photosensitive resins O.J. EPO 1995, 337; [1997] E.P.O.R. 478.

T647/93 HITACHI MAXELL/Procedural violation O.J. EPO 1995, 132; [1995] E.P.O.R. 195.

T840/93 PROCTOR II/Oral Composition O.J. EPO 1996, 335.

T926/93   MITSUBISHI/Gas laser device O.J. EPO 1997, 447; [1998] E.P.O.R. 94.

T986/93   EATON CORPORATION/Central tyre inflation system O.J. EPO 1996, 215; [1996] E.P.O.R. 486.

T1073/93   ALZA/Withdrawal of appeal February 11, 1993.

T97/94   CECA/Procedural timetable O.J. EPO 1998, 464.

T105/94   MOLNLYCKE July 29, 1997.

T522/94   TECHNO/Opposition admissibility O.J. EPO 1998, 421; [1992] E.P.O.R. 75.

T144/95   UNILEVER/Dishwashing process February 26, 1999

T154/95   GUILBERT EXPRESS January 27, 1998.

T274/95   MARS/Re-introduced ground of opposition O.J. EPO 1997, 99.

T389/95   MOTOROLA/Mobile phone October 15, 1997.

T460/95   SOMAB/Notice of appeal O.J. EPO 1998, 587.

T939/95   NCR/Time limit for rectification O.J. EPO 1998, 481.

T1002/95   FURUKAWA February 10, 1998.

T1007/95   PERSTORP/Appeal inadmissible O.J. EPO 1999, 733.

T501/96   March 3, 2000.

T570/96   ALLIED COLLOIDS August 20, 1998.

T898/96   HITACHI January 10, 1997.

T1/97   CROWN CORK/Naming of appellant March 30, 1999.

T315/97   3M/Reformatio in peius December 17, 1998, O.J. EPO (P).

T517/97   UNILEVER/Intervention O.J. EPO 2000, 515.

T722/97   JACOBS/Admissibility of appeal January 11, 1999.

Decisions of National Courts

Lenzing AG's European Patent (U.K.) [1997] R.P.C. 245
Buehler AG v. Chronos Richardson Ltd [1998] R.P.C. 609

CHAPTER 5

COMMON PROCEDURAL PROVISIONS

Contents

All references are to paragraph numbers

Cases Referred to in Chapter 5

A. Introduction

5–01 The three main proceedings which take place before the EPO are:-

(1) Examination proceedings before the Receiving Section and Examining Division (Part IV, Articles 90 to 98 EPC);
(2) Opposition proceedings before an Opposition Division (Part V, Articles 99 to 105 EPC);
(3) Appeal proceedings before a Board of Appeal (Part VI, Articles 106–112 EPC), in respect of a decision issued either by an Examining Division or by an Opposition Division.

5–02 Each of these proceedings is governed by its own specific procedural provisions which are set out in the corresponding parts of the EPC identified above and the Implementing Rules, and which are considered in Chapters 2, 3 and 4 above, respectively. Additionally, there are a number of procedural matters which are common to all proceedings before the EPO, and which are governed by common provisions of the EPC (in particular Part VII, Articles 113 to 125 EPC, which set out "Common provisions governing procedure"), and by subordinate legislation (see Chapter 1 at paragraphs 1–08 *et seq.*). Some of such common procedural provisions are considered below.

Proceedings before the EPO commonly involve procedural steps which have to be carried out within certain time limits. Such procedural steps normally involve the filing of documents or the payment of fees, or both.

B. Language

Article 14 EPC; Rule 6 EPC

(1) Language of an application as filed

5–03 A patent application must be filed in one of the three official languages of the EPO (English, French and German)—Article 14(1) EPC; this is subject to the provision in Article 14(2) EPC that "natural or legal persons having their residence or principal place of business" within a Contracting State having a language other than English, French or German as an official language may file an application in such official language, provided that a translation into English, French or German is filed within the relevant time limit set out in Rule 6 EPC.

5–03A According to the proposed revision of the EPC,[1] Article 14(2) EPC will be amended to allow a European patent application to be filed in any language, for the purpose of obtaining a filing date, provided that a translation into one of the three official languages is filed within a time

---

[1] See the Preface and Appendix 24.

limit provided in the Implementing Regulations. Article 14(3) EPC will also be amended to provide that the language of the proceedings (see below) will be the official language in which the European patent application is filed or translated.

(2) Language of EPO proceedings: use of other official languages

The official language of the EPO (English, French or German) in which a European patent application is filed becomes the "language of the proceedings" for all subsequent proceedings before the EPO concerning that application or any resulting European patent (Article 14(3) EPC). The significant language is that used for the description and claims (J7/80[2]), which must both be in the same language if the application is to be accorded a filing date (J18/96[3]). If the documents of an application are in more than one language, the application should be corrected by translation into the language of the description and claims (J7/80[4]). For example, if the text of the drawings is in a different official language from that of the description and claims, such text may be translated into the language of the proceedings (T382/94[5]). **5-04**

(a) Written proceedings

Nevertheless, in written proceedings any party may use any official language of the EPO (Rule 1(1) EPC). **5-05**

(b) Oral proceedings

Furthermore, in oral proceedings any party may use one of the other official EPO languages in place of the language of the proceedings, on condition that: either (i) the party gives notice to the EPO at least one month before the date appointed for the oral proceedings,
or (ii) the party makes provision for interpretation in the language of the proceedings (Rule 2(1) EPC). **5-06**

If (i) applies, the EPO makes provision at its own expense for interpretation into the language of the proceedings, or where appropriate into its other official languages (Rule 2(5) EPC).

"In the course of oral proceedings, the employees of the EPO may, in lieu of the language of the proceedings, use one of the other languages of the EPO" (Rule 2(2) EPC).

Furthermore: "If the parties and the EPO agree, any language may be used in oral proceedings" (Rule 2(4) EPC).

[2] J7/80 *SKF/Correction of mistakes—languages* O.J. EPO 1981, 137; [1979–85] E.P.O.R.: A: 36.
[3] J18/96 *N.N./Filing date* O.J. EPO 1998, 403; [1999] E.P.O.R. 9.
[4] J7/80 *SKF/Correction of mistakes—languages* O.J. EPO 1981, 137; [1979–85] E.P.O.R.: A.
[5] T382/94 *ZEISS/Documents as filed* O.J. EPO 1998, 24; [1998] E.P.O.R. 135.

(3) Use of other European languages: reduction in fees

(a) Filing an application

5–07　As mentioned in paragraph 5–04 above, "natural or legal persons having their residence or principal place of business" within a Contracting State having a language other than English, French or German as an official language may file an application in such official language (for example, Italian or Spanish), provided that a translation into an official EPO language (English, French or German) is filed within the time limit set out in Rule 6(1) EPC (Article 14(2) EPC).

(b) Filing "documents which have to be filed within a time limit"

5–08　Furthermore, such a person "may also file documents which have to be filed within a time limit" in such an official language of the Contracting State concerned, provided that a translation into the language of the proceedings (or a different official EPO language in certain cases) is filed within the time limit set out in Rule 6(2) EPC (Article 14(4) EPC).

(c) Entitlement of a party to use another European language

5–09　It is the residence or principal place of business of the party that is decisive under Article 14(2) and (4) EPC, not that of the party's professional representative (T149/85[6]).

(d) Effect of failure to file a translation in due time

5–10　If the translation of a document which is required under Article 14(2) or (4) EPC is not filed in due time, the document in question is deemed not to have been received, and the relevant fee is refunded (T193/87[7]).

(e) Entitlement to a reduction in fees

5–11　A reduction in the filing fee, examination fee, opposition fee or appeal fee (of 20 per cent: Article 12(1) R F) is allowed to an applicant, proprietor or opponent who "avails himself of the options" provided in Article 14(2) and (4) EPC (Rule 6(3) EPC).
　　The purpose of Article 14(2) and (4) EPC and Rule 6(1) and (2) EPC is:

> "to compensate at least in part for the disadvantages to nationals of Contracting States with non-EPO official languages of having to provide translations into an official EPO language. The main aim of Article 14 and Rule 6 EPC is thus to enable such parties to benefit from all EPC time limits for filing applications and subsequent items, and to allow them at least one month for translation purposes. The possibility of correcting any translation errors is also guaranteed" (G6/91[8]).

---

[6] T149/85 BREDERO/Inadmissible language of opposition O.J. EPO 1986, 143; [1986] E.P.O.R. 223.
[7] T193/87 ALFA LAVAL/Belated translation O.J. EPO 1993, 207; [1992] E.P.O.R. 63.
[8] G6/91 ASULAB II/Fee reduction O.J. EPO 1992, 491; [1993] E.P.O.R. 231.

A fee reduction is available if the "essential item of the first act" in filing, **5–12** examination, opposition or appeal proceedings is filed in an official language of the Contracting State concerned (G6/91[9]). Thus for an application, it is sufficient if the description and claims are filed in such a language (J4/88,[10] G6/91[11]). For an opposition at least the substantive part of the notice of opposition should be filed in such a language. For an appeal, the notice of appeal must be filed in such a language. Subsequent documents, such as the statement of grounds of appeal, may be filed in an official language of the EPO (G6/91[12]).

A fee reduction is precluded if "only inessential parts of the first act of the relevant proceedings" are filed in such a language (T905/90[13]). A fee reduction is not available if an application or other relevant document is first filed in an EPO official language and is subsequently filed in an official European language of the Contracting State concerned. Thus:

> "The person referred to in Article 14(2) EPC are entitled to the fee reduction under Rule 6(3) EPC if they file the essential item of the first act in filing, examination, opposition or appeal proceedings in an official language of the State concerned other than English, French or German, and supply the necessary translation *no earlier than simultaneously*" (G6/91[14]: emphasis added), and within the relevant time limit of Rule 6(1) or (2) EPC.

C. Representation of Parties

Articles 133 and 134 EPC   **5–13**

(1) Requirements for representation

A party to proceedings before the EPO may be either a natural or a legal **5–14** person.

Article 133 EPC provides a scheme of representation for parties to such proceedings. Article 133(1) provides that (subject to Article 133(2) EPC) "no person shall be compelled to be represented by a professional representative". Article 133(2) EPC provides that "a person not having either a residence or his principal place of business within the territory of a Contracting State to the EPC (that is, a 'non-European' person) must be represented by a professional representative and act through him in all proceedings" established by the EPC, "other than in filing the European patent application" (see Chapter 2 at paragraph 2–08). Article 133(2) EPC

---

[9] *Ibid.*
[10] J4/88 *GEO MECCANICA IDROTECNICA/Language of application* O.J. EPO 1989, 483; [1990] E.P.O.R. 69.
[11] G6/91 *ASULABII/Fee reduction* O.J. EPO 1992, 491; [1993] E.P.O.R. 231.
[12] *Ibid.*
[13] T905/90 *ALBRIGHT/Fee reduction* O.J. EPO 1994, 306; [1994] E.P.O.R. 585.
[14] *Ibid.*

also states that the Rules may provide other exceptions to the requirement for professional representation for non-European persons but no further exceptions have been made. Article 133(2) EPC provides that a person having his residence or principal place of business in the territory of one of the Contracting States (a "European" person) may act through an employee.

In other words, apart from when filing a European application, in proceedings before the EPO a non-European party must be represented by a professional representative. A European party may choose to be represented by a professional representative or may act on his own (if a natural person) or through one of his employees (G4/95[15]).

(2) Professional representatives

5–15 Article 134(1) EPC provides that a person may act as a professional representative if, being duly qualified, his name appears on the list maintained for this purpose by the EPO. Article 134(7) EPC provides that a "legal practitioner" as there defined may also act as a professional representative.

According to Article 134(2) EPC, a natural person may appear on that list if:

(a) he is a national of a Contracting State;
(b) he has his place of business or employment within a Contracting State; and
(c) he has passed the European qualifying examination.

Pursuant to Article 134(8) EPC, regulations were adopted by the Administrative Council setting up an Institute of Professional Representatives, and the European Qualifying Examination.

> "The purpose underlying such regulations is to ensure that proceedings before the EPO are conducted efficiently by properly qualified professional representatives, who are therefore fully knowledgeable in the law and practice under the EPC, and who are thus professionally competent to represent parties to such proceedings" (G4/95[16]).

(3) The function of a professional representative

5–16 "The appointment of a professional representative by a party involves the authorisation and identification of the professionally qualified person who is responsible for the presentation to the EPO of all submissions made by that party. Such presentation of a party's case is the essential core of the function of a professional representative under Article 133 EPC" (G4/95[17]).

---

[15] G4/95 BOGASKY II/Representation O.J. EPO 1996, 412; [1996] E.P.O.R. 333.
[16] Ibid.
[17] Ibid.

This applies during oral proceedings as well (see paragraphs 5–54 *et seq.* below).

(4) Authorisation

The requirements for authorisation of a professional representative are set **5–17** out in Rule 101 EPC. Cases where an authorisation is to be filed under Rule 101(1) EPC are determined by a decision of the President of the EPO. A signed authorisation may be required by the EPO within a specified period, and if it is not filed in due time "any procedural steps taken by the representative other than the filing of a European patent application shall be deemed not to have been taken" (Rule 101(4) EPC).

An "association of representatives" may be authorised. Such an association may consist of professional representatives who are not in private practice (Rule 101(9) EPC: Jl6/96[18]).

D. Objection to Members of the EPO: Suspected Partiality

Article 24 EPC

(1) Introduction

Article 24 EPC sets out a number of reasons for which a member of the **5–18** Board of Appeal may be excluded from participation in a particular appeal, or may be objected to by a party to a particular appeal, as well as the appropriate procedure to be followed. In contrast, there are no specific provisions in the EPC providing for exclusion of and objections to members of an Examining Division or an Opposition Division. Similar principles apply as regards an objection by a party, however, as will be discussed in section (3) at paragraph 5–24 below.

(2) Exclusion and objection: Boards of Appeal

(a) Exclusion of members

Article 24(1) EPC provides that members of the Board of Appeal may not **5–19** take part in a particular case:

- (a) "if they have any personal interest therein";
- (b) "if they have previously been involved as representatives of one of the parties";
- (c) "if they participated in the decision under appeal".

Article 24(2) EPC provides that either for one of the above reasons or "for any other reason", a member of a Board may inform the Board that he should not take part in a particular case. In such a circumstance, the procedure of Article 24(4) EPC is applied, namely that the remaining

---

[18] Jl6/96 *N.N./Association of representatives* O.J. EPO 1998, 347; [1999] E.P.O.R. 202.

members of the Board (in conjunction with a replacement member) decide whether or not to replace the member in question. No formal procedure is prescribed by the EPC in relation to the making of such a decision, and no formal decision is in practice issued.

(b) Objection to members

5–20 Members of a Board of Appeal may be objected to:

> (i) by a party, under Article 24(3) EPC;
> (ii) by other members of the Board, under the RPBA and the RPEBA.

5–21 **(i) Objection by a party.** The only grounds on which a party may object to one or more members are those set out in Article 24(1) EPC (see paragraph 5–19 above) or, if suspected of partiality (Article 24(3) EPC).

Furthermore, "An objection shall not be admissible if, while being aware of a reason for objection, the party has taken a procedural step"; and "No objection may be based upon the nationality of members" (Article 24(3) EPC).

If an objection is made to one or more members by a party, the Article 24(4) EPC decision process, described under paragraph 5–19 above, is applied. If necessary, a different composition will decide upon the objection. Oral proceedings may be appointed before the objection is decided (T1028/96[19]: see paragraph 5–28 below).

5–22 **(ii) Objection by other members.** Article 3 RPBA and RPEBA states that "If a Board has knowledge of a possible reason for exclusion or objection which does not originate from a member himself or from any party ... the procedure of Article 24(4) EPC shall be applied". In such a case: "The member concerned shall be invited to present his comments as to whether there is a reason for exclusion", and: "Before a decision is taken on the matter, there shall be no further proceedings in the case".

These provisions make it clear that there is a broad discretion given to members of the Boards of Appeal not to allow another member to take part in any particular case where they consider that there are good reasons why he should not take part. On general principles it is clearly better that a member should not participate in a particular case if there is any doubt as to the propriety of his doing so.

(c) Exclusion from file inspection of relevant documents

5–23 Rule 93(a) EPC provides that "the documents relating to the exclusion of or objections to members of the Boards of Appeal" shall, following publication of the application, be excluded from what is otherwise available for inspection in the files relating to a European patent application and a resulting patent, pursuant to Article 128(4) EPC.

---

[19] T1028/96 *DU PONT DE NEMOURS/Suspected partiality* O.J. EPO 2000, 475.

(3) Exclusion and objection: Examining and Opposition Divisions

According to the practice within the EPO, the director of the directorate 5–24 responsible for the technical field concerned selects the members of the Examining Division or Opposition Division for a particular case. In the event of an objection by a party to an examiner who is appointed by a member of an Examining Division or an Opposition Division in a particular case, such director takes an administrative decision as to whether or not to change that Examiner (G5/91[20]).

The provisions of Article 24 EPC relating to exclusion and objection apply only to members of the Boards of Appeal and the Enlarged Board of Appeal.

Nevertheless:

> "it must ... be considered as a general principle of law that nobody should decide a case in respect of which a party may have good reasons to assume partiality. The basic requirement of impartiality therefore applies also to employees of the departments of the first instance of the EPO taking part in decision-making activities affecting the rights of any party" (G5/91[21]).

Furthermore:

   (i) "There is no legal basis under the EPC for any separate appeal against an order of a director of a department of the first instance ... rejecting an objection to a member of the Division on the ground of suspected partiality";
  (ii) "the composition of [an Examining or Opposition Division] may be challenged on such a ground on appeal" against the decision of the Examining or Opposition Division" (G5/91).
 (iii) Furthermore, a Board of Appeal may consider such a ground of objection to a member of an Examining or Opposition Division of its own motion (G5/91[22]).

4. Suspected partiality: examples

The question of suspected partiality "can only be decided upon in the light 5–25 of the particular circumstances of each individual case," and has to be decided on an objective basis; are there good reasons for a "reasonable" party to the proceedings to suspect partiality in one or more members of an Examining Division, or an Opposition Division or a Board of Appeal?

   (a) In one case an objection to the primary examiner of an Opposition 5–26 Division was based upon the fact that this examiner was a former

---

[20] G5/91 DISCOVISION/Appealable decision O.J. EPO 1992, 617; [1993] E.P.O.R. 120.
[21] Ibid.
[22] Ibid.

employee of the opponent company, who had *inter alia* acted as representative of the opponent in a similar opposition case against another patent owned by the patentee about two years previously.

It was held that: "Disqualifying partiality presumes a preconceived attitude on the part of a deciding person . . . towards a party . . . to the case." On this basis, the Board proceeded to examine the file of the Opposition Division proceedings, and held that "When the content of the file . . . does not go beyond a normal discussion between the EPO and a party, and there is nothing manifestly unreasonable to be found in the reasoning, disqualifying partiality cannot be concluded". The objection of suspected partiality was therefore rejected (T261/88[23]).

This approach appears to be contrary to the general principle of law stated in G5/91[24] and quoted above. The correct principle to be applied is to enquire whether, at the time when a decision on the case is *about to be taken*, a reasonable party (having knowledge of the relevant circumstances) would *reasonably suspect* partiality from the deciding person in question; not whether, *after the decision has been taken*, the file shows any evidence of a preconceived attitude in the person who has made the decision.

5–27   (b) In another case, a Board of Appeal issued a substantive decision against the opponent, and remitted the case for further prosecution to the Opposition Division, who issued a further decision against the opponent on a different aspect of the case. The opponent appealed, and the second substantive appeal was assigned to the Board of Appeal with the same composition as previously. The opponent objected to all three members of the Board of Appeal deciding the second appeal, on the ground of suspected partiality.

A different composition of Board of Appeal was therefore appointed under Article 24 EPC to decide the issue of suspected partiality, *before the second appeal was decided*. In these circumstances the composition of the Board of Appeal appointed under Article 24 EPC applied the above stated general principle of law by considering whether the file of the proceedings in the first appeal indicated any evidence of a "preconceived attitude" in the conduct of the earlier Board of Appeal such as to justify a finding of disqualifying partiality which would require a change of composition of the Board of Appeal before the second substantive appeal was decided. The objection of suspected partiality was rejected (T843/91[25]).

5–28   (c) In a further case, the Opposition Division revoked a patent on the ground of insufficiency but the patent proprietor had not had an opportunity to comment upon this ground before issue of the decision, contrary to Article 113(1) EPC. The Board of Appeal set aside the decision of the Opposition Division, and ordered that the case be re-heard before a different composition of Opposition Division. The Board stated that:

[23] T261/88 DISCOVISION/Signal information O.J. EPO 1994 (1–2).
[24] G5/91 DISCOVISION/Appealable decision O.J. EPO 1992, 617; [1993] E.P.O.R. 120.
[25] T843/91 EASTMAN KODAK COMPANY/Partiality O.J. EPO 1994, 832; [1995] E.P.O.R. 126.

"the important point is not, whether the file record shows any previous evidence of actual partiality by the members of the Opposition Division during the previous conduct of the case, nor whether the present members of the Opposition Division would in fact be unprejudiced or partial if they re-heard the case, but whether a party ... would have reasonable ground to suspect that they would not receive a fair hearing if the case was re-heard before the same composition of Opposition Division (whether because of possible prejudice as to how the case should be decided, or because of possible partiality, or otherwise), since the Opposition Division has already issued a written decision containing reasons for revoking the patent ... The proprietor has reasonable grounds to suspect that the same composition of Opposition Division would have difficulty in re-hearing and deciding the case without being tainted by its previous decision (as reflected by the proprietor's request for rehearing before a different composition). It is therefore clearly in the interest of the proper administration of justice within the EPO that this case should be re-heard and re-decided by a different composition of Opposition Division" (T433/93[26]).

(d) In opposition appeal proceedings, a chairman of a Board of Appeal who has previously been a chairman or member of the Board of Appeal which decided upon the grant of the opposed patent may be excluded from such Board of Appeal, if the same issue or issues which were decided during the examination appeal lead to the grant of the opposed patent are to be decided again in opposition appeal proceedings (T1028/96[27]).

E. Auxiliary Requests: Amendment During Proceedings

An auxiliary request is a request for amendment which is contingent upon **5–29** the main request or any preceding auxiliary request being held to be unallowable (T153/85[28], T79/89[29], T169/96[30], T1105/96[31]).

Article 113(2) EPC states that the EPO shall consider and decide an application or patent "only in the text submitted to it, or agreed, by the applicant or proprietor".

In accordance with Legal Advice No 15/98[32], this is interpreted to mean that:

"the EPO is bound by the applicant's submissions. A European patent may however only be granted on the basis of a text which is without

[26] T433/93 *ATOTECH/Re-hearing* O.J. EPO 1997, 509; [1998] E.P.O.R. 135.
[27] T1028/96 *DU PONT DE NEMOURS/Suspected partiality* O.J. EPO 2000, 475.
[28] T153/85 *AMOCO/Alternative claims* O.J. EPO 1988, 1; [1988] E.P.O.R. 116.
[29] T79/89 *XEROX/Finality of decision* O.J. EPO 1992, 283; [1990] E.P.O.R. 558.
[30] T169/96 *ELF ATOCHEM/Main and auxiliary request* [1997] E.P.O.R. 209.
[31] T1105/96 *HAMAMATSU/Requests* O.J. EPO 1998, 249; [1998] E.P.O.R. 26.
[32] O.J. EPO 1998, 113; see Appendix 6.

formal or substantive deficiencies, and which has been submitted or agreed to by the applicant in its entirety. If the text submitted by the applicant contains deficiencies—even if the deficiencies relate to part of the application only—the application as a whole will be refused (Article 97(1) EPC)."

This is the basis of the practice of "auxiliary requests" (or "subsidiary" requests) which is applied in examination, opposition and appeal proceedings. This practice is in contrast to that in proceedings before the United Kingdom Patent Office and in appeals therefrom, where subsidiary claims are automatically considered as an alternative basis upon which a patent may be granted or maintained.

5–30   Consequently, in all such proceedings:

"When one or more auxiliary requests are filed in addition to the main request ..., the EPO is bound to these requests, and to their order. Before a decision can be made in relation to an auxiliary request, the main request and all preceding auxiliary requests must be examined and decided upon (Article 113(2) EPC ... T169/96[33]), so long as such preceding requests have not been withdrawn, and are therefore still pending" (T169/96,[34] T1105/96[35]).

In a case where the applicant or patent proprietor has filed main and auxiliary requests which are unallowable and which precede an auxiliary request which is allowable, the patent is granted or maintained in accordance with the allowable request. The decision must give reasons for rejecting each request which is unallowable and for allowing the one request. (Rule 68(2) EPC: T234/86[36]). A decision of an Opposition Division in such circumstances is an interlocutory decision under Article 106(3) EPC, which may be the subject of an appeal by either the patent proprietor or the opponent, or by both (see paragraph 3–82) (T234/86[37]; Legal Advice No. 15/98[38]).

F. Observations by Third Parties

5–31   Article 115 EPC provides, during pending proceedings before the EPO, that any person may file observations in writing concerning the patentability of an invention which is the subject of a European patent application, following publication of the application. The observations must include the grounds on which they are based.

---

[33] T169/96 *ELF ATOCHEM/Main and auxiliary requests* [1997] E.P.O.R. 209.
[34] *Ibid.*
[35] T1105/96 *HAMAMATSU/Requests* O.J. EPO 1998, 249; [1988] E.P.O.R. 26.
[36] T234/86 *SOMARTEC/Therapy with interference currents* O.J. EPO 1989, 79; [1989] E.P.O.R. 303.
[37] *Ibid.*
[38] O.J. EPO 1998, 113; see Appendix 6.

A person who files such observations is not a party to the proceedings before the EPO. Any such observations are communicated to the applicant or patent proprietor who may comment upon them. The EPO may of its own motion take up the contents of such observations as objections to the grant of a patent, under Article 114(1) EPC as a matter of discretion. The applicable principles when such discretion is exercised so as to introduce fresh grounds, facts or evidence into the proceedings before an Examining Division, an Opposition Division or a Board of Appeal are discussed in Chapters 2, 3, and 4 respectively.

The procedure under Article 115 EPC may in particular be useful if a competitor of the applicant knows of grounds of objection to a patent application which are not known to the EPO, and wishes such grounds to be considered by the EPO without having to wait for possible grant of the patent and the consequent opportunity to commence opposition proceedings.

G. Evidence

(1) Form and probative value: "free evaluation"

There are no rules as to the form or content of evidence and no line is drawn **5–32** between admissible and inadmissible evidence (as in the United Kingdom). All documents are admissible as evidence, and the probative value of any evidence in any form depends upon what it is, and the circumstances of each particular case. This is in accordance with the principle of "free appreciation of means of proof" (T482/89[39]), or "free evaluation of evidence" (T750/94[40]).

In accordance with this principle:

> "items of evidence relevant to a matter in issue must be given an appropriate weight, in order to reliably establish what is likely to have occurred. An unsigned statement by an unknown and unnamed person should in principle be given minimal weight" (T750/94[41]).

Oral evidence is admissible in the discretion of the EPO, and is considered in paragraph 5–60 below.

Cases are commonly decided simply upon the written submissions from the parties or their professional representatives, which may include information and statements of an evidential nature. A first instance department or a Board of Appeal, in deciding each case, will give such weight (if any) as it considers appropriate to all such evidence and submissions.

---

[39] T482/89 TÉLÉMECANIQUE/Electrical supply O.J. EPO 1992, 646; [1993] E.P.O.R. 259.
[40] T750/94 AT&T/Proof of publication O.J. EPO 1998, 32; [1997] E.P.O.R. 509.
[41] Ibid.

5–33   The EPO "must ascertain the relevance of evidence . . . before deciding to admit or reject it", save in exceptional circumstances (T142/97[42]), as to which, see Chapter 4 at paragraph 4–119, for example.

Having regard to the technical nature of most issues which have to be decided in EPO proceedings, and the technical expertise of those making the decisions in such proceedings, this approach works well in the majority of cases.

The application of this approach by the EPO to the assessment of evidence concerning an issue of fact, such as prior use, is commonly criticised, however, especially within the United Kingdom, where evidence of such a nature is normally the subject of oral examination and cross-examination. Such oral examination and cross-examination is well established within the adversarial system of litigation which is practised in the United Kingdom and Ireland, but is not normally practised in other Contracting States, under the investigative system of litigation which is applied in such States.

The determination within any kind of legal proceedings of what actually happened in the past is nevertheless always likely to be problematic, especially when such determination takes place many years after the events in questions and is at least partially dependent upon human memory: this is commonly the case in relation to allegations of prior use.

(2) Time of filing

5–33a   The EPC does not regulate the time of filing of facts and evidence in either *ex parte* or *inter partes* proceedings. Such timing is considered in the context of examination, opposition and appeal proceedings, in Chapters 2, 3 and 4 at paragraphs 2–40, 3–51 *et seq.* and 4–114 *et seq.*, respectively.

(3) Burden of proof

5–34   In accordance with normal principles, the initial burden of proof in establishing facts lies with whoever asserts such facts.

Thus in *examination* proceedings an Examining Division may assert that a document was *prima facie* published before the filing date of an application. If not challenged by the applicant, the Examining Division will proceed on the basis that the document is a prior publication. If the applicant challenges the fact of prior publication, investigations may be carried out which may or may not establish the fact of prior publication (see for example T750/94[43]).

In *opposition* proceedings the position has been stated as follows:

"If the parties to opposition proceedings make contrary assertions which they cannot substantiate and the EPO is unable to establish the

---

[42] T142/97 STOCKLI/Apparatus for separating disc-shaped objects O.J. EPO 2000, 358.
[43] T750/94 A.T.&T./Proof of publication O.J. EPO 1998, 32; [1997] E.P.O.R. 509.

facts of its own motion, the patent proprietor is given the benefit of the doubt" (T219/83[44]).

In other words, since the burden of proof lies on the opponent who is alleging invalidity on the basis of asserted facts, it is for the opponent to establish such facts to the required standard of proof (see below).

(4) Standard of proof

In relation to an issue of fact, such as prior publication of a document, or prior use of a product or process, the EPO must decide what happened, having regard to the available evidence on the balance of probabilities, as distinct from "beyond all reasonable doubt" or "absolute conviction": that is, it must decide what is more likely than not to have happened (T381/87[45], T182/89[46], T270/90[47]). Parties must therefore seek to prove facts alleged by it to that degree of proof (T270/90). **5–35**

In applying this principle:

> "When an issue of fact is being examined and decided by the EPO on the balance of probabilities, the more serious the issue the more convincing must the evidence be to support it. If a decision upon such an issue may result in refusal or revocation of a European patent, for example in a case concerning alleged prior publication or prior use, the available evidence in relation to that issue must be very critically and strictly examined. A European patent should not be refused or revoked unless the grounds for refusal or revocation (that is, the legal and factual reasons) are fully and properly proved" (T750/94[48]).

Although the standard of proof should be the same for all objections under Article 100 EPC, namely the balance of probabilities, if for example in a case concerning an alleged prior use practically all the evidence in support of the allegation "lies within the power and knowledge of the opponent the latter has to prove his case up to the hilt" (T472/92[49]). **5–36**

It has been stated that:

> "Where public prior use is cited, the assessment of probability which normally underlies the Board's opinion must cede to a stricter criterion close to absolute conviction. In other words, there should be a degree of certainty which is beyond all reasonable doubt" (T97/94[50]).

[44] T219/83 *BASF/Zeolites* O.J. EPO 1986, 211; [1986] E.P.O.R. 247.
[45] T381/87 *RESEARCH CORPORATION/Publication* O.J. EPO 1990, 213; [1989] E.P.O.R. 138.
[46] T182/89 *SUMITOMO/Extent of opposition* O.J. EPO 1991, 391; [1990] E.P.O.R. 438.
[47] T270/90 *ASAHI/Polyphenylene ether compositions* O.J. EPO 1993, 725; [1992] E.P.O.R. 365.
[48] T750/94 *A.T.&T./Proof of publication* O.J. EPO 1998, 32; [1997] E.P.O.R. 509.
[49] T472/92 *SEKISUI/Joint venture* O.J. EPO 1998, 161; [1997] E.P.O.R. 432.
[50] T97/94 *CECA/Timetable for procedure* O.J. EPO 1998, 467; [1992] E.P.O.R. 65

It seems difficult to justify such a high standard of proof for prior public use in particular, however.

(5) "Taking of Evidence"

5–37   Article 117 EPC and Rules 72 to 76 EPC "are solely concerned with setting out the procedure relevant to formal 'taking of evidence'" (G4/95). A number of decisions have referred to Article 117 EPC as providing a basis for the hearing of oral submissions and evidence in proceedings before the EPO (*e.g.* T482/89[51], T843/91[52]), but under the EPC, "the prescribed procedure does not contain any detailed regulations" controlling the filing of facts and evidence, which is "left to the discretionary control of the EPO" (see paragraph 3–51) and such decisions must be regarded as based upon an incorrect interpretation of the EPC in this respect.

A pre-condition for the use of the procedure of Article 117 EPC is the making of a decision by the EPC to "take evidence" in the sense of Article 117 EPC or to carry out an inspection, pursuant to Rule 71(1) EPC. The decision shall set out "the investigation which it intends to carry out, relevant facts to be proved and the date, time and place of the investigation".

The "taking of evidence" pursuant to Article 117 EPC may involve the hearing of oral evidence of witnesses and experts, either if the EPO considers it necessary or following a report from a party. In the latter case, the decision pursuant to Rule 72(1) EPC "shall determine the period of time within which the party filing the request must make known to the EPO the names and addresses of the witnesses and experts when it wishes to be heard".

5–38   The detailed regulation of the taking of evidence is set out in Article 117 and Rules 72 to 76 EPC. One important feature of this procedure is that a party, witness or expert who is summoned to give oral evidence may request that his evidence be heard "by a competent Court is his country of residence". The EPO may then request such a competent court under Article 131(2) EPC to hear such person, in its discretion, and may also request that the evidence is taken "on oath or in an equally binding form" (Article 117(4) EPC). A member of the EPO may attend the hearing before the court and may question such person, either through the court or directly (Article 117(6) EPC).

Furthermore, if a party, witness or expert is giving evidence before the EPO, before being heard "he shall be informed that the EPO may request the competent court in the country of residence of the person concerned to re-examine his evidence on oath or in an equally binding form" (Rule 72(3) EPC). Subsequently, the EPO may so request a competent court "if it considers it advisable" (Article 117(5) ERC).

Underlying these provisions is the fact that the EPO does not have

---

[51] T482/89 *TÉLÉMECANIQUE/Electrical supply* O.J. EPO 1992, 646; [1993] E.P.O.R. 259.
[52] T843/91 *EASTMAN KODAK COMPANY/Partiality* O.J. EPO 1994, 832; [1995] E.P.O.R. 126.

authority to administer oaths such as are normally administered to a witness giving evidence before a national court. Thus, in the event that a person gives false evidence before the EPO, no direct sanction is possible. Reference to a competent national court under the procedure discussed above provides an indirect sanction.

(6) Confidential evidence

(a) Request for confidentiality

Evidence which is filed by a party to proceedings before the EPO normally **5–38a** becomes part of the file relating to such proceedings, which is open to inspection upon request (Article 128(4) EPC). This is subject to the restrictions upon inspection which are set out in Rule 93 EPC.

If evidence is filed by a party during proceedings before a department of the EPO together with a request that it be maintained confidential, this request is decided by the President of the EPO, under Rule 93(d) EPC. If the request is refused by the President, the evidence is returned to the party without being examined by the department of the EPO (T516/89[53]).

(b) Documents filed in error in breach of confidentiality

"Documents filed as evidence may only be exceptionally and on a **5–38b** substantiated request remain unconsidered and be returned" to the party who filed them (T760/89[54]).

For example, in a case where documents has been placed under an order of confidentiality by a United States court but had been filed by the proprietor in opposition proceedings by error and in breach of such order, and the opponent agreed to their return to the proprietor, the documents were returned to the proprietor without consideration by the EPO, because "the interests of the filing party in having them returned unconsidered clearly prevail over the interests of any other party and the public interest" (T760/89[55]).

H. Oral Proceedings

(1) Introduction

The right to an oral hearing provided by Article 116 EPC is an important **5–39** procedural right. It is, of course, additional to what is set out in Article 113(1) EPC, namely that: "The decisions of the EPO may only be based on grounds or evidence on which the parties concerned have had an opportunity to present their comments." Nevertheless, both these provisions can be considered as essentially concerned with ensuring as far as possible that parties to proceedings before the EPO are treated fairly prior

---

[53] T516/89 *SCHERING/Confidential papers* O.J. EPO 1992, 436; [1992] E.P.O.R. 476.
[54] T760/89 *BURLINGTON/Return of documents* O.J. EPO 1994, 797; [1995] E.P.O.R. 224.
[55] *Ibid.*

to the making of a decision and particularly that they are given proper opportunity to present all relevant matters, *i.e.* facts, evidence and argument, in support of their case.

Oral proceedings may take place either following a decision to that effect by the EPO, or following a request from a party to proceedings before the EPO.

(a) Appointment by the EPO

5–40 Article 116(1) EPC provides that oral proceedings shall take place "at the instance of the EPO if it considers this to be expedient." However, as a matter of practice, it is rare for oral proceedings to be appointed either by a first instance department or by a Board of Appeal of its own motion and in the absence of a request from a party.

(b) Appointment upon request by a party

5–41 Generally a party to proceedings before any department or instance of the EPO has a *right* to an oral hearing under Article 116 EPC upon request. This is subject to two exceptions, when the appointment of such an oral hearing following a request from a party remains within the discretion of the competent department of the EPO.

(c) Discretionary power of the EPO in certain cases

5–42 **(i) Second or further requests.** If an oral hearing has already taken place in proceedings before a department of the EPO then, according to the second sentence of Article 116(1) EPC, "the EPO may reject a request for further oral proceedings before the same department where the parties and the subject of the proceedings are the same".

What exactly is meant by the phrase "the subject of the proceedings" has not yet been interpreted by the Board of Appeal. On a broad interpretation, the "subject" of proceedings could refer to the patent or application which is the subject of the proceedings. However, reference to the French and German corresponding texts indicates that a narrow interpretation is probably intended, namely when the same basic issue has already been considered at an oral hearing.

5–43 **(ii) Proceedings before the Receiving Section.** The Receiving Section is responsible for formal examination of an application after filing (see paragraphs 2–10 *et seq.*). The appointment of an oral hearing during proceedings before the Receiving Section is always discretionary, except when a *refusal* of the patent application in suit is envisaged.

The Receiving Section's powers to *refuse* an application are expressly provided for under Article 91(3) EPC. If the Receiving Section has to decide under Rule 69(2) EPC whether loss of rights (*i.e.* deemed withdrawal of the patent application for non-payment of a fee) has resulted from the EPC pursuant to Rule 69(1) EPC, the Receiving Section is not "envisaging refusing the application" within the meaning of Article 116(2) EPC. Thus in such a case the appointment of oral proceedings is discretionary (J Unnumbered[56]).

If the applicant has had a full opportunity to present facts, evidence and argument in support of his case, and the case is sufficiently clear for a decision to be taken, a request for oral proceedings may be rejected (J Unnumbered,[57] J20/89[58]).

(2) The right to oral proceedings upon request

Subject to the above exceptions pursuant to Article 116(1) EPC, a party who 5–44 requests oral proceedings is in principle entitled to such proceedings once as of right, *e.g.* (T299/86[59] and T19/87[60]).

Thus:

> "The right to be heard at oral proceedings under Article 116(1) EPC subsists so long as proceedings are pending before the EPO, and a request for oral proceedings which is must be granted (*i.e.* oral proceedings must be appointed) before any request for a party (whether procedural or substantive) is decided against that party so as to cause them a loss of rights" (T556/95[61]).

Article 116(1) EPC is in practice interpreted as being applicable so as to give a party a right to oral proceedings only if it is intended or envisaged that a decision will be issued which is adverse to that party. Requests for oral proceedings are normally made in that sense (for examine, "on an auxiliary basis").

Following a request for oral proceedings from a party, oral proceedings must be appointed before any request of that party, whether procedural or substantive, is decided against that party so as to cause a loss of rights (T556/95[62]).

(a) Requesting oral proceedings

(i) **Time of request.** Under Article 116 EPC, a party is entitled to make a 5–45 request for oral proceedings at any time during the course of proceedings before a particular department of Board of Appeal. A fresh request has to be filed in the event of an appeal, since this constitutes new proceedings (T34/90[63]).

If there is a possibility that oral proceedings will be desired in particular proceedings, it is clearly safer for a party to make such a request at the start

---

[56] J Unnumbered O.J. EPO 1985, 159; [1979–85] E.P.O.R.: A: 234.
[57] *Ibid.*
[58] J20/89 *Appellate jurisdiction (PCT cases)* O.J. EPO 1991, 375; [1991] E.P.O.R. 436.
[59] T299/86 *SECHER/Oral proceedings* O.J. EPO 1988, 88; [1988] E.P.O.R. 204.
[60] T19/87 *FUJITSU/Oral proceedings* O.J. EPO 1988, 268; [1988] E.P.O.R. 393.
[61] T556/95 *CHAUM/Undeniable system* O.J. EPO 1997, 205; [1997] E.P.O.R. 394.
[62] *Ibid.*
[63] T34/90 *UNILEVER/Viscosity reduction* O.J. EPO 1992, 454; [1992] E.P.O.R. 466.

of or at an early stage in the proceedings, since such a request can always subsequently be withdrawn (see paragraph 5–49 below):

"the right of a party to have oral proceedings is dependent upon such party filing a request for such proceedings: in the absence of such a request, a party has no right to such proceedings, and the EPO can issue a decision, whether adverse or not, without appointing such proceedings" (T299/86[64]).

Furthermore:

"unless and until (the party) has actually filed such a request, he runs the risk that an adverse decision may be issued without the appointment of such proceedings, if it is otherwise appropriate to do so ..." (T299/86[65]).

5–46   (ii) Contents of a request. If oral proceedings are required, it is essential that the form of the request should be clear. The need for clarity is especially necessary if misunderstandings are to be avoided, bearing in mind the multi-national membership of the EPO. Whether or not in a particular case there has been such a request is a matter of interpretation of the communication from the party in its context.

The sentence "I again request an interview, as a preliminary to oral proceedings" has been interpreted as containing both a request for an interview and a request for oral proceedings (T19/87[66]). The statement "I reserve my right to request oral proceedings under Article 116 EPC" has been interpreted in its context as not being a request for oral proceedings. The distinction was drawn between actually making such a request, and reserving the right to make such a request. It was pointed out that there is little point in a party reserving "his right" to request oral proceedings, in view of the fact that he is entitled to make such a request at any time during the proceedings. The sentence "probably there should be an appeal as soon as possible" has been interpreted in its context as a request for oral proceedings (T283/88[67]).

As a matter of practice, if there is any doubt in a particular case as to whether or not oral proceedings have been requested, it is clearly desirable that clarification should be sought by the EPO from the party concerned, before a decision is issued.

5–47   (iii) Effect of a request

"If on the proper interpretation of a communication from a party, it constitutes a request for oral proceedings, there is no power to issue an

---

[64] T299/86 SECHER/Oral proceedings O.J. EPO 1988, 88; [1988] E.P.O.R. 204.
[65] Ibid.
[66] T19/87 FUJITSU/Oral proceedings O.J. EPO 1988, 268; [1988] E.P.O.R. 393.
[67] T283/88 ABBOTT/Oral proceedings [1989] E.P.O.R. 225.

adverse decision without first appointing such oral proceedings" (T19/87[68]).

If a request for oral proceedings has been filed by a party to first instance proceedings, and a decision adverse to that party is issued without the appointment of an oral hearing in the event of an appeal the decision will be held void and set aside. Thus, in practice the proceedings before the first instance department which failed to appoint oral proceedings are continued by the appointment of an oral hearing before that department.

Such a situation constitutes a substantial procedural violation for the purpose of Rule 67 EPC, justifying refund of the appeal fee (see Chapter 4 at paragraphs 4–166 *et seq.* below).

If an admissible appeal is not filed against the first instance decision, neither the first instance department nor a Board of Appeal has the power to set aside such decision, which therefore exists with full effect (T371/92[69]).

(b) Oral proceedings compared with interview

In some cases, requests for interviews have become confused with requests **5–48** for oral proceedings (*e.g.* T19/87,[70] and T283/88[71]). Oral proceedings must be clearly distinguished from interviews. The practice in relation to the holding of interviews is clearly set out in the Guidelines (see, *e.g.* C-VI, 6), and is essentially a matter for the discretion of the Examining Division. The practice is set out in a Notice dated June 22, 1989.[72]

(c) Withdrawal of a request

A request for oral proceedings may be withdrawn at any time. However, it **5–49** is clearly desirable that such a withdrawal is made clearly and as early as possible in advance of the appointed day.

In *inter partes* proceedings, if one party withdraws a request for oral proceedings at a late stage and causes unnecessary expense to other parties, this could be a ground for an award of costs under Article 104 EPC (see Chapter 4 at paragraph 4–161).

> "If oral proceedings are appointed as a result of a party's request for such proceedings on an auxiliary basis, and if that party subsequently states that it will not be represented at the oral proceedings, such a statement should normally be treated as equivalent to withdrawal of the request for oral proceedings" (T3/90[73]).

---

[68] See note 66.
[69] T371/92 *FINA/Appeal not filed* O.J. EPO 1995, 324; [1995] E.P.O.R. 485.
[70] See note 66.
[71] See note 67.
[72] Notice of the Vice-President of DG2 concerning interview practice dated June 22, 1989: O.J. EPO 1989, 388.
[73] T3/90 *BRITISH TELECOMMUNICATIONS/Oral proceedings* O.J. EPO 1992 737; [1993] E.P.O.R. 366.

(3) Summons to oral proceedings

(a) Fixing the date

5–50   If oral proceedings are to take place, the parties are summoned on a particular date. At least two months notice of the summons must be given to the parties, unless they agree to a shorter period (Rule 71(1) EPC). However in special circumstances, a summons may be issued with less than two month's notice even without the agreement of the parties (J14/91[74]).

The procedure by which a date for oral proceedings is fixed is currently governed by a Notice dated September 1, 2000.[75] From November 1, 2000, one single date for oral proceedings will be fixed, without any pre-announcement by telephone or telefax. Oral proceedings as so appointed will only be cancelled or changed to another date if a party advances serious reasons which justify the fixing of a new date. A request to fix a different date must be filed as soon as possible after grounds preventing a party from attending the oral proceedings have arisen.

Examples of serious substantive reasons which may justify a change of date are set out in the Notice. Examples of reasons which will not normally justify a change of date are also given in the Notice, namely:

— a summons to other oral proceedings before the EPO or a national court notified after the summons in question.
— excessive work pressure.

Furthermore, every request for a change of date should contain a statement why another representative within the meaning of Article 133(3) or 134 EPC cannot take the place of the representative requesting a change of date.

(b) Preparing for oral proceedings: accompanying communications

5–51   Rule 71a EPC states that:

"(1) When issuing the summons, the European Patent Office shall draw attention to the points which in its opinion need to be discussed for the purposes of the decision to be taken. At the same time a final date for making written submissions in preparation for the oral proceedings shall be fixed. Rule 84 EPC ['Duration of time limits'] shall not apply. New facts and evidence presented after that date need not be considered, unless admitted on the grounds that the subject of the proceedings has changed.

(2) If the patent proprietor has been notified of the grounds prejudicing the grant or maintenance of the patent, he may be invited

---

[74] Notice of the Vice-Presidents of DG2 and DG3 dated September 1, 2000: O.J. EPO 2000, 456; see Appendix 9.
[75] J14/91 *ALT/Inspection of files* O.J. EPO 1993, 479; [1994] E.P.O.R. 184.

to submit, by the date specified in paragraph 1, second sentence, documents which reach the requirements of the Convention. Paragraph 1, third and fourth sentences, shall apply *mutatis mutandis.*"

This Rule is applicable to proceedings before first instance departments, but does not apply to the Boards of Appeal (G6/95[76]).

The subject of the proceedings is changed within the meaning of Rule 71a(1) and (?), *inter alia*, "where the Examining Division itself introduces a new document into the proceedings for the first time during oral proceedings" (T951/97[77]).

Rule 71a EPC gives the first instance departments a discretion to admit or refuse amendments (and other new material) prior to issuing a decision. However, the considerations underlying the exercise of such discretion are different in examination and opposition proceedings. A particular consideration in opposition proceedings is that other parties should not be taken by surprise. This does not apply in examination proceedings, where amendments proposed after the final date set under Rule 71a EPC may be admitted unless they are *clearly not allowable.* If amended claims are not admitted, the reasons therefor must be given (T755/96[78]).

Guidance to the conduct of oral proceedings during appeal proceedings is contained in "Guidance for Parties to Appeal Proceedings and their Representatives"[79]. It is there stated (paragraph 3.5.1.) that "Oral proceedings concentrate on the essential points of the appeal. The case should be ready for decision at the close of oral proceedings." This corresponds with Article 11(3) of the Rules of Procedure of the Boards of Appeal, which requires that "if oral proceedings take place, the Board shall endeavour to ensure that each case is ready for decision at the conclusion of the oral proceedings, unless there are special reasons to the contrary".

Both in relation to this requirement, and also to ensure that the decision **5–52** is based upon the grounds or evidence on which the parties have had a sufficient opportunity to present their comments (Article 113(1) EPC), a Board "may send with the summons to oral proceedings a communication under Article 11(1) RPBA" (see Chapter 4 at paragraph 4–89 above). Such a communication often plays an important part in shaping the course of oral proceedings.

Immediately prior to the oral proceedings, all the members of the Board will study the case. An important advantage of this aspect of the Board of Appeal procedure is that at the commencement of the oral proceedings all the members have a thorough knowledge of both the facts of the case and the issues which have to be decided: during the oral proceedings, the submissions and argument can thus be concentrated on the central issues,

---

[76] G6/95 GE CHEMICALS/Interpretation of Rule 71a(1) EPC O.J. EPO 1996, 649; [1997] E.P.O.R. 265.
[77] T951/97 CASIO/Change in subject matter of proceedings O.J. EPO 1998, 440; [1999] E.P.O.R. 160.
[78] T755/96 RESEARCH TRIANGLE INSTITUTE/Camptotheorin derivatives O.J. EPO 2000, 174.
[79] Guidance for Parties to Appeal Proceedings and their Representatives, O.J. EPO 1996, 342; see Appendix 8.

and there is no need for time to be spent on presenting the facts to the Board.

A possible criticism of the above procedure concerns the possibility that a Board of Appeal might be thought to pre-judge a case. However, the frequency with which decisions are issued which are contrary to the indications in a preceding communication tends to discount such a criticism.

(c) Duty to notify intended absence: costs

5–53   "There is an equitable obligation upon every party who is summoned to oral proceedings to inform the EPO as soon as it knows that it will not attend as summoned. This is the case whether or not that party has itself requested oral proceedings, and whether or not a communication has accompanied the summons to oral proceedings" (T930/92[80]).

Furthermore:

"If a party who has been summoned to oral proceedings fails to attend as summoned without notifying the EPO in advance that it will not attend, an apportionment of costs in favour of another party who has attended as summoned may be justified for reasons of equity in accordance with Article 104(1) EPC" (T930/92[81], T338/90[82]).

As to apportionment of costs in opposition proceedings, see Chapter 4 at paragraphs 4–156 *et seq.*

(4) Conduct of oral proceedings

(a) Representation and pleading: submissions by accompanying persons

5–54 As discussed in paragraph 5–14 above Article 133(2) EPC requires that a non-European "party to proceedings before the EPO must be represented by a professional representative and act through him in all proceedings" under the EPC. Additionally, a European party may choose to be represented by a professional representative.

Conflicting Board of Appeal decisions were issued concerning the interpretation of Article 133 EPC. Thus an early decision held that:

"An unqualified and unauthorised person who is not entitled to represent a party (under Articles 133 or 134 EPC) may not present part of the case of a party at oral proceedings, even under the direct supervision of that party's authorised representative" (T80/84[83]).

---

[80] T930/92 *HITACHI/Ion beam processing* O.J. EPO 1996, 191; [1997] E.P.O.R. 20.
[81] *Ibid.*
[82] T338/90 *DOW* October 21, 1993.
[83] T80/84 *MITA/Representation* O.J. EPO 1985, 269; [1979–85] E.P.O.R.: C: 946, [1986] E.P.O.R. 345.

This strict interpretation was not generally followed, however, and according to the general practice of the EPO assistants and experts accompanying an authorised representative were frequently allowed to contribute to a party's presentation of its case at oral proceedings.

This more liberal approach was reflected in a later decision: **5–55**

> "Article 133 EPC does not exclude the possibility of pleading by an assistant at oral proceedings in technical or legal matters, in addition to pleading by the professional representative, the authorised employee or the party himself, where he is a natural person, provided that the Board and the party for which the assistant speaks have given their permission and that the representative, employee or person continued to supervise the proceedings and bears full responsibility" (T598/91[84]).

Having regard to these and other conflicting decisions, questions of law were referred to the Enlarged Board of Appeal concerning whether a person other than the professional representative of a party (*i.e.* an "accompanying person") may make oral submissions on behalf of that party during oral proceedings under Article 116 EPC, in the context of *ex parte* appeal proceedings (G2/94[85]) and opposition and opposition appeal proceedings (G4/95[86]).

The main legal question underlying both cases was whether Article 133 **5–56** EPC excludes oral submissions by an accompanying person, or whether such oral submissions are allowable as a matter of discretion of the EPO.

The Enlarged Board held that a professional representative who is appointed by a non-European party "is responsible for the presentation to the EPO of all submissions made by that party" thus being "the essential core" of his function (see paragraph 5–16 above). In particular, during oral proceedings, "a professional representative is expected to present the entire case of the party that he represents", in any proceeding before the EPO.

As to whether an accompanying person may make oral submissions in addition to those made by the professional representative of a party, this is a matter of discretion for the EPO. When exercising such discretion, different considerations apply in *ex parte* and *inter partes* opposition proceedings.

(i) *Ex parte* appeal proceedings: G2/94.[87] This decision is in the context **5–57** of appeal proceedings, but its principles are equally applicable to first instance proceedings. It emphasises that the Board should control the proceedings, and that the professional representative should request

---

[84] T598/91 *VMI EPE/Tyre* O.J. EPO 1994, 912; [1995] E.P.O.R. 342.
[85] G2/94 *HAUTAU II/Pleading by an unauthorised representative* O.J. EPO 1996, 401; [1997] E.P.O.R. 115.
[86] G4/95 *BOGASKY II/Representation* O.J. EPO 1996, 412; [1996] E.P.O.R. 333.
[87] See note 85 above.

permission for an accompanying person to make any additional oral submissions in advance of the day appointed for oral proceedings. The request should state the name and qualifications of the accompanying person, and the subject-matter of the proposed submissions.

When exercising its discretion, the main criterion should be to ensure that the Board is fully informed of all relevant matters before deciding the case. Thus it can be expected that normally an accompanying person with appropriate qualifications would be allowed to make additional oral submissions. The Board should be satisfied that the oral submissions are made under the continuing responsibility and control of the professional representative.

5–58   **(ii) Opposition and opposition appeal proceedings: G4/95.**[88] The relevant considerations are the same in proceedings before an Opposition Division and before a Board of Appeal.

As in *ex parte* proceedings, permission for an accompanying person to make additional oral submissions should be requested in advance of the oral proceedings, and should state the name and qualifications of the person and the proposed subject-matter of his submissions; and the EPO should be satisfied that such oral submissions are made under the continuing responsibility and control of the professional representative.

The decision emphasises that in opposition proceedings generally it is a well recognised principle that each party should have a proper opportunity to reply to the case which is presented by an opposing party, accordingly:

(a) "The request should be made sufficiently in advance of the oral proceedings so that all opposing parties are able properly to prepare themselves in relation to the proposed oral submissions".

(b) "A request which is made shortly before or at oral proceedings should in the absence of special circumstance be refused unless each opposing party agrees to the making of the oral submissions requested."

(b) Representation and pleading by a former Board of Appeal member

5–59 A further question was raised in G2/94[89] as to whether in the exercise of discretion, a Board of Appeal should apply special criteria to former Board of Appeal members.

The decision is applicable to both *ex parte* and *inter partes* proceedings before a Board of Appeal and its principles are equally applicable to first instance proceedings. The same principles are also applicable to the making of oral submissions by a former Board of Appeal member, whether as an accompanying person or as a professional representative.

---

[88] See note 86 above.
[89] G2/94 *HAUTAU II/Pleading by an unauthorised representative* O.J EPO 1996, 401; [1995] E.P.O.R. 342.

The decision points out that if oral submissions are made by a former Board of Appeal member to a Board of Appeal, the Board of Appeal may be suspected of being inclined to favour such submissions, and that obviously, the problem cannot be resolved simply by changing the composition of the Board:

> "There is thus a potential conflict between what may be seen as a right of former Board of Appeal members to seek subsequent employment on the basis of their special knowledge by making oral submissions ... before the EPO, and the need for proceedings before the EPO to be conducted free from any suspicion of partiality".

It was held that "the above potential conflict must be resolved in the direction of avoiding any suspicion of partiality". Therefore:

> "A Board of Appeal should exercise its discretion ... by refusing permission for such oral submissions to be made, unless it is completely satisfied that a sufficient period of time has elapsed following termination of such former members' appointment to the Boards of Appeal, so that the Board ... could not reasonably be suspected of partiality in deciding the case, if it allowed such oral submissions ...."

Furthermore, such permission should normally be refused if less than three years have elapsed since termination of a former member's appointment, and should normally be granted after three years have elapsed.

(c) Oral evidence

The practice concerning the filing of written evidence is discussed in **5–60** connection with examination, opposition and appeal procedure (Chapters 2, 3 and 4 at paragraphs 2–40, 3–51 *et seq.* and 4–114 *et seq.*, respectively).

The making of oral submissions which involve the presentation of facts and evidence comes under the general discretionary power of the EPO to control the presentation of facts and evidence in the course of proceedings before it. Thus the presentation of facts and evidence orally on behalf of a party, by accompanying persons, in addition to the complete presentation of the party's case by the party himself, his employee or his professional representative, as the case may be, may be allowed during proceedings before the EPO, under the control of the party or his representative and under the overall discretionary control of the EPO. The principles which are applicable to the exercise of such discretion are discussed in paragraphs 5–57 and 5–58 above (G2/94[90], G4/95[91]).

If a party offers oral evidence from named witnesses concerning alleged

---

[90] *Ibid.*
[91] G4/95 *BOGASKY II/Representation* O.J. EPO 1996, 412; [1996] E.P.O.R. 333.

prior use in the notice of opposition, in conjunction with production of the alleged prior used apparatus for inspection at oral proceedings, the refusal to consider such evidence infringes that party's fundamental rights to free choice of evidence and to be heard (T142/97[92]).

The cross-examination of persons who have presented written or oral facts and evidence on behalf of a party, on behalf of an opposing party, is also a matter within the general discretionary control of the EPO.

(d) Voluntary absence of a party

5–61   Rule 71(2) EPC provides: "If a party who has been summoned to oral proceedings ... does not appear as summoned, the proceedings may continue without him". Nevertheless, Article 113(1) EPC states that "The decisions of the European Patent Office may only be based on grounds or evidence on which the parties concerned have had an opportunity to present their comments".

5–62   **(i) New facts, evidence and/or arguments.** Following conflicting Boards of Appeal decisions, the following question was considered by the Enlarged Board of Appeal in G4/92[93]:

> "If one party chooses not to attend to oral proceedings, can the decision handed down against that party be based on new facts, evidence and/or arguments put forward during those oral proceedings?"

The Enlarged Board distinguished between facts and evidence on the one hand, and arguments on the other hand. As to new facts or evidence, the Enlarged Board explained that if these are presented during oral proceedings in the absence of a party, a decision which is based upon such new facts or evidence and which is adverse to the absent party cannot be issued without first giving the absent party an opportunity to present its comments upon the new facts or evidence in writing, in accordance with Article 113(1) EPC. As regards new arguments, in so far as they do not change the ground on which the decision is based, they can in principle be used to support the reasoning of the decision without contravening Article 113(1)EPC.

The answers to the referred question were as follows:

> "1.   A decision against a party who has been duly summoned but who fails to appear at oral proceedings may not be based on facts put forward for the first time during those oral proceedings.
> 2.   Similarly, new evidence may not be considered unless it has been previously notified and it merely supports the assertions of the party who submits it, whereas new arguments may in principle be used to support the reasons for the decision."

---

[92] T142/97 *STOCKLI/Apparatus for separating disc-shaped objects* O.J. EPO 2000, 358.
[93] G4/92 *Basis for decisions* O.J. EPO 1994, 149; [1994] E.P.O.R. 392.

(ii) New ground of objection. It should be noted that G4/92[94] was only **5–63** concerned with new facts, evidence and/or arguments put forward during oral proceedings in the absence of a party, and did not deal with the situation when a new ground of objection is raised against maintenance of the patent, in the absence of the patent proprietor.

It would seem that such a situation is covered by Article 113(1) EPC, quoted above. In accordance with T951/92,[95] the word "grounds" in Article 113(1) EPC should be interpreted "as referring to the essential reasoning, both legal and factual, which leads to the refusal ..." However, in T341/92,[96] the patent was revoked by the Opposition Division, and the patent proprietor filed new claims in the appeal, but voluntarily did not appear at oral proceedings. The opponent argued for the first time during oral proceedings that the claims of the main request contravened Article 123(3) EPC. In its decision, the Board of Appeal refused the main request on this ground, which had not been notified to the patent proprietor "could have expected the question to be discussed was aware from the proceedings to date of the actual bases on which it would be judged".

In contrast, in T501/92[97] a new ground for revoking the patent was raised on appeal, for the first time during oral proceedings in the voluntary absence of the patent proprietor (it was submitted that the patent proprietor had made no request for maintenance of the patent and that the patent should be revoked for this reason). This submission was considered as a new "ground" within the meaning of Article 113(1) EPC, and it was held that "it would be contrary to Article 113(1) EPC and contrary to the principles underlying G4/92[98] to decide to allow the appeal (in the voluntary absence of the proprietor) on the basis of this new ground without first giving [the proprietor] an opportunity to comment thereon".

(e) Surrender of the right to be heard under Article 113(1) EPC

A party may in effect abandon his right to be heard under Article 113(1) **5–64** EPC (that is, his right to an opportunity to present comments on grounds or evidence on which a subsequent adverse decision is based), if he is voluntarily absent from oral proceedings, and in addition he surrenders such right: for example, by "declaring that it will take no further part in the proceedings" (T892/94[99]).

(f) Presentation of a party's case

Each party's case is normally presented on the basis of previously filed **5–65** written facts, evidence and arguments. "In principle, oral proceedings are appointed at a point in time in an opposition or opposition appeal

---

[94] *Ibid.*
[95] T951/92 *NEC/Opportunity to comment* O.J. EPO 1996, 53; [1996] E.P.O.R. 371.
[96] T341/92 *NEYNABER/Basic lead salts* O.J. EPO 1995, 373; [1995] E.P.O.R. 563.
[97] T501/92 *ARTHUR G. RUSSELL/Alpha-numeric display* O.J. EPO 1996, 261; [1996] E.P.O.R. 479.
[98] G4/92 *Basis for decisions* O.J. EPO 1994, 149; [1994] E.P.O.R. 392.
[99] T892/94 *ROBERTET/Deodorant compositions* O.J. EPO 2000, 1; [1999] E.P.O.R. 516.

procedure when the written submissions of all parties, including the written presentation of facts and evidence by all parties is complete"(G4/95[100]). The same applies in *ex parte* proceedings.

> "Appeal proceedings are normally examined and decided on the basis of facts and evidence filed during the proceedings before the Opposition Division" (G4/95[101]).

The above practice is subject to the exception that oral evidence may be presented under the discretionary control of the EPO at oral proceedings, as discussed in paragraph 5–60 above.

5–66   The presentation of *fresh facts and evidence* during oral proceedings is governed by the principles under which late-filed facts and evidence may be admitted into proceedings—see Chapters 3 and 4 at paragraphs 3–51 *et seq.* and 4–115 *et seq.*, respectively.

In general terms, the presentation of new arguments within the legal and factual framework set out in the preceding written submissions is allowable. However, in opposition proceedings:

> "A fair opposition procedure requires that an argument combining particular evidence with a particular prior document, even when such evidence and such document is already in the opposition file, should be presented in the notice of opposition or as soon as possible thereafter. Presentation of such an argument for the first time orally, during oral proceedings, is unfair to the opposing party and not normally allowable" (T124/87[102]).

(g) New facts, evidence and amendments, just before or during oral proceedings

5–67   **(i) First instance proceedings.** *General principles.* As explained in paragraph 5–51 above, when a summons to oral proceedings is issued to the parties to first instance proceedings, an accompanying communication under Rule 71a(1) EPC is issued, which sets a final date for written submissions from the parties. Furthermore:

> "New facts and evidence presented after that date need not be considered, unless admitted on the ground that the subject of the proceedings has changed" (Rule 71a(1) EPC).

Rule 71a(1) EPC applies *mutatis mutandis* to the filing of amendments by the applicant or proprietor (see Rule 71a(2) EPC).

Consequently, following issue of the communication under Rule 71a(1) EPC:

---

[100] G4/95 *BOGASKY II/Representation* O.J. EPO 1996, 412; [1996] E.P.O.R. 333.
[101] *Ibid.*
[102] T124/87 *DU PONT/Copolymers* O.J. EPO 1989, 491; [1989] E.P.O.R. 33.

"as a general rule [the first instance] is not obliged to admit new facts and evidence, or amendments as the case may be, but maintains its discretion to do so; however, if the subject of the proceedings has changed, it should exercise its discretion in favour of admitting them" (T951/97[103]).

Thus in relation to amendments:

"it would be contrary to the proper exercise of such discretion, if clearly allowable amendments overcoming the outstanding objections were not to be admitted into the proceedings" (T951/97[104]).

In practice, the first instance will be unlikely to admit either new facts and evidence, or amendments, into the proceedings after the Rule 71a(1) EPC communication has been issued, unless "the subject of the proceedings" is regarded as changed, because the object of this recent Rule is to reduce the amount of new material which is introduced immediately before and during oral proceedings.

Meaning of "the subject of the proceedings has changed". The practice under **5–68** Rule 71(a) EPC since it entered into force on June 1, 1995, is still to be developed. One example of a change in the subject of the proceedings is where an Examining Division introduced a new pertinent document into examination proceedings for the first time during oral proceedings (T951/97[105]). A similar example is: "Where the opponent files, before the indicated date [in the Rule 71a(1) EPC communication] pertinent new material, the patent proprietor must be given a chance to present his comments and submit amendments" (Guidelines E.III. 8.6; T951/97[106]).

(ii) Appeal proceedings. Since Rule 71a(1) EPC is not applicable to **5–69** appeal proceedings, the admission of new facts and evidence, and amendments, at a late stage of appeal proceedings is governed by the practice of the Boards of Appeal in this respect—see Chapter 4 at paragraphs 4–91 and 4–115 *et seq.*

(h) Recording oral proceedings

A Notice[107] dated February 25, 1986 states that: **5–70**

"No person other than an EPO employee is allowed to introduce any kind of sound recording device into the hearing room."

This is in accordance with the general practice in the Contracting States.

[103] T951/97 *CASIO/Change in subject of proceedings* O.J. EPO 1998, 440; [1999] E.P.O.R. 160.
[104] *Ibid.*
[105] *Ibid.*
[106] *Ibid.*
[107] Notice of the Vice-Presidents DG2 and 3 dated February 25 1986 concerning sound recording devices in oral proceedings before the EPO, O.J. EPO 1986, 63.

The EPO may record oral proceedings if requested to do so in advance of the fixed date, as a matter of discretion. Similarly, the EPO may allow the manual recording of oral proceedings upon prior request.

5–71   **(i) Filing observations after oral proceedings.** Normally, as previously discussed, a decision is issued orally at the close of oral proceedings, in which case any observations filed after such decision have no legal effect and are clearly inadmissible.

In a rare case where the decision is reserved, and therefore not issued at the end of the oral proceedings, any further observations filed by a party would be disregarded as inadmissible unless the case is re-opened, which is within the discretion of a Board of Appeal (T595/90[108]). Similar principles would be applied in first instance proceedings.

I. Decisions

(1) Introduction

5–72   Certain principles govern decisions of the EPO in both first instance and appeal proceedings. These are considered below. Otherwise, different considerations are applicable to first instance decisions (Examining and Opposition Divisions) and to decisions of the Boards of Appeal, and accordingly such decisions are considered separately in Chapters 2, 3 and 4 at paragraphs 2–70, 3–82 *et seq.* and 4–144 *et seq.*, respectively.

(2) The basis of decisions: Article 113 EPC

5–73   Article 113 EPC sets out certain basic principles which govern the making of a decision by any department or instance of the EPO as follows:

> "(1) The decisions of the EPO may only be based on grounds or evidence on which the parties concerned have had an opportunity to present their comments.
> (2) The EPO shall consider and decide upon the European patent application or the European patent only in the text submitted to it, or agreed, by the applicant for a proprietor of the patent."

Article 113(1) EPC reflects the right to a fair hearing which is one of the general legal principles of law discussed in Chapter 1 at paragraphs 1–78 *et seq.*

Any contravention of Article 113 EPC in the course of making a decision clearly constitutes a fundamental and substantial procedural violation, which may justify the decision being set aside as void by a Board of Appeal during appeal proceedings. The consequences of such a procedural violation are considered in Chapter 4 at paragraphs 4–154A and 4–166 *et seq.*

---

[108] T595/90 *KAWASAKI/Grain oriented silicon sheet* O.J. EPO 1994, 695; [1995] E.P.O.R. 36.

If a decision includes several grounds (for refusing an application for example), the requirements of Article 113(1) EPC must be met in respect of each of such grounds (T802/97[109]).

(3) Formal contents of a decision

A decision may be issued orally or in writing. If given orally: "sub- **5–73a** sequently the decision in writing shall be notified to the parties". Furthermore, all Rule 68(1) EPC written decisions must be reasoned (Rules 66(2)(g) and 68(2) EPC).

All decisions are thus required to consist of two essential parts—a statement as to what has been decided, and a statement of the reasons for what has been decided.

> "When a substantive decision is given orally during oral proceedings, such substantive decision must be formally completed by the giving of reasons for the decision in writing" (T390/86[110]).

In practice, all written decisions normally consists of a "Summary of Facts and Submissions" and "Reasons for the Decision", ending with a statement of what has been decided (the "Order").

Furthermore, Rule 68(2) EPC requires every decision which is open to appeal to be accompanied by a "written communication of the possibility of appeal", with the text of Articles 106 to 108 EPC attached. However, the omission of such a communication may not be invoked by the parties, and such omission does not by itself invalidate the decision if the other requirements of a decision are satisfied.

(4) Reasons for a decision: Rules 66(2) and 68(2) EPC

According to Rule 68(2), a decision of the EPO which is open to appeal **5–74** "shall be reasoned". Similarly, according to Rule 66(2) PC, a decision of a Board of Appeal shall contain "the reasons".

Failure of a first instance decision to satisfy Rule 68(2) PC in this respect constitutes a "substantial procedural violation" under Rule 67 EPC which may justify reimbursement of the appeal fee, and may justify the decision being set aside on appeal.

For example, a decision which only includes a formal acknowledgement of the applicant's submissions and does not deal with them in substance contravenes Rule 68(2) EPC and constitutes a substantial procedural violation (T291/94[111]).

It appears that if a Board of Appeal decision fails to contain reasons in accordance with Rule 66(2) EPC, the decision cannot be challenged or set

[109] T802/97 *LAMBDA ELECTRONICS* July 24, 1998.
[110] T390/86 *SHELL/Changed composition of division* O.J. EPO 1989, 30; [1989] E.P.O.R. 162.
[111] T291/94 October 7, 1997.

aside and remains final (G 1/97[112]): see Chapter 4 at paragraphs 4–154 and 4–154A as to the proposals to amend to EPC.

(5) Interlocutory and final decisions

5–75   A first instance decision may be either interlocutory or final. Article 106(3) EPC states that:

> "A decision which does not terminate proceedings as regards one of the parties [an interlocutory decision] can only be appealed together with the final decision, unless the decision allows separate appeal."

A first instance department has a discretion as to whether to issue a separate interlocutory decision and to allow separate appeal—see Guidelines E.X.6.

A decision of a Board of Appeal may also be interlocutory, in that it may (finally) decide upon certain issue(s) in dispute, and the case may then be remitted to the first instance for examination of other outstanding issues.

(6) Written and oral decisions

5–76   If no oral proceedings are appointed during proceedings before the EPO a written decision will be issued by the competent department.

If oral proceedings are held, the decision upon the issue(s) in dispute may be given orally (Rule 68(1) EPC) and will normally be given at the conclusions of the oral proceedings. In such cases, "the decision in writing shall be notified to the parties" (Rule 68(1) EPC). The written decision must include the reasons which lead to the decision but an oral announcement of a decision will not normally include reasons.

If a decision if given orally, Rule 68(1) EPC requires the *same decision* to be notified in writing subsequently. Any substantive deviation of the decision notified in writing from a decision which has been taken at oral proceedings and announced orally amounts to a substantial procedural violation; the decision will be set aside on appeal, and the appeal fee reimbursed (T425/97[113]).

(7) Finality of a decision

5–77   If a decision is given orally, it is final in respect of the issues which it decides (T390/86[114]).

Once a decision had been issued, whether in writing or orally, it is final in the sense that it cannot be cancelled or changed by the instance (*e.g.* Examining Division, Opposition Division, Board of Appeal) that issued it (except by the correction of errors under Rule 89 EPC—see Chapter 6 at

---

[112] G1/97 *ETA/Request with a view to revision* O.J. EPO 2000, 322.
[113] T425/97 *VEECH/Cardiac reperfusion* May 8, 1998.
[114] T390/86 *SHELL/Changed composition of division* O.J. EPO 1989 30; [1989] E.P.O.R. 162.

paragraphs 6–75 *et seq.*) (G4/91,[115] T390/86,[116] T212/88[117]). In the case of a first instance decision, if a party is adversely affected by such a decision, his only remedy is to file an appeal (G4/91,[118] T390/86[119]).

(8) Date of finality of the first instance written decision-making process—written decisions

"The decision-making process following written proceedings is completed **5–78** on the date the decision to be notified is handed over to the EPO postal services by the decision-taking department's formalities section" (G12/91[120]). After such date, therefore, a request for amendment or other submission from a party cannot be considered by the first instance department.

(9) Void decisions

In certain circumstances a first instance decision may be set aside by a **5–79** Board of Appeal in subsequent appeal proceedings as void and of no legal effect. Examples of such circumstances are:

(a) If the composition of the Opposition Division contravened Article 19(2)EPC—see Chapter 3 at paragraph 3–08.
(b) If the composition of an Examining or Opposition Division changes between announcement of an oral decision at oral proceedings and issue of the written decision—see Chapter 3 at paragraph 3–91.
(c) If a first instance decision is issued in circumstances where Article 113 EPC has been contravened—see paragraph 5–73.

In such circumstances, either a Board of Appeal or the first instance department has a discretion to decide that the case should be re-heard before a different, new composition of Examining or Opposition Division, in order to avoid suspected partiality on the part of one or more parties to the proceedings (see for example T433/93,[121] and paragraph 5–28 above).

(10) Correction of a decision

A decision of the EPO may be corrected in accordance with Rule 89 EPC **5–80** which states that:

"In decisions of the EPO, only linguistic errors, errors of transcription and obvious mistakes may be corrected."

---

[115] G4/91 *DOLEZYCH II/Intervention* O.J. EPO 1993, 707; [1993] E.P.O.R. 120.
[116] T390/86 *SHELL/Changed composition of division* O.J. EPO 1989 30; [1989] E.P.O.R. 162.
[117] T212/88 *BP/Theta-1* O.J. EPO 1992, 28; [1990] E.P.O.R. 518.
[118] See note 115 above.
[119] See note 116 above.
[120] G12/91 *NOVATOME II/Final decision* O.J. EPO 1994, 285; [1994] E.P.O.R. 309.
[121] T433/93 *ATOTECH/Re-hearing* O.J. EPO 1997, 509; [1998] E.P.O.R. 135.

Such corrections are considered in Chapter 6 at paragraphs 6–75 *et seq.*

Cases Referred to in Chapter 5

Board of Appeal Decisions

G4/91   DOLEZYCH II/Intervention O.J. EPO 1993, 707; [1993]
           E.P.O.R. 120.

G5/91   DISCOVISION/Appealable decision O.J. EPO 1992, 617;
           [1993] E.P.O.R. 120.

G6/91   ASULAB II/Fee reduction O.J. EPO 1992, 491; [1993]
           E.P.O.R. 231.

G12/91   NOVATOME II/Final decision O.J. EPO 1994, 285; [1994]
           E.P.O.R. 309.

G4/92   Basis for decisions O.J. EPO 1994, 149; [1997] E.P.O.R. 115.

G2/94   HAUTAU II/Pleading by an unauthorised representative
           O.J. EPO 1996, 401.

G4/95   BOGASKY II/Representation O.J. EPO 1996, 412; [1996]
           E.P.O.R. 333.

G6/95   GE CHEMICALS/Interpretation of Rule 71(a)(1) EPC O.J.
           EPO 1996, 649; [1997] E.P.O.R. 265.

G1/97   ETA/Request with a view to revision, O.J. EPO 2000, 322

J7/80   SKF/Correction of mistakes O.J. EPO 1981, 137; [1979–85]
           E.P.O.R. 36.

J4/88   GEO MECCANICA IDROTECNICA/Language of appli-
           cation O.J. EPO 1989, 483; [1990] E.P.O.R. 69.

J20/89   Appellate jurisdiction (PCT cases) O.J. EPO 1991, 375;
           [1991] E.P.O.R. 436.

J14/91   ALT/Inspection of files O.J. EPO 1993, 479; [1994] E.P.O.R.
           184.

J16/96   N.N./Association of representatives O.J. EPO 1998, 347;
           [1999] E.P.O.R. 202.

J18/96   N.N./Filing date O.J. EPO 1998, 403; [1999] E.P.O.R. 9.

T219/83   BASF/Zeolites O.J. EPO 1986, 211; [1986] E.P.O.R. 247.

T80/84   MITA/Representation O.J. EPO 1985, 269; [1979–85]
           E.P.O.R.: C: 946, [1986] E.P.O.R. 345.

T149/85   BREDERO/Inadmissible language of opposition O.J. EPO
           1986, 143; [1986] E.P.O.R. 223.

T153/85   AMOCO/Alternative claims O.J. EPO 1988, 1; [1988]
           E.P.O.R. 116.

T234/86   SOMARTEC/Therapy with interference currents O.J. EPO
           1989, 79; [1989] E.P.O.R. 303.

T299/86   SECHER/Oral proceedings O.J. EPO 1988, 88; [1988]
           E.P.O.R. 204.

T390/86   SHELL/Changed composition of division O.J. EPO 1989,
           30; [1989] E.P.O.R. 162.

T19/87   FUJITSU/Oral proceedings O.J. EPO 1988, 268; [1988] E.P.O.R. 393.

T124/87   DU PONT/Copolymers O.J. EPO 1989, 491; [1989] E.P.O.R. 33.

T193/87   ALFA LAVAL/Belated translation O.J. EPO 1993, 287; [1992] E.P.O.R. 63.

T381/87   RESEARCH CORPORATION/Publication O.J. EPO 1990, 213; [1989] E.P.O.R. 138.

T212/88   BP/Theta-1 O.J. EPO 1992, 28; [1990] E.P.O.R. 518.

T261/88   DISCOVISION/Appealable decision O.J. EPO 1992, 627.

T283/88   ABBOT/Oral proceedings [1989] E.P.O.R. 225.

T320/88   EXXON/Arranging oral proceedings O.J. EPO 1990, 359; [1989] E.P.O.R. 372.

T79/89   XEROX/Finality of decision O.J. EPO 1992, 283; [1990] E.P.O.R. 558.

T182/89   SUMITOMO/Extent of opposition O.J. EPO 1991, 391; [1990] E.P.O.R. 438.

T275/89   KLOSTERMANN/Steel radiators O.J. EPO 1992, 126; [1992] E.P.O.R. 260.

T482/89   TELEMECANIQUE/Prior use O.J. EPO 1992, 646; [1993] E.P.O.R. 249.

T760/89   BURLINGTON/Return of documents O.J. EPO 1994, 797; [1995] E.P.O.R. 224.

T3/90   BRITISH TELECOMMUNICATIONS/Oral proceedings O.J. EPO 1992, 737; [1996] E.P.O.R. 366.

T34/90   UNILEVER/Viscosity reduction O.J. EPO 1992, 454; [1992] E.P.O.R. 466.

T270/90   ASAHI/Polyphenylene ether compositions O.J. EPO 1993, 725; [1992] E.P.O.R. 365.

T338/90   DOW October 21, 1993.

T595/90   KAWASAKI/Grain oriented silicon sheet O.J. EPO 1994, 695; [1995] E.P.O.R. 36.

T905/90   ALBRIGHT/Fee reduction O.J. EPO 1994, 306; [1994] E.P.O.R. 585.

T598/91   VMI EPE/Tyre O.J. EPO 1994, 912; [1995] E.P.O.R. 342.

T843/91   EASTMAN KODAK COMPANY/Partiality O.J. EPO 1994, 832; [1995] E.P.O.R. 126.

T341/92   NEYNABER/Basic lead salts O.J. EPO 1995, 373; [1995] E.P.O.R. 563.

T371/92   FINA/Appeal not filed O.J. EPO 1995, 324; [1995] E.P.O.R. 485.

T472/92   SEKISUI/Joint venture O.J. EPO 1998, 161; [1997] E.P.O.R. 432.

T501/92   ARTHUR G. RUSSELL/Alpha-numeric display O.J. EPO 1996, 261; [1996] E.P.O.R. 479.

T930/92   HITACHI/Ion beam processing O.J. EPO 1996, 191; [1997] E.P.O.R. 20.

T433/93 ATOTECH/Re-hearing O.J. EPO 1997, 509; [1998] E.P.O.R. 135.

T97/94 CECA/Procedural timetable O.J. EPO 1998, 467.

T291/94 October 7, 1997.

T382/94 ZEISS/Documents as filed O.J. EPO 1998, 24; [1998] E.P.O.R. 200.

T750/94 AT & T/Proof of publication O.J. EPO 1998, 32; [1997] E.P.O.R. 509.

T892/94 ROBERTET/Deodorant compositions O.J. EPO 2000, 1; [1999] E.P.O.R. 516.

T556/95 SECURITY TECHNOLOGY/Undeniable system O.J. EPO 1997, 205; [1997] E.P.O.R. 394.

T169/96 ELF ATOCHEM/Main and auxiliary request [1997] E.P.O.R. 209.

T755/96 RESEARCH TRIANGLE INSTITUTE/Camptotheorin derivatives O.J. EPO 2000, 174.

T1028/96 DU PONT DE NEMOURS/Suspected partiality 2000, O.J. EPO 475.

T1105/96 HAMAMATSU/Requests O.J. EPO 1998, 249; [1998] E.P.O.R. 26.

T142/97 STOCKLI/Apparatus for separating disc-shaped objects O.J. EPO 2000, 358.

T425/97 VEECH/Cardiac reperfusion May 8, 1998.

T802/97 LAMBDA ELECTRONICS July 24 1998.

T951/97 CASIO/Change in subject of proceedings O.J. EPO 1998, 440; [1999] E.P.O.R. 160.

T169/98 AT&T/Anisotrophic deposition.

CHAPTER 6

PROCEDURAL REMEDIES

Rule 88 EPC, first sentence; Article 122 EPC; Rule 90 EPC;
Rule 89 EPC

Contents

All references are to paragraph numbers

A. Introduction

6–01 Within the system for granting and opposing European patents provided by the EPC, there are many procedural requirements coupled with time limits imposed upon parties to proceedings before the EPO, with accompanying sanctions if such requirements are not complied with in due time. In order to ensure that procedure before the EPO is efficient and runs smoothly, which is in the public interest, the sanctions are frequently severe: immediate loss of a patent application or patent, for example, or the loss of a right such as the right to appeal.

The EPC includes many provisions which alleviate the initial, necessarily strict, requirements in relation to time limits. These provisions fall into two classes, namely:

(1) those which allow an extension of time upon payment of a further fee or surcharge;
(2) those which allow relief in respect of certain procedural mistakes and omissions provided that particular mitigating circumstances are established.

(1) Extensions of time by further fee

(a) Further processing of an application

Article 121 EPC

6–02 During prosecution of an application, the EPO may set a time limit for replying to a communication (*e.g.* under Articles 91(2) and 110(2) EPC). Article 121(1) EPC) provides that:

"(1) If the European patent application is to be refused or is refused or deemed to be withdrawn following failure to reply within a time limit set by the European Patent Office, the legal consequences provided for shall not ensue or, if it has already ensued, shall be retracted if the applicant requests further processing of the application.

(2) The request shall be filed in writing within two months of the date on which either the decision to refuse the application or the communication that the application is deemed to be withdrawn was notified ..."

Thus if a time limit which is set by the EPO for filing a reply at the EPO is not complied with, Article 121 EPC provides for an extension of time of two months from the date defined in Article 121(2) EPC: the only requirements are that within such two months:

(i) a request for further processing in writing must be filed;
(ii) a prescribed fee must be paid;
(iii) the omitted act, *i.e.* the required reply, must be filed.

In practice the EPO usually sends a notification under Rule 69(1) EPC, advising the applicant as to the loss of rights and inviting a request for further processing within two months of the date of notification.

It should be noted that "further processing" under Article 121 EPC is only applicable to time limits which are *set by the EPO*, and is therefore not applicable to time limits which are laid down in the EPC itself (J47/92[1]). Furthermore, this provision is not applicable during opposition proceedings, since Article 121 EPC is only concerned with further processing of an *application*.

According to the proposed revision of the EPC, Article 121 EPC will be amended by broadening its scope so as to make further processing the standard legal remedy in cases of failure to observe time limits during pre-grant procedure. In particular, Article 121 will read: **6–02A**

> Article 121(1) EPC: "If an applicant fails to observe a time limit *vis-à-vis* the European Patent Office, he may request further processing of the European patent applications.
>
> (2) The EPO shall grant the request, provided that the requirements laid down in the Implementing Regulations are met. Otherwise, it shall reject the request.
>
> (3) If the request is granted, the legal consequences of the failure to observe the time limit shall be deemed not to have ensued.
>
> (4) Further processing shall be ruled out in respect of the time limits in Article 87(1), Article 108 and Article 112a(4), as well as the time limit for requesting further processing or re-establishment of rights. The Implementing Regulations may rule out further processing for other time limits."

The provisions of the present Article 121(2) and (3) EPC will be incorporated into the Implementing Regulations.

Thus further processing will replace the more complex "re-establishment of rights" (paragraphs 6–27 *et seq.* below) in pre-grant procedure.

(b) Late payment of fees: examples

(i) Filing, search, designation, national and examination fees. These fees may be paid late, *i.e.* within a grace period, as provided in Rules 85a and b EPC, together with a surcharge. **6–03**

(ii) Renewal fees. These fees may be paid together with an additional fee within six months of the due date, as provided in Article 86(2) EPC. **6–04**

(2) Procedural remedies in particular circumstances

In certain circumstances special remedies are provided by the EPC in the event of procedural mistakes, failures or omissions, namely: **6–05**

---

[1] *SILVER SYSTEMS/Further processing* O.J. EPO 1995, 180; [1995] E.P.O.R. 495.

(a) the correction of mistakes in formal documents (Rule 88 EPC first sentence);
(b) the re-establishment of rights (Article 122 EPC);
(c) the interruption of proceedings (Rule 90 EPC).

These remedies are considered separately below.

B. The Correction of Errors and Mistakes in Formal Documents

Rule 88 EPC, first sentence

(1) Introduction

6–06   The first sentence of Rule 88 EPC provides that "Linguistic errors, errors of transcription and mistakes in any document filed with the EPO may be corrected on request."

Although not explicit in this provision, the correction of such errors and mistakes is normally associated with the fact that the error or mistake has not been noticed before the expiry of a relevant time limit. If an error or mistake in a document is recognised before expiry of a time limit in relation to such document, a corrected document can normally be substituted within the time limit.

There are three main aspects of this provision in Rule 88 EPC:

(a) It must be established that either an error of the kind set out or a mistake was made;
(b) The error or mistake must be in a document;
(c) Correction of the error or mistake is discretionary.

These different aspects will be discussed separately below.

The second sentence of Rule 88 EPC, concerning the correction of errors and mistakes in a description, claims or drawings, is considered separately in Chapter 8 at paragraphs 8–80 *et seq.*

(2) Existence of an error or mistake

6–07   "For the purpose of Rule 88 EPC, a mistake may be said to exist ... if the document does not express the true intention of the person on whose behalf it was filed. The mistake may take the form of an incorrect statement or it may result from an omission. Correction, accordingly, can take the form of putting right an incorrect statement or adding omitted matter" (J8/80[2]).

---

[2] J8/80 *RIB LOC/Correction of mistakes* O.J. EPO 1980, 293; [1979–85] E.P.O.R.: A: 40.

(a) Evidence in support

"Before the EPO can accede to a request for correction of a mistake ... **6–08**
it must be satisfied that a mistake was made, what the mistake was
and what the correct should be. This is the necessary safeguard against
abuse of the provisions of Rule 88 EPC" (J8/80[3]).

In particular Rule 88 EPC cannot be used to give effect to a change of
mind, or a change in intention. For this reason the existence of a mistake
must be fully proved. Thus:

"It is the responsibility of the person requesting correction to put
evidence as to the relevant facts fully and frankly before the Office. In
cases where the making of the alleged mistake is not self-evident and
in cases where it is not immediately evident that nothing else would
have been intended than what is offered as the correct, the burden of
providing the facts must be a heavy one. If the evidence put forward is
incomplete, obscure or ambiguous, the request for correction should
be rejected. In particular, there should be no reasonable doubt as to the
true intention of the person on whose behalf the document was filed.
A mere statement of his intention which is not supported by evidence
as to what he said and did is almost certain to be insufficient.
Provisions designed to facilitate correction of mistakes cannot be
allowed to be used to enable a person to give effect to a change of his
mind or a subsequent development of his plans" (J1/80[4]).

(b) Time for filing evidence in support

Any evidence which a party wishes to rely upon in support of a request for **6–09**
correction of a mistake should be filed as soon as reasonably possible. The
EPO may fix a time limit for filing evidence.

"Where a department of the EPO is informed by an applicant's
representative that information and evidence will be submitted in
support of an application for correction under Rule 88 EPC as soon as
it is available, the department may commit a substantial procedural
violation if it issues a decision without having fixed a time limit for the
submission or having waited for a reasonable time" (J4/82[5]).

(3) A mistake must be in a document

Failure to pay a fee within a prescribed time limit is not a mistake which **6–10**
can be corrected under Rule 88 EPC (J21/84[6]: designation fee not paid;
T152/85[7]: opposition fee not paid).

---

[3] *Ibid.*
[4] J1/80 *SIEMENS/Filing priority documents* O.J. EPO 1980, 289; [1979–85] E.P.O.R.: A: 15.
[5] J4/82 *YOSHIDA KOGYO/Priority declaration* O.J. EPO 1982, 385; [1979–85] E.P.O.R.: A: 102.
[6] J21/84 *CONSUMERS GLASS/Late correction* O.J. EPO 1986, 75; [1986] E.P.O.R. 146.
[7] T152/85 *SANDVIK/Unpaid opposition fee* O.J. EPO 1987, 191; [1987] E.P.O.R. 258.

(4) The exercise of discretion

6–11 An important consideration which is taken into account by the EPO when exercising its discretion under Rule 88 EPC is whether third parties would be prejudiced by the correction of a particular mistake. For example, mistakes are sometimes made by applicants in completing the contents of the "Request for grant" of a European patent, this being a requirement for the filing of a European patent application (Article 78(1)(a) EPC). The contents of a "request for grant" are prescribed by Rule 26(2) EPC. Certain of these prescribed contents are important to the determination of the scope and validity of the European patent which may be granted pursuant to the application: in particular, the priority declaration (Rule 26(2)(g) EPC) and the designation of Contracting States (Rule 26(2)(h) EPC). Mistakes in such contents of the "Request for grant" are discussed in detail below. The allowability of corrections to such contents normally depends upon whether an application for correction is made in time to prevent third parties from being prejudiced by the uncorrected contents when the application (including the "Request for grant") is published under Article 93 EPC. Thus in particular, correction of a mistake in such contents is normally allowable if the correction can be made before the application is so published, because third parties will not then know of the uncorrected contents which contain a mistake. The correction of priority declarations and designations is considered in detail below, as well as the correction of other kinds of mistakes in formal documents filed at the EPO.

(5) Particular kinds of mistakes

(a) Naming the wrong applicant

6–12 Article 60(3) EPC states that "For the purposes of proceedings before the EPO, the applicant shall be deemed to be entitled to exercise the right to the European patent". This establishes the principle that the EPO assumes the applicant to be entitled to the European patent, and has no obligation to investigate the existence of the entitlement (J18/93[8]; see Chapter 2 at paragraphs 2–24 and 2–78).

However, the naming of the correct applicant on the request for grant may be important, especially for the purposes of a priority declaration (see Article 87 EPC and Chapter 10).

"A correction substituting the name of the applicant is allowable under Rule 83 EPC, if there is sufficient evidence to support the request for correction ..." (J18/93[9]; also J7/80[10]). The general principles for allowing the correction of mistakes which are set out in J1/80[11] and J8/80[12] (paragraphs 6–07, 6–08 above) are applicable in such a case (J18/93[13]).

[8] J18/93 CARDIAC/Correction of mistake O.J. EPO 1997, 91; [1998] E.P.O.R. 38.
[9] Ibid.
[10] J7/80 SKF/Correction of mistakes—languages O.J. EPO 1981, 137; [1979–85] E.P.O.R. 36.
[11] J1/80 SIEMENS/Filing priority documents O.J. EPO 1980, 289; [1979–85] E.P.O.R.: A: 15.
[12] J8/80 RIBLOC/Correction of mistakes O.J. EPO 1980, 293; [1979–85] E.P.O.R.: A: 40.
[13] See note 8.

(b) Naming the wrong opponent

Similarly: 6–13

> "if an opponent is not correctly identified in the notice of opposition, owing to a genuine mistake, in principle the mistake can be corrected even after expiry of the opposition period, under Rule 88 EPC" (T219/86[14]).

However:

> "Deliberate concealment of an opponent's identity must be regarded as intentional non-compliance with Rule 55(a) EPC and cannot be corrected as a 'mistake' under Rule 88 EPC at any time" (T219/86[15], explaining T25/85[16]).

(c) Mistakes in the designation of States

(i) Introduction. Article 79(1) and Rule 26(2)(h) EPC require that the 6–14 request for grant shall contain "the designation of the Contracting State or States in which protection of the invention is desired." (See Chapter 2 at paragraph 2–12) A number of cases involving corrections requested under Rule 88 EPC concern incorrect designations, particular States having allegedly been omitted by mistake. The correcting of such omissions has been of considerable importance in a number of cases, since allowing an additional designation after the date of filing is equivalent to a new national patent application.

(ii) General rule: time limitation. An addition of a designation of a 6–15 Contracting State is normally subject to a time limitation as follows:

> "A mistake in a designation of a Contracting State may be corrected in accordance with Rule 88 EPC only if a request has been made for correction sufficiently early for a warning to be included in the publication of the application [pursuant to Article 93 EPC] so that third parties can rely on the application as published" (J21/84[17]; also J7/90[18]).

This general rule applies:

> "... even where all other conditions to which such corrections are subject [see paragraph 6–08 above] ... have been met and, in particular even where the applicant has requested correction immediately upon

---

[14] T219/86 *ZOKOR/Naming of opponent* O.J. EPO 1988, 254; [1988] E.P.O.R. 407.
[15] *Ibid.*
[16] T25/85 *DEUTSCHE GELATINE FABRIKEN, STOESS & CO./Opponent-identifiability* O.J. EPO 1986, 81; [1986] E.P.O.R. 158.
[17] J21/84 *CONSUMERS GLASS/Late correction* O.J. EPO 1986, 75; [1986] E.P.O.R. 146.
[18] J7/90 *TOLEDO/Correction of designation* O.J. EPO 1993, 133; [1993] E.P.O.R. 329.

discovering his mistake" (J7/90[19]). In particular, the general rule applies even if inspection would have alerted third parties to the possibility of additional designations, because third parties "cannot be expected to undertake searches in case designations have been omitted" (J3/81[20]).

6–16 **(iii) An exception: failure by the EPO to publish a warning.** If the EPO receives a request for correction in good time to enable a warning to be included in the publication of the application but fails to publish such a warning in the application as published (in the case in question, until appeal proceedings were pending following refusal of the request by the Receiving Section), the correction is allowable, because the applicant has no control over the publication of the application (J12/80[21]).

Since Rule 88 EPC contains no provisions equivalent to Article 122(6) EPC (see paragraph 6–27 below) protecting third parties who may have relied upon the application as published, "the solution of any problem of third party rights in such a case must be left to the national courts competent jurisdiction" (J12/80[22]).

A mistake by the International Bureau in the interpretation of an international application under PCT, which results in the published application failing to mention a State which was properly designated in such application, is not a mistake to which Rule 88 EPC applies. There being no mistake in the Request for Grant form, "the EPO is bound by ... Article 153 EPC to act as the designated office for that Contracting State, even if the international application has been published ... without mentioning ... that State" (J26/87[23]).

It should be noted that if a Contracting State is designated by mistake, Article 79(3) EPC allows the designation of a Contracting State to be withdrawn at any time up to grant of a European patent. Designation fees are not refunded (see Chapter 2 at paragraph 2–22).

6–17 **(iv) Correction of a withdrawal of a designation.** Correction of a withdrawal of a designation:

"is allowable under Rule 88 EPC in appropriate circumstances, in particular if:

(a) the public has not been officially notified of the withdrawal by the EPO at the time the retraction of the withdrawal is applied for;
(b) the erroneous withdrawal is due to an excusable oversight;
(c) the requested correction does not result in a substantial delay of the proceedings; and

---

[19] *Ibid.*
[20] J3/81 *BODENRADER/International application* O.J. EPO 1982, 100; [1979–85] E.P.O.R.: A: 74.
[21] J12/80 *HOECHST/Correction of mistakes—published application* O.J. EPO 1981, 143; [1979–85] E.P.O.R.: A: 52.
[22] *Ibid.*
[23] J26/87 *McWHIRTER/PCT form* O.J. EPO 1989, 329; [1989] E.P.O.R. 430.

(d) the EPO is satisfied that the interests of third parties who may possibly have taken notice of the withdrawal by inspection of the file are adequately protected" (J10/87[24]).

As to (d), "individual persons having inspected the file and relying on the declaration of withdrawal of the ... designation could be protected by applying Article 122(6) EPC (see paragraph 6–27 below) *mutatis mutandis*" (J10/87[25]).

(d) Correction of a withdrawal of an application

The withdrawal of an application which was made in error may be **6–18** retracted by way of correction under Rule 88 EPC, in appropriate circumstances. The considerations which are set out in paragraph 6–17 above in relation to retraction of a withdrawal of a designation are applicable. "In particular, it has to be ascertained that the withdrawal was due to an excusable error and that the retraction of the withdrawal did not adversely affect the public interest or the interest of third parties" (J4/97[26]).

(e) Mistakes in claiming priority

(i) Introduction. Rule 26(2)(g) EPC requires that the request for grant **6–19** shall contain "where applicable, a declaration claiming the priority of an earlier application ...". (as to claiming priority, see Chapter 10). In some cases, such a claim to priority has been incomplete, or omitted altogether. Such an omission is clearly not of the same importance as the intended designation of States, but it is nevertheless something that the public is entitled to know as part of the information concerning a European patent application at the time when the application is published. "In principle, the public should be entitled to rely on the published information as being both accurate and complete" (J14/82[27]). Thus in principle, a time limitation applies in the same way as with a mistake in the designation of a Contracting State.

Neither Rule 41 EPC (concerning rectification of deficiencies in the application documents), nor any other provisions of the EPC prohibit a correction of a mistake in claiming priority. Furthermore, Article 4D of the Paris Convention is not inconsistent with such a correction being possible. Bodenhausen[28] has pointed out that "lack of ... publication (of particulars of the claim to priority) will not ... invalidate the right of priority."

(ii) General rule: time limitation   **6–20**

"If a mistake is made in a declaration of priority, it may be correct in

[24] J10/87 *INLAND STEEL/Retraction of withdrawal* O.J. EPO 1989, 323; [1989] E.P.O.R. 437.
[25] *Ibid.*
[26] J4/97 July 9, 1997.
[27] J14/82 *JOHNSON MATTHEY/Priority declaration* O.J. EPO 1983, 121; [1979–85] E.P.O.R.: A: 132.
[28] BODENHAUSEN: "Guide to the Application of the Paris Convention for the Protection of Industrial Property" (BIRPI, 1968): see paragraph 8–02.

accordance with Rule 88 EPC, provided that a request has been made for correction sufficiently early for a warning to be included in the publication of the application" (J4/82[29] and J14/82[30]).

Furthermore:

"If the effect of allowing correction of the mistake [in omitting to claim priority] would be to make the date for publication of the application prescribed by Article 93(1) EPC earlier, then the request for correction of the mistake must be received by the EPC in sufficient time for the application to be published on the appropriate date, including the necessary warning to the public that the request for correction has been made" (J3/82[31]).

Thus:

"In principle in the absence of any special circumstances, a request for correction of a priority claim by the addition of a first priority should be made sufficiently early for a warning to be included in the publication of the application" (J6/91[32]).

6–21   (iii) Exceptions: special circumstances

"If such a warning is not published, the question must be considered whether the public interest would be adversely affected by allowing the correction, taking into account any special circumstances of the case" (J14/82[33]). Thus: "The correction of priority data, not requested sufficiently early for a warning to be included in the publication of the application, is only allowable if it is justified by special circumstances" (J7/94[34]). "This applies also to the addition of a priority of later date than the priority claimed erroneously" (J7/94[35]).

Examples of special circumstances:

6–22   (a) *Failure by the EPO to publish a warning.* If a request for correction is made early enough for a warning to be included in the application as published, but the EPO fails to include such a warning, this is a special circumstance which may be taken into account, in combination with the fact that the applicant filed a second application with the correct priorities claimed for the same subject-matter in order to inform the public of the earlier mistake, so as to allow the request for correction (J14/82[36]).

---

[29] J4/82 *YOSHIDA KOGYO/Priority declaration* O.J. EPO 1982, 385; [1979–85] E.P.O.R.: A: 102.
[30] J14/82 *JOHNSON MATTHEY/Priority declaration* O.J. EPO 1983, 121; [1979–85] E.P.O.R.: A: 132.
[31] J3/82 *TAISHO/Correction-priority* O.J. EPO 1983, 171; [1979–85] E.P.O.R.: A: 99.
[32] J6/91 *DU PONT/Correction/Priority declaration* O.J. EPO 1994, 349; [1993] E.P.O.R. 318.
[33] See note 30.
[34] J7/94 *FONTECH/Priority declarations* O.J. EPO 1995, 817; [1996] E.P.O.R. 165.
[35] *Ibid.*
[36] See note 30.

(b) *No notification by the EPO of absence of claim to priority.* If the EPO **6–23** notes the absence of a formal claim to priority but fails to notify the applicant of this fact, this constitutes a lack of good faith by the EPO. In such circumstances, correction of the claim to priority is allowable, being "of greater importance than the interest of the public in being informed about the second priority claim ..." (J11/89[37]).

(c) *Apparent mistake on the face of the published application ("apparent* **6–24** *discrepancy").* An exception to the above general rule (as to the necessity for a warning in the published application) "may be allowed if it is apparent on the face of the published application that a first or only priority may be missing or wrong or that the date of a first or only priority is wrong. In such a case, the public interest is safeguarded by the fact that it was apparent from the published application that a mistake may have been or has been made with respect to the priority date claimed" (J6/91[38]: also J3/91,[39] J2/92[40]).

(d) *Notification to the public by second precautionary application.* "An **6–25** incomplete priority declaration may be corrected, by the addition of an omitted priority in special circumstances, even after publication of the European patent application without a warning to the public that a request for correction has been made, provided that the public has been informed about the full scope of European patent protection sought, by way of a second European or Euro-PCT patent application filed as a precautionary measure by the applicant in due time" (J11/92[41]).

(f) Wrong documents filed with an application

If the wrong description and claims are filed with an application it is not **6–26** allowable to correct such a mistake by substituting the correct description and claims, under either the first or the second sentence of Rule 88 EPC (G2/92[42]: see Chapter 8 at paragraph 8–85 below).

C. *Restitutio in Integrum*: Re-establishment of Rights

Article 122 EPC

(1) Introduction

Article 122 EPC provides a potential remedy for the majority of cases in **6–27** which loss of rights or means of redress is caused by the failure of a party to

---

[37] J11/89 *KYODO/Priority declaration* October 26, 1989.
[38] J6/91 *DU PONT/Correction/Priority declaration* O.J. EPO 1994 349; [1993] E.P.O.R. 318.
[39] J3/91 *UNI-CHARM/Priority declaration (correction)* O.J. EPO 1994, 365; [1994] E.P.O.R. 566.
[40] J2/92 *UNITED STATES/Priority declaration (correction)* O.J. EPO 1994, 375; [1994] E.P.O.R 547.
[41] J11/92 *BEECHAM/Priority declaration (correction)* O.J. EPO 1995, 25; [1996] E.P.O.R. 141.
[42] G2/92 *Non-payment of further search fees* O.J. EPO 1993, 591; [1994] E.P.O.R. 278.

proceedings before the EPO to comply with a time limit *vis-à-vis* the EPO, provided that certain mitigating circumstances are established.

> "The EPC provides for a number of procedural steps to be taken within time limits laid down either in the Convention itself or by the EPO.
> Failure to observe these time limits frequently involves the person concerned in an irrevocable loss of rights.
> This is particularly harsh when that person was not actually at fault and the failure was attributable to an oversight which occurred in spite of all due care required by the circumstances having been taken.
> *Restitutio in integrum* was instituted to mitigate this hardship ..." (G1/86[43]).

(a) Circumstances when re-establishment is available

6–27a   Article 122 EPC sets out both formal and substantive requirements which must be satisfied if re-establishment of rights is to be granted. These are discussed separately below. The substantive requirement is that "in spite of all due care required by the circumstances having been taken, [the application for re-establishment] was unable to observe a time limit ..." (see paragraph 6–48 below).

In contrast to Rule 88 EPC, which is limited in its effect to mistakes concerning documents (see paragraph 6–10 above), Article 122 EPC is potentially applicable to mistakes of fact, such as non-payment of a fee, as well. Furthermore, in contrast to Article 121 EPC, which provides for further processing of a European patent application only in a case of non-compliance with a time limit *set by the EPO* (see paragraph 6–02, above), Article 122 EPC also allows the re-establishment of rights which would otherwise be lost because of non-compliance with a time limit *laid down in the EPC itself.* Additionally, in contrast to Article 121 EPC, which only concerns the further processing of an *application*, Article 122 EPC is applicable in *opposition proceedings* as well (including, in certain circumstances as discussed in paragraph 6–30 below, re-establishment of an opponent's rights).

There are, however, certain specified time limits in respect of which re-establishment of rights under Article 122 EPC is not available (see paragraph 6–32 below).

(b) Consequences of re-establishment

6–27b   If an application for re-establishment is allowed, the rights which would otherwise have been lost as a result of the failure to meet a time limit are restored to the applicant, without any interruption. If the date of loss of rights has been entered in the European Patents Register under Rule 92(m)

---

[43] G1/86 *VOEST ALPINE/Re-establishment of opponent* O.J. EPO 1987, 447; [1987] E.P.O.R. 388.

or (r) EPC, the date or re-establishment of rights is entered in the Register under Rule 92(u) EPC.

Furthermore:

> "Any person who, in a designated Contracting State, in good faith has used or made effective and serious preparations for using an invention ... in the course of the period between the loss of rights ... and publication of the mention of re-establishment of those rights, may without payment continue such use in the course of his business or for the needs thereof" (Article 122(6) EPC).

(2) Whose rights may be re-established?

(a) Applicant or patent proprietor

Article 122(1) EPC specifies that "The applicant for or proprietor of" a European patent may have his rights re-established (upon application). **6–28**

(b) Other parties

The wording of Article 122(1) EPC would seem *prima facie* to exclude other parties to proceedings before the EPO, such as opponents. **6–29**

However:

> "Article 122 EPC is not to be interpreted as being applicable only to the applicant and patent proprietor" "as this would clearly have inequitable and logically unjustifiable consequences" (G1/86[44]).

(i) An opponent. (1) A potential opponent who has *failed to file a notice of* **6–30** *opposition* within the nine-month period under Article 99(1) EPC cannot obtain re-establishment of rights under Article 122 EPC (T25/85,[45] T152/85,[46] T702/89[47]).

(2) Similarly, following the issue of a decision by an Opposition Division, an opponent who has *failed to file a notice of appeal* within the two-month period under Article 108 EPC cannot obtain re-establishment of rights under Article 122 EPC (G1/86,[48] T210/89[49]). This follows from the wording of Article 122(1) EPC as well as the working papers leading to the EPC, and is justified by the fact that "the proprietor has a legitimate interest in not being left in the dark as to whether an appeal can still be filed" (G1/86[50]).

(3) However, the position of an opponent in appeal proceedings after the notice of appeal has been filed must be distinguished from his position before an appeal has been filed. In particular, "the legitimate interests of

---

[44] G1/86 *VOEST ALPINE/Re-establishment of opponent* O.J. EPO 1987, 447; [1987] E.P.O.R. 388.
[45] T25/85 *DEUTSCHE GELATINE-FABRIKEN STOESS & CO./Opponent identifiability* O.J. EPO 1986, 81; [1986] E.P.O.R. 158.
[46] T152/85 *SANDVIK/Unpaid opposition fee* O.J. EPO 1987, 191; [1987] E.P.O.R. 258.
[47] T702/89 *ALLIED SIGNAL INC/Proportioning valve* O.J. EPO 1994, 472; [1993] E.P.O.R. 580.
[48] See note 44.
[49] T210/89 *MARCONI/Restitution by opponent* O.J. EPO 1991, 433; [1991] E.P.O.R. 403.
[50] See note 44.

the patent proprietor do not ... justify refusing an opponent re-establishment of rights in respect of *the time limit for filing the statement of grounds of appeal*" (emphasis added). Thus:

> "An appellant as opponent may have his rights re-established under Article 122 EPC if he has failed to observe the time limit for filing the statement of grounds of appeal" (G1/86[51]).

This conclusion is justified under the general legal principle that "all parties to proceedings before a court must be accorded the same procedural rights"; this principle being applicable to proceedings before the Boards of Appeal because they "act as courts within the task of ensuring that the provisions of the EPC do not conflict with the law when applied in practice" (G1/86[52]).

6–31   **(ii) Other parties to proceedings before the EPO.** A professional representative in proceedings under Article 20 EPC, an inventor in proceedings under Rule 19 EPC, and a person who is not the applicant but who is entitled to a patent in proceedings under Article 61 EPC, may each apply for re-establishment, because "it is not clear on what grounds these persons should be excluded from re-establishment of rights" (G1/86[53]).

(3) Circumstances when re-establishment is not available

(a) Excluded time limits

6–32   Article 122(5) EPC identifies certain time limits set by the EPC to which re-establishment of rights is not applicable. These excluded time limits are in respect of:

> (i)   filing an application for *re-establishment*—Article 122(2) EPC itself;
>
> (ii)   paying *filing, search and examination fees* in respect of a *new European patent application* filed under Article 61(1)(b) EPC when it is found that a person other than the applicant is entitled to the grant of a patent;
>
> (iii) paying the *filing, search and examination fees* in respect of a *divisional application* under Article 76 EPC;
>
> (iv)   paying the *filing and search fees* in respect of a European patent application under Article 78(3) EPC (with period of grace under Rule 85(a) EPC);
>
> (v)   paying the *designation fee* in respect of a European patent application under Article 79(2) EPC (with period of grace under Rule 85(a) EPC);

---

[51] G1/86 *VOEST ALPINE/Re-establishment of opponent* O.J. EPO 1987, 447; [1987] E.P.O.R. 388.
[52] *Ibid.*
[53] *Ibid.*

(vi)   filing a European patent application within the *twelve-month priority period* in order to claim a right of priority from an earlier application under Article 87(1) EPC;

(vii) filing a *request for examination* (including paying the fee) in respect of a European patent application under Article 94(2) EPC (with period of grace under Rule 85(b) (EPC).

(1) European and Euro-PCT applications. The above excluded time **6–33** limits (in particular those time limits under (iv) and (vii) above) apply both to European applications and to "Euro-PCT applications" (international applications filed under the PCT—see Chapter 1 at paragraphs 1–42 *et seq.*) (G3/91[54], G6/92[55], G5/93[56]; overruling J6/79[57], J5/80[58]). Thus:

> "Article 122(5) EPC is applicable both to the time limits provided for in Article 78(2) and 79(2) EPC and to those provided for in Rule 104 b(1)(b) and (c) EPC in conjunction with Articles 157(2)(b) and 158(2) EPC"—the latter being those applicable to Euro-PCT applicants (G3/91[59] with respect to the time limits under (iv) and (v) above).
>
> "The time limit under Article 94(2) EPC is excluded from *restitutio in integrum* by the provisions of Article 1 22 EPC" (G6/92 with respect to the time limit under (vii) above for both European and Euro-PCT applications).

It may be noted that re-establishment of rights is available with respect **6–34** to the time limits for payment of claims fees under Rule 31 EPC (European applications) and Rule 104 b(1)(b)(iii) EPC (Euro-PCT applications). This follows from the omission of a reference to Rule 104 b(1)(b)(iii) EPC in G5/93[60].

Furthermore, having regard to Article 48(2)(a)PCT which reads:

> "Any Contracting State shall, as far as that State is concerned, excuse, for reasons admitted under its national law, any delay in meeting any time limit",
>
> "a Euro-PCT applicant who has not carried out a certain procedural act within the time limit prescribed in the PCT can take advantage of the relevant provisions of the EPC concerning re-establishment of rights in all cases where the direct European applicant too may invoke them if he fails to observe the relevant time limit" (T227/97[61]).

[54] G3/91 *FABRITIUS II/Re-establishment of rights* O.J. EPO 1993, 8; [1993] E.P.O.R. 361.
[55] G6/92 *DURIRON/Re-establishment* O.J. EPO 1994, 25; [1994] E.P.O.R. 381.
[56] G5/93 *NELLCOR/Re-establishment* O.J. EPO 1994, 447; [1994] E.P.O.R. 169.
[57] J6/79 *RHÔNE POULENC/International applications* O.J. EPO 1980, 225; [1979–85] E.P.O.R.: A: 10.
[58] J5/80 *SOCIÉTÉ PARISIENNE/Restitutio in integrum* O.J. EPO 1981, 343; [1979–85] E.P.O.R.: A: 31.
[59] G3/91 *FABRITIUS II/Re-establishment of rights* O.J. EPO 1993, 8; [1993] E.P.O.R. 361.
[60] G5/93 *NELLCOR/Re-establishment* O.J. EPO 1994, 447; [1994] E.P.O.R. 169.
[61] T227/97 *LINDAHL/Protein rib* O.J. EPO 1999, 495; [1999] E.P.O.R. 568.

6–35   (ii) Grace periods under Rule 85(a) and (b) EPC.

"Article 122(5) EPC excludes 'restitutio in integum' not only where the time limit provided for in the specifically mentioned [Articles 78(2), 79(2) and 94(2) are] not observed, but also where the period of grace laid down in [Rule 85a and b respectively], extending the normal period for [payment of the filing search and designation fees and filing a request for examination] respectively, is not observed" (J18/82[62], J12/82[63]; also J8/94[64]).

(b) Time limit not imposed upon an applicant

6–36   Article 122 EPC "provides only for restitution of rights where there has been a failure to observe a time limit which it has been for the applicant to observe" (J3/80[65]).

In this case a European patent application was filed at the United Kingdom Patent Office pursuant to Article 75 EPC, and the United Kingdom Patent Office issued a "secrecy direction" under section 22 of the 1977 U.K. Act. Despite accelerated processing by the Ministry of Defence, notification of revocation of the secrecy order was not issued until the date of expiry of the fourteen-month period from the priority date provided by Article 77(3) EPC, with the result that the application was not forwarded to the EPO by the United Kingdom Patent Office in due time, and was, therefore, deemed to be withdrawn under Article 77(5) EPC.

In these circumstances, re-establishment of the rights of the applicant was not possible, since the applicant was not responsible for observing the fourteen-month time limit, this responsibility resting solely upon the relevant central industrial property office (Article 77(1) EPC). An alternative course for the applicant was provided by Articles 135(1)(a) and 136(2) EPC, namely conversion of the European patent application into national patent applications.

(c) No rights lost as a direct consequence of non-observance of a time limit

6–37   If a failure to observe a time limit results in a "deficiency" which may be corrected after expiry of the time limit specified by the EPO, there is no loss of rights which can be re-established under Article 122 EPC until the applicant has been given an opportunity to correct the deficiency and has failed to take advantage of that opportunity (J1/80[66]).

In J1/80,[67] the applicant failed to file a priority document within the sixteen-month time limit of Rule 38(3) EPC. This was a deficiency which

---

[62] J18/82 *COCKERILL SAMBRE/Force majeure* O.J. EPO 1983, 441; [1979–85] E.P.O.R.: A: 140
[63] J12/82 *FLORIDIENNE/Late request for examination* O.J. EPO 1983, 221; [1979–85] E.P.O.R.: A: 125.
[64] J8/94 *PHOTOGRAPHIC SCIENCES/Re-establishment* O.J. EPO 1997, 17; [1997] E.P.O.R. 259.
[65] J3/80 *CHUBB/Failure to forward a European patent application* O.J. EPO 1980, 92; [1979–85] E.P.O.R.: A: 23.
[66] J1/80 *SIEMENS/Filing priority documents* O.J. EPO 1980, 289; [1979–85] E.P.O.R.: A: 15.
[67] *Ibid.*

could be corrected under Article 91(1)(d) and Rule 41(1) EPC, and which if so corrected, did not result in loss of a right.

"Article 122(1) EPC is so worded as to be applicable only where there is a loss of a right or a means of redress" (J1/80[68]).

(4) Time limits for re-establishment

(u) Filing an application for re-establishment

There are two aspects to the time limit for filing an application under Article 122(2) EPC:

6–38

(1) The application must be filed within two months from "the removal of the cause of non-compliance [with the original time limit]." The meaning of the phrase "removal of the cause of non-compliance" is considered in paragraphs 6–42 *et seq.* below.
(2) The application must also be filed within the year immediately following the expiry of the unobserved time limit.

There is one specific exception to this one year period provided in Article 122(2) EPC, namely in a case where a renewal fee is not paid before the due date under Article 86 EPC. In such a case the period of six months specified in Article 86(2) EPC, during which the renewal fee plus an additional fee may be paid, is deducted from the one year period of Article 122(2) EPC, with the result that an application for re-establishment must be filed within six months from the due date for payment of the renewal fee plus additional fee.

Having regard to the absolute nature of this one year time limit in the interest of legal certainty, an application for re-establishment must be rejected as inadmissible if filed more than one year after the expiry of the unobserved time limit, whatever the reason for the lateness of the application (J16/86[69]).

Both of the above two-month and one-year time limits are subject to the possibility of "interruption" under Rule 90 EPC, however (see below).

(b) Completion of the omitted act

The second sentence of Article 122(2) EPC states that "The omitted act must be completed within this period," that is, within the two month period which begins with the "removal of the cause of non-compliance" with the time limit.

6–39

This requirement "implies that the completed act also must meet the requirements of the EPC"; for example that the statement of grounds of appeal is admissible for the purpose of Article 108 (T167/97[70]).

---

[68] *Ibid.*
[69] J16/86 *PATIN/Restitutio* December 1, 1986.
[70] T167/97 *NN AG/Admissibility* O.J. EPO 1999, 488; [1999] E.P.O.R. 555.

Determination of the date of removal of the cause of non-compliance is frequently important in connection with the admissibility of appications for re-establishment, having regard to the non-extensibility of the time limits for filing such an application and completing the omitted act (subject to interruption under Rule 90 EPC—see paragraph 6–40 below).

(c) Interruption of time limits under Article 122 EPC

6–40 The only possibility of filing an admissible application for re-establishment after expiry of the above two-month and one-year time limits is in the case of an interruption of proceedings under Rule 90 EPC (see paragraphs 6–63 *et seq.* below).

(d) Purpose of the two-month period

6–41 "The two-month period laid down in Article 122 EPC was clearly designed to enable parties to carry out the necessary investigations and consultations, as well as to prepare the documentation for submission of a request under Article 122 EPC. The date of removal of the cause of non-compliance cannot, therefore, be set at the date when these preparations have been completed and the representative is about to submit a request for re-establishment, but must be a date before that" (J17/89[71]).

(e) Removal of the cause of non-compliance

6–42 As set out in paragraph 6–38 above, the starting point for the relatively short period of two months is defined by reference to the "removal of the cause of non-compliance." The determination of this starting date depends upon the particular circumstances involved. Thus "it is impossible to decide what is the cause of non-compliance with a time limit without considering the facts of each case" (J7/82[72]). Some particular circumstances in which such determinations have had to be made are considered below.

6–43 **(i) Notification of non-observance.** Frequently a party or his representative has intended to comply with a time limit and is unaware that the time limit was not in fact observed until receipt of a notification from the EPO (*e.g.* under Rule 69(1) EPC) to the effect that loss or rights has occurred as a result of non-observance. When determining the date of removal of the cause of non-compliance, "in a case in which receipt of a notification under Rule 69(1) EPC is relevant for the purpose of Article 122(2) EPC, it is the fact [*i.e.* the date] of *actual receipt* by the applicant which is significant, not ... the fact of despatch ... by the EPO" (J7/82[73]).

6–44 **(ii) Knowledge of non-observance before receipt of notification.** If the representative of an applicant has knowledge of non-observance of a time

---

[71] J17/89 *LION BREWERIES/Re-establishment* January 9, 1990.
[72] J7/82 *CATALDO/Cause of non-compliance* O.J. EPO 1982, 319; [1979–85] E.P.O.R.: A: 108.
[73] *Ibid.*

limit before receipt of a notification of non-observance from the EPC, the date of removal of the cause of non-compliance is the date of first knowledge of non-observance by the representative (J17/89[74]).

(iii) Knowledge of non-observance by the person responsible. In 6–45 principle:

> "the removal of the cause of non-compliance is a question of fact and occurs on the date on which the responsible person (*i.e.* the patent applicant or proprietor or his authorised agent, as the case may be) is made aware of the fact that a time limit has not been observed" (J27/88[75]; also T191/82[76], J9/86[77]).

Thus:

> "In the absence of circumstances to the contrary a communication under Rule 69(1) EPC to the professional representative qualified under Article 134 EPC and appointed in accordance with Article 133(2) EPC by the person entitled to the patent application removes the cause of non-compliance. This applies also when parties instruct the (European) professional representative via their (national) patent attorney" (J27/90[78]).

Furthermore:

> "The appointment of an independent service firm for the payment of renewal fees (a so-called 'renewal fee payment agency') does not constitute such circumstances to the contrary. The professional representative remains responsible for the application notwithstanding the fact that the applicants use such a payment agency" (J27/90[79]).

Following this approach: 6–46

> "If a party instructs the authorised representative not to pass on any further communication from the EPO it cannot then rely on the fact that information notified to the authorised representative and necessary for continuing the proceedings was lacking" (T840/94[80]).

It is knowledge "by the responsible person" which is crucial, however. For example:

---

[74] J17/89 *LION BREWERIES/Re establishment* January 9, 1990.
[75] J27/88 *UNIVERSITY OF CALIFORNIA/Re-establishment* July 5, 1989.
[76] T191/82 *FIBRE-CHEM/Re-establishment of rights* O.J. EPO 1985, 189; [1979–85] E.P.O.R. C: 701.
[77] J9/86 *SOLOW/Restitutio* March 17, 1987.
[78] J27/90 *BRUNSWICK/Restitutio* O.J. EPO 1993, 442; [1994] E.P.O.R. 82.
[79] *Ibid.*
[80] T840/94 *UNION CAMP/Revocation* O.J. EPO 1996, 680; [1997] E.P.O.R. 217.

"In a case in which non-compliance with a time limit leading to a loss of rights under the EPC is discovered by an employee of a representative, the cause of non-compliance, *i.e.* failure to appreciate that the time limit has not been complied with, cannot be considered to have been removed until the representative concerned has himself been made aware of the facts, since it must be his responsibility to decide whether an application for re-establishment of rights should be made and, if it is to be made, to determine the grounds and supporting facts to be presented to the EPO" (T191/82[81]).

Similarly, in a case where the applicant company had been informed that designations of two States had been lost through non-payment of the fees, the responsible person "was neither [the applicant] nor the European representative, but the United States patent attorney who was ... duly empowered to take all necessary measures to obtain [the desired designations]," in accordance with his instructions from the applicant (J27/88[82]).

6–47 In normal cases "a professional representative would be expected to know the circumstances in which a loss of rights occurs."

A distinction may exceptionally be drawn, however, between the responsible person having knowledge that a time limit has not been observed, and that person having knowledge that a loss of rights has occurred. Thus in one case it was recognised that:

"the true 'cause of non-compliance with the time limit' was not simply a failure by the appellant's representative to realise that, contrary to his intention, the excess claims fees had not in fact been paid; it was a failure by the representative to realise both that there had been an omission to pay the excess claims fees and that a loss of rights had already occurred, as a matter of law. In other words, on the evidence in the present case, ... during the [relevant] periods, the representative was not fully aware that there had been an omission that would cause loss of rights" (J29/86[83]).

Furthermore, "The fact that, after the tme limit expired ..., the representative completed the omitted act by paying the excess claims fees ..., does not mean that on that date he knew that there was necessarily a loss of rights, as a result of such omitted act" (J29/86[84]).

[81] T191/82 *FIBRE-CHEM/Re-establishment of rights* O.J. EPO 1985, 189; [1979–85] E.P.O.R.: C: 701.
[82] J27/88 *UNIVERSITY OF CALIFORNIA/Re-establishment* July 5, 1989.
[83] J29/86 *PACCAR/Excess claims fees* O.J. EPO 1988, 84; [1988] E.P.O.R. 194.
[84] *Ibid.*

(5) Contents of the application for re-establishment

(a) Basic principles

The application must establish that "in spite of all due care required by the **6–48** circumstances having been taken [the applicant for re-establishment] was unable to observe a time limit ..." (Article 122(1) EPC).

According to Article 122(2) and (3) EPC, the application for re-establishment must be in writing, must state "the grounds on which it is based", and must set out "the facts on which it relies". If these requirements are not complied with within the specified time limits, the application may be considered inadmissible.

However:

> "An application for re-establishment of rights may be considered as complying with the requirement that it must set out the facts on which it relies (Article 122(3) EPC) if the initially filed application in writing, which does not contain such facts, can be read together with a further document, which contains them and is filed before the expiry of the period within which the application has to be filed" (T287/84[85]).

(b) Multiple loss of rights

"Where time limits expiring independently of one another have been **6–49** missed ... each resulting in the application being withdrawn, a request for reestablishment has to be filed in respect of each unobserved time limit", and a fee has to be paid for each request (J26/95[86]).

(c) Exceptional cases

(i) **Grounds of appeal treated as an application for re-establishment.** In **6–50** exceptional circumstances, where the applicant has become confused as to the correct procedure to be followed after the issue of a decision of revocation under Article 102(4) and (5) EPC, Boards of Appeal have accepted a statement of grounds of appeal effectively setting out grounds for re-establishment as an application for re-establishment.

In one case, for example:

> "The patent proprietor filed the missing translations together with the appeal, requesting that the latter be allowed as non-observance of the time limit had been due to a stroke of bad luck. The appellant was thereby evidently requesting re-establishment to enable the omitted act to be deemed to have been completed within the time limit".

The formal deficiencies in the application for re-establishment were

---

[85] T287/84 BRUNSWICK/Re-establishment O.J. EPO 1985, 333; [1986] E.P.O.R. 46.
[86] J26/95 VPL/Bankruptcy O.J. EPO 1999, 668.

considered to be correctable having regard to the principle of good faith (see Chapter 1 at paragraphs 1–73 *et seq*).

> "The principle of good faith governing proceedings between the EPO and the parties involved requires that the applicant have his attention drawn to deficiencies in his application for re-establishment of rights which are obviously easy to correct (in this case: fee not paid and substantiation not supplied) if correct of the deficiencies can be expected within the two-month time limit for re-establishment of rights under Article 122(2) EPC" (T14/89[87]).

6–51   In another case the grounds of appeal were considered to be the application for re-establishment, and the appeal fee, being larger than the fee for re-establishment, was deemed to have been payment of the fee for re-establishment. This course had the effect that the application for re-establishment was filed in due time, and was again based on the principle of good faith (T522/88[88]).

Nevertheless the distinction between grounds for appeal and grounds for re-establishment must be emphasised:

> "Grounds of appeal are, as a matter of principle, the antithesis of grounds for re-establishment, since the former should be setting out a case why the appellant should not have lost rights or otherwise been 'adversely affected', and the latter should be setting out a case why in the particular circumstances rights which have been lost should be re-established" (T522/88[89]).

6–52   **(ii) Minimum content within the one-year time limit.**

> "To make a valid request for re-establishment of rights within the year immediately following the expiry of the unobserved time limit, it is sufficient if the files contain a clearly documented statement of intent from which any third party may infer that the applicant is endeavouring to maintain the patent application" (J6/90[90])

(6) Facts and evidence in support

6–53   It is not uncommon for the contents of an application for re-establishment to be supplemented after the two-month period has expired, for example to provide further information surrounding the non-observance of the time limit in response to communications from the EPO.

Similarly, as to the filing of evidence in support of re-establishment:

> "In order to comply with the two months time limit laid down in

---

[87] T14/89 *UHDE/Re-establishment* O.J. EPO 1990, 432; [1990] E.P.O.R. 656.
[88] T522/88 *SHELL/Gasification of solid fuel* [1990] E.P.O.R. 237.
[89] *Ibid*.
[90] J6/90 *BAXTER/One-year period* O.J. EPO 1993, 714; [1994] E.P.O.R. 304.

Article 122(2) EPC, it is not necessary that the application for re-establishment of rights provides any *prima facie* evidence for the facts set out in it, nor is it necessary that it indicates the means by which those facts are supported (*e.g.* medical certificates, sworn statements and the like). Such evidence may be submitted after the time limit, if so required" (T324/90[91]).

(7) "All due care required by the circumstances"

(a) Introduction

Article 122(1) EPC provides that if the party concerned "was unable to observe a time limit ... in spite of all due care required by the circumstances having been taken," then rights which are lost as a direct consequence of the non-observance shall be re-established.   6–54

Thus, the onus is upon an applicant for re-establishment of rights to prove that the non-observance of the time limit happened in spite of "all due care" having been taken to observe it. It should be emphasised that, "the word 'all' is important in this context," and furthermore that "the circumstances of each case must be considered as a whole" (T287/84[92]).

Determination of this question necessarily involves consideration of the particular facts of each case, and since the facts of a case are rarely exactly the same as a previous one, a detailed classification of the many Board of Appeal decisions concerning this matter would be inappropriate. Nevertheless, some particular factual circumstances which have occurred in previous cases are discussed below.

(b) Mistakes in a system

The majority of applications for re-establishment are consequential upon a mistake or error having been made either by the applicant or proprietor himself or by his representative. In many cases, the applicant, proprietor or representative is responsible for the prosecution of many patent applications or patents, and for observing many time limits in connection therewith, and something unusual happens so as to cause a particular time limit to be missed.   6–55

In such cases:

"Article 122 EPC is intended to ensure that in appropriate cases the loss of substantive rights does not result from an isolated procedural mistake within a normally satisfactory system" (J2, 3/86[93])

Thus, in cases of this type, the system of reminders, cross-checks, etc., which is used to ensure compliance with the relevant time limits will normally be examined.

---

[91] T324/90 *PHILLIPS PETROLEUM/Re-establishment* O.J. EPO 1993, 33; [1993] E.P.O.R. 507.
[92] T287 *BRUNSWICK/Re-establishment* O.J. EPO 1985, 333; [1986] E.P.O.R. 46.
[93] J2, 3/86 *MOTOROLA/Isolated mistake—restitutio* O.J. EPO 1987, 362; [1987] E.P.O.R. 394.

In one case, the applicant relied merely upon informal and voluntary reminders normally sent by the EPO in connection with the payment of renewal fees. It was held that "The applicant must ensure that renewal fees … are paid in time irrespective of whether [such a reminder] has been received," and consequently re-establishment was refused (J12/84[94]).

(c) Assistants

6–56 Applicants, proprietors and professional representatives commonly employ assistants to perform tasks which are part of the system for ensuring compliance with time limits. In such circumstances "it is encumbent upon the representative to choose for the work a suitable person, properly instructed in the tasks to be performed, and to exercise reasonable supervision over the work" (J5/80[95]).

Although "the same strict standards of care are not expected of the assistant as are expected of the applicant or his representative, nevertheless, if the representative delegates to an assistant a task which … normally falls to him, as for example the interpretation of laws and treaties," all due care would not have been established (J5/80[96]).

If an assistant is alleged to be responsible, "a conclusive case must be made, setting out and substantiating the facts, for the probability that such a wrongful act or omission [on the part of an assistant] was instrumental in the failure to meet the time limit" (T13/82[97]).

If the failure to observe a time limit is the responsibility of a substitute assistant of a professional representative:

> "The same standard of care must be exercised as regards the choice, instruction and supervision of the substitute as of the assistant himself" (J16/82[98]).

(d) Inadequate professional advice

6–57 "For an applicant who himself is lacking the necessary knowledge of … procedures, it is obviously necessary to consult a competent professional representative …" If an insufficiently competent professional representative is chosen by the applicant, the application for re-establishment may be refused (J23/87[99]).

(e) Financial difficulties

6–58 "Unavoidable financial difficulties which result in failure to observe time limits for payment of fees may constitute grounds for granting

---

[94] J12/84 *PROWECO/Restitutio in integrum* O.J. EPO 1985, 108; [1979–85] E.P.O.R.: A: 217.
[95] J5/80 *SOCIÉTÉ PARISIENNE/Restitutio in integrum* O.J. EPO 1981, 343; [1979–85] E.P.O.R.: A: 31.
[96] *Ibid.*
[97] J13/82 *GENERAL DATACOMM/Correction of description* O.J. EPO 1983, 12; [1979–85] E.P.O.R.: A: 129.
[98] J16/82 *THEURER/Assistant; substitute* O.J. EPO 1983, 262; [1979–85] E.P.O.R.: A: 137.
[99] J23/87 *K-CORPORATION OF JAPAN/Restitutio in integrum* [1988] E.P.O.R. 52.

re-establishment of rights, provided the requester has exercised all due care in seeking financial assistance" (J22/88[100]).

(f) One-person office

"In order to comply with the requirements under Article 122 EPC to **6–59** take all due care required by the circumstances, a professional representative who runs a one-person office must normally be expected to make appropriate arrangements so that, in the case of absence through illness, the observance of time-limits can be ensured with the help of other persons" (J41/92[101]).

(g) Proportionality

According to the principle of proportionality, which is one of the general **6–60** principles of law which is applied under European Community law (see Chapter 1 at paragraph 1–82a), "a procedural means used to achieve a given end (*e.g.* a sanction following a procedural non-compliance) should be no more than that which is appropriate and necessary to achieve that end" (T869/90[102], T111/92[103]).

In some cases a procedural non-compliance may involve the missing of a time limit by one day for example, in circumstances where the change of an interested member of the public becoming aware of the non-compliance is extremely remote, and where in any event such a member of the public would be protected under Article 122(6) EPC. In such a case, the loss of the right to a European patent for example, as a result of such a non-compliance, is very harsh. Especially in such cases, and "where there maybe some doubt as to whether or not all due care required by the circumstances was exercised it may be reasonable to have this principle in mind when deciding upon an application for re-establishment" (T869/90[104], T111/92[105]).

(8) The department competent to decide

According to Article 122(4) EPC, "The department competent to decide on **6–61** the omitted act shall decide upon the application" (for re-establishment). Thus, in the majority of cases, a first instance department of the EPO is responsible for deciding upon an application for re-establishment, and its decision may be the subject of an appeal in the usual way.

If a first instance department which was not "competent to decide on the omitted act" decides upon a request for re-establishment, the decision is void and will be set aside.

For example, in one case an application for re-establishment was made

[100] J22/88 *RADAKOVIC/Re-establishment of rights* O.J. EPO 1990, 244; [1990] E.P.O.R. 495.
[101] J41/92 *MARON BLANCO/Restitutio* O.J. EPO 1995, 93; [1994] E.P.O.R. 375.
[102] T869/90 *TEXACO/Restitution* [1994] E.P.O.R. 581.
[103] T111/92 *SONY/Restitution* August 3, 1992.
[104] See note 102.
[105] See note 103.

by the applicant in connection with the prosecution of the application during examination proceedings, and at the same time the applicant requested that a transfer of the application be recorded in the Register of European Patents, this being the responsibility of the Legal Division. The Legal Division proceeded to decide the application for re-establishment. In appeal proceedings the decision of the Legal Division concerning re-establishment was set aside, and the application for re-establishment was remitted to the Examining Division as the competent department (J10/93[106]).

When a time limit is not observed in the course of appeal proceedings, for example the two-month limit for filing a notice of appeal or the four-month time limit for filing a statement of grounds of appeal, the Board of Appeal to whom the appeal is assigned has exclusive competence to decide upon such an omitted act and consequently upon an application for re-establishment in connection therewith (T473/91[107]). There is only a single instance decision upon such an application for re-establishment, by the Board of Appeal itself, and there is no possibility of any appeal therefrom.

6–62   In a case where an applicant filed an application for re-establishment in respect of the late filing of a notice of appeal, a formalities officer of the Examining Division wrongly purported to decide the application for re-establishment in the context of considering the admissibility of the appeal under Article 109 EPC ("interlocutory revision"—see Chapter 4 at paragraphs 4–63 *et seq.*). However:

> "The admissibility question under Article 109 EPC only falls under the jurisdiction of the department of first instance when this question can be decided immediately on the basis of the appeal submissions themselves (notice of appeal and statement of grounds, date of payment of the appeal fee)" (T473/91[108]).

Consequently, the decision of the formalities officer on re-establishment was set aside, and the application for re-establishment was re-decided by the Board of Appeal.

D. Interruption of Proceedings

Rule 90 EPC

(1) Introduction

6–63   If certain events which are defined in Rule 90(1) EPC occur, "proceedings before the EPO shall be interrupted." In effect, time stops running as a

---

[106] J10/93 *COLLAPSIBLE BOTTLE OF AMERICA/Transfer* O.J. EPO 1997, 91; [1997] E.P.O.R. 491.
[107] T473/91 *WEGENEL/Jurisdiction* O.J. EPO 1993, 630; [1994] E.P.O.R. 292.
[108] *Ibid.*

result of such an interruption. Determination of the new time limits which apply after the proceedings are resumed is discussed in paragraphs 6–71 *et seq*. below.

(2) Events which result in interruption

These are specified in Rule 90(1) EPC as follows: **6–64**

(a) death or legal incapacity of the applicant or proprietor, or the person authorised by national law to act on his behalf;
(b) the applicant or proprietor being prevented by legal reasons from continuing the proceedings, as a result of some action being taken against his property;
(c) death or legal incapacity of the representative of the applicant or proprietor, or the representative being prevented by legal reasons from continuing the proceedings, resulting from action taken against his property.

Thus, it seems that opponents or other parties to proceedings before the EPO are not entitled to claim interruption of proceedings in which they are taking part.

In relation to Rule 90(1)(b) EPC: **6–65**

"The decisive criticism for interruption is whether the action against the property is such as to make it legally impossible for the applicant to continue with proceedings" (J26/95[109]).

Thus it is not the name or formal qualification of an action against property that is decisive. For example: "In the absence of specific circumstances ... proceedings against the applicant under Chapter 11—Bankruptcy of the United States code do not interrupt proceedings before the EPO", because "it is the very nature of proceedings under Chapter 11 that it is the debtor who continues to act for his business": this is in contrast to "cases where parties have been placed under receivership under French law (J7/83[110]) or have been declared bankrupt under Germany Bankruptcy Law" (J9/90[111], J26/95[112]).

(3) Automatic nature of an interruption

The EPO must apply Rule 90 EPC "of its own motion". Thus: **6–66**

"Rule 90 EPC must be applied automatically by the EPO; no specific formalities are required" (J .../87[113]).

[109] J26/95 *VPL/Bankruptcy* O.J. EPO 1999, 668.
[110] J7/83 *MOUCHET/Interruption of proceedings* O.J. EPO 1984, 211; [1979–85] E.P.O.R.: A: 174.
[111] J9/90 *DIETACHMAR/Restoration: bankruptcy of applicant* April 8, 1992.
[112] J26/95 See note 109.
[113] J .../87 *Incapacity* O.J. EPO 1988, 323; [1989] E.P.O.R. 73.

A Decision of the President of the EPO dated March 10, 1989 states *inter alia* that the sole responsibility for "Interruption and resumption of proceedings" in accordance with Rule 90 EPC is vested in the Legal Division of the EPO. Thus in any particular case the Legal Division must decide whether the facts establish that an interruption of proceedings has occurred, and in the light of its findings specify the time limits which may have been interrupted and began again on the date proceedings were resumed (J . . ./87[114]).

(4) The meaning of "legal incapacity"

6–67　The means of determining the legal incapacity of an applicant or proprietor on the one hand, and a representative on the other hand must be distinguished (J/unnumbered[115]).

(a) The applicant or proprietor—Rule 90(1)(a) EPC

6–68　"the (legal) capacity of the applicant or proprietor to carry out legal transactions relating to his application or patent must be determined according to a national system of law, since his interest in the application or patent is an interest in property (*cf.* Articles 74 and 2(2) EPC)" (J/Unnumbered[116]).

(b) The applicant or proprietor—Rule 90(1)(b) EPC

6–68a　In the circumstances . . . , proceedings against the applicant under Chapter 11—(Reorganisation) of the United States Banking Code do not cause an interruption under Rule 90(1)(b) EPC, because:

"The decisive criterion for interruption is whether the action against the property is such as to make it legally impossible for the applicant to continue with proceedings" (J26/95[117]).

(c) A representative—Rule 90(1)(c) EPC

6–69　In contrast to (a) and (b) above:

"The question of the capacity of a representative is clearly different. The relevant aspect of his legal incapacity for the purposes of Rule 90(1)(c) EPC is that of his incapacity to carry out professional work on behalf of a client. Since there is a unified European profession of representatives before the European Patent Office, it is justified to consider that there should be a uniform standard of judging legal incapacity, in order to avoid differences in the application of Rule

---

[114] *Ibid.*
[115] J/Unnumbered (March 1, 1985) O.J. EPO 1985, 159; [1979–85] E.P.O.R.: A: 234.
[116] *Ibid.*
[117] J26/95 *VPL/Bankruptcy* O.J. EPO 1999, 668.

90(1)(c) EPC depending on the nationality or domicile of the representative. The matter is, of course, completely separate from any question of a representative's legal incapacity to manage his own personal affairs, which, in accordance with the relevant national law will be governed by his nationality or domicile.

In these circumstances, the question of determining the legal incapacity of a representative for the purposes of Rule 90(1)(c) EPC is one for the EPO, applying its own standards, developed in the light of experience and taking into consideration principles applied in the national laws of Contracting States. The simple test proposed by the appellant seems a reasonable basis for developing such standards:

'was the representative concerned in a fit mental state to do the work required of him at the material time or did he lack the capacity to make rational decisions and to take necessary actions?'" (J/Unnumbered[118]); see also J .../86[119]).

In a case which was concerned specifically with the possible legal incapacity of a representative for the purpose of Rule 102(2) EPC (deletion from the list of professional representatives), it was stated that under Rule 90(1)(c) EPC as well as Rule 102(2)(a) EPC, incapacity to carry out professional work before the EPO "must be of a persistent nature" (J .../86[120]).

(5) The meaning of a "representative"

"A representative" within the meaning of Rule 90(1) PC must be a person **6–70** "authorised by national law to act" on behalf of the applicant or proprietor. A non-European patent attorney who acts on behalf of an applicant or proprietor is not authorised *by* national law (ie by operation of law) as required by Rule 90 EPC, but *under* national law (J23/88[121]).

In a case where such a non-European professional representative acts on behalf of an applicant with respect to the filing of a European patent application, and suffers legal incapacity in the course of filing the application, the non-European representative is "a representative" within the meaning of Rule 90(1) EPC, and accordingly interruption of proceedings may occur. This is because:

"Articles 133(2) and 134 EPC, dealing with the representation of natural or legal persons from outside the Contracting States, leave very limited scope for the application of Rule 90(1)(c) EPC to representatives other than professional representatives as defined in Article 134 EPC. However, that very limited scope is, in the Board's opinion, afforded by the last three lines of Article 133(2) EPC which

---

[118] J/Unnumbered (March 1, 1985) O.J. EPO 1988, 323; [1989] E.P.O.R. 73.
[119] J .../86 X/Professional representative—legal incapacity O.J. EPO 1987, 528; [1988] E.P.O.R. 129.
[120] Ibid.
[121] J23/88 WEBB/Interruption of proceedings [1989] E.P.O.R. 272.

provides a limited exception to the normal requirement for professional representation within the meaning of Article 134 EPC, in the case, and only in the case, of the filing of the European patent application. Such a filing can thus validly be made by the applicant himself or by any representative duly authorised by him.[122]"

(6) The effect of an interruption upon a time limit

(a) Introduction

6–71 Calculation of the time limits which have to be observed in the event of an interruption of proceedings depends upon the interpretation of Rule 90(1) and (4) EPC. Rule 90(4) EPC includes two exceptions in this respect, namely in connection with the time limits for making a request for examination and for paying renewal fees: these exceptions are considered separately below.

(b) General rule for determination of the new time limit

6–72 Rule 90(1) EPC "makes no explicit pronouncement as to the legal consequences of interruption of proceedings merely stating ... that "proceedings shall be interrupted" "when the specified events occur (J7/83[123]). Thus the relevant time limits cease to run on the date when an event occurs within the meaning of Rule 90(1)(a), (b) or (c) which causes the proceedings to be interrupted.

Rule 90(4)EPC states that "The time limits ... in force as regards the applicant for or proprietor of the patent at the date of interruption of the proceedings, shall begin again as from the day on which the proceedings are resumed".

Thus:

> "Rule 90(4) EPC deals with the point where interruption ends, or to be more precise what becomes of the interrupted time limits", and "does not constitute and exception to the general principle that all time limits are interrupted ... its sole purpose is to specify how time limits are to be calculated when proceedings resume" (J7/83[124]).

Consequently, apart from the two exceptions set out in Article 90(4) EPC and considered below, on the day when the proceedings are resumed, the period of the time limit also begins to run again.

(c) Two exceptions—request for examination and renewal fees

6–73   (i) **Request for examination.** If the time limit for making a request for examination is interrupted, "the interrupted time limit must necessarily resume for the remaining time only", except that, in accordance with the

---

[122] Ibid.
[123] J7/83 MOUCHET/Interruption of proceedings O.J. EPO 1984, 211; [1979–85] E.P.O.R.: A: 174.
[124] Ibid.

final sentence of Rule 90(4) EPC, "the time remaining to the applicant's disposal may in no circumstances be shorter than two months" (J7/83[125]).

(ii) Renewal fees. With respect to the payment of renewal fees: **6–74**

"the EPC does not prescribe a payment time limit but simply dates on which they fall due ... Therefore, the only time limit affecting renewal fees that may be suspended is the six-month period for paying the renewal fee together with a penalty fee referred to in Article 86 EPC, and Rule 90(4) EPC has to be interpreted as deferring, until the date proceedings are resumed, the payment date for renewal fees ...".

Accordingly:

"Rule 90(4) EPC has to be interpreted as deferring the payment date for renewal fees falling due during the period of incapacity of the applicant or his representative until the date proceedings are resumed" (J .../87[126]).

E. Correction of a Decision

(1) Introduction

Rule 89 EPC states that: **6–75**

"In decisions of the EPO, only linguistic errors, errors of transcription and obvious mistakes may be corrected".

In application of Rule 89 EPC:

"A decision cannot be cancelled by the instance which issued it, but can only be corrected under Rule 89 EPC" (T212/88[127]).

Furthermore: "The correction of a mistake in a decision under Rule 89 EPC has a retrospective effect" (T212/88[128]), in the sense that the corrected decision is considered to take the place of the original decision as of the original date of issue.

(2) Request for correction compared to an appeal

"... the difference between an appeal and a request for correction of a   **6–76** decision may be seen in the fact that in the first case the remedy is directed against the *substance* of the decision and in the latter case against the form in which the decision was expressed" (G8/95[129]).

---

[125] *Ibid.*
[126] J .../87 *Incapacity* O.J. EPO 1988, 323; [1989] E.P.O.R. 73.
[127] T212/88 *BP/Theta-1* O.J. EPO 1992, 28; [1990] E.P.O.R. 518.
[128] *Ibid.*
[129] G8/95 *US GYPSUM II/Correction of decision to grant* O.J. EPO 1996, 481.

(3) Correction of a decision to grant

6–77 Consequently, it can be within the scope of Rule 89 EPC to correct the text of the patent if it is not and cannot be in the form corresponding to the intention of the deciding instance (G8/95[130], T425/97[131]).

Cases Referred to in Chapter 6

Board of Appeal Decisions

G1/86	VOEST ALPINE/Re-establishment of opponent O.J. EPO 1987, 447; [1987] E.P.O.R. 388.
G3/91	FABRITIUS II/Re-establishment of rights O.J. EPO 1993, 8; [1993] E.P.O.R. 361.
G2/92	Non-payment of further search fees O.J. EPO 1993, 591; [1994] E.P.O.R. 278.
G6/92	DURIRON/Re-establishment O.J. EPO 1994, 25; [1994] E.P.O.R. 381.
G5/93	NELLCOR/Re-establishment O.J. EPO 1994, 447; [1994] E.P.O.R. 169.
G8/95	US GYPSUM II/ Correction of decision to grant O.J. EPO 1996, 481.
J6/79	RHÔNE-POULENC/International applications O.J. EPO 1980, 225 [1979–85] E.P.O.R.: A: 10.
J1/80	SIEMENS/Filing priority documents O.J. EPO 1980, 289; [1979–85] E.P.O.R.: A: 15.
J3/80	CHUBB/Failure to forward a European patent application O.J. EPO 1980, 92; [1979–85] E.P.O.R.: A: 23.
J5/80	SOCIÉTÉ PARISIENNE/Restitutio in integrum O.J. EPO 1981, 343; [1979–85] E.P.O.R.: A: 31.
J7/80	SKF/Correction of mistakes—languages O.J. EPO 1981, 137; [1979–85] E.P.O.R.: A: 36.
J8/80	RIB LOC/Correction of mistakes O.J. EPO 1980, 293; [1979–85] E.P.O.R.: A: 40.
J12/80	HOECHST/Correction of mistakes—published application O.J. EPO 1981, 143; [1979–85] E.P.O.R.: A: 52.
J3/81	BODENRADER/International application O.J. EPO 1982, 100; [1979–85] E.P.O.R.: A: 74.
J3/82	TAISHO/Correction—priority O.J. EPO 1983, 171; [1979–85] E.P.O.R.: A: 99.
J4/82	YOSHIDA KOGYO/Priority declaration O.J. EPO 1982, 385; [1979–85] E.P.O.R.: A: 102.
J7/82	CATALDO/Cause of non-compliance O.J. EPO 1982, 391; [1979–85] E.P.O.R.: A: 108.

---

[130] *Ibid.*
[131] T425/97 May 8, 1998.

J12/82   FLORIDIENNE/Late request for examination O.J. EPO 1983, 221; [1979–85] E.P.O.R.: A: 125.

J14/82   JOHNSON MATTHEY/Priority declaration O.J. EPO 1983, 121; [1979–85] E.P.O.R.: A: 132.

J16/82   THEURER/Assistant; substitute O.J. EPO 1983, 262; [1979–85] E.P.O.R.: A: 137.

J18/82   COCKERILL SAMBRE/Force majeure O.J. EPO 1983, 441; [1979–85] E.P.O.R.: A: 140.

J7/83   MOUCHET/Interruption of proceedings O.J. EPO 1984, 211; [1979–85] E.P.O.R.: A: 174.

J12/84   PROWECO/Restitutio in integrum O.J. EPO 1985, 108; [1979–85] E.P.O.R.: A: 217.

J21/84   CONSUMERS GLASS/Late correction O.J. EPO 1986, 75; [1986] E.P.O.R. 146.

J Unnumbered (March 1, 1985) O.J. EPO 1985, 159; [1979–85] E.P.O.R.: A: 234.

J.../86   X/Professional representative—legal incapacity O.J. EPO 1987, 528; [1988] E.P.O.R. 129.

J2, 3/86   MOTOROLA/Isolated mistake-restitution O.J. EPO 1987, 362; [1987] E.P.O.R. 394.

J9/86   SOLOW/Restitutio March 17, 1987.

J16/86   PATIN/Restitutio December 1, 1986.

J29/86   PACCAR/Excess claims fees O.J. EPO 1988, 84; [1988] E.P.O.R. 194.

J.../87   Incapacity O.J. EPO 1988, 323; [1989] E.P.O.R. 73.

J10/87   INLAND STEEL/Retraction of withdrawal O.J. EPO 1989, 323; [1989] E.P.O.R. 437.

J23/87   K-CORPORATION OF JAPAN/Restitutio in integrum [1988] E.P.O.R. 52.

J26/87   McWHIRTER/PCT form O.J. EPO 1989, 329; [1989] E.P.O.R. 430.

J22/88   RADAKOVIC/Re-establishment of rights O.J. EPO 1990, 244; [1990] E.P.O.R. 495.

J23/88   WEBB/Interruption of proceedings [1989] E.P.O.R. 272.

J25/88   NEW FLEX/Date of filing O.J. EPO 1989, 486; [1990] E.P.O.R. 59.

J27/88   UNIVERSITY OF CALIFORNIA/Re-establishment July 5, 1989.

J8/89   ISUZU/Mistake in designation [1990] E.P.O.R. 55.

J11/89   KYODO/Priority declaration October 26, 1989.

J17/89   LION BREWERIES/Re-establishment January 9, 1990.

J6/90   BAXTER/One-year period O.J. EPO 1993, 714; [1994] E.P.O.R. 304.

J7/90   TOLEDO/Correction of designation O.J. EPO 1993, 133; [1993] E.P.O.R. 329.

J9/90   DIETACHMAIR/Restoration: bankruptcy of applicant, April 8, 1992 .

J16/90   FABRITIUS/Re-establishment March 6, 1991 (P).

J27/90   BRUNSWICK/ Restitutio O.J. EPO 1993, 422; [1994] E.P.O.R.
            82.

J3/91   UNI-CHARM/Priority declaration (correction) O.J. EPO 1994,
            365; [1994] E.P.O.R. 566.

J6/91   DU PONT/Correction/Priority declaration O.J. EPO 1994,
            349; [1993] E.P.O.R. 318.

J2/92   UNITED STATES/Priority declaration (correction) O.J. EPO
            1994, 375; [1994] E.P.O.R. 547.

J11/92   BEECHAM/Priority declaration (correction) O.J. EPO 1995,
            25; [1996] E.P.O.R. 141.

J41/92   MARON BLANCO/Restitutio O.J. EPO 1995, 93; [1994]
            E.P.O.R. 375.

J47/92   SILVER SYSTEMS/Further processing O.J. EPO 1995, 180;
            [1995] E.P.O.R. 495.

J10/93   COLLAPSIBLE BOTTLE OF AMERICA/Transfer O.J. EPO
            1997, 91; [1997] E.P.O.R. 491.

J18/93   CARDIAC/Correction of mistake O.J. EPO 1997, 91; [1998]
            E.P.O.R. 38.

J7/94   FONTECH/Priority declarations (correction) O.J. EPO 1995,
            817; [1996] E.P.O.R. 165.

J8/94   PHOTOGRAPHIC SCIENCES/Re-establishment O.J. EPO
            1997, 17; [1997] E.P.O.R. 259.

J26/95   VPL/Bankruptcy O.J. EPO 1999, 668.

J4/97   XEROX/Retraction of withdrawal July 9, 1997.

T191/82   FIBRE-CHEM/Re-establishment of rights O.J. EPO 1985, 189;
            [1979–85] E.P.O.R. C: 701.

T287/84   BRUNSWICK/Re-establishment O.J. EPO 1985, 333; [1986]
            E.P.O.R. 46.

T25/85   DEUTSCHE GELATINE-FABRIKEN, STOESS & CO./
            Opponent-identifiability O.J. EPO 1986, 81; [1986] E.P.O.R.
            158.

T152/85   SANDVIK/Unpaid opposition fee O.J. EPO 1987, 191; [1987]
            E.P.O.R. 258.

T219/86   ZOKOR/Naming of opponent O.J. EPO 1988, 254; [1988]
            E.P.O.R. 407.

T212/88   BP/Theta-1 O.J.EPO 1992, 28; [1990] E.P.O.R. 518.

T522/88   SHELL/Gasification of solid fuel December 19, 1989; [1990]
            E.P.O.R. 237.

T14/89   UHDE/Re-establishment O.J. EPO 1990, 432; [1990] E.P.O.R.
            656.

T210/89   MARCONI/Restitution by opponent O.J. EPO 1991, 433;
            [1991] E.P.O.R. 403.

T702/89   ALLIED SIGNAL INC./Proportioning valve O.J. EPO 1994,
            472; [1993] E.P.O.R. 580.

T324/90   PHILLIPS PETROLEUM/Re-establisment O.J. EPO 1993, 33;
            [1993] E.P.O.R. 507.

T869/90 TEXACO/Restitution [1994] E.P.O.R. 581.
T473/91 WEGENER/Jurisdiction O.J. EPO 1993, 630; [1994] E.P.O.R.
         292.
T111/92 SONY/Restitution August 3, 1992.
T840/94 UNION CAMP/Revocation O.J. EPO 1996, 680; [1997]
         E.P.O.R. 217.
T850/95 US GYPSUM III/Correction of a decision to grant O.J. EPO
         1996, 455.
T167/97 NN AG/Admissibility O.J. EPO 1999, 488; [1999] E.P.O.R.
         555.
T227/97 LINDAHL/Protein rib O.J. EPO 1999, 495; [1999] E.P.O.R.
         568.
T425/97 May 8, 1998.

CHAPTER 7

THE CONTENTS OF A EUROPEAN PATENT APPLICATION

Articles 78, 83, 84 EPC; Rules 27 to 29 EPC

Contents

All references are to paragraph numbers

Cases Referred to in Chapter 7

A. Introduction

(1) Prescribed contents of the application

According to Article 78 EPC, a European patent application must contain: 7–01

    (a) a request for grant (see Chapter 2 at paragraphs 2–13 *et seq*.);
    (b) a description;
    (c) one or more claims;
    (d) any drawings referred to in the description or the claims;
    (e) an abstract.

Article 85 EPC makes the limited purpose of an abstract clear, namely that it "shall merely serve for use as technical information: it may not be taken into account for any other purpose, in particular not for the purpose of interpreting the scope of the protection sought nor for the purpose of applying Article 54(3) EPC".
Consequently:

> "there is a clear legal distinction between the abstract, on the one hand, and the description, the drawings (if any) and the claims, on the other. In fact, only the latter parts are to be considered as constituting the substantive contents of the European patent application to be taken into account for the purpose of judging what subject-matter is contained in the application as filed" (T407/86[1]).

(2) Substantive contents

This chapter is essentially concerned with the substantive contents of an 7–02 application: namely, those parts of the contents whose function is to *disclose* the technical subject-matter of the invention in such a way as to enable it to be carried out, and those parts whose function is to *define* the technical subject-matter which is to be protected.
The requirements for the substantive contents of an application (*i.e.* the description and the claims, and any drawings) will be considered below in two parts: first the description and the requirement of sufficiency; and secondly the claims and the requirements of clarity and support by the description.

(3) Functions of the description and claims

(a) Extent of protection

> "The main function of the description of a European patent is to 7–03 disclose the invention so that it may be carried out (Article 83 EPC). The function of the claims is to define the subject-matter which is to be

---

[1] T407/86 *FUJITSU/Memory circuit* [1988] E.P.O.R. 254.

protected in terms of its technical features (Article 84 EPC and Rule 29(1) EPC). If a technically meaningful feature is included in a claim of a granted patent, Article 69(1) EPC requires that such feature, in combination with the other technical features of the claim, should be taken into account by a national court when it determines the extent of protection conferred by the patent ... Article 69(1) EPC and the Protocol to Article 69 EPC allow reference to be made to the description for the purpose of interpreting the wording of such technical features of a claim and thus determining the subject-matter which is to be protected" (G1/93[2]: see also G2, 6/88,[3] T133/85,[4] and Chapter 13 below).

(b) Inter-relationship between description and claims: support

7–04 Although as stated above the main function of the description is to provide a sufficient disclosure to inform a skilled person how to carry out the invention (Article 83 EPC), a related function is to provide a disclosure which "supports" the claims (Article 84 EPC) There is therefore an important inter-relationship between the respective contents of the description and claims. The adequacy of the content of the description depends upon the extent of protection which is sought in the claims; and the allowable extent of protection conferred by the claims depends upon the extent of the disclosure contained in the description.

Thus:

"Although the requirements of sufficient disclosure of the invention (Article 83 EPC) and support by the description (Article 84 EPC) are related to different parts of the patent application, they give effect to the same legal principle that the patent monopoly should be justified by the technical contribution to the art. Therefore, the extent to which an invention is sufficiently disclosed is also highly relevant for the answer to the question of support" (T409/91[5]).

In other words :

"The extent of the patent monopoly, as defined by the claims, should correspond to the *technical contribution* to the art in order for it to be supported, or justified ... This means that the definitions in the claims should essentially correspond to the scope of the invention as disclosed in the description ... , the claims should not extend to subject-matter which, after reading the description, would still not be at the disposal of the person skilled in the art. Consequently, a technical feature which is described and highlighted in the description

---

[2] G1/93 *ADVANCED SEMICONDUCTOR PRODUCTS II/Conflicting requirements of Article 123(2) and (3) EPC* O.J. EPO 1994, 541; [1995] E.P.O.R. 97.
[3] G2, 6/88 *MOBIL OIL/BAYER/Friction reducing additive* O.J. EPO 1990, 93, 114; [1990] E.P.O.R. 73, 257.
[4] T153/85 *AMOCO/Alternative claims* O.J. EPO 1988, 1; [1988] E.P.O.R. 116.
[5] T409/91 *EXXON/Fuel oils* O.J. EPO 1994, 653; [1994] E.P.O.R. 149.

as being an essential feature of the invention must also be a part of the independent claim of claims defining this invention" (T409/91[6]; and see also T133/85[7]).

B. The Description and Sufficiency of Disclosure

(1) The description

(a) Prescribed contents

The contents of a description of a European patent are prescribed in detail **7–05** in Rule 27(1) EPC, the sub-paragraphs of which may be summarised as follows:

(a) Technical field of the invention;
(b) Background art;
(c) Disclosure of invention as claimed in terms of the technical problem and its solution, stating advantageous effects with reference to background art;
(d) Description of drawings;
(e) Description of at least one way of carrying out the invention;
(f) How the invention is capable of industrial exploitation.

With effect from June 1, 1991, Rule 27(1) EPC was amended by deleting sub-paragraph (a) ("Title") and re-lettering sub-paragraph (b) to (g) as (a) to (f) above. Decisions issued before that date therefore refer to the earlier letters. The above manner and order of the contents of the description should be followed unless the nature of the invention is such that a different manner or order "would afford a better understanding and a more economical presentation" (Rule 27(2) EPC). It follows that such prescribed contents are not mandatory as to their "manner or order". Nevertheless, individual requirements of this Rule have been held to be mandatory. Thus:

> "Rule 27 EPC ... is an integral part of the EPC ... and it is clear that any mandatory provisions it contains could only lawfully be disregarded in the case of conflict between [the EPC and the Rules]: Article 164(2) EPC" (T11/82[8]).

Similarly:

> "With regard to the application of Rule 27(1)(d) [now (c)] EPC, it should be first observed that the Board cannot share the opinion of the

---

[6] *Ibid.*
[7] T133/85 *XEROX/Amendments* O.J. EPO 1988, 441; [1989] E.P.O.R. 116.
[8] T11/82 *LANSING BAGNALL/Control circuit* O.J. EPO 1983, 479; [1979–85] E.P.O.R.: B: 385.

applicants that this rule is not of a mandatory character. Rule 27(2) EPC allows a 'different manner and order' of disclosure from that prescribed in paragraph 1 only when it 'because of the nature of the invention' would afford a 'better understanding and a more economic presentation'. This cannot imply any derogation from the essence of the requirement in Rule 27(1)(d) that the invention should be presented in such a way that the technical problem and its solution can be understood" (T26/81[9]).

(b) Background art

7–06 Rule 27(i)(b) EPC states that:

> "The description shall indicate the background art which, as far as known to the applicant, can be regarded as useful for understanding the invention, for drawing up the European search report and for the examination, and, preferably, all the documents reflecting such art." (T11/82[10])

In other words:

> "an application must point out or make known the background art known to him ... preferably by mentioning and/or quoting documents which reflect it" (T11/82[11]).

The expression "background art" has the same meaning as the more familiar expression "prior art" (T11/82).

7–07 Rule 27 EPC (especially Rule 27(1)(b) and (c) EPC) "recognises the needs of the public to be able to understand the invention and the advantageous effects it may have, from the description, at any time" (T11/82[12]). Thus the mere addition to the description of a reference to prior art does not contravene Article 123(2) EPC (T11/82,[13] T51/87,[14] T450/97,[15] and see Chapter 8 at paragraph 8–48), and it may be necessary, either in examination or opposition proceedings, to add a reference to prior art.

For example:

> "If a document is part of the common general knowledge and is the closest prior art, it may have to be introduced into the description during opposition proceedings" (T51/87[16]).

---

[9] T26/81 *ICI/Containers* O.J. EPO 1982, 211; [1979–85] E.P.O.R.: B: 362.
[10] T11/82 *LANSING BAGNALL/Control circuit* O.J. EPO 1983, 479; [1979–85] E.P.O.R.: B: 385.
[11] *Ibid.*
[12] *Ibid.*
[13] *Ibid.*
[14] T51/87 *MERCK/Starting compounds* O.J. EPO 1991, 177.
[15] T450/97 *PROCTER & GAMBLE/Shampoo composition* O.J. EPO 1999, 67; [1999] E.P.O.R. 324.
[16] See note 14.

Similarly:

> "After limitation of the claims, even at the opposition stage, a document which subsequently proves not only to be the closest state of the art, but also to be essential for understanding the invention within the meaning of Rule 27(i)(b) EPC, should be indicated in the amended description" (T450/97[17]).

(c) Disclosure of the invention—problem and solution

> "If it is impossible to satisfy the requirement of Rule 27(1)(d) [now (c)] **7–08** EPC that the invention should be disclosed in such terms that the technical problem and its solution can be understood—a requirement which is of a mandatory character—then it will be clear that an invention within the meaning of Article 52 EPC does not exist: but if it is accepted by an Examining Division that an independent claim defines a patentable invention, it must be possible to derive a technical problem from the application. Thus, the requirement of Rule 27(1)(d) EPC cannot be set up as a separate formal criterion independent of inventiveness" (T26/81[18]).

(d) Examples—at least one way of carrying out the invention

Under Rule 27(1)(e) EPC, normally one or more specific examples of how **7–09** to carry out a claimed invention are included in the description of an application.

> "Rule 27(1)(f) [now (e)] EPC specifically requires that the description of a European patent application shall 'describe in detail at least one way of carrying out the invention claimed using examples where appropriate …'. The description of the present application is conspicuous by the absence of any specific example setting out a way of carrying out the claimed invention, and of any specific details of the manner in which the vapour deposition of the alloy should be performed, especially with regard to certain parameters. But the requirement in Rule 27(1)(f) [now (e)] quoted above that there should be examples where appropriate must be interpreted in the sense that examples should be included when appropriate for the purpose of satisfying the requirement of sufficiency in Article 83 EPC" (T407/87[19]).

Thus the absence of any specific detailed example does not necessarily render the description insufficient (T407/87[20]).

---

[17] See note 15.
[18] *ICI/Containers* O.J. EPO 1982, 211; [1979–85] E.P.O.R.: B: 362.
[19] T407/87 *TOSHIBA/Semiconductor device* [1989] E.P.O.R. 470.
[20] *Ibid.*

(e) Functions of the description

7–10 With reference to the sub-paragraphs of Rule 27(1) EPC summarised in paragraph 7–05 above, Rule 27(1)(b) and (c) EPC are particularly relevant for providing a good basis for the requirement of disclosure of an invention involving an inventive step, and Rule 27(1)(e) EPC is significant in relation to the requirement of sufficient disclosure under Article 83 EPC, as discussed below. Furthermore, all three provisions in Rule 27(1)(b), (c) and (e) EPC are relevant to the requirement of Article 84 EPC that the description should support the claims.

The essential functions of the description are thus:

(a) to disclose an invention which satisfies Article 52 EPC;
(b) to provide a sufficient disclosure of how to carry out the invention (Article 83 EPC);
(c) to support the claims (Article 84 EPC).

(2) Sufficiency of disclosure

Article 83 EPC

(a) Introduction

7–11 Article 83 EPC states that:

> "The European patent application must disclose the invention in a manner sufficiently clear and complete for it to be carried out by a person skilled in the art."

The reference to a person skilled in the art ensures that it is unnecessary to include minor details of how to perform an invention, in that such a person inevitably has a body of knowledge in his art which can be applied as and when appropriate to the disclosure of an invention in a particular patent application.

In so far as it is the "application" which must sufficiently disclose the invention, such sufficient disclosure may be found in the description and claims (and drawings if any) in combination. In this connection only, the wording of Article 83 EPC differs from (and is broader than) that of Article 8(2) Strasbourg, which requires that "the description" shall sufficiently disclose the invention. Normally, it is the content of the description which is critical for sufficiency. Nevertheless, the broader wording of Article 83 EPC compared to Article 8(2) Strasbourg allows for special cases (such as the deposit of a micro-organism under Rule 28 EPC, see paragraphs 7–35 *et seq.* below), where an invention cannot by its nature be "described" in a way which enables it to be carried out.

(b) The basic principle

7–12 The basic principle in determining questions concerning sufficiency of disclosure is that the claimed invention must be capable of performance by a skilled person without "undue burden" (see paragraph 7–20 below) either on the basis of the information in the application on its own or supplemented when appropriate by information which is part of the common general knowledge of such a skilled person (see paragraph 7–14 below).

When applying this principle a number of subsidiary questions may arise in individual cases: in particular, what constitutes the common general knowledge of a skilled person; what constitutes "undue burden"; and what extent of disclosure as to how to carry out the invention is required having regard to the scope of the claimed invention. These and other matters relating to sufficiency of description are discussed below.

(c) Time limit for sufficiency

The disclosure in an application of how to carry out the claimed invention **7–13** must be sufficient within the meaning of Article 83 EPC at the filing date of the application. If this is not the case, the insufficiency cannot subsequently be cured by the addition of further information to the application without contravening Article 123(2) EPC (see Chapter 8).

For example, in a case where information concerning a culture deposit (as required by Rule 28(1)(c) EPC) was filed after the time limit of Rule 28(2)(a) EPC, it was held that:

> "Sufficiency of disclosure under Article 83 EPC requires *inter alia* that the subject-matter claimed in a European patent application be clearly identified. The requirement must be complied with as from the date of filing because a deficiency in a European patent application as filed consisting in an insufficient identification of the subject-matter claimed, cannot subsequently be cured without offending against Article 123(2) EPC which provides that the subject-matter content of a European patent application may not be extended" (G2/93[21]).

Comparison with United Kingdom law:
Similarly, under United Kingdom law the requirement for sufficiency of disclosure must be satisfied at the date of filing of an application. "An insufficient application could not become sufficient because of general developments in the state of the art after the filing date" (*Biogen Inc. v. Medeva*,[22] House of Lords).

(d) Common general knowledge

(i) Introduction. The common general knowledge of a skilled person in **7–14** the art with which the application is concerned is the knowledge which a person of appropriate skill and experience to whom the application is addressed would carry with him as his working knowledge, at the filing

[21] G2/93 *UNITED STATES OF AMERICA II/Hepatitis A virus* O.J. EPO 1994, 275; [1995] E.P.O.R. 437.
[22] [1997] R.P.C. 1.

date. The concept includes both what such a person would know without further reference, and what such a person could be expected to refer to in the course of his normal work.

When the sufficiency of disclosure of an application is being assessed, such a skilled person is expected to use his common general knowledge in order to carry out the invention to the best of his ability, and to be trying to succeed.

Neither the Guidelines (see Chapter 1 at paragraph 1–13) nor any Board of Appeal decision has attempted any comprehensive statement as to how to assess what common general knowledge comprises. Nevertheless some general principles have been developed, as discussed below.

If the description does not contain all the information necessary for performance of the claimed invention, and if "the missing information cannot be supplied from the general knowledge of a person skilled in the art", the invention is insufficiently disclosed and the requirements of Article 83 EPC are not complied with (T219/85[23]).

For example, if the manner in which a claimed function feature is carried out is critical to performance of the invention, but is neither described in the application nor apparent to a skilled person from his common general knowledge, the application contravenes Article 83 EPC (T219/85[24]).

7–15   On the other hand, incorrect or missing information which can be corrected or supplied by reference to common general knowledge does not cause insufficiency under Article 83 EPC. For example:

> "An error in the description (... an incorrect numerical value in the only example) is immaterial to the sufficiency of the disclosure if the skilled person could recognise and rectify it using his common general knowledge" (T171/84[25]).

> If a document necessary for carrying out the invention is not mentioned in the application as originally filed, the invention may nevertheless be sufficiently disclosed if the document is part of the common general knowledge" (T51/87[26]).

(ii) Textbooks and patent specifications: classical and new fields of research.

7–16   "It is normally accepted that common general knowledge is represented by basic handbooks and textbooks on the subject in question. The skilled person could well be expect to consult these to obtain clear advice as to what to do in the circumstances, since the skill of such persons not only includes knowledge about particular basic prior art but also knowledge as to where to find such information. Such books may indeed refer him to articles describing specifically how to act or at

[23] T219/85 HAKOUNE/Inadequate description O.J. EPO 1986, 376; [1987] E.P.O.R. 30.
[24] Ibid.
[25] T171/84 AIR PRODUCTS/Redox catalyst O.J. EPO 1986, 376; [1986] E.P.O.R. 210.
[26] T51/87 MERCK/Starting compounds O.J. EPO 1991, 177.

least giving a fairly generally applicable method for the purpose, which can be used without any doubt" (T206/83[27]).

On the other hand:

"Normally patent specifications are not part of the common general knowledge, and cannot therefore, cure apparent insufficiency" (T206/83[28]).

This applies at least within what can be regarded as the classical fields of **7–17** research and development. Thus two prior patent specifications were considered not to be part of the common general knowledge, even though they could have been identified by reference to "Chemical Abstracts", a well-known tool in the chemical industry, because:

"The indexes of 'Chemical Abstracts' cover virtually the whole state of the art, and represent, therefore, much more than what is assumed to be the common general knowledge ... Reliance on the contents of 'Chemical Abstracts' to rectify insufficiency might be tantamount to leaving the skilled reader to carry out a search in the whole state of the art which would be an unacceptable burden on the public" (T206/83[29]).

However, in new fields of research and technology, an individual patent specification may be recognised as part of the common general knowledge in appropriate circumstances, for example when it represents the ground-work for a new field of research:

"... the C–076 starting compounds are highly elaborated microbial metabolites opening a brand new field of research, so that any technical knowledge acquired in this field at the beginning through basic pioneering work had not yet been distilled into the form of textbooks. By contrast, in the prior Decision T206/83[30] the situation was quite a different one, namely that the man skilled in the art was a person working in the field of *classical* herbicide chemistry, which was *not* a new developing field like that of the chemistry of C–076 compounds. The man skilled in the art, therefore, cannot be presumed to possess the same common knowledge in both cases" (T51/87[31]).

Similarly, in new fields of technology specialist periodicals may be regarded as part of the common general knowledge. For example:

[27] T206/83 *ICI/Pyridine herbicides* O.J. EPO 1987, 5; [1986] E.P.O.R. 232.
[28] *Ibid.*
[29] *Ibid.*
[30] *Ibid.*
[31] T51/87 *MERCK/Starting compounds* O.J. EPO 1991, 177.

317

"In the absence of evidence to the contrary, ... [certain] publications which were not referred to in the specification were part of the common general knowledge. At that time, when there was considerable effort everywhere to achieve success in the manipulation of plasmids and genes, the cited papers represented important disclosures. ... Hence, it must be assumed that everybody concerned became aware of their teaching" (T292/85[32]).

7–18   **(iii) Comparison with United Kingdom Law.** A well-established summary of what constitutes common general knowledge is set out in *General Tire and Rubber Co. v. Firestone Tyre and Rubber Co. Ltd*,[33] as follows:

"The common general knowledge imputed to such an addressee must, of course, be carefully distinguished from what in patent law is regarded as public knowledge ... common general knowledge is a different concept derived from a common-sense approach to the practical question of what would in fact be known to an appropriately skilled addressee—the sort of man, good at his job, that could be found in real life. ...

... it is clear that individual patent specifications and their contents do not normally form part of the relevant common general knowledge, though there may be specifications which are so well known amongst those versed in the art upon evidence of that state of affairs they form part of such knowledge, and also there may occasionally be particular industries ... in which the evidence may show that all specifications form part of the relevant knowledge.

As regards scientific papers generally, it was said ... in *British Acoustic Films*[34]:

7–19   'In my judgment it is not sufficient to prove common general knowledge that a particular disclosure is made in an article, or series of articles, in a scientific journal, no matter how wide the circulation of that journal may be, in the absence of any evidence that the disclosure is accepted generally by those who are engaged in the art to which the disclosure relates. A piece of particular knowledge as disclosed in a scientific paper does not become common general knowledge merely because it is widely read, and still less because it is widely circulated. Such a piece of knowledge only becomes general knowledge when it is generally known and accepted without question by the bulk of those who are engaged in the particular art; in other words, when it becomes part of their common stock of knowledge relating to the art.'...

'It is certainly difficult to appreciate how the use of something which has in fact never been used in a particular art can ever be held to be common general knowledge in the art.'

---

[32] T292/85 *GENENTECH/Polypeptide expression* O.J. EPO 1989, 275; [1989] E.P.O.R. 1.
[33] [1972] R.P.C. 457.
[34] *British Acoustic Films Ltd v. Nettlefold Productions* (1936) 53 R.P.C. 221.

Those passages have often been quoted, and there has not been cited to us any case in which they have been criticised. We accept them as correctly stating in general the law on this point, though reserving for further consideration whether the words 'accepted without question' may not be putting the position rather high: for the purposes of this case we are disposed, without wishing to put forward any full definition, to substitute the words 'generally regarded as a good basis for further action'."

Such principles are applicable under the 1977 U.K. Act, (*e.g.* in *A.C. Edwards Ltd v. Acme Signs and Displays Ltd*[35]).

(e) "Undue burden"

A skilled person should be able to carry out an invention from the **7–20** disclosure of an application without "undue burden". Ideally, of course, the description of how to carry out the claimed invention should give the skilled person all he needs to achieve successful repetition with a minimum of effort. Nevertheless it is accepted that in some circumstances a certain amount of routine experimental work may be acceptable provided that this does not amount to an undue burden. The meaning of this concept of undue burden is illustrated as follows:

(1) Comparative results in the description showed occasional lack of **7–21** success in achieving the objective, notwithstanding strict adherence to the features as claimed. However:

> "occasional lack of success of a claimed process does not impair its feasibility in the sense of Article 83 EPC, if, for example, some experimentation is still to be done to transform the failure into success, provided that the experimentation is not undue and does not require inventive activity" (T14/83[36]).

In particular:

> "if, encouraging occasional lack of success notwithstanding strict adherences to the prescribed limits of [certain] variables, clear information contained in the description regarding the effects of individual variables on the properties of the product enables the person skilled in the art to bring about the desired properties quickly and reliably in such an event" (T14/83[37]).

It should be "possible to deduce from the description the action to be taken—which also cannot be precisely defined—by way of the tuning of the variables" (T14/83[38]).

---

[35] [1990] R.P.C. 621.
[36] T14/83 *SUMITOMO/Vinyl chloride resins* O.J. EPO 1984, 105; [1979–85] E.P.O.R.: C: 737.
[37] *Ibid.*
[38] *Ibid.*

7–22   (2) "Even though a reasonable amount of trial and error is permissible when it comes to the sufficiency of disclosure in an unexplored field or—as it is in this case—where there are many technical difficulties, there must then be available adequate instructions in the specification or on the basis of common general knowledge which would lead the skilled person necessarily and directly towards success through the evaluation of initial failures or through an acceptable statistical expectation rate in case of random experiments" (T226/85[39]).

7–22a   (3) On a similar basis:

"Relying on chance events for reproducibility amounts to undue burden in the absence of evidence that such chance events occur and can be identified frequently enough to guarantee success" (T727/95[40]).

7–23   (4) Furthermore:

"Information which can only be obtained after a comprehensive search is not to be regarded as part of common general knowledge" (T206/83[41]).

Thus, the concept of an "undue burden", can in some cases overlap with the determination of what constitutes common general knowledge.

(f) The extent of the disclosure of the invention

7–24   **(i) How many ways of carrying out the invention?**

(a) *Relationship with scope of claims: general principle.* A basic principle in relation to the content of an application is that:

"the need for a fair protection governs both the considerations of the scope of claims and of the requirements for sufficient disclosure" (T292/85[42]).

Having regard to the inter-relationship between the description and the claims required by Articles 83 and 84 EPC in order to give effect to the legal principle that the patent monopoly defined by the claims should be justified by the technical contribution to the art which is disclosed in the application in general and the description in particular (see paragraph 7–04 above), the general principle as regards the extent of disclosure of the invention is that:

"In order to fulfil the requirement of Article 83 EPC, the application as

---

[39] T226/85 *UNILEVER/Stable bleaches* O.J. EPO 1988, 336; [1989] E.P.O.R. 18.
[40] T727/95 *WEYERSHAEUSER/Cellulose* O.J. EPO 2001, 1.
[41] T206/83 *ICI/Pyridine herbicides* O.J. EPO 1987, 5; [1986] E.P.O.R. 232.
[42] T292/85 *GENETECH I/Polypeptide expression* O.J. EPO 1989, 275; [1989] E.P.O.R. 1.

filed must contain sufficient information to allow a person skilled in the art, using his common general knowledge, to carry out the invention within the *whole area* that is claimed" (T409/91[43]).

Similarly:

"... substantially any embodiment of the invention, as defined in the broadest claim, must be capable of being realised on the basis of the disclosure" (T226/85[44]).

Furthermore:

"the criteria for determining the sufficiency of the disclosure are the same for all inventions, irrespective of the way in which they are defined, be it by way of structural terms of their technical features or by their function. In both cases the requirement of sufficient disclosure can only mean that the whole subject-matter that is defined in the claims, and not only a part of it, must be capable of being carried out by the skilled person without the burden of an undue amount of experimentation or the application of inventive ingenuity" (T435/91[45]).

However, it is "the invention" which must be sufficiently disclosed: that **7–25** is, the claimed subject-matter which gives rise to the technical effect which provides the solution to the problem underlying the invention and thus provides a technical contribution to the art (see Chapter 12). In some cases, as discussed below, the required extent of disclosure may be less stringent for functional features which are not central to the invention.

Accordingly, the extent of disclosure (and in particular the number of ways of performing the invention) which the description must contain depends in each case upon the nature and extent of the invention which is claimed. In some cases the disclosure of one way of carrying out the claimed invention will be sufficient to enable a skilled person to carry out the invention across the full width of the claim, whereas in other cases more than one example of carrying out the invention will be necessary in order to satisfy Article 83 EPC, (and/or Article 84 EPC). Thus:

"the question whether the disclosure of one way of performing the invention is sufficient to enable a person skilled in the art to carry out the invention in the whole claimed range is a question of fact that must be answered on the basis of the available evidence and on the balance of probabilities in each individual case" (T409/91[46]).

[43] T409/91 *EXXON/Fuel oils* O.J. EPO 1994, 653; [1994] E.P.O.R. 149.
[44] T226/85 *UNILEVER/Stable bleaches* O.J. EPO 1988, 336; [1989] E.P.O.R. 18.
[45] T435/91 *UNILEVER/Detergents* O.J. EPO 1995, 188; [1995] E.P.O.R. 314.
[46] T409/91 *EXXON/Fuel oils* O.J. EPO 1994, 653; [1994] E.P.O.R. 149.

7–26   As mentioned in paragraph 7–05 above, Rule 27(1)(e) EPC requires the description to "describe in detail at least one way of carrying out the invention claimed . . .". Similarly: "An invention . . . is sufficiently disclosed if at least one way is clearly indicated enabling the person skilled in the art to carry out the invention" (T292/85[47]; see also T301/87,[48] T212/88,[49] T182/89,[50] T19/90[51] for example). This means that in the circumstances of particular cases, a disclosure of only one way of carrying out the invention may be sufficient for the purpose of Article 83 EPC, but clearly does not mean that "it is always enough that the description of the invention includes one example showing how to carry it out" (T694/91[52]).

For example, if a claimed invention defines the use of alternative components (vanadium or tungsten, for example) and the description only includes one example (using vanadium), "objections under Article 83 and 84 EPC could arise if carrying out the invention using tungsten in place of vanadium involved an undue burden for the skilled person" (T694/91[53]; and compare *Biogen*[54] see also paragraph 7–87 below: "if the claims include a number of discrete methods or products, the patentee must enable the invention to be performed in respect of each of them").

As already indicated, in view of the fact that Articles 83 and 84 EPC reflect the legal principle discussed above, according to the circumstances of each case a given set of facts may give rise to objections under Article 83 EPC or Article 84 EPC or both.

7–27   (b) *Functional features in the claims: future and inoperable variants.*
1. The inclusion of functional features in the claims, and the circumstances in which they may properly be used, is discussed in paragraph 7–69 below. The extent of disclosure of the invention in the description that is required under Article 83 EPC when functional features are included in the claims can be of considerable importance. As mentioned above, the requirement of sufficient disclosure under Article 83 EPC applies equally to both structural and functional features. Nevertheless, because of the open-ended scope of some functional features, the necessary extent of disclosure requires special consideration in the context of functional claims.

Any functional technical feature may embrace, in addition to known arrangements which achieve the defined function, variants on such arrangements which are not yet known. Thus functional features and terms "may cover an unlimited number of possibilities" and "may generically embrace the use of unknown or not yet envisaged possibilities,

---

[47] T292/85 GENENTECH I/Polypeptide expression O.J. EPO 1989, 275; [1989] E.P.O.R.I.
[48] T301/87 BIOGEN/Alpha-interferons O.J. EPO 1990, 335; [1990] E.P.O.R. 190.
[49] T212/88 BP/Theta-1 O.J. EPO 1992, 28; [1990] E.P.O.R. 518.
[50] T182/89 SUMITOMO/Extent of opposition O.J. EPO 1991, 391; [1990] E.P.O.R. 438.
[51] T19/90 HARVARD/Onco-mouse O.J. EPO 990, 476; [1990] E.P.O.R. 501.
[52] T694/91 TEKTRONIX/Schottky barrier diode [1995] E.P.O.R. 384.
[53] Ibid.
[54] Biogen Inc. v. Medeva plc [1997] R.P.C. 1.

including specific variants which might be provided or invented in the future ...".

"In appropriate cases ... it is only possible to define the invention (the matter for which protection is sought—Article 84 EPC) in a way which gives a fair protection having regard to the nature of the invention which has been described, by using functional terminology in the claims ... The need for a fair protection governs both the considerations of the scope of claims and of the requirements for sufficient disclosure" (T292/85[55]).

2. Thus in such cases, it is important to the determination of sufficiency   **7–28** under Article 83 EPC (as well as support under Article 84 EPC) whether or not the particular choice of variant within each functional term is relevant to achieving the defined result. If the same result is achieved irrespective of the particular choice of variant within a functional term, then:

> "the non-availability of some particular variants or unsuitability of some unspecified variants of a functionally defined component feature of the invention is immaterial to sufficiency as long as there are suitable variants known to the skilled person through the disclosure or common general knowledge which provide the same effect for the invention."[56]

This is because:

> "Unless variants of components are also embraced in the claims, which are now or later on, equally suitable to achieve the same effect in a manner which could not have been envisaged without the invention, the protection provided by the patent would be ineffectual" (T292/85[57]).

3. An additional important factor in such cases, where some variants   **7–29** within a functional feature may be unavailable or inoperable, is:

> "the relevance of such functional feature to the inventive step, *i.e.* its essentiality to the quality or quantity of the effect obtained and thereby to its distinguishing power against the relevant art. Some features may contribute to the core of the invention and others only assist their use, and the skilled person might ... be in a more difficult or an easier position to find suitable choices" (T292/85[58]).

Where the claimed subject-matter includes a functional feature defining a particular component in terms of the technical effect which it must achieve, and such technical effect is central to the claimed invention because it provides the claimed solution to the objective problem which

---

[55] T292/85 *GENETECH I/Polypeptide expression* O.J. EPO 1989, 275; [1989] E.P.O.R. 1.
[56] *Ibid.*
[57] *Ibid.*
[58] *Ibid.*

underlies the invention, a disclosure of only a small number of specific examples in the description which provide such technical effect may be an insufficient description under Article 83 EPC (and may provide insufficient support under Article 84 EPC).

7–30   For example:

> "The disclosure of an invention relating to a composition of matter, a component of which is defined by its function [... An additive which forces a detergent composition into the hexagonal liquid crystal phase] is not sufficient if the patent discloses only isolated examples, but fails to disclose, taking into account, if necessary, the relevant common general knowledge, any technical concept fit for generalisation, which would enable the skilled person to achieve the envisaged result without undue difficulty within the whole ambit of the claim containing the 'functional' definition" (T435/91[59]).

This is because in such a case, the functional definition (of the additive):

> "is not more than an invitation to perform a research programme in order to find other 'additives' which meet the 'functional requirements' in the claim. Such a functional definition is an attempt to claim 'not only the solution of the technical problem' [of providing surfactant compositions in the form of a hexagonal liquid crystal gel phase] made available to the person skilled in the art in the patent specification [*i.e.* two worked examples each with a specific additive] but in addition, all other possible solutions of this problem [which are based on the 'principle' of mixing a surfactant composition ... with a 'suitable additive' and water]" (T435/91[60]).

Thus if a description discloses only one or two ways of achieving a result which solves a problem as the "invention", such description may be insufficient with respect to a claim which seeks to protect all possible ways of solving the problem.

7–31   (c) *Extrapolation from specific examples.* If, for example, the description discloses how to carry out the invention with respect to one member of a class, or a limited number of members, the extent to which such a description sufficiently discloses the invention as required by Article 83 EPC in relation to a claim to a larger number of members of the class, or the whole class (and thus "supports" the claimed invention as required by Article 84 EPC) depends upon the circumstances of each case. As previously stated, in such a case the skilled person must be in a position to perform the invention over the full width of the claim.

For example, in one case the claimed invention concerned genetic alterations in mammals. The description only disclosed the invention

---

[59] T435/91 *UNILEVER/Detergents* O.J. EPO 1995, 188; [1995] E.P.O.R. 314.
[60] *Ibid.*

when carried out on mice, whereas the claims related to "non-human mammalian animals" in general. It was held that the application should not be refused "on the grounds that it involved an extrapolation from mice ... to mammals in general", because:

> "the mere fact that a claim is broad is not in itself a ground for considering the application as insufficient under Article 83 EPC. Only if there are serious doubts, substantiated by verifiable facts, may an application be objected to for lack of sufficient disclosure" (T19/90[61])

If there are serious doubts as to the validity of the extent of generalisation from the description to the claims, having regard to the evidence in the application as filed, the applicant or proprietor may be asked to provide further evidence in support of the generalisation and consequent scope of the claims (Guidelines C III 6).

(d) *Comparison with United Kingdom Law.* Similar principles to those discussed above were applied by the Patents Court in *America Home Products Corp. Inc. v. Novartis Pharmaceuticals U.K. Ltd*[62]:

> "If the claims of a patent extended further than the technical contribution made by the inventor, the specification in that respect did not disclose the invention clearly enough and completely enough for it to be performed by a person skilled in the art."
> "Patent law did not require precision where the technology made it impossible. A patent did not become invalid as a result of its scope covering ingredients and raw materials not yet produced or anticipated."

(ii) **Preparation of starting materials.** As previously mentioned, it is 7–32 "the invention" which must be sufficiently disclosed for the purposes of Article 83 EPC (paragraph 7–25 above). The question arises whether an application must also disclose how to obtain the starting materials for carrying out a claimed invention which necessarily starts from such materials.

In one case, the requirement for an "enabling disclosure" in a prior document for the purpose of novelty (see Chapter 11 at paragraph 11–67 below) was considered to be equivalent to the requirement of sufficiency under Article 83 EPC; and it was held that:

> "a document does not effectively disclose a chemical compound, even though it states the structure and the steps by which it is produced, if the skilled man is unable to find out from the document or from common general knowledge how to obtain the required starting materials or intermediates" (T206/83[63]).

---

[61] T19/90 *HARVARD/Onco-mouse* O.J. EPO 1990, 476; [1990] E.P.O.R. 501.
[62] [2000] R.P.C. 547.
[63] T206/83 *ICI/Pyridine herbicides* O.J. EPO 1987, 5; [1986] E.P.O.R. 232.

Thus it was assumed in this case that a sufficient disclosure of a claimed invention includes a requirement of access to starting materials which are necessary for carrying out the invention as such.

7–33   In another case, however, it was emphasised that Article 83 EPC "requires that the disclosure of the *invention* must be clear and complete so as to be sufficient ...", and it was considered that from the wording of the claims and the description it was clear "that the *invention* as such does not cover the preparation of starting compounds, as those were all assumed to be known compounds". Accordingly, the disclosure was held to be sufficient, even if a skilled person would not know how to obtain the necessary starting materials (T51/87[64]).

It was also held that a prior patent specification which disclosed the preparation of the starting compounds formed part of the common general knowledge (see paragraph 7–14), and should be included in the description (without contravening Article 123(2) EPC—see paragraph 7–07).

The above two cases point in different directions in relation to the question of whether or not (and if so in what circumstances) it is necessary for the description to contain a sufficient disclosure as to how to obtain the starting materials necessary for the performance of the claimed invention. Thus it is clearly safer for the description to contain such a disclosure.

7–34   **(iii) Exact repeatability not required.**

"There is no requirement under Article 83 EPC to the effect that a specifically described example of a process must be exactly repeatable. Variations in the constitution of an agent used in a process are immaterial to the sufficiency of a disclosure provided the claimed process reliably leads to the desired product" (T281/86[65]).

Accordingly, as long as the description of the process enables the invention to be put into practice, there is no lack of sufficiency.

This applies in a case where "the set of products was limited and all were obtainable as desired" (T281/86[66] as summarised in T292/85[67]) as well as in a case which is "one of general methodology which is fully applicable with any starting material ..." (T292/85[68]). Thus:

"generally applicable biological processes are not insufficiently described for the sole reason that some starting materials or genetic precursors therefore, *e.g.* a particular DNA or a plasmid, are not readily available to obtain each and every variant of the expected result of the invention, *e.g.* the product, provided the process as such is reproducible. In chemistry, widely applicable chemical reactions have

---

[64] T51/87 MERCK/Starting compounds O.J. EPO 1991, 177.
[65] T281/86 UNILEVER/Preprothaumatin O.J. EPO 1989, 202; [1989] E.P.O.R. 313.
[66] Ibid.
[67] T292/85 GENENTECH I/Polypeptide expression O.J. EPO 1989, 275; [1989] E.P.O.R. 1.
[68] Ibid.

been claimable without restrictions to irrelevant structural details. The same should be applicable to biochemical processes" (T292/85[69]).

(3) Microbiological inventions: the deposit of micro-organisms

Rule 28 EPC

(a) Introduction

During the period immediately preceding the signing of the EPC, it 7–35 became apparent that with certain inventions involving new strains of micro-organisms it was in practice impossible to describe the micro-organism in writing (and/or with drawings) in such a way that it could be obtained or reproduced by a skilled person, and the claimed invention thereby carried out.

Prior to the EPC, in the national patent laws of Contracting States, a description in writing of the invention was prescribed. It had been assumed that such a written description would always be capable of being sufficient in the sense of enabling the invention to be carried out. This assumption, however, proved to be wrong. For example, in a case under the 1949 U.K. Act (*American Cyanamid (Dann)'s Patent*[70]), the claimed invention was a new antibiotic and a process of making it, the process requiring a particular micro-organism as the starting material. The written description of this micro-organism was adequate to enable a skilled person to recognise it if he had it, but was insufficient to enable such a skilled person to get it. The micro-organism had been deposited in a culture collection before the filing date, but had not been available to the public until after both the filing date and the publication date. The House of Lords held that there was no obligation upon the patentee, under the existing law, to supply the micro-organism which he had described to the public, and the patent was, therefore, not invalid on the ground of insufficiency.

Similar problems arose in cases in the United States and Germany at 7–36 about that time, as a result of which the deposit of micro-organisms was recognised as a supplement to the written description for the purpose of satisfying the legal requirement of sufficiency.

In response to this situation, the EPC was drafted to include provisions in the rules, supplementing the requirement of Article 83 EPC, governing the deposit of micro-organisms in certain recognised institutions so as to supplement the written description of a European patent application. The combination of the written description and the deposited micro-organism was to provide the information necessary for the carrying out of the invention in appropriate cases.

The EPC was the first patent law to include specific provisions in respect of the deposit of micro-organisms as a supplement to the written description of an invention. It therefore constitutes new law compared to previously existing national laws.

[69] *Ibid.*
[70] [1971] R.P.C. 425.

(b) Relationship between Article 83 EPC and Rule 28 EPC

7–37   "With regard to an invention concerning a microbiological process or the product thereof and involving the use of a micro-organism which is not available to the public and which cannot be described in a European patent application in such a manner as to enable the invention to be carried out by a person skilled in the art, provisions have been included in Rule 28 EPC in order to implement the general principle of Article 83 EPC ... in view of the special character of such an invention" (G2/93[71]).

Furthermore:

"Rule 28(1) EPC refers to Article 83 EPC and serves to supplement the general requirements of Article 83 EPC for a specific group of inventions for which a mere written description is not sufficient to enable a person skilled in the art to carry out the invention. Therefore, the provisions of Rule 28 EPC are subordinate to the requirements of Article 83 EPC. For microbiological inventions making use of living matter which is not available to the public and which cannot be described in a reproducible way, these provisions set out a reliable framework for determining which indications are necessary in a European patent application and under which conditions the public may have access to a culture deposit. Consequently, the disclosure of an invention referred to in Rule 28(1) EPC has not only to comply with the provisions under Rule 28(1) EPC, but also with the requirements of Article 83 EPC" (G2/93[72]).

(c) Nature of an invention for which deposit is required

7–38 Rule 28 EPC applies to an invention which:

(a) concerns "a microbiological process or the product thereof";
(b) "and involves the use of a micro-organism which is not available to the public and which cannot be described ... in such a manner as to enable the invention to be carried out by a person skilled in the art".

In a case where the description gives details of the deposit of certain strains of a micro-organism which may be used in the claimed process, but the description also contains sufficient information as to how to obtain suitable strains for carrying out the invention without using the deposited strains, there is no insufficiency under Article 83 EPC, irrespective of any

---

[71] G2/93 *UNITED STATES OF AMERICA II/Hepatitis A virus* O.J. EPO 1995, 275; [1995] E.P.O.R. 437.
[72] *Ibid.*

non-compliance with Rule 28 EPC in relation to the deposited strains (T361/87[73]).

On the other hand, in one case the question at issue was whether the **7–39** claimed monoclonal antibody could be produced either from the description alone or from a deposited hybridoma. The description alone was considered insufficient because it was concerned with the known general process and a specific teaching for making the claimed antibody required the identity of the type of antigene.

Furthermore, with reference to the deposited hybridoma, it was held that:

"A disclosure provided by a deposit according to Rule 28 EPC is not regarded as being sufficient within the meaning of Article 83 EPC if and when it is only possible to reproduce the invention after repeated requests to the depository institution and by applying techniques considerably more sophisticated than those recommended by the depository institution" (T418/89[74]).

In such circumstances the claimed invention could not be carried out without "undue burden" (see paragraph 7–20 above).

A further question was whether the description was sufficient in relation **7–40** to claims defining monoclonal antibodies and hybridomas, and methods for preparing the monoclonal antibodies based simply on the deposited hybridoma. However, the true characteristics of such hybridoma when determined by analysis differed from the description. In this circumstance it was held that:

"A mere deposit number of hybridoma without any corresponding written description does not provide a sufficient disclosure of a technical teaching within the meaning of Article 83 EPC" (T418/89[75]).

(d) The requirements of Rule 28 EPC

The requirements of Rule 28 EPC in respect of an invention to which it **7–41** applies may be summarized as follows:

(a) The applicant must deposit a culture of the micro-organism with a recognised depositary institution not later than the filing date (Rule 28(1)(a) EPC).

(b) The application as filed must give "such relevant information as is available to the applicant on the characteristics of the micro-organism" (Rule 28(1)(b) EPC).

(c) The depositary institution and the accession number of the culture deposit must be stated in the application (Rule 28(1)(c) EPC) (this

[73] T361/87 *NABISCO/Micro-organisms* June 15, 1988.
[74] T418/89 *ORTHO/Monoclonal antibody* O.J. EPO 1993, 70; [1993] E.P.O.R. 338.
[75] *Ibid.*

information can be submitted after the filing date—see Rule 28(2) EPC discussed below).

(d) The deposited culture must be available upon request from the depositary institution, from the date of publication of the European application (Rule 28(3) EPC).

The requirement of availability of the culture is important, especially as regards when and to whom the deposited micro-organism is made available. The development of the legal requirements in these respects is discussed separately below.

The information required by Rule 28(1)(c) EPC—the depositary institution and the deposit accession number—is especially important because as stated in Rule 28(2) EPC, "The communication of this information shall be considered as constituting the unreserved and irrevocable consent of the applicant to the deposited culture being made available to the public ...".

(e) Time limit for stating the depositary institution and the accession number of deposit

7–42 The information required by Rule 28(1)(c) EPC concerning the depositary institution and the accession number of the culture deposit (which is to be stated in the patent application) may, according to Rule 28(2) EPC, be submitted after the filing of the application, provided it is submitted within the time limits there set out. In particular, in the absence of a request for early publication (Rule 28(2)(b) EPC) and of a communication that a right to inspect the files exists (Rule 28(2)(c) EPC), such information may be submitted within a period of sixteen months from the filing date (or the priority date if priority is claimed): "this time limit being deemed to have been met if the information is communicated before completion of the technical preparations for publication of the European Patent application" (Rule 28(2)(a) EPC as amended and in force on October 1, 1996). The significance of this information being submitted, in that it constitutes consent to the making available of the deposit, has been noted above.

7–43 "The indication of the [depository institution and accession] number of a culture deposit is ... *substantive* because it is instrumental in enabling a person skilled in the art to carry out the invention." Furthermore, the requirement of sufficiency under Article 83 EPC "must be complied with as from the date of filing" (see paragraph 7–13).

Consequently:

"The information concerning the [accession] number of a culture deposit according to Rule 28(l)(c) EPC may not be submitted after expiry of the time limit in Rule 28(2)(a) EPC" (G2/93[76]).

---

[76] G2/93 *UNITED STATES OF AMERICA II/Hepatitis A virus* O.J. EPO 1995, 275; [1995] E.P.O.R. 437.

The same time limit clearly applies to the identity of the depository institution. Compliance with this time limit "guarantees that the culture deposit is made available to the public at the same time as the corresponding European patent application is published" (G2/93[77]).

Failure to comply with this time limit therefore results in insufficiency under Article 83 EPC. This is subject to the possibility of re-establishment of rights under Article 122 EPC (T227/97,[78] and see Chapter 6 at paragraphs 6 27 et seq.).

(f) Deposit in an institution—The Budapest Treaty, 1977[79]

The deposit of a micro-organism for the purpose of a patent application 7–44 must be in an appropriate place and under appropriate control. While deposit for the purpose of a national patent application could appropriately be in a culture collection of the country concerned, that would be unsatisfactory in an international context. Recognition of this led to the signing of the Budapest Treaty concerning the Deposit of Micro-organisms ("Budapest") in 1977. The Treaty has been in force since 1980. It provides (in Article 3 Budapest) for the recognition by Contracting States of the deposit of a micro-organism in any "international depositary authority", by which is meant any depositary institution in a Contracting State which has acquired such status (Article 7 Budapest). The qualifications for such status are set out in Article 6 Budapest, and have now been attained by a considerable number of institutions in many countries.

So far as European patent applications are concerned, the deposit must be at a "recognised depositary institution"—see requirement (a) above and Rule 28(1)(a) EPC. A list of such recognised institutions is published in the Official Journal—see Rule 28(9) EPC. These include all the institutions which are "international depositary institutions" under the Budapest Treaty and other institutions with which the European Patent Organisation has concluded agreements for this purpose.

(i) The "Notice of the EPO dated July 18, 1986".[80] The purpose of this 7–45 Notice is to assist applicants with the drafting of applications concerning micro-organisms, as well as to explain the procedure concerning requests for samples of deposits and the issue of samples. In particular, the Notice explains the procedure for using a deposit which has been made for another purpose (e.g. in connection with a United States patent application) as a deposit for the purpose of the EPC: see paragraphs 7–53 et seq. below.

---

[77] Ibid.

[78] T227/97 LINDAHL/Protein rib O.J. EPO 1999, 495; [1999] E.P.O.R. 568.

[79] Treaty on the International Recognition of the Deposit of Micro-organisms for the purposes of patent procedure, signed Budapest 1977. See Appendix 20. Herein referred to as the "Budapest Treaty".

[80] Notice of the EPO dated July 18, 1986 concerning European patent applications and European patents in which reference is made to microorganisms, O.J. EPO 1986, 269. Reproduced in full at Appendix 10.

7–46   **(ii) Who must make the deposit.** "The applicant of an invention for a microbiological process and the depositor of a micro-organism must in principle be one and the same" (T118/87[81]).

This is because the legal fiction of Rule 28(2) EPC, whereby the communication of the required information concerning the culture deposit is considered to constitute "the unreserved and irrevocable consent of the applicant to the deposited biological material being made available to the public".

This provision "can only fulfil its legal purpose ... if applicant and depositor are one and the same ... If this is not the case suitable measures must be taken to ensure that the deposited culture is nevertheless available to the public in accordance with Rule 28 EPC ..." (see Rule 28(i)(d) EPC; T118/87[82]).

However:

> "Exceptionally it is justified to consider the parent company and subsidiary as one entity for the purposes of Rule 28 EPC, if the parent company has full control of the deposits made by the subsidiary company" (T118/87[83]).

(g) Availability of the deposited micro-organism

7–47   **(i) Introduction.** In a general sense, while the deposit of a micro-organism can be considered as corresponding to and supplementing the *description* of the claimed invention, the making available of what has been deposited to the public can be considered as corresponding to and supplementing the *publication* of the description. Thus, Rule 28(1)(a) EPC requires deposit not later than the date of filing of an application, and Rule 28(3) requires the deposited micro-organism to be available from the date of publication of the application.

7–48   **(ii) Persons to whom available—the "expert option".** Under the original text of Rule 28 EPC when the EPC came into force, a deposited micro-organism had to be made available upon request to "any person", without restriction, from the date of publication of the European patent application. Thus, availability of what was deposited was treated as corresponding exactly to publication of what had been described. Availability was effected by issue of a sample.

However, an amended version of Rule 28 EPC came into force on June 1, 1980, and is still in force, which allows a restriction to be placed upon the class of persons to whom a deposited micro-organism must be made available. In accordance with Rule 28(4) EPC, the applicant for a European patent may inform the EPO before "the technical preparations for publication of the application are deemed to have been completed" that availability "shall be effected only by the issue of a sample to an expert

---

[81] T118/87 *CPC/Amyloltic enzymes* O.J. EPO 1991, 474; [1990] E.P.O.R. 298.
[82] *Ibid.*
[83] *Ibid.*

nominated by the requester". This restriction may last until the date of grant (the date of publication of the mention of the grant of the European patent—Article 97(4) EPC) or until refusal, withdrawal or deemed withdrawal of the application. Furthermore, Rule 28(5) EPC places restrictions upon who may be nominated as such an expert, namely either:

(a) an expert approved by the applicant, or
(b) an expert recognised for the purpose by the EPO.

The procedure under Rule 28(4) EPC is known as the "expert option", and is described fully in a Notice of the President of the EPO dated July 28, 1981.[84]

(iii) Restrictions upon use. Whether or not the "expert option" has been **7–49** exercised, a deposited micro-organism is only made available by issue of a sample thereof (under Rule 28(3) or (4) EPC) subject to an undertaking as set out in Rule 28(3)(a) and (b) EPC, *i.e.*:

"(a) not to make the deposited culture or any culture derived therefrom available to any third party before the application has been refused or withdrawn or is deemed to be withdrawn or, if a patent is granted, before the expiry of the patent in the designated State in which it last expires;
(b) to use the deposited culture or any culture derived therefrom for experimental purposes only, until such time as the patent application is refused or withdrawn or is deemed to be withdrawn, or up to the date of publication of the mention of the grant of the European patent."

An undertaking as in (b) is not required if the requester has a compulsory licence (as defined) to use the culture.

(iv) Time of availability. (1) The timing of availability of a deposited **7–50** micro-organism is controversial. The heart of the difficulty stems from the concept of early publication of all European patent applications under the EPC (as discussed in Chapter 1 at paragraph 1–51), coupled with the treatment of the deposit of a micro-organism as if it was part of the description of the application. As discussed under (ii) above, this initially led to the requirement in the original Rule 28 EPC that a deposited micro-organism must be made available to the public without restriction, at the latest from the date of publication of the European patent application.

The result of this requirement was that an applicant was forced to make the deposited micro-organism available without restriction at a point in time before he knew whether a European patent would be granted

---

[84] Notice concerning the "expert option" dated July 28, 1981; O.J. EPO 1981, 358. The main text of the Notice is reproduced at Appendix 11.

pursuant to his application. While an applicant in respect of any invention has to accept publication of his description of that invention in his patent application before he knows whether a patent will be granted (under the concept of "early publication"), an applicant in respect of an invention involving a micro-organism was required under the original Rule to do rather more than this; namely in effect to supply something physical with which to perform the invention as well.

The amended (*i.e.* current) version of Rule 28 EPC enables the applicant for a European patent to protect himself against prejudicial use of samples of the deposited micro-organism during the period for which the claimed invention is not in the public domain, by making use of the "expert option" discussed above.

7–51 (2) However, there is another complication as regards the timing of availability of such deposited material; namely, the fact that in certain countries, in particular the United States, contrary to the system provided under the EPC, a deposited micro-organism need not be made available until the grant of a patent is made. Availability of the deposit to the public is then a "*quid pro quo*" for grant of the patent, and if no patent is granted the deposited micro-organism (like the description) is not made available, but remains secret. Under such a system, the applicant, by making a patent application, runs no risk of giving away what he has described and deposited, without concomitant grant of a patent which protects what has been described and deposited. This is obviously in contrast to the system under the EPC, where an applicant does run just such a risk.

(h) Consequence of non-availability

7–52 Cases have arisen in which, probably because of such different requirements in other countries, a deposited culture has not been available to the public during the period of time required under Rule 28(3) EPC.

7–53 (1) The micro-organisms which were required for the claimed process had not been available to the public from the collection in the United States where they had been deposited between the date of publication of the European patent application and the date of issue of a United States patent (a period of about three months).

The following matters were referred to as "special circumstances" in view of which refusal of the application under Article 83 EPC was not justified:

(a) The fact that the inherent risk of complications arising from a situation where a micro-organism was originally deposited for a different purpose (such as a national application) did not seem to have been foreseen during the initial years of the deposit system under the EPC. This conclusion was supported by the subsequent amendments made to the special agreements between the EPO and certain depositary institutions so as to provide for "conversion" of a deposit originally made for another purpose into a deposit for the purpose of Rule 28 EPC. Reference was made to the Notice dated July 18, 1986[85] in this connection, as it was the Notice which had, for the first time, made it clear to users of the deposit system that:

"the proper way of bringing a deposit originally filed for another purpose into line with the requirements of the EPC system is to formally convert the deposit into a deposit under Rule 28 EPC (in case of a deposit made on the basis of a special agreement between the EPO and the depositary institution) or into a deposit under the Budapest Treaty (which automatically covers Rule 28 EPC) as the case may be" (T239/87[86]).

The non-availability of the deposit had occurred before July 1986 (the date of the EPO Notice).

   (b) The short period of time (about three months) during which the deposited culture was not available.

   (c) The lack of evidence of any request for a sample of the deposit during that period (T239/87[87]).

(2) In a further case the deposit had been made for the purpose of a **7–54** United States patent application, and the application contained no indication that the deposit was made either under the Budapest Treaty or for the purpose of Rule 28 EPC. The deposit was not made available to the public until issue of the United States patent almost a year after publication of the European application.

"During this period there was no legal guarantee that the deposit would have been made available to the public as required by Rule 28(3) EPC. Although there is in the present case no reason to believe that the Appellant, had a request for the issue of a sample of the deposited organism actually been made, would not have given his consent to such release, it has to be kept in mind that one important purpose of Rule 28 EPC is just to make the availability of deposited organisms independent of any such subsequent consent by the depositor and to create a legal guarantee that the requirement for availability of such organisms from the date of publication of European patent applications is already fulfilled on the date of filing such applications. Thus, the Board is unable to accept the Appellant's argument that the deposit in this case fulfilled all the requirements under Rule 28 EPC." (T39/88[88])

[85] Notice dated July 18, 1986 concerning micro-organisms, O.J. EPO 1986, 269. See note 80 and Appendix 10.
[86] T239/87 *NABISCO/Micro-organisms* [1988] E.P.O.R. 311.
[87] *Ibid.*
[88] T39/88 *CPC/Micro-organisms* O.J. EPO 1989, 499; [1990] E.P.O.R. 41.

Thus:

> "There may be a deficiency in complying with Rule 28 EPC when the deposit of a culture of a micro-organism, originally made under other legislation, was not converted into a deposit under Rule 28 EPC or the Budapest Treaty before the filing of a European patent application.
>
> Nevertheless, due to the lack of clarity which was inherent in the system of deposits under Rule 28 EPC in that respect, it is not justified to refuse, on this sole ground, a European patent application filed before the publication of the clarifying Notice of the EPO dated July 18, 1986 . . . ."[89]

> "What really matters from a legal point of view is the inherent inclarity of the system under Rule 28 EPC . . . before the clarification made in 1986" (T39/88[90]).

by publication of the Notice dated July 18, 1986.[91]

T39/88[92] was followed in subsequent cases where the filing of the application in question also took place before publication of the Notice dated July 18, 1986.[93]

C. The Claims—Clarity and Support

Article 69 EPC, Article 84 EPC, Rule 29 EPC

(1) Their contents and function

(a) Central role—extent of protection

7–55 The EPC contains a single set of provisions which regulates both the contents of the claims of a European patent and the relative roles played by the claims and the description when the extent of protection conferred by the patent is to be determined. These provisions are applicable to all patents granted under the EPC, throughout their later life as national patents and have been summarised as follows:

> "Article 84 EPC provides that the claims of a European patent application 'shall define the matter for which protection is sought'. Rule 29(1) EPC further requires that the claims 'shall define the matter for which protection is sought in terms of the technical features of the invention'. The primary aim of the wording used in a claim must therefore be to satisfy such requirements, having regard to the

---

[89] Notice dated July 18, 1986 concerning micro-organisms, O.J. EPO 1986, 269. See note 80 and Appendix 10.
[90] T39/88 *CPC/Micro-organisms* O.J. EPO 1989, 49; [1990] E.P.O.R. 41.
[91] See note 89.
[92] See note 90.
[93] See note 89.

particular nature of the subject invention, and having regard also to the purpose of such claims.

The purpose of claims under the EPC is to enable the protection conferred by the patent (or patent application) to be determined (Article 69 EPC), and thus the rights of the patent owner within the designated Contracting States (Article 64 EPC), having regard to the patentability requirements of Articles 52 to 57 EPC" (G2, 6/88[94]).

The role of the claims of a European patent is thus central in defining the protection conferred. The determination of the precise extent of protection conferred by a European patent is discussed separately in Chapter 13.

(b) Allowable breadth of claims

As discussed in paragraph 7–04 above, the allowable breadth of a claim is   **7–56** essentially governed by the general legal principle that "the extent of the patent monopoly, as defined by the claims, should correspond to the *technical contribution* to the art ... This means that the definitions in the claims should essentially correspond to the scope of the invention as disclosed in the description" (T409/91[95]).

Consequently, when determining the allowable scope of the claim, it is first necessary to determine the technical contribution to the art which underlies the claimed invention and which has been disclosed to a skilled reader. The wording used in the claims may be appropriately generalised so as to correspond to such technical contribution.

The above stated principle has to be applied to all kinds of invention,   **7–57** whatever the scope and nature. Some inventions are quite specific in nature, having been devised in a narrow context, while others may have a more general scope and may be of broad application. The wording chosen to define the scope of protection sought should correspond to the nature of the invention to be protected, having regard to the technical contribution which underlies it.

"In assessing the subject-matter of a claim, the underlying invention has to be identified. In this respect, it is relevant how generic or specific the claimed invention is. An inventor who has invented fastening means characterised in that they consist of a specific material has invented neither a nail, nor a screw, nor a bolt. Rather his invention is directed to fastening means generally. That is not a question of form but of substance: the applicant may claim his invention in the broadest possible form, *i.e.* the most general form for which all patentability requirements are fulfilled. If he has made an invention of general applicability a generic claim is not the consequence of the verbal skill

---

[94] G2, 6/88 *MOBIL OIL/BAYER/Friction reducing additive* O.J. EPO 1990, 93, 114; [1990] E.P.O.R. 73, 257.
[95] T409/91 *EXXON/Fuel oils* O.J. EPO 1994, 653; [1994] E.P.O.R. 149.

of the attorney ... but of the breadth of application of the invention" (G1/98[96]).

In other words, an applicant is allowed to define the invention with broad wording, provided that the protection conferred corresponds to the technical contribution to the art as disclosed in the description (Articles 83 and 84 FPC), and provided that the claimed invention is novel and inventive (Articles 54, 56 EPC—see Chapters 11 and 12).

For example:

> "Where an invention relates to the actual realisation of a technical effect anticipated at a theoretical level in the prior art, a proper balance must be found between, on the one hand, the actual technical contribution to the art by which it is claimed, so that, if patent protection is granted, its scope is fair and adequate" (T694/92[97]).

(c) Contents: two-part claims

7–58 Rule 29(1) EPC requires that a claim should "where appropriate" contain two parts (a) the preamble or pre-characterising portion and (b) the characterising portion. The first part should contain those technical features "which are necessary for the definition of the claimed subject-matter, but which, in combination, are part of the prior art". The second part should contain the technical features "which, in combination ... , it is desired to protect".

The first part of the claim should therefore normally be based on the prior art document containing the most features in common with the claimed invention which is not necessarily prior art which is the closest concerned with the same problem as the claimed invention. A contention that the pre-characterising portion should be based on the closest prior art concerned with the same problem has been rejected as follows:

> "the purpose of the claims is to define the matter (*e.g.* an apparatus, a process) for which protection is sought (Article 84 EPC). The claims have to be formulated as prescribed by Rule 29 EPC. Neither the Article nor the Rule makes any reference to the necessity or desirability that 'the characterising portion of the claim should fairly set out the inventive step'. This contention by the Appellant seems to be based on the false conception that the inventive step resides in the characterising portion of the claims. It is, however, the subject-matter of the claim as a whole which embodies the invention and the inventive step involved" (T13/84[98]).

If the preamble to an orginally filed claim includes a combination of

[96] G1/98 *NOVARTIS II/Transgenic plant* O.J. EPO 1998, 509; [2000] E.P.O.R. 303.
[97] T694/92 *MYCOGEN/Modifying plant cells* O.J. EPO 1997, 408; [1998] E.P.O.R. 114.
[98] T13/84 *SPERRY/Reformulation of the problem* O.J. EPO 1986, 253; [1986] E.P.O.R. 289.

features based upon "in-house" prior art, which is not in fact part of the state of the art, appropriate amendment to the claim is allowable; and "the first version of the claim could not be considered a binding statement as to the common [lack of] novelty of these features" in the preamble (T6/81[99]).

A two-part claim is not always appropriate:

"A one-part claim is preferable to the two-part claim provided for in Rule 29(1) EPC if the subject matter for which protection is sought is thereby defined clearly and concisely by avoiding inappropriate and complex formulations ... However, it is then necessary to include in the description the information indicated in Rule 29(1)(a) EPC" (T170/84[100]).

In opposition proceedings, however:

"there is no need officially to insist on a change of wording of the claim simply because one feature in the preamble to a two-part claim does not belong to the state of art" (T99/85[101]).

(2) Types of claims

(a) Introduction: categories of claim: entity/activity

Each invention which is the subject of a European patent application **7–59**
should be defined in the claims in accordance with its nature and subject-matter in terms of its technical features.

"There are basically two different types of claim, namely a claim to a physical entity (e.g. product, apparatus) and a claim to a physical activity (e.g. method, process, use). These two basic types of claim are sometimes referred to as the two possible 'categories' of claim. ...

Within the above two basic types of claim various sub-classes are possible (e.g. a compound, a composition, a machine; or a manufacturing method, a process of producing a compound, a method of testing, etc.). Furthermore, claims including both features relating to physical activities and features relating to physical entities are also possible. There are no rigid lines of demarcation between the various possible forms of claim.

[The] technical features of a claim to a physical entity are the physical parameters of the entity, and the technical features of a claim to an activity are the physical steps which define such activity" (G2, 6/88[102]).

The protection available under the EPC is dependent to a large extent

[99] T6/81 SIEMENS/Electrode slide O.J. EPO 1982, 193; [1979–85] E.P.O.R.: B: 294.
[100] T170/84 BOSSERT KG/Two-part claim O.J. EPO 1986, 400; [1987] E.P.O.R. 82.
[101] T99/85 BOEHRINGER/Diagnostic agent O.J. EPO 1987, 413; [1987] E.P.O.R. 337.
[102] G2, 6/88 MOBIL OIL/BAYER/Friction reducing additive O.J. EPO 1990, 93, 114; [1990] E.P.O.R. 73, 257.

upon an appropriate choice of form and wording for the claims, according to the nature of the invention. The claims should define the invention in terms which provide an appropriately broad scope commensurate with a fair extent of protection having regard to the invention which is disclosed in the application.

(b) Product claims

7–60 A product claim includes a number of technical features which in combination define the product which is to be protected.

7–61 **(i) Machines, apparatus, etc.** In the case of a product such as a machine or apparatus, such technical features will define how it is construed, in terms of its component parts and their inter-relationship. The construction of a machine or apparatus will normally determine how it works, and indirectly, what its advantages are.

The protection which is conferred by such a product claim covers the machine or apparatus, however it is used, and whatever its context (see Chapter 13 at paragraph 13–27) The protection conferred by such construction of the machine or apparatus essentially determines how it is used.

7–62 **(ii) Chemical, pharmaceutical and food products.** Prior to the EPC, it was relatively unusual for national patent laws to allow patent protection for chemical, pharmaceutical and food products *per se*. In the United Kingdom, claims to such products were allowed before 1919, but were not permitted between 1919 and 1949, when such claims were re-introduced. In France, Germany and the Scandinavian countries, such patent protection was allowed by national patent laws for the first time during the late 1960s. From then on, other European countries also introduced such protection.

The Strasbourg Convention (1963) allowed Contracting Parties to reserve the right not to grant patents for food and pharmaceutical products as such for a limited period of ten years. The EPC allows claims to chemical, pharmaceutical and food products as such, but similarly provides in Article 167(2) EPC that each Contracting State may reserve the right (upon signature or ratification) to provide that European patents for such products may be ineffective or revocable under its national law, for a period of not more than ten years, subject to a possible five year extension.

Recent reservations under Article 167(2) EPC were implemented by Greece and Spain in October 1992, but European patents granted in these countries upon applications made before such date are subject to the reservations and are therefore ineffective or revocable in such countries.

In Contracting States where such reservations apply, such products are normally protected by claiming the process for making it (see below). However:

"The inclusion in a product claim of one or more process features may be permissible if their presence is desirable having regard to the impact of the national laws of one or more Contracting States" (T129/88[103]).

In the case of a product such as a new chemical substance or **7–63** pharmaceutical composition, the technical features of a claim to such a product will define how it is "constructed" in terms of its chemical structure or its constituents, for example. However, the structure of a chemical compound or the composition of a pharmaceutical product does not determine how it is used. The technical advantage which can be derived from such a product normally depends upon the environment in which it is used. Nevertheless, when claims to such chemical and pharmaceutical products were accepted in Europe in the 1960s, the protection conferred upon such products in accordance with national laws prior to the EPC was equivalent to that conferred upon other kinds of product, such as the mechanical and physical products discussed above. That is, claims to chemical and pharmaceutical products also conferred protection upon the product *per se* even though the technical advantages associated with such products could only be achieved when the products were used in a particular way. Although such "absolute protection" for product claims has sometimes been challenged, it has been accepted as underlying the EPC, and has been justified on the basis that the technical advantages associated with such products can only be achieved after the products *per se* have been invented (see also Chapter 13 at paragraph 13–27 below).

(c) Process claims: product-by-process claims

(i) Process or method claims. Process or method claims can be of two **7–64** kinds—those which treat something; and those which make something, and which therefore result in an end product, which may be either a new product or a known product.

Article 64(2) EPC provides that:

> "If the subject-matter of the European patent is a process, the protection conferred by the patent shall extend to the products directly obtained by such process."

The extent of protection conferred by a process claim is discussed in Chapter 13 at paragraph 13–23 below.

(ii) Product-by-process claims. Having regard to the extent of protec- **7–65** tion conferred by a process claim by virtue of Article 64(2) EPC:

> "Claims for products defined in terms of processes for their prep-
> aration (known as product-by-process claims) are admissible only if

---

[103] T129/88 *AKZO/Fibre* O.J. EPO 1993, 598; [1994] E.P.O.R. 176.

341

the products themselves fulfil the requirements for patentability and there is no other information available in the application which could enable the applicant to define the product satisfactorily by reference to its composition, structure or some other testable parameter" (T150/82[104]: see also T119/82,[105] T248/85[106]). (As to the novelty requirement for patentability in such circumstances, see Chapter 11 at paragraphs 11–79 *et seq.*)

A product-by-process claim is interpreted as a claim to the product *per se*, and the reference to the process for its preparation serves only to define the product (T20/94[107]).

(d) Use claims

7–66   **(i) Introduction.** Use claims provide protection for research into the further properties of known products, especially chemical and pharmaceutical products. Such a product when first prepared can be protected by a product claim. If further research reveals that such a product produces a new (*i.e.* previously unknown) and surprising technical effect in the context of a particular series of method steps, then that new effect can be protected by means of a method claim. But if further research reveals that such a product has new and surprising properties in the context of the same method steps in which the product has already been used, and can be used to produce a new and surprising technical effect in such context, the beneficial result of such research cannot be protected either by a product claim (the product is known) or by a method claim (the relevant method steps in combination with the product are known). The benefits of such research could only be protected by way of a use claim. Such a claim formulation reflects the essence of what has been invented, namely that a (known) product can be used (in a known method) to produce a previously unknown technical effect.

"The recognition or discovery of a previously unknown property of a known compound, such property providing a new technical effect, can clearly involve a valuable and inventive contribution to the art" (G2, 6/88[108]).

The status of a use claim as a distinct form of claim is recognised in Rule 29(2) EPC, not just in the specific context of chemical and pharmaceutical inventions, but generally.

7–67   **(ii) First medical use.** Furthermore, in the specific context of pharmaceutical inventions, Article 54(5) EPC envisages the patentability of a

[104] T150/82 *IFF/Claim categories* O.J. EPO 1984, 309; [1979–85] E.P.O.R. C: 629.
[105] T119/82 *EXXON/Gelation* O.J. EPO 1984, 217; [1979–85] E.P.O.R.: B: 566.
[106] T248/85 *BICC/Radiation processing* O.J. EPO 1986, 261; [1986] E.P.O.R. 311.
[107] T20/94 *ENICHEM/Amorphous TPM* November 4, 1998.
[108] G2, 6/88 *MOBIL OIL/BAYER/Friction reducing additive* O.J. EPO 1990, 93, 114; [1990] E.P.O.R. 73, 257.

known substance or composition for use in a medical or veterinary treatment, provided that its use for such a treatment is not part of a state of the art.

In other words, even if a compound is known in a non-therapeutic context, an invention consisting of the use of the same compound in a therapeutic treatment is to be regarded as novel.

(iii) Extent of claim to a first medical use

7–68

"Where a known compound is for the first time proposed and claimed for use in therapy, the fact that a specific use is disclosed in the specification does not in itself call for a restriction of the purpose-limited product claim to that use" (T128/82[109]).

Such a disclosure of a specific therapeutic use of a known product justifies a broad claim to all therapeutic uses on the basis that:

"If an inventor is granted absolute protection in respect of a new chemical compound for use in therapy [see Chapter 9 at paragraph 9–43] the principle of equal treatment would require that an inventor who for the first time makes a known compound available for therapy should be correspondingly rewarded for his service with a purpose-limited substance claim under Article 54(5) EPC to cover the whole field of therapy" (T128/82[110]).

The interpretation of use claims in the context of determining novelty is discussed in Chapter 11 at paragraphs 11–93 *et seq.* below.

(e) Functional features in claims

(i) **Introduction.** The inclusion of functional features in claims is **7–69** permissible in European patent applications and patents in certain circumstances, as discussed below. Clearly such claims provide a broader extent of protection than claims which only contain structural features.

"A functional feature is usually chosen out of the legitimate desire to couch the invention in the most general terms possible in order to secure adequate and reasonable protection" (T68/85[111]).

The allowability of functional claims is an aspect of claim definition and is primarily governed by the requirements of Article 84 EPC—not only that of clarity, but also that of support by the description. Furthermore,

[109] T128/82 HOFFMAN-LA ROCHE/Pyrrolidine derivatives O.J. EPO 1984, 164; [1979–85] E.P.O.R.: B: 591.
[110] Ibid.
[111] T68/85 CIBA-GEIGY/Synergistic herbicides O.J. EPO 1987, 228; [1987] E.P.O.R. 302.

questions of sufficiency of description under Article 83 EPC may also arise in relation to an application which contains functional claims (see paragraphs 7–27 *et seq.* above).

In so far as Rule 29(1) EPC prescribes that the definition of a claimed invention shall be "in terms of [its] technical features", a functional feature is a technical feature within the meaning of Rule 29 EPC (T68/85[112]).

7–70   A functional feature is a limitation by result. The limitation may be with respect to either a physical entity or a physical activity. For example, "a mechanical invention would be unlikely to refer to a nail or rivet, but to a fastening means" (T68/85[113]). In simple terms, either a product or a process, for example, may be limited by being defined as "such that" a particular result is achieved.

The extent to which a claim may include functional features is clearly related partly to the nature of the claimed invention and partly to the appropriate extent of protection which can properly be conferred upon it. It is generally recognised that a claim which defines an invention almost entirely in terms of functional features by covering all methods of achieving a desired result is not normally allowable. Where the line is drawn in allowing functional features in a particular case depends upon finding a proper balance between an appropriately wide protection for the patentee and sufficient legal certainty for competitors as to what is inside and what is outside the extent of protection conferred. Furthermore, broad functional features in claims commonly require an especially detailed description of how to carry out the claimed invention so as to allow what is claimed to be achieved without undue burden (again, see paragraph 7–27 *et seq.* above).

Accordingly, at a basic level the use of functional terms such as "fastening means" as technical features in claims is appropriate and necessary in order to obtain a fair and proper protection which is justifiably broader than the specific examples of an invention which the description may contain. In order to ensure that functional features in claims do not provide an unjustifiably wide protection compared to the scope of the invention which is described, however, the use of functional terms has to be properly regulated. Articles 83 and 84 EPC provide the primary means of regulation, together with their implementing Rules.

7–71   **(ii) Functional features.** The general rule in relation to the use of functional features is as follows:

> "Functional features defining a technical result are permissible in a claim if, from an objective viewpoint, such features cannot otherwise be defined more precisely without unduly restricting the scope of the invention, and if these features provide instructions which are sufficiently clear for the expert to reduce them to practice without

---

[112] *Ibid.*
[113] *Ibid.*

undue burden, if necessary with reasonable experiments" (T68/85[114]; see also T292/85[115]).

Furthermore, "the effort to define a feature in functional terms must stop short where it jeopardises the clarity of a claim as required by Article 84 EPC" (T68/85[116]).
On the other hand, it is well recognised that:

"In appropriate cases, . . . it is only possible to define the invention (the matter for which protection is sought—Article 84 EPC) in a way which gives a fair protection having regard to the nature of the invention which has been described, by using functional terminology in the claims" (T292/85[117]—see also T139/85[118]).

The claims in question in this case included functional terms such as "bacteria", "regulon" and "plasmid".

(iii) **Application of Articles 83 and 84 EPC.** See paragraphs 7–27 *et seq.* **7–72**

(3) Prescribed requirements for claims

Article 84 EPC requires that the claims shall be: **7–73**

    (a) clear and concise ("clarity")
    (b) supported by the description ("support").

These distinct requirements are considered separately in Sections (4) and (5) below. Such requirements must be fulfilled if a European patent is to be granted, and objections to grant during examination of an application will, therefore, arise if they are not fulfilled. However, objections to a European patent after grant may not be based on these requirements, because the requirements of Article 84 EPC do not constitute either a ground of opposition to the grant (Article 100 EPC) or a ground for evocation of a European patent in a national court (Article 138(1) EPC)—(see Chapter 3 at paragraph 3–26). Nevertheless, since as discussed above (paragraph 7–04) the requirements of Article 83 and 84 EPC both give effect to the same legal principle, objections to the scope of protection conferred by a claim of a European patent on the basis that the claim is not "supported by the description" can properly be raised within the ground of "insufficient disclosure" (Articles 100(b) and 138(1)(b) EPC (T435/91[119] for example: *Biogen*[120] in the United Kingdom—paragraph 7–87 below).

---

[114] T68/85 *CIBA-GEIGY/Synergistic herbicides* O.J. EPO 1987, 228; [1987] E.P.O.R. 302.
[115] T292/85 *GENENTECH I/Polypeptide expression* O.J. EPO 1989, 275; [1989] E.P.O.R. 1.
[116] See note 114.
[117] See note 115.
[118] T139/85 *EFAMOL/Pharmaceutical compositions* [1987] E.P.O.R. 229.
[119] T435/91 *UNILEVER/Detergents* O.J. EPO 1995, 188; [1995] E.P.O.R. 314.
[120] *Biogen Inc. v. Medeva plc* [1997] R.P.C. 1.

7–73A   Especially having regard to the close relationship between Articles 83 and 84 EPC as discussed throughout this Chapter (see, *e.g.* paragraphs 7–04, 7–26 and 7–84), there seems to be no good reason why the requirements of Article 84 EPC should be excluded as grounds for opposition under Article 100 EPC and as grounds for revocation by national courts under Article 138 EPC.

However, the proposed revision of the EPC does not include such amendments.

(4) Clarity

(a) Self-sufficiency of claims

7–74   Rule 29(6) EPC states that:

> "Claims shall not, except where absolutely necessary rely, in respect of technical features of the invention, on references to the description or drawings."

As a general principle, therefore, the claims should be self-sufficient in themselves. Furthermore:

> "the claims, *per se*, must be free of contradiction: it must be possible to understand them without reference to the description, especially as the description is not translated into all the official languages (Article 14(7) EPC" (T2/80[121]).

Nevertheless, it is clear from Article 69 EPC that reference can and should properly be made to the description in order to interpret the claims, and thus to understand the extent of protection sought. Thus:

> "The provision of Article 69 EPC, according to which the description and drawings shall be used to interpret the claims, applies also to the clarity requirement of Article 84 EPC, provided that the claims are not self-contradictory" (T860/93[122]).

It follows from the above that:

> "Claims relying on references to the description in the specification in respect of all their technical features (known in the patent practice of the United Kingdom as 'omnibus' claims) are unallowable as contrary to Rule 29(4) and 29(6) EPC, unless absolutely necessary, *e.g.* when a plurality of conditions would not lend themselves to verbal

---

[121] T2/80 *BAYER/Polyamide moulding compositions* O.J. EPO 1981, 431; [1979–85] E.P.O.R.: B: 257.

[122] T860/93 *AQUALON/Protective coating composition* O.J. EPO 1995, 47; [1995] E.P.O.R. 391.

expression without such a reference. The onus is on the applicant to show such exceptionality" (T150/82[123]).

In particular, *structural chemical formulae* cannot normally be set out in an **7–75** appendix to the claims because this would be contrary to Rule 29(6) EPC: they should normally be incorporated in the claims in the absence of "absolute necessity" (T271/88[124]).

Nevertheless, in some cases it may be "absolutely necessary" to rely on a reference to the description or drawings, as the Guidelines C111 4.10 recognises. In biotechnology, for example, claims concerning genes are often defined by reference to figures setting out *Div A sequences*.

Furthermore, *reference numerals and signs* should be included in a claim in **7–76** order to ensure lack of clarity, because such signs do not limit the extent of protection. Rule 29(7) EPC states that:

> "If the European patent application contains drawings, the technical features mentioned in the claims shall preferably, if the intelligibility of the claims can thereby be increased, be followed by reference signs relating to these features and placed in parentheses. These reference signs shall not be construed as limiting the claims."

Thus:

> "The purpose of reference signs in a claim (Rule 29(7)EPC) is to make the claims easier for all to understand. They do not limit the scope of the claim but they do affect its clarity and may enable it to be expressed more concisely that would otherwise be possible" (T237/84[125]).

A statement may be included in the description explaining the limited purpose of such signs in the claims, and making it clear that such signs do not limit the extent of protection. Such a statement is not "obviously irrelevant or unnecessary" within Rule 34(1)(c) EPC, since there is a possibility that a national court might regard the claims as limited by the signs (T237/84[126]).

(b) Definition of technical features

(i) Functional terms. These are discussed in paragraphs 7–69 *et seq.* **7–77** above.

(ii) Broad terms: clarity. **7–78**

---

[123] T150/82 *IFF/Claim categories* O.J. EPO 1984, 309; [1979–85] E.P.O.R.: C: 629.
[124] T271/88 *ICI/Chemical formulae* June 6, 1989.
[125] T237/84 *PHILIPS/Reference signs* O.J. EPO 1987, 309; [1987] E.P.O.R. 310.
[126] *Ibid.*

"The clarity of a claim is not diminished by the mere breadth of term of art (*e.g.* alkyl) contained in it, if the meaning of such term—either *per se* or in the light of the description—is unambiguous for a person skilled in the art" (T238/88[127]).

7–79   (iii) Relative terms.

"Since, in the absence of any unambiguous reference point, a relative term such as 'lower alkyl' in the field of organic chemistry does not have a generally accepted meaning with respect to its maximum number of carbon atoms, such a term is ambiguous and therefore not suitable for clearly defining the subject-matter for which protection is sought in a claim which is directed to a group of organic compounds *per se*" (T337/95[128]).

7–80   (iv) Measurement of parameters.

"Where a quality is expressed in a claim as being within a given numerical range, the method of measuring that quality must either be general technical knowledge, so that no explicit description is needed, or a method of measuring that quality needs to be identified. In contrast, where a claim specifies a relative quality, in this case that the products should be 'water-soluble', it is not normally necessary to identify any method for its determination provided it is sufficiently clear in its context to be understood by skilled workers" (T860/93[129]).

Furthermore, the requirements of Article 84 EPC "may be fulfilled in a claim to a product when the characteristics of the product are specified by parameters related to the physical structure of the product, provided that those parameters can be clearly and reliably determined by objective procedures which are usual in the art" (T94/82[130]).

7–81   (v) Constituents of a mixture. "Clarity, as regards claims for a mixture, demands that the proportions given for each constituent must add up to the requisite total (100 per cent in the case of percentages) for each composition claimed" (T2/80[131]).

The claim in question originally included five constituents with ranges of proportions such that, for example, if the minimum proportion of four of the constituents was combined with the maximum proportion of the fifth constituent, the total did not add up to 100 per cent. This contradiction was not mitigated by a stipulation in the claim that all the constituents must add up to 100 per cent. It was not enough for the purpose of Article 84 EPC

---

[127] T238/88 *KODAK/Crown ether* O.J. EPO 1992, 709; [1993] E.P.O.R. 100.
[128] T337/95 *NIHON NOHYAKU/Lower alkyl* O.J. EPO 1996, 628; [1997] E.P.O.R. 337.
[129] T860/93 *AQUALON/Protective coating compositions* O.J. EPO 1995, 47; [1995] E.P.O.R. 391.
[130] T94/82 *ICI/Gear crimped yarn* O.J. EPO 1984, 75; [1979–85] E.P.O.R. B: 513.
[131] T2/80 *BAYER/Polyamide moulding compositions* O.J. EPO 1981, 431; [1979–85] E.P.O.R.: B: 257.

that a skilled person would resolve the contradiction by referring to the description.

(c) Inclusion of essential technical features

> "Article 84 EPC requires amongst other thing that the claims, which **7–82**
> define the matter for which protection is sought (*i.e.* the object, of the
> invention as implied by Article 52(1) EPC) be clear …) this has to be
> interpreted as meaning not only that a claim from a technical point of
> view must be comprehensible, but also that it must define clearly the
> object of the invention, that is to say, indicate all the essential features
> thereof.
>   As essential features have to be regarded all features which are
> necessary to obtain the desired effect or, differently expressed, which
> are necessary to solve the technical problem with which the appli-
> cation is concerned" (T32/82[132]: see also T1055/92[133]).

This view of the first part of Article 84 EPC is complementary to the requirement of support by the description in the second sentence of Article 84 EPC which is considered below.
    Similarly:

> "the essential features of the invention, which must be used for
> defining the matter for which protection is sought in accordance with
> Article 84 EPC in combination with Rule 29(1) and (3) EPC, are all
> those technical features which are necessary to define an invention
> which is patentable under the EPC, including any feature which is
> necessary to define matter which also meets the requirement of
> sufficient disclosure pursuant to Article 83 EPC" (T409/91[134]).

(5) Support by the description

This requirement of Article 84 EPC defines the relationship between the **7–83**
description and the claims of a European patent application. In this
context, matters ancillary to the description should be considered as part of
it: in particular, the disclosure of drawings supplementary and additional
to that of the description should be considered as part of the description.
Furthermore, in the case of inventions concerning micro-organisms, the
information derived from a deposited micro-organism in accordance with
Rule 28 EPC supplements that of the description *per se* (see paragraphs
7–37 *et seq.* above).
    As discussed in paragraph 7–04 above, both Articles 83 and 84 EPC have **7–84**
the underlying purpose to give effect to "the same legal principle that the

---

[132] T32/82 *ICI/Control circuit* O.J. EPO 1984, 354; [1979–85] E.P.O.R. B: 426.
[133] T1055/92 *AMPEX CORPORATION/Clarity* O.J. EPO 1995, 214; [1995] E.P.O.R. 469.
[134] T409/91 *EXXON/Fuel oils* O.J. EPO 1994, 653; [1994] E.P.O.R. 149.

patent monopoly should be justified by the technical contribution to the art" (T409/91[135]). An expression of the same idea is that:

"The need for a fair protection governs both the considerations of the scope of claims and of the requirements for sufficient disclosure" (T292/85[136]).

Also as discussed above (paragraph 7–73), however, Article 84 EPC is a ground for objecting to the grant of a patent during examination proceedings, but is not a ground for opposition to a granted European patent.

An objection that a claimed invention is not supported by the description may therefore be raised during examination proceedings when the scope of protection sought by a claim does not appear to be justified by the extent of disclosure of the technical contribution to the art in the description.

"Thus the requirement in Article 84 EPC that the claims shall be supported by the description is of importance in ensuring that the monopoly given by a granted patent generally corresponds to the invention which has been described in the application. On the other hand, Article 84 EPC clearly envisages (by the use of the word 'supported') that the 'matter for which protection is sought' can be defined in generalised form compared to the specific description of the invention. The permissible extent of generalisation from the description to the claims, having regard to the requirement of Article 84 EPC, is a question of degree and has to be determined having particular regard to the nature of the invention which has been described, in each individual case" (T133/85[137]).

Consequently:

"Since most claims are generalisations of examples disclosed in the description, the purpose of [Article 84 EPC] must be seen as safe-guarding that the claims do not cover any subject-matter which, after reading the description, still would not be at the disposal of the skilled person. Undoubtedly, there may be cases where the lack of disclosure of a technical problem could lead to the conclusion that the claims lack support by the description" (T26/81[138]).

7–85   It follows that the extent of the description ultimately governs the matter for which protection may be sought in the claims. The requirement for support by the description also effectively determines the permissible

---

[135] *Ibid.*
[136] T292/85 *GENETECH I/Polypeptide expression* O.J. EPO 1989, 275; [1989] E.P.O.R. 1.
[137] T133/85 *XEROX/Amendments* O.J. EPO 1988, 441; [1989] E.P.O.R. 116.
[138] T26/81 *ICI/Containers* O.J. EPO 1982, 211; [1979–85] E.P.O.R.: B: 362.

width of the claims (in combination with the prior art). In general terms, the subject-matter of an invention as defined in the claims cannot be wider than the subject-matter of the invention which has been disclosed in the description. Nevertheless, generalisation in the claims of the subject-matter disclosed in the description is clearly permissible, in order to ensure that an appropriate extent of protection can be derived from the claims.

If during examination proceedings the scope of a claim is considered to be too wide and not supported by the description, the only remedy is to amend the claim by reducing its width, because the disclosure in the description cannot be expanded after filing in order to provide adequate support for the claim having regard to Article 123(2) EPC (see Chapter 8 at paragraph 8–50: T133/85[139]).

For example:

"In cases where the gist of the claimed invention consists in the achievement of a given technical effect by known techniques in different areas of application, and serious doubts exist as to whether this effect can readily be obtained for the whole range of applications claimed, ample technical details and more than one example may be necessary in order to support claims of a broad scope. Accordingly, claims of broad scope are not allowable if the skilled person, after reading the description, is not able to readily perform the invention over the whole area claimed without undue burden and without needing inventive skill" (T694/92[140]).

On the other hand: 7–86

"If a claim concerns a group of chemical compounds per se, an objection of lack of support by the description pursuant to Article 84 EPC cannot properly be raised for the sole reason that the description does not contain sufficient information in order to make it credible that an alleged technical effect (which is not however, a part of the definition of the claimed compounds) is obtained by all the compounds claimed" (T939/92[141]—and see Chapter 12 at paragraph 12–23).

(a) Comparison with United Kingdom Law

In *Biogen v. Medeva*,[142] the House of Lords referred to the principles set out 7–87
in T292/85[143] and T409/91[144] which are referred to above, and held that:

"There was more than one way in which the breadth of a claim might

[139] T133/85 *XEROX/Amendments* O.J. EPO 1988, 441; [1989] E.P.O.R. 116.
[140] T694/92 *MYCOGEN/Modifying plant cells* O.J. EPO 1997, 408; [1998] E.P.O.R. 114.
[141] T939/92 *AGREVO/Triazoles* O.J. EPO 1996, 309; [1996] E.P.O.R. 171.
[142] *Biogen Inc v. Medeva plc* [1997] R.P.C. 1.
[143] T292/85 *GENENTECH 1/Polypeptide expression* O.J. EPO 1989, 275; [1989] E.P.O.R. 1.
[144] T409/91 *EXXON/Fuel oils* O.J. EPO 1994, 653; [1994] E.P.O.R. 149.

exceed the technical contributions to the art embodied in the invention. The patent might claim results which did not enable, such as making a wide class of products, when it enabled only one of those products and disclosed no principle which would enable others to be made. Or it might claim every way of achieving a result when it enabled only one way and it was possible to envisage other ways of achieving that result which made no use of the invention."

Cases Referred to in Chapter 7

Board of Appeal Decisions

G2, 6/88   MOBIL OIL/Friction reducing additive O.J. EPO 1990, 93, 114; [1990] E.P.O.R. 73, 257.

G1/93   ADVANCED SEMICONDUCTOR PRODUCTS II/Conflicting requirements of Article 123(2) and (3) EPC O.J. EPO 1994, 541; [1995] E.P.O.R. 97.

G2/93   UNITED STATES OF AMERICA II/Hepatitus A virus O.J. EPO 1995, 275; [1995] E.P.O.R. 437.

G1/98   NOVARTIS II/Transgenic plant O.J. EPO 1998, 509; [2000] E.P.O.R. 303.

J1/80   SIEMENS/Filing priority documents O.J. EPO 1980, 289; [1979–85] E.P.O.R.: A: 15.

T2/80   BAYER/Polyamide moulding compositions O.J. EPO 1981, 431; [1979–85] E.P.O.R.: B: 257.

T6/81   SIEMENS/Electrode slide O.J. EPO 1982, 193; [1979–85] E.P.O.R.: B: 294.

T26/81   ICI/Containers O.J. EPO 1982, 211; [1979–85] E.P.O.R.: B: 362.

T11/82   LANSING BAGNALL/Control circuit O.J. EPO 1983, 479; [1979–85] E.P.O.R.: B: 385.

T32/82   ICI/Control circuit O.J. EPO 1984, 354; [1979–85] E.P.O.R.: B: 426.

T94/82   ICI/Gear crimped yarn O.J. EPO 1984, 75; [1979–85] E.P.O.R.: B: 513.

T119/82   EXXON/Gelation O.J. EPO 1984, 217; [1979–85] E.P.O.R. B: 566.

T128/82   HOFFMAN-LA ROCHE/Pyrrolidine derivatives O.J. EPO 1984, 164; [1979–85] E.P.O.R. B: 591.

T150/82   IFF/Claim categories O.J. EPO 1984, 309; [1979–85] E.P.O.R.: C: 629.

T14/83   SUMITOMO/Vinyl chloride resins O.J. EPO 1984, 105; [1979–85] E.P.O.R.: C: 737.

T206/83   ICI/Pyridine herbicides O.J. EPO 1987, 5; [1986] E.P.O.R. 232.

T13/84   SPERRY/Reformulation of the problem O.J. EPO 1986, 253; [1986] E.P.O.R. 289.

T170/84 BOSSERT KG/Two-part claim O.J. EPO 1986, 400; [1987] E.P.O.R. 82.

T171/84 AIR PRODUCTS/Redox catalyst O.J. EPO 1986, 376; [1986] E.P.O.R. 210.

T237/84 PHILIPS/Reference signs O.J. EPO 1987, 309; [1987] E.P.O.R. 310.

T68/85 CIBA-GEIGY/Synergistic herbicides O.J. EPO 1987, 228; [1987] E.P.O.R. 302.

T99/85 BOEHRINGER/Diagnostic agent O.J. EPO 1987, 413; [1987] E.P.O.R. 337.

T133/85 XEROX/Amendments O.J. EPO 1988, 441; [1989] E.P.O.R. 116.

T139/85 EFAMOL/Pharmaceutical compositions [1987] E.P.O.R. 229.

T150/85 ROMERO-SIERRA August 20, 1987.

T219/85 HAKOUNE/Inadequate description O.J. EPO 1986, 376; [1987] E.P.O.R. 30.

T226/85 UNILEVER/Stable bleaches O.J. EPO 1988, 336; [1989] E.P.O.R. 18.

T248/85 BICC/Radiation processing O.J. EPO 1986, 261; [1986] E.P.O.R. 311.

T292/85 GENENTECH I/Polypeptide expression O.J. EPO 1989, 275; [1989] E.P.O.R. 1.

T281/86 UNILEVER/Preprothaumatin O.J. EPO 1989, 202; [1989] E.P.O.R. 313.

T407/86 FUJITSU/Memory circuit [1988] E.P.O.R. 254.

T51/87 MERCK/Starting compounds O.J. EPO 1991, 177.

T118/87 CPC/Amylolytic enzymes O.J. EPO 1991, 474; [1990] E.P.O.R. 298.

T239/87 NABISCO/Micro-organisms [1988] E.P.O.R. 311.

T301/87 BIOGEN/Alpha-interferons O.J. EPO 1990 335; [1990] E.P.O.R. 190.

T361/87 NABISCO/Micro-organisms June 15, 1988.

T407/87 TOSHIBA/Semiconductor device [1989] E.P.O.R. 470.

T39/88 CPC/Micro-organisms O.J. EPO 1989, 499; [1990] E.P.O.R. 41.

T129/88 AKZO/Fibre O.J. EPO 1993, 598; [1994] E.P.O.R. 176.

T182/88 UNIVERSITY OF CALIFORNIA/Dimeric digopeptides O.J. EPO 1990, 287; [1989] E.P.O.R. 147.

T212/88 BP/Theta-1 O.J. EPO 1992, 28; [1990] E.P.O.R. 518.

T238/88 KODAK/Crown ether O.J. EPO 1992, 709; [1993] E.P.O.R. 100.

T271/88 ICI/Chemical formulae; June 6, 1989.

T182/89 SUMITOMO/Extent of opposition O.J. EPO 1991, 391; [1990] E.P.O.R. 438.

T418/89 ORTHO/Monoclonal antibody O.J. EPO 1993, 70; [1993] E.P.O.R. 338.

T19/90 HARVARD/Onco-mouse O.J. EPO 1990, 476; [1990] E.P.O.R. 501.

T409/91   EXXON/Fuel oils O.J. EPO 1994, 653; [1994] E.P.O.R. 149.
T435/91   UNILEVER/Detergents O.J. EPO 1995, 188; [1995] E.P.O.R.
          314.
T694/91   TEKTRONIX/Schottky barrier diode [1995] E.P.O.R. 384.
T694/92   MYCOGEN/Modifying plant cells O.J. EPO 1997, 408; [1998]
          E.P.O.R. 114.
T939/92   AGREVO/Triazoles O.J. EPO 1996, 309; [1996] E.P.O.R. 171.
T1055/92 AMPEX CORPORATION/Clarity O.J. EPO 1995, 214; [1995]
          E.P.O.R. 469.
T860/93   AQUALON/Protective coating compositions O.J. EPO 1995,
          47; [1995] E.P.O.R. 391.
T20/94   ENICHEM/Amorphous TPM November 4, 1998
T337/95   NIHON NOHYAKU/Lower alkyl O.J. EPO 1996, 628; [1997]
          E.P.O.R. 333.
T227/97   LINDAHL/Protein rib O.J. EPO 1999, 495; [1999] E.P.O.R.
          568.
T450/97   PROCTER & GAMBLE/Shampoo composition O.J. EPO 1999,
          67; [1999] E.P.O.R. 324.
T727/95   WEYERSHAEUSER/Cellulose O.J. EPO 2001, 1.

Decisions of National Courts

American Cyanamid (Dann's) Patent [1970] F.S.R. 443; [1971] R.P.C. 425.
Biogen Inc. v. Medeva plc (House of Lords) [1997] R.P.C. 1.
British Accoustic Films Ltd v. Nettlefold Productions (1936) 53 R.P.C. 221.
Edwards Ltd (A.C.) v. Acme Signs & Displays Ltd [1990] R.P.C. 621.
General Tire and Rubber Co. v. Firestone Tyre and Rubber Co. Ltd [1971]
    F.S.R. 417; [1972] R.P.C. 457.
Technograph Printed Circuits Ltd v. Mills & Rockley (Electronics) Ltd [1972]
    R.P.C. 346.

CHAPTER 8

AMENDMENT OF THE SPECIFICATION

Article 123(2) and (3) EPC; Rule 88 EPC second sentence

Contents

All references are to paragraph numbers

A. Introduction

8–01 The possibility of amending the description, claims and drawings of a patent application or patent, both after filing and after grant, is a matter of great practical importance. The description and claims of an application are commonly originally drafted without full knowledge either of all the prior art which may be used later to challenge its validity, or of all the ways in which the invention may be carried out. The wording of an application as originally drafted may not be as clear as it could be, especially because the draftsman is under pressure to file the application quickly. The information in an application as filed relating to the ways in which the invention can be carried out may not be as complete as it could be. In many circumstances, amendment offers the only possibility of curing invalidity, having regard to previously unknown prior art, for example, or of ensuring that the claims confer legal protection which corresponds to what has been invented and which is of commercial value.

8–02 Nevertheless, since the validity of a European patent is assessed as of its filing date, legal certainty requires that the possibility of amending the substantive contents of an application at any time after its filing date is very restricted. This is reflected in the provisions of Article 123 EPC. In particular, Article 123(2) EPC provides that a European patent application or patent "may not be amended in such a way that it contains subject-matter which extends beyond the content of the application as filed".

Similarly, in accordance with Article 76 EPC a divisional application may be filed having the notional date of filing of the earlier application (see Chapter 2 at paragraph 2–56) but "only in respect of subject-matter which does not extend beyond the content of the earlier application as filed".

Additionally, the extent to which the *claims* of a European patent may be amended *after grant* of the patent is restricted by Article 123(3) EPC, which provides that the claims of a European patent "may not be amended during opposition proceedings in such a way as to extend the protection conferred".

8–03 The prohibition under Article 123(2) EPC is reflected in Articles 100(c) and 138(1)(c) EPC, which respectively set out as a ground of opposition to or revocation of a patent that "the subject-matter of the European patent extends beyond the content of the application as filed, or, if the patent was granted on a divisional application or on a new application filed in accordance with Article 61 EPC, beyond the content of the earlier application as filed". In other words, this ground of opposition or revocation depends upon a finding by an Opposition Division or Board of Appeal in opposition proceedings or by a national court in revocation proceedings, that the application was allowed to be amended before grant in contravention of Article 123(2) EPC (or in the case of a divisional application or new application, that Article 76(1) EPC or Article 61 EPC were contravened, respectively). The effect of a successful opposition under Article 100(c) EPC and of a successful revocation action under Article 38(1)(c) EPC, in respect of a feature added to a claim before grant, in combination with the prohibition under Article 123(3) EPC, is considered in section D below (paragraphs 8–74 *et seq.*: "inescapable trap").

Legal certainty as to the content of the description, claims and drawings of an application following its filing is especially important having regard to the early publication of European patent applications pursuant to Article 93 EPC (see Chapter 1 at paragraph 1–51).

The practice as to the allowability of amendments and corrections to an **8–04** application or patent is governed by Article 123 EPC and Rules 86 to 88 EPC. The procedural aspects of amendment in proceedings before the Examining Divisions (*i.e.* pre-grant), the Opposition Divisions (*i.e.* post-grant) and the Boards of Appeal are considered above in Chapters 2, 3 and 4 respectively. The substantive aspects of amendment will be considered below under the following headings:

(a) Amendments after filing—Article 123(2) EPC;
(b) Amendments after grant—Article 123(3) EPC;
(c) Combination of Article 100(c) (123(2) EPC) and Article 123(3) EPC;
(d) Obvious corrections of errors and mistakes after filing—Rule 88 EPC;
(e) Late-filed or missing drawings.

This chapter is concerned with the substantive aspects of amendment or correction (that is, amendment to the description, claims and drawings), primarily in proceedings before the EPO. The possibility of amendment after grant in national proceedings is not governed by Articles 123(2) and (3) EPC, as such, but by provisions in national laws (which may or may not correspond exactly with the wording of Article 123 EPC). Some cases decided under United Kingdom law are considered below by way of comparison.

In fact, the wording of Article 123(2) EPC is appropriate to cover the whole of the subsequent life of an application or patent, both in proceedings before the EPO and before national courts, and amounts to a general principle prohibiting the addition of subject-matter after filing. The wording of Article 123(3) EPC is specific to "opposition proceedings" before the EPO, however, and leaves room for the possibility of other provisions governing the allowability of amendments in national proceedings.

The main purpose of Article 123(2) and (3) EPC "is to create a fair balance between the interests of applicants and patentees, on the one hand, and competitors and other third parties on the other. The problem . . . is . . . what constitutes such a fair balance in the circumstances of an individual case" (G1/93).[1]

This chapter examines the way in which this problem has been approached when deciding requests for amendment in the context of many individual cases.

---

[1] G1/93 *ADVANCED SEMI-CONDUCTOR PRODUCTS II/Conflicting requirements of Article 123(2) and (3) EPC* O.J. EPO 1994, 541; [1995] E.P.O.R. 97.

It may be mentioned that the requirements for allowability of amendments after filing under Article 123(2) EPC are in some respects analogous to the requirements for claiming priority from an earlier application "in respect of the same invention" under Article 87 EPC (see Chapter 10).

Thus after filing an initial application for a patent in respect of a particular invention in a Member State of the Paris Convention, an applicant may file an application for a European Patent within the Convention year and may wish to change ("amend") the description, claims or drawings as filed with the earlier application for the purposes of the European application. The question under Article 87 EPC is what changes ("amendments") an applicant may make to the specification of the European application without losing the right to priority from the filing date of the earlier application.

Article 123(2) EPC does not allow amendments to the description, claims and drawings as filed with a European application after such filing, which would extend the subject-matter beyond the context of the application as filed, because to do so would prejudice the right to the filing date (or the priority date) of the application.

8–04A According to the proposed revision of the EPC, new Articles 105a, 105b and 105c will be added to the EPC, whereby a patent proprietor may request limitation or revocation of a patent after grant, by means of a centralised procedure at the EPO. As mentioned in Chapter 3 at paragraph 3–11, at present the EPC does not contain any provision which allows a proprietor to initiate centralised proceedings before the EPO in order to request amendment of a granted European patent. Amendment of a European patent after grant is only possible within the context of opposition proceedings initiated by an opponent to grant of the patent (see Chapter 3, in particular at paragraph 3–11).

The new Article 105a EPC will read as follows:

"Request for limitation or revocation.

(1) At the request of the proprietor, the European patent may be revoked or be limited by an amendment of the claims. The request shall be filed with the European Patent Office in accordance with the Implementing Regulations. It shall not be deemed to have been filed until after the limitation or revocation fee has been paid.

(2) The request may not be filed while opposition proceedings in respect of the European patent are pending."

It will be noted that the only kind of limitation which will be permitted in such proceedings is a limitation "by an amendment of the claims".

Related procedure is set out in new Articles 105b and 105c EPC.

B. Amendments After Filing—No Added Subject-matter

Article 123(2) EPC

(1) Extent of applicability

The wording of Article 123(2) EPC (prohibition against added subject- **8–05** matter see paragraph 8–02 above) makes it clear that it applies to any amendment proposed after the initial filing of a European patent application (including a divisional application—see T873/94[2]), and, therefore, both in pre-grant and in post-grant proceedings before the EPO.

Furthermore, the same prohibition applies under Article 76(1) EPC in relation to the allowability of the filing of a divisional application (see Chapter 2 at paragraph 2–61), since the same wording is common to Article 123(2) EPC and Article 76(1) EPC.

(2) "Content of the application as filed": description, claims and drawings

The requirements of Article 78(1) EPC as regards the formal contents of a **8–06** European patent application, and the requirements of Article 80 EPC as regards the minimum contents of an application for a filing date to be allocated, are considered in Chapter 2.

Clearly, a European patent application when filed should include a description of the invention and one or more claims, as well as a request for grant of a patent, and it may also include other documents such as an abstract and/or documents relating to any claim to priority (see Chapter 10), for example a certified copy of an earlier application.

For the purpose of Article 123(2) EPC, the relevant "content of the application as filed" is the substantive content: namely, the description of the invention, the claim(s) and any drawings.

The term "content of the application" used in Article 123(2) EPC relates **8–07** to "the parts of a European patent application which determine the disclosure of the invention, namely the description, claims and drawings …" (G3/89[3])".

This is consistent with earlier decisions referred to below which were specifically concerned with whether the abstract and the priority documents respectively, were part of the content of the application as filed, or could be used to interpret it.

As to drawings, Article 78(1)(d) EPC requires an application to contain "any drawings referred to in the description or claims". However, it would seem that any drawings which are not referred to in the description or claims but which are included in the application documents as filed would be considered as part of the "content of the application as filed" for the

[2] T873/94 TOSHIBA/Amended divisional application O.J. EPO 1997, 456; [1998] E.P.O.R. 71.
[3] G3/89 Correction under Rule 88, second sentence, EPC O.J. EPO 1993, 117; [1993] E.P.O.R. 376.

purpose of Article 123(2) EPC (assuming that they are relevant to the described invention).

(a) Not the abstract

8–08   Article 78(1)(e) requires that an application shall contain an abstract. However, Article 85 EPC states that the abstract "shall merely serve as technical information; it may not be taken into account for any other purpose ...". Consequently, for the purpose of Article 123(2) EPC the content of the application as filed does not include the abstract (T407/86[4]).

> "The abstract is intended solely for documentation purposes and does not form part of the disclosure of the invention. It may not be used to interpret the content of the application for the purposes of Article 123(2) EPC" (T246/86[5]).

(b) Not priority documents

8–09   "It is clear from Article 78(1) EPC in conjunction with Articles 82 to 85 EPC (all in Chapter I of Part III EPC) that the substantive contents of a European patent application are the description and claims together with any drawings.
   As a separate matter, Chapter II of Part III EPC, containing Articles 87 to 89 EPC, concerns the priority of [an application]. From Article 88 and Rule 38 EPC it is clear that the filing of a copy of a previous application is required only for the purpose of claiming priority" (T260/85[6]).

Consequently:

> "for the purpose of Article 123(2) EPC the content of the application as filed does not include any priority documents, even if they were filed on the same day as the European patent application" (T260/85[7]).

8–10   **(i) Comparison with United Kingdom law.** The Patents Court has similarly held that a priority document is not part of an application for a patent, under sections 14 and 15, 1977 U.K. Act. In *Mitsui Engineering and Shipbuilding Ltd's Application*[8] in the context of consideration of a question concerning the requirement to file an English translation of a priority document, the Patents Court held that "the priority document was not one of the documents that made up an application for a patent".
   This judgment was followed by the Patents Court in *VEB Kombinat*

---

[4] T407/86 *FUJITSU/Memory circuit* [1988] E.P.O.R. 254.
[5] T246/86 *BULL/Identification system* O.J. EPO 1989, 199; [1989] E.P.O.R. 344.
[6] T260/85 *AMP/Coaxial connector* O.J. EPO 1989, 199; [1989] E.P.O.R. 403.
[7] *Ibid.*
[8] [1984] R.P.C. 471.

Walzlager and Normteile's Application[9] in the context of consideration of a question concerning whether a drawing filed as part of the priority documents was also a part of the application.

(c) Cross-referenced documents

A description filed with an application may include one or more **8–11** cross-references to other documents (which may or may not have been published before the filing date). Such cross-referenced documents are *prima facie* not part of the "content of the application as filed":

> "Features which are not disclosed in the description of the invention as originally filed but which are only described in a cross-referenced document which is identified in such description are prima facie to within [the content of the application as filed] for the purpose of Article 123(2) EPC" (T689/90[10]).

> "if this were not the case, the content of an application containing in its description numerous references to other documents … would become almost limitless …" (T689/90[11]).

The conditions under which features which are only described in a cross-referenced document may be used as a basis for amendment to the claims of an application are considered in paragraphs 8–37 *et seq.* below.

(3) Basic principles

The question to be considered in the case of any amendment which is **8–12** requested after the filing of an application is whether the amended application or patent "contains subject-matter which extends beyond the content of the application as filed" (Article 123(2) EPC).

Under Article 123(2) EPC:

> "the underlying idea is clearly that an applicant shall not be allowed to improve his position by adding subject-matter not disclosed in the application as filed, which would give him an unwarranted advantage and could be damaging to the legal security of third parties relying on the content of the original application" (G1/93[12]).

As to what is meant by adding subject-matter which would give the applicant an unwarranted advantage, this is explained in the context of amendment by addition of an undisclosed feature to a claim (see paragraphs 8–41 *et seq.* below).

[9] [1987] R.P.C. 405.
[10] T689/90 *RAYCHEM/Event detector* O.J. EPO 1993, 616; [1994] E.P.O.R. 157.
[11] *Ibid.*
[12] G1/93 *ADVANCED SEMI-CONDUCTOR PRODUCTS II/Conflicting requirements of Article 123(2) and (3) EPC* O.J. EPO 1994, 541; [1995] E.P.O.R. 97.

Having regard to the early publication of a European patent application pursuant to Article 93 EPC (Chapter 1 at paragraph 1–51), a further consideration underlying Article 123(2) EPC is that:

> "the reader of such a published application will be informed of the maximum extent of its subject-matter, and therefore its maximum content, sometime before the text of the application (including the claims) is finalised ... The content of the application as filed and as published ... , gives an indication to the public of the protection which may be granted.
> A further consideration underlying the relationship between the claims and the content of a European patent application is that, after appropriate amendment if necessary, the granted claims should give a fair protection for the inventive subject-matter which is contained in the application as filed" (T187/91[13]).

(a) Content of the application: express and implied disclosure

8–13   In the context of Article 123(2) EPC "the content of the application is the totality of the original disclosure; this constitutes, so as to speak, a reservoir from which the applicant can draw when amending the patent application" (T190/83[14]).

However, "the original application should be considered as a reservoir which cannot be expanded after the date of filing" (T133/85[15]).

In this connection, "the content of the application means the total information content of the disclosure. This includes the original statements as to the problem to be solved implying certain aims and effects ..." (T514/88[16]).

Thus the content of the application includes both the information which is expressly disclosed, and information which is implicit in the express disclosure (T151/84,[17] T201/83,[18] Guidelines C.VI.5.4.)

For example, "such content may, by implication, even include the relevant state of the art at the date of filing ..." (T201/83[19]).

(b) Comparison between application as filed and as amended: limited applicability of a "novelty test".

8–14   When determining whether a particular amendment is allowable, it is necessary to compare the total information content (both the express and implied disclosure) of the application as filed with the content of the application as proposed to be amended, and to decide whether the

---

[13] T187/91 *LELAND/Light source* O.J. EPO 1994, 572; [1995] E.P.O.R. 199.
[14] T190/83 *OTTO BOCK/Artificial knee joint*; [1998] E.P.O.R. 272.
[15] T133/85 *XEROX/Amendments* O.J. EPO 1988, 441; [1989] E.P.O.R. 116.
[16] T514/88 *ALZA/Infusor* O.J. EPO 1992, 570; [1990] E.P.O.R. 157.
[17] T151/84 *THOMSON-CSF* [1988] E.P.O.R. 29.
[18] T201/83 *SHELL/Lead alloys* O.J. EPO 1984, 481; [1979–85] E.P.O.R. C: 905.
[19] *Ibid.*

amended application contains "added subject-matter" over the content of the application as filed. Consequently, at least in some cases a simple kind of "novelty test" can be applied. If there is no new information in the application as proposed to be amended, so that the application as amended is "not new" compared to the application as filed, the application is allowable.

Such a novelty test must be applied with considerable caution, however, because as explained below with reference to decided cases, in various circumstances a novelty test is not properly applicable in order to determine allowability of a requested amendment.

(1)   "the test for compliance with Article 123(2) EPC is basically a novelty   **8–15**
       test, *i.e.* no new subject-matter must be generated by the amendment.
       Normally, the test for novelty calls for an inquiry whether or not a
       document ... contains sufficient information so that the person
       skilled in the art could derive the subject-matter directly and
       unambiguously, including any features implicit therein ... the
       requirement is not satisfied unless the skilled man could directly
       recognise [the proposed amendments] as a combination of features
       available from the document" (T201/83[20]).

(2)   The considerations in relation to a proposed amendment "are   **8–16**
       basically similar to those ... involved in relation to ... novelty", but
       "care is necessary when applying the law relating to novelty" to
       consideration of proposed amendments, since it is the words of
       Article 123(2) EPC "which must ultimately always be considered in
       each particular case" (T133/85[21]).

(3)   In particular, in the context of a request for amendment involving the   **8–17**
       generalisation of a particular feature of the claims as filed ("natural
       cellulose fibres" to be amended to "cellulose fibres"—the request
       was refused:

> "The ... argument that the original application could properly be cited
> against the novelty of a more generic claim to cellulose fibres, is based
> on incorrect application of the novelty test for allowability of an
> amendment. Otherwise it would follow that amendments involving a
> generalisation or the omission of a feature would always be allowable.
> The test for additional subject-matter corresponds to the test for
> novelty only insofar as both require assessment of whether or not
> information is directly and unambiguously derivable from that
> previously presented, in the originally filed application or in a prior
> document respectively. It follows that an amendment is not allowable
> if the resulting change in content of the application, in other words the
> subject-matter generated by the amendment, is novel when compared
> with the content of the original application or, looked at another way,

[20] *Ibid.*
[21] T133/85 *XEROX/Amendments* O.J. EPO 1988, 441; [1989] E.P.O.R. 116.

if the said change in content would be novelty-destroying for a hypothetical future claim when the original content would not be. It is important that it is the change in content which is tested, that is, the amended content minus the original content, so that the test is applicable also to amendment by generalisation or omission of a feature" (T194/84[22]).

(4) In the context of a request for amendment involving the addition of an undisclosed limiting feature to a claim:

"Where a proposal for amendment of an application involves the addition of a limiting feature to a claim, application of a 'novelty test' is not appropriate to determine whether or not the amendment complies with Article 123(2) EPC, because as explained in G1/93,[23] 'Whether or not the adding of an undisclosed feature limiting the scope of protection ... would be contrary to the purpose of Article 123(2) ... depends on the circumstances' (T873/94[24]: see also paragraphs 8–41 *et seq.* below)."

8–18   (5) The relationship of the novelty test to the question of "essentiality" is considered in paragraphs 8–26 *et seq.* below.

8–19   (6) The application of the novelty test to an amendment by generalisation is considered in paragraphs 8–29 *et seq.* below.

(c) Relationship between amendment and novelty

8–20   There is obviously no exact correspondence between the requirement of Article 123(2) EPC and the requirement for novelty having regard to a prior document, as defined in Article 54(2) EPC ("made available to the public"—see Chapter 10). The wording of the novelty requirement under Article 54 EPC is clearly different from the requirement for an allowable amendment under Article 123(2) EPC, and different considerations underlie Articles 54 and 123(2) EPC. What the two requirements do have in common is the necessity in each case to determine the content (or *disclosure*) of one or more documents. In the case of amendment, the disclosure of both the application as filed and the application as proposed to be amended must be determined, prior to assessing whether such content of the application as filed is extended by the amendment. In the case of novelty, the content or disclosure of a prior published document must be determined prior to assessing the novelty of a claimed invention.

A further important aspect of the relationship between amendment and novelty is that in principle, having regard to the requirement of Article 123(2) EPC that an amendment which adds subject-matter to the content of

[22] T194/84 *GENERAL MOTOR/Zinc electrodes* O.J. EPO 1990, 59; [1989] E.P.O.R. 351.
[23] G1/93 *ADVANCED SEMI-CONDUCTOR PRODUCTS II/Conflicting requirements of Article 123(2) and (3) EPC* O.J. EPO 1994, 541; [1995] E.P.O.R. 97.
[24] T873/94 *TOSHIBA/Amended divisional application* O.J. EPO 1997, 456; [1998] E.P.O.R. 71.

the application as filed is not allowable, it should not be possible for an application to be amended after filing in such a way that the "state of the art" within the meaning of Article 54(2) and (3) EPC is enlarged. Thus in particular, a subsequently claimed invention which was novel having regard to an earlier application as filed should not be deprived of novelty as a result of that application being amended after filing (T194/84[25]: paragraph 8–17 above).

Furthermore, in relation to the assessment of both novelty of a claimed invention (Article 54 EPC) and allowability of a proposed amendment (Article 123 (2) EPC) it is necessary to distinguish carefully between the content or disclosure (both express and implied) of a document, on the one hand, and what may be obvious to a skilled person having regard to the content or disclosure of the document, on the other hand. This distinction is considered and discussed in Chapter 10 in the context of the determination of novelty, and is considered below in the context of the determination of allowable amendments.

(4) Claim broadening before grant

(a) When permissible

It quite frequently happens that an application as filed contains a main **8–21** claim or claims which include one or more features which are recognised by the applicant after filing as unduly restricting the extent of protection conferred by such claims, having regard to the inventive subject-matter of the application. The applicant then wishes to broaden the protection conferred by such claims. In principle, claim broadening may be achieved in two ways:

  (a) deletion of one or more features;
  (b) replacement of a feature by a more generalised feature.

The deletion or generalisation of a feature in a claim is not in principle prohibited by Article 123(2) EPC. What matters is whether the claimed subject-matter after the amendment, whether by deletion or generalisation, extends beyond the content of the application as filed.

> "If a technical feature is deleted from a claim ... the broadening of the claim does not contravene Article 123(2) EPC as long as there is a basis for a claim lacking this feature in the application as filed. It is immaterial whether or not the feature in question is relevant to the inventive concept of the claimed subject-matter" (T66/85[26]).

Similarly: **8–22**

---

[25] T194/84 *GENERAL MOTORS/Zinc electrodes* O.J. EPO 1990, 59; [1989] E.P.O.R. 351.
[26] T66/85 *AMP/Connector* O.J. EPO 1989, 167; [1989] E.P.O.R. 283.

"it is possible without contravening Article 123(2) EPC to broaden a claim (*i.e.* to extend the protection conferred by it) provided that the subject-matter which is within the claims for the first time as a result of the amendment was alrady disclosed within the content of the original application as filed" (T133/85[27]).

Furthermore:

"The deletion of a feature in a claim is admissible if the sole purpose of such deletion is to clarify and/or resolve an inconsistency" (T172/82[28]).

The feature in question was shown in a drawing but not explained further in the description, and it was considered to be quite clear to a skilled reader that the presence of the feature was without importance for carrying out the invention and possibly inconsistent with it, in the technical context.

In other words, the claimed subject-matter without the deleted feature was considered to have been implicitly disclosed in the application as filed.

Further examples:

8–23   (1) The main claim as filed required "a plurality of light sources" (*i.e.* more than one) whereas the amended claim required "one or more light sources". In connection with the preferred embodiment which included three light sources, the description stated that "more or less light sources" could be used. The amendment was allowable because "there is no reason to regard the use of a plurality of light sources as essential to the invention in order to achieve its stated aims" (T187/91[29]).

"A specific example within a generic disclosure forming part of the description of the invention in an application as filed is part of the content of the application as filed for the purpose of Article 123(2) EPC if the skilled reader would seriously contemplate such specific example as a possible practical embodiment of the described invention, having regard to its context in the remainder of the application as filed, and subject to any understanding of the skilled reader to the contrary" (T187/91[30]).

Thus, what a skilled person would "seriously contemplate" within a generic disclosure may be considered as part of the implied disclosure or content of the application.

Comparison may be made in this case with cases relating to novelty having regard to a generic disclosure (Chapter 11 at paragraph 11–78).

8–24   (2) "The removal from a claim of a feature which 'does not provide a technical contribution to the subject-matter of the claimed invention'

---

[27] T133/85 *XEROX/Amendments* O.J. EPO 1988, 441; [1989] E.P.O.R. 116.
[28] T172/82 *CONTRAVES/Particle analyser* O.J. EPO 1983, 493; [1979–85] E.P.O.R.: C: 68.
[29] T187/91 *LELAND/Light source* O.J. EPO 1994, 572; [1995] E.P.O.R. 199.
[30] *Ibid.*

within the meaning of ... G1/93,[31] and which merely broadens the protection conferred by the claim, does not contravene Article 123(2) EPC" (T802/92[32]). (See also G1/93[33], paragraph 8–41 below.)

Such a case can be considered as one in which the claimed subject-matter without the deleted feature was within the implied disclosure or content of the application as filed.

(3) The application as filed disclosed a method for producing an effect **8–25** and a program corresponding to such method, and also implicitly disclosed a programmable apparatus by reference to a prior art document:

> "such an apparatus when suitably programmed for carrying out the method for producing said particular effect is considered as disclosed in the application as filed ...
>
> However, it is only this specific combination which is disclosed and not an apparatus being also suitable for carrying out other methods or for producing other effects" (T784/89[34]).

(b) Deletion of an essential feature not allowable

> "It is not permissible to delete from an independent claim a feature **8–26** which the application as originally filed consistently presents as being an essential feature of the invention, since this would constitute a violation of Article 123(2) EPC" (T260/85[35]).

In particular:

> "While it is true that under Article 123(2) EPC it is permissible to extend the scope of protection before grant, this is only possible within the content of the application as filed. In the present case, the application as originally filed contains no disclosure, express or implied, that the air space could be omitted. On the contrary, the reasons for its presence ... are given repeatedly" (T260/85[36]).

Furthermore, with reference to evidence filed by an expert witness:

> "There is nothing in the application as filed to suggest that the air space could be omitted. The fact that this particular expert could see that the air space was not essential for the function of the spring fingers does not mean that the application as filed discloses or implies that it could be omitted. It merely means that the expert had sufficient

---

[31] G1/93 *ADVANCED SEMI CONDUCTOR PRODUCTS/Conflicting requirements of Article 123(2) and (3) EPC* O.J. EPO 1993, 125; [1995] E.P.O.R. 97.
[32] T802/92 *COLORADO/Photovoltaic cell* O.J. EPO 1995, 379; [1996] E.P.O.R. 125.
[33] See note 31.
[34] T784/89 *GENERAL ELECTRIC/Disclosure of computer-related apparatus* O.J. EPO 1992, 438; [1992] E.P.O.R. 446.
[35] T260/85 *AMP/Coaxial connector* O.J. EPO 1989, 199; [1989] E.P.O.R. 403.
[36] *Ibid.*

imagination to conceive his own modifications of the disclosure, beyond the content of the application as originally filed" (T260/85[37]).

There is therefore a clear distinction between the (express and implied) disclosure or content of the application as filed, and what may be obvious to a skilled person having regard to such disclosure or content.

8–27 (1) When determining whether a feature is essential:

"The significance of a feature can only be assessed in the light of the application documents as a whole and in particular by taking into consideration the technical problem of the invention inferable from them. So if an application, for whatever reasons, originally clearly discloses an invention as a combination of features solving a particular problem, then one of those features, without which the problem can no longer be solved, cannot be regarded as obviously inessential to the original disclosure" (T401/88[38]).

8–28 (2) In relation to the "novelty test":

"... the considerations ... in relation to the question of broadening before grant by abandoning a feature, *i.e.* the test for essentiality (or inessentiality) on the one hand, and the novelty test on the other, are not contradictory but represent the same principle. In both cases, the relevant question is whether the amendment is consistent with the original disclosure.

... This means direct and unambiguous derivability from and no contradiction to the totality of the original disclosure. There should be such basis for the broadened claim in the original (or parent) application ... The basis need not be presented in express terms but it must be sufficiently clear to a person skilled in the art to be directly and unambiguously recognisable as such and not of a vague and general character" (T514/88[39]).

Furthermore:

"the omission of a feature and thereby the broadening of the scope of the claim may be permissible provided the skilled person could recognise that the problem-solving effect could still be obtained without it ... As to the critical question of essentiality in this respect, this is a matter of given feasibility of removal or replacement, as well as the manner of disclosure by the applicant" (T514/88[40]).

In particular:

[37] *Ibid.*
[38] T401/88 *BOSCH/Test piece* O.J. EPO 1990, 297; [1990] E.P.O.R. 640.
[39] T514/88 *ALZA/Infuser* O.J. EPO 1992, 570; [1990] E.P.O.R. 157.
[40] *Ibid.*

"the replacement or removal of a feature from a claim may not violate Article 123(2) EPC provided the skilled person would directly and unambiguously recognise that:

(1) the feature was not explained as essential in the disclosure,
(2) it is not, as such, indispensable for the function of the invention in the light of the technical problem it serves to solve, and
(3) the replacement or removal requires no real modification of other features to compensate for the change ... The feature in question may be inessential even if it was incidentally but consistently presented in combination with other features of the invention" (T331/87[41]).

(c) Generalisation of a claimed feature

The allowability of an amendment by which a particular feature in a claim **8–29** is generalised also depends upon the application of the principles discussed above, because such generalisation has the same effect as removal of a feature, namely broadening of the claim.

In principle, an amendment "which replaces a disclosed specified feature either by its function or by a more general term and thus incorporates undisclosed equivalents into the content of the application as filed" contravenes Article 123(2) EPC an is not allowable (T284/94[42]).

Examples of particular cases:

(1) The proposed amendment to the preamble to the claim was to change **8–30** the feature "rotatable disc" to "carrier". The amendment was allowed on the basis that the preamble of the claim was derived from a patent specification referred to in the description, which disclosed no rotatable disc, but a pivotal arm having a similar function. Thus:

"in the original document, a skilled person would not find any indication that it is of importance for the solution of the problem stated in the description to replace the pivotable arm ... by a rotatable disc ... he would understand immediately that the configuration of the carrier was of no consequence" (T52/82[43]).

(2) A proposed amendment consisting of the replacement of a described **8–31** specific aperture structure by its function was refused because:

"replacing a disclosed specific feature by a broad general expression constitutes an amendment inadmissible under Article 123(2) EPC where use of such a general expression for the first time explicitly associates with the subject-matter of the application specific features going beyond the initial disclosure" (T416/86[44]).

---

[41] T331/87 HOUDAILLE/*Removal of feature* O.J. EPO 1991, 22; [1991] E.P.O.R. 194.
[42] T284/94 PITNEY BOWES/*Electronic postage meter* O.J. EPO 1999, 464.
[43] T52/82 RIETER/*Winding apparatus* O.J. EPO 1983, 416; [1979–85] E.P.O.R.: B: 459.
[44] T416/86 BOEHRINGER/*Reflection photometer* O.J. EPO 1989, 308; [1989] E.P.O.R. 327.

8–32   (3) Similarly, a generalisation of the term "sealing bead" into the term "pressure seals" was refused by application of the "novelty test":

> "The amendment 'pressure seals' includes all the equivalents of the disclosed specific means 'sealing beads' into the content of the application, that is, subject-matter which is novel with regard to the application as filed. Hence, said amendment contradicts Article 123(2) EPC as a result of the novelty test" (T265/88[45]).

(5) Claim narrowing

(a) Claim narrowing before grant: danger of the "inescapable trap"

8–33   The basic principles which are applicable to claim narrowing are of course the same as those which apply to claim broadening before grant. There can be no extension of subject-matter beyond the content of the application as filed. However, there is in practice an important distinction between these two types of amendment, which relates to the legal consequences if an amendment is allowed during examination proceedings before grant, but is subsequently attacked during opposition proceedings under Article 100(c) EPC and is held not to have been allowable in such post-grant opposition proceedings.

The legal consequences in such a situation follow from Article 123(3) EPC, which prohibits amendments during opposition proceedings which "extend the protection conferred" (see paragraph 8–59). If, during opposition proceedings, claim narrowing amendments are held to have been wrongly allowed before grant, the claims cannot be re-amended so as to broaden the claims during such opposition proceedings after grant, and the patent has therefore to be revoked (an "inescapable trap"—see paragraphs 8–73 *et seq.* below).

The important point to be made at the outset of the following discussion of amendments which narrow the claims is therefore that it is potentially dangerous for an applicant to apply for claim narrowing amendments before grant which are not clearly allowable under Article 123(2) EPC, having regard to the existence of this inescapable trap (which is provided by the combination of Articles 100(c) and 123(2) and (3) EPC).

(b) Addition of a disclosed feature to a claim

8–34   In principle, if a feature, which is disclosed in the application as filed is to be added to a claim, the combination of features including the additional feature must have been disclosed in the application as filed, in the sense that such new claimed combination must not present information which was not disclosed in the application as filed.

Thus:

> "An objection does not necessarily arise when an amendment is

[45] T265/88 *LUNDIA/Diffusion device* [1990] E.P.O.R. 399.

proposed which involves combining separate features of the original subject-matter of an application. When considering whether different parts of the description ... may properly be read together, the state of the art may also be taken into account" (T54/82[46]).

"A technical feature taken in isolation from the application as filed can ... be introduced into a claim if the application as filed unmistakenly shows that the combination of technical features in the new claim ... is sufficient to produce the result sought in the application" (T17/86[47]).

Similarly: 8–35

"An amendment of a claim by the introduction of a technical feature taken in isolation from the description of a specific embodiment is not allowable under Article 123(2) EPC if it is not clear beyond any doubt for a skilled reader from the application documents as filed that the subject-matter of the claim thus amended provides a complete solution to a technical problem unambiguously recognisable from the application" (T284/94[48]).

"It is necessary to examine, in order to satisfy all the requirements under Article 123(2) EPC, whether undisclosed combinations of disclosed features are brought into the application as a result of the amendment. This is perfectly possible, particularly when features are omitted from a claim and others are added. The novelty test is helpful in deciding this point: if the original application had been published would it have to be prejudicial to the novelty of the amended claims in their entirety" (T190/83[49]).

However: "it is possible that features originally described as optional become essential in the sense that they are necessary to delimit the invention from the prior art". Thus:

"Whereas ... the deletion from a claim of features consistently described as essential is not permissible under Article 123(2) EPC [paragraphs 8–26 et seq. above], the converse is not true, so that any attempt to interpret Article 123(2) EPC in the sense that the introduction into a claim of features previously described as inessential would not be permissible, must fail" (T583/93[50]).

[46] T54/82 MOBIL/Disclosure O.J. EPO 1983, 446; [1979–85] E.P.O.R.: B: 469.
[47] T17/86 SATAM BRANDT/Refrigeration plant O.J. EPO 1989, 297; [1989] E.P.O.R. 347.
[48] T284/94 PITNEY BOWES/Electronic postage meter O.J. EPO 1999, 464.
[49] T190/83 OTTO BOCK/Artificial knee joint [1998] E.P.O.R. 272.
[50] T583/93 HYMO CORPORATION/Water-soluble polymer dispersion O.J. EPO 1996, 496; [1997] E.P.O.R. 129.

8–36   A claimed invention related to the improvement of prior art originally cited in the description. It was proposed to add a feature to the preamble of the claim. In this circumstance:

> "a feature [an activated support for a catalyst] described in broad terms in the cited document but not mentioned expressly in the invention is sufficiently disclosed if it is realised in the examples of the invention in the form of an embodiment also mentioned in the [cited] document [*i.e.* activation by grinding]" (T288/84[51]).

In contrast, a feature sought to be added was a "negative" feature (*i.e.* "with no internal fittings"). The only possible basis for this addition was the fact that the drawings of the apparatus which was the subject of the claims showed no internal fittings. The drawing in question was considered to be only schematic; thus "the mere absence of [the feature] ... does not make it unequivocally inferable that such a feature is to be excluded." The amendment was refused (T170/87[52]).

(c) Addition of a feature from a cross-referenced document

8–37   As explained in paragraph 8–11 above with reference to T689/90,[53] features which are only described in a cross-referenced document which is identified in the description are regarded as *prima facie* not within the content of the application as filed for the purpose of Article 123(2) EPC. In certain limited circumstances, however, it may be possible to introduce a feature from a cross-referenced document into the claims of an application.
There are two aspects to be considered:

(i) Sufficient identification of the cross-referenced document;
(ii) The conditions when amendment is allowable.

8–38   **(i) Identification of the cross-referenced document.** In the context that a cross-referenced document relates to the disclosure of the invention for the purpose of carrying it out (Article 83 EPC), the Guidelines require that the cross-reference must be in the application as filed and must clearly identify the document so that it can easily be retrieved. In particular, if the document was not available to the public at the filing date of the application it can only be taken into account if:

(1) a copy of the document was filed at the EPO on or before the filing date;
(2) the document was made available to the public no later than the date of publication of the application.

[51] T288/84 *STAMICARBON/Activated support* O.J. EPO 1986, 128; [1986] E.P.O.R. 217.
[52] T170/87 *SULZER/Hot gas cooler* O.J. EPO 1989, 441; [1990] E.P.O.R. 14.
[53] T689/90 *RAYCHEM/Event detector* O.J. EPO 1993, 616; [1994] E.P.O.R. 157.

These requirements are also applicable to a cross-referenced document which describes a feature which is proposed to be included in a claim by way of amendment (T689/90[54]).

Whether or not a cross-referenced document can be clearly identified and easily retrieved depends upon the facts of each case. If such is the case, a request to supplement a cross-reference to a document by the addition of its publication number is allowable under Article 123(2) EPC (T737/90[55]).

(ii) **The conditions when amendment is allowable.** Features of an **8–39** invention which are disclosed in a prior published cross referenced document:

> "may be incorporated into a patent claim if they unequivocably form part of the invention for which protection is sought. However, all the essential structural features thus disclosed which belong together must be incoporated into the claim. It is not permissible to single out a particular one of their number" (T6/84[56]).

In such a case the added features were already implicitly present in the claim (T689/90[57]).

Additional features which are only disclosed in a cross-referenced **8–40** document can be introduced by way of amendment into the claims of an application in the following circumstances, namely:

> "if the description of the invention as filed leaves no doubt to a skilled reader:
> (a) that protection is or may be sought for such features;
> (b) that such features contribute to achieving the technical aim of the invention and are thus comprised in the solution of the technical problem underlying the invention which is the subject of the application;
> (c) that such features implicitly clearly belong to the description of the invention contained in the application as filed (Article 78(1)(b) EPC) and thus to the content of the application as filed (Article 123(2) EPC);
> (d) that such features are precisely defined and identifiable within the total technical information within the reference document" (T689/90[58]).

For example, where the cross-referenced document is a prior art document:

> "When a patent application as filed discloses explicitly a method for

---

[54] T689/90 RAYCHEM/Event detector O.J. EPO 1993, 616; [1994] E.P.O.R. 157.
[55] T737/90 GENERAL ELECTRIC/Missing publication number September 9, 1993.
[56] T6/84 MOBIL/Amendment of claims O.J. EPO 1985, 238; [1979–85] E.P.O.R. C: 924.
[57] See note 54.
[58] See note 54.

producing a particular effect and a plurality of mathematical expressions and pulse sequences corresponding to a suitable program, and when it also discloses implicitly a programmable apparatus by reference to a prior art document, such an apparatus when suitably programmed for carrying out the method for producing said particular effect is ... disclosed in the application as filed ...
However, it is only this specific combination which is disclosed ..."
(T784/89[59]).

(d) Addition of an undisclosed feature: "mere disclaimer" with no technical contribution to the invention

8–41   As discussed in paragraphs 8–13 *et seq.* above, normally a feature can only be added to a claim if such feature has been expressly or implicitly disclosed in the application as filed. Exceptionally, however, as explained in G1/93[60] in the context of its consideration of the "inescapable trap" provided by the context of Article 123(2) EPC (see paragraph 8–73 below), an undisclosed feature may be added to a claim, provided that the effect of this addition is merely to limit the protection conferred by the claim, and the additional feature does not provide a "technical contribution to the invention":

> "Whether or not the adding of an undisclosed feature limiting the scope of protection conferred by the patent as granted would be contrary to the purpose of Article 123(2) EPC to prevent an applicant from getting an unwarranted advantage by obtaining patent protection for something he had not properly disclosed and may be not even invented on the date of filing of the application, depends on the circumstances. If such added feature, although limiting the scope of protection conferred by the patent, has to be considered as providing a technical contribution to the subject-matter of the claimed invention, it would in the view of the Enlarged Board, give an unwarranted advantage to the patentee contrary to the above purpose of Article 123(2) EPC. Consequently, such feature would constitute added subject-matter in the sense of that provision. A typical example of this seems to be the case, where the limiting feature is creating an inventive selection not disclosed in the application as filed or otherwise derivable therefrom. If, on the other hand, the feature in question merely excludes protection for part of the subject-matter of the claimed invention as covered by the application as filed, the adding of such feature cannot reasonably be considered to give any unwarranted advantage to the applicant. Nor does it adversely affect the interests of third parties. ..." (G1/93[61]).

[59] T784/89 *GENERAL ELECTRIC/Disclosure* O.J. EPO 1992, 438; [1992] E.P.O.R. 446.
[60] G1/93 *ADVANCED SEMICONDUCTOR PRODUCTS/Conflicting requirements of Article 123(2) and (3) EPC* O.J. EPO 1993, 125; [1995] E.P.O.R. 97.
[61] *Ibid.*

Consequently:

"A feature which has not been disclosed in the application as filed but which has been added to the application during examination and which, without providing a technical contribution to the subject-matter of the claimed invention, merely limits the protection conferred by the patent as granted by excluding protection for part of the subject-matter of the claimed invention as covered by the application as filed, is not to be considered as subject-matter which extends beyond the content of the application as filed in the sense of Article 123(2) EPC" (G1/93[62]).

Thus a distinction is clearly made between "the adding of an undis- **8–42** closed feature" (*i.e.* a feature which was not disclosed in the application as filed) which provides a technical contribution to the subject-matter of the claimed invention (not allowable in accordance with basic principles) and the addition of an undisclosed feature which provides no such technical contribution, but which merely limits the extent of protection conferred by the claim (allowable). This distinction is of considerable importance.

In relation to what is meant by an undisclosed feature which, "without providing a technical contribution to the subject-matter of the claimed invention merely limits the protection conferred ...":

"the assessment whether such an added feature is allowable 'should only rely on the technical relationship of the added feature with the content of the application as originally filed, as understood by a skilled reader'" and
"A feature should not be considered as merely limiting the protection conferred by the granted patent without providing a technical contribution to the invention as claimed, if it interacts with the remaining features of the claim in such terms that it influences the solution of the technical problem which can be understood from the application as originally filed" (T384/91[63]).

(e) Specific disclaimers

The circumstances in which such a disclaimer is allowable have been **8–43** defined as follows:

(1) This method of disclaimer can only be used "if the subject-matter remaining in the claim cannot be defined more clearly and concisely directly, *i.e.* by positive features (Article 84 EPC)" (T4/80[64]);
(2) This method may be used:

[62] *Ibid.*
[63] T384/91 *ADVANCED SEMI-CONDUCTOR PRODUCTS/"Conflict" between Article 123(2) and (3) EPC* O.J. EPO 1995, 745; [1996] E.P.O.R. 125.
[64] T4/80 *BAYER/Polyether polyols* O.J. EPO 1982, 149; [1979–85] E.P.O.R.: B: 260.

(a) to avoid loss of novelty (*e.g.* T4/80[65], T433/86[66], T597/92[67]);
(b) to avoid insufficiency (*e.g.* T313/86[68]) even if there is no specific basis for such an exclusion in the application as filed (see T170/87[69]).

(3) However, this method may not be used to create an inventive step:

"A disclaimer can be used to make an inventive teaching which overlaps with the prior state of the art novel but it cannot make an obvious teaching inventive" (T170/87[70]: T597/92[71]).

(4) Furthermore, there must be a specific reason for such a disclaimer. "A hypothetical novelty attack in possible proceedings before a national court ... is not a sufficient reason under the EPC for allowing a disclaimer" (T597/92[72]).

In this context, an amendment by way of a disclaimer in a claim is constituted by a statement in the claim whose effect is to subtract certain specified embodiments from the more general definition of the scope of the claim.

(f) Clarification and correction of a claim

8–44 (1) "An amendment to a claim to clarify an inconsistency does not contravene Article 123(2) EPC, if the amended claim has the same meaning as the unamended claim on its true construction in the context of the specification" (T271/84[73]).

8–45 (2) The correction of an erroneous calculation in a claim if percentage rates for components of a composition did not add up to 100 per cent is allowable:

"if the amendment would be regarded by the skilled reader as clearly implied by the disclosure of the application as filed. If more than one arithmetic possibility of correction can be envisaged, the correction must be the one which the application as a whole clearly implies" (T13/83[74]).

8–46 (3) The correction of an incorrect structural chemical formula of a substance in a claim, which is not an "obvious mistake" within the

---

[65] *Ibid.*
[66] T433/86 *ICI/Modified diisocyanates* [1988] E.P.O.R. 97.
[67] T597/92 *BLASCHIM/Rearrangement reaction* O.J. EPO 1996, 135; [1996] E.P.O.R. 456.
[68] T313/86 *CHEMISCHE WERKE* January 12, 1988.
[69] T170/87 *SULZER/Hot-gas cooler* O.J. EPO 1989, 441; [1990] E.P.O.R. 14.
[70] *Ibid.*
[71] See note 67.
[72] See note 67.
[73] T271/84 *AIR PRODUCTS/Removal of hydrogen sulphide and carnonyl sulphide* O.J. EPO 1987, 405; [1987] E.P.O.R. 23.
[74] T13/83 *ICI AMERICAS/Polyisocyanurates* O.J. EPO 1984, 428; [1979–85] E.P.O.R.: C: 732.

meaning of Rule 88 EPC (see paragraphs 8–80 *et seq.* below), cannot be corrected under Article 123(2) EPC.

However, if the application as filed unambiguously identifies the substance by other means, an appropriate claim may be formulated. In particular, if the application as filed discloses a method of producing the substance, a "product-by-process" claim defining the substance may be added, provided it contains *all* the process parameters which unambiguously define the substance as the inevitable result of the process (T552/91[75]).

(4) Amendment of the preamble to a claim in order to identify features **8–47** belonging to the closest prior art may be necessary in order to comply with Rule 29(1) EPC and is allowable under Article 123(2) EPC (T13/84[76]).

Similarly, a change in position of a feature from the preamble of a claim to the characterising portion is allowable in so far as it does not alter the meaning of the claim (T16/86[77]).

(6) Amendment of the description

(a) Addition of reference to prior art

The addition of a reference to prior art is allowable, and the addition of a **8–48** discussion of the advantages of the invention with reference to such prior art may be allowable depending upon the language used and the circumstances of the case (T11/82[78]).

(b) Clarification and additional explanation

The effect of a claimed feature may be clarified and explained if it can be **8–49** deduced by a skilled person from the application as filed (T37/82[79]).

(7) Relationship between Article 123(2) EPC and Article 84 EPC

If an amendment to the description or claims is proposed, the application **8–50** must be examined to ensure that the requirements of both Article 123(2) EPC and Article 84 EPC are met. An amendment may be allowable under Article 123(2) EPC but not allowable under Article 84 EPC (T133/85[80]).

(8) Amendments after filing: comparison with United Kingdom law
Section 76, 1977 U.K. Act

(a) Introduction

Section 76(2) 1977 U.K. Act provides that "No amendment of an appli- **8–51** cation for a patent shall be allowed ... if it results in the application

---

[75] T552/91 *MERCK/Chroman derivatives* O.J. EPO 1995, 100; [1995] E.P.O.R. 455.
[76] T13/84 *SPERRY/Reformulation of the problem* O.J. EPO 1986, 253; [1986] E.P.O.R. 289.
[77] T16/86 *THETFORD* February 4, 1988.
[78] T11/82 *LANSING BAGNALL/Control circuit* O.J. EPO 1983, 479; [1979–85] E.P.O.R.: B: 385.
[79] T37/82 *SIEMENS/Low-tension switch* O.J. EPO 1984, 71; [1979–85] E.P.O.R.: B: 437.
[80] T133/85 *XEROX/Amendments* O.J. EPO 1988, 441; [1989] E.P.O.R. 116.

disclosing matter extending beyond that disclosed in the application as filed." This section governs applications filed at the United Kingdom Patent Office, and is of similar effect as Article 123(2) EPC.

Section 76(3)(a) 1977 U.K. Act provides that "No amendment of the specification of a patent shall be allowed . . . , if it results in the specification disclosing addition matter." This section governs both United Kingdom patents and European patents (U.K.), the latter by virtue of section 77, 1977 U.K. Act. Again it seems that this section is of similar effect (after grant) as Article 123(2) EPC.

8–52　Furthermore, Section 72(1)(d) 1977 U.K. Act sets out a ground of revocation corresponding to Article 100(c) EPC, namely that "the matter disclosed in the specification of the patent extends beyond that disclosed in the application for the patent, as filed . . .".

Section 130(3) 1977 U.K. Act provides that "matter shall be taken to have been disclosed in any relevant application. . . , or in the specification of a patent if it was either claimed or disclosed (otherwise than by way of disclaimer or acknowledgment of prior art) in that application or specification".

Section 76 is not listed in section 130(7) of the 1977 U.K. Act as having been "framed so as to have . . . the same effects as the corresponding provisions of the EPC".

(b) Basic principles

8–53　The effect of section 76 was explained by the Patents Court in *Southco Inc. v. Dzus Fastener Europe Ltd*[81] as follows:

> "prior to grant the width of the claims can be extended but not thereafter, and in neither case is it permissible to make any amendment which has the result of the application or specification disclosing any matter which extends beyond that disclosed in the application as filed".

After referring to two previous cases (*Raychem Ltd's Application*[82] and *Re Harding's Patent*[83]), the Court stated that:

> "when amendment has been made pre-grant it is not material whether that amendment has the effect of widening or narrowing the monopoly claimed. The Act contemplates that amendments to claims will be made and therefore the ambit of the claim will be altered. What the Act is seeking to prevent is a patentee altering his claims in such a way that they claim a different invention from that which is disclosed in the application. Thus, provided the invention in the amended claim

---

[81] [1990] R.P.C. 587.
[82] [1986] R.P.C. 547.
[83] [1988] R.P.C. 515.

is disclosed in the application when read as a whole, it will not offend against section 76."

(i) Content of the application. The effect of section 130(3) 1977 U.K. Act 8–54 was considered in "*Southco*[84]". The word "matter" was considered to be "wide enough to cover both structural features and inventive concepts".

In *A. C. Edwards Ltd v. Acme Signs and Displays Ltd*[85] the Patents Court considered the effect of section 130(3) 1977 U.K. Act in greater depth, in relation to the disclosure of claims. Section 130(3) has no counterpart in this context in the EPC. The Court held that it was right "to take into account the different purpose of the claims and the specification...". Section 130(3) required "the claims to be considered as a separate disclosure to that of the specification, but a disclosure of the matter for which protection is sought but not a description of the invention". Thus, it was emphasised that:

"Not everything within a claim is disclosed, although it may fall within the ambit of the claim"; and:

"The fact that a claim is broad enough to cover a feature does not mean that it is disclosed."

(ii) Total information content: express and implied disclosure: com- 8–55 **parison between application as filed and as amended.** In *Bonzel v.* 8–56 *Intervention* (No. 3),[86] the Patents Court held that:

> "The decision as to whether there was an extension of disclosure must be made on a comparison of the two documents read through the eyes of a skilled addressee.
> The task of the court is threefold:
>
> (1) To ascertain through the eyes of the skilled addressee what is disclosed, both explicitly and implicitly in the application.
> (2) To do the same in respect of the patent as granted.
> (3) To compare the two disclosures and decide whether any subject-matter relevant to the invention has been added whether by deletion or addition. The comparison is strict in the sense that subject-matter will be added unless such matter is clearly and unambiguously disclosed in the application either explicitly or implicitly."

In *Richardson-Vicks Inc.'s Patent*,[87] the Patents Court followed *Bonzel*[88] (above) and held that "the test of added matter was whether a skilled man would, upon looking at the amended specification, learn anything about the invention which he could not learn from the unamended specification".

[84] [1990] R.P.C. 587.
[85] [1990] R.P.C. 621.
[86] [1991] R.P.C. 533.
[87] [1995] R.P.C. 568.
[88] See note 86.

8–57 **(iii) Limited applicability of a "novelty test".** In *A. C. Edwards*[89] the Patents Court stated that:

> "The EPO has found it useful to apply a novelty test to decide whether an amendment extends that disclosure. In that test the EPO considers the application as filed and decides whether it would render the claim as sought to be amended invalid because it would not be new. That can often be a useful test but should be applied with caution."

(c) Claim broadening before grant: generalisation of a feature

8–58 *Protoned B.V.'s Application*[90] was concerned with a proposed amendment to a claim by deleting the word "compression" from the feature "mechanical compression spring". The Patents Court upheld the decision of the Patent Office and refused the amendment on the ground that such a generalisation of the feature:

> "had the effect of adding notionally to the body of the specification a whole range of springs not described in the body of the specification."

The Court confirmed that:

> "the skilled person is not entitled to give a special broad meaning to a clear disclosure with an apparent, unambiguous meaning unless the context demands it, and this is not so in the present case."

C. Amendments After Grant

Article 123(3) EPC

(1) Introduction

8–59 The substantive provision set out in Article 123(3) EPC (prohibition of extension of protection) is specifically limited in its application to the amendment of *claims in opposition proceedings* before the EPO. ("The claims of the European patent may not be amended during opposition proceedings in such way as to extend the protection conferred.") Thus, the provision is not *prima facie* concerned with amendments to the description or drawings unless the protection conferred by the claims is affected. Amendments after grant continue to be controlled by Article 123(2) EPC (see paragraphs 8–05 to 8–50 above). In opposition proceedings, therefore, both Article 123(2) and (3) EPC are applicable.

When interpreting Article 123 EPC in general, and Article 123(3) EPC in particular, it is important to consider also the provisions of Article 138 EPC, which provides the grounds for revocation of a European patent under

[89] [1990] R.P.C. 621.
[90] [1983] F.S.R. 110.

national laws. In particular, Article 138(1)(c) and (d) EPC provide grounds of revocation of a European patent in proceedings before national courts which correspond to the requirements of Article 123(2) and (3) EPC. The extent of protection conferred by a European patent is determined in accordance with Article 69(1) EPC and its Protocol by the terms of the claims but also by reference to the description and drawings (see Chapter 13 at paragraph 13–04).

(2) Basic principles

"Once a European patent has been granted, an act by a third party which **8–60** would not infringe the patent as granted should not be able to become an infringing act as a result of amendment after grant." This is the essential purpose and guiding principle underlying Article 123(3) EPC (T1149/97[91]).

When considering Article 123(2) EPC the question of extension of subject-matter depends upon a comparison with the "application *as filed*" (emphasis added). When considering Article 123(3) EPC, however, the question of extension of protection depends upon a comparison with the claims *as granted*.

"Article 123(3) EPC is directly aimed at protecting the interests of third parties by prohibiting any broadening of the claims of a granted patent, even if there should be a basis for such broadening in the application as filed" (G1/93[92]).

(3) Relevant considerations

(a) "Protection conferred" (Article 123(3) EPC) distinguished from "rights conferred" (Article 64(1) EPC)

"The protection conferred by a patent is determined by the terms of **8–61** the claims (Article 69(1) EPC), and in particular by the categories of such claims and their technical features.

In contrast, the rights conferred on the proprietor of a European patent (Article 64(1) EPC) are the legal rights which the law of a designated Contracting State may confer upon the proprietor, for example, as regards what acts of third parties constitute infringement of the patent, and as regards the remedies which are available in respect of any infringement.

In other words ... determination of the "extent of the protection conferred' ... is a determination of *what* is protected, in terms of category plus technical features; whereas the 'rights conferred' ... are a matter solely for the designated Contracting States, and are related to *how* such subject-matter is protected" (G2, 6/88[93] emphasis added).

---

[91] T1149/97 *SOLATRON/Fluid transducer* O.J. EPO 2000, 259.
[92] G1/93 *ADVANCED SEMICONDUCTOR PRODUCTS/Conflicting requirements of Article 123(2) and (3) EPC* O.J. EPO 1993, 125; [1995] E.P.O.R. 97.
[93] G2, 6/88 *MOBIL OIL/BAYER/Friction reducing additive* O.J. EPO 1990, 93, 114; [1990] E.P.O.R. 73, 257.

Thus when deciding up on the allowability of amendments to claims under Article 123(3) EPC: "It is not necessary to consider the national laws of the Contracting States" (G2, 6/88[94]).

(b) Determination of "the protection conferred"

8–62   "The protection conferred by a patent is determined by the terms of the claims (Article 69(1) EPC), and in particular by the *categories* of such claims and their *technical features*. In this connection Article 69 EPC and its Protocol are to be applied, both in proceedings before the EPO and in proceedings within the Contracting States, whenever it is necessary to determine the protection which is conferred."

"when deciding upon the admissibility of any amendment to the claims of a patent which is proposed in opposition proceedings ... what has to be considered and decided is whether the subject-matter which is protected by the claims, as defined by their categories in combination with their technical features, is extended by the amendment".

"... a first step must be to determine the extent of protection which is conferred by the patent before the amendment".

"... the question to be considered ... is whether the subject-matter defined by the claims is more or less narrowly defined as a result of the amendment".

"... the subject-matter of a claimed invention involved two aspects: first, the category or type of the claim, and second, the technical features, which constitute its technical subject-matter".

"A proposed amendment may involve a change in category, or a change in the technical features of the invention or both. Each type of amendment requires separate consideration" (G2, 6/88[95]).

The above quotations are not in the order in which they occur in G2, 6/88.

8–63   "Although Article 123(2) EPC only addresses the claims of the European patent, amendments to the description and the drawings may also extend the protection conferred in accordance with Article 69(1) EPC" (T1149/97[96]: see Chapter 13 at paragraphs 13–07 and 13–08; see also paragraph 8–72a below).
        There is, of course, a basic distinction between determining the extent of protection conferred by a European patent in the context of infringement proceedings, and determining the question of extension of protection in

[94] G2, 6/88 *MOBIL OIL/BAYER/Friction reducing additive* O.J. EPO 1990, 93, 114; [1990] E.P.O.R. 73, 257.
[95] *Ibid.*
[96] T1149/97 *SOLATRON/Fluid transducer* O.J. EPO 2000, 259.

the context of opposition proceedings. In the former context, it is necessary to consider whether one or more specific acts of a defendant are within the extent of protection conferred. In the latter context, the question of extension of protection has to be decided in the abstract.

(c) Change of category

There are basically two different types of claim, namely a claim to a **8–64** physical entity (*e.g.* product, apparatus) and a claim to a physical activity (*e.g.* method, process use). These two basic types of claim are sometimes referred to as the two possible "categories" of claim ..." (G2, 6/88,[97] see also Chapter 7 at paragraph 7–59).

(i) **"Product" to "use".** This change of category was specifically **8–65** considered in G2, 6/88.[98]

After deciding that the protection conferred by a claim to a physical entity such as a compound, *per se*, is absolute, and extends to that compound "wherever it exists and whatever its context" (see Chapter 13 at paragraph 13–27), the Enlarged Board held that it follows that "a claim to a particular use of a compound is in effect a claim to the ... compound only when it is being used in the course of the particular physical activity (the use) ... Such a claim therefore confers less protection than a claim to the physical entity, *per se.*"

Consequently:

"An amendment to a European patent during opposition proceedings simply by way of change of category from a claim to a physical entity *per se* (*e.g.* a compound or composition), so as to include a claim to a physical activity involving the use of such physical entity, therefore does not extend the protection conferred by the patent, and is admissible" (G2, 6/88[99]).

(ii) **"Product-by-process" to "process".** On the application of similar **8–66** principles, such a change of category is allowable (T423/89[100]), because the product-by-process claim confers a wider (absolute) protection than the claim to the process.

(iii) **"Method of operating a physical entity (*e.g.* apparatus or device) to **8–67** a physical entity".** Following the above principles, a claim to a method of operating a physical entity only protects such physical entity *when in use*, whereas a claim to a physical entity confers absolute protection on such physical entity, *i.e. whether or not it is in use.* Thus:

"amendment of the claims of a patent during opposition proceedings

---

[97] G2, 6/88 *MOBIL OIL/BAYER/Friction reducing additive* O.J. EPO 1990, 93, 114; [1990] E.P.O.R. 73, 257.
[98] *Ibid.*
[99] *Ibid.*
[100] T423/89 *KONICA/Sensitising* June 10, 1992; [1994] E.P.O.R. 142.

by way of change of category from 'a method of operating a device' to 'a device' is in principle not allowable under Article 123(3) EPC" (T82/93[101]).

1. Example of "inescapable trap": Article 52(4) and 123(3) EPC
Consequently, in a case where a granted patent only contains claims to a method of operating a device (all device claims having been deleted before grant), and all such claims are successfully opposed on the ground that they each define "a method of medical treatment" which is excluded from patentability under Article 52(4) EPC (see Chapter 9 at paragraphs 9–36 *et seq.*, in particular paragraph 9–41), the combination of Articles 52(4) and 123(3) EPC operate as an "inescapable trap" resulting inevitably in revocation of the patent because:

"(a) the patent cannot be maintained as granted because its claims define subject-matter which is unpatentable having regard to Article 54(2) EPC;
(b) the patent cannot be maintained in amended form with claims which only define the device itself and which no longer contain features defining a therapeutic method of operating it ... because ... deletion of such "method features" would be contrary to Article 123 (3) EPC" (T82/93[102]).

2. Exceptional cases:
(a) It was held that a skilled person could deduce the apparatus suitable for carrying out the claimed process from the technical teaching of the patent, and that "the extent of protection (*cf.* Article 69 EPC) conferred by the process patent also encompasses the apparatus for carrying out the process". Thus the change of category was allowed (T378/86[103]—decided before G2, 6/88[104]).
(b) A change of category from "a method of operating a device" to "a device" was allowed on the basis that "the seeming change of category" was in fact a clarification (T426/89[105]).
Both these decisions are difficult to reconcile with the principles set out in G2, 6/88.[106]

8–68 **(iv) "Process" to "product".** Such a change of category from a physical activity to a physical entity is not allowable under Article 123(3) EPC, following the principles set out in G2, 6/88,[107] and having regard to the absolute protection which is conferred upon a claim to a physical entity (T20/94[108]).

---

[101] T82/93 TELECTRONICS/*Cardiac pacing* O.J. EPO 1996, 274; [1996] E.P.O.R. 409.
[102] *Ibid.*
[103] T378/86 MOOG/*Change of category* O.J. EPO 1988, 386; [1989] E.P.O.R. 85.
[104] G2, 6/88 MOBIL OIL/BAYER/*Friction reducing additive* O.J. EPO 1990, 93, 114; [1990] E.P.O.R. 73, 257.
[105] T426/89 SIEMENS/*Pacemaker* O.J. EPO 1992, 172; [1992] E.P.O.R. 149.
[106] See note 104.
[107] See note 104.
[108] T20/94 ENICHEM/*Amorphous TPM* November 4, 1998.

(v) "Process for preparing a product" to "product-by-process". A 8–69
product-by-process claim is interpreted as a claim to the product *per se*, and
the reference to the process for preparing the product serves only to define
it (see also Chapter 7 at paragraph 7–65) irrespective of how the claim is
worded. Consequently, such a claim confers absolute protection upon the
product which it defines, and confers such protection upon that product
regardless of the process by which it is prepared (T20/94[109]):

> "Where the granted claims are solely process claims, a change from a
> process claim for preparing a product to a product-by-process claim
> by way of amendment extends the protection conferred by the
> European patent to the same product obtained by a process for its
> preparation different to that defined in the granted process claim,
> contrary to the requirement of Article 123(3) EPC.
>
> Despite the fact that a product-by-process claim is characterised by
> the process for its preparation, it nevertheless belongs to the category
> of claim directed to a physical entity and is a claim directed to the
> product *per se*. Irrespective of whether the terms "directly obtained",
> "obtained" or "obtainable" are used in the product-by-process claim,
> it is still directed to the product *per se* and confers absolute protection
> upon the product" (T20/94[110]).

(vi) "Product" to "process for preparing the product". It is doubtful that 8–70
such a change of category is allowable having regard in particular to the
effect of Article 642) EPC in relation to such a process claim (T570/96[111]: see
also T958/90[112]).

(d) Change of technical features

(i) General principle.

> "In the case of a change in the technical features of the invention, if the 8–71
> technical features of the claimed invention after amendment are more
> narrowly defined, the extent of the protection conferred is less; and if
> such technical features are less narrowly defined as a result of
> amendment, the protection conferred is therefore extended. Clearly, if
> technical features are changed by an amendment, in that the technical
> subject-matter of the claims after amendment is outside the scope of
> the technical subject-matter before amendment, there is then neces-
> sarily an extension of protection" (G2, 6/88[113]).

(ii) Clarification and explanation of the extent of protection. Amend- 8–72
ment of a claim to clarify an inconsistency does not contravene Article

[109] *Ibid.*
[110] *Ibid.*
[111] T570/96 *ALLIED COLLOIDS* August 20, 1998.
[112] T958/90 *DOW/Sequestering agent* December 4, 1992; [1994] E.P.O.R. 1.
[113] G2, 6/88 *MOBIL OIL/BAYER/Friction reducing additive* O.J. EPO 1990, 93, 114; [1990]
E.P.O.R. 73, 257.

123(3) EPC if the amended claim has the same meaning as the unamended claim, on its true construction (T271/84[114]).

For example, in one case on a strict literal interpretation, the feature in the claim as granted ("... a transmission disposed in parallel with the engine ...") did not clearly embrace one of the described embodiments of the invention, whereas the feature as proposed to be amended ("... a transmission which is also transversely disposed ...") clearly did embrace all the described embodiments of the invention. Read in isolation, therefore, the amended claim could be considered as more broad than the claim as granted.

It was held that such an amendment was allowable, if the examination of the extent of protection conferred by the granted claim resulted in the following conclusions:

"(a) The restrictive term in the granted claim is not so clear in its technical meaning in the given context that it could be used to determine the extent of protection without interpretation by reference to the description and the drawings of the patent;

(b) It is quite clear from the description and the drawings of the patent and also from the examination procedure up to grant that the further embodiment belongs to the invention and that it was never intended to exclude it from protection conferred by the patent ..." (T371/88[115]).

In other words, if amendment is regarded merely as clarification and explanation of the protection conferred by the patent as granted, on a fair interpretation, there is no extension of protection.

Similarly:

"The amendment of a granted claim to replace an inaccurate technical statement, which is evidently inconsistent with the totality of the disclosure of the patent, by an accurate statement of the technical features involved, does not infringe Article 123(3) EPC" (T108/91[116]).

(e) Re-instating subject-matter deleted before grant

8–72a "If, in view of Articles 84 and 69 EPC, the application documents have been adapted to amended claims before grant, thereby deleting part of the subject-matter originally disclosed in order to avoid inconsistencies in the patent specification, as a rule subject-matter deleted for this reason can neither be re-inserted into the patent specification nor into the claims as granted without infringing Article 123(3) EPC. An analogous finding applies to subject-matter retained in the patent

---

[114] T271/84 *AIR PRODUCTS/Pressure swing adsorption* O.J. EPO 1988, 372; [1987] E.P.O.R. 23.
[115] T371/88 *FUJI/Transmission apparatus* O.J. EPO 1992, 157; [1992] E.P.O.R. 341.
[116] T108/91 *SEARS/Lockable closure* O.J. EPO 1994, 228; [1993] E.P.O.R. 407.

specification during such adaptation for reasons of comprehensibility, but indicated as not relating to the claimed invention" (T1149/97[117]).

D. Wrongful Addition of a Feature Before Grant: "Inescapable Trap"

Articles 100(c) and 138(1)(c) EPC; Article 123(2) and (3) EPC

(1) Introduction

During examination proceedings, the amendment of a claim may be **8–73** allowed by an Examining Division or a Board of Appeal, without any objection being taken under Article 123(2) EPC (or a divisional application may be filed, or a "new application" may be filed, without objections being raised under Article 76 or 61 EPC, respectively: the following discussion will be confined to the situation under Article 123(2) EPC, but the same principles apply in relation to Articles 76 and 61 RPC).

Subsequently, an opponent may object to such amendment having been allowed before grant, during opposition proceedings under Article 100(c) EPC. This ground of opposition requires the Opposition Division or Board of Appeal in the opposition proceedings to decide whether the Examining Division or Board of Appeal were right or wrong having regard to Article 123(2) EPC in allowing the amendment to be made during the examination proceedings.

During the opposition proceedings the patentee has the opportunity to propose further amendments having regard to the objection under Article 100(c). Thus if the amendment which is objected to under Article 100(c) EPC involved broadening of a claim by deletion of a feature, the patentee may in principle reinstate the feature during the opposition proceedings without contravening Article 123(3) EPC. However, if the amendment which is objected to under Article 100(c) EPC involved *narrowing a claim by addition of a feature*, the patentee cannot in principle broaden the claim by removing the feature in question during the opposition proceedings without contravening Article 123(3) EPC. The effect of the combination of Article 100(c) EPC (Article 123(2) EPC) and Article 123(3) EPC in opposition proceedings, in the case of the *addition of a feature to a claim before grant*, was considered by the Enlarged Board of Appeal in G1/93.[118]

(2) The "inescapable trap": G1/93

(a) The question of law which was considered was as follows: **8–74**
"If a European patent as granted contains subject-matter which extends beyond the content of the application as filed and also limits

---

[117] T1149/97 SOLATRON/Fluid Transducer O.J. EPO 2000, 259.
[118] G1/93 ADVANCED SEMI-CONDUCTOR PRODUCTS II/Conflicting requirements of Article 123(2) and (3) EPC O.J. EPO 1994, 541; [1995] E.P.O.R. 97

the scope of protection conferred by the claims, is it possible during the opposition proceedings to maintain the patent in view of paragraphs (2) and (3) of Article 123 EPC?"

In other words, the problem which was put to the Enlarged Board, in the context of an amendment before grant which narrows the protection conferred and which is held during opposition proceedings to have contravened Article 123(2) EPC, was whether revocation of the patent under Article 100(c) EPC inevitably follows such a finding.

8–75 (b) The Enlarged Board considered possible ways of avoiding the "conflict" between Article 123(2) and (3) EPC. In particular, against the background of a discussion of the purpose of these provisions, it was held that "there is no support under the EPC for the idea ... that there is a mutual relationship between paragraphs 2 and 3 of Article 123 EPC, the one to be applied as primary and the other as subsidiary depending on the facts of the individual case".

Furthermore, the Enlarged Board considered as a possible way of avoiding revocation of the patent the approach adopted by the German Federal Patents Court in a judgment concerning the same problem: namely to allow "a statement to be added to the description of the patent in suit to the effect that the undisclosed feature (which is maintained in the claim in order to avoid an extension of the protection conferred) represents an inadmissible extension from which no rights may be derived". However, it considered that there is no basis under the EPC for this so-called "footnote solution" which "would be incompatible with the European patent system..., and would go beyond the competence of the EPO within such system" (G1/93[119]).

8–76 (c) Consequently, paragraphs 2 and 3 of Article 123 EPC are mutually independent of each other. Thus, if a limiting feature is considered to fall under Article 123(2) EPC, it cannot be maintained in the patent in view of Article 100(c) EPC, nor can it be removed from the claims without violating Article 123(3) EPC. This is "the inescapable trap".

The only possibility of saving the patent in the situation where, during the opposition proceedings, a feature added before grant is considered to have violated Article 123(2) EPC was stated as follows:

"Only if the added feature can be replaced by another feature disclosed in the application as filed without violating Article 123(3) EPC, can the patent be maintained (in amended form). This may in practice turn out to be a rare case" (G1/93[120]).

Reference may be made to the cases discussed in paragraph 8–72 above in this respect.

8–77 (d) This result was recognised by the Enlarged Board as being unsatisfactory in the following words:

[119] *Ibid.*
[120] *Ibid.*

"In this sense, it must be admitted that Article 123(2) EPC in combination with Article 123(3) EPC can operate rather harshly against an applicant, who runs the risk of being caught in an inescapable trap and losing everything by amending his application, even if the amendment is limiting the scope of protection ... this hardship is not *per se* a sufficient justification for not applying Article 123(2) EPC as it stands in order to duly protect the interests of the public. Nor does it, in principle, matter, that such amendment has been approved by the Examining Division. The ultimate responsibility for any amendment of a patent application (or a patent) always remains that of the applicant (or the patentee)" (G1/93[121]).

(e) In so far as the national laws of the Contracting States are likely to **8–77A** include a provision corresponding to Article 123(3) EPC (see for example Section 76(3)(b) 1977 U.K. Act), a similar result will follow if a national court finds in an action for revocation of a European patent pursuant to Article 138(1)(c) EPC that such ground for revocation has been made out. There would similarly be no possibility of amending the patent so as to avoid revocation.

(3) Conclusion

It may be added here as comment upon the above paragraph: **8–78**

(i) as previously explained, a patentee runs the risk of "being caught in an inescapable trap and losing everything by amending his application *'even'* if the amendment is limiting the scope of protection." The word *"even"* used by the Enlarged Board rightly suggests that there is a lack of proportionality and balance in the result of the decision, in that in general it is in the public interest that a proprietor limits the scope of protection of his patent rather than broadens it, yet it is the proprietor who has so limited the protection that "runs the risk of losing everything". The patent proprietor who broadens the scope of protection before grant runs no such risk.

(ii) also as previously explained, a narrowing amendment may be **8–79** allowed before grant by a Board of Appeal (as well as by an Examining Division), and a (different) Board of Appeal during opposition proceedings may decide, contrary to the (pre-grant) Board of Appeal, that the amendment contravened Article 123(2) EPC and that the patent must therefore be revoked. Having regard to the fine line between violating and not violating Article 123(2) EPC in many cases, and also having regard to the fact that in the above situation it is a second Board of Appeal disagreeing with a first Board of Appeal which would lead to revocation of the patent, the legal situation which results from the combination of Article 123(2) and (3) EPC is unsatisfactory.

Nevertheless, having regard to the clear wording of these provisions, it

---

[121] *Ibid*.

would have been difficult for the Enlarged Board of Appeal to come to any other conclusion by way of interpretation of Article 123 EPC or otherwise.

In order to avoid the lack of balance and proportionality and the injustice which results from this "inescapable trap", an appropriate amendment of Article 123 EPC would be desirable (for example, so as to allow the patent proprietor to broaden the protection by removing the feature which was added before grant without contravening Article 123(3) EPC in this special situation (with appropriate protection for any competitors who have acted in good faith and would otherwise be prejudiced by the broadened protection).

8–79A   Regrettably, the proposed revision of the EPC does not include any amendment of Article 123 EPC in order to remove the effect of the "inescapable trap".

E. Obvious Corrections of the Description, Claims and Drawings

Rule 88 EPC second sentence

(1) Introduction

8–80 Rule 88 EPC states that:

> "Linguistic errors, errors of transcription and mistakes in any document filed with the European Patent Office may be corrected on request. However, if the request for such correction concerns a description, claims or drawings, the correction must be obvious in the sense that it is immediately evident that nothing else would have been intended than what is offered as the correction."

This chapter is concerned with the correction of such errors and mistakes in the description, claims or drawings (that is, the "content of the application") which is governed by the first sentence of Rule 88 EPC in combination with the more stringent requirement set out in the second sentence.

8–81   The correction of such errors and mistakes in documents other than the description, claims and drawings has been considered in Chapter 6 at paragraphs 6–06 et seq. above, where certain general aspects of Rule 88 EPC are pointed out. For present purposes, in particular:

(a) A mistake in a document may be said to exist if the document does not express the true intention of the person who filed it (J8/80[122]);

(b) An error or mistake "may take the form of an incorrect statement or it may result from an omission" (J8/80[122a]);

---

[122] J8/80 RIB LOC/Correction of mistakes O.J. EPO 1980, 293; [1979–85] E.P.O.R.: A: 40.
[122a] Ibid.

(c) Correction of an error or mistake is discretionary.

Paragraphs 6–07 *et seq.* refer (in the context of the first sentence of Rule 88 EPC) to the fact that the existence of an error or mistake must be established, if correction is to be allowed. In view of the more stringent requirement of the second sentence of Rule 88 EPC, which as discussed below requires both the existence of an error or mistake in the content of the application and its correction to be obvious to a skilled person, clearly the mere establishment that an error or mistake exists in the content of the application is not enough to satisfy the second sentence of Rule 88 EPC.

The interpretation of the second sentence of Rule 88 EPC has been controversial in that two questions of law concerning its interpretation have been considered by the Enlarged Board of Appeal, in G3/89[123] and G2/95.[124] These are discussed below.

(2) Relationship with Article 123(2) EPC: declaratory nature of a correction

A controversial question of interpretation has been whether the correction **8–82** of a mistake under Rule 88 EPC is one particular kind of amendment and therefore also governed by Article 123(2) EPC, or whether such a correction is different from an amendment so that its allowability is determined solely by Rule 88 EPC and not by Article 123(2) EPC. In other words, is Rule 88 EPC subsidiary to Article 123(2) EPC or independent of it? This question was referred to the Enlarged Board in G3/89,[125] which held that:

(a) correction of an error under Rule 88 EPC has the effect of amending the application as filed, and that such a correction is a special case of an amendment under Article 123 EPC, and is thus subject to the prohibition of extension set out in Article 123(2) EPC.

(b) Since a correction under Rule 88 EPC is only allowable if the corrected application or patent is declaratory of what a skilled person would derive from the application as filed, such a correction cannot violate Article 123(2) EPC.

The conditions under which a correction of the content of an application under Rule 88 EPC is allowable having regard to G3/89,[126] G2/95[127] and other decisions, are discussed below.

---

[123] G3/89 *Correction under Rule 88, second sentence,* EPC O.J. EPO 1993, 117; [1993] E.P.O.R. 376.
[124] G2/95 *ATOTECH/Replacement of application documents* O.J. EPO 1996, 55; [1999] E.P.O.R. 77.
[125] See note 123.
[126] See note 123.
[127] See note 124.

(3) Obviousness of the mistake and its correction

8–83 For a correction under Rule 88 EPC to be allowable:

  (a) The "content of the application as filed" must "contain such an *obvious* error that a skilled person is in no doubt that this information is not correct and—considered objectively—cannot be meant to read as such".
      Furthermore:
      "If, on the other hand , it is doubtful whether any information at all is incorrect, then a correction is ruled out."
  (b) The "content of the application as filed" must "further allow a skilled person—using the common general knowledge on the date of filing—directly and unequivocally to ascertain the precise content of the information" the applicant meant to give on the date of filing, "so that, for said skilled person, it is immediately evident that nothing else would have been intended than what is offered as the correction".

Furthermore: "If there is any doubt that nothing else would have been intended than what is offered as the correction, a correction cannot be made" (G3/89[128]).

8–84   Both the fact of the mistake and the obviousness of the correction must be apparent to a skilled person from the "content of the application as filed" on its own, and that other document "may only be used in so far as they are sufficient for proving the common general knowledge [of a skilled person] on the date of filing". In particular, documents such as "priority documents, the abstract and the like" may not be used in support of a correction under Rule 88 EPC "even if they were filed together with the European patent application" (G3/89[129]).

"Under certain circumstances the content of a document not belonging to the parts of a European patent application relating to the disclosure may be included, by means of reference, partially or wholly in the disclosure" (G3/89)—this is clearly directed at the possibility of the content of cross-referenced documents being used as a source for amendments, as discussed in paragraphs 8–11 and 8–37 *et seq.* above.

(4) Correction of an application filed with the wrong description and claims: not allowable

8–85 Following G3/89[129a], in one case an application was filed in respect of an invention described in the accompanying priority document, but the description and claims accompanying the application concerned different subject-matter, and drawings accompanying the application corresponded to those in the priority document but not to the description. Substitution of the correct description and claims was allowed by the Board of Appeal on

---

[128] G3/89 *Correction under Rule 28, second sentence EPC* O.J. EPO 1993, 117; [1993] E.P.O.R. 376.
[129] *Ibid.*
[129a] *Ibid.*

the basis that G3/89 was only concerned with cases where a mistake *within* the content of the application as filed has occurred, and did not cover a case where the entire description and claims were wrong; and that it was clear from the priority document what the correct description and claims should be (T726/93[130]).

Subsequently, the question was referred to the Enlarged Board whether the complete documents forming an application, that is, the description, claims and drawings could be replaced by way of correction under Rule 88 EPC by the documents which the applicant had intended to file. The Enlarged Board emphasised that the description, claims and drawings as first filed with the application are used as the basis for the accordance of a filing date in accordance with Article 80 EPC, and establish the "content of the application as filed" for the purpose of Article 123(2) EPC. Consequently:

> "the parts of the European patent application which determine the disclosure of the invention may thus not be replaced by other documents by way of a correction under Rule 88, second sentence EPC" (G2/95[131]).

T726/93[132] was therefore overruled.

(5) No estoppel from correction following approval of text

The fact that the applicant approved the text of the patent to be granted, 8–86 under Rule 51(4) EPC, does not estop the patentee from correcting an error in such text which is discovered during opposition proceedings after grant (T200/89[133]). This follows from the declaratory nature of a correction under Rule 88 EPC (see paragraph 8–82 above).

F. Late Filed or Missing Drawings

Rule 43 EPC

(1) Introduction

According to Rule 43 EPC, if upon formal examination of a European 8–87 patent application by the Receiving Section under Article 91(g) EPC (see Chapter 2 at paragraphs 2–10 *et seq.*) it is found that the drawings of the application were filed later than the date of filing or have not been filed, then:

> (a) in the former case, reference to the drawings shall be deemed to be deleted unless the applicant requests within one month of an

---

[130] T726/93 *RIETER/Textile machines* O.J. EPO 1995, 478; [1996] E.P.O.R. 72.
[131] G1/95 *ATOTECH/Replacement of application documents* O.J. EPO 1996, 55; E.P.O.R. 77.
[132] See note 130.
[133] T200/89 *BOEING/Obvious error in claims* O.J. EPO 1990, 10; [1990] E.P.O.R. 407.

invitation to do so that the application be re-dated to the date on which the drawings were filed.

(b) in the latter case, the drawings may be filed within one month of an invitation to do so, and if they are so filed, the application is re-dated to the date on which the drawings were filed: if they are not duly filed within the one month period all references to them in the application shall be deemed to be deleted.

(2) Relationship between Rules 43 and 88 EPC

8–88 "Rule 43 EPC does not constitute a *lex specialis* as compared with Rule 88 EPC, but merely complements its provisions" (J4/85[134]). Thus having regard to the declaratory nature of a correction under Rule 88 EPC, whereby the correction is only allowable if it expresses what a skilled person would derive from the application at its filing date (see paragraph 8–82 above), a request for a correction under Rule 88 EPC relating to the drawings of an application should be decided before the provisions of Rule 43 EPC are applied.

A request for correction of the drawings (or any other part of the content of an application) has to be decided by an Examining Division, whereas the provisions of Rule 43 EPC are decided by the Receiving Section (J4/85[135]).

(3) The extent of application of Rule 43 EPC

8–89 Rule 43 EPC states that if the examination of an application under Article 91(g) EPC reveals that "the drawings" were filed later than the date of filing, or were not filed, the consequences discussed in paragraph (1) above apply. *Prima facie*, the wording of Rule 43 EPC appears to apply only to cases where *all* the drawings referred to in the description or claims were filed late or are missing.

"If a part of a drawing identified as a Figure is missing, the missing part is not to be considered as a missing drawing for the purposes of Rule 43 EPC" (J19/80[136]). The correction of such a missing part of a drawing can therefore be considered only under the second sentence of Rule 88 EPC.

In a case where one sheet of drawings including two complete Figures was filed late:

"the late filing of one or more complete Figures is dealt with in Rule 43 EPC" (J1/82[137]).

Thus according to the above decisions, Rule 43 EPC is applicable (after any request for correction under the second sentence of Rule 88 EPC has been decided) in the case of a complete Figure which is filed late or is

---

[134] J4/85 *ÉTAT FRANÇAIS/Correction of drawings* O.J. EPO 1986, 205; [1986] E.P.O.R. 331.
[135] *Ibid.*
[136] J19/80 *FRANKLIN/Missing drawings* O.J. EPO 1981, 65; [1979–85] E.P.O.R.: A: 62.
[137] J1/82 *TEVA/Missing drawings* O.J. EPO 1982, 293; [1979–85] E.P.O.R.: A: 96.

missing (even if the other Figures referred to in the description or claims have been duly filed), but is not applicable in the case of part of a Figure being filed late or missing.

(4) Comparison with United Kingdom law

(a) Introduction

Section 117(1) of the 1977 U.K. Act[138] provides that: "The Comptroller may, **8–90** subject to any provision of rules, correct any error of translation of transcription, clerical error or mistake in any specification of a patent or application for a patent or any document filed in connection with a patent or such an application."

Rule 91(2) made under the 1977 U.K. Act provides that "Where ... a request relates to a specification no correction shall be made therein unless the correction is obvious in the sense that it is immediately evident that nothing else would have been intended than what is offered as the correction."

The combined effect of these two provisions is clearly closely similar to Rule 88 EPC.

Sections 15(2) and (3) of the 1977 U.K. Act contain provisions which are essentially the same as Rule 43 EPC except that such provisions refer to "any drawing" referred to in the application as filed, rather than "the drawings" (*cf.* paragraph 8–89 above).

Neither section 15 nor section 117, however, are included in section 130(7) of the 1977 U.K. Act as having been "framed so as to have ... the same effects as the corresponding provisions of the EPC".

(b) Relationship between Sections 15 and 117

In *Antiphon AB's Application*,[139] a sheet of drawings comprising Figures 5 to **8–91** 10 was filed later than the filing date.

The Patents Court held that:

> "Section 117(1) is expressed in general terms whereas section 15(2) is a particular enactment in the statute. Section 117(1) cannot be used to circumvent the clear mandatory requirements of section 15(2) and must be taken to affect only those other parts of the statute to which it may properly apply."

Furthermore:

> "Section 15(2) applies to any application for a patent, whether made initially in full compliance with the requirements of section 14(1) and (2) or initiated only by documents such as are specified in section 15(1), and is mandatory on the Comptroller whenever a drawing referred to in the application is filed later than the initial date of filing."

---

[138] See Appendix 21.
[139] [1984] R.P.C. 1.

Antiphon was followed in *VEB Kombinat Walzlager und Normteile's Application.*[140]

Thus, the Patents Court has taken the same approach as in J1/82,[141] and a contrary approach to that subsequently taken in J4/85.[142]

Although J4/85 had been published by the time that *VEB Kombinat Walzlager*[143] was heard by the Patents Court, it is not referred to in the judgment of the Patents Court.

Cases Referred to in Chapter 8

Board of Appeal Decisions

G2, 6/88 MOBIL/BAYER/Friction reducing additive O.J. EPO 1990, 93; [1990] E.P.O.R. 73.

G3/89 Correction under Rule 88, second sentence, EPC O.J. EPO 1993, 117; [1993] E.P.O.R. 376.

G1/93 ADVANCED SEMI CONDUCTOR PRODUCTS/Conflicting requirements of Article 123(2) and (3) EPC O.J. EPO 1993, 125; [1995] E.P.O.R. 97.

G2/95 ATOTECH/Replacement of application documents O.J. EPO 1996, 555; [1997] E.P.O.R. 77.

J8/80 RIB LOC/Correction of mistakes O.J. EPO 1980, 293; [1979–85] E.P.O.R.: A: 40.

J19/80 FRANKLIN/Missing drawings O.J. EPO 1981, 65; [1979–85] E.P.O.R.: A: 62.

J1/82 TEVA/Missing drawings O.J. EPO 1982, 293; [1979–85] E.P.O.R.: A: 96.

J4/85 ÉTAT FRANÇAIS/Correction of drawings O.J. EPO 1986, 205; [1986] E.P.O.R. 331.

T4/80 BAYER/Polyether polyols O.J. EPO 1982, 149; [1979–85] E.P.O.R.: B: 260.

T11/82 LANSING BAGNALL/Control circuit O.J. EPO 1983, 479; [1979–85] E.P.O.R.: B: 385.

T37/82 SIEMENS/Low-tension switch O.J. EPO 1984, 71; [1979–85] E.P.O.R.: B: 437.

T52/82 RIETER/Winding apparatus O.J. EPO 1983, 416; [1979–85] E.P.O.R.: B: 459.

T54/82 MOBIL/Disclosure O.J. EPO 1983, 446; [1979–85] E.P.O.R.: B: 469.

T172/82 CONTRAVES/Particle analyser O.J. EPO 1983, 493; [1979–85] E.P.O.R.: C: 668.

[140] [1987] R.P.C. 405.
[141] J1/82 *TEVA/Missing drawings* O.J. EPO 1982, 293; [1979–85] E.P.O.R. : A: 96.
[142] J4/85 *ÉTAT FRANÇAIS/Correction of drawings* O.J. EPO 1986, 205; [1986] E.P.O.R. 331.
[143] [1987] R.P.C. 405.

T13/83   ICI AMERICAS/Polyisocyanurates O.J. EPO 1984, 428;
          [1979–85] E.P.O.R.: C: 732.
T190/83   OTTO BOCK/Artificial knee joint, July 24, 1984; [1998]
          E.P.O.R. 272.
T201/83   SHELL/Lead alloys O.J. EPO 1984, 481; [1979–85] E.P.O.R.: C:
          905.
T6/84   MOBIL/Amendment of claims O.J. EPO 1985, 238; [1979–85]
          E.P.O.R.: C: 924.
T13/84   SPERRY/Reformulation of the problem O.J. EPO 1986, 253;
          [1986] E.P.O.R. 289.
T151/84   THOMSON-CSF [1988] E.P.O.R. 29.
T194/84   GENERAL MOTOR/Zinc electrodes O.J. EPO 1990, 59; [1989]
          E.P.O.R. 351.
T271/84   AIR PRODUCTS/Removal of hydrogen sulphide and car-
          bonyl sulphide O.J. EPO 1987, 405; [1987] E.P.O.R. 23.
T288/84   STAMICARBON/Activated support O.J. EPO 1986, 128;
          [1986] E.P.O.R. 217.
T66/85   AMP/Connector O.J. EPO 1989, 167; [1989] E.P.O.R. 283.
T133/85   XEROX/Amendments O.J. EPO 1988, 441; [1989] E.P.O.R.
          116.
T260/85   AMP/Coaxial connector O.J. EPO 1989, 199; [1989] E.P.O.R.
          403.
T16/86   THETFORD, February 4, 1988.
T17/86   SATAM BRANDT/Refrigeration plant O.J. EPO 1989, 297;
          [1989] E.P.O.R. 347.
T246/86   BULL/Identification system O.J. EPO 1989, 199; [1989]
          E.P.O.R. 344.
T313/86   CHEMISCHE WERKE, January 12, 1988.
T378/86   MOOG/Change of category O.J. EPO 1988, 386; [1989]
          E.P.O.R. 85.
T407/86   FUJITSU/Memory circuit [1988] E.P.O.R. 254.
T416/86   BOEHRINGER/Reflection photometer O.J. EPO 1989, 308;
          [1989] E.P.O.R. 327.
T433/86   ICI/Modified diisocyamates [1988] E.P.O.R. 97.
T170/87   SULZER/Hot gas cooler O.J. EPO 1989, 441; [1990] E.P.O.R.
          14.
T331/87   HOUDAILLE/Removal of feature O.J. EPO 1991, 22; [1991]
          E.P.O.R. 194.
T265/88   LUNDIA/Diffusion device [1990] E.P.O.R. 399.
T371/88   FUJI/Transmission apparatus, May 29, 1990 (P).
T401/88   BOSCH/Test piece O.J. EPO 1990, 297; [1990] E.P.O.R. 640.
T514/88   ALZA/Infusor [1990] E.P.O.R. 157.
T200/89   BOEING/Obvious error in claims O.J. EPO 1990, 10; [1990]
          E.P.O.R. 407.
T423/89   KONICA/Sensitising June 10, 1992; [1994] E.P.O.R. 142.
T426/89   SIEMENS/Pacemaker O.J. EPO 1992, 172; [1992] E.P.O.R. 149.

T784/89 GENERAL ELECTRIC/Disclosure of computer related apparatus O.J. EPO 1992, 438; [1992] E.P.O.R. 446.

T689/90 RAYCHEM/Event detector O.J. EPO 1993, 616; [1994] E.P.O.R. 157.

T737/90 GENERAL ELECTRIC/Missing publication number, September 9, 1993.

T958/90 DOW/Sequestering agent December 4, 1992; [1994] E.P.O.R. 1.

T187/91 LELAND/Light source O.J. EPO 1994, 572; [1995] E.P.O.R. 199.

T384/91 ADVANCED SEMI-CONDUCTOR PRODUCTS/"Conflict" between Article 123(2) and (3) EPC O.J. EPO 1995, 745; [1996] E.P.O.R. 125.

T522/91 MERCK/Chroman derivatives O.J. EPO 1995, 100; [1995] E.P.O.R. 455.

T597/92 BLASCHIM/Rearrangement reaction O.J. EPO 1996, 135; [1996] E.P.O.R. 456.

T802/92 COLORADO/Photovoltaic cell O.J. EPO 1995, 379; [1996] E.P.O.R. 125.

T82/93 TELECTRONICS/Cardiac pacing O.J. EPO 1996, 274; [1996] E.P.O.R. 409.

T583/93 HYMO CORPORATION/Water-soluble polymer dispersion O.J. EPO 1996, 496; [1997] E.P.O.R. 129.

T726/93 RIETER/Textile machines O.J. EPO 1995, 478; [1996] E.P.O.R. 72.

T20/94 ENICHEM/Amorphous TPM November 4, 1998.

T284/94 PITNEY BOWES/Electronic postage meter O.J. EPO 1999, 464.

T873/94 TOSHIBA/Amended divisional application O.J. EPO 1997, 456; [1998] E.P.O.R. 71.

T570/96 DOW/Sequestering agent [1994] E.P.O.R. 1.

T1149/97 SOLATRON/Fluid transducer O.J. EPO 2000, 259.

Decisions of National Courts

Antiphon AB's Application [1984] R.P.C. 1.
Edwards (A.C.) Ltd. v. Acme Signs & Displays Ltd [1990] R.P.C. 621.
Harding's Patent, Re [1988] R.P.C. 515.
Mitsui Engineering and Shipbuilding Ltd's Application [1984] R.P.C. 471.
Protoned BV's Application [1983] F.S.R. 110.
Raychem Ltd's Application [1986] R.P.C. 547.
Southco Inc. v. Dzus Fastener Europe Ltd [1990] R.P.C. 587.
VEB Kombinat Walzlager und Normteile's Application [1987] R.P.C. 405.

CHAPTER 9

PATENTABLE SUBJECT-MATTER

Articles 52, 53 and 57 EPC

Contents

All references are to paragraph numbers

A. Introduction

9–01 The nature of patentable inventions is governed by Articles 52 and 53 EPC.

(1) Positive requirements for patentability

9–02 Article 52(1) EPC sets out four criteria which must be met if a European patent application is to be granted:

    (a) there must be an invention;
    (b) the invention must be susceptible of industrial application;
    (c) the invention must be new;
    (d) the invention must involve an inventive step.

The meaning of requirement (a), the necessity for the presence of "an invention", has for the most part been considered by the Boards of Appeal in conjunction with the categories of excluded subject-matter set out in Article 52(2) EPC—see paragraphs 9–06 *et seq.* below. The Guidelines (C–IV, 1.1.) accept that consideration of requirement (a) is separate and distinct from requirements (b) to (d).

The requirement for "an invention" was the subject of discussion in *Genentech Inc.'s Patent,*[1] in the Court of Appeal of the United Kingdom.

Requirement (b), that the invention should be "susceptible of industrial application", is considered separately in section F of this chapter. Requirements (c) and (d), novelty and inventive step, are considered separately in Chapters 11 and 12.

If the above four criteria are met, the wording of Article 52(1) EPC is mandatory: European patents "shall be granted" for such inventions, subject only to the exclusions and exceptions set out in the remainder of Article 52 EPC and in Article 53 EPC, respectively, which are the subject of this chapter.

9–02A According to the proposed revision of the EPC, Article 52(1) EPC will be amended so as to read:

> 52(1) EPC: "European patents shall be granted for any inventions in all fields of technology, provided that they are new, involve an inventive step and are susceptible of industrial application."

This amendment is intended to bring Article 52(1) EPC into line with Article 27(1) TRIPS (see Chapter 1 at paragraph 1–55), and makes it plain that patent protection is available to *technical* inventions of all kinds. The legal tradition in Europe is to provide patent protection for creativity in a technical field, and claimed subject-matter must therefore have a technical character and involve a technical teaching with a view to solving a technical problem (see paragraphs 9–13 *et seq.* below).

---

[1] [1989] R.P.C. 147 at 262.

(2) Exclusions and exceptions from patentability

Articles 52 and 53 EPC identify various types of subject-matter which are **9–03**
not patentable uner the EPC, either by way of exclusion (Article 52 EPC) or
by way of exception (Article 53 EPC). In each case the effect is the same, *i.e.*
the subject-matter is not patentable.

(a) Article 52 EPC—exclusions

The scheme of Article 52 EPC is to set out in paragraphs (2) and (3) certain **9–04**
categories of subject-matter—the "mathematical" exclusions—which are
not to be regarded as "inventions" (requirement (a) above), and to set out
in paragraph (4) further categories of subject-matter—the "medical"
exclusions—which are not to be regarded as "inventions which are
susceptible of industrial application" (requirement (b) above). All such
categories of subject-matter are, therefore, excluded from patentability as a
matter of definition.

The difference between the "mathematical" and "medical" exclusions
under paragraphs (2) and (4) respectively of Article 52 EPC is explained as
follows:

> "The difference in wording between paragraphs (2) and (4) results
> from the nature of the subject-matters that are being excluded from
> patentability in the respective paragraphs. The subject-matters which
> are set out in paragraph (2) are excluded primarily because they have
> traditionally been regarded within national patent laws as more in the
> nature of ideas than industrial manufacturer. In contrast, the methods
> which are set out in paragraph (4) are excluded from patentability,
> even though such methods are capable of being applied industrially,
> as a matter of policy. Thus the wording of paragraph (4) is implicitly
> recognizing that such methods are susceptible of industrial appli-
> cation as a matter of reality, but provides that they 'shall not be
> regarded as inventions which are susceptible of industrial appli-
> cation', by way of legal fiction" (T116/85[2]).

(b) Article 53 EPC—exceptions

Article 53 EPC defines certain types of invention—the "morality" and **9–05**
"biological" exceptions—which by their nature cannot be the subject of a
granted European patent. The exceptions to patentability under Article 53
EPC may meet all of the requirements for patentability set out in Article 52
EPC, both in fact by way of definition, but are not patentable for reasons
which are essentially based on public policy.

---

[2] T116/85 *WELLCOME/Pigs I* O.J. EPO 1989, 13; [1988] E.P.O.R. 1.

(c) Classification of non-patentable subject-matter

9–06 The exclusions and exceptions from patentability provided by Articles 52 and 53 EPC are classified and considered separately under the following headings:

9–07 (1) *Discoveries, mathematical methods, computer programs, etc.* Article 52(2) excludes:

> "in particular:
>
> (a) discoveries, scientific theories and mathematical methods;
> (b) aesthetic creations;
> (c) schemes, rules and methods for performing mental acts, playing games or doing business, and programs for computers;
> (d) presentations of information."

The above exclusions are subject to the important qualification set out in Article 52(3) EPC, namely that such subject-matter and activities are excluded from patentability "only to the extent to which a European patent application or patent relates to such subject matter or activities *as such*" (emphasis added).

The question to be considered under this category of exclusions is therefore: "What is the nature of the claimed subject-matter?"

9–08 (2) *Methods of medical treatment, diagnostic methods.* Article 52(4) EPC excludes:

> "Methods for treatment of the human or animal body by
>
> (a) surgery; or
> (b) therapy.
>
> Diagnostic methods practised on the human or animal body."

The above exclusions are stated not to apply "to products, in particular substances or compositions, for use in any of these methods". Only inventions claimed in terms of methods are excluded.

The question to be considered under this category of exclusions in contrast to the question to be considered under category (1) above, is therefore: "What is the nature of the *protection* claimed?"

9–09 (3) *Inventions contrary to "ordre public" or morality.* Article 53(a) EPC excepts from patentability "Inventions the publication or exploitation of which would be contrary to *'ordre public'* or morality."

This is subject to the qualification that the "exploitation shall not be deemed to be so contrary merely because it is prohibited by law or regulation in some or all of the Contracting States".

The question to be considered under this category of exception, in contrast to the question to be considered under exclusion categories (1) and (2) above, is: "What is the effect of publication and exploitation of the claimed subject matter?"

(4) *Biological matter.* Article 53(b) EPC excepts from patentability: "Plant **9–10** or animal varieties; essentially biological processes for the production of plants or animals." This is subject to the qualification that "this provision does not apply to micro-biological processes or the products thereof".

The exclusions from patentability provided under the first two headings ("mathematical" and "medical") were new definitions in the EPC, although similar exclusions were found in various prior national laws of Contracting States, including the United Kingdom.

The question to be considered under this category of exception is therefore: "What is the nature of the claimed subject-matter?"

The exceptions from patentability under categories (3) and (4) ("moral" and "biological") are derived directly from Article 2 of the Strasbourg Convention[3] (see paragraphs 9–80 *et seq.* below).

The above categories of unpatentable subject-matter will be considered separately in detail below.

(3) Biotechnological inventions: E.U. Directive 98/44 and Rule 23b, c, d and e EPC

The protection of some biotechnological inventions raises difficult issues in **9.10a** relation to the exceptions to patentability under Article 53(a) and (b) EPC. In order to clarify the allowable scope of protection of such inventions in the light of the current state of development of such technology, a European Union Directive 98/44 was issued in 1998 concerning the legal protection of biotechnological inventions, which binds the Member States of the European Union, but not the EPO (see Chapter 1 at paragraph 1–26).

Subsequently, under Article 33(1)(b) EPC, the Administrative Council inserted a new Chapter VI containing new Rules 23b, 23c, 23d and 23e EPC into Part II of the Implementing Regulations, entitled "Biotechnological inventions", which entered into force on September 1, 1999. These new Rules correspond closely to the provisions of the E.U. Directive, and will be considered in relation to the provisions of Article 53(a) and (b) EPC below (paragraphs 9–72, 9–81 and 9–84 below).

According to new Rule 23b(1) EPC, "the relevant provisions of the EPC shall be applied and interpreted in accordance with the provisions of" the new Chapter VI, and the E.U. Directive 98/44 "shall be used as a supplementary means of interpretation".

---

[3] Convention on the "Unification of certain points of substantive law on Patents for Inventions": reproduced at Appendix 16.

B. Discoveries, Mathematical Methods, Computer Programs, etc.

Article 52(2) and (3) EPC

(1) Introduction

9–11   Article 52(2) EPC states that:

> "The following in particular shall not be regarded as inventions within the meaning of paragraph (1):
>
> (a) discoveries, scientific theories and mathematical methods;
> (b) aesthetic creations;
> (c) schemes, rules and methods for performing mental acts, playing games, or doing business and programs for computers;
> (d) presentations of information."

Articles 52(3) EPC emphasises that the above subject-matter and activities are excluded from patentability "only to the extent to which a European patent application or European patent relates to such subject-matter or activities *as such*" (emphasis added).

Clearly a most important specific exclusion from patentability is that of "programs for computers", and a number of cases which have developed the principles and practice of the Boards of Appeal discussed below have been concerned with this exclusion. The practice in relation to this exclusion, including recent important developments in such practice, are considered in paragraph 9–31 below.

A further potentially controversial area concerns the patentability of business methods, having regard to the expansion of internet business, but such cases have not yet been decided in the Boards of Appeal.

9–12   The first positive requirement for patentability under Article 52(1) EPC (see paragraph 9–02 above) is that the subject-matter must constitute an "invention". The concept of a patentable "invention" has always been notoriously difficult to define, and neither the Strasbourg Convention nor the EPC makes any attempt to do so. Article 52(2) goes further than the Strasbourg Convention, however, in setting out the above list of particular examples of subject-matter which are not regarded as within the concept of an "invention". It follows from the presence of the words "in particular" in Article 52(2) EPC that the various categories of subject-matter (a) to (d) are not intended as a complete definition of what is to be excluded. Subject-matter which is similar in nature to the defined categories could also be excluded.

Objections to patentability under Article 52(2) EPC commonly fall under more than one of the excluded categories of subject-matter set out in sub-paragraphs (a) to (d).

The words "as such" in Article 53(3) EPC narrow the scope of the excluded subject-matter and activities, as discussed below.

(2) Technical subject-matter of claimed invention

The requirement that a claimed invention must define technical subject- 9–13
matter was derived from the practice under the existing national patent
laws of at least the majority of Contracting States before the EPC came into
force. This requirement has been confirmed in the practice of the Boards of
Appeal.

Thus, with reference to the excluded subject-matter and activities under
Article 52(2)(a) to (d) EPC:

> "Whatever their differences, these exclusions have in common that
> they refer to activities which do not aim at any direct technical result
> but are rather of an abstract and intellectual character.
>
> The requirement that an invention must have a technical character,
> or in other words, must provide a technical contribution to the art, is at
> the basis of a long-standing legal practice in at least the majority of
> Contracting States of the EPO. Neither from the terms of Article 52
> EPC, nor from the legislative history of that Article as appearing from
> the preparatory documents, can it be deduced that these Contracting
> States would have intended to deviate from their national laws and
> jurisprudence in this respect. On the contrary, it seems to be borne out
> by the list of exceptions in Article 52(2)(a) to (d) EPC that they did not
> wish to do so" (T22/85[4]).

Similarly: 9–14

> "As the list of exclusions from patentability ... is not exhaustive in
> view of the phrase 'in particular' in Article 52(2) EPC, the exclusion
> might be arguably generalised to subject-matter which is essentially
> abstract in character and therefore is not characterised by technical
> features in the sense of Rule 29(1) EPC." (T163/85[5]).

> "Although Article 52 EPC does not use the word 'technical', neverthe-
> less ... the proper interpretation of the word 'inventions' as used in the
> plural in Article 52(1) EPC, requires a claimed subject-matter or
> activity to have a technical character, and thus in principle to be
> industrially applicable" (T854/90[6]; see also T22/85[7], T208/84[8]).

The above interpretation of Article 52(1) EPC is consistent with the
requirements of Rules 27 and 29 EPC. Rule 27(1)(c) EPC requires that
the *description* shall disclose the claimed invention in such terms that the
technical problem and its solution can be understood, while rule 29(1) EPC

---

[4] T22/85 *IBM/Document abstracting and retrieving* O.J. EPO 1990, 12; [1990] E.P.O.R. 98.
[5] T163/85 *BBC/Colour television signal* O.J. EPO 1990, 379; [1990] E.P.O.R. 599.
[6] T854/90 *IBM/Card reader* O.J. EPO 1993, 669; [1994] E.P.O.R. 89.
[7] See note 4.
[8] T208/84 *VICOM/Computer-related invention* O.J. EPO 1987, 14; [1987] E.P.O.R. 74.

requires the *claims* to define the matter for which protection is sought in terms of the *technical features* of the invention.

As indicated above the requirement for an invention to have a technical character implies a physical rather than an abstract or mental nature, and thus corresponds closely to the requirement for industrial applicability in Articles 52(1) and 57 EPC (see paragraph 9–98 below).

(3) Only excluded subject-matter "as such" is unpatentable

9–15   The distinction between technical and abstract subject-matter was emphasised in T208/84 (*Vicom*[9]) which is the leading case concerning Article 52(2) and (3) EPC, with particular reference to the words "as such" in Article 52(3) EPC. The application concerned an invention relating to digitally processing images in the form of a data array, as well as apparatus for carrying out such a method. Its patentability was considered with reference to Article 52(2)(a) EPC ("mathematical method") and Article 52(2)(c) EPC ("program for computers").

A distinction was drawn between a mathematical method or algorithm as such, and its use in a technical process, as follows:

> "There can be little doubt that any processing operation on an electric signal can be described in mathematical terms. The characteristic of a filter, for example, can be expressed in terms of a mathematical formula. A basic difference between a mathematical method and a technical process can be seen, however, in the fact that a mathematical method or a mathematical algorithm is carried out on numbers (whatever these numbers may represent) and provides a result also in numerical form, the mathematical method or algorithm being only an abstract concept prescribing how to operate on the numbers. No direct technical result is produced by the method as such. In contrast thereto, if a mathematical method is used in a technical process, that process is carried out on a physical entity (which may be a material object but equally an image stored as an electric signal) by some technical means implementing the method and provides as its result a certain change in that entity. The technical means might include a computer comprising suitable hardware or an appropriately programmed general purpose computer" (T208/84[10]).

Thus:

> "even if the idea underlying an invention may be considered to reside in a mathematical method, a claim directed to a technical process in which the method is used does not seek protection for the mathematical method as such.

[9] T208/84 *VICOM/Computer-related invention* O.J. EPO 1987, 14; [1986] E.P.O.R. 74.
[10] *Ibid.*

410

In contrast, a 'method for digitally filtering data', remains an abstract notion not distinguished from a mathematical method so long as it is not specified what physical entity is represented by the data and forms the subject of a technical process, *i.e.* a process which is susceptible of industrial application" (T208/84[11]).

Similarly, a distinction was drawn between a computer program as **9–16** such, and its use in a technical process, as follows:

"A claim directed to a technical process which process is carried out under the control of a program (whether by means of hardware or software), cannot be regarded as relating to a computer program as such ... claims which can be considered as being directed to a computer set up to operate in accordance with a specified program (whether by means of hardware or software) for controlling or carrying out a technical process cannot be regarded as relating to a computer program as such" (T208/84[12]).

In application of the above principles to computer programs, for **9–17** example:

"Even if the basic idea underlying an invention may be considered to reside in a computer program, a claim directed to its use in the solution of a technical problem cannot be regarded as seeking protection for the program as such within the meaning of Article 52(2)(c) and (3) EPC" (T115/85[13]).

Similarly, with reference to "discoveries", a "discovery as such" is normally considered to mean the mere recognition of what already exists. Human intervention or interaction with what has been discovered may therefore constitute a distinction between "discovery as such" and "inventing". Thus:

"In particular cases it may clearly be necessary to consider and decide whether a claimed invention is a discovery within the meaning of Article 52(2)(a) EPC. An essential first step in such consideration is to construe the claim so as to determine its technical features. If, after such determination, it is clear that the claimed invention relates to a discovery or other excluded subject-matter 'as such' (Article 52(3) EPC), then the exclusion of Article 52(2) EPC applies. In this connection, as was recognised in ... T208/84[14] (dealing there with a mathematical method rather than a discovery, but the same principle applies), the fact that the idea or concept underlying the claimed

---

[11] T208/84 *VICOM/Computer-related invention* O.J. EPO 1987, 14; [1986] E.P.O.R. 74.
[12] *Ibid.*
[13] T115/85 *IBM/Computer-related invention* O.J. EPO 1990, 30; [1990] E.P.O.R. 107.
[14] See note 11.

subject-matter resides in a discovery does not necessarily mean that the claimed subject-matter is a discovery 'as such'." (G2, 6/88[15]).

In summary of the above, therefore, whereas for example a discovery, mathematical method or a computer program "as such" is not patentable under Article 52(2) EPC, the practical application of such a discovery, mathematical method or computer program may be patentable if such practical application provides a technical contribution to the art.

(4) Consideration of the claimed invention as a whole

9–18 When determining the patentability of claimed subject-matter, it is necessary to consider the claimed invention as a whole:

> "Generally speaking, an invention which would be patentable in accordance with conventional patentability criteria should not be excluded from protection by the mere fact that, for its implementation, modern technical means in the form of a computer program are used. Decisive is what technical contribution the invention as defined in the claim *when considered as a whole* makes to the known art" (T208/84[16]— emphasis added).

Similarly:

> "an invention must be assessed as a whole. If it makes use of both technical and non-technical means, the use of non-technical means does not detract from the technical character of the overall teaching. The EPC does not ask that a patentable invention be exclusively or largely of a technical nature; in other words, it does not prohibit the patenting of inventions consisting of a mix of technical and non-technical elements" (T26/86[17])

Consequently:

> "In deciding whether a claim relates to a computer program as such, it is not necessary to give a relative weighting to its technical and non-technical features. If the invention defined in the claim uses technical means, it can be patented provided it meets the requirements of Articles 52 to 57 EPC" (T26/86[18]).

---

[15] G2, 6/88 *MOBIL OIL/BAYER/Friction reducing additive* O.J. EPO 1990, 93, 114; [1990] E.P.O.R. 73, 257.
[16] T208/84 *VICOM/Computer-aided invention* O.J. EPO 1987, 14; [1986] E.P.O.R. 74.
[17] T26/86 *KOCH & STERZEL/X-ray apparatus* O.J. EPO 1988, 19; [1988] E.P.O.R. 72.
[18] *Ibid.*

(5) Mixed technical and non-technical features: true nature of the invention

If a claimed invention includes both technical and non-technical features, its patentability has to be assessed against the requirements of Article 52(2) EPC. The presence of non-technical features (*i.e.* features lying within an excluded field) does not necessarily mean that the claimed invention is unpatentable, and the presence of technical features does not mean that it is patentable. In particular the mere "dressing up" of excluded subject-matter with technical features does not make such subject-matter patentable. 9–19

For example, in a case where the contribution to the art lies in an excluded field (*e.g.* abstracting, storing and retrieving documents in accordance with a set of rules), the inclusion of technical features in the claim in the form of conventional hardware which carries out such set of rules (*e.g.* conventional computer means controlled by a suitable program) does not avoid the exclusion from patentability under Article 52(2) EPC. In such a case:

> "The contribution to the art and the effects obtained are only in the area of the excluded activity and the true nature of the invention remains the same, whether or not a technical terminology is used in expressing it" (T22/85[19]).

Consequently: 9–20

> "The mere setting out of the sequence of steps necessary to perform an activity, excluded as such from patentability . . . , in terms of functions or functional means to be realised with the aid of conventional computer hardware elements does not impart any technical considerations and cannot therefore, lend a technical character to that activity and thereby overcome the exclusion from patentability" (T22/85[20]).

As another example:

> "The statement in a patent claim that technical means (in this case a visual display unit) are to be used to carry out a process is not alone sufficient to render patentable . . . a process which is in essence a computer program as such" (T158/88[21]).

Similarly:

> "A claim which, when taken as a whole, is essentially a business activity, does not have a technical character and is not a claim to a

---

[19] T22/85 *IBM/Document abstracting and retrieving* O.J. EPO 1990, 12; [1990] E.P.O.R. 98.
[20] *Ibid.*
[21] T158/88 *SIEMENS/Character form* O.J. EPO 1991, 566; [1992] E.P.O.R. 69.

patentable invention ..., even though the claimed method includes steps which include a technical component. The true nature of the claimed subject-matter remains the same even though some technical means are used to perform it" (T854/90[22]).

In summary:

"the subject-matter as a whole is excluded from patentability under Article 52(2) and (3) EPC if the mix does not make use of technical means in order to solve a technical problem" (T603/89[23]).

(6) Relationship between Articles 52(2) and 56 EPC

9–21 In cases where, with respect to a claimed invention issues arise both as to whether what is claimed constitutes an "invention" within the meaning of Article 52(1) EPC or is excluded from patentability under Article 52(2) EPC, and as to whether the claimed subject-matter involves an inventive step under Article 56 EPC, *prima facie* the issue of patentable subject-matter under Article 52(2) EPC should be examined and decided separately from the issue of inventiveness under Article 56 EPC (see for example T854/90[24], T1002/92[25] and T1173/97[26], paragraph 9–25 below).

In other words, in such cases the first question to be considered is whether or not the claimed subject-matter is excluded from patentability under Article 52(2) EPC. If the answer to such question is that the claimed subject-matter is not so excluded, a further and separate question then arises as to whether the claimed subject-matter involves an inventive step.

In many cases this approach has not been followed, however, as discussed below.

(7) Necessity for a contribution to the art in an unexcluded field

9–22 As discussed in paragraph 9–18 above, when determining whether claimed subject-matter is excluded from patentability:

"Decisive is what technical contribution the invention as defined in the claim when considered as a whole makes to the known art" (T208/84[27]).

Leaving aside in this context the requirement that the claim must be "considered as a whole", this statement also emphasises that the "contribution to the known art" must be "technical". The reference to a "contribution to the known art" necessarily implies some knowledge as to the state of the art, and in this connection it is relevant that Rule 27(1) EPC

---

[22] T854/90 *IBM/Card reader* O.J. EPO 1993, 669; [1994] E.P.O.R. 89.
[23] T603/89 *BEATTIE/Marker* O.J. EPO 1992, 230; [1992] E.P.O.R. 221.
[24] See note 22.
[25] T1002/92 *PETTERSON/Queueing system* O.J. EPO 1995, 605; [1996] E.P.O.R. 1.
[26] T1173/97 *IBM/Computer program product* O.J. EPO 1999, 609.
[27] T208/84 *VICOM/Computer-related invention* O.J. EPO 1987, 14; [1986] E.P.O.R. 74.

requires that the description of an application shall "indicate the background art which, as far as known to the applicant, can be regarded as useful for understanding the invention", and shall "disclose the invention ..., in such terms that the technical problem. ... and its solution can be understood".

Thus no claimed invention stands in complete isolation from the known background art. Such background prior art can properly be taken into account when determining the nature of the claimed invention and thus its relationship with the background art.

In a number of decisions, the idea that a patentable "invention" within 9–23 the meaning of Article 52(1) EPC must involve a technical contribution to the known art has been taken a stage further. In particular:

> "Since according to Article 52(3) EPC patentability is excluded only to the extent to which the patent application relates to subject-matter or activities summarised in Article 52(2) EPC as such, it appears to be the intention of the EPC to permit patenting in those cases in which the invention involves some contribution to the art in a field not excluded from patentability" (T38/86[28]).

Beyond this a number of subsequent Board of Appeal decisions have developed case law to the effect that:

> "from Article 52(3) EPC it would appear to be the intention of the EPC to permit patenting (only) in those cases in which the invention involves some contribution to the art in a field not excluded from patentability" (T833/91[29]).

In applying this criterion for assessing patentability: 9–24

> "the technical contribution to the art rendering a claimed invention an invention in the sense of Article 52(1) EPC, and thus patentable, may be either in the problem underlying and solved by the claimed invention, or in the means constituting the solution of the underlying problem or in the effects achieved in the solution of the underlying problem" (T833/91[30]).

In cases where the claimed invention involves a mixture of technical features and excluded subject-matter (see paragraph 9–18 above) (*e.g.* "a mix of computer hardware, *i.e.* technical, and of processing, *i.e.* functional features"):

> "in accordance with the Boards' case law (see T26/86[31]...), such a mix

---

[28] T38/86 *IBM/Text clarity processing* O.J. EPO 1990, 384; [1990] E.P.O.R. 181.
[29] T833/91 *IBM* April 16, 1993.
[30] *Ibid.*
[31] T26/86 *KOCH & STERZEL/X-ray apparatus* O.J. EPO 1988, 19; [1988] E.P.O.R. 72.

may or may not be patentable. If, for instance, a non-patentable (*e.g.* mathematical, mental or business) method is implemented by running a program on a general purpose computer, the fact above that the computer consists of hardware does not render the method patentable, if said hardware is purely conventional and no technical contribution to that (computer) art is made by the implementation. However, if a contribution to that art can be found either in a technical problem (to be) solved, or in a technical effect achieved by the solution, said mix may not be excluded from patentability under Articles 52(2) and (3) EPC, following T38/86[32] . . ." (T769/92[33]).

In particular:

"An invention comprising functional features implemented by software (computer programs) is not excluded from patentability ... if technical considerations concerning particulars of the solution of the problem the invention solves are required in order to carry out that same invention. Such technical considerations lend a technical nature to the invention in that they imply a technical problem to be solved by (implicit) technical features" (T769/92[34]).

In application of the above principles, a number of decisions have considered the issue of inventive step under Article 56 EPC at the same time as, and in the context of the issue of patentability under Article 52(2) EPC. However, patentability having regard to Article 52(2) EPC depends upon the presence of a technical character or effect associated with the claimed subject-matter (see paragraphs 9–13 *et seq.* above). The presence of such a technical character derived from a technical effect does not depend upon the state of the art at the filing date. For the purpose of determining the extent of the exclusion under Article 52(2) and (3) EPC, the technical effect which provides a technical character for the claimed subject-matter may be known in the prior art. In such a case the claimed subject-matter is potentially patentable subject-matter within the meaning of Article 52(1), (2) and (3) EPC but lacks novelty (and/or inventive step).

Determining the technical contribution an invention achieves with respect to the prior art is therefore more appropriate for the purpose of examining novelty and inventive step than for deciding on possible exclusion under Article 52(2) and (3) EPC (T1173/97[35]).

---

[32] T38/86 *IBM/Text clarity processing* O.J. EPO 1990, 384; [1990] E.P.O.R. 72.
[33] T769/92 *SOHEI/General purpose management system* O.J. EPO 1995, 525; [1996] E.P.O.R. 253.
[34] *Ibid.*
[35] T1173/97 *IBM/Computer program product* O.J. EPO 1999, 609.

(8) Examples of the excluded categories: particular cases

(a) Discoveries, scientific theories and mathematical methods

(1) The invention concerned a method of generating a data analysis of the **9–25** cyclical behaviour of a curve represented by a plurality of plots relating two parameters to one another. The analysis of the cyclical behaviour of a curve was regarded as a mathematical method and therefore excluded from patentability (T953/94[36]).

(b) Aesthetic creations

The claimed invention was a flexible plastic disc jacket having a colour **9–26** outer surface (other than black). A suggested technical advantage of resistance to finger-print marking was rejected as purely aesthetic (Article 52(2)(b) EPC):

> "The feature of having a specific colour or any of a specified range of colours does cause an otherwise known invention to be excluded from patentability when the effects produced by that feature in its combination with said known invention constitute a contribution to the prior art solely within the fields excluded from patentabilty" (T119/88[37]).

(c)(i) Schemes, rules and methods for performing mental acts

(1) The claimed invention was a method of abstracting and storing **9–27** documents in an information storage and retrieval system, using conventional hardware controlled by new software which put into effect a specific set of rules for the above activities. The claimed method fell within Article 52(2)(c) EPC:

> "The mere setting out of the sequence of steps ..., in terms of functions or functional means to be realised with the aid of conventional computer hardware does not impart any technical considerations ..." (T22/85[38]).

(2) The claimed invention was a method for automatically detecting and **9–28** replacing difficult linguistic expressions with mere readily understandable synonyms. The claimed operating steps were considered to be exactly equivalent to the mental steps which a person would take, wishing to achieve the same result, but according to the claim, such steps were instead controlled by a computer. The claimed method was excluded from patentability under Article 52(2)(c) EPC (T38/86[39]).

---

[36] T953/94 July 15, 1996.
[37] T119/88 FUJI/Coloured disk jacket O.J. EPO 1990, 395; [1990] E.P.O.R. 615.
[38] T22/85 IBM/Document abstracting and retrieving O.J. EPO 1990, 12; [1990] E.P.O.R. 98.
[39] T38/86 IBM/Text clarity processing O.J. EPO 1990, 384; [1990] E.P.O.R. 181.

9–29   (3) The claimed invention concerned a process for protecting sound-recording carriers and their labels and packaging against counterfeiting, by marking such materials with coded marks derived from the individual data as individual carriers:

> "Procedural steps involved in applying a coded distinctive mark to an object, providing the object with characteristic data and forming the distinctive mark by coding the characteristic data, may be carried out in any desired manner.
>
>   If a claim focuses solely on such procedural steps without indicating or presupposing technical means for carrying them out, a process of this kind will come under the heading of matter excluded from patentability by Article 52(2)(c) ..." (T51/84[40]).

(c)(ii) Methods of doing business

9–30 The claimed invention concerned an automatic self-service machine operable upon presentation of a card carrying identification data, and was based on the idea that a person wishing to carry out transactions on the machines does not need a special card issued by the machine owner as authorisation, but may use a card already in his possession following authorisation by another organisation, in the first instance in order to apply for authorisation to the machine owner. The card which is presented for the first time to the machine is therefore equivalent to an application form, for authorisation by the machine owner.

   The claimed invention was essentially a business operation, did not have a technical character and was not a claim to a patentable invention (T854/90[41]).

(c)(iii) Programs for computers

9–31 A computer program is a series of instruction to a control processing unit. A computer program as such is abstract and mental in nature and therefore specifically excluded from patentability. In other words, Articles 52(2) and (3) EPC are interpreted as meaning that "programs for computers cannot be considered as having a technical character for the very reason that they are programs for computers" (T1173/97[42]). The question then arises as to the circumstances in which a computer program can be considered as having a technical character for the purposes of Article 52(2) and (3) EPC, and thus as to the circumstances in which a claimed invention involving a computer program is patentable.

---

[40] T51/84 *STOCKBURGER/Coded distinctive mark* O.J. EPO 1986, 226; [1986] E.P.O.R. 229.
[41] T854/90 *IBM/Card reader* O.J. EPO 1993, 669; [1994] E.P.O.R. 89.
[42] T1173 *IBM/Computer program product* O.J. EPO 1999, 609.

A technical character cannot be attributed to a computer program for the sole reason that the program is destined to be used in a technical apparatus, namely a computer (T1173/97[43], and see, *e.g.* T208/84[44]).

Similarly, "physical modifications of the hardware drawing from the execution of the instructions of a computer program cannot per se constitute the technical character of programs for computers" (T1173/97[45] and see, *e.g.* T22/85[46]).

However, a claimed invention may be patentable "when the basic idea underlying the invention resides in the computer program itself". For example, "A claim directed to the use of a computer program for the solution of a technical problem cannot be regarded as seeking protection for the program as such...", even if the basic idea underlying the invention lies in the computer program (T208/84[47]; T115/85[48], T1173/97[49] and see paragraph 9–16 above).

For example, as discussed in paragraphs 9–13 *et seq.* above, the fact that technical considerations were required in order to arrive at the invention may provide sufficient technical character to avoid exclusion from patentability (T769/92[50]).

In a number of cases a computer program *per se* was regarded as **9–32** excluded from patentability under Article 52(2) EPC, independently of its contents, and in particular, regardless of what the program would do when used in a computer (see for example T26/86[51], T110/90[52], T164/92[53], T204/93[54]).

However, distinguishing the above decisions, claims to a *computer program product* are now allowed on the basis that:

> "A computer program product is not excluded from patentability ... if, when it is run on a computer, it produces a further technical effect which goes beyond the 'normal' physical interactions between program (software) and computer (hardware)" (T1173/97[55]).

Such a "further technical effect" is regarded as giving a technical character to a claimed invention so as to avoid exclusion from patentability under Article 52(2) and (3) EPC.

Thus where such further effects "have a technical character or where

---

[43] T1173/97 IBM/*Computer program product* O.J. EPO 1999, 109.
[44] T208/84 VICOM/*Computer-related invention* O.J. EPO 1987, 14; [1986] E.P.O.R. 74.
[45] See note 43.
[46] T22/85 IBM/*Document abstracting and retrieving* O.J. EPO 1990, 12; [1990] E.P.O.R. 98.
[47] See note 44.
[48] T115/85 IBM/*Computer related invention* O.J. EPO 1990, 30; [1990] E.P.O.R. 107.
[49] See note 43.
[50] T769/92 SOHEI/*General purpose management system* O.J. EPO 1995, 525; [1996] E.P.O.R. 253.
[51] T26/86 KOCH & STERZEL/*x-ray apparatus* O.J. EPO 1988, 19; [1988] E.P.O.R. 72.
[52] T110/90 IBM/*Editable document prm* O.J. EPO 1994, 557; [1995] E.P.O.R. 185.
[53] T164/92 ROBERT BOSCH/*Electronic computer components* O.J. EPO 1995, 305; [1995] E.P.O.R. 585.
[54] T204/93 AT&T October 29, 1993.
[55] See note 43.

they cause the software to solve a technical problem, an invention which brings about such an effect ... can ... in principle be the subject-matter of a patent", and "a patent may be granted ... in every case where a program for a computer is the only means, or one of the necessary means of obtaining a technical effect within the meaning specified above, where, for instance, a technical effect of that kind is achieved by the internal functioning of a computer itself under the influence of said program".

9-33   "In other words, on condition that they are able to produce a technical effect in the above sense, all computer programs must be considered as inventions within the meaning of Article 52(1) EPC, and may be the subject-matter of a patent if the other requirements provided for by the EPC are satisfied" (T1173/97[56]).

The technical character of such a computer program product is derived from the "further technical effect" in the sense of the "potential technical effect" which the program possesses and reveals when it is run on a computer.

It should be mentioned that the decision to allow claims in the form of computer programs products to be patented in accordance with the principles set out above was taken in the context of the TRIPS Agreement (see Chapter 1 at paragraph 1–55). In this connection, "although TRIPS may not be applied directly to the EPC ... it [is] appropriate to take it into consideration, since it is aimed at setting common standards and principles ..." (T1173/97[57]).

Having regard to Article 27 TRIPS, "it is the clear intention of TRIPS not to exclude from patentability ..., in particular ... programs for computers as mentioned in and excluded under Article 52(2)(c) EPC" (T1173/97[58]).

9-33A   The proposed revision of the EPC does not include any amendment of Article 52(2) EPC. Particularly, in relation to the exclusion of computer programs, this will be considered in a further revision Conference (see Chapter 1 at paragraph 1–06, and Appendix 24).

(d) Presentations of information

9-34   (1) The claimed invention was a flexible disc jacket having a coloured outer surface (other than black) (see paragraph 9–26 above). A suggested advantage that such jackets could be classified according to colour was rejected as constituting "presentation of information" (T119/88[59]).

9-35   (2) The claimed invention was a colour television signal characterised by features of the transmitting and receiving system in which it was to be used, which were therefore technical in nature. Such technical information was distinguished from, for example, picture information transmitted within the system, and the transmission of such technical information was

---

[56] T1173/97 IBM/*Computer program product* O.J. EPO 1999, 609.
[57] *Ibid.*
[58] *Ibid.*
[59] T119/88 FUJI/*Coloured disc jacket* O.J. EPO 1990, 395; [1990] E.P.O.R. 615.

420

therefore not a "presentation of information" within Article 52(2)(d) EPC (T163/85[60]; see also T110/90[61], T1194/97[62]).

C. Medical Treatment and Diagnosis

Article 52(4) EPC

(1) Introduction

Article 52(4) EPC states that: 9–36

> "Methods for treatment of the human or animal body by surgery or therapy and diagnostic methods practised on the human or animal body shall not be regarded as inventions which are susceptible of industrial application within the meaning of [Article 52(1) EPC]. This provision shall not apply to products, in particular substances or compositions for use in any of these methods".

The above defined methods will be referred to as "methods of medical treatment".

The wording of the first sentence of Article 52(4) EPC emphasises that, in contrast to Article 52(2) EPC (which excludes certain subject-matter as not being regarded as "inventions"—see paragraph 9–04 above), the excluded methods of medical treatment may constitute an "invention", but are not to be regarded as "susceptible of industrial application", by way of legal fiction. This distinction between the mechanisms of exclusion in Articles 52(2) and (4) EPC is essentially academic in view of the way in which Article 52(4) EPC has been interpreted, namely that even if a method of medical treatment is novel, inventive and susceptible of industrial application as a matter of reality, such a method is still excluded from patentability as a matter of legal fiction (see below).

The second sentence of Article 52(4) EPC emphasises "out of an 9–37 abundance of caution" (G5/83[63]) that the exclusion from patentability only applies to *methods*, and does not apply to products. This reflects the fact that pharmaceutical products in general (as well as chemical and food products) are not excluded from patent protection (subject to any past reservations by individual Contracting States for a limited period of time under Article 167 EPC: according to the Basic Proposal Article 67 EPC will be deleted).

If an excluded method of medical treatment involves a further medical use of a known product, it may still be protected by means of a "Swiss form

---

[60] T163/85 *BBC/Colour television signal* O.J. EPO 1990, 379; [1990] E.P.O.R. 599.
[61] T110/90 *IBM/Editable document form* O.J. EPO 1994, 557; [1995] E.P.O.R. 185.
[62] T1194/97 *PHILIPS/Data structure* O.J. EPO (P).
[63] G5/83 *EISAI/Second medical indication* O.J. EPO 1985, 64; [1979–85] E.P.O.R.: B: 241.

of claim" (see Chapter 11 at paragraphs 11–86 *et seq.*; G5/83; and see for example T19/86[64], T290/86[65], T655/92[66]).

It has been suggested that in accordance with general principles, because Article 52(4) EPC is an exclusion clause, it should be interpreted narrowly (T385/86[67]).

However, the proper extent of these exclusions is in practice normally considered having particular regard to their purpose, namely to prevent medical and veterinary practitioners from being restricted by patents in the treatment of their patients.

Article 52(4) EPC excludes three specific kinds of method from patentability:

(i) Methods of treatment by surgery;
(ii) Methods of treatment by therapy;
(iii) Diagnostic methods.

These will be considered separately below.

9–37A   According to the proposed revision of the EPC, the provisions of Article 52(4) EPC will become Article 53(c) EPC. Accordingly, the legal fiction that "methods of medical treatment" are not to be regarded as "susceptible of industrial application" will cease, and such provisions will become an exception to patentability, in parallel with Article 53(a) and (b) EPC (see paragraphs 9–73 *et seq.* below).

See also paragraph 9–38A.

(2) The nature of these exclusions

(a) Only methods excluded

9–38 These exclusions only concern inventions claimed in terms of a method:

"The intention of Article 52(4) EPC ... is only to free from restraint non-commercial and non-industrial medical and veterinary activities" (G5/83[68]).

"The exclusion of such methods from patentability is not a new provision under the EPC. Prior to the coming into force of the EPC, such methods were excluded from patentability under the national laws of many European countries. The policy behind the exclusion of such methods is clearly in order to ensure that those who carry out such methods as part of the medical treatment of humans or the veterinary treatment of animals should not be inhibited by patents" (T116/85[69]).

[64] T19/86 DUPHAR/Pigs II O.J. EPO 1989, 24; [1988] E.P.O.R. 10.
[65] T290/86 ICI/Cleaning plaque O.J. EPO 1992, 414; [1991] E.P.O.R. 157.
[66] T655/92 NYCOMED/Contrast agent for NMR imaging O.J. EPO 1998, 17; [1998] E.P.O.R. 206.
[67] T385/86 BRUKER/Non invasive measurement O.J. EPO 1988, 398; [1988] E.P.O.R. 357.
[68] G5/83 EISAI/Second medical indication O.J. EPO 1985, 64; [1979–85] E.P.O.R.: B: 241.
[69] T116/85 WELLCOME/Pigs I O.J. EPO 1989, 13; [1988] E.P.O.R. 1.

Such policy can be seen as a compromise between opposing interests, namely, on the one hand, the need to encourage research in relation to medical compositions and, on the other hand, the need not to restrict the medical and veterinary treatments normally carried out by physicians.

Nevertheless, the avoidance of legal restrictions upon medical veterinary practitioners could be achieved without excluding such methods of treatment from patentability, and furthermore, it is in the public interest to encourage inventive research equally for both medical products and medical methods of treatment. Having regard also to the complications surrounding the protection of further medical uses of known products (see Chapter 11 at paragraphs 11–86 *et seq.*), it would seem desirable for Article 52(4) EPC to be deleted from the EPC.

According to the proposed revision of the EPC, however, Article 52(4) **9–38A**
EPC will not be deleted: see paragraph 9–37A above.

(b) Necessity for interaction with the human or animal body

Accordingly to Article 52(4) EPC methods of medical treatment are not **9–39**
excluded from patentability unless, in the case of surgery or therapy, they involve "treatment of the human or animal body", and in the case of diagnostic methods, they are "practised on the human or animal body".

The preparatory papers for Article 52(4) EPC provide pointers to its meaning and purpose in the context of diagnostic methods:

> "According to an initial proposal, processes used in the laboratory for the purpose of diagnosis were definitely not to be patentable where they involved treatment by doctors.... The subsequent proposal of a general exclusion of all diagnostic methods brought objections from interested circles who claimed that advances in technology had indeed led to the evolving of diagnostic methods which were not of a specifically medical nature.... Following a proposal from the French delegation, the term 'diagnostic methods' was later defined more precisely by the addition of the words 'applied to the human or animal body....' Moreover, in the 'Grounds given with regard to the ratification of international patent conventions' it is stated that the exclusion made by article 52(4) EPC is in line with existing case law and literature and was ethically motivated...." (T385/86[70]).

(c) Treatments of human and animal bodies equally excluded

The wording of Article 52(4) EPC regards the medical treatment of both **9–40**
human and animal bodies as equally deserving of exclusion from patentability.

At the Intergovernmental Conference leading to the EPC, it had been proposed that the medical treatment of animal bodies should be considered as patentable. However, the present wording of the Article was

---

[70] T385/86 *BRUKER/Non-invasive measurement* O.J. EPO 1988, 398; [1988] E.P.O.R. 357.

adopted on ethical grounds, although it was accepted that wording of the exclusion was in broad terms and would be the subject of interpretation by the Boards of Appeal and national courts.

(d) Claims with one "method of treatment" step included

9–41 A claim which only includes one method step which is a method of treatment of a human or animal body as a technical feature of the claim is sufficient to exclude such claim from patentability.
Thus:

> "Under Article 52(4) EPC, a claim is not allowable if it includes at least one feature defining a physical activity or action (*e.g.* a method step) which constitutes 'a method of treatment of the human ... body by therapy' ... Whether or not the claim includes features directed to a technical object is legally irrelevant to the application of Article 52(4) EPC" (T82/93[71]).

For example, even if the overall effect of a claimed treatment is not therapeutic, "a method claim falls under the prohibition of Article 52(4) EPC ... if the purpose of the administration of one of the substances is a treatment by therapy, and the administration of this substance is a feature of the claim" (T820/92[72]).

Similarly, a claim which includes a number of features defining a device, and which also includes at least one technical feature defining a method of therapeutic treatment, is excluded under Article 52(4) EPC (T82/93[73]).

(3) Treatment by surgery

9–42 Following the principles set out in paragraph 9–41 above:

> "The presence of a surgical step in a multi-step method for treatment of the human or animal body normally confers a surgical character on that method"

and thus excludes the method from patentability (T182/90[74]).

For example, a claimed method which includes a step of accessing the pericardial space between the heart and the pericardium of a human being, by penetrating through the wall of the right auricle with a catheter or an electrode, is a method for treatment of the human body by surgery which is therefore excluded from patentability (T35/99[75]).

> "However, a method which includes a surgical step practised on a

---

[71] T82/93 *TELECTRONICS/Cardiac pacing* O.J. EPO 1996, 274; [1996] E.P.O.R. 409.
[72] T820/92 *GENERAL HOSPITAL/Contraceptive method* O.J. EPO 1995, 113; [1995] E.P.O.R. 446.
[73] See note 71.
[74] T182/90 *SEE-SHELL/Blood flow* O.J. EPO 1994, 641; [1994] E.P.O.R. 320.
[75] T35/99 *GEORGETOWN UNIVERSITY/Pericordial access* O.J. EPO (P).

living laboratory animal, and, in addition, a step of sacrificing said animal, which step is also necessary to carry out the method, cannot be regarded in its entirety as a method for treatment of the animal by surgery in the sense of Article 52(4) EPC" (T182/90[76]).

A method of treatment which deliberately ends in the death of the treated subject is not *by its nature* a method of surgical treatment, irrespective of whether it comprises one or more surgical steps (T182/90[77], T35/99[78]), and carrying it out would not interfere with medical or veterinary practitioners.

(4) Treatment by therapy

(a) The nature of therapy

Therapy "covers any non-surgical treatment which is designed to cure, **9–43** alleviate, remove or lessen the symptom of, or prevent or reduce the possibility of contracting any malfunction of the human or animal body . . . and also relates to the treatment of a disease in general or to a curative treatment in the narrow sense, as well as the alleviation of the symptoms of pain and suffering (T58/87[79]: see also T144/83[80]).
    Thus:

"the concept of therapy should not be confined narrowly. There are many chemical agents which are used by physicians to relieve pain, discomfort and incapacity. Although at least some of such and similar experiences may have been caused by natural circumstances (*e.g.* menstruation, pregnancy or age, etc., or by a reaction to situations in the human environment (*e.g.* atmospheric conditions provoking tiredness, headaches, etc.), these overlap with and are often indistinguishable from symptoms of a disease or an injury. The biochemical effects and mechanisms which medicaments generate in order to restore the normal, capable and painless state for the body are often very similar or identical in these instances and in cases of diseases, irrespective of the nature of the real cause.
    It would be impossible and undesirable to distinguish between **9–44** basic and symptomatic therapy, *i.e.* healing or cure and mere relief. The use of medicaments may be called for whenever the human body is suffering from a disease, illness, pain or discomfort or incapacity, and the administration thereof could provide or contribute to either full or partial healing, or relief or restoration of fitness. These are part of the everyday therapeutic activities of the medical profession. . . .
    Contrary to other situations where the boundaries with the

[76] T182/90 SEE-SHELL/Blood flow O.J. EPO 1994, 641; [1994] E.P.O.R. 320.
[77] Ibid.
[78] T35/99 GEORGETOWN UNIVERSITY/Pericordial access O.J. EPO (P).
[79] T58/87 SALMINEN/Pigs III O.J. EPO 1988, 347; [1989] E.P.O.R. 125.
[80] T144/83 DU PONT/Appetite suppressant O.J. EPO 1986, 301; [1987] E.P.O.R. 6.

non-medical handling of the human body are not at all clear in view of the involvement of different specialists (*cf.* cosmeticians), the treatment of pain normally is a matter exclusively reserved for the physician" (T81/84[81]).

9–45 Consequently, "irrespective of the origin of pain, discomfort or incapacity, its relief, by the administration of an appropriate agent, is to be construed as 'therapy' or 'therapeutic use' in the sense of Article 52(4) EPC..." (T81/84[82]).
In summary therefore:

(a) the concept of therapy should not be narrowly construed; but
(b) a distinction should be drawn between the treatment of pain (which constitutes medical treatment and, therefore, therapy) and the treatment of other conditions where the boundary between medical and non-medical treatment is not so clear, *e.g* cosmetic treatments, considered below).

(b) Prophylactic treatment is therapy

9–46 Following the above definition "both prophylactic and curative treatments of disease should be regarded as falling within the meaning of the word 'therapy' in the sense that the word is used in Article 52(4) EPC, since both are directed to the same objective, *i.e.* the maintenance or restoration of health" (T19/86[83]). Thus:
"all prophylaxis serves to maintain health and therefore comes under the provisions of Article 52(4) EPC" (T780/89[84]).

(c) External and internal treatment is therapy

9–47 External treatment of a body, such as treatment of an external ectoparasitic infestation, constitutes therapy. There is no legal basis under Article 52(4) EPC for distinguishing between the treatment of ectoparasites and endoparasites, for example (T116/85[85]).

(d) Treatment of temporary or permanent conditions is therapy

9–48 For example, the treatment of both temporary and permanent ectoparasites constitues therapy (T116/85[86]).
Similarly, a treatment for the discomfort of women during periods of menstruation constitutes therapy (T81/84[87]).

[81] T81/84 *ROKER/Dysmenorrhea* O.J. EPO 1988, 207; [1988] E.P.O.R. 297.
[82] *Ibid.*
[83] T19/86 *DUPHAR/Pigs II* O.J. EPO 1989, 24; [1988] E.P.O.R. 10.
[84] T780/89 *BAYER/Immunostimulant* O.J. EPO 1993, 440; [1993] E.P.O.R. 377.
[85] T116/85 *WELLCOME/Pigs I* O.J. EPO 1989,13; [1998] E.P.O.R. 1.
[86] *Ibid.*
[87] T81/84 *RORER/Dysmenorrhea* O.J. EPO 1988, 207; [1988] E.P.O.R. 297.

(e) Contraceptive methods: not therapy

Pregnancy is not an illness and therefore its prevention by a method of 9–49
contraception is not in general within the meaning of therapy and is not
excluded from patentability under Article 52(4) EPC (T74/93[88]).

An individual contraceptive method may fall within Article 57 EPC
(T74/93[89]: see paragraph 9–98 below).

(f) The prevention of accidents: not therapy

For example, a method of preventing piglets from suffocating under their 9–50
dam, by sensing when the dam stands up, and creating conditions under
her to discourage the piglets from that area, cannot be regarded as a
treatment by therapy on the bodies of the piglets, but is more analogous to
preventing a worker from trapping his hand in machinery (T58/87[90]).

(g) Treatment by or under supervision of a physician

> "A method for treatment of the human body can normally be said to 9–51
> fall within the exclusion of . . . Article 52(4) EPC at least in those cases
> where, in view of the health risks connected with such a treatment, it
> has to be performed by a physician or under his supervision"
> (T24/91[91]).

Thus: "A process for re-profiling the anterior surface of a synthetic
lenticule secured to the cornea of the human eye for correcting vision, by
ablating (*i.e.* removing) with a laser portions of the said lenticule . . . is
excluded from patentability". . . (T24/91[92]) This is in spite of the fact that
the claimed method was not actually performed on a human body, but
upon a synthetic attachment to the human body.

However: "The need for a medical practitioner to perform a measure on
the human body or supervise such an operation is not the sole criterion by
which a method step has to be assessed . . . under Article 52(4) EPC. The
purpose and inevitable effect of the step at issue are much more important"
(T329/94[93]).

Thus if a claimed method step clearly does not involve therapeutic 9–52
treatment, the fact that it is performed by or under the supervision of a
medical practitioner does not cause the method to be excluded from
patentability.

For example: "If the claimed subject-matter is actually confined to
operating an apparatus for performing a method with the technical aim of

[88] T74/93 *BRITISH TECHNOLOGY GROUP/Contraceptive method* O.J. EPO 1995, 712; [1995] E.P.O.R. 279.
[89] *Ibid.*
[90] T58/87 *SALMINEN/Pigs III* O.J. EPO 1988, 347; [1989] E.P.O.R. 125.
[91] T24/91 *THOMPSON/Cornea* O.J. EPO 1995, 512; [1996] E.P.O.R. 19.
[92] *Ibid.*
[93] T329/94 *BAXTER/Blood extraction method* O.J. EPO 1998, 241; [1998] E.P.O.R. 363.

facilitating blood flow towards a blood extraction point, the operating method has no therapeutic purpose or effect and ... is not excluded from patentability" (T329/94[94]).

The factual situations in these two cases can be clearly distinguished. In T24/91[95], the claimed method had a therapeutic purpose (correcting vision), even if it was literally performed upon a synthetic attachment to the human body, whereas in T329/94[96] the claimed method had no therapeutic purpose as such.

(h) Methods interacting with a body without a therapeutic effect not excluded

9–53 As discussed above with reference to T329/94[97], a claimed method which has no therapeutic purpose or effect is not excluded from patentability (even if carried out by or under a medical practitioner).
Thus:

"A method ... does not fall within ... Article 52(4) EPC if there is no functional link and hence no physical causability between its constituent steps carried out in relation to a therapy device and the therapeutic effect produced on the body by the device" (T245/87[98]).

For example:

"A method of measuring the flow of small quantities of liquid is not automatically excluded from patentability ..., even if used in an implanted device for controlled drug administration, as long as there is no functional link between the method claimed and the dosing of the drug administered by means of the devices" (T245/87[99]).

In this case, the claimed method steps, although carried out upon a device implanted in a human body, represented "no more than a method of measuring the efficiency of the pump fitted in the device", in order to check the operation of the implanted device.

(5) Concurrent veterinary and therapeutic treatment in agriculture: the relationship between Articles 52(4) and 57 EPC

9–54 The question has arisen in some cases whether a veterinary therapeutic treatment carried out on herds of animals in farms (for example, prophylactic or other treatment leading to healthy animals and consequent greater yields of meat, *etc*), is excluded from patentability under Article

---

[94] T329/94 *BAXTER/Blood extraction method* O.J. EPO 1998, 241; [1998] E.P.O.R. 363.
[95] T24/91 *THOMPSON/Cornea* O.J. EPO 1995, 512; [1996] E.P.O.R. 19.
[96] See note 94.
[97] *Ibid.*
[98] T245/87 *SIEMENS/Flow measurement* O.J. EPO 1989, 171; [1989] E.P.O.R. 241.
[99] *Ibid.*

52(4) EPC having regard to the provision of Article 57 EPC, which states that:

> "An invention shall be considered as susceptible of industrial application if it can be made or used in any kind of industry, including agriculture."

"The particular problem which arises . . . is that the method which is defined by the claims can be applied either to individual animals or to herds of animals. When the method is applied to individual animals it has the nature of a veterinary treatment, and when applied to herds of animals it also has the nature of an industrial activity. There is, of course, no doubt that the rearing of live stock such as herds of pigs is a farming activity, and that farming is in the broad sense a part of agriculture and, therefore, in turn an industrial activity. . . . Thus it is easy, as such, to draw the distinction between individual veterinary treatment on the one hand and large-scale treatment activities normally carried out by a farmer on the other hand—as was put forward by the Appellant. Nevertheless, if the method defined in the claims covers both forms of activity. . . . Article 52(4) EPC excludes the methods therein defined from patentability.

It must be recognised that any therapeutic treatment of a farm animal can also be considered as an industrial activity, insofar as farming is clearly an industrial activity, and the medical treatment of disease in both individual farm animals and herds of farm animals is intended to increase the efficiency of such industrial activity. To prevent the death of a farmyard pig from disease by a medical treatment, or to cure it of a disease by such treatment and thus to increase its yield of meat, is in each case both an industrial activity and a therapeutic treatment. Clearly, the therapeutic treatment of animals is commonly an aspect of agriculture" (T116/85[100]).

The relationship between Articles 52(4) and 57 EPC is explained as **9–55** follows:

> "Article 57 EPC defines and explains the nature of the requirement in Article 52(i) EPC that the subject-matter is 'susceptible of industrial application', in particular, this Article makes it quite clear that under the EPC, agriculture is a kind of industry; and that agricultural methods are therefore, in general, methods which are susceptible of industrial application.
>
> However, the scheme of Articles 52 to 57 as set out above makes it quite clear that even though agricultural methods in general are potentially patentable subject-matter, the particular methods defined in Article 52(4) EPC are excluded from patentability. In other words,

---

[100] T116/85 WELLCOME/Pigs I O.J. EPO 1989, 13; [1988] E.P.O.R. 1.

for the particular methods defined in Article 52(4) EPC, Article 52(4) takes precedence over Article 57 EPC" (T116/85[101]).

9–56 Thus, a claimed method which by its terms is susceptible of industrial application, but which by its terms also falls within the wording of Article 52(4) EPC, must be regarded as not susceptible of industrial application and, therefore, excluded from patentability.

"A method which constitutes a therapeutic treatment cannot be patented" (T780/89[102]).

For example, a claimed invention which involved "immunostimulation of the body's own defences by the use of particular compounds, in conjunction with specific prophylaxis against certain infections, is to be classed as therapeutic treatment" within Article 52(4)EPC. Furthermore:

> "If an increase in meat production is merely the consequence of improved health and a lower death rate because of therapeutic treatment with a specific substance, this secondary effect does not deprive the use invention of the character of a therapeutic treatment" (T780/89[103]).

(6) Associated therapeutic and cosmetic treatment

(a) Introduction

9–57 A somewhat analogous question to that considered in paragraphs 9–54 to 9–56 above has arisen in cases involving a product which can be used for both therapeutic and cosmetic treatment, as to whether the cosmetic treatment is patentable; in particular where the therapeutic and cosmetic effects overlap to a greater or lesser extent.

The situation is complicated by the fact that, if the compound *per se* is already known, then in the case of a non-medical (*e.g.* cosmetic) effect, the method of treatment or use may be claimed as such, but in the case of a medical effect, the further medical use may only be claimed "in the Swiss form"—("use of a substance for the manufacture of a medicament for a specified therapeutic application") (see paragraph 9–38 above, and Chapter 11 at paragraphs 11–86 *et seq.*).

It is recognised that in appropriate cases an application or patent may contain claims in appropriate form both to a medical and a non-medical (*e.g.* cosmetic) effect. The question to be considered below is what kind of invention constitute such appropriate cases justifying patent protection, in the light of Article 52(4)EPC in particular.

"Whether or not a claimed invention is excluded from patentability

---

[101] *Ibid.*
[102] T780/89 *BAYER/Immuno stimulant* O.J. EPO 1993, 440; [1993] E.P.O.R. 377.
[103] *Ibid.*

under Article 52(4) EPC depends in particular upon the wording of the claim in question" (T290/86[104]).

(b) Separate protection of medical and non-medical (e.g. cosmetic) treatment

In a case involving medical and non-medical (*e.g.* cosmetic) uses of a **9–58** compound, appropriate wording of the claims may allow separate protection of both such uses.
Thus:

"Where a product is shown to have various properties, a right of protection may be accorded for various uses. A product's first use in a method of treatment of the human or animal body by therapy and also its use cosmetically may therefore be claimed in one and the same application. The cosmetic indication of a product having medical indications as well does not fall within the scope of Article 52(4) EPC and may be patentable" (T36/83[105]).

In particular, the cosmetic use of such a product may be patentable if the wording of the claim is such that "it clearly covers a method of cosmetic use and is unrelated to the therapy of human or animal body in the ordinary sense" (T144/83[106]; also T36/83[107]). This applies even if "the cosmetic treatment according to the application may also incidentally involve a medical treatment" (T36/83[108]).
For example, in both of the above cases the claimed non-medical treatment was considered to be in practice distinct from a medical treatment.

(c) Inevitable concurrent medical and non-medical treatment excluded

In contrast to the above cases: **9–59**

"If the claimed invention is not directed solely to a cosmetic effect, but is also necessarily defining a treatment of the human body by therapy as well such a claim is excluded from patentability ..." (T290/86[109]).

In this case, the claims were directed to "A method of cleaning plaque and/or stains from human teeth ..." by applying a composition including a particular ingredient. The description recognised that plaque is a dominant factor in cavities and peridontal disease. Thus the claimed invention would "always inevitably have a therapeutic effect (at least in

[104] T290/86 *ICI/Cleaning plaque* O.J. EPO 1992, 414; [1991] E.P.O.R. 157.
[105] T36/83 *ROUSSEL-UCLAF/Thenoyl peroxide* O.J. EPO 1986, 295; [1987] E.P.O.R. 1.
[106] T144/83 *DU PONT/Appetite suppressant* O.J. 1986, 301; [1987] E.P.O.R. 6.
[107] See note 105.
[108] *Ibid.*
[109] See note 104.

the prophylactic sense) as well as a cosmetic effect", and was therefore "not directed solely to a cosmetic effect, but is also necessarily defining" a therapeutic treatment as well.

This is in contrast to T144/83[110] above, where "a cosmetically beneficial loss of weight by treatment (in accordance with the invention) of a person who is not suffering from obesity in the medical sense would not necessarily be beneficial to the health of that person, and therefore would not be a therapeutic treatment of that person" (T290/86[111]).

The distinction between T290/86[112] and T144/83[113] is a fine one. In the latter case, the invention was in fact protected by a "Swiss form of claim".

(7) Diagnostic methods

9–60 The proper extent of this exclusion is indicated by the preparatory papers for Article 52(4) EPC. The original proposed wording—a general exclusion of all diagnostic methods—was subsequently more precisely defined in the present wording of the Article, by the addition of the words "applied to the human or animal body".

Against this background, and having regard to the intention underlying Article 52(4) EPC which is to ensure that "no-one can be hampered in the practice of medicine by patent legislation":

> "As any exclusion clause, Article 52(4) EPC, first sentence, must be narrowly construed. A diagnostic method is practised on the human body ... only if both examination and establishing the symptoms on the basis of the examination results are performed on a living human or animal body" (T385/86[114]).

Consequently, in accordance with the established practice:

> "The only diagnostic methods to be excluded from patent protection are those whose results immediately make it possible to decide on a particular course of medical treatment. Methods providing only interim results are thus [not excluded], even if they can be utilised in making a diagnosis" (T385/86[115]).

9–61 Thus "methods for obtaining chemical/physical data from inside the living body by means of diagnostic apparatus registering these data or reproducing images ... do not fall within the exclusion of Articles 52(4) EPC". This is "based on the consideration that in such methods the step sequence for which protection is sought does not include any stage having the character of medical diagnostic activity or medical treatment or any

---

[110] T144/83 *DU PONT/Appetite suppressant* O.J. EPO 1986, 301; [1987] E.P.O.R. 6.
[111] T290/86 *ICI/Cleaning plaque* O.J. EPO 1992, 414; [1991] E.P.O.R. 157.
[112] *Ibid.*
[113] See note 110.
[114] T385/86 *BRUKER/Non-invasive measurement* O.J. EPO 1988, 398; [1988] E.P.O.R. 357.
[115] *Ibid.*

measure requiring a doctor to carry them out. Rather [such methods] could be carried out by a technician in order to provide a basis for the doctors' subsequent activity of diagnosis" (T655/92[116]).

"However, the diagnostic character of a process within the meaning of Article 52(4) EPC may be recognised [if] such a process for which protection is sought does include essential steps which are to be implemented by medical staff or under the responsibility of a doctor. A different interpretation would be in clear conflict with the spirit of Article 52(4) EPC" (T655/92[117]; and compare paragraphs 9–51 and 9–52 above).

For example, an invasive *in vivo* NMR imaging technique using contrast agents, which involves a risk of side effects which are sufficiently serious as to require supervision by medical staff, is excluded from patentability under Article 52(4) EPC (T655/92[118]).

D. Inventions Contrary to "Ordre Public" or Morality

Article 53(a) EPC

(1) Introduction

According to Article 53(a) EPC: 9–62

"European patents shall not be granted in respect of: inventions the publication or exploitation of which would be contrary to 'ordre public' or 'morality'."

This is subject to the proviso that:

"the exploitation shall not be deemed to be so contrary merely because it is prohibited by law or regulation in some or all of the contracting States."

The Guidelines (Section C–IV, 3.1) indicate that few inventions are likely to be excluded on this basis. Thus, it is stated that "A fair test to apply is to consider whether it is probable that the public in general would regard the invention as so abhorrent that the grant of patent rights would be inconceivable." The purpose of the exclusion is said to be to exclude "inventions likely to induce riot or public disorder, or to lead to criminal or other generally offensive behaviour."

It has frequently been said that the assessment of what is contrary to 9–63 public order or morality should not be a matter to be decided by a patent office such as the EPO, and that accordingly Article 53(a) EPC should be deleted from the EPC. However, in the first place Article 53(a) EPC itself recognises that activities which are potentially within the exception of

---

[116] T655/92 *NYCOMED/Contract agent for NMR imaging* O.J. EPO 1998, 17; [1998] E.P.O.R. 206.
[117] *Ibid.*
[118] *Ibid.*

Article 53(a) EPC are frequently regulated by other laws and other regulations of individual countries within Europe. The purpose of Article 53(a) EPC is not to regulate such activities as such, but merely to regulate the patentability of such activities.

Secondly, every legal system is based upon public order and morality. The European patent system is part of the European legal system. A European patent application in respect of a particular entity or activity frequently represents a first contact with the legal system, since an application for a patent with respect to an entity or activity will precede its publication and exploitation. Article 53(a) EPC allows objections to be raised to European patent applications or patents, having regard to the publication and exploitation of the inventions which are the subject of such applications, at an early stage in the life of such inventions, either by the EPO itself or by third parties in the context of opposition proceedings.

In these circumstances, the presence of Article 53(a) EPC within the EPC plays a useful role in general, and particularly having regard to the widespread public concerns in relation to biotechnology. Oppositions to the grant of patents in the field of biotechnology under Article 53(a) EPC have already provided clarification as to the proper practice in this connection, as discussed below.

9–63A According to the proposed revision of the EPC, Article 53(a) EPC will remain part of the EPC and will be amended to read as follows:

> 53 EPC: "European patents shall not be granted in respect of:
>
> (a) inventions the commercial exploitation of which would be contrary to 'ordre public' or morality ... (ie 'publication' is deleted)."

Such an amendment will bring Article 53(a) EPC into line with both the TRIPS Agreement (Chapter 1 at paragraph 1–55) and Article 6.1 of European Directive 98/44 (Chapter 1 at paragraph 1–26), and would not change the current EPO practice.

(2) Applicable principles: genetically modified living matter

9–64 Especially in connection with the genetic engineering of living matter, certain principles have been established concerning the application of Article 53(a) EPC in the cases discussed below:

(a) Animals: T19/90[119] ("Onco-mouse"): "Ordre public" and Morality

9–65 The Examining Division refused the application (which concerned genetic manipulation of animals) on other grounds, but specifically concluded that "patent law is not the right legislative tool for regulating problems which may arise in view of [possible dangers arising from such manipulation]," and consequently did not reject the application under Article 53(a) EPC.

---

[119] T19/90 *HARVARD/Onco-mouse* O.J. EPO 1990, 476; [1990] E.P.O.R. 501.

However, the Board of Appeal considered that "precisely in a case of this kind there are compelling reasons" to consider Article 53(a) EPC in relation to patentability, and went on to say:

"The genetic manipulation of mammalian animals is undeniably problematical in various respects, particularly where activated onco-genes are inserted to make an animal abnormally sensitive to carcinogenic substances and stimuli and consequently prone to develop tumours, which necessarily cause suffering. There is also a danger that genetically manipulated animals, if released into the environment, might entail unforeseeable and irreversible adverse effects. Misgivings and fears of this kind have been expressed by a number of persons who have filed observations with the Board under Article 115 EPC. Considerations of precisely this kind have also led a number of Contracting States to impose legislative control on genetic engineering. The decision as to whether or not Article 53(a) EPC is a bar to patenting the present invention would seem to depend mainly on a careful *weighing up of the suffering of animals and possible risks to the environment on the one hand, and the invention's usefulness to mankind on the other*" (T19/90[120]: emphasis added).

The application was, therefore, remitted to the Examining Division for further examination and decision *inter alia* in the light of such considerations.

Subsequently, the Examining Division issued a communication under Rule 51(4) EPC[120a] indicating that it intended to grant the patent, and at the same time it took the unusual step of commenting on the issues involved, in view of the importance of and public interest in the case.

In relation to Article 53(a) EPC, the Examining Division commented in **9–66** particular that "the development of new technologies is normally afflicted with new risks", and against this background "possible detrimental effects and risks have to be weighed and balanced against the merits and advantages aimed at", for each individual invention. In the case in question three different interests were involved: "there is a basic interest of mankind to remedy widespread and dangerous diseases, on the other hand the environment has to be protected against the uncontrolled dissemination of unwanted genes and, moreover, cruelty to animals has to be avoided". As to the invention in suit, "its usefulness to mankind cannot be denied", since "in cancer research animal test models are at present considered indispensable". Furthermore, in relation to possible risks to the environment, the "mere fact that ... uncontrollable acts are conceivable cannot be a major determinant" for deciding upon patentability, especially since the "regulations of the handling of dangerous material is not the task of the EPO ... but is rather the business of specialised governmental authorities".

[120] *Ibid.*
[120a] O.J. EPO 1992, 589.

In the overall balance, therefore, the invention in suit was not considered to be immoral or contrary to public order. The Examining Division stressed, however, that such considerations "apply solely to the present case and that other cases of transgenic animals are conceivable for which a different conclusion might be reached in applying Article 53(a) EPC".

Following grant of this patent, many oppositions were filed and the case is currently being examined by an Opposition Division, pursuant to Article 101 EPC. Having regard also to the likelihood of opposition appeal proceedings in this case, a final decision cannot be expected for several years yet.

(b) Plants: T356/93[121] *("Plant Genetic Systems")*

9–67 The opposed patent was concerned with genetically modified plants. The following principles and conclusions are set out:

9–68 **(i)** *"Ordre public"*. "It is generally accepted that the concept of '**ordre public**' covers the protection of public security and the physical integrity of individuals as part of society. This concept encompasses also the protection of the environment. Accordingly, under Article 53(a) EPC, inventions the exploitation of which is likely to breach public peace, or social order (for example, through acts of terrorism) or to seriously prejudice the environment are to be excluded from patentability as being contrary to 'ordre public'."

9–69 **(ii)** *Morality*. "The concept of **morality** is related to the belief that some behaviour is right and acceptable whereas other behaviour is wrong, this belief is founded on the totality of the accepted norms which are deeply rooted in a particular culture. For the purposes of the EPC, the culture in question is the culture inherent in European society and civilisation. Accordingly, under Article 53(a) EPC, inventions the exploitation of which is not in conformity with the culture are to be excluded from patentability as being contrary to morality".

(iii) Living matter

9–70 Especially having regard to the "preparatory papers" for the EPC, "seeds and plants *per se* shall not constitute an exception to patentability under Article 53(a) EPC merely because they represent living matter, or ... (on the ground that plant genetic resources should remain the 'common heritage of mankind'".

Under Article 53(a) EPC "the relevant question is not whether living organisms are excluded as such, but rather whether or not the publication or exploitation of an invention related to particular living organisms is to be considered contrary to 'ordre public' or morality".

As to the patentability of living matter, see paragraphs 9–76 *et seq.* below.

---

[121] T356/93 *PLANT GENETIC SYSTEMS/Plant cells* O.J. EPO 1995, 545; [1995] E.P.O.R. 357.

(iv) Conclusion

With regard to *"ordre public"*: "no conclusive evidence has been presented **9–71**
... showing that the exploitation of the claimed subject-matter is likely to
seriously prejudice the environment".
    With regard to morality:

> "none of the claims ..., refer to subject-matter which relates to a
> misuse or destructive use of plant biotechnological techniques
> because they concern activities (production of plants and seeds,
> protection of plants from weeds or fungal diseases) and products
> (plant cells, plants, seeds) which cannot be considered to be wrong as
> such in the light of conventionally accepted standard of conduct of
> European culture".

Thus, the claimed invention was not excluded from patentability under
Article 53(a) EPC.

(3) The European Union Biotechnology Directive: Rule 23d EPC

The legal effect of this Directive is considered in Chapter 1 at paragraph **9–72**
1–26. Rule 23d EPC corresponds to Article 6.2 of the Directive.
    In relation to Article 53(a) EPC, Recitals 20 to 25 recognise that
"inventions must be excluded from patentability where their commercial
exploitation offends against public policy or morality", and sets out certain
kinds of biotechnological activity which would so offend. Article 6.2 of the
Directive and Rule 23d EPC set out particular activities which "shall be
considered unpatentable".

"(a)   procedures for human reproductive cloning;
 (b)   processes for modifying the germ line genetic identity of human
        beings;
 (c)   methods in which human embryos are used;
 (d)   processes for modifying the genetic identity of animals which are
        likely to cause them suffering without any substantial medical
        benefit to man or animal and also animals resulting from such
        processes."

Furthermore, Article 7 of the Directive provides that: "The Commission's
Group of Advisers on the Ethical Implications of Biotechnology shall
assess all ethical aspects of biotechnology".

E. Plant and Animal Varieties, and Essentially Biological Processes

Article 53(b) EPC

(1) Introduction

9–73 According to Article 53(b) EPC:

> "European patents shall not be granted in respect of:
> plant or animal varieties or essentially biological processes for the production of plants or animals: this provision does not apply to microbiological processes or the products thereof".

All of the exceptions under Article 53(b) EPC are derived directly from Article 2 of the Strasbourg Convention[122]. At the time when the Strasbourg Convention was prepared and signed (1963), the potential importance of biotechnology could not have been predicted. The relatively recent growth of this area of technology has made determination of the scope of the provisions in Article 53(b) EPC increasingly critical.

These exceptions can be classified and sub-divided as follows:

(a) Plant and animal varieties, *i.e.*

    (i) Plant varieties
    (ii) Animal varieties.

(b) Essentially biological processes for the production of plants and animals, *i.e.*

    (i) such processes for the production of plants;
    (ii) such processes for the production of animals;

(this provision not being applicable to microbiological processes or the products thereof).

9–74 These exceptions will be considered separately.

So far as the wording of the exception is concerned, no distinction is drawn between plants and animals, both forms of living matter being treated in parallel. For reasons which will become apparent hereafter, separate consideration of the different kinds of excepted subject-matter is necessary, especially in connection with plant varieties as compared to animal varieties, having regard to the legal context of the exception from patentability of plant varieties.

The inter-relationship between the first and second halves of Article 53(b) EPC is not entirely clear as a matter of language. In particular, with

---

[122] Reproduced at Appendix 16.

reference to the sentence which follows the semi-colon—"this provision does not apply to microbiological processes or the processes or the product thereof", it is questionable whether "this provision" refers to everything which precedes the semi-colon, namely "plant and animal varieties" and "essentially biological processes ...", or whether it refers only to "essentially biological processes".

On one view, Article 53(b) EPC could be interpreted as contrasting "essentially biological processes for the production of plant or animals" (which are excepted from patentability) with "microbiological processes or the products thereof" (which are not excepted from patentability, and are therefore patentable in accordance with normal principles).

As discussed in paragraph 9–96 below, however, the Boards of Appeal **9–75** have interpreted Article 53(b) EPC as an overall "exception to an exception", in that everything defined before the semi-colon is excepted from patentability, except that "microbiological processes of the products thereof" are patentable.

In contrast to such interpretation, Article 4 of the E.U. Directive states that the non-patentability of "essentially biological processes" (only) is "without prejudice to the patentability of 'microbiological inventions'". Beyond this, new Rule 23 c(c) provides that "Biological inventions shall also be patentable if they concern: (c) a microbiological or other technical process, or a product obtained by means of such a process other than a plant or animal variety".

Clearly, according to the E.U. Directive and Rule 23c EPC, whereas essentially biological processes are not patentable, microbiological processes are patentable. This distinction is discussed further in paragraph 9–95 below. Thus the "exception to an exception" principle is more narrow than earlier Board of Appeal practice.

(2) The patentability of living matter

(a) Historical background

Historically, before the EPC came into force, living matter had not **9–76** generally been considered as patentable subject-matter or otherwise protectable by intellectual property rights. Plant varieties constituted a limited exception to this, in that since 1961 the provision of a form of intellectual property right for plant varieties had been agreed by a number of major industrial countries, as discussed below. Under earlier national patent laws of the Contracting States, living matter was excluded from patentability either by express provision or by case law. The underlying reason for this was an ethical objection to intellectual property protection for any form of life.

(b) Applicable principles

In principle living matter is not excluded from patentability under the **9–77** EPC. In particular, living matter is not excluded from patentability under

439

Article 53(a) EPC (T356/93) and plants and animals *per se* are not within the exception of Article 53(b) EPC. Thus, "no general exclusion of inventions in the sphere of animate nature can be inferred from the EPC" (T49/83[123]).

In relation to plants:

"The very wording of Article 53(b) EPC before the semi-colon precludes the equation of plants and plant varieties" (T49/83[124]).

Similarly in relation to animals:

"The exception to patentability under Article 53(b) EPC applies to certain categories of animals but not to animals as such" (T19/90[125]).

(c) The European Union Biotechnology Directive: Rule 23c EPC

9–78 The legal effect of this Directive is considered in Chapter 1 at paragraph 1–26 above. In relation to the patentability of living matter, Article 4(2) provides that:

"Inventions which concern plants or animals may be patented if the application of the invention is not technically confined to a particular plant or animal variety".

Rule 23(c) EPC corresponds to Article 4(2) and reads:

"Biotechnological inventions shall also be patentable if they concern:

(b) plants or animals if the technical feasibility of the invention is not confined to a particular plant or animal variety".

Rule 23b(2) EPC defines "biotechnological inventions as "inventions which concern a product consisting of or containing biological material or a process by means of which biological material is produced, processed or used".

Rule 23b(3) EPC also defines "biological material" as "any material containing genetic information and capable of reproducing itself or being reproduced in a biological system".

The term "plant variety" is also defined in Rule 23b(4) EPC: see paragraph 9–81 below.

9–79 Furthermore, Article 5 provides in relation to gene sequences that:

"1.   The human body, at the various stages of its formation and development, and the simple discovery of one of its elements including the sequence or partial sequence of a gene, cannot constitute patentable inventions.

---

[123] T49/83 *CIBA-GEIGY/Propagating material* O.J. EPO 1984, 112; [1979–85] E.P.O.R. 758.
[124] *Ibid.*
[125] T19/90 *HARVARD/Onco-mouse* O.J. EPO 1990, 476; [1990] E.P.O.R. 501.

2. An element isolated from the human body or otherwise produced by means of a technical process including the sequence or partial sequence of a gene may constitute a patentable invention, even if the structure of that element is identical to that of a natural element.
3. The function of a sequence or a partial sequence of a gene must be disclosed in the patent application".

Rule 23b EPC has the same wording as Article 5, except that "industrial application" replaces "function" in paragraph 3.

(3) Plant and animal varieties

(a) Plant varieties

(i) **Background to this exception.** Just prior to the signing of the 9–80 Strasbourg Convention[126] in 1963, another international Convention had been signed whose subject-matter concerned this exclusion, namely the International Convention for the protection of New Varieties of Plants, 1961 (known as the "UPOV Convention"). There is a considerable overlap between the signatory States of these two Conventions, especially so far as the major European industrial countries are concerned (of the Contracting States to the EPC, only Greece and Luxembourg are currently not Member States of the UPOV Convention).

The UPOV Convention recognises monopoly rights for new plant varieties, such rights being provided under appropriate national laws: in the United Kingdom the relevant laws are the Plant Varieties and Seeds Act, 1964, as amended by the Plant Varieties Act, 1983. It is also relevant that, by virtue of Article 2(1) of the UPOV Convention, the Member States agreed in principle to prohibit "double protection" in respect of the rights recognised by the Convention: either a special "plant breeders right" may be granted, or patent protection, but not both, in respect of plant varieties to which the Convention applies. While the exact extent of this prohibition and its application in individual countries is a matter for specific consideration and is not relevant here, nevertheless, its existence is indirectly relevant to the interpretation of Article 53(b) EPC. In particular, it has been recognised that Article 2 Strasbourg and consequently Article 53(b) EPC express a general intention to exclude patent protection for subject-matter capable of protection within the UPOV Convention.

(ii) **The meaning of "plant varieties": the E.U. Directive and Rule 9–81 23b, c EPC.** As discussed in paragraphs 9–77 and 9–78 above, it is well established that the exception of "plant varieties" from patentability does not mean that plants in general are excluded from patentability (T49/ 83[126a]). This is reflected in Article 4 of the E.U. Directive and Rule 23c(b) EPC:

---

[126] Reproduced at Appendix 16.
[126a] T49/83 *CIBA-GEIGY/Propagating material* O.J. EPO 1984, 112; [1979–85] E.P.O.R. 758.

"The skilled person understands the term 'plant varieties' to mean a multiplicity of plants which are largely the same in their characteristics and remain the same within specific tolerances after every propagation or every propagation cycle. This definition is reflected in the [UPOV Convention], which is intended to give the breeder of a new plant variety a protective right (Article 1(1)) extending both to the reproductive or vegetative propagating material and also to the whole plant (Article 5(1)). Plant varieties in this sense are all cultivated varieties, clones, lines, strains and hybrids which can be grown in such a way that they are clearly distinguishable from other varieties, sufficiently homogenous, and stable in their essential characteristics (Article 2(2) in conjunction with Article 6(1) (a), (c) and (d)). The legislator did not wish to afford patent protection under the European Patent Convention to plant varieties of this kind, whether in the form of propagating material or of the plant itself" (T49/83[127]).

Consequently, possession of both these characteristics of "homogeneity" and "stability" would be a prerequisite for a "plant variety" (T320/87[128]).

The concept of "plant variety" is defined in the revised UPOV Convention 1991, in Article 2 of the E.U. Directive by reference to Article 5(2) of the E.C. Regulation on Community Plant Variety Rights, and in Rule 23(4)b EPC in substantially identical terms:

"Plant variety" means a plant grouping within a single botanical taxon of the lowest known rank, which grouping, irrespective of whether the conditions for the grant of plant variety are fully met, can be:

(a) defined by the expression of the characteristics that results from a given genotype or combination of genotypes;
(b) distinguished from any other plant grouping by the expression of at least one of the said characteristics, and
(c) considered as a unit with regard to its suitability for being propagated unchanged".

The reference to the expression of the characteristics that results from a given genotype or combination of genotypes is a reference to the entire constitution of a plant or a set of genetic information" (G1/98[129]).

(iii) Particular cases

9–82   **(1) T49/83**[130]. The claimed invention concerned propagating material (*i.e.* seeds) for cultivated plants, treated with a chemical agent of defined formula. Such treatment was for the purpose of increasing resistance to agricultural chemicals. Claims to such treated propagating material were

---

[127] T49/83 *CIBA-GEIGY/Propagating material* O.J. EPO 1984, 112; [1979–85] E.P.O.R. 758.
[128] T320/87 *LUBRIZOL/Hybrid plant* O.J. EPO 1990, 771; [1990] E.P.O.R. 173.
[129] G1/98 *NOVARTIS II/Transgenic plant* O.J. EPO 1998, 509; [2000] E.P.O.R. 303.
[130] T49/83 *CIBA-GEIGY/Propagation material* O.J. EPO 1984, 112; [1979–85] E.P.O.R. 758.

rejected by the Examining Division under Article 53(b) EPC, on the basis that since the exception to patentability applied to new plant varieties, it applied also to known plant varieties in seed form even if such seeds had received chemical treatment.

The Board of Appeal distinguished the claimed invention as not lying "within the sphere of plant breeding, which is concerned with the genetic modification of plants." The claimed chemically treated propagating material was not concerned with providing plant varieties, and there was no conflict between the UPOV Convention and patent protection so far as the claimed material was concerned. Patent protection was the only possible kind of protection for the claimed invention, which was not within the exception from patentability under Article 53(b) EPC.

(2) T320/87[131]. The application included "product-by-process" claims to   **9–83** seeds which had been produced by a process including defined steps of selection of parent plants, crossing and cloning, and repetition to produce hybrid seed yielding phenotypically uniform hybrid plants; a claim to plants produced from such hybrid seed was also included.

The claimed products were distinguished from "plant varieties" within Article 53(b) on the basis that, considered as a whole generation population, such seeds and plants were not stable in the sense required by the definition of plant variety; on the contrary, such stability was not aimed at, and in accordance with the claims it was necessary to go back repeatedly to the parent plants for further propagation by cloning. The claimed invention was not, therefore, within the exception to patentability.

(3) T356/93[132]: **G3/95**[133] **("Plant Genetic Systems").** The invention   **9–84** claimed in the opposed patent concerned the genetic modification of plants in order to make them herbicide-resistant; this characteristic was stable in succeeding generations. The patent included certain claims to plants which had been genetically modified in accordance with the invention. The working examples in the patent described the genetic modifications of specifically named known plant varieties.

The Board of Appeal defined "plant varieties" as set out in paragraph 9–81 above, and then stated:

"A product claim which embraces within its subject-matter 'plant varieties' as just defined is not patentable. Having regard to the fact that the working examples of the opposed patent were carried out upon specific known plant varieties, this appears to be at least part of the basis for rejection of the claims defining genetically modified plants."

Furthermore, the Board of Appeal held that:

[131] T320/87 *LUBRIZOL/Hybrid plant* O.J. EPO 1990, 771; [1990] E.P.O.R. 173.
[132] T356/93 *PLANT GENETIC SYSTEMS/Plant cells* O.J. EPO 1995, 545; [1995] E.P.O.R. 357.
[133] G3/95 *Inadmissible referral* O.J. EPO 1996, 169; [1996] E.P.O.R. 505.

"a claim defining genetically modified plants having a distinct, stable herbicide-resistance genetic characteristic was not allowable under Article 53(b) EPC because the claimed genetic modification itself made the modified or transformed plant a 'plant variety' within the meaning of Article 53(b) EPC" (G3/95[134]).

A question of law concerning Article 53(b) EPC was referred to the Enlarged Board of Appeal by the President of the EPO under Article 112(1)(b) EPC (see Chapter 4 at paragraph 4–187) but the question was held to be inadmissible because 'two Boards of Appeal have not given different (*i.e.* conflicting) decisions' on that question (G3/95[135]). In particular, there was no conflict between what was decided in T49/83[136] and T19/90[137], and what was decided in T356/93.[138]

9–85   **(4) T1054/96[139]; G1/98[140] ("Transgenic plant").** The claimed invention concerned "transgenic plants" comprising in their genomes specific foreign genes, the expression of which results in the production of antipathorgenically active substances, and to methods of preparing such plants" (G1/98[141]). The claims therefore "covered plants which might or might not belong to a plant variety".

Having regard to widely expressed doubts as to the correctness of the findings in T356/93[142], and in the light of challenges to such findings by the appellant in T1054/96[143] the following questions of law were referred to the Enlarged Board of Appeal under Article 112(1)(a) EPC (see Chapter 4 at paragraph 4–183: there is no requirement that "two Boards of Appeal have been given different decisions" in order that the referred questions should be admissible under Article 112(1)(a) EPC):

(1) To what extent should the instances of the EPO examine an application in respect of whether the claims are allowable in view of the provision of Article 53(b) EPC that patents shall not be granted in respect of plant varieties or essentially biological processes for the production of plants, which provisions does not apply to microbiological processes or the products thereof, and how should a claim be interpreted for this purpose?

(2) Does a claim which relates to plants but wherein specific plant varieties are not individually claimed *ipso facto* avoid the prohibition on patenting in Article 53(b) EPC even though it embraces plant varieties?

---

[134] *Ibid.*
[135] *Ibid.*
[136] T49/83 *CIBA-GEIGY/Propagating material* O.J. EPO 1984, 112; [1979–85] E.P.O.R. 758.
[137] T19/90 *HARVARD/Onco-mouse* O.J. EPO 1990, 476; [1990] E.P.O.R. 501.
[138] T356/93 *PLANT GENETIC SYSTEMS/Plant cells* O.J. EPO 1995, 545; [1995] E.P.O.R. 357.
[139] T1054/96 *NOVARTIS/Transgenic plant* O.J. EPO 1998, 511; [1999] E.P.O.R. 123.
[140] G1/98 *NOVARTIS II/Transgenic plant* O.J. EPO 2000, 111; [2000] E.P.O.R. 303.
[141] *Ibid.*
[142] See note 138.
[143] T1054/96 *NOVARTIS/Transgenic plant* O.J. EPO 1998, 511; [1999] E.P.O.R. 123.

(3) Should the provision of Article 64(2) EPC be taken into account when considering what claims are allowable?

(4) Does a plant variety, in which each individual plant of that variety contains at least one specific gene introduced into an ancestral plant by recombinant gene technology, fall outside the provision of Article 53(b) EPC that patents shall not be granted in respect of plant varieties or essentially biological processes for the production of plants, which provision does not apply to microbiologiocal processes or the products thereof?"

In so far as questions (1) and (4) relate to "essentially biological processes   9–86 for the production of plants 'and' microbiological processes or the products thereof", they are considered in paragraph 9–97 below.

T1054/96[144] itself contains a discussion of some of the issues that arise in relation to such questions.

G1/98[145] explains that question (1) is very broad, and that the answers to questions (2), (3) and (4) demonstrate that a separate answer to question (1) is not required. Questions (2) to (4) were answered essentially as follows:

Question (2)

(a) In relation to Article 53(b) EPC "it is not the wording but the substance   9–87 of a claim which is decisive in assessing the subject-matter to which the claims is directed ... In assessing the subject-matter of a claim, the underlying invention has to be identified" (G1/98[146]).

In contrast to the definition of "plant variety" in the UPOV Convention and elsewhere (see paragraph 9–81 above), "a plant defined by single recombinant DNA sequences is not an individual plant grouping to which an entire constitution can be attributed. ... It is not a concrete living being or grouping of concrete living being but an abstract and open definition embracing an indefinite number of individual entities defined by a part of its genotype or by a property bestowed on it by that part" (G1/98[147]).

The claimed invention defines plant "by certain characteristics allowing the plants to inhibit the growth of plant pathogens. ... The taxonomic category ... to which the claimed plants belong is not specified, let alone the further characteristics necessary to assess the homogeneity and stability of varieties within a given species. Hence, it would appear that the claimed invention neither expressly nor implicitly defines a plant variety" ... according to the above definitions. "In the absence of the identification of specific varieties in the product claims, the subject-matter of the claimed invention is neither limited nor even directed to a variety or varieties".

(b) Article 53(b) EPC was derived from Article 2(b) of the Strasbourg

[144] *Ibid.*
[145] G1/98 *NOVARTIS II/Transgenic plant* O.J. EPO 2000, 111; [2000] E.P.O.R. 303.
[146] *Ibid.*
[147] *Ibid.*

Convention[147a] (see Chapter 1 at paragraph 1–41) according to which "the Contracting States shall not be bound to provide for the grant of patents in respect of plant varieties."

9–88   The background to the EPC suggests that "the purpose of Article 53(b) EPC corresponds to the purpose of Article 2(b) Strasbourg: European patents should not be granted for subject-matter for which the grant of patents was confirmed was excluded under the ban on dual protection in the UPOV Convention 1961 ... The idea that the exclusion in the EPC should correspond to the availability of protection in UPOV" can be derived from the background papers to the EPC.

> "This historical background shows at least an intention to protect by plant breeders' rights system biological developments for which the plant system was less suited ... and to keep technical inventions related to plants within the patent system".

Thus:

> "The extent of the exclusion for patents is the obverse of the availability of plant variety rights. The latter are only granted for specific plant varieties and not for technical teachings which can be implemented in an indefinite number of plant varieties" (G1/98[148]).

> (c) Consequently, the answer to question (2) is that:

> "A claim [which related to plants] wherein specific plant varieties are not individually claimed is not excluded from patentability under Article 53(b) EPC, even though it may embrace plant varieties" (G1/98[149]).

Question (3)

9–89   In the light of the answer to question (2), question (3) was answered in accordance with the established Board of Appeal case law in relation to Article 64(2) EPC (see Chapter 13 at paragraph 13–22).

> "When a claim to a process for the production of a plant variety is examined, Article 64(2) EPC is not to be taken into consideration" (G1/98[150]).

Question (4)

9–90   In relation to this question, the meaning of "microbiological processes" in relation to processes of genetic engineering was considered (see paragraph 9–97 below).

[147a] See Appendix 16.
[148] G1/98 *NOVARTIS II/Transgenic plant* O.J. EPO 2000, 111; [2000] E.P.O.R. 303.
[149] *Ibid.*
[150] *Ibid.*

As discussed under question (2) above: "The exclusion in Article 53(b) EPC was made to serve the purpose of excluding from patentability subject-matter which is eligible for protection under the plant breeder's rights system".

In this connection "it does not make any difference under the UPOV Convention or under the Regulations on Plant Variety Rights how a variety was obtained. Whether a plant variety is the result of traditional breeding techniques, or whether genetic engineering was used to obtain a distinct plant grouping, does not matter for the criteria of distinctiveness, homogenecity and stability and the Examination thereof".

Consequently, the answer to question (4) is that:

> "The exception to patentability in Article 53(b) EPC, first half-sentence applies to plant varieties irrespective of the way in which they were produced. Therefore, plant varieties containing genes introduced into an ancestral plant by recombinant gene technology are excluded from patentability" (G1/98[151]).

(b) Animal varieties

(i) **Background to this exception.** In contrast to plant varieties, which is 9–91 discussed above may receive legal protection as a result of the UPOV Convention, no alternative form of legal protection is available for animal varieties.

(ii) **The meaning of "animal varieties".** As discussed in paragraphs 9–92 9–77 and 9–78 above, it is well established that the exception of "animal varieties" from patentability does not mean that animals in general are excluded from patentability (T19/90[152]: E.U. Directive, Rule 23c EPC).

Beyond this, although as stated above the background to the exception of "animal varieties" does not correspond to that of "plant varieties", having regard to the wording of Article 53(b) EPC it is logically difficult to distinguish between the interpretation of plant and animal varieties as a matter of principle. The concept of "plant and animal varieties" is clearly an integrated one.

Neither the E.U. Directive nor Rule 23 EPC contains a definition of "animal varieties". However, it appears that the meaning of "animal varieties" should correspond *mutatis mutandis* to that of "plant varieties" (see paragraph 9–81 above).

(4) Essentially biological processes for the production of plants and animals

(a) The distinction between biological and non-biological processes

(i) **The meaning of "essentially biological processes".** A process for the 9–93 production of plants or animals (which is not a microbiological process, as

---

[151] *Ibid.*
[152] T19/90 *HARVARD/Onco-mouse* O.J. EPO 1990, 476; [1990] E.P.O.R. 501.

to which see paragraph 9–97 below) will be inside or outside the exception to patentability depending upon "the extent to which there is intervention by man in the process" (Guidelines, GIV, 3.4). This "has to be judged on the basis of the essence of the invention taking into account the totality of human intervention and its impact on the result achieved". This is "not a matter simply of whether such intervention is of a quantitative or qualitative character" (T320/87[153]).

For example, in a case where "the claimed processes for the preparation of hybrid plant represent an essential modification of known biological and classical breeders processes, and the efficiency and high yield associated with the product ... show important technological character", such processes fall outside the exception of Article 53(b) EPC, and are patentable (T320/87[154]).

Thus in this context "biological" may be contrasted with "technical" or "technological"; and "a process for the production of plants comprising at least one essential technical step, which cannot be carried out without human intervention and which has a decisive impact on the final result does not fall under the exception to patentability under Article 53(b) EPC" (T356/93[155]).

9–94   **(ii) The E.U. Directive: Rule 23b, c EPC.** This Directive and Rule 23c EPC contain provisions which are reasonably consistent with the above approach. The following provisions are particularly relevant:

Article 2(2): "A procedure for the breeding of plants or animals shall be defined as essentially biological if it is based on crossing and selection".

Rule 23b EPC: "A process for the production of plants or animals is essentially biological if it consists entirely of natural phenomena such as crossing or selection".

Article 4(1)(b) (2) and (3): 1(b). The following shall not be patentable:

1. Essentially biological procedures for the breeding of plants and animals.
2. Inventions which concern plants or animals may be patented if the application of the invention is not technically confined to a particular plant or animal variety.
3. Paragraph 1(b) shall be without prejudice to the patentability of inventions which concern a microbiological or other technical procedure or a product obtained by means of such a procedure.

9–95   **(iii) The distinction between biology and microbiology.** The importance of this distinction derives from the final part of Article 53(b) EPC, which provides that the previously defined exceptions to patentability "do not apply to microbiological processes or the products thereof." Thus, the EPC specifically makes it clear that, at least at the microbe level, living matter is in principle patentable. Consequently, European patents are

---

[153] T320/87 *LUBRIZOL/Hybrid plant* O.J. EPO 1990, 771; [1990] E.P.O.R. 173.
[154] *Ibid.*
[155] T356/93 *PLANT GENETIC SYSTEMS/Plant cells* O.J. EPO 1995, 545; [1995] E.P.O.R. 357.

commonly granted for micro-organisms *per se*, whether merely isolated from nature or when genetically changed, as well as for their components, *i.e.* specific DNA sequences, plasmids, etc.

Scientifically, however, there is no clear line between biology and microbiology.

(5) Microbiological processes and the products thereof

(a) An "exception to an exception"

As discussed in paragraph 9–74 above, the interrelationship between the **9–96** second half of Article 53(b) EPC, after the semi-colon, and the first half of which sets out unpatentable subject-matter, is not at all clear as a matter of language.

Accordingly to the cases decided so far, the second half of Article 53(b) EPC is an "exception to an exception", in that subject-matter which is defined in the first half as excepted from patentability (that is, including "plant and animal varieties") becomes patentable if it falls within the second half. Thus:

> "Article 53(b) EPC, first half-sentence, is an exception to the general principles of patentability contained in Article 52(1) EPC. The second half-sentence is an *'exception to this exception'* ensuring that the patentability bar does not cover microbiological processes or the products thereof" (T19/90[156]: followed in T356/93[157]).

Consequently, "animal varieties are patentable if they are the product of microbiological process within the meaning of Article 53(b) EPC, second-half sentence ... this principle applies *mutatis mutandis* to plant varieties" (T356/93[158]).

This interpretation of Article 53(b) EPC is questionable, however, especially when applied to "plant or animal varieties". Having regard to the historical background to Article 53(b) EPC (discussed in paragraph 9–80 above), in particular its derivation from the Strasbourg Convention of 1963, it seems unlikely that such an "exception to an exception" was the intended meaning of Article 53(b) EPC.

(b) The meaning of "microbiological processes or the products thereof"

In the light of the preparatory papers to the EPC, the specific statement in **9–97** Article 53(b) as to the patentability of such processes and the products thereof "may be explained by the legislators' intention to make it absolutely clear that the EPC must provide patent protection for industrially applicable processes involving micro-organisms and their products". This clarification was most certainly considered useful in order to

---

[156] T19/90 *HARVARD/Onco-mouse* O.J. EPO 1990, 476; [1990] E.P.O.R. 501.
[157] T356/93 *PLANT GENETIC SYSTEMS/Plant cells* O.J. EPO 1995, 545; [1995] E.P.O.R. 357.
[158] *Ibid.*

prevent the exclusion from patentability from being extended to processes using eucaryotic micro-organisms which could be fitted into the pattern of the plant or animal kingdoms (*e.g.* some fungi, plant cells, animal cells) (T356/93[159]).

According to the current practice of the EPO, the term "micro-organism" includes not only bacteria and yeasts, but also fungi, algae, protozoa and human, animal and plant cells, *i.e.* all generally unicellular organisms with dimensions beneath the limits of vision which can be propagated and manipulated in a laboratory. Plasmids and viruses are also considered to fall under this definition (see Guidelines ... (G.IV, 3.5.)), (T356/93[160]).

> "... cells and parts thereof are treated like organisms under the current practice of the EPO. This appears justified since modern biotechnology has developed from traditional microbiology and cells are comparable to unicellular organisms" (G1/98[161]).

"The term microbiological processes [in Article 53(b) EPC] was used as synonymous with processes using micro-organisms. Micro-organisms are different from the parts of living beings used for the genetic modification of plants".

Consequently:

> "Processes of genetic engineering ... are not identical with microbiological processes" (G1/98[162]).

Similarly, genetically modified plants are not treated as products of microbiological processes within Article 53(b) EPC.

It follows that a genetically engineered plant variety is a plant variety within the meaning of the first half-sentence of Article 53(b) EPC and is excluded from patentability (not being the product of a microbiological process and therefore not being an "exception to an exception").

F. Susceptible of Industrial Application

Article 57 EPC

9–98 In explanation of Article 52(1) EPC, which requires that an invention shall be "susceptible of industrial application" if it is to be patentable, Article 57 EPC states that:

> "An invention shall be considered as susceptible of industrial application if it can be made or used in any kind of industry, including agriculture."

[159] *Ibid.*
[160] *Ibid.*
[161] G1/98 *NOVARTIS II/Transgenic plant* O.J. EPO 2000, 111; [2000] E.P.O.R. 303.
[162] *Ibid.*

The requirement that a claimed invention be susceptible of industrial application in order to be patentable has been considered in some Board of Appeal decisions which were primarily concerned with possible exclusions under Article 52 EPC and which have already been referred to in this chapter.

For example, an invention which "can be used by enterprises whose object is to beautify the human or animal body" is patentable, because: "Such enterprises in the cosmetic field—such as cosmetic salons and beauty parlours—are part of industry". This concept "implies that an activity is carried out continuously, independently and for financial gain" (T144/83[163]: also T36/83[164]).

An invention concerning a method involving interaction with a human body to produce results which would subsequently be used by a doctor in diagnosis "is susceptible of industrial application if it can be used with the desired result by a technician without specialist medical knowledge and skills" (T385/86[165]).

A method of contraception may in general be susceptible of industrial application. However, according to one view the invention as claimed must satisfy Article 57 EPC. Thus:

"A method of contraception which is to be applied in the private and personal sphere of a human being shall not be considered as susceptible of industrial application" (T74/93[166]).

It is suggested that this view is too restrictive. Article 57 EPC is **9–99** concerned with the subject-matter to which the claim is directed. "In assessing the subject-matter of a claim, the underlying invention has to be identified" (G1/98[167]). In the case in question, the underlying invention was the novel compound to be applied for contraceptive purposes, not the method of application.

In assessing whether the requirement of Article 57 EPC is satisfied, the question to be considered is:

"What is the nature of the claimed subject-matter?"

Cases Referred to in Chapter 9

Board of Appeal Decisions

G5/83   EISAI/Second medical indication O.J. EPO 1985, 64; [1979–85] E.P.O.R.: B: 241.

[163] T144/83 DU PONT/Appetite suppressant O.J. EPO 1986, 301; [1987] E.P.O.R. 6.
[164] T36/83 ROUSSEL-UCLAF/Thenoyl peroxide O.J. EPO 1986, 295; [1987] E.P.O.R. 1.
[165] T385/86 BRUKER/Non-invasive measurement O.J. EPO 1988, 398; [1988] E.P.O.R. 357.
[166] T74/93 BRITISH TECHNOLOGY GROUP/Contraceptive method O.J. EPO 1995, 712; [1995] E.P.O.R. 279.
[167] G1/98 NOVARTIS II/Transgenic plant O.J. EPO 2000, 111; [2000] E.P.O.R. 303.

G2/88   MOBIL OIL/Friction reducing additive O.J. EPO 1990, 93,
          114; [1990] E.P.O.R. 73, 257.
G3/95   Inadmissible referral O.J. EPO 1996, 169; [1996] E.P.O.R. 505.
G1/98   NOVARTIS II/Transgenic plant O.J. EPO 2000, 111; [2000]
          E.P.O.R. 303.

T36/83   ROUSSEL-UCLAF/Thenoyl peroxide O.J. EPO 1986, 295;
          [1987] E.P.O.R. 1.
T49/83   CIBA-GEIGY/Propagating material O.J. EPO 1984, 112;
          [1979–85] E.P.O.R.: C: 758.
T144/83   DU PONT/Appetite suppressant O.J. EPO 1986, 301; [1987]
          E.P.O.R. 6.
T51/84   STOCKBURGER/Coded distinctive mark O.J. EPO 1986, 226;
          [1986] E.P.O.R. 229
T81/84   RORER/Dysmenorrhea O.J. EPO 1988, 207; [1988] E.P.O.R.
          297.
T208/84   VICOM/Computer-related invention O.J. EPO 1987, 14;
          [1986] E.P.O.R. 74.
T22/85   IBM/Document abstracting and retrieving O.J. EPO 1990, 12;
          [1990] E.P.O.R. 98.
T52/85   IBM/Semantically-related linguistic expressions [1989]
          E.P.O.R. 454.
T115/85   IBM/Computer related invention O.J. EPO 1990, 30; [1990]
          E.P.O.R. 107.
T116/85   WELLCOME/Pigs I O.J. EPO 1989, 13; [1988] E.P.O.R. 1.
T163/85   BBC/Colour television signal O.J. EPO 1990, 379; [1990]
          E.P.O.R. 599.
T19/86   DUPHAR/Pigs II O.J. EPO 1989, 24; [1988] E.P.O.R. 10.
T26/86   KOCH & STERZEL/X-ray apparatus O.J. EPO 1988, 19;
          [1988] E.P.O.R. 72.
T38/86   IBM/Text clarity processing O.J. EPO 1990, 384; [1990]
          E.P.O.R. 181.
T290/86   ICI/Cleaning plaque O.J. EPO 1992, 414; [1991] E.P.O.R. 157.
T385/86   BRUKER/Non-invasive measurement O.J. EPO 1988, 398;
          [1988] E.P.O.R. 357.
T58/87   SALMINEN/Pigs III O.J. EPO 1988, 347; [1989] E.P.O.R. 125.
T245/87   SIEMENS/Flow measurement O.J. EPO 1989, 171; [1989]
          E.P.O.R. 241.
T320/87   LUBRIZOL/Hybrid plants O.J. EPO 1990, 771; [1990] E.P.O.R.
          173.
T119/88   FUJI/Coloured disk jacket O.J. EPO 1990, 395; [1990] E.P.O.R.
          615.
T158/88   SIEMENS/Character form O.J. EPO 1991, 566; [1992] E.P.O.R.
          69.
T603/89   BEATTIE/Marker O.J. EPO 1992, 230; [1992] E.P.O.R. 221.
T780/89   BAYER/Immunostimulant O.J. EPO 1993, 440; [1993]
          E.P.O.R. 377.

T19/90   HARVARD/Onco-mouse O.J. EPO 1990, 476; [1990] E.P.O.R.
           501.
           HARVARD ("Onco-mouse") Examining Division decision,
           O.J. EPO 1989, 451; [1990] E.P.O.R. 4; communication under
           Article 51(4) EPC upon grant, after remittal by Board of
           Appeal, O.J. EPO 1992, 589; [1991] E.P.O.R. 525.
T110/90   IBM/Editable document form O.J. EPO 1994, 557; [1995]
           E.P.O.R. 185.
T182/90   SEE-SHELL/Blood flow O.J. EPO 1994, 641; [1994] E.P.O.R.
           320.
T854/90   IBM/Card reader O.J. EPO 1993, 669; [1994] E.P.O.R. 89.
T24/91   THOMPSON/Cornea O.J. EPO 1995, 512; [1996] E.P.O.R. 19.
T833/91   IBM April 16, 1993.
T164/92   ROBERT BOSCH/Electronic computer components O.J. EPO
           1995, 305; [1995] E.P.O.R. 585.
T655/92   NYCOMED/Contrast agent for NMR imaging O.J. EPO 1998,
           17; [1998] E.P.O.R. 206.
T769/92   SOHEI/General purpose management system O.J. EPO 1995,
           525; [1996] E.P.O.R. 253.
T820/92   THE GENERAL HOSPITAL/Contraceptive method O.J. EPO
           1995, 113; [1995] E.P.O.R. 446.
T1002/92   PETTERSON/Queueing system O.J. EPO 1995, 605; [1996]
           E.P.O.R. 1.
T74/93   BRITISH TECHNOLOGY GROUP/Contraceptive method
           O.J. EPO 1995, 712; [1995] E.P.O.R. 279.
T82/93   TELECTRONICS/Cardiac pacing O.J. EPO 1996, 274; [1996]
           E.P.O.R. 409.
T204/93   AT&T October 29, 1993.
T356/93   PLANT GENETIC SYSTEMS/Plant cells O.J. EPO 1995, 545;
           [1995] E.P.O.R. 357.
T329/94   BAXTER/Blood extraction method O.J. EPO 1998, 241; [1998]
           E.P.O.R. 363.
T873/94   TOSHIBA/Amended divisional application.
T953/94   July 15, 1996.
T1173/97   IBM/Computer program product O.J. EPO 1999, 609.
T1194/97   PHILIPS/Data structure O.J. EPO (P).
T35/99   GEORGETOWN UNIVERSITY/Pericordial access O.J. EPO
           (P).

Decisions of National Courts

"Flugkostenminimierung" BGH Case No. X ZR 65/85 G.R.U.R. 1986, 531
Genentech Inc's Patent [1989] R.P.C. 147, CA.
Merrill Lynch's Application [1989] R.P.C. 561, CA.; reversing [1988] R.P.C. 1
Unilever Ltd's (Davis) Application [1983] R.P.C. 219

CHAPTER 10

PRIORITY

Articles 87 to 89 EPC; Rule 38 EPC

Contents

All references are to paragraph numbers

A. Introduction

(1) Priority under the EPC

10–01 An applicant for a European patent may claim priority for his application from the filing date of an earlier application in an individual country, filed within the previous 12 months. The success or otherwise of such a claim to priority determines whether the claimed invention, the subject of the European application, is examined for novelty and inventive step at the filing date of the earlier application or at the filing date of the European application. The principles which govern the claiming of priority are therefore discussed first, in this chapter, and the principles governing the determination of novelty and inventive step are then respectively considered in Chapters 11 and 12.

The system of priority rights under the EPC, and the effects of this system, are governed by Articles 87 to 89 and Rule 38 EPC, which:

> "together form a complete, self-contained code of rules of law on the subject of claiming priority for the purpose of filing a European patent application. The language of some of these provisions is, to a large extent, taken from that used in Article 4 of the Paris Convention.[1] However, this code of rules of law is, and was designed to be, independent of the Paris Convention" (J15/80[2]).

Nevertheless, since the system of priority rights under the EPC is closely related to and partly directly derived from Article 4 of the Paris Convention, an understanding of the provisions of Article 4 Paris is essential background to the interpretation of Articles 87 to 89 EPC.

(2) Relationship between the EPC and the Paris Convention

10–02 The EPO cannot be directly bound by Article 4 Paris, since the European Patent Organisation is not a party to the Paris Convention, even though the Contracting States of the EPC are each individually parties to the Paris Convention (J15/80,[3] which contains considerable discussion and background information concerning the relationship between the EPC and the Paris Convention).

The preamble to the EPC states that the Contracting States were "desiring ... to conclude a Convention ... which constitutes a special agreement within the meaning of Article 19 Paris ...". Article 19 Paris provides that the Union countries may make special agreements between themselves for the protection of industrial property "insofar as these agreements do not contravene the provisions of this Convention".

Thus the EPC constitutes a special agreement within the meaning of

---

[1] Paris Convention for the Protection of Industrial Property; see Appendix 14.
[2] J15/80 *ARENHOLD/Priority right* O.J. EPO 1981, 213; [1979–85] E.P.O.R. 56.
[3] *Ibid.*

Article 19 Paris, whose relevant provisions are clearly intended not to contravene the basic principles of priority laid down in the Paris Convention (J15/80[4] and T301/87[5]). Articles 87 to 89 and Rule 38 EPC should thus be construed on this basis. A short commentary upon Article 4 Paris and its relationship to Articles 87 to 89 EPC is therefore included here. This section should be considered within the context of the general comments upon the Paris Convention which are set out in Chapter 1 above.

A full commentary upon the whole of the Paris Convention is contained in Bodenhausen, *Guide to the Application of the Paris Convention for the Protection of Industrial Property* (BIRPI, 1968), which is a well-recognised authority.

B. Article 4 of the Paris Convention

Article 4 Paris is divided into nine sections, A to I, which are discussed **10–03** individually below. For convenience, the more important of the sections will be set out in the text, but the whole of Article 4 is also reproduced as part of Appendix 14.

(1) Section A

"**A.** (1) Any person who has duly filed an application for a patent, or **10–04** for the registration of a utility model, or of an industrial design, or of a trademark, in one of the countries of the Union, or his successor in title, shall enjoy, for the purpose of filing in the other countries, a right of priority during the periods hereinafter fixed.

(2) Any filing that is equivalent to a regular national filing under the domestic legislation of any country of the Union or under bilateral or multilateral treaties concluded between countries of the Union shall be recognised as giving rise to the right of priority.

(3) By a regular national filing is meant any filing that is adequate to establish the date on which the application was filed in the country concerned, whatever may be the subsequent fate of the application."

(a) Right of priority from a duly filed application

Paragraph (1) above provides that what is called "a right of priority" is **10–05** derived *inter alia* from a "duly filed" application for a patent. Although the subject-matter of the priority application is not specifically referred to in paragraph A(1), it appears to be implicit that the right of priority attaches to such subject-matter. The nature of this right to priority will be discussed more fully below.

What is meant by a "duly filed" application is set out further in paragraphs A(2) and (3), which are generally self-explanatory. The final phrase of paragraph A(3), "whatever may be the subsequent fate of the

---

[4] J15/80 *ARENHOLD/Priority right* O.J. EPO 1981, 213; [1979–85] E.P.O.R.: A: 56.
[5] T301/87 *BIOGEN/Alpha-interferons* O.J. EPO 1990, 335; [1990] E.P.O.R. 190.

application", is of considerable importance to the priority system under the Paris Convention. It emphasises that under this priority system the outcome of the first filed priority application is irrelevant: the only thing that matters is the subject-matter that it discloses.

It is to be noted that paragraph A(1) is also silent as to the subject-matter of the later filed applications in other countries. In particular the possibility of a later filing of a different species of industrial property from the earlier filing is here left open.

(b) Successors in title

10–06 The right of priority belongs in the first place to the original applicant ("Any person who has duly filed …"). Being a legal right, it is assignable in law, as is recognised in paragraph A(1) by the reference to "his successor in title".

The validity of an assignment of a priority right is a matter for the law in the country where the assignment is made, on general principles.

(2) Section B

10–07 "**B.** Consequently, any subsequent filing in any of the other countries of the Union before the expiration of the periods referred to above shall not be invalidated by reason of any acts accomplished in the interval, in particular, another filing, the publication or exploitation of the invention, the putting on sale of copies of the design, or the use of the mark, and such acts cannot give rise to any third party right or any right of personal possession. Rights acquired by third parties before the date of the first application that serves as the basis for the right of priority are reserved in accordance with the domestic legislation of each country of the Union."

(a) Effect of priority right

10–08 The first sentence of this paragraph sets out in general terms the consequence and effect of the "right of priority" provided in paragraph A(1). The broad statement of the effect of the right of priority is that "*any* subsequent filing" within the priority period "shall not be invalidated by reason of *any* acts accomplished in the interval" (emphasis added). If considered in isolation this statement is of course far too broad to make sense. There must be an assumption underlying sections A and B that (as far as patents are concerned) the earlier filing and the subsequent filing are by the same person (or his successor in title) and in respect of essentially the same subject-matter, and that similarly "any acts accomplished in the interval" are acts in respect of the same subject-matter. The subsequent example given in section B, "as, for instance, … the publication or exploitation of the invention", brings out the underlying assumption, namely, that there is a particular invention which is common to the earlier and subsequent filings and to the "acts" which may be accomplished in the interval.

(b) Identity of subject-matter

The Paris Convention is silent as to the degree of identity of subject-matter **10–09** that is required between the first and the subsequently filed applications in order that a priority right should arise. It was presumably intended that this should be left to be developed within the context of the national laws of the "Union countries" that are parties to the Paris Convention.

Bodenhausen[6] simply refers to the fact that the subsequent filing "must concern the same subject as the first filing on which the right of priority is based", and later refers to this as "identity of subject".

(c) Acts accomplished in the interval

Subject to what is said above, the wording which is concerned with the **10–10** nature of the intervening and non-invalidating acts is also of broad scope, and makes no distinction between the performance of such acts by the applicant himself or persons associated therewith or by persons independent of the applicant (who may have devised such subject-matter themselves, for example).

(3) Section C

Paragraphs C(1), (2) and (3) set out time limits for the periods during which **10–11** a right of priority is enjoyed (twelve months for patents and utility models, compared with six months for industrial designs and trademarks), and explain how the time limits are to be calculated.

(a) Twelve-month priority period

As to the twelve-month period for patents, the extension of this period **10–12** from six months to twelve months took place at the 1900 Revision Conference; since then there has been no change.

This twelve-month priority period, or Convention year as it is often called, is primarily intended to provide a sufficiently long period of protection (in the sense of Article 4B as discussed above) to enable the maker of a first application to decide upon the number of additonal countries in which he wishes to apply for correponding patents. As is apparent from the discussion of section B above, the effect of the right of priority period is that time stops running as far as subsequent Convention applications in respect of the same invention are concerned. Such Convention applications are "back-dated" to the date of the first filed application. So far as each subsequent Convention application is concerned, its claim to priority is thus a retrospective claiming of a date earlier than its filing date in its own country or territory.

Clearly, it is in the public interest that the period within which such retroactivity can take place should be kept to a minimum.

On the other hand, if the priority period is to be meaningful for the

---

[6] Bodenhausen, *Guide to the Application of the Paris Convention for the Protection of Industrial Property* (BIRPI, 1968).

applicant, it must be long enough for him to form a reasonable idea as to the extent of geographical protection which he will need. As with many other aspects of patent law, there can be no single answer which is fair for each individual case. The nature of each invention and the circumstances surrounding its exploitation necessarily vary widely.

A period of one year seems a reasonable balance between an applicant's interest in having a reasonable time in which to decide upon the extent of protection that he desires, and the public interest in certainty as to where patent protection may be applied for.

(b) From the first application

10–13 The twelve-month period starts from the date of filing of the "first application" in respect of specific subject-matter. Identification of this "first application" may sometimes be of crucial importance to the allowability of a claim to priority—see paragraph 10–49 below.

Paragraph C(4) reads as follows:

> "(4) A subsequent application concerning the same subject as a previous first application within the meaning of paragraph (2) above, filed in the same country of the Union, shall be considered as the first application, of which the filing date shall be the starting point of the period of priority, if, at the time of filing the subsequent application, the said previous application has been withdrawn, abandoned or refused, without having been laid open to public inspection and without leaving any rights outstanding, and if it has not yet served as a basis for claiming a right of priority. The previous application may not thereafter serve as a basis for claiming a right of priority."

This provision was introduced into the Paris Convention as late as 1958. The general principle was previously that once a first application had been made in respect of certain subject-matter, the priority period could not thereafter be extended. As mentioned above, time ran from the date of filing of the first application.

While this remains the general principle, paragraph C(4) provides a mechanism by which an applicant can, in effect, substitute a later "first applicant" for his original first application (for example, in order to improve the disclosure of his "first application"). The original first application has to have been withdrawn, abandoned or refused without having been published, without leaving any rights outstanding, and without having been the subject of a claim to priority. A corresponding provision is set out in Article 87(4) EPC.

(4) Section D: Formalities of claiming priority

10–14 This section sets out provisions and requirements in relation to the formal aspects of claiming priority (cf. Article 88(1) and Rule 38 EPC).

(5) Section E: Priority from a utility model

E(1) This paragraph is not relevant to patents.   10–15

E(2) This paragraph provides that priority for a patent application may be claimed from a utility model, and vice versa.

(6) Section F

"**F.** No country of the Union may refuse a priority or a parent **10–16** application on the ground that the applicant claims multiple priorities, even if they originate in different countries, or on the ground that an application claiming one or more priorities contains one or more elements that were not included in the application or applications whose priority is claimed, provided that, in both cases, there is unity of invention within the meaning of the law of the country.

With respect to the elements not included in the application or applications whose priority is claimed, the filing of the subsequent application shall give rise to a right of priority under ordinary conditions."

(a) Multiple and partial priorities

The first paragraph of section F deals with both multiple and partial **10–17** priorities. These provisions date basically from 1925 but were clarified subsequently.

The priority period for claiming priority being 12 months, clearly it frequently happens that the subject-matter of the first application is improved or added to within this period. Alternatively the wording by which such subject-matter is described or defined may be improved. Two consequences follow, in relation to possible patent protection:

(i) Multiple priorities. During the priority period the applicant may **10–18** follow up his first application with additional and separate applications in respect of additional or improved subject-matter, either in the same country as the first application or in a different country. According to the provisions of the first paragraph of section F, at the end of the priority period he may then file an application in which priority is claimed from the various "multiple" earlier applications; neither the application itself nor the claimed priorities may be refused on the ground that there are multiple priorities claimed, provided there is unity of invention in such application (according to the law of the country where that application is made).

(ii) Partial priorities. Improvements or additions to the subject-matter of **10–19** the first application may only be devised towards the end of the priority period, and may therefore be too late to be included in separate applications; or for other reasons such improvements or additions may not be the subject of separate applications during the priority period. The new "elements" of such improvements or additions which are not the subject of separate intervening applications may, according to the provisions of section F, be included in a final application claiming priority either from the first application alone (partial priority) or from the first and subsequent applications (multiple and partial priorities); in such a case neither the application itself nor the claimed priorities may be refused on the ground that there are additional "element(s)" in the final application, provided there is unity of invention in such final application (according to the law of the country where the final application is made).

(b) Further priority rights

10–20   The second paragraph of section F provides that in relation to such additional elements which have not previously been included in "priority applications", the filing of the "final" application including such elements shall give rise to a separate right of priority in respect of those elements. In other words, a later application filed within 12 months of the "final" application may claim priority from such "final" application in respect of the additional elements, and the "final" application becomes the first application for the purpose of the additional elements.

The general effect of Article 4F Paris is reflected in Article 88(2) and (3) EPC, as to which see below.

(7) Section G: Divisional applications: priority rights preserved

10–21   This section provides primarily that if an application contains more than one invention and there is therefore no unity of invention, divisional application(s) may be filed by the applicant, either as a requirement during examination (with the sanction that the application may otherwise be refused) or upon the applicant's own initiative. The filing of a European divisional application is allowed under article 676 EPC. The only relevance of this section to priority is that it is provided that in both cases where a divisional application is filed, the benefit of priority is preserved notwithstanding the filing of the divisional application.

(8) Section H: Disclosure in first application as a whole

10–22   "H. Priority may not be refused on the ground that certain elements of the invention for which priority is claimed do not appear among the claims formulated in the application in the country of origin, provided that the application documents as a whole specifically disclose such elements."

This provision dates from 1934. It is closely related to and explanatory of, sections A and B above which as mentioned previously, together set up the basic framework for the priority system.

The main point of the provision is to ensure that the subject-matter of the first application, to which the priority right attaches under section A, does not depend upon what is within the claims (if any) of the first application: the subject-matter of the invention in respect of which a priority right is enjoyed is to be determined by reference to "the application documents as a whole". The necessity for this provision derives primarily from the fact that different countries have different requirements for the contents of the claims of a patent application (if any). Furthermore, it is of course common in many countries for subject-matter to be added to the claims during prosecution of the priority application, or subsequently, provided there is support for such additional subject-matter in the disclosure of the application as a whole.

The effect of the provision is thus that all elements of an invention constituting the subject-matter of the first application enjoy the priority right, whether or not such elements are set out in claims in such first application, provided that such elements are "specifically disclosed" in the first application.

The statement "provided that the application documents as a whole specifically disclose such elements" is not intended to add to the basic substantive conditions set out in sections A and B above concerning the provision of a priority right (in particular, the necessity for identity of subject-matter). The general effect of section H is reflected in Article 88(4) EPC.

(9) Section I: Priority from an inventor's certificate

"I. (1) This paragraph provides for a right of priority for a patent application, claimed from an application for an inventor's certificate in a country where an applicant has an option to apply either for such a certificate or for a patent." **10–23**

(10) Summary

It is clear from the above discussion that the Paris Convention was intended to present a broad scheme for an international priority system, thus allowing later legislation within individual countries or groups of countries to provide more specific provisions according to individual requirements. **10–24**

In particular, as stated previously, section B makes no specific mention of the subject-matter of the subsequent application. Thus the degree of identity of subject-matter between a first application and a subsequent "Convention application" is a matter for interpretation. It would seem, however, that a degree of flexibility was intended in this respect, having regard in particular to the variations between countries as to what could constitute patentable subject-matter (*e.g.* chemical and pharmaceutical products, medical methods, etc.), and the consequent variations in the drafting and content of patent applications (especially at the time when the Paris Convention was first drafted).

As these basic aspects of patent law become more standardised and harmonised internationally, however, it may be that the need for flexibility in this respect becomes less important.

C. The Priority System under the EPC

(1) Nature of the earlier application

(a) Introduction

10–25 Article 87(1) EPC provides a priority right during a period of 12 months for a person who has duly filed an application in a Convention country for one of the following species of industrial property:

    (a) a patent;
    (b) a registration of a utility model;
    (c) a utility certificate;
    (d) an inventor's certificate.

10–25A   According to the proposed revision of the EPC, Article 87(1) EPC will be amended to align it with Article 2 TRIPS (see Chapter 1 at paragraph 1–55), which requires that priority rights also be extended to first filings made in any member state of the World Trade Organisation.

Furthermore, the reference to inventor's certificates will be deleted because this is now obsolete.

(b) No priority right from an industrial design application

10–26 Article 4 Paris provides a priority right in respect of an application for an industrial design, if a subsequent application for an industrial design is made within the appropriate priority period (six months).

In respect of a European patent application, Article 87(1) EPC sets out the only kinds of prior applications that can give rise to a right of priority, however. Accordingly, since Article 87(1) EPC does not provide that a person who has deposited an industrial design shall enjoy a priority right in respect of a subsequently filed European patent application, such a priority right is not recognised under the EPC. This is consistent with the Paris Convention (J15/80[7]).

(2) Ownership of the priority right

10–27 Under Article 87(1) EPC a right of priority belongs in the first instance to a person who has duly filed an application in a Convention country for one of the species of intellectual property set out in paragraph 10–25 above, or to his successor in title. Being a legal right, a priority right is assignable in law. The validity of an assignment of a priority right is a matter for the law of the country in which the assignment is made on general principles.

---

[7] J15/80 *ARENHOLD/Priority right* O.J. EPO 1981, 213; [1979–85] E.P.O.R. 56.

Accordingly, in proceedings before the EPO any relevant national law has to be established and proved by suitable evidence (J19/87[8]).

(3) Entitlement to priority—background

When considering priority, the following factors need to be borne in mind **10–28** as general background:

(a) Having filed a first application in respect of an invention in one country, an applicant has one year in which to decide in what other countries he desires patent protection. This decision is commonly related to commercial prospects, and in order to assess and promote such commercial prospects, the subject-matter of his first application may need to be disclosed, without putting at risk the potential international patent protection in respect of the invention.

(b) During the priority year following a first application the inventive subject-matter commonly becomes improved and refined, and such improvements may or may not justify being made the subject of ancillary patent applications during the year. This situation is recognised by the possibility of multiple and partial priorities provided for both in the Paris Convention and in the EPC.

There may be cases, however, where such an improvement or refinement is within the general disclosure of the earlier application, but not fully worked out at that time. The question is then whether a claim which includes such improvement is still entitled to claim priority from the general disclosure in the earlier application.

(c) It is also part of the normal course of events that an applicant has a **10–29** much better idea of the proper scope of his claimed invention one year after the filing of the basic application, both in relation to the prior art and in relation to obtaining a fair protection for what has been invented.

(d) Regardless of scope, the actual wording used in the claims to define the invention can also often be improved. Bearing in mind that the subject-matter of a patent application commonly comprises creative thinking, it is not always immediately easy to describe and define such subject-matter in the most appropriate way, especially when under pressure to file a patent application as soon as possible in order to establish the earliest possible priority date.

(e) As mentioned in Chapter 8 at paragraph 8–04, the requirements for claiming priority from an earlier application in respect of the same invention are somewhat analogous to the requirements for allowable amendments to the specification of a European application after filing. In both cases the essential question to be

---

[8] J19/87 BURR-BROWN/Assignment [1988] E.P.O.R. 350.

decided is what changes (amendments) can be made to a specification as previously filed (the specification of the earlier application or the European application as filed) without losing entitlement to the priority date of the earlier application or invalidating the European application, respectively.

Nevertheless, the wording of the legal requirement for entitlement to priority ("the same invention" – Article 87(1) EPC) differs from that for an allowable amendment ("no added subject-matter" – Article 123(2) EPC: see Chapter 8 at paragraphs 8–05 *et seq.*)

(4) Articles 87 to 89 EPC: corresponding provisions of the Paris Convention

10–30   Articles 87 to 89 EPC are closely related to corresponding provisions in the Paris Convention, as the following table shows:

EPC Article	Corresponding Paris Article
87(1)	4A(1)
(2)	(2)
(3)	(3)
(4)	4C(4)
(5)	—
88(1)	4D
88(2)	4F
(3)	4F
(4)	4H
89	4B
76(1)	4G

(5) Effect of priority right

(a) Basic principles

10–31   Article 89 EPC states that:

"The right of priority shall have the effect that the date of priority shall count as the date of filing of the European patent application for the purposes of Article 54(2) and (3) EPC and Article 60(2) EPC."

Accordingly, having regard to Article 54(2) and (3) EPC, if a claim to priority is allowable for individual claims of a European application, the novelty and inventiveness of each such claim is assessed under Article 54 and 56 EPC respectively having regard to the state of the art at the date of priority (instead of at the filing date of the European application in the absence of a claim to priority).

Furthermore, under Article 60(2) EPC the right to a European patent in respect of an invention which is made independently by two or more persons belongs to the person whose European application has the earliest filing date (either the actual filing date or the notional filing date having regard to Article 89 EPC). This reflects the "first-to-file" aspect of the European patent system.

(b) Intervening publication and disclosure

A question arises as to the extent to which the priority system under the **10–32** EPC provides protection to an applicant who has duly filed an application in a Convention country in respect of an invention, and who thereafter wishes to publish or disclose the invention during the 12 months Convention period prior to filing a European application in respect of the invention (that is, an "intervening publication" of the invention).

(1) In a case where all the claims of the European application are entitled **10–33** to claim priority from the date of filing of the earlier application, such an intervening publication is not part of the state of the art with respect to such claims and the applicant is therefore protected by the priority system from any possible adverse effect upon the validity of such claims as a result of such intervening publication.

(2) However, in a case where the European application contains claims **10–34** which are not entitled to priority under Article 87 EPC, for example as a result of the invention having been developed during the Convention year beyond what is disclosed in the priority document of the earlier application, such an intervening publication of the subject-matter of the priority document does form part of the state of the art with respect to any such claims which are not entitled to priority from the earlier application and whose filing date is accordingly that of the European application. Thus such an intervening publication could form the basis for an attack upon the validity of such claims on the ground of lack of inventive step under Article 56 EPC.

In other words, "A document published during the priority interval, the technical contents of which correspond to that of the priority document, constitutes prior art citable under Article 54(2) EPC against a European patent application claiming that priority to the extent such priority is not validly claimed" (G3/93[9]).

A claim to priority will be invalid, for example, "if the priority document and the subsequent European application do not concern the same invention because the European application claims subject-matter not disclosed in the priority document". It is a condition precedent to the effect of a priority right set out in Article 89 EPC that the European application is "in respect of the same invention" as disclosed in the priority document (G3/93[10]).

The requirements for "identity of invention" and consequent entitle- **10–35** ment to priority are discussed in paragraphs 10–38 *et seq.* below.

It should be noted that the above conclusions concerning the effect of an

---

[9] G3/93 *Priority interval* O.J. EPO 1995, 18; [1994] E.P.O.R. 521.
[10] *Ibid.*

intervening publication are contrary to the "*obiter dictum*" contained in T301/87,[11] to the effect that when priority is claimed for a European application, such an intervening publication or disclosure "cannot be used as state of the art against any claim" such as European application. This *obiter dictum* in T301/87[12] was overrruled in G3/93.[13]

Accordingly, applicants should avoid any public disclosure of the invention disclosed in a priority document until after a European patent application in respect of that invention has been filed. Any developments during the Convention year of the invention disclosed in a priority document which could become the subject-matter of separate claims of a European application filed at the end of the Convention year should either form the subject-matter of separate applications filed during the Convention year ("multiple priorities", see paragraph 10–18) or such developments may be included in the European application filed at the end of the Convention year, in which case the European application is a "first application" in respect of such subject-matter which itself gives rise to a priority right ("partial priorities" see paragraph 10–19).

(6) Multiple and partial priorities

10–36 Article 88(2) and (3) EPC reflects the provisions in Article 4F of the Paris Convention concerning multiple and partial priorities (see paragraphs 10–17 *et seq.* above).

(7) Disclosure in the priority document as a whole

10–37 Article 88(4) EPC corresponds to Article 4H Paris, which is discussed in paragraph 10–22 above. This provision emphasises the necessity for disclosure of all the elements of the claimed invention in the priority document—if such elements are not in the claims of the priority document, at least the priority document "as a whole" must "specifically disclose such elements".

(a) Entitlement to priority

(a) Introduction: disclosure of the same invention

10–38 There is one important qualification in Article 87(1) EPC as compared to Article 4A(1) Paris, namely that an applicant for a European patent is only entitled to claim priority from an earlier filed application if the European application is "in respect of the same invention" (*cf.* Bodenhausen's "identity of subject", see paragraph 10–09). Thus what is implicit in Articles 4A(1) and B Paris has been made explicit in Article 87(1) EPC.

The degree of correspondence required between what is claimed in the European application and what is disclosed in a priority application, if the claim to priority is to be upheld, is therefore a matter of interpretation of

---

[11] T301/87 *BIOGEN/Alpha-interferons* O.J. EPO 1990, 335; [1990] E.P.O.R. 190.
[12] *Ibid.*
[13] G3/93 *Priority interval* O.J. EPO 1995, 18; [1994] E.P.O.R. 521.

the words "in respect of the same invention". This is of course a question of substance, not form. In assessing whether the subject-matter of a claim of a European application is entitled to priority from an earlier application, the underlying invention has to be identified.

(i) The basic question: disclosure of all claimed features? In the majority of decisions of the Boards of Appeal concerning the right to priority, the relevant basic question which has been considered is whether there is a disclosure of all the claimed features of the invention in the priority document. In relation to the question of disclosure, the same principles have often been applied as are applied in relation to novelty. In particular, the disclosure may be express or implied.

Thus, many Board of Appeal decisions have followed the approach set out in the "Guidelines" (section C—V, 24), namely that the basic test to determine whether a claim is entitled to the date of a priority document is the same as the test of whether an amendment to an application satisfies Article 123(2) EPC, which in turn is the same as the test for novelty: that is, is the subject-matter of the claim directly and unambiguously derivable from the disclosure in the priority document?

If yes, the claim of the European application and the priority document are "in respect of the same invention", and the claim to priority is allowable.

This approach is satisfactory in simple cases.

(ii) Mere change in protection. On the other hand, in accordance with 10–39 the established practice of the Boards of Appeal, even if a claimed feature has not been disclosed in the priority document, a claim to priority may still be allowable if the undisclosed claimed feature is not a feature of the invention as such, but merely affects and changes the extent of protection. In such a case the undisclosed feature does not affect the essential character and nature of the invention, and its omission from the priority document does not affect the fact that the same invention is both disclosed in the priority document and defined in the claim for which priority is sought. This is discussed further below (see paragraphs 10–45 *et seq.*).

In Board of Appeal decisions, there is normally an emphasis upon whether or not features which are related to the character and technical effect of the invention (*i.e.* the essential features) have been disclosed in the priority document: the implication is that this consideration is normally central to determining whether the claims are "in respect of the same invention" as the disclosure in the priority document. Such a consideration helps to focus upon the main criterion in respect of the claiming of priority, namely whether the claimed invention is disclosed in the priority document as a matter of substance.

(iii) Referral to the Enlarged Board. In July 1998, the President of the 10–39a EPO referred the following questions to the Enlarged Board of Appeal, pursuant to Article 112(1)(b) EPC:

"1(a) Does the requirement of the 'same invention' in Article 87(1) EPC mean that the extent of the right to priority derivable from a priority application for a later application is determined by, and at the same time limited to, what is at least implicitly disclosed in the priority application?

1(b) Or can a lesser degree of correspondence between the priority application and the subject-matter claimed in the later application be sufficient in this respect and still justify a right to priority?

2 If question 1(b) is answered in the affirmative, what are the criteria to be applied in assessing whether the claim in the later application is in respect of the same invention as is in the priority application?

3 In particular, where features not disclosed, even implicitly, in the priority application have been added in the relevant claim of the later application, or where features defined in broader terms in the priority application have been more specifically or more narrowly defined in the later application, can a right to priority nevertheless be derived from the priority application and, if so, what are the criteria which must be met to justify the priority in such cases?"

The case is pending as G2/98.[14] At the time of writing the opinion of the Enlarged Board is awaited.

The above referred questions appear in part at least indirectly to question the practice of the Boards of Appeal in relation to "mere change in protection" (paragraphs 10–39 above and 10–45 *et seq.* below), in relation to which there appears to be no real conflict between any decisions: clearly "the same invention" can be claimed in different claims with different extents of protection.

(b) Express or implied disclosure of essential features

10–40 The essential requirements for claiming priority from an earlier application are as follows:

> "the subject-matter of the claims of the European application must be clearly identifiable in the documents of the previous application as a whole, [and] the disclosure of the essential elements, *i.e.* features of the invention in the priority document must either be express, or be directly and unambiguously implied by the text as filed. Missing elements which are to be recognised as essential only later on are thus not part of the disclosure. ... the argument that the skilled person would supplement the disclosure from his common general knowledge to make it work, should any difficulty be encountered, is no

---

[14] G2/98 Not yet issued: O.J. EPO (P).

excuse when this is a feature of the definition of the invention, and is missing, not envisaged by the inventor and not implied in the description. Adding such feature later on would be to change the character of the invention itself ..." (T81/87[15]).

This clearly sets out the distinction between what the applicant has disclosed in the priority document (either expressly or by direct and unambiguous implication) and what a skilled reader might add to such disclosure from his common general knowledge. Thus the disclosure of the inventive subject-matter in the priority document may be considered as evidence of what the inventor had invented at the claimed priority date.

There is some flexibility in the requirement of identity of invention between a claim of a European application and the disclosure of the priority document, in that a claimed feature need not be explicitly and expressly mentioned in the priority document, provided that a skilled person would clearly infer the claimed feature as being implicitly present in the priority document on the basis of his common general knowledge (T136/95[16]).

(c) Role of the skilled person: priority, novelty and inventive step compared

The role of the skilled person in the determination of priority, novelty and inventive step can be compared as follows: **10–41**

(i) When determining a claim to priority, what matters is what a skilled person would consider that the applicant put into the priority document, as compared to the subject-matter of the claim for which priority is claimed;

(ii) When determining novelty of a claim, what matters is what the content of the prior document discloses to a skilled person, compared to the subject-matter of the claimed invention (see Chapter 11).

In most cases in practice, the "result" of (i) and (ii) will be the same. However, there is a difference of emphasis between (i) and (ii) which in some cases may lead to a different "result":

(iii) When determining inventive step, on the other hand, what matters is what a skilled person would consider obvious to do using a combination of the disclosure of the prior document and his common general knowledge (see Chapter 12).

In many cases the result of (iii) will be different from (i) and (ii).

[15] T81/87 *COLLABORATIVE/Preprorennin* O.J. EPO 1990, 250; [1990] E.P.O.R. 361.
[16] T136/95 *JUSTAMENTE/Waste compactor* O.J. EPO 1998, 198; [1993] E.P.O.R. 301.

(d) General disclosures

10–42 A number of cases have dealt with the question whether a general or generic disclosure in a priority document can properly provide a basis for a claim to priority in respect of a claim of a subsequent European application whose subject-matter is directed to a specific aspect of such general disclosure.

The principle which is applied to the determination of the novelty of a specific chemical compound having regard to a generic disclosure of a group of compounds which includes such specific compound, namely that a general disclosure does not disclose specific individual compounds or entities within it (see Chapter 11 at paragraph 11–69) is equally applicable to the determination of a claim to priority (T85/87[17]), having regard to the principles discussed in paragraph 10–41 above.

Thus:

> "if an entity itself is disclosed to the skilled person, this does not necessarily mean that a component part is also disclosed for the purpose of priority if this is not envisaged directly and unambiguously as such, and requires considerable investigation to reveal its identity" (T301/87[18]).

10–43 The above principle has also been applied in a case where a general disclosure in a priority document encompassed two possible alternative processes, only one of which was claimed in the subsequent European application. The claimed alternative process had an improved effect compared to the other alternative, and was therefore considered as a necessary functional limitation for the claimed invention, which reflected "the discovery that not all variants of the priority document work, or work adequately to the newly set degree". The claimed alternative was held not to be "clearly and unequivocally implied by the priority document", and priority was therefore refused (T61/85[19]).

The above principle is also applied in cases where a claim in a priority document embraces more specific claimed subject-matter in a European application, but does not expressly disclose such subject matter.

> "The invention which is the subject of the priority document has to be determined from a consideration of the priority document as a whole, as read by a skilled person.
>
> When considering what is disclosed by a claim of a priority document it is relevant that the purpose of the claim is to define the protection which is sought. The fact that a claim in a priority document is broad enough to cover specific subject-matter claimed for the first time in a European patent application cannot by itself be

[17] T85/87 *CSIRO/Arthropedicidal compounds* [1989] E.P.O.R. 24.
[18] T301/87 *BIOGEN/Alpha-interferons* O.J. EPO 1990, 335; [1990] E.P.O.R. 190.
[19] T61/85 *ICI/Polyester crystallisation* [1988] E.P.O.R. 20.

sufficient evidence that such subject-matter has already been disclosed in the priority document so as to establish identity of invention for the purpose of claiming priority under Article 87 EPC" (T409/90[20]).

On the other hand, in a case where the priority document defines a feature generally and functionally, in terms of the desired result, a claim in the subsequent European application which defines such feature structurally may be entitled to priority, provided that a skilled person wishing to carry out the invention in accordance with the priority document would be guided by the functional definition of such feature to construct the invention in accordance with the claimed structural definition. In such a case, even though there is no express disclosure of the claimed structural feature, such feature is implicit in the disclosure of the priority document because a skilled person would infer it "when performing simple operations to carry out the invention" (T136/95[21]).

(e) Specific disclosure cf. general claim

In some cases, a specific disclosure of a particular structure or arrangement **10–44** in the priority document may be the basis for a priority claim in respect of broader, for example, functional subject-matter, in a claim of a European application. However, in such a case it is important to distinguish between an applicant who has "only" invented and put in to the disclosure of the priority document the particular structure or arrangement, and an applicant who has invented the broader concept and disclosed that at the filing date of the priority document, the particular arrangement clearly being merely an example within the general concept. This distinction is not always easy to draw, especially if there are hints of the general concept within the description of the specific arrangement.

Clearly, however, in such a case the principles which are applicable to the determination of novelty are not applicable when determining the allowability of the right to priority. In relation to novelty, a prior specific disclosure would normally destroy the novelty of a claim to general subject-matter including such specific disclosure (see paragraph 11–69). In contrast, a specific disclosure in a priority document would not *per se* justify a claim to priority in respect of a more general claim in a European application.

(f) Mere change in protection

It should be emphasised that whether or not a European applicant is **10–45** entitled to claim priority from an earlier application under Article 87EPC depends upon whether or not the claims are "in respect of the same invention" as the earlier application. The individual claims of an application may (or may not) all relate to the same invention as that disclosed in

---

[20] T409/90 *FUJITSU/Avalanche photo diodes* O.J. EPO 1993, 40; [1991] E.P.O.R. 423.
[21] T136/95 *JUSTAMENTE/Waste compactor* O.J. EPO 1998, 198; [1998] E.P.O.R. 301.

the priority document, even though individually they each provide a different extent of protection. Thus variations in the extent of protection conferred by individual claims of a European application do not *per se* affect the entitlement to priority of all such claims, provided of course that they are each "in respect of the same invention" as the priority document.

It follows that the presence of a feature in a claim of a European application, which feature is not disclosed in the priority document, will not cause loss of priority if the effect of such undisclosed feature is merely to change the extent of protection conferred by the claim. Thus "the inclusion of a technical feature in a claim which is an essential feature for the purpose of determining the scope of protection conferred is not necessarily an essential feature for the purpose of determining priority" (T73/88[22]).

10–46   "Whether a particular claimed feature is essential for the purpose of priority, and therefore needs to be specifically disclosed in the priority document, depends upon its relationship to the function and effect of the invention, and therefore to the character and nature of the invention." (T73/88[23])

In a case where a feature in a claim is not related to the function and effect of the invention, such feature is not related to the character and nature of the invention, and the absence of such feature from the disclosure of the priority document does not cause loss of priority, provided the claim is otherwise in substance in respect of the same invention as that disclosed in the priority document (T73/88[24]).

10–47   Accordingly, the presence of a feature in a claim, which feature is not disclosed in the priority document, but which does not constitute an essential technical element of the invention and "represents simply a voluntary restriction of the scope of that claim", does not cause loss of priority (T16/87[25]).

The addition of a feature in the claim of a European application as compared to the disclosure of the priority document—such as discussed above—is in a general sense analogous to the amendment of a claim of a European application after filing by the addition of a feature which restricts the scope of the claimed invention, see paragraph 10–29 above, and Chapter 8 at paragraph 8–04. Consequently, similar principles as are discussed above when determining a claim to priority are also applicable when determining the allowability of an amendment under Article 123(2) EPC (G1/93[26]: see Chapter 8 at paragraph 8–41).

---

[22] T73/88 *HOWARD/Snackfood* O.J. EPO 1990, 5; [1990] E.P.O.R. 112.
[23] *Ibid.*
[24] *Ibid.*
[25] T16/87 *PROCATALYSE/Catalyst* O.J. EPO 1992, 212; [1992] E.P.O.R. 305.
[26] G1/93 *ADVANCED SEMICONDUCTOR PRODUCTS II/Conflict between requirements of Article 123(2) and (3) EPC* O.J. EPO 1994, 541; [1995] E.P.O.R. 97.

(g) Necessity for an enabling disclosure

A priority document should contain a disclosure which enables the **10–48** claimed invention which is the subject of the European application to be carried out by a skilled person, if the claim to priority is to be allowable. If this were not so, it could become a misuse of the priority system if an applicant in a competitive priority situation was allowed to jump ahead of other applicants on the basis of mere speculation in a priority document, without sufficient disclosure enabling a skilled person to perform the invention (T81/87[27]).

(h) Priority application not the first filing

Objection to the claiming of priority may be based upon the ground that **10–49** the priority application was not the first filed application in respect of the invention, and that an earlier application in respect of the same invention had been filed more than 12 months before the European application, by the same applicant (or his predecessors in title).

The same principles as regards the question of identity of invention discussed above are applied in such cases also (T184/84[28], T295/87[29]).

> "In particular, a patent application cannot serve as a basis for claiming priority under Article 87(1) EPC where an application has been filed prior to the said application and this subsequent application is distinguished from the previous application only by a limitation of the scope of protection (*e.g.* a disclaimer) which does not change the nature of the invention (T255/91[30], following T73/88[31])."

D. Comparison with United Kingdom law

1977 U.K. Act, ss.5 and 6

The wording of sections 5 and 6 of the 1977 U.K. Act[32] is totally different **10–50** from that in Articles 87 to 89 EPC, but nevertheless sections 5 and 6 are expressly referred to in section 130(7) as having been drafted "so ... as to have, as nearly as practicable, the same effects" as the corresponding provisions of the EPC.

(1) Effect of priority right: intervening publication

Section 6 1977 U.K. Act appears to state that an intervening publication of **10–51** the subject-matter of a priority document such as discussed in paragraphs

---

[27] T81/87 COLLABORATIVE/*Preprorennin* O.J. EPO 1990, 250; [1990] E.P.O.R. 361.
[28] T184/84 NGK INSULATORS/*Ferrite crystal* [1986] E.P.O.R. 169.
[29] T295/87 ICI/*Polyetherketones* O.J. EPO 1990, 470; [1991] E.P.O.R. 56.
[30] T255/91 AIR PRODUCTS AND CHEMICALS/*Priority* O.J. EPO 1993, 318; [1993] E.P.O.R. 544.
[31] T73/88 HOWARD/*Snackfood* O.J. EPO 1990, 5; [1990] E.P.O.R. 112.
[32] See Appendix 21.

10–32 *et seq.* above cannot be used as part of the state of the art to invalidate a subsequent application claiming priority from such priority document (even if the claims of the subsequent application do not define the same invention as that disclosed in the priority document).

In *Beloit Technologies Inc. v. Valmet Paper Machinery Inc.,*[33] however, the Patents Court interpreted section 6(1) of the 1977 U.K. Act as referring only to an **effective** claim for priority (not to a mere claim *per se* for priority). The Patents Court recognised that the language of section 6(1) ("declaration is made in accordance with section 5(2)") "does not readily admit" such an interpretation, but that "it is possible, just", to read the words of section 6(1) in that way. Furthermore, such an interpretation is in conformity with the interpretation of Article 87 EPC by the Enlarged Board of Appeal in G3/93[34] (see paragraph 10–34 above), and is therefore also in conformity with the stated intention of section 130(7) of the 1977 U.K. Act that section 6 has, "as nearly as practicable, the same effects" as Articles 87 to 89 EPC.

Thus, section 6(1) 1977 U.K. Act has been judicially harmonised with Article 87 EPC, notwithstanding the linguistic difficulties in achieving this.

(2) Entitlement to priority

10–52 The requirement in section 5(2)(a) is that the "invention to which the application in suit relates is supported by matter disclosed" in the earlier application. This compares with the requirement of "fairly based" in section 5(4) of the 1949 U.K. Act, which was recognised by the Court of Appeal in *Asahi Kasei Kogyo KK's Application*[35] as being "no longer relevant law under the [1977] Act and the EPC ... Section 5(4) of the 1949 Act [having] no direct parallel in the 1977 Act". On this basis it appears that judicial interpretations of "fairly based" such as in *Mond Nickel Co. Ltd's Application*[36] are similarly no longer relevant law (although the requirement of "fairly based" was also intended to conform with the Paris Convention).

(3) Enabling disclosure

10–53 In *Asahi Kasei Kogyo K.K.'s Application*[37] the House of Lords followed the same principles as set out in T81/87[38] (paragraph 10–48 above).

[33] [1995] R.P.C. 705.
[34] G3/93 *Priority interval* O.J. EPO 1994, 541; [1995] E.P.O.R. 97.
[35] [1991] R.P.C. 485; [1990] F.S.R. 465, CA.
[36] [1956] R.P.C. 189.
[37] [1991] R.P.C. 485, HL, reversing [1990] F.S.R. 465; [1991] R.P.C. 485, CA.
[38] T81/87 *COLLABORATIVE/Preprorennin* O.J. EPO 1990, 250; [1990] E.P.O.R. 361.

Cases Referred to in Chapter 10

Board of Appeal Decisions

G1/93   ADVANCED SEMICONDUCTOR PRODUCTS II/Conflicting requirements of Article 123(2) and (3) EPC O.J. EPO 1995, 745; [1995] E.P.O.R. 97.

G3/93   Priority interval O.J. EPO 1994, 541; [1995] E.P.O.R. 97.

G2/98   Not yet issued: O.J. EPO (P).

J15/80   ARENHOLD/Priority Right O.J. EPO 1981, 213; [1979–85] E.P.O.R.: A: 56.

J19/87   BURR-BROWN/Assignment [1988] E.P.O.R. 350.

T184/84   NGK INSULATORS/Ferrite crystal [1986] E.P.O.R. 169.

T61/85   ICI/Polyester crystallisation [1988] E.P.O.R. 20.

T16/87   PROCATALYSE/Catalyst O.J. EPO 1992, 212; [1992] E.P.O.R. 305.

T81/87   COLLABORATIVE/Preprorennin O.J. EPO 1990, 250; [1990] E.P.O.R. 361.

T85/87   CSIRO/Arthropodicidal compounds [1989] E.P.O.R. 24.

T295/87   ICI/Polyetherketones O.J. EPO 1990, 470; [1991] E.P.O.R. 56.

T301/87   BIOGEN/Alpha-interferons O.J. EPO 1990, 335; [1990] E.P.O.R. 190.

T73/88   HOWARD/Snackfood O.J. EPO 1992, 557; [1990] E.P.O.R. 112.

T409/90   FUJITSU/Avalanche photo diodes O.J. EPO 1993, 40; [1991] E.P.O.R. 423.

T255/91   AIR PRODUCTS AND CHEMICALS/Priority O.J. 1993, 318.

T136/95   JUSTAMENTE/Waste compactor O.J. EPO 1998, 198; [1998] E.P.O.R. 301.

Decisions of National Courts

Asahi Kasei Kogyo K.K.'s Application [1991] R.P.C. 485, HL, reversing [1990] F.S.R. 465; [1991] R.P.C. 485, CA

Beloit Technologies Inc. v. Valmet Paper Machinery Inc. [1995] R.P.C. 705.

Mond Nickel Co. Ltd's Application [1956] R.P.C. 189.

CHAPTER 11

NOVELTY

Articles 54 and 55 EPC

Contents

All references are to paragraph numbers

Cases Referred to in Chapter 11

A. Introduction

(1) Preliminary considerations

11–01 A novelty requirement for patentability is generally basic to all national patent systems. Prior to the EPC, however, novelty requirements under different national laws varied considerably in certain respects. As will be seen, aspects of the law relating to novelty under the EPC have developed differently from those relating to many previous national laws, including that of the United Kingdom. In fact this area of law under the EPC has surprised some practitioners within national systems who had grown accustomed to regarding the law of novelty as well settled.

It can be questioned whether a requirement of novelty in patent law is really necessary. Since subject-matter which does not involve an inventive step is not patentable, a single requirement of inventive step could be sufficient. Lack of novelty is equivalent to a zero level of inventiveness. Thus "if a document destroys the novelty of the claimed subject matter, such subject-matter obviously cannot involve an inventive step. Therefore, a finding of lack of novelty in such circumstances inevitably results in such subject-matter being unallowable on the ground of lack of inventive step" (G1, 7/95[1]).

It will be seen below that the problem areas in relation to substantive novelty commonly occur in situations where an inventive step in the sense of a contribution to human knowledge, or an advance in the art, can be recognised as present within a patent application or patent, but where difficulties arise in drafting claims which give adequate protection to the advance in the art and yet are also novel.

11–02 There is, of course, a basic contradiction in the idea of refusing patentability for a claimed invention on the ground of lack of novelty in the light of a particular disclosure, if it would have required an inventive step to derive the claimed invention from such disclosure. This principle is supported by the scheme of Articles 54 and 56 EPC, which deal respectively with the requirements of novelty and inventive step as prerequisites for patentability.

The first step in relation to both requirements is the determination of what constitutes the state of the art, as defined in Article 54(2) and (3) EPC. The second step in relation to the requirement of novelty is to determine whether the subject-matter claimed in the European patent application or patent "forms part of the state of the art" (Article 54(1) EPC). The second step in relation to the requirement of inventive step is to determine whether the claimed subject-matter was or was not "obvious to a person skilled in the art" having regard to the state of the art defined in Article 54(2) EPC (Article 56 EPC, and see Chapter 12). The latter determination pre-supposes that the claimed subject-matter is not part of the state of the art.

---

[1] G1, 7/95 *DE LA RUE/ETHICON/Fresh grounds for opposition* O.J. EPO 1996, 615, 626; [1996] E.P.O.R. 601.

(2) What constitutes "the state of the art"

The state of the art comprises:

   (i) everything made available to the public ... before the date of filing **11–03** of the European patent application" (Article 54(2) EPC: see paragraphs 11–07 to 11–40); and

  (ii) "prior rights": that is "the content of European patent applications as filed", which were filed before and published on or after the date of filing of the European patent application (Article 54(3) EPC: see paragraphs 11–41 to 11–48). The determination of what constitutes the state of the art under both these headings is considered in detail in Section B below.

(3) Novelty and inventive step distinguished

A claimed invention is new "if it does not form part of the state of the art" **11–04** (Article 54(1) EPC), as defined in Article 54(2) and (3) EPC): namely, everything "made available to the public" and "prior rights", respectively.

A claimed invention involves an inventive step if it is not obvious to a skilled person having regard to the state of the art as defined in Article 54(2) EPC: namely, everything "made available to the public" (Article 56 EPC).

Thus documents which are prior rights "are not to be considered in deciding whether there has been an inventive step" (Article 56 EPC, second sentence).

As previously stated, the determination of whether a claimed invention involves an inventive step presupposes that the claimed invention has not previously been "made available to the public", and that there is therefore a step to be taken between the prior art which has been "made available to the public" and the claimed invention.

In each case:

> "a line must be drawn between what is in fact made available, and what remains hidden or otherwise has not been made available ... information equivalent to a claimed invention may be 'made available' (lack of novelty), or may not have been made available but obvious (novel, but lack of inventive step), or not made available and not obvious (novel and inventive). Thus, in particular, what is hidden may still be obvious" (G2, 6/88[2]).

(4) The requirements for novelty

Article 54 EPC states as follows: **11–05**

> "(1) An invention shall be considered to be new if it does not form part of the state of the art.

---

[2] G2, 6/88 *MOBIL OIL/BAYER/Friction reducing additive* O.J. EPO 1990, 93, 114; [1990] E.P.O.R. 73, 257.

   (2) The state of the art shall be held to comprise everything made available to the public by means of a written or oral description, by use, or in any other way, before the date of filing of the European patent application.

   (3) Additionally, the content of European patent applications as filed, of which the dates of filing are prior to the date referred to in paragraph (2) and which were published under Article 93 on or after that date, shall be considered as comprised in the state of the art."

The essence of Article 54(1) EPC in conjunction with Article 52(1) EPC is that what already forms part of the state of the art cannot be patented, because it is not new. The state of the art is constituted by all information which has been "made available to the public" (Article 54(2) EPC) together with the contents of (unpublished) European patent applications as defined in Article 54(3) EPC ("prior rights").

In relation to the question of novelty of a claimed invention, there are in principle two quite distinct matters to be considered:

   (1) *What is the prior art* that comprises "the state of the art"?
   (2) *Is the claimed invention novel* over the state of the art?

These two questions are discussed in sections B and C below, respectively entitled "The State of the Art" and "Substantive Novelty."

(5) The dual concept of "made available to the public"

11–06   "Whatever the means of disclosure (written description, oral description, use by sale, etc.), availability in the sense of Article 54(2) EPC involves two separate stages: availability of the means of disclosure, and availability of information which is accessible and derivable from such means" (T952/92[3]). Two separate and sequential inquiries as to what was "made available to the public" before the filing date may require consideration, namely:

   (a) What source of information has been made available to the public in the physical sense (by physical means such as a book, a prior used machine, an oral lecture, etc)?
   (b) What actual information in the form of a technical teaching has been made available to a skilled person, as a result of the source of information having been made available in the sense of (a) above?

The first question is considered in section B, "The State of the Art", and the second question is considered in section C, "Substantive Novelty", below.

---

[3] T952/92 *PACKARD/Supersolve* O.J. EPO 1995, 755; [1997] E.P.O.R. 457.

Section D is concerned with the special considerations of substantive novelty which arise in connection with inventions relating to further uses of known products.

B. The State of the Art

(1) Published prior art

Article 54(2) EPC

(a) Introduction

The word "published" is used here in its original, general sense as meaning **11–07** "made public", and is applicable not only to written documents, in the literary sense, but also to all other forms of public availability. It is therefore used here as a convenient shorthand for the phrase used in Article 54(2) EPC—"made available to the public".

It is not necessary that any particular member of the public actually received information about an invention. What matters is whether such information was made available. The concept of "made available to the public" is discussed in paragraphs 11–41 *et seq.*, below with reference to particular different means of publication.

(b) Absence of limitations as to publication

The breadth of the concept of published prior art under Article 54(2) EPC is **11–08** an important legal innovation under the EPC.

(i) Language. The language in which information is made available is **11–09** irrelevant, in the case of a written or oral description. However, for the purpose of proceedings before the EPO, a translation into an official language may be required (Rule 1(2) EPC).

(ii) Scale. The scale on which information has been made available to the **11–10** public is in principle irrelevant, for example a single copy of a document that has been placed on the shelves of a library on a particular date forms part of the state of the art for the purpose of Article 54 EPC on that date (T381/87[4]).

Similarly a single sale is sufficient to make the subject of the sale **11–11** available to the public for the purpose of Article 54(2) EPC (T482/89[5]).

"The public" in this context therefore means one or more members of the public.

Evidence of scale could be relevant, however, for example in order to establish that there was no intention to keep the information confidential to certain specific persons (see paragraphs 11–30, 11–31 below).

---

[4] T381/87 *RESEARCH CORPORATION/Publication* O.J. EPO 1990, 213; [1989] E.P.O.R. 138.
[5] T482/89 *TÉLÉMÉCANIQUE/Electrical supply* O.J. EPO 1992, 646; [1993] E.P.O.R. 259.

11–12 **(iii) Territory.** Information which is "made available to the public" anywhere in the world "forms part of the state of the art" and is therefore part of the published prior art for the purpose of Article 54 EPC.

This is in contrast to the previous law under Section 32(1)(e) 1949 U.K. Act, which provided that only what was known or used in the United Kingdom could be taken into account.

11–13 **(iv) Time.** Information may become part of the published prior art for the purpose of Article 54 EPC at any point in time before the filing date.

This is in contrast to section 50(1) 1949 U.K. Act, which provided that patent specifications more than 50 years old cannot be taken into account for novelty purposes. Other countries, in particular Germany, provided a similar temporal limit under their national laws.

11–14 **(v) Means of publication.** Information may become part of the published prior art by any means for the purpose of Article 54 EPC.

This is in contrast to the previous position under certain national laws, in particular Austria and Germany, which provided that only printed publications or use could be taken into account.

Article 54(2) EPC sets out possible means of publication in the following categories:

(1) written description;
(2) oral description;
(3) use;
(4) any other way.

"Article 54(2) EPC does not make any distinction between the different means by which any information is made available to the public. Thus, information deriving from a use is governed in principle by the same conditions as is information disclosed by oral or written description" (G1/92[6]).

"In other words, the disclosure of a written description is the information which a skilled person can learn by reading it, the disclosure of an oral description is the information which a skilled person can learn by hearing it, and the disclosure of a product which has been used is the information which a skilled person can learn from it, either visually or by analysis for example" (T952/92[7]).

Furthermore:

"whatever the physical means by which information is made available to the public (*e.g.* written description, oral description, use, pictorial description on a film or in a photograph, etc, or a combination of such

---

[6] G1/92 *Availability to the public* O.J. EPO 1993, 277; [1993] E.P.O.R. 241.
[7] T152/92 *PACKARD/Supersolve* O.J. EPO 1995, 755; [1997] E.P.O.R. 457.

means), the question of what has been made available to the public is one of fact in each case" (G2, 6/88[8]).

In particular, an initial question of fact may arise as to whether a physical means such as a written description was itself "made available to the public". Such a question of fact is decided on the balance of probabilities (see Chapter 5 at paragraph 5 35).

(c) Publication by written description

In this case, where the written description is in the form of a patent **11–15** specification or any other document, the content of the document is prior art if before the filing date the document was in a place to which at least one member of the public had access. Thus, a document which is proved to have been on the shelves of a public library is prior art, regardless of whether any person looked at it (T381/87[9]).

Particular examples:

(a) A document which is posted before the filing date but which is not received by the addressee before the filing date is not prior art (T381/87[9a]);

(b) A document which is posted and delivered to the addressee before the filing date is prior art (T381/87[10], T750/94[11]);

(c) A document which is placed on the shelves of a library one day before the filing date, and which was "available on that day to anyone who requested to see it", is prior art (T381/87[12]);

(d) A document which is available on demand from the publishers of document before the filing date is prior art (T750/94[13]);

(e) A document for which permission to publish has been given to a publisher is not prior art merely as a result of such permission (T842/91[14]).

(d) Publication by "oral description"

The same principles are applicable to an oral description, which could be a **11–16** lecture at a meeting for example (T534/88[15]).

In the absence of a record of an oral description, difficulties may often arise in determining what was made available to the public.

---

[8] G2, 6/88 *MOBIL OIL/BAYER/Friction reducing additive* O.J. EPO 1990, 93, 114; [1990] E.P.O.R. 73, 257.
[9] T381/87 *RESEARCH CORPORATION/Publication* O.J. EPO 1990, 213; [1989] E.P.O.R. 138.
[9a] *Ibid.*
[10] *Ibid.*
[11] T750/94 *AT&T/Proof of prior publication* O.J. EPO 1998, 32; [1997] E.P.O.R. 509.
[12] See note 9.
[13] See note 11.
[14] T842/91 *BILFINGER/Sealing screen* [1999] E.P.O.R. 192.
[15] T534/88 *IBM/Ion etching* [1991] E.P.O.R. 18.

(e) Publication by use

11–17 While the same principles are applicable to the determination of what is the state of the art having regard to an allegation of prior use, in that "information deriving from a use is governed in principle by the same conditions as is information disclosed by oral or written description" (G1/92[16]), the situation is complicated by the large number of factual circumstances which may arise.

11–18   **(i) Intrinsic and extrinsic characteristics of an object distinguished.** In relation to any prior use of a physical object, a distinction must be drawn between the availability of information concerning its "intrinsic" and "extrinsic" properties or characteristics. The intrinsic proprieties of an object are those concerning its composition or structure, whereas its extrinsic properties are concerned with how it reacts under particular conditions.
Thus

> "a commercially available product *per se* does not implicitly disclose anything beyond its composition or internal structure. Extrinsic characteristics, which are only revealed when the product is exposed to interaction with specifically chosen outside conditions, *e.g.* reactants or the like, in order to provide a particular effect or result or to discover potential results or capabilities, therefore point beyond the product *per se* as they are dependant on deliberate choices being made. Typical examples are the application as a pharmaceutical product of a known substance or composition (*cf.* Article 54(5) EPC) and the use of a known compound for a particular purpose, based on a new technical effect (*cf.* G2, 6/88[17] ...). Thus, such characteristics cannot be considered as already having been made available to the public" (G1/92[18]).

In other words, the logic which underlies this distinction is that the intrinsic characteristics of an object exist and are in principle ascertainable, and accordingly make information corresponding to such characteristics "available to the public"; whereas the extrinsic properties of an object are not in principle ascertainable from an examination of the object, and may or may not be "made available to the public" in the context of any previous use of the object.

11–19   **(ii) The availability of information concerning intrinsic characteristics.** In all cases of prior use of a physical object the circumstances of the prior use must be such that information concerning the structure of the object (intrinsic characteristics) corresponding to the subject-matter of

---

[16] G1/92 *Availability to the public* O.J. EPO 1993, 277; [1993] E.P.O.R. 241.
[17] G2, 6/88 *MOBIL OIL/BAYER/Friction reducing additive* O.J. EPO 1990, 93, 114; [1990] E.P.O.R. 73, 257.
[18] G1/92 *Availability to the public* O.J. EPO 1993, 277; [1993] E.P.O.R. 241.

the claimed invention must be "made available to the public", if the prior use is to constitute prior art.

a *Visually available information.*   **11–20**

1   Prior public use of a product or process. In a simple case, a product or process which has been used in public may, in the course of such use, visually communicate information as to its structure to any members of the public who see it. The visually available information is prior art (T84/83[19], T87/90[20]).

On the other hand, apparatus used on a site to which the public did not have access does not make any information visually or otherwise available concerning the construction of the apparatus available to the public (T245/88[21]). Similarly if a product has been exhibited in public in circumstances where members of the public could not have obtained information concerning the construction of the product either visually or otherwise, its construction is not prior art (T363/90[22], T461/88[23]).

The above principles also apply to the prior public use of a process.

2   Prior sale of a product.   If a product is sold to a member of the **11–21** public, the buyer may receive certain information concerning the product and how it is constructed merely by looking at it. Such visual information is prior art (T482/89[24]).

Furthermore, the buyer as owner of the product can do whatever he wants with it. In particular, he may take it apart in order to ascertain visually how it is constructed, and the visual information that is accessible to the buyer in this way is prior art (irrespective of whether such an exercise has actually been carried out).

b *Information available by analysis.* In accordance with the principles **11–22** discussed above, the intrinsic characteristics of a product, such as its chemical composition or structure, are part of the state of the art when the product as such is made available to the public (for example, by sale) and can be analysed so as to reveal such characteristics (G1/92[25]). In this regard, there is no "distinction between chemical products and other products such as mechanical or electrical articles" (G1/92[26]).

This is the case "irrespective of whether or not particular reasons can be identified for analysing the composition" (G1/92[27]).

On general principles, the information about a product which is made available as a result of such analysis must be sufficient to enable a skilled

---

[19] T84/83 *LUCHTENBERG/Rear-view mirror* [1979–85] E.P.O.R.: C: 796.
[20] T87/90 September 26, 1991.
[21] T245/88 *UNION CARBIDE/Atmospheric vaporizer* [1991] E.P.O.R. 373.
[22] T363/90 February 25, 1992.
[23] T461/88 *HEIDELBERGER DRUCKSMASCHINEN/Micro-chip* O.J. EPO 1993, 295; [1993] E.P.O.R. 529.
[24] T482/89 *TELÉMECANIQUE/Electrical Supply* O.J. EPO 1992, 646; [1993] E.P.O.R. 259.
[25] G1/92 *Availability to the public* O.J. EPO 1993, 277; [1993] E.P.O.R. 241.
[26] *Ibid.*
[27] *Ibid.*

person to be able to reproduce such product (G1/92[28]) (see paragraph 11–67).

11–23   In particular:

> "Information as to the composition or internal structure of a prior sold product is made available to the public and becomes part of the state of the art in the sense of Article 54(2) EPC if direct unambiguous access to such information is possible by means of known analytical techniques which were available for use by a skilled person before the relevant filing date" (T952/92[29]).
>
> "The likelihood or otherwise of a skilled person analysing such a prior sold product, and the degree of burden (*i.e.* the amount of work and time involved in carrying out such an analysis) is in principle irrelevant to the determination of what constitutes the state of the art" (T952/92[30]):
>
> > "Where it is possible for the skilled person to discover the composition or the internal structure of the product and to reproduce it without undue burden, then both the product and its composition or internal structure become state of the art" (G1/92[31]). However: the above quoted passage in G1/92 "is not entirely clear as a matter of grammar, since the phrase 'without undue burden' could qualify the reproduction of the product, or it could qualify both the discovery of its composition or internal structure and its reproduction." (T952/92[32])

It appears that the first possibility is the correct interpretation, and the phrase without "undue burden" only qualifies the reproducibility of the product, and not the discovery of its composition or internal structure (T952/92[33]) (see also Chapter 7 at paragraphs 7–22 *et seq.*).

Nevertheless, the question whether or not information as the composition of a product for example is "made available" in circumstances where access to such information is extremely difficult is discussed in the following paragraph.

11–24   **(iii) Drawing the line between what is "available" or "hidden".** In some extreme cases, information as to the intrinsic characteristics of a prior sold or used product or article may be accessible to a skilled person in theory, but the circumstances of the prior sale or use are such that such information may be considered as "hidden" rather than "made available to the public".

Particular examples:

---

[28] *Ibid.*
[29] T952/92 *PACKARD/Supersolve* O.J. EPO 1995, 755; [1997] E.P.O.R. 457.
[30] *Ibid.*
[31] G1/92 *Availability to the public* O.J. EPO 1993, 277; [1993] E.P.O.R. 241.
[32] T952/92 *PACKARD/Supersolve* O.J. EPO 1995, 755; [1997] E.P.O.R. 457.
[33] *Ibid.*

Prior use of a "gene bank". A gene bank (a public collection of DNA **11–25** fragments which could notionally be considered as somewhat equivalent to a "library" of such fragments) does not destroy novelty of polynucleotides, even when the gene bank contains DNA sequences which coded for such polynucleotides (amongst a multitude of other DNA sequences) (T301/87[34]).

> "The assumed presence of some fragments satisfying the criteria of the claim is not like the incidental availability of an unindexed book in a library. The interrogation of a library material is, at least for some members of the public, a direct mental procedure. The collection in the present case must be interrogated by physical interactions, and a consequent biochemical process in each case. Although any vial containing the relevant phage is a separate entity here, it is impossible to get to the vial without working through tens of thousands of samples. The circumstances are such as if the material were under lock and where the key has to be first manufactured and applied. If anything, the situation resembles that prevailing with natural substances, since the availability of phages is not direct, and is rather like the isolation of a component or bacterium from soil, where the same exists in admixture with other useless materials. Thus, the idea that the gene bank itself would once and for all anticipate an invention relating to a nucleotide sequence which may be contained therein somewhere, cannot be sustained.
>
> Accordingly, the mere existence of a DNA sequence coding for a polypeptide of the IFN-α type, within the multitude of clones of 'Lawn's gene bank' cannot automatically mean that the chemical compound (polynucleotide) concerned does become part of the state of the art. The latter would only then be the case if the existence of the compound concerned had recognisably been made publicly available" (T301/87[35]).

This case was decided before G1/92[36], and can be considered as an example of a prior "hidden use", because the "making available" of the relevant sequences within the gene bank would have been extremely burdensome.

Prior use of a control procedure on a microchip. In this case, a single printing **11–26** machine had been sold, delivered, installed and used for about a year before the relevant filing date. The machine included a microchip on which a program was stored. The program was written in machine language and realised a control procedure in accordance with the claimed invention.

The control procedure could be derived from the microchip by an expensive and difficult form of "reverse engineering". Nevertheless, the claimed control procedure "does not form part of the state of the art . . . if no

---

[34] T301/87 *BIOGEN/Alpha-interferons* O.J. EPO 1990, 335; [1990] E.P.O.R. 190.
[35] *Ibid.*
[36] G1/92 *Availability to the public* O.J. EPO 1993, 277; [1993] E.P.O.R. 241.

logic diagrams and block diagrams are available to skilled members of the interested public, if the principle underlying the control procedure is not discernible by inspection, and if moreover, the technical possibility exists of ascertaining the contents of the program but experience suggests that under the circumstances, especially in view of cost-benefit considerations, this cannot have occurred" (T461/88[37]).

This case was also decided before G1/92[38], and can also be considered as an example of prior hidden use, because the making available of information concerning the claimed control procedure by a skilled person would have been extremely burdensome and extremely unlikely in the circumstances of the prior used machine. The claimed control procedure of the microchip can also be considered as an "extrinsic" characteristic of the microchip (paragraph 11–18 above).

11–27   **(iv) Comparison with United Kingdom law.** The concept of "made available to the public" was a part of the United Kingdom statute law concerning novelty immediately prior to the 1977 U.K. Act, but only in the specific and limited context of what constituted published prior art for the purpose of oppositions (1949 U.K. Act, section 101, as applied to section 14(1)(*b*)).

The direct application of this concept to the determination of what constitutes "the state of the art" is a new aspect of the law of novelty since the coming into force of the EPC and the 1977 U.K. Act, which has caused a major change in the law of "prior use" compared to the 1949 U.K. Act.

Under the 1949 Act, two principles were applicable:

"The first ... was that the Crown could not grant a patent which would enable the patentee to stop another trader from doing what he had done before. It did not matter that he had been doing it secretly or otherwise uninformatively [see, *e.g. Bristol-Myers Company (Johnson's) Application*[39]].

11–28   The second was that the test for anticipation before the priority date was in this respect co-extensive with the test for infringement afterwards. If the use would have been an infringement afterwards, it must have been an anticipation before. For the purposes of infringement, it was not necessary that the defendant should have realised that he was doing an infringing art. Such knowledge was therefore equally unnecessary for anticipation.

"[In contrast to the 1949 U.K. Act, Article 54 EPC] makes it clear that to be part of the state of the art, *the invention* must have been made available to the public. An invention is a piece of information. Making matter available to the public within the meaning of section 2(2) [1977 U.K. Act] therefore requires the communication of information. The use of a product makes the invention part of the state of the art only so far as that use makes available the necessary information" (*Merrell Dow Pharmaceutical Inc. v. H.N. Norton & Co. Ltd*[40]).

---

[37] T461/88 *HEIDELBERGER DRUCKSMASCHINEN/Micro-chip* O.J. EPO 1993, 295; [1993] E.P.O.R. 529.
[38] G1/92 *Availability to the public* O.J. EPO 1993, 277; [1993] E.P.O.R. 241.
[39] [1975] R.P.C. 127, HL.
[40] [1996] R.P.C. 76, HL.

As discussed previously in this chapter, Article 54 EPC has always been interpreted in this sense, in proceedings before the EPO.

Neither of the above two principles are therefore applicable under the **11–29** 1977 U.K. Act:

> "The 1977 Act ... introduced a substantial qualification into the old principle that a patent cannot be used to stop someone doing what he has done before. If the previous use was secret or uninformative, then subject to section 64, it can. Likewise, a gap has opened between the tests for infringement and anticipation. Acts done secretly or without knowledge of the relevant facts, which would amount to infringements after the grant of the patent, will not count as anticipations before" (*Merrell Dow*[41]).

(f) Public availability compared with confidentiality

For the purpose of determining what is published prior art, the words "to **11–30** the public" clearly distinguish information which has been made public from information which is private, confidential or secret.

Thus, information which is published without restriction as to its subsequent use is part of the state of the art.

Whether particular information is private or secret, or has been made available in confidence, and subject to restrictions as to its further disclosure and use, must be determined according to the individual facts and circumstances of each case.

Clearly, if a disclosure of information concerning an invention is made **11–31** by the inventor or his successor in title under an express written agreement of secrecy or confidentiality which forbids further disclosure by the recipient, such information has not been made available to the public. Difficulties frequently arise, however, when there is no such express written agreement. "A secrecy agreement which rules out availability to the public does not necessarily have to be a contract made in writing" (T830/90[42]). A disclosure of information does not make such information available to the public "if there is an express or tacit agreement on secrecy which has not been broken" (see also paragraph 11–33 below) "or if the circumstances of the case are such that such secrecy derives from a relationship of good faith or trust. Good faith or trust are factors which may occur in contractual or commercial relationships" (Guidelines, D.V. 3.1.3.2, and see for example T799/91[43], T1085/92[44], T365/93[45]). Confidentiality through good faith or trust may also arise through the circumstances of any other human relationship.

For example: "The content of a business meeting is not deemed to have

---

[41] *Ibid.*
[42] T830/90 *MACOR MARINE SYSTEMS/Confidentiality agreement* O.J. EPO 1994, 713; [1995] E.P.O.R. 21.
[43] T799/91 February 3, 1994.
[44] T1085/92 *ROBERT BOSCH/Electrical machine* [1996] E.P.O.R. 381.
[45] T365/93 July 27, 1995.

been made available to the public ... if the parties concerned understood it to be secret and no breach of secrecy has been established" (T830/90[46]).

(g) Exclusions from the published prior art

Article 55 EPC

11–32   **(i) Non-prejudicial disclosures.** Article 55 EPC sets out two circumstances in which information that has become part of the published prior art is nevertheless excluded from consideration for the purpose of Article 54 EPC.

These circumstances arise when, during the six months immediately preceding the filing of a European patent application (as to which, see paragraph 11–35 below), a "disclosure of the invention" takes place "due to, or in consequence of":

(a) "an evident abuse in relation to the applicant or his legal predecessor";
(b) a display of the invention at an official international exhibition.

These two provisions of Article 55 EPC are derived directly from Article 4 of the Strasbourg Convention[47] (see Chapter 1 at paragraph 1–41 above). Provision (b) is also in accordance with, and follows from, Article 11 of the Paris Convention[48] (see Chapter 1 at paragraph 1–37 above).

11–33   a *Evident Abuse.* Article 55(1)(a) EPC states *inter alia* that:

"For the application of Article 54 EPC a disclosure of the invention shall not be taken into consideration ... if it was due to or in consequence of, an evident abuse in relation to the applicant or his legal predecessor ... "

The expression "an evident abuse" is intended to cover cases such as when an inventor discloses an invention in confidence, but the invention is subsequently made available to the public in breach of confidence. The adjective "evident" seems unnecessary: as a matter of law, it would seem that if an invention is wrongly disclosed in breach of confidence, there has been an "abuse" which ought to be enough for the purpose of the Article. Nevertheless, the word "evident" may be intended to limit application of the Article to clear cases of abuse.

For example:

"there would be evident abuse if it emerged clearly and unquestionably that a third party had not been authorised to communicate the

---

[46] T830/90 *MACOR MARINE SYSTEMS/Confidentiality agreement* O.J. EPO 1994, 713; [1995] E.P.O.R. 21.
[47] Reproduced in full at Appendix 16.
[48] Reproduced at Appendix 14.

information received to other persons there would be abuse not only when there is intention to cause harm, but also when a third party, knowing full well that he is not authorised to do so, acts in such a way as to risk causing harm to the inventor, or again when this third party fails to honour the declaration of mutual trust binding him to the inventor" (T173/83[49]).

However, according to one view, when determining whether a disclosure of the invention constituted an evident abuse within the meaning of Article 55(1)(a) EPC, the state of mind of the "abuser" is of importance. Thus: "Where a patent application is published early by a government agency as a result of an error, this is not of necessity an abuse in relation to the applicant ... however unfortunate and detrimental its consequences may turn out to be". Such a disclosure made by mistake by "a recipient of information who does not stand in any personal or specific contractual relationship to the discloser" does not constitute "evident abuse" (T585/92[50], and see also T436/92[51]).

b *Display at an official international exhibition.* Disclosure "due to, or in **11–34** consequence *of*" such a display is also excluded from consideration as prior art under Article 55(1)(b) EPC.
The display of the invention must be:

(a) by the applicant or his legal predecessor; and
(b) at an official or officially recognised international exhibition; the exhibition must fall within the terms of the Paris Convention on International Exhibitions, 1928 (as amended, Paris 1972). A list of international exhibitions which have been registered under the Paris Convention is published in the Official Journal from time to time.[52]

Furthermore:

(c) when filing the patent application, the applicant must state that the invention has been so displayed; and
(d) within four months of the filing date, the applicant must file a supporting certificate in accordance with Rule 23 EPC, together with an identification of the invention, authenticated by the authority at the exhibition which issued the certificate.

It is apparent that the exclusion from the published prior art for previously displayed inventions is very closely restricted.

[49] T173/83 TELECOMMUNICATIONS/*Anti-oxidant* O.J. EPO 1987, 465; [1988] E.P.O.R. 133.
[50] T585/92 UNILEVER/*Deodorant detergent* O.J. EPO 1996, 129; [1996] E.P.O.R. 579.
[51] T436/92 March 20, 1995.
[52] See *e.g.* O.J. EPO 1996, 246.

11–35 **(ii) Time period for non-prejudicial disclosures.** Article 55(1) EPC provides that a disclosure of the invention in accordance with sub-paragraph (a) or (b) shall not be taken into consideration "if it occurred no earlier than six months preceding the filing of the European patent application ...." A controversial question has been whether "the filing of the European patent application" should be interpreted as referring to the actual filing date of the application which is accorded under Article 80 EPC, or to the date of priority of the application, if priority is claimed under Articles 87 to 89 EPC. In this connection Article 89 EPC states that "The right of priority shall have the effect that the date of priority shall count as the date of filing" of the application for the purposes of Article 54(2) and (3) EPC and Article 60(2) EPC—and thus does not refer to Article 55 EPC. *Prima facie*, therefore, it would appear that "the filing of the European patent application" refers to the actual date of filing of the application, not the priority date. This result is consistent with the preparatory documents of the EPC (T173/83[53]), and has recently been confirmed by the Enlarged Board of Appeal:

> "For the calculation of the six-month period referred to in Article 55(1) EPC, the relevant date is the date of the actual filing of the European Patent application: the date of priority is not to be taken account of in calculating this period" (G3/98[54], G2/99[55]).

11–36 **(iii) Scope of the exclusions from the prior art.** Article 55(1) EPC provides that a disclosure of the invention "due to, or in consequence of" either of the two circumstances discussed above shall not be taken into consideration "for the application of Article 54 EPC". On a literal interpretation it might therefore be thought that such a disclosure is only excluded from the published prior art for the purpose of novelty considerations and not for considerations of inventiveness. This would, however, lead to an unduly narrow scope for the exclusions. It seems more reasonable to interpret Article 55(1) EPC as providing for the exclusion of such a disclosure from "the state of the art", this being "the application of Article 54 EPC." It would then follow that such a disclosure is excluded from the published prior art for both novelty (Article 54 EPC) and inventiveness (Article 56 EPC) considerations. No Board of Appeal decision, however, has so far considered this point.

11–37 **(iv) Comparison with previous United Kingdom law (1949 U.K. Act).** The two exclusions provided for in Article 55(1)(a) and (b) EPC correspond approximately to similar forms of exclusion under the 1949 U.K. Act, as follows:

> 55(1)(a)—see 1949 U.K. Act, s.51(2);

---

[53] T173/83 *TELECOMMUNICATIONS/Anti-oxidant* O.J. EPO 1987, 465; [1988] E.P.O.R. 133.
[54] G3/98 *Six months period* O.J. EPO (P).
[55] G2/99 *DEWERT/Six months period* O.J. EPO (P).

55(1)(b)—see 1949 U.K. Act, s.50(2) and (3).

The 1949 U.K. Act also provided for exclusions in circumstances where the EPC contains no corresponding provisions as follows:

a *Protection of experimental use.* The 1949 U.K. Act included an exclusion **11–38**
for experimental use, provided it was either secret (section 32(2)(a), or fell within the provisions of section 51(3) (*i.e.* public working of the invention by or with the consent of the applicant "if the working was affected for the purpose of reasonable trial only and if it was reasonably necessary, having regard to the nature of the invention, that the working for that purpose should be effected in public"). As to secret use, under the EPC this does not form part of the published prior art, whether or not it is experimental, because the use has by definition not been made available to the public. As to "reasonably necessary experimental use in public", this was a valuable protection for a particular type of invention, especially having regard to the broad scope of the concept of prior use under the 1949 U.K. Act. However, under the EPC and the 1977 U.K. Act the absence of a corresponding exclusion for this type of invention is to a large extent mitigated by the more narrow scope of the concept of prior public use (being limited to what is made available as a result of such use, as previously discussed). Thus, if it is necessary to test an invention experimentally in public prior to filing a European patent application, care should be taken as far as possible to ensure that the public is unable to ascertain the nature of the invention which is the subject of the experimental use.

Anomalously, in *Prout v. British Gas plc*[56] the Patents County Court held that the effect of the change between the 1949 U.K. Act and the 1977 U.K. Act was to revive the pre-existing common law, according to which public experimental prior use by or on behalf of the inventor was not destructive of novelty.

b *Protection of Government use.* Under section 51(1) and (4) of the 1949 **11–39**
U.K. Act, a communication of the invention to a Government department, or to a person authorised by a Government department, in order to investigate the invention or its merits, and anything done for the purpose of the investigation, could not be used to invalidate a patent for that invention.

Such an exclusion was clearly provided in order to further the national interest, but finds no counterpart in the EPC or in the 1977 U.K. Act.

c *Priority protection.* Under section 52 of the 1949 U.K. Act, any matter **11–40**
disclosed in a priority application (either a provisional specification or an earlier application in a Convention country), if "used or published" at any

---

[56] [1992] F.S.R. 428.

time after the filing of the priority application, could not be used to invalidate a patent filed in pursuance of the priority application.

Such exclusion of the published matter did not depend upon the later application successfully claiming priority from the priority application (see, *e.g. Terrell on the Law of Patents* (Sweet & Maxwell, 13th ed.), paragraphs 3.49 and 5.81, and *Letraset Ltd v. Rexel Ltd*[57]). This provision of the 1949 U.K. Act therefore enabled an applicant, having filed his basic application for an invention, to have complete freedom in disclosing to the public what he had already described in such application, without fear that he could thereby invalidate subsequent applications in respect of that invention (or developments of it).

Section 6 of the 1977 U.K. Act corresponds generally to section 52 of the 1949 U.K. Act.

However, in *Beloit Technologies Inc v. Valmet Paper Machinery Inc*[58] the Patents Court interpreted section 6(1) as referring only to an effective claim for priority (not to a mere claim to priority *per se*) (see Chapter 10 at paragraph 10–51 above).

(2) Prior rights

Article 54(3) EPC

(a) Introduction

11–41 A European patent application which has a filing date earlier than the filing date of a second European application, but which has been published after the filing date of the second European application, is clearly not a part of the state of the art under Article 54(2) EPC in respect of the second application; but it constitutes a "prior right". Such a prior right forms part of the state of the art by reason of a legal fiction set out in Article 54(3) EPC, and may, therefore, form the basis for an objection to grant or maintenance of a European patent on the ground of lack of novelty. The object of Article 54(3) EPC is to avoid the grant of more than one European patent in respect of an invention. Prior to the EPC, within the European countries that were later to become Contracting States, there were traditionally two ways of determining such a prior right effect upon a later filed patent application: the "prior claim" approach, whereby the claims of a later application were only prejudiced by identical claims in an earlier filed application; and the "whole contents" approach, whereby the entire contents of the earlier filed application were treated as part of the state of the art in respect of a consideration of novelty of the claims of the later filed application. The EPC adopted the "whole contents" approach as set out in Article 54(3) EPC discussed below. However, at the time of signing the EPC, it was not clear whether all the Contracting States would adopt the same approach for their national laws.

---

[57] [1976] R.P.C. 51 at 59–60.
[58] [1995] R.P.C. 705.

(b) Prior art in relation to novelty, not obviousness

Article 54(3) EPC provides that if a European patent application has a filing **11–42** date prior to the filing date of another European patent application (or patent), but has been published on or after the latter's filing date, the content of the former European application as filed "shall be considered as comprised in the state of the art" in relation to the latter application (or patent). The first filed application is a "European prior right", and forms part of the state of the art in accordance with the "whole contents" approach. However, this legal fiction in respect of prior filed European patent applications is only for the purpose of novelty considerations under Article 54(1) EPC. The contents of applications which become part of "the state of the art" by virtue of Article 54(3) EPC are expressly excluded from consideration in deciding whether there has been an inventive step—see Article 56, second sentence.

(c) National prior rights not within Article 54(3) EPC

Article 54(3) EPC specifically refers only to prior filed "European patent **11–43** applications" *i.e.* "European prior rights". A prior national patent application or "national prior right" is not a European patent application within the meaning of Article 54(3) EPC, and is accordingly not comprised in the state of the art." Thus, only prior filed European patent applications (European prior rights) are comprised in the state of the art, for the purpose of proceedings within the EPO.

The prior right effects of national patent applications and patents upon European patent applications and patents and vice versa are governed by Article 139(1) and (2) EPC. In each such case, the national law as to prior right effects is applicable. In Switzerland in particular, the "prior claim" approach is used to determine such conflicts, although the "whole contents" approach is used in the majority of Contracting States.

Nevertheless, Rule 87 EPC states *inter alia* that if the EPO is informed of **11–44** the existence of one or more national prior rights, "the European patent application or European patent may contain for such State or States claims, and if the EPO considers it necessary, a description and drawings which are different from those for the other designated Contracting States".

(d) Common designated Contracting States

A basic principle of Article 54(3) EPC, as already stated, is to avoid (as far as **11–45** possible) the granting of more than one European patent in respect of exactly the same invention. Article 54(4) EPC limits the application of Article 54(3) EPC to situations where the same Contracting States are designated in both European patent applications. For any particular designated Contracting State, Article 54(3) EPC thereby prevents the grant of a patent in respect of an invention which has been described in another European patent application which has not been published but which has an earlier filing date, and which designates the same Contracting State(s). The "collision" of European patents is thus generally avoided.

In this connection "a European patent application shall be considered as comprised in the state of the art under Article 74(3) and (4) EPC only if the designation fees under Article 79(2) EPC have been validly paid" (Rule 23a EPC).

11–45A   According to the proposed revision of the EPC, Article 54(4) EPC will be deleted, as a consequence of the introduction of a ceiling for the payment of designation fees whereby upon payment of seven designation fees, all 20 Contracting States are deemed to be validly designated. Most European applications now designate all Contracting States (see Chapter 1). In view of Rule 23a EPC above, the time at which Article 54(3) EPC prior art can be determined is at least six months from the publication of the application, which may be after the application is ready for grant. Accordingly, Rule 87 EPC will be amended and Rule 23a EPC will be deleted.

(e) PCT applications as prior art

11–46   An international application under the PCT for which the EPO is a designated office is comprised in the state of the art under Article 54(3) EPC from the date when it is filed at the EPO in accordance with Article 158(2) EPC (in an official language, accompanied by payment for the national fee). The prior art effect is limited to common designated States in the European patent application and the earlier PCT application when it enters the European phase (T404/93[59]) (but see paragraph 11–45A).

(f) Avoidance of "self-collision"

11–47   The fact that the contents of prior filed patent applications are only considered from the point of view of novelty, and not as regards inventive step, makes the distinction between novelty and inventive step an important one (see paragraphs 11–62 *et seq.* below).

The exclusion of inventive step from consideration in relation to prior filed applications is particularly important in relation to the avoidance of so-called "self-collision".

Thus, having filed a first application, an applicant may subsequently file one or more subsequent applications in respect of developments to the subject-matter of the first application, before publication of the basic application. Provided that the claimed subject-matter of each such later application is novel over the contents of each of the earlier applications, such claimed subject-matter is separately patentable, and there is no "self-collision" (see also paragraph 11–61 below).

(g) Applications having the same filing date

11–48   Article 54(3) EPC refers to European patent applications of *earlier* filing date, and there is nothing in the EPC to prevent the grant of two or more

---

[59] T404/93 September 28, 1994.

European patent applications, designating the same Contracting States, and having exactly the same subject-matter, in the unlikely but possible event that they have the same filing date.

What happens when there is "collision" between a European patent application or patent and a national patent application or patent having the same priority date is left to the law of each Contracting State, under Article 139(3) EPC.

C. Substantive Novelty

(1) Introduction: a comparison

This section is concerned with the question set out in paragraph 11–05 **11–49** above: is the claimed invention novel over the state of the art? Determination of novelty thus involves a comparison between the information, or technical teaching, which is within the state of the art, and the claimed invention. While such a comparison has to be made whatever the physical means by which the information is made available to the public, the cases considered in this section are primarily concerned with the assessment of information which has been made available in published documents.

Whatever the physical means of making information available:

> "A claimed invention lacks novelty unless it includes at least one essential technical feature which distinguishes it from the state of the art. When deciding upon the novelty of a claim, a basic initial consideration is therefore to construe the claim in order to determine its technical features" (G2, 6/88[60]).

Having thus determined the technical features of the claimed invention, the further question to be considered when determining novelty is whether what has been "made available to the public" includes all of the claimed technical features:

> "The word 'available' carried with it the idea that, for lack of novelty to be found, all the technical features of the claimed invention in combination must have been communicated to the public, or laid open for inspection" (G2, 6/88[61]).

Various aspects of the question of substantive novelty are considered below.

---

[60] G2, 6/88 MOBIL OIL/BAYER/Friction reducing additive O.J. EPO 1990, 93, 114; [1990] E.P.O.R. 73, 257.
[61] Ibid.

(2) The prior art to be compared

(a) Individual documents in isolation

11–50 "When assessing novelty, the disclosure of a particular prior document must always be considered in isolation; in other words it is only the actual content of a document (as understood by a skilled man) which destroys novelty. It is not permissible to combine separate items of prior art together" (T153/85[62]).

"The literal disclosure of a prior published document *prima facie* stands on its own when assessing novelty. This is the general rule" (T77/87[63]).

For example, "the literal disclosure of a prior published abstract, considered *per se* without the corresponding original document, forms *prima facie* part of the prior art (T77/87[64]).

This principle is clearly equally applicable to other physical means which provide an individual source of information, such as a prior use or oral description.

(b) Incorporation by reference

11–51 Nevertheless, "where there is a specific reference in one prior document (the 'primary document') to a second prior document, when construing the primary document (*i.e.* determining its meaning to the skilled man) the presence of such specific reference may necessitate that part or all of the disclosure of the second document be considered as part of the disclosure of the primary document" (T153/85[65]).

Whether or not a reference in a primary document to a second document is to be construed as incorporating the second document or a part of it clearly depends upon the relevant wording and circumstances of each particular case.

Again, this principle would be equally applicable to other physical means of making information available: for example, an oral lecture might incorporate information from another lecture, or from a written description, into its content.

(c) Consideration of a document in its entirety

11–52 "The technical teaching in a prior art document should be considered in its entirety, as it would be done by a person skilled in the art. It is not justified arbitrarily to isolate parts of such document from their context in order to derive therefrom a technical information which would be distinct from or even in contradiction with the integral teaching of the document". (T56/87[66]).

---

[62] T153/85 *AMOCO/Alternative claims* O.J. EPO 1988, 1; [1988] E.P.O.R. 116.
[63] T77/87 *ICI/Latex composition* O.J. EPO 1990, 280; [1989] E.P.O.R. 246.
[64] *Ibid.*
[65] T153/85 *AMOCO/Alternative claims* O.J. EPO 1988, 1; [1988] E.P.O.R. 116.
[66] T56/87 *SCANDITRONIX/Ion chamber* O.J. EPO 1990, 188; [1990] E.P.O.R. 352.

(d) Erroneous disclosures

(i) Inconsistency within a prior document. If part of the disclosure of a 11–53
prior document, when read literally, would deprive a claimed invention of
novelty, but it is clear from the remainder of its disclosure that such part is
erroneous and would be corrected by a skilled person as a matter of course,
the erroneous literal disclosure should be disregarded (T89/87[67]).

(ii) Inconsistency of an abstract with the original document. As stated 11–54
in paragraph 11–50 above, the literal disclosure *per se* of a prior published
abstract from an original document *prima facie* forms part of the state of the
art and may be cited as such. However: "When it is clear from related
contemporaneously available evidence that the literal disclosure of a
document is erroneous and does not represent the intended technical
reality, such an erroneous disclosure should not be considered as part of
the state of the art" (T77/87[68]).
Thus:

> "When a published abstract contains a cross-reference to its original
> document which is contemporaneously available, and the literal
> disclosure of the abstract is inconsistent with the disclosure of the
> original document, the abstract should be interpreted by reference to
> the original document [—which is 'the primary source of what has
> been made available as a technical teaching'—] for the purpose of
> ascertaining the technical reality of what has been disclosed. If it is
> then clear that the disclosure in the abstract is erroneous, such
> erroneous disclosure should not be considered as part of the state of
> the art." (T77/87[69])

(e) Disclosure in drawings

For the purpose of Article 54(2) EPC a "written description" may take the 11–55
form of a drawing with or without an accompanying description in words.
"Features shown solely in a drawing form part of the state of the art when a
person skilled in that art is able, in the absence of any other description, to
derive a technical teaching from them".
When a feature is shown solely in a drawing without any other clarifying
description it has to be determined whether the mere diagrammatic
representation enables a person skilled in the art to derive a practical
technical teaching therefrom. It is impossible to lay down general rules as
to how this should be done, because in each case the technical teaching will
depend on the knowledge of the person skilled in the art and the way in
which the feature is shown in the drawing (T204/83[70]).
A diagrammatic representation is confined to the essential features of

---

[67] T89/87 *WAVIN* December 20, 1989.
[68] T77/87 *ICI/Latex composition* O.J. EPO 1990, 280; [1989] E.P.O.R. 246.
[69] *Ibid.*
[70] T204/83 *CHARBONAGE/Venturi* O.J. EPO 1985, 310; [1986] E.P.O.R. 1.

the object shown. A considerable latitude is allowed in its practical realisation, and such a representation cannot therefore be regarded as a disclosure of the exact dimensions of the subject-matter.

A technical feature which can be derived from or based on dimensions obtained from a diagrammatic representation, but which technically contradicts the teaching of the description, does not form part of the disclosure of the document (T56/87[71]).

(3) General principles of comparison

(a) Date of interpretation of a prior document

11–56 "The technical content of a document is what is disclosed to a skilled person at the time when it was written and published" (T677/91[72]).

For the purpose of deciding novelty, the disclosure of a prior published document must be interpreted and determined at the date of its publication, in the light of the common general knowledge of a skilled person at that date (T229/90[73], T205/91[74], T677/91[75]). Common general knowledge which did not exist at the date of publication but which only became available at a later date cannot be used to interpret a document (T229/90[76]).

(b) Technical teaching

11–57 A prior art disclosure must be considered as a matter of substance:

> "The concept of novelty must not be given such a narrow interpretation that only what has already been described in the same terms is prejudiced to it" (T12/81[77]). "A difference in wording is insufficient to establish novelty" (T198/84[78], T114/86[79]).

As emphasised in the following quotations, the technical teaching of a prior art disclosure to a skilled person has to be compared with the claimed subject-matter.

> "Since novelty is an absolute concept, a definition of an invention which differs only in wording is insufficient; what has to be established in the examination as to novelty is whether the state of the art is likely to reveal the content of the invention's subject-matter to the skilled person in a technical teaching" (T198/84[80]): that is,
> "... whether the state of the art is such as to make available the

---

[71] T56/87 SCANDITRONIX/Ion chamber O.J. EPO 1990, 188; [1990] E.P.O.R. 352.
[72] T677/91 FINNIGAN/Mass selective ejection November 13, 1992.
[73] T229/90 KONICA/Monodisperse emulsions October 28, 1992.
[74] T205/91 June 16, 1992.
[75] See note 72.
[76] See note 73.
[77] T12/81 BAYER/Diastereomers O.J. EPO 1982, 296; [1979–85] E.P.O.R.: B: 308.
[78] T198/84 HOECHST/Triochloroformates O.J. EPO 1985, 209; [1979–85] E.P.O.R.: C: 987.
[79] T114/86 ERIKSSON/Foam plastics filter O.J. EPO 1987, 485; [1988] E.P.O.R. 25.
[80] See note 78.

subject-matter of the invention to the skilled person in a technical teaching" (T124/87[81]).

In summary:

"Article 54(1) EPC does not allow what already forms part of the state of the art to be patented. When part of the state of the art is a written document, what has to be considered is whether the disclosure of the document as a whole is such as to make available to a skilled man as a technical teaching the subject-matter for which protection is sought in the claims of the disputed patent" (T124/87[82]).

In particular:

"What is 'made available to the public' by specific detailed examples included in a document is not necessarily limited to the exact details of such specific examples but depends in each case upon the technical teaching which is 'made available' to a skilled reader. Thus if a prior document includes a specific composition falling within the claimed composition, the amendment of the claim by including a disclaimer to such specific detailed example may not render the claim novel" (T290/86[83]: see also T188/83[84]).

Similarly: **11–58**

"The teaching of a cited document is not confined to the detailed information given in the examples of how the invention is carried out, but embraces any information in the claims and description enabling a person skilled in the art to carry out the invention" (T12/81[85]: see paragraph 11–65 below; see also T124/87[86] and paragraph 11–76 below).

In a case where the claimed invention is a known compound having a particular level of purity:

"Since, as a rule, conventional methods for the purification of low molecular organic compounds are within [the skilled person's] common general knowledge, a document disclosing a low molecular chemical compound and its manufacture normally makes available this compound to the public in the sense of Article 54 EPC in all desired grades of purity" (T990/96[87]).

[81] T124/87 DU PONT/Copolymers O.J. EPO 1989, 491; [1991] E.P.O.R. 33.
[82] Ibid.
[83] T290/86 ICI/Cleaning plaque O.J. EPO 1992, 414; [1991] E.P.O.R. 175.
[84] T188/83 FERNHOLZ/Vinyl acetate O.J. EPO 1984, 555; [1979–85] E.P.O.R.: C: 891.
[85] T12/81 BAYER/Diastereomers O.J. EPO 1982, 296; [1979–85] E.P.O.R.: B: 308.
[86] T124/87 DU PONT/Copolymers O.J. EPO 1989, 491; [1991] E.P.O.R. 33.
[87] T990/96 NOVARTIS/Erythro compounds O.J. EPO 1998, 489; [1998] E.P.O.R. 441.

(c) Clear and unmistakable disclosure

11–59 Furthermore, for lack of novelty to be found, the prior art must contain a "clear and unmistakable disclosure" of the claimed subject-matter (T450/89[88], T465/92[89]). The claimed subject-matter must be "derivable directly and unambiguously" from the prior art (T204/83[90], T56/87[91]).

This principle is applicable not only to written descriptions, where the literal or diagrammatic technical meaning must be clear and unmistakable as a matter of language, but also to cases of prior art, where the results of an analysis must similarly be clear and unmistakable.

(d) Express and implied disclosure: inventive step distinguished

11–60 "The term 'available' clearly goes beyond literal or diagrammatic description, and implies the communication, express or implicit, of technical information by other means as well" (T666/89[92]).

Nevertheless, it is important to distinguish between what is implicitly *disclosed* in a prior document or other prior art (and is therefore present *in* the document) and what may be obvious to a skilled person even though it is not either expressly or implicitly disclosed in the document. The latter consideration goes beyond the determination of novelty, and involves an assessment of inventive step (T572/88[93], T763/89[94], T71/93[95]).

Thus "novelty must be decided by reference to the total information content of a cited prior document, and in assessing the content for the purpose of deciding whether or not a claim is novel legal concepts [may be employed] that are similar to those used in deciding issues of obviousness, without, however, thereby confusing or blurring the distinction between these separate statutory grounds of objection" (T666/89[96]).

In this connection similar principles are applied when determining priority (see Chapter 10 at paragraph 10–41) and when determining the state of the art for novelty purposes. Thus it is necessary to make a strict distinction between a modification which might be regarded as an obvious alternative to the specific disclosure of the priority document [—prior document] and a modification which is actually *disclosed* in the sense of "a specific teaching with regard to technical action" (T85/87[97]—see also paragraph 11–70).

---

[88] T450/89 *ENTHONE/Zinc plating* [1994] E.P.O.R. 326
[89] T465/92 *ALCAN/Aluminium alloys* O.J. EPO 1996, 32; [1995] E.P.O.R. 501.
[90] T204/83 *CHARBONNAGES/Venturi* O.J. EPO 1985, 310; [1986] E.P.O.R. 1
[91] T56/87 *SCANDITRONIX/Ion chamber* O.J. EPO 1990, 188; [1990] E.P.O.R. 352.
[92] T666/89 *UNILEVER/Washing composition* O.J. EPO 1993, 495; [1992] E.P.O.R. 501.
[93] T572/88 *HOECHST/Reactive dye* February 27, 1991.
[94] T763/89 July 10, 1991.
[95] T71/93 *MONSANTO/Rheological testing* [1998] E.P.O.R. 402.
[96] T666/89 *UNILEVER/Washing composition* O.J. EPO 1993, 495; [1992] E.P.O.R. 501.
[97] T85/87 *CSIRO/Arthropodicidal compounds* [1989] E.P.O.R. 24.

(e) Equivalents: not part of the implicit disclosure

Following the above principle, "when considering novelty, it is not correct **11–61** to interpret the teaching of a document as embracing well-known equivalents which are not disclosed in the document: this is a matter for obviousness" (Guidelines C.IV 7.2: T167/84[98]). Well-known equivalents are therefore not part of the implicit disclosure of a document.

This strict approach to novelty is justified in order to reduce the risk of "self-collision" (T167/84[99]. and see paragraph 11–47 above).

(f) Importance of the distinction between novelty and obviousness

In many cases, it is not essential to draw a line between novelty and **11–62** obviousness. If for example a prior document discloses the subject-matter of a claimed invention except that there is some doubt as to identity of disclosure of one feature of the claim, in many cases the claimed subject-matter will be held to be lacking an inventive step, on the basis that even if that one feature is not actually disclosed in the prior document, the claimed subject-matter including that one feature is nevertheless, not inventive having regard to the teaching of the prior document.

There are, however, certain circumstances when the distinction between novelty and inventive step is particularly important. Two examples are given below.

(i) Under Article 54(3) EPC. When the prior art to be considered is not **11–63** published prior art, but a prior filed European application (*i.e.* a prior right), then as stated in paragraph 11–42 above the only applicable ground of objection is lack of novelty having regard to the content of that application. In this context, therefore, the distinction between lack of novelty and lack of inventive step can be crucial to the granting or maintenance of a European patent (T167/84[100], see paragraph 11–61).

(ii) "Accidental anticipation." In a case where a prior document in the **11–64** published prior art is not concerned with the same technical field as the claimed subject-matter, but nevertheless "accidentally" discloses (or comes close to disclosing) all the features claimed, the determination of novelty may also be of crucial importance. A particular prior document may in such circumstances be considered as the closest prior art from the point of view of novelty determination, but not in relation to the question of inventive step. Thus, if the claimed invention is held to be novel over such a prior document, the prior documents may be considered as irrelevant to the question of inventive step (see also Chapter 12 at paragraph 12–07).

"In cases where an anticipation is of a chance nature, in that what is

[98] T167/84 *NISSAN/Fuel injector valve* O.J. EPO 1987, 369; [1987] E.P.O.R. 344.
[99] *Ibid.*
[100] *Ibid.*

disclosed in a prior document would accidentally fall within the wording of a claim without there being a common technical problem, a particularly careful comparison has to be made between what can fairly be considered to fall within the wording of the claim and what is effectively shown in the document" (T161/82[101]).

(g) Inevitable result: part of the implicit disclosure

11-65 A disclosure may go beyond the literal or diagrammatic description in a document. "One example of the available information content of a document extending beyond this literal or diagrammatic content is the case where the carrying out of a process, specifically or literally described in a prior art document, inevitably results in a product not so described. In such a case, the prior art document will destroy the novelty of a claim covering the product" (T666/89[102]), because "the information which the written description actually contains, teaching the carrying out of a process for example, also makes available further information which is the inevitable result of carrying out such teaching" (G2, 6/88[103]).

For example, if a prior document describes a number of processes each described by reference to the starting material and the process, a particular substance which is the inevitable result of one such process will lack novelty. In such a situation "it is not necessary for the starting compound or the process variant to be given special prominence. The essential point is what a person skilled in the art, carrying out the invention, could be expected to deduce from it" (T12/81[104]).

A prior disclosure of identical starting materials and process reaction conditions to those which produced a claimed product will destroy the novelty in such product, because processes identical in these respects must inevitably yield identical products (T303/86[105]).

A distinction should be drawn, however, between combinations of starting material and process, and combinations of two starting materials, as a matter of disclosure. In the first case, as previously stated, "the disclosure ... of the starting substance as well as the reaction process is always prejudicial to novelty because those data unalterably establish the end product". In the second case, if "two classes of starting materials are required to prepare the end product and examples of individual entities in each class are given in two lists of some length, then a substance resulting from the reaction of a specific pair from the two lists can nevertheless be regarded as new" (T12/81[106], T7/86[107]: see also the discussion of generic disclosures in paragraph 11-70 below).

[101] T161/82 *AMP/Electrical contact* O.J. EPO 1984, 551; [1979–85] E.P.O.R.: C: 660.
[102] T666/89 *UNILEVER/Washing composition* O.J. EPO 1993, 495; [1992] E.P.O.R. 501.
[103] G2, 6/88 *MOBIL OIL/BAYER/Friction reducing additive* O.J. EPO 1990, 93, 114; [1990] E.P.O.R. 73, 257.
[104] T12/81 *BAYER/Diasteromers* O.J. EPO 1982, 296; [1979–85] E.P.O.R. B: 250.
[105] T303/86 *CPC/Flavour concentrates* [1989] E.P.O.R. 95.
[106] T12/81 *BAYER/Diastereomers* O.J. EPO 1982, 296; [1979–85] E.P.O.R.: B: 308.
[107] T7/86 *DRACO/Xanthines* O.J. EPO 1988, 381; [1989] E.P.O.R. 65.

(g^1) Comparison with United Kingdom law

In *Merrell Dow Pharmaceutical Inc. v. H.N. Norton & Co. Ltd*[108], the House of **11–66** Lords held that "at least for some purposes, products need not be known under their chemical description in order to be part of the state of the art", and that "if the recipe which inevitably produces the substance is part of the state of the art so is the substance as made by the recipe" (reference being made to T12/81[109], T303/86[110], G1/92[111]).

The case concerned allegations of lack of novelty having regard to both prior written description and prior use of a compound whose acid metabolite was subsequently claimed. In finding no lack of novelty having regard to the prior use, but lack of novelty over the prior written description, it was held that:

> "In both cases no one was aware that the acid metabolite was being made. In the case of anticipation by use, however, the acts relied upon conveyed no information which would have enabled anyone to work the invention. Anticipation by disclosure, on the other hand, relies upon the communication to the public of information which enables it to do an act having the inevitable consequence of making the acid metabolite. Under the description the acid metabolite was part of the state of the art" (*Merrell Dow*[112]).

(h) Enabling disclosure

A prior disclosure by any means will only deprive a claimed invention of **11–67** novelty if what is disclosed is sufficient to enable a skilled person to carry out the claimed invention (in this respect see also *Merrell Dow*[113] in paragraph 11–66 above). If this was not the case, a purely speculative disclosure (for example, of the mere structure of an unknown chemical compound) would destroy the novelty of such compound, when claimed in a subsequent patent in conjunction with full details as to how to prepare it.

Thus:

> "A compound defined by its chemical structure can only be regarded as being disclosed in a particular document if it has been 'made available to the public' in the sense of Article 54(2) EPC in the field of chemistry, this requirement is, for instance, satisfied if a reproducible method is described in the same document. This need for an enabling disclosure not only applies to documents cited under Article 54(2) EPC but is also in conformity with the principle expressed in Article 83

---

[108] *Merrell Dow Pharmaceutical Inc. v. H.N. Norton & Co. Ltd* [1996] R.P.C. 76, HL.
[109] T12/81 *BAYER/Diastereomers* O.J. EPO 1982, 296; [1979–85] E.P.O.R.: B: 250.
[110] T303/86 *CPC/Flavour concentrates* [1989] E.P.O.R. 95.
[111] G1/92 *Availability to the public* O.J. EPO 1993, 277; [1993] E.P.O.R. 241.
[112] See note 108.
[113] See note 108.

EPC for patent applications which must, accordingly, 'disclose the invention in a manner sufficiently clear and complete for it to be carried out by a person skilled in the art'. The requirements as to the sufficiency of disclosure are, therefore, identical in all these instances" (T206/83[114]: see also T12/81[115]).

In particular:

"a document does not effectively disclose a chemical compound, even though it states the structure and the steps by which it is produced, if the skilled person is unable to find out from the document or from common general knowledge how to obtain the required ... starting materials or intermediates" (T206/83[116]).

(h¹) Comparison with United Kingdom law

11–68 In *Asahi Kasei Kogyo K.K.'s Application*,[117] the House of Lords similarly held that an enabling disclosure in a prior document is necessary in order to establish lack of novelty (reference being made to T206/83[118], T12/81[119]).

(i) Generic disclosures compared to specific disclosures: selection inventions

11–69 In many cases (especially but not only chemical cases) the subject-matter of a claim (for example a particular compound) is embraced by a general prior disclosure covering a larger area of subject-matter (for example a class of compounds of which the particular compound is a member). Alternatively, a prior disclosure may contain specific examples, which fall within a subsequent claim.

The general principle which is applicable in such cases is that "... a generic disclosure does not usually take away the novelty of any specific example falling within the terms of that disclosure", where "a specific disclosure does take away the novelty of a generic claim embracing that disclosure" (Guidelines C.IV. 7.4).

For example, if the ratio of the reactants of a claimed process is defined in terms of a range, "the novelty of this range is destroyed if the previous description contains examples which fall within it" (T188/83). Similarly "... a designated compound is anticipated state of the art, whatever its purpose may be" (T181/82[120]).

This approach to a generic disclosure allows for the possibility of a so-called "selection inventions", where inventiveness lies in a particular selection from a known field—see paragraph 11–77 below. Literally and logically, it is of course possible to regard a generic disclosure as taking

---

[114] T206/83 *ICI/Pyridine herbicides* O.J. EPO 1987, 5; [1986] E.P.O.R. 232.
[115] T12/81 *BAYER/Diastereomers* O.J. EPO 1982, 296; [1979–85] E.P.O.R.: B: 250.
[116] See note 114.
[117] *Asahi Kasei Kogyo K.K.'s Application* [1991] R.P.C. 485.
[118] See note 114.
[119] T12/81 *BAYER/Diastereomers* O.J. EPO 1982, 296; [1979–85] E.P.O.R.: B: 250.
[120] T181/82 *CIBA-GEIGY/Spiro compounds* O.J. EPO 1984, 401; [1979–85[E.P.O.R.: C: 672.

away the novelty of every specific example within it, but such a literal approach would result in a finding of lack of novelty in circumstances where an inventive contribution to the art can be recognised in the particular selection of a specific example.

(j) Generic disclosures

(i) Individualisation and sub-ranges. The above principle that a generic **11–70** disclosure *per se* does not disclose specific individual examples within it is consistent with the concept discussed in paragraph 11–65 above, to the effect that if a prior document discloses two lists of co-reactant starting materials, specific combinations of pairs of starting materials (and consequently the resultant reactant products) are regarded as novel (T12/81[121]), because such combinations are not individually disclosed.

This principle can also be extended so as to provide novelty for a sub-range within a generic disclosure. For example a disclosed broad range does not represent a disclosure for all the values within the range, and does not necessarily disclose a selected sub-range if the sub-range is narrow and sufficiently far removed from the *known range as illustrated* by examples (T198/84[122]).

"The sub-range is novel not by virtue of an effect which occurs only within it: but this effect permits the inference that what is involved is not an abitrarily chosen specimen from the prior art but another invention (purpose selection)" (T198/84[123]).

In this connection, when determining the state of the art "a strict distinction must be drawn between [the] purely intellectual content of the definitions and their information content in the sense of a specific teaching with regard to technical action" (T181/82[124]; and see T85/87[125] paragraph 11–60 above).

Thus, if a prior document discloses di-substituted compounds wherein **11–71** the substituents are to be chosen from two different lists, a particular compound having a specific combination of substituents is novel. More generally:

"A class of chemical compounds defined only by a general structural formula having at least two variable groups does not specifically disclose each of the "individual compounds which would result from the combination of all possible variants within such groups" (T7/86[126]).

As a specific example, a prior disclosure of a racemate defined by a chemical formula, containing a (single) asymetrical carbon atom does not

[121] T12/81 *BAYER/Diastereomers* O.J. EPO 1982, 296; [1979–85] E.P.O.R.: B: 250.
[122] T198/84 *HOECHST/Triochloroformates* O.J. EPO 1985, 209; [1979–85] E.P.O.R.: C: 987.
[123] *Ibid.*
[124] T181/82 *CIBA-GEIGY/Spiro componds* O.J EPO 1984, 401; [1979–85] E.P.O.R.: C: 672.
[125] T85/87 *CSIRO/Arthropodicidal compounds* [1989] E.P.O.R. 24.
[126] T7/87 *DRACO/Xanthines* O.J. EPO 1988, 381; [1989] E.P.O.R. 65.

disclose the D and L enantiomers, which are specific spatial configurations resulting from the asymetrical carbon atom, because such configurations are not disclosed in individualised form. Thus a prior disclosure of a specific racemate does not anticipate the D enantiomer, for example, even though both the D and L enantiomers would actually exist unseparated in the racemate (T296/87[127]).

11–72   **(ii) Individual compounds and families of compounds distinguished.** If the prior art discloses a family of compounds, a distinction is drawn between the following two kinds of claimed subject-matter:

(1) a specific compound within the prior art family of compounds, but not specifically and explicitly disclosed: the specific compound is novel;

(2) a second family of compounds which fall within or overlap with the prior art family of compounds the claimed subject-matter may lack novelty. This distinction arises because the concept of individualisation which has been discussed above only applies to the structural definition of a single compound (T12/90[128], T133/92[129]).

11–73   **(iii) Overlapping ranges and sub-ranges.** The technical teaching which can fairly be said to be derivable by a skilled person from a general disclosure such as a range of values for a parameter depends upon a careful examination in each particular case of what is really taught in the prior document. As previously indicated, a disclosure of a broad range of values does not necessarily disclose a sub-range within it. The following quotations and examples illustrate this.

a *Examples within claimed range*

11–74   "If for the purpose of a chemical production process previously described a certain ratio of reactants, defined in terms of a range, is chosen, the said ratio being covered by the conventional teaching but not mentioned in it, this may involve a new invention. The novelty of this range is destroyed if the previous description contains examples which fall within it. The range is not rendered novel by the fact that the values calculated from the examples are excepted by means of a disclaimer, at least not if these values cannot be regarded as individual on the basis of the broader previously known teaching in the light of general knowledge of the art" (T188/83[130]).

b *Preferred range overlaps with claimed range*

11–75   "If the preferred numerical range in a citation in part anticipates '(*i.e.* overlaps with) a range claimed in an application, the said claimed range cannot be regarded as novel, at least in cases where the values in

---

[127] T296/87 *HOECHST/Enantiomers* O.J. EPO 1990, 195; [1990] E.P.O.R. 337.
[128] T12/90 August 23, 1990.
[129] T133/92 *AKZO/Bleaching activator*, October 18, 1994.
[130] T188/83 *FERNHOLZ/Vinyl acetate* O.J. EPO 1984, 555; [1979–85] E.P.O.R.: C: 891.

the examples given in the citation lie just outside the claimed range and teach the skilled person that it is possible to use the whole of this range" (T17/85[131]).

c *General teaching covers claimed range*

"If a prior document describes a process for the production of a class of **11–76** compounds, the members of the class being defined as having any combination of values of particular parameters within numerical ranges for each of those parameters, and if all the members of the defined class of compounds can be prepared by a skilled man following such teaching, all such members are thereby made available to the public and form part of the state of the art; and a claim which defines a class of compounds which overlaps the described class lacks novelty" (T124/87[132]).

d *Selection of a sub-range*. The requirements if the selection of a sub-range **11–77** from a broad range disclosed in the prior art is to be held novel:

"(a) the selected sub-range should be narrow;
(b) the selected sub-range should be sufficiently far removed from the known range illustrated by means of examples;
(c) the selected area should not provide an arbitrary specimen from the prior art, in other words not a mere embodiment of the pre-description, but another invention (purposive selection)" (T279/89[133], following T198/84[134]—see paragraph 11–70 above).

e *"Seriously contemplate"*. Patent specifications are often drafted so as to **11–78** define the limits of protection as broadly as possible. Thus some of a broadly claimed range may be speculative and of less practical relevance.

Since the disclosure of a prior art document depends upon its technical teaching to a skilled person, "in assessing the novelty of the invention compared to the prior art in a case where overlapping ranges of a certain parameter exist, it has to be considered whether the person skilled in the art would, in the light of the technical facts, seriously contemplate applying the technical teaching of the prior art document in the range of overlap. If it can be fairly assumed that he would do so it must be concluded that no novelty exists" (T26/85[135], T666/89[136]).

"If there exists in a prior art document disclosing a range of parameters a reasoned statement dissuading the person skilled in the art from practising the technical teaching of the document in a certain part of the range, such part has to be regarded as novel ..." (T26/85[137]).

[131] T17/85 *PLÜSS-STAUFER/Filler* O.J. EPO 1986, 406; [1987] E.P.O.R. 66.
[132] T124/87 *DU PONT/Copolymers* O.J. EPO 1989, 491; [1989] E.P.O.R. 33.
[133] T279/89 July 3, 1991.
[134] T198/84 *HOECHT/Trichloroformates* O.J. EPO 1985, 209; [1979–85] E.P.O.R.: C: 987.
[135] T26/85 *TOSHIBA/Thickness of magnetic layers* O.J. EPO 1989, 6; [1990] E.P.O.R. 267.
[136] T666/89 *UNILEVER/Washing composition* O.J. EPO 1993, 495; [1992] E.P.O.R. 501.
[137] See note 135.

(k) Product-by-process claims

(i) New process for making a known product: protection of the product

Article 64(2) EPC

11–79 The invention of a new process for making a known product is properly protected by a process claim in which the result of carrying out the process steps is the production of the known product.

However, the protection for such an invention needs to extend to the known product when produced by the new process, for example to prevent importation, use and sale of such products which have been made outside the territory of the patent. The need for such protection is implicitly recognised by Article 5 *quater* of the Paris Convention[138] (see Chapter 1 at paragraph 1–36): this leaves the exact manner in which products are protected to the legislation of individual countries or groups of countries.

Article 64(2) EPC is within the framework of Article 5 *quater* Paris, and prescribes that "If the subject-matter of the European patent is a process, the protection conferred by the patent shall extend to the products directly obtained by such process". Article 64(2) EPC is directed only to a patent whose subject-matter is a process of manufacture of a product (to be distinguished from a patent whose subject-matter is the use of a process or method to achieve an effect, for example) (G2, 6/88[139]).

Having regard to such product protection provided by a process claim pursuant to Article 64(2) EPC, "product-by-process" claims are not accepted in respect of inventive subject-matter consisting of a process of manufacture for a known product (in the absence of novelty in the product). Thus:

> "Claims for products defined in terms of processes for their prep-aration (known as 'product-by-process' claims) are admissible only if the products themselves fulfil the requirements for patentability ..." (T150/82[140]).

11–80 Similarly:

> "Article 64(2) EPC does not confer novelty upon a claim which is formulated as a 'product-by-process' when no novelty exists in such product *per se*, and does not entitle or enable an applicant for a European patent to include such claims in his patent which do not satisfy the requirements for patentability of Article 52(1) EPC" (T248/85[141]).

[138] See Appendix 14.
[139] G2, 6/88 *MOBIL OIL/BAYER/Friction reducing additive* O.J. EPO 1990, 93, 114; [1990] E.P.O.R. 73, 257.
[140] T150/82 *IFF/Claim categories* O.J. EPO 1984, 309; [1979–85] E.P.O.R.: C: 629.
[141] T248/85 *BICC/Radiation processing* O.J. EPO 1986, 261; [1986] E.P.O.R. 311.

In other words, novelty is not conferred upon a product merely by reason of the history of its origin. If the product of a new process is in all respects identical with the product of a known process, there is no novelty either in a claim to the product *per se* of the new process, or in a claim to the product-by-(new) process.

For example:

> "The polymer product of a known chemical process is not new automatically as a result of the said process being modified. If such a chemical product cannot be defined by structural characteristics (substance parameters) but only by its method of manufacture (process parameters), novelty can be established only if evidence is provided that modification of the process parameters results in other products. It is sufficient for this purpose if it is shown that distinct differences exist in the properties of the products" (T205/83[142]).

(ii) A known process for making a new product—an analogy process. 11–81
Such an invention may be protected by a claim which defines the (known) process steps, the final step being the production of the new product. In such a case:

> "the character of the product, including its novelty (and obviousness) ... has a decisive role in the assessment of the inventive step for the process. The effect of a process manifests itself in the result, *i.e.* in the product in chemical cases .... It is well established that analogy processes, *i.e.* which are themselves otherwise non-inventive, are patentable insofar as they provide a novel (and inventive) product" (T119/82[143]).

In Contracting States where claims to certain categories of product (chemical, pharmaceutical and food) have not been allowed under reservations pursuant to Article 167(2) EPC (see Chapter 13 at paragraph 13–26), an invention for such a new product is commonly protected by claiming the product by means of such an analogy process. Such a method of claiming is necessarily artificial in nature.

D. Further Uses of a Known Product

(1) Introduction: use claims and their interpretation

The need for and rationale underlying use claims has been discussed in 11–82
Chapter 7 at paragraph 7–66. In particular, use claims are frequently proposed in order to seek protection for a previously unknown effect

---

[142] T205/83 *HOECHST/Vinyl ester-crotonic acid copolymers* O.J. EPO 1985, 363; [1986] E.P.O.R. 57.
[143] T119/82 *EXXON/Gelation* O.J. EPO 1984, 217; [1979–85] E.P.O.R.: B: 566.

which is obtained when a known product is used in context of known method steps.

When determining novelty, the basic principle which is set out in paragraph 11–49 above is that:

"A claimed invention lacks novelty unless it includes at least one essential technical feature which distinguishes it from the state of the art. When deciding upon the novelty of a claim, a basic initial consideration is therefore to construe the claim in order to determine its technical features" (G2, 6/88[144]).

The crucial question when determining the novelty of a use claim concerning a further use of a known product is whether or not the claimed invention includes a technical feature which distinguishes it from the prior art.

When construing such a use claim, having regard to Article 69 EPC and its Protocol "where a particular effect which underlies such use is described in the patent ... the proper interpretation of the claim will require that a functional feature should be implied into the claim, as a technical feature: for example, that the compound actually achieves the particular [described] effect" (G2, 6/88[145]).

Consequently, in accordance with the basic principle set out above, the novelty of such a claim will normally depend upon whether such a functional technical feature (in combination with the other claimed features) has been "made available to the public."

(2) First medical use of a known product

(a) The effect of Article 54(5) EPC

11–83 While methods of treatment of the human or animal body are excluded from patentability under Article 52(4) (on the basis that they are not inventions which are susceptible to industrial application, see Chapter 9 at paragraph 9–36), nevertheless, it is specifically stated there that "This provision shall not apply to products, in particular substances or compositions, for use in any of these methods". This sentence "appears to be a statement of the self-evident made out of an abundance of caution" (G5/83[146]). Furthermore, Article 54(5) EPC provides that a substance or composition for use in such a medical or veterinary method does not lack novelty, even when the substance or composition is itself part of the state of the art, "provided that its use for any [such medical or veterinary] method is not comprised in the state of the art". Thus, purpose-limited product protection of such an invention may be sought in the claims of a European

---

[144] G2, 6/88 *MOBIL OIL/BAYER/Friction reducing additive* O.J. EPO 1990, 93, 114; [1990] E.P.O.R. 73, 257.
[145] *Ibid.*
[146] G5/83 *EISAI/Second medical indication* O.J. EPO 1985, 64; [1979–85] E.P.O.R.: B: 241.

patent, so as to avoid a finding of lack of novelty by reason of the fact that the product itself is known. It follows that the novelty in such a claim is derived, in accordance with Article 54(5) EPC itself, from its new purpose, namely use in a medical or veterinary method of treatment: that is, "from the new pharmaceutical use" (G5/83[147]).

It would seem that the clear intention of Article 54(5) EPC is twofold: to emphasise the distinction between a pharmaceutical method and a pharmaceutical product from the point of view of patentability, and to provide an exception to the exclusion from patentability for pharmaceutical methods contained in Article 52(4) EPC, for a claim to a use of a known product in such a method.

Unlike Articles 54(1) to (3) EPC, Article 54(5) EPC is not based on a corresponding provision of the Strasbourg Convention, nor is it based on a generally recognised concept in the Contracting States of the EPC prior to 1978; it is based on a specific form of French patent for medical preparations which was allowed under French law prior to 1978.

(b) Extent of protection for a first medical use

If a European application discloses a specific therapeutic effect as the first **11–84** therapeutic use of a known product, such disclosure justifies claiming the invention in terms of a broad statement of therapeutic purpose, not limited to the specifically disclosed individual therapeutic purpose, since such first specific therapeutic use is novel as a therapeutic use in general. The novelty of such a broad claim to a first therapeutic use would be destroyed by a prior disclosure of any therapeutic use, not just the specifically disclosed therapeutic use (T128/82[148]).

(c) Protection of a "kit-of-parts" for medical use

In a case which concerned a claimed invention comprising a combination **11–85** of two individually known pharmaceutical agents, defined "as a combined preparation for simultaneous, separate or sequential use in cytostatic therapy", claims to pharmaceutical compositions containing both agents were accepted as novel and involving an inventive step. The above-quoted indication of purpose meant that the components are not necessarily present in a composition. Nevertheless:

> "Combined preparations the individual components of which represent known therapeutic agents may be protected in a formulation corresponding to Article 54(5) EPC even when claimed as a kit-of-parts, providing those components form a functional unity (true combination) through a purpose-directed application" (T9/81[149]).

[147] *Ibid.*
[148] T128/82 *HOFFMAN-LA ROCHE/Pyrrolidine derivatives* O.J. EPO 1984, 164; [1979–85] E.P.O.R.: B: 591.
[149] T9/81 *ASTA/Cytostatic combination* O.J. EPO 1983, 372; [1979–85] E.P.O.R.: B: 303.

(3) Further medical uses of a known product

(a) Introduction

11–86 Prima facie, the wording of Article 54(5) EPC in its final sentence: "... provided that [the product's] use for any method referred to in [Article 52(4) EPC] is not comprised in the state of the art", could be interpreted as meaning that if the product in question has already been used or disclosed for use in any pharmaceutical method (*i.e.* a pharmaceutical use of the product is already part of the state of the art), a claim to a second or further pharmaceutical use of the product would lack novelty.

However, especially having regard to the recognition in Article 54(5) EPC of the novelty of a first therapeutic use of a known product, second and further therapeutic uses of a known product are also considered allowable from the point of view of novelty, when claimed in the proper form (G5/83[150]).

(b) Allowable form of claim

The problem in relation to the form of claim is caused by Article 52(4) EPC which excludes "methods of therapeutic treatment" from patentability. In this connection, whether such a method of treatment is claimed as a "method" of carrying out a therapeutic activity as a sequence of steps, or as the use of a product for a stated therapeutic purpose, makes no difference of substance: both forms of claim are regarded as excluded from patentability under Article 52(4) EPC.

11–87 However, a claim directed to "the use of a substance or composition for the manufacture of a medicament for a specified new and inventive therapeutic application" is allowable, because such a claim does not define a method of therapeutic treatment within Article 52(4) EPC (G5/83[151]). Such a claim is essentially "directed to the preliminary production (manufacture) of a medicament intended for the new application" (T958/94[152]), and thus does not fall within the exclusion of Article 52(4) EPC.

A claim to a further medical use which is allowable in accordance with G5/83[153] "may be claimed in the form either of the application (or use) of a substance or composition for the manufacture of a medicament, or of a process (or method) to manufacture a medicament characterised in the use of said substance" (T958/94[154]). The "determining factor is not the wording or category chosen for the claim but its substance, namely the technical feature which forms the essence of the invention claimed (use of the substance in question)" (T958/94[155]).

---

[150] G5/83 *EISAI/Second medical indication* O.J. EPO 1985, 64; [1979–85] E.P.O.R.: B: 241.
[151] *Ibid.*
[152] T958/94 *THERAPEUTIQUES SUBSTITUTIVES/Anti-tumoral agent* O.J. EPO 1997, 241; [1997] E.P.O.R. 417.
[153] See note 150.
[154] See note 152.
[155] See note 152.

"A claim directed to the use of a substance or composition for the production of a medicament for a therapeutic application does not conflict with Articles 52(4) or 57 EPC (see G5/83[156]) irrespective of the purpose (protection of a first medical use of a substance or composition, or protection of a further medical use) served by that claim. Accordingly, prior evidence of a further medical use is not required for this form of claim to be included in a patent application" (T143/94[157]).

In summary, therefore:

(a) claims directed to the use of a product for the treatment of an illness in a human or animal body (when such use is the second or subsequent medical use) are considered as equivalent to claims for a method of treatment of the human or animal body, and therefore excluded from patentability by Article 52(4) EPC;

whereas:

(b) claims directed to the use of a product for the manufacture of a medicament for a specified new therapeutic use (the "Swiss form of claim") do not lack in novelty for the purpose of Article 54 EPC.

Consequently: 11–88

"1. A European patent with claims directed to the use may not be granted for the use of a substance or composition for the treatment of the human or animal body by therapy.
2. A European patent may be granted with claims directed to the use of a substance or composition for the manufacture of a medicament for a specified new and inventive therapeutic application" (G5/83[158]).

The justification for this extension of patent protection to second and subsequent medical uses clearly lies fundamentally in a reluctance to draw the line for patentability at the first medical use, there being no reason in equity or logic for so doing. Furthermore:

"No intention to exclude second (and further) medical indications generally from patent protection can be deduced from the terms of the EPC; nor can it be deduced from the legislative history of the Articles in question" [i.e. the working papers of the conferences leading to the EPC]" (G5/83[159]).

---

[156] G5/83 EISAI/Second medical indication O.J. EPO 1985, 64; [1979–85] E.P.O.R.: B: 241.
[157] T143/94 MAI/Trigonelline O.J. EPO 1996, 430; [1996] E.P.O.R. 613.
[158] See note 156.
[159] See note 156.

The *ratio decidendi* of G5/83[160] "is essentially confined to the proper interpretation of Articles 52(4) and 54(5) EPC in their context". Thus:

> "G5/83[161] was concerned with making a limited exception to the general rules for novelty in cases of second and subsequent therapeutic use, but expressly indicated that such a special approach to the derivation of novelty could only be applied to claims to the use of substances or compositions intended for use in a method referred to in Article 52(4) EPC" (G2, 6/88[162]).

Moreover:

> "G5/83[163] has the effect of giving to the inventor of a new use for a known medicament a protecton analogous to but restricted in comparison with the protection normally allowable for a new non-medical use. The patentability of a second non-medical, new and non-obvious use of a product is clearly recognised in principle . . . . The patentability of 'the (second or subsequent) use of a substance or composition for the manufacture of a medicament for a specified new and inventive therapeutic application' was accepted, because although the exclusion of therapeutic methods from patentability provided in Article 52(4) EPC (on the ground that then these are not susceptible of industrial application) has the effect of excluding from patentability a claim directed to the use of a substance for therapy, this type of claim would be clearly allowable (as susceptible of industrial application) for a non-medical use. . . . Compare: 'The use of X for treating disease A mammals' (not allowed) with 'The use of X for treating disease B in cereal crops (allowed)'" (G2, 6/88[164]).

(c) Extent of protection for a further medical use

11–89 Having regard to the fact that a first medical use may be claimed generally (see paragraph 11–84 above), the patentability of a second or further (specific) medical use has to be considered in accordance with the principles of selection inventions (see paragraph 11–69). The second or subsequent medical use has to be specifically set out in the claim and the extent of protection is thus limited.

(d) The nature of novelty in a first or further medical use: new technical effect

11–90 As discussed above, the novelty of a second or subsequent medical use for a known product is derived "from the new therapeutic use of the

---

[160] G5/83 *EISAI/Second medical indication* O.J. EPO 1985, 64; [1979–85] E.P.O.R.: B: 241.
[161] *Ibid.*
[162] G2, 6/88 *MOBIL OIL/BAYER/Friction reducing additive* O.J. EPO 1990, 93, 114; [1990] E.P.O.R. 73, 257.
[163] See note 160.
[164] See note 162.

medicament", by analogy with the novelty of a first medical use under Article 54(5) EPC. It is important to recognise that, in contrast to "normal" product claims where a pre-requisite for novelty is that the product as defined in the claim has at least one physical parameter which distinguishes it from previously known products, in the case of a claim to "a product for use in a first or subsequent medical use" (whatever the exact form of the claim), the product *per se* as defined in the claim does not need to be physically distinguishable from previously known products in order for the claim to be novel. A "special concept of novelty" is involved (T128/82[165]).

Novelty is derived from the new technical effect which is associated with the first or further medical use. In this connection an enhanced (known) effect is to be distinguished from a new technical effect.

An example of a new medical technical effect is as follows:

"When a prior document and a claimed invention are both concerned with a similar treatment of the human body for the same therapeutic purpose (here: prevention of tooth decay), the claimed invention represents a further medical indication as compared to the prior document within the meaning of G5/83, if it is based upon a different technical effect which is both new and inventive over the disclosure of the prior document (here: use of compositions including lanthanum salts to reduce the solubility of tooth enamel *cf.* use of such compositions to improve the removal of plaque from teeth)" (T290/86[166]).

However:

"The use of a substance or composition for the manufacture of a preparation to be used in a specific method may derive its novelty from the subsequent use of the preparation in this specific method only if said method is one of those excluded from patentability by virtue of Article 52(4) EPC (see G5/83[167])" (T655/92[168]).

(e) No novelty in a new surgical use of a known instrument

A surgical use of an instrument is not analogous to a first therapeutic use **11–91** under Article 54(5) EPC, or a further therapeutic use within the meaning of G5/83[169], because a surgical instrument can be repeatedly used whereas a medicament is expended during use. Consequently:

"The purpose of a surgical use alone cannot render the subject-matter

[165] T128/82 *HOFFMAN-LA ROCHE/Pyrrolidine derivatives* O.J. EPO 1984, 164; [1979–85] E.P.O.R. B: 591.
[166] T290/86 *ICI/Cleaning plaque* O.J. EPO 1992, 414; [1991] E.P.O.R. 175.
[167] G5/83 *EISAI/Second medical indication* O.J. EPO 1985, 64; [1979–85] E.P.O.R.: B: 241.
[168] T655/92 *NYCOMED/Contrast agent* O.J. EPO 1998, 17; [1998] E.P.O.R. 206.
[169] See note 167.

of a claim relating to the use of the components of a known instrument for its manufacture, *i.e.* assembly, novel" (T227/91[170]).

(4) Further (non-medical) uses of a known product

(a) Introduction

11–92   In connection with non-medical inventions, there is obviously no potential difficulty in claiming new methods of using a known product where the method steps themselves are new, *i.e.* where there is novelty in the physical activity defined by the claim.

Difficulty arises as far as the question of novelty is concerned, however, when there is no novelty in the physical activity required for the carrying out of a new use of a known product, *i.e.* when a known product is used to achieve a new purpose or effect. In this case, no "special concept" of novelty can be derived from the EPC (*cf.* Article 54(5) EPC, discussed above).

On the other hand (as with medical inventions concerning further medical uses of a known product), when a product is known to have a particular use, there is, in principle, a proper basis for a patentable invention in the discovery of a further new and non-obvious use of the same product. Whether the carrying out of such a further use requires the same or a different physical activity is essentially an artificial distinction, which does not go to the heart of the question of patentability of this kind of invention.

(b) Relevant considerations: "made available" compared to "inherent"

11–93   As discussed in paragraph 11–82 above, when determining the novelty of a use claim, the first step is to construe the claim in the manner there discussed in order to determine its technical features. In particular, for a use claim defining a new use (*i.e.* purpose) for a known product, it is important to determine the functional technical feature corresponding to the technical effect which underlies the new use.

If, on its interpretation in accordance with Article 69 EPC, a claim to a further use of a known entity includes such a functional technical feature, the novelty of the claim will depend upon whether this functional technical feature (in combination with the other claimed features) has been "made available to the public".

In this connection, it is important to distinguish between what has been "made available" by the prior art, and what may be "inherent" in the prior art.

Thus:

> "under Article 54(2) EPC the question to be decided is what has been 'made available' to the public: the question is not what may have been 'inherent' in what was made available (by a prior written description,

---

[170] T227/91 *CODMAN/Second surgical use* O.J. EPO 1994, 491; [1995] E.P.O.R. 82.

or in what has previously been used (prior use), for example). Under the EPC, a hidden or secret use, because it had not been made available to the public, is not a ground of objection to validity of a European patent" (G2, 6/88[171]).

Consequently, the fact that a particular product has been used, or disclosed **11–94** for use, for a particular previously known purpose based upon a known technical effect of that product, does not destroy the novelty in a claim which (on its proper interpretation in accordance with Article 69 EPC) includes a functional feature defining a new use for a new purpose in accordance with a technical effect which was inherently achieved during the prior use for the previously known purpose, provided that such technical effect underlying the new use remained hidden during such prior use and was, therefore, not made available to the public.

> "If [a functional technical feature reflected a newly discovered technical effect] has not been previously made available to the public by any of the means as set out in Article 54(2) EPC, then the claimed invention is novel, even though such technical effect may have inherently taken place in the course of carrying out what has previously been made available to the public" (G2, 6/88[172]).

The formal answer to the referred question of law was as follows:

> "A claim to the use of a known compound for a particular purpose, which is based on a technical effect which is described in the patent, should be interpreted as including that technical effect as a functional technical feature, and is accordingly not open to objection under Article 54(1) EPC provided that such technical feature has not previously been made available to the public" (G2, 6/88[173]).

Although the referred question of law, and therefore the answer by the Enlarged Board, was framed in terms of a new non-medical use of a known "compound", the principles set out in G2, 6/88[174] are clearly equally applicable to claims defining the use of any kind of product, and for any purpose, whether medical or non-medical.

(c) Novelty of purpose: summary

In accordance with G2, 6/88[175], the main legal considerations governing **11–95** the novelty of a use claim defining a further non-medical use of a known compound are the following:

---

[171] G2, 6/88 *MOBIL OIL/BAYER/Friction reducing additive* O.J. EPO 1990, 93, 114; [1990] E.P.O.R. 73, 257.
[172] *Ibid.*
[173] *Ibid.*
[174] *Ibid.*
[175] *Ibid.*

(a) The claimed use of the known compound must be based upon a technical effect which accompanies and underlies the new use;

(b) Such a technical effect is a technical feature forming part of the subject-matter of such a use claim;

(c) The presence of such a technical feature in a claim may make the claimed subject-matter novel; this depends upon whether or not the underlying technical effect was "made available to the public" by the disclosure of a previously known use of the known compound.

11–96 The subject-matter of a use claim is considered to be novel when the only novel feature in the claim is the purpose of the defined use ("mere new use"), provided that the technical effect which underlies the purpose has not been "made available to the public". The novel subject-matter of such a claim (and therefore the protected subject-matter) is the technical effect. This holds whatever the technical field of the claimed subject-matter, whether medical or non-medical (see, *e.g.* T290/86[176] at paragraph 11–90 above, and the examples in paragraphs 11–98 *et seq.* below).

The logic of the above conclusion follows naturally from a consideration of the nature of an invention under the EPC as interpreted within the EPO. An invention is usually regarded as being based upon technical subject-matter which reflects a new solution of a new or existing problem, and thus as constituting a new technical teaching: in other words, a technical contribution to the art. Patents are granted in respect of subject-matter which reflects new and inventive technical teaching, whatever the technical nature of such teaching, in order to encourage inventors and to reward innovative research in all technical fields.

Potential difficulties in determining what constitutes infringement of a claim to the use of a known product for a new purpose have sometimes been put forward as a reason for regarding such a claim as lacking novelty (see for example *Bristol-Myers Squibb v. Baker Norton Pharmaceuticals*[177]). Patentability in general, and the determination of novelty in particular, is of course an entirely different question from the determination of infringement. The question of infringement of such a claim is considered in Chapter 13 at paragraphs 13–30 *et seq.*

(d) The nature of novelty in a new (non-medical) use of a known product; new technical effect

11–97 As with first and subsequent medical use claims (paragraphs 11–83 *et seq.* above), the product *per se*, which is defined in the claim, does not need to be physically distinguishable from previously known products in order for the claim to be novel. Similarly, the method of use of the known product which is defined in the claim, does not need to be distinguishable from the previously known method of use of the known product.

[176] T290/86 *ICI/Cleaning plaque* O.J. EPO 1992, 414; [1991] E.P.O.R. 175.
[177] [1999] R.P.C. 253.

524

In contrast to first and subsequent medical use claims, the novelty in a "new (non-medical) use" claim is not derived either directly or analogously from the provision of Article 54(5) EPC, but is derived from the general principle that a claim is novel if it includes at least one technical feature that distinguishes it from the state of the art because such technical feature has not been "made available to the public" (G2, 6/88[178]).

In the case of a new technical effect underlying a claimed new use of a known product, such new technical effect is a technical feature of the claim. This applies whether the new technical effect is medical or non-medical.

> "It is a basic consideration in G2/88[179] that the recognition or discovery of a previously unknown property of a compound, such property providing a new technical effect, can involve a valuable and inventive contribution to the art . . . . This is apparently the reason why the Enlarged Board accepted that the use related to such a property may be regarded as a technical feature appropriate for establishing novelty" (T254/93[180]).

(e) Meaning of a new technical effect

A new technical effect within the meaning of G2, 6/88[181] normally requires **11–97a** the realisation of a new technical mechanism which solves a technical problem. By way of contrast, an increase in activity resulting from a known technical effect, or further information or explanation concerning a known technical effect, does not constitute a new technical effect from which novelty can be derived.

(i) Examples of the presence of a new technical effect   **11–98**
(a) A compound x had been previously known and used as a plant growth regulator: the claimed invention was the use of compound x as a plant fungicide. The method of use was the same for both uses or purposes, namely appropriate application of the compound to plants. The claimed use was novel, because it involved a new technical effect:

> "the fact of a substance being known cannot preclude the novelty of a hitherto unknown use of that substance, even if the new use does not require any technical realisation other than for a hitherto known use of the same substance" (T231/85[182]).

(b) The claimed invention was the use of certain compounds as friction **11–99** reducing additives in lubricant compositions. A prior document disclosed

[178] G2, 6/88 *MOBIL OIL/BAYER/Friction reducing additive* O.J. EPO 1990, 93, 114; [1990] E.P.O.R. 73, 257.
[179] *Ibid.*
[180] T254/93 *ORTHO/Prevention of skin atrophy* O.J. EPO 1998, 285; [1999] E.P.O.R. 1.
[181] G2, 6/88 *MOBILOIL/BAYER/Friction reducing additive* O.J. EPO 1990, 93, 114; [1990] E.P.O.R. 73, 257.
[182] T231/85 *BASF/Triazole derivatives* O.J. EPO 1989, 74; [1989] E.P.O.R. 293.

the use of the claimed compounds in lubricant compositions for the purpose of rust inhibition, and did not contain any technical teaching that the disclosed compounds would reduce friction.

In general:

"whether a previously undisclosed technical effect which in fact inevitably occurs when a previously disclosed technical teaching in a written description is carried out has been made available to the public by reason of the teaching in the written description is a question of fact which has to be decided in the context of each individual case" (T59/87[183]).

On the facts of the case the claimed invention was novel because:

"the skilled person would remain unaware that [the disclosed compounds] not only prevent rust formation in lubricant compositions but also serve as friction reducing additives" (T59/87[184], referred to the Enlarged Board of Appeal as G2, 6/88[185]).

11–100   (c) The claimed invention was the use of certain compounds as plant growth regulators, whereas a prior document disclosed the use of the claimed compounds as fungicides (a new technical effect). The claimed invention had not been unequivocally disclosed in the prior document, and was therefore novel (T208/88[186], referred to the Enlarged Board of Appeal as G6/88[187]).

11–101   (d) The claimed invention was the use of a substance as an emulsion stabiliser in a food product. A prior document disclosed the use of the substance in a food product in combination with other named substances which were stated to act as emulsion stabilisers, and did not refer to the use of the claimed substances as an emulsion stabiliser (a new technical effect). The claim was novel (T267/89[188]).

Even if the claimed substance did in fact act as an emulsion stabiliser in the food product disclosed in the prior document, such use would have been a "hidden" use (see G2, 6/88[189]), which would not have been recognised, because the other named substances acted as emulsion stabilisers (T112/92[190]).

(ii) Examples of the absence of a new technical effect
11–102   (a) An increase of activity of a known use is not a new technical effect within the meaning of G2, 6/88[191]: "a known effect cannot become novel for

[183] T59/87 MOBIL IV/Friction reducing additive O.J. EPO 1991, 561; [1990] E.P.O.R. 514.
[184] Ibid.
[185] G2/88 MOBIL OIL/Friction reducing additive O.J. EPO 1990, 93; [1990] E.P.O.R. 73.
[186] T208/88 BAYER/Plant growth regulation O.J. EPO 1992, 22; [1992] E.P.O.R. 74.
[187] G6/88 BAYER/Plant growth regulating agent O.J. EPO 1990, 114; [1990] E.P.O.R. 257.
[188] T267/89 MARS August 28, 1990.
[189] See notes 185 and 187.
[190] T112/92 MARS II/Glucomannan O.J. EPO 1994, 192; [1994] E.P.O.R. 249.
[191] See notes 185 and 187.

the sole reason that it is present to a hitherto unknown (greater) extent" (T958/90[192]).

The claimed invention was the use of a mixture of two components, I and N, as a sequestering agent. A prior document disclosed the use of such a mixture for that purpose. It was argued that the claimed invention was directed to "the use of I for the new purpose of increasing the ability of N to sequester calcium or magnesium ions". However, it was held that the only new information in the patent was that the sequestering activity of the known mixture was better than that of N on its own, and that "a known effect cannot become novel for the sole reason that it is present to a hitherto unknown extent". Thus:

> "The use of a known physical entity for a known purpose does not represent a new technical teaching in the sense of G2/88[193], if a hitherto unknown increase in activity occurs" (T958/90[194]).

(b) The claimed invention was directed to the use of a first compound in **11–103** a process for preparing a second compound, and was distinguished from the disclosure of a prior document by the words "in order to reduce the formation of isomelamine impurities". This wording was considered to define a mere discovery (namely, "noticing that an old product has the properties of less isomelamine impurities or, as a consequence thereof, a lighter colour"), and not a new technical effect as required by G2/88[195]. In order "to show the characteristic of a new technical effect ... the use referred to in the claim would have to be some new use of the product which exploits the discovery for some new technical purpose" (T279/93[196]).

(c) The claimed invention related in particular to a combined corticoste- **11–104** riodretinoid preparation, which was applied for the treatment of dermaoses in the same way as previously known identical products. The alleged technical effect which provided novelty was the prevention of skin atrophy. However, this effect would have been visually recognised as a consequence of the application of previously known identical products. Consequently:

> "the pharmaceutical feature of preventing skin atrophy does not represent a new technical effect within the meaning of G2, 6/88[197] ...",

because:

> "The mere explanation of an effect obtained when using a compound in a known composition, even if the effect was not known to be due to

---

[192] T958/90 DOW/Sequestering agent December 4, 1992; [1994] E.P.O.R. 1.
[193] G2/88 MOBIL OIL/Friction reducing additive O.J. EPO 1990, 93; [1990] E.P.O.R. 73.
[194] See note 192.
[195] See note 193.
[196] T279/93 AMERICAN CYANAMIDE/Melamine derivative [1999] E.P.O.R. 88.
[197] G2, 6/88 MOBIL OIL/BAYER/Friction reducing additive O.J. EPO 1990, 93, 114; [1990] E.P.O.R. 73, 257.

this compound in the known composition, cannot confer novelty on a known process if the skilled person was already aware of the occurrence of the desired effect" (T254/93[198]).

11–104a (d) The claimed invention concerned the use of aromatic esters in a deodorant composition. Such use was disclosed in a prior document, which, however, was silent about the explanation for the effect of the aromatic esters. The claimed invention defined the effect of the aromatic esters "as an inhibitor of esterase producing micro-organisms".

The claimed invention lacked novelty because:

> "a *newly discovered technical effect* does not confer novelty on a claim directed to the use of a known substance for a known non-medical purpose if the newly discovered technical effect already underlies the known use of the known substance" (T892/94[199]).

(5) Comparison with United Kingdom and other national laws

(a) Further medical uses of a known products

11–105 The question of novelty of such further medical uses has been considered in a number of national contexts, both before and after the issue of G5/83[200] by the Enlarged Board of Appeal

(i) Before G5/83[201]

11–106 (a) The German Federal Court of Justice decided that a second medical use was patentable under German national law (equivalent to the relevant provisions of the EPC) by means of a claim directed to "the use of a product to treat an illness".

As mentioned in paragraph 11–86 above, this form of claim was considered to be unallowable in G5/83[202], as being contrary to Article 52(4) EPC.

11–107 (b) The Swiss Federal Intellectual Property Office had issued a "Legal Advice" concerning "use" claims in accordance with which a claim to "the use of a substance or composition (the active ingredient) for the manufacture of a medicament (ready for administration) for a specified (new) therapeutic application (the "Swiss form of claim").

As mentioned in paragraph 11–87 above, this Swiss form of claim was considered to be allowable in G5/83[203].

[198] T254/93 ORTHO/Prevention of skin atrophy O.J. EPO 1998, 285; [1999] E.P.O.R. 1.
[199] T892/94 ROBERTET/Deodorant composition O.J. EPO 2000, 1; [1999] E.P.O.R. 516.
[200] G5/83 EISAI/Second medical indication O.J. EPO 1985, 64; [1979–85] E.P.O.R.: B: 241.
[201] Ibid.
[202] Ibid.
[203] Ibid.

(ii) After G5/83[204]

(a) *United Kingdom.* In a corresponding cases in the United Kingdom the **11–108** Patents Court followed G5/83[205] in allowing further medical uses to be protected under the "Swiss form of claim".

In reaching this conclusion, the Patent Court stated that:

> "... had the matter to be considered on the wording of [the 1977 U.K. Act] and without regard to the position, as it has developed, under the corresponding provisions of the EPC, we think the better views would be that a claim in the Swiss form ... would not be patentable as lacking the required novelty .... It would have been a simple matter to provide for the patenting of such an invention directed to a second medical use by the omission of the word 'any' in section 2(6) [corresponding to Article 54(5) EPC], if it had been the intention of the legislature that a novel second or further use of a known pharmaceutical should be patentable".

Notwithstanding this opinion, however, the Patents Court adopted the approach to the novelty of such a further medical use set out in G5/83[206] "having regard to the desirability of achieving conformity" which is indicated by sections 91(1) and 130(7) of the 1977 UK Act.

(b) *Sweden.* In a corresponding case in Sweden, the Court of Patent **11–109** Appeals also followed G5/83[207], because such an approach was in line with earlier Swedish patent law, and because of the importance of harmonisation of the application of Swedish law with EPO practice.

(c) *The Netherlands.* In a corresponding case before the Appeal Division **11–110** of the Netherlands Patent Office, it was recognised that:

> "A patent may in principle be granted in response to an application based on the discovery of a second medical use, since such a discovery is essentially no different from the initial discovery of a new property of a known substance that renders it suitable for a (first) medical use."

However, G5/83[208] was not followed, on the basis that:

> "Novelty does not derive from the mere fact that the known compound has a new therapeutic use."

(d) *France.* In a case in France, the Court of Appeal accepted that a further **11–111** medical use of a known compound was new and involved an inventive step, but the Cour de Cassation held that the Court of Appeal had violated

---

[204] *Ibid.*
[205] *Ibid.*
[206] *Ibid.*
[207] *Ibid.*
[208] *Ibid.*

the law on the ground that "A second medical use of a known medicine is not patentable.[209]"

(b) Further non-medical uses of a known product

11–112 No case concerning the novelty of a claim to a further non-medical use has been decided in the United Kingdom.

In *Merrell Dow*[210], it was held that: "The use of a product made the invention part of the state of the art only so far as that use made available the necessary information." Consequently, "a patent could be used, subject to Section 64 1977 U.K. Act, to stop someone doing what he had done before if the previous use was secret or uninformative".

The statement in G2, 6/88[211] which distinguishes what has been "made available" from what is "inherent" in what has been made available (see paragraph 11–93 above) was therefore approved.

Cases Referred to in Chapter 11

Board of Appeal Decisions

G1/83	BAYER/Second medical indication O.J. EPO 1985, 60
G5/83	EISAI/Second medical indication O.J. EPO 1985, 64; [1979–85] E.P.O.R.: B: 241
G2/88	MOBIL OIL/Friction reducing additive O.J. EPO 1990, 93; [1990] E.P.O.R. 73
G6/88	BAYER/Plant growth regulating agent O.J. EPO 1990, 114; [1990] E.P.O.R. 257
G1/92	Availability to the public O.J. EPO 1993, 277; [1993] E.P.O.R. 241
G1/95	DE LA RUE/Fresh grounds for opposition O.J. EPO 1996, 615
G2/98	Six months period O.J. EPO (P).
G2/99	DEWERT/Six months period O.J. EPO (P).
T9/81	ASTA/Cytostatic combination O.J. EPO 1983, 372; [1979–85] E.P.O.R.: B: 303.
T12/81	BAYER/Diastereomers O.J. EPO 1982, 296; [1979–85] E.P.O.R.: B: 308.
T119/82	EXXON/Gelation O.J. EPO 1984, 217; [1979–85] E.P.O.R.: B: 566.
T128/82	HOFFMAN-LA ROCHE/Pyrrolidine derivatives O.J. EPO 1984, 164; [1979–85] E.P.O.R.: B: 591.
T150/82	IFF/Claim categories O.J. EPO 1984, 309; [1979–85] E.P.O.R.: C: 629.

---

[209] *Alfuzosine*, Cour de Cassation O.J. EPO 1995, 252.
[210] *Merrell Dow Pharmaceutical Inc. v. H.N. Norton & Co. Ltd* [1996] R.P.C. 76, HL.
[211] G2, 6/88 *MOBIL OIL/BAYER/Friction reducing additive* O.J. EPO 1990, 93, 114; [1990] E.P.O.R. 73, 257.

T181/82	CIBA-GEIGY/Spiro compounds O.J. EPO 1984, 401; [1979–85] E.P.O.R.: C: 672.
T84/83	LUCHTENBERG/Rear-view mirror [1979–85] E.P.O.R.: C: 796.
T173/83	TELECOMMUNICATIONS/Anti-oxidant O.J. EPO 1987, 465; [1988] E.P.O.R. 133.
T188/83	FERNHOLZ/Vinyl acetate O.J. EPO 1984, 555; [1979–85] E.P.O.R.: C: 891.
T204/83	CHARBONNAGE/Venturi O.J. EPO 1985, 310; [1986] E.P.O.R. 1.
T205/83	HOECHST/Vinyl ester-crotonic acid copolymers O.J. EPO 1985, 363; [1986] E.P.O.R. 57.
T206/83	ICI/Pyridine herbicides O.J. EPO 1987, 5; [1986] E.P.O.R. 232.
T167/84	NISSAN/Fuel injector valve O.J. EPO 1987, 369; [1987] E.P.O.R. 344.
T198/84	HOECHST/Triochloroformates O.J. EPO 1985, 209; [1979–85] E.P.O.R.: C: 987.
T17/85	PLÜSS-STAUFER/Filler O.J. EPO 1986, 406; [1987] E.P.O.R. 66.
T26/85	TOSHIBA/Thickness of magnetic layers O.J. EPO 1989, 6; [1990] E.P.O.R. 267.
T153/85	AMOCO/Alternative claims O.J. EPO 1988, 1; [1988] E.P.O.R. 116.
T231/85	BASF/Triazole derivatives O.J. EPO 1989, 74; [1989] E.P.O.R. 293.
T248/85	BICC/Radiation processing O.J. EPO 1986, 261; [1986] E.P.O.R. 311.
T7/86	DRACO/Xanthines O.J. EPO 1988, 381; [1989] E.P.O.R. 65.
T114/86	ERIKSSON/Foam plastic filter, O.J. EPO 1987, 485; [1988] E.P.O.R. 25.
T290/86	ICI/Cleaning plaque, O.J. EPO 1992, 414; [1991] E.P.O.R. 175.
T303/86	CPC/Flavour concentrates [1989] E.P.O.R. 95.
T56/87	SCANDITRONIX/Ion chamber O.J. EPO 1990, 188; [1990] E.P.O.R. 352.
T59/87	MOBIL IV/Friction reducing additive O.J. EPO 1991, 561; [1990] E.P.O.R. 514.
T77/87	ICI/Latex composition O.J. EPO 1990, 280; [1989] E.P.O.R. 246.
T85/87	CSIRO/Arthropodicidal compounds, [1989] E.P.O.R. 24.
T89/87	WAVIN, December 20, 1989.
T124/87	DU PONT/Copolymers O.J. EPO 1989, 491; [1989] E.P.O.R. 33.
T296/87	HOECHST/Enantiomers O.J. EPO 1990, 195; [1990] E.P.O.R. 337.

T301/87	BIOGEN/Alpha-interferons O.J. EPO 1990, 335; [1990] E.P.O.R. 190.
T381/87	RESEARCH CORPORATION/Publication O.J. EPO 1990, 213; [1989] E.P.O.R. 138.
T208/88	BAYER/Plant growth regulation O.J. EPO 1992, 22; [1992] E.P.O.R. 74.
T245/88	UNION CARBIDE/Atmospheric vaporizer [1991] E.P.O.R. 373.
T297/88	BAYER/Nimodipin II December 5, 1989.
T461/88	HEIDELBERGER DRUCKMASCHINEN/Micro-chip O.J. EPO 1993, 295; [1993] E.P.O.R. 529.
T523/88	SULZER-ESCHER WYSS/Rolling mill February 26, 1991.
T534/88	IBM/Ion etching [1991] E.P.O.R. 18.
T572/88	HOESCHT/Reactive dye, February 27, 1991.
T93/89	HOECHST/Polyvinyl ester dispersion November 15, 1990 (P).
T267/89	MARS August 28, 1990.
T279/89	July 3, 1991.
T450/89	ENTHONE/Zinc plating [1994] E.P.O.R. 326.
T482/89	TÉLÉMÉCANIQUE/Electrical supply, O.J. EPO 1992, 646; [1993] E.P.O.R. 259.
T666/89	UNILEVER/Washing composition O.J. EPO 1993, 495; [1992] E.P.O.R. 501.
T763/89	July 10, 1991.
T87/90	September 26, 1991.
T229/90	KONICA/Monodisperse emulsions October 28, 1992.
T363/90	February 25, 1992.
T830/90	MACOR MARINE SYSTEMS/Confidentiality agreement O.J. EPO 1994, 713; [1995] E.P.O.R. 21.
T205/91	June 16, 1992.
T227/91	CODMAN/Second surgical use O.J. EPO 1994, 491; [1995] E.P.O.R. 82.
T677/91	FINNEGAN/Mass selective ejection November 13, 1992.
T799/91	February 3, 1994.
T842/91	BILFINGER/Sealing screen [1999] E.P.O.R. 192.
T112/92	MARS II/Glucomannan O.J. EPO 1994, 192.
T133/92	AKZO/Bleaching activator October 18, 1994.
T436/92	March 20, 1995.
T465/92	ALCAN/Aluminium alloy O.J. EPO 1996, 32; [1995] E.P.O.R. 501.
T585/92	UNILEVER/Deodorant detergent O.J. EPO 1996, 129; [1996] E.P.O.R. 579.
T655/92	NYCOMED/Contrast agent O.J. EPO 1998, 17; [1998] E.P.O.R. 206.
T952/92	PACKARD/Supersolve O.J. EPO 1995, 755.
T1085/92	ROBERT BOSCH/Electrical machine [1996] E.P.O.R. 381.
T71/93	MONSANTO/Rheological testing [1998] E.P.O.R. 402.

T254/93	ORTHO/Prevention of skin atrophy O.J. EPO 1998, 285; [1999] E.P.O.R. 1.
T279/93	AMERICAN CYANIMIDE/Melamine derivative [1999] E.P.O.R. 88.
T365/93	July 27, 1995.
T404/93	September 28, 1994.
T143/94	MAI/Trigonelline O.J. EPO 1996, 430; [1996] E.P.O.R. 613.
T750/94	AT&T/Proof of prior publication O.J. EPO 1998, 32; [1997] E.P.O.R. 509.
T892/94	ROBERTET/Deodorant compositions O.J. EPO 2000, 1; [1999] E.P.O.R. 516.
T958/94	THERAPEUTIQUES SUBSTITUTIVES/Anti-tumoral agent O.J. EPO 1997, 241; [1997] E.P.O.R. 417.
T990/96	NOVARTIS/Erythro compounds O.J. EPO 1998, 489; [1998] E.P.O.R. 441.

Decisions of National Courts

Alfuzosine; Judgment of the Cour de Cassation, France, O.J. EPO 1995, 252.
Asahi Kasei Kogyo K.K.'s Application [1991] R.P.C. 485, HL.
Bristol-Myers Company (Johnson's) Application [1975] R.P.C. 127.
Bristol-Myers Squibb Co. v. Baker Norton Pharmaceuticals Inc. [1999] R.P.C. 253.
"Hydropyridine", BGH Decision XYZB 4/83, Germany, O.J. EPO 1984, 26.
"Hydropyridine", Court of Patent Appeals, Sweden, O.J. EPO 1988, 198.
John Wyeth and Brother Ltd's/Schering A.G.'s Application [1985] R.P.C. 545.
Lane-Fox v. The Kensington & Knightsbridge Electric Lighting Co. Ltd (1892) R.P.C. 413; [1892] 3 Ch. 424.
Letraset v. Rexel Ltd [1975] F.S.R. 62; [1976] R.P.C. 51, CA.
Merrell Dow Pharmaceutical Inc. v. H.N. Norton & Co. Ltd [1996] R.P.C. 76, HL.
Monsanto Co. (Brignac's) Application [1971] R.P.C. 153.
Prout v. British Gas plc [1992] F.S.R. 428.
Quantel Ltd v. Spaceward Microsystems Ltd [1990] R.P.C. 83.
"Second medical use/NL"; Decision dated September 30, 1987, Appeal Division, Netherlands Patent Office, O.J. EPO 1988, 405.

CHAPTER 12

INVENTIVE STEP

Articles 56 EPC

Contents

All references are to paragraph numbers

Cases Referred to in Chapter 12

A. Introduction

(1) Principles of assessment

12–01 As discussed in Chapter 11 at paragraphs 11–01 and 11–03, determination of the question whether a claimed invention involves an inventive step only arises if it has been established that the combination of claimed technical features is not part of the state of the art, and that the claimed invention is therefore novel. Inventiveness is assessed having regard to the state of the art as defined in Article 54(2) EPC (*i.e.* the published prior art). To be inventive, a claimed invention must provide a solution to an objective technical problem in a non-obvious way.

The practice of the Examining and Opposition Divisions in assessing inventive step is set out comprehensively in the Guidelines, Section C-IV, 9.

The majority of appeals which are decided by the Technical Boards of Appeal are concerned with the assessment of inventive step, and are decided upon their individual facts. Nevertheless a number of decisions of the Boards of Appeal have emphasised points of legal principle which underlie the assessment of inventive step in accordance with the EPC, and which should be taken into account in particular cases. The most important and distinctive principle which has been generally applied by the Boards of Appeal from the beginning of their activities is referred to as the "problem-and-solution" approach to the assessment of inventive step. This approach is considered in detail below. It is of course commonplace that:

> "The problem and solution approach is no more than one possible route for the assessment of inventiveness. Accordingly, its use is not a *sine qua non* when deciding inventiveness under Article 56 EPC" (T465/92[1]).

Furthermore, the problem-and-solution approach can be criticised because it relies on the results of a search made with actual knowledge of the claimed invention, and is therefore inherently based on hindsight, and care in its application is required in some circumstances (T465/92[2]).

Nevertheless, the problem-and-solution approach is applied as the official policy in the first instance departments of the EPO, and is almost always applied in the Boards of Appeal.

In view of the very large number of issued decisions concerning inventive step, it is only possible to refer to a representative selection of the more important decisions in this chapter.

---

[1] T465/92 *ALCAN/Aluminium alloys* O.J. EPO 1996, 32; [1995] E.P.O.R. 501.
[2] *Ibid.*

(2) Time of assessment

Article 56 EPC states that "An invention shall be considered as involving **12–02** an inventive step if, having regard to the state of the art, it is not obvious to a person skilled in the art." This wording corresponds closely that of Article 5 Strasbourg,[3] but with the addition of the reference to "a person skilled in the art."

Since the "state of the art" is defined in Article 54(2) EPC as comprising "everything made available to the public ... before the date of filing of the European patent application," the date at which the state of the art has to be assessed for inventive step is the filing date. The filing date of an application is either the actual filing date, or if the application is entitled to a right of priority under Article 87 EPC (see Chapter 10), then the date of priority counts as the filing date by virtue of Article 89 EPC.

As to what constitutes the state of the art under Article 54(2) EPC, or "published prior art", see paragraphs 11–07 et seq.

> "When examining for inventive step, the state of the art must be assessed from the point of view of the man skilled in the art at the time of priority relevant for the application" (T24/81[4]).

Similarly:

> "the guiding consideration in assessing inventive step is the knowledge of the skilled person before the date of priority or filing" (T268/89[5]).

(3) Standard of inventiveness

In general: **12–03**

> "patents granted under the EPC should have inventive step sufficient to ensure to the patentees a fair degree of certainty that if contested the validity of the patent will be upheld by a national court. The standard should anyhow not be below what may be considered an average amongst the standards presently applied by the Contracting States" (T1/81[6]).

---

[3] Strasbourg Convention on the Unification of Certain Points of Substantive Law on Patents for Invention; reproduced in full at Appendix 16.
[4] T24/81 *BASF/Metal refining* O.J. EPO 1983, 133; [1979–85] E.P.O.R.: B: 354.
[5] T268/89 *LATZKE/Magnetic plaster* O.J. EPO 1994, 50; [1994] E.P.O.R. 469.
[6] T1/81 *AECI/Thermoplastics sockets* O.J. EPO 1981, 439; [1979–85] E.P.O.R.: B: 273.

B. The Problem-and-Solution Approach

(1) Basic principles

12–04   The legislative basis for the problem-and-solution approach is in Rule 27(1)(d) EPC, which requires that the description of a European patent application shall "disclose the invention, as claimed, in such terms that the technical problem (even if not expressly stated as such) and its solution can be understood. ..." This requirement is mandatory (T26/81[7]—see Chapter 7 at paragraph 7–05).

The basic principles of the approach were developed in a number of early cases which came before the Boards of Appeal. In particular, "Assessment of inventive step of a chemical invention ... has to be preceded by determination of the technical problem based on objective criteria" (T1/80[8]). Such determination of the technical problem "requires the assessment of the technical success *vis-à-vis* the state of the closest art" (T20/81[9]).

Furthermore:

"the inventive step may be considered as a step from the technical problem to its solution. If, therefore, the requirements of the above Rule 27(1)(d) EPC are neither satisfied by the original description nor ... by an amendment, it will emerge that an invention within the meaning of Article 52 EPC does not exist. On the other hand, if the subject-matter ... is judged as being inventive in character, it must always be possible to derive a technical problem from the application" (T20/81[10]).

12–05   These principles were further developed as follows:

"Objectivity in the assessment of inventive step is achieved by starting out from the objectively prevailing [*i.e.* closest] state of the art, in the light of which the problem is determined which the invention addresses and solves from an objective point of view ... Consideration is given to the question of the obviousness of the disclosed solution to this problem as seen by the man skilled in the art ..." (T24/81[11]).

Thus the basic sequence of the problem-and-solution approach may be summarised as follows:

(a) With reference to the claimed invention to be assessed, the "closest prior art" is determined (for example, the prior document which comes closest to disclosing the invention).

---

[7] T26/81 *ICI/Containers* O.J. EPO 1982, 211; [1979–85] E.P.O.R.: B: 362.
[8] T1/80 *BAYER/Carbonless copying paper* O.J. EPO 1981, 206; [1979–85] E.P.O.R.: B: 250.
[9] T20/81 *SHELL/Amyloxybenzaldehydes* O.J. EPO 1982, 217; [1979–85] E.P.O.R.: B: 335.
[10] *Ibid.*
[11] T24/81 *BASF/Metal refining* O.J. EPO 1983, 133; [1979–85] E.P.O.R.: B: 354.

(b) Starting from this closest prior art and the technical results or effect achieved thereby, and by comparison with the technical effect achieved by the claimed invention, the objective technical problem to be solved in progressing from the closest prior art to the claimed invention is determined.

(c) The obviousness or otherwise of the proposed solution to this problem to a person skilled in the art starting from the closest prior art is assessed.

(2) Characteristics

Particular characteristics of this problem-and-solution approach are as **12–06** follows:

(a) The assessment of inventive step is essentially objective.

(b) The presence or absence of an inventive step is predominantly determined on the basis of a technical assessment of the inventiveness of the advance made from the closest prior art to the claimed invention.

(c) Having assessed inventive step starting from the closest prior art, there should be no need for further consideration of inventiveness starting from other less relevant prior art.

An advantage of the regular use of the problem-and-solution approach to the assessment of inventive step in proceedings before the EPO, as opposed to a more random consideration of various potentially relevant factors indicating the presence or absence of inventive step which may arise on a case-to-case basis, is that a consistent standard of inventiveness as a criterion for the grant or maintenance of European patents in such proceedings should thereby be developed.

The adoption of a consistent standard of inventiveness for European patents has been regarded as highly important for the operation of the EPO, in order that public confidence in the inventive merit underlying the subject-matter of such patents should be sustained.

C. Identification of the Closest Prior Art

(1) General considerations

"An objective assessment of inventive step starting from the closest prior **12–07** art implies that the latter has been positively identified and considered" (T248/85[12]).

The closest prior art is that which forms the best starting point within the state of the art from which the claimed invention could have been made, *i.e.* the most promising springboard towards the invention which was

---

[12] T248/85 *BICC/Radiation processing* O.J. EPO 1986, 261; [1986] E.P.O.R. 311.

available to the skilled person at the filing date (T254/86[13]). Generally the prior art which has the most technical features in common with the claimed invention and which is in the same technical field of application will be the closest prior art. In many cases, however, the prior art which is the most closely concerned with the problem underlying the claimed invention will be considered as the closest prior art.

In a few cases there is controversy as to what should be considered as the closest prior art document (see *e.g.* T69/83[14]); and it may then be sensible to assess inventive step from more than one document in the alternative.

The fact that a particular prior document is the closet prior art document with respect to novelty, since it discloses many techncial features in common with the claimed invention, does not mean that it is the closest prior art with respect to the assessment of inventive step. Such common features "may be of a rather incidental nature if . . . the prior art in question is not concerned with a similar technical problem and does not relate to the same specific technical field as the claimed invention" (T267/88[15]).

(2) Identifying the closest prior art: a practical view

12–08 The closest prior art must be selected from the objective practical view of a skilled person in the art at the filing date. A particular prior art document should be identified as the closest prior art of the skilled person would have had good reason to select it as the basis of further development. Thus a prior art document published long before the filing date may be rejected as the objective "closest prior art" if it does not meet this criterion (see T495/91[16], T741/91[17], T334/92[18], T1002/92[19]; and compare T964/92[20]).

(3) Patent publications compared with commercial state of the art

12–09 A number of decisions have emphasised that commercial publications and products are to be assessed at the same level as patent and other technical literature when identifying the closest prior art, even though the former may represent current actual practice.

When looking for the solution to a problem the skilled person is pressured to study patent publications in the relevant patent classes with particular interest (T1/81[21]).

This is in accordance with commercial practice, since patent specifications are recognised in industry as a most important source of technical information.

---

[13] T254/86 *SUMITOMO/Yellow dyes* O.J. EPO 1989, 115; [1989] E.P.O.R. 257.
[14] T69/83 *BAYER/Thermoplastic moulding* O.J. EPO 1984, 357; [1979–85] E.P.O.R.: C: 771.
[15] T267/88 *FUJI/Photographic materials* [1991] E.P.O.R. 168.
[16] T495/91 *TARKETT PEGULAN/Floor covering* July 20, 1993; [1995] E.P.O.R. 516.
[17] T741/91 *UENO/Bon-3-acid* O.J. EPO 1993, 630; [1995] E.P.O.R. 533.
[18] T334/92 *EISAI/Benzodioxane derivatives* March 23, 1994.
[19] T1002/92 *PETTERSON/Queueing system* O.J. EPO 1995, 605; [1996] E.P.O.R. 1.
[20] T964/92 *EISAI/Benzodioxanes* [1997] E.P.O.R. 201.
[21] T1/81 *AECI/Thermoplastics sockets* O.J. EPO 1981, 439; [1979–85] E.P.O.R.: B: 273.

D. Formulation of the Problem

(1) The objective technical problem *vis-à-vis* the closest prior art: reformulation of the problem

The objective nature of the examination for inventive step in accordance **12–10** with the problem-and-solution approach has been stressed in a number of decisions, and subjective evidence as to the problems facing the inventor and the history of the making of the invention is frequently disregarded. For example:

> "When assessing inventive step . . ., it is not a question of the subjective achievement of the inventor, so that the case history of the invention . . . is irrelevant . . ." (T24/81[22]).

It often happens that an invention which is the subject of a European patent application is described and claimed having regard to prior art known to the inventor at the time that the invention was made. In the course of examination or opposition proceedings, further more relevant prior art commonly becomes known, with the result that the problem which the inventor sees himself as having solved is not the same as the objective problem defined by following the problem-and-solution approach, and in particular by comparing the technical result of the invention with that achieved by the closest prior art. In such circumstances the history of the making of the invention is clearly not relevant to the assessment of inventive step having regard to the objective problem to be solved (see T13/84,[23] for example).

In such circumstances the objective problem has to be reformulated. Thus:

> ". . . the nature of the problem has to be determined on the basis of objective facts, in particular as appearing in the prior art revealed in the course of the proceedings, which may be different from the prior art of which the inventor was actually aware at the time the application was filed. A reformulation of the problem which then may become necessary is not precluded by Article 123(2) EPC . . ." (T13/84[24]).

The problem may also be reformulated in the light of further knowledge of the technical effect underlying the invention (*e.g.* T1/80,[25] T184/82[26]). However, such a reformulation "should not contradict earlier statements in the application about the general purpose and effect of the invention". Thus it is "not acceptable to rely on an effect which has previously been

---

[22] T24/81 *BASF/Metal refining* O.J. EPO 1983, 133; [1979–85] E.P.O.R.: B: 354.
[23] T13/84 *SPERRY/Reformulation of the problem* O.J. EPO 1986, 253; [1986] E.P.O.R. 289.
[24] *Ibid.*
[25] T1/80 *BAYER/Carbonless copying paper* O.J. EPO 1981, 206; [1979–85] E.P.O.R.: B: 250.
[26] T184/82 *MOBIL/Poly (p-methylstyrene) articles* O.J. EPO 1984, 261; [1979–85] E.P.O.R.: C: 690.

described as undesirable ... as possibly representing an advantage from another point of view, and thereby to imply that the technical problem ... should take this reversal into account" (T155/85[27]).

12-11   On the other hand, the technical problem cannot be reformulated to take into account the inefficacy of the prior art disclosures, if this has only been recognised and alleged after the filing date. This applies especially where a "problem invention" is alleged—paragraph 12–48 below (T268/89[28]).

In summary, therefore:

> "The technical problem as originally presented, in accordance with Rule 27(1)(c) EPC, in the application or patent in suit, which is to be regarded as the 'subjective' technical problem, may require reformulation on the basis of objectively more relevant elements originally not taken into account ... This reformulation yields a definition of the 'objective' technical problem. The latter represents the ultimate residue (effect), corresponding to the objective contribution provided by the subject-matter defined in the relevant claims (features)" (T39/93[29]).

Examples:

12-12   (1) In T1/80[30], the Examining Division held that a claimed invention was obvious on the basis that the only distinguishing feature of the claimed copying papers over a prior art document (selection of a particular more precisely defined compound) produced no surprising effect. In the absence of a surprising effect, the problem could be seen as the mere preparation of another carbonless copying paper. However, comparative experiments filed during the appeal showed that the claimed invention produced superior results, with the consequence that the objective problem *vis-à-vis* the nearest prior art could be redefined as "not just preparing other copying papers but improved copying papers." On the basis of this problem, the claimed invention was held not to have been obvious.

12-13   (2) In T184/82[31] it was recognised that when there is doubt as to the validity of technical effects originally claimed for an invention, the presence of related improvements could support inventive step on the basis of an "appropriate re-statement of the problem based on a less ambitious goal ... success at a more general level could replace failure at a specific level regarding the effect of the invention, provided the skilled man would recognise the same as implied or related to the problem initially suggested."

---

[27] T155/85 *PHILLIPS PETROLEUM/Passivation of catalyst* O.J. EPO 1988, 87; [1988] E.P.O.R. 164.
[28] T268/89 *LATZKE Magnetic blaster* O.J. EPO 1994, 50.
[29] T39/93 *ALLIED COLLOIDS/Polymer powders* O.J. EPO 1997, 134; [1997] E.P.O.R. 347.
[30] T1/80 *BAYER/Carbonless copying paper* O.J. EPO 1981, 206; [1979–85] E.P.O.R.: B: 250.
[31] T184/82 *MOBIL/Poly (p-methylstyrene) articles* O.J. EPO 1984, 261; [1979–85] E.P.O.R.: C: 690.

(2) Defining the problem

(a) Avoiding hindsight

Many decisions emphasise the danger of using knowledge of the claimed **12–14** invention when assessing inventive step. For example:

> "Examination with regard to inventive step is limited to the question of obviousness in the overall light of the state of the art and from the viewpoint of the closest prior art (looking forward) and not from that of the invention (looking backward)" (T181/82[32]).

In accordance with the problem-and-solution approach, knowledge of the claimed invention and its effect is necessarily used both when determining what is the closest prior art and when defining the problem to be solved by the skilled person *vis-à-vis* such closest prior art. The avoidance of hindsight when following the problem-and-solution approach depends primarily upon an objective definition of the problem to be solved. The objective technical problem is the problem which a skilled person would objectively recognise as the problem when comparing the closest prior art with the technical effect of the claimed invention.

The importance of a fair approach to the definition of the objective problem to be solved, following comparison between the effect of the closest prior art and that of the claimed invention, has frequently been emphasised. For example:

> "[the prevention of deformation] can certainly be considered as a problem common to the prior document and the application, but the actual problem explicitly indicated in the prior document ... does not correspond to the problem proper of the application ... and does not suggest it either. Thus, it cannot be said that the invention resides only in [replacement of a cooling process as in the prior document with a direct cooling process as in another prior document]. Such a conclusion would merely be the result of *a posteriori* analysis, *i.e.* an interpretation of the prior documents as influenced by the problem solved by the invention, while the problem was neither mentioned or suggested by ... those documents nor known to ... the person skilled in the art" (T5/81[33]).

(b) Avoiding pointers to the solution

The objective technical problem must be formulated in such a way that it **12–15** does not contain pointers to the solution or partially anticipate the solution. Thus:

---

[32] T181/82 *CIBA-GEIGY/Spiro compounds* O.J. EPO 1984, 401; [1979–85] E.P.O.R.: C: 672.
[33] T5/81 *SOLVAY/Production of hollow thermoplastic objects* O.J. EPO 1982, 249; [1979–85] E.P.O.R.: B: 287.

"The technical problem to be solved by an invention must be so formulated as not to contain pointers to the solution ... since including part of a solution offered by an invention in the statement of the problem must, when the state of the art is assessed in terms of that problem, necessarily result in an *ex post facto* view being taken of inventive activity" (T229/85[34]: and see T422/93[35]).

Similarly:

"In order to assess inventive step, the problem must be defined objectively in such a way that it does not partially anticipate the solution" (T99/85[36]).

(c) Avoiding artificial and unrealistic problems

12–16 A practical approach should be followed when defining the objective technical problem underlying the claimed invention. Normally the problem recognised in the European patent application should be used as the technical problem, in the absence of reasons such as discussed above for defining a different objective problem by way of reformulation.

Thus:

"A comparison of the problem indicated in the application with that indicated in a prior document must avoid an excessively abstract approach far removed from the practical thinking of the person skilled in the art.

12–17   The teaching of a document may have narrower implications for a person skilled in the art and broader implications for a potential inventor who first perceives the problem which is future invention is intended to solve. The assessment of inventive step must look at the situation solely from the practical view point of the person skilled in the art" (T5/81[37]).

Furthermore:

"a proper application of the ... problem-and-solution approach requires the avoidance of formulating artificial and unrealistic technical problems, and that to this end, the technical problem as defined in the patent in suit should be the basis for evaluation of inventive step, provided that no-re-definition is necessary in view of the true state of the art or in the light of an inadequate solution". (T495/91[38] and see

---

[34] T229/85 *SCHMID/Etching process* O.J. EPO 1987, 237; [1987] E.P.O.R. 279.
[35] T422/93 *JALON/Luminescent security fibres* O.J. EPO 1997, 24; [1999] E.P.O.R. 486.
[36] T99/85 *BOEHRINGER/Diagnostic agent* O.J. EPO 1987, 413; [1987] E.P.O.R. 337.
[37] T5/81 *SOLVAY/Production of hollow thermoplastic objects* O.J. EPO 1982, 249; [1979–85] E.P.O.R.: B: 287.
[38] T495/91 *TARKETT PEGULAN* July 20, 1993; [1995] E.P.O.R. 516.

T741/91,[39] where a prior document published long before the filing date was rejected as the closest prior art in favour of more up-to-date prior art which was available to the skilled person at the filing date; and the objective technical problem was formulated in relation to the up-to-date prior art).

E. Assessment of Inventive Step

Having established the objective problem to be solved *vis-à-vis* the closest   **12–18** prior art, the question whether or not the claimed invention was obvious to a "person skilled in the art" has to be considered in every case.

(1) Technical considerations

(a) Nature of the skilled person

When assessing inventive step, "the starting point for defining the   **12–19** appropriate skilled person is the technical problem to be solved on the basis of what the closest prior art discloses, irrespective of any other definition of the skilled person suggested in the contested patent" (T422/93[40]).

In some cases the notional skilled person has been regarded as a team of appropriate specialists (see T141/87[41], T424/90[42], T99/89[43], for example).

The practical orientation of a skilled person within the meaning of Article 56 EPC has frequently been emphasised. For example:

"The comparison of a problem indicated in or deriving from a prior document with that indicated in the application must avoid an excessively abstract approach; as the degree of abstraction increases so does the likelihood of discovering points of similarity, but at the same time the approach becomes further removed from the thinking of the person skilled in the art, which, being oriented towards practicalities, means that the points suggested to him by a prior document remain relatively limited in scope. Therefore, the teaching of a document may have narrower implications for a person skilled in the art and broader implications for a potential inventor who first recognises the problem on which his future invention is to be based. The assessment of inventive step must consider solely the limited teaching for the person skilled in the art" (T5/81[44]).

It may be appropriate in some cases to consider the problem with the

---

[39] T741/91 *UENO/Bon-3-acid* O.J. EPO 1993, 630; [1995] E.P.O.R. 533.
[40] T422/93 *JALON/Luminescent security fibres* O.J. EPO 1997, 24; [1999] E.P.O.R. 486.
[41] T141/87 *BOSCH/Diagnostic test system for motor vehicles* [1996] E.P.O.R. 570.
[42] T424/90 December 11, 1991.
[43] T99/89 *BOSCH/Optical display* March 5, 1991.
[44] T5/81 *SOLVAY/Production of hollow thermoplastic objects* O.J. EPO 1982, 249; [1979–85] E.P.O.R.: B: 287.

specialised knowledge of a person skilled in a different art from that which forms the subject-matter of the claimed invention. Thus:

"If the problem prompts the person skilled in the art to seek its solution in another technical field, the specialist in that field is the person qualified to solve the problem. The assessment of whether the solution involves an inventive step must therefore be based on that specialist's knowledge and ability" (T32/81[45]; and see also T164/92[46]).

12–20   However:

"Since the technical problem addressed by an invention must be so formulated as not to anticipate the solution [paragraph 12–15 above], the skilled person to be considered cannot be the appropriate expert in the technical field to which the proposed solution belongs if this technical field is different to the one considered when formulating the technical problem" (T422/93[47]).

In particular:

"The appropriate skilled person's basic knowledge does not include that of a specialist in the different technical field to which the proposed solution belongs if the closest prior art gives no indication that the solution is to be sought in this other technical field" (T422/93[48]).

Finally,

"generally accepted definitions of the notional 'skilled person in the art' . . . have one thing in common, namely that none of them suggests that he is possessed of any inventive capability" (T39/93[49]).

(b) Common general knowledge

12–21 A person skilled in the art carries within him the common general knowledge of the particular art in which he is skilled. As to what constitutes such common general knowledge, reference can be made to Chapter 7 at paragraphs 7–14 *et seq.* and the decisions referred to there (in particular T206/83[50]). Clearly handbooks and textbooks are generally recognised as forming part of the common general knowledge. The language of such a textbook does not affect its relevance (T426/88[51]).

[45] T32/81 *FIVES-CAIL BABCOCK/Cleaning apparatus for conveyor belt* O.J. EPO 1982, 225; [1979–85] E.P.O.R.: B: 377.
[46] T164/92 *ROBERT BOSCH/Electronic computer components* O.J. EPO 1995, 305; [1995] E.P.O.R. 585.
[47] T422/93 *JALON/Luminescent security fibres* O.J. EPO 1997, 24; [1999] E.P.O.R. 486.
[48] *Ibid.*
[49] T39/93 *ALLIED COLLOIDS/Polymer powders* O.J. EPO 1997, 134; [1997] E.P.O.R. 347.
[50] T206/83 *ICI/Pyridine herbicides* O.J. EPO 1987, 5; [1986] E.P.O.R. 232.
[51] T426/88 *LUCAS INDUSTRIES/Combustion engine* O.J. EPO 1992, 427; [1992] E.P.O.R. 458.

Common general knowledge which is exemplified in one field, may be applied in a different field, in appropriate circumstances. Thus:

"When books, representing common general knowledge, describe a basic general technical theory or methodology and exemplify the same with specific applications in certain technical fields only, these do not limit the general scope and relevance of such disclosures so as to exclude possible applications in other fields" (T426/88[52]).

In many technical fields, however, the common general knowledge is not available in written form, *e.g.* textbooks (see T69/89,[53] for example). In such cases, the extent of common general knowledge has to be assessed on the basis of the available evidence.

The basic principles which form part of the common general knowledge   **12–22** in a particular technology will frequently be known to the parties and the EPO without specific proof. In appropriate cases, however, substantiation as to what constitutes common general knowledge may be necessary: for example:

"The ground of objection relied upon by the Examining Division that the use of microcrystalline cellulose as an additive in plastics is common general knowledge was not substantiated, nor has the Board such knowledge of its own. Therefore, in the absence of proper substantiation this ground must be set aside" (T157/87[54]).

Direct evidence as to what constitutes the common general knowledge in a particular field is not often filed by parties to proceedings before the EPO, although there is no reason why such evidence should not be filed, and such evidence might frequently be of assistance.

(c) The technical features to be considered: technical effect in relation to scope of claim

In principle: **12–23**

"In the absence of any indication to the contrary in the wording of a claim, it must be assumed, when examining for inventive step, that the claim is directed solely to the simultaneous application of all its features" (T175/84[55]).

Nevertheless:

"In assessing the inventive step of a combination of features, consideration must be given to a feature only if the applicant has

[52] *Ibid.*
[53] T69/89 *SURGIKOS/Disinfection* [1990] E.P.O.R. 632.
[54] T157/87 *KUBAT/Cellulose composites* [1989] E.P.O.R. 221.
[55] T175/84 *KABELMETAL/Combination claim* O.J. EPO 1989, 71; [1989] E.P.O.R. 181.

provided evidence that it contributes, either independently or in conjunction with one or more of the other features, to the solution of the problem set in the description" (T37/82[56]).

Thus the inclusion in a claim of features which do not contribute to the solution of the objective problem to be solved cannot make a claimed invention inventive if it is otherwise obvious.

For example, if the applicant acknowledges that certain claimed features were not intended to provide an inventive step, then:

"these features and any advantages resulting therefrom can be disregarded in assessing the inventive step and investigation as to non-obviousness can be confined to the remaining features of the claim" (T22/81[57]).

Furthermore:

"Whenever an invention resides in the modification of a known article in order to improve its known capability, the modifying feature should not only characterise the invention in the claim, *i.e.* distinguish it from the prior art, but must contribute causally to the improvement ... thereby achieved" (T192/82[58]).

Thus, inventiveness is assessed having regard to the essential features of the invention, namely those claimed features which contribute to the achievement of the technical effect underlying the invention.

As discussed in Chapter 7 at paragraphs 7–04 and 7–56 for example, it is "a generally accepted legal principle that the extent of the patent monopoly should correspond to and be justified by the technical contribution to the art".

This principle also governs the assessment of inventive step, because "everything falling within a valid claim has to be inventive. If this is not the case, the claim must be amended so as to exclude obvious subject-matter in order to justify the monopoly" (T939/92[59]).

Thus if a claim concerns a group of chemical compounds *per se*, and the description does not contain sufficient information to make it credible that an alleged technical effect (for example, herbicidal activity—which is not a part of the definition of the claimed compounds) is obtained by all the claimed compounds, objection may arise under Article 56 EPC, if such technical effect is the sole reason for the alleged inventiveness (T939/92[60]). This is because, if some claimed

---

[56] T37/82 SIEMENS/*Low-tension switch* O.J. EPO 1984, 71; [1979–85] E.P.O.R.: B: 437.
[57] T22/81 LUCAS/*Ignition system* O.J. EPO 1983, 226; [1979–85] E.P.O.R.: B: 348.
[58] T192/82 BAYER/*Moulding compositions* O.J. EPO 1984, 415; [1979–85] E.P.O.R.: C: 705.
[59] T939/92 AGREVO/*Triazoles* O.J. EPO 1996, 309; [1996] E.P.O.R. 171.
[60] *Ibid.*

compounds must be assumed not to have any technically useful property, the making of such compounds would be purely arbitrary and therefore non-inventive (see also paragraph 12–39 below).

(d) Combinations of teachings

A combination of teachings from different prior art documents or sources, **12–24** including the "closest prior art," may result in a finding of lack of inventive step, if such a combination was obvious to a skilled person at the filing date. It is normally regarded as part of the skill of a skilled person that, being aware of the literature in his own and related fields, he is in principle capable of seeking and recognising technical developments which can be derived from simple combinations of documents within such literature. In the majority of cases before the EPO in which a finding of lack of inventive step is made, the finding is based upon a combination of teachings from documents.

For example:

> "A process developed in the light of a need which arose relatively shortly before the application is not deemed to involve inventive step if this need could be readily met by an obvious combination of teachings from the state of the art" (T24/81[61]).

Furthermore:

> "When examining for inventive step, the state of the art must be assessed from the point of view of the man skilled in the art at the time of priority relevant for the application. Consequently all previously published embodiments must be taken into consideration which offered a suggestion to the skilled practitioner for solving the problem addressed, even where those embodiments were not particularly emphasised" (T24/81[62]).

> "When a feature, which is lacking from the closest prior art document, **12–25** is known from a document in the same specialised field, and solves the same problem, then the fact that the skilled person would not encounter difficulties in applying this known feature to the disclosure of the closest prior art document demonstrates that the documents are not conflicting and that an inventive step is lacking" (T142/84[63]).

For example, in a case where the claimed invention concerned a reflecting device including a foil whose purpose was to protect the mirror glass against stress, constituted the only distinguishing feature over the closest prior art document, which disclosed a layer of flexible material having the same purpose as the claimed foil. A further document showed a flexible

---

[61] T24/81 *BASF/Metal refining* O.J. EPO 1983, 133; [1979–85] E.P.O.R.: B: 354.
[62] *Ibid.*
[63] T142/84 *BRITAX/Inventive step* O.J. EPO 1987, 112; [1987] E.P.O.R. 148.

foil support for a different arrangement of mirror glass. It was held that "the use of a foil in place of an elastic intermediate layer of some other kind can no longer constitute an inventive step" (T6/80[64]).

It is considered as forming part of the normal activities of the person skilled in the art to select from the materials which are known to him as suitable for a certain purpose the most appropriate one, and this also in the case where he is presented with no more than an unreasoned preference for a specific material in the clost prior art document (T21/81[65]).

Similarly, if a skilled person who operated apparatus according to the closest prior art document would undoubtedly discover certain deficiencies in a part of it, and he does not possess the technical knowledge to overcome such deficiencies, "he can be expected to consult the relevant prior art for components which perform the same function and are better able to meet the requirements" and to combine a further document with the closest prior art accordingly (T15/81[66]).

(e) Unforeseeable or unsuggested results

12–26 On the other hand, unrelated or conflicting documents cannot be combined in order to deny an inventive step, and unforeseeable advantageous results achieved from a combination of known features from different prior art documents may indicate the presence of an inventive step (T2/81,[67] T39/82[68]).

For example, inventive step cannot be denied solely on the ground that a particular measure characterising the claimed invention was known in a publication in the same special field. To assess inventive step properly, it is necessary to examine whether the prior art gave an indication to apply the measure in accordance with the claimed invention. "Such an indication does not have to be given *express is verbis*. It can reside in the fact that the purpose of the known measure in the known case is the same as in the case to be decided. It therefore has to be investigated what problems are solved in the known case and the case in suit ..." (T39/82[69]).

(f) No pointer: feature disclosed for a different purpose

12–27 The use of a feature which is described in the closest prior art document for a different purpose than that described, in order to achieve an unexpected effect, may involve an inventive step, if the relevant disclosure gives no pointer to the claimed solution of the objective problem.

In particular, "in examining inventive step on the basis of a single

[64] T6/80 *MAN/Intermediate layer for reflector* O.J. EPO 1981, 434; [1979–85] E.P.O.R. B: 265.
[65] T21/81 *ALLEN-BRADLEY/Electromagnetically operated switch* O.J. EPO 1983, 15; [1979–85] E.P.O.R.: B: 342.
[66] T15/81 *KRAFWERK UNION/Eddy-current testing device* O.J. EPO 1982, 2; [1979–85] E.P.O.R.: B: 316.
[67] T2/81 *MOBAY/Methylenebis (phenyl isolyanate)* O.J. EPO 1982, 394; [1979–85] E.P.O.R.: B: 280.
[68] T39/82 *AUER-SOG/Light-reflecting slats* O.J. EPO 1982, 419; [1979–85] E.P.O.R.: B: 441.
[69] *Ibid*

document, the purpose which a known technical feature serves can become crucial". In a case where the features of a test were described as being carried out after completion of a process for verification purposes, to confirm the desired result, the incorporation of the features of the test as a final step in the process in order to achieve a surprising technical effect was held to involve an inventive step, because the relevant disclosure was confined to test procedure and gave no pointer to the claimed solution of the problem (T4/83[70]).

(g) Need for a series of steps

"If in order to proceed from the known art to the invention a series of **12–27a** steps are needed, this may be considered as a significant indicator of the presence of inventiveness, particularly in a case where the last decisive step has neither been proved to be known from the prior art nor is derivable therefrom, although this last step may at first sight seem to be a very simple one" (T113/82[71]).

(h) Simplification

When a claimed invention is characterised by its simplicity, there is an **12–28** inevitable risk that it appears obvious in retrospect. However, such invention must be assessed without the benefit of hindsight.
  For example:

"What at first sign appears to be an obvious step of incorporating a known device in a known machine may not be such if there is evidence that this results in simplification of design coupled with improved performance in use and the solution of a long-standing problem. There is a danger that the difficulty of developing a simple solution without sacrifice of quality will be disregarded when obviousness is assessed with the benefit of hindsight. Care must be taken not to destroy applications for lack of inventive step when persons in the related industry would recognise that it is very surprising that no one had ever hit upon the simple solution before" (T106/84[72]).

The simplicity of a claimed invention may often indicate inventiveness. Thus:

"A further such indication [of inventive step] is the notable simplicity of the solution proposed, which despite the considerable amount of activity in this field has escaped those concerned"(T229/85[73]).

Similarly:

[70] T4/83 EXXON/Purification of sulphonic acids O.J. EPO 1983, 498; [1979–85] E.P.O.R.: C: 721.
[71] T113/82 IBM/Recording apparatus O.J. EPO 1984, 10; [1979–85] E.P.O.R.: B: 553.
[72] T106/84 MICHAELSEN/Packing machine O.J. EPO 1985, 132; [1979–85] E.P.O.R.: C: 959.
[73] T229/85 SCHMID/Etching process O.J. EPO 1987, 237; [1987] E.P.O.R. 279.

"In a technical field of commercial importance to which considerable attention is directed the simplicity of a proposed solution may indicate inventiveness" (T9/86[74]).

(i) Neighbouring versus remote fields of technology

12–29 The relevant state of the art to be considered when examining for inventive step is not limited to the specific field with which the claimed invention is directly concerned but extends at least to relevant art in neighbouring fields and in general technical fields. In particular, it is normally regarded as part of the skill of the skilled person that when confronted with a problem he will consider relevant developments within fields of technology which are adjacent to his own (sometimes after enlisting the help of a specialist in such a neighbouring field).

Consequently:

"The state of the art to be considered ... includes, as well as that in the specific field of the application, the state of any relevant art in neighbouring fields and/or a broader general field of which the specific field is a part, that is to say any field in which the same problem or one similar to it arises and of which the person skilled in the art of the specific field must be expected to be aware" (T176/84[75])

12–30 For example:

"A skilled person working in the area of genetic engineering (*e.g.* expression in yeast) would regard a means found possible in a neighbouring area of genetic engineering (*e.g.* the bacterial art) as being usable in his own area, if this transfer of technical knowledge appears to be easy and to involve no obvious risks" (T455/91[76]).

However, if the introduction to the application refers to a prior art document in a field, which cannot objectively be classified as a neighbouring field, such a reference will not be taken into consideration when assessing inventive step, if the reference resulted from "an association of ideas ... which the applicant had obviously made [and which] only existed in his own private domain" (T28/87[77]).

Thus:

"the question of what is a neighbouring field is one of fact and ... depends ... on whether the person skilled in the art seeking a solution to a given problem would take into account developments in the neighbouring field ..."(T176/84[78]).

[74] T9/86 *BAYER/Polymide-6* O.J. EPO 1988, 12; [1988] E.P.O.R. 83.
[75] T176/84 *MÖBIUS/Pencil sharpener* O.J. EPO 1986, 50; [1986] E.P.O.R. 117.
[76] T455/91 *GENENTEEN/Expression in yeast* O.J. EPO 1995, 684; [1996] E.P.O.R. 85.
[77] T28/87 *KERBER/Wire link bands* O.J. EPO 1989, 383; [1989] E.P.O.R. 377.
[78] See note 75.

Furthermore:

> "solutions of general technical problems in non-specific (general) fields must be considered to form part of the general technical knowledge which *a priori* is to be attributed to those skilled persons versed in any specific technical field" (T195/84[79]).

In particular, if a book described a general technical theory or method- **12–31** ology with examples in certain fields, this does not limit the relevance of such a disclosure so as to exclude its possible application on other fields (T426/88[80]).

In special circumstances a skilled person may be expected to consult a technical field which is neither a neighbouring field nor a broader general field.

Thus:

> "A person skilled in the art who is confronted with a technical problem in a specific technical field would consider consulting another technical field where the same problem is well known to the general public owing to widespread debate thereon [health risks associated with asbestos], even if this other field is neither a neighbouring field nor a broader general field, provided that there exists a relationship between the kinds of material used in the specific field and those used in this other field" (T560/89[81]).

(j) Unexpected technical progress

A number of decisions have relied upon unexpected progress, or an **12–32** unexpected technical effect, compared to the closest prior art as a sufficient indication of inventive step. Thus: "An effect which may be said to be unexpected can be regarded as an indication of inventive step" (T181/82[82]).

For example:

> "Where, because of an existing need, an applicant sets himself the task of developing an economically and technologically advantageous new complete chemical process for the preparation of known and desired end products ..., the solution ... may be inventive if—despite the choice of the same starting materials as for the nearest comparable process in the prior art—the advantageous result actually achieved [higher overall yield] is surprising (in this case quantitatively)" (T22/82[83]).

[79] T195/84 *BOEING/General technical knowledge* O.J. EPO 1986, 121; [1986] E.P.O.R. 190.
[80] T426/88 *LUCAS/Combustion engine* O.J. EPO 1992, 427; [1992] E.P.O.R. 458.
[81] T560/89 *N.I. INDUSTRIES/Filler mass* O.J. EPO 1992, 725; [1994] E.P.O.R. 120.
[82] T181/82 *CIBA-GEIGY/Spiro compounds* O.J. EPO 1984, 401; [1979–85] E.P.O.R.: C: 672.
[83] T22/82 *BASF/Bis-epoxy ethers* O.J. EPO 1982, 341; [1979–85] E.P.O.R.: B: 414.

Even small improvements may imply the presence of inventive step. For example:

> "The achievement of a numerically small improvement of a process commercially used on a large scale (here an enhanced yield of 0.5 per cent.) represents a worthwhile technical problem which must not be disregarded in assessing the inventive step of its solution as claimed" (T38/84[84]).

12–33 Similarly, in T20/83[85] the fact that the claimed compounds had an anti-allergic effect was considered to be "qualitatively surprising, so that the question of surprising quantitative superiority can be left aside ...". The substantial modifications to the molecule of the claimed compounds, compared to the prior art, in combination with the fact that the modified compounds were still anti-allergic, was held to be a new and surprising finding which supported inventiveness.

On the other hand, if the claimed invention provides technical progress in comparison with the closest prior art, but such progress would be expected to be achieved in the light of the objective problem to be considered, such progress does not support inventive step. For example:

> "the considerable technical effect here claimed provides no basis for the presence of inventive step, if only because it is not surprising, but was on the contrary certainly to be expected in view of the problem facing the skilled practitioner" (T24/81[86]).

12–34 Similarly:

> "If an article is known as a combination or mixture of components fulfilling known functions, the generation and application of an improved novel component for the same purpose may be patentable as such, and also as an improved article incorporating the same. If the component in question forms, on the other hand, part of the state of the art together with its relevant properties, the incorporation thereof in the same article will be obvious in view of its predictable beneficial effect ('analogous substitution')" (T192/82[87]).

The use of a known material on the basis of its known properties and in a known manner to obtain a known effect in a new combination is not normally inventive ("similar use") in the absence of special circumstances (T130/89[88]).

---

[84] T38/84 STAMICARBON/Oxidation of toluene O.J. EPO 1984, 368; [1979–85] E.P.O.R.: C: 931.
[85] T20/83 CIBA-GEIGY/Benzothiopyran derivatives O.J. EPO 1983, 419; [1979–85] E.P.O.R.: C: 746.
[86] T24/81 BASF/Metal refining O.J. EPO 1983, 133; [1979–85] E.P.O.R.: B: 354.
[87] T192/82 BAYER/Moulding compositions O.J. EPO 1984, 415; [1979–85] E.P.O.R.: C: 705.
[88] T130/89 KOMMERLING/Profile member O.J. EPO 1991, 514; [1992] E.P.O.R. 98.

It is sometimes necessary to balance a surprising advantage against concurrent disadvantages. Thus:

"An invention which relies on a substantial and surprising improvement of a particular property need not also show advantages over the prior art with regard to other properties relevant to its use, provided the latter are maintained at a reasonable level so that the improvement is not completely offset by disadvantages in other respects to an unacceptable degree or in a manner which contradicts the disclosure of the invention fundamentally" (T254/86[89]).

Furthermore, in some cases it may be necessary to assess the overall **12–35** effect of tests under varying conditions. For example in T57/84[90] the claimed invention was a fungicide, which is required to be effective under various conditions. In relation to evidence of comparative tests under various conditions which were intended to show the superiority of the claimed compounds. It was held that:

"it is their combined results that have to be considered. The decisive factor is whether the invention out-performs the substance used for comparison in the tests as a whole . . ., even if [that] substance proves better in one of the tests" (T254/86[91]).

(k) Comparative tests

In some cases, as discussed above, the surprising result achieved by the **12–36** claimed invention can be shown by means of evidence in the form of comparative tests: unexpected technical progress has to be demonstrated for the claimed invention in comparison with the closest prior art.

Such evidence may be filed during proceedings before the EPO after the filing date of the application, in order to establish the technical effect of the claimed invention as asserted in the application as filed, or closely related technical effect which is implied by the technical problem underlying the claimed invention as set out in the application as filed (see T184/82[92] for example). Such evidence can be regarded as confirming the technical effect of the invention which is disclosed either expressly or implicitly in the application as filed.

For example:

"An effect which may be said to be unexpected can be regarded as an **12–37** indication of inventive step; where comparative tests are submitted as evidence of this, there must be the closest possible structural

---

[89] T254/86 *SUMITOMO/Yellow dyes* O.J. EPO 1989, 115; [1989] E.P.O.R. 257.
[90] T57/84 *BAYER/Tolyfluanid* O.J. EPO 1987, 53; [1987] E.P.O.R. 131.
[91] T254/86 *SUMITOMO/Yellow dyes* O.J. EPO 1989, 115; [1989] E.P.O.R. 257.
[92] T184/82 *MOBIL/Poly (p-methylstyrene) articles* O.J. EPO 1984, 261; [1979–85] E.P.O.R.: C: 690.

approximation—in a comparable type of use—to the subject-matter of the invention. ... the only tests suitable for this are those which are concerned with the structural closeness to the invention, because it is only here that the factor of unexpectedness is to be sought" (T181/82[93]).

Furthermore:

"In the case where comparative tests are chosen to demonstrate an inventive step with an improved effect over a claimed area, the nature of the comparison with the closest state of the art must be such that the effect is convincingly shown to have its origin in the distinguishing feature of the invention. For this purpose it may be necessary to modify the elements of comparison so that they differ only by such a distinguishing feature" (197/86[94], supplementing T181/82[95]).

It should also be noted that:

"Technical progress shown in comparison with marketed products as an alleged support for inventive step cannot be a substitute for the demonstration of inventive step with regard to the relevant closest state of the art (T164/83[96]).

Comparative tests may be superfluous. Thus:

"Where an alleged invention is *prima facie* obvious having regard to the prior art, nevertheless it is sometimes possible to prove inventiveness by comparative tests showing a significant improvement over the closest prior art. That situation is to be contrasted with ... cases such as the present ... in which it is not *prima facie* obvious to make the claimed compounds at all, and therefore comparative tests are not essential to establish inventiveness" (T390/88[97]).

(l) No necessity for technical progress

12–38 Whereas technical superiority may be indicative of inventive step as discussed above, technical progress is not a requirement for inventiveness and patentability under the EPC (T181/82[98] and T164/83[99]) This is in contrast to the earlier German law in which technical progress was a "criterion of patentability in addition to that of inventive step" (T164/83[100]).

---

[93] T181/82 *CIBA-GEIGY/Spiro compounds* O.J. EPO 1984, 401; [1979–85] E.P.O.R.: C: 672.
[94] T197/86 *KODAK/Photographic couplers* O.J. EPO 1989, 371; [1989] E.P.O.R. 395.
[95] See note 93.
[96] T164/83 *EISAI/Antihistamines* O.J. EPO 1987, 149; [1987] E.P.O.R. 205.
[97] T390/88 *KONISHIROKU/Photographic film* [1990] E.P.O.R. 417.
[98] T181/82 *CIBA-GEIGY/Spiro compounds* O.J. EPO 1984, 401; [1979–85] E.P.O.R.: C: 672.
[99] See note 96.
[100] See note 96.

(m) Lack of technical progress

Nevertheless, lack of technical progress may well indicate a lack of **12–39** inventive step.

For example, a mere structural difference from the known prior art in new chemical intermediate compounds is not sufficient to support inventive step in the absence of "a valuable property in the widest sense" resulting from such difference (T22/50[101] and see paragraph 12–50 below).

Furthermore:

> "The argument that alternative routes should be considered to be the less obvious the odder, or perhaps even the more disadvantageous, they are, cannot be sustained. The rhetorical question why the skilled man should have contemplated such detour at all, would equally apply, if someone tried to patent the least attractive further analogy processes for the making of a known compound. Obviousness is not only at hand when the skilled man would have seen all the advantages of acting in a certain manner but also when he could clearly see why he should not act in the suggested manner in view of its predictable disadvantages or absence of improvement, provided he was indeed correct in his assessment of all the consequences" (T119/82[102]).

Thus:

> "There can be no invention in merely worsening the prior art, especially if such consequence is substantially foreseeable, ... even if some aspect of the results may not be accurately predictable" (T155/85[103]).

(n) Additional unexpected (bonus) effects: one way street

It sometimes happens that a claimed invention not only shows improved **12–40** properties that would be expected, but also an additional, unexpected property or advantage. Since the improved but expected properties would be part of routine development by a skilled person, the claimed invention can be regarded as obvious on this basis and therefore effectively in the public domain; but the question may arise whether the presence of additional unexpected effects can provide a basis for a finding of inventive step.

For example:

(1) The claimed invention concerned an electro-magnetic device, whose modified construction in relation to the closest prior art was regarded as within the normal activities of a skilled person faced with solving well-known problems within the state of the art. It was held that:

[101] T22/82 *BASF/Bis-epoxy ethers* O.J. EPO 1982, 341; [1979–85] E.P.O.R.: B: 414.
[102] T119/82 *EXXON/Gelation* O.J. EPO 1984, 217; [1979–85] E.P.O.R.: B: 566.
[103] T155/85 *PHILLIPS PETROLEUM/Passivation of catalyst* O.J. EPO 1988, 87; [1988] E.P.O.R. 164.

"If, having regard to the state of the art, something falling within the terms of the claim would have been obvious to a person skilled in the art, because the combined teaching of the prior art documents could be expected to produce an advantageous effect, such claim lacks inventive step, regardless of the fact that an extra effect (possibly unforeseen) is obtained" (T21/81[104]).

12–41   (2) The claimed invention concerned moulding compositions comprising specified polymers, having improved moulding properties. Such compositions fell within the general scope of the closest prior art document. The state of the art included little choice of suitable materials apart from the closest prior art document, so it was "all the more likely that the skilled man would have inevitably turned to the [disclosed] materials with excellent published properties" (T192/82[105]).

In cases where unexpected additional properties are relied upon, a distinction may be drawn between cases where many options are available to the skilled person and cases where the choice available to the skilled person is restricted.

Thus:

"The skilled man must be free to employ the best means already available for his purposes, although the use of means leading to some expected improvements may well be patentable if [reliance is placed] on an additional effect, provided this involves a choice from a multiplicity of possibilities. The lack of alternatives in this respect may ... create a 'one-way-street' situation leading to predictable advantages which remain obvious in spite of the existence of some unexpected 'bonus' effect" (T192/82[106]).

12–42   Similarly:

"Where, because of an essential part of the technical problem being addressed, the state of the art obliges a skilled person to adopt a certain solution, that solution is not automatically rendered inventive, by the fact that it also unexpectedly solves part of the problem" (T69/83[107]).

Furthermore:

"Once it is established that a *particular* solution to a [realistic technical] problem *would* have been envisaged by a person skilled in the art in the light of the relevant state of the art then this solution lacks an

---

[104] T21/81 *ALLEN-BRADLEY/Electromagnetically operated switch* O.J. EPO 1983, 15; [1979–85] E.P.O.R.: B: 342.
[105] T192/82 *BAYER/Moulding compositions* O.J. EPO 1984, 415; [1979–85] E.P.O.R.: C: 705.
[106] *Ibid.*
[107] T69/83 *BAYER/Thermoplastic moulding compositions* O.J. EPO 1984, 357; [1979–85] E.P.O.R.: C: 771.

inventive step, and this assessment cannot be altered by the fact that the claimed invention inherently also solves further technical problems" (T936/96[108]). This applies even if "an additional problem had been effectively solved in a manner not suggested by the state of the art relevant in respect of the solution to this problem" (T936/96[109]).

The presence of unexpected properties for a claimed invention must therefore be balanced against the freedom of a skilled person to use that which is already obvious from the state of the art.

(o) Obvious to try: expectation of success

"If, for a particular application of a known process, the skilled person **12–42a** could obviously use a material generally available on the market and suitable for the purpose, and was also highly likely to use it for reasons irrespective of its characteristics, the usage should not be considered inventive on account of those characteristics alone" (T513/90[110]).

"Even if the availability of such material is not exclusive but common enough to be reasonably likely to be tried for the purpose simply by chance, such choice should remain in the public domain. This should not, of course, diminish the right to obtain coverage for a novel product of such process, if that turns out to be inventive *per se*" (T513/90[111]).

In a case concerning genetic engineering:

"Inventive step may be acknowledged ... if there is no reasonable expectation of success that the cloning and expression of a given gene can be carried out. However, in a case where ... a skilled person can expect to perform the cloning and expression of a gene in a fairly straightforward manner, and the cloning, although requiring much work, does not pose such problems as to prove that the expectation of success was ill-founded, inventive step cannot be acknowledged" (T386/94[112]).

The above approach is equally applicable in any field of technology.

(p) "Could" versus "would"

In assessing inventive step the question is whether a skilled person *would* **12–43** have arrived at the claimed solution to a problem (as compared to whether he *could* have done so). In other words, the assessment of inventive step

---

[108] T936/96 *KANEGAFUCHI/Absorbent for LDL* June 11, 1999.
[109] *Ibid.*
[110] T513/90 *JAPAN STYRENE/Foamed articles* O.J. EPO 1994, 154; [1994] E.P.O.R. 129.
[111] *Ibid.*
[112] T386/94 *UNILEVER/Chymosin* O.J. EPO 1996, 658; [1997] E.P.O.R. 184.

depends upon the extent to which a skilled person would have been technically motivated towards the claimed invention.

For example:

> "In a case where the applicant had supplemented a known layered tablet by the provision of a barrier between the layers, ... the proper question to be asked was not whether the skilled man could have provided the barrier but whether he would have done so in expectation of some improvement or advantage ... Since the [known] tablet was ... a satisfactory answer to the problem of undesirable migration, the addition of a barrier would have appeared superfluous, wasteful and devoid of any technical effect. In view of the recognition that a barrier has, after all, a substantial effect, the outcome was not predictable, and the claimed modification involves an inventive step. ..." (T2/83[113]).

Similarly:

> "While [the skilled person] *could* have found by mere change or extensive research and testing ... variants in the areas [disclosed in prior documents], he had no good reason to move in such direction ... in the absence of any expectation of improvement. The assumption must therefore be that he *would* not have done so in the circumstances. ..." (T265/84[114]).

(2) Circumstantial or secondary indications

12–44 In some cases what are sometimes called "secondary indications" may support inventive step (*i.e.* long-felt want, overcoming a prejudice, commercial success). Nevertheless, as a generality such potential indications of an inventive step are regarded as secondary compared to the technical considerations discussed in the previous section. In some cases what are sometimes called "secondary indications" may support inventive step (*i.e.* long-felt want, overcoming a prejudice, commercial success). Nevertheless, as a generality such potential indications of a inventive step are regards as secondary compared to the technical considerations discussed in the previous section (in particular, "whether the skilled person would have solved the existing technical problem" T270/84[115]).

Thus: "a mere investigation for indications of the presence of inventive step is no substitute for the technically skilled assessment of the invention *vis-à-vis* the state of the art, pursuant to Article 56 EPC. Where such indications are present, the overall picture of the state of the art and consideration of all significant factors may show that inventive step is involved, but will not necessarily do so ..." (T24/81[116]).

---

[113] T2/83 RIDER/Simethicane tablet O.J. EPO 1984, 265; [1979–85] E.P.O.R.: C: 715.
[114] T265/84 ALLIED/Cobalt foils [1987] E.P.O.R. 193.
[115] T270/84 ICI/Fusecord [1987] E.P.O.R. 357.
[116] T24/81 BASF/Metal refining O.J. EPO 1983, 133; [1979–85] E.P.O.R.: B: 354.

Similarly: "such so-called secondary indicia in support of an inventive step represent auxiliary considerations which can in certain cases facilitate a decision ... However, [their] presence does not mean that an inventive step must be recognised" (T270/84[117]).

(a) Long-felt want: the time factor

A few decisions refer to the fact that a problem has awaited solution for a **12–45** long period of time as an indication of inventive step.
Thus:

> "The fact that the state of the art has been inactive over a long period prior to the invention may be an indication that an inventive step is involved if during that time an urgent need for improvement has demonstrably existed" (T109/82[118]).

Similarly:

> "If a process has been performed successfully on a commercial scale for more than 20 years in spite of economic disadvantages associated with it, and the claimed invention provides a solution to the technical problem of avoiding such economic disadvantages, this supports a finding of inventive step" (T271/84[119]).

Normally such a "time factor" in a field of technical interest and commercial importance is used in decisions as corroboration of a finding of inventive step which has already been deduced on the basis of other reasoning.
On the other hand:

> "A process developed in the light of a need which arose relatively shortly before the application is not deemed to involve inventive step if this need could be readily met by an obvious combination of teachings from the state of the art" (T24/81[120]).

(b) Overcoming a prejudice

The existence of a prejudice in the art may be an indication that an **12–46** inventive step was required in order to overcome it (see *e.g.* T18/81[120a]). However, those "who wish to rely on a prejudice which might have diverted the skilled man away from the invention have the onus of demonstrating the existence of such prejudice" (T119/82[121]).
Furthermore:

[117] T270/89 *ICI/Fusecord* [1987] E.P.O.R. 193.
[118] T109/82 *BOSCH/Hearing aid* O.J. EPO 1984, 473; [1979–85] E.P.O.R.: B: 539.
[119] T271/84 *AIR PRODUCTS/Removal of hydrogen sulphide and carbonyl sulphide* O.J. EPO 1987, 405; [1987] E.P.O.R. 23.
[120] T24/81 *BASF/Metal refining* O.J. EPO 1983, 133; [1979–85] E.P.O.R.: B: 354.
[120a] T18/81 *SOLVAY/Olefine polymers* O.J. EPO 1985, 166.
[121] T119/82 *EXXON/Gelation* O.J. EPO 1984, 217; [1979–85] E.P.O.R.: B: 566.

"Where a patent specification is used to support an assertion of prejudice, it must be borne in mind that technical information in a patent specification may be based on special premises or on the view of the drafter ... such information can often be accorded general validity only where further corroboration is available ..." (T19/81[122]).

Thus:

"it is indeed permissible to consider various documents together mosaically in order to prove a prejudice or a general trend pointing away from the invention" (T2/81[123]).

On the other hand:

"A process developed in the light of a need which arose relatively shortly before the application is not deemed to involve inventive step if this need could be readily met by an obvious combination of teachings from the state of the art" (T24/81[124]).

(c) Commercial success

12–47 It is fairly rare for evidence of commercial success to play a major role in the assessment of inventive step. Occasionally, commercial success has been relied on as an additional indication supporting a finding of inventive step especially if it can be established that "the commercial success stems from the technical advantages of the claimed invention," and is combined with evidence of a long felt want (see for example T106/84[125]). Furthermore:

"in certain cases, commercial success may be an indication for inventive step if it can be shown by evidence that this success clearly derives from a technical feature claimed" (T191/82,[126] and see also T677/91[127]).

(3) Special cases

(a) Perceiving the problem

12–48 "The discovery of an unrecognised problem may in certain circumstances give rise to patentable subject-matter in spite of the fact that the claimed solution is retrospectively trivial and in itself obvious" (T2/83[128]).

---

[122] T19/81 *RÖHM/Film coating* O.J. EPO 1982, 51; [1979–85] E.P.O.R.: B: 330.
[123] T2/81 *MOBAY/Methylenebis (phenyl isolyanate)* O.J. EPO 1982, 394; [1979–85] E.P.O.R.: B: 280.
[124] T24/81 *BASF/Metal refining* O.J. EPO 1983, 133; [1979–85] E.P.O.R.: B: 354.
[125] T106/84 *MICHAELSEN/Packing machine* O.J. EPO 1985, 132; [1979–85] E.P.O.R.: C: 959.
[126] T191/82 *FIBRE-CHEM/Re-establishment of rights* EPO 1985, 189; [1979–85] E.P.O.R.: C: 701.
[127] 677/91 *FINNEGAN/Mass selective ejection* November 13, 1992.
[128] T2/83 *RIDER/Simethicone tablet* O.J. EPO 1984, 265; [1979–85] E.P.O.R.: C: 715.

This kind of invention is outside the mechanism of the problem-and-solution approach to the assessment of inventive step (see paragraphs 12–04 *et seq.*), since the problem cannot be identified without hindsight.

Thus, the claimed subject-matter is inventive in a case where "the perception of the problem has to be considered as being the main contribution to the inventive merits ..."(T225/84[129]).

> "the perception of the problem has to be considered as being the main contribution to the inventive merits ..." (T225/84[130]).

On the other hand:

> "The posing of a new problem does not represent a contribution to the inventive merits of the solution if it could have been posed by the average person skilled in the art. Such is the case where a problem consists solely of eliminating deficiencies in an object which comes to light when it is in use" (T109/82[131]).

Of course, problems which are no more than obvious *desiderata* in a given situation cannot contribute to inventiveness. The assessment of whether or not the discovery of a particular problem is inventive is carried out against the background that "the elimination of deficiencies and achievement of improvements is a constant preoccupation in technical circles" and that "the overcoming of drawbacks and the achievement of improvements resulting therefrom must be considered as the normal task of the skilled person" (T195/84[132]).

(b) Analogy processes

Since claims to chemical products have in the past not been accepted in **12–49** some Contracting States pursuant to reservation under Article 167 EPC (see paragraph 13–26), such products are sometimes protected by claims to an "analogy process," *i.e.* defining a known process for producing the new product. Thus "analogy processes are patentable in so far as they provide a novel and inventive product" because:

> "the character of the product, including its novelty and obviousness in the light of the state of the art, has a decisive role in the assessment of the inventive step for the purpose. The effect of the process manifests itself in the result, *i.e.* in the product ..." (T119/82[133]).

The reverse is also true: an analogy process leading to a known or obvious product is normally regarded as not inventive.

[129] T225/84 BOEING/Spoiler device [1986] E.P.O.R. 263.
[130] Ibid.
[131] T109/82 BOSCH/Hearing aid O.J. EPO 1984, 473; [1979–85] E.P.O.R.: B: 539.
[132] T195/84 BOEING/General technical knowledge O.J. EPO 1986, 121; [1986] E.P.O.R. 190.
[133] T119/82 EXXON/Gelation O.J. EPO 1984, 217; [1979–85] E.P.O.R.: B: 566.

However:

"A product which can be envisaged as such with all the characteristics determining its identity including its properties in use, i.e. an otherwise obvious entity, may become obvious and claimable as such, if there is no known way or applicable (analogy) method in the art to make it and the claimed methods for its preparation are the first to achieve this in an inventive manner" (T595/90[134]).

(c) Chemical intermediates

12–50 (1) If a new intermediate product is prepared in the course of an inventive process for the production of a known end-product, such intermediate product may itself be inventive and may therefore be the subject of a separate claim.
Thus:

"'the process effect' will also support the inventive step for the intermediates themselves, without which the advantageous complete process is not conceivable ... new chemical intermediates still satisfy the patentability criterion of inventive step if their being made available opens the way to a new chemical process for preparing known and desired end products, itself involving an inventive step" (T22/82[135]).

"A new chemical intermediate product is not inventive merely because it is prepared in the course of an inventive multi-stage process and is further processed to a known end product. Such a product is however at any rate patentable when its further processing is inventive" (T163/84[136]).

12–51 (2) If a new intermediate product is prepared in the course of a non-inventive process for the preparation of a new and inventive, end-product (*i.e.* an "analogy process"—see paragraph 12–49), such intermediate product may itself be inventive (and may therefore be the subject of a separate claim) if it provides a structural contribution to the subsequent end-product. However, such an intermediate is not unconditionally inventive, "*i.e.* not without taking the state of the art into consideration". The state of the art in relation to intermediates may be found in two different areas, namely "close to the intermediate" and "close to the product" prior art (T65/82[137]). In other words "claimed intermediates must themselves be based on an inventive step to be patentable". For

[134] T595/90 KAWASAKI STEEL/Grain-oriented silicon sheet O.J. EPO 1994, 695; [1995] E.P.O.R. 36.
[135] T22/82 BASF/Bis-epoxy ethers O.J. EPO 1982, 341; [1979–85] E.P.O.R.: B: 414.
[136] T163/84 BAYER/Acetophenone derivatives O.J. EPO 1987, 301; [1987] E.P.O.R. 284.
[137] T65/82 BAYER/Cyctopropane O.J. EPO 1983, 327; [1979–85] E.P.O.R.: B: 484.

example in a case where the subsequent end-products are either not novel or not inventive, then:

> "The superior effect of subsequent products which are neither novel nor inventive is not sufficient to render the intermediates inventive" (T18/88[138]).

(3) In general, therefore: **12–52**

> "The same criteria which are generally decisive for determining whether the preparation of a new chemical substance is to be regarded as inventive should in principle also be applied when the substance in question is an intermediate. Here the sole determining factor is whether or not its preparation enhances the art in a non-obvious way.
>
> An intermediate intended for the preparation of a known end product is deemed to be inventive if its preparation takes place in connection with inventive preparation or inventive further processing, or in the course of an inventive complete process" (T648/88[139]).

Thus:

> "it can no longer matter whether the preparation of the said intermediate resulting in that enhancement occurred in connection with its inventive manner of preparation, or within the scope of an inventive complete process for preparing the end product" (T648/88[140]).

(d) Novel further use of known product: technical link with previous use

If a claimed invention is based upon a further use of a known compound, **12–52a** and such further use was novel because the previous known use did not disclose the further use (as for example in T59/87[141]: see Chapter 11 at paragraph 11–100), such further use "will yet lack inventive step if the prior art indicates a well-established link between the earlier and later uses" (T112/92[142]).

Thus if a prior document disclosed the use of a substance as a thickening agent for emulsions, and if it was part of the common general knowledge that a substance which acted as a thickener for emulsions would be likely also to be effective as a stabiliser, such a technical link would establish a

---

[138] T18/88 *DOW/Pyrimidines* O.J. EPO 1092, 107; [1992] E.P.O.R. 184.
[139] T648/88 *BASF/(R,R,R)-alpha-toco-pherol* O.J. EPO 1991, 292; [1991] E.P.O.R. 305.
[140] *Ibid.*
[141] T59/87 *MOBIL OIL IV/Friction reducing additive* O.J. EPO 1991, 561; [1990] E.P.O.R. 514.
[142] T112/92 *MARS II/Glucomannan* O.J. EPO 1994, 192; [1994] E.P.O.R. 249.

lack of inventive step in the use of such a substance as an emulsion stabiliser (T112/92[143]).

F. Comparison with United Kingdom Law

12–53 There are many differences in practice between the assessment of inventive step by the Patent Office and courts of the United Kingdom and by the Boards of Appeal.

Although the wording of section 3 of the 1977 U.K. Act[144] is virtually the same as Article 56 EPC, and is "framed so as to have, as nearly as practicable, the same effect" by virtue of section 130(7) of the 1977 U.K. Act, there is no Rule in the United Kingdom corresponding to Rule 27(1)(d) EPC, which forms a legislative basis for the problem-and-solution approach to the assessment of inventive step within the Boards of Appeal, as discussed in paragraph 12–04 above. The problem-and-solution approach discussed in the preceding sections is not applied as such in the United Kingdom.

There is also a much greater willingness within the EPO, both at first instance and at Board of Appeal level, to combine teachings from different documents, on the basis that this is what a skilled person would have done when faced with the objective problem to be solved (see paragraph 12–24 above): in the United Kingdom such "mosaicing" of prior documents rarely provides the basis for a finding of lack of inventive step.

12–54 Within the United Kingdom the normal practice is to base an obviousness attack on a particular prior document in combination with evidence of the "common general knowledge" in the art. In oppositions before the EPO, direct evidence of such common general knowledge is rarely filed.

As mentioned in paragraphs 12–44 *et seq.* above, so-called "secondary indicia" in connection with inventive step do not feature very often in decisions of the Boards of Appeal; in contrast, matters such as commercial success often play a major part in the assessment of inventive step in the courts in the United Kingdom. Especially as regards commercial success, this distinction may be partly because, in the United Kingdom, the validity of a patent is commonly assessed in the context of an infringement action at a relatively late stage in the life of a patent, and normally only commercially successful inventions merit the expense of an infringement action, whereas opposition proceedings before the EPO take place immediately after grant.

In addition, the assessment of inventive step within the EPO, including the Board of Appeal, is as a generality more technically based than in the corresponding assessment in the United Kingdom. This no doubt partly derives from the fact that every Technical Board of Appeal includes a majority of technically qualified members (see Chapter 4 at paragraph

[143] *Ibid.*
[144] See Appendix 21.

4–17), who have considerable expertise in the specific technology of the case.

Cases Referred to in Chapter 12

Board of Appeal Decisions

T1/80	BAYER/Carbonless copying paper O.J. EPO 1981, 206; [1979–85] E.P.O.R.: B: 250.
T6/80	MAN/Intermediate layer for reflector O.J. EPO 1981, 434; [1979–85] E.P.O.R.: B: 265.
T1/81	AECI/Thermoplastics sockets O.J. EPO 1981, 439; [1979–85] E.P.O.R.: B: 273.
T2/81	MOBAY/Methylenebis (phenyl isocyanate) O.J. EPO 1982, 394; [1979–85] E.P.O.R.: B: 280.
T5/81	SOLVAY/Production of hollow thermoplastic objects O.J. EPO 1982, 249; [1979–85] E.P.O.R.: B: 287.
T15/81	KRAFTWERK UNION/Eddy-current testing device O.J. EPO 1982, 2; [1979–85] E.P.O.R.: B: 316.
T18/81	SOLVAY/Olefine polymers O.J. EPO 1985, 166.
T19/81	RÖHM/Film coating O.J. EPO 1982, 51; [1979–85] E.P.O.R.: B: 330.
T20/81	SHELL/Amyloxybenzaldehydes O.J. EPO 1982, 217; [1979–85] E.P.O.R.: B: 335.
T21/81	ALLEN-BRADLEY/Electromagnetically operated switch O.J. EPO 1983, 15; [1979–85] E.P.O.R.: B: 342.
T22/81	LUCAS/Ignition system O.J. EPO 1983, 226; [1979–85] E.P.O.R.: B: 348.
T24/81	BASF/Metal refining O.J. EPO 1983, 133; [1979–85] E.P.O.R.: B: 354.
T26/81	ICI/Containers O.J. EPO 1982, 211; [1979–85] E.P.O.R.: B: 362.
T32/81	FIVES-CAIL BABCOCK/Cleaning apparatus for conveyor belt O.J. EPO 1982, 225; [1979–85] E.P.O.R.: B: 377.
T22/82	BASF/Bis-epoxy ethers O.J. EPO 1982, 341; [1979–85] E.P.O.R.: B: 414.
T37/82	SIEMENS/Low-tension switch O.J. EPO 1984, 71; [1979–85] E.P.O.R.: B: 437.
T39/82	AUER-SOG/Light reflecting slats O.J. EPO 1982, 419; [1979–85] E.P.O.R.: B: 441.
T65/82	BAYER/Cyctopropane O.J. EPO 1983, 327; [1979–85] E.P.O.R.: B: 484.
T109/82	BOSCH/Hearing aid, O.J. EPO 1984, 473; [1979–85] E.P.O.R.: B: 539.
T113/82	IBM/Recording apparatus O.J. EPO 1984, 10; [1979–85] E.P.O.R.: B: 553.
T119/82	EXXON/Gelation O.J. EPO 1984, 217; [1979–85] E.P.O.R.: B: 566.

T181/82   CIBA-GEIGY/Spiro compounds O.J. EPO 1984, 401; [1979–85]
E.P.O.R.: C: 672.

T184/82   MOBIL/Poly (p-methylstyrene) articles O.J. EPO 1984, 261;
[1979–85] E.P.O.R.: C: 690.

T191/82   FIBRE-CHEM/Re-establishment of rights O.J. EPO 1985, 189;
[1975–85] E.P.O.R.: C: 701.

T192/82   BAYER/Moulding compositions O.J. EPO 1984, 415;
[1979–85] E.P.O.R.: C: 705.

T2/83   RIDER/Simethicone tablet O.J. EPO 1984, 265; [1979–85]
E.P.O.R.: C: 715.

T4/83   EXXON/Purification of sulphuric acids O.J. EPO 1983, 498;
[1979–85] E.P.O.R.: C: 721.

T20/83   CIBA-GEIGY/Benzothiopyran derivatives O.J. EPO 1983, 419;
[1979–85] E.P.O.R.: C: 746.

T69/83   BAYER/Thermoplastic moulding O.J. EPO 1984, 357;
[1979–85] E.P.O.R.: C: 771.

T164/83   EISAI/Antihistamines O.J. EPO 1987, 149; [1987] E.P.O.R. 205.

T206/83   ICI/Pyridine herbicides O.J. EPO 1987, 5; [1986] E.P.O.R. 232.

T13/84   SPERRY/Reformulation of the problem O.J. EPO 1986, 253;
[1986] E.P.O.R. 289.

T38/84   STAMICARBON/Oxidation of toluene O.J. EPO 1984, 368;
[1979–85] E.P.O.R.: C: 931.

T57/84   BAYER/Tolylfluanid O.J. EPO 1987, 53; [1987] E.P.O.R. 131.

T106/84   MICHAELSEN/Packing machine O.J. EPO 1985, 132;
[1979–85] E.P.O.R.: C: 959.

T142/84   BRITAX/Inventive step O.J. EPO 1987, 112; [1987] E.P.O.R.
148.

T163/84   BAYER/Acetophenone derivatives O.J. EPO 1987, 301; [1987]
E.P.O.R. 284.

T175/84   KABELMETAL/Combination claim O.J. EPO 1989, 71; [1989]
E.P.O.R. 181.

T176/84   MÖBIUS/Pencil sharpener O.J. EPO 1986, 50; [1986] E.P.O.R.
117.

T195/84   BOEING/General technical knowledge O.J. EPO 1986, 121;
[1986] E.P.O.R. 190.

T225/84   BOEING/Spoiler device [1986] E.P.O.R. 263.

T265/84   ALLIED/Cobalt foils [1987] E.P.O.R. 193.

T270/84   ICI/Fusecord [1987] E.P.O.R. 357.

T271/84   AIR PRODUCTS/Removal of hydrogen sulphide and
carbonyl sulphide, O.J. EPO 1987, 405; [1987] E.P.O.R. 23.

T99/85   BOEHRINGER/Diagnostic agent O.J. EPO 1987, 413; [1987]
E.P.O.R. 337.

T155/85   PHILLIPS PETROLEUM/Passivation of catalyst O.J. EPO
1988, 87; [1988] E.P.O.R. 164.

T229/85   SCHMID/Etching process O.J. EPO 1987, 237; [1987] E.P.O.R.
279.

T248/85 BICC/Radiation processing O.J. EPO 1986, 261; [1986]
         E.P.O.R. 311.
T9/86   BAYER/Polyamide-6 O.J. EPO 1988, 12; [1988] E.P.O.R. 83.
T197/86 KODAK/Photographic couplers O.J. EPO 1989, 371; [1989]
         E.P.O.R. 395.
T254/86 SUMITOMO/Yellow dyes O.J. EPO 1989, 115; [1989] E.P.O.R.
         257.
T28/87   KERBER/Wire link bands O.J. EPO 1989, 383; [1989] E.P.O.R.
         377.
T59/87   MOBIL OIL IV/Friction reducing additive O.J. EPO 1991, 561;
         [1990] E.P.O.R. 514.
T141/87 BOSCH/Diagnostic test system for motor vehicles [1996]
         E.P.O.R. 570.
T157/87 KUBAT/Cellulose composites [1989] E.P.O.R. 221.
T18/88   DOW/Pyrimidines O.J. EPO 1992, 107; [1992] E.P.O.R. 184.
T267/88 FUJI/Photographic materials [1991] E.P.O.R. 168.
T390/88 KONISHIROKU/Photographic film [1990] E.P.O.R. 417.
T426/88 LUCAS INDUSTRIES/Combustion engine, O.J. EPO 1992,
         427; [1992] E.P.O.R. 458.
T648/88 BASF/(R,R,R)-Alpha-toco-pherol O.J. EPO 1991, 292; [1991]
         E.P.O.R. 301.
T69/89   SURGIKOS/Disinfection [1990] E.P.O.R. 632.
T99/89   BOSCH/Optical display March 5, 1991.
T130/89 KOMMERLING/Profile member O.J. EPO 1991, 514; [1992]
         E.P.O.R. 98.
T268/89 LATZKE/Magnetic plaster O.J. EPO 1994, 50.
T560/89 N.I. INDUSTRIES/Filler mass O.J. EPO 1992, 725; [1994]
         E.P.O.R. 120.
T424/90 December 11, 1991.
T513/90 JAPAN STYRENE/Foamed articles O.J. EPO 1994, 154; [1994]
         E.P.O.R. 129.
T595/90 KAWASAKI/Grain oriented silicon sheet O.J. EPO 1994, 695;
         [1995] E.P.O.R. 36.
T455/91 GENENTEEN/Expression in yeast O.J. EPO 1995, 684; [1996]
         E.P.O.R. 85.
T495/91 TARKETT PEGULAN/Floor covering July 20, 1993; [1995]
         E.P.O.R. 516.
T677/91 FINNEGAN/Mass selective ejection November 13, 1992.
T741/91 UENO/Bon-3-acid O.J. EPO 1993, 630; [1995] E.P.O.R. 533.
T112/92 MARS II/Glucomannan O.J. EPO 1994, 192.
T164/92 ROBERT BOSCH/Electronic computer components O.J. EPO
         1995, 305; [1995] E.P.O.R. 585.
T334/92 EISAI/Benzodioxane derivatives March 23, 1994.
T465/92 ALCAN/Aluminium alloys O.J. EPO 1996, 32; [1995] E.P.O.R.
         501.
T939/92 AGREVO/Triazoles O.J. EPO 1996, 309; [1996] E.P.O.R. 171.
T964/92 EISAI/Benzodioxanes [1997] E.P.O.R. 201.

T1002/92 PETTERSON/Queueing system O.J. EPO 1995, 605; [1996] E.P.O.R. 1.

T39/93 ALLIED COLLOIDS/Polymer powders O.J. EPO 1997, 134; [1997] E.P.O.R. 347.

T422/93 JALON/Luminescent security fibres O.J. EPO 1997, 24; [1999] E.P.O.R. 486.

T936/96 KANEGAFUCHI/Absorbent for LDL June 11, 1999.

CHAPTER 13

THE EXTENT OF PROTECTION

Article 69 EPC

Contents

All references are to paragraph numbers

Cases Referred to in Chapter 13

A. Historical Background and its Effect Upon Claim Drafting

(1) Protection under national patents

Prior to the entry into force of the EPC, there was no uniformity of 13–01 approach in Europe to the determination of the extent of protection which was conferred by a national patent and thus to the determination of what constituted infringement of such a patent. Each country developed and followed its own jurisprudence on such matters, although there were spheres of influence within neighbouring countries and countries with common legal backgrounds. Thus, national patents with essentially the same text describing and claiming the same invention could confer a markedly different extent of protection upon the patentee, with respect to the same alleged infringement.

In particular, the role played by the wording of the claims of a patent in such determination varied widely from country to country.

At one extreme, English law emphasised the necessity of "claims defining the scope of the invention claimed". The requirement for such a definition was interpreted by the courts in the sense that:

> "The function of the claims is to define clearly and with precision the monopoly claimed, so that others may know the exact boundaries of the area within which they will be trespassers ... What is not claimed is disclaimed ... the forbidden field must be found in the language of the claims and not elsewhere" (*EMI v. Lissen*).[1]

In other words, the patentee was required to formulate in precise language in the claims of his patent application a legal definition which would thereafter be decisive for the determination of infringement. The wording was all important. The nature of the inventive step underlying the claimed invention was relatively unimportant.

At the other extreme, in countries such as Holland, Germany and 13–02 Switzerland, the scope of protection conferred by a national patent was commonly determined in accordance with what was considered by a court to be the essence of the patented invention, that is, the general inventive concept disclosed in the patent as a whole. Little attention was focused upon the wording of the claims as such. The scope of the inventive concept to be protected could often be expanded to the maximum extent allowable having regard to the prior art, regardlness of the precise way in which the invention was described and claimed.

An intermediate position was adopted in particular by the Nordic countries (Denmark, Finland, Norway and Sweden), where their Patent Acts[2] provided that "the scope of protection of a patent ... is dependent on

---

[1] (1939) 56 R.P.C. 23.
[2] Danish, Finnish, Norwegian and Swedish Patent Acts, 1968, s.39.

the claims", and that "the description may be referred to for interpreting the claims".

These different approaches to the determination of the extent of protection reflect the basic conflict which is inherent in any patent system, between the idea of suitably protecting an inventor in accordance with the real breadth of his technical advance, and the idea of promoting freedom of competition between commercial enterprises, with all temporary monopolies from patent protection being clearly defined in advance in the interest of legal certainty.

(2) Traditional claim drafting in Contracting States

13–03 These different national approaches to the determination of protection necessarily influenced the way in which patent specifications were drafted in different countries.

> "Prior to the entry into force of the EPC in 1978, the role of patent claims in determining the protection conferred by a patent had developed differently within the national patent systems of the countries that are now Contracting States. Such different development reflected somewhat different national philosophies underlying the concept of patent protection.
>
> In particular, the extent to which the wording of the claims determined the scope of protection varied considerably from country to country, and this factor significantly affected drafting practice.
>
> In some countries, in particular Germany, in practice the protection conferred by a patent depended more upon what was perceived to be the inventor's contribution to the art, as disclosed in the patent, by way of the general inventive concept, than upon the wording of the claims. In other countries, in particular the United Kingdom, the precise wording of the claims were regarded as crucial, because the claims were required to define the boundary between what was protected and what was not, for purposes of legal certainty.
>
> The manner in which claims were drafted naturally developed differently in the different countries, depending upon the relative importance of their function. Clearly in a country such as the United Kingdom, the wording of a claim had to provide a much more precise definition of what was sought to be protected than in countries such as Germany, where a statement of the essence of the inventive concept was more appropriate.
>
> Despite the entry into force of the EPC, European patent applications originating the different Contracting States have continued commonly to include claims drafted in accordance with the traditional practices of such Contracting States discussed above.
>
> However, the requirements for drafting and amending claims in respect of inventions which are the subject of European patent applications and patents, and the patentability of such inventions, are

all matters which must be decided upon the basis of the law under the EPC. The function of the claims is central to the operation of the European patent system" (G2, 6/88)[3].

The drafting of claims in individual Contracting States is also to some extent affected by the fact that the extent of the protection conferred by European patents is determined by national courts of the Contracting States, and the judges of such national courts are primarily trained in accordance with national practice, and consequently tend to interpret claims in accordance with such national practice, as will be seen in the remainder of this chapter.

Thus the legacy from the different national backgrounds is still working its way through the current European patent system.

B. The Interpretation of Claims under the EPC

The EPC contains a set of provisions (Article 84 and Rule 29(1) EPC in **13–04** conjunction with Article 69 EPC and its Protocol) which reflect the central importance of the claims of a European patent application or patent for determining the extent of protection conferred by it (see also Chapter 7 at paragraph 7–03).

Determination of the extent of protection has to be carried out in accordance with Article 69(1) EPC and its Protocol. The main role of the claims is emphasised in the first sentence of Article 69(1) EPC. The subsidiary role of the description and drawings is set out in the second sentence.

The nature of the relationship between the claims on the one hand, and the description and drawings on the other hand, is further explained in the Protocol to Article 69 EPC, which is an integral part of the EPC, and which provides a guide to the manner in which the technical features of the claim are to be interpreted. The background to and purpose of this Protocol are as follows:

> "The Protocol was adopted by the Contracting States as an integral part of the EPC in order to provide a mechanism for harmonisation of the various national approaches to the drafting and interpretation of claims discussed in paragraph 2.1 above. The central role of the claims under the EPC would clearly be undermined if the protection and consequently the rights conferred within individual designated Contracting States varied widely as a result of purely national traditions of claim interpretation: and the Protocol was added to the EPC as a supplement primarily directed to providing an intermediate method of interpretion of claims of European patents throughout their life, as a compromise between the various national approaches to

---

[3] G2, 6/88 *MOBIL OIL/BAYER/Friction reducing additive* O.J. EPO 1990, 93, 114; [1990] E.P.O.R. 73, 257.

interpretation and determination of the protection conferred ('... so as to combine a fair protection for the patentee with a reasonable degree of certainty for third parties').

The object of the Protocol is clearly to avoid too much emphasis on the literal wording of the claims when considered in isolation from the remainder of the text of the patent in which they appear; and also to avoid too much emphasis upon the general inventive concept disclosed in the text of the patent as compared to the relevant prior art, without sufficient regard also to the wording of the claims as a means of definition" (G2, 6/88[3a]).

Thus, the Protocol represents an attempt to set out an intermediate approach to determination of the extent of protection conferred, in particular between what have been traditionally regarded as the opposite extremes of Germany and the United Kingdom.

13–04A   According to the proposed revision of the EPC, the Protocol to Article 69 EPC ("Extent of protection") will be amended by the addition of a new Article 2 reading as follows:

> "Article 2
> Equivalents
> For the purpose of determining the extent of protection conferred by a European patent, due account shall be taken of any element which is equivalent to an element specified in the claims."

13–05   This shift in emphasis as regards German law has been clearly recognised in decisions of the German Federal Court of Justice. For example, in its Decision "*Formstein*"[4] in an infringement action, the Federal Court of Justice corrected the legal approach of the *Oberlandgericht* (Court of Appeal) concerning the question whether the defendant had made an equivalent use of the claimed invention, stating that:

> "[the legal reasons of the Court of Appeal] are based on legal error ...
> the extent of the protection conferred by a patent is to be determined in accordance ... [with] the Patent Law 1981. In contrast to the legal situation until 1978, the claims are not now merely the starting point but rather the essential basis for determining the extent of protection. Under ... the Patent Law 1981, the terms of the claims have to be determined by interpretation, taking the description and drawings into consideration. As the Protocol ... shows, the interpretation does not only serve the purpose of resolving an ambiguity found in the claims but also of clarifying the technical terms used in the claims as well as the limits and bounds of the invention described therein. ...
> the Federal Government referred to this Protocol and emphasised that the principles expressed therein should also be applicable under

---

[3a] *Ibid.*

[1] *Formstein* (*Moulded Curbstone* BGH Case No. XZ R28/85, O.J. EPO 1987, 551.

German law ...; only in this way could the goal of as uniform a determination as possible of the extent of protection of patents in Europe, aimed at by the introduction of the new provision, be achieved."

C. The Relationship Between the Extent of Protection and Infringement

This relationship is as follows: 13–06

"... the protection conferred by a patent is to be determined by interpretation of the terms of the claims, and the rights of the patent proprietor flow from the protection which is conferred. There is a clear distinction between the protection which is conferred and the rights which are conferred by a European patent, however. The protection conferred by a patent is determined by the terms of the claims (Article 69(1) EPC), and in particular by the categories of such claims and their technical features. In this connection, Article 69 EPC and its Protocol are to be applied, both in proceedings before the EPO and in proceedings within the Contracting States, whenever it is necessary to determine the protection which is conferred.

In contrast, the rights conferred on the proprietor of a European patent (Article 64(1) EPC) are the legal rights which the law of a designated Contracting State may confer upon the proprietor, for example, as regards what acts of third parties constitute infringement of the patent, and as regards the remedies which are available in respect of any infringement.

In other words, in general terms, determination of the 'extent of the protection conferred' by a patent under Article 69(1) EPC is a determination of *what* is protected, in terms of category plus technical features; whereas the 'rights conferred' by a patent are a matter solely for the designated Contracting States, and are related to *how* such subject-matter is protected" (G2, 6/88[5]).

Attention must also be drawn to Article 64(3) EPC: "Any infringement of a European patent shall be dealt with by national law."

D. The Interpretation of Claims within the EPO

During examination and opposition proceedings within the EPO, claims 13–07
are necessarily constantly interpreted in the context of determination of patentability, in particular novelty and inventive step, in accordance with Article 69 EPC and its Protocol. The importance of the relationship

---

[5] G2, 6/88 *MOBIL OIL/BAYER/Friction reducing additive* O.J. EPO 1990, 93, 114; [1990] E.P.O.R. 73, 257.

between description and claims has also been recognised with regard to the requirement of support in Article 84 EPC.
Thus:

> "the relationship between the description and the claims is important, because, *inter alia*, the description shall be used to interpret the claims (Article 69(1) EPC) and because the claims shall be supported by the description (Article 84 EPC). The Protocol on the interpretation of Article 69 EPC underlines the significance of the description when the extent of protection conferred by a European patent is being determined. It is in accordance with the expressed policy of maintaining a just balance between a fair protection for the patentee and a reasonable degree of certainty for third parties, that the European Patent Office must ensure that applicants comply properly with the requirements of *inter alia* Rule 27 EPC" (T11/82[6]; see also T150/85[7]).

13–08   For example, in the context of determining inventive step:

> "If the description on its proper interpretation specifies a feature to be an overriding requirement of the invention, following Article 69 EPC and its Protocol the claims may be interpreted as requiring this as an essential feature, even though the wording of the claims when read in isolation does not specifically require such a feature" (T416/87[8]).

The idea that determination "of the extent of protection conferred in accordance with Article 69 EPC and the relevant Protocol is not a matter for the examining opposition and appeal bodies of the EPO" (T175/84[9]) is clearly incorrect. On the contrary, determination of the scope of a claim and thus the extent of protection conferred is always determined in accordance with the principles of Article 69 EPC and its Protocol, whenever and in whatever context it may be necessary to determine such scope (see for example G2, 6/88[10]).

E. The Interpretation of Claims in the United Kingdom

13–09   Prior to 1978 (under the 1949 U.K. Act), the leading case concerning the question of interpretation of a patent in the context of infringement was *Catnic Components Ltd v. Hill and Smith Ltd ("Catnic")*,[11] where the principle is stated that:

[6] T11/82 *LANSING BAGNALL/Control circuit* O.J. EPO 1983, 479; [1979–85] E.P.O.R.: B: 385.
[7] T150/85 *ROMERO-SIERRA* August 20, 1987.
[8] T416/87 *JSR/Block copolymer* O.J. EPO 1990, 415; [1991] E.P.O.R. 25.
[9] T175/84 *KABELMETAL/Combination claim* O.J. EPO 1989, 71; [1989] E.P.O.R. 181.
[10] G2, 6/88 *MOBIL OIL/BAYER/Friction reducing additive* O.J. EPO 1990, 93, 114; [1990] E.P.O.R. 73, 257.
[11] [1982] R.P.C. 183.

"A patent specification should be given a purposive construction rather than a purely literal one."

Under the 1977 U.K. Act, essentially the same approach is followed (see also *Anchor Building Products Ltd v. Redland Roof Tiles Ltd*,[12] *Kastner v. Rizla Ltd*[13]). Thus in *Improver Corporation v. Remington Consumer Products Ltd* ("*Improver*"),[14] with reference to Article 69 EPC (equivalent to section 125) and its Protocol it is stated that:

"So far as the development of English law is concerned, the latest decision is [*Catnic*[15]]. It seems ... that the well-known speech of Lord Diplock in that case correctly indicates the same approach to construction as is indicated in the Protocol."

Thus the traditional approach in English law to determination of the **13–10** extent of protection as represented in particular by the passage in *EMI v. Lissen*[16] quoted in paragraph 13–01 above is no longer to be applied. The current approach, therefore, is to follow the passage from the speech of Lord Diplock in *Catnic*[17] set out below:

"... a patent specification is a unilateral statement by the patentee, in words of his own choosing, addressed to those likely to have a practical interest in the subject-matter of the invention (*i.e.* 'skilled in the art'), by which he informs them what he claims to be the essential features of the new product or process for which the letters patent grant him a monopoly. It is those novel features only that he claims to be essential that constitute the so-called 'pith and marrow' of the claim. A patent specification should be given a purposive construction rather than a purely literal one derived from applying to it the kind of meticulous verbal analysis in which lawyers are too often tempted by their training to indulge. The question in each case is: whether persons with practical knowledge and experience of the kind of work in which the invention was intended to be used, would understand that strict compliance with a particular descriptive word or phrase appearing in a claim was intended by the patentee to be an essential requirement of the invention so that any variant would fall outside the monopoly claimed, even though it could have no material effect upon the way the invention worked.

The question, of course, does not arise where the variant would in fact have a material effect upon the way the invention worked. Nor does it arise unless at the date of publication of the specification it

---

[12] [1990] R.P.C. 283.
[13] [1995] R.P.C. 585, CA.
[14] [1989] R.P.C. 69.
[15] [1982] R.P.C. 183.
[16] [1939] 56 R.P.C. 23.
[17] [1982] R.P.C. 183.

would be obvious to the informed reader that this was so. Where it is not obvious, in the light of the then-existing knowledge, the reader is entitled to assume that the patentee thought at the time of the specification that he had good reason for limiting his monopoly so strictly and had intended to do so, even though subsequent work by him or others in the field of the invention might show the limitation to have been unnecessary. It is to be answered in the negative only when it would be apparent to any reader skilled in the art that a particular descriptive word or phrase used in a claim cannot have been intended by a patentee, who was also skilled in the art, to exclude minor variants which, to the knowledge of both him and the reades to whom the patent was addressed, could have no material effect upon the way in which the invention worked."

F. The Interpretation of Claims in Germany

13–11 The above approach to the interpretation of claims in the United Kingdom can be compared with that of the German Federal Court of Justice in *Formstein*[18]:

"In accordance with this Protocol (to Article 69 EPC) the extent of the protection conferred by a patent is not confined to what is defined by the strict literal meaning of the wording used in the claims. This opens the way for extending the scope of protection beyond the wording of the claim to encompass modifications of the invention as claimed. The extension of the scope of protection beyond the wording of the claim to include equivalent embodiments, corresponds in the opinion of this Court, to the intention of the Member States of the EPC, although significant differences regarding both the approach of determining the extent of protection of patents and the scope of the protection granted, still exist.

The extent of protection of a patent filed after January 1, 1978, is determined as regards the equivalent use of the invention, by the terms of the claims to be ascertained by interpretation. What must be considered is the scope of the invention as it may be recognised by a person skilled in the art. It has to be examined whether a person skilled in the art, based on the invention as claimed, is able to solve the problem solved by the invention as claimed with equivalent means, *i.e.* to achieve the desired result with different means also leading to that result. Means which the average person skilled in the art, due to his knowledge and skill and based on considerations oriented on the invention as claimed, can identify as being equivalent are generally covered by the extent of the protection conferred by the patent. This is required by the goal of fair remuneration for the inventor under consideration of the aspect of legal certainty."

[18] *Formstein/Moulded curbstone* BGH Case No. XZ R28/85, O.J. EPO 1987, 551; [1991] R.P.C. 597.

While there are considerable similarities between the statements in *Catnic*[19] and *Formstein*,[20] there is perhaps a greater freedom given to the skilled person (*i.e.* the Court's view of what the skilled person would think) in *Formstein* than in *Catnic*. This reflects the traditional approaches in Germany as compared to the United Kingdom: broadly speaking, in Germany a court is more concerned to determine objectively the extent of protection which it thinks the patentee ought to have, having regard to what has actually been invented, while in the United Kingdom a court is more concerned to determine objectively the extent of protection which it thinks the patentee has told the public that he wants, having regard to what he thought he had invented when the patent was applied for.

The Protocol aims for a position somewhere in between these two approaches.

G. The Interpretation of Claims in National Infringement Proceedings—A Comparative Example

An examination of the judgments delivered by national courts in Germany, the United Kingdom, Hong Kong and the Netherlands in parallel infringement cases concerning the same European patent designating *inter alia* Germany, the Netherlands and the United Kingdom (the relevant United Kingdom designated patent being registered in Hong Kong), and the same allegedly infringing device, provides some further illustration of the different national approaches still existing in national courts concerning the interpretation of claims for the purpose of determining the extent of protection conferred by a patent. The patent proprietor and plaintiff was the same in each case: *i.e.* Improver Corporation. The patent was concerned with an electrically driven mechanical depilatory device for removing unwanted human hair from the body by the action of a helical spring. The allegedly infringing device obtains the same result by the mechanical action of an arcuate rubber roll provided with radial slits.

13–12

Applications for interlocutory injunctions or summary judgment were made in all of the above jurisdictions, with results that varied from country to country and between first and second instances. Since the legal considerations involved in the determination of such applications go beyond mere determination of the extent of protection of the patent, the judgments delivered pursuant to these applications are only of limited relevance. It is worth pointing out, however, that in its judgment on the interlocutory application in *Improver Corporation v. Remington Consumer Products Ltd*[21] the United Kingdom Court of Appeal specifically endorsed the relevant passages of *Catnic* (see paragraph 13–10 above), while in the interlocutory judgments of the courts of both first and second instance in

[19] *Catnic Components Ltd v. Hill and Smith Ltd* [1982] R.P.C. 183.
[20] *Formstein/Moulded curbstone BGH* Case No. XZ R28/85, O.J. EPO 1987, 551; [1991] R.P.C. 597.
[21] [1989] R.P.C. 69.

581

Düsseldorf, Germany, (*Improver Corporation v. Remington Products Inc.*[22]), reliance was placed upon the relevant passages in *Formstein* (see paragraph 13–11 above).

In opposition proceedings before the EPO, the Opposition Division revoked the European patent on the ground of lack of inventive step, but the Board of Appeal set aside such decision and maintained the patent as granted (T754/89[23]).

(1) The judgments in the infringement actions

13–13 (1) In the first instance trial of the case in Germany,[24] the Court held that the patent had been infringed. In reaching this conclusion the Court followed the legal considerations set out in the *Formstein*[25] judgment and held that a skilled person could arrive at the infringing device from consideration of the claims, description and drawings of the patent using his technical knowledge. It was stated that

> "To this end, merely the finding was necessary that, in the context of the patent claim, the helical spring stands for an arcuate cylindrical body in which wedge-shaped gaps are opened and closed during the rotational motion, and the reflection that such a body is also formed by a rubber roll provided with cuts. This reflection was possible for the expert without an inventive effort being necessary."

13–14 (2) In the first instance trial of the case before the Patents Court in the United Kingdom,[26] the Court considered that the passages previously quoted from the *Catnic* judgment were binding upon it, having regard in particular to the judgment of the Court of Appeal in *Anchor Building Products*[27] (paragraph 13–09 above).

With reference to a passage in the description of the patent (the "equivalent clause") including the statement that "all variations which come within the meaning and range of equivalency of the claims are therefore intended to be embraced therein", the Court held that this passage meant no more than that the claims must be interpreted in accordance with the *Catnic* judgment and the Protocol to Article 69 EPC.

The Court went on to hold that, so interpreted, the term "helical spring" in the claims of the patent could not reasonably be given a wide generic construction. A skilled reader of the patent:

> "would be entitled to think that the patentee had good reasons for limiting himself, as he obviously appeared to have done, to a helical coil. To derive a different meaning solely from the equivalent clause

---

[22] Judgments delivered July 19 and October 27, 1988, respectively.
[23] T754/89 *IMPROVER/Depilatory device* [1993] E.P.O.R. 153.
[24] Judgment delivered December 30, 1988.
[25] *Formstein/Moulded curbstone BGH case No. XZ R28/85* O.J. EPO 1987, 551; [1991] R.P.C. 597.
[26] Judgment delivered May 16, 1989.
[27] *Anchor Building Products Ltd v. Redland Roof Tiles Ltd* [1989] R.P.C. 69.

would ... be denying third parties that reasonable degree of certainty to which they are entitled under the Protocol."

(3) In the first instance trial of the case before the High Court in Hong **13–15** Kong,[28] the Court held that the patent had not been infringed. In its judgment the Court began by stating that:

"It is evident from a reading of the Protocol that what the negotiating parties have attempted to achieve is a balance between what was perceived to be the rather literal approach of the English courts on the one part and the more purposive or functional approach of some continental systems including the German one on the other part. I would hasten to add that it is not an entirely simple matter to attempt to reconcile these two approaches."

The Court considered that the *Catnic*[29] judgment was "entirely consistent with the Protocol", and it had no doubt that the United Kingdom Patents Court was right to follow closely the guidelines laid down in *Catnic*.
As to the German case, the Court stated that:

"On reading the German judgment[30] it is difficult not to gain the impression that the court was far more disposed to treat the patent specification merely as a guide than an English court would. There is also not much assistance as to how the court arrived at the conclusion it did. They gave no reason why they considered a rubber rod with slits would be the equivalent of a helical spring. One is driven to a conclusion that they were unduly pre-occupied with questions of function and had insufficient regard to the text of the specification.
I was also concerned as to the exact nature of the test they applied to determine what would have been either evident or obvious to 'a person skilled in the art'. It is even possible that they applied their own technical knowledge to the matter and reached a conclusion on a subjective basis."

(a) In the Netherlands, following a summary judgment at first instance **13–16** which ordered the defendant Remington not to infringe the European patent, a judgment of The Hague Court of Appeals[31] considered the principles which govern determination of infringement.
The Court held that the question of infringement should not be answered by first determining and formulating "the essence of the invention" (as had been contended by the defendant) On the contrary, while the essential aspects of the invention should not be disregarded, a court must:

[28] *Improver Corporation v. Raymond Industrial Ltd* [1990] F.S.R. 422.
[29] [1982] R.P.C. 183.
[30] Judgment delivered December 30, 1988.
[31] Judgment delivered February 20, 1992.

"(i) investigate the nature of operation and the function of the feature ... in the patent claim ... which the third party has replaced in its device ... and (ii) establish ... (the function of) that feature within the complex of the features in the claim. Subsequently ... having regard to the state of the art, it must be determined (a) to what extent the inventor is, in fairness, entitled to a certain measure of abstraction regarding the features described by him, and (b) to what extent this abstraction is not unfair towards third parties who are entitled to base their actions ... On the belief that these actions will not be retroactively prohibited."

13–17   As to (b), this "must be determined on the basis of what scope of protection an expert in the Netherlands should expect" this expectation being "based on earlier decisions by the Dutch courts". It was considered that such an approach "renders it more difficult to arrive at a uniform 'European scope of protection', but it does not violate the Protocol to Article 69 EPC".

An opinion of the Special Division of the Dutch Patent Office was regarded as an indication of "the view of Dutch experts on the patent's scope of protection". On the basis of this opinion, the "obvious mechanical equivalence" and the above mentioned considerations of fairness, the defendant's device was considered to fall within the scope of protection of the European patent.

(2) The different approaches to determining infringement

13–18   The different approaches to the determination of the extent of protection conferred by the patent in Germany and the Netherlands on the one hand, and in the United Kingdom and Hong Kong on the other hand, appear to reflect traditional national approaches, in spite of the fact that all three judgments are based directly upon Article 69 EPC and, more particularly, its Protocol. In particular, it seems that in the United Kingdom and Hong Kong judgments a greater emphasis is placed upon what the patentee must have intended the patent to cover (having regard especially to the wording of the claims): such a consideration is basic to the construction of any written document under English law. In contrast, in the German and Dutch judgments, no mention is made of what the patentee is presumed to have intended: determination of the extent of protection is governed to a major extent by consideration of the technical functional equivalence of the allegedly infringing device to the claimed device, from the point of view of the skilled reader of the patent.

(3) Future need for uniformity

13–19   As mentioned in the judgment in Hong Kong, reconciliation of the traditional literal approach of English Courts with the more functional approach of German Courts is "not an entirely simple matter". Nevertheless, while uniformity of result is obviously desirable, it can only be made more likely by a greater uniformity of legal approach than exists at present.

It remains to be seen how far the proposed revision of the EPC with **13–19A** respect to the Protocol to Article 69 EPC (see paragraph 13–04A above) will help to achieve greater uniformity.

H. The Extent of Protection of Products

1. Introduction

In connection with a product, at least three different kinds of invention **13–20** can be distinguished:

(a) a new process for making a known product;
(b) a new product as such;
(c) a new use for a known product.

The extent of the protection which may be conferred upon each of such kinds of invention is considered below.

The justifiable scope of protection for chemical inventions is always a more delicate matter when compared to other technologies, having regard to the possibility of generalising chemical inventions both as regards definition of technical features and as regards the technical effect achieved. Thus, the subsequent discussion is based upon a consideration of chemical inventions. However, the discussion is equally applicable to inventions concerning non-chemical products, and apparatus, so far as the underlying principles are concerned.

Each of the above kinds of invention require an appropriate extent of protection, so that the benefits of the invention in each case cannot unlawfully be taken by others, and investment in research is properly rewarded. The extent of protection conferred by a patent should correspond to the nature and scope of the invention which has been made. However, the protection of these different kinds of inventions in each case raises a different legal problem, as follows:

(a) The question here arises as to the extent to which the products of the new process are themselves protected, having regard to Article 64(2) EPC, which states that the protection conferred by a European patent for a process shall extend to "the products directly obtained by" such process.
(b) When a claimed invention is a new product as such it can be questioned whether the protection conferred is "absolute" or "purpose-limited" to the use of the product which has been described in the patent.

(c) The patentability of this kind of invention in both medical and non-medical cases has been confirmed by G5/83[32] and G2, 6/88[33] respectively, even when the mode of using the product is previously known (see Chapter 11 at paragraphs 11–82 *et seq.*). However, questions may arise as to whether a previously known use of a product could be held to infringe a subsequently granted European patent claiming a new use for that product.

These matters are discussed below.

2. Specific kinds of invention

(a) New process for making a known product

13–21 **(i) Article 64(2) EPC.** With such an invention, both the novelty and the inventive step reside primarily in the particular process described in the patent and defined in its claims, and there is no difficulty in drafting process claims to such a physical activity, which normally set out a starting material, one or more process steps and the final product. Patent protection for such subject-matter has been widely recognised internationally for many years.

However, an inventor of such a process does not only need protection against competing manufacturers who may carry out the new process. He also needs to protect the products which have been made by his new process, otherwise a competitor may manufacture the products by the patented process in a country where there is no patent, and sell the products where there are patents for the process, thus taking the commercial benefit of the invention. The need for such protection is implicitly recognised by Article 5 *quater* Paris. This Article was introduced into the Paris Convention during the Revision Conference at Lisbon in 1958. According to Bodenhausen,[34] the original proposal at the Conference was a stipulation that a patent for a process of manufacture would be infringed by the importation, sale or use of products made by such process in another country. This proposal was not accepted, however, and the final version of the Article is considerably weaker than the original proposal, and essentially leaves the nature of such product protection to the legislation of individual countries and groups of countries.

Article 64(2) EPC describes that "if the subject-matter of the European patent is a process, the protection conferred by the patent shall extend to the products directly obtained by such process". Similar provisions appear in the national laws of the Contracting States to the EPC.

13–22 In the EPO Article 64(2) EPC is interpreted as being directed only to a patent whose subject-matter is a process of manufacture of a product (and as not being directed to a patent whose subject-matter is the use of a

---

[32] G5/83 *EISAI/Second medical indication* O.J. EPO 1985, 64; [1979–85] E.P.O.R.: B: 241.
[33] G2, 6/88 *MOBIL OIL/BAYER/Friction reducing additive* O.J. EPO/1990, 93, 114; [1990] E.P.O.R. 73, 257.
[34] Bodenhausen, *Guide to the Application of the Paris Convention for the Protection of Industrial Property*, BIRPI, 1968.

process to achieve an effect, as in a "use" claim, for example) (G2, 6/88[35]). Such interpretation is clearly in line with Article 5 *quater* Paris, which specifically refers to "a patent protecting a process of manufacture of the said product".

As discussed in Chapter 11 at paragraph 11–79, the Boards of Appeal have refused to accept "product-by-process" claims in European patent applications whose inventive subject-matter is a process of manufacture for a known product, on the ground of lack of novelty.

Thus, European patents will not be granted including product-by-process claims, unless the product is itself patentable.

(ii) The extent of protection conferred by a process claim. For European 13–23 patents whose claimed subject-matter is a new process for making a known product, the extent of protection conferred by such a patent is determined by national courts having regard to Article 64(2) EPC and corresponding national provisions.

In this connection, the question arises in relation to Article 64(2) EPC, as to what is meant by the phrase "directly obtained by" a patented process. The particular meaning of that phrase will in individual cases determine the extent of protection conferred by a patent, and, therefore, what constitutes infringement. Under Article 64(3) EPC, "Any infringement of a European patent shall be dealt with by national law". Article 64(2)EPC was the model for Section 60(1) 1977 U.K. Act, which states that "where the invention is a process" there is infringement *inter alia* when a product is disposed of which was "obtained directly by means of that process".

In straightforward cases where the subject matter of an alleged infringement is the immediate end-product of the claimed process, no difficulty arises. The immediate end-product of the process is clearly "directly obtained by" the claimed process according to the natural meaning of these words, and consequently, protection extends to such end-product by operation of law under Article 64(2) EPC and the equivalent national provisions.

Thus: 13–24

> "The product obtained directly by means of a patented process was the product with which the process ended" (*Pioneer Electronics Capital Inc. v. Warner Music*[36]).
>
> Furthermore, if such immediate end product of a patented process is subjected to further processing, the product of such further processing may also infringe the patented process if there is no "loss of identity".

Thus:

> "The product obtained directly by means of a patented process [was the product with which the process ended; it] did not cease to be the

[35] G2/88 *MOBIL OIL/Friction reducing additive* O.J. EPO 1990, 93; [1990] E.P.O.R. 73. G6/88 *BAYER/Plant growth regulating agent* O.J. EPO 1990, 114; [1990] E.P.O.R. 257.
[36] [1997] R.P.C. 755, CA.

product so obtained if it was subjected to further processing which did not cause it to lose its identity, there being no such loss where it retained its essential characteristics." (*Pioneer Electronics Capital Inc. v. Warner Music*[36a]).

Such "loss of identity" test is derived from the relevant German authorities in interpretation of the German patent law, which has used the word "unmittelbar" (corresponding to "directly" in Article 64(2)EPC) since 1891. The relevant Dutch, Swiss, Danish and Austrian authorities have also adopted the "loss of identity" test, which can therefore be taken to represent the test adopted by European law. This test is one of fact and degree in each particular case.

The United Kingdom patent law prior to 1977 is of historical interest, but does not throw light upon the true construction of Section 60(1) 1977 U.K. Act. (*Pioneer Electronics Capital Inc. v. Warner Music*[37].)

(b) A new product per se

13–25 **(i) Historical background.** Until comparatively recently, it was unusual for European national patent laws to permit the inclusion in a patent of claims to a chemical product or substance *per se*. For example, in the United Kingdom, such claims were permitted up until 1919, but were not permitted between 1919 and 1949. In 1949, the possibility of including claims to chemical substances and products was reintroduced (but coupled with compulsory licence provisions in respect of patented food and medicines). In France, Germany and the Scandinavian countries, the possibility of patents includng claims to chemical products was introduced into their national laws for the first time during the late 1960s. From this time onwards, the trend in European countries was towards increasing protection for chemical products in general, including pharmaceutical products.

Furthermore, the Strasbourg Convention[38] (1963) (Chapter 1 at paragraphs 1–40 *et seq.*) provided in Article 12 for the possibility that each Contracting Party could temporarily reserve the right, for a limited period of 10 years from the entry into force of the Convention for that country, not to provide for the grant of patents in respect of food and pharmaceutical products as such. Only Italy and Switzerland made such reservations upon signature of the Convention. The provision of such a limited period for such reservations confirms the international acceptance within Europe of increasing patent protection for pharmaceutical products in particular.

13–26 The EPC (1973) permits the inclusion of claims to chemical products as such in European patents.

However, Article 167(2) EPC provides that each Contracting State may reserve the right (upon signature or ratification) to provide that European patents for chemical, pharmaceutical and food products as such may be ineffective or revocable under its national law, for a period of not more

---

[36a] *Ibid.*
[37] *Ibid.*
[38] Reproduced in full at Appendix 16.

than 10 years, subject to a possible five-year extension. A reservation by Austria in this respect expired in 1987 and similar reservations by Greece and Spain expired after extension in 1992. Such reservations apply to all European patent applications which designate a Contracting State having made such a reservation and which are filed before expiry of the reservation.

According to the proposed revision of the EPC, Article 167 EPC will be **13–26A** deleted. Reservations made when Article 167 EPC was in force would be effective for European patents granted on applications which were filed while the reservation was in force.

(ii) The extent of protection conferred by a product claim.   **13–27**
(1) The inventive step underlying such a claimed invention can be regarded (at least in part) as the bringing into existence of a substance or product that did not previously exist. It is assumed that the new product has useful properties: a totally useless product would be devoid of technical effect (and consequently lacking an inventive step).

As a matter of language, a claim to a product *per se* confers protection upon the product as such, however it is used. This is commonly referred to as "absolute protection".

Countries such as Germany, the United Kingdom and France have accepted such absolute protection for products at least since the late 1960s. In other countries, however, such as Sweden and Italy, product protection before 1978 was closely limited to the uses which were included in the claims or at least mentioned in the description.

Within the EPO:

> "It is generally accepted as a principle underlying the EPC that a patent which claims a physical entity *per se* confers absolute protection upon such physical entity; that is, wherever it exists and whatever its context (and therefore for all uses of such physical entity, whether known or unknown)" (G2, 6/88[39]).

It follows that, at least in proceedings before the EPO, the protection conferred by a European patent having claims to a product *per se* will be considered to extend to all uses of that product, whether or not such uses have been disclosed in the description of the patent. This is relevant, for example, to the determination of whether a proposed amendment violates Article 123(3) EPC (G2, 6/88[40]; and see Chapter 8 at paragraphs 8–65 *et seq.*).

(2) In countries which do not permit the filing of claims to a chemical **13–28** product *per se*, it is normal to claim a new product in terms of a process for making it. The process may be known in general terms, but the novelty and inventive step may lie in the use of a known process by analogy to produce the new product (see T119/82[41]).

---

[39] G2, 6/88 *MOBIL OIL/BAYER/Friction reducing additive* O.J. EPO 1990, 93, 114; [1990] E.P.O.R. 73, 257.
[40] *Ibid.*
[41] T119/82 *EXXON/Gelation* O.J. EPO 1984, 217; [1979–85] E.P.O.R.: B: 566.

(c) A new use of a known product

13–29   **(i) Background.** The development under the EPC of the possibility of patenting inventions concerning new uses of known products has been discussed in Chapter 11 at paragraphs 11–82 *et seq.* above). In summary, a first medical use of a known product is patentable by a product claim (Article 54(5) EPC); a second or further medical use of a known product is patentable by the "Swiss form of claim" (use of a product to manufacture a composition for the medical use: G5/83[42]; and a second or further non-medical use of a known product is patentable by a claim to the use of the product for the new purpose (G2, 6/88[43]). G5/83 and G2, 6/88 were both concerned with patents where a "statement of purpose" was included in the claims as such. As explained in G5/83, novelty in the Swiss form of claim is derived from the new medical use, so that the statement of purpose included in that form of claim is crucial to its patentability. Similarly, as explained in G2, 6/88, the statement of purpose in the claim, when coupled with the description of the technical effect underlying such purpose, affects the interpretation of the claim so as to include a functional technical feature reflecting the new use or purpose, and is, therefore, again decisive for patentability.

13–30   **(ii) The extent of protection conferred by a purpose-limited use claim.** The above method of interpretation of such claims not only determines the technical features of the claim for the purpose of determining novelty, but also necessarily determines the protection sought by the patentee, having regard to Article 84 and Rule 29(1) EPC, for the purpose of infringement proceedings in national courts.

In cases such as those discussed above, both in the medical and non-medical fields, protection is sought by the patentee for an invention where the only novel technical feature of the claimed invention is the ability of the claimed product to achieve a particular desired effect (A). The physical form of the product is the same as before. The product may have been previously known and used to achieve other particular desired effects (B, C, etc.), but the ability of the product to achieved effect (A) had not been made available to the public (Article 54 EPC), nor was it obvious (Article 56 EPC). In such circumstances, the Enlarged Board has recognised the justification for granting a European patent in respect of an inventive contribution to the art. Nevertheless, practical situations could arise where the proper extent of the rights of the patentee in enforcing such a European patent before a national court is not so easy to determine.

In particular, before the filing of a European patent, a person may have used the patented product for purposes other than that which is the subject of the European patent, and may, in the course of such use, have in fact also achieved the technical effect which is the basis of the European patent, without knowing it, and without making such effect "available to the

[42] G5/83 EISAI/Second medical indication O.J. EPO 1985, 64; [1979–85] E.P.O.R.: B: 241.
[43] G2, 6/88 MOBIL OIL/BAYER/Friction reducing additive O.J. EPO 1990, 93, 114; [1990] E.P.O.R. 73, 257.

public" and without, therefore, destroying its novelty under Article 54 EPC. A question to be considered is whether such a prior use would be an infringement of the European patent if continued after its grant.

As is recognised in G2, 6/88[44], Article 38 of the Community Patent Convention[45] refers to the possibility of national laws within Contracting States and the European Community providing vested rights, for example to continue to do acts which would otherwise infringe or lead to infringement of a patent and which were commenced before the filing of the patent. Thus, a person who has used the same product for a purpose other than that protected by the European patent before the filing thereof may acquire vested rights under national laws which protect him against an allegation of infringement.

So far as the United Kingdom is concerned, section 64 of the 1977 U.K. **13–31** Act[46] provides that if the alleged infringing acts have been commenced or prepared for before the filing date of the European patent, such acts may be continued and "shall not amount to infringement of the patent concerned".

In cases where section 64 is not applicable, if a document such as a published patent discloses a first use of a product, a question could arise as to whether a patent proprietor of a subsequently filed European patent claiming a second use of that product could successfully allege infringement by the first patentee (or by a licensee of the first patent proprietor), if the carrying out of such first use also necessarily and unavoidably involves carrying out the second use as well. This question could arise in either a medical or non-medical context.

Depending upon the exact facts, it would seem that in certain circumstances a finding of infringement could result. A further question could then arise as to the extent of relief that a court would grant, having regard in particular to section 61(6) of the 1977 U.K. Act,[47] and having regard to the technical nature of the infringing acts. Clearly specific factual situations will require separate consideration.

Any difficulties that may arise in such cases are more likely to be connected with the facts than with the legal principles involved.

Since G5/83 and G2, 6/88 were issued, a considerable number of European patents have been granted in respect of further medical and non-medical uses, and their value in industrial patent portfolios and otherwise is well recognised. However, no infringement cases before national courts concerning such patents are known so far in which difficulties have arisen in relation to the determination of infringement.

It may be that the courts which are responsible for the determination of infringement will need to develop further common principles in relation to such use claims. In any event, any difficulty in relation to the determination of infringement in particular cases is hardly a reason for not granting European patents for this kind of invention.

[44] *Ibid.*
[45] See Appendix 19.
[46] See Appendix 21.
[47] See Appendix 21.

3. Conclusion

13–32 For each of the three types of invention referred to above, it would seem that statements made in a European patent concerning the purpose of a product may be of considerable importance, both in relation to the obtaining of a European patent and in relation to enforcing it. This is in accordance with common sense, since the value of a product depends upon its utility, and the need for patent protection for such a product is obviously directly related to its value.

Cases Referred to in Chapter 13

Board of Appeal Decisions

G5/83   EISAI/Second medical indication O.J. EPO 1985, 64; [1979–85] E.P.O.R.: B: 241.

G2, 6/88 MOBIL OIL/Friction reducing additive O.J. EPO 1990, 93, 114; [1990] E.P.O.R. 73, 257.

T11/82   LANSING-BAGNALL/Control circuit O.J. EPO 1983, 479; [1979–85] E.P.O.R.: B: 385.

T119/82   EXXON/Gelation O.J. EPO 1984, 217; [1979–85]: E.P.O.R.: B: 566.

T175/84   KABELMETAL/Combination claim O.J. EPO 1989, 71; [1989] E.P.O.R. 181.

T150/85   ROMERO-SIERRA, August 20, 1987.

T416/87   JSR/Block-copolymer O.J. EPO 1990, 415; [1991] E.P.O.R. 25.

T754/89   IMPROVER/Depilatory device [1993] E.P.O.R. 153.

Decisions of National Courts

Anchor Building Products Ltd v. Redland Rooftiles Ltd [1990] R.P.C. 283, CA.

Beecham Group v. Bristol Laboratories [1978] R.P.C. 153; [1977] F.S.R. 215, HL.

Catnic Components Ltd v. Hill and Smith Ltd [1981] F.S.R. 60; [1982] R.P.C. 183.

E.M.I. v. Lissen (1939) 56 R.P.C. 23.

Formstein/Moulded Curbstone, BGH Case No. XZ R28/85, O.J. EPO 1987, 551; [1991] R.P.C. 597.

Improver Corporation v. Remington Consumer Products Ltd [1989] R.P.C. 69.

Improver Corporation v. Raymond Industrial Ltd [1990] F.S.R. 422.

Kastner v. Rizla [1995] R.P.C. 585, CA.

Pioneer Electronics Capital Inc. v. Warner Music Manufacturing Europe GmbH [1997] R.P.C. 755, CA.

Saccharin Corp. v. Anglo-Continental Chemical Works (1900) 17 R.P.C. 307; [1901] 1 Ch. 414.

CHAPTER 14

THE COMMUNITY PATENT CONVENTION

Contents

All references are to paragraph numbers

A. Introduction

The previous chapters have considered the background to and main **14–01** developments of European patent law with reference to the case law established by the Boards of Appeal of the EPO during the last 20 years. The analysis has concentrated upon the procedural and substantive law relating to the grant of and opposition to European patents under the EPC.

The present chapter considers the earlier proposals for development of the European patent system as set out in the Community Patent Convention[1] ("the CPC") and the Agreement relating to Community Patents[2] signed on December 15, 1989 ("the 1989 Agreement"). The historical background to the CPC and the 1989 Agreement has been described in Chapter 1 at paragraph 1–53.

The CPC provides a system for a judicial harmonisation of European patent law, so that the divergences between national patent laws sometimes noted in the preceding chapters could eventually be brought into conformity. This system of jurisdiction is considered in outline below.

However, this proposed system of jurisdiction is widely recognised as unsatisfactory and is consequently very unlikely to be adopted. It is of course generally agreed that some kind of "supreme court of patent appeals" should be created in order to provide an ultimate authority on the interpretation of European patent law, but the practical aspects of creating such a court are very complicated, both politically and in the determination of the position of such a court in an international judicial structure.

The CPC also contains a number of important provisions of substantive law concerning both infringement and validity of Community patents, as well as administrative and procedural provisions, which mainly date from 1975, with some subsequent amendments in 1985 and 1989.

The 1989 Agreement provides a link between the general legal order of the European Community on the one hand, and the European patent system under the EPC and the CPC, including the Community patent, on the other.

The future of the CPC has in recent years been the subject of considerable consultation and discussion. Numerous recommendations and proposals have been put forward, following the issue in 1997 of a Green Paper on the Community patent and the patent system in Europe by the European Commission. More recently, a proposal for a Community Patent Regulation has been published by the Commission. This proposal is based upon the 1989 Agreement but contains substantial improvements concerning languages and the system of jurisdiction. However, at the time of writing it is unclear what the ultimate text of the Regulation will be. In the circumstances, this chapter remains essentially unchanged from the previous edition of this book, because further discussion would necessarily be speculative.

[1] See Appendix 19.
[2] See Appendix 19.

B. The Community Patent

(1) Designation

14–02　Article 79 EPC provides for the designation of Contracting States as part of the "request for grant" of a European patent: as stated in Chapter 1 at paragraph 1–50 above, upon grant a European patent becomes a bundle of national patents in each of the designated Contracting States, pursuant to Articles 2(2) and 64(1) EPC. Article 142 EPC provides that:

> "Any group of Contracting States, which has provided by a special agreement that a European patent granted for those States has a unitary character throughout their territories, may provide that a European patent may only be granted jointly in respect of all those States."

Furthermore, Article 149 EPC provides in connection with such a group of Contracting States that:

> "The group ... may provide that these States may only be designated jointly and that the designation of one or some only of such States shall be deemed to constitute the designation of all the States of the group."

These latter provisions of the EPC foreshadow the provisions of the CPC concerning designation of a Community patent. Article 3 CPC provides that:

> "Designation of the States parties to this Convention in accordance with Article 79 EPC shall be effected jointly. Designation of one or some only of these States shall be deemed to be designation of all of these States."

Nevertheless, amongst the Transitional Provisions in Part VIII of the CPC, Article 81 CPC allows an option between a Community patent and a European patent. An applicant for a European patent (within a prescribed time limit, namely "before or when the applicant approves ... the text in which the patent is to be granted"—Rule 32 CPC) may file a statement "indicating that he does not wish to obtain a Community patent" and designating specific Contracting States. The statement shall not be deemed to have been filed until a prescribed fee has been paid. Such a statement may not subsequently be withdrawn.

(2) Characteristics

14–03　A Community patent is a European patent which is granted for the Contracting States to the CPC.

According to Article 2(2) CPC, Community patents have a unitary character, and have equal effect throughout the territories of the Community. They may only be granted, transferred, revoked or allowed to lapse in respect of all such territories. The same applies *mutatis mutandis* for European patent applications with appropriate designations.

Furthermore, according to Article 2(3) CPC, Community patents have an autonomous character. They are subject only to the CPC and "those provisions of the EPC which are binding upon every European patent", and which are, therefore, "deemed to be provisions of the CPC".

(3) Administration

A Patent Administration Division of the EPO will be set up pursuant to **14–04** Articles 4(a), 6(a) and 7 CPC, having responsibility for all administrative aspects of Community patents that are not already the responsibility of departments of the EPO under relevant provisions of the EPC. In particular, the Parent Administration Division will decide upon entries in a Register of Community Patents.

(4) As an object of property

Part II, Chapter IV of the CPC contains in Articles 38 to 44 CPC a series of **14–05** provisions concerning the Community patent as an object of property.

In particular, according to Article 38(1) and (2) CPC, a Community patent "shall be dealt with in its entirety, and for the whole of the territories in which it is effective", as a national patent of the Contracting State in which, at the date of filing of the European patent application:

(1) the applicant had his residence or principal place of business;
(2) or if (1) is inapplicable, in which the applicant had a place of business;
(3) or if both (1) and (2) are inapplicable, in which the applicant's representative who was entered first in the Register of European patents had his place of business on the date of entry.

If none of the above are applicable, the Community patent shall be dealt with as a national patent of Germany.

Article 42 CPC deals with contractual licensing and provides that a Community patent "may be licensed in whole or in part for the whole or part of the territories in which it is effective", and the licence may be exclusive or non-exclusive.

Article 43 CPC provides for "licences of right", if the proprietor of a Community patent files a written statement as prescribed, in return for "appropriate compensation" to be determined by a Revocation Division of the EPO (see paragraph 14–17 below) if not agreed. Renewal fees are reduced following receipt of such a statement.

C. The 1989 Agreement[3]

(1) Preamble

14–06 The preamble sets out the background to and aims of the Contracting Parties, namely the Member States of the European Community. In particular:

(i) The Agreement is a special agreement under Article 142 EPC and within Article 19 Paris, as well as being a regional parent treaty within Article 45(1) PCT.

(ii) The Agreement is intended to integrate the European patent system with the European Community interest in the elimination of distortion of competition and the abolition of obstacles to the free movement of goods, by linking the Community patent system with the Community legal order.

(iii) The Agreement recognises that the uniform application of the law on infringement and validity of Community patents requires the setting up of a Community patent appeal court common to the Contracting States (the Common Appeal Court, COPAC).

(2) Contents of the 1989 Agreement

14–07 As set out in Article 1, the 1989 Agreement has the following annexes which are an integral part of it:

(i) The CPC as signed in 1975 and amended by the 1989 Agreement;

(ii) Protocol on the settlement of Litigation concerning the infringement and validity of Community patents (the "Protocol on Litigation" or simply "Protocol");

(iii) Protocol on privileges and immunities of the Common Appeal Court;

(iv) Protocol on the statute of the Common Appeal Court.

The contents of the 1989 Agreement, in particular the Protocol on Litigation, provide the system of jurisdiction for Community patents which is discussed below.

D. The System of Jurisdiction

(1) General characteristics

(a) First instance

14–08 Litigation at first instance concerning Community patents is divided between Revocation Divisions of the EPO and designated national courts,

[3] The 1989 Agreement, the CPC, its Implementing Regulations and the Protocol on Litigation are all reproduced at Appendix 19.

which are called Community patent courts. The Revocation Divisions have exclusive jurisdiction concerning actions for limitation and revocation of Community parents, and the national Community patent courts have exclusive jurisdiction concerning other proceedings involving infringement and validity of Community patents, as discussed below.

(b) Second instance

A Common Appeal Court, called COPAC, will be set up as the second **14–09** instance, hearing appeals from Revocation Divisions, and hearing all issues concerning infringement and validity of Community patents arising in appeals from the first instance national Community patent courts.

The relevant "patent issues" in appeals from a national first instance court to a national second instance court will be referred to COPAC for judgment thereon. Non-patent issues will remain to be decided by national second instance courts. Such "non-patent" issues will include, for example, questions concerning the amount of damages for patent infringement, as well as separate issues such as infringement of copyright.

(c) Third instance

The system of jurisdiction under the CPC does not provide a third instance **14–10** in respect of the "patent issues" of an action brought before a national Community patent court. In accordance with Article 29 Protocol, non-patent issues in such an action may be the subject of an appeal to a third instance court, if national law permits (for example, an appeal to the House of Lords in the United Kingdom on the amount of damages to be awarded in respect of patent infringement).

(d) European Court of Justice (ECJ)

The ECJ may give preliminary rulings on the interpretation of provisions **14–11** relating to the applicable jurisdiction in relation to an action concerning a Community patent, and in connection with any provisions of the 1989 Agreement which may conflict with the EEC Treaty,[4] so as to ensure continuity of the Community legal order (Articles 2 and 3 1989 Agreement).

(2) National proceedings

(a) Community patent courts

Each Contracting State will designate courts and tribunals at first and **14–12** second instance having jurisdiction with respect to Community patents. According to Article 1 Protocol, each State should designate "as limited a number as possible" of such courts, the object being to promote specialisation in patent matters in certain courts in each State. Of course, such courts may also have jurisdiction with respect to non-patent matters.

[4] Treaty establishing the European Economic Community—signed Rome, March 25, 1957.

A list of such courts in the Contracting States is included in an Annex to the Protocol on Litigation. In the United Kingdom, the current designated courts of first instance are:

England and Wales	The Patents County Court
	The Patents Court
Scotland	The Outer House to the
	Court of Session
Northern Ireland	The High Court

The designated courts of second instance are:

England and Wales	The Court of Appeal
Scotland	The Inner House of the
	Court of Session
Northern Ireland	The Court of Appeal.

(b) Jurisdiction of Community patent courts

14–13   **(i) Jurisdiction with respect to subject-matter.** *First instance courts.* The jurisdiction of the first instance Community patent courts is dealt with in Part III of the Protocol on Litigation; in particular, Article 15 Protocol. Such courts have exclusive jurisdiction in relation to Community patents:

(a) For all infringement actions and counterclaims for revocation (including actions in respect of threatened infringement, if permitted under national law).

(b) For actions for declarations of non-infringement (if permitted under national law).

(c) For all actions for compensation for use of an invention which is the subject of a European patent application for a Community patent, pursuant to Article 32(1) CPC.

An action before a first instance Community patent court may also involve issues concerning non-Community patent matters; for example, breach of contract, trade mark infringement, etc.

With reference to (a) above, an important aspect of the first instance jurisdiction under the 1989 Agreement, as compared to the provisions of the CPC as originally worded in the 1975 version, is the joint hearing before the first instance national Community patent courts of counterclaims for revocation in conjunction with infringement actions. Under the 1975 CPC, these issues were to be decided separately: infringement actions were to be heard and decided separately: infringement actions were to be heard and decided in national courts, on the assumption that the patent was valid, and revocation actions were to be decided by the Revocation Divisions of the EPO. Such a separation of these issues has been abandoned in the 1985 and 1989 versions of the CPC. Under the 1989 Agreement, if a defendant to an infringement action wishes to challenge the validity of the patent by way of defence, he must do this by way of a counterclaim for revocation. Unless the validity of the patent is put in issue by a counterclaim for revocation, "the Community patent courts of first instance shall treat the Community patent as valid"—Article 15(2) Protocol.

In the event of a counterclaim for revocation before a first instance Community patent court, three results are possible (Article 19(1) Protocol, *cf.* Article 102 EPC concerning opposition proceedings before the EPO):

(a) Revocation of the patent;
(b) Maintenance of the patent in amended form;
(c) Rejection of the application for revocation.

Second instance courts. This jurisdiction is dealt with in Part IV of the **14–14** Protocol on Litigation. An appeal lies to such appeal courts from judgments of the first instance Community patent courts in respect of the issues within their jurisdiction as discussed above.

However, as considered below, Article 22 Protocol provides that the Common Appeal Court has exclusive jurisdiction over the "patent issues" in such an appeal. Thus, in accordance with Article 23 Protocol, when such an appeal raises issues within the exclusive jurisdiction of the Common Appeal Court, the second instance national court must "stay its proceedings in so far as they require a judgment on such issues and refer them to the Common Appeal Court for judgment".

The second instance national court "may continue its proceedings provided that there is no possibility of the judgment of the Common Appeal Court being prejudged", in connection with other issues raised; but it "may not render a final judgment before the judgment of the Common Appeal Court has been given".

"A judgment given by the Common Appeal Court shall be binding in the further proceedings of the case"—Article 27 Protocol.

(ii) Jurisdiction with respect to parties and acts of infringement. The **14–15** Protocol on Litigation provides rules for determining where an action in respect of a Community patent (*i.e.* "proceedings governed by this Protocol", Article 13(1) Protocol) may be commenced.

The system set out in Articles 13 and 14 Protocol is interlinked with the Brussels Convention on Jurisdiction and Enforcement of judgments[5] ("Brussels"), identified in Article 13(1) Protocol. As provided by Article 13(1) Protocol, the provisions of the Brussels Convention apply "Unless otherwise specified in this Protocol."

Under the Brussels Convention, proceedings in respect of a tort such as **14–16** patent infringement may be brought either in the national courts of the

---

[5] Convention on Jurisdiction and the Enforcement of Judgments in Civil and Commercial Matters—signed Brussels, September 23, 1968 and subsequently amended—Appendix 17 contains Articles 17 and 18 Brussels.

State where the defendant is domiciled (Article 2 Brussels) or in the courts of the State where the act complained of occurred (the *"forum delicti commissi"*) (Article 5(3) Brussels). The Protocol on Litigation provides a more developed system of rules in this respect, in order to take into account *inter alia* that an alleged infringer of a patent may be domiciled outside the Contracting States.

Thus, Article 14(1) Protocol specifies that, subject to other provisions of the Protocol and applicable provisions of the Brussels Convention, proceedings governed by the Protocol shall be brought in the national courts of the State "in which the defendant is domiciled", or if he is not domiciled in any of the Contracting States, in the national courts of the State "in which he has an establishment" (Article 14(1) Protocol).

If neither of these criteria apply to the defendant, the proceedings shall be brought in the State "in which the plaintiff is domiciled", or if he is not domiciled in any of the Contracting States, in the State "in which he has an establishment" (Article 14(2) Protocol).

If neither of these criteria are applicable either, then the proceedings shall be brought in the State "where the Common Appeal Court has its seat" (*i.e.* probably Luxembourg, see paragraph 14–21 below) (Article 14(3) Protocol).

Alternatively, if the parties agree that a different Community patent court shall have jurisdiction, Article 17 Brussels[6] applies. If the defendant enters an appearance before a different Community patent court, Article 18 Brussels applies.

Additionally, Article 14(5) Protocol provides that except for an action for a declaration of non-infringement, proceedings may also be brought in the national courts of the State in which the act of infringement has been committed or threatened (or in which the act has been committed, in respect of which compensation is claimed pursuant to Article 32(1) CPC—see paragraph 14–13, sub-paragraph (c), above).

An action for a declaration of non-infringement must be brought either in the courts of the Contracting State where the patent proprietor (*i.e.* the defendant) is domiciled or in which he has an establishment, in accordance with Article 14(1) Protocol (or otherwise in accordance with Article 14(2) or (3) Protocol).

(3) Revocation Divisions of the EPO

14–17 These Divisions will be set up within the EPO, pursuant to Articles 4(a), 6(b) and 8 CPC, to decide upon requests for limitation (*i.e.* amendment by the patent proprietor) and applications for revocation of Community patents. They will also have a special jurisdiction under Article 43(5) CPC to determine or review the appropriate compensation for a licence of right under a Community patent.

A Revocation Division will consist of three members, namely a legally qualified Chairman and two technically qualified members.

---

[6] See Appendix 17.

(a) Requests for limitation

The proprietor of a Community patent may request amendments to its **14–18** description, claims or drawings. The request must be in writing and the prescribed fee paid.

Such a request may not be filed either during the period during which an opposition to the Community patent may be filed (*i.e.* the nine-month period under Article 99 EPC), or while opposition or revocation proceedings are pending. Applications for amendment may be made in the course of such proceedings (Articles 57 to 59 CPC, respectively).

Thus, the CPC provides the possibility of a centralised procedure for amendment of a Community patent, which is not possible in respect of a European patent under the EPC.

When examining such a request for amendment, the Revocation Division shall examine whether the grounds for revocation under Article 56(1)(a) to (d) CPC prejudice maintenance of the Community patent. Since Article 56(1)(c) and (d) CPC contains provisions corresponding respectively to Article 123(2) and (3) EPC (and Article 76(1) EPC in respect of divisional applications)—prohibiting the addition of subject-matter after filing, and the extension of the protection conferred after grant, respectively—the same considerations will apply as discussed in relation to the above Articles of the EPC in Chapter 5. Furthermore, Article 56(1)(a) and (b) CPC contains provisions corresponding respectively to Articles 52 to 57 EPC and Article 83 EPC.

Article 53 CPC contains provisions concerning approval of the amended text, payment of a printing fee and the filing of translations, which are analogous to the provisions of Article 102(3), (4) and (5) EPC concerning amendment of a European patent during opposition proceedings (except that if the requirements for paying a printing fee and filing translations are not complied with in due time, the sanction is that the request for limitation is deemed to be withdrawn, instead of the patent being revoked).

(b) Applications for revocation

"Any person" may file such an application for revocation of a Community **14–19** patent (except in the case where the ground for revocation is as set out in Article 56(1)(e) CPC, as to which see below). The application must be filed in a written reasoned statement (*cf.* a notice of opposition under Article 99 EPC, discussed in Chapter 3 at paragraphs 3–19 *et seq.* above), and the prescribed revocation fee must be paid.

Such an application may not be filed on the grounds set out in Article 56(1)(a) to (d) CPC (see below), during the period during which an opposition may be filed (*i.e.* the nine-month period under Article 99 EPC), or while opposition proceedings are pending.

The possible grounds for revocation are set out in Article 56(1) CPC. Sub-paragraphs (a) to (e) correspond to the grounds set out in Article 138(1) EPC, namely:

603

    (a) the subject-matter of the patent is not patentable, under Articles 52 to 57 EPC;

    (b) insufficiency under Article 83 EPC;

    (c) added subject-matter by amendment;

    (d) extension of protection by amendment;

    (e) the proprietor not being entitled to the patent under Article 60(1) EPC.

When the ground of revocation is as set out in Article 56(1)(e) CPC, only the person or persons who are so entitled may apply for revocation.

In addition to the above grounds of revocation corresponding to Article 138(1)(a) to (e) EPC, Article 56(1)(f) provides for revocation of a Community patent on the ground that the subject-matter of the patent is not patentable having regard to the existence of a national prior right (Article 36(1) CPC); see paragraph 14–30 below and compare Chapter 11 at paragraph 11–43 above, concerning the fact that a national prior right does not constitute a ground of objection to a European patent application or patent under Article 54(3) EPC.

The procedure in connection with an application for revocation is set out in Articles 57 to 60 CPC, and corresponds generally to the procedure before an Opposition Division under Articles 101 to 104 EPC.

14–19A   According to the proposed revision of the EPC, new Articles 105a, b and c EPC will be added which will allow the proprietor to request limitation or revocation of a patent in a centralised procedure before the EPO (see Chapter 8 at paragraph 8–04A above). Such a procedure will clearly replace that proposed in the CPC.

(4) Staying proceedings at first instance

14–20 Article 34 Protocol provides rules for staying actions in the event of more than one action being commenced at first instance.

Thus, a first instance national Community patent court hearing an action concerning a Community patent as set out in paragraph 14–13 above (except an application for a declaration of non-infringement) must, at the request of one party and after hearing the other parties, stay the proceedings if the validity of the patent is already in issue before another Community patent court or before COPAC, or where an opposition or an application for revocation or a request for limitation has already been filed at the EPO,—"unless there are special grounds for continuing the hearing."

Similarly, the EPO must stay an application for revocation or a request for limitation on the same basis, if the validity of the patent is already in issue in proceedings before a Community patent court or COPAC.

Thus, the normal rule is that subsequent actions concerning a Community patent are to be stayed, to prevent a multiplicity of actions in relation to a particular patent.

In any event, harmonisation of decisions will result from the fact that the highest court in relation to the validity and effect of a Community patent will be COPAC, as discussed below.

(5) COPAC—the Common Appeal Court

(a) Introduction

COPAC will be established by the Protocol on Litigation and will perform **14–21** the functions which are assigned to it by the Protocol (Article 2(1) Protocol).

Under the Protocol, COPAC will have jurisdiction in respect of the following matters:

(a) Issues in respect of which it has exclusive jurisdiction under Article 22 Protocol, and which are referred to it by a second instance national Community patent court under Article 23 Protocol (see paragraph 14–14 above).

(b) Appeals from the Revocation Divisions and the Patent Administration Divisions of the EPO, under Article 28 Protocol.

(c) Giving certain preliminary rulings concerning the interpretation of the 1989 Agreement and concerning the validity and interpretation of provisions enacted in implementation of the 1989 Agreement (to the extent that they are not national provisions), under Article 30(1) Protocol.

COPAC will be constituted as an independent jurisdictional body. Its seat will be determined by the Governments of the signatory States, in accordance with Article 2(2) Protocol, and is likely to be in Luxembourg. It will be independent from the ECJ at Luxembourg, however. The Protocol, therefore, necessarily includes a series of provisions concerning the legal status of the judges and various administrative and financial matters.

(b) Issues referred by a second instance national court

COPAC "shall examine all the issues of which it is seised and give a ruling **14–22** on fact and law" (Article 24 Protocol). The national second instance court must stay its proceedings in relation to such issues.

In a judgment on such issues, COPAC "shall find whether the Community patent or the European patent application has or has not the effects at issue" (Article 25(1) Protocol). Such a judgment of COPAC will be binding in the further proceedings of the case, before national Community patent courts (Article 27 Protocol).

The jurisdictional position of COPAC in relation to national Community patent courts is thus very different from the position of the Enlarged Board of Appeal in relation to the other Boards of Appeal under the EPC (see

Chapter 4 at paragraphs 4–175 *et seq.* above). Whereas under Article 112(1)(a) EPC, the Enlarged Board of Appeal *may be asked* to decide upon a point of law that arises in an appeal to a Board of Appeal, under the Protocol, COPAC *must* decide upon all substantive issues of infringement and validity, in relation to questions both of fact and law, that arise in each appeal to a second instance national Community patent court. COPAC will thus function as a specialist patent appeal court for all appeals which are lodged in the Contracting States from first instance actions in national Community patents courts concerning infringement and validity of Community patents.

The jurisdictional position of COPAC is thus also quite different from the "preliminary ruling" procedure under Article 177 of the EEC Treaty.[7]

(c) Appeals from the Revocation and Parent Administration Divisions

14–23 COPAC will decide upon appeals from decisions of the Revocation and Patent Administration Divisions of the EPO in accordance with Article 28 Protocol.

The procedure in relation to such appeals is governed by Article 61(2) CPC, which provides that "Articles 106 to 109 EPC, shall apply *mutatis mutandis* ... insofar as the Rules of Procedure of the Common Appeal Court or the Rules relating to Fees do not provide otherwise". Thus, the jurisprudence of the Boards of Appeal concerning Articles 106 to 109 EPC, which has been discussed in Chapter 2 above, will be generally applicable to such appeals.

(d) Preliminary rulings

14–24 COPAC will have jurisdiction in accordance with Article 30 Protocol to give preliminary rulings concerning:

> "(a) The interpretation of the 1989 Agreement in respect of matters not falling within its exclusive jurisdiction as provided in Article 22 Protocol;
>
> (b) the validity and interpretation of provisions enacted in implementation of the 1989 Agreement, to the extent to which they are not national provisions."

Requests for preliminary rulings on these matters will be brought before COPAC via proceedings in national courts. Such a court *may*, "if it considers that a decision on the question is necessary to enable it to give judgment", request a ruling from COPAC—Article 30(2) Protocol. Furthermore, where such a question is raised in a case pending before such a court "against whose decisions there is no judicial remedy under national law", that court "*shall* bring the matter" before COPAC (emphasis added).

---

[7] Appendix 15 contains Article 177 EEC Treaty.

(e) Preliminary rulings from the ECJ

Pursuant to Article 2(2) 1989 Agreement: **14–25**

> "In order to ensure the uniformity of the Community legal order,
> COPAC ... shall request the ECJ to give a preliminary ruling (in
> accordance with Article 177 EEC Treaty[8]) whenever there is a risk of
> an interpretation of the 1989 Agreement being inconsistent with the
> EEC Treaty."

E. Applicable Law

In accordance with Article 26 Protocol, COPAC "shall apply the provisions   **14–26**
of the 1989 Agreement", which, as discussed in paragraph 14–07 above,
includes the CPC itself and the Protocol on Litigation.

The CPC contains provisions of substantive patent law complementary
to the EPC, governing, in particular, infringement and validity of
Community patents. Thus, COPAC will be able to ensure uniform
application of the law on infringement and validity of Community patents.

F. Particular Aspects of Substantive Law Under the CPC

(1) Effect of a Community patent—infringing acts

Articles 25 and 26 CPC contain provisions which respectively concern the   **14–27**
prohibition of direct and indirect use of the invention. Article 27 CPC sets
out a number of acts and circumstances which do not constitute infringement of a Community patent, and which are, therefore, exceptions to the
above prohibitions of direct and indirect use.

Since Articles 25 to 27 CPC were part of the 1975 CPC, these provisions
were taken into account by subsequent national patent laws, including the
1977 U.K. Act: section 60 contains provisions corresponding to Articles 25
to 27 CPC.

(2) Exhaustion of rights

Article 28 CPC contains a codification of jurisprudence of the European   **14–28**
Court of Justice concerning the exhaustion of rights conferred by a patent,
which will be directly applicable to Community patents.

(3) Burden of proof in infringement proceedings relating to a process patent for a new product

Article 35 CPC contains a special provision which in effect reverses the   **14–29**
burden of proof in relation to proving infringement of a patent whose

---

[8] *Ibid.*

subject-matter is a process of manufacturing a new product. In the absence of proof to the contrary, the same product shall "be deemed to have been obtained by the patented process".

(4) National prior rights

14–30 Article 36 CPC provides that a prior national application or patent will have the same prior art effect with regard to a Community patent as a prior European patent application has with regard to a European patent under Article 54(3) EPC (*cf.* Chapter 11 at paragraphs 11–43 *et seq.* above).

(5) Vested rights from prior use or possession

14–31 Article 27 CPC provides that any person will have the same rights in respect of a Community patent as he would have under the national law of a Contracting State in respect of a national patent for the same invention, having regard to his prior use or personal possession of the invention (see for example section 64 of the 1977 U.K. Act).

G. Conclusion

14–32 Even if the CPC ever comes into force in modified form, it would take some years before the legal order under the CPC could begin to become effective in practice. Community patents would have to be designated, examined, granted and then litigated, both at first instance (before national Community patent courts or Revocation Divisions), and then on appeal to COPAC in the course of second instance proceedings as discussed above, before the delivery of judgments by COPAC on such patent issues could begin to harmonise previous national jurisprudence.

The CPC allows the creation of a uniform and harmonised European patent law to be envisaged, in which European patents covering the territories of the European Community will be effective in accordance with a common system of European patent law and procedure, integrated with European Community law. The actual creation of such a system is still in the future, however.

APPENDICES

APPENDIX 1

EUROPEAN PATENT CONVENTION

Convention of October 5, 1973   A1–01
as amended by Decision of the Administrative Council of the European Patent
Organisation
of December 21, 1978 (O.J. EPO 1979, 3)

Contents of Convention

PART V. OPPOSITION PROCEDURE

PART VI. APPEALS PROCEDURE

PART VII. COMMON PROVISIONS

Chapter I. Common provisions governing procedure

Chapter II. Information to the public or offical authorities

APPENDIX 1

PART XI. TRANSITIONAL PROVISIONS

PART XII. FINAL PROVISIONS

Convention on the Grant of European Patents (Euopean Patent Convention)

Munich, 5 October 1973

text as amended by the act revising Article 63 EPC of 17 December 1991 and by decisions of the Administrative Council of the European Patent Organisation of 21 December 1978, 13 December 1994, 20 October 1995, 5 December 1996 and 10 December 1998

Preamble

The Contracting States,

Desiring to strengthen co-operation between the States of Europe in respect of the protection of inventions.

Desiring that such protection may be obtained in those States by a single procedure for the grant of patents, and by the establishment of certain standard rules governing patents so granted.

Desiring, for this purpose, to conclude a Convention which establishes a European Patent Organisation and which constitutes a special agreement within the meaning of Article 19 of the Convention for the Protection of Industrial Property, signed in Paris on 20 March 1883 and last revised on 14 July 1967, and a regional patent treaty within the meaning of Article 45, paragraph 1, of the Patent Co-operation Treaty of 19 June 1970.

Have agreed on the following provisions:

Part I. General and Institutional Provisions

Chapter I. General provisions

ARTICLE 1

European law for the grant of patents

A system of law, common to the Contracting States, for the grant of patents for invention is hereby established.

ARTICLE 2

European patent

(1) Patents granted by virtue of this Convention shall be called European patents.

(2) The European patent shall, in each of the Contracting States for which it is granted, have the effect of and be subject to the same conditions as a national patent granted by that State, unless otherwise provided in this Convention.

617

ARTICLE 3

Territorial effect

The grant of a European patent may be requested for one or more of the Contracting States.

ARTICLE 4

European Patent Organisation

(1) A European Patent Organisation, hereinafter referred to as the Organisation, is established by this Convention. It shall have administrative and financial autonomy.

(2) The organs of the Organisation shall be:

    (a) a European Patent Office;
    (b) an Administrative Council.

(3) The task of the Organisation shall be to grant European patents. This shall be carried out by the European Patent Office supervised by the Administrative Council.

Chapter II. The European Patent Organisation

ARTICLE 5

Legal status

(1) The Organisation shall have legal personality.

(2) In each of the Contracting States, the Organisation shall enjoy the most extensive legal capacity accorded to legal persons under the national law of that State; it may in particular acquire or dispose of movable and immovable property and may be a party to legal proceedings.

(3) The President of the European Patent Office shall represent the Organisation.

ARTICLE 6

Seat

(1) The Organisation shall have its seat at Munich.

(2) The European Patent Office shall be set up at Munich. It shall have a branch at The Hague.

ARTICLE 7

Sub-offices of the European Patent Office

By decision of the Administative Office, sub-offices of the European Patent Office may be created if need be, for the purpose of information and liaison, in the Contracting States and with inter-governmental organisations in the field of industrial property, subject to the approval of the Contracting State or organisation concerned.

ARTICLE 8

Privileges and immunities

The Protocol on Privileges and Immunities annexed to this Convention shall define the conditions under which the Organisation, the members of the Administrative Council, the employees of the European Patent Office and such other persons specified in that Protocol as take part in the work of the Organisation, shall enjoy, in the territory of each Contracting State, the privileges and immunities necessary for the performance of their duties.

ARTICLE 9

Liability

(1) The contractual liability of the Organisation shall be governed by the law applicable to the relevant contract.

(2) The non-contractual liability of the Organisation in repsect of any damage caused by it or by the employees of the European Patent Office in the performance of their duties shall be governed by the provisions of the law of the Federal Republic of Germany. Where the damage is caused by the branch at The Hague or a sub-office or employees attached thereto, the provisions of the law of the Contracting State in which such branch or sub-office is located shall apply.

(3) The personal liability of the employees of the European Patent Office towards the Organisation shall be laid down in their Service Regulations or conditions of employment.

(4) The courts with jurisdiction to settle disputes under paragraphs 1 and 2 shall be:

(a) for disputes under paragraph 1, the courts of competent jurisdiction in the Federal Republic of Germany, unless the contract concluded between the parties designates the courts of another State;

(b) for disputes under paragraph 2, either the courts of competent jurisdiction in the Federal Republic of Germany, or the courts of competent jurisdiction in the State in which the branch or sub-office is located.

Chapter III. The European Patent Office

ARTICLE 10

Direction

(1) The European Patent Office shall be directed by the President who shall be responsible for its activities to the Administrative Council.

(2) To this end, the President shall have in particular the following functions and powers:

(a) he shall take all necessary steps, including the steps of internal administrative instructions and the publication of guidance for the public, to ensure the functioning of the European Patent Office;

(b) in so far as this Convention contains no provisions in this respect, he shall prescribe which transactions are to be carried out at the European Patent Office at Munich and its branch at The Hauge respectively;

(c) he may place before the Administrative Council any proposal for amending this Convention and any proposal for general regulations or decisions which come within the competence of the Administrative Council;

(d) he shall prepare and implement the budget and any amending or supplementary budget;

(e) he shall submit a management report to the Administrative Council each year;

(f) he shall exercise supervisory authority over the personnel;

(g) subject to the provisions of Article 11, he shall appoint and promote the employees;

(h) he shall exercise disciplinary authority over the employees other than those referred to in Article 11, and may propose disciplinary action to the Administrative Council with regard to employees referred to in Article 11, paragraphs 2 and 3;

(i) he may delegate his functions and powers.

(3) The President shall be assisted by a number of Vice-Presidents. If the President is absent or indisposed, one of the Vice-Presidents shall take place in accordance with the procedure laid down by the Administrative Council.

ARTICLE 11

Appointment of senior employees

(1) The President of the European Patent Office shall be appointed by decision of the Administrative Council.

(2) The Vice-Presidents shall be appointed by decision of the Administrative Council after the President has been consulted.

(3) The members, including the Chairman, of the Boards of Appeal and of the Enlarged Board of Appeal shall be appointed by decision of the Administrative Council, taken on a proposal from the President of the European Patent Office. They may be re-appointed by decision of the Administrative Council after the President of the European Patent Office has been consulted.

(4) The Administrative Council shall exercise disciplinary authority over the employees referred to in paragraphs 1 to 3.

ARTICLE 12

Duties of office

The employees of the European Parent Office shall be bound, even after the termination of their employment, neither to disclose nor to make use of information which by its nature is a professional secret.

ARTICLE 13

Disputes between the Organisation and the employees of the European Parent Office

(1) Employees and former employees of the European Patent Office or their successors in title may apply to the Administrative Tribunal of the International Labour Organisation in the case of disputes with the European Patent Organisation in accordance with the Statute of the Tribunal and within the limits and subject to the conditions laid down in the Service Regulations for permanent employees or the Pension Scheme Regulations or arising from the conditions of employment of other employees.

(2) An appeal shall only be admissible if the person concerned has exhausted

such other means of appeal as are available to him under the Service Regulations, the Pension Scheme Regulations or the conditions of employment, as the case may be.

ARTICLE 14

Languages of the European Patent Office

(1) The official language of the European Patent Office shall be English, French and German, European patent applications must be filed in one of these languages.

(2) However, natural or legal persons having their residence or principal place of business within the territory of the Contracting State having a language other than English, French or German as an official language, and nationals of that State who are resident abroad, may file European patent applications in an official language of that State. Nevertheless, a translation in one of the official languages of the European Patent Office must be filed within the time limit prescribed in the Implementing Regulations; throughout the proceedings before the European Patent Office, such translation may be brought into conformity with the original text of the application.

(3) The official language of the European Patent Office in which the European patent application is filed or, in the case referred to in paragraph 2, that of the translation, shall be used as the language of the proceedings in all proceedings before the European Patent Office concerning the application or the resulting patent, unless otherwise provided in the Implementing Regulations.

(4) The persons referred to in paragraph 2 may also file documents which have to be filed within a time limit in an official language of the Contracting State concerned. They must however file a translation in the language of the proceedings within the time limit prescribed in the Implementing Regulations; in the cases provided for in the Implementing Regulations, they may file a translation in a different official language of the European Patent Office.

(5) If any document, other than those making up the European patent application, is not filed in the language prescribed by this Convention, or if any translation required by virtue of this Convention is not filed in due time, the document shall be deemed not to have been received.

(6) European patent applications shall be published in the language of the proceedings.

(7) The specifications of European patents shall be published in the language of the proceedings; they shall include a translation of the claims in the two other official languages of the European Patent Office.

(8) There shall be published in the three official languages of the European Patent Office:

    (a) the European Patent Bulletin;
    (b) the Official Journal of the European Patent Office.

(9) Entries in the Register of European Patents shall be made in the three official languages of the European Patent Office. In cases of doubt, the entry in the language of the proceedings shall be authentic.

ARTICLE 15

The departments charged with the procedure

For implementing the procedures laid down in this Convention, there shall be set up within the European Patent Office:

(a) a Receiving Section;
(b) Search Divisions;
(c) Examining Divisions;
(d) Opposition Divisions;
(e) a Legal Division;
(f) Boards of Appeal;
(g) an Enlarged Board of Appeal.

ARTICLE 16

Receiving Section

The Receiving Section shall be in the branch at The Hague. It shall be responsible for the examination on filing and the examination as to formal requirements of each European patent application up to the time when a request for examination has been made or the applicant has indicated under Article 96, paragraph 1, that he desires to proceed further with his application. It shall also be responsible for the publication of the European patent application and of the European search report.

ARTICLE 17

Search Divisions

The Search Divisions shall be in the branch at The Hague. They shall be responsible for drawing up European search reports.

ARTICLE 18

Examining Divisions

(1) An Examining Division shall be responsible for the examination of each European patent application from the time when the Receiving Section ceases to be responsible.

(2) An Examining Division shall consist of three technical examiners. Nevertheless, the examination prior to a final decision shall, as a general rule, be entrusted to one member of the Division. Oral proceedings shall be before the Examining Division itself. If the Examining Division considers that the nature of the decision so requires, it shall be enlarged by the addition of a legally qualified examiner. In the event of parity of votes, the vote of the Chairman of the Division shall be decisive.

ARTICLE 19

Opposition Divisions

(1) An Opposition Division shall be responsible for the examination of oppositions against any European patent.

(2) An Opposition Division shall consist of three technical examiners, at least two of them shall not have taken part in the proceedings for grant of the patent to which the opposition relates. An examiner who has taken part in the proceedings for the grant of the European patent shall not be the Chairman. Prior to the taking of a final decision on the opposition, the Opposition Division may entrust the examination of the opposition to one of its members. Oral Proceedings shall be before the

Opposition Division itself. If the Opposition Division considers that the nature of the decision so requires, it shall be enlarged by the addition of a legally qualified examiner who shall not have taken part in the proceedings for grant of the patent. In the event of parity of votes, the vote of the Chairman of the Division shall be decisive.

ARTICLE 20

Legal Division

(1) The Legal Division shall be responsible for decisions in respect of entries in the Register of European Patents and in respect of registration on, and deletion from, the list of professional representatives.

(2) Decisions of the Legal Division shall be taken by one legally qualified member.

ARTICLE 21

Boards of Appeal

(1) The Boards of Appeal shall be responsible for the examination of appeals from the decisions of the Receiving Section, Examining Divisions, Opposition Divisions and of the Legal Division.

(2) For appeals from a decision of the Receiving Section or the Legal Division, a Board of Appeal shall consist of three legally qualified members.

(3) For appeals from a decision of an Examining Division, a Board of Appeal shall consist of:

(a) two technically qualified members and one legally qualified member, when the decision concerns the refusal of a European patent application or the grant of a European patent and was taken by an Examining Division consisting of less than four members;

(b) three technically qualified members and two legally qualified members, when the decision was taken by an Examining Division consisting of four members or when the Board of Appeal considers that the nature of the appeal so requires;

(c) three legally qualified members in all other cases.

(4) For appeals from a decision of an Opposition Division, a Board of Appeal shall consist of:

(a) two technically qualified members and one legally qualified member, when the decision was taken by an Opposition Division consisting of three members;

(b) three technically qualified members and two legally qualified members, when the decision was taken by an Opposition Division consisting of four members or when the Board of Appeal considers that the nature of the appeal so requires.

ARTICLE 22

Enlarged Board of Appeal

(1) The Enlarged Board of Appeal shall be responsible for:

(a) deciding points of law referred to it by Boards of Appeal;

(b) giving opinions on points of law referred to it by the President of the European Patent Office under the conditions laid down in Article 112.

(2) For giving decisions or opinions, the Enlarged Board of Appeal shall consist of five legally qualified members and two technically qualified members. One of the legally qualified members shall be the Chairman.

ARTICLE 23

Independence of the members of the Boards

(1) The members of the Enlarged Board of Appeal and of the Boards of Appeal shall be appointed for a term of five years and may not be removed from office during this term, except if there are serious grounds for such removal and if the Administrative Council, on a proposal from the Enlarged Board of Appeal, takes a decision to this effect.

(2) The members of the Boards may not be members of the Receiving Section, Examining Divisions, Opposition Divisions or of the Legal Division.

(3) In their decisions the members of the Boards shall not be bound by any instructions and shall comply only with the provisions of this Convention.

(4) The Rules of Procedure of the Boards of Appeal and the Enlarged Board of Appeal shall be adopted in accordance with the provisions of the Implementing Regulations. They shall be subject to the approval of the Administrative Council.

ARTICLE 24

Exclusion and objection

(1) Members of the Boards of Appeal or of the Enlarged Board of Appeal may not take part in any appeal if they have any personal interest therein, if they have previously been involved as representatives of one of the parties, or if they participated in the decision under appeal.

(2) If, for one of the reasons mentioned in paragraph 1, or for any other reason, a member of a Board of Appeal or of the Enlarged Board of Appeal considers that he should not take part in any appeal, he shall inform the Board accordingly.

(3) Members of a Board of Appeal or of the Enlarged Board of Appeal may be objected to by any party for one of the reasons mentioned in paragraph 1, or if suspected of partiality. An objection shall not be admissible if, while being aware of a reason for objection, the party has taken a procedural step. No objection may be based upon the nationality of members.

(4) The Boards of Appeal and the Enlarged Board of Appeal shall decide as to the action to be taken in the cases specified in paragraphs 2 and 3 without the participation of the member concerned. For the purposes of taking this decision the member objected to shall be replaced by his alternate.

ARTICLE 25

Technical opinion

At the request of the competent national court trying an infringement or revocation action, the European Patent Office shall be obliged, against payment of

624

an appropriate fee, to give a technical opinion concerning the European patent which is the subject of the action. The Examining Divisions shall be responsible for the issue of such opinions.

Chapter IV. The Administrative Council

ARTICLE 26

Membership

(1) The Administrative Council shall be composed of the Representatives and the alternate Representatives of the Contracting States. Each Contracting State shall be entitled to appoint one Representative and one alternate Representative to the Administrative Council.

(2) The members of the Adminstrative Council may, subject to the provisions of its Rules of Procedure, be assisted by advisers or experts.

ARTICLE 27

Chairmanship

(1) The Administrative Council shall elect a Chairman and a Deputy Chairman from among the Representatives and alternate Representatives of the Contracting States. The Deputy Chairman shall *ex officio* replace the Chairman in the event of his being prevented from attending to his duties.

(2) The duration of the terms of office of the Chairman and the Deputy Chairman shall be three years. The terms of office shall be renewable.

ARTICLE 28

Board

(1) When there are at least eight Contracting States, the Administrative Council may set up a Board composed of five of its members.

(2) The Chairman and the Deputy Chairman of the Administrative Council shall be members of the Board *ex officio*; the other three members shall be elected by the Administrative Council.

(3) The term of office of the members elected by the Administrative Council shall be three years. This term of office shall not be renewable.

(4) The Board shall perform the duties given to it by the Administrative Council in accordance with the Rules of Procedure.

ARTICLE 29

Meetings

(1) Meetings of the Administrative Council shall be convened by its Chairman.

(2) The President of the European Patent Office shall take part in the deliberations of the Administrative Council.

(3) The Administrative Council shall hold an ordinary meeting once each year. In addition, it shall meet on the initiative of its Chairman or at the request of one-third of the Contracting States.

(4) The deliberations of the Administrative Council shall be based on an agenda, and shall be held in accordance with its Rules of Procedure.

(5) The provisional agenda shall contain any question whose inclusion is requested by any Contracting State in accordance with the Rules of Procedure.

ARTICLE 30

Attendance of observers

(1) The World Intellectual Property Organization shall be represented at the meetings of the Administrative Council, in accordance with the provisions of an agreement to be concluded between the European Patent Organisation and the World Intellectual Property Organization.

(2) Any other inter-governmental organisation charged with the implementation of international procedures in the field of patents with which the Organisation has concluded an agreement shall be represented at the meetings of the Administrative Council, in accordance with any provisions contained in such agreement.

(3) Any other inter-governmental and international non-governmental organisations exercising an activity of interest to the Organisation may be invited by the Administrative Council to arrange to be represented at its meetings during any discussion of matters of mutual interest.

ARTICLE 31

Languages of the Administrative Council

(1) The languages in use in the deliberations of the Administrative Council shall be English, French and German.

(2) Documents submitted to the Administrative Council, and the minutes of its deliberations, shall be drawn up in the three languages mentioned in paragraph 1.

ARTICLE 32

Staff, premises and equipment

The European Patent Office shall place at the disposal of the Administrative Council and any body established by it such staff, premises and equipment as may be necessary for the performance of their duties.

ARTICLE 33

Competence of the Administrative Council in certain cases

(1) The Administrative Council shall be competent to amend the following provisions of this Convention:

(a) the time limits laid down in this Convention; this shall apply to the time limit laid down in Article 94 only in the conditions laid down in Article 95;
(b) the Implementing Regulations.

(2) The Administrative Council shall be competent, in conformity with this Convention, to adopt or amend the following provisions:

    (a) the Financial Regulations;

    (b) the Service Regulations for permanent employees and the conditions of employment of other employees of the European Patent Office, the salary scales of the said permanent and other employees, and also the nature, and rules for the grant, of any supplementary benefits;

    (c) the Pension Scheme Regulations and any appropriate increases in existing pensions to correspond to increases in salaries;

    (d) the Rules relating to Fees;

    (e) its Rules of Procedure.

(3) Notwithstanding Article 18, paragraph 2, the Administrative Council shall be competent to decide, in the light of experience, that in certain categories of cases Examining Divisoins shall consist of one technical examiner. Such decisions may be rescinded.

(4) The Administrative Council shall be competent to authorise the President of the European Patent Office to negotiate and, with its approval, to conclude agreements on behalf of the European Patent Organisation with States, with inter-governmental organisations and with documentation centres set up by virtue of agreements with such organisation.

Article 34

Voting rights

(1) The right to vote in the Administrative Council shall be restricted to the Contracting States.

(2) Each Contracting State shall have one vote, subject to the application of the provisions of Article 36.

Article 35

Voting rules

(1) The Administrative Council shall take its decisions other than those referred to in paragraph 2 by a simple majority of the Contracting States represented and voting.

(2) A majority of three-quarters of the votes of the Contracting States represented and voting shall be required for the decisions which the Administrative Council is empowered to take under Article 7, Article 11, paragraph 1, Article 33, Article 39, paragraph 1, Article 40, paragraphs 2 and 4, Article 46, Article 87, Article 95, Article 134, Article 151, paragraph 3, Article 154, paragraph 2, Article 155, paragraph 2, Article 156, Article 157, paragraphs 2 to 4, Article 160, paragraph 1, second sentence, Article 162, Article 163, Article 166, Article 167 and Article 172.

(3) Abstentions shall not be considered as votes.

Article 36

Weighting of votes

(1) In respect of the adoption or amendment of the Rules relating to Fees and, if the financial contribution to be made by the Contracting States would thereby be

increased, the adoption of the budget of the Organisation and of any amending or supplementary budget, any Contracting State may require, following a first ballot in which each Contracting State shall have one vote, and whatever the result of this ballot, that a second ballot be taken immediately, in which votes shall be given to the States in accordance with paragraph 2. The decision shall be determined by the result of this second ballot.

(2) The number of votes that each Contracting State shall have in the second ballot shall be calculated as follows:

(a) the percentage obtained for each Contracting State in respect of the scale of the special financial contributions, pursuant to Article 40, paragraphs 3 and 4, shall be multiplied by the number of Contracting States and divided by five;

(b) the number of votes thus given shall be rounded upwards to the next higher whole number;

(c) five additional votes shall be added to this number;

(d) nevertheless no Contracting State shall have more than 30 votes.

Chapter V. Financial provisions

ARTICLE 37

Cover for expenditure

The expenditure of the Organisation shall be covered:

(a) by the Organisation's own resources;

(b) by payments made by the Contracting States in respect of renewal fees for European patents levied in these States;

(c) where necessary, by special financial contributions made by the Contracting States;

(d) where appropriate, by the revenue provided for in Article 146.

ARTICLE 38

The Organisation's own resources

The Organisation's own resources shall be the yield from the fees laid down in this Convention, and also all receipts, whatever their nature.

ARTICLE 39

Payments by the Contracting States in respect of renewal fees for European patents

(1) Each Contracting State shall pay to the Organisation in respect of each renewal fee received for a European patent in that State an amount equal to a proportion of that fee, to be fixed by the Administrative Council; the proportion shall not exceed 75 per cent and shall be the same for all Contracting States. However, if the said proportion corresponds to an amount which is less than a uniform minimum amount fixed by the Administrative Council, the Contracting State shall pay that minimum to the Organisation.

(2) Each Contracting State shall communicate to the Organisation such information as the Administrative Council considers to be necessary to determine the amount of its payments.

(3) The due dates for these payments shall be determined by the Administrative Council.

(4) If a payment is not remitted fully by the due date, the Contracting State shall pay interest from the due date on the amount remaining unpaid.

ARTICLE 40

Level of fees and payments—Special financial contributions

(1) The amounts of the fees referred to under Article 38 and the proportion referred to under Article 39 shall be fixed at such a level as to ensure that the revenue in respect thereof is sufficient for the budget of the Organisation to be balanced.

(2) However, if the Organisation is unable to balance its budget under the conditions laid down in paragraph 1, the Contracting States shall remit to the Organisation special financial contributions, the amount of which shall be determined by the Administrative Council for the accounting period in question.

(3) These special financial contributions shall be determined in respect of any Contracting State on the basis of the number of patent applications filed in the last year but one prior to that of entry into force of this Convention, and calculated in the following manner:

(a) one half in proportion to the number of patent applications filed in that Contracting State;

(b) one half in proportion to the second highest number of patent applications filed in the order Contracting State by natural or legal persons having their residence or principal place of business in that Contracting State.

However, the amount to be contributed by States in which the number of patent applications filed exceeds 25,000 shall then be taken as a whole and a new scale drawn up determined in proportion to the total number of patent applications filed in these States.

(4) Where, in respect of any Contracting State, its scale position cannot be established in accordance with paragraph 3, the Administrative Council shall, with the consent of that State, decide its scale position.

(5) Article 39, paragraphs 3 and 4, shall apply *mutatis mutandis* to the special financial contributions.

(6) The special financial contributions shall be repaid together with interest at a rate which shall be the same for all Contracting States. Repayments shall be made in so far as it is possible to provide for this purpose in the budget; the amount thus provided shall be distributed among the Contracting States in accordance with the scale mentioned in paragraphs 3 and 4 above.

(7) The special financial contributions remitted in any accounting period shall be wholly repaid before any such contributions or parts thereof remitted in any subsequent accounting period are repaid.

ARTICLE 41

Advances

(1) At the request of the President of the European Patent Office, the Contracting States shall make advances to the Organisation, on account of their payments and contributions, within the limit of the amount fixed by the Administrative Council. Such advances shall be apportioned in proportion to the amounts due by the Contracting States for the accounting period in question.

(2) Article 39, paragraphs 3 and 4, shall apply *mutatis mutandis* to the advances.

ARTICLE 42

Budget

(1) Income and expenditure of the Organisation shall form the subject of estimates in respect of each accounting period and shall be shown in the budget. If necessary, there may be amending or supplementary budgets.

(2) The budget shall be balanced as between income and expenditure.

(3) The budget shall be drawn up in the unit of account fixed in the Financial Regulations.

ARTICLE 43

Authorisation for expenditure

(1) The expenditure entered in the budget shall be authorised for the duration of one accounting period, unless any provisions to the contrary are contained in the Financial Regulations.

(2) Subject to the conditions to be laid down in the Financial Regulations, any appropriations, other than those relating to staff costs, which are unexpended at the end of the accounting period may be carried forward, but not beyond the end of the following accounting period.

(3) Appropriations shall be set out under different headings according to type and purpose of the expenditure and subdivided, as far as necessary, in accordance with the Financial Regulations.

ARTICLE 44

Appropriations of unforeseeable expenditure

(1) The budget of the Organisation may contain appropriations for unforeseeable expenditure.

(2) The employment of these appropriations by the Organisation shall be subject to the prior approval of the Administrative Council.

ARTICLE 45

Accounting period

The accounting period shall commence on 1 January and end on 31 December.

ARTICLE 46

Preparation and adoption of the budget

(1) The President of the European Patent Office shall lay the draft budget before the Administrative Council not later than the date prescribed in the Financial Regulations.

(2) The budget and any amending or supplementary budget shall be adopted by the Administrative Council.

ARTICLE 47

Provisional budget

(1) If, at the beginning of the accounting period, the budget has not been adopted by the Administrative Council, expenditures may be effected on a monthly basis per heading or other division of the budget, according to the provisions of the Financial Regulations, up to one-twelfth of the budget appropriations for the preceding accounting period, provided that the appropriations thus made available to the President of the European Patent Office shall not exceed one-twelfth of those provided for in the draft budget.

(2) The Administrative Council may, subject to the observance of the other provisions laid down in paragraph 1, authorise expenditure in excess of one-twelfth of the appropriations.

(3) The payments referred to in Article 37, sub-paragraph (b), shall continue to be made, on a provisional basis, under the conditions determined under Article 39 for the year preceding that to which the draft budget relates.

(4) The Contracting States shall pay each month, on a provisional basis and in accordance with the scale referred to in Article 40, paragraphs 3 and 4, any special financial contributions necessary to ensure implementation of paragraphs 1 and 2 above. Article 39, paragraph 4, shall apply *mutatis mutandis* to these contributions.

ARTICLE 48

Budget implementation

(1) The President of the European Patent Office shall implement the budget and any amending or supplementary budget on his own responsibility and within the limits of the allocated appropriations.

(2) Within the budget, the President of the European Patent Office may, subject to the limits and conditions laid down in the Financial Regulations, transfer funds as between the various headings or sub-headings.

ARTICLE 49

Auditing of accounts

(1) The income and expenditure account and a balance sheet of the Organisation shall be examined by auditors whose independence is beyond doubt, appointed by the Administrative Council for a period of five years, which shall be renewable or extensible.

(2) The audit, which shall be based on vouchers and shall take place, if necessary, *in situ*, shall ascertain that all income has been received and all expenditure effected in a lawful and proper manner and that the financial management is sound. The auditors shall draw up a report after the end of each accounting period.

(3) The President of the European Patent Office shall annually submit to the Administrative Council the accounts of the preceding accounting period in respect of the budget and the balance sheet showing the assets and liabilities of the Organisation togetherwith the report of the auditors.

(4) The Administrative Council shall approve the annual accounts together with the report of the auditors and shall give the President of the European Patent Office a discharge in respect of the implementation of the budget.

631

ARTICLE 50

Financial Regulations

The Financial Regulations shall in particular establish:

(a) the procedure relating to the establishment and implementation of the budget and for the rendering and auditing of accounts;
(b) the method and procedure whereby the payments and contributions provided for in Article 37 and the advances provided for in Article 41 are to be made available to the Organisation by the Contracting States;
(c) the rules concerning the responsibilities of accounting and paying officers and the arrangements for their supervision;
(d) the rates of interest provided for in Articles 39, 40 and 47;
(e) the method of calculating the contributions payable by virtue of Article 146;
(f) the composition of and duties to be assigned to a Budget and Finance Committee which should be set up by the Administrative Council.

ARTICLE 51

Rules relating to Fees

The Rules relating to Fees shall determine in particular the amounts of the fees and the ways in which they are to be paid.

Part II. Substantive Patent Law

Chapter I. Patentability

ARTICLE 52

Patentable inventions

(1) European patents shall be granted for any inventions which are susceptible of industrial application, which are new and which involve an inventive step.

(2) The following in particular shall not be regarded as inventions within the meaning of paragraph 1:

(a) discoveries, scientific theories and mathematical methods;
(b) aesthetic creations;
(c) schemes, rules and methods for performing mental acts, playing games or doing business, and programs for computers;
(d) presentations of information.

(3) The provisions of paragraph 2 shall exclude patentability of the subject-matter or activities referred to in that provision only to the extent to which a European patent application or European patent relates to such subject-matter or activities as such.

(4) Methods for treatment of the human or animal body by surgery or therapy and diagonistic methods practised on the human or animal body shall not be regarded as inventions which are susceptible of industrial application within the meaning of paragraph 1. This provision shall not apply to products, in particular substances or compositions, for use in any of these methods.

ARTICLE 53

Exceptions to patentability

European patents shall not be granted in respect of:

(a) inventions the publication or exploitation of which would be contrary to "ordre public" or morality, provided that the exploitation shall not be deemed to be so contrary merely because it is prohibited by law or regulation in some or all of the Contracting States;

(b) plant or animal varieties or essentially biological processes for the production of plants or animals; this provision does not apply to microbiological processes or the products thereof.

ARTICLE 54

Novelty

(1) An invention shall be considered to be new if it does not form part of the state of the art.

(2) The state of the art shall be held to comprise everything made available to the public by means of a written or oral description, by use, or in any other way, before the date of filing of the European patent application.

(3) Additionally, the content of European patent applications as filed, of which the dates of filing are prior to the date referred to in paragraph 2 and which were published under Article 93 on or after that date, shall be considered as comprised in the state of the art.

(4) Paragraph 3 shall be applied only in so far as a Contracting State designated in respect of the later application, was also designated in respect of the earlier application as published.

(5) The provisions of paragraph 1 to 4 shall not exclude the patentability of any substance or composition, comprised in the state of the art, for use in a method referred to in Article 52, paragraph 4, provided that its use for any method referred to in that paragraph is not comprised in the state of the art.

ARTICLE 55

Non-prejudicial disclosures

(1) For the application of Article 54 a disclosure of the invention shall not be taken into consideration if it occurred no earlier than six months preceding the filing of the European patent application and if it was due to, or in consequence of:

(a) an evident abuse in relation to the applicant or his legal predecessor, or

(b) the fact that the applicant or his legal predecessor has displayed the invention at an official, or officially recognised, international exhibition falling within the terms of the Convention on international exhibitions signed at Paris on 22 November 1928 and last revised on 30 November 1972.

(2) In the case of paragraph 1(b), paragraph 1 shall apply only if the applicant states, when filing the European patent application, that the invention has been so displayed and files a supporting certificate within the period and under the conditions laid down in the Implementing Regulations.

ARTICLE 56

Inventive step

An invention shall be considered as involving an inventive step if, having regard to the state of the art, it is not obvious to a person skilled in the art. If the state of the art also includes documents within the meaning of Article 54, paragraph 3, these documents are not to be considered in deciding whether there has been an inventive step.

ARTICLE 57

Industrial application

An invention shall be considered as susceptible of industrial application if it can be made or used in any kind of industry, including agriculture.

Chapter II. Persons entitled to apply for and obtain European patents— Mention of the inventor

ARTICLE 58

Entitlement to file a European patent application

A European patent application may be filed by any natural or legal person, or any body equivalent to a legal person by virtue of the law governing it.

ARTICLE 59

Multiple applicants

A European patent application may also be filed either by joint applicants or by two or more applicants designating different Contracting States.

ARTICLE 60

Right to a European patent

(1) The right to a European patent shall belong to the inventor or his successor in title. If the inventor is an employee the right to the European patent shall be determined in accordance with the law of the State in which the employee is mainly employed; if the State in which the employee is mainly employed cannot be determined, the law to be applied shall be that of the State in which the employer has his place of business to which the employee is attached.

(2) If two or more persons have made an invention independently of each other, the right to the European patent shall belong to the person whose European patent application has the earliest date of filing; however, this provision shall apply only if this first application has been published under Article 93 and shall only have effect in respect of the Contracting States designated in that application as published.

(3) For the purposes of proceedings before the European Patent Office, the applicant shall be deemed to be entitled to exercise the right to the European patent.

ARTICLE 61

European patent applications by persons not having the right to a European patent

(1) If by a final decision it is adjudged that a person referred to in Article 60, paragraph 1, other than the applicant, is entitled to the grant of a European patent, that person may, within a period of three months after the decision has become final, provided that the European patent has not yet been granted, in respect of those Contracting States designated in the European patent application in which the decision has been taken or recognised, or has to be recognised on the basis of the Protocol on Recognition annexed to this Convention:

(a) prosecute the application as his own application in place of the applicant.
(b) file a new European patent application in respect of the same invention, or
(c) request that the applicant be refused.

(2) The provisions of Article 76, paragraph 1, shall apply *mutatis mutandis* to a new application filed under paragraph 1.

(3) The procedure to be followed in carrying out the provisions of paragraph 1, the special conditions applying to a new application filed under paragraph 1 and the time limit for paying the filing, search and designation fees on it are laid down in the Implementing Regulations.

ARTICLE 62

Right of the inventor to be mentioned

The inventor shall have the right, *vis-à-vis* the applicant for or proprietor of a European patent, to be mentioned as such before the European Patent Office.

Chapter III. Effects of the European patent and the European patent application

ARTICLE 63

Term of the European patent

(1) The Term of the European patent shall be 20 years as from the date of filing of the application.

(2) Nothing in the preceding paragraph shall limit the right of a Contracting State to extend the term of a European patent, or to grant corresponding protection which follows immediately on expiry of the term of the patent, under the same conditions as those applying to national patents:

(a) in order to take account of a state of war or similar emergency conditions affecting that State;
(b) if the subject-matter of the European patent is a product or a process of manufacturing a product or a use of a product which has to undergo an administrative authorisation procedure required by law before it can be put on the market in that State.

(3) Paragraph 2 shall apply *mutatis mutandis* to European patents granted jointly for a group of Contracting States in accordance with Article 142.

(4) A Contracting State which makes provision for extension of the term or corresponding protection under paragraph 2(b) may, in accordance with an

agreement concluded with the Organisation, entrust to the European Patent Office tasks associated with implementation of the relevant provisions.

ARTICLE 64

Rights conferred by a European patent

(1) A European patent shall, subject to the provisions of paragraph 2, confer on its proprietor from the date of publication of the mention of its grant, in each Contracting State in respect of which it is granted, the same rights as would be conferred by a national patent granted in that State.

(2) If the subject-matter of the European patent is a process, the production conferred by the patent shall extend to the products directly obtained by such process.

(3) Any infringement of a European patent shall be dealt with by national law.

ARTICLE 65

Translation of the specification of the European patent

(1) Any Contracting State may prescribe that if the text, in which the European Patent Office intends to grant a European patent or maintain a European patent as amended for that State, is not drawn up in one of its official languages, the applicant for or proprietor of the patent shall supply to its central industrial property office a translation of this text in one of its official langauges at his option or, where that State has prescribed the use of one specific official language, in that language. The period for supplying the translation shall end three months after the date on which the mention of the grant of the European patent or of the maintenance of the European patent is amended is published in the European Patent Bulletin, unless the State concerned prescribes a longer period.

(2) Any Contracting State which has adopted provisions pursuant to paragraph 1 may prescribe that the applicant for or proprietor of the patent must pay all or part of the costs of publication of such translation within a period laid down by that State.

(3) Any Contracting State may prescribe that in the event of failure to observe the provisions adopted in accordance with paragraphs 1 and 2, the European patent shall be deemed to be void *ab initio* in that State.

ARTICLE 66

Equivalence of European filing with national filing

A European patent application which has been accorded a date of filing shall, in the designated Contracting States, be equivalent to a regular national filing, where appropriate with the priority claimed for the European patent application.

ARTICLE 67

Rights conferred by a European patent application after publication

(1) A European patent application shall, from the date of its publication under Article 93, provisionally confer upon the applicant such protection as is conferred by Article 64, in the Contracting States designated in the application as published.

(2) Any Contracting State may prescribe that a European patent application shall not confer such protection as is conferred by Article 64. However, the protection attached to the publication of the European patent application may not be less than that which the laws of the State concerned attach to the compulsory publication of unexamined national patent applications. In any event, every State shall ensure at least that, from the date of publication of a European patent application, the applicant can claim compensation reasonable in the circumstances from any person who has used the invention in the said State in circumstances where that person would be liable under national law for infringement of a national patent.

(3) Any Contracting State which does not have as an official language the language of the proceedings, may prescribe that provisional protection in accordance with paragraphs 1 and 2 above shall not be effective until such time as a translation of the claims in one of its official languages at the option of the applicant or, where that State has prescribed the use of one specific official language, in that language:

(a) has been made available to the public in the manner prescribed by national law, or

(b) has been communicated to the person using the invention in the said State.

(4) The European patent application shall be deemed never to have had the effects set out in paragraphs 1 and 2 above when it has been withdrawn, deemed to be withdrawn or finally refused. The same shall apply in respect of the effects of the European patent application in a Contracting State the designation of which is withdrawn or deemed to be withdrawn.

ARTICLE 68

Effect of revocation of the European patent

The European patent application and the resulting patent shall be deemed not to have had, as from the outset, the effects specified in Articles 64 and 67, to the exent that the patent has been revoked in opposition proceedings.

ARTICLE 69

Extent of protection

(1) The extent of the protection conferred by a European patent or a European patent application shall be determined by the terms of the claims. Nevertheless, the description and drawings shall be used to interpret the claims.

(2) For the period up to grant of the European patent, the extent of the protection conferred by the European patent application shall be determined by the latest filed claims contained in the publication under Article 93. However, the European patent as granted or as amended in opposition proceedings shall determine retroactively the protection conferred by the European patent application, in so far as such protection is not thereby extended.

[Although not originally part of the main text of the Convention, the Protocol relating to the interpretation of Article 69 is included here for ease of reference:

Protocol on the interpretation of Article 69 of the convention

Article 69 should not be interpreted in the sense that the extent of the protection conferred by a European patent is to be understood as that defined by the strict, literal meaning of the wording used the claims, the description and drawings being employed only for the purpose

637

of resolving an ambiguity found in the claims. Neither should it be interpreted in the sense that the claims serve only as a guideline and that the actual protection conferred may extend to what, from a consideration of the description and drawings by a person skilled in the art, the patentee has contemplated. On the contrary, it is to be interpreted as defining a position between these extremes which combines a fair protection for the patentee with a reasonable degree of certainty for third parties.]

ARTICLE 70

Authentic text of a European patent application or European patent

(1) The text of a European patent application or a European patent in the langauge of the proceedings shall be the authentic text in any proceedings before the European Patent Office and in any Contracting State.

(2) However, in the case referred to in Article 14, paragraph 2, the original text shall, in proceedings before the European Patent Office, constitute the basis for determining whether the subject-matter of the application or patent extends beyond the content of the application as filed.

(3) Any Contracting State may provide that a translation, as provided for in this Convention, in an official language of that State, shall in that State be regarded as authentic, except for revocation proceedings, in the event of the application or patent in the language of the translation conferring protection which is narrower than that conferred by it in the language of the proceedings.

(4) Any Contracting State which adopts a provision under paragraph 3:

    (a) must allow the applicant for or proprietor of the patent to file a corrected translation of the European patent application or European patent. Such corrected translation shall not have any legal effect until any conditions established by the Contracting State under Article 65, paragraph 2, and Article 67, paragraph 3, have been complied with *mutatis mutandis*;

    (b) may prescribe that any person who, in that State, in good faith is using or has made effective and serious preparations for using an invention the use of which would not constitute infringement of the application or patent in the original translation may, after the corrected translation takes effect, continue such use in the course of his business or for the needs thereof without payment.

Chapter IV. The European patent application as an object of property

ARTICLE 71

Tranfer and constitution of rights

A European patent application may be transferred or give rise to rights for one or more of the designated Contracting States.

ARTICLE 72

Assignment

An assignment of a European patent application shall be made in writing and shall require the signature of the parties to the contract.

ARTICLE 73

Contractual licensing

A European patent application may be licensed in whole or in part for the whole or part of the territories of the designated Contracting States.

ARTICLE 74

Law applicable

Unless otherwise specified in this Convention, the European patent application as an object of property shall, in each designated Contracting State and with effect for such State, be subject to the law applicable in that State to national patent applications.

Part III. Application for European Patents

Chapter I. Filing and requirements of the European patent application

ARTICLE 75

Filing of the European patent application

(1) A European patent application may be filed:

(a) at the European Patent Office at Munich or its branch at The Hague, or
(b) if the law of the Contracting State so permits, at the central industrial property office or other competent authority of that State. An application filed in this way shall have the same effect as if it had been filed on the same date at the European Patent Office.

(2) The provisions of paragraph 1 shall not preclude the application of legislative or regulatory provisions which, in any Contracting State:

(a) govern inventions which, owing to the nature of their subject-matter may not be communicated abroad without the prior authorisation of the competent authorities of that State, or
(b) prescribe that each application is to be filed initially with a national authority or make direct filing with another authority subject to prior authorisation.

(3) No Contracting State may provide for or allow the filing of European divisional applications with an authority referred to in paragraph 1(b).

ARTICLE 76

European divisional applications

(1) A European divisional application must be filed directly with the European Patent Office at Munich or its branch at The Hague. It may be filed only in respect of subject-matter which does not extend beyond the content of the earlier application as filed; in so far as this provision is complied with, the divisional application shall be deemed to have been filed on the date of filing of the earlier application and shall have the benefit of any right to priority.

639

(2) The European divisional application shall not designate Contracting States which were not designated in the earlier application.

(3) The procedure to be followed in carrying out the provisions of paragraph 1, the special conditions to be complied with by a divisional application and the time limit for paying the filing, search and designation fees are laid down in the Implementing Regulations.

ARTICLE 77

Forwarding of European patent applications

(1) The central industrial property office of a Contracting State shall be obliged to forward to the European Patent Office, in the shortest time compatible with the application of national law concerning the secrecy of inventions in the interests of the State, any European patent applications which have been filed with that office or with other competent authorities in that State.

(2) The Contracting States shall take all appropriate steps to ensure that European patent applications, the subject of which is obviously not liable to secrecy by virtue of the law referred to in paragraph 1, shall be forwarded to the European Patent Office within six weeks after filing.

(3) European patent applications which require further examination as to their liability to secrecy shall be forwarded in such manner as to reach the European Patent Office within four months after filing, or, where priority has been claimed, fourteen months after the date of priority.

(4) A European patent application, the subject of which has been made secret, shall not be forwarded to the European Patent Office.

(5) European patent applications which do not reach the European Patent Office before the end of the fourteenth month after filing or, if priority has been claimed, after the date of priority, shall be deemed to be withdrawn. The filing, search and designation fees shall be refunded.

ARTICLE 78

Requirements of the European patent application

(1) A European patent application shall contain:

(a) a request for the grant of a European patent;
(b) a description of the invention;
(c) one or more claims;
(d) any drawings referred to in the description or the claims:
(e) an abstract.

(2) A European patent application shall be subject to the payment of the filing fee and the search fee within one month after the filing of the application.

(3) A European patent application must satisfy the conditions laid down in the Implementing Regulations.

ARTICLE 79

Designation of Contracting States

(1) The request for the grant of a European patent shall contain the designation of the Contract State or States in which protection for the invention is desired.

(2) The designation of a contracting state shall be subject to the payment of the

designation fee. The designation fees shall be paid within six months of the date on which the European Patent Bulletin mentions the publication of the European search report.

(3) The designation of a Contracting State may be withdrawn at any time up to the grant of the European patent. Withdrawal of the designation of all the Contracting States shall be deemed to be a withdrawal of the European patent application. Designation fees shall not be refunded.

ARTICLE 80

Date of filing

The date of filing of a European patent application shall be the date on which documents filed by the applicant contain:

(a) an indication that a European patent is sought;
(b) the designation of at least one Contracting State;
(c) information identifying the applicant;
(d) a description and one or more claims in one of the languages referred to in Article 14, paragraphs 1 and 2, even though the description and the claims do not comply with the other requirements of this Convention.

ARTICLE 81

Designation of the inventor

The European patent application shall designate the inventor. If the applicant is not the inventor or is not the sole inventor, the designation shall contain a statement indicating the origin of the right to the European patent.

ARTICLE 82

Unity of invention

The European patent application shall relate to one invention only or to a group of inventions so linked as to form a single general inventive concept.

ARTICLE 83

Disclosure of the invention

The European patent application must disclose the invention in a manner sufficiently clear and complete for it to be carried out by a person skilled in the art.

ARTICLE 84

The claims

The claims shall define the matter for which protection is sought. They shall be clear and concise and be supported by the description.

APPENDIX 1

ARTICLE 85

The abstract

The abstract shall merely serve for use as technical information; it may not be taken into account for any other purpose, in particular not for the purpose of interpreting the scope of the protection sought nor for the purpose of applying Article 54, paragraph 3.

ARTICLE 86

Renewal fees for European patent applications

(1) Renewal fees shall be paid to the European Patent Office in accordance with the Implementing Regulations in respect of European patent applications. These fees shall be due in respect of the third year and each subsequent year, calculated from the date of filing of the application.

(2) When a renewal fee has not been paid on or before the due date, the fee may be validly paid within six months of the said date, provided that the additional fee is paid at the same time.

(3) If the renewal fee and any additional fee have not been paid in due time the European patent application shall be deemed to be withdrawn. The European Patent Office alone shall be competent to decide this.

(4) The obligation to pay renewal fees shall terminate with the payment of the renewal fee due in respect of the year in which the mention of the grant of the European patent is published.

Chapter II. Priority

ARTICLE 87

Priority right

(1) A person who has duly filed in or for any State party to the Paris Convention for the Protection of Industrial Property, an application for a patent or for the registration of a utility model or for a utility certificate or for an inventor's certificate, or his successors in title, shall enjoy, for the purpose of filing a European patent application in respect of the same invention, a right of priority during a period of twelve months from the date of filing of the first application.

(2) Every filing that is equivalent to a regular national filing under the national law of the State where it was made or under bilateral or multilateral agreements, including this Convention, shall be recognised as giving rise to a right of priority.

(3) By a regular national filing is meant any filing that is sufficient to establish the date on which the application was filed, whatever may be the outcome of the application.

(4) A subsequent application for the same subject-matter as a previous first application and filed in or in rsepect of the same State shall be considered as the first application for the purposes of determining priority, provided that, at the date of filing the subsequent application, the previous application has been withdrawn, abandoned or refused, without being open to public inspection and without leaving any rights outstanding, and has not served as a basis for claiming a right of priority. The previous application may not thereafter serve as a basis for claiming a right of priority.

(5) If the first filing has been made in a State which is not a party to the Paris Convention for the Protection of Industrial Property, paragraphs 1 to 4 shall apply only in so far as that State, according to a notification published by the Administrative Council, and by virtue of bilateral or multilateral agreements, grants on the basis of a first filing made at the European Patent Office as well as on the basis of a first filing made in or for any Contracting State and subject to conditions equivalent to those laid down in the Paris Convention, a right of priority having equivalent effect.

ARTICLE 88

Claiming priority

(1) An applicant for a European patent desiring to take advantage of the priority of a previous application shall file a declaration of priority, a copy of the previous application and, if the language of the latter is not one of the official languages of the European Patent Office, a translation of it in one of such official languages. The procedure to be followed in carrying out these provisions is laid down in the Implementing Regulations.

(2) Multiple priorities may be claimed in respect of a European patent application, notwithstanding the fact that they originated in different countries. Where appropriate, multiple priorities may be claimed for any one claim. Where multiple priorities are claimed, time limits which run from the date of priority shall run from the earliest date of priority.

(3) If one or more priorities are claimed in respect of a European patent application, the right of priority shall cover only those elements of the European patent application which are included in the application or applications whose priority is claimed.

(4) If certain elements of the invention for which priority is claimed do not appear among the claims formulated in the previous application, priority may nonetheless be granted, provided that the documents of the previous application as a whole specifically disclose such elements.

ARTICLE 89

Effect of priority right

The right of priority shall have the effect that the date of priority shall count as the date of filing of the European patent application for the purposes of Article 54, paragraphs 2 and 3, and Article 60, paragraph 2.

Part IV. Procedure up to Grant

ARTICLE 90

Examination on filing

(1) The Receiving Section shall examine whether:

   (a) the European patent application satisfies the requirements for the accordance of a date of filing;

643

(b) the filing fee and the search fee have been paid in due time;

(c) in the case provided for in Article 14, paragraph 2, the translation of the European patent application in the language of the proceedings has been filed in due time.

(2) If a date of filing cannot be accorded, the Receiving Section shall give the applicant an opportunity to correct the deficiencies in accordance with the Implementing Regulations. If the deficiencies are not remedied in due time, the application shall not be dealt with as a European patent application.

(3) If the filing fee and the search fee have not been paid in due time or, in the case provided for in Article 14, paragraph 2, the translation of the application in the language of the proceedings has not been filed in due time, the application shall be deemed to be withdrawn.

ARTICLE 91

Examination as to formal requirements

(1) If a European patent application has been accorded a date of filing, and is not deemed to be withdrawn by virtue of Article 90, paragraph 3, the Receiving Section shall examine whether:

(a) the requirements of Article 133, paragraph 2, have been satisfied;

(b) the application meets the physical requirements laid down in the Implementing Regulations for the implementation of this provision;

(c) the abstract has been filed;

(d) the request for the grant of a European patent satisfies the mandatory provisions of the Implementing Regulations concerning its content and, where appropriate, whether the requirements of this Convention concerning the claim to priority have been satisfied;

(e) the designation fees have been paid;

(f) the designation of the inventor has been made in accordance with Article 81;

(g) the drawing referred to in Article 78, paragraph 1(d), were filed on the date of filing of the application.

(2) Where the Receiving Section notes that there are deficiencies which may be corrected, it shall give the applicant an opportunity to correct them in accordance with the Implementing Regulations.

(3) If any deficiencies noted in the examination under paragraph 1(a) to (d) are not corrected in accordance with the Implementing Regulations, the application shall be refused; where the provisions referred to in paragraph 1(d) concern the right of priority, this right shall be lost for the application.

(4) Where, in the case referred to in paragraph 1(e), the designation fee has not been paid in due time in respect of any designated State, the designation of that State shall be deemed to be withdrawn.

(5) Where, in the case referred to in paragraph 1(f), the omission of the designation of the inventor is not, in accordance with the Implementing Regulations and subject to the exceptions laid down therein, corrected within 16 months after the date of filing of the European patent application or, if priority is claimed, after the date of priority, the application shall be deemed to be withdrawn.

(6) Where, in the case referred to in paragraph 1(g), the drawings were not filed on the date of filing of the application and no steps have been taken to correct the deficiency in accordance with the Implementing Regulations, either the application shall be re-dated to the date of filing of the drawings or any reference to the drawings in the application shall be deemed to be deleted, according to the choice exercised by the applicant in accordance with the Implementing Regulations.

ARTICLE 92

The drawing up of the European search report

(1) If a European patent application has been accorded a date of filing and is not deemed to be withdrawn by virtue of Article 90, paragraph 3, the Search Division shall draw up the European search report on the basis of the claims, with due regard to the description and any drawings, in the form prescribed in the Implementing Regulations.

(2) Immediately after it has been drawn up, the European search report shall be transmitted to the applicant together with copies of any cited documents.

ARTICLE 93

Publication of a European patent application

(1) A European patent application shall be published as soon as possible after the expiry of a period of eighteen months from the date of filing or, if priority has been claimed, as from the date of priority. Nonetheless, at the request of the applicant the application may be published before the expiry of the period referred to above. It shall be published simultaneously with the publication of the specification of the European patent when the grant of the patent has become effective before the expiry of the period referred to above.

(2) The publication shall contain the description, the claims and any drawings as filed and, in an annex, the European search report and the abstract, in so far as the latter are available before the termination of the technical preparations for publication. If the European search report and the abstract have not been published at the same time as the application, they shall be published separately.

ARTICLE 94

Request for examination

(1) The European Patent Office shall examine, on written request, whether a European patent application and the invention to which it relates meet the requirements of this Convention.

(2) A request for examination may be filed by the applicant up to the end of six months after the date on which the European Patent Bulletin mentions the publication of the European search report. The request shall not be deemed to be filed until after the examination fee has been paid. The request may not be withdrawn.

(3) If no request for examination has been filed by the end of the period referred to in paragraph 2, the application shall be deemed to be withdrawn.

ARTICLE 95

Extension of the period within which requests for examination may be filed

(1) The Administrative Council may extend the period within which requests for examination may be filed if it is established that European patent applications cannot be examined in due time.

(2) If the Administrative Council extends the period, it may decide that third parties will be entitled to make requests for examination. In such cases, it shall determine the appropriate rules in the Implementing Regulations.

645

(3) Any decision of the Administrative Council to extend the period shall apply only in respect of applications filed after the publication of such decision in the Official Journal of the European Patent Office.

(4) If the Administrative Council extends the period, it must lay down measures with a view to restoring the original period as soon as possible.

ARTICLE 96

Examination of the European patent application

(1) If the applicant for a European patent has filed the request for examination before the European search report has been transmitted to him, the European Patent Office shall invite him after the transmission of the report to indicate, within a period to be determined, whether he desires to proceed further with the European patent application.

(2) If the examination of a European patent application reveals that the application or the invention to which it relates does not meet the requirements of this Convention, the Examining Division shall invite the applicant, in accordance with the Implementing Regulations and as often as necessary, to file his observations within a period to be fixed by the Examining Division.

(3) If the applicant fails to reply in due time to any invitation under paragraph 1 or paragraph 2, the application shall be deemed to be withdrawn.

ARTICLE 97

Refusal or grant

(1) The Examining Division shall refuse a European patent application if it is of the opinion that such application or the invention to which it relates does not meet the requirements of this Convention, except where a different sanction is provided for by this Convention.

(2) If the Examining Division is of the opinion that the application and the invention to which it relates meet the requirements of this Convention, it shall decide to grant the European patent for the designated Contracting States provided that:

(a) it is established, in accordance with the provisions of the Implementing Regulations, that the applicant approves the text in which the Examining Division intends to grant the patent;

(b) the fees for grant and printing are paid within the time limit prescribed in the Implementing Regulations;

(c) the renewal fees and any additional fees already due have been paid.

(3) If the fees for grant and printing are not paid in due time, the application shall be deemed to be withdrawn.

(4) The decision to grant a European patent shall not take effect until the date on which the European Patent Bulletin mentions the grant. This mention shall be published at least 3 months after the start of the time limit referred to in paragraph 2(b).

(5) Provision may be made in the Implementing Regulations for the applicant to file a translation, in the two official languages of the European Patent Office other than the language of the proceedings, of the claims appearing in the text in which the Examining Division intends to grant the Patent. In such case, the period laid

down in paragraph 4 shall be at least five months. If the translation has not been filed in due time, the application shall be deemed to be withdrawn.

(6) At the request of the applicant, mention of grant of the European patent shall be published before expiry of the time limit under paragraph 4 or 5. Such request may only be made if the requirements pursuant to paragraphs 2 and 5 are met.

ARTICLE 98

Publication of a specification of the European patent

At the same time as it publishes the mention of the grant of the European patent, the European Patent Office shall publish a specification of the European patent containing the description, the claims and any drawings.

Part V. Opposition Procedure

ARTICLE 99

Opposition

(1) Within nine months from the publication of the mention of the grant of the European patent, any person may give notice to the European Patent Office of opposition to the European patent granted. Notice of opposition shall be filed in a written reasoned statement. It shall not be deemed to have been filed until the opposition fee has been paid.

(2) The opposition shall apply to the European patent in all the Contracting States in which that patent has effect.

(3) An opposition may be filed even if the European patent has been surrendered or has lapsed for all the designated States.

(4) Opponents shall be parties to the opposition proceedings as well as the proprietor of the patent.

(5) Where a person provides evidence that in a Contracting State, following a final decision, he has been entered in the patent register of such State instead of the previous proprietor, such person shall, at his request, replace the previous proprietor in respect of such State. By derogation from Article 118, the previous proprietor and the person making the request shall not be deemed to be joint proprietors unless both so request.

ARTICLE 100

Grounds for opposition

Opposition may only be filed on the grounds that:

(a) the subject-matter of the European patent is not patentable within the terms of Articles 52 to 57;
(b) the European patent does not disclose the invention in a manner sufficiently clear and complete for it to be carried out by a person skilled in the art;
(c) the subject-matter of the European patent extends beyond the content of the application as filed, or, if the patent was granted on a divisional

application or on a new application filed in accordance with Article 61, beyond the content of the earlier application as filed.

ARTICLE 101

Examination of the opposition

(1) If the opposition is admissible, the Opposition Division shall examine whether the grounds for opposition laid down in Article 100 prejudice the maintenance of the European patent.

(2) In the examination of the opposition, which shall be conducted in accordance with the provisions of the Implementing Regulations, the Opposition Division shall invite the parties, as often as necessary, to file observations, within a period to be fixed by the Opposition Division, on communications from another party or issued by itself.

ARTICLE 102

Revocation or maintenance of the European patent

(1) If the Opposition Division is of the opinion that the grounds for opposition mentioned in Article 100 prejudice the maintenance of the European patent, it shall revoke the patent.

(2) If the Opposition Division is of the opinion that the grounds for opposition mentioned in Article 100 do not prejudice the maintenance of the patent unamended, it shall reject the opposition.

(3) If the Opposition Division is of the opinion that, taking into consideration the amendments made by the proprietor of the patent during the opposition proceedings, the patent and the invention to which it relates meet the requirements of this Convention, it shall decide to maintain the patent as amended, provided that:

    (a) it is established, in accordance with the provisions of the Implementing Regulations, that the proprietor of the patent approves the text in which the Opposition Division intends to maintain the patent;

    (b) the fee for the printing of a new specification of the European patent is paid within the time limit prescribed in the Implementing Regulations.

(4) If the fee for the printing of a new specification is not paid in due time, the patent shall be revoked.

(5) Provision may be made in the Implementing Regulations for the proprietor of the patent to file a translation of any amended claims in the two official languages of the European Patent Office other than the language of the proceedings. If the translation has not been filed in due time the patent shall be revoked.

ARTICLE 103

Publication of a new specification of the European patent

If a European patent is amended under Article 102, paragraph 3, the European Patent Office shall, at the same time as it publishes the mention of the opposition decision, publish a new specification of the European patent containing the description, the claims and any drawings, in the amended form.

ARTICLE 104

Costs

(1) Each party to the proceedings shall meet the costs he has incurred unless a decision of an Opposition Division or Board of Appeal, for reasons of equity, orders, in accordance with the Implementing Regulations, a different apportionment of costs incurred during taking of evidence or in oral proceedings.

(2) On request, the registry of the Opposition Division shall fix the amount of the costs to be paid under a decision apportioning them. The fixing of the costs by the registry may be reviewed by a decision of the Opposition Division on a request filed within the period laid down in the Implementing Regulations.

(3) Any final decision of the European Patent Office fixing the amount of costs shall be dealt with, for the purpose of enforcement in the Contracting States, in the same way as a final decision given by a civil court of the State in the territory of which enforcement is to be carried out. Verification of such decisions shall be limited to its authenticity.

ARTICLE 105

Intervention of the assumed infringer

(1) In the event of an opposition to a European patent being filed, any third party who proves that proceedings for infringement of the same patent have been instituted against him may, after the opposition period has expired, intervene in the opposition proceedings, if he gives notice of intervention within three months of the date on which the infringement proceedings were instituted. The same shall apply in respect of any third party who proves both that the proprietor of the patent has requested that he cease alleged infringement of the patent and that he has instituted proceedings for a court ruling that he is not infringing the patent.

(2) Notice of intervention shall be filed in a written reasoned statement. It shall not be deemed to have been filed until the opposition fee has been paid. Thereafter the intervention shall, subject to any exceptions laid down in the Implementing Regulations, be treated as opposition.

Part VI. Appeals Procedure

ARTICLE 106

Decisions subject to appeal

(1) An appeal shall lie from decisions of the Receiving Section, Examining Divisions, Opposition Divisions and the Legal Division. It shall have suspensive effect.

(2) An appeal may be filed against the decision of the Opposition Division even if the European patent has been surrendered or has lapsed for all the designated States.

(3) A decision which does not terminate proceedings as regards one of the parties can only be appealed together with the final decision, unless the decision allows separate appeal.

(4) The apportionment of costs of opposition proceedings cannot be the sole subject of an appeal.

(5) A decision fixing the amount of costs of opposition proceedings cannot be appealed unless the amount is in excess of that laid down in the Rules relating to Fees.

ARTICLE 107

Persons entitled to appeal and to be parties to appeal proceedings

An party to proceedings adversely affected by a decision may appeal. Any other parties to the proceedings shall be parties to the appeal proceedings as of right.

ARTICLE 108

Time limit and form of appeal

Notice of appeal must be filed in writing at the European Patent Office within two months after the date of notification of the decision appealed from. The notice shall not be deemed to have been filed until after the fee for appeal has been paid. Within four months after the date of notification of the decision, a written statement setting out the grounds of appeal must be filed.

ARTICLE 109

Interlocutory revision

(1) If the department whose decision is contested considers the appeal to be admissible and well founded, it shall rectify its decision. This shall not apply where the appellant is opposed by another party to the proceedings.

(2) If the appeal is not allowed within one month after receipt of the statement of grounds, it shall be remitted to the Board of Appeal without delay, and without comment as to its merit.

ARTICLE 110

Examination of appeals

(1) If the appeal is admissible, the Board of Appeal shall examine whether the appeal is allowable.

(2) In the examination of the appeal, which shall be conducted in accordance with the provisions of the Implementing Regulations, the Board of Appeal shall invite the parties, as often as necessary, to file observations, within a period to be fixed by the Board of Appeal, on communications from another party or issued by itself.

(3) If the applicant fails to reply in due time to an invitation under paragraph 2, the European patent application shall be deemed to be withdrawn, unless the decision under appeal was taken by the Legal Division.

ARTICLE 111

Decision in respect of appeals

(1) Following the examination as to the allowability of the appeal, the Board of Appeal shall decide on the appeal. The Board of Appeal may either exercise any

power within the competence of the department which was responsible for the decision appealed or remit the case to that department for further prosecution.

(2) If the Board of Appeal remits the case for further prosecution to the department whose decision was appealed, that department shall be bound by the *ratio decidendi* of the Board of Appeal, in so far as the facts are the same. If the decision which was appealed emanated from the Receiving Section, the Examining Division shall similarly be bound by the *ratio decidendi* of the Board of Appeal.

ARTICLE 112

Decision or opinion of the Enlarged Board of Appeal

(1) In order to ensure uniform application of the law, or if an important point of law arises:

(a) the Board of Appeal shall, during proceedings on a case and either of its own motion or following a request from a party to the appeal, refer any question to the Enlarged Board of Appeal if it considers that a decision is required for the above purposes. If the Board of Appeal rejects the request, it shall give the reasons in its final decision;

(b) the President of the European Patent Office may refer a point of law to the Enlarged Board of Appeal where two Boards of Appeal have given different decisions on that question.

(2) In the cases covered by paragraph 1(a) the parties to the appeal proceedings shall be parties to the proceedings before the Enlarged Board of Appeal.

(3) The decision of the Enlarged Board of Appeal referred to in paragraph 1(a) shall be binding on the Board of Appeal in respect of the appeal in question.

Part VII. Common Provisions

Chapter I. Common provisions governing procedure

ARTICLE 113

Basis of decisions

(1) The decisions of the European Patent Office may only be based on grounds or evidence on which the parties concerned have had an opportunity to present their comments.

(2) The European Patent Office shall consider and decide upon the European patent application of the European patent only in the text submitted to it, or agreed, by the applicant for or proprietor of the patent.

ARTICLE 114

Examination by the European Patent Office of its own motion

(1) In proceedings before it, the European Patent Office shall examine the facts of its own motion; it shall not be restricted in this examination to the facts, evidence and arguments provided by the parties and the relief sought.

(2) The European Patent Office may disregard facts or evidence which are not submitted in due time by the parties concerned.

651

APPENDIX 1

ARTICLE 115

Observations by third parties

(1) Following the publication of the European patent application, any person may present observations concerning the patentability of the invention in respect of which the application has been filed. Such observations must be filed in writing and must include a statement of the grounds on which they are based. That person shall not be a party to the proceedings before the European Patent Office.

(2) The observations referred to in paragraph 1 shall be communicated to the applicant for or proprietor of the patent who may comment on them.

ARTICLE 116

Oral proceedings

(1) Oral proceedings shall take place either at the instance of the European Patent Office if it considers this to be expedient or at the request of any party to the proceedings. However, the European Patent Office may reject a request for further oral proceedings before the same department where the parties and the subject of the proceedings are the same.

(2) Nevertheless, oral proceedings shall take place before the Receiving Section at the request of the applicant only where the Receiving Section considers this to be expedient or where it envisages refusing the European patent application.

(3) Oral proceedings before the Receiving Section, the Examining Divisions and the Legal Division shall not be public.

(4) Oral proceedings, including delivery of the decision, shall be public, as regards the Boards of Appeal and the Enlarged Board of Appeal, after publication of the European patent application, and also before the Opposition Divisions, in so far as the department before which the proceedings are taking place does not decide otherwise in cases where admission of the public could have serious and unjustified disadvantages, in particular for a party to the proceedings.

ARTICLE 117

Taking of evidence

(1) In any proceedings before an Examining Division, an Opposition Division, the Legal Division or a Board of Appeal the means of giving or obtaining evidence shall include the following:

  (a) hearing the parties;
  (b) requests for information;
  (c) the production of documents;
  (d) hearing the witnesses;
  (e) opinions by experts;
  (f) inspection;
  (g) sworn statements in writing.

(2) The Examining Division, Opposition Division or Board of Appeal may commission one of its members to examine the evidence adduced.

(3) If the European Patent Office considers it necessary for a party, witness or expert to give evidence orally, it shall either:

  (a) issue a summons to the person concerned to appear before it, or

(b) request, in accordance with the provisions of Article 131, paragraph 2, the competent court in the country of residence of the person concerned to take such evidence.

(4) A party, witness or expert who is summoned before the European Patent Office may request the latter to allow his evidence to be heard by a competent court in his country of residence. On receipt of such a request, or if there has been no reply to the summons by the expiry of a period fixed by the European Patent Office in the summons, the European Patent Office may, in accordance with the provisions of Article 131, paragraph 2, request the competent court to hear the persons concerned.

(5) If a party, witness or expert gives evidence before the European Patent Office, the latter may, if it considers it advisable for the evidence to be given on oath or in an equally binding form, request the competent court in the country of residence of the person concerned to re-examine his evidence under such conditions.

(6) When the European Patent Office requests a competent court to take evidence, it may request the court to take the evidence on oath or in an equally binding form and to permit a member of the department concerned to attend the hearing and question the party, witness or expert either through the intermediary of the court or directly.

ARTICLE 118

Unity of the European patent application or European patent

Where the applicants for or proprietors of a European patent are not the same in respect of different designed Contracting States, they shall be regarded as joint applicants or proprietors for the purposes of proceedings before the European Patent Office. The unity of the application or patent in these proceedings shall not be affected; in particular the text of the application or patent shall be uniform for all designated Contracting States unless otherwise provided for in this Convention.

ARTICLE 119

Notification

The European Patent Office shall, as a matter of course, notify those concerned of decisions and summonses, and of any notice or other communication from which a time limit is reckoned, or of which those concerned must be notified under other provisions of this Convention, or of which notification has been ordered by the President of the European Patent Office. Notifications may, where exceptional circumstances so require, be given through the intermediary of the central industrial property offices of the Contracting States.

ARTICLE 120

Time limits

The Implementing Regulations shall specify:

(a) the manner of computation of time limits and the conditions under which such time limits may be extended, either because the European Patent Office or the authorities referred to in Article 75, paragraph 1(b), are not open to receive documents or because mail is not delivered in the localities in which the European Patent Office or such authorities are situated or because postal services are generally interrupted or subsequently dislocated;

(b) the minima and maxima for time limits to be determined by the European Patent Office.

ARTICLE 121

Further processing of the European patent application

(1) If the European patent application is to be refused or is refused or deeemed to be withdrawn following failure to reply within a time limit set by the European Patent Office, the legal consequence provided for shall not ensue or, if it has already ensued, shall be retracted if the applicant requests further processing of the application.

(2) The request shall be filed in writing within two months of the date on which either the decision to refuse the application or the communication that the application is deemed to be withdrawn was notified. The omitted act must be completed within this time limit. The request shall not be deemed to have been filed until the fee for further processing has been paid.

(3) The department competent to decide on the omitted act shall decide on the request.

ARTICLE 122

Restitutio in integrum

(1) The applicant for or proprietor of a European patent who, in spite of all due care required by the circumstances having been taken, was unable to observe a time limit *vis-à-vis* the European Patent Office shall, upon application, have his rights re-established if the non-observance in question has the direct consequence, by virtue of this Convention, of causing the refusal of the European patent application, or of a request, or the deeming of the European patent application to have been withdrawn, or the revocation of the European patent, or the loss of any other right or means of redress.

(2) The application must be filed in writing within two months from the removal of the cause of non-compliance with the time limit. The omitted act must be completed within this period. The application shall only be admissible within the year immediately following the expiry of the unobserved time limit. In the case of non-payment of a renewal fee, the period specified in Article 86, paragraph 2, shall be deducted from the period of one year.

(3) The application must state the grounds on which it is based, and must set out the facts on which it relies. It shall not be deemed to be filed until after the fee for re-establishment of rights has been paid.

(4) The department competent to decide on the omitted act shall decide upon the application.

(5) The provisions of this Article shall not be applicable to the time limits referred to in paragraph 2 of this Article, Article 61, paragraph 3, Article 76, paragraph 3, Article 78, paragraph 2, Article 79, paragraph 2, Article 87, paragraph 1, and Article 94, paragraph 2.

(6) Any person who, in a designated Contracting State, in good faith has used or made effective and serious preparations for using an invention which is the subject of a published European patent application or a European patent in the course of the period between the loss of rights referred to in paragraph 1 and publication of the mention of re-establishment of those rights, may without payment continue such use in the course of his business or for the needs thereof.

(7) Nothing in this Article shall limit the right of a Contracting State to grant *restitutio in integrum* in respect of time limits provided for in this Convention and to be observed *vis-à-vis* the authorities of such State.

ARTICLE 123

Amendments

(1) The conditions under which a European patent application or a European patent may be amended in proceedings before the European Patent Office are laid down in the Implementing Regulations. In any case, an applicant shall be allowed at least one opportunity of amending the description, claims and drawings of his own volition.

(2) A European patent application or a European patent may not be amended in such a way that it contains subject-matter which extends beyond the content of the application as filed.

(3) The claims of the European patent may not be amended during opposition proceedings in such a way as to extend the protection conferred.

ARTICLE 124

Information concerning national patent applications

(1) The Examining Division or the Board of Appeal may invite the applicant to indicate, within a period to be determined by it, the States in which he has made applications for national patents for the whole or part of the invention to which the European patent application relates, and to give the reference numbers of the said applications.

(2) If the applicant fails to reply in due time to an invitation under paragraph 1, the European patent application shall be deemed to be withdrawn.

ARTICLE 125

Reference to general principles

In the absence of procedural provisions in this Convention, the European Patent Office shall take into account the principles of procedural law generally recognised in the Contracting States.

ARTICLE 126

Termination of financial obligations

(1) Rights of the Organisation to the payment of a fee to the European Patent Office shall be extinguished after four years from the end of the calendar year in which the fee fell due.

(2) Rights against the Organisation for the refunding by the European Patent Office of fees or sums of money paid in excess of a fee shall be extinguished after four years from the end of the calendar year in which the right arose.

(3) The period laid down in paragraphs 1 and 2 shall be interrupted in the case covered by paragraph 1 by a request for payment of the fee and in the case covered by paragraph 2 by a reasoned claim in writing. On interruption it shall begin again immediately and shall end at the latest six years after the end of the year in which it

originally began, unless, in the meantime, judicial proceedings to enforce the right have begun; in this case the period shall end at the earliest one year after the judgment enters into force.

Chapter II. Information to the public or official authorities

ARTICLE 127

Register of European Patents

The European Patent Office shall keep a register, to be known as the Register of European Patents, which shall contain those particulars the registration of which is provided for by this Convention. No entry shall be made in the Register prior to the publication of the European patent application. The Register shall be open to public inspection.

ARTICLE 128

Inspection of files

(1) The files relating to European patent applications, which have not yet been published, shall not be made available for inspection without the consent of the applicant.

(2) Any person who can prove that the applicant for a European patent has invoked the rights under the application against him may obtain inspection of the files prior to the publication of that application and without the consent of the applicant.

(3) Where a European divisional application or a new European patent application filed under Article 61, paragraph 1, is published, any person may obtain inspection of the files of the earlier application prior to the publication of that application and without the consent of the relevant applicant.

(4) Subsequent to the publication of the European patent application, the files relating to such application and the resulting European patent may be inspected on request, subject to the restrictions laid down in the Implementing Regulations.

(5) Even prior to the publication of the European patent application, the European Patent Office may communicate the following bibliographic data to third parties or publish them:

   (a) the number of the European patent application;
   (b) the date of filing of the European patent application and, where the priority of a previous application is claimed, the date, State and file number of the previous application;
   (c) the name of the applicant;
   (d) the title of the invention;
   (e) the Contracting States designated.

ARTICLE 129

Periodical publications

The European Patent Office shall periodically publish:

   (a) a European Patent Bulletin containing entries made in the Register of European Patents, as well as other particulars the publication of which is prescribed by this Convention;

(b) an Official Journal of the European Patent Office, containing notices and information of a general character issued by the President of the European Patent Office, as well as any other information relevant to this Convention or its implementation.

ARTICLE 130

Exchanges of information

(1) The European Patent Office and, subject to the application of the legislative or regulatory provisions referred to in Article 75, paragraph 2, the central industrial property office of any Contracting State shall, on request, communicate to each other any useful information regarding the filing of European or national patent applications and regarding any proceedings concerning such applications and the resulting patents.

(2) The provisions of paragraph 1 shall apply to the communication of information by virtue of working agreements between the European Patent Office and:

(a) the central industrial property office of any State which is not a party to this Convention;

(b) any inter-governmental organisation entrusted with the task of granting patents;

(c) any other organisation.

(3) The communications under paragraphs 1 and 2(a) and (b) shall not be subject to the restrictions laid down in Article 128. The Administrative Council may decide that communications under paragraph 2(c) shall not be subject to such restrictions, provided that the organisation concerned shall treat the information communicated as confidential until the European patent application has been published.

ARTICLE 131

Administrative and legal co-operation

(1) Unless otherwise provided in this Convention or in national laws, the European Patent Office and the courts of authorities of Contracting States shall on request give assistance to each other by communicating information or opening files for inspection. Where the European Patent Office lays files open to inspection by courts, Public Prosecutors' Offices or central industrial property offices, the inspection shall not be subject to the restrictions laid down in Article 128.

(2) Upon receipt of letters rogatory from the European Patent Office, the courts or other competent authorities of Contracting States shall undertake, on behalf of that Office and within the limits of their jurisdiction, any necessary enquiries or other legal measures.

ARTICLE 132

Exchange of publications

(1) The European Patent Office and the central industrial property offices of the Contracting States shall despatch to each other on request and for their own use one or more copies of their respective publications free of charge.

(2) The European Patent Office may conclude argreements relating to the exchange or supply of publications.

APPENDIX 1

Chapter III. Representation

ARTICLE 133

General principles of representation

(1) Subject to the provisions of paragraph 2, no person shall be compelled to be represented by a professional representative in proceedings established by this Convention.

(2) Natural or legal persons not having either a residence or their principal place of business within the territory of one of the Contracting States must be represented by a professional representative and act through him in all proceedings established by this Convention, other than in filing the European patent application; the Implementing Regulations may permit other exceptions.

(3) Natural or legal persons having their residence or principal place of business within the territory of one of the Contracting States may be represented in proceedings established by this Convention by an employee, who need not be a professional representative but who must be authorised in accordance with the Implementing Regulations. The Implementing Regulations may provide whether and under what conditions an employee of such a legal person may also represent other legal persons which have their principal place of business within the territory of one of the Contracting States and which have economic connections with the first legal person.

(4) The Implementing Regulations may prescribe special provisions concerning the common representation of parties acting in common.

ARTICLE 134

Professional representatives

(1) Professional representation of natural or legal persons in proceedings established by this Convention may only be undertaken by professional representatives whose names appear on a list maintained for this purpose by the European Patent Office.

(2) Any natural person who fulfils the following conditions may be entered on the list of professional representatives:

(a) he must be a national of one of the Contracting States;
(b) he must have his place of business or employment within the territory of one of the Contracting States;
(c) he must have passed the European qualifying examination.

(3) Entry shall be effected upon request, accompanied by certificates which must indicate that the conditions laid down in paragraph 2 are fulfilled.

(4) Persons whose names appear on the list of professional representatives shall be entitled to act in all proceedings established by this Convention.

(5) For the purpose of acting as a professional representative, any person whose name appears on the list referred to in paragraph 1 shall be entitled to establish a place of business in any Contracting State in which proceedings established by this Convention may be conducted, having regard to the Protocol on Centralisation annexed to this Convention. The authorities of such State may remove that entitlement in individual cases only in application of legal provisions adopted for the purpose of protecting public security and law and order. Before such action is taken, the President of the European Patent Office shall be consulted.

(6) The President of the European Patent Office may, in special circumstances, grant exemption from the requirement of paragraph 2(a).

(7) Professional representation in proceedings established by this Convention may also be undertaken, in the same way as by a professional representative, by any legal practitioner qualified in one of the Contracting States and having his place of business within such State, to the extent that he is entitled, within the said State, to act as a professional representative in patent matters. Paragraph 5 shall apply *mutatis mutandis*.

(8) The Administrative Council may adopt provisions governing:

(a) the qualifications and training required of a person for admission to the European qualifying examination and the conduct of such examination;

(b) the establishment or recognition of an institute consituted by the persons entitled to act as professional representatives by virtue of either the European qualifying examination or the provisions of Article 163, paragraph 7;

(c) any disciplinary power to be exercised by that institute or the European Patent Office on such persons.

Part VIII. Impact on National Law

Chapter I. Conversion into a national patent application

ARTICLE 135

Request for the application of national procedure

(1) The central industrial property office of a designated Contracting State shall apply the procedure for the grant of a national patent only at the request of the applicant for or proprietor of a European patent, and in the following circumstances:

(a) when the European patent application is deemed to be withdrawn pursuant to Article 77, paragraph 5, or Article 162, paragraph 4;

(b) in such other cases as are provided for by the national law in which the European patent application is refused or withdrawn or deemed to be withdrawn, or the European patent is revoked under this Convention.

(2) The request for conversion shall be filed within three months after the European patent application has been withdrawn or after notification has been made that the application is deemed to be withdrawn, or after a decision has been notified refusing the application or revoking the European patent. The effect referred to in Article 66 shall lapse if the request is not filed in due time.

ARTICLE 136

Submission and transmission of the request

(1) A request for conversion shall be filed with the European Patent Office and shall specify the Contracting States in which application of the procedure for the grant of a national patent is desired. The request shall not be deemed to be filed until the conversion fee has been paid. The European Patent Office shall transmit the request to the central industrial property offices of the Contracting States

specified therein, accopanied by a copy of the files relating to the European patent application or the European patent.

(2) However, if the applicant is notified that the European patent application has been deemed to be withdrawn pursuant to Article 77, paragraph 5, the request shall be filed with the central industrial property office with which the application has been filed. That office shall, subject to the provisions of national security, transmit the request, together with a copy of the European patent application, directly to the central industrial property offices of the Contracting States specified by the applicant in the request. The effect referred to in Article 66 shall lapse if such transmission is not made within twenty months after the date of filing or, if a priority has been claimed, after the date of priority.

ARTICLE 137

Formal requirements for conversion

(1) A European patent application transmitted in accordance with Article 136 shall not be subjected to formal requirements of national law which are different from or additional to those provided for in this Convention.

(2) Any central industrial property office to which the application is transmitted may require that the applicant shall, within not less than two months:

(a) pay the national application fee;
(b) file a translation in one of the official languages of the State in question of the original text of the European patent application and, where appropriate, of the text, as amended during proceedings before the European Patent Office, which the applicant wishes to submit to the national procedure.

Chapter II. Revocation and prior rights

ARTICLE 138

Grounds for revocation

(1) Subject to the provisions of Article 139, a European patent may only be revoked under the law of a Contracting State, with effect for its territory, on the following grounds:

(a) if the subject-matter of the European patent is not patentable within the terms of Articles 52 to 57;
(b) if the European patent does not disclose the invention in a manner sufficiently clear and complete for it to be carried out by a person skilled in the art;
(c) if the subject-matter of the European patent extends beyond the content of the application as filed or, if the patent was granted on a divisional application or on a new application filed in accordance with Article 61, beyond the content of the earlier application as filed;
(d) if the protection conferred by the European patent has been extended;
(e) if the proprietor of the European patent is not entitled under Article 60, paragraph 1.

(2) If the grounds for revocation only affect the European patent in part, revocation shall be pronounced in the form of a corresponding limitation of the said patent. If the national law so allows, the limitation may be effected in the form of an amendment to the claims, the description or the drawings.

ARTICLE 139

Rights of earlier date or the same date

(1) In any designated Contracting State a European patent application and a European patent shall have with regard to a national patent application and a national patent the same prior right effect as a national patent application and a national patent.

(2) A national patent application and a national patent in a Contracting State shall have with regard to a European patent in which that Contracting State is designated the same prior right effect as they have with regard to a national patent.

(3) Any Contracting State may prescribe whether and on what terms an invention disclosed in both a European patent application or patent and a national application or patent having the same date of filing or, where priority is claimed, the same date of priority, may be protected simultaneously by both applications or patents.

Chapter III. Miscellaneous effects

ARTICLE 140

National utility models and utility certificates

Article 66, Article 124, Articles 135 to 137 and Article 139 shall apply to utility models and utility certificates and to applications for utility models and utility certificates registered or deposited in the Contracting States whose laws make provision for such models or certificates.

ARTICLE 141

Renewal fees for European patents

(1) Renewal fees in respect of a European patent may only be imposed for the years which follow that referred to in Article 86, paragraph 4.

(2) Any renewal fees falling due within two months after the publication of the mention of the grant of the European patent shall be deemed to have been validly paid if they are paid within that period. Any additional fee provided for under national law shall not be charged.

Part IX. Special Agreements

ARTICLE 142

Unitary patents

(1) Any group of Contracting States, which has provided by a special agreement that a European patent granted for those States has a unitary character throughout their territories, may provide that a European patent may only granted jointly in respect of all those States.

(2) Where any group of Contracting States has availed itself of the authorisation given in paragraph 1, the provisions of this Part shall apply.

APPENDIX 1

ARTICLE 143

Special departments of the European Patent Office

(1) The group of Contracting States may give additional tasks to the European Patent Office.

(2) Special departments common to the Contracting States in the group may be set up within the European Patent Office in order to carry out the additional tasks. The President of the European Patent Office shall direct such special departments; Article 10, paragraphs 2 and 3, shall apply *mutatis mutandis.*

ARTICLE 144

Representation before special departments

The group of Contracting States may lay down special provisions to govern representation of parties before the departments referred to in Article 143, paragraph 2.

ARTICLE 145

Select committee of the Administrative Council

(1) The group of Contracting States may set up a select committee of the Administrative Council for the purpose of supervising the activities of the special departments set up under Article 143, paragraph 2; the European Patent Office shall place at its disposal such staff, premises and equipment as may be necessary for the performance of its duties. The President of the European Patent Office shall be responsible for the activities of the special departments to the select committee of the Administrative Council.

(2) The composition, powers and functions of the select committee shall be determined by the group of Contracting States.

ARTICLE 146

Cover for expenditure for carrying out special tasks

Where additional tasks have been given to the European Patent Office under Article 143, the group of Contracting States shall bear the expenses incurred by the Organisation in carrying out these tasks. Where special departments have been set up in the European Patent Office to carry out these additional tasks, the group shall bear the expenditure on staff, premises and equipment chargeable in respect of these departments. Article 39, paragraphs 3 and 4, Article 41 and Article 47 shall apply *mutatis mutandis.*

ARTICLE 147

Payments in respect of renewal fees for unitary patents

If the group of Contracting States has fixed a common scale of renewal fees in respect of European patents the proportion referred to in Article 39, paragraph 1, shall be calculated on the basis of the common scale; the minimum amount referred to in Article 39, paragraph 1, shall apply to the unitary patent. Article 39, paragraphs 3 and 4, shall apply *mutatis mutandis*.

ARTICLE 148

The European patent application as an object of property

(1) Article 74 shall apply unless the group of Contracting States has specified otherwise.

(2) The group of Contracting States may provide that a European patent application for which these Contracting States are designated may only be transferred, mortgaged or subjected to any legal means of execution in respect of all the Contracting States of the group and in accordance with the provisions of the special agreement.

ARTICLE 149

Joint designation

(1) The group of Contracting States may provide that these States may only be designated jointly, and that the designation of one or some only of such States shall be deemed to constitute the designation of all the States of the group.

(2) Where the European Patent Office acts as a designated Office under Article 153, paragraph 1, paragraph 1 shall apply if the applicant has indicated in the international application that he wishes to obtain a European patent for one or more of the designated States of the group. The same shall apply if the applicant designates in the international application one of the Contracting States in the group, whose national law provides that the designation of that State shall have the effect of the application being for a European patent.

Part X. International Application Pursuant to the Patent Co-operation Treaty

ARTICLE 150

Application of the Patent Co-operation Treaty

(1) The Patent Co-operation Treaty of 19 June 1970, hereinafter referred to as the Co-operation Treaty, shall be applied in accordance with the provisions of this Part.

(2) International applications filed under the Co-operation Treaty may be the subject of proceedings before the European Patent Office. In such proceedings, the provisons of that Treaty shall be applied, supplemented by the provisions of this Convention. In case of conflict, the provisions of the Co-operation Treaty shall prevail. In particular, for an international application the time limit within which a request for examination must be filed under Article 94, paragraph 2, of this Convention shall not expire before the time prescribed by Article 22 or Article 39 of the Co-operation Treaty as the case may be.

(3) An international application, for which the European Patent Office acts as designated Office or elected Office, shall be deemed to be a European patent application.

(4) Where reference is made in this Convention to the Co-operation Treaty, such reference shall include the Regulations under that Treaty.

ARTICLE 151

The European Patent Office as a receiving Office

(1) The European Patent Office may act as a receiving Office within the meaning of Article 2(xv) of the Co-operation Treaty if the applicant is a resident or national or a Contracting State to this Convention in respect of which the Co-operation Treaty has entered into force.

(2) The European Patent Office may also act as a receiving Office if the applicant is a resident or national of a State which is not a Contracting State to this Convention, but which is a Contracting State to the Co-operation Treaty and which has concluded an agreement with the Organisation whereby the European Patent Office acts as a receiving Office, in accordance with the provisions of the Co-operation Treaty, in place of the national office of that State.

(3) Subject to the prior approval of the Administrative Council, the European Patent Office may also act as a receiving Office for any other applicant, in accordance with an agreement concluded between the Organisation and the International Bureau of the World Intellectual Property Organization.

ARTICLE 152

Filing and transmittal of the international application

(1) If the applicant chooses the European Patent Office as a receiving Office for his international application, he shall file it directly with the European Patent Office. Article 75, paragraph 2, shall nevertheless apply *mutatis mutandis*.

(2) In the event of an international application being filed with the European Patent Office through the intermediary of the competent central industrial property office, the Contracting State concerned shall take all necessary measures to ensure that the application is transmitted to the European Patent Office in time for the latter to be able to comply in due time with the conditions for transmittal under the Co-operation Treaty.

(3) Each international application shall be subject to the payment of the transmittal fee, which shall be payable within one month after receipt of the application.

ARTICLE 153

The Europeran Patent Office as a designated Office

(1) The European Patent Office shall act as a designated Office within the meaning of Article 2(xiii) of the Co-operation Treaty for those Contracting States to this Convention in respect of which the Co-operation Treaty has entered into force and which are designated in the international application if the applicant informs the receiving Office in the international application that he wishes to obtain a European patent for these States. The same shall apply if, in the international application, the applicant designates a Contracting State of which the national law provides the designation of that State shall have the effect of the application being for a European patent.

(2) When the European Patent Office acts as a designated Office, the Examining

Division shall be competent to take decisions which are required under Article 25, paragraph 2(a), of the Co-operation Treaty.

ARTICLE 154

The European Patent Office as an International Searching Authority

(1) The European Patent Office shall act as an International Searching Authority within the meaning of Chapter I of the Co-operation Treaty for applicants who are residents or nationals of a Contracting State in respect of which the Co-operation Treaty has entered into force, subject to the conclusion of an agreement between the Organisation and the International Bureau of the World Intellectual Property Organization.

(2) Subject to the prior approval of the Administrative Council, the European Patent Office shall also act as an International Searching Authority for any other applicant, in accordance with an agreement concluded between the Organisation and the International Bureau of the World Intellectual Property Organization.

(3) The Boards of Appeal shall be responsible for deciding on a protest made by an applicant against an additional fee charged by the European Patent Office under the provisions of Article 17, paragraph 3(a), of the Co-operation Treaty.

ARTICLE 155

The European Patent Office as an International Preliminary Examining Authority

(1) The European Patent Office shall act as an International Preliminary Examining Authority within the meaning of Chapter II of the Co-operation Treaty for applicants who are residents or nationals of a Contracting State bound by that Chapter, subject to the conclusion of an agreement between the Organisation and the International Bureau of the World Intellectual Property Organization.

(2) Subject to the prior approval of the Administrative Council, the European Patent Office shall also act as an International Preliminary Examining Authority for any other applicant, in accordance with an agreement concluded between the Organisation and the International Bureau of the World Intellectual Property Organization.

(3) The Boards of Appeal shall be responsible for deciding on a protest made by an applicant against an additional fee charged by the European Patent Office under the provisions of Article 34, paragraph 3(a), of the Co-operation Treaty.

ARTICLE 156

The European Patent Office as an elected Office

The European Patent Office shall act as an elected Office within the meaning of Article 2(xiv) of the Co-operation Treaty if the applicant has elected any of the designated States referred to in Article 153, paragraph 1, or Article 149, paragraph 2, for which Chapter II of that Treaty has become binding. Subject to the prior approval of the Administrative Council, the same shall apply where the applicant is a resident or national of a State which is not a party to that Treaty or which is not bound by Chapter II of that Treaty, provided that he is one of the persons whom the Assembly of the International Patent Co-operation Union has decided to allow, pursuant to Article 31, paragraph 2(b), of the Co-operation Treaty, to make a demand for international preliminary examination.

ARTICLE 157

International search report

(1) Without prejudice to the provisions of paragraphs 2 to 4, the international search report under Article 18 of the Co-operation Treaty or any declaration under Article 17, paragraph 2(a), of that Treaty and their publication under Article 21 of that Treaty shall take the place of the European search report and the mention of its publication in the European Patent Bulletin.

(2) Subject to the decisions of the Administrative Council referred to in paragraph 3:

  (a) a supplementary European search report shall be drawn up in respect of all international applications;
  (b) the applicant shall pay the search fee, which shall be paid at the same time as the national fee provided for in Article 22, paragraph 1, or Article 39, paragraph 1, of the Co-operation Treaty. If the search fee is not paid in due time the application shall be deemed to be withdrawn.

(3) The Administrative Council may decide under what conditions and to what extent:

  (a) the supplementary European search report is to be dispensed with;
  (b) the search fee is to be reduced.

(4) The Administrative Council may at any time rescind the decisions taken pursuant to paragraph 3.

ARTICLE 158

Publication of the international application and its supply to the European Patent Office

(1) Publication under Article 21 of the Co-operation Treaty of an international application for which the European Patent Office is a designated Office shall, subject to paragraph 3, take the place of the publication of a European patent application and shall be mentioned in the European Patent Bulletin. Such an application shall not however be considered as comprised in the state of the art in accordance with Article 54, paragraph 3, if the conditions laid down in paragraph 2 are not fulfilled.

(2) The international application shall be supplied to the European Patent Office in one of its official languages. The applicant shall pay to the European Patent Office the national fee provided for in Article 22, paragraph 1, or Article 39, paragraph 1, of the Co-operation Treaty.

(3) If the international application is published in a language other than one of the official languages of the European Patent Office, that Office shall publish the international application, supplied as specified in paragraph 2. Subject to the provisions of Article 67, paragraph 3, the provisional protection in accordance with Article 67, paragraphs 1 and 2, shall be effective from the date of that publication.

Part XI. Transitional Provisions

ARTICLE 159

Administrative Council during a transitional period

(1) The States referred to in Article 169, paragraph 1, shall appoint their representatives to the Administrative Council; on the invitation of the Government of the Federal Republic of Germany, the Administrative Council shall meet no later than two months after the entry into force of this Convention, particularly for the purpose of appointing the President of the European Patent Office.

(2) The duration of the term of office of the first Chairman of the Administrative Council appointed after the entry into force of this Convention shall be four years.

(3) The terms of office of two of the elected members of the first Board of the Administrative Council set up after the entry into force of this Convention shall be five and four years respectively.

ARTICLE 160

Appointment of employees during a transitional period

(1) Until such time as the Service Regulations for permanent employees and the conditions of employment of other employees of the European Patent Office have been adopted, the Administrative Council and the President of the European Patent Office, each within their respective powers, shall recruit the necessary employees and shall conclude short-term contracts to that effect. The Administrative Council may lay down general principles in respect of recruitment.

(2) During the transitional period, the expiry of which shall be determined by the Administrative Council, the Administrative Council, after consulting the President of the European Patent Office, may appoint a members of the Enlarged Board of Appeal or of the Boards of Appeal technically or legally qualified members of national courts and authorities of Contracting States who may continue their activities in their national courts or authorities. They may be appointed for a term of less than five years, though this shall not be less than one year, and may be reappointed.

ARTICLE 161

First accounting period

(1) The first accounting period of the Organisation shall extend from the date of entry into force of this Convention to 31 December of the same year. If that date falls within the second half of the year, the accounting period shall extend until 31 December of the following year.

(2) The budget for the first accounting period shall be drawn up as soon as possible after the entry into force of this Convention. Until contributions provided for in Article 40 due in accordance with the first budget are received by the Organisation, the Contracting States shall, upon the request of and within the limit of the amount fixed by the Administrative Council, make advances which shall be deducted from their contributions in respect of that budget. The advances shall be determined in accordance with the scale referred to in Article 40. Article 39, paragraphs 3 and 4, shall apply *mutatis mutandis* to the advances.

ARTICLE 162

Progressive expansion of the field of activity of the European Patent Office

(1) European patent applications may be filed with the European Patent Office from the date fixed by the Administrative Council on the recommendation of the President of the European Patent Office.

(2) The Administrative Council may, on the recommendation of the President of the European Patent Office, decide that, as from the date referred to in paragraph 1, the processing of European patent applications may be restricted. Such restriction may be in respect of certain areas of technology. However, examination shall in any event be made as to whether European patent applications can be accorded a date of filing.

(3) If a decision has been taken under paragraph 2, the Administrative Council may not subsequently further restrict the processing of European patent applications.

(4) Where, as a result of the procedure being restricted under paragraph 2, a European patent application cannot be further processed, the European Patent Office shall communicate this to the applicant and shall point out that he may make a request for conversion. The European patent application shall be deemed to be withdrawn on receipt of such communication.

ARTICLE 163

Professional representatives during a transitional period

(1) During a transitional period, the expiry of which shall be determined by the Administrative Council, notwithstanding the provisions of Article 134, paragraph 2, any natural person who fulfils the following conditions may be entered on the list of professional representatives:

(a) he must be a national of a Contracting State;
(b) he must have his place of business or employment within the territory of one of the Contracting States;
(c) he must be entitled to represent natural or legal persons in patent matters before the central industrial property office of the Contracting State in which he has his place of business or employment.

(2) Entry shall be effected upon request, accompanied by a certificate furnished by the central industrial property office, which must indicate that the conditions laid down in paragraph 1 are fulfilled.

(3) When, in any Contracting State, the entitlement referred to in paragraph 1(c) is not conditional upon the requirement of special professional qualifications, persons applying to be entered on the list who act in patent matters before the central industrial property office of the said State must have habitually so acted for at least five years. However, persons whose professional qualification to represent natural or legal persons in patent matters before the central industrial property office of one of the Contracting States is officially recognised in accordance with the regulations laid down by such State shall not be subject to the condition of having exercised the profession. The certificate furnished by the central industrial property office must indicate that the applicant satisfies one of the conditions referred to in the present paragraph.

(4) The President of the European Patent Office may grant exemption from:

(a) the requirement of paragraph 3, first sentence, if the applicant furnishes proof that he has acquired the requisite qualification in another way;
(b) the requirement of paragraph 1(a) in special circumstances.

(5) The President of the European Patent Office shall grant exemption from the requirement of paragraph 1(a) if on 5 October 1973 the applicant fulfilled the requirements of paragraph 1(b) and (c).

(6) Persons having their places of business or employment in a State which acceded to this Convention less than one year before the expiry of the transitional period referred to in paragraph 1 or after the expiry of the transitional period may, under the conditions laid down in paragraphs 1 to 5, during a period of one year calculated from the date of entry into force of the accession of that State, be entered on the list of professional representatives.

(7) After the expiry of the transitional period, any person whose name was entered on the list of professional representatives during that period shall, without prejudice to any disciplinary measures taken under Article 134, paragraph 8(c), remain thereon, or, on request, be restored thereto, provided that he then fulfils the requirement of paragraph 1(b).

Part XII. Final Provisions

ARTICLE 164

Implementing Regulations and Protocols

(1) The Implementing Regulations, the Protocol on Recognition, the Protocol on Privileges and Immunities, the Protocol on Centralisation and the Protocol on the Interpretation of Article 69 shall be integral parts of this Convention.

(2) In the case of conflict between the provision of this Convention and those of the Implementing Regulations, the provisions of this Convention shall prevail.

ARTICLE 165

Signature—Ratification

(1) This Convention shall be open for signature until 5 April 1974 by the States which took part in the Inter-Governmental Conference for the setting up of a European System for the Grant of Patents or were informed of the holding of that conference and offered the option of taking part therein.

(2) This Convention shall be subject to ratification; instruments of ratification shall be deposited with the Government of the Federal Republic of Germany.

ARTICLE 166

Accession

(1) This Convention shall be open to accession by:

   (a) the States referred to in Article 165, paragraph 1;
   (b) any other European State at the invitation of the Administrative Council.

(2) Any State which has been a party to the Convention and has ceased so to be as a result of the application of Article 172, paragraph 4, may again become a party to the Convention by acceding to it.

(3) Instruments of accession shall be deposited with the Government of the Federal Republic of Germany.

APPENDIX 1

ARTICLE 167

Reservations

(1) Each Contracting State may, at the time of signature or when depositing its instruments of ratification or accession, make only the reservations specified in paragraph 2.

(2) Each Contracting State may reserve the right to provide that:

(a) European patents, in so far as they confer protection on chemical, pharmaceutical or food products, as such, shall, in accordance with the provisions applicable to national patents, be ineffective or revocable; this reservation shall not affect protection conferred by the patent in so far as it involves a process of manufacture or use of a chemical product or a process of manufacture of a pharmaceutical or food product;

(b) European patents, in so far as they confer protection on agricultural or horticultural processes other than those to which Article 53, sub-paragraph (b), applies, shall, in accordance with the provisions applicable to national patents, be ineffective or revocable;

(c) European patents shall have a term shorter than twenty years, in accordance with the provisions applicable to national patents;

(d) it shall not be bound by the Protocol on Recognition.

(3) Any reservation made by a Contracting State shall have effect for a period of not more than ten years from the entry into force of this Convention. However, where a Contracting State has made any of the reservations referred to in paragraph 2(a) and (b), the Administrative Council may, in respect of such State, extend the period by not more than five years for all or part of any reservation made, if that State submits, at the latest one year before the end of the ten-year period, a reasoned request which satisfies the Administrative Council that the State is not in a position to dispense with that reservation by the expiry of the ten-year period.

(4) Any Contracting State that has made a reservation shall withdraw this reservation as soon as circumstances permit. Such withdrawal shall be made by notification addressed to the Government of the Federal Republic of Germany and shall take effect one month from the date of receipt of such notification.

(5) Any reservation made in accordance with paragraph 2(a), (b) or (c) shall apply to European patents granted on European patent applications filed during the period in which the reservation has effect. The effect of the reservation shall continue for the term of the patent.

(6) Without prejudice to paragraphs 4 and 5, any reservation shall cease to have effect on expiry of the period referred to in paragraph 3, first sentence, or, if the period is extended, on expiry of the extended period.

ARTICLE 168

Territorial field of application

(1) Any Contracting State may declare in its instrument of ratification or accession, or may inform the Government of the Federal Republic of Germany by written notification any time thereafter, that this Convention shall be applicable to one or more of the territories for the external relations of which it is responsible. European patents granted for that Contracting State shall also have effect in the territories for which such a declaration has taken effect.

(2) If the declaration referred to in paragraph 1 is contained in the instrument of ratification or accession, it shall take effect on the same date as the ratification or

670

accession; if the declaration is made in a notification after the deposit of the instrument of ratification of accession, such notification shall take effect six months after the date of its receipt by the Government of the Federal Republic of Germany.

(3) Any Contracting State may at any time declare that the Convention shall cease to apply to some or to all of the territories in respect of which it has given a notification pursuant to paragraph 1. Such declaration shall take effect one year after the date on which the Government of the Federal Republic of Germany received notification thereof.

ARTICLE 169

Entry into force

(1) This Convention shall enter into force three months after the deposit of the last instrument of ratification or accession by six States on whose territory the total number of patent applications filed in 1970 amounted to at least 180,000 for all the said States.

(2) Any ratification or accession after the entry into force of this Convention shall take effect on the first day of the third month after the deposit of the instrument of ratification or accession.

ARTICLE 170

Initial contribution

(1) Any State which ratifies or accedes to this Convention after its entry into force shall pay to the Organisation an initial contribution, which shall not be refunded.

(2) The initial contribution shall be 5 per cent. of an amount calculated by applying the percentage obtained for the State in question, on the date on which ratification or accession takes effect, in accordance with the scale provided for in Article 40, paragraphs 3 and 4, to the sum of the special financial contributions due from the other Contracting States in respect of the accounting periods preceding the date referred to above.

(3) In the event that special financial contributions were not required in respect of the accounting period immediately preceding the date referred to in paragraph 2, the scale of contributions referred to in that paragraph shall be the scale that would have been applicable to the State concerned in respect of the last year for which financial contributions were required.

ARTICLE 171

Duration of the Convention

The present Convention shall be of unlimited duration.

ARTICLE 172

Revision

(1) This Convention may be revised by a Conference of the Contracting States.

(2) The Conference shall be prepared and convened by the Administrative

Council. The Conference shall not be deemed to be validly constituted unless at least three-quarters of the Contracting States are represented at it. In order to adopt the revised text there must be a majority of three-quarters of the Contracting States represented and voting at the Conference. Abstentions shall not be considered as votes.

(3) The revised text shall enter into force when it has been ratified or acceded to by the number of Contracting States specified by the Conference, and at the time specified by that Conference.

(4) Such States as have not ratified or acceded to the revised text of the Convention at the time of its entry into force shall cease to be parties to this Convention as from that time.

ARTICLE 173

Disputes between Contracting States

(1) Any dispute between Contracting States concerning the interpretation or application of the present Convention which is not settled by negotiation shall be submitted, at the request of one of the States concerned, to the Administrative Council, which shall endeavour to bring about agreement between the States concerned.

(2) If such agreement is not reached within six months from the date when the Administrative Council was seized of the dispute, any one of the States concerned may submit the dispute to the International Court of Justice for a binding decision.

ARTICLE 174

Denunciation

Any Contracting State may at any time denounce this Convention. Notification of denunciation shall be given to the Government of the Federal Republic of Germany. Denunciation shall take effect one year after the date of receipt of such notification.

ARTICLE 175

Preservation of acquired rights

(1) In the event of a State ceasing to be a party to this Convention in accordance with Article 172, paragraph 4, or Article 174, rights already acquired pursuant to this Convention shall not be impaired.

(2) A European patent application which is pending when a designated State ceases to be party to the Convention shall be processed by the European Patent Office, in so far as that State is concerned, as if the Convention in force thereafter were applicable to that State.

(3) The provisions of paragraph 2 shall apply to European patents in respect of which, on the date mentioned in that paragraph, an opposition is pending or the opposition period has not expired.

(4) Nothing in this Article shall affect the right of any State that has ceased to be a party to this Convention to treat any European patent in accordance with the text to which it was a party.

ARTICLE 176

Financial rights and obligations of a former Contracting State

(1) Any State which has ceased to be a party to this Convention in accordance with Article 172, paragraph 4, or Article 174, shall have the special financial contributions which it has paid pursuant to Article 40, paragraph 2, refunded to it by the Organisation only at the time and under the conditions whereby the Organisation refunds special financial contributions paid by other States during the same accounting period.

(2) The State referred to in paragraph 1 shall, even after ceasing to be a party to this Convention, continue to pay the proportion pursuant to Article 39 of renewal fees in respect of European patents remaining in force in that State, at the rate current on the date on which it ceased to be a party.

ARTICLE 177

Languages of the Convention

(1) This Convention, drawn up in a single original, in the English, French and German languages, shall be deposited in the archives of the Government of the Federal Republic of Germany, the three texts being equally authentic.

(2) The texts of this Convention drawn up in official languages of Contracting States other than those referred to in paragraph 1 shall, if they have been approved by the Administrative Council, be considered as official texts. In the event of conflict on the interpretation of the various texts, the texts referred to in paragraph 1 shall be authentic.

ARTICLE 178

Transmission and notifications

(1) The Government of the Federal Republic of Germany shall draw up certified true copies of this Convention and shall transmit them to the Governments of all signatory or acceding States.

(2) The Government of the Federal Republic of Germany shall notify to the Governments of the States referred to in paragraph 1:

(a) any signature;
(b) the deposit of any instrument of ratification or accession;
(c) any reservation or withdrawl of reservation pursuant to the provisions of Article 167;
(d) any declaration or notification received pursuant to the provisions of Article 168;
(e) the date of entry into force of this Convention;
(f) any denunciation received pursuant to the provisions of Article 174 and the date on which such denunciation comes into force.

(3) The Government of the Federal Republic of Germany shall register this Convention with the Secretariat of the United Nations.

In witness whereof, the Plenipotentiaries authorised thereto, having presented their Full Powers, found to be in good and due form, have signed this Convention.

Done at Munich this fifth day of October one thousand nine hundred and seventy-three.

Signatures

Austria
Belgium
Switzerland
Cyprus
Germany
Denmark
Spain
Finland
France
Greece
Ireland
Italy
Liechtenstein
Luxembourg
Monaco
Netherlands
Portugal
Sweden

APPENDIX 2

IMPLEMENTING REGULATIONS TO THE EUROPEAN PATENT CONVENTION

Regulations of October 5, 1973
as amended by Decisions of the Administrative Council of the European
Patent Organisation
of December 7, 1990 and July 5, 1991

(O.J. EPO 1991, 4 *et seq.* and 421 *et seq.*)

A2–01

Contents

675

Part I. Implementing Regulations to Part I of the Convention

Chapter I. Languages of the European Patent Office

RULE 1

Derogations from the provisions concerning the language of the proceedings in written proceedings

(1) In written proceedings before the European Patent Office any party may use any official language of the European Patent Office. The translation referred to in Article 14, paragraph 4, may be filed in any official language of the European Patent Office.

(2) Amendments to a European patent application or European patent must be filed in the language of the proceedings.

(3) Documents to be used for purposes of evidence before the European Patent Office, and particularly publications, may be filed in any language. The European Patent Office may, however, require that a translation be filed, within a given time limit of not less than one month, in one of its official languages.

RULE 2

Derogations from the provisions concerning the language of the proceedings in oral proceedings

(1) Any party to oral proceedings before the European Patent Office may, in lieu of the language of the proceedings, use one of the other official languages of the European Patent Office, on condition either that such party gives notice to the European Patent Office at least one month before the date laid down for such oral proceedings or makes provision for interpreting into the language of the proceedings. Any part may likewise use one of the official languages of the Contracting States, on condition that he makes provision for interpretation into the language of the proceedings. The European Patent Office may permit derogations from the provisions of this paragraph.

(2) In the course of oral proceedings, the employees of the European Patent Office may, in lieu of the language of the proceedings, use one of the other official languages of the European Patent Office.

(3) In the case of taking of evidence, any party to be heard, witness or expert who is unable to express himself adequately in one of the official languages of the European Patent Office or the Contracting States may use another language. Should the taking of evidence be decided upon following a request by a party to the proceedings, parties to be heard, witnesses or experts who express themselves in languages other than the official languages of the European Patent Office may be heard only if the party who made the request makes provision for interpretation into the language of the proceedings; the European Patent Office may, however, authorise interpretation into one of its other official languages.

(4) If the parties and the European Patent Office agree, any language may be used in oral proceedings.

(5) The European Patent Office shall, if necessary, make provision at its own expense for interpretation into the language of the proceedings, or, where appropriate, into its other official languages, unless this interpretation is the responsibility of one of the parties to the proceedings.

(6) Statements by employees of the European Patent Office, by parties to the proceedings and by witnesses and experts, made in one of the official languages of

the European Patent Office during oral proceedings shall be entered in the minutes in the language employed. Statements made in any other language shall be entered in the official language into which they are translated. Amendments to the text of the description or claims of a European patent application or European patent shall be entered in the minutes in the language of the proceedings.

RULE 3 (deleted)

RULE 4

Language of a European divisional application

European divisional applications or, in the case referred to in Article 14, paragraph 2, the translations thereof, must be filed in the language of the proceedings for the earlier European patent application.

RULE 5

Certification of translations

When a translation of any document must be filed, the European Patent Office may require the filing of a certificate that the translation corresponds to the original text within a period to be determined by it. Failure to file the certificate in due time shall lead to the document being deemed not to have been received unless the Convention provides otherwise.

RULE 6

Time limits and reduction of fees

(1) The translation referred to in Article 14, paragraph 2, must be filed within three months after the filing of the European patent application, but no later than thirteen months after the date of priority. Nevertheless, if the translation concerns a European divisional application or a new European patent application under Article 61, paragraph 1(b), the translation may be filed at any time within one month of the filing of such application.

(2) The translation referred to in Article 14, paragraph 4, must be filed within one month of the filing of the document. Where the document is a notice of opposition or an appeal, this period shall be extended where appropriate to the end of the opposition period or appeal period.

(3) A reduction in the filing fee, examination fee, opposition fee or appeal fee shall be allowed an applicant, proprietor or opponent, as the case may be, who avails himself of the options provided in Article 14, paragraphs 2 and 4. The reduction shall be fixed in the Rules relating to Fees at a percentage of the total of the fees.

RULE 7

Legal authenticity of the translation of the European patent application

Saving proof to the contrary, the European Patent Office may, for the purposes of determining whether the subject-matter of the European patent application or European patent extends beyond the content of the European patent application as filed, assume that the translation referred to in Article 14, paragraph 2, is in conformity with the original text of the application.

Chapter II. Organisation of the European Patent Office

RULE 8

Patent classification

(1) The European Patent Office shall use:

    (a) the classification referred to in Article 1 of the European Convention on the International Classification of Patents for Invention of 19 December 1954 until the entry into force of the Strasbourg Agreement concerning the International Patent Classification of 24 March 1971;

    (b) the classification referred to in Article 1 of the afore-mentioned Strasbourg Agreement, after the entry into force of that Agreement.

(2) The classification referred to in paragraph 1 is hereinafter referred to as the international classification.

RULE 9

Allocation of duties to the departments of the first instance

(1) The President of the European Patent Office shall determine the number of Search Divisions, Examining Divisions and Opposition Divisions. He shall allocate duties to these departments by reference to the international classification and shall decide where necessary on the classification of a European patent application or a European patent in accordance with that classification.

(2) In addition to the responsibilities vested in them under the Convention, the President of the European Patent Office may allocate further duties to the Receiving Section, Search Divisions, Examining Divisions, Opposition Divisions and the Legal Division.

(3) The President of the European Patent Office may entrust to employees who are not technically or legally qualified examiners the execution of individual duties falling to the Examining Divisions or Opposition Divisions and involving no technical or legal difficulties.

(4) The President of the European Patent Office may grant exclusive responsibilities to one of the registries of the Opposition Divisions for fixing the amount of costs as provided for in Article 104, paragraph 2.

RULE 10

Allocation of duties to the departments of the second instance and designation of their members

(1) Duties shall be allocated to the Boards of Appeal and the regular and alternate members of the various Boards of Appeal and the Enlarged Board of Appeal shall be designated before the beginning of each working year. Any member of a Board of Appeal may be designated as a member of more than one Board of Appeal. These measures may, where necessary, be amended during the course of the working year in question.

(2) The measures referred to in paragraph 1 shall be taken by an authority

consisting of the President of the European Patent Office, who shall act as Chairman, the Vice-President responsible for appeals, the Chairmen of the Boards of Appeal and three other members of the Boards of Appeal, elected by the full membership of these Boards for the working year in question. This authority may only take a decision if at least five of its members are present; these must include the President or a Vice-President of the European Patent Office and the Chairmen of two Boards of Appeal. Decisions shall be taken by a majority vote; in the event of parity of votes, the vote of the Chairman shall be decisive.

(3) The authority referred to in paragraph 2 shall decide on conflicts regarding the allocation of duties between two or more Boards of Appeal.

(4) The Administrative Council may allocate duties under Article 134, paragraph 8(c), to the Boards of Appeal.

RULE 11

Rules of Procedure of the departments of the second instance

The authority referred to in Rule 10, paragraph 2, shall adopt the Rules of Procedure of the Boards of Appeal. The Enlarged Board of Appeal shall adopt its own Rules of Procedure.

RULE 12

Administrative structure of the European Patent Office

(1) The Examining Divisions and the Opposition Divisions shall be grouped together administratively so as to form Directorates, the number of which shall be laid down by the President of the European Patent Office.

(2) The Directorates, the Legal Division, the Boards of Appeal and the Enlarged Board of Appeal, and the administrative services of the European Patent Office shall be grouped together administratively so as to form Directorates-General. The Receiving Section and the Search Divisions shall be grouped together administratively so as to form a Directorate-General.

(3) Each Directorate-General shall be directed by a Vice-President. The appointment of a Vice-President to a Directorate-General shall be decided upon by the Administrative Council, after the President of the European Patent Office has been consulted.

Part II. Implementing Regulations to Part II of the Convention

Chapter I. Procedure where the applicant or proprietor is not entitled

RULE 3

Suspension of proceedings

(1) If a third party provides proof to the European Patent Office that he has opened proceedings against the applicant for the purpose of seeking a judgment that he is entitled to the grant of the European patent, the European Patent Office shall stay the proceedings for grant unless the third party consents to the

continuation of such proceedings. Such consent must be communicated in writing to the European Patent Office; it shall be irrevocable. However, proceedings for grant may not be stayed before the publication of the European patent application.

(2) Where proof is provided to the European Patent Office that a decision which has become final has been given in the proceedings concerning entitlement to the grant of the European patent, the European Patent Office shall communicate to the applicant and any other party that the proceedings for grant shall be resumed as from the date stated in the communication unless a new European patent application pursuant to Article 61, paragraph 1(b), has been filed for all the designated Contracting States. If the decision is in favour of the third party, the proceedings may only be resumed after a period of three months of that decision becoming final unless the third party requests the resumption of the proceedings for grant.

(3) When giving a decision on the suspension of proceedings or thereafter the European Patent Office may set a date on which it intends to continue the proceedings pending before it regardless of the stage reached in the proceedings referred to in paragraph 1 opened against the applicant. The date is to be communicated to the third party, the applicant and any other party. If no proof has been provided by that date that a decision which has become final has been given, the European Patent Office may continue proceedings.

(4) If a third party provides proof to the European Patent Office during opposition proceedings or during the opposition period that he has opened proceedings against the proprietor of the European patent for the purpose of seeking a judgment that he is entitled to the European patent, the European Patent Office shall stay the opposition proceedings unless the third party consents to the continuation of such proceedings. Such comment must be communicated in writing to the European Patent Office; it shall be irrevocable. However, the suspension of the proceedings may not be ordered until the Opposition Division has deemed the opposition admissible. Paragraphs 2 and 3 shall apply *mutatis mutandis*.

(5) The time limits in force at the date of suspension other than time limits for payment of renewal fees shall be interrupted by such suspension. The time which has not yet elapsed shall begin to run as from the date on which proceedings are resumed; however, the time still to run after the resumption of the proceedings shall not be less than two months.

RULE 14

Limitation of the option to withdraw the European patent application

As from the time when a third party proves to the European Patent Office that he has initiated proceedings concerning entitlement and up to the date on which the European Patent Office resumes the proceedings for grant, neither the European patent application nor the designation of any Contracting State may be withdrawn.

RULE 15

Filing of a new European patent application by the person entitled to apply

(1) Where the person adjudged by a final decision to be entitled to the grant of the European patent files a new European patent application pursuant to Article 61, paragraph 1(b), the original European patent application shall be deemed to be

withdrawn on the date of filing of the new application for the Contracting States designated therein in which the decision has been taken or recognised.

(2) The filing fee and search fee shall be payable in respect of the new European patent application within one month after the filing thereof. The designation fees shall be payable within six months of the date on which the European Patent Bulletin mentions the publication of the European search report drawn up in respect of the new European patent application.

(3) The time limits for forwarding European patent applications provided for in Article 77, paragraphs 3 and 5, shall, for the new European patent application, be four months as from the actual filing date of that application.

RULE 16

Partial transfer of right by virtue of a final decision

(1) If by a final decision it is adjudged that a third party is entitled to the grant of a European patent in respect of only part of the matter disclosed in the European patent application, Article 61 and Rule 15 shall apply *mutatis mutandis* to such part.

(2) Where appropriate, the original European patent application shall contain, for the designated Contracting States in which the decision was taken or recognised, claims, a description and drawings which are different from those for the other designated Contracting States.

Chapter II. Mention of the inventor

RULE 17

Designation of the inventor

(1) The designation of the inventor shall be filed in the request for the grant of a European patent. However, if the applicant is not the inventor or is not the sole inventor, the designation shall be filed in a separate document; the designation must state the family name, given names and full address of the inventor and the statement referred to in Article 81 and shall bear the signature of the applicant or his representative.

(2) The European Patent Office shall not verify the accuracy of the designation of the inventor.

(3) If the applicant is not the inventor or is not the sole inventor, the European Patent Office shall inform the designated inventor of the data in the document designating him and the further data mentioned in Article 128, paragraph 5.

(4) The applicant and the inventor may invoke neither the omission of the notification under paragraph 3 nor any errors contained therein.

RULE 18

Publication of the mention of the inventor

(1) The person designated as the inventor shall be mentioned as such in the published European patent application and the European patent specification, unless the said person informs the EPO in writing that he waives his right to be thus mentioned.

(2) In the event of a third party filing with the European Patent Office a final decision whereby the applicant for or proprietor of a patent is required to designate him as the inventor, the provisions of paragraph 1 shall apply.

RULE 19

Rectification of the designation of an inventor

(1) An incorrect designation of an inventor may not be rectified save upon request, accompanied by the consent of the wrongly designated person and, in the event of such request not being filed by the applicant for or proprietor of the European patent, by the consent of that party. The provisions of Rule 17 shall apply *mutatis mutandis*.

(2) In the event of an incorrect mention of the inventor having been entered in the Register of European Patents or published in the European Patent Bulletin such entry or publication shall be corrected.

(3) Paragraph 2 shall apply *mutatis mutandis* to the cancellation of an incorrect designation of the inventor.

Chapter III. Registering transfers, licences and other rights

RULE 20

Registering a transfer

(1) A transfer of a European patent application shall be recorded in the Register of European Patents at the request of an interested party and on production of documents satisfying the European Patent Office that the transfer has taken place.

(2) The request shall not be deemed to have been filed until such time as an administrative fee has been paid. It may be rejected only in the event of failure to comply with the conditions laid down in paragraph 1.

(3) A transfer shall have effect *vis-à-vis* the European Patent Office only when and to the extent that the documents referred to in paragraph 1 have been produced.

RULE 21

Registering of licences and other rights

(1) Rule 20, paragraphs 1 and 2, shall apply *mutatis mutandis* to the registration of the grant or transfer of a licence, the establishment or transfer of a right *in rem* in respect of a European patent application and any legal means of execution of such an application.

(2) The registration referred to in paragraph 1 shall be cancelled upon request, which shall not be deemed to have been filed until an administrative fee has been paid. Such request shall be supported either by documents establishing that the right has lapsed, or by a declaration whereby the proprietor of the right consents to the cancellation of the registration; it may be rejected only if these conditions are not fulfilled.

RULE 22

Special indications for the registration of a licence

(1) A licence in respect of a European patent application shall be recorded in the Register of European Patents as an exclusive licence if the applicant and the licensee so require.

(2) A licence in respect of a European patent application shall be recorded in the Register of European Patents as a sub-licence where it is granted by a licensee whose licence is recorded in the said Register.

Chapter IV. Certification of exhibition

RULE 23

Certificate of exhibition

The applicant must, within four months of the filing of the European patent application, file the certificate referred to in Article 55, paragraph 2, issued at the exhibition by the authority responsible for the protection of industrial property at that exhibition, and stating that the invention was in fact exhibited there. This certificate shall also state the opening date of the exhibition and, where the first disclosure of the invention did not coincide with the opening date of the exhibition, the date of the first disclosure. This certificate must be accompanied by an identification of the invention, duly authenticated by the above-mentioned authority.

Chapter V. Prior European Applications

RULE 23A

Prior application as state of the art

A European patent application shall be considered as comprised in the state of the art under Article 54, paragraphs 3 and 4, only if the designation fees under Article 79, paragraph 2, have been validly paid.

Chapter VI. Biological inventions

RULE 23B

General and definitions

(1) For European patent applications and patents concerning biotechnological inventions, the relevant provisions of the Convention shall be applied and interpreted in accordance with the provisions of this chapter. Directive 98/44/EC of 6 July 1998 on the legal protection of biotechnological inventions shall be used as a supplementary means of interpretation.

(2) "Biotechnological inventions" are inventions which concern a product consisting of or containing biological material or a process by means of which biological material is produced, processed or used.

(3) "Biological material" means any material containing genetic information and capable of reproducing itself or being reproduced in a biological system.

(4) "Plant variety" means any plant grouping within a single botanical taxon of the lowest known rank, which grouping, irrespective of whether the conditions for the grant of a plant variety right are fully met, can be:

(a) defined by the expression of the characteristics that results from a given genotype or combination of genotypes,

(b) distinguished from any other plant grouping by the expression of at least one of the said characteristics, and

(c) considered as a unit with regard to its suitability for being propagated unchanged.

(5) A process for the production of plants or animals is essentially biological if it consists entirely of natural phenomena such as crossing or selection.

(6) "Microbiological process" means any process involving or performed upon or resulting in microbiological material.

RULE 23C

Patentable biotechnological inventions

Biotechnological inventions shall also be patentable if they concern:

    (a) biological material which is isolated from its natural environment or produced by means of a technical process even if it previously occurred in nature;

    (b) plants or animals if the technical feasibility of the invention is not confined to a particular plant or animal variety;

    (c) microbiological or other technical process, or a product obtained by means of such a process other than a plant or animal variety.

RULE 23D

Exceptions to patentability

Under Article 53(a), European patents shall not be granted in respect of biotechnological inventions which, in particular, concern the following:

    (a) processes for cloning human beings;

    (b) processes for modifying the germ line genetic identity of human beings;

    (c) uses of human embryos for industrial or commercial purposes;

    (d) processes for modifying the genetic identity of animals which are likely to cause them suffering without any substantial medical benefit to man or animal, and also animals resulting from such processes.

RULE 23E

The human body and its elements

(1) The human body, at the various stages of its formation and development, and the simple discovery of one of its elements, including the sequence or partial sequence of a gene, cannot constitute patentable inventions.

(2) An element isolated from the human body or otherwise produced by means of a technical process, including the sequence or partial sequence of a gene, may constitute a patentable invention, even if the structure of that element is identical to that of a natural element.

(3) The industrial application of a sequence or a partial sequence of a gene must be disclosed in the patent application.

Part III. Implementing Regulations to Part III of the Convention

Chapter I. Filing of the European patent application

RULE 24

General provisions

(1) European patent applications may be filed in writing with the authorities referred to in Article 75 either directly or by post. The President of the European Patent Office may permit European patent applications to be filed by other means of communication and lay down conditions governing their use. He may, in particular, require that within such period as the European Patent Office shall specify written confirmation be supplied reproducing the contents of applications so filed and complying with the requirements of these implementing Regulations.

(2) The authority with which the European patent application is filed shall mark the documents making up the application with the date of their receipt. It shall issue without delay a receipt to the applicant which shall include at least the application number, the nature and number of the documents and the date of their receipt.

(3) If the European patent application is filed with an authority mentioned in Article 75, paragraph 1(b), it shall without delay inform the European Patent Office of receipt of the documents making up the application. It shall inform the European Patent Office of the nature and date of receipt of the documents, the application number and any priority date claimed.

(4) When the European Patent Office has received a European patent application which has been forwarded by a central industrial property office of a Contracting State, it shall inform the applicant accordingly, indicating the date of its receipt at the European Patent Office.

RULE 25

Provisions for European divisional applications

(1) Up to the approval of the text, in accordance wtih Rule 51, paragraph 4, in which the European patent is to be granted, the applicant may file a divisional application on the pending earlier European patent application.

(2) The filing fee, search fee and designation fees must be paid in respect of each European divisional application within one month after the filing thereof. The designation fees shall be payable within six months of the date on which the European Patent Bulletin mentions the publication of the European search report drawn up in respect of the European divisional application.

Chapter II. Provisions governing the application

RULE 26

Request for grant

(1) The request for the grant of a European patent shall be filed on a form drawn up by the European Patent Office. Printed forms shall be made available to applicants free of charge by the authorities referred to in Article 75, paragraph 1.

(2) The request shall contain:

(a) a petition for the grant of a European patent;

(b) the title of the invention, which shall clearly and concisely state the technical designation of the invention and shall exclude all fancy names;

(c) the name, address and nationality of the applicant and the State in which his residence or principal place of business is located. Names of natural persons shall be indicated by the person's family name and given name(s), the family name being indicated before the given name(s). Names of legal entities, as well as companies considered to be legal entities by reason of the legislation to which they are subject, shall be indicated by their official designations. Addresses shall be indicated in such a way as to satisfy the customary requirements for prompt postal delivery at the indicated address. They shall in any case comprise all the relevant administrative units, including the house number, if any. It is recommended that the telegraphic and telex address and telephone number be indicated;

(d) if the applicant has appointed a representative, his name and the address of his place of business under the conditions contained in sub-paragraph (c);

(e) where appropriate, indication that the application constitutes a European divisional application and the number of the earlier European patent application;

(f) in cases covered by Article 61, paragraph 1(b), the number of the original European patent application;

(g) where applicable, a declaration claiming the priority of an earlier application and indicating the date on which and the country in or for which the earlier application was filed;

(h) designation of the Contracting State or States in which protection of the invention is desired;

(i) the signature of the applicant or his representative;

(j) a list of the documents accompanying the request. This list shall also indicate the number of sheets of the description, claims, drawings and abstract filed with the request;

(k) the designation of the inventor where the applicant is the inventor.

(3) If there is more than one applicant, the request shall preferably contain the appointment of one applicant or representative as common representative.

RULE 27

Content of the description

(1) The description shall:

(a) specify the technical field to which the invention relates;

(b) indicate the background art which, as far as known to the applicant, can be regarded as useful for understanding the invention, for drawing up the European search report and for the examination, and, preferably, cite the documents reflecting such art;

(c) disclose the invention, as claimed, in such terms that the technical problem (even if not expressly stated as such) and its solution can be understood, and state any advantageous effects of the invention with reference to the background art;

(d) briefly describe the figures in the drawings, if any;

(e) describe in detail at least one way of carrying out the invention claimed using examples where appropriate and referring to the drawings, if any;

(f) indicate explicitly, when it is not obvious from the description or nature of the invention, the way in which the invention is capable of exploitation in industry.

(2) The description shall be presented in the manner and order specified in paragraph 1, unless because of the nature of the invention, a different manner or a different order would afford a better understanding and a more economic presentation.

RULE 27A

Requirements of European patent applications relating to nucleotide and amino acid sequences

(1) If nucleotide or amino acid sequences are disclosed in the European patent application the description shall contain a sequence listing conforming to the rules laid down by the President of the European Patent Office for the standardised representation of nucleotide and amino acid sequences.

(2) The President of the European Patent Office may require that, in addition to the written application documents, a sequence listing in accordance with paragraph 1 be submitted on a data carrier prescribed by him accompanied by a statement that the information recorded on the data carrier is identical to the written sequence listing.

(3) If a sequence listing is filed or corrected after the date of filing, the applicant shall submit a statement that the sequence listing so filed or corrected does not include matter which goes beyond the content of the application as filed.

(4) A sequence listing filed after the date of filing shall not form part of the description.

RULE 28

Deposit of a biological material

(1) If an invention involves the use of or concerns biological material which is not available to the public and which cannot be described in the European patent application in such a manner as to enable the invention to be carried out by a person skilled in the art, the invention shall only be regarded as being disclosed as prescribed in Article 83 if:

    (a) a sample of the biological material has been deposited with a recognised depositary institution not later than the date of filing of the application;

    (b) the application as filed gives such relevant information as is available to the applicant on the characteristics of the biological material;

    (c) the depositary institution and the accession number of the deposited biological material are stated in the application, and

    (d) where the biological material has been deposited by a person other than the applicant, the name and address of the depositor are stated in the application and a document is submitted satisfying the European Patent Office that the latter has authorised the applicant to refer to the deposited biological material in the application and has given his unreserved and irrevocable consent to the deposited material being made available to the public in accordance with this Rule.

(2) The information referred to in paragraph 1(c) and, where applicable, (d) may be submitted

    (a) within a period of sixteen months after the date of filing of the application or, if priority is claimed, after the priority date, this time limit being deemed to have been met if the information is communicated before completion of the technical preparations for publication of the European patent application;

(b) up to the date of submission of a request for early publication of the application;

(c) within one month after the European Patent Office has communicated to the applicant that a right to inspect the files pursuant to Article 128, paragraph 2, exists. The ruling period shall be the one which is the first to expire. The communication of this information shall be considered as constituting the unreserved and irrevocable consent of the applicant to the deposited biological material being made available to the public in accordance with this Rule.

(3) The deposited biological material shall be available upon request to any person from the date of publication of the European patent application and to any person having the right to inspect the files pursuant to Article 128, paragraph 2, prior to that date. Subject to paragraph 4, such availability shall be effected by the issue of a sample of the biological material to the person making the request (hereinafter referred to as "the requester").

Said issue shall be made only if the requester has undertaken *vis-à-vis* the applicant for or proprietor of the patent not to make the biological material or any biological material derived therefrom available to any third party and to use that material for experimental purposes only, until such time as the patent application is refused or withdrawn or deemed to be withdrawn, or before the expiry of the patent in the designated State in which it last expires, unless the applicant for or proprietor of the patent expressly waives such an undertaking.

The undertaking to use the biological material for experimental purposes only shall not apply in so far as the requester is using that material under a compulsory licence. The term "compulsory licence" shall be construed as including *ex officio* licences and the right to use patented inventions in the public interest.

(4) Until completion of the technical preparations for publication of the application, the applicant may inform the European Patent Office that

(a) until the publication of the mention of the grant of the European patent or, where applicable,

(b) for twenty years from the date of filing if the application has been refused or withdrawn or deemed to be withdrawn, the availability referred to in paragraph 3 shall be effected only by the issue of a sample to an expert nominated by the requester.

(5) The following may be nominated as an expert:

(a) any natural person provided that the requester furnishes evidence, when filing the request, that the nomination has the approval of the applicant;

(b) any natural person recognised as an expert by the President of the European Patent Office.

The nomination shall be accompanied by a declaration from the expert *vis-à-vis* the applicant in which he enters into the undertaking given pursuant to paragraph 3 until either the date on which the patent expires in all the designated States or, where the application has been refused, withdrawn or deemed to be withdrawn, until the date referred to in paragraph 4(b), the requester being regarded as a third party.

(6) For the purposes of paragraph 3, derived biological material shall mean any material which still exhibits those characteristics of the deposited material which are essential to carrying out the invention. The undertaking referred to in

paragraph 3 shall not impede any deposit of derived biological material necessary for the purpose of patent procedure.

(7) The request provided for in paragraph 3 shall be submitted to the European Patent Office on a form recognised by that Office. The European Patent Office shall certify on the form that a European patent application referring to the deposit of the biological material has been filed, and that the requester or the expert nominated by him is entitled to the issue of a sample of that material. After grant of the European patent, the request shall also be submitted to the European Patent Office.

(8) The European Patent Office shall transmit a copy of the request, with the certification provided for in paragraph 7, to the depositary institution as well as to the applicant for or the proprietor of the patent.

(9) The President of the European Patent Office shall publish in the Official Journal of the European Patent Office the list of depositary institutions and experts recognised for the purpose of this Rule.

RULE 28A

New deposit of biological material

(1) If biological material deposited in accordance with Rule 28, paragraph 1, ceases to be available from the institution with which it was deposited because:

(a) the biological material is no longer viable, or

(b) for any other reason the depositary institution is unable to supply samples, and if no sample of the biological material has been transferred to another depositary institution recognised for the purposes of Rule 28, from which it continues to be available, an interruption in availability shall be deemed not to have occurred if a new deposit of the biological material originally deposited is made within a period of three months from the date on which the depositor was notified of the interruption by the depositary institution and if a copy of the receipt of the deposit issued by the institution is forwarded to the European Patent Office within four months from the date of the new deposit stating the number of the application or of the European patent.

(2) In the case provided for in paragraph 1(a), the new deposit shall be made with the depositary institution with which the original deposit was made; in the cases provided for in paragraph 1(b), it may be made with another depositary institution recognised for the purposes of Rule 28.

(3) Where the institution with which the original deposit was made ceases to be recognised for the purposes of Rule 28, either entirely or for the kind of biological material to which the deposited sample belongs, or where that institution discontinues, temporarily or definitively, the performance of its functions as regards deposited biological material, and the notification referred to in paragraph 1 from the depositary institution is not received within six months from the date of such event, the three-month period referred to in paragraph 1 shall begin on the date on which this event is announced in the Official Journal of the European Patent Office.

(4) Any new deposit shall be accompanied by a statement signed by the depositor certifying that the newly deposited biological material is the same as that originally deposited.

(5) If the new deposit has been made under the provisions of the Budapest Treaty on the International Recognition of the Deposit of Microorganisms for the Purposes of Patent Procedure of 28 April 1977, the provisions of that Treaty shall prevail.

RULE 29

Form and content of claims

(1) The claims shall define the matter for which protection is sought in terms of the technical features of the invention. Wherever appropriate, claims shall contain:

(a) a statement indicating the designation of the subject-matter of the invention and those technical features which are necessary for the definition of the claimed subject-matter but which, in combination, are part of the prior art;

(b) a characterising portion—preceded by the expression "characterised in that" or "characterised by"—stating the technical features which, in combination with the features stated in sub-paragraph (a), it is desired to protect.

(2) Subject to Article 82, a European patent application may contain two or more independent claims in the same category (product, process, apparatus or use) where it is not appropriate, having regard to the subject-matter of the application, to cover this subject-matter by a single claim.

(3) Any claim stating the essential features of an invention may be followed by one or more claims concerning particular embodiments of that invention.

(4) Any claim which includes all the features of any other claim (dependent claim) shall contain, if possible at the beginning, a reference to the other claim and then state the additional features which it is desired to protect. A dependent claim shall also be admissible where the claim it directly refers to is itself a dependent claim. All dependent claims referring back to a single previous claim, and all dependent claims referring back to several previous claims, shall be grouped together to the extent and in the most appropriate way possible.

(5) The number of the claims shall be reasonable in consideration of the nature of the invention claimed. If there are several claims, they shall be numbered consecutively in arabic numerals.

(6) Claims shall not, except where absolutely necessary, rely, in respect of the technical features of the invention, on references to the description of drawings. In particular, they shall not rely on such references as: "as described in part ... of the description", or "as illustrated in figure ... of the drawings".

(7) If the European patent application contains drawings, the technical features mentioned in the claims shall preferably, if the intelligibility of the claim can thereby be increased, be followed by reference signs relating to these features and placed between parentheses. These reference signs shall not be construed as limiting the claim.

RULE 30

Unity of invention

(1) Where a group of inventions is claimed in one and the same European patent application, the requirement of unity of invention referred to in Article 82 shall be fulfilled only when there is a technical relationship among those inventions involving one or more of the same or corresponding special technical features. The expression "special technical features" shall mean those technical features which define a contribution which each of the claimed inventions considered as a whole makes over the prior art.

(2) The determination whether a group of inventions is so linked as to form a single general inventive concept shall be made without regard to whether the inventions are claimed in separate claims or as alternatives within a single claim.

RULE 31

Claims incurring fees

(1) Any European patent application comprising more than ten claims at the time of filing shall, in respect of each claim over and above that number, incur payment of a claims fee. The claims fee shall be payable within one month after the filing of the application. If the claims fees have not been paid in due time they may still be validly paid within a period of grace of one month of notification of a communication pointing out the failure to observe the time limit.

(2) If a claims fee is not paid within the period referred to in paragraph 1, the claim concerned shall be deemed to be abandoned. Any claims fee duly paid shall be refunded only in the case referred to in Article 77, paragraph 5.

RULE 32

Form of the drawings

(1) On sheets containing drawings, the usable surface area shall not exceed 26.2 cm × 17 cm. These sheets shall not contain frames round the usable or used surface. The minimum margins shall be as follows:

top	2.5 cm
left side	2.5 cm
right side	1.5 cm
bottom	1 cm

(2) Drawings shall be executed as follows:

(a) Drawings shall be executed in durable, black, sufficiently dense and dark, uniformly thick and well-defined, lines and strokes without colourings.

(b) Cross-sections shall be indicated by hatching which should not impede the clear reading of the reference signs and leading lines.

(c) The scale of the drawings and the distinctness of their graphical execution shall be such that a photographic reproduction, obtained electronically or photographically, with a linear reduction in size to two-third would enable all details to be distinguished without difficulty. If, as an exception, the scale is given on a drawing, it shall be represented graphically.

(d) All numbers, letters, and reference signs, appearing on the drawings, shall be simple and clear. Brackets, circles or inverted commas shall not be used in association with numbers and letters.

(e) All lines in the drawings shall, ordinarily, be drawn with the aid of drafting instruments.

(f) Elements of the same figure shall be in proportion to each other, unless a difference in proportion is indispensable for the clarity of the figure.

(g) The height of the numbers and letters shall not be less than 0.32 cm. For the lettering of drawings, the Latin and, where customary, the Greek alphabets shall be used.

(h) The same sheet of drawings may contain several figures. Where figures drawn on two or more sheets are intended to form one whole figure, the figures on the several sheets shall be so arranged that the whole figure can be assembled without concealing any part of the partial figures. The different figures shall be arranged without wasting space, preferably in an upright position, clearly separated from one another. Where the figures are not arranged in an upright position, they shall be presented sideways with the top of the figures at the left side of the sheet. The different figures

695

shall be numbered consecutively in arabic numerals, independently of the numbering of the sheets.

(i) Reference signs not mentioned in the description and claims shall not appear in the drawings, and *vice versa*. The same features, when denoted by reference signs, shall, throughout the application, be denoted by the same signs.

(j) The drawings shall not contain text matter, except, when absolutely indispensable, a single word or words such as "water," "steam," "open," "closed," "section on AB," and, in the case of electric circuits and block schematic or flow sheet diagrams, a few short catchwords indispensable for understanding. Any such words shall be placed in such a way that, if required, they can be replaced by their translations without interfering with any lines of the drawings.

(3) Flow sheets and diagrams are considered drawings.

Rule 33

Form and content of the abstract

(1) The abstract shall indicate the title of the invention.

(2) The abstract shall contain a concise summary of the disclosure as contained in the description, the claims and any drawings; the summary shall indicate the technical field to which the invention pertains and shall be drafted in a way which allows the clear understanding of the technical problem, the gist of the solution of that problem through the invention and the principal use or uses of the invention. The abstract shall, where applicable, contain the chemical formula which, among those contained in the application, best characterises the invention. It shall not contain statements on the alleged merits or value of the invention or on its speculative application.

(3) The abstract shall preferably not contain more than one hundred and fifty words.

(4) If the European patent application contains drawings, the applicant shall indicate the figure or, exceptionally, the figures of the drawings which he suggests should accompany the abstract when the abstract is published. The European Patent Office may decide to publish one or more other figures if it considers that they better characterise the invention. Each main feature mentioned in the abstract and illustrated by a drawing shall be followed by a reference sign, placed between parentheses.

(5) The abstract shall be so drafted that it constitutes an efficient instrument for purposes of searching in the particular technical field particularly by making it possible to assess whether there is a need for consulting the European patent application itself.

Rule 34

Prohibited matter

(1) The European patent application shall not contain:

(a) statements or other matter contrary to "ordre public" or morality;

(b) statements disparaging the products or processes of any particular person other than the applicant, or the merits or validity of applications or patents of any such persons. Mere comparisons with the prior art shall not be considered disparaging *per se*;

(c) any statement or other matter obviously irrelevant or unnecessary under the circumstances.

(2) If a European patent application contains prohibited matter within the meaning of paragraph 1(a), the European Patent Office shall omit it when publishing the application, indicating the place and number of words or drawings omitted.

(3) If a European patent application contains statements within the meaning of paragraph 1(b), the European Patent Office may omit them when publishing the application. It shall indicate the place and number of words omitted, and shall furnish, upon request, a copy of the passages omitted.

RULE 35

General provisions governing the presentation of the application documents

(1) Translations mentioned in Article 14, paragraph 2, shall be considered to be included in the term "documents making up the European patent application."

(2) The documents making up the European patent application shall be filed in three copies. The President of the European Patent Office may, however, determine that the documents shall be filed in fewer than three copies.

(3) The documents making up the European patent application shall be so presented as to admit of direct reproduction by photography, electrostatic processes, photo offset and micro-filming, in an unlimited number of copies. All sheets shall be free from cracks, creases and folds. Only one side of the sheet shall be used.

(4) The documents making up the European patent application shall be on A4 paper (29.7 cm × 21 cm) which shall be pliable, strong, white, smooth, matt and durable. Subject to the provisions of Rule 32, paragraph 2(h), and paragraph 11 of this Rule, each sheet shall be used with its short sides at the top and bottom (upright position).

(5) Each of the documents making up the European patent application (request, description, claims, drawings and abstract) shall commence on a new sheet. The sheets shall be connected in such a way that they can easily be turned over, separated and joined together again.

(6) Subject to Rule 32, paragraph 1, the minimum margins shall be as follows:

top	2 cm
left side	2.5 cm
right side	2 cm
bottom	2 cm

The recommended maximum for the margins quoted above is as follows:

top	4 cm
left side	4 cm
right side	3 cm
bottom	3 cm

(7) The margins of the documents making up the European patent application, when submitted, must be completely blank.

(8) All the sheets contained in the European patent application shall be numbered in consecutive arabic numerals. These shall be placed at the top of the sheet, in the middle, but not in the top margin.

(9) The lines of each sheet of the description and of the claims shall preferably be numbered in sets of five, the numbers appearing on the left side, to the right of the margin.

(10) The request for the grant of a European patent, the description, the claims

and the abstract shall be typed or printed. Only graphic symbols and characters and chemical or mathematical formulae may, if necessary, be written by hand or drawn. The typing shall be 1½ spaced. All text matter shall be in characters, the capital letters of which are not less than 0.21 cm high, and shall be in a dark, indelible colour.

(11) The request for the grant of a European patent, the description, the claims and the abstract shall not contain drawings. The description, the claims and the abstract may contain chemical or mathematical formulae. The description and the abstract may contain tables. The claims may contain tables only if their subject-matter makes the use of tables desirable. Tables and chemical or mathematical formulae may be placed sideways on the sheet if they cannot be presented satisfactorily in an upright position thereon; sheets on which tables or chemical or mathematical formulae are presented sideways shall be so presented that the tops of the tables or formulae are at the left side of the sheet.

(12) Physical values shall be expressed in the units recognised in international practice, wherever appropriate in terms of the metric system using SI units. Any data not meeting this requirement must also be expressed in the units recognised in international practice. For mathematical formulae the symbols in general use shall be employed. For chemical formulae the symbols, atomic weights and molecular formulae in general use shall be employed. In general, use should be made of the technical terms, signs and symbols generally accepted in the field in question.

(13) The terminology and the signs shall be consistent throughout the European patent application.

(14) Each sheet shall be reasonably free from erasures and shall be free from alterations, overwritings and interlineations. Non-compliance with this rule may be authorised if the authenticity of the content is not in question and the requirements for good reproduction are not in jeopardy.

RULE 36

Documents filed subsequently

(1) The provisions of Rules 27, 29 and 32 to 35 shall apply to documents replacing documents making up the European patent application. Rule 35, paragraphs 2 to 14, shall also apply to the translation of the claims referred to in Rule 51, paragraph 6.

(2) All documents other than those referred to in the first sentence of paragraph 1 shall normally be typewritten or printed. There must be a margin of about 2.5 cm on the left-hand side of each page.

(3) All documents, with the exception of annexed documents, filed after filing of the European patent application must be signed. If a document has not been signed, the European Patent Office shall invite the party concerned to do so within a time limit to be laid down by that Office. If signed in due time, the document shall retain its original date of receipt; otherwise it shall be deemed not to have been received.

(4) Such documents as must be communicated to other persons or as relate to two or more European patent applications or European patents, must be filed in a sufficient number of copies. If the party concerned does not comply with this obligation in spite of a request by the European Patent Office, the missing copies shall be provided at the expense of the party concerned.

(5) Notwithstanding paragraphs 2 to 4 the President of the European Patent Office may permit documents filed after filing of the European patent application to be transmitted to the European Patent Office by other means of communication and lay down conditions governing their use. He may, in particular, require that

within a period laid down by him written confirmation be supplied reproducing the contents of documents so filed and complying with the requirements of these Implementing Regulations; if such confirmation is not supplied in due time, the documents shall be deemed not to have been received.

Chapter III. Renewal fees

RULE 37

Payment of renewal fees

(1) Renewal fees for the European patent application in respect of the coming year shall be due on the last day of the month containing the anniversary of the date of filing of the European patent application. Renewal fees may not be validly paid more than one year before they fall due.

(2) An additional fee shall be deemed to have been paid at the same time as the renewal fee within the meaning of Article 86, paragraph 2, if it is paid within the period laid down in that provision.

(3) Renewal fees already due in respect of an earlier application up to the date on which a European divisional application is filed must also be paid for the divisional application and fall due when the latter is filed. These fees and any renewal fee falling due within a period of four months from the filing of the divisional application may be paid without an additional fee within that period. If payment is not made in due time, the renewal fees may still be validly paid within six months of the due date, provided that the additional fee under Article 86, paragraph 2, is paid at the same time.

(4) Renewal fees shall not be payable for a new European patent application filed pursuant to Article 61, paragraph 1(b), in respect of the year in which it was actually filed and any preceding year.

Chapter IV. Priority

RULE 38

Declaration of priority and priority documents

(1) The declaration of priority referred to in Article 88, paragraph 1, shall state the date of the previous filing and the State in or for which it was made and shall indicate the file number.

(2) The date and State of the previous filing must be stated on filing the European patent application; the file number shall be indicated before the end of the sixteenth month after the date of priority.

(3) The copy of the previous application required for claiming priority shall be filed before the end of the sixteenth month after the date of priority. The copy must be certified as an exact copy of the previous application by the authority which received the previous application and shall be accompanied by a certificate issued by that authority stating the date of filing of the previous application.

(4) The copy of the previous application shall be deemed duly filed if a copy of that application available to the European Patent Office is to be included in the file of the European patent application under the conditions laid down by the President of the European Patent Office.

(5) The translation of the previous application required under Article 88, paragraph 1, must be filed within a time limit to be set by the European Patent Office but at the latest within the time limit under Rule 51, paragraph 6.

Alternatively, a declaration may be submitted that the European patent application is a complete translation of the previous application. Paragraph 4 shall apply *mutatis mutandis*.

(6) The particulars stated in the declaration of priority shall appear in the published European patent application and also on the European patent specification.

Part IV. Implementing Regulations to Part IV of the Convention

Chapter I. Examination by the Receiving Section

RULE 39

Communication following the examination on filing

If the European patent application fails to meet the requirements laid down in Article 80, the Receiving Section shall communicate the disclosed deficiencies to the applicant and inform him that the application will not be dealt with as a European patent application unless he remedies the disclosed deficiencies within one month. If he does so, he shall be informed of the date of filing.

RULE 40

Examination for certain physical requirements

The physical requirements which the European patent application must satisfy pursuant to Article 91, paragraph 1(b), shall be those prescribed in Rule 32, paragraphs 1 and 2, Rule 35, paragraphs 2 to 11 and 14, and Rule 36, paragraphs 2 and 4.

RULE 41

Rectification of deficiencies in the application documents

(1) If the examination provided for in Article 91, paragraph 1(a) to (d), reveals deficiencies in the European patent application, the Receiving Section shall inform the applicant accordingly and invite him to remedy the deficiencies within such period as it shall specify. The description, claims and drawings may be amended only to an extent sufficient to remedy the disclosed deficiencies in accordance with the observations of the Receiving Section.

(2) Paragraph 1 shall not apply where the applicant, while claiming priority, has omitted to indicate on filing the European patent application the date or State of first filing.

(3) Paragraph 1 shall not apply where the examination reveals that the date of the first filing given on filing the European patent application precedes the date of filing of the European patent application by more than one year. In this event the Receiving Section shall inform the applicant that there will be no right of priority for the application unless, within one month, the applicant indicates a corrected date, lying within the year preceding the date of filing of the European patent application.

RULE 42

Subsequent identification of the inventor

(1) If the examination provided for in Article 91, paragraph 1(f), reveals that the inventor has not been identified in accordance with the provisions of Rule 17, the Receiving Section shall inform the applicant that the European patent application shall be deemed to be withdrawn unless this deficiency is corrected within the period prescribed by Article 91, paragraph 5.

(2) In the case of a European divisional application or a new European patent application filed pursuant to Article 61, paragraph 1(b), the time limit for identifying the inventor may in no case expire before two months after the communication referred to in paragraph 1, which shall state the time limit.

RULE 43

Late-filed or missing drawings

(1) If the examination provided for in Article 91, paragraph 1(g), reveals that the drawings were filed later than the date of filing of the European patent application, the Receiving Section shall inform the applicant that the drawings and the references to the drawings in the European patent application shall be deemed to be deleted unless the applicant requests within a period of one month that the application be re-dated to the date on which the drawings were filed.

(2) If the examination reveals that the drawings were not filed, the Receiving Section shall invite him to file them within one month and inform him that the application will be re-dated to the date on which they are filed, or, if they are not filed in due time, any reference to them in the application shall be deemed to be deleted.

(3) The applicant shall be informed of any new date of filing of the application.

Chapter II. European search report

RULE 44

Content of the European search report

(1) The European search report shall mention those documents, available to the European Patent Office at the time of drawing up the report, which may be taken into consideration in deciding whether the invention to which the European patent application relates is new and involves an inventive step.

(2) Each citation shall be referred to the claims to which it relates. If necessary, the relevant parts of the documents cited shall be identified (for example, by indicating the page, column and lines or the diagrams).

(3) The European search report shall distinguish between cited documents published before the date of priority claimed, beween such date of priority and the date of filing, and on or after the date of filing.

(4) Any document which refers to an oral disclosure, a use or any other means of disclosure which took place prior to the date of filing of the European patent application shall be mentioned in the European search report, together with an indication of the date of publication, if any, of the document and the date of the non-written disclosure.

(5) The European search report shall be drawn up in the language of the proceedings.

(6) The European search report shall contain the classification of the subject-

701

matter of the European patent application in accordance with the international classification.

RULE 45

Incomplete search

If the Search Division considers that the European patent application does not comply with the provisions of the Convention to such an extent that it is not possible to carry out a meaningful search into the state of the art on the basis of all or some of the claims, it shall either declare that search is not possible or shall, so far as is practicable, draw up a partial European search report. The declaration and the partial report referred to shall be considered, for the purposes of subsequent proceedings, as the European search report.

RULE 46

European search report where the invention lacks unity

(1) If the Search Division considers that the European patent application does not comply with the requirement of unity of invention, it shall draw up a partial European search report on those parts of the European patent application which relate to the invention, or the group of inventions within the meaning of Article 82, first mentioned in the claims. It shall inform the applicant that if the European search report is to cover the other inventions, a further search fee must be paid, for each invention involved, within a period to be fixed by the Search Division which must not be shorter than two weeks and must not exceed six weeks. The Search Division shall draw up the European search report for those parts of the European patent application which relate to inventions in respect of which search fees have been paid.

(2) Any fee which has been paid under paragraph 1 shall be refunded if, during the examination of the European patent application by the Examining Division, the applicant requests a refund and the Examining Division finds that the communication referred to in the said paragraph was not justified.

RULE 47

Definitive content of the abstract

(1) At the same time as drawing up the European search report, the Search Division shall determine the definitive content of the abstract.

(2) The definitive content of the abstract shall be transmitted to the applicant together with the European search report.

Chapter III. Publication of the European patent application

RULE 48

Technical preparations for publication

(1) The President of the European Patent Office shall determine when the technical preparations for publication of the European patent application are to be deemed to have been completed.

(2) The European patent application shall not be published if it has been finally

refused or withdrawn or deemed to be withdrawn before the termination of the technical preparations for publication.

Rule 49

Form of the publication of European patent applications and European search reports

(1) The President of the European Patent Office shall prescribe the form of the publication of the European patent application and the data which are to be included. The same shall apply where the European search report and the abstract are published separately. The President of the European Patent Office may lay down special conditions for the publication of the abstract.

(2) The designated Contracting States shall be specified in the published European patent application.

(3) If, before the termination of the technical preparations for publication of the European patent application, the claims have been amended pursuant to Rule 86, paragraph 2, the new or amended claims shall be included in the publication in addition to the original claims.

Rule 50

Information about publication

(1) The European Patent Office shall communicate to the applicant the date on which the European Patent Bulletin mentions the publication of the European search report and shall draw his attention in this communication to the provisions of Article 94, paragraphs 2 and 3.

(2) The applicant may not invoke the omission of the communication provided for in paragraph 1. If a later date than the date of the mention of the publication is specified in the communication, the later date shall be the decisive date as regards the time limit for filing the request for examination unless the error is apparent.

Chapter IV. Examination by the Examining Division

Rule 51

Examination procedure

(1) In the invitation pursuant to Article 96, paragraph 1, the European Patent Office shall invite the applicant, if he wishes, to comment on the European search report and to amend, where appropriate, the description, claims and drawings.

(2) In any invitation pursuant to Article 96, paragraph 2, the Examining Division shall, where appropriate, invite the applicant to correct the disclosed deficiencies and, where necessary, to file the description, claims and drawings in an amended form.

(3) Any communication pursuant to Article 96, paragraph 2, shall contain a reasoned statement covering, where appropriate, all the grounds against the grant of the European patent.

(4) Before the Examining Division decides to grant the European patent, it shall inform the applicant of the text in which it intends to grant it and shall request him to indicate, within a period to be set by it which may not be less than two months or more than four months, his approval of the text notified. The period shall be

extended once by a maximum of two months provided the applicant so requests before it expires.

(5) If the applicant fails to communicate his approval within the period according to paragraph 4, the European patent application shall be refused. If within this period the applicant proposes amendments to the claims, description or drawings to which the Examining Division does not consent under Rule 86, paragraph 3, the Examining Division shall, before taking a decision, request the applicant to submit his observations within a period it shall specify and shall state its reasons for so doing.

(6) If it is established that the applicant approves the text in which the Examining Division, taking account of any proposed amendments (Rule 86, paragraph 3), intends to grant the European patent, it shall invite him to pay, within a non-extendable period to be set by it which may not be less than two months or more than three months, the fees for grant and printing and shall also invite him to file within the same period a translation of the claims in the two official languages of the European Patent Office other than the language of the proceedings.

(7) If the European patent application in the text in which the Examining Division intends to grant the European patent comprises more than ten claims, the Examining Division shall invite the applicant to pay claims fees in respect of each additional claim within the period laid down in paragraph 6 unless the said fees have already been paid in accordance with Rule 31, paragraph 1.

(8) If the fee for grant, the fee for printing or the claims fees are not paid in due time or if the translation is not filed in due time, the European patent application is deemed to be withdrawn.

(9) If a renewal fee becomes due after the invitation referred to in paragraph 6 has been notified and before the next possible date for publication of the mention of the grant of the European patent, the mention shall not be published until the renewal fee has been paid. The applicant shall be notified accordingly.

(10) The communication of the Examining Division under paragraph 6 shall indicate the designated Contracting States which require a translation pursuant to Article 65, paragraph 1.

(11) The decision to grant the European patent shall state which text of the European patent application forms the basis for the grant of the European patent.

Rule 52

Grant of the European patent to different applicants

Where different persons are entered in the Register of European Patents as applicants in respect of different Contracting States, the Examining Division shall grant the European patent for each Contracting State to the applicant or applicants registered in respect of that State.

Chapter V. The European patent specification

Rule 53

Technical preparations for publication and form of the specification of the European patent

Rules 48 and 49, paragraphs 1 and 2, shall apply *mutatis mutandis* to the specification of the European patent. The specification shall also contain an indication of the time limit for opposing the European patent.

RULE 54

Certificate for a European patent

(1) As soon as the specification of the European patent has been published the European Patent Office shall issue to the proprietor of the patent a certificate for a European patent, to which the specification shall be annexed. The certificate shall certify that the patent has been granted, in respect of the invention described in the patent specification, to the person named in the certificate, for the Contracting States designated in the specification.

(2) The proprietor of the patent may request that duplicate copies of the European patent certificate be supplied to him upon payment of an administrative fee.

Part V. Implementing Regulations to Part V of the Convention

RULE 55

Content of the notice of opposition

The notice of opposition shall contain:

   (a) the name and address of the opponent and the State in which his residence or principal place of business is located, in accordance with the provisions of Rule 26, paragraph 2(c);

   (b) the number of the European patent against which opposition is filed, and the name of the proprietor and title of the invention;

   (c) a statement of the extent to which the European patent is opposed and of the grounds on which the opposition is based as well as an indication of the facts, evidence and arguments presented in support of these grounds;

   (d) if the opponent has appointed a representative, his name and the address of his place of business, in accordance with the provisions of Rule 26, paragraph 2(c).

RULE 56

Rejection of the notice of opposition as inadmissible

(1) If the Opposition Division notes that the notice of opposition does not comply with the provisions of Article 99, paragraph 1, Rule 1, paragraph 1, and Rule 55, sub-paragraph (c), or does not provide sufficient identification of the patent against which opposition has been filed, it shall reject the notice of opposition as inadmissible unless these deficiencies have been remedied before expiry of the opposition period.

(2) If the Opposition Division notes that the notice of opposition does not comply with provisions other than those mentioned in paragraph 1, it shall communicate this to the opponent and shall invite him to remedy the deficiencies noted within such period as it may specify. If the notice of opposition is not corrected in good time the Opposition Division shall reject it as inadmissible.

(3) Any decision to reject a notice of opposition as inadmissible shall be communicated to the proprietor of the patent, together with a copy of the notice.

705

RULE 57

Preparation of the examination of the opposition

(1) The Opposition Division shall communicate the opposition to the proprietor of the patent and shall invite him to file his observations and to file amendments, where appropriate, to the description, claims and drawings within a period to be fixed by the Opposition Division.

(2) If several notices of opposition have been filed, the Opposition Division shall communicate them to the other opponents at the same time as the communication provided for under paragraph 1.

(3) The observations and any amendments filed by the proprietor of the patent shall be communicated to the other parties concerned who shall be invited by the Opposition Division, if it considers it expedient, to reply within a period to be fixed by the Opposition Division.

(4) In the case of a notice of intervention in opposition proceedings the Opposition Division may dispense with the application of paragraphs 1 to 3.

RULE 57A

Amendment of the European Patent

Without prejudice to Rule 87, the description, claims and drawings may be amended, provided that the amendments are occasioned by grounds for opposition specified in Article 100, even if the respective ground has not been invoked by the opponent.

RULE 58

Examination of opposition

(1) All communications issued pursuant to Article 101, paragraph 2, and all replies thereto shall be communicated to all parties.

(2) In any communication to the proprietor of the European patent pursuant to Article 101, paragraph 2, he shall, where appropriate, be invited to file, where necessary, the description, claims and drawings in amended form.

(3) Where necessary, any communication to the proprietor of the European patent pursuant to Article 101, paragraph 2, shall contain a reasoned statement. Where appropriate, this statement shall cover all the grounds against the maintenance of the European patent.

(4) Before the Opposition Division decides on the maintenance of the European patent in the amended form, it shall inform the parties that it intends to maintain the patent as amended and shall invite them to state their observations within a period of two months if they disapprove of the text in which it is intended to maintain the patent.

(5) If disapproval of the text communicated by the Opposition Division is expressed, examination of the opposition may be continued; otherwise, the Opposition Division shall, on expiry of the period referred to in paragraph 4, request the proprietor of the patent to pay, within three months, the fee for the printing of a new specification of the European patent and to file a translation of any amended claims in the two official languages of the European Patent Office other than the language of the proceedings.

(6) If the acts requested under paragraph 5 are not performed in due time they may still be validly performed within two months of notification of a communication pointing out the failure to observe the time limit, provided that within this two-month period a surcharge equal to twice the fee for printing a new specification of the European patent is paid.

(7) The communication of the Opposition Division under paragraph 5 shall indicate the designated Contracting States which require a translation pursuant to Article 65, paragraph 1.

(8) The decision to maintain the European patent as amended shall state which text of the European patent forms the basis for the maintenance therof.

RULE 59

Requests for documents

Documents referred to by a party to opposition proceedings shall be filed together with the notice of opposition or the written submissions in two copies. If such documents are neither enclosed nor filed in due time upon invitation by the European Patent Office, it may decide not to take into account any arguments based on them.

RULE 60

Continuation of the opposition proceedings by the European Patent Office of its own motion

(1) If the European patent has been surrendered or has lapsed for all the designated States, the opposition proceedings may be continued at the request of the opponent filed within two months as from a notification by the European Patent Office of the surrender or lapse.

(2) In the event of the death or legal incapacity of an opponent, the opposition proceedings may be continued by the European Patent Office of its own motion, even without the participation of the heirs or legal representatives. The same shall apply when the opposition is withdrawn.

RULE 61

Transfer of the European patent

Rule 20 shall apply *mutatis mutandis* to any transfer of the European patent made during the opposition period or during opposition proceedings.

RULE 61A

Documents in opposition proceedings

Part III, Chapter II, of the Implementing Regulations shall apply *mutatis mutandis* to documents filed in opposition proceedings.

707

APPENDIX 2

RULE 62

Form of the new specification of the European patent in opposition proceedings

Rule 49, paragraphs 1 and 2, shall apply *mutatis mutandis* to the new specification of the European patent.

RULE 62A

New certificate for a European patent

Rule 54 shall apply *mutatis mutandis* to the new specification of the European patent.

RULE 63

Costs

(1) Apportionment of costs shall be dealt with in the decision on the opposition. Such apportionment shall only take into consideration the expenses necessary to assure proper protection of the rights involved. The costs shall include the remuneration of the representatives of the parties.

(2) A bill of costs, with supporting evidence, shall be attached to the request for the fixing of costs. The request shall only be admissible if the decision in respect of which the fixing of costs is required has become final. Costs may be fixed once their credibility is established.

(3) The request for a decision by the Opposition Division on the awarding of costs by the registry, stating the reasons on which it is based, must be filed in writing to the European Patent Office within one month after the date of notification of the awarding of costs. It shall not be deemed to be filed until the fee for the awarding of costs has been paid.

(4) The Opposition Division shall take a decision on the request referred to in paragraph 3 without oral proceedings.

Part VI. Implementing Regulations to Part VI of the Convention

RULE 64

Content of the notice of appeal

The notice of appeal shall contain:

(a) the name and address of the appellant in accordance with the provisions of Rule 26, paragraph 2(c);
(b) a statement identifying the decision which is impugned and the extent to which amendment or cancellation of the decision is requested.

RULE 65

Rejection of the appeal as inadmissible

(1) If the appeal does not comply with Articles 106 to 108 and with Rule 1, paragraph 1, and Rule 64, sub-paragraph (b), the Board of Appeal shall reject it as inadmissible, unless each deficiency has been remedied before the relevant time limit laid down in Article 108 has expired.

(2) If the Board of Appeal notes that the appeal does not comply with the provisions of Rule 64, sub-paragraph (a), it shall communicate this to the appellant and shall invite him to remedy the deficiencies noted within such period as it may specify. If the appeal is not corrected in good time, the Board of Appeal shall reject it as inadmissible.

RULE 66

Examination of appeals

(1) Unless otherwise provided, the provisions relating to proceedings before the department which has made the decision from which the appeal is brought shall be applicable to appeal proceedings *mutatis mutandis*.

(2) The written decision shall be signed by the Chairman of the Board of Appeal and by the competent employee of the registry of the Board of Appeal. The decision shall contain:

    (a) a statement that it is delivered by the Board of Appeal;

    (b) the date when the decision was taken;

    (c) the names of the Chairman and of the other members of the Board of Appeal taking part;

    (d) the names of the parties and their representatives;

    (e) a statement of the issues to be decided;

    (f) a summary of the facts;

    (g) the reasons;

    (h) the order of the Board of Appeal, including, where appropriate, a decision on costs.

RULE 67

Reimbursement of appeal fees

The reimbursement of appeal fees shall be ordered in the event of interlocutory revision or where the Board of Appeal deems an appeal to be allowable, if such reimbursement is equitable by reason of a substantial procedural violation. In the event of interlocutory revision, reimbursement shall be ordered by the department whose decision has been impugned and, in other cases, by the Board of Appeal.

Part VII. Implementing Regulations to Part VII of the Convention

Chapter I. Decisions and communications of the European Patent Office

RULE 68

Form of decisions

(1) Where oral proceedings are held before the European Patent Office, the decision may be given orally. Subsequently the decision in writing shall be notified to the parties.

(2) Decisions of the European Patent Office which are open to appeal shall be reasoned and shall be accompanied by a written communication of the possibility of appeal. The communication shall also draw the attention of the parties to the provisions laid down in Articles 106 to 108, the text of which shall be attached. The parties may not invoke the omission of the communication.

RULE 69

Noting of loss of rights

(1) If the European Patent Office notes that the loss of any right results from the Convention, without any decision concerning the refusal of the European patent application of the grant, revocation or maintenance of the European patent, or the taking of evidence, it shall communicate this to the person concerned in accordance with the provisions of Article 119.

(2) If the person concerned considers that the finding of the European Patent Office is inaccurate, he may, within two months after notification of the communication referred to in paragraph 1, apply for a decision on the matter by the European Patent Office. Such decision shall be given only if the European Patent Office does not share the opinion of the person requesting it; otherwise the European Patent Office shall inform the person requesting the decision.

RULE 70

Signature, name, seal

(1) Any decision, communication and notice from the European Patent Office is to be signed by and to state the name of the employee responsible.

(2) Where the documents mentioned in paragraph 1 are produced by the employee responsible using a computer, a seal may replace the signature. Where the documents are produced automatically by a computer the employee's name may also be dispensed with. The same applies to pre-printed notices and communications.

Chapter II. Oral proceedings and taking of evidence

RULE 71

Summons to oral proceedings

(1) The parties shall be summoned to oral proceedings provided for in Article 116 and their attention shall be drawn to paragraph 2 of this Rule. At least two months' notice of the summons shall be given unless the parties agree to a shorter period.

(2) If a party who has been duly summoned to oral proceedings before the European Patent Office does not appear as summoned, the proceedings may continue without him.

RULE 71A

Preparation of oral proceedings

(1) When issuing the summons, the European Patent Office shall draw attention to the points which in its opinion need to be discussed for the purposes of the decision to be taken. At the same time a final date for making written submissions in preparation for the oral proceedings shall be fixed. Rule 84 shall not apply. New facts and evidence presented after that date need not be considered, unless admitted on the grounds that the subject of the proceedings has changed.

(2) If the applicant or patent proprietor has been notified of the grounds prejudicing the grant or maintenance of the patent, he may be invited to submit, by the date specified in paragraph 1, second sentence, documents which meet the requirements of the Convention. Paragraph 1, third and fourth sentences, shall apply *mutatis mutandis*.

RULE 72

Taking of evidence by the European Patent Office

(1) Where the European Patent Office considers it necessary to hear the oral evidence of parties, witnesses or experts or to carry out an inspection, it shall make a decision to this end, setting out the investigation which it intends to carry out, relevant facts to be proved and the date, time and place of the investigation. If oral evidence of witnesses and experts is requested by a party, the decision of the European Patent Office shall determine the period of time within which the party filing the request must make known to the European Patent Office the names and addresses of the witnesses and experts whom it wishes to be heard.

(2) At least two months' notice of a summons issued to a party, witness or expert to give evidence shall be given unless they agree to a shorter period. The summons shall contain:

(a) an extract from the decision mentioned in paragraph 1, indicating in particular the date, time and place of the investigation ordered and stating the facts regarding which parties, witnesses and experts are to be heard;

(b) the names of the parties to the proceedings and particulars of the rights which the witnesses or experts may invoke under the provisions of Rule 74, paragraphs 2 to 4;

(c) an indication that the party, witness or expert may request to be heard by the competent court of his country of residence and a requirement that he

711

inform the European Patent Office within a time limit to be fixed by the Office whether he is prepared to appear before it.

(3) Before a party, witness or expert may be heard, he shall be informed that the European Patent Office may request the competent court in the country of residence of the person concerned to re-examine his evidence on oath or in an equally binding form.

(4) The parties may attend an investigation and may put relevant questions to the testifying parties, witnesses and experts.

RULE 73

Commissioning of experts

(1) The European Patent Office shall decide in what form the report made by an expert whom it appoints shall be submitted.

(2) The terms of reference of the expert shall include:

 (a) a precise description of his task;
 (b) the time limit laid down for the submission of the expert report;
 (c) the names of the parties to the proceedings;
 (d) particulars of the rights which he may invoke under the provisions of Rule 74, paragraphs 2 to 4.

(3) A copy of any written report shall be submitted to the parties.

(4) The parties may object to an expert. The department of the European Patent Office concerned shall decide on the objection.

RULE 74

Costs of taking of evidence

(1) The taking of evidence by the European Patent Office may be made conditional upon deposit with it, by the party who requested the evidence to be taken, of a sum the amount of which shall be fixed by reference to an estimate of the costs.

(2) Witnesses and experts who are summoned by and appear before the European Patent Office shall be entitled to appropriate reimbursement of expenses for travel and subsistence. An advance for these expenses may be granted to them. The first sentence shall apply to witnesses and experts who appear before the European Patent Office without being summoned by it and are heard as witnesses or experts.

(3) Witnesses entitled to reimbursement under paragraph 2 shall also be entitled to appropriate compensation for loss of earnings, and experts to fees for their work. These payments shall be made to the witnesses and experts after they have fulfilled their duties or tasks.

(4) The Administrative Council shall lay down the details governing the implementation of the provisions of paragraphs 2 and 3. Payment of amounts due pursuant to these paragraphs shall be made by the European Patent Office.

RULE 75

Conservation of evidence

(1) On request, the European Patent Office may, without delay, hear oral evidence or conduct inspections, with a view to conserving evidence of facts liable to affect a decision which it may be called upon to take with regard to an existing European patent application of a European patent, where there is reason to fear that it might subsequently become more difficult or even impossible to take evidence. The date on which the measures are to be taken shall be communicated to the applicant for or proprietor of the patent in sufficient time to allow him to attend. He may ask relevant questions.

(2) The request shall contain:

    (a) the name and address of the person filing the request and the State in which his residence or principal place of business is located, in accordance with the provisions of Rule 26, paragraph 2(c);

    (b) sufficient identification of the European patent application or European patent in question;

    (c) the designation of the facts in respect of which evidence is to be taken;

    (d) particulars of the way in which evidence is to be taken;

    (e) a statement establishing a *prima facie* case for fearing that it might subsequently become more difficult or impossible to take evidence.

(3) The request shall not be deemed to have been filed until the fee for conservation of evidence has been paid.

(4) The decision on the request and any resulting taking of evidence shall be incumbent upon the department of the European Patent Office required to take the decision liable to be affected by the facts to be established. The provisions of the Convention with regard to the taking of evidence in proceedings before the European Patent Office shall be applicable.

RULE 76

Minutes of oral proceedings and of taking of evidence

(1) Minutes of oral proceedings and of the taking of evidence shall be drawn up containing the essentials of the oral proceedings or of the taking of evidence, the relevant statements made by the parties, the testimony of the parties, witnesses or experts and the result of any inspection.

(2) The minutes of the testimony of a witness, expert or party shall be read out or submitted to him so that he may examine them. It shall be noted in the minutes that this formality has been carried out and that the person who gave the testimony approved the minutes. If his approval is not given, his objections shall be noted.

(3) The minutes shall be signed by the employee who drew them up and by the employee who conducted the oral proceedings or taking of evidence, either by their signature or by any other appropriate means.

(4) The parties shall be provided with a copy of the minutes.

Chapter III. Notifications

RULE 77

General provisions on notifications

(1) In proceedings before the European Patent Office, any notification to be made shall take the form either of the original document, a copy thereof certified by, or bearing the seal of, the European Patent Office or a computer print-out bearing such seal. Copies of documents emanating from the parties themselves shall not require such certification.

(2) Notification shall be made:

    (a) by post in accordance with Rule 78;

    (b) by delivery on the premises of the European Patent Office in accordance with Rule 79;

    (c) by public notice in accordance with Rule 80, or

    (d) by such technical means of communication as determined by the President of the European Patent Office and under the conditions laid down by him governing their use.

(3) Notification through the central industrial property office of a Contracting State shall be made in accordance with the provisions applicable to the said office in national proceedings.

RULE 78

Notification by post

(1) Decisions incurring a time limit for appeal, summonses and other documents as decided on by the President of the European Patent Office shall be notified by registered letter with advice of delivery. All other notifications by post, except those referred to in paragraph 2, shall be by registered letter.

(2) Where notification is effected by registered letter, whether or not with advice of delivery, this shall be deemed to be delivered to the addressee on the tenth day following its posting, unless the letter has failed to reach the addressee or has reached him at a later date; in the event of any dispute, it shall be incumbent on the European Patent Office to establish that the letter has reached its destination or to establish the date on which the letter was delivered to the addressee, as the case may be.

(3) Notification by registered letter, whether or not with advice of delivery, shall be deemed to have been effected even if acceptance of the letter has been refused.

(4) To the extent that notification by post is not covered by the provisions of this Rule, the law of the State on the territory of which the notification is made shall apply.

RULE 79

Notification by delivery by hand

Notification may be effected on the premises of the European Patent Office by delivery by hand of the document to the addressee, who shall on delivery acknowledge its receipt. Notification shall be deemed to have taken place even if the addressee refuses to accept the document or to acknowledge receipt thereof.

RULE 80

Public notification

(1) If the address of the addressee cannot be established, or if notification in accordance with Rule 78, paragraph 1, has proved to be impossible even after a second attempt by the European Office, notification shall be effected by public notice.

(2) The President of the European Patent Office shall determine how the public notice is to be given and the beginning of the period of one month on the expiry of which the document shall be deemed to have been notified.

RULE 81

Notification to representatives

(1) If a representative has been appointed, notifications shall be addressed to him.

(2) If several such representatives have been appointed for a single interested party, notification to any one of them shall be sufficient.

(3) If several interested parties have a common representative, notification of a single document to the common representative shall be sufficient.

RULE 82

Irregularities in the notification

Where a document has reached the addressee, if the European Patent Office is unable to prove that it has been duly notified, or if provisions relating to its notification have not been observed, the document shall be deemed to have been notified on the date established by the European Patent Office as the date of receipt.

Chapter IV. Time limits

RULE 83

Calculation of time limits

(1) Periods shall be laid down in terms of full years, months, weeks or days.

(2) Computation shall start on the day following the day on which the relevant event occurred, the event being either a procedural step or the expiry of another period. Where the procedural step is a notification, the event considered shall be the receipt of the document notified, unless otherwise provided.

(3) When a period is expressed as one year or a certain number of years, it shall expire in the relevant subsequent year in the month having the same name and on the day having the same number as the month and the day on which the said event occurred, provided that if the relevant subsequent month has no day with the same number the period shall expire on the last day of that month.

(4) When a period is expressed as one month or a certain number of months, it shall expire in the relevant subsequent month on the day which has the same number as the day on which the said event occurred, provided that if the relevant subsequent month has no day with the same number the period shall expire on the last day of that month.

(5) When a period is expressed as one week or a certain number of weeks, it shall expire in the relevant subsequent week on the day having the same name as the day on which the said event occurred.

RULE 84

Duration of time limits

Where the Convention or these Implementing Regulations specify a period to be determined by the European Patent Office, such period shall be not less than two months nor more than four months; in certain special circumstances it may be up to six months. In certain special cases, the period may be extended upon request, presented before the expiry of such period.

RULE 84A

Late receipt of documents

(1) A document received late at the European Patent Office shall be deemed to have been received in due time if it was posted, or delivered to a recognised delivery service, in due time before the expiry of the time limit in accordance with the conditions laid down by the President of the European Patent Office, unless the document was received later than three months after expiry of the time limit.

(2) Paragraph 1 shall apply *mutatis mutandis* to the time limits provided for in the Convention where transactions are carried out with the competent authority in accordance with Article 75, paragraph 1(b) or paragraph 2(b).

RULE 85

Extension of time limits

(1) If a time limit expires on a day on which one of the filing offices of the European Patent Office in the sense of Article 75, paragraph 1(a) is not open for receipt of documents or on which, for reasons other than those referred to in paragraph 2, ordinary mail is not delivered there, the time limit shall extend until the first day thereafter on which all the filing offices are open for receipt of documents and on which ordinary mail is delivered.

(2) If a time limit expires on a day on which there is a general interruption or subsequent dislocation in the delivery of mail in a Contracting State or between a Contracting State and the European Patent Office, the time limit shall extend to the first day following the end of the period of interruption or dislocation for parties resident in the State concerned or who have appointed representatives with a place of business in that State. The first sentence shall apply *mutatis mutandis* to the period referred to in Article 77, paragraph 5. In the case where the State concerned is the State in which the European Patent Office is located, this provision shall apply to all parties. The duration of the above-mentioned period shall be as stated by the President of the European Patent Office.

(3) Paragraphs 1 and 2 shall apply *mutatis mutandis* to the time limits provided for in the Convention in the case of transactions to be carried out with the competent authority within the meaning of Article 75, paragraph 1(b).

(4) If an exceptional occurrence such as a natural disaster or strike interrupts or dislocates the proper functioning of the European Patent Office so that any communication from the Office to parties concerning the expiry of a time limit is delayed, acts to be completed within such a time limit may still be validly completed within one month after the notification of the delayed communication. The date of commencement and the end of any such interruption or dislocation shall be as stated by the President of the European Patent Office.

Rule 85a

Period of grace for payment of fees

(1) If the filing fee, the search fee, a designation fee or the national basic fee have not been paid within the time limits provided for in Article 78, paragraph 2, Article 79, paragraph 2, Rule 15, paragraph 2, Rule 25, paragraph 2, or Rule 107, paragraph 1(c), (d), and (e), they may still be validly paid within a period of grace of one month of notification of a communication pointing out the failure to observe the time limit, provided that within this period a surcharge is paid.

(2) Designation fees in respect of which the applicant has dispensed with notification under paragraph 1 may still be validly paid within a period of grace of two months of expiry of the normal time limits referred to in paragraph 1, provided that within this period a surcharge is paid.

Rule 85b

Period of grace for the filing of the request for examination

If the request for examination has not been filed within the time limit provided for in Article 94, paragraph 2, or Rule 107, paragraph 1(c), (d) and (e), it may still be validly filed within a period of grace of one month of notification of a communication pointing out the failure to observe the time limit, provided that within this period a surcharge is paid.

Chapter V. Amendments and corrections

Rule 86

Amendment of the European patent application

(1) Before receiving the European search report the applicant may not amend the description, claims or drawings of a European patent application where otherwise provided.

(2) After receiving the European search report and before receipt of the first communication from the Examining Division, the applicant may, of his own volition, amend the description, claims and drawings.

(3) After receipt of the first communication from the Examining Division the applicant may, of his own volition, amend once the description, claims and drawings provided that the amendment is filed at the same time as the reply to the communication. No further amendment may be made without the consent of the Examining Division.

(4) Amended claims may not relate to unsearched subject-matter which does not combine with the originally claimed invention or group of inventions to form a single general inventive concept.

Rule 87

Different claims, description and drawings for different States

If the European Patent Office notes that, in respect of one or some of the designated Contracting States, the content of an earlier European patent application forms part of the state of the art pursuant to Article 54, paragraphs 3 and 4 or if it is informed of the existence of prior right under Article 139, paragraph 2, the European patent application or European patent may contain for such State or States claims and, if the European Patent Office considers it necessary, a description and drawings which are different from those for the other designated Contracting States.

Rule 88

Correction of errors in documents filed with the European Patent Office

Linguistic errors, errors of transcription and mistakes in any document filed with the European Patent Office may be corrected on request. However, if the request for such correction concerns a description, claims or drawings, the correction must be obvious in the sense that it is immediately evident that nothing else would have been intended than what is offered as the correction.

Rule 89

Correction of errors in decisions

In decisions of the European Patent Office, only linguistic errors, errors of transcription and obvious mistakes may be corrected.

Chapter VI. Interruption of proceedings

Rule 90

Interruption of proceedings

(1) Proceedings before the European Patent Office shall be interrupted:

(a) in the event of the death or legal incapacity of the applicant for or proprietor of a European patent or of the person authorised by national law to act on his behalf. To the extent that the above events do not affect the authorisation of a representative appointed under Article 134, proceedings shall be interrupted only on application by such representative;

(b) in the event of the applicant for or proprietor of a European patent, as a result of some action taken against his property, being prevented by legal reasons from continuing the proceedings before the European Patent Office;

(c) in the event of the death or legal incapacity of the representative of an applicant for or proprietor of a European patent or of his being prevented for legal reasons resulting from action taken against his property from continuing the proceedings before the European Patent Office.

(2) When, in the cases referred to in paragraph 1(a) and (b), the European Patent Office has been informed of the identity of the person authorised to continue the proceedings before the European Patent Office, the European Patent Office shall

communicate to such person and to any interested third party that the proceedings shall be resumed as from a date to be fixed by the European Patent Office.

(3) In the case referred to in paragraph 1(c), the proceedings shall be resumed when the European Patent Office has been informed of the appointment of a new representative of the applicant or when the European Patent Office has notified to the other parties the communication of the appointment of a new representative of the proprietor of the patent. If, three months after the beginning of the interruption of the proceedings, the European Patent Office has not been informed of the appointment of a new representative, it shall communicate to the applicant for or proprietor of the patent:

(a) where Article 133, paragraph 2, is applicable, that the European patent application will be deemed to be withdrawn or the European patent will be revoked if the information is not submitted within two months after this communication is notified, or

(b) where Article 133, paragraph 2, is not applicable, that the proceedings will be resumed with the applicant for or proprietor of the patent as from the date on which this communication is notified.

(4) The time limits, other than the time limit for making a request for examination and the time limit for paying the renewal fees, in force as regards the applicant for or proprietor of the patent at the date of interruption of the proceedings, shall begin again as from the day on which the proceedings are resumed. If such date is less than two months before the end of the period within which the request for examination must be filed, such a request may be filed up to the end of two months after such date.

Chapter VII. Waiving of enforced recovery procedures

RULE 91

Waiving of enforced recovery procedures

The President of the European Patent Office may waive action for the enforced recovery of any sum due if the sum to be recovered is minimal or if such recovery is too uncertain.

Chapter VIII. Information to the public

RULE 92

Entries in the Register of European Patents

(1) The Register of European Patents shall contain the following entries:

(a) number of the European patent application;
(b) date of filing of the European patent application;
(c) title of the invention;
(d) classification code given to the European patent application;
(e) the Contracting States designated;
(f) family name, given names, address and the State in which the residence or principal place of business of the applicant for or proprietor of the European patent is located;
(g) family name, given names and address of the inventor designated by the applicant for or proprietor of the patent unless he has renounced his title as inventor under Rule 18, paragraph 1;
(h) family name, given names and address of the place of business of the representative of the applicant for or proprietor of the patent referred to in

Article 134; in the case of several representatives only the family name, given names and address of the place of business of the representative first named, followed by the words "and others", shall be entered; however, in the case of an association referred to in Rule 101, paragraph 9, only the name and address of the association shall be entered;

(i) priority data (date, State and file number of the previous application);
(j) in the event of a division of the European patent application, the numbers of the European divisional applications;
(k) in the case of European divisional applications and a new European patent application under Article 61, paragraph 1(b), the information referred to under sub-paragraphs (a), (b) and (i) with regard to the earlier European patent application;
(l) date of publication of the European patent application and where appropriate date of the separate publication of the European search report;
(m) date of filing of the request for examination;
(n) date on which the European patent application is refused, withdrawn or deemed to be withdrawn;
(o) date of publication of the mention of the grant of the European patent;
(p) date of lapse of the European patent in a Contracting State during the opposition period and, where appropriate, pending a final decision on opposition;
(q) date of filing opposition;
(r) date and purport of the decision on opposition;
(s) dates of suspension and resumption of proceedings in the cases referred to in Rule 13;
(t) dates of interruption and resumption of proceedings in the case referred to in Rule 90;
(u) date of re-establishment of rights provided that an entry has been made in accordance with sub-paragraph (n) or sub-paragraph (r);
(v) the filing of a request to the European Patent Office pursuant to Article 135;
(w) rights and transfer of such rights over a European patent application or European patent where these are recorded pursuant to these Implementing Regulations.

(2) The President of the European Patent Office may decide that entries other than those referred to in paragraph 1 shall be made in the Register of European Patents.

(3) Extracts from the Register of European Patents shall be delivered on request on payment of an administrative fee.

RULE 93

Parts of the file not for inspection

The parts of the file which shall be excluded from inspection pursuant to Article 128, paragraph 4, shall be:

(a) the documents relating to the exclusion of or objections to members of the Boards of Appeal or of the Enlarged Board of Appeal;
(b) draft decisions and opinions, and all other documents, used for the preparation of decisions and opinions, which are not communicated to the parties;
(c) the designation of the inventor if he has renounced his title as inventor under rule 18, paragraph 1;
(d) any other document excluded from inspection by the President of the European Patent Office on the ground that such inspection would not

serve the purpose of informing the public about the European patent application or the resulting patent.

RULE 94

Procedures for the inspection of files

(1) Inspection of the files of European patent applications and of European patents shall either be of the original documents, or of copies thereof, or of technical means of storage if the files are stored in this way. The means of inspection shall be determined by the President of the European Patent Office. Inspection of files shall be subject to the payment of an administrative fee.

(2) The inspection shall take place on the premises of the European Patent Office and, for such time as the file is with the central industrial property office of a Contracting State pursuant to an agreement concluded under the Protocol on Centralisation, on the premises of the latter office. However, on request, inspection of the files shall take place on the premises of the central industrial property office of the Contracting State in whose territory the person making the request has his residence or principal place of business.

(3) On request, inspection of the files shall be effected by means of issuing copies of file documents. Such copies shall incur fees.

(4) The European Patent Office shall issue on request certified copies of the European patent application upon payment of an administrative fee.

RULE 95

Communication of information contained in the files

Subject to the restrictions provided for in Article 128, paragraphs 1 to 4, and in Rule 93, the European Patent Office may, upon request, communicate information concerning any file of a European patent application or European patent subject to the payment of an administrative fee. However, the European Patent Office may require the exercise of the option to obtain inspection of the file itself should it deem this to be appropriate in view of the quantity of information to be supplied.

RULE 95A

Constitution, maintenance and preservation of files

(1) The European Patent Office shall constitute, maintain and preserve files relating to all European patent applications and patents.

(2) The President of the European Patent Office shall determine the form in which the files relating to European patent applications and patents shall be constituted, maintained and preserved.

(3) Documents incorporated in an electronic file shall be considered to be originals.

(4) Files relating to European patent applications and patents shall be preserved for at least five years from the end of the year in which:

(a) the application is refused or withdrawn or is deemed to be withdrawn;

(b) the patent is revoked pursuant to opposition proceedings; or

(c) the patent or the extended term or corresponding protection under Article 63, paragraph 2, lapses in the last of the designated States.

721

(5) Without prejudice to paragraph 4, files relating to European patent applications which have given rise to divisional applications under Article 76 or new applications under Article 61, paragraph 1(b), shall be preserved for at least the same period as the files relating to any one of these last applications. The same shall apply to files relating to any resulting European patents.

RULE 96

Additional publications by the European Patent Office

(1) The President of the European Patent Office may provide that, and in what form, the data referred to in Article 128, paragraph 5, shall be communicated to third parties or published.

(2) The President of the European Patent Office may provide for the publication of new or amended claims received after the time mentioned in Rule 49, paragraph 3, the form of such publication and the entry in the European Patent Bulletin of particulars concerning such claims.

Chapter IX. Legal and administrative co-operation

RULE 97

Communications between the European Patent Office and the authorities of the Contracting States

(1) Communications between the European Patent Office and the central industrial property offices of the Contracting States which arise out of the application of the Convention shall be effected directly between these authorities. Communications between the European Patent Office and the courts or other authorities of the Contracting States may be effected through the intermediary of the above central industrial property offices.

(2) Expenditure in respect of communications under paragraph 1 shall be chargeable to the authority making the communications, which shall be exempt from fees.

RULE 98

Inspection of files by or via courts or authorities of the Contracting States

(1) Inspection of the files of European patent applications or of European patents by courts or authorities of the Contracting States shall be of the original documents or of copies thereof; Rule 94 shall not apply.

(2) Courts or Public Prosecutors' Offices of the Contracting States may, in the course of their proceedings, communicate to third parties files or copies thereof transmitted to them by the European Patent Office. Such communications shall be effected in accordance with the conditions laid down in Article 128; they shall not incur the payment of the administrative fee.

(3) The European Patent Office shall, at the time of transmission of the files or copies thereof to the courts or Public Prosecutors' Offices of the Contracting States, indicate such restrictions as may, under Article 128, paragraphs 1 and 4, be applicable to the communication to third parties of files concerning a European patent application or a European patent.

RULE 99

Procedure for letters rogatory

(1) Each Contracting State shall designate a central authority which will undertake to receive letters rogatory issued by the European Patent Office and to transmit them to the authority competent to execute them.

(2) The European Patent Office shall draw up letters rogatory in the language of the competent authority or shall attach to such letters rogatory a translation into the language of that authority.

(3) Subject to the provisions of paragraphs 5 and 6, the competent authority shall apply its own law as to the procedures to be followed in executing such requests. In particular, it shall apply appropriate measures of compulsion in accordance with its own law.

(4) If the authority to which the letters rogatory are transmitted is not competent to execute them, the letters rogatory shall be sent forthwith to the central authority referred to in paragraph 1. That authority shall transmit the letters rogatory either to the competent authority in that State, or to the European Patent Office where no authority is competent in that State.

(5) The European Patent Office shall be informed of the time when, and the place where, the enquiry or other legal measure is to take place and shall inform the parties, witnesses and experts concerned.

(6) If so requested by the European Patent Office, the competent authority shall permit the attendance of members of the department concerned and allow them to question any person giving evidence either directly or through the competent authority.

(7) The execution of letters rogatory shall not give rise to any reimbursement of fees or costs of any nature. Nevertheless, the State in which letters rogatory are executed has the right to require the Organisation to reimburse any fees paid to experts and interpreters and the costs incurred by the procedure of paragraph 6.

(8) If the law applied by the competent authority obliges the parties to secure evidence and the authority is not able itself to execute the letter rogatory, that authority may, with the consent of the European Patent Office, appoint a suitable person to do so. When seeking the consent of the European Patent Office, the competent authority shall indicate the approximate costs which would result from this procedure. If the European Patent Office gives its consent, the Organisation shall reimburse any costs incurred; without such consent, the Organisation shall not be liable for such costs.

Chapter X. Representation

RULE 100

Appointment of a common representative

(1) If there is more than one applicant and the request for the grant of a European patent does not name a common representative, the applicant first named in the request shall be considered to be the common representative. However, if one of the applicants is obliged to appoint a professional representative this representative shall be considered to be the common representative unless the first named applicant has appointed a professional representative. The same shall apply *mutatis mutandis* to third parties acting in common in filing notice of opposition or intervention and to joint proprietors of a European patent.

(2) If, during the course of proceedings, transfer is made to more than one person,

723

and such persons have not appointed a common representative, paragraph 1 shall apply. If such application is not possible, the European Patent Office shall require such persons to appoint a common representative within two months. If this request is not complied with, the European Patent Office shall appoint the common representative.

RULE 101

Authorisations

(1) Representatives acting before the European Patent Office shall upon request file a signed authorisation within a period to be specified by the European Patent Office. The President of the European Patent Office shall determine the cases where an authorisation is to be filed. The authorisation may cover one or more European patent applications or European patents and shall be filed in the corresponding number of copies. Where the requirements of Article 133, paragraph 2, have not been satisfied, the same period shall be specified for the notification of the appointment of a representative and for the filing of the authorisation.

(2) A general authorisation enabling a representative to act in respect of all the patent transactions of the party making the authorisation may be filed. A single copy shall be sufficient.

(3) The President of the European Patent Office may determine and publish in the Official Journal of the European Patent Office the form and content of:

(a) an authorisation in so far as it relates to the representation of persons as defined in Article 133, paragraph 2;
(b) a general authorisation.

(4) If the authorisation is not filed in due time, any procedural steps taken by the representative other than the filing of a European patent application shall, without prejudice to any other legal consequences provided for in the Convention, be deemed not to have been taken.

(5) The provisions of paragraphs 1 and 2 shall apply *mutatis mutandis* to a document withdrawing an authorisation.

(6) Any representative who has ceased to be authorised shall continue to be regarded as the representative until the termination of his authorisation has been communciated to the European Patent Office.

(7) Subject to any provisions to the contrary contained therein, an authorisation shall not terminate *vis-à-vis* the European Patent Office upon the death of the person who gave it.

(8) If several representatives are appointed by a party, they may, notwithstanding any provisions to the contrary in the notification of their appointment or in the authorisation, act either jointly or singly.

(9) The authorisation of an association of representatives shall be deemed to be authorisation of any representative who can establish that he practises within that association.

RULE 102

Amendment of the list of professional representatives

(1) The entry of a professional representative shall be deleted from the list of professional representatives if he so requests or if, despite due reminder, he fails to

pay the annual subscription to the Institute of Professional Representatives before the European Patent Office for two years in succession.

(2) After the expiry of the transitional period provided for in Article 163, paragraph 1, and without prejudice to any disciplinary measures taken under Article 134, paragraph 8(c), the entry of any professional representative may be deleted automatically in the following cases only:

(a) in the event of the death or legal incapacity of the professional representative;

(b) in the event of the professional representative no longer being a national of one of the Contracting States, unless he was entered on the list during the transitional period or was granted exemption by the President of the European Patent Office in accordance with Article 134, paragraph 6;

(c) in the event of the professional representative no longer having his place of business or employment within the territory of one of the Contracting States.

(3) A person whose entry has been deleted shall, upon request, be re-entered in the list of professional representatives if the conditions for deletion no longer exist.

Part VIII. Implementing Regulations to Parts VIII

RULE 103

Information to the public in the event of conversion

(1) The documents which, in accordance with Article 136, accompany the request for conversion shall be communicated to the public by the central industrial property office under the same conditions and to the same extent as documents relating to national proceedings.

(2) The printed specifications of the national patent resulting from the conversion of a European patent application must mention that application.

Part IX. Implementing Regulations to Part X of the Convention

RULE 104

The European Patent Office as a receiving Office

(1) When the European Patent Office acts as a receiving Office under the Cooperation Treaty, the international application shall be filed in English, French or German. It shall be filed in three copies; the same applies to any of the documents referred to in the check list provided for in Rule 3.3(a)(ii) of the Regulations under the Cooperation Treaty except the receipt for the fees paid or the cheque for the payment of the fees.

(2) If the provisions of paragraph 1, second sentence, are not complied with, the missing copies shall be prepared by the European Patent Office at the expense of the applicant.

(3) If an international application is filed with an authority of a Contracting State for transmittal to the European Patent Office as the receiving Office, the

Contracting State must ensure that the application reaches the European Patent Office not later than two weeks before the end of the thirteenth month after filing or, if priority is claimed, after the date of priority.

RULE 105

The European Patent Office as an International Searching Authority or International Preliminary Examining Authority

(1) In the case of Article 17, paragraph 3(e), of the Cooperation Treaty, an additional fee equal to the amount of the search fee shall be payable for each further invention for which an international search is to be carried out.

(2) In the case of Article 34, paragraph 3(a), of the Cooperation Treaty, an additional fee equal to the amount of the preliminary examination fee shall be payable for each further invention for which the international preliminary examination is to be carried out.

(3) Without prejudice to Rules 40.2(e) and 68.3(e) of the Regulations under the Cooperation Treaty, where an additional fee has been paid under protest, the European Patent Office shall review whether the invitation to pay the additional fee was justified and, if it does not so find, shall refund the additional fee. If the European Patent Office after such a review considers the invitation to be justified, it shall inform the applicant accordingly and shall invite him to pay a fee for the examination of the protest ("protest fee"). If the protest fee is paid in due time, the protest shall be referred to the Board of Appeal for a decision.

RULE 106

The National Fee

The national fee provided for in Article 158, paragraph 2, shall comprise the following fees:

(a) a national basic fee equal to the filing fee provided for in Article 78, paragraph 2, and

(b) the designation fees provided for in Article 79, paragraph 2.

RULE 107

The European Patent Office as a designated or elected office

(1) In the case of an international application as referred to in Article 150, paragraph 3, the applicant must perform the following acts within a period of twenty-one months, where Article 22, paragraphs 1 and 2, of the Cooperation Treaty apply, or thirty-one months where Article 39, paragraph 1(a), of the Cooperation Treaty applies, from the date of filing of the application, or, if priority has been claimed, from the priority date:

(a) supply, where applicable, the translation of the international application required under Article 158, paragraph 2;

(b) specify the application documents, as originally filed or in amended form, on which the European grant procedure is to be based;

(c) pay the national basic fee provided for in Rule 106(a);

(d) pay the designation fees if the time limit specified in Article 79, paragraph 2, has expired earlier;

(e) pay the search fee provided for in Article 157, paragraph 2(b), where a supplementary European search report has to be drawn up;

(f) file the request for examination provided for in Article 94, if the time limit specified in Article 94, paragraph 2, has expired earlier;

(g) pay the renewal fee in respect of the third year provided for in Article 86, paragraph 1, if the fee has fallen due earlier under Rule 37, paragraph 1;

(h) file, where applicable, the certificate of exhibition referred to in Article 55, paragraph 2, and Rule 23.

(2) Where the European Patent Office has drawn up an international preliminary examination report the examination fee shall be reduced as laid down in the Rules relating to Fees. If the report was established on certain parts of the international application in accordance with Article 34, paragraph 3(c), of the Cooperation Treaty, the reduction shall be allowed only if examination is to be performed on the subject-matter covered by the report.

RULE 108

Consequence of non-payment of the national fee

(1) If the national basic fee is not paid in due time, the European patent application shall be deemed to be withdrawn.

(2) The designation of any Contracting State in respect of which the designation fee has not been paid in due time shall be deemed to be withdrawn.

RULE 109

Amendment of the application

Without prejudice to Rule 86, paragraphs 2 to 4, the application may be amended once, within a non-extendable period of one month as from notification of a communication informing the applicant accordingly. The application as amended shall serve as the basis for any supplementary search which has to be performed under Article 157, paragraph 2.

RULE 110

Claims incurring fee Consequence of non-payment

(1) If the application documents on which the European grant procedure is to be based comprise more than ten claims, a claims fee shall be payable for the eleventh and each subsequent claims within the period provided for in Rule 107, paragraph 1.

(2) Any claims fees not paid in due time may still be validly paid within a non-extendable period of grace of one month as from notification of a communication pointing out the failure to pay. If within this period amended claims are filed, the claims fees due shall be computed on the basis of such amended claims.

(3) Any claims fees paid within the period provided for in paragraph 1 and which are in excess of those due under paragraph 2, second sentence, shall be refunded.

(4) Where a claims fee is not paid in due time, the claim concerned shall be deemed to be abandoned.

727

Rule 111

Examination of certain formal requirements by the European Patent Office

(1) If the data concerning the inventor prescribed in paragraph 1, have not yet been submitted at the expiry of the period provided for in Rule 107, paragraph 1, the European Patent Office shall invite the application to furnish the data within such period as it shall specify.

(2) Where the priority of an earlier application is claimed and the file number or copy provided for in Article 88, paragraph 1, and Rule 38, paragraphs 1 to 3, have not yet been submitted at the expiry of the period provided for in Rule 107, paragraph 1, the European Patent Office shall invite the applicant to furnish the number or copy of the earlier application within such period as it shall specify. Rule 38, paragraph 4, shall apply.

(3) If at the expiry of the period provided for in Rule 107, paragraph 1, a sequence listing as prescribed in Rule 5.2 of the Regulations under the Cooperation Treaty is not available to the European Patent Office, or does not conform to the prescribed standard, or has not been filed on the prescribed data carrier, the applicant shall be invited to file a sequence listing conforming to the prescribed standard or on the prescribed data carrier within such period as the European Patent Office shall specify.

Rule 112

Consideration of unity by the European Patent Office

If only a part of the international application has been searched by the International Searching Authority because that Authority considered that the application did not comply with the requirement of unity of invention, and the applicant did not pay all additional fees according to Article 17, paragraph 3(a), of the Cooperation Treaty within the prescribed time limit, the European Patent Office shall consider whether the application complies with the requirement of unity of invention. If the European Patent Office considers that this is not the case, it shall inform the applicant that a European search report can be obtained in respect of those parts of the international application which have not been searched if a search fee is paid for each invention involved within a period specified by the European Patent Office which may not be shorter than two weeks and may not exceed six weeks. The Search Division shall draw up a European search report for those parts of the international application which relate to inventions in respect of which search fees have been paid. Rule 46, paragraph 2, shall apply *mutatis mutandis*.

APPENDIX 3

RULES RELATING TO FEES

Rules of October 20, 1977

A3–01

(O.J. EPO 1978, 21 *et seq.* and 81) as last amended by Decisions of the Administrative Council of the European Patent Organisation of December 7, 1990 (O.J. EPO 1991, 4 *et seq.* and 11 *et seq.*)

Contents

THE ADMINISTRATIVE COUNCIL OF THE EUROPEAN PATENT ORGANISATION,
HAVING REGARD to the European Patent Convention and in particular Article 33, paragraph 2(d), thereof,
HAS ADOPTED THE FOLLOWING RULES RELATING TO FEES:

ARTICLE 1

General

The following shall be levied in accordance with the provisions contained in these Rules:

(a) fees due to be paid to the European Patent Office (hereinafter referred to as the Office) as provided for in the Convention and in the Implementing Regulations and the fees and costs which the President of the Office lays down pursuant to Article 3, paragraph 1;

(b) fees and costs pursuant to the Patent Cooperation Treaty (hereinafter referred to as the PCT), the amounts of which may be fixed by the Office.

ARTICLE 2

Fees provided for in the Convention and in the Implementing Regulations

The fees due to be paid to the Office under Article 1 shall be as follows:

	EUR
1. Filling fee (Article 78, paragraph 2)	127
2. Search fee in repsect of	
— a European or supplementary European search (Article 78, paragraph 2, Rule 46, paragraph 1, and 112, paragraph 4, and Article 157, paragraph 2(b))	690
— an international search (Rule 16.1 PCT and Rule 105, paragraph 1)	945
3. Designation fee for each Contracting State designated (Article 79, paragraph 2) designation fees being deemed paid for all contracting states upon payment of seven times the amount of this fee	76
3a. Joint designation fee for the Swiss Confederation and the Principality of Leichtenstein	76
3b. Surcharge on the filing fee, the search fee, a designation fee or the national basic fee (Rule 85a)	50% of the relevant fee or fees, but not to exceed a total of EUR 715
4. Renewal fees for European patent applications (Article 86, paragraph 1), calculated in each case from the date of filing of the application	
— for the 3rd year	383
— for the 4th year	409

— for the 5th year	434
— for the 6th year	715
— for the 7th year	741
— for the 8th year	766
— for the 9th year	971
for the 10th and each subsequent year	1022

5. Additional fee for belated payment of a renewal fee for the European patent application (Article 86, paragraph 2)   10% of the belated renewal fee

6. Examining fee (Article 94, paragraph 2)   1431

7. Surcharge for late filing of the request for examination (rule 85b)   50% of the examination fee

8. Fee for grant including fee for printing the European patent specification (Article 97, paragraph 2(b)), where the application documents to be printed comprise:

8.1 not more than 35 pages   715

8.2 more than 35 pages   715 plus EUR 1020 for the 36th and each subsequent page

9. Fee for printing a new specification of the European patent (Article 102, paragraph 3(b))—flat-rate fee   51

10. Opposition fee (Article 99, paragraph 1, and Article 105, paragraph 2)   613

11. Fee for appeal (Article 108)   1022

12. Fee for further processing (Article 121, paragraph 2)   76

13. Fee for re-establishment of rights (Article 122, paragraph 3)   76

14. Conversion fee (Article 136, paragraph 1, and Article 140)   51

15. Claims fee for the eleventh and each subsequent claim (Rule 31, paragraph 1, and Rule 51, paragraph 7 and Rule 110, paragraph 1)   40

16. Fee for the awarding of costs (Rule 63, paragraph 3)   51

17. Fee for the conservation of evidence (Rule 75, paragraph 3)   51

18. Transmittal fee for an international application (Article 152, paragraph 3)   102

19. Fee for the preliminary examination of an international application (Rule 58 PCT and Rule 105, paragraph 2)   1533

20. Fee for a technical opinion (Article 25)   3066

21. Protest fee (Rules 40.2(e) and 68.3(e) PCT, Rule 105, paragraph 3)

ARTICLE 3

Fees, costs and prices laid down by the President of the Office

(1) The President of the Office shall lay down the amount of the administrative fees provided for in the Implementing Regulations and, where appropriate, the amount of the fees and costs for any services rendered by the Office other than those specified in Article 2.

(2) He shall also lay down the prices of the publications referred to in Articles 93, 98, 103 and 129 of the Convention.

(3) The amounts of the fees provided for in Article 2 and of the fees and costs laid down in accordance with paragraph 1 shall be published in the Official Journal of the European Patent Office.

ARTICLE 4

Due date for fees

(1) Fees in respect of which the due date is not specified in the provisions of the Convention or of the PCT or of the Implementing Regulations thereto shall be due on the date of receipt of the request for the service incurring the fee concerned.

(2) The President of the Office may decide not to make services within the meaning of paragraph 1 dependent upon the advance payment of the corresponding fee.

ARTICLE 5

Payment of fees

(1) Subject to the provisions of Article 6, the fees due to the Office shall be paid in euro or in a currency freely convertible into euro:

(a) by payment or transfer to a bank account held by the Office,
(b) by payment or transfer to a Giro account held by the Office,
(c) by delivery or remittance of cheques which are made payable to the Office.

(2) The President of the Office may allow other methods of paying fees than those set out in paragraph 1.

ARTICLE 6

Currencies

(1) Payments in accordance with Article 5, paragraph 1(a) and (b), shall be made in euro or in the currency of the State in which the bank or Giro account is held.

(2) Payments in accordance with Article 5, paragraph 1(c), shall be made in euro or in the currency of the State where the banking establishment on which the cheque is drawn is located, provided that the equivalents of the amounts of fees expressed in euro have been laid down in that currency by the President of the Office.

(3) For payments to the Office made in currencies other than euro, the President of the Office shall, after consulting the Budget and Finance Committee if appropriate, lay down the equivalents in such other currencies of the fees in euro payable pursuant to these Rules. In doing so, he shall ensure that fluctuations in monetary rates of exchange are not prejudicial to the Office. The amounts determined in this way shall be published in the Official Journal of the European Patent Office. Revised amounts shall be binding on payments for fees which are made on or after the date laid down by the President of the Office.

ARTICLE 7

Particulars concerning payments

(1) Every payment must indicate the name of the person making the payment and must contain the necessary particulars to enable the Office to establish immediately the purpose of the payment.

(2) If the purpose of the payment cannot immediately be established, the Office shall require the person making the payment to notify it in writing of this purpose within such period as it may specify. If he does not comply with this request in due time the payment shall be considered not to have been made.

ARTICLE 8

Date to be considered as the date on which the payment is made

(1) The date on which any payment shall be considered to have been made to the Office shall be as follows:

(a) in the cases referred to in Article 5, paragraph 1(a) and (b): the date on which the amount of the payment or of the transfer is actually entered in a bank account or a Giro account held by the Office;

(b) in the case referred to in Article 5, paragraph 1(c): the date of receipt of the cheque at the Office, provided that the cheque is met.

(2) Where the President of the Office allows, in accordance with the provisions of Article 5, paragraph 2, other methods of paying fees than those set out in Article 5, paragraph 1, he shall also lay down the date on which such payments shall be considered to have been made.

(3) Where, under the provisions of paragraphs 1 and 2, payment of a fee is not considered to have been made until after the expiry of the period in which it should have been made, it shall be considered that this period has been observed if evidence is provided to the Office that the person who made the payment.

(a) fulfilled one of the following conditions in a Contracting State within the period within which the payment should have been made:
    (i) he effected the payment through a banking establishment or a post office;
    (ii) he duly gave an order to a banking establishment or a post office to transfer the amount of the payment;

(iii) he despatched at a post office a letter bearing the address of the Office and containing a cheque within the meaning of Article 5, paragraph 1(c), provided that the cheque is met, and

(b) paid a surcharge of 10% on the relevant fee or fees, but not exceeding EUR 153; no surcharge is payable if a condition according to sub-paragraph (a) has been fulfilled not later than ten days before the expiry of the period for payment.

(4) The Office may request the person who made the payment to produce evidence as to the date on which a condition according to paragraph 3(a) was fulfilled and, where required, pay the surcharge referred to in paragraph 3(b), within a period to be specified by it. If he fails to comply with this request or if the evidence is insufficient, or if the required surcharge is not paid in due time, the period for payment shall be considered not to have been observed.

ARTICLE 9

Insufficiency of the amount paid

(1) A time limit for payment shall in principle be deemed to have been observed only if the full amount of the fee has been paid in due time. If the fee is not paid in full, the amount which has been paid shall be refunded after the period for payment has expired. The Office may, however, in so far as this is possible within the time remaining before the end of the period, give the person making the payment the opportunity to pay the amount lacking. It may also, where this is considered justified, overlook any small amounts lacking without prejudice to the rights of the person making the payment.

(2) Where the request for grant of a European patent designates more than one Contracting State in accordance with Article 79, paragraph 1, of the Convention, and the amount paid is insufficient to cover all the designation fees, the amount paid shall be applied according to the specifications made by the applicant at the time of payment. If the applicant makes no such specifications at the time of payment, these fees shall be deemed to be paid only for as many designations as are covered by the amount paid and in the order in which the Contracting States are designated in the request.

ARTICLE 10

Refund of the fee for the European search report

The search fee shall be refunded fully or in part if the European search report is based on an earlier search report already prepared by the Office on an application whose priority is claimed for the European patent application or which is the earlier application within the meaning of Article 76 of the Convention or the original application within the meaning of Rule 15 of the Implementing Regulations thereto.

(2) The amount of any refund allowed under paragraph 1 shall be 25, 50, 75 or 100% of the search fee, depending upon the extent to which the Office benefits from the earlier search report.

(3) The search fee shall be fully refunded if the European search report relates to a European divisional application and is based entirely on an earlier search report on the earlier application.

(4) The search fee shall be fully refunded if the European patent application is withdrawn or refused or deemed to be withdrawn at a time when the Office has not yet begun to draw up the European search report.

ARTICLE 10A

Refund of the fee for a technical opinion

An amount of 75% of the fee for a technical opinion under Article 25 of the Convention shall be refunded if the request for a technical opinion is withdrawn at a time when the Office has not yet begun to draw up the technical opinion.

ARTICLE 10B

Refund of examination fee

The examination fee provided for in Article 94, paragraph 2, of the Convention shall be refunded:

(a) in full if the European patent application is withdrawn, refused or deemed to be withdrawn before the Examination Divisions have assumed responsibility;

(b) at a rate of 75% if the European patent application is withdrawn, refused or deemed to be withdrawn after the Examining Divisions have assumed responsibility but before substantive examination has begun.

ARTICLE 10C

Refund of insignificant amounts

Where too large a sum is paid to cover a fee, the excess shall not be refunded if the amount is insignificant and the party concerned has not expressly requested a refund. The President of the Office shall determine what constitutes an insignificant amount.

ARTICLE 11

Decisions fixing costs which are subject to appeal

In accordance with Article 106, paragraph 5, of the Convention, decisions fixing the amount of costs of opposition proceedings may be appealed if the amount is in excess of the fee for appeal.

ARTICLE 12

Reduction of fees

(1) The reduction laid down in Rule 6, paragraph 3, of the Convention shall be 20% of the filing fee, examination fee, opposition fee and fee for appeal.

(2) The reduction laid down in Rule 107, paragraph 2, of the Convention shall be 50% of the examination fee.

ARTICLE 13

Notification

The President of the European Patent Office shall forward a certified copy of these Rules to all the signatory States to the Convention and to the States which accede thereto.

ARTICLE 14

Entry into force

These Rules shall enter into force on 20 October 1977.
DONE at Munich, 20 October 1977.

APPENDIX 4

RULES OF PROCEDURE OF THE BOARDS OF APPEAL

Rules adopted with effect from June 6, 1980 (O.J. EPO 1980, 171), amended with effect from December 10, 1982 (O.J. EPO 1983, 7) and further amended with effect from July 7, 1989 (O.J. EPO 1989, 361)

A4–01

Contents

The authority referred to in Rule 10, paragraph 2, of the Implementing Regulations to the European Patent Convention, hereby adopts, under Rule 11 thereto, the following Rules of Procedure:

ARTICLE 1

Business distribution scheme

(1) The authority referred to in Rule 10, paragraph 2, shall at the beginning of each working year draw up a scheme for the distribution among the Boards of Appeal of all appeals that may be filed during the year, designating the members who may serve on each Board and their respective alternatives. The scheme may be amended during the working year.

(2) The authority may delegate to the Chairman of each Board the task of designating members responsible for the examination of each appeal assigned to his Board as and when it is received by the Registry of the Boards of Appeal.

ARTICLE 2

Replacement of members

(1) Reasons for replacement by alternatives shall in particular include sickness, excessive workload, and commitments which cannot be avoided.

(2) Any member requesting to be replaced by an alternative shall inform the Chairman of the Board concerned of his unavailability without delay.

ARTICLE 3

Exclusion and objection

(1) If a Board has knowledge of a possible reason for exclusion or objection which does not originate from a member himself or from any party to the proceedings, then the procedure of Article 24, paragraph 4, of the Convention shall be applied.

(2) The member concerned shall be invited to present his comments as to whether there is a reason for exclusion.

(3) Before a decision is taken on the exclusion of the member, there shall be no further proceedings in the case.

ARTICLE 4

Rapporteurs

(1) The Chairman of each Board shall for each appeal designate a member of his Board, or himself as rapporteur.

(2) The rapporteur shall carry out a preliminary study of the appeal and may prepare communications to the parties subject to the direction of the Chairman of the Board. Communications shall be signed by the rapporteur on behalf of the Board.

(3) The rapporteur shall make the preparations for meetings of the Board and for oral proceedings.

(4) The rapporteur shall draft decisions.

(5) If a rapporteur considers that his knowledge of the language of the proceedings is insufficient for drafting communications or decisions, he may draft

these in one of the other official languages. His drafts shall be translated by the European Patent Office into the language of the proceedings and the translations shall be checked by the rapporteur or by another member of the Board concerned.

ARTICLE 5

Registries

(1) Registries shall be established for the Boards of Appeal. Registrars shall be responsible for the discharge of the functions of the Registries. One of the Registrars shall be designated Senior Registrar.

(2) The authority referred to in Rule 10(2) may entrust to the Registrars the execution of functions which involve no technical or legal difficulties, in particular in relation to arranging for inspection of files, issuing summonses to oral proceedings and notifications and granting requests for further processing of applications.

(3) The Registrar shall report to the Chairman of the Board concerned on the admissibility of each newly filed appeal.

(4) Minutes of oral proceedings and of the taking of evidence shall be drawn up by the Registrar or such other employees of the Office as the Chairman may designate.

ARTICLE 6

Attendance of interpreters

If required, the Chairman of the Board shall make arrangements for interpretation during oral proceedings, the taking of evidence or the deliberations of his Board.

ARTICLE 7

Change in the composition of a Board

(1) If the composition of a Board is changed after oral proceedings, the parties to the proceedings shall be informed that, at the request of any party, fresh oral proceedings shall be held before the Board in its new composition. Fresh oral proceedings shall also be held if so requested by the new member and if the other members of the Board concerned have given their agreement.

(2) The new member shall be bound to the same extent as the other members by an interim decision which has already been taken.

(3) If, when a Board has already reached a final decision, a member is unable to act, he shall not be replaced by an alternate. If the Chairman is unable to act, the member of the Board concerned having the longer or longest service on the Boards of Appeal, or in the case where members have the same length of service, the elder or eldest member, shall sign the decision on behalf of the Chairman.

ARTICLE 8

Enlargement of a Board of Appeal

If a Board of Appeal consisting of two technically qualified members and one legally qualified member considers that the nature of the appeal requires that the

Board should consist of three technically qualified members and two legally qualified members, the decision to enlarge the Board shall be taken at the earliest possible stage in the examination of that appeal.

ARTICLE 9

Consolidation of appeal proceedings

(1) If several appeals are filed from a decision, these appeals shall be considered in the same proceedings.

(2) If appeals are filed from separate decisions and all the appeals are designated to be examined by one Board in a common composition, that Board may deal with those appeals in consolidated proceedings with the consent of the parties.

ARTICLE 10

Remission to the department of first instance

A Board shall remit a case to the department of first instance if fundamental deficiencies are apparent in the first instance proceedings, unless special reasons present themselves for doing otherwise.

ARTICLE 11

Oral proceedings

(1) If oral proceedings are to take place, the Board concerned shall endeavour to ensure that the parties have provided all relevant information and documents, before the hearing.

(2) The Board may send with the summons to oral proceedings a communication drawing attention to matters which seem to be of special significance, or to the fact that questions appear no longer to be contentious, or containing other observations that may help concentration on essentials during the oral proceedings.

(3) If oral proceedings take place, the Board shall endeavour to ensure that each case is ready for decision at the conclusion of the oral proceedings, unless there are special reasons to the contrary.

ARTICLE 12

Communications to the parties

If a Board deems it expedient to communicate with the parties regarding a possible appreciation of substantive or legal matters, such communication shall be made in such a way as not to imply that the Board is in any way bound by it.

ARTICLE 12A

[inserted July 7, 1989]

The Board may, on its own initiative or at the written, reasoned request of the President of the European Patent Office, invite him to comment in writing or orally on questions of general interest which arise in the course of proceedings pending before it. The parties shall be entitled to submit their observations on the President's comments.

ARTICLE 13

Deliberations preceding decisions

If the members of a Board are not all of the same opinion, the Board shall meet to deliberate regarding the decision to be taken. Only members of the Board shall participate in the deliberations: the Chairman may, however, authorise other officers to attend. Deliberations shall be secret.

ARTICLE 14

Order of voting

(1) During the deliberations between members of a Board, the opinion of the rapporteur shall be heard first and, if the rapporteur is not the Chairman, the Chairman's last.

(2) If voting is necessary, votes shall be taken in the same sequence, save that if the Chairman is also the rapporteur, he shall vote last. Abstentions shall not be permitted.

ARTICLE 15

Deviations from an earlier decision of any Board or from the Guidelines

(1) Should a Board consider it necessary to deviate from an interpretation or explanation of the Convention given in an earlier decision of any Board, the grounds for this deviation shall be given, unless such grounds are in accordance with an earlier opinion or decision of the Enlarged Board of Appeal. The President of the European Patent Office shall be informed of the Board's decision.

(2) If, in its decision, a Board gives a different interpretation of the Convention to that provided for in the Guidelines, it shall state the grounds for its action if it considers that this decision will be more readily understood in the light of such grounds.

ARTICLE 16

Deviation from an earlier decision or opinion of the Enlarged Board of Appeal

Should a Board consider it necessary to deviate from an interpretation or explanation of the Convention contained in an earlier opinion or decision of the Enlarged Board of Appeal, the question shall be referred to the Enlarged Board of Appeal.

ARTICLE 17

Referral of a question to the Enlarged Board of Appeal

(1) If a point is to be referred to the Enlarged Board of Appeal, a decision to this effect shall be taken by the Board concerned.

(2) The decision shall contain the items specified in Rule 66, paragraph 2(*a*), (*b*), (*c*), (*d*) and (*f*) and the point which the Board refers to the Enlarged Board of Appeal. The context in which the point originated shall also be stated.

(3) The decision shall be communicated to the parties.

ARTICLE 18

Binding nature of the Rules of Procedure

These Rules of Procedure shall be binding upon the Boards of Appeal, provided that they do not lead to a situation which would be incompatible with the spirit and purpose of the Convention.

ARTICLE 19

Entry into force

These Rules of Procedure shall enter into force on the date on which they are approved by the Administrative Council of the European Patent Organisation. Simultaneously with their entry into force, the Rules of Procedure of the Legal Board of Appeal, adopted by the authority referred to in Rule 10, paragraph 2, on 27 April 1978, and approved by the Administrative Council of the European Patent Organisation by a Decision of 3 June 1978, shall cease to have effect.

APPENDIX 5

RULES OF PROCEDURE OF THE ENLARGED BOARD OF APPEAL

Rules adopted December 10, 1982 (O.J. EPO 1983, 3), amended July 7, 1989 (O.J. EPO 1989, 362), June 8, 1994 (O.J. EPO 1994, 443).

A5–01

Contents

The Enlarged Board of Appeal hereby adopts under Rule 11 of the Implementing Regulations to the European Patent Convention, the following Rules of Procedure:

ARTICLE 1

Business distribution scheme

(1) Before the beginning of each working year the authority referred to in Rule 10, paragraph 2, shall draw up a business distribution scheme for all points of law that shall be referred during the year. The scheme may be amended during the working year.

(2) In proceedings before the Enlarged Board of Appeal at least four of the members shall not have taken part in the proceedings before the Board of Appeal referring to the point of law.

ARTICLE 2

Replacement of members

(1) Reasons for replacement by alternates shall in particular include sickness, excessive workload, and commitments which cannot be avoided.

(2) Any member who wishes to be replaced by an alternate shall inform the Chairman of the Board of his unavailability without delay.

ARTICLE 3

Exclusion and objection

(1) If a Board has knowledge of a possible reason for exclusion or objection which does not originate from a member himself or from any party to the proceedings, then the procedure of Article 24, paragraph 4, of the Convention shall be applied.

(2) The member concerned shall be invited to present his comments as to whether there is a reason for exclusion.

(3) Before a decision is taken on the exclusion of the member, there shall be no further proceedings in the case.

ARTICLE 4

Rapporteurs

(1) The Chairman of the Board shall for each point of law designate a member of the Board, or himself, as rapporteur. The Chairman may appoint an additional rapporteur.

(2) If an additional rapporteur is appointed, the steps referred to in paragraphs 3 to 5 shall be taken by the rapporteur and additional rapporteur jointly unless the Chairman directs otherwise.

(3) The rapporteur shall carry out a preliminary study of the point of law and may prepare communications to the parties subject to the direction of the Chairman of the Board. Communications shall be signed by the rapporteur on behalf of the Board.

(4) The rapporteur shall make the preparations for meetings of the Board and for oral proceedings.

(5) The rapporteur shall draft decisions.

(6) If a rapporteur or additional rapporteur considers that his knowledge of the language of the proceedings is sufficient for drafting communications or decisions, he may draft these in one of the other official languages. His drafts shall be translated by the European Parent Office into the language of the proceedings and the translations shall be checked by the rapporteur or by another member of the Board.

ARTICLE 5

Registry

(1) A Registry shall be established for the Enlarged Board of Appeal. The Senior Registrar of the Board of Appeal shall be responsible for the discharge of its functions.

(2) The authority referred to in Rule 10(2) may entrust to the Senior Registrar tasks which involve no technical or legal difficulties, in particular in relation to arranging for inspection of files, issuing summonses to oral proceedings and notifications and granting requests for further processing of applications.

(3) Minutes of oral proceedings and of the taking of evidence shall be drawn up by the Senior Registrar or such other employee of the Office as the Chairman may designate.

ARTICLE 6

Attendance of interpreters

If required, the Chairman of the Board shall make arrangements for interpreting during oral proceedings, the taking of evidence or the deliberations of the Board.

ARTICLE 7

Change in the composition of a Board

(1) If the composition of a Board is changed after oral proceedings, the parties to the proceedings shall be informed that, at the request of any party, fresh oral proceedings shall be held before the Board in its new composition. Fresh oral proceedings shall also be held if so requested by the new member and if the other members of the Board have given their agreement.

(2) The new member shall be bound to the same extent as the other members by an interim decision which has already been taken.

(3) If, when the Board has already reached a final decision, a member is unable to act, he shall not be replaced by an alternate. If the Chairman is unable to act, the legally qualified member of the Board having the longest service on the Board or, in the case where members have the same length of service, the eldest member shall sign the decision on behalf of the Chairman.

ARTICLE 8

Consolidation of points of law

If two or more points of law have been submitted with the same or similar subject-matter, the Board may consider them in consolidated proceedings.

745

ARTICLE 9

Oral proceedings

(1) If oral proceedings are to take place, the Board shall endeavour to ensure that the parties have provided all relevant information and documents before the hearing.

(2) The Board may send with the summons to oral proceedings a communication drawing attention to matters which seem to be of special significance, or to the fact that questions appear no longer to be contentious, or containing other observations that may help concentration on essentials during the oral proceedings.

(3) If oral proceedings take place, the Board shall endeavour to ensure that each case is ready for decision at the conclusion of the oral proceedings, unless there are special reasons to the contrary.

ARTICLE 10

Communications to the parties

If the Board deems it expedient to communicate with the parties regarding a possible appreciation of substantive or legal matters, such communication shall be made in such a way as not to imply that the Board is in any way bound by it.

ARTICLE 11

Deliberations preceding decisions

Only members of the Board shall particpate in deliberations: the Chairman may, however, authorise other officers to attend. Deliberations shall be secret.

ARTICLE 11A

EPO Presidents' right to comment

[Inserted July 7, 1989]

The Board may, on its own initiative or at the written, reasoned request of the President of the European Patent Office, invite him to comment in writing or orally on questions of general interest which arise in the course of proceedings pending before it. The parties shall be entitled to submit their observations on the President's comments.

ARTICLE 11B

Statements by third parties

[Inserted June 8, 1994]

(1) In the course of proceedings before the Board, any written statement concerning the points of law raised in such proceedings which is sent to this Board by a third party may be dealt with as the Board thinks fit.

(2) The Board may announce further provisions concerning such statements in the Official Journal of the European Patent Office if it seems appropriate.

ARTICLE 12

Order of voting

(1) During the deliberations between members of the Board, the opinion of the rapporteur shall be heard first, followed by that of the additional rapporteur if one has been appointed and, if the rapporteur is not the Chairman, the Chairman's last.

(2) If voting is necessary, votes shall be taken in the same sequence, even if the Chairman is the rapporteur, he shall vote last. Abstentions shall not be permitted.

ARTICLE 12A

Reasons for the decision

[Inserted June 8, 1994]

The decision of the Board shall be in accordance with the votes of the majority of its members. If a majority of the members of the Board agrees, the reasons for such decision may also indicate the opinions held by a minority of the members.

Neither the decision nor its reasons may indicate either the names of the members forming any such minority or the size of such minority.

ARTICLE 13

Opinions on points of law

The foregoing provisions shall apply *mutatis mutandis* to opinons on points of law referred to the Board by the President of the EPO pursuant to Article 112(1)(b) of the Convention.

ARTICLE 14

Binding nature of the Rules of Procedure

These Rules of Procedure shall be binding upon the Enlarged Board of Appeal, provided that they do not lead to a situation which would be incompatible with the spirit and purpose of the Convention.

ARTICLE 15

Entry into force

These Rules of Procedure shall enter into force on the date on which they are approved by the Administrative Council of the European Patent Organisation.

APPENDIX 6

LEGAL ADVICE FROM THE EPO—HEADNOTES

A6–01 [The headnote for each Legal Advice so far issued by the EPO is set out below, unless it has been cancelled. The following Legal Advices have been cancelled, being either superceded or no longer relevant: 1/79, 2/79, 7/80, 9/81, 12/82 (O.J. EPO 1998, 359). The full texts are set out in the Official Journal of the EPO, as indicated. Each Legal Advice should be read in the light of any subsequent changes in the EPC Implementating Regulations and any subsequent Board of Appeal decisions.]

Contents

Legal Advice No. 3/85 rev. O.J. EPO 1985, 347
Rule 31 EPC
Claims fees—multiple sets of claims

In multiple sets of claims, fees are incurred under Rule 31 EPC only for the set with the greatest number of claims. If the set which originally had the greatest number is reduced with the result that another set then has the greatest number, the number of claims in the latter set has to be reduced to the same number as the former set if no claims fees have been paid.

Legal Advice No. 4/80 O.J. EPO 1980, 48
Article 167(2)(a) EPC
Rule 86 EPC
Period for submitting a separate set of claim for Austria

If different claims for Austria have not already been presented in the European patent application itself, they may be presented after the European search report has been received and before the reply to the first communciation from the Examining Division, without the Examining Division's consent. Subsequently, however, they may only be presented with the Examining Division's consent.

Legal Advice No. 5/93 rev. O.J. EPO 1993, 229
Rules 83(4), 85 and 85a(2) EPC
Calculation of aggregate time limits

Where a time limit starts to run immediately following the expiry of an earlier time limit, the date on which the earlier time limit expires must first be determined in order to calculate the expiry date of the second time limit.

In such cases, the relevant events (Rule 83 EPC) for calculating the second time limit is the expiry of the earlier time limit. At present this applies to the period of grace for payment of designation fees provided for in Rule 85a(2) EPC and, by way of exception in the case of Euro-PCT applications to which Article 39(1) PCT applies, to the additional period under Article 86(2) EPC for payment of the renewal fee with additional fee in respect of the third year if the fee under Rule 37(1) EPC would have fallen due before the expiry of the 31-month time limit under Rule 104b(1)(e) EPC.

Legal Advice No. 6/91 (revised) O.J. EPO 1991, 573
Articles 7(1) and 8(3) Rules relating to Fees
Articles 133 and 134(7) EPC
Payment of Fees; Refunds of fees or other sums

1. Fees can be validly paid to the European Patent Office by any person.
2. Refunds of fees or other sums are made to the party or to a representative authorised to receive payments.

Legal Advice No. 8/80 O.J. EPO 1981, 6
Article 78(1)(a), EPC
Withdrawal of European patent application

The withdrawal of a European patent application is binding on an applicant.

Legal Advice No. 10/92 rev. O.J. EPO 1992, 662
Articles 153 and 94(2) EPC
Consolidation of a European patent application with a Euro-PCT application
Refund of the examination fee

1. A European patent application and an international application for which the EPO acts as designated Office or elected Office may be consolidated at

749

the request of the applicant for the purpose of joint proceedings up to grant before the Examining Division. The filing and priority dates of the application to be consolidated must be the same and the text of the description and the claims must be identical, as also must be the drawings.

2. The decision to consolidate cannot be taken until the Examining Division has become responsible for both applications in accordance with Article 18(1) EPC.

3. If the request for the proceedings to be consolidated is made before the Examining Division has become responsible for both applications in accordance with Article 18(1) EPC, the effect of the decision to consolidate is that no separate examination proceedings will be initiated for one of the applications: the examination fee paid for the European application will be refunded (by analogy with Article 10b(a) of the Rules relating to Fees). If the request for the proceedings to be consolidated is made after the Examining Division has become responsible for both applications in accordance with Article 18(1) EPC but before the substantive examination for the second applications has begun, 75% of the examination fee paid for the European application will be refunded (by analogy with Article 10b(b) of the Rules relating to Fees).

Legal Advice No. 11/82 O.J. EPO 1982, 57
Articles 68, 102 and 113 EPC
Revocation of the European patent during opposition proceedings

If the applicant states that he no longer approves the text in which the patent was granted and does not submit an amended text, the patent must be revoked. This also applies when the proprietor requests that the patent be revoked. The revocation always has retroactive effect.

Legal Advice No. 13/82 O.J. EPO 1982, 196
Article 121 EPC
Further processing of the European patent application

The request for further processing may be filed immediately after expiry of a time limit within which to reply set by the European Patent Office.

Legal Advice No. 14/83 O.J. EPO 1983, 189
Article 10(1), Rules relating to Fees
Article 8(2) of the Agreement between WIPO and the EPO concerning the PCT
Refund of the European search fee
Refund of the international search fee where a European patent application and an international application are filed simultaneously

I. *Interpretation of Article 10(1) of the Rules relating to Fees*

The fee refunded is the "European search fee", *i.e.* the fee for the European search (Article 78(2) EPC), the fee for further European searches (Rule 46(1) EPC) or the fee for the supplementary European search (Article 157(2)(b) EPC; Rule 104(b)(3) EPC).

The term "an earlier search report already prepared by the Office on an application" covers not only European search reports (Article 92 EPC), international search reports drawn up by the EPO as an International Searching Authority (Article 18 PCT) and EPO search reports on national applications by virtue of its obligations under the Agreement on the setting up of the International Patent Institute (Section 1(1)(b), second sentence, of the Protocol on Centralisation), but also searches on patent applications performed to the same standards as apply to European searches (standard searches).

A pre-condition for the refund of the European search fee is that the patent application on which the "earlier search report" was drawn up by the EPO has indeed given rise to the priority right claimed.

II. *Interpretation of the Agreement between WIPO and the EPO concerning the PCT*

If a European patent application and an international application for which the EPO is the International Searching Authority are filed on the same day, the question of refunding the fee is governed by Rule 41 PCT in conjunction with Article 8 of the Agreement between WIPO and the EPO concerning the PCT. The applicant is entitled to a refund of the international search fee.

Legal Advice No. 15/98 O.J. EPO 1998, 113
Articles 97, 102, 113 EPC
Auxiliary requests in examination and opposition proceedings

The Examining Division must refuse European patent applications (Article 97(1) EPC) and the Opposition Division must revoke European patents (Article 102(1) EPC) if the text of the application or patent as a whole does not meet the requirements of the EPC. Filing an alternative version as an auxiliary request may, in certain cases, clarify the procedural position and expedite the procedure without the applicant or patent proprietor being required to abandon his position. This legal advice explains various aspects and procedural consequences of filing a set of claims as an auxiliary request during examination or opposition proceedings.

Legal Advice No. 16/85 O.J. EPO 1985, 141
Rule 69 EPC
Request for a decision after the noting of loss of rights

If the European Patent Office communicates the loss of any right in accordance with Rule 69(1) in conjunction with Article 119 EPC, the party concerned may, within two months after notification of the communication, apply for a decision on the matter by the European Patent Office (Rule 69(2) EPC). The communication in itself is not appealable under Article 106 EPC. If the time limit under Rule 69(2) EPC is not observed, the only legal possibility left open is that of *restitutio in integrum*; under Article 122 EPC.

Legal Advice No. 17/90 O.J. EPO 1990, 260
Article 70(1), 97(2) and (4), 98 EPC
Authentic text of a granted patent when the specification contains misprints

Mistakes in the specification of a European patent arising in the course of its production have no effect on the content of the patent granted. For this, only the text on which the decision to grant the patent is based is authentic.

Legal Advice No. 18/92
Articles 22(1), (3), 39(1), 37(7), 49 PCI
Articles 133(2), 150, 153(1), 156, Rule 104b EPC
Procedural steps a "non-resident" Euro-PCT applicant may himself take
before the EPO as designated or elected Office

I. A Euro-PCI applicant with neither a residence nor his principal place of business in an EPC Contracting State ("non-resident applicant") must be represented in the regional phase before the EPO as designated or elected Office by a professional representative entitled to practice before the EPO and act through him.

II. The applicant himself however may initiate processing of the international application, provided he does so before expiry of the 21st or 31st month as from the priority date.

III. The applicant's representative in the international phase may act before the EPO as designated or elected Office only if he is also entitled to practice before the EPO (Article 49 PCT, 133(2) EPC).

IV. Fees may be paid by any person, and thus also by a non-resident applicant or his representative in the international phase (*cf.* Legal Advice No. 6/91 rev. O.J. EPO 1991, 573).

Legal Advice No. 19/99
Article 88(1) EPC, Rule 38(4) EPC
Filing of a translation of the previous application or a declaration under Rule 38(4) EPC

When a European patent application claims the priority of a previous application, the language of which is not one of the official languages of the European Patent Office, the applicant must file either a translation of the previous application in one of the official languages or a declaration that the European patent application is a complete translation of the previous application ("priority application"). Such a "declaration is acceptable only if the text of the European patent application is a complete translation of the previous application. Either one must be filed within a time limit to be set by the European Patent Office, but at the latest within the time limit under Rule 51(6) EPC.

NOTICES CONCERNING THE DUTIES OF FORMALITIES OFFICERS

A. Duties Normally the Responsibility of the Examining Divisions

Notice of the Vice-President of Directorate-General 2 of the EPO concerning the entrustment to formalities officers of certain duties normally the responsibility of the Examining Divisions of the EPO, dated 15 June 1984.   A7–01

O.J. EPO 1984, 317 as amended by Notice dated February 1, 1989
(O.J. EPO 1989, 178).

By virtue of the powers transferred to me by order of the President of the EPO of 6 March 1979, under Rule 9(3) EPC the following provisions shall apply:

The notice of 11 February 1983 concerning the entrustment to formalities officers of certain duties normally the responsibility of the Examining Divisions of the EPO shall be amended in what concerns points 11, 13 and 22 and supplemented by the addition of points 23 to 26 and shall now read as follow:

Within the framework of the responsibilities of the Examining Divisions of the EPO, certain employees (formalities officers) who are not technically or legally qualified examiners shall be entrusted with the following duties normally the responsibility of the Examining Divisions:

1. Examination as to formal deficiencies under Article 91 EPC.
2. Examination of documents submitted under Rule 32(1) and (2), Rule 35(2) to (11) and (14) as well as Rule 36(2) to (4) EPC in as far as this is not covered in number 1 above.
3. Examination under Rule 104(b)(1) and (2) EPC.
4. Examination of duly made appointments of representatives and authorisations as well as communications under Rule 101(4) EPC.
5. Communications under Article 96(2) EPC in cases 1 to 4 referred to above.
6. Refusal of the European patent application in as far as this has to take place in cases 1 to 4 referred to above.
7. Communications concerning loss of rights under Rule 69(1) EPC.
8. Decisions under Rule 69(2) EPC.
9. Examination and communications under Rule 51(4), (6) to (10) EPC; extension of time limits under Rule 51(4); issuing decisions whereby European patents are granted (Rule 51(11) EPC).
10. Decisions on requests under Article 121 EPC in cases where
   (a) the application is deemed withdrawn under Article 96(3) or Rule 51(8) EPC; or
   (b) the application has been refused on grounds covered by points 6 or 21.

11. Decisions as to applications under Article 122(4) EPC where the application can be dealt with without further taking of evidence under Rule 72 EPC.

12. Request to the applicant to comment on an application for inspection of files under Article 128(1) EPC.

13. Allowing inspection of files in cases covered by Article 128(2) to (4) EPC and provision of information from the files under Rule 95 EPC.

14. Summons to oral proceedings under Rule 71(1) EPC following request by the Examining Division.

15. Summons to give evidence before the European Patent Office under Rule 72(2) EPC following request by the Examining Division.

16. Decision concerning notification under Article 119 in conjunction with Rules 77 *et seq.* EPC and examination of proof of notification.

17. Extension of a time limit under Rule 84 EPC.

18. Issue of a certificate for a European patent and issue of duplicate copies of the certificate under Rule 54 EPC.

19. Decision to consolidate a European patent application with a Euro-PCT application pursuant to Legal Advice No. 10/1981 (O.J. 9/1981, pp. 349–355).

20. Correction of the deisgnation of Contracting States where the designation is withdrawn after a decision to grant a European patent and before the decision takes effect.

21. Refusal of European patent applications under Article 97(1), Rule 51(5), first sentence, EPC.

22. Decisions to refund fees, with the exception of the European search fee and the fee for appeal. The decision to refund the appeal fee shall be taken by the formalities officer where it is part of his duty to rectify the decision.

23. Decisions concerning the correction of errors in documents filed with the European Patent Office, with the exception of the description, claims and drawings (Rule 88 EPC).

24. (*Deleted*).

25. Decisions of the European Patent Office as designated Office under Article 25(2)(a) of the Cooperation Treaty (Article 153(2) (EPC).

26. Examination of an application for evidence to be taken under Rule 75(2)(a) and (b) and (3) EPC and notification that the taking of evidence has been ordered.

27. Registering transfers and changes of name until such time when an adverse decision seems likely (Articles 71, 72 and 74, Rules 20 and 61 EPC; *cf.* O.J. EPO 1987, 215).

28. Rectification of the designation of an inventor until such time when an adverse decision seems likely (Rule 19 EPC; *cf.* O.J. EPO 1987, 215, 226 points 6.3 and 6.4).

B. Duties Normally the Responsibility of the Opposition Divisions

Notice of the Vice-President of Directorate-General 2 of the EPO concerning the entrustment to formalities officers of certain duties normally the responsibility of the Opposition Divisions of the EPO, dated 15 June 1984.

O.J. EPO 1984, 319, as amended by Notice dated February 1, 1989
(O.J. EPO 1989, 178).

By virtue of the powers transferred to me by order of the President of the EPO of 6 March 1979, under Rule 9(3) EPC the following provisons shall apply:

The notice of 8 January 1982 concerning the entrustment to formalities officers of certain duties normally the responsibility of the Opposition Divisions of the EPO shall be amended in what concerns points 12, 17, 18 and 19 and supplemented by the addition of points 20 to 23 and shall now read as follows:

Within the framework of the responsibilities of the Opposition Divisions of the EPO, certain employees (formalities officers) who are not technically or legally qualified examiners shall be entrusted with the following duties normally the responsibility of the Examining Divisions:

1. Examination as to formal deficiencies, under Rule 32(1) and (2), Rule 35(2) to (11) and (14) and Rule 36(2) to (5) EPC on the basis of Rule 61(a) EPC, of the notice of opposition, the amendments of the European patent made by the proprietor and the documents filed.

2. Examination of duly-made appointments of representatives and authorisations as well as communications under Rule 101(4) EPC.

3. Communication of documents to the parties and invitation to state observations or to file documents in routine cases or on the instructions of the Opposition Division.

4. Communications under Rule 69(1) and decisions under Rule 69(2) EPC.

5. Communication to the opponent concerning deficiencies under Rule 56(1) and (2) EPC.

6. Decisions in *ex parte* proceedings on the admissibility of the opposition and the intervention of the assumed infringer with the exception of the cases provided for in Rule 55(c) EPC.

7. Communications under Rule 58(4) and (5) EPC on the instructions of the Opposition Division and communications under Rule 58(6) EPC (*cf.* O.J. EPO 1989, 1).

8. Issue of a decision on the maintenance of the European patent as amended under Article 102(3) EPC.

9. Issue of a new certificate for a European patent as amended under Rule 62(a) EPC and issue of duplicate copies of the certificate under Rule 54 EPC.

10. Revocation of the European patent in accordance with Article 102(4) EPC.

11. Revocation of the European patent in accordance with Article 102(5) EPC.

12. Decisions as to applications under Article 122(4) EPC when the appplication can be dealt with without further evidence being taken under Rule 72 EPC.

13. Granting of inspection of files in cases covered by Article 128(2) to (4) EPC and provision of information contained in the files under Rule 95 EPC.

14. Summons to oral proceedings under Rule 71(1) EPC following request by the Opposition Division.

15. Summons to give evidence before the European Patent Office under Rule 72(2) EPC following request by the Opposition Division.

16. Notification as required under Article 119 in conjunction with Rule 77 *et seq.* EPC and examination of proof of notification.

17. Extension of time limits under Rule 84 EPC.

18. (*Deleted*).

19. Decisions concerning discontinuance of the opposition proceedings in cases covered by Rule 60 EPC where such proceedings are not continued by the Opposition Division of its own motion.

20. Decisions concerning the refund of fees, with the exception of the appeal fee.

21. Decisions concerning the correction of errors in documents filed with the European Parent Office with the exception of the description, claims and drawings (Rule 88 EPC).

22. Examination of an application for evidence to be taken under Rule 75(2)(a) , (b) and (3) EPC and notification that the taking of evidence has been ordered.

23. Revocation of a European patent during opposition proceedings in accordance with Legal Advice No. 11/1982 (O.J. EPO 1982, 57) where the patent proprietor states that he no longer approves the text in which the patent was granted and does not submit an amended text or where the proprietor requests that the patent be revoked.

24. Authorising changes in the language of proceedings under Rule 3(1) EPC where the other parties have raised no objection.

25. Registering transfers and changes of name until such time when an adverse decision seems likely (Articles 71, 72 and 74, Rules 20 and 61 EPC; *cf.* O.J. EPO 1987, 215).

26. Rectification of the designation of an inventor until such time when an adverse decision seems likely (Rule 19 EPC; *cf.* O.J. EPO 1987, 215, 226 points 6.3 and 6.4).

C. Supplemental Notice to A. and B.

Notice dated 1 February 1989 from the Vice-President Directorate-General 2 of the EPO concerning the entrustment to non-examining staff of certain duties normally the responsibility of the Examining or Opposition Divisions.

This notice follows the notices of 15 June 1984 (O.J. EPO 1984, 317 and 319) which are revised and supplemented as follows.

I and II. [... *The revision made to the notices of 15 June 1984 are incorporated into the texts reproduced immediately above.*]

III. Delegation of such a duty to an employee who is not a technically or legally qualified examiner shall not affect the competence of the Examining or Opposition Division to take decisions itself.

APPENDIX 8

GUIDANCE FOR PARTIES TO APPEAL PROCEEDINGS AND THEIR REPRESENTATIVES[1]

(O.J. EPO 1996, 342)   A8–01

Preliminary remarks

These notes have been written to assist parties to appeal proceedings and their representatives in filing appeals under Articles 21 and 106 EPO and pursuing their rights in proceedings before the boards of appeal. They are intended to expedite the appeal procedure and take account of the relevant board of appeal case law.

Additional information is available from the following DG 3 (Appeals) publications:

- Regulations implementing the European Patent Convention—1996
- Case law of the boards of appeal of the European Patent Office 1987–1997[2] (3rd edition 1998).

Annual EPO board of appeal case law reports (annual special edition of the Official Journal of the European Patent Office).

Queries should be addressed to the head of the Boards of Appeal Registry, European Patent Office, Erhardtstrasse 27, D–80331 Munich (Tel.: (+49–89)–2399–3910 or 3921; telex 523 656 epmu d; Fax: (+49 89) 2399–4465).

1. Filing an appeal

1.1 Admissibility

A board of appeal can only consider the merits of an appeal (see section 3) if it is admissible (see below). The board will not begin its examination until reply to the appeal has been received or the deadline for replying (usually 4 months) has expired.

1.1.1 Decisions subject to appeal

The appeal must be against a decision of the Receiving Section, an examining division, an opposition division or the Legal Division (Art. 106(1), first sentence, EPC; see also G 1/90. O.J. EPO 1991, 275). A decision is usually identified as such and, in accordance with Rule 68(2) EPC, indicates that an appeal is possible.

Interlocutory decisions which do not terminate proceedings as regards one of

---

[1] These notes for parties to appeal proceedings and their representatives replace the previous versions (see O.J. EPO 1989, 395; 1981, 175).
[2] This publication is updated at regular intervals.

the parties can only be appealed if the decision allows separate appeal (Art. 106(3) EPC).

A mere communication, an interim communication issued in preparation for a decision, or a communication notifying a loss of rights under Rule 69(1) EPC, does not give rise to a right of appeal. Under Rule 69(2) EPC a decision by the EPO may be applied for in response to a communication notifying a loss of rights. Attention is drawn to the possibility of a re-establishment of rights and the deadline for filing the application under Article 122(2) EPC (see 1.5).

1.1.2 Entitlement to appeal

An appeal may only be lodged by a party to the proceedings in which the decision was given. The applicant must be **adversely affected** by the decision (Art. 107 EPC).

A party is **adversely affected** if the decision does not correspond to what the party had expressly requested. This is also the case, for example, where only the auxiliary request, but not the main request, was granted.

1.1.3 Other parties to the proceedings

Under Article 107, second sentence, EPC, any other parties to the proceedings who are not adversely affected by the contested decision or who have not lodged an appeal are also parties to the appeal proceedings as of right. They do not however have any independent right to continue the proceedings if, for example, the appeal is deemed not to have been filed because the appellant did not pay the appeal fee, if the appeal is inadmissible or if it is withdrawn (see G 2/91, O.J. EPO 1992, 206). In such cases, only a party having lodged an appeal may continue the proceedings.

Parties to the proceedings under Article 107, second sentence, EPC are asked by the Boards of Appeal Registry whether or not they wish to receive any further communications in connection with the appeal proceedings (EPO Form 3349). This declaration may be revoked at any time.

Third parties may intervene in appeal proceedings under Article 105 EPC as long as appeal proceedings are still pending (G 4/91, O.J. EPO 1993, 707; G 1/94, O.J. EPO 1994, 787).

1.1.4 Appeal period, appeal fee

The appeal must be lodged with the EPO in the form of **a notice of appeal** (see 1.19) **within two months** of the date of notification[3] of the decision appealed from (Art. 108, first sentence, EPC). **The time limit cannot be extended**. The decisive date in assessing whether the time limit has been adhered to is the date of receipt of the notice of appeal by the EPO.

The notice of appeal is not deemed to have been filed until after the appeal fee[4] has been paid within the two-months appeal period (Art. 108, second sentence, EPC). Payment can be made by any of the methods described in Article 5 of the

---

[3] See in particular paragraphs 3 and 4 of Rule 78 EPC:
  (3) Where notification is effected by registered letter, whether or not with the advice of delivery, this shall be deemed to be delivered to the addressee on the tenth day following its posting, unless the letter has failed to reach the addressee or has reached him at a later date; in the event of any dispute, it shall be incumbent on the European Patent Office to establish that the letter has reached its destination or to establish the date on which the letter was delivered to the addressee, as the case may be,
  (4) Notification by registered letter, whether or not with advice of delivery, shall be deemed to have been affected even if acceptance of the letter has been refused.
[4] Regarding the amount see Article 2, No. 11, Rules relating to Fees of 20 October 1977 (O.J. EPO 1978, 21ff), most recently amended by the decision of the Administrative Council of the European Patent Organisation dated 13 December 1994 (O.J. EPO 1995, 9ff).

Rules relating to Fees (RFees). The date of payment is determined by Article 8 RFees.

Appellants from contracting states having a language other than English, French or German as an official language, and nationals of these states who are resident abroad (Art. 14(2), first sentence, EPC) are entitled to a reduction **in the appeal fee** of 20% if they file at least the notice of appeal—the essential document at the first stage in appeal proceedings—in that language (R. 6(3) EPC in conjunction with Art. 12(1) RFees). This reduction may however only be claimed if the translation required under Article 14(4), second sentence, and Rule 6(2) EPC is filed no earlier than simultaneously with the notice of appeal itself (see G 6/91, O.J. EPO 1992, 491). A reduction in the filing fee under Rule 6(1) EPC does not automatically result in a reduction in the examination or appeal fee (G 6/91 *op. cit.*).

1.1.5 Reimbursement of appeal fees

The appeal fee is reimbursed under Rule 67 EPC if the appeal is deemed allowable, there has been a substantial procedural violation and reimbursement is equitable.

The appeal fee is also refunded if it was paid with no legal basis, such as when the appeal is deemed not to have been filed for legal reasons (Art. 108, second sentence, EPC: late payment of the appeal fee; Art. 14(5) EPC: documents not filed in an EPC official language in due time; R. 101(4) EPC: authorisation not filed in due time).

The appeal fee is not refundable if the appeal, although validly filed, is inadmissible unsubstantiated or subsequently withdrawn.

If an appeal is lodged by **several parties** to the proceedings at first instance, the appeal fee is not refunded simply because another party has filed an appeal and paid the fee. Each appellant must pay an appeal fee (G 2/91, O.J. EPO 1992, 206).

1.1.6 Form of the appeal

Article 108 EPC requires that the notice of appeal and the statement of grounds of appeal be filed in writing. They may also be filed by **telex, telegram or fax** (see R. 36(5) EPC). The Boards of Appeal Registry will request **written confirmation** if the quality of the document filed is deficient. Details on supplying written confirmation and on other matters relating to the use of technical means of communication for filing documents *e.g.* signing of documents and establishing the date of receipt) are set out in the decisions of the President of the European Patent Office dated 26 May 1992 (O.J. EPO 1992, 299) and 2 June 1992 (O.J.) EPO 1992, 306).

See Rule 36(4) EPC concerning the filing of **additional copies** of documents.

1.1.7 Language

An appeal may be filed **in any official language of the EPO** (English, French, German) (Rule 1(1), first sentence, EPC).

Appellants from contracting states in which a language other than English, French or German is the official language, and nationals of these states resident abroad (Art. 14(2), first sentence, EPC) may file the appeal in **an official language of that state** (Art. 14(2) EPC). The translation required under Article 14(4) EPC may be filed in any official language of the EPO.

The one-month **time limit for filing the translation** may be extended to the end of the appeal period (R. 6(2) EPC). If the translation is not filed in due time, under Article 14(5) EPC the notice of appeal is deemed not to have been filed, in which case the appeal fee is refunded.

Documents intended for use **as evidence** before the EPO—in particular publications—may be filed in any language. The EPO may however require that a translation be filed, within a given time limit of not less than one month, in one of the EPO's offical languages (R. 1(3) EPC).

1.1.8 Filing office, registration

In order to expedite the procedure it is recommended that appeals be sent to the **filing office** at the European Patent Offices main building in Munich (point 2.2 of the Notice of the President of the European Patent Office dated 2 June 1992, O.J. EPO 1992, 306).[5] Attention is also drawn to the possibility of using the automatic night letter-box.[6]

The Boards of Appeal Registry gives each appeal a separate reference number which is to be used in all correspondence with the board of appeal and the Registry throughout the appeal proceedings.

1.1.9 Content of the notice of appeal

The content of the notice of appeal referred to in Article 108, first sentence, EPC is laid down in Rule 64 EPC. The notice of appeal must contain the name and address of the appellant in accordance with the provisions of Rule 25(2)(c) EPC; and a statement sufficiently identifying the decision contested and the extent to which it is contested.

1.2 Statement of grounds of appeal

An appeal cannot be considered on its merits until the statement of grounds is received.

A statement of grounds of appeal must be filed **in writing within four months** of the date of notification of the decision appealed from (Art. 108, third sentence, EPC). The statement of grounds may also be filed by **telex, telegraph or fax** (see 1.1.6). If the statement of grounds of appeal is not filed in due time and the requirements for re-establishment of rights have not been met (see 1.5), the appeal must be rejected as inadmissible. The appeal fee is not then refunded (see 1.1.5).

1.2.1 Content of the statement of grounds

The statement of grounds must indicate the points of law and of fact on which the contested decision should be set aside or the appeal allowed. Its content should not be restricted simply to stating that the contested decision is incorrect. It is not therefore sufficient merely to restate points made during proceedings before the department of first instance. Appellants should always state what in their view are the issues in dispute and give sufficient grounds for their view.

The statement of grounds should be a succinct but full statement of the appellant's arguments. Ideally it should follow a logical sequence—for example, with numbered paragraphs, each dealing with a separate issue, and with underlined sub-headings, etc. Passages which are necessarily lengthy should be concluded with a brief summary.

1.2.2 New submissions

If any allegations of fact or law are being made that were not argued in the previous proceedings, this should be made clear. Since it lies within the board of appeal's discretion whether or not to admit late-filed facts and evidence into the

[5] The Vienna sub-office is not a filing office for the purpose of Article 75(1)(a) EPC (Notice from the European Patent Office dated 4 March 1992, O.J. EPO 1992, 183).
[6] Munich main building, Erhardtstrasse, by te barrier on te cornellusstrasse (see notice in O.J. EPO 1987, 38); "Pachorr-H le" building, at the entrance at Zollatrasse 3 (see notice in O.J. EPO 1991, 577).

proceedings, the appellant should indicate why the new submission was not filed earlier. New grounds for opposition cannot as a matter of principle be submitted at the appeal stage (see 3.1.2).

1.2.3 Quotations and references

Reference may be made to the decision appealed against, the European Patent Convention, the Implementing Regulations, the Rules of Procedure of the Boards of Appeal, the Guidelines for Examination, the patent application in suit or any other document contained in the file of the case. References should only be cited in detail to the extent that this is necessary to the development of the argument.

If reference is made to international treaties (other than the European Patent Convention, the Patent Cooperation Treaty and the Paris Convention), national law (other than the patent laws of the contracting states) or the judgment of any national or international court, a complete copy of the treaty, law or judgment in question should be provided unless the board of appeal concerned agrees that extracts will be sufficient.

1.2.4 Submission of documents, samples, models, etc.

The purpose of introducing any new documents into the proceedings should be stated briefly and a legible copy of each such document should be appended to the statement of grounds and identified as an appendix. No copies need be supplied of European patent applications or European patent specifications. Similarly, graphs, diagrams, photographs, tables of figures and the like should not be incorporated into the text but placed in an appendix. Where handwritten documents are submitted, they should be accompanied by typewritten copies.

Any party wishing to submit objects such as modes, samples or documents that cannot conveniently be placed in an appendix should consult the Registry about how best they should be submitted.

1.3 Correction of errors

If, after filing a notice of appeal or statement of grounds, the appellant notices errors in them within the meaning of Rule 88 EPC, the Registry should be informed without delay.

If the appeal does not comply with Articles 106 to 108, Rule 1(1) or Rule 64(b) EPC, the error may only be corrected within the period for appeal or the period for filing the statement of grounds under Article 108 EPC (R. 65(1) EPC).

If the appellant's name and address have not been given correctly, a time limit is set for correcting this error.

1.4 Interlocutory revision

Under Article 109 EPC interlocutory revision of an appeal is conducted by the department which issued the contested decision. If this department does not allow the appeal, it is remitted to the board of appeal without delay and without comment as to its merit (Article 109(2) EPC).

1.5 Binding time limits, re-establishment of rights

The time limits for filing the notice of appeal, paying the appeal fee and filing the statement of grounds may not be extended. Under the conditions laid down in Article 122 EPC, however, **the appellant or proprietor of a European patent** who, in spite of all due care required by the circumstances having been taken, was unable to observe a time limit, may apply for a re-establishment of rights (*restitutio in integrum*). The opponent may not apply for re-establishment of rights with respect to the two-month appeal period, but re-establishment under Article 122 EPC is possible where the opponent has failed to observe the four-month time limit for filing the statement of grounds of appeal (G 1/86, O.J. EPO 1987, 447).

2. Withdrawal of the appeal

An appeal may be withdrawn at any time while appeal proceedings are pending. The appeal fee is not refunded, even where the appeal is withdrawn after the notice of appeal has been correctly filed and the appeal fee paid in due time, but before the statement of grounds has been filed.

If an appeal is filed by only one party and that party withdraws the appeal, the proceedings are terminated in so far as they relate to the substantive issues settled by the contested decision at first instance (see G 8/91, O.J. EPO 1993, 346, 478). The decision of the department of first instance accordingly becomes final.

Where several parties have filed an appeal, proceedings are only terminated by all appeals being withdrawn. Where this is not the case, appeal proceedings continue with the remaining appeals (see G 2/91, O.J. EPO 1992, 206).

2.1 Withdrawal of the opposition by the appellant

The filing by an opponent, who is sole appellant, of a statement withdrawing the opposition immediately and automatically terminates the appeal proceedings, because the withdrawal of the opposition is also a withdrawal of the appeal (see G 8/93, O.J. EPO 1994, 887). This renders the decision of the opposition division final.

2.2 Withdrawal of the opposition by the respondent

Where the patent proprietor is the appellant and the opposition is withdrawn by the respondent during appeal proceedings, the appeal proceedings continue without the opponent/respondent. However, the status of the opponent/respondent as a party to proceedings with regard to the awarding of costs under Article 104 EPC remains unaffected.

3. Examination of the appeal

3.1 Scope of examination

As a judicial procedure, appeal proceedings differ significantly from examination and opposition proceedings (see G 7/91 and G 8/91, O.J. EPO 1993, 346, 356, 478). The procedure before the boards of appeal offers an opportunity to **examine the contested decision of the department of first instance within the scope of the parties' request** and offers the appellant the possibility of recourse **to a further instance competent to rule on the facts of the case.**

3.1.1 *Ex parte* proceedings

In *ex parte* appeal proceedings the board of appeal is restricted neither to examination of the grounds for the contested decision of the examining division nor to the facts and evidence on which this decision was based. The board incorporates into the proceedings patentability requirements which the examining division did not take into consideration or held to have been met but which the board has reason to believe may not have been met (G 10/93, O.J. EPO 1995, 172).

3.1.2 Opposition appeal proceedings (*inter partes* proceedings)

In opposition appeal proceedings the board of appeal's examination of the contested decision is in principle restricted **to the extent** to which the European patent is opposed pursuant to Rule 55(c) EPC. However, **claims dependent** on a

762

claim which has not been allowed may be examined, even if they have not been explicitly opposed, provided their validity is **prima facie in doubt** on the basis of information already available (G 9/91, O.J. EPO 1993, 408).

Grounds for opposition referred to in Article 100 EPC which have not been properly submitted during opposition proceedings in accordance with Article 99(1) in conjunction with Rule 55(c) EPC are not as a rule considered in opposition appeal proceedings. The position is somewhat different however if the patent proprietor agrees to this and the ground in question is considered by the board to be **prima facie highly relevant** (G 9/91 and G 10/91, O.J. EPO 1993, 408, 420).

3.1.3 Prohibition of *reformatio in peius*

If the patent proprietor is the sole appellant, neither the opponent after expiry of the period for appeal nor the board of appeal may challenge the version of the patent as approved by the opposition division (G 9/92 and G 4/93, O.J. EPO 1994, 875).

If the opponent is the sole appellant against an interlocutory decision maintaining a patent in amended form, the patent proprietor is primarily restricted to defending the patent in the form in which it was maintained by the opposition division. Amendments proposed by the patent proprietor as a party to the proceedings under Article 107, second sentence, EPC, may be rejected by the board if they are neither appropriate nor necessary. Amendments may well be considered appropriate if they have arisen from the appeal (G 9/92 and G 4/93, O.J. EPO 1994, 875).

3.2 Written procedure

The appeal procedure is primarily a written procedure. Parties should therefore always develop their arguments in writing and not reserve them for a possible oral hearing. After the statement of grounds and any observations by the other parties have been received the board of appeal will give any necessary directions for the parties to present further arguments.

3.3 Submission of amendments, auxiliary requests

The submission of amendments to the description, claims or drawings of a patent application or patent is regulated by Article 123 EPC in general terms, Rules 51 and 86 EPC for the examination procedure and Rules 57 and 57a EPC for the opposition procedure.

A party wishing to submit amendments to the patent documents in appeal proceedings should do so as early as possible. It should be borne in mind that the board concerned may disregard amendments which are submitted after a time limit set by the board has expired or are not submitted in good time prior to oral proceedings (as a rule four weeks before the date set for the oral proceedings).

Auxiliary requests should be filed as early as possible.

3.4 Evidence

Evidence should, wherever possible, already have been made available to the department of first instance. While evidence may still be introduced at the appeal stage, the board may disregard evidence not submitted in due time (Art. 114(2) EPC).

If evidence is not submitted until the appeal proceedings, it should indicate the facts it is intended to elucidate and state the name and exact address of witnesses.

If the evidence is not in documentary form, the board should be notified of the nature of the evidence and the boards directions sought before it is submitted.

3.5 Oral proceedings

3.5.1 Reaching the decision-making stage

Oral proceedings concentrate on the essential points of the appeal. The case should be ready for decision at the close of oral proceedings. The parties involved and their representatives should therefore be prepared to deal with any problems that may arise during the hearing (see Art. 11(3) Rules of Procedure of the Board of Appeal).

3.5.2 Fixing a date for oral proceedings

Requests for oral proceedings should be submitted as early as possible. Parties requesting oral proceedings to consider individual points only (*e.g.* admissibility of the appeal) should make this clear when filing the request. A request for oral proceedings made before the department of first instance does not also apply to appeal proceedings. A separate request must therefore be made if a party desires oral proceedings before the board of appeal.

The procedure for fixing a date for oral proceedings is set out in the Notice of the Vice-Presidents Directorates-General 2 and 3 dated 14 February 1989 (O.J. EPO 1989, 132).

Parties invited to attend oral proceedings must inform the European Patent Office as early as possible if they are unable to attend, regardless of whether they themselves requested oral proceedings or not. Failure to provide timely notification can justify the awarding of costs under Article 104 EPC to the party attending tried proceedings.

3.5.3 Simultaneous interpreting

If a language other than the language of proceedings is to be used at oral proceedings, the Registry must be informed at least one month before the date set for oral proceedings, if the party concerned is not making provision for interpreting into the language of proceedings (R. 2(1), first sentence, EPC). In proceedings before the boards of appeal this **obligation to give notice** also applies if the party concerned has already lawfully used an alternative language to that of the proceedings in oral proceedings before the department of first instance (Communication from the Vice-President Directorate-General 3 of the European Patent Office dated 19 May 1995, O.J. EPO 1995, 489).

3.5.4 Notice of summons, acknowledgment of receipt

The period for issuing the summons to oral proceedings is at least two months unless the parties agree to a shorter period (R. 71 EPC).

The summons to oral proceedings is sent with an advice of delivery and accompanied by an acknowledgment of receipt (EPO Form 2936). This should be returned to the Registry without delay in order to ensure that oral proceedings can be held on the date fixed (see Notice in O.J. EPO 1991, 577).

3.5.5 Submission of information and documents

The parties should provide all relevant information and documents in good time, *i.e.* at the latest one month before the hearing (see Art. 11(1) Rules of Procedure of the Boards of Appeal).

If the board concerned considers it unnecessary to pursue certain lines of argument or deal with certain aspects of a case, it will, whenever possible, advise the parties to that effect in advance of the hearing, or, at the latest, at the commencement of the hearing (Art. 11(2) Rules of Procedure of the Boards of Appeal).

3.5.6 Conduct of the oral proceedings

Arguments presented at oral proceedings should be succinct and limited to the points at issue or those raised by the board.

It is within the board's discretionary powers to decide whether or not to disregard **new facts or evidence** which could have been submitted in good time prior to oral proceedings (Art. 114(2) EPC). If a party has been duly summoned but fails to appear, the decision issued may not be based on facts put forward for the first time during those oral proceedings. In these circumstances new evidence may not be considered unless it has been previously notified and it merely supports the assertions of the party who submits it. New arguments, on the other hand, may in principle be used to support the reasons for the decision (G 4/92, O.J. EPO 1994, 149).

3.5.7 Sound recording devices

At oral proceedings before a board of appeal only EPO employees may bring any kind of sound recording device into the hearing room (see Notice of the Vice-Presidents Directorates-General 2 and 3 dated 25 February 1986, O.J. EPO 1986, 63).

3.6 Representation

If a party to appeal proceedings is represented, the representative must meet the requirements of Article 134 EPC.

Professional representatives within the meaning of Article 134 EPC need only file an authorisation in certain circumstances,[7] in particular if there is a change of representative and the EPO is not notified of the previous representatives authorisation having terminated.

The Boards of Appeal Registry must be notified of any change of representative as early as possible and the relevant documents must be submitted.

---

[7] See Decision of the President of the European Patent Office dated 18 December 1991 (O.J. EPO 1991, 489).

APPENDIX 9

ORAL PROCEEDINGS

A9–01 Notice of the Vice-Presidents Directorates-General 2 and 3 dated 1 September 2000 concerning Oral Proceedings before the EPO

(O.J. EPO 2000, 456)

1. The current practice for fixing the date of oral proceedings, both before the departments of first instance and before the boards of appeal, was published in O.J. EPO 1997, 469.

1.1 Experience has shown that the present practice of proposing a first date and an alternative one is not satisfactory. In view of the large proportion of appeal cases in which oral proceedings are requested, current practice gives rise to complex organisational problems involving the availability in advance of rooms and facilities, and of the legally qualified members of the boards of appeal (who, as a rule, serve on several boards) for the fixed dates. Proposing a first date and an alternative date for oral proceedings means that for the two dates the use of the meeting room is blocked for about two weeks during this stage of summoning the parties. No other reservation of the respective room is possible during this period. The same is true for the availability of the legally qualified members. If the proposed dates are not suitable for the parties, the complicated co-ordination process must re-start. Dates near to the originally proposed ones have by then often been attributed to other cases, so that further delay in appointing oral proceedings in the case in question is caused.

1.2 Cancellations of oral proceedings at a later stage, in particular, if requested shortly before the fixed date, result, as a rule, in a considerable prolongation of the appeal proceedings. Another date must be found where all the necessary parameters mentioned above can be met. It is seldom possible to fill gaps since the time period for summoning to oral proceedings is at least two months, unless the parties waive the time limit.

1.3 Further it is to be noted that parties occasionally do not feel obliged to indicate any reasons or to submit sufficiently substantiated reasons as to why they cannot agree to the proposed dates.

1.4 Similar problems arise in proceedings before the departments of first instance.

1.5 In general, the present system impedes the aim of streamlining procedures before the EPO.

2. On the initiative of the boards of appeal, in co-operation with DG 2 and after discussion in the Standing Advisory Committee before the EPO (SACEPO), it has been decided to implement **as from 1 November 2000 a new procedure for fixing the dates of oral proceedings**:

2.1 The departments of first instance and the boards of appeal will as of 1 November 2000 **fix one single date for oral proceedings**. The pre-announcement of the date by phone or fax will no longer be made.

2.2 Oral proceedings appointed by the EPO will be **cancelled and another date fixed** at the request of a party **only if** the party concerned can advance **serious reasons which justify the fixing of a new date**. The request to fix another date shall be filed **as soon as possible** after the grounds preventing the party concerned from attending the oral proceedings have arisen. The request shall be accompanied by a sufficiently substantiated written statement indicating these reasons.

2.3 Serious substantive reasons to request the change of the date for oral proceedings may be, for instance:

— a **previously** notified summons to oral proceedings of the same party in other proceedings before the EPO or a national court,
— serious illness,
— a case of death within the family,
— the marriage of a person whose attendance in oral proceedings is relevant,
— military service or other obligatory performance of civic duties,
— holidays which have already been firmly booked before the notification of the summons to oral proceedings.

2.4 Grounds which, as a rule, are not acceptable are, for instance:

— a summons to oral proceedings before the EPO or a national court notified **after** the summons in the relevant proceedings,
— excessive work pressure.

2.5 Every request for fixing another date for oral proceedings should contain a statement why another representative within the meaning of Articles 133(3) or 134 EPC cannot substitute the representative prevented from attending the oral proceedings.

APPENDIX 10

MICRO-ORGANISMS

A10–01 **Notice of the European Patent Office dated 18 July 1986 concerning European Patent Applications and European Patents in which reference is made to Micro-organisms**

(O.J. EPO 1986, 269)

I. PURPOSE OF THE NOTICE

1. Where, in disclosing the invention, a European patent application refers to one or more micro-organisms deposited with depositary institutions, applicants are strongly advised to indicate **clearly** in the application as filed the legal status of the micro-organism deposit.

If this is done the EPO, when examining the application for compliance with Article 83 EPC concerning disclosure of the invention in conjunction, where applicable, with Rule 28(1) and (2) EPC, will not need to communicate with applicants on the matter. **Equally important, it will enable the public to determine the procedure for gaining access to the micro-organism.**

2. The form entitled "Request for Grant of a European Patent" (EPO Form 1001) includes a section headed "Micro-organisms" which must be completed when the patent application refers to a micro-organism deposited in accordance with Rule 28 EPC.

This section of the Request for Grant form contains a box which must be crossed if the invention refers to one or more micro-organisms deposited in accordance with Rule 28 EPC and requires the applicant to indicate where in the technical documents of the European patent application particulars of the depositary institution and the file number of the deposit are given or to indicate that such particulars will be furnished at a later date.

Applicants frequently fail to complete this part of the Request for Grant form or do so incorrectly.

The purpose of this notice is to assist applicants with the drafting of their applications and to facilitate completion of the "Micro-organisms" section of the Request for Grant form where the European patent application refers to one or more micro-organisms deposited in accordance with Rule 28 EPC (Chapter II below).

3. Where the European patent application refers to a micro-organism deposited in accordance with Rule 28(1) EPC, the issue of a sample of the micro-organism is governed by Rule 28(3) to (8) which requires submission to the EPO of a request for furnishing of a sample made on the appropriate form. The EPO certifies the request before transmitting it to the depositary institution which is then authorised to issue the sample.

4. Copies of the forms to be used for requesting the furnishing of a sample of a micro-organism deposited in accordance with Rule 28 EPC are available from the EPO.

Another purpose of this Notice is to explain the request form and the sample-issue procedure (Chapter III below).

II. GUIDANCE ON COMPLETING THE "MICRO-ORGANISMS" SECTION OF THE REQUEST FOR GRANT FORM

5. Deposited micro-organisms referred to in a European patent application generally belong to one of the two following categories which will be considered in turn below:

A. Micro-organisms which are not available to the public and which cannot be described sufficiently;

B. Micro-organisms which are available to the public.

In case A, the "Micro-organisms" section of the Request for Grant Form is to be completed, but not in case B.

A. Micro-organisms not available to the public and which cannot be described sufficiently

6. A typical example of a European patent application referring to a micro-organism not available to the public on the date the application is filed and which cannot be described in such a manner as to meet the requirements of Article 83 EPC (Disclosure of the invention) is where the invention relates to a new micro-organism obtained by mutation from known strains available to the public.

7. To meet the requirements of Article 83 in conjunction with Rule 28 EPC a culture of this new micro-organism **must** have been deposited **with** a recognised depositary institution not later than the date of filing of the European patent application, **in accordance with the legal statute on the basis of which the insitution is recognised.**

Two situations arise here:

—either the deposit is made direct in accordance with the Budapest Treaty or, where appropriate, in accordance with the bilateral agreement between the EPO and the institution concerned, in which case the requirements of Rule 28 EPC are automatically met;

—or the deposit was made previously in accordance with a legal statute other than the Budapest Treaty or bilateral agreement (for example, in accordance with a specific national law), in which case, the deposit must be converted to a deposit in accordance with the Budapest Treaty or the bilateral agreement **not later than the date on which the European patent application is filed.**

The depositary institution and the file number of the culture deposit must be submitted to the EPO **within the period applying under Rule 28(2) EPC. Furthermore,** in disclosing the invention the application **as filed** must give such relevant information as is available to the applicant on the characteristics of the micro-organism.

8. Where a European patent application claims the priority of a previous application in accordance with Articles 87 to 89 EPC, the general conditions covering disclosure of the invention in the previous application apply to the micro-organism.

In particular, if an invention, in order to be sufficiently disclosed, requires the deposit of a micro-organism culture to supplement the written description, the culture must hve been deposited not later than the date of filing of the previous application. The depository institution and the legal statute under which the micro-organism is deposited must comply with the requirements of the country in which the previous application has been filed.

The previous application must also refer to this deposit in a manner enabling it to be identified.

Where the micro-organism deposit referred to in the European patent application is not the same as the deposit referred to in the previous application, it is up to the applicant, if the EPO considers it necessary to provide evidence that the two micro-organisms themselves are identical.

9. **The section relating to micro-organisms in the Request for Grant Form (1001) must be completed where the application refers to that category A of micro-organisms.**

10. Rule 28 EPC does not expressly require the depositor to indicate the date of deposit of the micro-organism or to produce the deposit receipt issued by the recognised depositary institution in accordance with Rule 7 of the Budapest Treaty or point 17 of the relevant bilateral agreement as the case may be.

To enable the EPO to ascertain, at the time of substantive examination of the application, whether the micro-organism deposited in accordance with Rule 28(3) EPC is available, the Office must have proof that the requirements laid down in Rule 28(1) and (2) have in fact been complied with.

The EPO accordingly recommends the applicant to furnish upon filing of the European patent application or within the time limit referred to in Rule 28(2) EPC the deposit receipt issued by the international depositary institution or, where appropriate, by the depositary institution recognised in accordance with the bilateral agreement. Unless the deposit receipt or equivalent proof has been furnished by the time examination of the European patent application commences, the examiner will ask for it in the course of examination.

B. Micro-organisms available to the public

11. The second category of micro-organisms to which reference may be made in a European patent application is that of known micro-organisms which are accessible to the public without restriction and typically used as a means for carrying out the invention to which the European patent application relates.

Examples are strains held in the public collections of the recognised depositary institutions within the meaning of Rule 28(9) EPC and available without restriction.

12. **The section relating to micro-organisms in the Request for Grant Form (1001) does not apply to this category of deposited micro-organisms.**

III. FORMS TO BE USED WHEN REQUESTING SAMPLES OF MICRO-ORGANISMS DEPOSITED IN ACCORDANCE WITH RULE 28 EPC

A. Obligation to file a request using the appropriate form

13. Where a European patent application or patent refers to a micro-organism deposited in accordance with Rule 28(1) and (2) EPC, the public may obtain samples subject to the conditions of Rule 28(3) to (8).

In particular, a sample will be issued only when a request has been made to the EPO which, after certification, transmits the request to the depositary institution (Rule 28(8) EPC and Rule 11(3)(a) of the Budapest Treaty).

Copies of the forms to be used when requesting the furnising of a sample are available free of charge from the EPO.

14. **EPO Form 1140a/1141 must be used where the micro-organism has been deposited under the Budapest Treaty and EPO form 1140/1141 where the micro-organism has been deposited under a bilateral agreement between the European Patent Organisation and the depositary institution.**

B. Procedure to be followed

15. Forms are provided with notes, which it is advisable to read carefully, explaining how they are to be completed and the procedure that is to be followed.

Only one form may be used to request samples of different micro-organisms referred to **in one and the same European patent application or patent.**

16. **EPO Forms 1140a** and **1140** are the request forms proper which must be completed and signed by the person making the request in all cases. EPO Form 1140a complies with the requirements of Rule 11.4(d) of the Budapest Treaty in conjunction with Rule 11.3(a) relating to the furnishing of samples to parties legally entitled.

17. **EPO Form 1141** contains the wording of the undertakings which the requester must enter into *vis-à-vis* the applicant for or proprietor of the European patent pursuant Rule 28(3) EPC. It must be completed and signed in addition to the request proper **where**:

   (i) the European patent application has not been refused or withdrawn and is not deemed to be withdrawn;
   (ii) the European patent has not lapsed in all the designated Contracting States.

18. Where the requester of samples of micro-organisms deposited in accordance with Rule 28 EPC **appoints a professional representative before the EPO (Article 134 EPC)** to deal with the formalities associated with the filing of the request for samples, the following should be noted:

   (a) the request forms proper—**EPO Forms 1140a** or **1140**—may be signed by the professional representative; a specific authorisation or a reference to a general authorisation is required;
   (b) **EPO Form 1141** containing the wording of the undertakings which the requester must enter into *vis-à-vis* the applicant for or proprietor of the European patent **must be signed by the requester personally**; it may not be signed by the professional representative since these undertakings are not entered *vis-à-vis* the EPO.

19. On receiving a request for the furnishing of samples the EPO checks that the prescribed forms have been correctly completed and signed:

   (a) if they have, the EPO certifies the request and transmits it to the depositary institution; a copy is also sent to the applicant for or proprietor of the European patent.
   (b) if the request does not fully comply with the requirements the EPO informs the requester and invites him to remedy matters.

20. The EPO makes no charge for certifying the request. Fees fixed by the depositary institutions for the furnishing of samples must be paid direct to them. The amounts of such fees are published in the Official Journal of the EPO.

C. Application of Rule 28(4) EPC concerning the "expert" option

21. Where a request is made for samples of deposited micro-organisms to be furnished prior to grant of the European patent **and** provided the application has not been refused or withdrawn or is not deemed to be withdrawn, requesters are advised to check whether the appliant has availed himself of the "expert" option provided for in Rule 28(4) EPC.

If such is the case, until one of the aforementioned events (grant, refusal or withdrawal of the application) takes place, the availability of the culture of the deposited micro-organism may be effected only by the issue of a sample to an expert nominated by the requester. This fact is made known in the published European patent application on a separate form.

22. Under Rule 28(5) EPC, the following may be nominated as an expert: any natural person provided that the requester furnishes evidence, when submitting the request, that the nomination has the approval of the applicant, or an expert recognised by the President of the EPO (*cf.* the list of recognised expert published in the Official Journal of the EPO).

23. Where the "expert" option applies, **EPO Form 1142** entitled "Request to make a deposited micro-organism available by issuing a sample to an expert" should be used for the purpose of nominating an expert. The form is available on request from the EPO free of charge.

24. In this case, only **EPO Form 1142** needs to be signed by the requester whereas "**EPO Form 1140**" or "**EPO Form 1140a**" and "**EPO Form 1141**" (see point 14 above) must be signed by the expert.

25. Where the requester **and** the recognised expert act through **a professional representative before the EPO (Article 134 EPC)**, a separate representative must be appointed for each one of them. However, "**EPO Form 1141**" (Undertakings *vis-à-vis* the applicant for or the proprietor of the European patent) **must** be **signed by the recognised expert personally** (see point 18 above).

APPENDIX 11

THE "EXPERT OPTION"

Notice of the President of the EPO dated 28 July 1981 concerning the Procedure for Informing the EPO that the "Expert Option" (Rule 28, paragraph 4, EPC) has been chosen, and the publication of that fact

A11–01

(O.J. EPO 1981, 358)

1. As provided for in Rule 28, paragraph 4, of the European Patent Convention, until the date on which the technical preparations for publication of the European patent application are deemed to have been completed, the applicant may inform the European Patent Office that, until the publication of the mention of the grant of the European patent or until the date on which the application has been refused or withdrawn or is deemed to be withdrawn, the availability of the micro-organism deposited for the purpose of the said Rule shall be effected only by the issue of a sample to an expert.

2. The information referred to in point 1 of this Notice must be supplied in the form of a written statement addressed to the EPO and separate from the description and claims of the European patent application. It may be submitted in the request for the grant of a European patent referred to in Rule 26 of the European Patent Convention.

3. If the statement is admissible, the fact that it has been made will be mentioned in the published European patent application, on a separate form (EPA/EPO/OEB Form 1165).

Recognition of microbiological experts for the purpose of Rule 28 EPC

By Decision of 28 July 1981, the President of the European Patent Office recognised, in accordance with Rule 28(5)(b) EPC, a first batch of experts in the field of microbiology as experts for the purposes of Rule 28 EPC. The first list of these experts, containing all the relevant information, is published in Part III below pursuant to Rule 28(9) EPC.

The recognition of experts for the purposes of Rule 28 occurs on the basis of and in accordance with the "General Conditions set by the President of the European Patent Office for the recognition of experts in accordance with Rule 28(5)(b) of the European Patent Convention (EPC)" and the "Declaration for the purposes of recognition as an expert by the President of the European Patent Office in accordance with Rule 28(5)(b) of the European Patent Convention (EPC)" which has to be supplied by each applicant for recognition. These two texts are given in Parts I and II below.

I. General Conditions set by the President of the European Patent Office for the Recognition of Experts in Accordance with Rule 28, paragraph 5(b), of the European Patent Convention (EPC)

Preamble

Rule 28 EPC as amended by Decision of the Administrative Council of 30 November 1979 (Official Journal 11–12/1979, p. 447), entered into force on 1 June 1980. It lays down special requirements for European patent applications concerning certain inventions in the field of microbiology. If such an invention involves the use of a micro-organism which is not available to the public and which cannot be described in the European patent application in such a manner as to enable the invention to be carried out by a person skilled in the art, the invention is only regarded as being sufficiently disclosed within the meaning of Article 83 EPC if a culture of the micro-organism has been deposited with a depositary institution recognised by the European Patent Office (EPO) not later than the date of filing of the application, and if the application gives certain information necessary for characterising and identifying the micro-organism (Rule 28, paragraph 1).

The deposited culture of the micro-organism is available upon request to any person at the latest from the date of publication of the European patent application. Such availability is effected by the issue of a sample to the requester, provided that the latter has undertaken, *vis-à-vis* the applicant for or proprietor of the patent, not to make the deposited culture or any culture derived therefrom available to any third party and to use them for experimental purposes only, until such time as certain events specified in Rule 28, paragraph 3, take place (grant of the patent or some other outcome of the patent application).

However, until the date on which the technical preparations for publication of the application are deemed to have been completed, the applicant may inform the EPO that, until such time as certain events specified in Rule 28, paragraph 4, take place (grant of the patent or some other outcome of the patent application), the availability of the deposited culture shall be effected only by the issue of a sample to an *expert* nominated by the requester.

In accordance with Rule 28, paragraph 5, the requester may nominate as an expert any *natural person* whose nomination has the approval of the applicant or who is *recognised as an expert by the President of the EPO*. The list of experts recognised for the purpose of Rule 28 shall be published in the Official Journal of the EPO (Rule 28, paragraph 9).

The following conditions and requirements apply with regard to *recognition as an expert for the purpose of Rule 28 EPC* (hereinafter referred to as "recognised expert.")

General prerequisites for recognition as an expert

1. Any natural person may be recognised as an expert for the purpose of Rule 28 EPC, provided that person is able to demonstrate that he has sufficient scientific and practical experience in the field of microbiology in its widest sense to qualify him to deliver, on the basis of taxonomic, practical or other kinds of analyses, experiments or tests, expert opinions regarding micro-organisms deposited for the purpose of Rule 28 EPC, and provided that he possesses or has access to the equipment, appliances and facilities necessary for delivering such opinions.

These prerequisites may apply in respect of one or more kinds of micro-organisms and one or more kinds of analyses, experiments or tests.

2. A person cannot be recognised as an expert unless he provides sufficient guarantee that he possesses the personal independence and impartiality expected of an expert. As a means of asserting his independence and impartiality, the applicant for recognition shall declare to the President of the EPO that to the best of

his knowledge and belief there are no reasons which might give rise to justified doubts as to his independence and impartiality as an expert or which might conflict in any other way with his recognition as an expert.

3. A person cannot be recognised as an expert unless he undertakes *vis-à-vis* the President of the EPO that he is prepared to deliver expert opinions for any person upon request in respect of micro-organisms deposited for the purpose of Rule 28 EPC, under the conditions prescribed by Rule 28 and in particular paragraph 3 thereof, if the micro-organism concerned belongs to one of the kinds of micro-organisms specified by him and notified to the President of the EPO. However, a recognised expert's acceptance or refusal in individual cases of requests for an opinion is governed solely by points 7 to 10 of these Conditions.

4. A person cannot be recognised as an expert unless he undertakes *vis-à-vis* the President of the EPO to enter into and comply, *vis-à-vis* any applicant for or proprietor of a patent who for the purpose of Rule 28 EPC has deposited a micro-organism a sample of which is to be or has been supplied to him, in his capacity as a recognised expert, for the purpose of an expert opinion at the request of a third party, with the obligations under Rule 28, paragraph 3(a) and (b), EPC—paragraph 7 of the latter Rule being observed and the requester (person commissioning the opinion) being regarded as a third party within the meaning of Rule 28, paragraph 3, EPC.

5. Any person applying for recognition as an expert shall preferably specify what particular kinds of analyses, experiments or tests—*e.g.* taxonomic, practical or other—he is prepared or, as the case may be, not prepared to carry out.

6. A person cannot be recognised as an expert unless he declares to the President of the EPC that he has taken note of these Conditions and unless he undertakes to comply with the obligations thereunder for the duration of his status as recognised expert and, where applicable, after he ceases to hold such status.

Acceptance or refusal by a recognised expert of requests for an expert opinion

7. Subject to an agreement with the requester (person commissioning the opinion) concerning special requirements attaching to his work, including reasonable remuneration thereof, the recognised expert shall deliver the opinion required by the requester (person commissioning the opinion) unless he is obliged under point 8 of these Conditions, or entitled under point 9 thereof to refuse the request.

8. The recognised expert shall be obliged to refuse a request for an expert opinion if

(i) its subject, on thorough examination, lies outside the range of his expertise;

(ii) he does not possess the equipment, appliances or facilities necessary for carrying out the commission for an opinion (in particular that necessary for performing the required analyses, experiments or tests), or has access to such equipment, appliances or facilities only on conditions incompatible with his undertaking not to make the sample he has received of the deposited culture available to any third party, as prescribed by Rule 28, paragraph 3(a), EPC;

(iii) if there are circumstances which might give rise to justified doubts as to his independence and impartiality, *e.g.* because of conflict of interests;

(iv) in accepting or performing the commission for an opinion, the recognised expert would infringe, as a result of the agreement desired by the requester (person commissioning the opinion), his obligations under these Conditions or under Rule 28 EPC.

9. The recognised expert shall be entitled to refuse a request for an expert opinion, if

(i) the micro-organism to which the request relates does not belong to one of the kinds of micro-organisms specified by him in accordance with point 3 of these conditions or if the opinion desired by the requester (person commissioning the opinion) requires analyses, experiments or tests which the recognised expert, by virtue of a declaration under point 5 of these Conditions, is not prepared to carry out;

(ii) as a result of personal circumstances, *e.g.* illness, overwork or lengthy absence, he cannot deliver the opinion or cannot do so within a reasonable period of time.

10. If the recognised expert refuses to accept a request for an opinion, he shall inform the requester (person commissioning the opinion) and the President of the EPO immediately, giving the reasons for refusal.

Performance of commissions for an opinion by the recognised expert

11. The performance of commissions by the recognised expert is governed by the content of the agreements between the recognised expert and the requester (person commissioning the opinion) and by the law applicable to such agreements.

12. The recognised expert shall observe the principles of objectivity and impartiality in performing the commission and making known its results to the requester (person commissioning the opinion).

13. Without prejudice to his undertaking under Rule 28, paragraph 3(a), EPC, the recognised expert shall, when performing the commission, take all necessary measures to prevent the micro-organism samples received and further samples derived therefrom being made available to third parties.

14. The recognised expert shall as far as possible perform the commission and, in particular, the necessary analyses, experiments or tests in person and must not appoint a proxy for the purpose. However, he may, in so far as is necessary, make use of the services of assistants and other persons under his personal direction and supervision. Such persons are not to be regarded as "third parties" within the meaning of Rule 28, paragraph 3(a), EPC and point 13 of these Conditions.

15. Liability on the part of the recognised expert, including liability for persons engaged by him in accordance with point 14 of these Conditions, *vis-à-vis* persons other than the requester (person commissioning the opinion) and in particular *vis-à-vis* the applicant for or proprietor of a patent, arising out of a breach of contractual or statutory obligations and the resulting damages, is governed by the law applicable.

Termination of status as recognised expert

16. The status as recognised expert ceases when the recognised expert is deleted from the list of recognised experts. This shall occur

(i) at any time upon request by the recognised expert;

(ii) *ex officio*, if the prerequisites for recognition as an expert are not met at the time of recognition or cease to be met, or for any other important reason, *e.g.* if the recognised expert infringes his obligations under Rule 28 EPC or under these Conditions.

Other conditions and requirements

17. There is no automatic legal right to recognition as an expert for the purpose of Rule 28 EPC, even if the applicant meets all the prerequisites for recognition specified in these Conditions.

18. The recognised expert shall in his capacity, and particularly when performing commissions for an opinion, observe the generally recognised rules and principles of professional conduct applicable to his field of expertise.

19. The recognised expert shall inform the President of the EPO of any change in

his personal, professional or other circumstances which is of importance to or may have an effect on his recognition or work as recognised expert.

20. The European Patent Office shall supply the recognised expert with any information which he needs in order to perform his work as recognised expert.

21. The President of the EPO shall publish in the Official Journal the list of recognised experts and any changes therein. This list shall give the name and address of each recognised expert, the kinds of micro-organisms specified by him in accordance with point 3 of these Conditions and, where applicable, the particular kinds of analyses, experiments or tests he is or is not prepared to carry out and which he has specified in accordance with point 5 of these Conditions.

22. These Conditions shall apply for the duration of the status as recognised expert and, where applicable, after this status ceases to exist. The obligations incurred by the recognised expert under Rule 28, paragraph 3 EPC *vis-à-vis* the applicant for or proprietor of the patent shall remain unaffected.

[Part II of the Notice, concerning specimen declaration forms, and Part III, a list of recognised experts, are not included here. For the full text, see O.J. EPO 1981, 358.]

OPPOSITION PROCEDURE IN THE EPO

A12–01   (O.J. EPO 1989, 417)

1. The following is a new version of the note on EPO opposition procedure set out in OJ EPO 1985, 272 *et seq*. The note has been substantially revised in the light of experience and taking account of discussions with interested circles. The new version places particular emphasis on ways in which the opposition procedure can be expedited.

General principles

2. The EPO's aim remains to establish as rapidly as possible, in the interests of both the public and the parties to the opposition proceedings, whether or not the patent may be maintained given the opponent's submissions. It seeks to achieve this by means of a speedy and streamlined procedure, which implies firm control by the Opposition Division at all stages. This requirement must however be balanced against the need to allow the parties to present their case adequately so that the correct decision can be made.

Summary of the procedure

3. (A) Procedural steps taken before or after expiry of the opposition period, as the case may be:

(a) Communication of the notice of opposition to the patent proprietor, immediately after its filing at the EPO.

(b) Examination of the opposition for admissibility, and invitation to the opponent to furnish within two months the facts or evidence indicated, if not already submitted with the notice of opposition (see point 8 below).

(B) Procedural steps taken after expiry of the opposition period:

(c) Immediately after expiry of the opposition period or of the time limit set by the Opposition Division in a communication under Rule 56(2) or in the invitation referred to in point 3(b) above (whichever is the later), the formalities officer invites the proprietor to file within a specified period (four months) his observations (facts, evidence and arguments) and any amendments—Rule 57(1).

(d) The observations and any amendments filed by the proprietor are immediately communicated by the formalities officer to the opponent— Rule 57(3).

   If the proprietor responds to the notice of the opposition by filing amended patent documents, the formalities officer's communication to the opponent also invites him to comment within a specified period (normally four months; *cf.* Guidelines D–IV, 5.4, para. 1). If the proprietor does not file amended documents, his observations are forwarded for information to the opponent, who at the same time is given the opportunity to comment within a specified period (normally two months).

The procedure described in the preceding paragraph will not apply in cases where both the proprietor and the opponent have requested oral proceedings. In such a case, the dossier is forwarded immediately to the Opposition Division who will decide on the next step (*e.g.* inviting the parties to file further observations or fixing a date for the oral proceedings).

If during the proceedings the Opposition Division considers further clarification of the position or observations from one party on matters raised by the other to be necessary, the party in question is invited to comment within a specified period (normally four months) on such points as are material to the maintenance of the European patent (*cf.* Guidelines D–VI, 3.1 and 4.1).

If oral proceedings are requested by one of the parties or considered expedient by the Opposition Division itself, and if the questions at issue have been clarified sufficiently to suggest that hearing the parties would bring the opposition proceedings to a rapid conclusion, a date for oral proceedings is fixed (see Notice published in OJ EPO 1989, 132). With the summons to oral proceedings, the parties also receive a communication setting out, and if need be explaining, the issues which in the Opposition Division's view must be discussed at the oral proceedings (*cf.* Guidelines D–VI, 3.2 and E–III, 5), unless the issues are clear enough for a reference in the summons to certain parts of the file to suffice. Any further written observations from either party should be submitted to the EPO—and directly to the other party—at least one month before the oral proceedings.

(e) In oral proceedings, the opponent generally speaks first and the proprietor second. Each party is given two opportunities to speak, the first to make an opening statement and the second to reply to the other party. The Opposition Division may question the parties to clarify matters. At the end of the oral proceedings, usually after a brief adjournment for deliberation, the Chairman normally makes a statement summarising the decision reached by the Opposition Division. This decision is subsequently notified to the parties in writing (Rule 68(1), second sentence).

4. The above summary assumes only a single opposition. Where more than one opposition is filed against the same European patent, it is obviously best to deal with them together if possible. The procedure is essentially the same, but the notices of opposition and all subsequent documents in the proceedings must be communicated to all the opponents.

5. If no oral proceedings are to be held it may be possible in clear-cut cases to issue a decision after expiry of the specified period referred to in point 3(c) above, which will substantially reduce the time involved. This presupposes however that the decision is based only on grounds on which the parties have had an opportunity to comment (Article 113(1)).

6. Some important aspects of the procedure will now be considered in more detail.

The notice of opposition and reply of the proprietor

7. Opponents should use Form 2300 for the notice of opposition (see OJ EPO 1989, 239). The notice may be filed by facsimile. Opponents should also file, **with** the notice of opposition, all relevant papers including copies of new documents cited (even those available in the EPO documentation), translations of those documents not in an EPO official language, and, wherever possible, a copy of any evidence indicated in the notice.

8. Under Rule 55(c), the notice of opposition must contain an "indication" of the facts, evidence and arguments in support of the grounds of opposition. This

requirement is to be interpreted as meaning that the notice of opposition must at least indicate clearly to the proprietor the case he has to answer, *i.e.* within the nine-month period the opponent must give at least one ground for opposition under Article 100 and indicate the facts, evidence and arguments adduced in support of the ground(s). If he fails to do so in respect of at least one ground, the opposition is rejected as inadmissible.

An opposition may be considered admissible even when the opponent fails to submit the documents containing the indicated facts or evidence within the nine-month period. In such a case, he is allowed a short period (two months) to complete his opposition in this respect, as indicated in point 3(b) above (see also Guidelines D–IV, 1.2.2.1(f)).

9. After the nine-month period and any time limit under Rule 56(2) or point 3(b) above, the proprietor is invited to reply within four months. Within this period the proprietor must submit a full response to the opposition, *i.e.* all the facts, evidence and arguments in support of his case. He should also submit any amendments he considers necessary to meet the grounds of opposition; he should not however submit any "tidying-up" or other unnecessary amendments not related to those grounds. Any requests for amendment submitted at a later stage of the proceedings may be refused.

Documents which must be communicated to other parties

10. Parties are reminded of the need to file such documents in a sufficient number of copies (*cf.* Rule 36(4)). This applies also when filing by telegram, telex or facsimile (see Notice in OJ EPO 1989, 219).

11. In response to the wishes of interested circles, the practice of allowing extensions of time on request up to a total period of six months will be maintained for the time being. However, a request for a longer extension will be allowed only in exceptional circumstances (see Notice in OJ EPO 1989, 180).

Facts and evidence not submitted in due time

12. The Opposition Division may disregard facts or evidence which are not submitted in due time by the parties concerned (Article 114(2)). However if late-filed facts or evidence are obviously crucial to the decision, they have to be taken into consideration no matter what stage the procedure has reached.

13. In order to expedite proceedings, parties should, in principle, submit all facts, evidence and requests at the beginning of the procedure. Where this is not possible, the facts, evidence or requests must be submitted at the earliest opportunity. If relevant facts or evidence are submitted by a party only at a late stage of the proceedings without very good reason and if, as a consequence, unnecessary costs are incurred by another party, this will be taken into account in apportionment of costs (see point 20 below).

Oral proceedings

14. There are many cases in which the written procedure puts the Opposition Division in full possession of the facts, evidence and arguments needed to arrive at a correct decision. Parties should therefore refrain from systematically and automatically requesting oral proceedings. Nevertheless any party has the right to oral proceedings on a request made under Article 116(1) EPC.

Before the summons to the oral proceedings is issued, efforts are usually made to set a date convenient to all the parties. Once set, the date is altered only if unexpected and exceptional circumstances arise (for details see Notice in OJ EPO 1989, 132).

15. When oral proceedings take place, they should normally be concluded by a decision based on the parties' final submissions and requests voiced during the oral proceedings. Therefore the representatives of the parties should, in principle, come

to the oral proceedings fully prepared with possible fall-back positions and armed with the authority to take a stand on behalf of their clients on any developments which are likely to occur in the course of the proceedings.

16. The subject of the oral proceedings is the crucial issues listed in the communication referred to in point 3(d) above, but the parties are not confined to those issues alone, provided they are able to convince the Opposition Division that their additional submissions are relevant. The parties are not permitted to read extensively from documents. Passages from documents already forming part of the proceedings and which are being referred to again may only be read out where their precise wording is of importance.

At the oral proceedings parties are not allowed to introduce new facts or evidence (such as a new document) unless the Opposition Division concludes upon briefly reading the document through that it is so important that it must exercise its discretion and admit it under Article 114(2). In such circumstances the proceedings may be briefly interrupted to enable the other parties to study the new document, which may then—subject to the other party's consent—be considered at the proceedings. If this consent is not forthcoming the proceedings may be adjourned.

17. At the oral proceedings the members of the Opposition Division endeavour to be helpful and constructive and to make clear their line of thought so that the parties know the points on which they must concentrate in their arguments.

Oral evidence

18. Oral proceedings must be held if one of the parties requests them, but oral evidence is taken only if the Opposition Division considers it necessary (Rule 72). However, the Opposition Division normally allows (and may itself require) oral evidence to be given at least in cases where the evidence on a crucial issue depends on the memory or credibility of a witness. This could apply, for example, in cases of prior use. Clearly, such evidence must be examined especially critically.

Costs

19. The normal rule is that each party bears its own costs, but under Article 104(1) the costs may be otherwise apportioned "for reasons of equity". This however is limited to "costs incurred during taking of evidence or in oral proceedings", which means for example that the proprietor is unable to recover the costs involved in replying to the notice of opposition even if the opposition subsequently proves to be wholly unfounded.

20. However, within the limits imposed by Article 104(1) the Office endeavours to apportion costs in such a way as to discourage delaying tactics and other unreasonable conduct by any party.

21. The "taking of evidence" includes written as well as oral evidence, as is clear from Article 117. If a party presents facts or evidence after expiry of the nine-month period pursuant to Article 99, such late-filed material, irrespective of whether it is admitted into the proceedings or not, may justify an order for apportionment of those costs to the other party which would not have been incurred by him if such material had been presented in time.

22. If a party fails to appear, without adequate excuse, at oral proceedings arranged at his request he bears the full costs incurred by the other party, provided these are reasonable in the circumstances. Other examples of special apportionment of costs are given in the Guidelines at D–IX, 1.4.

Intervention of the assumed infringer

23. A third party may intervene under Article 105 at any time before the decision of the Opposition Division becomes final; if the intervention is properly filed and

781

admissible, it must be treated as an opposition. This means that regardless of the stage at which he enters the proceedings the intervener enjoys essentially the same rights as any other party to the proceedings.

24. If the intervener introduces into the proceedings new facts and evidence which appear to be crucial, the proceedings may need to be prolonged to enable them to be adequately considered. In other cases, however, (*i.e.* where the intervener adds nothing of substance to the case of the existing opponent(s)), the Opposition Division does not allow the intervention to delay the proceedings, with the sole exception that if the intervention occurs after oral proceedings with the other parties, the Opposition Division cannot refuse a request for oral proceedings by the intervener; such a request can be refused only where the parties as well as the subject of the proceedings are the same (Article 116(1), second sentence).

Examination by the opposition division of its own motion

25. Under Article 114(1), the Opposition Division is not restricted to the submissions of the parties. In practice, however, the examination of an opposition is usually confined to the grounds raised by the opponent. The Opposition Division goes beyond this only where clearly necessary, and certainly does not treat the opposition as an opportunity for a complete re-examination of the patent specification.

If a sole opposition or all oppositions are withdrawn, the opposition proceedings may be continued by the Office of its own motion. This must be done if it appears that the patent cannot be maintained unamended, provided that the examination necessary for the decision has already been concluded, or can be concluded without the participation of the opponent(s) (*cf.* Guidelines D–VII,6.3). It must equally be done if the proprietor has himself submitted amendmetns (*cf.* Article 113(2)).

Appendix 13

ACCELERATED PROCESSING

Notice from the President of the EPO dated 19 May 1998 concerning Accelerated Processing of Oppositions where Infringement Proceedings have been instituted

A13–01

(O.J. EPO 1998, 361)

1. In cases where an infringement action in respect of a European patent is pending before a national court of a contracting state a party to the oppositions may request accelerated processing. The request may be filed at any time. It must be filed in written reasoned form. The Office will then make every effort to issue the next procedural action (*e.g.* communication, summons to oral proceedings) within three months of receipt of the request or where the request is already filed within the opposition period, within three months after receipt of the patent proprietor's response to the notice of opposition (whichever is the later).

2. In addition, the EPO will also accelerate the processing of the opposition if it is informed by the national court of competent authority of a contracting state that infringement actions are pending.

3. However, the EPO has to rely on the co-operation of the parties to the proceedings who are expected in particular to make their submissions promptly and in full and in any case strictly to adhere to the time limits set by the EPO for replying to communications or commenting on written submissions from the other parties. Requests to extend time limits over and above the normal four-month period can only be granted in exceptional, duly substantiated cases.

Notice from the Vice-President Directorate-General 3 dated 19 May 1998 concerning Accelerated Processing before the Boards of Appeal

(O.J. EPO 1998, 362)

Parties with a legitimate interest may ask the boards of appeal to deal with their appeals rapidly. The boards can speed up an appeal as far as the procedural regulations allow.

Requests for accelerated processing must be submitted to the competent board either at the beginning of or during proceedings. They should contain reasons for the urgency together with relevant documents; no particular form is required.

This option is also available to the courts and competent authorities of the contracting states.

By way of example, the following circumstances could justify an appeal being dealt with particularly rapidly:

— where infringement proceedings have been brought or are envisaged
— where the decision of potential licensees of the patent in suit, that is the patent which is the subject of an appeal, hinges upon the outcome of the appeal proceedings
— where an opposition which is to be given accelerated processing (see Notice of the President of the EPO dated 19 May 1998, O.J. EPO 1998, 361) has been made the subject of an appeal.

By way of exception, the board may accelerate the procedure *ex officio*, for example in view of the disadvantages which could ensue from the suspensive effect of the appeal in the case in question.

Whether or not a particular case is regarded as urgent will depend on the nature of the case and not merely on whether accelerated processing is requested by the parties.

If, in view of the circumstances, the reasons given and the documents provided, the board decides to grant accelerated processing, this will involve in particular giving the appeal priority, and/or—with due respect for the parties' right to be heard and the fair administration of justice—adopting a strict framework for the procedure, for example concerning the time limits available before the final decision.

APPENDIX 14

PARIS CONVENTION

Paris Convention for the Protection of Industrial Property   A14–01

of March 20, 1883,

as revised
at BRUSSELS on December 14, 1900, at WASHINGTON on June 2, 1911, at THE
HAGUE on November 6, 1925, at LONDON on June 2, 1934, at LISBON on
October 31, 1958,

and at STOCKHOLM on July 14, 1967

(Relevant Parts)

ARTICLE 1

[Establishment of the Union; Scope of Industrial Property]

(1) The countries to which this Convention applies constitute a Union for the
protection of industrial property.

(2) The protection of industrial property has as its object patents, utility models,
industrial designs, trademarks, service marks, trade names, indications of source
or appellations of origin, and the repression of unfair competition.

(3) Industrial property shall be understood in the broadest sense and shall apply
not only to industry and commerce proper, but likewise to agricultural and
extractive industries and to all manufactured or natural products, for example,
wines, grain, tobacco leaf, fruit, cattle, minerals, mineral waters, beer, flowers, and
flour.

(4) Patents shall include the various kinds of industrial patents recognised by the
laws of the countries of the Union, such as patents of importation, patents of
improvement, patents and certificates of addition, etc.

ARTICLE 2

[National Treatment for Nationals of Countries of the Union]

(1) Nationals of any country of the Union shall, as regards the protection of
industrial property, enjoy in all the other countries of the Union the advantages that
their respective laws now grant, or may hereafter grant, to nationals; all without
prejudice to the rights specially provided for by this Convention. Consequently,
they shall have the same protection as the latter, and the same legal remedy against

any infringement of their rights, provided that the conditions and formalities imposed upon nationals are complied with.

(2) However, no requirement as to domicile or establishment in the country where protection is claimed may be imposed upon nationals of countries of the Union for the enjoyment of any industrial property rights.

(3) The provisions of the laws of each of the countries of the Union relating to judicial and administrative procedure and to jurisdiction, and to the designation of an address for service or the appointment of an agent, which may be required by the laws on industrial property are expressly reserved.

ARTICLE 3

[Same Treatment for Certain Categories of Persons as for Nationals of Countries of the Union]

Nationals of countries outside the Union who are domiciled or who have real and effective industrial or commercial establishments in the territory of one of the countries of the Union shall be treated in the same manner as nationals of the countries of the Union.

ARTICLE 4

[A to I. Patents, Utility Models, Industrial Designs, Marks, Inventors' Certificates: Right of Priority.—G. Patents: Division of the Application]

A(1) Any person who has duly filed an application for a patent, or for the registration of a utility model, or of an industrial design, or of a trademark, in one of the countries of the Union, or his successor in title, shall enjoy, for the purpose of filing in the other countries, a right of priority during the periods hereinafter fixed.

(2) Any filing that is equivalent to a regular national filing under the domestic legislation of any country of the Union or under bilateral or multilateral treaties concluded between countries of the Union shall be recognised as giving rise to the right of priority.

(3) By a regular national filing is meant any filing that is adequate to establish the date on which the application was filed in the country concerned, whatever may be the subsequent fate of the application.

B. Consequently, any subsequent filing in any of the other countries of the Union before the expiration of the periods referred to above shall not be invalidated by reason of any acts accomplished in the interval, in particular, another filing, the publication or exploitation of the invention, the putting on sale of copies of the design, or the use of the mark, and such acts cannot give rise to any third-party right or any right of personal possession. Rights acquired by third parties before the date of the first application that serves as the basis for the right of priority are reserved in accordance with the domestic legislation of each country of the Union.

C(1) The periods of priority referred to above shall be twelve months for patents and utility models, and six months for industrial designs and trademarks.

(2) These periods shall start from the date of filing of the first application; the day of filing shall not be included in the period.

(3) If the last day of the period is an official holiday, or a day when the Office is not open for the filing of applications in the country where protection is claimed, the period shall be extended until the first following working day.

(4) A subsequent application concerning the same subject as a previous first application within the meaning of paragraph (2), above, filed in the same country of the Union, shall be considered as the first application, of which the filing date shall be the starting point of the period of priority, if, at the time of filing the subsequent

786

application, the said previous application has been withdrawn, abandoned, or refused, without having been laid open to public inspection and without leaving any rights outstanding, and if it has not yet served as a basis for claiming a right of priority. The previous application may not thereafter serve as a basis for claiming a right of priority.

D(1) Any person desiring to take advantage of the priority of a previous filing shall be required to make a declaration indicating the date of such filing and the country in which it was made. Each country shall determine the latest date on which such declaration must be made.

(2) These particulars shall be mentioned in the publications issued by the competent authority, and in particular in the patents and the specifications relating thereto.

(3) The countries of the Union may require any person making a declaration of priority to produce a copy of the application (description, drawings, etc.) previously filed. The copy, certified as correct by the authority which received such application, shall not require any authentication, and may in any case be filed, without fee, at any time within three months of the filing of the subsequent application. They may require it to be accompanied by a certificate from the same authority showing the date of filing, and by a translation.

(4) No other formalities may be required for the declaration of priority at the time of filing the application. Each country of the Union shall determine the consequences of failure to comply with the formalities prescribed by this Article, but such consequences shall in no case go beyond the loss of the right of priority.

(5) Subsequently, further proof may be required.

Any person who avails himself of the priority of a previous application shall be required to specify the number of that application; this number shall be published as provided for by paragraph (2), above.

E(1) Where an industrial design is filed in a country by virtue of a right of priority based on the filing of a utility model, the period of priority shall be the same as that fixed for industrial designs.

(2) Furthermore, it is permissible to file a utility model in a country by virtue of a right of priority based on the filing of a patent application, and vice versa.

F. No country of the Union may refuse a priority or a patent application on the ground that the applicant claims multiple priorities, even if they originate in different countries, or on the ground that an application claiming one or more priorities contains one or more elements that were not included in the application or applications whose priority is claimed, provided that, in both cases, there is unity of invention within the meaning of the law of the country.

With respect to the elements not included in the application or applications whose priority is claimed, the filing of the subsequent application shall give rise to a right of priority under ordinary conditions.

G(1) If the examination reveals that an application for a patent contains more than one invention, the applicant may divide the application into a certain number of divisional applications and preserve as the date of each the date of the initial application and the benefit of the right of priority, if any.

(2) The applicant may also, on his own initiative, divide a patent application and preserve as the date of each divisional application the date of the initial application and the benefit of the right of priority, if any. Each country of the Union shall have the right to determine the conditions under which such division shall be authorised.

H. Priority may not be refused on the ground that certain elements of the invention for which priority is claimed do not appear among the claims formulated in the application in the country of origin, provided that the application documents as a whole specifically disclose such elements.

I(1) Applications for inventors' certificates filed in a country in which applicants have the right to apply at their own option either for a patent or for an inventor's certificate shall give rise to the right of priority provided for by this Article, under the same conditions and with the same effects as applications for patents.

(2) In a country in which applicants have the right to apply at their own option either for a patent or for an inventor's certificate, an applicant for an inventor's certificate shall, in accordance with the provisions of this Article relating to patent applications, enjoy a right of priority based on an application for a patent, a utility model, or an inventor's certificate.

ARTICLE 4bis

[Patents: Independence of Patents Obtained for the Same Invention in Different Countries]

(1) Patents applied for in the various countries of the Union by nationals of countries of the Union shall be independent of patents obtained for the same invention in other countries, whether members of the Union or not.

(2) The foregoing provision is to be understood in an unrestricted sense, in particular, in the sense that patents applied for during the period of priority are independent, both as regards the grounds for nullity and forfeiture, and as regards their normal duration.

(3) The provision shall apply to all patents existing at the time when it comes into effect.

(4) Similarly, it shall apply, in the case of the accession of new countries, to patents in existence on either side at the time of accession.

(5) Patents obtained with the benefit of priority shall, in the various countries of the Union, have a duration equal to that which they would have, had they been applied for or granted without the benefit of priority.

ARTICLE 4ter

[Patents: Mention of the Inventor in the Patent]

The inventor shall have the right to be mentioned as such in the patent.

ARTICLE 4quater

[Patents: Patentability in Case of Restrictions of Sale by Law]

The grant of a patent shall not be refused and a patent shall not be invalidated on the ground that the sale of the patented product or of a product obtained by means of a patented process is subject to restrictions or limitations resulting from the domestic law.

ARTICLE 5

[A. Patents: Importation of Articles; Failure to Work or Insufficient Working; Compulsory Licenses.—B. Industrial Designs: Failure to Work; Importation of Articles.—C. Marks: Failure to Use; Different Forms; Use by Co-proprietors.— D. Patents, Utility Models, Marks, Industrial Designs: Marking]

A(1) Importation by the patentee into the country where the patent has been granted of articles manufactured in any of the countries of the Union shall not entail forfeiture of the patent.

(2) Each country of the Union shall have the right to take legislative measures providing for the grant of compulsory licenses to prevent the abuses which might result from the exercise of the exclusive rights conferred by the patent, for example, failure to work.

(3) Forfeiture of the patent shall not be provided for except in cases where the grant of compulsory licences would not have been sufficient to prevent the said abuses. No proceedings for the forfeiture or revocation of a patent may be instituted before the expiration of two years from the grant of the first compulsory license.

(4) A compulsory license may not be applied for on the ground of failure to work or insufficient working before the expiration of a period of four years from the date of filing of the patent application or three years from the date of the grant of the patent, whichever period expires last; it shall be refused if the patentee justifies his inaction by legitimate reasons. Such a compulsory license shall be non-exclusive and shall not be transferable, even in the form of the grant of a sub-license, except with that part of the enterprise or goodwill which exploits such license.

(5) The foregoing provisions shall be applicable, *mutatis mutandis*, to utility models.

B. The protection of industrial designs shall not, under any circumstance, be subject to any forfeiture, either by reason of failure to work or by reason of the importation of articles corresponding to those which are protected.

C(1) If, in any country, use of the registered mark is compulsory, the registration may be cancelled only after a reasonable period, and then only if the person concerned does not justify his inaction.

(2) Use of a trademark by the proprietor in a form differing in elements which do not alter the distinctive character of the mark in the form in which it was registered in one of the countries of the Union shall not entail invalidation of the registration and shall not diminish the protection granted to the mark.

(3) Concurrent use of the same mark on identical or similar goods by industrial or commercial establishments considered as co-proprietors of the mark according to the provisions of the domestic law of the country where protection is claimed shall not prevent registration or diminish in any way the protection granted to the said mark in any country of the Union, provided that such use does not result in misleading the public and is not contrary to the public interest.

D. No indication or mention of the patent, of the utility model, of the registration of the trademark, or of the deposit of the industrial design, shall be required upon the goods as a condition of recognition of the right to protection.

ARTICLE 5*bis*

[All Industrial Property Rights: Period of Grace for the Payment of Fees for the Maintenance of Rights; Patents: Restoration]

(1) A period of grace of not less than six months shall be allowed for the payment of the fees prescribed for the maintenance of industrial property rights, subject, if the domestic legislation so provides, to the payment of a surcharge.

(2) The countries of the Union shall have the right to provide for the restoration of patents which have lapsed by reason of non-payment of fees.

ARTICLE 5*ter*

[Patents: Patented Devices Forming Part of Vessels, Aircraft, or Land Vehicles]

In any country of the Union the following shall not be considered as infringements of the rights of a patentee:

789

1. the use on board vessels of other countries of the Union of devices forming the subject of his patent in the body of the vessel, in the machinery, tackle, gear and other accessories, when such vessels temporarily or accidentally enter the waters of the said country, provided that such devices are used there exclusively for the needs of the vessel;
2. the use of devices forming the subject of the patent in the construction or operation of aircraft or land vehicles of other countries of the Union, or of accessories of such aircraft or land vehicles, when those aircraft or land vehicles temporarily or accidentially enter the said country.

ARTICLE 5*quater*

[Patents: Importation of Products Manufactured by a Process Patented in the Importing Country]

When a product is imported into a country of the Union where there exists a patent protecting a process of manufacture of the said product, the patentee shall have all the rights, with regard to the imported product, that are accorded to him by the legislation of the country of importation, on the basis of the process patent, with respect to products manufactured in that country.

* * *

ARTICLE 11

[Inventions, Utility Models, Industrial Designs, Marks: Temporary Protection at Certain International Exhibitions]

(1) The countries of the Union shall, in conformity with their domestic legislation, grant temporary protection to patentable inventions, utility models, industrial designs, and trademarks, in respect of goods exhibited at official or officially recognised international exhibitions held in the territory of any of them.

(2) Such temporary protection shall not extend the periods provided by Article 4. If, later, the right of priority is invoked, the authorities of any country may provide that the period shall start from the date of introduction of the goods into the exhibition.

(3) Each country may require, as proof of the identity of the article exhibited and of the date of its introduction, such documentary evidence as it considers necessary.

ARTICLE 12

[Special National Industrial Property Services]

(1) Each country of the Union undertakes to establish a special industrial property service and a central office for the communication to the public of patents, utility models, industrial designs, and trademarks.

(2) This service shall publish an official periodicial journal. It shall publish regularly:

(a) the names of the proprietors of patents granted, with a brief designation of the inventions patented;
(b) the reproductions of registered trademarks.

* * *

ARTICLE 19

[Special Agreements]

It is understood that the countries of the Union reserve the right to make separately between themselves special agreements for the protection of industrial property, in so far as these agreements do not contravene the provisions of this Convention.

*   *   *

[The above excerpts from the Paris Convention are reproduced in the Official English translation of the original French text. The Articles have been given titles to facilitate their identification—there are no titles in the signed text.]

Appendix 15

EUROPEAN ECONOMIC COMMUNITY TREATY

A15–01 Treaty Establishing the European Economic Community

Rome, March 25, 1957

(Relevant Parts)

FOUNDATIONS OF THE COMMUNITY

Title I—Free Movement of Goods

Chapter 2—Elimination of Quantitative Restrictions between Member States

*   *   *

Article 30

Quantitative restrictions on imports and all measures having equivalent effect shall, without prejudice to the following provisions, be prohibited between Member States.

*   *   *

Article 34

1. Quantitative restrictions on exports, and all measures having equivalent effect, shall be prohibited between Member States.
2. Member States shall, by the end of the first stage at the latest, abolish all quantitative restrictions on exports and any measures having equivalent effect which are in existence when this Treaty enters into force.

*   *   *

ARTICLE 36

The provisions of Articles 30 to 34 shall not preclude prohibitions or restrictions on imports, exports or goods in transit justified on grounds of public morality, public policy or public security; the protection of health and life of humans, animals or plants; the protection of national treasures possessing artistic, historic or archaeological value; or the protection of industrial and commercial property. Such prohibitions or restrictions shall not, however, constitute a means of arbitrary discrimination or a disguised restriction on trade between Member States.

* * *

POLICY OF THE COMMUNITY

Title I—Common Rules

CHAPTER 1—RULES ON COMPETITION

SECTION 1

Rules Applying to Undertakings

ARTICLE 85

1. The following shall be prohibited as incompatible with the common market: all agreements between undertakings, decisions by associations of undertakings and concerted practices which may affect trade between Member States and which have as their object or effect the prevention, restriction or distortion of competition within the common market, and in particular those which:

(a) directly or indirectly fix purchase or selling prices or any other trading conditions;
(b) limit or control production, markets, technical development, or investment;
(c) share markets or sources of supply;
(d) apply dissimilar conditions to equivalent transactions with other trading parties, thereby placing them at a competitive disadvantage;
(e) make the conclusion of contracts subject to acceptance by the other parties of supplementary obligations which, by their nature or according to commercial usage, have no connection with the subject of such contracts.

2. Any agreements or decisions prohibited pursuant to this Article shall be automatically void.

3. The provisions of paragraph 1 may, however, be declared inapplicable in the case of:

— any agreement or category of agreements between undertakings;
— any decision or category of decisions by associations of undertakings;
— any concerted practice or category of concerted practices;

which contributes to improving the production or distribution of goods or to promoting technical or economic progress, while allowing consumers a fair share of the resulting benefit, and which does not:

(a) impose on the undertakings concerned restrictions which are not indispensable to the attainment of these objectives;

793

(b) afford such undertakings the possibility of eliminating competition in respect of a substantial part of the products in question.

ARTICLE 86

Any abuse by one or more undertakings of a dominant position within the common market or in a substantial part of it shall be prohibited as incompatible with the common market in so far as it may affect trade between Member States. Such abuse may, in particular, consist in:

(a) directly or indirectly imposing unfair purchase or selling prices or other unfair trading conditions;
(b) limiting production, markets or technical development to the prejudice of consumers;
(c) applying dissimilar conditions to equivalent transactions with other trading parties, thereby placing them at a competitive disadvantage;
(d) making the conclusion of contracts subject to acceptance by the other parties of supplementary obligations which, by their nature or according to commercial usage, have no connection with the subject of such contracts.

* * *

ARTICLE 177

The Court of Justice shall have jurisdiction to give preliminary rulings concerning:

(a) the interpretation of this Treaty;
(b) the validity and interpretation of acts of the institutions of the Community;
(c) the interpretation of the statutes of bodies established by an act of the Council, where those statutes so provide.

Where such a question is raised before any court or tribunal of a Member State, that court or tribunal may, if it considers that a decision on the question is necessary to enable it to give judgment, request the Court of Justice to give a ruling thereon.

Where any such question is raised in a case pending before a court or tribunal of a Member State, against whose decisions there is no judicial remedy under national law, that court or tribunal shall bring the matter before the Court of Justice.

* * *

GENERAL AND FINANCIAL PROVISIONS

Setting up of the Institutions

ARTICLE 222

This Treaty shall in no way prejudice the rules in Member States governing the system of property ownership.

* * *

APPENDIX 16

STRASBOURG CONVENTION

Convention on the Unification of Certain Points of Substantive Law on Patents for Invention

A16–01

Strasbourg, November 27, 1963

The Member States of the Council of Europe, signatory hereto;

Considering that the aim of the Council of Europe is to achieve a greater unity between its Members for the purpose, among others, of facilitating their economic and social progress by agreements and common action in economic, social, cultural, scientific, legal and administrative matters;

Considering that the unification of certain points of substantive law on patents for invention is likely to assist industry and inventors, to promote technical progress and contribute to the creation of an international patent;

Having regard to Article 15 of the Convention for the Protection of Industrial Property signed at Paris on 20 March 1883, revised at Brussels on 14 December 1900, at Washington on 2 June 1911, at The Hague on 6 November 1925, at London on 2 June 1934, and at Lisbon on 31 October 1958;

Have agreed as follows:

ARTICLE 1

In the Contracting States, patents shall be granted for any inventions which are susceptible of industrial application, which are new and which involve an inventive step. An invention which does not comply with these conditions shall not be the subject of a valid patent. A patent declared invalid because the invention does not comply with these conditions shall be considered invalid *ab initio*.

ARTICLE 2

The Contracting States shall not be bound to provide for the grant of patents in respect of

(a) inventions the publications or exploitation of which would be contrary to "*ordre public*" or morality, provided that the exploitation shall not be deemed to be so contrary merely because it is prohibited by a law or regulation;

(b) plant or animal varieties or essentially biological processes for the production of plants or animals; this provision does not apply to microbiological processes and the products thereof.

ARTICLE 3

An invention shall be considered as susceptible of industrial application if it can be made or used in any kind of industry including agriculture.

ARTICLE 4

1. An invention shall be considered to be new if it does not form part of the state of the art.

2. Subject to the provisions of paragraph 4 of this Article, the state of the art shall be held to comprise everything made available to the public by means of a written or oral description, by use, or in any other way, before the date of the patent application or of a foreign application, the priority of which is validly claimed.

3. Any Contracting State may consider the contents of applications for patents made, or of patents granted, in that State, which have been officially published on or after the date referred to in paragraph 2 of this Article, as comprised in the state of the art, to the extent to which such contents have an earlier priority date.

4. A patent shall not be refused or held invalid by virtue only of the fact that the invention was made public, within six months preceding the filing of the application, if the disclosure was due to, or in consequence of:

(a) an evident abuse in relation to the applicant or his legal predecessor, or
(b) the fact that the applicant or his legal predecessor has displayed the invention at official, or officially recognised, international exhibitions falling within the terms of the Convention on international exhibitions signed at Paris on 22nd November 1928 and amended on 10th May 1948.

ARTICLE 5

An invention shall be considered as involving an inventive step if it is not obvious having regard to the state of the art. However, for the purposes of considering whether or not an invention involves an inventive step, the law of any Contracting State may, either generally or in relation to particular classes of patents or patent applications, for example patents of addition, provide that the state of the art shall not include all or any of the patents or patent applications mentioned in paragraph 3 of Article 4.

ARTICLE 6

Any Contracting State which does not apply the provisions of paragraph 3 of Article 4 shall nevertheless provide that no invention shall be validly protected in so far as it includes matter which is or has been validly protected by a patent in that State which, though not comprised in the state of the art, in respect of that matter, an earlier priority date.

ARTICLE 7

Any group of Contracting States who provide for a common patent application may be regarded as a single State for the purposes of paragraph 3 of Article 4, or of Article 6.

ARTICLE 8

1. The patent application shall contain a description of the invention with the necessary drawings referred to therein and one or more claims defining the protection applied for.

2. The description must disclose the invention in a manner sufficiently clear and complete for it to be carried out by a person skilled in the art.

3. The extent of the protection conferred by the patent shall be determined by the terms of the claims. Nevertheless, the description and drawings shall be used to interpret the claims.

ARTICLE 9

1. This Convention shall be open for signature by the member States of the Council of Europe. It shall be subject to ratification or acceptance. Instruments of ratification or acceptance shall be deposited with the Secretary-General of the Council of Europe.

2. This Convention shall enter into force three months after the date of deposit of the eight instrument of ratification or acceptance.

3. In respect of a signatory State ratifying or accepting subsequently, the Convention shall come into force three months after the date of deposit of its instrument of ratification or acceptance.

ARTICLE 10

1. After the entry into force of this Convention, the Committee of Ministers of the Council of Europe may invite any Member of the International Union for the Protection of Industrial Property which is not a Member of the Council of Europe to accede thereto.

2. Such accession shall be effected by depositing with the Secretary-General of the Council of Europe an instrument of accession which shall take effect three months after the date of its deposit.

ARTICLE 11

1. Any Contracting Party may at the time of signature or when depositing its instrument of ratification, acceptance or accession, specify the territory or territories to which this Convention shall apply.

2. Any Contracting Party may, when depositing its instrument of ratification, acceptance or accession or at any later date, by notification addressed to the Secretary-General of the Council of Europe, extend this Convention to any other territory or territories specified in the declaration and for whose international relations it is responsible or on whose behalf it is authorised to give undertakings.

3. Any declaration made in purusuance of the preceding paragraph may, in respect of any territory mentioned in such declaration, be withdrawn according to the procedure laid down in Article 13 of this Convention.

ARTICLE 12

1. Notwithstanding anything in this Convention, each Contracting Party may, at the time of signature or when depositing its instrument of ratification, acceptance or accession, temporarily reserve, for the limited period stated below, the right:

797

(a) not to provide for the grant of patents in respect of food and pharmaceutical products, as such, and agricultural or horticultural processes other than those to which paragraph (b) of Article 2 applies;

(b) to grant valid patents for inventions disclosed within six months preceding the filing of the application, either apart from the case referred to in paragraph 4(b) of Article 4, by the inventor himself or, apart from the case referred to in paragraph 4(a) of Article 4, by a third party as a result of information derived from the inventor.

2. The limited period referred to in paragraph 1 of this article shall be ten years in the case of sub-paragraph (a) and five years in the case of sub-paragraph (b). It shall start from the entry into force of this Convention for the Contracting Party considered.

3. Any Contracting Party which makes a reservation under this Article shall withdraw the said reservation as soon as circumstances permit. Such withdrawal shall be made by notification addressed to the Secretary-General of the Council of Europe and shall take effect one month from the date of receipt of such notification.

ARTICLE 13

1. This Convention shall remain in force indefinitely.

2. Any Contracting Party may, in so far as it is concerned, denounce this Convention by means of a notification addressed to the Secretary-General of the Council of Europe.

3. Such denunciation shall take effect six months after the date of receipt by the Secretary-General of such notification.

ARTICLE 14

The Secretary-General of the Council of Europe shall notify the member States of the Council, any State which has acceded to this Convention and the Director of the International Bureau for the Protection of Industrial Property of:

(a) any signature;

(b) any deposit of an instrument of ratification, acceptance or accession;

(c) any date of entry into force of this Convention;

(d) any declaration and notification received in pursuance of the provisions of paragraphs 2 and 3 of Article 11;

(e) any reservation made in pursuance of the provisions of paragraph 1 of Article 12;

(f) the withdrawal of any reservation carried out in pursuance of the provisions of paragraph 3 of Article 12;

(g) any notification received in pursuance of the provisions of paragraph 2 of Article 13 and the date on which denunciation takes effect.

In witness whereof the undersigned, being duly authorized thereto, have signed this Convention.

Done at Strasbourg, this 27th day of November 1963 in English and in French, both texts being equally authoritative, in a single copy which shall remain deposited in the archives of the Council of Europe.

BRUSSELS CONVENTION

Convention on Jurisdiction and the Enforcement of Judgments in Civil and Commercial Matters

A17–01

Brussels, September 23, 1968

(Relevant Parts)

Preamble

The High Contracting Parties to the Treaty establishing the European Economic Community,

Desiring to implement the provisions of Article 220 of that Treaty by virtue of which they undertook to secure the simplification of formalities governing the reciprocal recognition and enforcement of judgments of courts or tribunals;

Anxious to strengthen in the Community the legal protection of persons therein established;

Considering that it is necessary for this purpose to determine the international jurisdiction of their courts, to facilitate recognition and to introduce an expeditious procedure for securing the enforcement of judgments, authentic instruments and court settlements;

Have decided to conclude this Convention and to this end have designated as their Plenipotentiaries:

[Designations of Plenipotentiaries of the original six Contracting States]

Have agreed as follows:

Title I

Scope

ARTICLE 1

This Convention shall apply in civil and commercial matters whatever the nature of the court or tribunal. It shall not extend, in particular, to revenue, customs or administrative matters.

The Convention shall not apply to:
1. the status or legal capacity of natural persons, rights in property arising out of a matrimonial relationship, wills and succession;

799

2. bankruptcy, proceedings relating to the winding-up of insolvent companies or other legal persons, judicial arrangements, compositions and analogous proceedings;
3. social security;
4. arbitration.

Title II

Jurisdiction

*   *   *

Section 5. Exclusive jurisdiction

ARTICLE 16

The following courts shall have exclusive jurisdiction, regardless of domicile:
  (1) in proceedings which have as their object rights *in rem* in, or tenancies of, immovable property, the courts of the Contracting State in which the property is situated;
  (2) in proceedings which have as their object the validity of the constitution, the nullity or the dissolution of companies or other legal persons or associations of natural or legal persons, or the decisions of their organs, the courts of the Contracting State in which the company, legal person or association has its seat;
  (3) in proceedings which have as their object the validity of entries in public registers, the courts of the Contracting State in which the register is kept;
  (4) in proceedings concerned with the registration or validity of patents, trade marks, designs, or other similar rights required to be deposited or registered, the court of the Contracting State in which the deposit or registration has been applied for, has taken place or is under the terms of an international convention deemed to have taken place;
  (5) in proceedings concerned with the enforcement of judgments, the courts of the Contracting State in which the judgment has been or is to be enforced.

Section 6. Prorogation of jurisdiction

ARTICLE 17

If the parties, one or more of whom is domiciled in a Contracting State, have agreed that a court or the courts of a Contracting State are to have jurisdiction to settle any disputes which have arisen or which may arise in connection with a particular legal relationship, that court or those courts shall have exclusive jurisdiction. Such an agreement conferring jurisdiction shall either be in writing or evidenced in writing or, in international trade or commerce, in a form which accords with practices in that trade or commerce of which the parties are or ought to have been aware. Where such an agreement is concluded by parties, none of whom is domiciled in a Contracting State, the courts of other Contracting States shall have no jurisdiction over their dispute unless the court or courts chosen have declined jurisdiction.

The court or courts of a Contracting State on which a trust instrument has conferred jurisdiction shall have exclusive jurisdiction in any proceedings brought against a settlor, trustee or beneficiary, if relations between these persons or their rights or obligations under the trust are involved.

Agreements or provisions of a trust instrument conferring jurisdiction shall have no legal force if they are contrary to the provisions of Article 12 or 15, or if the courts whose jurisdiction they purport to exclude have exclusive jurisdiction by virtue of Article 16.

If an agreement conferring jurisdiction was concluded for the benefit of only one of the parties, that party shall retain the right to bring proceedings in any other court which has jurisdiction by virtue of this Convention.

ARTICLE 18

Apart from jurisdiction derived from other provisions of this Convention, a court of a Contracting State before whom a defendant enters an appearance shall have jurisdiction. This rule shall not apply where appearance was entered solely to contest the jurisdiction, or where another court has exclusive jurisdiction by virtue of Article 16.

*   *   *

APPENDIX 18

VIENNA CONVENTION

A18–01   ## Convention on the Law of Treaties

Vienna, May 22, 1969

(Relevant parts)

Preamble

The states parties to the present convention,

Considering the fundamental role of treaties in the history of international relations,

Recognizing the ever-increasing importance of treaties as a source of international law and as a means of developing peaceful co-operation among nations, whatever their constitutional and social systems,

Noting that the principle of free consent and of good faith and the "pacta sunt servanda" rule are universally recognized.

Affirming that disputes concerning treaties, like other international disputes, should be settled by peaceful means and in conformity with the principles of justice and international law,

Recalling the determination of the peoples of the United Nations to establish conditions under which justice and respect for the obligations arising from treaties can be maintained,

Having in mind the principles of international law embodied in the Charter of the United Nations, such as the principles of the equal rights and self-determination of peoples, of the sovereign equality and independence of all states, of non-interference in the domestic affairs of states, of the prohibition of the threat or use of force and of universal respect for, and observance of, human rights and fundamental freedoms for all.

Believing that the codification and progressive development of the law of treaties achieved in the present convention will promote the purposes of the United Nations set forth in the Charter, namely, the maintenance of international peace and security, the development of friendly relations and the achievement of co-operation among nations,

Affirming that the rules of customary international law will continue to govern questions not regulated by the provisions of the present convention,

Have agreed as follows:

Part I. Introduction

ARTICLE 1

Scope of the present convention

The present convention applies to treaties between states.

ARTICLE 2

Use of terms

1. For the purposes of the present convention:
   (a) "treaty" means an international agreement concluded between states in written form and governed by international law, whether embodied in a single instrument or in two or more related instruments and whatever its particular designation;
   [(b) to (f) are not reproduced]
   (g) "party" means a state which has consented to be bound by the treaty and for which the treaty is in force;
   (h) "third state" means a state not a party to a treaty;
   (i) "international organization" means an inter-governmental organization.

2. The provisions of paragraph 1 regarding the use of terms in the present convention are without prejudice to the use of those terms or to the meanings which may be given to them in the internal law of any state.

ARTICLE 3

International agreements not within the scope of the present convention

The fact that the present convention does not apply to international agreements concluded between states and other subjects of international law or between such other subjects of international law, or to international agreements not in written form, shall not affect:

   (a) the legal force of such agreements;
   (b) the application to them of any of the rules set forth in the present convention to which they would be subject under international law independently of the convention;
   (c) the application of the convention to the relations of states as between themselves under international agreements to which other subjects of international law are also parties.

ARTICLE 4

Non-retroactivity of the present convention

Without prejudice to the application of any rules set forth in the present convention to which treaties would be subject under international law independently of the convention, the convention applies only to treaties which are concluded by states after the entry into force of the present convention with regard to such states.

ARTICLE 5

*Treaties constituting international organizations and treaties adopted within an
international organization*

The present convention applies to any treaty which is the constituent instrument
of an international organization and to any treaty adopted within an international
organization without prejudice to any relevant rules of the organization.

*   *   *

Part III. Observance, Application and Interpretation of Treaties

Section 1. Observance of treaties

ARTICLE 26

Pacta sunt servanda

Every treaty in force is binding upon the parties to it and must be performed by
them in good faith.

ARTICLE 27

Internal law and observance of treaties

A party may not invoke the provisions of its internal law as justification for its
failure to perform a treaty. This rule is without prejudice to Article 46.

Section 2. Application of treaties

ARTICLE 28

Non-retroactivity of treaties

Unless a different intention appears from the treaty or is otherwise established,
its provisions do not bind a party in relation to any act or fact which took place or
any situation which ceased to exist before the date of the entry into force of the
treaty with respect to that party.

ARTICLE 29

Territorial scope of treaties

Unless a different intention appears from the treaty or is otherwise established, a
treaty is binding upon each party in respect of its entire territory.

ARTICLE 30

Application of successive treaties relating to the same subject matter

1. Subject to Article 103 of the Charter of the United Nations, the rights and obligations of states parties to successive treaties relating to the same subject matter shall be determined in accordance with the following paragraphs.

2. When a treaty specifies that it is subject to, or that it is not to be considered as incompatible with, an earlier or later treaty, the provisions of that other treaty prevail.

3. When all the parties to the earlier treaty are parties also to the later treaty but the earlier treaty is not terminated or suspended in operation under Article 59, the earlier treaty applies only to the extent that its provisions are compatible with those of the later treaty.

4. When the parties to the later treaty do not include all the parties to the earlier one:

(a) as between states parties to both treaties the same rule applies as in paragraph 3;

(b) as between a state party to both treaties and a state party to only one of the treaties, the treaty to which both states are parties governs their mutual rights and obligations.

5. Paragraph 4 is without prejudice to Article 41, or to any question of the termination or suspension of the operation of a treaty under Article 60 or to any question of responsibility which may arise for a state from the conclusion or application of a treaty the provisions of which are incompatible with its obligations towards another state under another treaty.

Section 3. Interpretation of treaties

ARTICLE 31

General rule of interpretation

1. A treaty shall be interpreted in good faith in accordance with the ordinary meaning to be given to the terms of the treaty in their context and in the light of its object and purpose.

2. The context for the purpose of the interpretation of a treaty shall comprise, in addition to the text, including its preamble and annexes:

(a) any agreement relating to the treaty which was made between all the parties in connection with the conclusion of the treaty;

(b) any instrument which was made by one or more parties in connection with the conclusion of the treaty and accepted by the other parties as an instrument related to the treaty.

3. There shall be taken into account, together with the context:

(a) any subsequent agreement between the parties regarding the interpretation of the treaty or the application of its provisions;

(b) any subsequent practice in the application of the treaty which establishes the agreement of the parties regarding its interpretation;

(c) any relevant rules of international law applicable in the relations between the parties.

4. A special meaning shall be given to a term if it is established that the parties so intended.

ARTICLE 32

Supplementary means of interpretation

Recourse may be had to supplementary means of interpretation, including the preparatory work of the treaty and the circumstances of its conclusion, in order to confirm the meaning resulting from the application of Article 31, or to determine the meaning when the interpretation according to Article 31:

(a) leaves the meaning ambiguous or obscure; or
(b) leads to a result which is manifestly absurd or unreasonable.

ARTICLE 33

Interpretation of treaties authenticated in two or more languages

1. When a treaty has been authenticated in two or more languages, the text is equally authoritative in each language, unless the treaty provides or the parties agree that, in case of divergence, a particular text shall prevail.

2. A version of the treaty in a language other than one of those in which the text was authenticated shall be considered an authentic text only if the treaty so provides or the parties so agree.

3. The terms of the treaty are presumed to have the same meaning in each authentic text.

4. Except where a particular text prevails in accordance with paragraph 1, when a comparison of the authentic texts discloses a difference of meaning which the application of Articles 31 and 32 does not remove, the meaning which best reconciles the texts, having regard to the object and purpose of the treaty, shall be adopted.

*   *   *

Appendix 19

COMMUNITY PATENT CONVENTION

[This appendix sets out in full the 1989 Agreement relating to Community   **A19–01** Patents, the Community Patent Convention, its Implementing Regulations and the Protocol on Litigation, in that order.]

Agreement Relating to Community Patents

Luxembourg, December 15, 1989

(89/695/EEC)

Preamble

The High Contracting Parties to the Treaty establishing the European Economic Community;

Desiring to give unitary and autonomous effect to European patents granted in respect of their territories under the Convention on the Grant of European Patents of 5 October 1973;

Anxious to establish a Community patent system which contributes to the attainment of the objectives of the Treaty establishing the European Economic Community and in particular to the elimination within the Community of the distortion of competition which may result from the territorial aspect of national protection rights;

Considering that one of the fundamental objectives of the Treaty establishing the European Economic Community is the abolition of obstacles to the free movement of goods;

Considering that one of the most suitable means of ensuring that this objective will be achieved, as regards the free movement of goods protected by patents, is the creation of a Community patent system;

Considering that the creation of such a Community patent system is therefore inseparable from the attainment of the objectives of the Treaty and thus linked with the Community legal order;

Considering that it is necessary for these purposes for the High Contracting Parties to conclude an Agreement which constitutes a special agreement within the meaning of Article 142 of the Convention on the Grant of European Patents, a regional patent treaty within the meaning of Article 45(1) of the Patent Cooperation Treaty of 19 June 1970, and a special agreement within the meaning of Article 19 of the Convention of the Protection of Industrial Property, signed in Paris on 20 March 1883 and last revised on 14 July 1967;

Considering that the achievement of a common market which offers conditions

807

similar to those of a national market necessitates the creation of legal instruments which enable enterprises to adapt their production and distribution activities to European scales;

Considering that the problem of dealing effectively with actions relating to Community patents and the problems arising from the separation of jurisdiction created by the Community Patent Convention as signed at Luxembourg on 15 December 1975 in respect of infringement and validity of Community patents will best be solved by giving jurisdiction in actions for infringement of a Community patent to national courts of first instance designated as Community patent courts which can at the same time consider the validity of the patent in suit and, where necessary, amend or revoke it; and that an appeal to national courts of second instance designated as Community patent courts should lie from judgments of these courts;

Considering, however, that uniform application of the law on infringement and validity of Community patents requires the setting up of a Community patent appeal court common to the Contracting States (Common Appeal Court) to hear on appeal referrals on questions of infringement and validity from the Community patent courts of second instance;

Considering that the same requirement of uniform application of the law leads to conferral upon the Common Appeal Court of jurisdiction to decide on appeals from the Revocation Divisions and the Patent Administration Division of the European Patent Office, thus replacing the Revocation Boards provided for in the Community Patent Convention as signed on 15 December 1975;

Considering that it is essential that the application of this Agreement must not operate against the application of the provisions of the Treaty establishing the European Economic Community and that the Court of Justice of the European Communities must be able to ensure the uniformity of the Community legal order;

Anxious to promote the completion of the internal market and the establishment of a European technological community by means of the Community patent;

Convinced therefore that the conclusion of this Agreement is necessary to facilitate the achievement of the tasks of the European Economic Community,

Have agreed as follows:

Article 1

Contents of the Agreement

1. The Convention for the European Patent for the common market signed at Luxembourg on 15 December 1975, hereinafter referred to as "the Community Patent Convention," as amended by this Agreement, shall be annexed hereto.

2. The Community Patent Convention shall be supplemented by the following Protocols annexed to this Agreement:

— Protocol on the Settlement of Litigation concerning the Infringement and Validity of Community Patents, hereinafter referred to as "the Protocol on Litigation,"
— Protocol on Privileges and Immunities of the Common Appeal Court,
— Protocol on the Statute of the Common Appeal Court.

3. The Annexes to this Agreement shall form an integral part thereof.

4. On entry into force of this Agreement, it shall replace the Community Patent Convention in the form signed at Luxembourg on 15 December 1975.

ARTICLE 2

Relationship with the Community legal order

1. No provision of this Agreement may be invoked against the application of the Treaty establishing the European Economic Community.

2. In order to ensure the uniformity of the Community legal order, the Common Appeal Court established by the Protocol on Litigation shall request the Court of Justice of the European Communities to give a preliminary ruling in accordance with Article 177 of the Treaty establishing the European Economic Community whenever there is a risk of an interpretation of this Agreement being inconsistent with that Treaty.

3. Where a Member State or the Commission of the European Communities considers that a decision of the Common Appeal Court which closes the procedure before it does not comply with the principle stated in the foregoing paragraphs, it may request the Court of Justice of the European Communities to give a ruling. The ruling given by the Court of Justice in response to such request shall not affect the decision by the Common Appeal Court which gave rise to the request. The Registrar of the Court of Justice shall give notice of the request to the Member States, to the Council and, if the request is made by a Member State, the Commission of the European Communities; they shall then be entitled within two months of the notification to submit statements of case or written observations to the Court. No fees shall be levied or any costs of expenses awarded in respect of the proceedings provided for in this paragraph.

ARTICLE 3

Interpretation of provisions on jurisdiction

1. The Court of Justice of the European Communities shall have jurisdiction to give preliminary rulings concerning the interpretation of the provisions on jurisdiction applicable to actions relating to Community patents brought before national courts, contained in Part VI, Chapter I, of the Community Patent Convention and in the Protocol on Litigation.

2. The following courts shall have the power to request the Court of Justice to give a preliminary ruling on any question of interpretation as defined in paragraph 1:

(a) — in Belgium: la Cour de cassation (het Hof van Cassatie) and le Conseil d'État (de Raad van State),
— in Denmark: Højesteret,
— in the Federal Republic of Germany: die obersten Gerichtshöfe des Bundes,
— in Greece: τα ανώτατα Δικαστήρια,
— in Spain: el Tribunal supremo,
— in France: la Cour de cassation and le Conseil d'État,
— in Ireland: an Chúirt Uachtarach (the Supreme Court),
— in Italy: la Corte suprema di cassazione,
— in Luxembourg: la Cour supérieure de justice when sitting as Cour de cassation,
— in the Netherlands: de Hoge Raad,
— in Portugal: o Supremo Tribunal de Justiça,
— in the United Kingdom: the House of Lords;

(b) the courts of the Contracting States when ruling on appeals.

809

3. Where such a question is raised in a case before one of the courts listed in paragraph 2(a), that court must, if it considers that a decision on the question is necessary to enable it to give a judgment, request the Court of Justice to give a ruling thereon.

4. Where such a question is raised before one of the courts referred to in paragraph 2(b), that court may, under the conditions laid down in paragraph 1, request the Court of Justice to give a ruling thereon.

ARTICLE 4

Rules of Procedure of the Court of Justice

1. The Protocol on the Statute of the Court of Justice of the European Economic Community and the Rules of Procedure of the Court of Justice shall apply to any proceedings referred to in Articles 2 and 3.

2. The Rules of Procedure shall be adapted and supplemented, as necessary, in conformity with Article 188 of the Treaty establishing the European Economic Community.

ARTICLE 5

Jurisdiction of the Common Appeal Court

Subject to Articles 2 and 3, the Common Appeal Court shall ensure uniform interpretation and application of this Agreement and of the provisions enacted in implementation thereof, to the extent to which these are not national provisions.

ARTICLE 6

Signing—Ratification

1. This Agreement shall be open until 21 December 1989 for signing by the States parties to the Treaty establishing the European Economic Community.

2. This Agreement shall be subject to ratification by the 12 signatory States. Instruments of ratification shall be deposited with the Secretary-General of the Council of the European Communities.

ARTICLE 7

Accession

1. This Agreement shall be open to accession by States becoming Member States of the European Economic Community.

2. Instruments of accession to this Agreement shall be deposited with the Secretary-General of the Council of the European Communities. Accession shall take effect on the first day of the third month following the deposit of the instrument of accession, provided that the ratification by the State concerned of the Convention of the Grant of European Patents, hereinafter referred to as "the European Patent Convention," or its accession thereto has become effective.

3. The signatory States hereby recognise that any State which becomes a member of the European Economic Community must accede to this Agreement.

4. A special agreement may be concluded between the Contracting States and the acceding State to determine the details of application of this Agreement necessitated by the accession of that State.

ARTICLE 8

Participation of third States

The Council of the European Communities may, acting by a unanimous decision, invite a State party to the European Patent Convention which forms a customs union or a free trade area with the Europeran Economic Community to enter into negotiations with a view to enabling that third State to participate in this Agreement on the basis of a special agreement, to be concluded between the Contracting States to this Agreement and the third State concerned, determining the conditions and details for applying this Agreement to that State.

ARTICLE 9

Application to the sea and submarine areas

This Agreement shall apply to the sea and submarine areas adjacent to a territory to which the Agreement applies in which one of the Contracting States exercises sovereign rights or jurisdiction in accordance with international law.

ARTICLE 10

Entry into force

To enter into force this Agreement must be ratified by the 12 signatory States. It shall enter into force on the first day of the third month following deposit of the instrument of ratification by the last such State to take this step. However, if the European Patent Convention enters into force on a subsequent date in respect of any signatory State to this Agreement, the latter shall enter into force on the latest subsequent date.

ARTICLE 11

Observers

As long as this Agreement has not entered into force in respect of a Member State of the European Economic Community which is not a signatory to this Agreement, that State may take part as an observer in the Select Committee of the Administrative Council of the European Patent Organization, hereinafter referred to as "the Select Committee" and in the Administrative Committee of the Common Appeal Court, hereinafter referred to as "the Administrative Committee," and may appoint a representative and an alternative representative to each of these bodies for this purpose.

811

ARTICLE 12

Duration of the Agreement

This Agreement is concluded for an unlimited period.

ARTICLE 13

Revision

If a majority of the Member States of the European Economic Community requests the revision of this Agreement, a revision conference shall be convened by the President of the Council of the European Communities. The conference shall be prepared by the Select Committee or by the Administrative Committee, each acting within the limits of its own competence.

ARTICLE 14

Disputes between Contracting States

1. Any dispute between Contracting States concerning the interpretation or application of this Agreement which is not settled by negotiation shall be submitted, at the request of one of the States concerned, to the Select Committee or to the Administrative Committee as the case may be. The body to which the dispute is submitted shall endeavour to bring about agreement between the States concerned.

2. If agreement is not reached within six months from the date when the Select Committee or the Administrative Committee was seised of the dispute, any one of the States concerned may submit the dispute to the Court of Justice of the European Communities.

3. If the Court of Justice finds that a Contracting State has failed to fulfil an obligation under this Agreement, that State shall be required to take the necessary measures to comply with the judgment of the Court of Justice.

ARTICLE 15

Definition

For the purposes of this Agreement "Contracting State" means a State for which the Agreement is in force.

ARTICLE 16

Original of the Agreement

This Agreement, drawn up in a single original in the Danish, Dutch, English, French, German, Greek, Irish, Italian, Portuguese and Spanish languages, all 10 texts being equally authentic, shall be deposited in the archives of the General Secretariat of the Council of the European Communities. The Secretary-General shall transmit a certified copy to the Government of each Member State of the European Economic Community.

ARTICLE 17

Notification

The Secretary-General of the Council of the European Communities shall notify the Member States of the European Community of:

(a) the deposit of each instrument of ratification and accession:
(b) the date of entry into force of this Agreement;
(c) any reservation or withdrawal of reservation pursuant to Article 83 of the Community Patent Convention;
(d) any notification received pursuant to Article 1(2) and (3) of the Protocol on Litigation.

Convention for the European Patent for the Common Market

(Community Patent Convention)

as revised, Luxembourg, 15 December 1989

Part I. General and Institutional Provisions

Chapter I. General provisions

ARTICLE 1

Common system of law for patents

1. A system of law, common to the Contracting States, concerning patents for invention is hereby established.
2. The common system of law shall govern the European patents granted for the Contracting States in accordance with the Convention on the Grant of European Patents, hereinafter referred to as "the European Patent Convention," and the European patent applications in which such States are designated.

ARTICLE 2

Community patent

1. European patents granted for the Contracting States shall be called Community patents.
2. Community patents shall have a unitary character. They shall have equal effect throughout the territories to which this Convention applies and may only be granted, transferred, revoked or allowed to lapse in respect of the whole of such territories. The same shall apply *mutatis mutandis* to applications for European patents in which the Contracting States are designated.
3. Community patents shall have an autonomous character. They shall be subject only to the provisions of this Convention and those provisions of the European Patent Convention which are binding upon every European patent and which shall consequently be deemed to be provisions of this Convention.

813

ARTICLE 3

Joint designation

Designation of the States parties to this Convention in accordance with Article 79 of the European Patent Convention shall be effected jointly. Designation of one or some only of these States shall be deemed to be designation of all of these States.

ARTICLE 4

Setting up of special departments

The following bodies common to the Contracting States shall implement the procedures laid down in this Convention:

(a) special departments which are set up within the European Patent Office and whose work shall be supervised by a Select Committee of the Administrative Council of the European Patent Organisation;

(b) the Common Appeal Court established by the Protocol on the Settlement of Litigation concerning the Infringement and Validity of Community Patents, hereinafter referred to as "the Protocol on Litigation."

ARTICLE 5

National patents

This Convention shall be without prejudice to the right of the Contracting States to grant national patents.

Chapter II. Special departments of the European Patent Office

ARTICLE 6

The special departments

The special departments shall be as follows:

(a) a Patent Administration Division;

(b) one or more Revocation Divisions.

ARTICLE 7

Patent Administration Division

1. The Patent Administration Division shall be responsible for all acts of the European Patent Office relating to Community patents, in so far as these acts are not the responsibility of other departments of the Office. It shall in particular be responsible for decisions in respect of entries in the Register of Community Patents.

2. Decisions of the Patent Administration Division shall be taken by one legally qualified member.

3. The members of the Patent Administration Division may not be members of the Boards of Appeal or the Enlarged Board of Appeal set up under the European Patent Convention.

ARTICLE 8

Revocation Divisions

1. The Revocation Divisions shall be responsible for the examination of requests for the limitation of and applications for the revocation of Community patents, and for determining compensation under Article 43(5).

2. A Revocation Division shall consist of one legally qualified member who shall be the Chairman, and two technically qualified members. Prior to the taking of a final decision on the request or application, the Revocation Division may entrust the examination of the request or application to one of its members. Oral proceedings shall be before the Revocation Division itself.

ARTICLE 9

Exclusion and objection

1. Members of the Revocation Divisions may not take part in any proceedings if they have any personal interest therein, if they have previously beeen involved as representatives of one of the parties, or if they have participated in the final decision on the case in the proceedings for grant or opposition proceedings.

2. If, for one of the reasons mentioned in paragraph 1 or for any other reason, a member of a Revocation Division considers that he should not take part in any proceedings, he shall inform the division accordingly.

3. Members of a Revocation Division may be objected to by any party for one of the reasons mentioned in paragraph 1, or if suspected of partiality. An objection shall not be admissible if, while being aware of a reason for objection, the party has taken a procedural step. No objection may be based upon the nationality of members.

4. The Revocation Divisions shall decide as to the action to be taken in the cases specified in paragraphs 2 and 3 without the participation of the member concerned. For the purpose of taking this decision the member objected to shall be replaced by his alternate.

ARTICLE 10

Languages for proceedings and publications

1. The official languages of the European Patent Office shall also be the official languages of the special departments.

2. Throughout the proceedings before the special departments, a translation filed in accordance with Article 14(2), second sentence, of the European Patent Convention may be brought into conformity with the original text of the European patent application.

3. The official language of the European Patent Office in which the Community patent is granted shall be used as the language of the proceedings in all proceedings before the special departments concerning the Community patent, unless otherwise provided in the Implementing Regulations.

4. However, natural or legal persons having their residence or principal place of business within the territory of a Contracting State having a language other than one of the official languages of the European Patent Office as an official language, and nationals of that State who are resident abroad, may file documents which have to be filed within a time limit in an official language of the Contracting State concerned. They must, however, file a translation in the language of the

815

proceedings within the time limit prescribed in the Implementing Regulations; in the cases provided for in the Implementing Regulations, they may file a translation in a different official language of the European Patent Office.

5. If any document is not filed in the language prescribed by this Convention, or if any translation required by virtue of this Convention is not filed in due time, the document shall be deemed not to have been received.

6. New specifications of Community patents published following limitation or revocation proceedings shall be published in the language of the proceedings; they shall include a translation of the amended claims in one of the official languages of each of the Contracting States which do not have as an official language the language of the proceedings.

7. The Community Patent Bulletin shall be published in the three official languages of the European Patent Office.

8. Entries in the Register of Community Patents shall be made in the three official languages of the European Patent Office. In cases of doubt, the entry in the language of the proceedings shall be authentic.

9. No State party to this Convention may avail itself of the authorisations given in Articles 65, 67(3) and 70(3) of the European Patent Convention.

Chapter III. The Select Committee of the Administrative Council

ARTICLE 11

Membership

1. The Select Committee of the Administrative Council shall be composed of the Representatives of the Contracting States, the Representative of the Commission of the European Communities and their alternate Representatives. Each Contracting State and the Commission shall be entitled to appoint one Representative and one alternate Representative to the Select Committee The same members shall represent the Contracting States on the Administrative Council and on the Select Committee.

2. The members of the Select Committee may, subject to the provisions of its Rules of Procedure, be assisted by advisers or experts.

ARTICLE 12

Chairmanship

1. The Select Committee of the Administrative Council shall elect a Chairman and a Deputy Chairman from among the Representatives and alternate Representatives of the Contracting States. The Deputy Chairman shall *ex officio* replace the Chairman in the event of his being prevented from attending to his duties.

2. The duration of the terms of office of the Chairman and the Deputy Chairman shall be three years. The terms of office shall be renewable.

ARTICLE 13

Board

1. The Select Committee of the Administrative Council may set up a Board composed of five of its members.

2. The chairman and the deputy chairman of the Select Committee shall be members of the board *ex officio;* the other three members shall be elected by the Select Committee.

3. The term of office of the members elected by the Select Committee shall be three years. This term of office shall be three years. This term of office shall not be renewable.

4. The board shall perform the duties given to it by the Select Committee in accordance with the Rules of Procedure.

ARTICLE 14

Meetings

1. Meetings of the Select Committee of the Administrative Council shall be convened by its chairman.

2. The President of the European Patent Office shall take part in the deliberations of the Select Committee.

3. The Select Committee shall hold an ordinary meeting once each year. In addition, it shall meet on the initiative of its chairman or a the request of one-third of the Contracting States.

4. The deliberations of the Select Committee shall be based on an agenda, and shall be held in accordance with its Rules of Procedure.

5. The provisional agenda shall contain any question whose inclusion is requested by any Contracting State in accordance with the Rules of Procedure.

ARTICLE 15

Languages of the Select Committee

1. The languages in use in the deliberations of the Select Committee of the Administrative Council shall be English, French and German.

2. Documents submitted to the Select Committee, and the minutes of its deliberations, shall be drawn up in the three languages mentioned in paragraph 1.

ARTICLE 16

Competence of the Select Committee in certain cases

1. The Select Committee of the Administrative Council shall be competent to amend the following provisions of this Convention:

  (a) the time limits laid down in the Convention which are to be observed *vis-à-vis* the European Patent Office;
  (b) the Implementing Regulations.

2. The Select Committee shall be competent, in conformity with this Convention, to adopt or amend the following provisions:

  (a) the Financial Regulations;
  (b) the Rules relating to Fees;
  (c) its Rules of Procedure.

817

APPENDIX 19

ARTICLE 17

Voting rights

1. The right to vote in the Select Committee of the Administrative Council shall be restricted to the Contracting States.
2. Each Contracting State shall have one vote, subject to the application of the provisions of Article 19.

ARTICLE 18

Voting rules

1. The Select Committee of the Administrative Council shall take its decisions other than those referred to in paragraph 2 by a simple majority of the Contracting States represented and voting.
2. A majority of three-quarters of the votes of the Contracting States represented and voting shall be required for the decisions which the Select Committee is empowered to take under Article 16 and Article 21(a).
3. Abstentions shall not be considered as votes.

ARTICLE 19

Weighting of votes

In respect of the adoption or amendment of the rules relating to fees and, if the financial contribution to be made by the Contracting States would thereby be increased, the approval referred to in Article 21(a), voting shall be conducted according to Article 36 of the European Patent Convention. The term "Contracting States" in that Article shall be understood as meaning the States parties to this Convention.

Chapter IV. Financial provisions

ARTICLE 20

Financial obligations and benefits

1. The amount payable by the States parties to this Convention pursuant to Article 146 of the European Patent Convention shall be covered by financial contributions determined in respect of each State in accordance with the scale laid down in paragraph 3.
2. Both the revenue derived from fees paid in accordance with the rules relating to fees, less the payments to the European Patent Organisation pursuant to Articles 39 and 147 of the European Patent Convention, and all other receipts of the European Patent Organisation obtained in implementation of this convention shall be distributed among the States parties to this convention in accordance with the scale laid down in paragraph 3.
3. The scale referred to in paragraphs 1 and 2 shall be as follows:

Belgium	5,25%
Denmark	5,20%

Germany	20,40%
Greece	4,40%
Spain	6,30%
France	12,80%
Ireland	3,45%
Italy	7,00%
Luxembourg	3,00%
Netherlands	11,80%
Portugal	3,50%
United Kingdom	16,90%

4. The scale laid down in paragraph 3 may be amended by decision of the Council of the European Communities, acting on a proposal from the Commission of the European Communities, or on a request from at least three Contracting States, following a review to be conducted by the Select Committee of the Administrative Council of the European Patent Organisation five years after the entry into force of the Agreement relating to Community Patents.

5. The decision referred to in paragraph 4 shall require:

(a) unanimity from the sixth to the 10th year inclusive from the date of entry into force of the Agreement relating to Community Patents;
(b) after the expiry of that period, a qualified majority; this majority shall be that specified in the first indent of the second subparagraph of Article 148(2) of the Treaty establishing the European Economic Community.

6. Five years after the entry into force of the Agreement relating to Community Patents the necessary work shall be commenced in order to examine under what conditions and at what date the system of financing provided for in paragraphs 1 to 5 may be replaced by another system based, having regard to developments in the European Communities, on Community financing. This system may include the amounts payable by the States parties to this Convention pursuant to the European Patent Convention and the amounts accruing to these States pursuant to that Convention. When this work has been concluded, this Article and, if appropriate, Article 19 may be amended by a decision of the council of the European Communities acting unanimously on a proposal from the Commission.

ARTICLE 21

Powers of the Select Committee of the Administrative Council in budgetary matters

The Select Committee of the Administrative Council shall:

(a) approve annually the forecasts of expenditure and revenue relating to the implementation of this Convention and any amendments or additions made to these forecasts, submitted to it by the President of the European Patent Office, and supervise the implementation thereof;
(b) grant the authorisation provided for in Article 47(2) of the European Patent Convention, in so far as the expenditure involved relates to the implementation of this Convention;
(c) approve the annual accounts of the European Patent Organisation which relate to the implementation of this Convention and that part of the report of the auditors appointed under Article 49(1) of the European Patent Convention which relates to these accounts, and give the President of the European Patent Office a discharge.

819

Rules relating to Fees

The Rules relating to Fees shall determine in particular the amounts of the fees and the ways in which they are to be paid.

Part II. Substantive Patent Law

Chapter I. Right to the Community patent

ARTICLE 23

Claiming the right to the Community patent

1. If a Community patent has been granted to a person who is not entitled to it under Article 60(1) of the European Patent Convention, the person entitled to it under that provision may, without prejudice to any other remedy which may be open to him, claim to have the patent transferred to him.

2. Where a person is entitled to only part of the Community patent, that person may, in accordance with paragraph 1, claim to be made a joint proprietor.

3. Legal proceedings in respect of the rights specified in paragraphs 1 and 2 may be instituted only within a period of not more than two years after the date on which the European Patent Bulletin mentions the grant of the European patent. This provision shall not apply if the proprietor of the patent knew, at the time when the patent was granted or transferred to him, that he was not entitled to the patent.

4. The fact that legal proceedings have been instituted shall be entered in the Register of Community Patents. Entry shall also be made of the final decision in, or of any other termination of, the proceedings.

ARTICLE 24

Effect of change of proprietorship

1. Where there is a complete change of proprietorship of a Community patent as a result of legal proceedings under Article 23, licences and other rights shall lapse upon the registration of the person entitled to the patent in the Register of Community Patents.

2. If, before the institution of legal proceedings has been registered,

(a) the proprietor of the patent has used the invention within the territory of any of the Contracting States or made effective and serious preparations to do so, or

(b) a licensee of the patent has obtained his licence and has used the invention within the territory of any of the Contracting States or made effective and serious preparations to do so,

he may continue such use provided that he requests a non-exclusive licence of the patent from the new proprietor whose name is entered in the Register of Community Patents. Such request must be made within the period prescribed in the Implementing Regulations. The licence shall be granted for a reasonable period and upon reasonable terms.

3. Paragraph 2 shall not apply if the proprietor of the patent or the licensee, as the case may be, was acting in bad faith at the time when he began to use the invention or to make preparations to do so.

Chapter II. Effects of the Community patent and the European patent application

ARTICLE 25

Prohibition of direct use of the invention

A Community patent shall confer on its proprietor the right to prevent all third parties not having his consent:

(a) from making, offering, putting on the market or using a product which is the subject-matter of the patent, or importing or stocking the product for these purposes;

(b) from using a process which is the subject-matter of the patent or, when the third party knows, or it is obvious in the circumstances, that the use of the process is prohibited without the consent of the proprietor of the patent, from offering the process for use within the territories of the Contracting States;

(c) from offering, putting on the market, using, or importing or stocking for these purposes the product obtained directly by a process which is the subject-matter of the patent.

ARTICLE 26

Prohibition of indirect use of the invention

1. A Community patent shall also confer on its proprietor the right to prevent all third parties not having his consent from supplying or offering to supply within the territories of the Contracting States a person, other than a party entitled to exploit the patented invention, with means, relating to an essential element of that invention, for putting it into effect therein, when the third party knows, or it is obvious in the circumstances, that these means are suitable and intended for putting that invention into effect.

2. Paragraph 1 shall not apply when the means are staple commercial products, except when the third party induces the person supplied to commit acts prohibited by Article 25.

3. Persons performing the acts referred to in Article 27(a) to (c) shall not be considered to be parties entitled to exploit the invention within the meaning of paragraph 1.

ARTICLE 27

Limitation of the effects of the Community patent

The rights conferred by a Community patent shall not extend to:

(a) acts done privately and for non-commercial purposes;

(b) acts done for experimental purposes relating to the subject-matter of the patented invention;

(c) the extemporaneous preparation for individual cases in a pharmacy of a medicine in accordance with a medical prescription nor acts concerning the medicine so prepared;

(d) the use on board vessels of the countries of the Union of Paris for the Protection of Industrial Property, other than the Contracting States, of the patented invention, in the body of the vessel, in the machinery, tackle, gear and other accessories, when such vessels temporarily or accidentally enter the waters of Contracting States, provided that the invention is used there exclusively for the needs of the vessel;

(e) the use of the patented invention in the construction or operation of aircraft or land vehicles of countries of the Union of Paris for the Protection of Industrial Property, other than the Contracting States, or of accessories to such aircraft or land vehicles, when these temporarily or accidentally enter the territory of Contracting States;

(f) the acts specified in Article 27 of the Convention on International Civil Aviation of 7 December 1944, where these acts concern the aircraft of a State, other than the Contracting States, benefiting from the provisions of that Article.

ARTICLE 28

Exhaustion of the rights conferred by the Community patent

The rights conferred by a Community patent shall not extend to acts concerning a product covered by that patent which are done within the territories of the Contracting States after that product has been put on the market in one of these States by the proprietor of the patent or with his express consent, unless there are grounds which, under Community law, would justify the extension to such acts of the rights conferred by the patent.

ARTICLE 29

Translation of the claims in examination or opposition proceedings

1. The applicant shall file with the European Patent Office within the time limits prescribed in the Implementing Regulations a translation of the claims on which the grant of the European patent is to be based in one of the official languages of each of the Contracting States which does not have English, French or German as an official language.

2. Paragraph 1 shall apply *mutatis mutandis* in respect of claims which are amended during opposition proceedings.

3. The translations of the claims shall be published by the European Patent Office.

4. The applicant for or proprietor of the patent shall pay the fee for the publication of the translation of the claims within the time limits prescribed in the Implementing Regulations.

5. If the translations prescribed in paragraph 1 are not filed in due time or if the fee for the publication of the translations of the claims is not paid in due time the European patent application shall be deemed to be withdrawn in respect of the designated Contracting States. If the translations prescribed in paragraph 2 are not filed in due time or if the fee for the publication of the translations of the claims is not paid in due time the Community patent shall be revoked.

6. Where a translation of the claims prescribed in paragraph 1 or 2, or a translation of the claims in the two official languages of the European Patent Office which are not the language of the proceedings, is defective, the applicant for or the proprietor of the patent may file a corrected translation with the European Patent

Office. The corrected translation shall not have any legal effect until the conditions prescribed in the Implementing Regulations have been complied with.

7. Where the translation of the claims in one of the official languages of a Contracting State is defective, any person who, in that State, is using or has made effective and serious preparations for using an invention the use of which would not constitute infringement of the patent in the defective translation of the claims, may, after the corrected translation takes effect, continue such use without payment. This shall not apply if it is established that the person concerned did not act in good faith.

ARTICLE 30

Translation of the specification of the Community patent

1. In addition to the translations prescribed in Article 29(1) the applicant shall file with the European Patent Office, before the end of the period prescribed in the Implementing Regulations, a translation of the text of the application which forms the basis for the grant of the Community patent in one of the official languages of each of the Contracting States in which the language of the proceedings is not an official language.

2. Paragraph 1 shall apply *mutatis mutandis* to the text of the Community patent which forms the basis for its maintenance in amended form during opposition proceedings.

3. The European Patent Office shall, within the time limit laid down in the Implementing Regulations, forward to each of the central industrial property offices of the Contracting States which have so requested a copy of the translations referred to in paragraphs 1 and 2 in the relevant language or languages. The applicant must for that purpose file a sufficient number of copies of the translations.

4. The translations prescribed in paragraphs 1 and 2 shall be made available to the public by the European Patent Office and shall be forwarded in due time and free of charge to the central industrial property offices of the Contracting States concerned in a suitable form for adequate and inexpensive dissemination.

5. If the translations prescribed in paragraph 1 are filed in due time, the proprietor of the patent may avail himself from the date of publication of the mention of the grant of the patent of the rights conferred by the patent.

6. If the translations prescribed in paragraphs 1 or 2 are not filed in due time, the Community patent shall be deemed to be void *ab initio*. However, the proprietor may, instead of the Community patent, obtain a European patent for the Contracting States for which he has filed translations in due time. He must for that purpose notify his intention in writing to the European Patent Office within a period of two months from the expiry of the applicable time limit and pay within the same period the fees referred to in Article 81(1).

7. Article 29(6) and (7) shall apply *mutatis mutandis* to the translations prescribed in paragraphs 1 and 2.

ARTICLE 31

Status of translations

The translations provided for in Articles 29 and 30 which have been carried out by persons authorised under the law of a Contracting State shall be deemed in that State to be in conformity with the original, until proved to the contrary.

ARTICLE 32

Rights conferred by a European patent application after publication

1. Compensation reasonable in the circumstances may be claimed from a third party who, in the period between the date of publication of a European patent application in which the Contracting States are designated and the date of publication of the mention of the grant of the European patent, has made any use of the invention which, after that period, would be prohibited by virtue of the Community patent.

2. Any Contracting State which does not have as an official language the language of the proceedings of a European patent application in which the Contracting States are designated may prescribe that such application shall not confer, in respect of use of the invention within its territory, the right referred to in paragraph 1 until such time as the applicant, at his option, has:

  (a) supplied a translation of the claims in one of its official languages to the competent authority of that State and the translation has been published in accordance with the law of that State; or
  (b) communicated such a translation to the person using the invention within that State.

3. Any Contracting State referred to in paragraph 2 may prescribe that, where the applicant avails himself of the option provided for in subparagraph 2(b), the right conferred by the application in respect of use of the invention within the territory of the State concerned may be invoked only if the applicant supplies a copy of the translation to the competent authority of that State within 15 days after it has been communicated to the person using the invention within that State. The Contracting State may prescribe that the authority shall publish the translation, in accordance with the law of that State.

4. Any Contracting State which adopts a provision under paragraph 2 may prescribe that, where the translation of the claims is defective, any person who, in that State, has used or made effective and serious preparations for using the invention the use of which would not constitute infringement of the application in the original translation of the claims shall be liable for reasonable compensation in accordance with paragraph 1 only from the moment when the corrected translation of the claims has been published or has been received by him, unless it is established that he did not act in good faith, in which case he shall be liable for reasonable compensation in accordance with paragraph 1 from the moment when the requirements of paragraph 2 were fulfilled.

ARTICLE 33

Effect of revocation of the Community patent

1. A European patent application in which the Contracting States are designated and the resulting Community patent shall be deemed not to have had, as from the outset, the effects specified in this Chapter, to the extent that the patent has been revoked.

2. Subject to the national provisions relating either to claims for compensation for damage caused by negligence or lack of good faith on the part of the proprietor of the patent, or to unjust enrichment, the retroactive effect of the revocation of the patent as a result of opposition or revocation proceedings shall not affect:

  (a) any decision on infringement which has acquired the authority of a final decision and been enforced prior to the revocation decision;

(b) any contract concluded prior to the revocation decision, in so far as it has been performed before that decision; however, repayment, to an extent justified by the circumstances, of sums paid under the relevant contract, may be claimed on grounds of equity.

ARTICLE 34

Complementary application of national law regarding infringement

1. The effects of a Community patent shall be governed solely by the provisions of this Convention. In other respects, infringement of a Community patent shall be governed by the national law relating to infringement of a national patent, in accordance with and subject to the provisions of the Protocol on Litigation.

2. Paragraph 1 shall apply *mutatis mutandis* to a European patent application which may result in the grant of a Community patent.

ARTICLE 35

Burden of proof

1. If the subject-matter of a Community patent is a process for obtaining a new product, the same product when produced by any other party shall, in the absence of proof to the contrary, be deemed to have been obtained by the patented process.

2. In the adduction of proof to the contrary, the legitimate interests of the defendant in protecting his manufacturing and business secrets shall be taken into account.

Chapter III. National rights

ARTICLE 36

National prior right

1. With regard to a Community patent having a date of filing or, where priority has been claimed, a date of priority later than that of a national patent application or national patent made public in a Contracting State on or after that date, the national patent application or patent shall, for that Contracting State, have the same prior right effect as a published European patent application designating that Contracting State.

2. If, in a Contracting State, a national patent application or patent, which is unpublished by reason of the national law of the State concerning the secrecy of inventions, has a prior right effect with regard to a national patent in that State having a later date of filing, or where priority has been claimed a later date of priority, the same shall apply in that State with regard to a Community patent.

ARTICLE 37

Right based on prior use and right of personal possession

1. Any person who, if a national patent had been granted in respect of an invention, would have had, in one of the Contracting States, a right based on prior use of that invention or a right of personal possession of that invention, shall enjoy,

in that State, the same rights in respect of a Community patent for the same invention.

2. The rights conferred by a Community patent shall not extend to acts concerning a product covered by that patent which are done within the territory of the State concerned after that product has been put on the market in that State by the person referred to in paragraph 1, in so far as the national law of that State makes provision to the same effect in respect of national patents.

Chapter IV. The Community patent as an object of property

ARTICLE 38

Dealing with the Community patent as a national patent

1. Unless otherwise specified in this Convention, a Community patent as an object of property shall be dealt with in its entirety, and for the whole of the territories in which it is effective, as a national patent of the Contracting State in which, according to the Register of European Patents provided for in the European Patent Convention:

   (a) the applicant for the patent had his residence or principal place of business on the date of filing of the European patent application;
   (b) where subparagraph (a) does not apply, the applicant had a place of business on that date; or
   (c) where neither subparagraph (a) nor subparagraph (b) applies, the applicant's representative whose name is entered first in the Register of European Patents had his place of business on the date of that entry.

2. Where subparagraphs (a), (b), and (c) of paragraph 1 do not apply, the Contracting State referred to in that paragraph shall be the Federal Republic of Germany.

3. If two or more persons are mentioned in the Register of European Patents as joint applicants, paragraph 1 shall apply to the joint applicant first mentioned; if this is not possible, it shall apply to the joint applicant next mentioned in respect of whom it is applicable. Where paragraph 1 does not apply to any of the joint applicants, paragraph 2 shall apply.

4. If in a Contracting State as determined by the preceding paragraphs a right in respect of a national patent is effective only after entry in the national patent register, such a right in respect of a Community patent shall be effective only after entry in the Register of Community Patents.

ARTICLE 39

Transfer

1. An assignment of a Community patent shall be made in writing and shall require the signature of the parties to the contract, except when it is a result of a judgment.

2. Subject to Article 24(1) a transfer shall not affect rights acquired by third parties before the date of transfer.

3. A transfer shall, to the extent to which it is verified by the papers referred to in the Implementing Regulations, only have effect *vis-à-vis* third parties after entry in the Register of Community Patents. Nevertheless, a transfer, before it is so entered, shall have effect *vis-à-vis* third parties who have acquired rights after the date of the transfer but who knew of the transfer at the date on which the rights were acquired.

ARTICLE 40

Enforcement proceedings

The courts and other authorities of the Contracting State determined in accordance with Article 38 shall have exclusive jurisdiction in respect of proceedings relating to judgments or other official acts in so far as they are being enforced against Community patents.

ARTICLE 41

Bankruptcy or like proceedings

1. Until such time as common rules for the Contracting States in this field enter into force, the only Contracting State in which a Community patent may be involved in bankruptcy or like proceedings shall be that in which such proceedings are opened first.

2. Paragraph 1 shall apply *mutatis mutandis* in the case of joint proprietorship of a Community patent to the share of the joint proprietor.

ARTICLE 42

Contractual licensing

1. A Community patent may be licensed in whole or in part for the whole or part of the territories in which it is effective. A licence may be exclusive or non-exclusive.

2. The rights conferred by the Community patent may be invoked against a licensee who contravenes any restriction in his licence which is covered by paragraph 1.

3. Article 39(2) and (3) shall apply *mutatis mutandis* to the grant or transfer of a licence in respect of a Community patent.

ARTICLE 43

Licences of right

1. Where the proprietor of a Community patent files a written statement with the European Patent Office that he is prepared to allow any person to use the invention as a licensee in return for appropriate compensation, the renewal fees for the Community patent which fall due after receipt of the statement shall be reduced; the amount of the reduction shall be fixed in the rules relating to fees. Where there is a complete change of proprietorship of the patent as a result of legal proceedings under Article 23, the statement shall be deemed withdrawn upon the entry of the name of the person entitled to the patent in the Register of Community Patents.

2. The statement may be withdrawn at any time upon written notification to this effect to the European Patent Office, provided that no-one has informed the proprietor of the patent of his intention to use the invention. Such withdrawal shall take effect from the date of its notification. The amount by which the renewal fees were reduced shall be paid within one month after withdrawal; Article 48(2) shall apply, but the six-month period shall start upon expiry of the above period.

3. The statement may not be filed while an exclusive licence is recorded in the Register of Community Patents or a request for the recording of such a licence is before the European Patent Office.

4. On the basis of the statement, any person shall be entitled to use the invention as a licensee under the conditions laid down in the Implementing Regulations. A licence so obtained shall, for the purposes of this Convention, be treated as a contractual licence.

5. On written request by one of the parties, a Revocation Division shall determine the appropriate compensation or review it if circumstances have arisen or become known which render the compensation determined obviously inappropriate. The provisions governing revocation proceedings shall apply *mutatis mutandis*, unless they are inapplicable as a result of the particular nature of revocation proceedings. The request shall not be deemed to have been made until such time as an administrative fee has been paid.

6. No request for recording an exclusive licence in the Register of Community Patents shall be admissible after the statement has been filed, unless it is withdrawn or deemed withdrawn.

ARTICLE 44

The European patent application as an object of property

1. Articles 38 to 42 shall apply *mutatis mutandis* to a European patent application in which the Contracting States are designated, the reference to the Register of Community Patents being understood as referring to the Register of European Patents provided for in the European Patent Convention.

2. The rights acquired by third parties in respect of a European patent application referred to in paragraph 1 shall continue to be effective with regard to the Community patent granted upon that application.

Chapter V. Compulsory licences in respect of a Community patent

ARTICLE 45

Compulsory licences

1. Any provisions in the law of a Contracting State for the grant of compulsory licences in respect of national patents shall be applicable to Community patents. The extent and effect of compulsory licences granted in respect of Community patents shall be restricted to the territory of the State concerned. Article 28 shall not apply.

2. Each Contracting State shall, at least in respect of compensation under a compulsory licence, provide for a final appeal to a court of law.

3. As far as practicable national authorities shall notify the European Patent Office of the grant of any compulsory licence in respect of a Community patent.

4. For the purposes of this Convention, the term "compulsory licences" shall be construed as including official licences and any right to use patented inventions in the public interest.

ARTICLE 46

Compulsory licences for lack or insufficiency of exploitation

A compulsory licence may not be granted in respect of a Community patent on the ground of lack or insufficiency of exploitation if the product covered by the patent, which is manufactured in a Contracting State, is put on the market in the territory of any other Contracting State, for which such a licence has been requested, in sufficient quantity to satisfy needs in the territory of that other Contracting State. This provision shall not apply to compulsory licences granted in the public interest.

ARTICLE 47

Compulsory licences in respect of dependent patents

Any provision in the law of a Contracting State for the grant of compulsory licences in respect of earlier patents in favour of subsequent dependent patents shall be applicable to the relationship between Community patents and national patents and to the relationship between Community patents themselves.

Part III. Renewal, Lapse, Limitation and Revocation of the Community Patent

Chapter I. Renewal and lapse

ARTICLE 48

Renewal fees

1. Renewal fees in respect of Community patents shall be paid to the European Patent Office in accordance with the Implementing Regulations. These fees shall be due in respect of the years following the year referred to in Article 86(4) of the European Patent Convention, provided that no renewal fees shall be due in respect of the first two years, calculated from the date of filing of the application.

2. When a renewal fee has not been paid on or before the due date, the fee may be validly paid within six months of that date, provided that the additional fee is paid at the same time.

3. Any renewal fee in respect of a Community patent falling due within two months after the publication of the mention of the grant of the European patent shall be deemed to have been validly paid if it is paid within that period. No additional fee shall be charged.

ARTICLE 49

Surrender

1. A Community patent may be surrendered only in its entirety.

2. Surrender must be declared in writing to the European Patent Office by the proprietor of the patent. It shall not have effect until it is entered in the Register of Community Patents.

3. Surrender will be entered in the Register of Community Patents only with the agreement of any third party who has a right *in rem* recorded in the Register or in respect of whom there is an entry in the Register pursuant to Article 23(4), first sentence. If a licence is recorded in the Register, surrender will be entered only if the proprietor of the patent proves that he has previously informed the licensee of his

829

intention to surrender; this entry will be made on expiry of the period laid down in the Implementing Regulations.

ARTICLE 50

Lapse

1. A Community patent shall lapse:

    (a) at the end of the term laid down in Article 63 of the European Patent Convention;
    (b) if the proprietor of the patent surrenders it in accordance with Article 49;
    (c) if a renewal fee and any additional fee have not been paid in due time.

2. The Community patent shall lapse on the date mentioned in Article 53(4) to the extent that it is not maintained.

3. The lapse of a patent for failure to pay a renewal fee and any additional fee within the due period shall be deemed to have occurred on the date on which the renewal fee was due.

4. The lapse of a Community patent shall, if necessary, be decided by the Patent Administration Division or, if proceedings in respect of that patent are pending before it, a Revocation Division.

Chapter II. Limitation procedure

ARTICLE 51

Request for limitation

1. At the request of the proprietor, a Community patent may be limited in the form of an amendment to the claims, the description or the drawings. Limitation in respect of one or some of the Contracting States may be requested only where Article 36(1) applies.

2. The request may not be filed during the period within which an opposition may be filed or while opposition proceedings or revocation proceedings are pending.

3. The request shall be filed in writing with the European Patent Office. It shall not be deemed to have been filed until the fee for limitation has been paid.

4. Article 49(3) shall apply *mutatis mutandis* to the filing of the request.

5. Where an application for revocation of the Community patent is filed during limitation proceedings, the Revocation Division shall stay the limitation proceedings until a final decision is given in respect of the application for revocation.

ARTICLE 52

Examination of the request

1. The Revocation Division shall examine whether the grounds for revocation mentioned in Article 56(1)(a) to (d) would prejudice the maintenance of the Community patent as amended.

2. In the examination of the request, which shall be conducted in accordance with the Implementing Regulations, the Revocation Division shall invite the proprietor of the patent, as often as necessary, to file observations, within a period to be fixed by the Revocation Division, on communications issued by itself.

3. If the proprietor of the patent fails to reply in due time to any invitation under paragraph 2, the request shall be deemed to be withdrawn.

ARTICLE 53

Rejection of the request or limitation of the Community patent

1. If, following the examination provided for in Article 52, the Revocation Division is of the opinion that the amendments are not acceptable, it shall reject the request.

2. If the Revocation Division is of the opinion that, taking into consideration the amendments made by the proprietor of the patent during the limitation proceedings, the grounds for revocation mentioned in Article 56 do not prejudice the maintenance of the Community patent, it shall decide to limit the patent accordingly, provided that:

    (a) it is established, in accordance with the Implementing Regulations, that the proprietor of the patent approves the text in which the Revocation Division intends to limit the patent;

    (b) a translation of all amendments to the patent specification in one of the official languages of each of the Contracting States which does not have as an official language the language of the proceedings is filed within the time limit prescribed in the Implementing Regulations;

    (c) the fee for the printing of a new specification is paid within the time limit prescribed in the Implementing Regulations.

3. If a translation is not filed in due time or if the fee for the printing of a new specification is not paid in due time, the request shall be deemed to be withdrawn, unless these acts are done and the additional fee is paid within a further period as prescribed in the Implementing Regulations.

4. The decision to limit a Community patent shall not take effect until the date on which the Community Patent Bulletin mentions the limitation.

ARTICLE 54

Publication of a new specification following limitation proceedings

If a Community patent is limited under Article 53(2) the European Patent Office shall, at the same time as it publishes the mention of the decision to limit, publish a new specification of the Community patent containing the description, the claims and any drawings, in the amended form. Article 30(3) and (4) shall apply *mutatis mutandis*.

Chapter III. Revocation procedure

ARTICLE 55

Application for revocation

1. Any person may file with the European Patent Office an application for revocation of a Community patent; however, in the case specified in Article 56(1)(e) the application may be filed only by a person entitled to be entered in the Register of Community Patents as the sole proprietor of the patent or by all the persons entitled to be entered as joint proprietors of it in accordance with Article 23 acting jointly.

2. The application may not be filed in the cases specified in Article 56(1)(a) to (d) during the period within which an opposition may be filed or while opposition proceedings are pending.

3. An application may be filed even if the Community patent has lapsed.

4. The application shall be filed in a written reasoned statement. It shall not be deemed to have been filed until the revocation fee has been paid.

5. Applicants shall be parties to the revocation proceedings as well as the proprietor of the patent.

6. If the applicant has neither his residence nor his principal place of business within the territory of one of the Contracting States, he shall, at the request of the proprietor of the patent, furnish security for the costs of the proceedings. The Revocation Division shall fix at a reasonable figure the amount of the security and the period within which it must be deposited. If the security is not deposited within the period specified, the application shall be deemed to be withdrawn.

ARTICLE 56

Grounds for revocation

1. An application for revocation of a Community patent may be filed only on the grounds that:

   (a) the subject-matter of the patent is not patentable within the terms of Articles 52 to 57 of the European Patent Convention;
   (b) the patent does not disclose the invention in a manner sufficiently clear and complete for it to be carried out by a person skilled in the art;
   (c) the subject-matter of the patent extends beyond the content of the European patent application as filed, or, if the patent was granted on a European divisional application or on a new European application filed in accordance with Article 61 of the European Patent Convention, beyond the content of the earlier application as filed;
   (d) the protection conferred by the patent has been extended;
   (e) the proprietor of the patent is not, having regard to a decision which has to be recognised in all the Contracting States, entitled under Article 60(1) of the European Patent Convention;
   (f) the subject-matter of the patent is not patentable within the terms of Article 36(1).

2. If the grounds for revocation affect the patent only partially, revocation shall be pronounced in the form of a corresponding limitation of the patent. The limitation may be effected in the form of an amendment to the claims, the description or the drawings.

3. In the case specified in paragraph 1(f), revocation shall be pronounced only in respect of the Contracting State in which the national patent application or national patent has been made public.

ARTICLE 57

Examination of the application

1. If the application for revocation of the Community patent is admissible, the Revocation Division shall examine whether the grounds for revocation mentioned in Article 56 prejudice the maintenance of the patent.

2. In the examination of the application, which shall be conducted in accordance with the Implementing Regulations, the Revocation Division shall invite the

parties, as often as necessary, to file observations, within a period to be fixed by the Revocation Division, on communications from another party or issued by itself.

ARTICLE 58

Revocation or maintenance of the Community patent

1. If the Revocation Division is of the opinion that the grounds for revocation mentioned in Article 56 prejudice the maintenance of the Community patent, it shall revoke the patent.

2. If the Revocation Division is of the opinon that the grounds for revocation mentioned in Article 56 do not prejudice the maintenance of the patent unamended, it shall reject the application.

3. If the Revocation Division is of the opinion that, taking into consideration the amendments made by the proprietor of the patent during the revocation proceedings, the grounds for revocation mentioned in Article 56 do not prejudice the maintenance of the patent, it shall decide to maintain the patent as amended, provided that:

(a) it is established, in accordance with the Implementing Regulations, that the proprietor of the patent approves the text in which the Revocation Division intends to maintain the patent;

(b) a translation of all amendments to the patent specification in one of the official languages of each of the Contracting States which does not have as an official language the language of the proceedings is filed within the time limit prescribed in the Implementing Regulations;

(c) the fee for the printing of a new specification is paid within the time limit prescribed in the Implementing Regulations.

4. If a translation is not filed in due time or if the fee for the printing of a new specification is not paid in due time, the patent shall be revoked, unless these acts are done and the additional fee is paid within a further period as prescribed in the Implementing Regulations.

ARTICLE 59

Publication of a new specification following revocation proceedings

If a Community patent is amended under Article 58(3) the European Patent Office shall, at the same time as it publishes the mention of the decision on the application for revocation, publish a new specification of the Community patent containing the description, the claims and any drawings, in the amended form. Article 30(3) and (4) shall apply *mutatis mutandis*.

ARTICLE 60

Costs

1. Each party to revocation proceedings shall meet the costs he has incurred unless a decision of a Revocation Division in accordance with the Implementing Regulations or of the Common Appeal Court in accordance with its Rules of Procedure, for reasons of equity, orders a different apportionment of costs incurred during taking of evidence or in oral proceedings. A decision on the apportionment

of the costs may also be taken on request when the application for revocation is withdrawn or when the Community patent lapses.

2. On request, the registrar of the Revocation Division shall fix the amount of the costs to be paid under a decision apportioning them. The fixing of the costs by the registry may be reviewed by a decision of the Revocation Division on a request filed within the period laid down in the Implementing Regulations.

3. Article 104(3) of the European Patent Convention shall apply *mutatis mutandis*.

Part IV. Appeals Procedure

ARTICLE 61

Appeal

1. An appeal shall lie from decisions of the Revocation Division and the Patent Administration Division.

2. Articles 106 to 109 of the European Patent Convention shall apply *mutatis mutandis* to this appeals procedure in so far as the Rules of Procedure of the Common Appeal Court or the Rules relating to Fees do not provide otherwise.

Part V. Common Provisions

ARTICLE 62

Common provisions governing procedure and representation

1. The provisions of Part VII, Chapters I and III, of the European Patent Convention, other than Article 124, shall apply *mutatis mutandis* to this Convention, subject to the following:

(a) Article 114(1) shall apply only to the Revocation Divisions;
(b) Article 116(2) and (3) shall apply only to the Patent Administration Division, and paragraph 4 shall apply only to the Revocation Divisions;
(c) Article 122 shall also apply to all other parties to proceedings before the special departments;
(d) Article 123(3) shall apply to limitation and revocation proceedings before the Revocation Divisions;
(e) the term "Contracting States" shall be understood as meaning the States parties to this Convention.

2. Notwithstanding paragraph 1(e), a person whose name appears on the list of professional representatives maintained by the European Patent Office who is not a national of one of the States parties to this Convention or does not have his place of business or employment within the territory of one of these States, shall be entitled to act as a professional representative for a party to proceedings relating to a Community patent before the special departments, provided that:

(a) he was, according to the Register of European Patents, the person last authorised to act as the professional representative for the same party or his predecessor in title in proceedings pursuant to the European Patent

Convention which relate to this Community patent or to the European patent application on which it is based; and

(b) the State of which he is a national or within the territory of which he has his place of business or employment applies rules, as regards representation before the central industrial property office of the State concerned, which comply, in respect of reciprocity, with such conditions as the Select Committee of the Administrative Council may prescribe.

ARTICLE 63

Register of Community Patents

The European Patent Office shall keep a register, to be known as the Register of Community Patents, which shall contain those particulars the registration of which is provided for by this Convention. The Register shall be open to public inspection.

ARTICLE 64

Community Patent Bulletin

The European Patent Office shall periodically publish a Community Patent Bulletin containing entries made in the Register of Community Patents, as well as other particulars, the publication of which is prescribed by this Convention.

ARTICLE 65

Information to the public or official authorities

Articles 128(4) and 130 to 132 of the European Patent Convention shall apply *mutatis mutandis*, the term "Contracting States" being understood as meaning the States parties to this Convention.

Part VI. Jurisdiction and Procedure in Actions Relating to Community Patents other than those Governed by the Protocol on Litigation

Chapter I. Jurisdiction and enforcement

ARTICLE 66

General provisions

Unless otherwise specified in this Convention, the Convention on Jurisdiction and Enforcement of Judgments in Civil and Commercial Matters, signed at Brussels on 27 September 1968, as amended by the Conventions on the Accession to that Convention of the States acceding to the European Communities, the whole of which Convention and of which Conventions of Accession are hereinafter referred to as the "Convention on Jurisdiction and Enforcement," shall apply to actions relating to Community patents, other than those to which the Protocol on Litigation applies, and to decisions given in respect of such actions.

ARTICLE 67

Jurisdiction of national courts concerning actions relating to Community patents

The following courts shall have exclusive jurisdiction:

(a) in actions relating to compulsory licences in respect of a Community patent, the courts of the Contracting State the national law of which is applicable to the licence;

(b) in actions relating to the right to a patent in which an employer and an employee are in dispute, the courts of the Contracting State under whose law the right to a European patent is determined in accordance with Article 60(1), second sentence, of the European Patent Convention. Any agreement conferring jurisdiction shall be valid only in so far as the national law governing the contract of employment allows the agreement in question.

ARTICLE 68

Supplementary provisions on jurisdiction

1. Within the Contracting State whose courts have jurisdiction under Articles 66 and 67, those courts shall have jurisdiction which would have jurisdiction *ratione loci* and *ratione materiae* in the case of actions relating to a national patent granted in that State.

2. Articles 66 and 67 shall apply to actions relating to a European patent application in which the Contracting States are designated, except in so far as the right to the grant of a European patent is claimed.

3. Actions relating to a Community patent for which no court has jurisdiction under Articles 66 and 67 and paragraphs 1 and 2 may be heard before the courts of the Federal Republic of Germany.

ARTICLE 69

Supplementary provisions on recognition and enforcement

1. Article 27(3) and (4) of the Convention on Jurisdiction and Enforcement shall not apply to decisions relating to the right to the Community patent.

2. In the case of irreconcilable decisions relating to the right to a Community patent given in proceedings between the same parties, only the decision of the court first seised of the matter shall be recognised. Neither party may invoke any other decision even in the Contracting State in which it was given.

ARTICLE 70

National authorities

For actions relating to the right to a Community patent or to compulsory licences in respect of a Community patent the term "courts" in this Convention and the

Convention on Jurisdiction and Enforcement shall include authorities which, under the national law of a Contracting State, have jurisdiction to decide such actions relating to a national patent granted in that State. The Contracting State concerned shall notify the European Patent Office of any authority on which such jurisdiction is conferred and the European Patent Office shall inform the other Contracting States accordingly.

Chapter II. Procedure

ARTICLE 71

Rules of procedure

Unless otherwise specified in this Convention, the actions referred to in Articles 66 to 68 shall be subject to the national rules of procedure governing the same type of action relating to a national patent.

ARTICLE 72

Obligation of the national court

A national court which is dealing with an action relating to a Community patent, other than the actions governed by the Protocol on Litigation, shall treat the patent as valid.

ARTICLE 73

Stay of proceedings

1. If the decision in an action before a national court relating to a European patent application which may result in the grant of a Community patent, other than an action governed by the Protocol on Litigation, depends upon the patentability of the invention, that decision may be given only after the European Patent Office has granted a Community patent or refused the European patent application. Paragraph 2 shall apply after the grant of the Community patent.
2. Where an opposition has been filed or a request for the limitation or an application for the revocation of a Community patent has been made, the national court may, at the request of one of the parties and after hearing the other parties, stay proceedings relating to the Community patent, in so far as its decision depends upon validity. At the request of one of the parties the court shall instruct that the documentary evidence of the opposition, limitation or revocation proceedings be communicated to it, in order to give a ruling on the request for a stay of proceedings.

ARTICLE 74

Penal sanctions for infringement

The national penal provisions in the matter of infringement shall be applicable in the case of infringement of a Community patent, to the extent that like acts of infringement would be punishable if they similarly affected a national patent.

Part VII. Impact on National Law

ARTICLE 75

Prohibition of simultaneous protection

1. Where a national patent granted in a Contracting State relates to an invention for which a Community patent has been granted to the same inventor or to his successor in title with the same date of filing, or, if priority has been claimed, with the same date of priority, that national patent shall be ineffective to the extent that it covers the same invention as the Community patent, from the date on which:

(a) the period for filing an opposition to the Community patent has expired without any opposition being filed;
(b) the opposition proceedings are concluded with a decision to maintain the Community patent; or
(c) the national patent is granted, where this date is subsequent to the date referred to in subparagraph (a) or (b), as the case may be.

2. The subsequent lapse or revocation of the Community patent shall not affect the provisions of paragraph 1.

3. Each Contracting State may prescribe the procedure whereby the loss of effect of the national patent is determined and, where appropriate, the extent of that loss. It may also prescribe that the loss of effect shall apply as from the outset.

4. Prior to the date applicable under paragraph 1, simultaneous protection by a Community patent or a European patent application and a national patent or a national patent application shall exist unless any Contracting State provides otherwise.

ARTICLE 76

Exhaustion of the rights conferred by a national patent

1. The rights conferred by a national patent in a Contracting State shall not extend to acts concerning a product covered by that patent which are done within the territory of that Contracting State after that product has been put on the market in any Contracting State by the proprietor of the patent or with his express consent, unless there are grounds which, under Community law, would justify the extension to such acts of the rights conferred by the patent.

2. Paragraph 1 shall also apply with regard to a product put on the market by the proprietor of a national patent, granted for the same invention in another Contracting State, who has economic connections with the proprietor of the patent referred to in paragraph 1. For the purpose of this paragraph, two persons shall be deemed to have economic connections where one of them is in a position to exert a decisive influence on the other, directly or indirectly, with regard to the exploitation of a patent, or where a third party is in a position to exercise such an influence on both persons.

3. The preceding paragraph shall not apply in the case of a product put on the market under a compulsory licence.

ARTICLE 77

Compulsory licences in respect of national patents

Article 46 shall apply *mutatis mutandis* to the grant of compulsory licences for lack of insufficiency of exploitation of a national patent.

ARTICLE 78

Effect of unpublished national applications or patents

1. Where Article 36(2) applies, the Community patent shall be ineffective in the Contracting State concerned to the extent that it covers the same invention as the national patent application or patent.
2. The procedure confirming that, pursuant to paragraph 1, the Community patent is ineffective in the Contracting State shall, in that State, be that according to which, if the Community patent had been a national patent, it could have been revoked or made ineffective.

ARTICLE 79

National utility models and utility certificates

1. Articles 36, 75 and 76 shall apply to utility models and utility certificates and to applications for utility models and utility certificates in the Contracting States whose laws make provision for such models or certificates.
2. If a Contracting State provides in its law that a person may not exercise the rights conferred by a patent so long as there exists a utility model having an earlier date of filing or, where priority has been claimed an earlier date of priority, the same shall, notwithstanding paragraph 1, apply also to the Community patent in that State.

Part VIII. Transitional Provisions

ARTICLE 80

Application of the Convention on Jurisdiction and Enforcement

The provisions of the Convention on Jurisdiction and Enforcement rendered applicable by the preceding Articles shall not have effect in respect of any Contracting State for which that convention has not yet entered into force until such entry into force.

ARTICLE 81

Option between a Community patent and a European patent

1. This Convention shall, subject to paragraph 3, not apply to a European patent application filed during a transitional period nor to any resulting European patent provided that, within the time limit prescribed in the Implementing Regulations, the applicant files with the European Patent Office a statement indicating that he does not wish to obtain a Community patent and identifying the Contracting States the designation of which is to be maintained. The statement shall not be deemed to be filed until after the prescribed fees have been paid. The statement may not be withdrawn.
2. Article 54(3) and (4) of the European Patent Convention shall apply where a European patent application in which the Contracting States are designated or a

Community patent has a date of filing or, where priority has been claimed, a date of priority later than that of a European patent application in which one or some of the Contracting States are designated. In the event of limitation or revocation of the Community patent on this ground, limitation or revocation shall be pronounced only in respect of the Contracting States designated in the earlier European patent application as published.

3. Articles 75 to 77 and 79 shall apply to a European patent as referred to in paragraph 1, the references in Articles 75 and 79 to a Community patent and the references in Articles 76 and 77 to a national patent being understood as references to such a European patent.

4. The transitional period referred to in paragraph 1 may be terminated by decision of the Council of the European Communities, acting on a proposal from the Commission of the European Communities or from a Contracting State.

5. The decision referred to in paragraph 4 shall require unanimity.

ARTICLE 82

Subsequent choice of a Community patent

This Convention shall apply to a European patent granted in respect of a European patent application in which all the Contracting States are designated and which is filed prior to the entry into force of this Convention, provided that prior to the expiry of the time limit mentioned in Article 97(2)(b) of the European Patent Convention the applicant files with the European Patent Office a written statement that he wishes to obtain a Community patent.

ARTICLE 83

Reservation in respect of compulsory licences

1. Any signatory State may, at the time of signature or when depositing its instrument of ratification, declare that it reserves the right to provide that Articles 46 and 77 shall not apply within its territory to Community patents or to European patents granted for, or to national patents granted by, that State.

2. Any reservation made by a signatory State under paragraph 1 shall have effect until the end of the 10th year at the latest after the entry into force of the Agreement relating to Community Patents. However, the Council of the European Communities may, acting by a qualified majority on a proposal from a signatory State, extend the period in respect of a signatory State making such a reservation by not more than five years. This majority shall be that specified in the second indent of the second subparagraph of Article 148(2) of the Treaty establishing the European Economic Community.

3. Any reservation made under paragraph 1 shall cease to apply when common rules on the granting of compulsory licences in respect of Community patents have become operative.

4. Any signatory State that has made a reservation under paragraph 1 may withdraw it at any time. Such withdrawal shall be made by notification addressed to the Secretary-General of the Council of the European Communities and shall take effect one month from the date of receipt of such notification.

5. Termination of the effect of the reservation shall not affect compulsory licences granted before the date on which the reservation ceased to have effect.

ARTICLE 84

Other transitional provisions

1. Articles 159, 161 and 163 of the European Patent Convention shall apply *mutatis mutandis*, subject to the following:

(a) the first meeting of the Select Committee of the Administrative Council shall be on the invitation of the Secretary-General of the Council of the European Communities;

(b) the term "Contracting State" shall be understood as meaning the States parties to this Convention.

2. Notwithstanding paragraph 1(b), Article 62(2) shall apply.

Part IX. Final Provisions

ARTICLE 85

Implementing Regulations

1. The Implementing Regulations shall be an integral part of this Convention.
2. In the case of conflict between the provisions of this Convention and those of the Implementing Regulations, the provisions of this Convention shall prevail.

Implementing Regulations to the Convention for the European Patent for the Common Market

Part I. Implementing Regulations to Part I of the Convention

Chapter I. Organisation of the special departments

RULE 1

Allocation of duties to the departments of the first instance

1. The President of the European Patent Office shall determine the number of Revocation Divisions. He shall allocate duties to these departments by reference to the international classification.

2. The President of the European Patent Office shall, with the agreement of the Select Committee of the Administrative Council, determine in detail the duties for which the Patent Administration Division is responsible pursuant to Article 7.

3. In addition to the responsibilities vested in them under the Convention, the President of the European Patent Office may allocate further duties to the Patent Administration Division and the Revocation Divisions.

4. The President of the European Patent Office may entrust to employees who are not technically or legally qualified members the execution of individual duties falling to the Patent Administration Division or the Revocation Divisions, and involving no technical or legal difficulties.

RULE 2

Administrative structure of the special departments

1. The Revocation Divisions may be grouped together administratively with the Examining Divisions and Opposition Divisions so as to form directorates, or may form a directorate together with the Patent Administration Division.
2. The special departments may be grouped together administratively with other departments of the European Patent Office so as to form Directorates-General or may form a separate Directorate-General; in the latter case, Rule 12(3) of the Implementing Regulations to the European Patent Covention shall apply, but the appointment of a vice-president to the Directorate-General shall be decided upon by the Select Committee of the Administrative Council.

Chapter II. Languages of the special departments

RULE 3

Language of the proceedings

1. Rules 1 to 3, 5, 6(2) and 7 of the Implementing Regulations to the European Patent Convention shall apply *mutatis mutandis* to proceedings before the special departments.
2. A reduction in the limitation fee, revocation fee or appeal fee shall be allowed the proprietor of a patent or an applicant for revocation who avails himself of the options provided for in Article 10(4). The reduction shall be fixed in the Rules relating to Fees at a percentage of the total of the fees.

Part II. Implementing Regulations to Part II of the Convention

RULE 4

Suspension of proceedings

Rule 13 of the Implementing Regulations to the European Patent Convention shall apply *mutatis mutandis* to limitation proceedings and revocation proceedings.

RULE 5

Entries regarding claims to the right to Community patents

The entries referred to in Article 23(4) shall be made:

(a) at the request of the registrar of the court before which the proceedings are instituted;

(b) at the request of the claimant or any other interested person.

Rule 6

Filing of translations and payment of fees in examination or opposition proceedings

1. When sending the invitation referred to in Rule 51(6) of the Implementing Regulations to the European Patent Convention, the European Patent Office shall also invite the applicant for the patent to file, within the period set by it, the translations prescribed in Article 29(1) and to pay, within the same period, the fee for the publication of the translations of the claims.

2. When sending the invitation referred to in Rule 58(5) of the Implementing Regulations to the European Patent Convention, the European Patent Office shall also invite the proprietor of the patent to file, within the period referred to in the said paragraph, the translations prescribed in Article 29(2) and to pay the fee for the publication of the translations of the claims.

3. The period for filing the translations prescribed in Article 30(1) and (2) shall be three months from the date of publication in the Community Patent Bulletin of the mention of the grant of the Community patent or, as the case may be, of the decision on the maintenance of the Community patent in amended form.

4. If the acts required by paragraph 2 are not performed in due time they may still be validly performed within two months of notification of the communication pointing out the failure to observe the time limit, provided that within this two-month period an additional fee in accordance with the Rules relating to Fees is paid.

Rule 7

Forwarding of translations

The European Patent Office shall enter in the Register of Community Patents the date on which the translations prescribed in Article 30 are filed. Copies of the translations shall be forwarded to the central industrial property offices of the Contracting States concerned by post within the three days following the expiry of the period laid down in Rule 6(3).

Rule 8

Revision of the translation

The corrected translation provided for in Article 29(6) shall not have any legal effect until the fee for its publication has been paid.

Rule 9

Registering transfers, licences and other rights

1. Rules 20 to 22 of the Implementing Regulations to the European Patent Convention shall apply *mutatis mutandis* to entries made in the Register of Community Patents.

2. The request provided for in Article 24(2) must, in the case of subparagraph (a), be made within two months, or in the case of subparagraph (b), within four months, of receipt of notification from the European Patent Office that the name of a new proprietor has been entered in the Register of Community Patents.

3. Where a Community patent is involved in bankruptcy or like proceedings, an entry to this effect shall be made in the Register of Community Patents on request of the competent national authority. The entry shall not incur a fee.

4. The entry referred to in paragraph 3 shall be deleted at the request of the competent national authority. The request shall not incur a fee.

5. Where a European patent application in which the Contracting States are designated is involved in bankruptcy or like proceedings, paragraphs 3 and 4 shall apply *mutatis mutandis* but the reference to the Register of Community Patents shall be understood as being a reference to the Register of European Patents provided for in the European Patent Convention.

RULE 10

Licences of right

1. Any person who wishes to use the invention after a statement provided for in Article 43(1) has been filed, shall declare his intention to the proprietor of the patent by registered letter. The declaration shall be deemed to have been made one week after posting of the registered letter. A copy of this declaration, stating the date upon which the declaration was posted, shall be sent to the European Patent Office. Failing this, the European Patent Office shall, in the event of withdrawal of the statement, consider the declaration not to have been made.

2. The declaration shall state how the invention is to be used. After the declaration has been made, the person making it shall be entitled to use the invention in the way he has stated.

3. The licensee shall be obliged at the end of every quarter of a calendar year to report to the proprietor of the patent on the use made thereof and to pay the compensation therefor. If this obligation is not complied with, the proprietor of the patent may lay down a further suitable time limit for this purpose. If the time limit is not complied with the licence shall expire.

4. A request for review of the compensation determined by the Revocation Division may be made only after the expiry of one year from the last determination of compensation.

Part III. Implementing Regulations to Part III of the Convention

Chapter I. Renewal fees

RULE 11

Payment of renewal fees

1. Rule 37(1) and (2) of the Implementing Regulations to the European Patent Convention shall apply to the payment of renewal fees for Community patents.

2. An additional fee shall be deemed to have been paid at the same time as the renewal fee within the meaning of Article 48(2) if it is paid within the period laid down in that provision.

RULE 12

Period for the entry of surrender

The period referred to in Article 49(3) shall be three months from the date on which the proprietor of the patent has proved to the European Patent Office that he has informed the licensee of his intention to surrender. If, before expiry of the period, the proprietor of the patent proves to the European Patent Office that the licensee agrees to the surrender, it may be entered immediately.

Chapter II. Limitation procedure

RULE 13

Period for the filing of the request for limitation

Rule 12 shall apply *mutatis mutandis* to the filing of the request for limitation of the Community patent.

RULE 14

Content of the request for limitation

The request for limitation of a Community patent shall contain:

(a) the number of the Community patent which it is sought to limit, the name of the proprietor and the title of the invention;
(b) the amendments sought;
(c) if the proprietor of the patent has appointed a representative, his name and the address of his place of business in accordance with Rule 26(2)(c) of the Implementing Regulations to the European Patent Convention.

RULE 15

Rejection of the request for limitation as inadmissible

If the Revocation Division notes that the request for limitation of a Community patent does not comply with Article 51(1) and (3) and Rule 14, it shall communicate this to the proprietor of the patent and shall invite him to remedy the deficiencies noted within such a period as it may specify. If the request for limitation is not corrected in good time, the Revocation Division shall reject it as inadmissible.

RULE 16

Examination of the request for limitation

1. If the request for limitation of the Community patent is admissible, the proprietor of the patent shall, in any communication pursuant to Article 52(2), where appropriate, be invited to file the description, claims and drawings in amended form.
2. Where necessary, any communication pursuant to Article 52(2) shall contain a

reasoned statement. Where appropriate, this statement shall cover all the grounds against the limitation of the patent.

3. Before the Revocation Division decides on the limitation of the patent, it shall inform the proprietor of the extent to which it intends to limit the patent, and shall request him to pay within three months the fee for printing a new patent specification and to file the translation prescribed in Article 53(2)(b) within the same period. If within that period the proprietor has communicated his disapproval of the patent being limited to this extent, the communication of the Revocation Division shall be deemed not to have been made, and the limitation proceedings shall be resumed.

4. The further period referred to in Article 53(3) shall be two months.

5. The decision to limit the patent shall state the text of the patent as limited.

RULE 17

Resumption of limitation proceedings

Where limitation proceedings have been stayed because of revocation proceedings which result in a decision under Article 58(2) or (3), the Revocation Division, after the publication of the mention of such decision, shall communicate to the proprietor of the patent that the proceedings will be resumed after notification of this communication to the proprietor. Rule 13(5) of the Implementing Regulations to the European Patent Convention shall apply *mutatis mutandis*.

RULE 18

Different claims, description and drawings in the case of limitation

Where it is decided to limit a Community patent in respect of one or some of the Contracting States, the Community patent may, where appropriate, contain, for that State or States, claims and, if the Revocation Division considers it necessary, a description and drawings which are different from those for the other Contracting States.

RULE 19

Form of the new specification following limitation proceedings

The President of the European Patent Office shall prescribe the form of the publication of the new specification of the Community patent and the data which are to be included.

Chapter III. Revocation procedure

RULE 20

Content of the application for revocation

An application for revocation of a Community patent shall contain:

(a) the name and address of the applicant for revocation and the State in which his residence or principal place of business is located, in accordance with Rule 26(2)(c) of the Implementing Regulations to the European Patent Convention;

(b) the number of the patent in respect of which revocation is applied for, the name of the proprietor and the title of the invention;

(c) a statement of the extent to which revocation is applied for and of the grounds on which the application is based as well as an indication of the facts, evidence and arguments presented in support of these grounds;

(d) if the applicant has appointed a representative, his name and the address of his place of business, in accordance with Rule 26(2)(c) of the Implementing Regulations to the European Patent Convention.

RULE 21

Security for the costs of proceedings

The security for the costs of the proceedings shall be deposited in a currency in which fees may be paid. It must be deposited with a financial or banking establishment included in the list drawn up by the President of the European Patent Office. The national law of the Contracting State in which the establishment has its place of business shall apply to any such security.

RULE 22

Rejection of the application for revocation as inadmissible

1. The Revocation Division shall communicate the application for revocation to the proprietor of the patent who may comment on its admissibility within one month.

2. If the Revocation Division notes that the application for revocation does not comply with Article 55(1) and (4) and Rule 20, as well as Rule 3 of these Implementing Regulations in conjunction with Rule 1(1) of the Implementing Regulations to the European Patent Convention, it shall communicate this to the proprietor and to the applicant and shall invite the applicant to remedy the deficiencies noted within such period as it may specify. If the application for revocation is not corrected in good time, the Revocation Division shall reject it as inadmissible.

3. Any decision to reject an application for revocation as inadmissible shall be communicated to the proprietor of the patent.

RULE 23

Preparation of the examination of the application for revocation

1. If the application for revocation is admissible, the Revocation Division shall invite the proprietor of the patent to file his observations and to file amendments, where appropriate, to the description, claims and drawings within a period to be fixed by the Revocation Division.

2. The observations and any amendments filed by the proprietor of the patent shall be communicated to the applicant who shall be invited by the Revocation Division, if it considers it expedient, to reply within a period to be fixed by the Revocation Division.

RULE 24

Examination of the application for revocation

1. All communications issued pursuant to Article 57(2) and all replies thereto shall be communicated to all parties.

2. In any communication from the Revocation Division to the proprietor of the patent pursuant to Article 57(2), he shall, where appropriate, be invited to file the description, claims and drawings in amended form.

3. Where necessary, any communication from the Revocation Division to the proprietor of the patent pursuant to Article 57(2) shall contain a reasoned statement. Where appropriate, this statement shall cover all the grounds against the maintenance of the Community patent.

4. Before the Revocation Division decides on the maintenance of the patent in the amended form, it shall inform the parties that it intends to maintain the patent as amended and shall invite them to state their observations within a period of one month if they disapprove of the text in which it is intended to maintain the patent.

5. If disapproval of the text communicated by the Revocation Division is expressed, examination of the revocation may be continued; otherwise, the Revocation Division shall, on expiry of the period referred to in paragraph 4, request the proprietor of the patent to pay within three months the fee for the printing of a new specification and to file the translations prescribed in Article 58(3)(b) within the same period.

6. The further period referred to in Article 58(4) shall be two months.

7. The decision to maintain the patent as amended shall state which text of the patent forms the basis for the maintenance thereof.

RULE 25

Joint processing of applications for revocation

1. The Revocation Division may order that two or more applications for revocation pending before it and relating to the same Community patent be dealt with jointly in order to carry out a joint investigation and take a joint decision.

2. The Revocation Division may rescind an order given pursuant to paragraph 1.

RULE 26

Different claims, description and drawings in the case of revocation

Where revocation of a Community patent is pronounced in respect of one or more of the Contracting States, Rule 18 shall apply *mutatis mutandis*.

RULE 27

Form of the new specification following revocation proceedings

Rule 19 shall apply to the new specification of the Community patent referred to in Article 59.

Other provisions applicable to revocation proceedings

Rules 59, 60 and 63 of the Implementing Regulations to the European Patent Convention shall apply *mutatis mutandis* to requests for documents, continuation of revocation proceedings by the European Patent Office of its own motion and costs in revocation proceedings.

Part IV. Implementing Regulations to Part V of the Convention

RULE 29

Entries in the Register of Community Patents

1. Rule 92(1)(a) to (l), (o), (q) to (u) and (w), (2) and (3) of the Implementing Regulations to the European Patent Convention shall apply *mutatis mutandis* to the Register of Community Patents.
2. The Register of Community Patents shall also contain the following entries:

  (a) date of lapse of the Community patent in the cases provided for in Article 50(1)(b) and (c);
  (b) date of filing of the statement provided for in Article 43;
  (c) date of receipt of a request for limitation of the Community patent;
  (d) date and purport of the decision on the request for limitation of the Community patent;
  (e) date of receipt of an application for revocation of the Community patent;
  (f) date and purport of the decision on the application for revocation of the Community patent;
  (g) particulars of matters referred to in Article 23(4);
  (h) a record of the information communicated to the European Patent Office concerning proceedings under the Protocol on Litigation.

RULE 30

Additional publications by the European Patent Office

The President of the European Patent Office shall determine in what form the translations filed pursuant to the Convention by the applicant for or proprietor of a patent and, where appropriate, corrected translations, shall be published and whether particulars of such translations and corrected translations should be entered in the Community Patent Bulletin.

RULE 31

Other common provisions

Rules 36 and 106 and the provisions of Part VII of the Implementing Regulations to the European Patent Convention, with the exception of Rules 85(3), 86, 87, 92 and 96, shall apply *mutatis mutandis* subject to the following:

(a) Rule 69 shall not apply to decisions on requests for limitation or on applications for revocation of the Community patent;
(b) the Select Committee of the Administrative Council shall determine the details of the application of Rule 74(2) and (3);
(c) the term "Contracting States" shall be understood as meaning the States parties to this Convention.

Part V. Implementing Regulations to Part VIII of the Convention

RULE 32

Option between a Community patent and a European patent

1. The statement referred to in Article 81(1) must be filed, and the fees paid, before or when the applicant approves, in accordance with Rule 51(4) of the Implementing Regulations to the European Patent Convention, the text in which the patent is to be granted.
2. The prescribed fees referred to in Article 81(1) shall consist of:

(a) an additional fee in accordance with the Rules relating to Fees; and
(b) if the designation of more than three Contracting States is to be maintained, the currently prescribed designation fee for each additional Contracting State over and above the first three.

Protocol on the Settlement of Litigation Concerning the Infringement and Validity of Community Patents

(Protocol on Litigation)

Part I. General Provisions

ARTICLE 1

Community patent courts

1. The Contracting States shall designate in their territories as limited a number as possible of national courts and tribunals of first and second instance, hereinafter referred to as "Community patent courts," which shall perform the functions assigned to them by this Protocol.
2. The names of the Community patent courts and their territorial jurisdiction are specified in the Annex to this Protocol. However, as regards the Kingdom of Spain and the Portuguese Republic, the names of these courts and their territorial jurisdiction shall be notified to the Secretary-General of the Council of the European Communities at the latest at the time of ratification of the Agreement relating to Community Patents.

3. Any change in the number, the names or territorial jurisdiction of the courts shall be notified by the Contracting State concerned to the Secretary-General of the Council of the European Communities.

ARTICLE 2

Common Appeal Court

1. A Community patent appeal court, common to the Contracting States, hereinafter referred to as "the Common Appeal Court," shall be established by the present Protocol. The Common Appeal Court shall perform the functions assigned to it by this Protocol.

2. The seat of the Common Appeal Court shall be determined by common accord of the Governments of the signatory States.

ARTICLE 3

Legal status

1. The Common Appeal Court shall have legal personality.

2. In each of the Contracting States, the Common Appeal Court shall enjoy the most extensive legal capacity accorded to legal persons under the national law of that State; it may in particular acquire or dispose of movable and immovable property and may be a party to legal proceedings.

3. The President of the Common Appeal Court shall represent the Common Appeal Court.

ARTICLE 4

Privileges and immunities

The Protocol on Privileges and Immunities of the Common Appeal Court shall define the conditions under which the Common Appeal Court, its judges, the members of the Administrative Committee, the officials and other servants of the Common Appeal Court and such other persons specified in that Protocol as take part in the work of the Common Appeal Court shall enjoy, in the territory of each Contracting State, the privileges and immunities necessary for the performance of their duties.

ARTICLE 5

Plenum and registry

1. The Common Appeal Court shall be constituted by the necessary number of judges to be determined by the Administrative Committee, acting unanimously, after consulting the Common Appeal Court; this number shall be at least equal to the number of Contracting States.

2. The Common Appeal Court shall sit in plenary session. It may, however, form chambers, each consisting of the number of judges set out in its Rules of Procedure.

3. The Common Appeal Court shall have a registry.

ARTICLE 6

Appointment of the judges of the Common Appeal Court

1. The Judges of the Common Appeal Court shall be chosen from persons who possess the qualifications required for appointment to judicial office in their respective State and experience in patent law; they shall be appointed by common accord of the representatives of the Governments of the Contracting States, for a term of six years.
2. Retiring judges shall be eligible for reappointment.

ARTICLE 7

President of the Common Appeal Court

1. The Judges shall elect the President of the Common Appeal Court from among their number for a term of three years. He may be re-elected.
2. If the President is absent or indisposed, another member of the Court shall take his place, in order of seniority.

ARTICLE 8

Management

The Common Appeal Court shall be managed by its President. For the administration of the Common Appeal Court, its financial management and its accounts, the President shall be responsible to the Administrative Committee.

ARTICLE 9

Administrative Committee

1. The Administrative Committee shall be composed of the representatives of the Contracting States, the representative of the Commission of the European Communities and their alternate representatives. Each Contracting State and the Commission shall be entitled to appoint one representative and one alternate representative to the Administrative Committee. Where appropriate, the President of the Common Appeal Court shall take part in the deliberations of the Administrative Committee.
2. Articles 11(2), 12, 13, 14(1), (3), (4) and (5), 16(2), 17, 18 and 19 of the Community Patent Convention shall apply *mutatis mutandis* to the Administrative Committee.

ARTICLE 10

Cover of expenditure

1. Expenditure of the Common Appeal Court shall be covered:

   (a) by the Common Appeal Court's own resources;
   (b) by financial contributions from the Contracting States, the amount of which shall be determined in accordance with the scale resulting from Article 20 of the Community Patent Convention.

2. Each Contracting State may ask the European Patent Office to pay to the Common Appeal Court the contribution which that State is bound to make pursuant to paragraph 1(b) by drawing from the revenue due to that State pursuant to Article 20(2) of the Community Patent Convention.

3. The provisions laid down in paragraph 1 shall also be included in the examination of the system of financing for the special departments of the European Patent Office provided for in Article 20(6) of the Community Patent Convention. When this examination has been concluded this Article may also be amended by a unanimous decision of the Council of the European Communities acting on a proposal by the Commission.

4. Articles 42 to 48 of the European Patent Convention shall apply to the Common Appeal Court, the Administrative Committee acting in place of the Administrative Council of the European Patent Organization and the President of the Common Appeal Court acting in place of the President of the European Patent Office.

5. The income and expenditure account and a balance sheet of the Common Appeal Court shall be examined by the Court of Auditors of the European Communities. The audit, which shall be based on vouchers and shall take place, if necessary, on the spot, shall ascertain that all income has been received and all expenditure effected in a lawful and proper manner and that the financial management is sound. The Court of Auditors shall draw up a report after the end of each accounting period.

6. The President of the Common Appeal Court shall annually submit to the Administrative Committee the accounts of the preceding accounting period in respect of the budget and the balance sheet showing the assets and liabilities of the Common Appeal Court together with the report of the Court of Auditors.

7. The Administrative Committee shall approve the annual accounts together with the report of the Court of Auditors and shall give the President of the Common Appeal Court a discharge in respect of the implementation of the budget.

ARTICLE 11

Remuneration of the members of the Common Appeal Court and Staff Regulations

1. The Administrative Committee shall determine the salaries, allowances and pensions of the President and judges of the Common Appeal Court. It shall also determine any payment to be made instead of remuneration.

2. The Administrative Committee shall lay down the Staff Regulations of the officials of the Common Appeal Court and the Conditions of Employment of other servants of the Common Appeal Court.

3. A majority of three-quarters of the votes of the Contracting States represented and voting shall be required for the decisions which the Administrative Committee is empowered to take under this Article. Abstentions shall not be considered as votes.

ARTICLE 12

Rules of Procedure of the Common Appeal Court

The Common Appeal Court shall adopt its rules of Procedure which shall, *inter alia*, lay down the language arrangements of the Court. The Rules of Procedure shall be subject to the unanimous approval of the Administrative Committee.

Part II. Provisions on International Jurisdiction and Enforcement

ARTICLE 13

Application of the Convention on Jurisdiction and Enforcement

1. Unless otherwise specified in this Protocol, the Convention on Jurisdiction and the Enforcement of Judgments in Civil and Commercial Matters, signed in Brussels on 27 September 1968, as amended by the Conventions on the Accession to that Convention of the States acceding to the European Communities, the whole of which Convention and of which Conventions of Accession are hereinafter referred to as "the Convention on Jurisdiction and Enforcement," shall apply to proceedings governed by this Protocol.

2. Articles 2, 4, 5(1), (3), (4), (5) and 24 of the Convention on Jurisdiction and Enforcement shall not apply to proceedings governed by this Protocol. Articles 17 and 18 of that Convention shall apply subject to the limitations in Article 14(4) of this Protocol.

3. For the purpose of applying the Convention on Jurisdiction and Enforcement to proceedings governed by this Protocol, the provisions of Title II of that Convention which are applicable to persons domiciled in a Contracting State shall also be applicable to persons who do not have a domicile in any Contracting State but have an establishment therein.

ARTICLE 14

Jurisdiction

1. Subject to the provisions of this Protocol as well as to any provisions of the Convention on Jurisdiction and Enforcement applicable by virtue of Article 13, proceedings governed by this Protocol shall be brought in the courts of the Contracting State in which the defendant is domiciled or, if he is not domiciled in any of the Contracting States, in which he has an establishment.

2. If the defendant neither is domiciled nor has an establishment in any of the Contracting States, such proceedings shall be brought in the courts of the Contracting State in which the plaintiff is domiciled or, if he is not domiciled in any of the Contracting States, in which he has an establishment.

3. If neither the defendant nor the plaintiff is so domiciled or has such an establishment, such proceedings shall be brought in the courts of the Contracting State where the Common Appeal Court has its seat.

4. Notwithstanding the provisions of paragraphs 1 to 3 above:

(a) Article 17 of the Convention on Jurisdiction and Enforcement shall apply if the parties agree that a different Community patent court shall have jurisdiction;

(b) Article 18 of that Convention shall apply if the defendant enters an appearance before a different Community patent court.

5. The proceedings governed by this Protocol, with the exception of actions for a declaration of non-infringement of a Community Patent, may also be brought in the courts of the Contracting State in which the act of infringement has been committed or threatened, or in which an act within the meaning of Article 15(1)(c) has been committed.

Part III. First Instance

ARTICLE 15

Jurisdiction over infringement and validity

1. The Community patent courts of first instance shall have exclusive jurisdiction:

   (a) for all infringement actions and—if they are permitted under national law—actions in respect of threatened infringement relating to Community patents;

   (b) for actions for a declaration of non-infringement, if they are permitted under national law;

   (c) for all actions in respect of the use made of the invention during the period specified in Article 32(1) of the Community Patent Convention;

   (d) for counterclaims for revocation of the Community patent pursuant to paragraph 2.

2. The Community patent courts of first instance shall treat the Community patent as valid unless its validity is put in issue by the defendant with a counterclaim for revocation of the Community patent. The counterclaim may only be based on the grounds for revocation mentioned in Article 56(1) of the Community Patent Convention. The second phrase of Article 55(1) and Article 55(2), (3) and (6) of the Community Patent Convention shall apply.

3. If the counterclaim is brought in a legal action to which the proprietor of the patent is not already a party, he shall be informed thereof and may be joined as a party to the action in accordance with the conditions set out in national law.

4. The validity of a Community patent may not be put in issue in an action for a declaration of non-infringement.

ARTICLE 16

Information to the European Patent Office

The Community patent court of first instance with which a counterclaim for revocation of the Community patent has been filed shall inform the European Patent Office of the date on which the counterclaim for revocation was filed. The latter shall record this fact in the Register of Community Patents.

ARTICLE 17

Territorial jurisdiction

1. A Community patent court of first instance whose jurisdiction is based on Article 14(1) to (4) shall have jurisdiction in respect of:

   — acts of infringement committed or threatened within the territory of any of the Contracting States,

   — acts within the meaning of Article 15(1)(c) committed within the territory of any of the Contracting States.

2. A Community patent court of first instance whose jurisdiction is based on

Article 14(5) shall have jurisdiction only in respect of acts committed or threatened within the territory of the State in which that court is situated.

ARTICLE 18

Stay of proceedings

If the judgment in an action before a Community patent court of first instance relating to a European Patent application which may result in the grant of a Community patent depends upon the patentability of the invention, that judgment may be given only after the European Patent Office has granted a Community patent or refused the European patent application.

ARTICLE 19

Judgments on validity

1. Where, in a proceeding before the Community patent courts of first instance, the validity of a Community patent has been put in issue,

    (a) if any of the grounds for revocation mentioned in Article 56(1) of the Community Patent Convention are found to prejudice the maintenance of the Community patent, the court shall order the revocation of the patent;

    (b) if none of the grounds for revocation mentioned in Article 56(1) of the Community Patent Convention is found to prejudice the maintenance of the Community patent, the court shall reject the application for revocation;

    (c) if, taking into consideration the amendments made by the proprietor of the patent during the course of the action, none of the grounds for revocation mentioned in Article 56(1) of the Community Patent Convention is found to prejudice the maintenance of the Community patent, the court shall order the patent to be maintained as amended.

2. Where a Community patent court of first instance has given a judgment which has become final on a counterclaim for revocation of the Community patent, it shall send a copy of the judgment to the European Patent Office. Any party may request information about such transmission.

3. Where a Community patent court of first instance, by a judgment which has become final, has decided to maintain the Community patent as amended, it shall send a copy of the judgment to the European Patent Office with the text of the patent as amended as a result of the proceedings. Any party may request information about such transmission. The European Patent Office shall publish the text provided that:

    (a) a translation of all amendments to the patent specification in one of the official languages of each of the Contracting States which does not have as an official language the language of proceedings of the court is filed within a time limit identical to that referred to in Article 58(3)(b) of the Community Patent Convention;

    (b) the fee for the printing of a new specification is paid within a time limit identical to that referred to in Article 58(3)(c) of the Community Patent Convention.

4. If a translation is not filed in due time or if the fee for the printing of a new specification is not paid in due time, the European Patent Office shall, notwithstanding the decision of the Community patent court, revoke the Community

patent unless these acts are done and the additional fee is paid within a further period identical to that referred to in Article 58(4) of the Community Patent Convention.

ARTICLE 20

Effect of judgments on validity

When it has become final, a judgment of a Community patent court of first instance revoking or amending a Community patent shall have, subject to Article 56(3) of the Community Patent Convention, in all Contracting States the effects specified in Article 33 of that Convention.

Part IV. Second Instance

ARTICLE 21

Jurisdiction of the Community patent courts of second instance

1. An appeal to the Community patent courts of second instance shall lie from judgments of the Community patent courts of first instance in respect of proceedings referred to in Article 15(1).
2. The conditions under which an appeal may be lodged with a Community patent court of second instance shall be determined by the national law of the Contracting State in which that court is located.

ARTICLE 22

Jurisdiction of the Common Appeal Court in respect of issues raised on appeal before Community patent courts of second instance

The Common Appeal Court shall have exclusive jurisdiction to determine issues raised on appeal before the Community patent courts of second instance concerning:

    (a) the effects of the Community patent and the European patent application as provided in Articles 25 to 33 inclusive of the Community Patent Convention, in so far as questions of national law are not involved;
    (b) the validity of the Community patent put in issue pursuant to Article 15(2).

ARTICLE 23

Referrals from the Community patent courts of second instance to the Common Appeal Court

1. Where an appeal to a Community patent court of second instance raises issues in respect of which the Common Appeal Court has exclusive jurisdiction pursuant to Article 22, the court of second instance shall stay its proceedings in so far as they require a judgment on such issues and refer them to the Common Appeal Court for a judgment. A decision to stay proceedings and refer any of the issues mentioned in Article 22 to the Common Appeal Court may be taken without oral proceedings taking place.

2. However, the Community patent court of second instance may continue its proceedings provided that there is no possibility of the judgment of the Common Appeal Court being prejudged.

3. The Community patent court of second instance may not render a final judgment before the judgment of the Common Appeal Court has been given.

ARTICLE 24

Nature of proceedings before the Common Appeal Court

The Common Appeal Court shall examine all the issues of which it is seised and give a ruling on fact and law.

ARTICLE 25

Judgments of the Common Appeal Court

1. Where a judgment is given by the Common Appeal Court on an issue referred to in Article 22(a) it shall find whether the Community patent or the European patent application has or has not the effects at issue.

2. Where a judgment is given by the Common Appeal Court on an issue referred to in Article 22(b), Articles 19 and 20 shall apply *mutatis mutandis*.

ARTICLE 26

Applicable law

The Common Appeal Court shall apply the provisions of the Agreement relating to Community Patents.

ARTICLE 27

Effect of the judgment

A judgment given by the Common Appeal Court shall be binding in the further proceedings of the case.

ARTICLE 28

Supplementary jurisdiction of the Common Appeal Court

1. The Common Appeal Court shall decide on appeals from decisions of the Revocation Divisions and the Patent Administration Division of the European Patent Office.

2. If proceedings in respect of a Community patent are pending before it, the Common Appeal Court shall, if necessary, decide on the lapse of that patent.

3. Where the Common Appeal Court has given a judgment pursuant to paragraph 1 or 2 it shall send a copy of the judgment to the European Patent Office. Any party may request information about such transmission.

Part V. Third Instance and Preliminary Ruling Procedure

ARTICLE 29

Further appeal to national courts

The national rules concerning further appeal shall be applicable in respect of judgments of Community patent courts of second instance on matters upon which the Common Appeal Court does not have exclusive jurisdiction under Article 22.

ARTICLE 30

Preliminary ruling procedure before the Common Appeal Court

1. The Common Appeal Court shall have, in accordance with Article 5 of the Agreement relating to Community Patents, jurisdiction to give preliminary rulings concerning:

   (a) the interpretation of the Agreement in respect of matters not falling within its exclusive jurisdiction as provided in Article 22 of this Protocol;
   (b) the validity and interpretation of provisions enacted in implementation of the Agreement, to the extent to which they are not national provisions.

2. Where such a question is raised before a national court, that court may, if it considers that a decision on the question is necessary to enable it to give judgment, request the Common Appeal Court to give a ruling thereon.

3. Where any such question is raised in a case pending before a national court against whose decisions there is no judicial remedy under national law, that court shall bring the matter before the Common Appeal Court.

4. The term "courts" shall include the authorities referred to in Article 70 of the Community Patent Convention.

Part VI. Common Provisions for the Community Patent Courts of First and Second Instance

ARTICLE 31

Qualifications of judges

The judges of the Community patent courts shall be persons who possess experience of patent law.

ARTICLE 32

Applicable law

1. The Community patent courts shall apply the provisions of the Agreement relating to Community Patents.

2. On all matters not covered by the Agreement relating to Community Patents a Community patent court shall apply its national law, including its private international law.

ARTICLE 33

Procedure

1. Unless otherwise specified in the Agreement relating to Community Patents, a Community patent court shall apply the rules of procedure governing the same type of action relating to a national patent in the Contracting State where it has its seat.

2. Paragraph 1 shall apply *mutatis mutandis* in the case of a European patent application which may result in the grant of a Community patent.

3. The Community patent court shall record in writing at least the essentials of the oral proceedings, including the testimony given and the summary examination of the items produced in evidence; it shall attach the procedural acts and written statements.

ARTICLE 34

Specific rules on related actions

1. A Community patent court hearing an action referred to in Article 15(1), other than an action for a declaration of non-infringement, shall, unless there are special grounds for continuing the hearing, at the request of one of the parties and after hearing the other parties, stay the proceedings where the validity of the Community patent is already in issue before another Community patent court or before the Common Appeal Court, or where opposition to the Community patent has already been lodged or an application for revocation or a request for limitation of the Community patent has been filed at the European Patent Office.

2. The European Patent Office, when hearing an application for revocation or a request for limitation of a Community patent shall, unless there are special grounds for continuing the hearing, at the request of one of the parties and after hearing the other parties, stay the proceedings where the validity of the Community patent is already in issue before a Community patent court or before the Common Appeal Court.

ARTICLE 35

Sanctions

1. Where a Community patent court finds that the defendant has infringed or threatened to infringe a Community patent, it shall, unless there are special reasons for not doing so, issue an order prohibiting the defendant from proceeding with the acts which infringed or would infringe the Community patent. It shall also take such measures in accordance with its national law as are aimed at ensuring that this prohibition is complied with.

2. In all other respects the Community patent court shall apply the law of the Contracting State in which the acts of infringement or threatened infringement were committed.

ARTICLE 36

Provisional, including protective measures

1. Application may be made to the courts of a Contracting State, including Community patent courts, for such provisional, including protective, measures in respect of a Community patent as may be available under the law of that State in respect of a national patent, even if, under this Protocol, a Community patent court of another Contracting State has jurisdiction as to the substance of the matter.

2. A Community patent court whose jurisdiction is based on Article 14(1), (2), (3) or (4) shall have jurisdiction to grant provisional, including protective, measures which, subject to any necessary procedure for recognition and enforcement pursuant to Title III of the Convention on Jurisdiction and Enforcement, are applicable in the territory of any Contracting State. No other court shall have such jurisdiction.

3. The Common Appeal Court shall not be competent to order provisional, including protective, measures and no appeal may be made to the Common Appeal Court against a judgment ordering such measures.

Part VII. Transitional Provisions

ARTICLE 37

Proceedings to which the Protocol applies

This Protocol shall only apply to proceedings initiated after the entry into force of the Agreement relating to Community Patents.

ARTICLE 38

Application of the Convention on Jurisdiction and Enforcement

The provisions of the Convention on Jurisdiction and Enforcement rendered applicable by the preceding Articles shall not have effect in respect of any Contracting State for which that Convention has not yet entered into force until such entry into force.

ARTICLE 39

Appointment of judges to the Common Appeal Court during a transitional period

1. During a transitional period, the expiry of which shall be determined by the Administrative Committee, that Committee may, in accordance with the conditions set out in Article 5(1), determine a number of judges of the Common Appeal Court which is smaller than the number of Contracting States.

2. During the transitional period referred to in paragraph 1, the representatives of the Governments of the Contracting States may appoint as judges of the Common Appeal Court persons who possess the qualifications required for appointment to judicial office in their respective States and experience in patent law. The judges may continue their activities in their respective States or in international organisations. They may be appointed for a term of less than six years, though this shall not be less than one year. They may be reappointed.

[Note: the Protocol on privileges and immunities of the Common Appeal Court, the Protocol on the Statute of the Common Appeal Court, and the Protocol on the possible modification of the conditions of entry into force of the 1989 Agreement are not reproduced here; see E.C. Official Journal [1991] O.J. L401/45 et seq.]

BUDAPEST TREATY AND EPO DECLARATION RELATING THERETO

Treaty on the International Recognition of the Deposit of A20–01
Micro-organisms for the Purposes of Patent Procedure

Budapest, April 28, 1977

(Relevant Parts)

Introductory Provisions

ARTICLE 1

Establishment of a Union

The States party to this Treaty (hereinafter called "the Contracting States")
constitute a Union for the international recognition of the deposit of micro-
organisms for the purposes of patent procedure.

ARTICLE 2

Definitions

For the purposes of this Treaty and the Regulations:

(i)   references to a "patent" shall be construed as references to patents for
inventions, inventors' certificates, utility certificates, utility models,
patents or certificates or addition, inventors' certificates of addition, and
utility certificates of addition;

(ii) "deposit of a micro-organism" means, according to the context in which
these words appear, the following acts effected in accordance with this
Treaty and the Regulations; the transmittal of a micro-organism to an
international depositary authority, which receives and accepts it, or the
storage of such a micro-organism by the international depositary
authority or both the said transmittal and the said storage;

(iii) "patent procedure" means any administrative or judicial procedure
relating to a patent application or a patent;

(iv) "publication for the purposes of patent procedure" means the official
publication , or the official laying open for public inspection, of a patent
application or a patent;

(v)   "inter-governmental industrial property organisation" means an organisation that has filed a declaration under Article 9(1);

(vi)   "industrial property office" means an authority of a Contracting State or an inter-governmental industrial property organisation competent for the grant of patents;

(vii) "depositary institution" means an institution which provides for the receipt, acceptance and storage of micro-organisms and the furnishing of samples thereof;

(viii) "international depositary authority" means a depositary institution which has acquired the status of international depositary authority as provided in Article 7;

(ix)   "depositor" means the natural person or legal entity transmitting a micro-organism to an international depositary authority, which receives and accepts it, and any successor in title of the said natural person or legal entity;

(x)   "Union" means the Union referred to in Article 1;

(xi)   "Assembly" means the Assembly referred to in Article 10;

(xii) "Organisation" means the World Intellectual Property Organisation;

(xiii) "International Bureau" means the International Bureau of the Organisation and, as long as it subsists, the United International Bureau for the Protection of Intellectual Property (BIRPI);

(xiv) "Director-General" means the Director-General of the Organisation;

(xv)   "Regulations" means the Regulations referred to in Article 12.

Chapter I. Substantive provisions

ARTICLE 3

Recognition and effect of the deposit of micro-organisms

(1)(a) Contracting States which allow or require the deposit of micro-organisms for the purposes of patent procedure shall recognise, for such purposes, the deposit of a micro-organism with any international depositary authority. Such recognition shall include the recognition of the fact and date of the deposit as indicated by the international depositary authority as well as the recongition of the fact that what is furnished as a sample is a sample of the deposited micro-organism.

(b) Any Contracting State may require a copy of the receipt of the deposit referred to in subparagraph (a), issued by the international depositary authority.

(2) As far as matters regulated in this Treaty and the Regulations are concerned, no Contracting State may require compliance with requirements different from or additional to those which are provided in this Treaty and the Regulations.

ARTICLE 4

New deposit

(1)(a) Where the international depositary authority cannot furnish samples of the deposited micro-organisms for any reason, in particular,

(i)   where such micro-organism is no longer viable, or

(ii) where the furnishing of samples would require that they be sent abroad and the sending or the receipt of the samples abroad is prevented by export or import restrictions,

that authority shall, promptly after having noted its inability to furnish samples, notify the depositor of such inability, indicating the cause thereof, and the depositor, subject to paragraph (2) and as provided in this paragraph, shall have the right to make a new deposit of the micro-organism which was originally deposited.

(b) The new deposit shall be made with the international depositary authority with which the original deposit was made, provided that:

(i) it shall be made with another international depositary authority where the institution with which the original deposit was made has ceased to have the status of international depositary authority, either entirely or in respect of the kind of micro-organism to which the deposited micro-organism belongs, or where the international depositary authority with which the original deposit was made discontinued, temporarily or definitively, the performance of its functions in respect of deposited micro-organisms;

(ii) it may be made with another international depositary authority in the case referred to in subparagraph (a)(ii).

(c) Any new deposit shall be accompanied by a statement signed by the depositor alleging that the newly deposited micro-organism is the same as that originally deposited. If the allegation of the depositor is contested, the burden of proof shall be governed by the applicable law.

(d) Subject to subparagraphs (a) to (c) and (e), the new deposit shall be treated as if it has been made on the date on which the original deposit was made where all the preceding statements concerning the viability of the originally deposited micro-organism indicated that the micro-organism was viable and where the new deposit was made within three months after the date on which the depositor received the notification referred to in subparagraph (a).

(e) Where subparagraph (b)(i) applies and the depositor does not receive the notification referred to in subparagraph (a) within six months after the date on which the termination, limitation or discontinuance referred to in subparagraph (b)(i) was published by the International Bureau, the three-month time limit referred to in subparagraph (d) shall be counted from the date of the said publication.

(2) The right referred to in paragraph (1)(a) shall not exist where the deposited micro-organism has been transferred to another international depositary authority as long as that authority is in a position to furnish samples of such micro-organism.

ARTICLE 5

Export and import restrictions

Each Contracting State recognises that it is highly deisirable that, if and to the extent to which the export from or import into its territory of certain kinds of micro-organisms is restricted, such restriction should apply to micro-organisms deposited, or destined for deposit, under this Treaty only where the restriction is necessary in view of national security or the dangers for health or the environment.

ARTICLE 6

Status of international depositary authority

(1) In order to qualify for the status of international depositary authority, any depositary institution must be located on the territory of a Contracting State and must benefit from assurances furnished by that State to the effect that the said institution complies and will continue to comply with the requirements specified in

865

paragraph (2). The said assurances may be furnished also by an inter-governmental industrial property organisation; in that case, the depositary institution must be located on the territory of a State member of the said organisation.

(2) The depositary institution must, in its capacity of international depositary authority:

(i)   have a continuous existence;

(ii)   have the necessary staff and facilities, as prescribed in the Regulations, to perform its scientific and administrative tasks under this Treaty;

(iii)   be impartial and objective;

(iv)   be available, for the purposes of deposit, to any depositor under the same conditions;

(v)   accept for deposit any or certain kinds of micro-organisms, examine their viability and store them, as prescribed in the Regulations;

(vi)   issues a receipt to the depositor, and any required viability statement, as prescribed in the Regulations;

(vii)   comply, in respect of the deposited micro-organisms, with the requirement of secrecy, as prescribed in the Regulations;

(viii)   furnish samples of any deposited micro-organism under the conditions and in conformity with the procedure prescribed in the Regulations.

(3) The Regulations shall provide the measures to be taken:

(i)   where an international depositary authority discontinues, temporarily or definitively, the performance of its functions in respect of deposited micro-organisms or refuses to accept any of the kinds of micro-organisms which it should accept under the assurances furnished;

(ii)   in case of the termination or limitation of the status of international depositary authority of an international depositary authority.

Article 7

Acquisition of the status of international depositary authority

(1)(a) A depositary institution shall acquire the status of international depositary authority by virtue of a written communication addressed to the Director-General by the Contracting State on the territory of which the depositary institution is located and including a declaration of assurances to the effect that the said institution complies and will continue to comply with the requirements specified in Article 6(2). The said status may be acquired also by virtue of a written communication addressed to the Director-General by an inter-governmental industrial property organisation and including the said declaration.

(b) The communication shall also contain information on the depositary institution as provided in the Regulations and may indicate the date on which the status of international depositary authority should take effect.

(2)(a) If the Director-General finds that the communication includes the required declaration and that all the required information has been received, the communication shall be promptly published by the International Bureau.

(b) The status of international depositary authority shall be acquired as from the date of publication of the communication or, where a date has been indicated under paragraph (1)(b) and such date is later than the date of publication of the communication, as from such date.

(3) The details of the procedure under paragraphs (1) and (2) are provided in the Regulations.

ARTICLE 8

Termination and limitation of the status of international depositary authority

(1)(a) Any Contracting State or any inter-governmental industrial property organisation may request the Assembly to terminate, or to limit to certain kinds of micro-organisms, any authority's status of international depositary authority on the ground that the requirements specified in Article 6 have not been or are no longer complied with. However, such a request may not be made by a Contracting State or inter-governmental industrial property organisation in respect of an international depositary authority for which it has made the declaration referred to in Article 7(1)(a).

(b) Before making the request under subparagraph (a), the Contracting State or the inter-governmental industrial property organisation shall, through the inter- mediary of the Director-General, notify the reasons for the proposed request to the Contracting State or the inter-governmental industrial property organisation which has made the communication referred to in Article 7(1) so that that State or organisation may, within six months from the date of the said notification, take appropriate action to obviate the need for making the proposed request.

(c) Where the Assembly finds that the request is well founded, it shall decide to terminate, or to limit to certain kinds of micro-organisms, the status of international depositary authority of the authority referred to in subparagraph (a). The decision of the Assembly shall require that a majority of two-thirds of the votes cast be in favour of the request.

(2)(a) The Contracting State or inter-governmental industrial property organis- ation having made the declaration referred to in Article 7(1)(a) may, by a communication addressed to the Director-General, withdraw its declaration either entirely or in respect only of certain kinds of micro-organisms and in any event shall do so when and to the extent that its assurances are no longer applicable.

(b) Such a communication shall, from the date provided for in the Regulations, entail, where it relates to the entire declaration, the termination of the status of international depositary authority or, where it relates only to certain kinds of micro-organisms, a corresponding limitation of such status.

(3) The details of the procedure under paragraphs (1) and (2) are provided in the Regulations.

ARTICLE 9

Inter-governmental industrial property organisations

(1)(a) Any inter-governmental organisation to which several States have entrusted the task of granting regional patents and of which all the member States are members of the International (Paris) Union for the Protection of Industrial Property may file with the Director-General a declaration that it accepts the obligation of recognition provided for in Article 3(1)(a), the obligation concerning the requirements referred to in Article 3(2) and all the effects of the provisions of this Treaty and the Regulations applicable to inter-governmental industrial property organisations. If filed before the entry into force of this Treaty according to Article 16(1), the declaration referred to in the preceding sentence shall become effective on the date of the said entry into force. If filed after such entry into force, the said declaration shall become effective three months after its filing unless a later date has been indicated in the declaration. In the latter case, the declaration shall take effect on the date thus indicated.

(b) The said organisation shall have the right provided for in Article 3(1)(b).

(2) Where any provision of this Treaty or of the Regulations affecting inter-governmental industrial property organisations is revised or amended, any inter-governmental industrial property organisation may withdraw its declaration referred to in paragraph (1) by notification addressed to the Director-General. The withdrawal shall take effect:

(i) where the notification has been received before the date on which the revision or amendment enters into force, on that date;

(ii) where the notification has been received after the date referred to in (i), on the date indicated in the notification or, in the absence of such indication, three months after the date on which the notification was received.

(3) In addition to the case referred to in paragraph (2), any inter-governmental industrial property organisation may withdraw its declaration referred to in paragraph (1)(a) by notification addressed to the Director-General. The withdrawal shall take effect two years after the date on which the Director-General has received the notification. No notification of withdrawal under this paragraph shall be receivable during a period of five years from the date on which the declaration took effect.

(4) The withdrawal referred to in paragraph (2) or (3) by an inter-governmental industrial property organisation whose communication under Article 7(1) has led to the acquisition of the status of international depositary authority by a depositary institution shall entail the termination of such status one year after the date on which the Director-General has received the notification of withdrawal.

(5) Any declaration referred to in paragrpah (1)(a), notification of withdrawal referred to in paragraph (2) or (3), assurances furnished under Article 6(1), second sentence, and included in a declaration made in accordance with Article 7(1)(a), request made under Article 8(1) and communication of withdrawal referred to in Article 8(2) shall require the express previous approval of the supreme governing organ of the inter-governmental industrial property organisation whose members are all the States members of the said organisation and in which decisions are made by the official representatives of the governments of such States.

*   *   *

Declaration by the European Patent Organisation relating to obligations under Article 3(1)(a) and (2) of the Budapest Treaty

(O.J. EPO 1980, 380)

On 26 August 1980, the President of the EPO, acting on behalf of the European Patent Organisation, filed with the Director-General of the WIPO the declaration specified in Article 9 of the Budapest Treaty on the International Recognition of the Deposit of Micro-organisms for the Purposes of Patent Procedures. This declaration states that the organisation accepts the obligation of recognition provided for in Article 3(1)(a) of the Budapest Treaty, the obligation concerning the requirements referred to in Article 3(2) of the treaty and all the effects of the provisions of that treaty and the regulations applicable to inter-governmental industrial property organisations.

The declaration will become effective from 26 November 1980.

In accordance with the declaration, the EPO will recognise, as from that date, for the purposes of Rules 28 and 28a EPC, the deposit of micro-organisms with any international depositary authority. Such recognition will include the recognition of the fact and date on the deposit as indicated by the international depositary authority as well as the recognition of the fact that what is furnished as a sample is a sample of the deposited micro-organism.

At the date of this notice going to print, no depositary institution had yet acquired the status of international depositary authority under Article 7 of the Budapest Treaty. However, several institutions are expected to acquire such status in the near future and immediate announcement will be made of this in the Journal.

Therefore, under Rule 28(9) EPC the depositary institutions recognised for the purpose of Rules 28 and 28a EPC are at present only those mentioned in Official Journals 1978, 401 and 1980, 4 to 6.

PATENTS ACT 1977 (U.K.)

A21–01 **Patents Act 1977**

(1977 c.37)

(Relevant Parts)

An Act to establish a new law of patents applicable to future patents and application for patents; to amend the law of patents applicable to existing patents and applications for patents; to give effect to certain international conventions on patents; and for connected purposes.

Patentability

Patentable inventions

1.—(1) A patent may be granted only for an invention in respect of which the following conditions are satisfied, that is to say—

    (a) the invention is new;
    (b) it involves an inventive step;
    (c) it is capable of industrial application;
    (d) the grant of a patent for it is not excluded by subsections (2) and (3) below;

and references in this Act to a patentable invention shall be construed accordingly.

(2) It is hereby declared that the following (among other things) are not inventions for the purposes of this Act, that is to say, anything which consists of—

    (a) a discovery, scientific theory or mathematical method;
    (b) a literary, dramatic, musical or artistic work or any other aesthetic creation whatsoever;
    (c) a scheme, rule or method for performing a mental act, playing a game or doing business, or a program for a computer;
    (d) the presentation of information;

but the foregoing provision shall prevent anything from being treated as an invention for the purposes of this Act only to the extent that a patent or application for a patent relates to that thing as such.

(3) A patent shall not be granted—

    (a) for an invention the publication or exploitation of which would be generally expected to encourage offensive, immoral or anti-social behaviour;

(b) for any variety of animal or plant or any essentially biological process for the production of animals or plants, not being a micro-biological process or the product of such a process.

(4) For the purposes of subsection (3) above behaviour shall not be regarded as offensive, immoral or anti-social only because it is prohibited by any law in force in the United Kingdom or any part of it.

(5) The Secretary of State may by order vary the provisions of subsection (2) above for the purpose of maintaining them in conformity with developments in science and technology; and no such order shall be made unless a draft of the order has been laid before, and approved by resolution of, each House of Parliament.

Novelty

2.—(1) An invention shall be taken to be new if it does not form part of the state of the art.

(2) The state of the art in the case of an invention shall be taken to comprise all matter (whether a product, a process, information about either, or anything else) which has at any time before the priority date of that invention been made available to the public (whether in the United Kingdom or elsewhere) by written or oral description, by use or in any other way.

(3) The state of the art in the case of an invention to which an application for a patent or a patent relates shall be taken also to comprise matter contained in an application for another patent which was published on or after the priority date of that invention, if the following conditions are satisfied, that is to say—

(a) that matter was contained in the application for that other patent both as filed and as published; and

(b) the priority date of that matter is earlier than that of the invention.

(4) For the purposes of this section the disclosure of matter constituting an invention shall be disregarded in the case of a patent or an application for a patent if occurring later than the beginning of the period of six months immediately preceding the date of filing the application of the patent and either—

(a) the disclosure was due to, or made in consequence of, the matter having been obtained unlawfully or in breach of confidence by any person—
   (i) from the inventor or from any other person to whom the matter was made available in confidence by the inventor or who obtained it from the inventor because he or the inventor believed that he was entitled to obtain it; or
   (ii) from any other person to whom the matter was made available in confidence by any person mentioned in sub-paragraph (i) above or in this sub-paragraph or who obtained it from any person so mentioned because he or the person from whom he obtained it believed that he was entitled to obtain it:

(b) the disclosure was made in breach of confidence by any person who obtained the matter in confidence from the inventor or from any other person to whom it was made available, or who obtained it from the inventor; or

(c) the disclosure was due to, or made in consequence of the inventor displaying the invention at an international exhibition and the applicant states, on filing the application, that the invention has been so displayed and also, within the prescribed period, files written evidence in support of the statement complying with any prescribed conditions.

(5) In this section references to the inventor include references to any proprietor of the invention for the time being.

(6) In the case of an invention consisting of a substance or composition for use in a method of treatment of the human or animal body by surgery or therapy or of

diagnosis practised on the human or animal body, the fact that the substance or composition forms part of the state of the art shall not prevent the invention from being taken to be new if the use of the substance or composition in any such method does not form part of the state of the art.

Inventive step

3. An invention shall be taken to involve an inventive step if it is not obvious to a person skilled in the art, having regard to any matter which forms part of the state of the art by virtue only in section 2(2) above (and disregarding section 2(3) above).

Industrial application

4.—(1) Subject to subsection (2) below, an invention shall be taken to be capable of industrial application if it can be made or used in any kind of industry, including agriculture.

(2) An invention of a method of treatment of the human or animal body by surgery or therapy or of diagnosis practised on the human or animal body shall not be taken to be capable of industrial application.

(3) Subsection (2) above shall not prevent a product consisting of a substance or composition being treated as capable of industrial application merely because it is invented for use in any such method.

Priority date

5.—(1) For the purposes of this Act the priority date of an invention to which an application for a patent relates and also of any matter (whether or not the same as the invention) contained in any such application is, except as provided by the following provisions of this Act, the date of filing the application.

(2) If in or in connection with an application for a patent (the application in suit) a declaration is made, whether by the applicant or any predecessor in title of his, complying with the relevant requirements of rules and specifying one or more earlier relevant applications for the purposes of this section made by the applicant or a predecessor in title of his and each having a date of filing during the period of twelve months immediately preceding the date of filing the application in suit, then—

(a) if an invention to which the application in suit relates is supported by matter disclosed in the earlier relevant application or applications, the priority date of that invention shall instead of being the date of filing the application in suit be the date of filing the relevant application in which that matter was disclosed or, if it was disclosed in more than one relevant application, the earliest of them;

(b) the priority date of any matter contained in the application in suit which was also disclosed in the earlier relevant application or applications shall be the date of filing the relevant application in which that matter was disclosed or, if it was disclosed in more than one relevant application, the earliest of them.

(3) Where an invention or other matter contained in the application in suit was also disclosed in two earlier relevant applications filed by the same applicant as in the case of the application in suit or a predecessor in title of his and the second of those relevant applications was specified in or in connection with the application in suit, the second of those relevant applications shall, so far as concerns that invention or matter, be disregarded unless—

(a) it was filed in or in respect of the same country as the first; and

(b) not later than the date of filing the second, the first (whether or not so specified) was unconditionally withdrawn, or was abandoned or refused, without—

  (i) having been made available to the public (whether in the United
      Kingdom or elsewhere);
 (ii) leaving any rights outstanding; and
(iii) having served to establish a priority date in relation to another
      application, wherever made.

(4) The foregoing provisions of this section shall apply for determining the
priority date of an invention for which a patent has been granted as they apply for
determining the priority date of an invention to which an application for that
patent relates.

(5) In this section "relevant application" means any of the following applications
which has a date of filing, namely—

(a) an application for a patent under this Act;
(b) an application in or for a convention country (specified uner section 90
    below) for protection in respect of an invention or an application which, in
    accordance with the law of a convention country or a treaty or inter-
    national convention to which a convention country is a party, is equivalent
    to such an application.

Disclosure of matter, etc., between earlier and later applications

6.—(1) It is hereby declared for the avoidance of doubt that where an application
(the application in suit) is made for a patent and a declaration is made in accordance
with section 5(2) above in or in connection with that application specifying an
earlier relevant application, the application in suit and any patent granted in
pursuance of it shall not be invalidated by reason only of relevant intervening acts.

(2) In this section—

"relevant application" has the same meaning as in section 5 above; and
"relevant intervening acts" means acts done in relation to matter disclosed in
an earlier relevant application between the dates of the earlier relevant
application and the application in suit, as for example, filing another
application for the invention for which the earlier relevant application was
made, making information available to the public about that invention or that
matter or working that invention, but disregarding any application, or the
disclosure to the public of matter contained in any application, which is itself
to be disregarded for the purposes of section 5(3) above.

*   *   *

Applications

Making of application

14.—(1) Every application for a patent—

(a) shall be made in the prescribed form and shall be filed at the Patent Office
    in the prescribed manner; and
(b) shall be accompanied by the free prescribed for the purposes of this
    subsection (hereafter in this Act referred to as the filing fee).

(2) Every application for a patent shall contain—

(a) a request for the grant of a patent;
(b) a specification containing a description of the invention, a claim or claims
    and any drawing referred to in the description or any claim; and
(c) an abstract;

but the foregoing provision shall not prevent an application being initiated by
documents complying with section 15(1) below.

(3) The specification of an application shall disclose the invention in a manner which is clear enough and complete enough for the invention to be performed by a person skilled in the art.

(4) Without prejudice to subsection (3), above, rules amy prescribe the circumstances in which the specification of an application which requires for its performance the use of a micro-organism is to be treated for the purposes of this Act as complying with that subsection.

(5) The claim or claims shall—

    (a) define the matter for which the applicant seeks protection;

    (b) be clear and concise;

    (c) be supported by the description; and

    (d) relate to one invention or to a group of inventions which are so linked as to form a single inventive concept.

(6) Without prejudice to the generality of subsection (5)(d) above, rules may provide for treating two or more inventions as being so linked as to form a single inventive concept for the purposes of this Act.

(7) The purpose of the abstract is to give technical information and on publication it shall not form part of the state of the art by virtue of section 2(3) above, and the comptroller may determine whether the abstract adequately fulfils its purpose and, if it does not, may reframe it so that it does.

(8) Rules may require a person who has made an application for a patent for an invention which requires for its performance the use of a micro-organism not to impose or maintain in the prescribed circumstances any restrictions on the availability to the public of samples of the micro-organism and the uses to which they may be put, subject, however, to any prescribed exceptions, and rules may provide that in the event of a contravention of any provision included in the rules by virtue of this subsection the specification shall be treated for the purposes of this Act as not disclosing the invention in a manner required by subsection (3) above.

(9) An application for a patent may be withdrawn any any time before the patent is granted and any withdrawal of such an application may not be revoked.

Date of filing applications

15.—(1) The date of filing an application for a patent shall, subject to the following provisions of this Act, be taken to be the earliest date on which the following conditions are satisfied in relation to the application, that is to say—

    (a) the documents filed at the Patent Office contain an indication that a patent is sought in pursuance of the application;

    (b) those documents identify the applicant or applicants for the patent;

    (c) those documents contain a description of the invention for which a patent is sought (whether or not the description complies with the other provisions of this Act and with any relevant rules); and

    (d) the applicant pays for the filing fee.

(2) If any drawing referred to in any such application is filed later than the date which by virtue of subsection (1) above is to be treated as the date of filing the application, but before the beginning of the preliminary examination of the application under section 17 below, the comptroller shall give the applicant an opportunity of requesting within the prescribed period that the date on which the drawing is filed shall be treated for the purposes of this Act as the date of filing the application and—

    (a) if the applicant makes any such request, the date of filing the drawing shall be so treated; but

    (b) otherwise any reference to the drawing in the application shall be treated as omitted.

(3) If on the preliminary examination of an application under section 17 below it is found that any drawing referred to in the application has not been filed, then—

    (a) if the drawing is subsequently filed within the prescribed period, the date on which it it filed shall be treated for the purposes of this Act as the date of filing the application; but

    (b) otherwise any reference to the drawing in the application shall be treated as omitted.

(3A) Nothing in subsection (2) or (3) above shall be construed as affecting the power of the comptroller under section 117(1) below to correct errors or mistakes with respect to the filing of drawings.

(4) Where, after an application for patent has been filed and before the patent is granted, a new application is filed by the original applicant or his successor in title in accorance with rules in respect of any part of the matter contained in the earlier application and the conditions mentioned in sub-section (1) above are satisfied in relation to the new application (without the new application contravening section 76 below) the new application shall be treated as having, as its date of filing, the date of filing the earlier application.

(5) An application which has a date of filing by virtue of the foregoing provisions of this section shall be taken to be withdrawn at the end of the relevant prescribed period, unless before that end the applicant—

    (a) files at the Patent Office one or more claims for the purposes of the application and also the abstract; and

    (b) makes a request for a preliminary examination and search under the following provisions of this Act and pays the search fee.

*   *   *

Information prejudicial to defence of realm or safety of public

22.—(1) Where an application for a patent is filed in the Patent Office (whether under this Act or any treaty or international convention to which the United Kingdom is a party and whether before or after the appointed day) and it appears to the comptroller that the applicant contains information of a description notified to him by the Secretary of State as being information the publication of which might be prejudicial to the defence of the realm, the comptroller may give directions prohibiting or restricting the publication of that information or its communication to any specified person or description of persons.

*   *   *

Infringement

Meaning of infringement

60.—(1) Subject to the provisions of this section, a person infringes a patent for an invention if, but only if, while the patent is in force, he does any of the following things in the United Kingdom in relation to the invention without the consent of the proprietor of the patent, that is to say—

    (a) where the invention is a product, he makes, disposes of, offers to dispose of, uses or imports the product or keeps it whether for disposal or otherwise;

    (b) where the invention is a process, he uses the process or he offers it for use in the United Kingdom when he knows, or it is obvious to a reasonable person in the circumstances, that its use there without the consent of the proprietor would be an infringement of the patent;

875

(c) where the invention is a process, he disposes of, offers to dispose of, uses or imports any product obtained directly by means of that process or keeps any such product whether for disposal or otherwise.

(2) Subject to the following provisions of this section, a person (other than the proprietor of the patent) also infringes a patent for an invention if, while the patent is in force and without the consent of the proprietor, he supplies or offers to supply in the United Kingdom a person other than a licensee or other person entitled to work the invention with any of the means, relating to an essential element of the invention, for putting the invention into effect when he knows, or it is obvious to a reasonable person in the circumstances, that those means are suitable for putting, and are intended to put, the invention into effect in the United Kingdom.

(3) Subsection (2) above shall not apply to the supply or offer of a staple commercial product unless the supply or the offer is made for the purpose of inducing the person supplied or, as the case may be, the person to whom the offer is made to do an act which constitutes an infringement of the patent by virtue of subsection (1) above.

(4) Without prejudice to section 86 below, subsctions (1) and (2) above shall not apply to any act which, under any provision of the Community Patent Convention relating to the exhaustion of the rights of the proprietor of a patent, as that provision applies by virtue of that section, cannot be prevented by the proprietor of the patent.

(5) An act which, apart from this subsection, would constitute an infringement of a patent for an invention shall not do so if—

(a) it is done privately and for purposes which are not commercial;
(b) it is done for experimental purposes relating to the subject-matter of the invention;
(c) it consists of the extemporaneous preparation in a pharmacy of a medicine for an individual in accordance with a prescription given by a registered medical or dental practitioner or consists of dealing with a medicine so prepared;
(d) it consists of the use, exclusively for the needs of a relevant ship, of a product or process in the body of such a ship or in its machinery, tackle, apparatus or other accessories, in a case where the ship has temporarily or accidentally entered the internal or territorial waters of the United Kingdom;
(e) it consists of the use of a product or process in the body or operation of a relevant aircraft, hovercraft or vehicle which has temporarily or accidentally entered or is crossing the United Kingdom (including the air space above it and its territorial waters) or the use of accessories for such a relevant aircraft, hovercraft or vehicle;
(f) it consists of the use of an exempted aircraft which has lawfully entered or is lawfully crossing the United Kingdom as aforesaid or of the importation into the United Kingdom, or the use or storage there, of any part or accessory for such an aircraft.

(6) For the purposes of subsection (2) above a person who does an act in relation to an invention which is prevented only by virtue of paragraph (a), (b) or (c) of subsection (5) above from constituting an infringement of a patent for the invention shall not be treated as a person entitled to work the invention, but—

(a) the reference in that subsection to a person entitled to work an invention includes a reference to a person so entitled by virtue of section 55 above, and
(b) a person who by virtue of section 28A(4) or (5) above or section 64 below is entitled to do an act in relation to the invention without it constituting such an infringement shall, so far as concerns that act, be treated as a person entitled to work the invention.

(7) In this section—

"relevant ships" and "relevant aircraft, hovercraft or vehicle", mean respectively a ship and an aircraft, hovercraft or vehicle registered in, or belonging to, any country, other than the United Kingdom, which is a party to the Convention for the Protection of Industrial Property signed at Paris on 20th March 1883; and

"exempted aircraft" means an aircraft to which section 53 of the Civil Aviation Act 1949 (aircraft exempted from seizure in respect of patent claims) applies.

Proceedings for infringement of patent

61.—(1) Subject to the following provisions of this Part of this Act, civil proceedings may be brought in the court by the proprietor of a patent in respect of any act alleged to infringe the patent and (without prejudice to any other jurisdiction of the court) in those proceedings a claim may be made—

(a) for an injunction or interdict restraining the defendant or defender from any apprehended acts of infringement;

(b) for an order for him to deliver up or destroy any patented product in relation to which the patent is infringed or any article in which that product is inextricably comprised;

(c) for damages in respct of the infringement;

(d) for an account of the profits derived by him from the infringement;

(e) for a declaration or declarator that the patent is valid and has been infringed by him.

* * *

(6) Subject to the following provisions of this Part of this Act, in determining whether or not to grant any kind of relief claimed under this section and the extent of the relief granted the court or the comptroller shall apply the principles applied by the court in relation to that kind of relief immediately before the appointed day.

* * *

The right to continue use begun before priority date

64.—(1) Where a patent is granted for an invention, a person who in the United Kingdom before the priority date of the invention—

(a) does in good faith an act which would constitute an infringement of the patent if it were in force, or

(b) makes in good faith effective and serious preparations to do such an act,

has the right to continue to do the act or, as the case may be, to do the act, notwithstanding the grant of the patent; but this right does not extend to granting a licence to another person to do the act.

(2) If the act was done, or the preparations were made, in the course of a business, the person entitled to the right conferred by subsection (1) may—

(a) authorise the doing of that act by any partners of his for the time being in that business, and

(b) assign that right, or transmit it on death (or in the case of a body corporate on its dissolution), to any person who acquires that part of the business in the course of which the act was done or the preparations were made.

(3) Where a product is disposed of to another in exercise of the rights conferred by subsection (1) or (2), that other and any person claiming through him may deal with the product in the same way as if it had been disposed of by the registered proprietor of the patent.

* * *

Revocation of patents

Power to revoke patents on application

72.—(1) Subject to the following provisions of this Act, the court or the comptroller may on the application of any person by order revoke a patent for an invention on (but only on) any of the following grounds, that is to say—

(a) the invention is not a patentable invention;

(b) that the patent was granted to a person who was not entitled to be granted that patent;

(c) the specification of the patent does not disclose the invention clearly enough and completely enough for it to be performed by a person skilled in the art;

(d) the matter disclosed in the specification of the patent extends beyond that disclosed in the application for the patent, as filed, or, if the patent was granted on a new application filed under section 8(3), 12, or 37(4) above or as mentioned in section 15(4) above, in the earlier application, as filed;

(e) the protection conferred by the patent has been extended by an amendment which should not have been allowed.

* * *

76.—(1) An application for a patent which—

(a) is made in respect of matter disclosed in an earlier application, or in the specification of a patent which has been granted, and

(b) discloses additional matter, that is, matter extending beyond that disclosed in the earlier application, as filed, or the application for the patent, as filed.

may be filed under section 8(3), 12 or 37(4) above, or as mentioned in section 15(4) above, but shall not be allowed to proceed unless it is amended so as to exclude the additional matter.

(2) No amendment of an application for a patent shall be allowed under section 17(3), 18(3) or 19(1) if it results in the application disclosing matter extending beyond that disclosed in the application as filed.

(3) No amendment of the specification of a patent shall be allowed under section 27(1), 73 or 75 if it—

(a) results in the specification disclosing additional matter, or

(b) extends the protection conferred by the patent.

* * *

Extent of invention

125.—(1) For the purposes of this Act an invention for a patent for which an application has been made or for which a patent has been granted shall, unless the context otherwise requires, be taken to be that specified in a claim of the specification of the application or patent, as the case may be, as interpreted by the description and any drawings contained in that specification, and the extent of the protection conferred by a patent or application for a patent shall be determined accordingly.

(2) It is hereby declared for the avoidance of doubt that where more than one invention is specified in any such claim, each invention may have a different priority date under section 5 above.

(3) The Protocol on the Interpretation of Article 69 of the European Patent Convention (which Article contains a provision corresponding to subsection (1) above) shall, as for the time being in force, apply for the purposes of subsection (1) above as it applies for the purposes of that Article.

* * *

Interpretation

130.—(3) For the purposes of this Act matter shall be taken to have been disclosed in any relevant application within the meaning of section 5 above or in the specification of a patent if it was either claimed or disclosed (otherwise than by way of disclaimer or acknowledgment of prior art) in that application or specification.

* * *

(7) Whereas by a resolution made, on the signature of the Community Patent Convention the governments of the member states of the European Economic Community resolved to adjust their laws relating to patents so as (among other things) to bring those laws into conformity with the corresponding provisions of the European Patent Convention, the Community Patent Convention and the Patent Co-operation Treaty, it is hereby declared that the following provisions of this Act, that is to say, sections 1(1) to (4), 2 to 6, 14(3), (5) and (6), 37(5), 54, 60, 69, 72(1) and (2), 74(4), 82, 83, 88(6) and (7), 100 and 125, are so framed as to have, as nearly as practicable, the same effects in the United Kingdom as the corresponding provisions of the European Patent Convention, the Community Parent Convention and the Patent Co-operation Treaty have in the territories to which those Conventions apply.

* * *

APPENDIX 22

AGREEMENT ON TRADE-RELATED ASPECTS OF INTELLECTUAL PROPERTY RIGHTS

A22–01   Members,

Desiring to reduce distortions and impediments to international trade, and taking into account the need to promote effective and adequate protection of intellectual property rights, and to ensure that measures and procedures to enforce intellectual property rights do not themselves become barriers to legitimate trade;

Recognizing to this end, the need for new rules and disciplines concerning:

(a) the applicability of the basic principles of GATT 1994 and of relevant international intellectual property agreements or conventions;

(b) the provisions of adequate standards and principles concerning the availability, scope and use of trade-related intellectual property rights;

(c) the provision of effective and appropriate means for the enforcement of trade-related intellectual property rights, taking into account differences in national legal systems;

(d) the provision of effective and expeditious procedures for the multilateral prevention and settlement of disputes between governments; and

(e) transitional arrangements aiming at the fullest participation in the results of the negotiations;

Recognizing the need for a multilateral framework of principles, rules and disciplines dealing with international trade in counterfeit goods;

Recognizing that intellectual property rights are private rights;

Recognizing the underlying public policy objectives of national systems for the protection of intellectual property, including developmental and technological objectives;

Recognizing also the special needs of the least-developed country. Members in respect of maximum flexibility in the domestic implementation of laws and regulations in order to enable them to create a sound and viable technological base;

Emphasizing the importance of reducing tensions by reaching strengthened commitments to resolve disputes on trade-related intellectual property issues through multilateral procedures;

Desiring to establish a mutually supportive relationship between the WTO and the World Intellectual Property Organization (referred to in this Agreements "WIPO") as well as other relevant international organizations;

HEREBY AGREE AS FOLLOWS:

PART 1

GENERAL PROVISIONS AND BASIC PRINCIPLES

ARTICLE 1

Nature and scope of obligations

1. Members shall give effect to the provisions of this Agreement. Members may, but shall not be obliged to, implement in their law more extensive protection than is required by this Agreement, provided that such protection does not contravene the provisions of this Agreement. Members shall be free to determine the appropriate method of implementing the provisions of this Agreement within their own legal system and practice.

Section 5

PATENTS

ARTICLE 27

Patentable Subject Matter

1. Subject to the provisions of paragraphs 2 and 3, patents shall be available for any inventions, whether products or processes, in all fields of technology, provided that they are new, involve an inventive step and are capable of industrial application. Subject to paragraph 1 of Article 65, paragraph 8 of Article 70 and paragraph 3 of this Article, patents shall be available and patent rights enjoyable without discrimination as to the place of invention, the field of technology and whether products are imported or locally produced.

2. Members may exclude from patentability inventions, the prevention within their territory of the commercial exploitation of which is necessary to protect *ordre public* or morality, including to protect human, animal or plant life or health or to avoid serious prejudice to the environment, provided that such exclusion is not made merely because the exploitation is prohibited by their law.

3. Members may also exclude from patentability:

   (a) diagnostic, therapeutic and surgical methods for the treatment of humans or animals;
   (b) plants and animals other than micro organisms, and essentially biological processes for the production of plants or animals other than non-biological and microbiological processes. However, Members shall provide for the protection of plant varieties either by patents or by an effective *sui generis* system or by any combination thereof. The provisions of this subparagraph shall be reviewed four years after the date of entry into force of the WTO Agreement.

881

ARTICLE 28

Rights Conferred

1. A patent shall confer on its owner the following exclusive rights:

(a) where the subject matter of a patent is a product, to prevent third parties not having the owner's consent from the acts of: making, using, offering for sale, selling, or importing[1] for these purposes that product;

(b) where the subject matter of a patent is a process, to prevent third parties not having the owner's consent from the act of using the process, and from the acts of: using, offering for sale, selling, importing for these purposes at least the product obtained directly by that process.

2. Patent owners shall also have the right to assign, or transfer by succession, the patent and to conclude licensing contracts.

ARTICLE 29

Conditions on Patent Applicants

1. Members shall require that an applicant for a patent shall disclose the invention in a manner sufficiently clear and complete for the invention to be carried out by a person skilled in the art and may require the applicant to indicate the best mode for carrying out the invention known to the inventor at the filing date or, where priority as claimed, at the priority date of the application.

2. Members may require an applicant for a patent to provide information concerning the applicant's corresponding foreign applications and grants.

ARTICLE 32

Revocation/Forfeiture

An opportunity for judicial review of any decision to revoke or forfeit a patent shall be available.

ARTICLE 33

Term of Protection

The term of protection available shall not end before the expiration of a period of twenty years counted from the filing date.

ARTICLE 34

Process. Patents: Burden of Proof

1. For the purposes of civil proceedings in respect of the infringement of the rights of the owner referred to in paragraph 1(b) of Article 28, if the subject matter of

[1] This right, like all other rights conferred under this Agreement in respect of the use, sale, importation or other distribution of goods, is subject to the provisions of Article 6.

a patent is a process for obtaining a product, the judicial authorities shall have the authority to order the defendant to prove that the process to obtain an identical product is different from the patented process. Therefore, Members shall provide, an at least one of the following circumstances, that any identical product when produced without the consent of the patent owner shall, in the absence of proof to the contrary, be deemed to have been obtained by the patented process:

    (a) the product obtained by the patent process is new;
    (b) if there is a substantial likelihood that the identical product was made by the process and the owner of the patent has been unable through reasonable efforts to determine the process actually used.

2. Any Member shall be free to provide that the burden of proof indicated in paragraph 1 shall be on the alleged infringer only if the condition referred to in subparagraph (a) is fulfilled or only if the condition referred to in subparagraph (b) is fulfilled.

3. In the adduction of proof to the contrary, the legitimate interests of defendants in protecting their manufacturing and business secrets shall be taken into account.

PART III

ENFORCEMENT OF INTELLECTUAL PROPERTY RIGHTS

Section 1

GENERAL OBLIGATIONS

ARTICLE 41

1. Members shall ensure that enforcement procedures as specified in this Part are available under their law so as to permit effective action against any act of infringement of intellectual property rights covered by this Agreement, including expeditious remedies to prevent infringements and remedies which constitute a deterrent to further infringements. These procedures shall be applied in such a manner as to avoid the creation of barriers to legitimate trade and to provide for safeguards against their abuse.

2. Procedures concerning the enforcement of intellectual property rights shall be fair and equitable. They shall not be unnecessarily complicated or costly, or entail unreasonable time limits or unwarranted delays.

3. Decisions on the merits of a case shall preferably be in writing and reasoned. They shall be made available at least to the parties to the proceeding without undue delay. Decisions on the merits of a case shall be based only on evidence in respect of which parties were offered the opportunity to be heard.

4. Parties to a proceeding shall have an opportunity for review by a judicial authority of final administrative decision, and, subject to jurisdictional provisions in a Member's law concerning the importance of a case, of at least the legal aspects of initial judicial decisions on the merits of a case. However, there shall be no obligation to provide an opportunity for review of acquittals in criminal cases.

5. It is understood that this Part does not create any obligation to put in place a judicial system for the enforcement of intellectual property rights distinct from that for the enforcement of law in general, nor does it affect the capacity of Members to enforce their law in general. Nothing in this Part creates any obligation with respect to the distribution of resources as between enforcement of intellectual property rights and the enforcement of law in general.

APPENDIX 22

Section 2

CIVIL AND ADMINISTRATIVE PROCEDURES AND REMEDIES

ARTICLE 42

Fair and Equitable Procedures

Members shall make available to right holders' civil judicial procedures—concerning the enforcement of any intellectual property right covered by this Agreement. Defendants shall have the right to written notice which is timely and contains sufficient detail, including the basis of the claims. Parties shall be allowed to be represented by independent legal counsel, and procedures shall not impose overly burdensome requirements concerning mandatory personal appearances. All parties to such procedures shall be duly entitled to substantiate their claims and to present all relevant evidence. The procedure shall provide a means to identify and protect confidential information, unless this would be contrary to existing constitutional requirements.

ARTICLE 43

Evidence

1. The judicial authorities shall have the authority, where a party has presented reasonably available evidence sufficient to support its claims and has specified evidence relevant to substantiation of its claims which lies in the control of the opposing party, to order that this evidence be produced by the opposing party, subject in appropriate cases to conditions which ensure the protection of confidential information.

2. In cases in which a party to a proceeding voluntarily and without good reason refuses access to, or otherwise does not provide necessary information within a reasonable period, or significantly impedes a procedure relating to an enforcement action, a Member may accord judicial authorities the authority to make preliminary and final determinations, affirmative or negative, on the basis of the information presented to them, including the complaint or the allegation presented by the party adversely affected by the denial of access to information, subject to providing the parties an opportunity to be heard on the allegations or evidence.

APPENDIX 23

EUROPEAN UNION BIOTECHNOLOGY DIRECTIVE

Directive 98/44/EC of the European Parliament and of the Council of 6 July 1998 on the legal protection of biotechnological inventions

(Relevant parts)

THE EUROPEAN PARLIAMENT AND THE COUNCIL OF THE EUROPEAN **A23–01**
UNION,

Having regard to the Treaty establishing the European Community, and in particular Article 100a thereof,

Having regard to the proposal from the Commission,[1]

Having regard to the opinion of the Economic and Social Committee,[2]

Acting in accordance with the procedure laid down in Article 189b of the Treaty[3]

(1) Whereas biotechnology and genetic engineering are playing an increasingly important role in a broad range of industries and the protection of biotechnological inventions will certainly be of fundamental importance for the Community's industrial development;

(2) Whereas, in particular in the field of genetic engineering, research and development require a considerable amount of high-risk investment and therefore only adequate legal protection can make them profitable;

(3) Whereas effective and harmonised protection throughout the Member States is essential in order to maintain and encourage investment in the field of biotechnology;

(4) Whereas following the European Parliament's rejection of the joint text, approved by the Conciliation Committee, for a European Parliament and Council Directive on the legal protection of biotechnological inventions[4], the European Parliament and the Council have determined that the legal protection of biotechnological inventions requires clarification;

(5) Whereas differences exist in the legal protection of biotechnological inventions offered by the laws and practices of the different Member States; whereas

---

[1] O.J. C 296, 8.10.1996, p. 4 and O.J. C311, 11.10.1997, p. 12.
[2] O.J. C 295,7.10.1996, p. 11.
[3] Opinion of the European Parliament of 16 July 1997 (O.J. C 286, 22.9.1997, p.87). Council Common Position of 26 February 1998 (O.J. C 110. 8.4.1998, p. 17) and Decision of the European Parliament of 12 May 1998 (O.J. C 167, 1.6.1998). Council Decision of 16 June 1998.
[4] O.J. C 68, 20.3.1995, p. 26.

such differences could create barriers to trade and hence impede the proper functioning of the internal market;

(6) Whereas such differences could well become greater as Member States adopt new and different legislation and administrative practices, or whereas national case-law interpreting such legislation develops differently;

(7) Whereas uncoordinated development of national laws on the legal protection of biotechnological inventions in the Community could lead to further disincentives to trade, to the detriment of the industrial development of such inventions and of the smooth operation of the internal market;

(8) Whereas legal protection of biotechnological inventions does not necessitate the creation of a separate body of law in place of the rules of national patent law; whereas the rules of national patent law remain the essential basis for the legal protection of biotechnological inventions given that they must be adapted or added to in certain specific respects in order to take adequate account of technological developments involving biological material which also fulfil the requirements for patentability;

(9) Whereas in certain cases, such as the exclusion from patentability of plant and animal varieties and of essentially biological processes for the production of plants and animals, certain concepts in national laws based upon international patent and plant variety conventions have created uncertainty regarding the protection of biotechnological and certain microbiological inventions; whereas harmonisation is necessary to clarify the said uncertainty;

(10) Whereas regard should be had to the potential of the development of biotechnology for the environment and in particular the utility of this technology for the development of methods of cultivation which are less polluting and more economical in their use of ground; whereas the patent system should be used to encourage research into, and the application of, such processes;

(11) Whereas the development of biotechnology is important to developing countries, both in the field of health and combating major epidemics and endemic diseases and in that of combating hunger in the world; whereas the patent system should likewise be used to encourage research in these fields; whereas international procedures for the dissemination of such technology in the Third World and to the benefit of the population groups concerned should be promoted;

(12) Whereas the Agreement on Trade-Related Aspects of Intellectual Property Rights (TRIPs)[5] signed by the European Community and the Member States, has entered into force and provides that patent protection must be guaranteed for products and processes in all areas of technology;

(13) Whereas the Community's legal framework for the protection of biotechnological inventions can be limited to laying down certain principles as they apply to the patentability of biological material as such, such principles being intended in particular to determine the difference between inventions and discoveries with regard to the patentability of certain elements of human origin, to the scope of protection conferred by a patent on a biotechnological invention, to the right to use a deposit mechanism in addition to written descriptions and lastly to the option of obtaining non-exclusive compulsory licenses in respect of interdependence between plant varieties and inventions, and conversely;

(14) Whereas a patent for invention does not authorise the holder to implement that invention, but merely entitles him to prohibit third parties from exploiting it for industrial and commercial purposes; whereas, consequently, substantive patent law cannot serve to replace or render superfluous national, European or international law which may impose restrictions or prohibitions or which concerns the monitoring of research and of the use or commercialisation of its results, notably from the point of view of the requirements of public health, safety,

[5] O.J. L 336, 223.12.1994, p. 213.

environmental protection, animal welfare, the preservation of genetic diversity and compliance with certain ethical standards;

(15) Whereas no prohibition or exclusion exists in national or European patent law (Munich Convention) which precludes a priori the patentability of biological matter;

(16) Whereas patent law must be applied so as to respect the fundamental principles safeguarding the dignity and integrity of the person; whereas it is important to assert the principle that the human body, at any stage in its formation or development, including germ cells, and the simple discovery of one of its elements or one of its products, including the sequence or partial sequence of a human gene, cannot be patented; whereas these principles are in line with the criteria of patentability proper to patent law, whereby a mere discovery cannot be patented;

(17) Whereas significant progress in the treatment of diseases has already been made thanks to the existence of medicinal products derived from elements isolated from the human body and/or otherwise produced, such medicinal products resulting from technical processes aimed at obtaining elements similar in structure to those existing naturally in the human body and whereas, consequently, research aimed at obtaining and isolating such elements valuable to medicinal production should be encouraged by means of the patent system;

(18) Whereas, since the patent system provides insufficient incentive for encouraging research into and production of biotechnological medicines which are needed to combat rare or "orphan" diseases, the Community and the Member States have a duty to respond adequately to this problem;

(19) Whereas account has been taken of Opinion No. 8 of the Group of Advisers on the Ethical Implications of Biotechnology to the European Commission;

(20) Whereas, therefore, it should be made clear that an invention based on an element isolated from the human body or otherwise produced by means of a technical process, which is susceptible of industrial application, is not excluded from patentability, even where the structure of that element is identical to that of a natural element, given that the rights conferred by the patent do not extend to the human body and its elements in their natural environment;

(21) Whereas such an element isolated from the human body or otherwise produced is not excluded from patentability since it is, for example, the result of technical processes used to identify, purify and classify it and to reproduce it outside the human body, techniques which human beings alone are capable of putting into practice and which nature is incapable of accomplishing by itself;

(22) Whereas the discussion on the patentability of sequences or partial sequences of genes is controversial; whereas, according to this Directive, the granting of a patent for inventions which concern such sequences or partial sequences should be subject to the same criteria of patentability as in all other areas of technology: novelty, inventive step and industrial application; whereas the industrial application of a sequence or partial sequence must be disclosed in the patent application as filed;

(23) Whereas a mere DNA sequence without indication of a function does not contain any technical information and is therefore not a patentable invention;

(24) Whereas, in order to comply with the industrial application criterion it is necessary in cases where a sequence or partial sequence of a gene is used to produce a protein or part of a protein, to specify which protein or part of a protein is produced or what function it performs;

(25) Whereas, for the purposes of interpreting rights conferred by a patent, when sequences overlap only in parts which are not essential to the invention, each sequence will be considered as an independent sequence in patent law terms;

(26) Whereas if an invention is based on biological material of human origin or if it uses such material, where a patent application is filed, the person from whose

body the material is taken must have had an opportunity of expressing free and informed consent thereto, in accordance with national law;

(27) Whereas if an invention is based on biological material of plant or animal origin or if it uses such material, the patent application should, where appropriate, include information on the geographical origin of such material, if known; whereas this is without prejudice to the processing of patent applications or the validity of rights arising from granted patents;

(28) Whereas this Directive does not in any way affect the basis of current patent law, according to which a patent may be granted for any new application of a patented product;

(29) Whereas this Directive is without prejudice to the exclusion of plant and animal varieties from patentability; whereas on the other hand inventions which concern plants or animals are patentable provided that the application of the invention is not technically confined to a single plant or animal variety;

(30) Whereas the concept 'plant variety' is defined by the legislation protecting new varieties, pursuant to which a variety is defined by its whole genome and therefore possesses individuality and is clearly distinguishable from other varieties;

(31) Whereas a plant grouping which is characterised by a particular gene (and not its whole genome) is not covered by the protection of new varieties and is therefore not excluded from patentability even if it comprises new varieties of plants;

(32) Whereas, however, if an invention consists only in genetically modifying a particular plant variety, and if a new plant variety is bred, it will still be excluded from patentability even if the genetic modification is the result not of an essentially biological process but of a biotechnological process;

(33) Whereas it is necessary to define for the purposes of this Directive when a process for the breeding of plants and animals is essentially biological;

(34) Whereas this Directive shall be without prejudice to concepts of invention and discovery, as developed by national, European or international patent law;

(35) Whereas this Directive shall be without prejudice to the provisions of national patent law whereby processes for treatment of the human or animal body by surgery or therapy and diagnostic methods practiced on the human or animal body are excluded from patentability;

(36) Whereas the TRIPs Agreement provides for the possibility that members of the World Trade Organisation may exclude from patentability inventions, the prevention within their territory of the commercial exploitation of which is necessary to protect ordre public or morality, including to protect human, animal or plant life or health or to avoid serious prejudice to the environment, provided that such exclusion is not made merely because the exploitation is prohibited by their law;

(37) Whereas the principle whereby inventions must be excluded from patentability where their commercial exploitation offends against ordre public or morality must also be stressed in this Directive;

(38) Whereas the operative part of this Directive should also include an illustrative list of inventions excluded from patentability so as to provide national courts and patent offices with a general guide to interpreting the reference to ordre public and morality; whereas this list obviously cannot presume to be exhaustive; whereas processes, the use of which offend against human dignity, such as processes to produce chimeras from germ cells or totipotent cells of humans and animals, are obviously also excluded from patentability;

(39) Whereas ordre public and morality correspond in particular to ethical or moral principles recognised in a Member State, respect for which is particularly important in the field of biotechnology in view of the potential scope of inventions

in this field and their inherent relationship to living matter; whereas such ethical or moral principles supplement the standard legal examinations under patent law regardless of the technical field of the invention;

(40) Whereas there is a consensus within the Community that interventions in the human germ line and the cloning of human beings offends against ordre public and morality; whereas it is therefore important to exclude unequivocally from patentability processes for modifying the germ line genetic identity of human beings and processes for cloning human beings;

(41) Whereas a process for cloning human beings may be defined as any process, including techniques of embryo splitting, designed to create a human being with the same nuclear genetic information as another living or deceased human being;

(42) Whereas, moreover, uses of human embryos for industrial or commercial purposes must also be excluded from patentability; whereas in any case such exclusion does not affect inventions for therapeutic or diagnostic purposes which are applied to the human embryo and are useful to it;

(43) Whereas pursuant to Article F(2) of the Treaty on European Union, the Union is to respect fundamental rights, as guaranteed by the European Convention for the Protection of Human Rights and Fundamental Freedoms signed in Rome on 4 November 1950 and as they result from the constitutional traditions common to the Member States, as general principles of Community law;

(44) Whereas the Commission's European Group on Ethics in Science and New Technologies evaluates all ethical aspects of biotechnology; whereas it should be pointed out in this connection that that Group may be consulted only where biotechnology is to be evaluated at the level of basic ethical principles, including where it is consulted on patent law;

(45) Whereas processes for modifying the genetic identity of animals which are likely to cause them suffering without any substantial medical benefit in terms of research, prevention, diagnosis or therapy to man or animal, and also animals resulting from such processes, must be excluded from patentability;

(46) Whereas, in view of the fact that the function of a patent is to reward the inventor for his creative efforts by granting an exclusive but time-bound right, and thereby encourage inventive activities, the holder of the patent should be entitled to prohibit the use of patented self-reproducing material in situations analogous to those where it would be permitted to prohibit the use of patented, non-self-reproducing products, that is to say the production of the patented product itself;

(47) Whereas it is necessary to provide for a first derogation from the rights of the holder of the patent when the propagating material incorporating the protected invention is sold to a farmer for farming purposes by the holder of the patent or with his consent; whereas that initial derogation must authorise the farmer to use the product of his harvest for further multiplication or propagation on his own farm; whereas the extent and the conditions of that derogation must be limited in accordance with the extent and conditions set out in Council Regulation (EC) No. 2100/94 of 27 July 1994 on Community plant variety rights[6];

(48) Whereas only the fee envisaged under Community law relating to plant variety rights as a condition for applying the derogation from Community plant variety rights can be required of the farmer;

(49) Whereas, however, the holder of the patent may defend his rights against a farmer abusing the derogation or against a breeder who has developed a plant variety incorporating the protected invention if the latter fails to adhere to his commitments;

(50) Whereas a second derogation from the rights of the holder of the patent must authorise the farmer to use protected livestock for agricultural purposes;

(51) Whereas the extent and the conditions of that second derogation must be

---

[6] O.J. L 227, 1.9.1994, p. 1. Regulation as amended by Regulation (EC) No. 2506/95 (O.J. L 258, 28.10.1995, p. 3).

determined by national laws, regulations and practices, since there is no Community legislation on animal variety rights;

(52) Whereas, in the field of exploitation of new plant characteristics resulting from genetic engineering, guaranteed access must, on payment of a fee, be granted in the form of a compulsory licence where, in relation to the genus or species concerned, the plant variety represents significant technical progress of considerable economic interest compared to the invention claimed in the patent;

(53) Whereas, in the field of the use of new plant characteristics resulting from new plant varieties in genetic engineering, guaranteed access must, on payment of a fee, be granted in the form of a compulsory licence where the invention represents significant technical progress of considerable economic interest;

(54) Whereas Article 34 of the TRIPs Agreement contains detailed provisions on the burden of proof which is binding on all Member States; whereas, therefore, a provision in this Directive is not necessary;

(55) Whereas following Decision 93/626/EEC[7] the Community is party to the Convention on Biological Diversity of 5 June 1992; whereas, in this regard, Member States must give particular weight to Article 3 and Article 8(j), the second sentence of Article 16(2) and Article 16(5) of the Convention when bringing into force the laws, regulations and administrative provisions necessary to comply with this Directive;

(56) Whereas the Third Conference of the Parties to the Biodiversity Convention, which took place in November 1996, noted in Decision 111/17 that "further work" is required to help develop a common appreciation of the relationship between intellectual property rights and the relevant provisions of the TRIPs Agreement and the Convention on Biological Diversity, in particular on issues relating to technology transfer and conservation and sustainable use of biological diversity and the fair and equitable sharing of benefits arising out of the use of genetic resources, including the protection of knowledge, innovations and practices of Indigenous and local communities embodying traditional lifestyles relevant for the conservation and sustainable use of biological diversity,

HAVE ADOPTED THIS DIRECTIVE:

CHAPTER I

Patentability

ARTICLE 1

1. Member States shall protect biotechnological inventions under national patent law. They shall, if necessary, adjust their national patent law to take account of the provisions of this Directive.

2. This Directive shall be without prejudice to the obligations of the Member States pursuant to international agreements, and in particular the TRIPs Agreement and the Convention on Biological Diversity.

ARTICLE 2

1. For the purposes of this Directive,

(a) "biological material" means any material containing genetic information and capable of reproducing itself or being reproduced in a biological system;

[7] O.J. L 309, 31.12.1993, p. 1.

(b) "microbiological process" means any process involving or performed upon or resulting in microbiological material.

2. A process for the production of plants or animals is essentially biological if it consists entirely of natural phenomena such as crossing or selection.

3. The concept of "plant variety" is defined by Article 5 of Regulation (EC) No. 2 100/94.

ARTICLE 3

1. For the purposes of this Directive, inventions which are new, which involve an inventive step and which are susceptible of industrial application shall be patentable even if they concern a product consisting of or containing biological material or a process by means of which biological material is produced, processed or used.

2. Biological material which is isolated from its natural environment or produced by means of a technical process may be the subject of an invention even if it previously occurred in nature.

ARTICLE 4

1. The following shall not be patentable:

(a) plant and animal varieties;
(b) essentially biological processes for the production of plants or animals.

2. Inventions which concern plants or animals shall be patentable if the technical feasibility of the invention is not confined to a particular plant or animal variety.

3. Paragraph 1(b) shall be without prejudice to the patentability of inventions which concern a microbiological or other technical process or a product obtained by means of such a process.

ARTICLE 5

1. The human body, at the various stages of its formation and development, and the simple discovery of one of its elements, including the sequence or partial sequence of a gene, cannot constitute patentable inventions.

2. An element isolated from the human body or otherwise produced by means of a technical process, including the sequence or partial sequence of a gene, may constitute a patentable invention, even if the structure of that element is identical to that of a natural element.

3. The industrial application of a sequence or a partial sequence of a gene must be disclosed in the patent application.

ARTICLE 6

1. Inventions shall be considered unpatentable where their commercial exploitation would be contrary to ordre public or morality; however, exploitation shall not be deemed to be so contrary merely because it is prohibited by law or regulation.

2. On the basis of paragraph 1, the following, in particular, shall be considered unpatentable:

(a) processes for cloning human beings;
(b) processes for modifying the germ line genetic identity of human beings;

(c) uses of human embryos for industrial or commercial purposes;
(d) processes for modifying the genetic identity of animals which are likely to cause them suffering without any substantial medical benefit to man or animal, and also animals resulting from such processes.

ARTICLE 7

The Commission's European Group on Ethics in Science and New Technologies evaluates all ethical aspects of biotechnology.

CHAPTER II

Scope of protection

ARTICLE 8

1. The protection conferred by a patent on a biological material possessing specific characteristics as a result of the invention shall extend to any biological material derived from that biological material through propagation or multiplication in an identical or divergent form and possessing those same characteristics.
2. The protection conferred by a patent on a process that enables a biological material to be produced possessing specific characteristics as a result of the invention shall extend to biological material directly obtained through that process and to any other biological material derived from the directly obtained biological material through propagation or multiplication in an identical or divergent form and possessing those same characteristics.

ARTICLE 9

The protection conferred by a patent on a product containing or consisting of genetic information shall extend to all material, save as provided in Article 5(1), in which the product is incorporated and in which the genetic information is contained and performs its function.

ARTICLE 10

The protection referred to in Articles 8 and 9 shall not extend to biological material obtained from the propagation or multiplication of biological material placed on the market in the territory of a Member State by the holder of the patent or with his consent, where the multiplication or propagation necessarily results from the application for which the biological material was marketed, provided that the material obtained is not subsequently used for other propagation or multiplication.

ARTICLE 11

1. By way of derogation from Articles 8 and 9, the sale or other form of commercialisation of plant propagating material to a farmer by the holder of the patent or with his consent for agricultural use implies authorisation for the farmer to use the product of his harvest for propagation or multiplication by him on his own farm, the extent and conditions of this derogation corresponding to those under Article 14 of Regulation (EC) No. 2 100/94.

2. By way of derogation from Articles 8 and 9, the sale or any other form of commercialisation of breeding stock or other animal reproductive material to a farmer by the holder of the patent or with his consent implies authorisation for the farmer to use the protected livestock for an agricultural purpose. This includes making the animal or other animal reproductive material available for the purposes of pursuing his agricultural activity but not sale within the framework or for the purpose of a commercial reproduction activity.

3. The extent and the conditions of the derogation provided for in paragraph 2 shall be determined by national laws, regulations and practices.

CHAPTER III

Compulsory cross-licensing

ARTICLE 12

1. Where a breeder cannot acquire or exploit a plant variety right without infringing a prior patent, he may apply for a compulsory licence for non-exclusive use of the invention protected by the patent inasmuch as the licence is necessary for the exploitation of the plant variety to be protected, subject to payment of an appropriate royalty. Member States shall provide that, where such a licence is granted, the holder of the patent will be entitled to a cross-licence on reasonable terms to use the protected variety.

2. Where the holder of a patent concerning a biotechnological invention cannot exploit it without infringing a prior plant variety right, he may apply for a compulsory licence for non-exclusive use of the plant variety protected by that right, subject to payment of an appropriate royalty. Member States shall provide that, where such a licence is granted, the holder of the variety right will be entitled to a cross-licence on reasonable terms to use the protected invention.

3. Applicants for the licences referred to in paragraphs 1 and 2 must demonstrate that:

(a) they have applied unsuccessfully to the holder of the patent or of the plant variety right to obtain a contractual licence;
(b) the plant variety or the invention constitutes significant technical progress of considerable economic interest compared with the invention claimed in the patent or the protected plant variety.

4. Each Member State shall designate the authority or authorities responsible for granting the licence. Where a licence for a plant variety can be granted only by the Community Plant Variety Office, Article 29 of Regulation (EC) No. 2100/94 shall apply.

CHAPTER IV

Deposit, access and re-deposit of a biological material

ARTICLE 13

1. Where an invention involves the use of or concerns biological material which is not available to the public and which cannot be described in a patent application in such a manner as to enable the invention to be reproduced by a person skilled in the art, the description shall be considered inadequate for the purposes of patent law unless:

893

(a) the biological material has been deposited no later than the date on which the patent application was filed with a recognised depositary institution. At least the international depositary authorities which acquired this status by virtue of Article 7 of the Budapest Treaty of 28 April 1977 on the international recognition of the deposit of micro-organisms for the purposes of patent procedure, hereinafter referred to as the 'Budapest Treaty', shall be recognised;

(b) the application as filed contains such relevant information as is available to the applicant on the characteristics of the biological material deposited;

(c) the patent application states the name of the depository institution and the accession number.

2. Access to the deposited biological material shall be provided through the supply of a sample:

(a) up to the first publication of the patent application, only to those persons who are authorised under national patent law;

(b) between the first publication of the application and the granting of the patent, to anyone requesting it or, if the applicant so requests, only to an independent expert;

(c) after the patent has been granted, and notwithstanding revocation or cancellation of the patent, to anyone requesting it.

3. The sample shall be supplied only if the person requesting it undertakes, for the term during which the patent is in force:

(a) not to make it or any material derived from it available to third parties; and

(b) not to use it or any material derived from it except for experimental purposes, unless the applicant for or proprietor of the patent, as applicable, expressly waives such an undertaking.

4. At the applicant's request, where an application is refused or withdrawn, access to the deposited material shall be limited to an independent expert for 20 years from the date on which the patent application was filed. In that case, paragraph 3 shall apply.

5. The applicant's requests referred to in point (b) of paragraph 2 and in paragraph 4 may only be made up to the date on which the technical preparations for publishing the patent application are deemed to have been completed.

ARTICLE 14

1. If the biological material deposited in accordance with Article 13 ceases to be available from the recognised depositary institution, a new deposit of the material shall be permitted on the same terms as those laid down in the Budapest Treaty.

2. Any new deposit shall be accompanied by a statement signed by the depositor certifying that the newly deposited biological material is the same as that originally deposited.

CHAPTER V

Final provisions

ARTICLE 15

1. Member States shall bring into force the laws, regulations and administrative provisions necessary to comply with this Directive not later than 30 July 2000. They shall forthwith inform the Commission thereof.

When Member States adopt these measures, they shall contain a reference to this Directive or shall be accompanied by such reference on the occasion of their official publication. The methods of making such reference shall be laid down by Member States.

2. Member States shall communicate to the Commission the text of the provisions of national law which they adopt in the field covered by this Directive.

ARTICLE 16

The Commission shall send the European Parliament and the Council:

(a) every five years as from the date specified in Article 15(1) a report on any problems encountered with regard to the relationship between this Directive and international agreements on the protection of human rights to which the Member States have acceded;

(b) within two years of entry into force of this Directive, a report assessing the implications for basic genetic engineering research of failure to publish, or late publication of, papers on subjects which could be patentable;

(c) annually as from the date specified in Article 15(1), a report on the development and implications of patent law in the field of biotechnology and genetic engineering.

ARTICLE 17

This Directive shall enter into force on the day of its publication in the Official Journal of the European Communities.

ARTICLE 18

This Directive is addressed to the Member States.

Done at Brussels, 6 July 1998.

For the European Parliament
The President
J.M. GIL-ROBLES

For the Council
The President
R. EDLINGER

APPENDIX 24

REVISION OF THE EUROPEAN PATENT CONVENTION: BACKGROUND AND OUTLINE OF PROPOSALS

Reforming the European patent system

Less than 30 years after the signing of the European Patent Convention, the European Patent Organisation has initiated a major process of reform, aimed at establishing a patent system in Europe that will be efficient, user-friendly and fully equipped to meet the challenges of the future.

The reforms concern three main areas:

- Revision of the European Patent Convention (EPC)—
- Reduction of patent translation costs and the introduction of common judicial arrangements for patents in Europe—
- Introduction of a Community patent.

The introduction of the Community patent is the responsibility of the EU, but the other two reform projects are the result of an initiative by the 20 Member States of the European Patent Organisation. However, all three projects are closely linked, the intention being that the existing European patent and the prospective Community patent should eventually form a fully integrated patent system in Europe. The success of the efforts to reform the existing European patent system will have lasting consequences for the next step: the creation of a single patent valid throughout the EU.

Why a reform of the European patent system?

The development of the European patent system has been influenced by many factors, including the political and economic integration of Europe, the rapid expansion of world trade, the emergence of new technologies and the growing pace of economic competition. Promoting innovation is a cornerstone of economic policy, and industry has come to regard effective patent protection as strategically vital.

The World Trade Organization (WTO) also attaches great importance to the protection of intellectual property and has laid down a set of general standards for this in the Agreement on Trade-Related Aspects of Intellectual Property Rights (TRIPs). This has significantly strengthened the institutional basis for industrial property rights, especially for patents. The emergence of new, research-based technologies, with a strong market presence, has clearly increased the practical relevance of patenting.

Together, these factors have led to dynamic growth of the European patent system and an unexpectedly high demand for patents:

- *Geographical growth*
  The European Patent Organisation, founded 23 years ago, now has 20 Member States.
  Six further countries, the so-called extension states, recognise European patents as valid within their borders but are not members of the Organisation. Eight countries of central and eastern Europe have been invited by the Organisation's Administrative Council to accede to the European Patent Convention with effect from July 2002.
- *Development of the European Patent Office*
  Rapid rise in staff numbers, from 940 permanent employees in 1978 to a current total of nearly 5,000.
  Four locations (Munich, The Hague, Berlin and Vienna), with major building programmes in Munich and The Hague. Increase in budget from DEM 98m in 1978, when the Office first opened its doors, to nearly DEM 2bn in 2001.
- *Increase in workload*
  The number of patent applications has risen from 3,600 in 1978 to an expected 140,000 this year—over four times the maximum of 30,000 anticipated when the Organisation was set up. Applications have increased by 70% since 1995.
  The Office plays a key part in handling international patent applications under the Patent Cooperation Treaty (PCT)—around 60% of searching and substantive examination under the PCT is carried out by the EPO.
  The office has taken numerous steps to boost efficiency and help to cope with its rapidly growing workload. One such measure is the BEST project (**B**ringing **S**earch and **E**xamination **T**ogether).
- *Developments in patent law*
  Since the drafting of the EPC in the early 1970s, technical innovations have emerged which at that time would have belonged to the realm of science fiction. Information technology, e-business, biotechnology and genetic engineering are the new growth areas. The Office, in granting patents, and its boards of appeal, in deciding on matters concerning the application of patent law, have to find appropriate solutions to the problems of protecting these new technologies.
  The European patent system is also affected by international legal developments, to which it must respond quickly and flexibly.
  Less than 30 years after the signing of the European Patent Convention in Munich on 5 October 1973, the 20 Member States of the European Patent Organisation have embarked on a wide-ranging reform of the European patent system. The centrepiece of the reform project is the revision of the Convention at the Diplomatic Conference 2000. Its aim is to ensure that the European patent procedure can continue to function in a way that fully meets the needs of its users and is responsive to ongoing legal and technological developments.

Reform components

(A) COST REDUCTION AND ARRANGEMENTS FOR SETTLING LITIGATION

Two crucial tasks for the future are the reduction of the cost of translating European patents and the creation of a common system of courts for post-grant litigation. Initiatives in these two areas were launched by the Member States of the European Patent Organisation at an intergovernmental conference in Paris in June 1999, and significant further steps were taken at a second conference in London in October 2000.

Regarding the *cost issue*, an optional agreement was concluded in London enabling Member States to waive, wholly or in part, the requirement for translations of European patents into their official languages. A translation is no longer required where the patent is granted for states which have one of the three EPO languages as an official language. In other states, a translation of the description no longer needs to be filed if the European patent is granted in an EPO language designated by the country in question or has been translated into that language. When the agreement takes effect, the cost of translation will be reduced by as much as 50%. Eight countries—Denmark, Germany, Liechtenstein, Monaco, the Netherlands, Sweden, Switzerland and the United Kingdom—signed the agreement in London; three further states have announced their intention to sign by the end of the year. The agreement is subject to ratification and can only enter into force when it has been ratified by eight states, including the three for which the EPO granted the largest number of European patents in 1999.

Improving the conditions for *litigation concerning European patents* after grant by the EPO is a particularly important aspect of the reforms. Up to now, issues of infringement and—except in European opposition proceedings—validity have been decided by the national courts of the individual countries for which the patent is granted. There is no common European patent court. This makes the enforcement of rights in several counties difficult and costly, with legal procedures and approaches differing considerably from one country to another—national courts may come to dissimilar conclusions about whether a European patent is valid or has been infringed.

The Paris and London intergovernmental conferences have opened the way for concentrating all litigation involving European patents on a small number of courts and ultimately creating an integrated judicial system in Europe. This, too, is to be achieved by an optional agreement between the Member States of the European Patent Organisation. A working party has been entrusted with the task of drafting such an agreement, which is to be finalised by the end of 2001 and signed at a further intergovernmental conference (probably in 2002).

(B) COMMUNITY PATENT

The idea of supplementing the European patent system with a Community patent for the Member States of the EU has been on the stocks for many years, but attempts to put it into practice have hitherto been unsuccessful. On 1 August, the EU Commission published a proposal to introduce the Community patent via a Council Regulation. Under the proposal, Community patents would be granted by the EPO on the basis of the EPC for the entire territory of the Community and centrally administered. The effects of the Community patent and the judicial arrangements for enforcement and the settling of questions relating to validity are laid down in the Regulation on a unitary, Community-wide basis.

The Commission's proposal is based on an earlier agreement concluded in 1989 between the then 12 EU Member States. However, it contains substantial improvements concerning two aspects, the language issue and the judicial system, which had obstructed previous attempts to create a Community patent. Here, too, the translation of patents granted in an EPO official language—English, French or German—into a Community language is to be optional only: *i.e.* the filing of a translation is no longer required for the patent to be valid. Exclusive jurisdiction for litigation concerning Community patents is to be given to a newly created central Community court with chambers of first instance and appeal.

The creation of a Community patent on the basis of a Regulation under Article 308 of the EC Treaty requires the unanimous approval of the EU Member States. Discussion of the Commission's proposal has only just begun and is likely to take some time.

The European patent and the Community patent are complementary aspects of the future European patent system. Community patents will be granted, like

European patents, according to the provisions of the EPC. The difference is that, after grant, the unitary EU patent will no longer be subject to the national law of the Member States, but only to Community law in the form of the Council Regulation. The forthcoming revision of the EPC therefore has no immediate bearing on the plans for the Community patent. The structure for the latter has to be established before the connections between the European and Community patents can be defined and anchored in the EPC. This will require a further round of EPC revision, and will also involved the question whether the European Community should become a member of the European Patent Organisation.

(c) Revision of the European Patent Convention

The revision of the EPC, the focal point for the reform of the European patent system, is the subject of the Diplomatic Conference 2000 in Munich. Its purpose is to bring about a judicious modernisation of European patent law, preserving those features of the system which have stood the test of time but ensuring that it can continue to function efficiently and flexibly as an instrument for industry and inventors in Europe.

With this aim, and in view of the impending expansion of the European Patent Organisation to a total of 28 Member States, the Paris intergovernmental conference in June 1999 called on the Organisation to hold a Diplomatic Conference before the end of 2000 to revise the EPC. The Basic Proposal, approved by the Organisation's Administrative Council and placed before the Conference for adoption, contains over 90 draft amendments to the provisions of the Convention, taking account of suggestions from users of the European patent system as well as the needs of the Organisation and the European Patent Office itself. The proposals for revision differ in scope but involve nearly every aspect of the EPC: from institutional provisions and substantive patent law through to proceedings before the EPO and its boards of appeal, and including the post-grant phase. The bringing together of search and substantive examination is to be anchored in the EPC, with the intention of simplifying and speeding up the patent grant procedure.

The main points for revision are as follows:

- **Safeguarding the adaptability of the EPC**
  Rapid technological change, globalisation and the information society have not only increased the demand for patent protection; they also call for measures to ensure that the European patent system is equipped to keep pace with new developments. To this end, so that the EPC can quickly be brought into line with international agreements or Community law relating to the patent system, the Administrative Council of the European Patent Organisation is to be authorised to implement necessary amendments to the EPC without needing to go through a long and elaborate process of revision. In view also of the accession of eight new Member States, this has a considerable importance for the efficient functioning of the European patent system.
- **Amendments of substantive patent law**
  The key items in this area are the proposed amendments concerning patent protection for computer software and pharmaceutical substances, in accordance with the TRIPs Agreement.
- **Clarifying the extent of protection conferred by European patents**
- **Extending the means of redress in proceedings before the EPO**
- **Central limitation proceedings for European patents**

Issues still pending

A number of issues which have yet to be debated in full have been omitted from the Basic Proposal and are not on the conference agenda. This concerns amendments to the EPC in view of the future Community patent, the introduction of a grace period for prior disclosure, and the protection of biotechnological inventions. These questions, however, will be subjected to further examination once the present reform has been concluded, and may be submitted to a subsequent revision conference.

Regarding patent protection for biotechnological inventions, it should be noted that the grant of patents in this field is now subject to Community law, following the incorporation in September 1999 of the EU Biotechnology Directive into the EPC Implementing Regulations. The provisions of the Directive are strictly observed.

Perspectives for the future

With the implementation of its reform projects, in particular the revision of the EPC, the European Patent Organisation is making a major contribution to the further development of the European patent system, whose authority and influence extend far beyond the boundaries of Europe. The reduction of patenting costs, the harmonisation of the judicial system and the substantial improvements in European patent law will make the European patent system more efficient and enhance its attractiveness for industry in Europe and elsewhere.

The proposal to make a conference of ministers of the contracting states a permanent institution under the EPC will give the European patent system a stronger political context as far as the Member States of the European Patent Organisation are concerned. The extension of the powers granted to the Organisation's Administrative Council will make it possible to adapt the Convention quickly and flexibly to changing conditions and will ensure that the European patent system remains capable in the long term of learning and evolving.

INDEX

All references are to paragraph numbers

INDEX

Inventive step—*cont.*
introduction—*cont.*
standard of inventiveness, 12–03
time of assessment, 12–02
novelty, and, 11–04
prior art, and, 12–02
problem-and-solution approach
basic principles, 12–04—12–05
characteristics, 12–06
formulation of problem, 12–10—
12–17
identification of closest prior art,
12–07—12–09
introduction, 12–01
secondary indications
commercial success, 12–47
generally, 12–44
long-felt want, 12–45
overcoming a prejudice, 12–46
skilled person, role of
assessment of inventive step,
12–02, 12–18
common general knowledge,
12–21
introduction, 10–41
nature of, 12–19—12–20
special cases
analogy processes, 12–49
chemical intermediates, 12–50—
12–52
novel further use of known
compound, 12–52a
perceiving the problem, 12–48
state of the art, and, 12–02
standard of inventiveness, 12–03
technical considerations
combination of teachings,
12–24—12–25
common general knowledge,
12–21—12–22
comparative tests, 12–36—12–37
could/would, 12–43
expectation of success, 12–42a
feature disclosed for different
purpose, 12–27
field of technology, 12–29—
12–31
nature of skilled person, 12–19—
12–20
need for series of steps, 12–27a

Inventive step—*cont.*
technical considerations—*cont.*
series of steps, 12–27
simplification, 12–28
technical features, 12–23
technical progress, 12–38—12–39
unexpected bonus effects, 12–40—
12–42
unexpected technical progress,
12–32—12–35
unforeseeable results, 12–26
would/could, 12–43
time of assessment, 12–02
U.K. law, comparison with, 12–53—
12–54
Inventiveness
patentability, and, 9–21
standard of, 12–03
Inventors rectification of designation
restitutio in integrum, and, 6–31
Invitation to amend patent
examinations of objections arising,
3–62—3–63
generally, 3–59—3–61
Invitation to reply
failure to reply in due time,
2–41
generally, 2–39
Invitation to reply further
discretion, 2–45—2–46
generally, 2–43—2–44
Language
applications, of
generally, 2–29
introduction, 2–09
official languages, 5–03—5–03A
other European languages, 5–07
claim, of, 2–29
description, of, 2–29
EPO proceedings, of
generally, 5–04
official languages, 5–03—5–03A
oral proceedings, in, 5–06
written proceedings, in, 5–05
official languages, use of, 5–03—
5–03A
other European languages, use of
application, in, 5–07
documents having a time limit, in,
5–08

925